# HUEY LONG

# HUEY

 *Vintage Books*

# LONG

*T. Harry Williams*

*A Division of Random House · New York*

First Vintage Books Edition, September 1981
Copyright © 1969 by Alfred A. Knopf, Inc.

Library of Congress Cataloging in Publication Data
Williams, T. Harry (Thomas Harry), 1909–
Huey Long.

Includes bibliographical references and index.
1. Long, Huey Pierce, 1893–1935.
2. Louisiana—Politics and government—1865–1950.
3. United States—Politics and government—1933–1945.
4. Legislators—United States—Biography.
5. United States. Congress. Senate—Biography.
6. Louisiana—Governors—Biography.
E748.L86W48   1981   976.3′062′0924 [B]   81-40091
ISBN 0-394-74790-9   AACR2

Manufactured in the United States of America

789

Cover photograph courtesy of Wide World Photos

*for* Mai Frances *and* Nils

# PREFACE

SOMETIMES THE GENESIS OF A BOOK becomes somewhat vague to an author, particularly if the research and writing stretch over a long time. This book was begun over ten years ago, but I am very clear as to how it was born.

During the early 1950's I became greatly interested in the project in Oral History being conducted at Columbia University. The sponsors of the project had an idea that seemed eminently sensible to me. They were concerned with preserving the history of the recent past, roughly the period since 1930, but they emphasized that to do the job properly, a new research technique would have to be utilized, the tape-recorded interview with persons still living. This technique was necessary because of the impact of modern technology on communications. For example, a politician in the nineteenth century who had to get in touch with a colleague would write that man a letter, whereas a politician of today's era in a similar situation would telephone his friend, and most probably the conversation was not recorded. Therefore, said the Columbia people, the historians of the recent past would not have available, at least in abundance, the principal sources hitherto relied on by historians—letters and diaries. These historians should get busy and tape the recollections of individuals who figured in recent history and have the conversations reduced to typescripts, and thus rescue a history that would otherwise disappear.

As I thought about the Columbia plan, I was seized with an idea (living in Louisiana I almost had to have it): someone should use the technique of oral history as basic research for a biography of

Huey P. Long. A quick check of various sources told me that no one was contemplating such a biography, apparently because no significant collection of Long manuscripts was known to exist. At about the same time I received a letter from United States Senator Russell B. Long, Huey's son. He wished to tell me that a friend had presented him with a copy of my recently published *P.G.T. Beauregard: Napoleon in Gray*, which I had autographed in a Baton Rouge bookstore, and that he liked the book because he admired biography. I was so impressed by his appreciation of the scholarly approach to biography that I wrote to ask him if he did not think the time had come when an objective life of his father should be written. I added that I would like to attempt the task and explained that unless he possessed a large body of Long papers I would have to rely on the method of oral history.

His reply was instant and warm. He had long desired that a biography of his father be written and he had hoped that it would be done by a scholar. He grasped the utility of oral history and thought it would have to be my main research source, as he did not have any Long papers. But he believed that I would be able to secure rich and intimate reminiscences from the friends of his father, and he promised to ask these men to talk to me frankly. I stressed to him that I would have to have an absolutely free hand in interpreting the facts, and he readily agreed to this condition, signing a statement that my conclusions were not subject to his "editing or censorship in any manner." He has scrupulously observed the agreement, although he has naturally tried to influence my opinion of his father and has strong objections to some of my generalizations. I owe him a large debt of gratitude, since many of the Long followers would not have talked to me without his intercession.

My arrangements with Senator Long were completed late in 1955, and in the following year I began research on the book. In part the research was conducted in conventional sources: state and federal government documents, newspapers, magazine and periodical articles, and manuscripts. But most of the information, and that which was most valuable, was secured from men and women who knew Long: members of his family, politicians who held high places in his organization and lesser leaders, politicians who opposed him, and businessmen, educators, musicians, football coaches and players, and other individuals, many of them obscure but all having something significant to contribute to the Long story. Altogether, the reminiscences of two hundred and ninety-five individuals were gathered. Their statements were in nearly every case tape-recorded and later placed in typescript form. As I continued with the research, I became increasingly convinced of the validity of oral history. Not only was it a necessary tool in compiling the history of the recent past, but it also provided an unusually intimate look into that past. I found that the politicians were astonishingly frank in detailing their dealings, and often completely realistic in viewing themselves. But they had not trusted a record of these dealings to paper, and it would not have occurred to them to transcribe their experiences at a later time. Anybody who heard them would have to conclude that the full and inside story of politics is not in *any* age committed to the documents.

Those interviewed understood that I was gathering material for a book and that I would cite their names as sources in my footnotes. Only a few asked that their names not be used, and others requested that they not be named in connection with certain statements. I have respected their wishes, and in place of their names have employed the phrase "confidential communication." Some academic readers may object to the introduction of unidentified sources, but the practice is sometimes necessary in taking testimony from living persons. However, I have placed my typescripts in the Louisiana State University library under a time seal, and eventually they will be available to other scholars.

As I proceeded with the research, various persons asked me if I was going to write a pro-Long or an anti-Long book. I expected the question from Louisianians. Huey Long aroused among his people extreme feelings—love or hate—and they still find it difficult to view him neutrally. I was surprised, however, that many persons outside the state also asked the question, indicating that they too reacted to Long in terms of extremes. Long was obviously the type of leader who excites violent antithetical emotions in people, even in those not closely associated with him. He has inspired such emotions in those writers who have treated him, most of whom have been repelled by him. I have tried to regard him objectively, cutting through the myths that have grown up about him and trying to see the real man, and I hope that I have succeeded.

I should add, however, that I have certain concepts about Long and leaders like him, and these have influenced what I have written here. I believe that some men, men of power, can influence the course of history. They appear in response to conditions, but they may alter the conditions, may give a new direction to history. In the process they may do great good or evil or both, but whatever the case they leave a different kind of world behind them. Their accomplishment should be recognized. I believe that Huey Long was this kind of man.

I also agree with what I understand to be the thesis of Robert Penn Warren in *All the King's Men:* that the politician who wishes to do good may have to do some evil to achieve his goal. This was the course that was forced on the hero of Warren's novel, Willie Stark, who was a politician much like Long. It is also the course that Long, faced with a relentless opposition, felt he had to follow. Stark was in the end possessed by the evil or the method and was destroyed. Long did not come to such a dramatic fate. But in striving to do good he was led on to grasp for more and more power, until finally he could not always distinguish between the method and the goal, the power and the good. His story is a reminder, if we need one, that a great politician may be a figure of tragedy.

During the course of my research I received assistance from many persons and incurred many obligations. I have tried to acknowledge these debts at appropriate places in the footnotes and bibliography, and if I have omitted anyone, it is an oversight of the mind and not the heart. I have here to record my gratitude to T. N. McMullan, V. L. Bedsole, and other members of the Louisiana State University library staff, who gave me unfailing cooperation; to Fred Benton, Jr., an attorney friend who read the manuscript with an expert legal eye; to Professor Frank Freidel, who shared with me his intimate knowledge of the era of Franklin D. Roosevelt; to Mrs. Thomas Smylie, an expert editor who improved many chapters; and to Ben C. Toledano, who searched energetically for pictures of Long. A special vote of thanks goes to my editor at the house of Knopf, Ashbel Green. For research grants that enabled me to take off needed time in the initial stages of my study I am grateful to the American History Research Center (Senator Russell Long, wishing to aid my work but determined to avoid the appearance of subvention, contributed to this fund) and the John Simon Guggenheim Memorial Foundation.

T. HARRY WILLIAMS

*Baton Rouge, Louisiana*

*January 1969*

# CONTENTS

# ILLUSTRATIONS

# HUEY LONG

# CHAPTER 1

# *Not Even a Horse*

**T**HE STORY SEEMS TOO GOOD TO BE TRUE—but people who should know swear that it is true. The first time that Huey P. Long campaigned in rural, Latin, Catholic south Louisiana, the local boss who had him in charge said at the beginning of the tour: "Huey, you ought to remember one thing in your speeches today. You're from north Louisiana, but now you're in south Louisiana. And we got a lot of Catholic voters down here." "I know," Huey answered. And throughout the day in every small town Long would begin by saying: "When I was a boy, I would get up at six o'clock in the morning on Sunday, and I would hitch our old horse up to the buggy and I would take my Catholic grandparents to mass. I would bring them home, and at ten o'clock I would hitch the old horse up again, and I would take my Baptist grandparents to church." The effect of the anecdote on the audiences was obvious, and on the way back to Baton Rouge that night the local leader said admiringly: "Why, Huey, you've been holding out on us. I didn't know you had any Catholic grandparents." "Don't be a damn fool," replied Huey. "We didn't even have a horse."[1]

Some people would say today, as some said then, that the incident was characteristic of Huey P. Long, that it revealed all the cynicism and contempt of democracy and all the scheming ruthlessness of the man who seemed in the 1930's to be the first American dictator, the first great native fascist, who was compared to Hitler and Mussolini, who finally commanded one of the largest mass fol-

[1] Confidential communications.

lowings in the country and appeared to be on the verge of taking over the national government as he had his own state. And he was a new type of leader on the American scene—this man whose reddish-brown hair dipped rebelliously over his forehead, whose full and facile face could in a moment shift from its usual expression of mischief to one of consuming anger, who could act like a rustic clown off the platform and turn into a magnetic spellbinder when he stepped on it. A pudgy pixie who could suddenly become a demon, he was different—and yet in many ways he was completely traditional. His many enemies missed the latter aspect. They saw in him only the singular and the ominous, and they gave him such sinister titles as "despot of the delta" or "Caesar of the bayous." But not even they could deny that something made him surpassingly interesting; something set him apart from other leaders of his time.

He had that quality that political scientists call charism, of being able to excite people merely by appearing before them, which all the great mass leaders in history—for example, Hitler, Gandhi, Lincoln, Franklin D. Roosevelt, John F. Kennedy—have had. He excited people and he excited emotions, arousing in his relatively short but explosive career every feeling in the political spectrum—amazement and admiration, disbelief and disgust, love and hatred, and, with many individuals, cold apprehension.

He burst on the Louisiana scene in the mid-1920's, and nothing in that hitherto placid and planter-ruled state would ever be the same again. After a spectacular stint on the state Public Service Commission, where he made his name a household word by enforcing the law on the previously sacrosanct big corporations, he won the governorship in 1928, when he was not quite thirty-five years old. He won it by promising to enact an expansive program of economic and political reform. His victory was a new departure in Louisiana, which since Reconstruction had lived submissively under the sway of the upper-income groups. But nobody worried very much that Long would put through his program, least of all the ruling hierarchy, which would suffer its impact. After all, he was just another demagogue and demagogues promised much but delivered little—and usually nothing. He could be easily handled, as his counterparts in other Southern states had been handled. The way you dealt with a demagogue was to defeat his bills in the legislature or deflect him into forays against harmless objectives or, if things got really bad, absorb him into your own organization. Whatever the method, the end was the same. The demagogue, in helpless frustration, would go to cussing "niggers" or "Yankees"—and life would continue as before, and the right people would still monopolize the profits and the prestige.

That should have been the story, but this time it was different, startlingly so. As governor, Long broke completely with the established pattern for leaders of his type—the promising demagogue who forgot his promises or the idealistic liberal or progressive governor who permitted reactionary elements to stall and then sabotage his program. He put through the whole of his program and even added to it as he went along. And because from the first he faced an unrelenting and sometimes an unreasoning opposition, and because he was fascinated with power and its usage and became more fascinated as he grasped more of it, he erected a machine whose like had never existed before in American politics and has not existed since. Other Southern mass leaders on reaching the governor's office had attempted to form their own machine or to come to some kind of terms with the opposition organization. But they organized merely to protect their own place, wishing only to contain the opposition. They never attempted to destroy the ruling hierarchy. They did not think it could be destroyed; and even if the possibility had occurred to them, they would have shrunk from it. Despite their violent and extreme rhetoric, they were essentially reasonable and moderate men; and as politicians, they were, notwithstanding a certain flamboyance in manner, conventional and unimaginative users of power. They lacked not only the ability but, more important, the will to destroy the opposition. The inevitable result was that the opposition survived and turned back the demagogues and their programs or, at least, seriously blunted the cutting edge of the reform drives.

Long created a machine of his own, and a very effective one, but he went much further. He was the first Southern leader, and very possibly the first American leader, to set out not to contain the opposition or to impose certain conditions on it, but to force it out of existence. Deliberately, he grasped the control of all existing boards and other agencies, and then just as deliberately, by creating new agencies to perform new functions, he continually enlarged the patronage at his disposal. His control of patronage gave him control of the legislature, and his control of the legislature enabled him to have laws enacted that invested him with imperial authority over every level of local government. He became so powerful finally that he could deny the opposition almost all political sustenance, and if he wished, destroy it. But with the finesse of a great political artist he preferred to do it another way, if his foes would accept his way. What he was working on before his death, and in effect had brought off, was creating an arrangement in which the only remaining opposition faction would have to come into his organization to survive. It would have a place and obtain rewards, but he would define the place and assign the rewards. Controlling the executive and legislative branches and also the judicial branch—he campaigned to elect sympathetic justices—he dominated the whole power structure of the state. If the system had been perfected, and if it had endured—which is the bigger "if"—it would have been the most daring and dangerous concentration of power ever established in an American state government.

At the midpoint in his governorship, in 1930, Long had run for a seat in the United States Senate and had easily defeated the incumbent, a venerable planter-statesman of the old school. He did not, however, take his seat immediately. His legislative program was still encountering opposition, and he did not want to leave the completion of it to lesser men. Moreover, he had broken with his lieutenant governor, and under no circumstances would he let this man step into his seat. Not until January 1932, when he finally arranged a satisfactory succession, did he feel that he could leave for Washington. Even then he departed the Louisiana scene only in a ceremonial sense. The state was his base of operations for larger aspirations, and he had no intention of relinquishing his control over it. It was, in fact, in the senatorial period that he extended his power structure to its widest limit. In 1932 he secured the election of a completely compliant governor, along with his whole slate of other officeholders, and thereafter he increased the number of his followers in the legislature until he commanded more than a two-thirds majority in both houses, which enacted any law he asked for. He asked for many. Still intent on extending his reform program, still insistent on weakening an evaporating opposition, he would storm back from Washington and, through his governor, summon without advance notice a special session of the legislature. At these numerous meetings laws would be passed at a breathtaking rate and without much regard for such parliamentary niceties as committee hearings or floor debate. In seven special sessions between August 1934 and September 1935 a total of 226 bills was turned out, and at one especially memorable session 44 bills were enacted within five days.

A secure and safe Louisiana was necessary to Long as a base for the national operations he planned. He went to Washington with the conviction that his destiny would lead him to the presidency, just as from youth he planned step by step the career that would lead him to the highest office. He entered the Senate as a liberal Democrat, a supporter of men and measures to curb big business. In 1932 he advocated that his party nominate as its presidential candidate Franklin D. Roosevelt, the progressive governor of New York, and at the Democratic convention that year he helped Roosevelt get the nomination by holding important Southern votes in line at critical moments. Long stumped vigorously for Roosevelt in the campaign, and after the latter's election there was a brief period when it seemed that the two were going to make an unusually effective combination, the Eastern and the Southern liberals working together for liberal reform. That possibility evaporated almost immediately. Long seems to have actually thought for a time that he could control the President and use Roosevelt to further his own presidential ambitions. He had had only casual contacts with Roosevelt before the latter's inauguration, and he was convinced from these meetings that the New Yorker was only a genial dilettante who could be easily influenced. But a closer acquaintance with the President impressed a new image on him. He realized that Roosevelt was a man who had a will fully as strong as his own and who was also just as great a politician. Returning from an interview with Roosevelt, he said to a close friend: "I found a man as smart as I am. I don't know if I can travel with him." Recounting the episode, the friend added a comment that dozens of others have echoed: "Huey couldn't be second to anybody."[2]

He could not be second . . . and therefore he had to break with Roosevelt. There were other reasons that led to the separation—Long came to despise Roosevelt personally, and he sincerely felt that the President was moving far too slowly toward the goal of economic democracy—but essentially this was a contest that had to be fought, a power struggle between two great politicians. Franklin D. Roosevelt could not be second either. The battle between them was waged in the Senate and in presidential press conferences and over the radio and in the press, and eventually it reached such epic proportions that it threatened to tear the Democratic party to pieces. In the fight Roosevelt had many advantages. His mastery of the art of politics was the equal of Long's, and he operated from an even stronger base, the presidency and the immense prestige of that office. However, Long won some victories. Thundering that Roosevelt's New Deal was inadequate to meet the crisis of the Great Depression, he put forward his own, more radical, program under the title Share Our Wealth. He shouted that to help the suffering masses the New Deal must turn to the left—he had no hesitation in adopting the leftist label—and his voice and the very evident, large following that listened to him were the most potent factors that did force Roose-

[2] Confidential communication.

velt to shift, in part, to the left in 1935. Roosevelt responded to what
he thought was a dangerous possibility—if the New Deal failed to
solve the problems of capitalism, the restless factions of the American left might erupt into some kind of revolution under Long's
leadership.[3]

Roosevelt also feared what Long might accomplish as a conventional political operator, as a rival who might unseat him from
the presidency. On the eve of the election of 1936 most of the talk at
Democratic headquarters concerned Long's intentions, and it was
scared talk. Would Huey be a presidential candidate on a third-
party ticket? And if he were, would he take enough votes away from
Roosevelt to throw the election to the Republicans? Some of the best
party strategists feared that he might command enough strength to
make the election a close one. Long himself had a somewhat different plan. According to the testimony of intimates, he intended to
run some liberal Democrat as a third-party entry and so divide the
liberal vote that the Republican candidate would win. The Republicans would be incapable of dealing with the depression, the economic system would go to pieces, and by 1940 the country would be
crying for a strong leader to save it. That savior could be only one
man. Then Huey Long would take over and put the pieces together
—as he wanted to put them.[4]

There was no doubt in Long's mind that all would go as he had
planned it. Of Roosevelt he said scornfully: "I can take him. He's a
phony. . . . He's scared of me. I can outpromise him, and he knows
it. People will believe me and they won't believe him. His mother's
watchin' him, and she won't let him go too far, but I ain't got no
mother left, and if I had, she'd think anything I said was all right.
He's livin' on an inherited income. I got nothin', so I don't have to
bother about that."[5] Conceivably, it might have happened just as he
thought it would. Just as conceivably, it might not have. Long might
well have foundered on the rock of the two-party system, as other
gifted political rebels before him had done. Instead of grasping the
supreme success he saw as his destiny, he might have lived out his
life as a frustrated and embittered secondary politican. What might
have been can never be known. Fate, which has shattered the dreams
of other strong men, suddenly intervened. On a warm September
night in 1935 Huey Long, at the height of his power, apparently invincible, was shot down by an assassin in his capitol at Baton Rouge.

[3] Rexford G. Tugwell: *The Democratic Roosevelt* (New York, 1957), pp. 348–51.
[4] Confidential communications.
[5] Arthur Krock, memoir in Oral History Project, Columbia University.

When he died, his ambitions and his powers and his machine died with him. But not his program or his philosophy or his hopes for a better life for the masses. These lived on, in Louisiana, in the South, and, espoused by other men, in the nation.

Nor did the enigma of Huey Long die. What, exactly, was he? Dictator, demagogue, or democrat? An incipient fascist, an American boss, a supreme power artist? Whatever the label may be, he was undeniably a great leader, one of the breed who has to move and drive ordinary men, one of those who break the pattern of their time and then shape it anew. He conforms perfectly to Jacob Burckhardt's delineation of the type: "He appears complete in every situation, but every situation at once seems to cramp him. He does not merely fill it. He may shatter it. . . . Confronted with parliaments, senates, assemblies, press, public opinion, he knows at any moment how far they are real or only imaginary, and makes frank use of them. . . . He will curb his impatience and know no flinching." No one can yet explain why such men appear at given moments in history or what forces shape them to be what they are. But certainly a part of the answer lies in Huey Long's background, in those family origins he delighted to belittle as being so humble and inconsequential.

ALTHOUGH AT TIMES it seemed that Long talked about the poverty of his family out of mischief or sheer perversity, he was acting, naturally enough, out of political motives to secure a political advantage. If for no other reason, he wanted to impress on the rural voters of Louisiana that he was one of them, a product of the same kind of hard, hand-to-mouth way of life that they endured, but also a spectacular reminder that that kind of life could be escaped. In addition, he wanted to emphasize to reporters and interviewers, especially those from the big-city press of the North, that in his career he embodied the best of the American tradition, the rise from nothing to greatness, the ascent from the log cabin to the governor's mansion, with possibly the White House itself beckoning at the end of the saga. To one of these inquiring journalists, in the course of a number of remarks that were not completely frank on many points, Long spoke of the soil on his father's farm in Winn parish (county). "Poor land, hard to farm," he reminisced. "Wasn't alluvial, wasn't timbered, wasn't anything. Just hard work." He had had to work hard even as a small boy, he continued, and often he did not have enough to eat. With a shiver, he recalled that the family had had to subsist for long periods on a diet of blackstrap molasses and corn pone, but, he added hastily, in an apparent attempt to be objective: "We had a little better food than that most of the time."[6]

In the course of his career Huey created a myth—expanded by his brother Earl, who subsequently would have a career almost as sensational as Huey's—that the Longs were abjectly poor and lacked education, culture, and opportunity. Huey Long formed and fostered the myth with such artistry, sometimes even acting with consummate skill the role of a boor or a bumpkin, that it was accepted not only by his own generation but also by later ones as well, and finally by history. Writings about the Longs almost universally depict them as representing the very lowest stratum of Southern white society, the poor white or hillbilly type, crude, coarse, and comic.

So plausible did Long make the myth appear that only a few have challenged it. The most violent dissenters are the feminine members of the Long family, Huey's sisters, who survived him and have had to live with his legend. Although they recognize, with a realism common to the whole family, that politics sometimes compels its practitioners to exaggerate, they nonetheless feel that Huey, and also Earl, overplayed the theme of the log cabin. "Huey warped things for political reasons," said one of them with resigned resentment. Another said with an air of pride that only faintly concealed a sense of outrage: "We were taught to think that we were somebody, that we had a message, a purpose." The sisters are determined women—"They all should have been men," remarked a not unfriendly critic—and they have devoted a good deal of energy and time to collecting material showing that the family background was quite different from Huey's public version. Their research has been invaluable, and their version of the family's standing is more accurate than their brother's. But in their understandable zeal to redress the balance, they stress too much the other extreme. Huey's presentation was not completely wrong. There is much exaggeration but some truth in the Long myth, as is the case with most myths and with the pretensions of most American families.[7]

ON THE DAY before Christmas in 1859 John Murphy Long, a sturdy, blond man, whose dancing blue eyes evinced the gaiety within him, drove a team of oxen and a wagon into Winn parish in north-central

[6] Mildred Adams: "Huey the Great," *Forum*, LXXXIX (February 1933), 72.

[7] Charlotte Long Davis (Mrs. Robert Davis); Clara Long Knott (Mrs. W. M. Knott); Lucille Long Hunt (Mrs. Stewart Hunt); Olive Long Cooper (Mrs. E. R. Cooper).

Louisiana. With him were his wife and a brood of children that would eventually total fourteen. The Longs had come from Smith county, Mississippi, and now, bypassing the village of Winnfield, the parish seat, they were making for a settlement called Tunica, about five miles southeast, where a brother of John's, James D., and some other migrants from Smith county, had preceded them two years before. Late in the afternoon John halted his team. Both ox team and children needed a little rest, he announced. It had been a long trip from central Mississippi, at least 275 miles, over rough and wearing roads. The only excitement for the children had been the ferry crossing at Natchez. Eager to release their pent-up energies, the children now piled out of the wagon and played in a clearing near a large log house that was under construction. The third son, who was seven and a half years old, Huey Pierce Long (he would eventually become Huey Pierce Long, Sr.), would remember this house. Years later he would move his own family into it.

Shortly John Long collected his offspring and went on to Tunica. He had thought when he began his journey that he might go to Texas, but on reaching Tunica and finding his brother and other friends well settled, he decided to stay. He acquired title to some land and, like everybody else who had come to the community, turning to farming. Soon another brother, Michael, came out from Mississippi to join the colony, giving Tunica still more the character of a Long center. Even if John had considered leaving after that, he could not have moved. In 1861 the Civil War intervened, and all normal migration in the South was halted. The Longs would remain in Louisiana, and henceforth their life would be inextricably bound up in the strange and stark region that as a political subdivision was called Winn parish.[8]

Winn parish was a recent creation when John M. Long moved to it. It had been carved out of four adjoining parishes in 1852, as a result of the machinations of one of the most remarkable men in the area, Dennis Mackie, who was assisted by his brother Thomas and other associates. Dennis Mackie was born in Georgia of Irish extraction, and he and other members of his family had moved to

[8] Huey P. Long, Sr., quoted in John Klorer, ed.: *The New Louisiana* (New Orleans, 1936), pp. 20–1; Lucille Long Hunt; Clara Long Knott; Julius T. Long; Harley B. Bozeman. Mr. Bozeman, the historian of Winn parish, thinks that probably the Long family was traveling with a caravan of migrants from Mississippi. It is his surmise, and also mine, that John Long used oxen, the usual means of animal power at that time for journeys where many people and much equipment had to be transported. Tunica had been founded by Mississippians, who named the settlement for a Tunica in their home state.

Louisiana in the 1830's. He was probably the largest landowner in that part of the state, its recognized political boss, and a powerful and domineering personality (through marriage this strong Mackie blood would eventually enter the Long strain). Dennis and his associates decided that they could profit politically and economically by manipulating the creation of new parishes out of existing large ones, which would enable them to speculate in land titles, and they persuaded a compliant state legislature to authorize the formation of Winn. When representatives of the various settlements in the new parish began to squabble about where the seat of government should be located, Dennis characteristically stepped in to settle the argument. He proposed that the parish seat should be placed away from any community with a name, at a small and untitled spot which by a process that seemed logical became Winnfield. At the time of its creation the parish had a population of only 2,600 persons, but by the time John Long arrived, increasing migration had swelled the number to 5,700.[9]

Before the 1850's settlers had avoided the area because, for one reason, it had no nearby local government that could protect property rights. The formation of the parish undoubtedly helped stimulate immigration. But even the triple increase in population of the next decade was comparatively moderate for virtually an open frontier region. The main reason settlers shunned Winn was that it was known as poor farming country. Situated on the rim of the fertile Red River Valley, it was in what was then, and still is, called the Louisiana hill country. In its approximately 970 square miles there were some attractions—dense pine and hardwood forests, pleasant streams, expanses of prairie grass, and some rich river-bottom land. But most of its rolling surface was covered by a thin soil that shaded in color from reddish brown to gray, a type common to coastal plains. The environment of Winn was not conducive to a plantation economy, and although most of its inhabitants had come from other Southern states—Georgia, the Carolinas, Alabama, Mississippi—

[9] The parish was named after a central Louisiana figure of prominence. Local legend identifies at least three men who fit the role. It was probably Colonel Walter Winn of Alexandria. Harley B. Bozeman: "Winn Parish As I Have Known It," in *Winn Parish Enterprise*, June 2, 1960, January 3, 10, May 9, 1963; hereafter cited as Bozeman, in *Winn Parish Enterprise*. On October 2, 1956, Mr. Bozeman began writing a weekly article for the local newspaper; at the present date the series is still continuing. Partly personal reminiscence, partly conventional history, the articles form a valuable collection of information on Winnfield and Winn parish and on the Long family and the early life of Huey P. Long. See also *Winn Parish Enterprise*, Centennial Edition, 1952.

only a small number owned large tracts of land or many slaves. However, the parish counted in 1860 some two hundred slave-owners and something over a thousand Negroes. The majority of the whites were small farmers.[1]

All the whites, whatever their economic standing, were in a very real sense shut out of the mainstream of Southern culture. Scattered over a large rural area, isolated from more advanced centers and able to communicate with these only over poor roads and capricious rivers, and identified but lightly with the institution of slavery, the Winnians were different from most Southerners, and they thought differently. They manifested this separation in striking fashion in the secession crisis of 1860–1 and during the Civil War that followed. The Winn voters instructed their delegate to the Louisiana secession convention, David Pierson, to oppose all proposals to take the state out of the Union. Pierson was an usually able and attractive person. Of recent Georgia origin and only twenty-one years of age, he had become in a short time a leading lawyer and a popular political figure in Winn. Personally opposed to secession, he went to the convention with the added incentive of representing faithfully the wishes of his people. He was one of seventeen delegates who voted against the ordinance of secession and one of seven who even after it was passed refused to sign it. But then, although he believed that a tragic mistake had been made, he returned home to raise an infantry company to fight for the Confederate cause.

Pierson enlisted his unit and served throughout the war with distinction, and three and possibly five companies from Winn went into the Confederate or state home guard service. But it could not be said that the parish flamed into war fever once the issue was joined, as did other Southern hill areas that had opposed secession. Among the farmers there was a definite feeling that this was not their war, that it was, as one of them put it later, a fight for "the other man's niggers." Some of them remembered that rather than be conscripted into the Confederate army, they had "laid" out in the woods for long

[1] Robert O. Trout: "The People of the North Central Louisiana Hill Country" (unpublished Ph.D. dissertation, Louisiana State University, 1954), *passim*; John M. Price: "Slavery in Winn Parish," *Louisiana History*, VIII (1967), 137–48. The parish was somewhat larger in 1860 than it is today; then it included a part of present Grant parish. On the social configuration of Winn, see also Bozeman, in *Winn Parish Enterprise*, November 17, 1960; Roger W. Shugg: *Origins of Class Struggle in Louisiana* (Baton Rouge, 1939), p. 322. For an account of how a typical family from a Southern state, in this case Georgia, moved to Winn in this period, see John Pinckney Durham: *Biography of James Lucius Durham* (Shreveport, 1961), pp. 5–6, 82–3.

periods—joined, in a local phrase, the forces of "General Green." Their memories may have exaggerated somewhat the extent of opposition to the war. Still, it seems obvious that a large proportion of the population simply sat the war out and hoped for a Union victory. It was the first but it would not be the last time Winn parish would demonstrate that it was not afraid to dissent from the majority.[2]

One of the Winn dissenters was John M. Long. He did not enlist in the Confederate or state service, although his brothers James and Michael did—at least, for limited periods. The reasons John remained at home are not entirely clear, obscured by the vagueness of family legend and surviving evidence. Some members of the family would like to believe that he passively supported the Confederate cause, and that he avoided service because he was incapacitated by a hernia. They resent particularly an imputation that has gained some currency, that John was of the poor farmer class and opposed the war because he was jealous of the rich planters. This interpretation first appeared in an interview that his son, Huey P. Long, Sr., purportedly gave as an old man. According to the reporter's account, John and his whole family had a violent "poor white" psychology and burned with hatred for the aristocrats.[3]

The interview is open to a good deal of suspicion. Both the sentiments and the language of the speaker seem exaggerated and do not square with other statements made by Huey, Sr., or the known facts about his father. John Long was not a slaveholder or a planter, but neither was he a poor white. He was an average Southern farmer, and although it is very possible that during the war and after he indulged in the common complaint of his class that it was a rich man's war and a poor man's fight, the reasons for his abstention from the Confederate cause were other than economic. His Yankee ancestry may have had something to do with it. He was born in Springfield, Ohio, although his forebears were border-state Southern. His father, James, was from Maryland, where the first American Longs who can be identified appeared before the Revolution. These Maryland Longs were apparently people of some substance in

[2] Bozeman, in *Winn Parish Enterprise*, April 9, 1959, January 7, 1960, April 27, May 11, 1961; David Pierson to his father, W. N. Pierson, April 22, 1861, letter in possession of R. Hunter Pierson, Alexandria, La.; *Winn Parish Enterprise*, Centennial Edition, 1952; Ralph Wooster: "The Louisiana Secession Convention," *Louisiana Historical Quarterly*, XXXIV (1951), 103–33; Jefferson Davis Bragg: *Louisiana in the Confederacy* (Baton Rouge, 1941), pp. 61–2; James Rorty: "Callie Long's Boy Huey," *Forum*, XCIV (August 1935), 126.

[3] Clara Long Knott; Julius T. Long; Rorty: "Callie Long's Boy Huey," *Forum*, August 1935, p. 78.

Baltimore and properly were Episcopalians. James Long became a Methodist, however, and a minister of that faith as well. He was also a practicing physician, with a degree from a Baltimore college, but increasingly he subordinated his medical labors to his clerical ones. A preaching assignment caused him to leave Baltimore and go to "the West" (Ohio), and another call led him in 1841 to transfer to the South, to Smith county, Mississippi, where he reared his family and whence three of his sons emigrated to Louisiana.[4]

John M. Long was approximately sixteen years old when his father left Ohio, and apparently he had already developed strong nationalist attachments, which he continued to maintain against all Southern pressures. In another, more reliable, interview, Huey, Sr., touched on this likelier interpretation of his father's motivation: "He was a Yankee. He was with the North during the war, but he stayed here and kept his mouth shut." The implication was that John closed his mouth for fear of reprisals, as may have been the case, but he had also a personal reason for being prudent. His wife, a Wingate from Mississippi, was sympathetic to the Confederacy. They agreed that reticence on the part of both was the only way to preserve family tranquillity.[5]

There remains yet another possible explanation of John Long's course. Although entirely speculative, it is wholly plausible and probably closer to the truth than any other. It accords with the known nature of the Long family, with what might be called a Long way of acting, and it also resolves some of the apparent contradictions in the statements of Huey, Sr. If one quality stands out above others in the family over the years, it is a hard, cold realism. The Longs have never embraced romantic, quixotic, or lost causes—they have, in fact, been contemptuous of such causes. John Long certainly embodied this characteristic. What he thought about the war for Southern independence and what he probably said about it that his son remembered was that it was a foolish conflict started by foolish men who should have known that they could not win.

John Long lived until 1901, long enough to know for several years the grandson of his who would become one day as ruthless a winner as American politics has produced. Directly or indirectly he imparted to the boy something of his scorn of the Southern adventure

[4] Genealogical data based on church, legal, and census records, furnished by Clara Long Knott; family tree data, furnished by Lucille Long Hunt.
[5] Frederick W. Carr: "Huey Long's Father Relates the Story of the Senator's Boyhood," in *Christian Science Monitor*, September 11, 1935; Huey P. Long, Sr., quoted in Klorer, ed.: *The New Louisiana*, p. 21.

of the 1860's. It is of great significance that in his rise to power Huey P. Long, unlike other Southern politicians of his time, did not oratorically employ and exploit the Confederate tradition. In an era when most Southern politicans preferred to distract their audiences of rural poor with the magnificent irrelevancy of how their grandpappies had charged up the slope at Gettysburg, Long talked about crucial economic issues of the present. On the rare occasions when he did refer to the legend still cherished in Southern hearts, he spoke of it in mocking or humorous terms. Once in a Senate speech he boasted of his ancestors who had been "Southern patriots." They got to be patriots, he said, because the sheriff arrested them and forced them into Confederate service. He had other ancestors who had fought on the Northern side, he confessed, and he had some who had wanted to fight on both sides.[6]

Of John Long's numerous progeny, one is of particular interest to the historian. The third son, Huey Pierce Long, Sr.,[7] commands attention because he sired one of the most remarkable political families in America—one son, Huey P., Jr., who became a national figure; another, Earl K., who was the only three-time governor of Louisiana and a superb state politician; still another, George S., who was a member of the Oklahoma legislature and a Congressman from Louisiana; and a grandson, Russell B., the son of Huey, who succeeded to his father's seat in the Senate. Huey, Sr., although something of a figure in his own right, intrigues the historian as a symbol, as a case example of cause and effect. Why was his family so remarkable? Was it all the result of heredity? Or was it something arising out of the social and political climate of Winn parish—or was it pure accident?

Huey, Sr., was raised on his father's farm below Winnfield. He had litttle formal education, attending neighborhood schools at sporadic intervals and receiving a measure of private tutoring, most of it from his mother, who was a person of some education. As a youth, he nourished hopes of becoming a physician and saved money to enter medical school, but as the time of decision approached, a brother, George P. Long, who had become president of a Winnfield bank, cautioned him that doctors did not receive good incomes. While he hesitated, a family matter intervened to change his plans

[6] Forrest Davis: *Huey Long: A Candid Biography* (New York, 1935), p. 46 *n.*

[7] The name Huey was given in honor of a physician friend of John Long's in Mississippi, a Dr. Huey, and the name Pierce in honor of another local friend. Lucille Long Hunt; Carr: "Huey Long's Father," in *Christian Science Monitor*, September 11, 1935.

completely. John Long was a gay, friendly man who did not devote all his attention to farming. He liked people and spent much of his time in Winnfield, and he loved good horses and kept them and raced them at local meets. By an inevitable process, young Huey had gradually taken over the supervision of his father's farm. Then John became so ill that he had to retire from active work, and his son became the actual operator. Huey ran the farm expertly and made money, so much so that he soon was able to acquire tracts of land of his own, and finding that he liked farming, he settled into it as a career.[8]

He did well because he realized the limits of farming in the parish. There were two kinds of farmers in Winn—"row-crop" men and stockmen. The first went in for cotton, the second for hogs and cattle. The cotton men had their troubles. The soil, except on the river bottoms, would not produce good crops, and in the years after the Civil War, when the world price of cotton fluctuated madly, cotton producers found it difficult to show a consistent profit even on fertile soil. Huey was a stockman. He ran hundreds of cattle and hogs on his lands, letting the animals feed in the woods during the long warm months and during the winter providing them with corn, which he raised himself. He also grew various vegetables for home consumption, and being one of the few fruit fanciers in the parish, he experimented with orchards—apple, pear, and peach. He was, like his father, a lover of fine horses, and he maintained several, including the first blooded stallion in the area.[9]

Forced to take on a man's work at an early age, Huey matured rapidly in character and appearance. He was one of those individuals who because of their bearing and manner always seem older than they are. People who knew him referred to him (the surviving ones still do) as "Uncle Hugh," "Mr. Hugh," but usually, "Old Hugh." Whatever the title, they nearly always spell it Hu. Six feet in height, big-boned (although his hands and feet were small), with gold-brown hair that later turned iron-gray, and with flashing brown eyes, he was undeniably an impressive figure of a man. With this fine presence and his roaring voice he dominated any group he was in. One man who knew him said: "You always knew two blocks before you got there that he was there." But the respect that he commanded was based on more than appearance and vocal volume. Even people who

[8] Mrs. Robert Parrott; Clara Long Knott; Bozeman, in *Winn Parish Enterprise*, July 11, 1957.
[9] Jesse Roberts, H. P. Long's caretaker; Matt Milam, Sr.; Charlotte Long Davis; Lucille Long Hunt; Julius T. Long.

privately professed otherwise publicly accepted his leadership. Any-body who talked with Old Hu could recognize that although the discipline of a formal education was lacking, he had an extremely keen intelligence, coupled with a friendly and ingratiating personality. But a perceptive observer would also note that under the surface there were strains of passion, violence, and power that might at any time erupt to dominate lesser men.[1]

Soon after he started farming on his own, Old Hu felt well enough established to take a wife. In 1875 he married fifteen-year-old Caledonia Tison, also of Winn parish. Five feet five inches tall but weighing less than a hundred pounds, with large hazel eyes set in a face framed by coal-black hair, she looked very much like the child that she was. Her parents had died, and she was living with two half-sisters when Hu married her. He was moved as much by pity for her as by love. According to one account, after the ceremony they rode off on a mule, she sitting behind and clinging to him, which may be true, but which seems odd in view of Hu's penchant for fine horses.[2]

The marriage brought a number of disparate and important strains into the Long line of descent. Caledonia Tison's mother was an Albright (probably originally Albrecht), and other names in her ancestral cluster were Vince (French Huguenot), Fleming, and Mackie. The Tisons and Albrights had been in Louisiana much longer than the Longs, arriving there before 1820, and were a cut higher economically, having risen to the status of slaveholders. Although several religious denominations were represented in Caledonia's forebears, she herself was a Baptist, as Old Hu's mother had been. He too adhered to that church, and Baptist doctrine henceforth became the faith of the Longs.

Old Hu cherished his genteel wife, but he never indicated in the slightest way that he was overcome by her more impressive background. He rendered to such a matter as aristocratic ancestry a typical Long deference—which was to give it as much respect as it deserved. He did like to say, when his children revealed a common quality of stubborn combativeness, that they must have got it from the Mackies. Anybody who had a drop of Mackie blood wanted to be boss, opined Old Hu. He spoke more mischievously than seri-

[1] Lucille Long Hunt; confidential communication; Rorty: "Callie Long's Boy Huey," *Forum*, August 1935, p. 78; Carr: "Huey Long's Father," in *Christian Science Monitor*, September 11, 1935.

[2] Lucille Long Hunt; Clara Long Knott; W. M. Hallack; H. P. Long, Sr., quoted in Klorer, ed.: *The New Louisiana*, p. 21; confidential communication.

ously. Himself an expert at bossing, he knew exactly from whom his offspring had inherited their domineering spirit. His famous son would later refer to other aspects of the family background in the same bantering spirit. The Longs were an amalgam of almost every blood in America—English, Scotch, Irish, German, French—Huey P. Long frequently reminded the voters. He knew that his audiences would recognize this ethnic boasting for what he meant it to be—a bit of captivating political byplay. But it became too much for his older brother Julius, who had an inordinate amount of Long belligerence but an un-Longlike streak of seriousness. Julius sneered that Huey would claim he had Negro blood if he thought it would get him any colored votes in the North.[3]

This brother Julius, who would have a pervasive influence on the early career of Huey, was the second of four children born to Old Hu and Caledonia on the farm southeast of Winnfield. The others were a sister, Charlotte, the oldest child, another sister, Helen, who died in infancy, and another brother, George. As his family grew, Hu expanded his landholdings. In 1886 he bought 320 acres of a tract near Winnfield (part of the present city of Winnfield is located on his property) and moved his family there, onto what was known as the Pipes property and, by an interesting coincidence, into the log house that he remembered having passed as a boy in 1859. The place had been developed by David Pipes, a wealthy sugar planter from West Baton Rouge parish, who in the Civil War had "refugeed" farther north when the Federals occupied south Louisiana. There, by another interesting twist of history, David Pierson, the secession convention delegate whose views on the war coincided so closely with those of the Longs, met and married a Pipes girl. Eventually the estate passed into other hands, and it was the southern half of it that Old Hu purchased, from a man named Little.

The log house was a large and sturdy structure and would have been a comfortable place had it not been very drafty. One of the Long girls remembers it as the "biggest, coldest house" she ever saw. Built of split logs, it had a center hall twelve feet wide, with two rooms on either side and an L-shaped back wing, containing a kitchen and a dining room. Three more Long children were born in

---

[3] Genealogical data, furnished by Clara Long Knott; family tree data, furnished by Lucille Long Hunt; Lucille Long Hunt; Harley B. Bozeman; Julius T. Long: "What I Know About My Brother, United States Senator Huey Long," *Real America*, II (September 1933), 34–7; ["Scaramouche"]: "Senator Huey P. Long, Clown and Knave," *Real America*, I (July 1933), 71.

this house, two girls, Olive and Clara, and on August 30, 1893, a boy who was given the name of his father. Huey P. Long, Jr., could legitimately utter the politician's stock boast, that he had been born in a log house. But he was not consistent in his descriptions of the dwelling. Writing in his autobiography, he said correctly that it was a "comfortable, well-built" house. In his speeches over the years, however, it appeared as something quite different, something much more humble. And then, after his death, admiring orators decreased its size even more than he had. Finally, when a speaker at a dedication ceremony in his honor made the expected reference, one of his sisters snorted and remarked audibly: "Every time I hear of that cabin it gets smaller and smaller.[4]

Its very size, as a matter of fact, coupled with its style of construction, made the log house difficult to heat. Mrs. Long especially, who was small and frail, suffered from the drafts that whistled through the walls in the winter. Therefore, about a year after Huey's birth, Old Hu moved the family to a new house that he had had built on the same property, a smaller but warmer structure, which is remembered in the family as the "salt-box" house. Here the Longs lived for thirteen years, and here three more children were born, Earl, Caledonia, and Lucille. Then in 1907 Hu moved the salt-box house to another location and built on its site a large, graceful colonial-style house of two stories and ten rooms. It was one of the most impressive residences in Winnfield.[5]

Old Hu was able to build such a house because he prospered after moving to Winnfield. His increased affluence was tied up with the growth of the town. At the turn of the century Winnfield entered a period still remembered there today as the boom years. In 1901 the Arkansas Southern Railroad extended its line to the town, locating its depot on Old Hu's property, and other roads soon followed, giving Winnfield and the parish for the first time adequate connections with outside markets. Lumber companies came in to exploit the area's rich timber resources and built their noisy sawmills and their ugly towns. The result of all this economic expansion was a movement of people

[4] Harley B. Bozeman; R. Hunter Pierson; Julius T. Long; Lucille Long Hunt; Clara Long Knott; H. P. Long, Sr., quoted in Klorer, ed.: *The New Louisiana*, p. 20; Huey P. Long: *Every Man a King* (New Orleans, 1933), p. 2. Long confused the date of the family's move to Winnfield, putting it in 1892. The house where he was born is no longer standing.

[5] Lucille Long Hunt; Clara Long Knott; Rupert S. Whitley; Jess Nugent; Bozeman, in *Winn Parish Enterprise*, July 11, 1957. The colonial-style house was destroyed by fire in the 1920's. The "salt box" stood until about 1962, when it was torn down to enlarge the Earl K. Long State Memorial Park.

from other parishes into Winn and a movement of people within the parish into the principal town, Winnfield. As the population grew, so did the demand for homes, and Old Hu, holding property in the area toward which the town would logically grow, was able to dispose of parts of it as residential subdivisions at good prices. In 1900, when the boom began, he owned 348 acres in the parish. The parish assessment rolls for that year listed eighteen Longs as landowners, the largest holder being George, the Winnfield bank president, with 2,300 acres.[6]

Very few families in Winn owned more land than the Longs. (One was the Millings, a clan that the Longs had some argument with at an early date, causing thereafter every Long to mark every Milling as an enemy to be destroyed.) Nor did any family live any better or more proudly. Old Hu and his wife were proud that they had a big house, that they set a good table, and that they were financially independent. They were even prouder that they were people who had genuine intellectual pretensions, who read books and magazines, and who talked about things they read. It was a mark of distinction in Winnfield to read anything beyond a newspaper. Books and magazines were hard to come by. The town had no library, and only a few families owned many books. The Longs were among the literary elite. According to the memories of surviving family members, they had access to the works of Shakespeare, Dickens, Poe, and other English and American classics, and to such periodicals as the *Saturday Evening Post*, the *Progressive Farmer*, and the *Youth's Companion*. The most often-read book was the Bible, if only because Mrs. Long insisted on reading aloud from it at evening gatherings. Second in popularity was a history of the world by John Clark Ridpath. A colorful although superficial work, it stressed the role of powerful leaders. It became one of the favorites of young Huey, who also manifested a consuming interest in a biography of Napoleon.

Old Hu exercised a close and prideful supervision over the family's reading. At meals he would lead off a discussion of some book then being passed around or steer the conversation into a political argument, encouraging everybody present to speak his mind. He wanted his children to be educated, he would say, and not like those of the common people who lived on Cohobbin or, as he preferred to call it, Cohabiting Street. He was insistent that every one of his children get some kind of college education, and he helped each on the way as much as he could. Julius attended Louisiana Polytechnic In-

---

[6] Winn parish assessment rolls, 1900, in state capitol, Baton Rouge.

stitute at Ruston and Tulane University. George received a dental degree from an institution in Quincy, Illinois. Huey spent brief interludes at the University of Oklahoma and Tulane. Earl, who came of college age when his father had more money than when Julius and Huey were young, went to Polytechnic, Louisiana State University, and Loyola University in New Orleans. All the girls took the two-year teacher training course at the state normal school at Natchitoches, and all taught in secondary or grade schools for varying periods. One, Olive, eventually received a master's degree from Columbia University and became a member of the faculty of the normal school (now Northwestern State College at Natchitoches, La.).[7]

The owners of wide acres and a big house, known as good providers and good hosts, and people of culture—the Longs stood high in Winn parish. But it would be a mistake to read too much into their status. In a richer parish, a plantation area, a family like the Longs would have occupied a lower position, would have been ranked in the middle class. Old Hu owned a fair amount of property, and from that property he was able to furnish his family with a good living, a measure of creature comforts, and a few luxuries. He did it by producing on his land nearly everything the family needed, buying almost nothing. He had little to buy with. His only consistent cash income came from the sale of his cattle and hogs, and usually it was small. In operating on a slender economic margin, Old Hu was no different from thousands of other farmers in the South in the years between the close of the Civil War and the turn of the century. He was different only in that he made a go of it. Most farmers found it difficult to turn any kind of profit, and many lapsed into tenantry or sought employment in the sawmills or other newly born industries. Thus in Louisiana and throughout the South the number of small farms owned by their operators decreased, and the number of large plantations and tenants increased. Winn, for instance, counted 209 farms of under fifty acres in 1860, but only 53 in 1880; in the same span, the number of plantations of over 500 acres jumped from 3 to 120.[8]

Farmers in Winn, with its thin soil, had a rougher time than those in most other parishes. Even by the standards of rural Louisiana, Winn was poor—pathetically, almost sensationally poor, so

[7] Confidential communications; Fred Francis; Jess Nugent; Clara Long Knott; Lucille Long Hunt; Charlotte Long Davis. Here it may be noted that one of the sisters, Caledonia, later was stricken with tuberculosis and had to move to the West, hence leaving the Long story.

[8] Shugg: *Origins of Class Struggle*, pp. 241, 269, 326–7.

much so that its condition became a byword in the state. "Over there," said a later condescending critic from a plantation parish, "any woman who had seven or eight hens and a cow could support a husband." The people had a wry saying about their poverty—they said they made a living by taking in each other's washing. But they did not accept their lot as something ordained by higher economic law or by people higher on the economic scale; they did not see it as something that had to be endured without complaint. They were Winnians, and, like their ancestors of the Civil War period, they were entirely ready to dissent from established views and, if the need arose, to embark on new and rebellious political paths. The need seemed acute in the depression-ridden 1890's, whose hard times struck with special fierceness the farmers of the South and the prairie West. In those sections a third party, the Populist, or People's, party, emerged to speak for the agricultural interests and to win large numbers of supporters. Appealing frankly to the farmers' sense of class identity, the Populists just as frankly proposed a radical remedy for the economic ills of the time—a program of national governmental control over the economy. Nothing like Populism had appeared before in American politics, and its doctrine frightened conservative people everywhere, including some farmers. But as extreme as it appeared, the new party did not repel the farmers of Winn. They hailed it as a savior and embraced it with a religious fervor. The parish became the center of Populist strength in the state and furnished most of the party's leaders. In the election of 1892 the Populist candidate for governor was a resident of Winnfield. He swept the parish by a margin of almost five to one, though failing in the state, and the Populists carried every election in Winn until 1900, when the party went out of existence.[9]

Old Hu did not join the Populist movement, nor apparently did any Long, except a great-uncle of Huey's. At first thought, it would seem natural and logical that the Longs should be Populists, for this allegiance would fit in neatly with the Long legend—Huey, the great representative of the family and the bitter foe of the big corporations, carrying on the democratic tradition of his father and his parish. But the truth of history is never that neat or simple. Nor were the Longs simple people. The reasons why they did not adhere to Populism have to be conjectured. It is possible that Old Hu, somewhat more prosperous than the mass of farmers, simply was not at-

[9] Confidential communications; Lucia Elizabeth Daniel: "The Louisiana People's Party," *Louisiana Historical Quarterly,* XXVI (1943), 1077, 1127; *Winn Parish Enterprise,* Centennial Edition, 1952.

tracted by the tenets of the third party. It is more probable that with
the usual Long realism, he avoided association with a movement that
he realized would ultimately have to fail—or with a party that was
not smart enough to ask him to be one of its leaders. If he did not
support Populism, neither did he prominently oppose it. He sympathized, in fact, with its broad philosophy and its broad purposes.
Young Huey Long, as he grew up, heard plenty of Populist talk,
some of it from his father, more from other elders in Winnfield. The
things he heard subtly shaped his own thinking. He knew that in
significant ways Winn was different from most other parishes in
Louisiana, that it had an unequaled record for dissent and that it was
poorer than other parishes. If his own family was well-to-do by Winn
standards, he came to realize that those standards were not those of
the aristocrats of the plantation belt or of New Orleans and other
cities. He came to realize too—and it is impossible to say what effect
the knowledge had on his inner self—that patrician Louisianians
would regard him as a hillbilly or a hick, as somebody who did not
quite belong. In the caste society of the South, he and everybody
else in Winn stood outside, perhaps not very far, but still outside the
select circle. The fact is of vital importance in explaining him, what
he became and what he did. If he sometimes seemed to hate rich
people, if he often tried to humiliate them, if he always advocated
programs that struck at their interests, the explanation lies in part
in his family's place in the stratified social order of his state and his
section. The myth that he created about his early environment reflected his awareness of his status, and it was not entirely without
foundation.

# CHAPTER 2

# *There He Goes Again*

O N A DAY IN LATE DECEMBER 1905, fourteen-year-old Harley Bozeman went into the Grand Leader Dry Goods store, one of the leading emporiums of Winnfield, to buy some shoes. Young Bozeman's family was moving to the parish seat from the smaller town of Dodson, and as yet he knew few people in the new location. He had looked at several pairs of shoes and was on the point of buying one that the clerk assured him was waterproof when he heard a voice say: "Hold on, don't buy that pair of shoes, unless you want to get cheated." He looked up and saw a boy with frizzly hair, slightly younger and smaller than himself. The clerk, in a rage, bellowed at the boy to get out and leave his customers alone, then turning to Bozeman said: "Don't pay any attention to him. That's nobody except little Huey Long, who is always butting in, where he has no business." The nobody stood his ground, however, and stated positively that he knew the shoes would leak. Bozeman finally bought them, largely because he feared that if he did not the clerk would bodily throw little Huey out of the store. This eased the situation, but Huey did not stop talking. He fired a volley of questions at Bozeman: What's your name? That your new house being built on our old field? What grade you in? What books 've you read? Bozeman, who would become Huey's closest friend in Winnfield, left this first meeting with feelings of incredulity and uneasy admiration. It was the reaction that most people experienced when they met Huey Long as a boy.[1]

[1] Bozeman, in *Winn Parish Enterprise*, January 24, 1957.

People who knew him then, whether they were in his own age group or older, have some trouble when they try to describe what he was like. They say that he was intelligent, "bright," extremely active, and always interesting. They also say other things that are not so complimentary. A schoolmate rolled off the following characterization: "Belligerent, ornery, that's the best word, disputatious, officious, bossy, a show-off." A man who was a young lawyer in Winnfield in the early 1900's confirms the show-off label. He relates that a circus came to town when Huey was twelve years old. Everybody was watching the parade and, with especially rapt attention, the elephants. It was too much for Huey, who ran out on the street, got a stone, and threw it at one of the animals. "He would do anything to attract even unfavorable attention," concluded this individual. Everybody agrees. "If Huey couldn't pitch, he wouldn't play," is a common saying in Winnfield. Everybody agrees too that he could be highly irritating, that he was, in a phrase of the town mothers, "a pesterance." Most of those who attempt to describe him end helplessly by saying: "He was just different."[2]

Without fully appreciating it, his contemporaries touch on one of the qualities that made him different—a feverish and almost abnormal energy, united with an encompassing curiosity. Huey Long walked at the age of nine months. But before he could walk, he would, if left alone, roll off the porch of the Long home, crawl to the gate of the yard, and climb up and by some means unlatch it. (It became a saying in the family that he had a gift for undoing things meant to restrain him.) Once outside he sat on the side of the road and solemnly observed passers-by. Whenever it was discovered that he had escaped, his mother would shout at Olive, the sister designated to watch him, "Run, Ollie, run! There he goes again!"

After he learned to walk, he went everywhere. He was eight years old when the first train came to Winnfield, and he commemorated the event by crawling under one of the cars to inspect it. The train had to be held up until he was liberated. Not impressed by the trouble he had created, he continued to examine other trains from the underside. It became a regular feature of life in Winnfield to see Huey Long pulled out from beneath a car by somebody. A relative once told Mrs. Long that a good whipping would cure the habit. She replied that she would have to whip him to death to stop him.

[2] Confidential communications; James Rorty: "Callie Long's Boy Huey," *Forum,* XCIV (August 1933), 127; Bozeman, in *Winn Parish Enterprise,* July 11, 1957.

His younger brother Earl, who sometimes accompanied him to the trains but never crawled under, recalled: "He was nervous, curious about everything. Our father used to say that he'd jump in the well to see what it was like if it wasn't kept covered. He wouldn't stay still." Every member of the family stresses this intense desire to find out about everything and the excessive energy that he threw into every activity. Huey ran to school, he ran back from school, he ran to play, and twice he ran away from home, once going all the way to Alexandria, fifty miles, on the train.[3]

Although his enterprise led him into many activities not attempted by other boys, and into some dangerous spots, it did not impel him into physical fights with his fellows. On the contrary, he avoided such encounters, often precipitately leaving the scene. The testimony on this point is almost universal and is so strong that out of it has grown a myth that Huey Long was a physical coward all the years of his life, as a boy and also as a man. As governor and senator, he was customarily surrounded by bodyguards, and one speculation is that he had them merely because he feared somebody would attempt to lay hands on him. But even as a boy, some people say, he resorted to the device of a protector—he induced his brother Earl, two years younger but heavier and stronger, to do his fighting for him. According to Julius Long, Huey would start fights by insulting other boys and then leave the actual battling to Earl. On one occasion, Julius recalled, two larger boys who had suffered the sting of Huey's tongue cornered him and proceeded to give him a sound drubbing. Suddenly Earl appeared with a broomstick and lit into the assailants, who turned their attention to him. In a lull in the engagement Earl looked around to find what support Huey was providing. He saw Huey disappearing down the road in a cloud of dust.[4]

There is no doubt that Earl intervened in numerous affairs to protect Huey. The two boys, close in age in a large family that contained many older brothers and sisters, had an unusually intimate relationship. They slept together, played together, and acted together generally, with Huey, quick and daring, playing the part of

[3] Mrs. Robert Parrott; Charlotte Long Davis; Lucille Long Hunt; George S. Long, quoted in Harvey G. Fields: *A True History of the Life, Works, Assassination and Death of Huey P. Long* (Silver Spring, Md., 1944), p. 23; Earl K. Long, as recorded in "Earl Long: Last of the Red Hot Papas," edited by Brooks Read and Bud Hebert (News Records, Inc., Baton Rouge). All statements hereafter attributed to Earl Long are from this recording or additional recordings made available to me by the editors.

[4] Confidential communications; Julius T. Long: "What I Know About My Brother," *Real America*, II (September 1933), 39.

planner and leader, and Earl, slower mentally but abler physically, being the follower and the executor. Earl fought for Huey out of sheer admiration and perhaps because fighting was the one thing he could do better than his dominating brother. But Huey did not have to persuade Earl to fight. Earl fought for the sheer pleasure of combat, with savage and joyful passion. He delighted in the clash of bodies, and he battled with every weapon in his possession, including his teeth. Earl was the same way all the years of his active life. Even as a mature leader, he would fly into uncontrollable rages, leading into unplanned conflicts that sometimes ended as physical encounters. He thereby violated one of the cardinal rules of the politician—never quarrel in anger; if you quarrel, do it deliberately, with a cool head and steady courage.

It is significant that the adult Huey Long, although he was not above using Earl's bellicose talents to his own advantage, always expressed condescending amusement at his brother's antics. "Earl been fighting again?" he would ask, as if to say: Why should anyone be fool enough to fight when he can get what he wants without doing it? His attitude as a boy, though not fully rationalized, was much the same. He simply saw no need, in most situations, to engage in physical combat. Whether this reluctance constituted cowardice or an ability, rare in one of his years, to plan for advantage to self, is a matter of definition. "He wasn't a coward," insisted one of his sisters; "he just got bored and walked off." "Huey did not believe in physical violence," argued a man who knew him intimately from youth. Perhaps Earl Long, who had a peculiar knowledge of the problem, best understood Huey's attitude. "I don't think Huey liked to fight, " said Earl.[5]

But on one occasion Huey did fight, long and gamely and fiercely, and the story of that battle confounds the myth that he always ran away from combat. When he was fifteen, he worked up a great crush on a girl in his class. Every afternoon he would wait for her to come out from school and would take her books and walk her home. The affair progressed tenderly until another boy, Harry Davis, set his eyes on the girl. One day, while Huey yearned in the yard, Davis went inside the building and emerged with the girl and her books. The later Huey would have admired such enterprise in an adversary. But the young Huey knew only jealous fury. He bumped Davis, the schoolboy's traditional challenge to battle, and then struck him—and received a prompt blow in return. Before the engagement

[5] Lucille Long Hunt; Rose Long McFarland (Mrs. Osman McFarland); Mrs. Robert Parrott; Earl K. Long; Charles L. Smith; Jess Nugent.

could develop further, an older boy proposed that the rivals settle their difference in a boxing bout in the school gymnasium the next day. A formal meeting would be more dignified, he suggested, and tickets could be sold and the participants could split the proceeds.

Everybody in school bought a ticket, including the girl for whose favor Huey and Davis were willing to battle. They were to fight, according to the rules laid down by the arranger of the encounter, who also acted as referee, with bare knuckles and for twenty rounds of three minutes each, with a minute's rest between rounds. Although the bout had been set up with great regard for the conventions of scientific boxing, it was surely one of the most unscientific meetings in pugilistic history. Each contestant thought only of hitting the other and evinced no interest in protecting himself. For ten rounds they took turns knocking one another down. They spent, in fact, more time on the floor than upright. Finally, at the end of the tenth round, when the combatants, bloody and bruised of face, could barely stand, the referee stopped the fight, announcing that it was a draw. The aftermath was enough to make even a less introspective person than Huey cynical about letting passion rule him. The girl stopped dating both boys and two years later married a third one. And the referee, after giving a part of the proceeds to the school baseball team, pocketed the major share for his services. All Winnfield laughed at the two boys who had fought so gallantly—for nothing.[6]

The Winnfield of Huey's youth was a small enough place to take delighted notice of such an episode as a fight between two boys. Not that Winnfield considered itself small or provincial. An unincorporated village with an undetermined population before 1900, it experienced a healthy growth in the boom years when the railroads and the sawmills moved in. This expansion slowed somewhat after 1907, largely because the lumber companies, having exhausted the timber reserves, transferred operations to other areas; but although the town's physical development, as measured by the construction of business buildings, came to a halt, its human resources continued to increase. By the end of the decade Winnfield could boast of a population of 2,900 persons. And there were other things to be proud of—two hotels, one of the largest lumber mills in the state, a stave manufacturing plant, a brickyard, and seven brick buildings in the business district.

These were the material signs of the town's status in the parish,

[6] Meigs O. Frost, article in New Orleans *States*, January 4, 1931; Harry Davis.

the tokens that indicated it was the metropolis of Winn. There were others that pointed up that it was also the political and cultural center. It was the parish seat, the courthouse town. It contained a flourishing bar of able lawyers. It had stores that specialized in the sale of one or two products, such as shoes or drygoods. It had drugstores, a "photographic gallery" presided over by a professional "picture taker," a weekly newspaper called the *Southern Sentinel*, poolrooms, and restaurants. The restaurants listed "chili con carne" as their chief culinary delicacy, and young bloods of Huey's age thought it was the height of urban elegance to saunter into one of the eateries and order "a chili."

Winnfield boosters could have bragged of another urban quality, although this was one they usually chose to ignore. The town had a more cosmopolitan population than any other in the parish—a half dozen Italian families, who operated fruit stands; two hundred Mexican laborers, who had been imported to work on the railroads or in the sawmills; one or two Jewish businessmen; two clans of Syrian foot peddlers, who appeared on the streets at regular intervals to hawk their exotic wares; a few French "Cajuns" from South Louisiana; and several Chinese, who ran a laundry. These groups constituted patches of alien and colorful culture affixed to the predominantly Anglo-Saxon, Protestant surface of Winnfield. They intrigued the natives, without necessarily awakening feelings of understanding or respect. The most common reactions to them were amusement and perplexity. Huey Long, having heard that Chinese regarded rats as the finest food, once trundled a wheelbarrow full of dead rodents down to the Chinese laundry and offered to sell them to the proprietor. He was utterly astounded when the Oriental chased him out of the shop, brandishing a flatiron and screaming: "Git out, git out. Chinee no eat rats."

But despite some undeniable advantages, Winnfield was, for all its pretensions, a small, drab, provincial, Southern town, differing only in detail from hundreds of others scattered over the region. It might brag about its seven brick buildings in the business district, but most of its stores and shops were housed in frame edifices, and some in nothing more than tents. In no part of the town were there any concrete sidewalks. People walked on the dirt or sand streets, which in rainy weather became deep with mud. At all times they had to dodge the cows, hogs, and goats that ran the streets, for Winnfield had no stock law regulating the enclosure of animals. As there was no municipal water system, each home had to have its own well or cistern. Neither was there a public utility system. The only electric lights were in a few stores, the current being provided by one of the lumber companies.

Residents of Winnfield hardly ever traveled very far from it. They had little direct knowledge of the outside world and were incredulous of those of its marvels that came within their confines—the first automobile or ice-cream cone or telephone. When the first telephone was installed in town, in a store, some boys incited Huey to go in and try it. Curious as always, he entered and took down the receiver. "Number, please," came the voice of the operator. "I just wanted to see how it sounds," Huey answered. "Sounds funny, don't it? Goodbye." Such a boy as Huey—inquisitive, original, intellectually curious—could find entertainment in observing Winnfield, and by studying its people he could, as sharp small-town boys have always done, learn a lot about people. But he could not get from the town itself the things he really wanted—intellectual stimulation, a knowledge of the larger society around him and its ways, and some intimation of how a boy from Winnfield might ascend to that society. These he would have to extract from other sources, from, as a beginning, books and school.[7]

IN EVERYTHING THAT has been written about Huey Long there are immense contradictions about every aspect of his life. They appear even in discussions of what he read as a child and a youth. People who knew him well, like political and personal associates and knowing reporters, reproduce the same disagreement—Huey read much and widely; no, Huey read little except newspapers, magazines, and law books until he entered the Senate. Condescending patricians sniff that the man was an ignoramus who stole his knowledge of what was in books, as he did everything else, from other people. Long himself added to the confusing testimonies, in typical fashion, by stating at different times differing estimates of what he had read. But he never neglected to say that his main literary fare had always been the Bible. "I don't know how many times I've read it through," he would muse. Some would deny him the mastery of even this one book. Julius Long

[7] Bozeman, in *Winn Parish Enterprise*, November 1, 1956, January 31, February 7, 14, and 28, March 14 and 28, May 9, November 21, 1957, February 20, 1958; George M. Wallace. It is necessary to say, in fairness to Mr. Bozeman, whose valuable articles form the basis for the above sketch, that he would not agree with much of the characterization of Winnfield.

always insisted that all Huey knew of the Bible was what he had heard their mother read at family gatherings.[8]

It is now possible to speak with authority on the nature of Huey's reading. The evidence is available—indeed, some of it was before— and it comes down on the side of those who have thought that he read a great deal, that he was, in fact, for his time and place, an exceptionally well-read man. Although it is impossible to pinpoint everything that he read, most of the items can be identified, and the influence of some of them upon him can be fairly speculated. Every book that he read he went through rapidly and easily. "Huey could tell what was in a book fast," one of his sisters recalled. "I never saw him study." He read wherever he could find a relatively quiet spot, in his room or on the end of the porch, and, in his characteristically nervous way, he often read while walking around town or in the woods.[9]

A more acute problem than finding a place to read was finding books. Neither the town nor the high school had a library in Huey's youth, and a boy who wanted to delve into the wonders of literature had to go to some trouble to locate material. Huey was fortunate in that he could utilize the not inconsiderable resources of the family library, and he was also able to borrow some books from other families. But he took advantage of every opportunity to add to his hoard. He once heard that a man near the neighboring town of Sikes had a set of James Fenimore Cooper's *Leatherstocking Tales* that he would give to anybody who would carry them away, and young Long, in Abraham Lincoln fashion, made his way there and collected the volumes in a wheelbarrow.

A new and abundant source opened when his brother Julius, fourteen years older, enrolled at Louisiana Polytechnic. Julius believed in reading, and when he came home on weekends he would bring books from the school library. Although Julius was proud that all members of the family would read the books, he took special pride in the aptitude of his bright younger brother, and Huey, who idolized Julius and tried to imitate him in every way, devoured every book that Julius recommended. Thus from an early age Huey had access to a wide and fairly good literary selection. It is certain that he read the following works and authors—the Ridpath multi-volumed *History of the World*; Shakespeare, Dickens, Poe, Longfellow, and Balzac; Scott's *Ivanhoe*, Goldsmith's *The Deserted*

[8] Confidential communication; Frost, article in New Orleans *States*, August 28, 1927; Hermann B. Deutsch, column, ibid., February 25, 1959; Julius T. Long.
[9] Charlotte Long Davis.

*Village*, and Hugo's *Les Miserables*; the lurid novels of the Reconstruction period by Thomas Dixon, *The Klansmen* and *The Leopard's Spots*; the writings of the Jewish historian Josephus; Alexandre Dumas's *The Count of Monte Cristo*; the poem "Invictus," by William E. Henley; the autobiography of the sixteenth-century Florentine artist, Benvenuto Cellini; and biographies of Napoleon and Julius Caesar.[1]

It is not so certain, however, how old he was when he read some of these works, especially those that might be called the more mature items. These he probably got into in 1908, when he was approaching fifteen. That year a Texas book dealer came to Winnfield with a collection ranging from trashy books to the finest literary and scholarly works and proceeded to sell the volumes at daily public auctions. Huey and Harley Bozeman, who was also an eager reader, immediately induced the dealer to hire them as his assistants, agreeing to take their pay in books. When the Texan closed out his Winnfield stand, he left a bulky consignment of books to the two boys. That summer they tried to peddle them in the small towns of central Louisiana, carrying their wares from door to door or hawking them at auction. Success was small until Huey traded someone a book for a mandolin. He explained to Bozeman that he could play the instrument well enough to get by, and that by singing as he played, he could attract larger crowds to the auctions. Thereafter the boys would set up shop in front of a country store, and Huey would break into "Pretty Red Wing," "Old Black Joe," or some other song that he knew and thought his auditors would like. As he had foreseen, the crowds came, and soon the young merchants were able to dispose of most of their stock. They had a nice profit for their summer's work, and, more important, they had had access to some good books that otherwise they would never have seen. They had read all the books consigned to them, and they kept some volumes that they considered especially intriguing for future study.[2]

Certain books appealed to the young Huey more than others. He read them over and over, and being easily able to photograph mentally whole pages of a printed work, he memorized long sections of them and carried their import with him all his life. Although the books did influence his thinking, they cannot be credited with shaping him into what he became. He seemed already to know what he would become, and he sought to learn from the books a knowledge

[1] Clara Long Knott; Lucille Long Hunt; Charlotte Long Davis; Julius T. Long; Harley B. Bozeman; Fields: *Long*, p. 14.
[2] Bozeman, in *Winn Parish Enterprise*, July 25, 1957; Edmund E. Talbot.

of the crafts that would help him on his way. He was fascinated with anything that dealt with personal power, with the strong leader and with the techniques of leadership—such as every book about Napoleon he could lay hands on, the autobiography of Cellini, and the Ridpath history, which also emphasized the social evil inherent in concentrated wealth. He gloried in the indomitable hero of Henley's "Invictus" and seized on every occasion to proclaim: "I am the master of my fate, I am the captain of my soul." At some point— it is impossible to say exactly when—he read a good deal about the history of the Reconstruction period in Louisiana and about the carpetbag governor, Henry Clay Warmoth, a minor political genius who for a period ruled the state with almost dictatorial authority.

But by far his favorite work was *The Count of Monte Cristo*, whose hero meted out harsh revenge to all his enemies. Years later, when he was a United States senator he was walking down a street in New York City with a friend and spied the book in the window of a shop. He announced that he was going in to buy a copy and asked the friend if he wanted one. This man replied that he had read the book as a boy. "I read it then too," Huey said, "but I read it every year. That man in that book knew how to hate and until you learn how to hate you'll never get anywhere in this world."[3] He understood, and apparently at an early age, one of the qualities that a leader who hopes to move the masses must have—a capacity to hate his opponents, or to seem to hate them and act as if he did, being in either case able to destroy them.

The boy Huey may have had only a dim perception that his destiny was to lead others, but deliberately or not he read works that would help equip him for this role. His literary fare, like that of the young Lincoln, may have been narrow, but it was the kind that somebody deliberately preparing to be a politician might well have chosen. For what he was going to be, Huey Long derived more

---

[3] Harley B. Bozeman; Huey P. Long, in *American Progress*, September 14, 1933; confidential communications. This is a convenient point to dispel a Long myth that has gained some standing. It is that Long drew all his ideals about politics—and especially the concept that a master of ballyhoo could easily deceive the people— from a series of sketches by Samuel G. Blythe that appeared in the *Saturday Evening Post* in 1914. The sketches also appeared as a book, *The Fakers* (New York, 1914). The claim that Long was influenced by Blythe was first advanced in an early biography by T. O. Harris called *The Kingfish: Huey P. Long, Dictator* (New Orleans, 1938), pp. 16–18. Although Long probably read the articles, any notion that he was impressed by them is preposterous. Blythe's hero was a rather inept politician who ended as a failure and was not likely to inspire anybody to emulate him. On this issue, see Deutsch, column in New Orleans *States*, February 25, 1959.

value from his program of self-education than he did from the Winn-field educational system.

Huey began his school days in a flimsy, unprepossessing two-story wooden building. The Winnfield school was, in the language of the state department of education, "unaccredited," which meant that it was ranked as a "grade" school rather than as a "high school." It added enough classes to rise to an accredited status in 1906, just as Huey was finishing the sixth grade, and two years later it moved into a handsome three-story brick edifice built by the town. Of Huey's earliest school years there is almost no record. People who knew him then recall that he always seemed to be busy at something, that he could have made good grades but usually did not, that his stand-ing in "deportment" was bad. "I remember him as an active boy, mentally and physically active," said one classmate with an air of disapproval. "I guess he was smart." In his textbooks he wrote his name as "Hon. Huey P. Long." People expected him to do brash things like that. Around town he was known as a "smart-aleck kid" who was always butting in to tell everybody what to do. Whereas other properly raised boys in Winfield never spoke in the presence of older people without being asked, Huey intervened whenever he felt like it. He advised his elders even on what political opinions to adopt, and he drove them to sputtering rage by instructing them on what moves to make in checker games, which were a favorite public recreation.[4] He gave a typical demonstration of his impudence when the Winnfield school was placed on an accredited basis.

Under the new system, grades one through seven constituted the elementary school. The eighth, ninth, tenth, and eleventh grades made up the high school. Huey, studying the effect of the new curriculum, decided there was no point in his wasting a year in the seventh grade. So he promoted himself to the eighth grade! He did it by the simple expedient of presenting himself for admission to that group when school opened. Some of the students complained loudly that Huey was skipping a whole grade, but the teacher of the eighth, Miss Ophelia Stone, an unusual woman who was capable of doing the un-conventional herself, saw nothing improper in Huey's action. If he could do the work he ought to be promoted, she declared, and after subjecting him to a casual quizzing in history, civics, and English she enrolled him as an eighth-grader.

Most of the Winnfield faculty disregarded the niceties of educa-tional procedure whenever the rules stood in the way of education.

[4] Clara Long Knott; Charles L. Smith; Mrs. Robert Parrott; confidential com-munication; Bozeman, in *Winn Parish Enterprise*, July 18, 1957.

Their attitude was largely a reflection of the views of the principal, W. C. Robinson, a real educational maverick for his time. Something of an authority on mathematics, he believed that a teacher should teach only the subjects he knew best. Accordingly, he abolished the custom of having one instructor handle all the subjects in a high-school grade and assigned each teacher to present specified subjects to every grade. He taught some classes himself, and students watched in awe as before each session he took a healthy chew of tobacco and then proceeded through the forty-five-minute period without ever having to spit and without betraying any impediment in his speech. His greatest innovation was to add to the curriculum, contrary to the wishes of the state board of education, a twelfth grade, which included some courses normally taught then only in colleges. By the time Huey got to high school, Winnfield students had to struggle with such knotty subjects as Latin, plane and solid geometry, and trigonometry.

Not all the students approved the new courses, and some of them resorted to time-honored schoolboy tricks to avoid the work required of them. In Huey's Latin class, for instance, a "pony" of the reader, *Caesar's Gallic Wars*, was obtained and put to wide though secret use. Huey had access to the pony, but he could not possibly have employed it as his associates did, quietly and effectively. One day the teacher asked him to translate a paragraph from the first chapter. He stated the paragraph in Latin and then gave the English translation. The startled teacher asked him to render the next paragraph, which he did. What impressed her was not Huey's correctness of translation but her sudden discovery that he had no textbook on his desk. Reasonably, she inquired how Huey could read without a reader. "That's easy," he replied. "I got X-ray eyes." Thinking to puncture his pretense, she asked him to try his eyes on the rest of the chapter. He sailed through it easily and at the teacher's request started on the next one. Quickly she stopped him and commanded him to skip forward three chapters. Huey had not memorized this far and sat silent. But he was still able to carry off the situation. When the teacher asked what had happened to his wonderful eyes, he answered: "I think they got short-circuited. I musta blown a fuse."

It was a striking demonstration of his gift to photograph whole pages in his mind, and it impressed his youthful auditors mightily. They naturally did not see some of the deeper meanings in the episode. It had also been a condescending commentary on the educational system and an open, almost brutal, affront to the rules of the school, the whole of it done so entertainingly that the amused onlookers missed the essence of what was happening. The Latin incident was only one of a number of such exhibitions. When teachers in the social science classes organized mock trials, to give their charges a notion of the judicial process, Huey always managed to appear as one of the lawyers. When the literary society staged a program, Huey directed it and cast himself in the starring role. The threat of a smallpox epidemic caused a mass inoculation, and Huey went around with a sign pinned to his sleeve: "Do not touch this arm, Vaccinated." Frequently on Sunday afternoon he would go up to neighboring Dodson and pain the mores of that community by ostentatiously dating its high-school teachers, years older than he.[5]

In these and similar doings, the teenaged Huey was revealing most of the characteristics of the later leader. He was intensely and solely interested in himself. He had to dominate every scene he was in and every person around him. He craved attention and would go to almost any length to get it. He knew that an audacious action, although it was harsh and even barbarous, could shock people into a state where they could be manipulated. He knew too that laughter could be a weapon of manipulation; most people would accept incredible actions if they were entertained by the actor. If he disliked existing rules, he was quite ready to make up his own. These are qualities that make an ordinary person the opposite of endearing— but in a politician they are called genius.

Huey gave a striking display of these developing qualities in his senior year, when he represented Winnfield in declamation at the annual state high-school "rally" at Baton Rouge, an event that brought together youth from throughout the state in literary and athletic competition. For most extracurricular activities Huey evinced a condescending scorn. He was a good runner and jumper and sometimes worked out with the track team, but he avoided the rougher contact sports of football and basketball. He was fascinated with debate and declamation, however, and entered every contest involving these arts. In the spring of 1909, his junior year, he and Harley Bozeman represented Winnfield in debate at the rally and to their chagrin got no further than the preliminaries. By the time of the next year's meeting the rules had been changed to allow only one entrant from each school in a particular event. Bozeman continued in debate, but Huey switched to declamation, choosing an oration by Henry W. Grady, Georgian advocate of the New South, for his effort. Huey practiced the delivery of his address for weeks, going out in

[5] Bozeman, in *Winn Parish Enterprise*, March 28, April 11, June 27, July 4 and 18, 1957; confidential communications.

the woods every day after school to mount a stump and speak it at Bozeman, and he headed for Baton Rouge with full confidence that he would carry off the first prize.

When they arrived on the campus of Louisiana State University, the site of the rally, Bozeman went to the building where the debate preliminaries were held and Huey to the one where the orators were screened. Later, while Bozeman was waiting to hear the decision on the debate question, "Should women be given the right to vote?" an enraged Huey burst in upon him. He had lost out in the declamation, Huey announced, and for the unfair reason that the judges were awarding all the honors to girls. Suddenly, in the midst of his tirade, he stopped to tell Bozeman an idea that had just come to him—he would ask the professor in charge of the debate to let him enter and speak against letting women vote. "They got too many rights, right now," he growled; "that's why no boy ain't gonna win nothing here."

Locating the presiding professor, Huey pulled him out in the hall and let loose a flood of arguments on why he should be permitted to participate in the debate. The astonished chairman mumbled that it would be irregular but he would let the boy in. Fired with anger at all women, Huey gave an impromptu speech that brought down the house. He was named as one of the four finalists, the only boy chosen, and that night he placed third and won a scholarship to attend the university. Later he told Bozeman that from the episode he had learned an important lesson: the most effective way to speak was not to orate but to "level down" and talk naturally.[6] He did not mention that he had applied another lesson that he had already learned. His entrance into the debate, a second event, was illegal. But he had forced it, as he knew he could, by the sheer effrontery of his demand.

It was the custom of Baton Rouge residents to take into their homes participants in the rally. Huey and the other Winnfield representatives were assigned to the home of T. H. Harris, state superintendent of education. Harris, a skilled politician who would dominate the school system for years, never forgot the brash boy from Winnfield. Huey came swaggering into the house, leaving the baggage for his associates to carry, and introduced himself to everybody in the family, including the Negro cook. He was always late for meals and left his clothes strewn all over the bathroom floor. When Harris asked how he thought he would do in the declamation, Huey answered:

---

[6] Bozeman, in *Winn Parish Enterprise*, April 25, 1957; Huey P. Long: *Every Man a King* (New Orleans, 1933), p. 7; Lucille Long Hunt. In his autobiography, Long gave a short and not completely accurate account of his part in the rally.

"If I get justice, I'll win." When he returned from the contest, he told Harris: "The committee was ignorant, or bought, and gave me third place." Just before departing for Winnfield, Huey thanked his hostess: "Mrs. Harris, you have been mighty good to us, and when I get to be Governor, United States Senator, and President of the United States, I am going to do something for you." Harris was startled and amused, but with the politician's instinct he recognized that he was dealing with an unusual person, and he was also impressed.[7]

Huey said many times later that at the rally he fell in love with Louisiana State University—LSU to everyone in the state—and there is no reason to doubt the sincerity of his statement. But he was not able to use the scholarship he had won to attend LSU, and he would never step on its campus as a student. He did not, in fact, finish his education at the Winnfield high school. In 1910, his senior year, he abruptly left school. The reasons for his action are not entirely clear. According to one version of events, Huey's eleventh grade thought it would graduate as the senior class of that year. But Principal Robinson insisted that the group had to take another year, the twelfth grade that he had installed, and he refused to certify Huey and his classmates, even though the state department of education insisted that he must. The upshot of the affair was that Robinson, under state and local pressure, resigned; his requirement stood, however, and Huey, who had denounced the concept of a twelfth grade almost from the beginning, refused to return for another year.[8]

Another and more sensational version states that Huey did not leave the school but was expelled and that the expulsion had nothing to do with the curriculum but was the outcome of a personal and political fight between Huey, supported by some of his classmates, and the principal and the faculty. Huey himself vouched for this interpretation in recalling the affair years later for a reporter. "We had formed a secret society," he said, "a sort of circle that was to run things, laying down certain rules the students would have to follow; and if they followed the faculty instead of our rules, we kept them off the baseball team, or the debating team. But the faculty members ruled it out of order. . . . I was the one they had it in for, because I had published a sheet attacking the faculty members, every now and then, so I was the one they expelled." He had retaliated by carrying around town a petition demanding the removal of

[7] T. H. Harris: *The Memoirs of T. H. Harris* (Baton Rouge, 1963), p. 125.
[8] Bozeman, in *Winn Parish Enterprise*, April 11 and May 2, 1957.

the principal, which a majority of the citizens signed, he went on; but he had not come back to school even though as a result of his efforts Robinson was ousted.

Huey was quite capable of either exaggerating or obscuring his role in any episode, but his explanation of his course in this controversy is creditable. Audacious and arrogant as he was, and afflicted with a precocious urge for power, he probably did pretty much what he claimed. It is certain that throughout his high-school years his relations with the faculty steadily worsened. Undoubtedly part of the reason was that the administration and the teachers did not know how to deal with a gifted boy like Huey; in a later educational era he would have been placed in special advanced classes and special efforts would have been made to channel his talents into constructive activities. Not understanding him, the operators of the system were only puzzled and irritated by him. But if the system did not act to accommodate itself to Huey, he showed no disposition at all to cooperate with the system. Rather, his reaction was to bend it to his purpose. His father, thinking he was justifying Huey, inadvertently revealed the truth. "The teachers had it in for him; he dictated to them," said Old Hu, without realizing the implication of his words. "They were a sorry bunch of teachers, some of them. Huey always had trouble with them." Huey transferred to a high school in Shreveport, in the northwestern section of the state, where he stayed with an aunt. But the teachers there were no more pliable than those in Winnfield, and after a brief period he dropped out. He would never have a diploma from any high school.[9]

One device the Winnfield faculty might have employed to interest and influence Huey would have had sure effects—an appeal to his love of music, a passion that appeared in him early and stayed with him all his life. He liked to listen to the sound of music, and even more he liked to render the sounds himself. The Long family did a lot of singing, and Huey had picked up enough words at the age of four to join in the collective "sings" and to attempt some solo efforts in a quavery tenor. As he grew older, he enlarged his repertoire—he could remember the words of any song he heard once—and soon he took over the starring part in every family gathering, warbling such favorites as "Rose Marie" or "Three Little Words" while his

[9] Hermann B. Deutsch: "Prelude to a Heterocrat," *Saturday Evening Post*, CCVII (September 7, 1935), 6–7; H. P. Long, Sr., quoted in John Klorer, ed.: *The New Louisiana* (New Orleans, 1936), p. 20; Charlotte Long Davis; Lucille Long Hunt; Bozeman, in *Winn Parish Enterprise*, August 22, 1957. Huey's sisters cited here believe that he founded some kind of secret society, and they affirm that he was expelled; but they are not clear as to what specific action led to his expulsion.

sister Olive accompanied him on the piano. He and Olive, who could master an air as quickly as Huey could words, put on impromptu shows in the Long home and other residences, and some members of the family thought Huey would become a great musician or actor.[1]

Huey's mother believed that he could be a great preacher of God —and she set her heart on his entering the ministry. She liked to think that she could choose the right careers for her sons. Thus she urged Julius to be a lawyer and George a doctor. Both of them followed her advice, although George varied it a little by going into dentistry. Just why Mrs. Long thought Huey was fitted for the life of a cleric is something of a mystery. Probably it was because she was impressed by his forensic abilities and reasoned that oratory was the primary qualification of a preacher. But even a fond mother would have had trouble in discovering much evidence of a deep inner spiritual urge in Huey's nature.

It was not that he ignored the rules and rites of the Baptist church. On the contrary, he observed all of them. He applied for admission to the church and was immersed in Crawford's fishpond; he attended Sunday service and Sunday school and prayer meeting; and he took the temperance pledge, several times, and tried to refrain from swearing at home. He even enjoyed some of the functions. He liked the group singing, and he observed with a professional interest the speaking techniques of the preachers. But he did everything as an obvious duty, as a formality, and because, as he candidly admitted later, he was under compulsion. He was not going to revolt against the church as he did against the school—he was too smart to do that—but neither was he going to put his heart into the exercise of religion. He never had any intention of becoming a man of the cloth. On several occasions, it is true, he spoke about entering the ministry—he must have noticed that preachers could influence people and exert power—but he was doing no more than toying with the idea.[2] He shied away from the disciplined study and laborious preparation his mother would have wanted him to undertake before ascending to the pulpit.

As a boy, Huey never worked at anything he did not like. He disliked most of the work on the farm, on the land his father retained near Winnfield or on another farm Old Hu operated farther

[1] Clara Long Knott; Charlotte Long Davis; Lucille Long Hunt; Olive Long Cooper.

[2] Mrs. Robert Parrott; Lucille Long Hunt; Charlotte Long Davis; Bozeman, in *Winn Parish Enterprise*, February 14, 1957; Frost, article in New Orleans *States*, August 28, 1927; Long: *Every Man a King*, pp. 6–7.

back in the country. In later years Huey often described for the voters and reporters how much he knew about farm life and how hard he had worked when he was a boy. In these presentations, he had risen before the sun and labored until dark, he had planted sweet-potato slips in the spring and picked the tubers at harvest time, he had hoed and picked cotton, he had rounded up hogs in the woods, he had shelled corn by hand, and he had plowed many a hard furrow. He would admit, in rare frank moments, that he had hated every part of it.[3]

He did these autobiographical bits so well—the conditions of farm life were painted in faithful and realistic detail—that he deceived everybody but himself and people in Winnfield. Those who had known him as a boy snorted derisively, although being Winnians and Louisianians and hence instinctive politicians they could not help admiring the artistry of his words. Those who were most contemptuous were those who knew him best, the members of his family. "Huey never got near a plow unless somebody else was using it," said one of his sisters. "If he ever did plow," said another, "it was all he could do to get to the end of the row." Still another sister recalled that when Huey was sent out to bring in an armful of wood for the fire, she always went out and brought in another, just to be sure of having some. Once at cotton-picking time Old Hu offered money to every child who could pick a hundred pounds. His brothers and sisters performed their task. But Huey came in with his sack dragging and half empty, and the others had to pitch in and fill it for him. It became a Winnfield myth that other farmers who hired Huey to pick cotton insisted on paying him on a flat rate rather than on weight—because he had once slipped a watermelon into his bag.[4]

Huey avoided farm work for two reasons: he hated the dirt and the monotony of the labor; and he feared that if he got involved in it he would in some way be committed to stay with it, that he would not be able to embark on other and more appealing projects that might take him away from the farm and Winnfield altogether. He was not lazy or afraid of physical endeavor, as evidenced by his willingness to work at jobs away from home. One summer he drove a bakery wagon from daylight to dark six days a week, receiving each

[3] Frost, article in New Orleans *States*, August 28, 1957; Deutsch: "Prelude to a Heterocrat," *Saturday Evening Post*, September 7, 1935, p. 6; Long, in *American Progress*, July, 1935; Long: *Every Man a King*, p. 6.

[4] Charlotte Long Davis; Clara Long Knott; Lucille Long Hunt; Harley B. Bozeman; Associate Press dispatch, quoted in Webster Smith: *The Kingfish* (New York, 1933), p. 16 *n*.

Saturday the sum of three dollars for his long hours. Another summer he acted as a water boy for a construction gang and carried refreshments to the bricklayers until a falling brick knocked him unconscious and out of the job.

When he was thirteen, he learned how to set type and in his free time from school worked at the offices of the *Southern Sentinel,* the town's weekly, or the *Baptist Guardian,* a local monthly publication. It was an age when on small-town newspapers all type was set by hand. Good typesetters were at a premium, and a man who could produce three galleys a day was considered good. Huey, with his remarkable ability to see things mentally, could turn out four. In addition to setting type, he also wrote some news items and possibly a few editorials. He liked the work and learned from it some things he never forgot—a realization of the importance of the press as a medium to influence mass opinion and a knowledge of the techniques of newspaper persuasion. But there is no record that he ever considered journalism as a profession or the editorial chair as a satisfactory base from which to exercise the role of leadership that he increasingly felt was his destiny.[5]

There was only one profession for Huey Long, and he knew what it was at an early age. His recognition of it was intuitive rather than intellectual. He was drawn to the great art of politics as if by an irresistible magnet, and even at his first political experience he acted with the instinctive skill of the natural politician. "All I remember is that the first time I knew anything about it, I was in it," he once recalled. He was referring to an episode in the gubernatorial election of 1908, when he was not quite fifteen. His brother Julius, who had emerged as one of the Winn bosses, was supporting Theo Wilkinson against Jared Y. Sanders in the Democratic primary, the only one that counted in one-party Louisiana. It was a hot contest in Winn, but Julius had no hesitation in entrusting to his younger brother a polling precinct. Huey justified the confidence. Although "J.Y." was one of the giants of the day, Huey carried the box against him by three hundred votes. Later that year the political elders of the parish gave Huey a more spectacular assignment. They asked him and Harley Bozeman to represent the Democratic party in a debate with a touring Socialist lecturer at Mineral Springs, in the country between Sikes and Dodson. The Socialist had challenged the state senator

[5] Bozeman, in *Winn Parish Enterprise,* July 25, August 1, 1957; Deutsch: "Prelude to a Heterocrat," *Saturday Evening Post,* September 7, 1935, p. 6; Frost, article in New Orleans *States,* August 28, 1927; Long: *Every Man a King,* p. 7; Mrs. Theo Terzia; Rupert Peyton.

and representative to meet him, but for some reason these men preferred to dodge the issue. They suggested instead that Huey and Bozeman should speak for the party. The Socialist, who did not think that two high-school boys were suitable opponents, reluctantly agreed to the switch.

This was to be no mere academic discussion with a representative of a minor party that did not matter. The Socialists mattered very much in Winn and other upland parishes, which had been devastated by the lumber industry. In these parishes a swelling sentiment of farmer resentment threatened to elevate Socialism to the status of a major party. The Socialists of Winn, for example, had elected half of the parish officers in 1908 and had won a number of ward posts as well. This was a better showing than the party made in any other parish, but it was not surprising that Winn should be the center of Socialist strength. It had earlier been the center of Populism, and its support of Socialism was only a reaffirmation of devotion to the older doctrine, which now bore a new label. There was, in fact, a direct connection between Populism and the whole Louisiana Socialist movement. The Socialists of Winn and other parishes were not Marxists at all. They were protesting farmers, small capitalists who felt the big capitalists were taking over the country, and they embraced Socialism, as they had Populism, because they were looking for a convenient weapon of protest. Nevertheless, it was significant that so many Winnians were not afraid to wear the name of Socialist, a title which was not popular in the rural South. Huey and Bozeman faced a critical audience of their neighbors when they stood up in the school house at Mineral Springs.[6]

Unfortunately, there is no clear surviving record of what Huey, who carried the argument for his side, said that night. He apparently bore down hard on the lessons of history and the laws of economics, and as he had taken an instant dislike to the Socialist speaker, he was probably adequately personal. It is possible, however, to offer a likely reconstruction of his remarks. He defended capitalism as a general concept but attacked the big corporations and monopolies. He rejected Socialism but advocated the Populist program of placing

[6] Frost, article in New Orleans *States*, August 28, 1957; Long, in *American Progress*, January 4, 1934; Bozeman, in *Winn Parish Enterprise*, August 1, 1957; Rorty: "Callie Long's Boy Huey," *Forum*, August, 1935, p. 127; Perry H. Howard: *Political Tendencies in Louisiana, 1812–1952* (Baton Rouge, 1957), pp. 112–15; Grady McWhiney: "Louisiana Socialists in the Early Twentieth Century: A Study of Rustic Radicalism," *Journal of Southern History*, XX (1954), 316–19. In 1912 Eugene Debs, the Socialist candidate for the presidency, received almost thirty-six per cent of the popular vote in Winn.

restraints on big business. In short, he voiced the same rustic radicalism, the same small-capitalist philosophy that his audience really
believed in, and they heard him with pleasure and applause. But he
did not speak as he did just to curry the favor of the crowd. Huey
Long believed in the things he said. He would always believe in
them, and he would never cease his efforts to lift the small and the
poor to a better life.

It was ingrained in him, something he felt when he saw farmers'
homes sold to satisfy debts or witnessed the lumber companies slash-
ing their ruthless swaths across the countryside and then moving on
to new conquests. It was instilled in him by everything he heard as a
boy, by the arguments of Populists and Socialists and, most of all, by
the pragmatic counsel of his father. Old Hu was no more a Socialist
than he had been a Populist. He preferred to make his fight from a
vantage point where he could win. But he was bitterly hostile to the
ambitions of corporate wealth, and completely capable of dealing
corporate power a damaging blow when the situation warranted.
Thus once a railroad executive named William Edenborn, president
of the Louisiana Railway and Navigation Company, proposed to
build a spur line to Winnfield if the town would vote a tax to compensate him. All the local leaders endorsed the project as a boon to
the town and called for an election to ratify the tax. Only Old Hu
denounced the proposal. It smelled, he proclaimed. Edenborn
would construct but a tap line and take it up when the timber was
gone, whereas if the tax was defeated, he would build the road anyway to reap quick profits. Almost singlehanded, the old man, using
Huey as his chief lieutenant, beat the tax when it came up in the
election.[7]

But this particular story did not end on a simple note of virtue
triumphing over greed and the small putting down the powerful.
Years later, when Huey had power of his own as a member of the
Public Service Commission, Edenborn would have cause to regret
that he had ever run afoul of the Longs. His undoubtedly inefficient
railroad drew constant and brutal attention from the Commission.
And therein lies an important revelation about Huey Long. He was
not satisfied just to win a victory of principle over an opponent,
not content merely to establish his principle as a matter of law. Such
behavior would have violated every rule of his training. He was educated in a peculiar school of politics. It was a school that emphasized

[7] Long: *Every Man a King*, pp. 3–4; Rose Lee: "Senator Long at Home," *New Republic*, LXXIX (May 30, 1934), 67; Fields: *Long*, p. 12; H. P. Long, Sr., quoted in Klorer, ed.: *The New Louisiana*, p. 21.

the personal element in the political art. You remembered your friends, you repaid your enemies. It stressed above all the desirability and the necessity of personal power. You must have power to do anything good. You may have ideals, such as a love of the poor, but first you get the power. You may have to do some things you don't like to get it, but you do them. That was the Winnfield school. Winnfield, said one who knew it well, was "a hotbed of feuding and fussing, and Huey was raised right in the middle of it. He was away ahead of everybody in knowing how to trade and traffic."[8] It was a good school for one who aspired to be a leader of the masses and who would encounter strong and cunning foes along his way. Huey would learn some new lessons about the political trade in the life that he entered after leaving Winnfield at the end of his high-school career.

[8] Confidential communication.

# CHAPTER 3

# *High Popalorum and*
# *Low Popahirum*

O NE DAY, WHILE HE WAS STILL IN HIGH SCHOOL, Huey Long, lounging on the street with some of his fellows, suddenly announced that he could sell anything on earth to anybody. Noting that he had aroused the interest of his audience and also their skepticism, he said that a real salesman could look a prospective customer in the eye and easily lead him on to a sale. He pointed to an old Negro man standing nearby and said he would sell him a secondhand coffin to keep for his funeral. Followed by the other boys, Huey went up to the elderly man and said that he was selling coffins and that any sensible man of advanced age should provide himself with a burial receptacle right now. Startled, the Negro listened wonderingly to the flood of arguments that Huey proceeded to unloose. When Huey wound up his pitch by quoting from the Scriptures, both he and the old man were in tears, and the latter insisted on securing his coffin immediately. Huey, exhilarated by his own oratory, prolonged the situation as long as possible. He led the customer and the crowd to the barn at his home, where he said the coffin was waiting, and not until then did he reveal to the Negro that he had been a figure in an experiment. In the course of the exhortation the onlookers probably had become convinced that Huey really did have a coffin in the barn.[1]

The realization that he was good at selling did not come to Huey suddenly on that day. He had known for some time before the coffin incident that he had a talent for selling. He had demonstrated

---

[1] Harvey G. Fields: *A True History of the Life, Works, Assassination and Death of Huey P. Long* (Silver Spring, Md., 1944), p. 24.

this when he and Harley Bozeman peddled books through the little towns of central Louisiana and again, on a different level, when he debated the Socialist lecturer at Mineral Springs. In fact, Huey had been selling something ever since his grade-school days—he had been selling himself, to his teachers and to school administrators, to his fellow students, to the townspeople of Winnfield and to the voters of Winn, to, indeed, anybody who would listen to him expound on any subject that interested him at the moment. Up to the time he left high school, his persuasive efforts had been dictated more by motives of personal pleasure than by pecuniary profit. He had sold whatever he chose to offer because he was challenged by the possible resistance of the buyers, because he derived a feeling of power when he overcame that resistance. But now, in 1910, when he realized that he was not going to graduate from the Winnfield school and was faced with the prospect of having to make his own living, he decided to make selling his profession. He became a "traveling salesman," the name used by rural America for the practitioners of a trade considered to be among the most romantic of occupations.

Huey, in his autobiography, dismissed his entrance into the traveling profession almost casually. He said that he needed a job and secured one with a supply house and went to selling. The real story was more complicated. His friend Harley Bozeman, who was another one of the nongraduating seniors and who was thus in a like predicament, had earlier taken a job with the N. K. Fairbank Company of New Orleans, a concern that specialized in marketing a product called Cottolene, a lard substitute. Bozeman had taken a two-week training course in New Orleans and then had gone on the road in north Louisiana as a "junior salesman." These juniors went from town to town soliciting orders from housewives and then turned the orders over to a local retail grocer. They also took orders from the grocers for cases of Cottolene, which were then shipped from some nearby wholesale company. The salesmen had to overcome a good deal of customer resistance before they could get an order. Most of the women they called on were accustomed to using hog lard or cow butter in their frying and baking. Cottolene had a cottonseed-oil base and was a strange and therefore suspect product. For their efforts junior salesmen received a starting salary of nineteen dollars a week. They also were reimbursed for their travel expenses, such as train transportation, but they had to pay their own hotel bills.[2]

[2] Huey P. Long: *Every Man a King* (New Orleans, 1933), p. 8. The home office of the Fairbank Company was in Chicago. Besides Cottolene, the concern also

In north Louisiana Bozeman joined a road crew working under the supervision of a man named Victor Thorsson. Bozeman soon decided that he liked the traveling life, and he knew that if he liked it, Huey would too. So when two of the crew quit in July, Bozeman asked Thorsson to give Huey a job. The supervisor assented and told Bozeman to notify Huey to join the group at Monroe, a small city in the northeastern part of the state. Huey went there immediately when he got the word, traveling by train and arriving late on a Sunday afternoon. He was hatless and tieless and carried what few personal belongings he had in a shoe box. Thorsson was horrified when he met his prospective new salesman. Taking Bozeman aside, the manager said that this raw country boy would not do, that the company required its salesmen to present a neater appearance. Bozeman begged that Huey be given a week's trial and promised to get his friend some better clothes the first thing in the morning. Thorsson agreed reluctantly. Early the next day Huey showed up more suitably attired and reported to Thorsson for instructions. Rather patronizingly, the supervisor announced that he would have to take Huey and another new salesman, Louis Grieff, a former actor, on a day's training course. The two apprentices were to trail along and study Thorsson's techniques as he talked to the customers.

After the trio had made three or four house calls, Huey startled Thorsson by saying: "Mr. Thorsson, I got the hang of this selling racket. How about me cutting loose, working one side of a street and you and Mr. Grieff the other side?" So annoyed by this brashness that he showed it, Thorsson answered that if Long thought he was that smart, he should get going. That night the salesmen reported on their efforts to Thorsson at his hotel room. Fifteen house sales a day was considered good for a junior salesman, and anything over twenty was rated tops. Huey turned in twenty-six slips. Thorsson and Grieff, working the same area, had made only fourteen sales.

After Thorsson overcame his surprise, he was delighted. He realized that unwittingly he had acquired a star salesman. His satisfaction deepened into a sense of personal pride in his discovery as the junior crew moved on from Monroe to other towns and Huey continued to lead the sales record. In later years, when he had retired from the business and Huey was a famous political figure, Thorsson would try to recall for interviewers just what it was that made Huey so good. It was partly his "gift of gab," Thorsson thought,

---

marketed Gold Dust washing powder and bath and laundry soaps. When "junior" salesmen graduated to "regular," they sold all the company's products and called only on retail and wholesale grocers.

but mostly it was his personality—everybody remembered him after one meeting. Huey did have the qualities Thorsson ascribed to him, and they were important ones in a salesman. But Huey did not roll up sales merely because of his personality. He seemed to know intuitively most of the appeals that would move a customer, and he deliberately studied other methods that came to his notice. From Grieff the actor he learned the value of advertising and particularly of display advertising, and he always carried with him a trunk full of posters and cookbooks. By setting up an exhibit of these items, along with his Cottolene, in stores, he secured extra orders not only from consumers but also from grocers. He was tireless in soliciting house sales and would go to almost any length to persuade reluctant housewives that Cottolene was superior to lard. Thoroughly familiar with the religious principles and prejudices of his customers, he often employed a theological assault. Citing the Bible, he would intone that the Lord had forbidden the Israelites to use anything from the flesh of swine for food. In his interpretation the injunction did not apply to the meat itself but to derivatives from it. Lard was clearly on the prohibited list, whereas cottonseed oil, a vegetable product, was not, and besides, it was purer. If this and other arguments failed, he would as a last resort go into the kitchen and bake a cake or cook supper for the whole family.[3]

After working Monroe and surrounding towns, the junior crew headed for Alexandria. There Thorsson received instructions from the New Orleans office to stage a cake-baking contest among the local housewives. The cakes had to be baked, of course, with Cottolene. The company sent Thorsson detailed directions on the organization of such a contest and supplied him with a large number of cookbooks and pie plates, all stamped with the name Cottolene, to give away. But the company informed the supervisor that he would have to provide the prizes himself! He was to go out and ask businessmen to put them up in return for having their names appear on the advertising for the contest. Thorsson could not do it. A courteous and rather sensitive man, he did not have the gall to solicit something valuable for something worth relatively little, and apparently he shrank from meeting the rebuffs he knew he would encounter. However, he had to arrange the contest. In desperation, he asked his

[3] Bozeman, in *Winn Parish Enterprise*, August 8, 1957; Thorsson, quoted in Associated Press dispatch, n.d., in Linnie B. Persac Scrapbook, Louisiana State University Library; Frost, article in New Orleans *States*, August 28, 1927; Hermann B. Deutsch: "Prelude to a Heterocrat," *Saturday Evening Post*, CCVII (September 7, 1935), 7; W. Harry Talbot.

top salesman to get the prizes. Huey accepted the assignment without a qualm. Gall was one of his specialties, and rebuffs did not affect him at all. In two days he accumulated enough prizes to stock a number of contests. He came in with several sacks of flour, a ham, buckets of coffee, a miscellany of other grocery items, a rocking chair, a floor lamp, and an electric iron. He could have had a case of beer, offered by a local dealer who was impressed by the Long oratory, but he had rejected it, after some consideration, as being an unsuitable award for feminine contestants.

The Alexandria cake contest proved so successful an advertising device that the company directed Thorsson to stage several of them in the larger city of Shreveport when he took his crew there. The group reached Shreveport in September, and Thorsson and Huey put on a number of their competitions. The two now worked as a team on the arrangements, with Huey drumming up the prizes and Thorsson acting as master of ceremonies. Huey also acted a a judge at the affairs. At a contest in the west end he encountered a different kind of challenge to his selling powers. Moving among the tables trying to get some orders from the housewives, he came to a petite, dark-haired, dark-eyed contestant. Her name was Rose McConnell, and she was a stenographer for a local insurance concern. Her mother, originally from south Louisiana, was steeped in the tradition of French cookery and had imparted her knowledge to Rose. Both mother and daughter had entered cakes—Huey's sisters still claim that the mother baked them—and both were winners.

Huey's judging at this contest was cursory and not altogether objective. He showed great interest in Rose's product but only because he wanted to meet the baker. "I bet you didn't make this cake," he challenged her. "Yes, I did," she replied. "How about having a date and proving it?" he came back. They had several meetings and decided they liked each other. Rose was impressed by the quickness of his mind and his retentive memory for everything that he had read. She noted tenderly that he was small for his age and that his clothes were too big for him; being a little over a year older, she was probably moved in part by an urge to mother him. Huey seemed overwhelmed by her physical charms. She was the most beautiful thing he had ever seen, he confided to members of his family, and he told Bozeman that he had found the girl he was going to marry.

Marriage was not to come immediately, however. It would be two and a half years, in fact, before Huey and Rose would say their vows. Huey's insecure economic status was supposedly the cause of the delay; he did not earn enough money to support a wife. But

there were other hindering forces at work. Despite Huey's apparently complete capitulation, he was not quite as smitten as he
seemed. At an early stage in the courtship he gave Rose a diamond
ring. It was a very small ring—not "the size of a pinhead but of a
pin point," she recalls—which he said he had borrowed from one
of his sisters. Later, however, he requested the ring back. She asked
him why. He said that there was another girl whom he might marry;
at least, he was going to see her. Still later, he returned the ring.
Rose wanted to know what had happened with the other girl. He answered that she did not look the same when he saw her again. It is
very possible that there was no other girl, that Huey were merely
playing the lover's game of making himself appear sought after. It is
just as possible that there was someone else. In after years he told one
of his most trusted friends that as a youth he had loved a girl of the
upper class. But he came to realize that he could not have her—she
could not understand the crudities of his nature, and she would not
be able to follow him on the path he intended to go. If there was
calculation in this, there was also some in his admiration for Rose.
Although for one of the rare times in his life he was letting himself
be ruled by emotion, he could still measure qualities in her that he
could use at the right time. He liked to tell her that she had the
talents he lacked: she could take shorthand and type expertly, and
she had the practical, common touch. It was as if he was ticking off
desirable characteristics in a politician's wife. He never forgot at any
time in his salesman days what he intended to be at a later day.
Whenever people asked him the occupation he hoped to follow ultimately, he answered that he expected to go into politics.[4]

If Huey did nurture plans for a quick marriage, he saw them
dashed soon after the cake contest. The junior crew finished working Shreveport and the surrounding area late in September. As they
wondered where they would move next, letters from the Fairbank
Company arrived announcing the termination of the services of
Thorsson and all the salesmen except Huey and Bozeman, who were
assigned to cover the whole of north Louisiana by themselves. The
mass dismissal should have indicated to the two young men that the

[4] Bozeman, in *Winn Parish Enterprise*, August 15, 1957; Frost, article in New
Orleans *States*, August 28, 1927 (the same issue also contains the recipe for Rose's
cake); Rose McConnell Long (Mrs. Huey P. Long); Charlotte Long Davis; Lucille
Long Hunt; Clara Long Knott; confidential communication. Huey's sisters believe
that he met Rose before the cake contest, while attending high school at Shreveport,
but since he did not enroll at this school until January 1911, they are evidently
confused as to the time sequence of the courtship. Huey himself fell into the same
error in his autobiography; *Every Man a King*, p. 14.

company would do anything to cut costs. Instead, they took it as a mark of confidence in them. They were certain that their retention meant that the company had marked them for promotion—if they performed well, they would be raised to "regular" salesmen and would draw up to $175 a month plus all expenses and would be able to put up at the best hotels. Fired by these visions of impending affluence, they started to work their circuit with special diligence. As a reward for their efforts, they received letters in the middle of November terminating their services. They headed for Winnfield for the Thanksgiving holidays without very much money but with an added measure of cynicism. They had known that politicians would make promises, outright or implied, to get votes and then repudiate their pledges. Now they realized that a corporation, in exactly the same way, could hold out the promise of a reward to get maximum work out of its employees and then back out of its assurance.[5]

It was a dissatisfied and restless Huey who came back to Winnfield. He had no intention of staying in the town, and he bent every effort to getting out as soon as he could. He and Bozeman wrote letters to every company they knew of asking for jobs as salesmen, but all the replies were discouraging—no increase in the sales force was contemplated at the present. His brother Julius, now well established as a lawyer, urged him to settle down and go to a law school, preferably the one at Tulane University, which Julius had attended. Huey was willing enough to consider the idea. He expected to be a lawyer someday; the law was, as everybody knew who knew anything, the obvious and best springboard from which to jump into politics. But to be accepted as a regular student in an accredited law school in Louisiana, he would have to have a high-school diploma, and he would not, he told Julius and the family, return to the Winnfield school under any conditions. So they pressed him to enroll at the high school in Shreveport, where he could stay with an aunt. Huey finally agreed to try. Early in January 1911 he left for Shreveport, probably swayed more by the prospect of being able to see Rose McConnell every day than by any very serious plans to pursue an education.

Bozeman, in the meantime, continued to write letters of application, and late in February he received an offer from the Houston

---

[5] Bozeman, in *Winn Parish Enterprise*, August 15, 1957; Long: *Every Man a King*, p. 8. In his autobiography Huey merely stated that he "dropped out" of employment of the company. For some reason, in this book he passed lightly over the whole story of his salesman days, and he did not mention Bozeman or the latter's part in helping him secure jobs.

Packing Company. On his way to Houston he had a long layover in Shreveport and decided to look up Huey. To while away the afternoon hours while waiting for school to let out, he sought out an old acquaintance. In the course of their conversation this man volunteered the information that Huey was going to school only in the mornings and was working in the afternoons as a stenographer for a plumbing company. Bozeman could not believe what he heard. He was naturally surprised that Huey was not taking full-time school work, but what confounded him was the picture of Huey, who knew nothing of shorthand, acting as a stenographer. He went down to the office of the plumbing company to see for himself. Sure enough, there sat the owner dictating letters—and across the desk was Huey, busily taking notes on a pad. Huey looked up and recognized Bozeman but made frantic signs for him to get out. Bozeman did, but he telephoned Huey later and they arranged to meet after work.

That evening Huey told Bozeman a revealing story. He said that the Shreveport administrators would not let him be graduated in the spring because he had not been in school the first semester. So he had dropped all classes except those that met in the morning and had looked around for a job. (This was a repetition of the Winnfield experience—he would ignore rules he did not like.) He had noticed a newspaper advertisement of the plumbing company for a part-time stenographer and had applied for the job. When the owner asked for references, Huey countered by suggesting that he demonstrate his competence by taking some letters. The man dictated a half dozen or so letters, and a short time later Huey, who had learned a little about typing in high school, placed copies on his desk. The renditions were so good that the plumber exclaimed: "Them's the best written letters I ever dictated to a stenographer. You get the job." But how, Bozeman asked, had Huey learned to be a stenographer so quickly? Huey answered that he knew nothing about shorthand. His note pad was merely for effect. He had invented a few symbols for his own guidance, and he wrote down the key points and any figures cited in a dictation. But mainly he depended on his phenomenal memory to recall the text of each letter. He was making only nine dollars a week, he told Bozeman, and he wanted to get back to selling. If Bozeman could get him a job with the Houston Packing Company he would leave Shreveport immediately.

Bozeman soon found an opportunity for Huey. The Houston Packing Company was an independent concern that nourished dreams of expansion. Its "specialty" salesmen, of whom Bozeman was one, sold its cured meats, lard, and canned goods to whole-sale distributors, who resold the goods to retailers. Bozeman lined up so many orders the first week that his manager asked him if he could recommend another young man who could produce in the same way. Bozeman mentioned Huey, and the manager agreed to hire him. After receiving a letter from his friend, Huey was in Houston by the next Sunday ready to go to work.[6]

Huey was first assigned to work the Austin area. While he was familiarizing himself with the company's policies and products, the company was studying him. After a week the sales manager concluded that the new salesman was a real find. Huey was thereupon sent to Little Rock to supervise sales in the whole Arkansas area. He continued to pile up orders, and when in July the company decided to open a new office in Memphis it unhesitatingly named Huey to head it. He was to introduce the company's products in all of west Tennessee and north Mississippi. It was a broad sales territory to entrust to a boy not quite turned eighteen, and when Huey arrived in Memphis and installed himself in the plushy Gayosa Hotel he felt that he was definitely on the road to success. He would have a rough and almost immediate awakening. Memphis was, in salesman parlance, a highly competitive town; that is, most of the big packers had offices there and were represented by aggressive salesmen. To make matters worse for somebody trying to break in, a drought in 1911 heralded a bad cotton year, and when the cotton crop in the Delta region was poor, all business was poor. Huey, with all his persuasive powers, was unable to secure any significant orders. On the last weekend in August, as he checked in at the Gayosa from a fruitless trip, he found a letter from the company ending his employment and asking him to submit his latest expenses. He requested that his salary and expenses be sent to the Gayosa. He liked Memphis and hoped to line up another job with a local company.[7]

He also liked the luxury of the Gayosa and remained there while he looked for employment. Everywhere he met the same answer—there was no opening for an additional salesman. After a week his money began to run out, and he realized that he would have to seek cheaper quarters. He paid his bill at the Gayosa and with nine dollars in his pocket moved to a rooming house whose rates were a dollar a day, payable every morning. Still he could not find a job. On his third morning at the rooming house, when the proprietor came to collect the rent Huey had only $2.30 in his possession. He asked the

[6] Bozeman, in *Winn Parish Enterprise*, August 22, 1957.
[7] Ibid., August 29, 1957.

owner for a few days' credit. The man consented surlily but insisted on taking Huey's suitcase, which contained his slender stock of clothes, as security. Two mornings later, when Huey could not pay again the proprietor would allow no more concessions. He escorted Huey downstairs to the door and shoved him out. Vainly Huey begged that he be permitted to get some clean clothes out of his suitcase. The landlord shouted: "Git going, you little bum, I don't never want to see no more of you."

Huey hit the streets with less than a dollar in his pocket. His problem now was not to find a job but to survive. For sleeping quarters he resorted to a bench in a park near the Gayosa. For food he relied on the free lunches that saloons then allowed to customers who bought a nickel beer. Sometimes a generous bartender would be impressed by Huey's account of his plight and would let him eat without buying a drink. One member of this fraternity told Huey he knew of a painting contractor who needed laborers to paint a house and gave him a nickel for trolley fare out to the job. Huey, showing up without overalls or any equipment, had a little trouble convincing the contractor he was a painter. Nevertheless, the man handed him a brush and told him to get to work. Huey watched the other painters and stirred up his mixture as they did theirs. But he started to paint the wall assigned to him from the bottom up! When the boss noticed this display of amateurism, he was more amused than angry. He told Huey he admired his nerve—but to get out of a job he knew nothing about.

That night Huey repaired again to his park bench, whose hard contours were becoming all too familiar. Toward morning a policeman aroused him with a stick and questions. Huey related his misfortunes so eloquently that the official took him to the Salvation Army home instead of to jail. Huey stayed at the home for several days and nights and earned a little money working at odd jobs that the directors got for him. Then he heard of an opening in a foundry near the railroad yards on the edge of Memphis. He walked out to the place and got the job. But he had not anticipated the kind of work he was given. He was set to mauling boxcars to pieces. It was backbreaking labor, and the pay was poor, so poor, in fact, that he economized on lodging costs by sleeping in an abandoned boxcar. After several days of this he could stand it no longer. He had always said that no matter how low he sank, he would never admit to his family that he had failed, would never ask them for help. But now he was in straits too desperate to think of pride. He informed his family of his situation. His mother, although she was touched by the news, saw in it an opportunity to achieve her dream that Huey would become a minister. His older brother George, called "Shan" from his middle name, Shannon, was practicing dentistry in Shawnee, Oklahoma, where a Baptist seminary was located. She asked Shan to send for Huey so that he could enter the school. Both Shan and Huey agreed to the arrangement, and Shan sent Huey enough money to pay his train fare. Huey immediately proceeded to spend most of the money, however, and had to get Bozeman to wire him some more before he could leave. He left Memphis late in September.[8]

Huey's arrival in Shawnee, as recalled by Dr. Long, was about as unpropitious an event as could be imagined. He had no money, he was wearing a frayed suit (the only clothes he had), and he was carrying his few personal possessions wrapped up in a newspaper. He was rapidly regaining his brashness, however; he bragged that if Shan had not sent for him he would have been able to come on his own: he had been on the way back up when Shan invited him. The next day Dr. Long bought him some new clothes and paid his admission fee to the Oklahoma Baptist University. Huey, obedient to the wishes of his mother and the agreement he had made with his brother, attended this school until the end of the semester, which came during the Christmas holidays. So Dr. Long thought, and so think surviving friends and members of the family. But did he? The archives of the institution show no record that he was enrolled. It is possible that these records are incomplete or that there is some confusion about his name—people always tried to make that odd appellation Huey into something else. But it seems more likely that the records are right, that he did not enroll at the school. How then did he deceive people into thinking that he did? What probably happened is that he went out to the campus frequently and sat in on some classes. He had never had any serious intention of becoming a minister and had gone into the arrangement with his mother and his brother only to get money to leave Memphis. At Shawnee he went through the motions of observing his agreement and then backed out of it as soon as he could. During the holidays he told Shan that he had decided he was not cut out to be a preacher. He wanted to be a lawyer, he said, and if Shan would advance the necessary money he

---

[8] Ibid., September 5, 1957; Long: *Every Man a King*, pp. 9–10; Deutsch: "Prelude to a Heterocrat," *Saturday Evening Post*, September 7, 1935, p. 7. Neither in his autobiography nor in his account to Deutsch did Long give a very full or a very accurate description of this Memphis interlude. It has to be inferred from the above sources that Huey wrote his family about his troubles.

would enter the law school of the University of Oklahoma at Norman. Dr. Long gave him a hundred dollars.[9]

Huey journeyed to Norman by way of Oklahoma City. Apparently, he went to the state's largest town to enjoy a few days of high living before he settled down to student life. Near the hotel where he stayed, he found a gambling den, and on the last day of the year, in one fling at the roulette wheel, he lost practically all of the money he had. This was not the first time he had been attracted to gambling, nor would it be the last. When and why he acquired the habit is not certain. The lure may have been nothing more than a country boy's fascination with urban sin. A more probable explanation is that Huey was simply trying to follow the example of admired older brother Julius, who in his youth had gambled in the back rooms of various establishments with excellent results. In fact, at one sojourn in Monroe Julius had picked up enough money to enable him to enter the Tulane law school, after which he never touched a card again. Huey certainly knew about Julius's activities, and when he went into the place in Oklahoma City, he must have had in mind emulating Julius's exploit. Instead he woke up on the morning of January 1, 1912, to find that he was almost broke. He had no money to pay for registration, books, or even the hotel bill.

Huey went for a walk to consider his problem. As he passed the stores in the business section he had a saving inspiration. He would try to get a job as sales representative of one of the Oklahoma City wholesale grocery concerns in Norman. Boldly he marched into the office of the Dawson Produce Company, one of the largest in the city, and asked for the manager. To this man, K. W. Dawson, he told an almost honest story. He said that he was going to attend the university law school but needed some extra money, that he had had experience as a salesman and was good at it—and would Mr. Dawson give him a job selling the company's goods in Norman on a commission basis? The earnest plea and the forlorn look of the pleader moved Dawson. He asked the boy to come back later. At this second meeting the manager told Huey that he could have the job; the company needed a man to work Norman and three smaller towns nearby. Although Dawson undoubtedly thought that he was getting an adept agent, he was probably moved in large part by altruism: he though he was helping a deserving youth get an education.

[9] Bozeman, in *Winn Parish Enterprise*, September 12, 1957, quoting George S. Long; Charlotte Long Davis; L. E. Solomon, dean and registrar, Oklahoma Baptist University.

It was late in the afternoon when Huey left the office of the Dawson Company. He now had some assurance that he could support himself when he got to Norman. But first he had to get there, and he decided he had better start immediately, so that he could execute his enrollment at the university and try to earn a few commissions. He had to pawn his overcoat to raise the money for his hotel bill. After spending thirty cents for supper, he had only twenty-five cents left, not enough to pay the fare on the railroad that traversed the eighteen miles between Oklahoma City and Norman. Darkness was coming on, and the chill of a January night was descending on the Oklahoma plains. Again Huey had to make a hard decisions—whether to call Shan and and ask for help or walk to Norman. He could not bring himself to appeal to his brother. Hunching up in his thin suit, he started down the tracks. He never forgot the horror of that night, the loneliness of the dark landscape and the numbing cold that struck through him like a knife. Toward two o'clock in the morning he reached the railroad yards in Norman. He saw a lone light burning in a cottonseed-oil mill. He entered and asked the watchman if he could warm himself by the stove. The man, touched by the sight of the shivering youth, readily consented. When Huey asked if there was a place where he could catch a little sleep, the watchman pointed to a cottonseed bin. Huey fell into it and slept until daylight. Then he got up, straightened his clothes and brushed off the lint, and sallied forth to look for customers.

Making his way to the business section, he called first at the grocery store of S. H. McCall. McCall gave him an order for a carload of potatoes. Delighted at this easy initial success, Huey went to the store phone and placed a call to Dawson collect. To his surprise the company refused to accept the call. He then used the twenty-five cents he had on him to place the call again. Excitedly he told Dawson about his order. Dawson said that he could not fill the order, that he had no potatoes. This was too much for Huey. Throwing aside all prudence, he shouted: "The list you gave me yesterday has got spuds on it. If you did not have any spuds, why didn't you mark them off the list? You caused me to spend my last two bits on this damn phone call." McCall, who was listening to the conversation, intervened. He said that there were several other items he needed and that as long as Huey had Dawson on the phone he might as well have the order made up. The list comprised a respectable total and mollified Dawson, who otherwise might have discharged Huey on the spot. Huey then visited other stores and succeeded in securing orders at all of them. Near the end of the day he counted up an impressive number of sales. But his financial troubles were far from over. He would not receive the commissions on the sales for a week. In the meantime he had to eat and sleep and get himself registered at the university. The hopelessness of the situation plunged him into a fit of depression. He might as well leave Norman, he decided. He wandered over to the railroad station.

Apparently he went to the station because it was the only point of departure he knew. He had walked into town on the tracks, and he would walk out the same way. But there must have been some indecision in his mind, for he lingered on the platform a while. Near him stood an older, well-dressed man who was waiting for a train. His name was Ralph Jackson, a salesman who worked in and out of Norman a great deal. He and Huey soon fell into a conversation. It is highly probable that Huey made the first approach and made it with a measure of calculation. At any rate, Jackson was soon listening to Huey's story, which was straightforward for the most part, though containing some embroidery: Huey was trying to work his way through college; he was broke and had not eaten all day; and he was afraid that he was going to have to give up his dream of getting an education. Jackson's sympathies were quickly aroused, and he found himself liking the boy. He broke in to say: "Son, I'll stand good for your room and board until you can pay me, and here is twenty dollars for you." Huey refused the twenty. He said that if he could get by at all, he could do it with five dollars, which amount he would accept as a loan. As Jackson handed him a five, Huey said that if he never repaid the loan he had at least saved his benefactor fifteen dollars. He had recovered his impudence now that he had money in his pocket again.

What Huey meant by saying that five dollars would be enough is something of a mystery. With this sum he could do no more than make a token payment on his registration fee and perhaps subsist until he received his commissions. But the whole story of this Norman episode, obviously a crucial one in his life, is wrapped in ambiguities, all of them resulting from various versions of it that he later supplied. He said, but never clearly and flatly, that Jackson paid his room and board bill for a period. He did state flatly that Jackson arranged for him to buy law books on credit and asked local merchants to give him orders. But he also said that it was grocer McCall who approached the merchants in his behalf. In one account, he had found his benefactor in a hotel lobby instead of on a railroad platform and had deliberately worked on the man's sympathies so that he could get some money out of him. Running through all the versions was one theme: a friendless youth had survived a hard time, partly because he had chanced upon generous strangers, but mainly because he had been industrious and also, on occasion, downright cunning. In none of his public presentations did Huey ever say anything about George Long's helping him or even mention that Dr. Long was living in Oklahoma. So great was his egotism that he could not admit that he even once had to depend on a member of his family. Yet it was this brother more than anybody else who rescued him at this critical moment. Huey registered at the law school on January 3, the day after he met Jackson. Then, having achieved a partial success, he felt that he could phone Shan for aid. Unexpected and extra expenses required for registration had consumed his money, he said, and Shan would have to send him seventy-five dollars more. Dr. Long came through again.[1]

With the acquisition of this money, Huey had no more financial worries. He was, in fact, soon living what was for a student a life of affluence. His commissions for his work with the Dawson Company brought him on an average one hundred dollars a month. He worked hard to earn these commissions. He had to solicit orders in Norman and in three nearby towns as well. Each of these towns was about nine miles from Norman. Usually he traveled to them by train, but sometimes, when he could not make connections, he walked. Once he came to an eight o'clock class late. When the professor reprimanded him, Huey explained that he had risen before daylight to walk to Moore and had been delayed in returning. As rewarding as his commissions were, he soon developed another source of income that was probably even more lucrative. He renewed his gambling contacts in Oklahoma City, and this time his luck was much better. It was so good, in fact, that he took to spending most of his weekends in the city. And he became so good at the art that one of the places employed him as a dealer and dice man.[2]

The records of the university list him as Hugh Pierce Long, Jr., and his birth date as 1891, two years before the actual date. The

[1] Bozeman, in *Winn Parish Enterprise*, September 12, 1957; confidential communications; Long: *Every Man a King*, pp. 10–14; Frost, article in New Orleans *States*, August 28, 1927; Ralph Jackson, quoted in Associated Press dispatch, n.d., in Persac Scrapbook. There are other minor discrepancies in the sources cited; the text account is a reconstruction of the probable truth. Of one thing there can be no doubt—Ralph Jackson extended some kind of help to Huey, and this Huey never forgot. Years later, when Long was a senator, Jackson fell upon hard times. He notified Long, who brought him to Louisiana and got him a job in New Orleans.

[2] Long: *Every Man a King*, pp. 13–14; Charles L. Orr; Fred E. Tarman; confidential communication; Mildred Adams: "Huey the Great," *Forum*, LXXXIX (February 1933), 72.

mistake with his first name was a natural one for strangers to make. The error in his birth date may have been a deliberate deception on his part to create an impression of maturity. He earned no credits in the first semester. Registering almost at its end, he could only enroll as an auditor in four classes: property, elementary law, torts, and contracts. In the second semester he took domestic relations, a special one-hour lecture course, criminal law, common law proceedings, and contracts. He made C grades in the first three, a W (withdrawn, passing) in common law, and an E (condition) in contracts. Although this was far from an outstanding performance, it was not a bad one for somebody who was studying law only in odd moments between two busy careers in selling and gambling. He did attend classes regularly, and he did try to do what his teachers asked of him, but he showed little enthusiasm for anything. He went at his studies sullenly, as if he was determined to prove, if only to himself, that he could submit to the discipline of others.[3]

Only once did his real nature flame forth, revealing his compulsion to manipulate people to his own ends. The issue that drew him out was politics, always his deepest passion. During the second semester the excitement of the approaching presidential campaign gripped the students at the University of Oklahoma as it did other colleges. The two leading contenders for the Democratic nomination in 1912 were Governor Woodrow Wilson of New Jersey and Champ Clark of Missouri, speaker of the House of Representatives. On the Norman campus many students were enthusiastic for Wilson, possibly because of his university background, and under the leadership of fraternity men the Wilson supporters formed a Wilson for President club. The fraternity men assumed the major offices in the organization. Immediately the independents were in an uproar. If the "Greeks" were for Wilson, then the "Barbs" were going to be for Clark. The Barbs indulged in a lot of loud talk, but they took no concrete action. Unorganized socially, they did not know how to act politically. Suddenly a leader appeared to tell them what to do— Huey put himself at their head. In projecting himself into the controversy, Huey was not swayed by any fundamental political philosophy. And he had no great preference for either Wilson or Clark. He acted initially only because he was piqued that the Wilson group

[3] Transcript of Long's record, furnished by the University of Oklahoma. In his autobiography Huey said that he had intended to complete his law studies at Norman. It is unlikely that he ever had this purpose in mind—unless he meant to live and practice in Oklahoma. The training he received at Norman would not have equipped him to practice in Louisiana, where the Napoleonic Code prevails.

had not included him on its roster of officers. But once he was in the contest, he had to go all the way. Huey Long would dominate the Clark movement, and Huey Long would defeat the Wilson crowd.

As a first move in his campaign, he wrote and had printed for distribution all over the campus a one-sheet document that was a concentrated attack on Wilson. Bearing intriguing headlines that charged that Wilson had been successful only as a schoolteacher, it called for a mass meeting of the Barbs to organize a Clark for President club. Although Huey had seen similar sheets used in campaigns in Winn parish, this was the first time that he himself employed the device of the printed circular, a weapon that he would make famous in later Louisiana contests. Enough of the independents responded to the call to enable Huey to hold his meeting. These students voted to form a Clark club, and, not surprisingly, elected Huey as its president. The appearance of this rival organization so shocked the leaders of the Wilson group that they decided to call a campus "national convention" to demonstrate support for their candidate.

As the convention was about to meet, Huey rallied his followers to attend. He found to his dismay that he did not have enough people to make a majority. Either there were fewer members of the Clark club than he had thought or the members were not sufficiently interested to go to the convention. Frantically he sought to swell his ranks by calling in some young fellows he knew from the town. But the Wilson leaders, probably recognizing the trick, moved to call the roll. Huey realized that the result would disqualify many of his delegates. There was only one thing to do. He announced that the Clark people were bolting the meeting. Solemnly Huey's crowd marched to the courthouse square and proceeded to hold their own convention. But he left two of his representatives in the original meeting under instructions to vote to the last for the respected elder statesman of the Democrats, William Jennings Bryan. When reports of the two conventions appeared, they painted a picture foreseen by Huey and really set up by him. One group had unanimously and enthusiastically nominated Clark. The other had nominated Wilson, but its decision had followed much wrangling and was not unanimous. Huey liked to cite this incident later as an example of what a politician with weak support should do. "In a political fight, when you've got nothing in favor of your side," he would say, "start a row in the opposition camp."

Huey had clearly won the battle of the Norman conventions. The candidate for whom he had fought, however, did not do nearly so well in the Democratic national convention. When the Democrats convened in Baltimore in June, they nominated Wilson. Huey, demonstrating that his efforts for Clark had been an expression of his own ego, did everything he could to help the Wilson cause in Oklahoma. He and some other students formed an organization they called the Young Democratic League. It spread rapidly and may have been the first state unit of what ultimately became a national society. The Oklahoma convention of the Young Democrats recognized Huey's role by electing him vice-president for the district in which Norman was located. At the same time he was involved in a local political fight. When the school term ended in May, Huey went to stay with Dr. Long, who had moved to another town and was already mixing in its politics. His brother was backing a friend who was running for Congress and needed Huey's aid. For a good part of the summer Huey labored for Shan's candidate. He devoted most of his energy to writing circulars, a form of political activity for which he decided he had a special talent. But for all his frenzied work, he was really bored with what he was doing. He was bored too with his law studies. Suddenly he felt that he had to get away from Oklahoma. All during his stay in the state he had kept up a correspondence with Bozeman, who was now working in Louisiana as a salesman for the Faultless Starch Company of Kansas City. He wrote to Bozeman and asked if he could get him a job with the company.

Bozeman took the request to his supervisor, John Nesbitt, and backed it up with a glowing description of Huey's selling career and ability. Nesbitt was interested. The company was considering opening up a new sales office in Memphis to supervise business in several states. This colorful and dynamic youth might be just the man to head up the office. He decided to have Huey meet him in Texarkana in two weeks. He would take the applicant out on the road for a week's trial to see if he was good enough to have the Memphis job. About the time Huey received this good news from Bozeman, Dr. Long decided to visit the family in Winnfield. Huey traveled with his brother as far as Shreveport, where he stopped off to see Rose McConnell. He then went to Texarkana to meet Nesbitt. The supervisor required hardly a week to decide that he had found his man. He took Huey to Memphis and offered him the division office, giving him carte blanche to work the territory as he wanted and to hire what personnel he needed to get the orders. It was a heavy responsibility to thrust on a nineteen-year-old boy, but Nesbitt believed he had discovered a great salesman. Still he was a little puzzled by

Huey. He later told Bozeman: "He is the damnedest character I ever met. I don't know whether he is crazy or a genius."[4]

Huey assumed his managerial duties late in the summer. Immediately he installed himself in the Gayosa Hotel, which he had departed from a little less than a year before almost penniless. There was a revealing symbolism in his return to the Gayosa. He had become a salesman again for just one reason. He told Bozeman quite frankly what this reason was—he wanted to make a lot of money. He talked often at this time of carving out a career in the business world, but it is unlikely that he meant it. He was quite sincere, however, when he admitted his desire for money. He had had a taste of high living in Oklahoma and had liked it. Now, at least for a period, he was going to devote himself to earning enough money to continue living in his former style. He gave every promise in the last months of 1912 that he would accomplish this new ambition. He directed efficiently a crew of salesmen and advertising men who fanned out over four states. One of the salesmen was his younger brother Earl, who came up from Winnfield at Huey's request. The sales volume of the division climbed steadily, and the mounting orders drew expressions of praise from the company's executives. Huey's salary also increased, until he was getting $125 a month and expenses, the largest stipend he had ever received. In the glow of this prosperity he forgot any plans he might have harbored of pursuing an education. He almost forgot even politics, but his fascination with the art was too great for him to get away from it completely. Thus on one occasion he plunged into a fist-swinging election brawl that had started around one of the polling places and managed to get himself arrested. Shrewdly, he had swung on the side of supporters of the mayor, "Boss" Ed Crump, and Crump himself, when he heard of the fracas, came down to police headquarters to arrange for Huey's release. Crump told his young champion that if he could ever return the favor he would.[5]

In December the company announced that it was rewarding its salesmen with a long Christmas holiday. Huey immediately headed

[4] Deutsch: "Prelude to a Heterocrat," *Saturday Evening Post*, September 7, 1935, p. 7; Bozeman, in *Winn Parish Enterprise*, September 19, 1957; Fields: *Long*, pp. 23–4.

[5] Long: *Every Man a King*, p. 14; Frost, article in New Orleans *States*, August 28, 1927; manuscript reminiscence of Marvin Pope, Crump's secretary, furnished by William D. Miller; Miller: *Mr. Crump of Memphis* (Baton Rouge, 1964), p. 62. Miller erroneously dates this incident as occurring in 1907, years before Huey came to Memphis; it may have happened either at the time cited above or during his first stay in the city.

for Shreveport. He went resolved to persuade Rose McConnell to marry him. Now he could tell her that he was making enough money to support a wife, and he thought that he should act before some other suitor pushed him aside. He spent a pleasant week courting Rose. One evening they attended a performance of *Lohengrin* at the Grand Opera House. After it ended, they rode the streetcar to Rose's house, where Huey stayed for a time to talk with her family. He left just in time to catch the last streetcar going back to the business section. As he stepped off it near his hotel, he found several policemen waiting for him. They put him under arrest and took him off to the city jail. To his shock, he learned that he was charged with having shot at two citizens earlier on the street. Witnesses had seen a young man do the shooting, and they had furnished a description that fitted Huey. He was lodged in a cell for the night and denied the opportunity to notify anybody of his predicament. The next day, however, word of the arrest began to spread around town, and Bozeman, who was passing through on his way to Winnfield, and other friends heard about it. With some difficulty, they secured permission to talk to Huey. When they heard his story, they realized how weak the case against him was. He had an almost perfect alibi. Various witnesses could attest that at the time of the shooting Huey had been at the opera or at the McConnell home. Fortunately, Rose had kept their ticket stubs as souvenirs.

Even with this evidence before them, the local authorities were strangely reluctant to release Huey or to even give him a hearing. Bozeman finally had to post bond to get him out. On the day after he won his freedom, Huey went to Winnfield to spend the holidays with his family. He told Julius about the episode, and the older brother, who was now district attorney of Winn, was able to get the charges dropped. But Huey would always remember his arrest and his treatment by the police. He decided that he had been the victim of a frame-up. Later he thought that maybe the police had mistaken him for a youth in Winnfield who resembled him. Whatever the conclusion, the experience was not one to leave him with any great respect for the efficiency of local officials or the vaunted freedom of local government.[6]

The incident drew Huey and Rose closer together, and surer than ever now that he would win her, Huey invited her down to meet his family during the holidays. She came—and endured the critical scrutiny of his mother and his sisters. She was a nice girl, they ad-

[6] Long: *Every Man a King*, pp. 14–15; Frost, article in New Orleans *States*, August 28, 1927; Bozeman, in *Winn Parish Enterprise*, September 26, 1957.

mitted to Huey after she left. But they also insisted that he was too young to get married. Huey brushed their objections aside. He could not, however, persuade Rose to marry him and go back to Memphis with him. She had lingering doubts that he was really making enough money to support two, and she may have been influenced by her knowledge of his family's opposition. Irritated by her attitude, Huey went off to Memphis in a huff, and she was hurt. For a time they corresponded only at rare intervals, and friends thought the affair was over. Then in the spring Huey started bombarding her with telegrams and telephone calls, all of them voicing frantic appeals to marry him. She decided that he must be drinking heavily and took the train to Memphis to save him from himself.

When she met him, she realized that his only trouble was a bad case of lovesickness. This time she could not resist him. They were married on the day she arrived, April 12, 1913, by a Baptist minister in the Gayosa Hotel. As they stood up together, she looked much more mature than Huey, and although she was a small woman, she seemed more robust. Huey looked boyish, spindly, and callow. At the close of the ceremony an embarrassing moment ensued. Huey's monthy salary check had not arrived, and he did not have enough money on him to reward the preacher. Rose had to pay the fee out of the eleven dollars she had brought with her. The incident was revealing as to the character of the man she had married, but it probably did not surprise her. No matter how much money Huey made, he would never keep any if left to himself. He cared for money only because with it he could do things that gave him pleasure. He had the same attitude toward all of life—he was a man of unrestrained desires. Rose brought a needed element of discipline to the way he lived. She brought other gifts as well. She was gentle, tactful, calm— qualities noticeably absent in Huey. She made a quietly attractive background for his brilliance, and remaining by preference in the background, she could manage him, sometimes.[7]

After the ceremony the young couple went looking for a place to live. They found a satisfactory apartment, where they stayed until October. Early in that month Huey's mother died, and soon after that he had to endure another loss, a severe reduction in his professional status. His company entered on a period of economic difficulty and had to reduce its sales force. Although the management still had every confidence in Huey, it had to close the Memphis office and or-

[7] Rose McConnell Long; Lucille Long Hunt; Mrs. Gaston Porterie; Frost, article in New Orleans *States*, August 28, 1927; Bozeman, in *Winn Parish Enterprise*, September 26, 1957.

der Huey back to Louisiana. He and Rose decided to cut expenses by taking up residence in the Long family home. Now, instead of directing other salesmen, Huey had to go on the road himself, working north Louisiana and, for the first time, south Louisiana as well. Worse conditions soon afflicted the company. Early in 1914 the founder and owner of Faultless Starch died, and pending the settlement of his estate in the corporation, the company cut all its salesmen off. Huey was without a job again.

He caught onto another one immediately. He agreed to work north Louisiana for the Chattanooga Medicine Company, a concern owned by the Patten family of Chattanooga and directed by the colorful "Bome" Patten. It was a patent medicine house whose list featured such concoctions as Wine of Cardui (which was supposed to stimulate the blood and if taken in sufficient quantity, the whole system) and Black Draught (a laxative). Huey easily made the transition from selling starch to selling medicine. One man who met him at this time remembered that he was "hicky but nervy" and highly persuasive, whether he was talking about pills, politics, or the Bible. Although Huey compiled a good sales record, he was only with the company for a short time. The outbreak of war in Europe in the summer of 1914 caused a depression of prices in the United States and particularly of cotton prices in the South. As business fell off, most companies had to cut their sales force, and the medicine company was no exception. Huey received his dismissal notice at the Bentley Hotel in Alexandria. Depressed by the unexpected news, he telephoned Julius in Winnfield to ask for advice. Julius said that this was the time for Huey to resume his law studies. If Huey would agree to enter the Tulane law school, Julius would arrange to finance his and Rose's expenses while there. Huey accepted the offer.[8]

Huey had spent four years of his life as a salesman. These years had not brought him the riches he had yearned for nor even any economic security. He was almost as destitute when he stopped selling medicine as he had been when he started selling Cottolene. But they were far from wasted years. His experience as a salesman was, in fact, about as valuable a training for his ultimate profession as he could have had. He knew this and took advantage of it. His travels took him into every section of the state and gave him an unrivaled knowledge of the nature and the needs of the people in each area. On a trip into south Louisiana, for example, he learned that the

[8] Bozeman, in *Winn Parish Enterprise*, October 3 and 17, 1957; Rose McConnell Long; Long: *Every Man a King*, p. 15; *Standard Remedies*, XXI (1935), 14, note furnished by J. Harvey Young; Frank Odom.

French "Cajuns" of that area were very different from the Anglo-Saxon farmers of his own northern hills. These Cajuns were easy-going people who would not be hurried into anything. Huey irritated them with his brash, quick ways until he learned how to handle them—that he must relax with them, "pass a good time," before getting down to the business of the moment. In all parts of the state he met hundreds of people from all walks of life. With his remarkable memory, he could recall the names of every one of them. These personal contacts would help him in many ways when he got into politics, but the largest benefit he derived from them was that he learned what ordinary people were like and what they wanted from life. He liked to say later that mere knowledge of law or politics would not make a great lawyer or a great politician. The great leader had to know what made people "tick," and the best way to learn this secret was to be a house-to-house salesman.

Wherever he traveled, in Louisiana or in other states, he attended every political meeting he could, and he studied carefully the speaking techniques of famous orators. In Arkansas he listened with rapt attention to the speeches of Jeff Davis, a flamboyant man who won the governorship and a United States senatorship by denouncing the corporations and "the potbellied, pussle-gutted" bankers and by appealing for the votes of the "rednecks" and "hillbillies," the "one-gallus boys" who lived at the "forks of the creek." Huey observed with interest that the voters did not resent the terms Davis applied to them. Rather, they relished them as showing that their leader was one of them and yet somehow above them. Huey told associates that he could rally the hillbillies of Louisiana behind him in the same way. "They all come from the same stock," he said.

In Mississippi he watched the antics of two other mass leaders, James K. Vardaman, the "Great White Chief," former governor and then aspirant for the Senate, who always dressed in immaculate white and who rode to rallies on a lumber wagon pulled by white oxen, and red-necktied Theodore Bilbo, a diminutive demagogue who was Vardaman's heir and on the way up. Vardaman's attire did not offend the ragged farmers, Huey noticed. In fact, they followed him more trustingly because he dressed like the planters he denounced. Huey voiced a personal distaste for Bilbo, but he admitted that the man had one imaginative tactic. In every town where he spoke, he would begin by denouncing in violent language the wealthiest citizen or citizens. Huey noted that the device always stirred the interest of Bilbo's hearers—and then their envy. He was equally interested in the methods of an entirely different type of politician, Senator John Sharp Williams, often called "the last of the planter statesmen." Polished, scholarly, dignified, Williams looked like a figure out of the past. Yet he could hold his own in debate with anybody. Huey admired particularly his rapier-like wit and his ability to express his thoughts in crystal-clear language that could not be misunderstood.

A leader of the people had to be able to speak in several languages, Huey decided. He had to address the masses in such a way that even his most subtle distinctions came through to them. He could reach them only by using figures of speech that were a part of their experience. From his salesman days Huey drew one of his most telling expressions, a phrase that he would later use with devastating effect to characterize political opponents who had no real difference between them. He would tell how the patent medicine men used to concoct a mixture to sell to Negroes as a hair-straightener, an "anti-kink" medicine. The makers called it "high popalorum" or "low popahirum," depending on how they manufactured it. They made the first by tearing the bark of a tree down, and the second by tearing the bark up. When Huey dismissed two political rivals by comparing them to the two compounds, his amused rural listeners knew exactly what he was talking about. They liked the fact that Huey talked like them, that he was so obviously one of them. But this level of appeal could be overdone. The masses also wanted their leader to be different from them, to be in some ways superior, to talk sometimes in a language they but dimly understood. When he talked in the cultured cadences of a planter-statesman, they could believe that here indeed was a man who was fitted to lead them, a man who was of the people and who yet knew the smooth ways of the lordly ones, a man who could defeat the planter masters at their own game. All these vagaries of the popular psychology Huey knew before he was twenty-one, and he learned most of them while he was a salesman. Those four years on the road were invaluable to him, said one especially analytical associate; they gave him a "jump on everybody else" he would encounter in politics.[9]

[9] Bozeman, in *Winn Parish Enterprise*, October 17 and April 17, 1957; W. Harry Talbot; Joseph Fisher. The phrase employed by Huey was an old one in Winn Parish, spelled in different ways but always meaning the same thing. Huey's version was simply a salesman's variation.

# CHAPTER 4

# All the Law Business
# I Could Handle

JULIUS LONG HAD almost a paternal feeling for Huey. The much older brother, who, with his large, domed head, looked like the intellectual that he was, regarded himself as the guardian of all the younger members of the family. But he showed a special interest in Huey. He tried to guide Huey's intellectual development—to map out his reading, to keep him in school, to form his mind, in essence. Julius was the first member of the family to sense that there was something great in Huey. Julius decided this quality had to be nurtured and brought out, and it was significant that he thought he was the only person who could do the developing. In the plans that he harbored for Huey there was undoubtedly an unconscious projection of self. Through this brilliant younger brother Julius would express his own ambitions and accomplish things he could not achieve on his own. But if Julius's attitude suggested a father who wanted to be reborn in his son, this father did not intend to sit in reflected glory. Julius fully intended to create a great man in Huey, but he also wanted to dominate his creation.

Huey, for his part, had worshipped Julius since childhood and had tried to emulate him. But just as there was an unconscious element of self in Julius's regard for Huey, so there was in Huey's feeling for Julius. Huey might imitate Julius—but he might also want to surpass him. One thing was certain to Huey: he was not always going to submit to Julius's domination. No Long could subordinate himself indefinitely to any other person and especially to another Long. Every Long had to command those around him and all other members of the family. "The desire for power is inherent in the family,"

remarked one veteran Long supporter. "They were nervous men, under tension." Said another: "If I was to go to see Earl now the conversation would start out all right. But pretty soon he'd be telling
me on everything. That's the way the Longs are." One result of this
urge to power has been that throughout its history the family has
periodically divided into warring factions, occasionally into warring
individuals. Sometimes these feuds were patched up in the face of
political exigencies or outside enemies. More often, they were fought
out bitterly and, to the fascinated edification of all Louisiana,
publicly. In thus exposing their differences the Longs violated one
of the canons of Southern hill folk. "They were not typical hill people in their emotions," concluded one observer. "Other families did
not talk about their feuds even though they might be killing each
other. The Longs advertised theirs." When Julius and Huey came to
the fated break, it was inevitable that the younger brother, the
stronger character of the two, would assume the ascendant role. It
was just as inevitable that the older brother would be unable to accept his subordination.[1]

But in the fall of 1914 relations between the brothers still stood
on the original basis. Huey, out of a job and discouraged and at
loose ends, looked to Julius for advice and material help. Julius,
paternal and protective and determined to redeem his promise to
their mother on her deathbed to see that Huey got an education,
offered both. He told Huey that he would plan his course of study at
the Tulane law school and finance his expenses to the sum of fifty
dollars a month for nine months. One condition Julius laid down.
Knowing Huey's splendid ability to spend money and his inability
to save any, Julius insisted that Rose accompany Huey and that the
couple live on a tight monthly budget, to be worked out beforehand
and to be administered by Rose. Huey agreed to the terms, as indeed
he had to. But it was characteristic of him that he would go to New
Orleans with more money than Julius advanced as a starter, money
that Julius did not know about. One of the characters of Winnfield
was State Senator S. J. Harper, who in addition to being a politician
and a cotton buyer, was also an amateur scholar and hence qualified
as an eccentric. Huey went into Harper's store one day and
announced that he was going to Tulane. He must have coupled the
statement with some kind of plea, for Harper asked how much money
he needed. Huey said that he thought $250 would do, whereupon
Harper unhesitatingly wrote him out a check for that amount. When

[1] Lucille Long Hunt; Julius T. Long; confidential communications.

Huey left, Harper's daughter asked if Huey would ever repay the money. Harper answered simply that Huey had a brilliant mind and needed help. Then he added that if he ever required a good lawyer, Huey would help him.[2]

For some reason, probably to show that he had something to say about the arrangement, Huey went down to New Orleans ahead of Rose to rent a place to stay. He took some rooms on Prytania Street that he thought would be ideal for light housekeeping. When Rose arrived, she was horrified to learn that he had agreed to pay a rental of twenty-five dollars a month, a sum that would strain their agreed-on budget to the breaking point. She vetoed his selection and went hunting for a cheaper place. She found one on Carrollton Avenue, a large kitchen and a breakfast room that she secured for only fifteen dollars a month. They used the breakfast nook as a bedroom and turned the kitchen into a study for Huey and a sitting room. On September 28 Huey registered in the Tulane college of law. Once again college bureaucrats rendered his name as Hugh Pierce Long, Jr.[3]

Out of Huey's tenure at Tulane a myth has arisen, the most famous of many that have clustered around his career. It is that he completed the tough three-year law course in one year. The story has been perpetuated endlessly by newspapers, magazines, radio commentators, and almost every writer who has dealt with the Long theme. Curiously, the people who have most readily accepted it are those who were his worst enemies. Yes, they say, Huey did that, but it shows only how devilishly clever the man was. Just how the tale originated is a mystery. It is not certain that Huey invented it, but he never denied it. When he wrote his autobiography, he practically said that he did three years' work in one—but he so qualified the statement that it could also be otherwise interpreted.

No myth could be more at variance with the facts. It was a physical impossibility for a student to cram three years of courses into one year. Even Huey, with all his phenomenal powers of memory, could not have done it. And if he could have, the rules of the school would have prohibited him. Tulane required of its degree candidates three years of resident study, or one year if two years of residence had been taken at another university. To register for a degree as a "regular" student, an aspirant had to possess a high-school diploma.

[2] Lucille Long Hunt; Julius T. Long; Bozeman, in *Winn Parish Enterprise*, October 3, 1957; Maud H. Harper.

[3] Rose McConnell Long; Frost, article in New Orleans *States*, August 28, 1927; E. J. Oakes.

Huey, who could show no record of having finished high school, was therefore ineligible to register for the three-year curriculum. He had to enroll as a "special" student. A special student could not earn a degree, but when he left school, he was given a certificate listing what he had accomplished. Usually a special student registered for fewer classes than a degree candidate. Thus Huey during his year of residence carried a schedule that constituted about a third of the normal load of a regular student. He enrolled in four two-semester courses: Louisiana civil code, Louisiana practice, constitutional law, and successions. He took in addition two one-semester courses: corporation law in the first semester and federal practice in the second. These one-semester courses were the only ones in which he took examinations, however, and hence were the only ones in which he received credit.[4]

This apparently light schedule is as deceptive in its own way as is the myth of the three-in-one performance. It did not mean that Huey was acting irresponsibly or avoiding work. On the contrary, he adopted the one sensible procedure that would get him admitted to the bar quickly. The only way that a student without a law degree could secure admittance was to pass an examination by a committee of lawyers. Most of the lawyers in Louisiana, including Huey's brother Julius, had won their entrance by this method. It was a method that called for a diet of concentrated cramming before the examination. That was what Huey was doing, cramming everything he could into the short period of study available to him. By registering for courses in which he did not seek credit, he picked up a lot of knowledge from the lectures and had more time to study other areas of law. He also sat in on at least one class outside the law school—a political science course. For the first time in his life he was doing something systematically. Only once did he diverge from his stern regime. He went out for the debating team. The coach told him that he had a bad public speaking form: he waved his arms and yelled too much.

In all his classes Huey tried to wring every drop of information he could from the teacher. A fellow student recalled that when the bell rang, Huey always had one more question to ask. Frequently, he

[4] Huey P. Long: *Every Man a King* (New Orleans, 1933), p. 15; Professor Eugene A. Nabors, of the School of Law, Tulane University; excerpts from the Tulane University College of Law Bulletin, 1914–15; transcript of Long's student record, and certificate dated April 26, 1915, of work he accomplished, furnished by the Tulane School of Law. For providing me with these Tulane documents, I am grateful to Mrs. Alexander W. Norman and Mrs. D. F. Yost of the law school staff.

would contradict a professor to stimulate him to continued discussion—or to gratify his own ego. Thus he once said to the venerable Charles Payne Fenner, authority on the civil code: "I can't believe that's the law." On this occasion the technique misfired. Fenner, dignified and humorless, snapped back: "Mr. Long, for the benefit of your future clients, tell them that is the law and reserve your opinions to yourself."

But it was from his own reading that he learned most of his law. He later claimed that he studied from sixteen to twenty hours a day, and he did not exaggerate much. He read all the books that were used as texts in his courses. Not satisfied with this considerable accomplishment, he also read every book that he could get the professors or other lawyers to recommend to him. As soon as he got home from classes, he started reading, and except to stop to eat, he read until a little after midnight. Then he would walk to a nearby saloon, buy a half gallon of beer, bring it back to the room, and by drinking it, try to induce sleep. Sometimes he varied the routine by walking around the block with Rose. When he finished a book, he would sit Rose down at a typewriter they had acquired and dictate to her what he considered the essence of the volume. "I would extract that book from hell to breakfast while it was fresh in my mind," he recalled later, "and I would practically memorize the extract."[5]

He provided a revealing glimpse into his method of self-instruction in a document he wrote years later when he was governor of the state. One day a young man came to Long's suite at the Roosevelt Hotel in New Orleans and asked to see the governor. He told Long that he was too poor to attend a law school and that he wanted somebody to outline for him a course of study that would enable him to pass the bar examination. His earnestness immediately impressed Huey, who walked over to a desk and sketched out a program. As Long wrote, he must have had his experience at Tulane in mind. He advised the youth to study from casebooks and textbooks the following areas of law in order: torts, criminal law, and evidence and the civil code at the same time. Evidence and criminal law should receive special attention; the student must synopsize each case and what the parties contended the law to be, summarize the court's holding, and render his own opinion on the ruling and the reasons why it was right or wrong. Then he was to take up corporation law, briefing the

[5] Charles E. Dunbar; H. Lester Hughes; Long: *Every Man a King*, p. 15; Frost, article in New Orleans *States*, August 28, 1927; George E. Sokolsky: "Huey Long," *Atlantic Monthly*, CLVI (1935), 525–6; Hermann B. Deutsch: "Prelude to a Heterocrat," *Saturday Evening Post*, CCVII (September 7, 1935), 84.

cases as he had for evidence and criminal law; equity, mastering particularly the principles and maxims; constitutional law, again briefing the cases; the revised statutes of Louisiana; and the code of practice.

Throughout the list Long sprinkled injunctions: "read carefully," "never stop studying this," "study hard, article by article," and twice he revealingly wrote: "don't get discouraged." Also revealing was his counsel that the student read some good books, "so that your head will stay open to absorb." He recommended his favorite books, Dumas's *Count of Monte Cristo*, three of Victor Hugo's novels, and Shakespeare's *Julius Caesar, Hamlet,* and *The Merchant of Venice*. These were all works that Huey had read and mastered before he began to study law.

He wrote the suggested reading list at the top of one of the pages of hotel stationery, as though it was an afterthought and something he did not consider absolutely vital. But one piece of outside reading he thought was important enough to put in his program of study. In between the civil code and corporation law on the schedule he inserted a lengthy exhortation to study the Bible. Start in at Genesis and read several pages a day, he commanded. Keep reading, no matter how "wearsome it becomes;" keep the "begats" in mind "just enough to trace generations." But "when you get to the Hebrew Law study carefully all the way: It's the basis of all law."[6]

Huey meant that the Hebraic code provided a philosophical and political foundation for other law. He was so obsessed with this notion that it became almost a fixation with him, a concept that he thought should be installed in every law school. His own introduction to Hebrew law came when he was a student at Tulane, and it was, although he did not fully realize it then, one of the most important things that ever happened to him. It began, apparently, when he heard Professor Fenner deliver in the civil code class one day a lecture on the Louisiana law concerning inheritance. Louisiana followed the Napoleonic or French code, one of whose provisions stipulated "forced heirship" in the transmission of an estate: all heirs, male and female, must receive a certain share of the property. Fenner stressed that the Louisiana law made for a more equitable division than the law of other states and was a most practical way of preventing the concentration of wealth. Huey was so impressed by the lecture that when he saw Fenner leave the campus on a street-

[6] James Thomas Connor, former dean of the law school at Loyola University in New Orleans, told me of this incident and furnished me with a photostatic copy of the document.

car, he got on the car with him and engaged the professor in discussion throughout the ride downtown.

In the conversation, either Fenner remarked that the Hebrew law had a lot to say about the redistribution of property or Huey recalled as he listened that he had heard something about the law in the Bible readings he had been subjected to in childhood. Whatever the case, Huey immediately began to study the Bible, giving particular attention to the books of Leviticus and Deuteronomy that expounded the law of Moses. The whole code impressed him as an admirable set of principles, but what struck him particularly were the commandments that every seven years there should be a release of debts and that every fiftieth year, the "Jubilee" year, there should be a return of possessions to every man. He would later claim that these economic provisions moved him to write a letter to his Congressman pointing out that the present inequities in income in America would bring about a depression in fifteen years, but it is doubtful that he was as precise as he remembered. There can be no doubt, however, that through the study of law his attention was directed as it never had been before to the question of the distribution of wealth. This was not the first time that he had heard the question raised. It had been posed in the Ridpath history he had read as a boy, and it had been a staple item in the political discussions he had listened to as a youth. But now it was brought before him in a peculiarly authoritative and institutional way. He would never forget the lesson. It was ironic that he should have learned it at such a citadel of conservatism as Tulane University.[7]

At Tulane he liked everything he was doing, the classes themselves and the opportunity to study and speculate. But in May, as the end of the second semester approached, Huey faced up to the realization that the allotment of money Julius had advanced him would soon come to an end. He would have to take the bar examination very soon if he expected to be a lawyer. Reluctantly, he sent Rose home to her mother. She could not help him any more, and her departure would lighten living expenses. Then he took a room in a boardinghouse and made his final preparations for the coming ordeal. As a first and major step, he decided to get someone to coach him. At that time it was a common practice for a bar aspirant to solicit the aid of a lawyer who had recently passed the examination and who hence knew what questions the examiners were likely to ask. Nearly always the new lawyers responded favorably; they considered it a duty to coach a worthy candidate. Such was the reaction of Charles J. Rivet, the lawyer Huey sought out. But Rivet, a man with a razor-sharp mind and a somewhat sardonic manner, who later became one of Louisiana's ablest lawyers, was astonished when Huey volunteered that he was from Winnfield. He told Huey that he could not take the examination in New Orleans, that for him to do so would violate one of the firmest rules of the state supreme court, which passed on the admittance of all lawyers. The court maintained examining committees of elder lawyers in the respective judicial districts of the state, Rivet explained, and a candidate had to take the test in the district where he intended to practice. Therefore, Huey would have to take the examination in Shreveport.

No, said Huey, he was going to take it in New Orleans. "And when I insisted that he couldn't," Rivet recalled, "he insisted that he could." Huey ended the argument with a simple proposal: he would take care of the examination if Rivet would coach him. Although Rivet did not believe that Huey could get around the rule, he consented to help. He went to Huey's boardinghouse several nights a week over a period of two or three weeks and gave the candidate the benefit of his knowledge and experience. He passed on to Huey a number of practical hints. For instance, one of the examiners, Edward T. Merrick, liked to have the candidate miss a part of a question so that he could correct him. Always leave out something with Mr. Merrick, Rivet cautioned.

Huey, when he thought that he had had enough coaching, went before the New Orleans examing committee, just as he had told Rivet he would. Later he explained that he simply went to Chief Justice Frank A. Monroe of the supreme court and asked for an early examination. He was married, he said, and he was poor; he did not have enough money to stay in New Orleans until June, when the bar examinations were scheduled. Monroe was sympathetic and advised him to go to the committee and repeat his request. If the committee passed him, the court would admit him immediately. Huey sought out the committee and was easily able to arrange a meeting. That was his story, and it is probably for the most part true. It would have been characteristic of him to go right to the top, to request the intercession of the chief justice. But his account left out how he explained away his ineligibility to take the test in New Orleans. He doubtless neglected to mention that he intended to practice in another district. The busy lawyers who had to take time out to sit on the examining committee were likely to assume that any candidate who appeared before them was qualified to appear. Some years later, when politician Long was offending every belief of conservative Louisianians, Edward T. Merrick asked Rivet how "that creature" had ever got admitted to the bar. Rivet replied that Merrick had been chairman of the examining committee. Even when the shocked Merrick verified the information by checking his records, he was incredulous. How, he asked helplessly, could Huey ever have fooled so many people?

Whatever deception Huey may have employed in arranging the examination, he used none when he came before the committee. He was well prepared and serious, and he answered the questions in a straightforward manner and with accuracy. Only once did he resort to impudence, and he did it knowing that a brash answer would please the interrogator. George H. Terriberry, an expert on admiralty law, asked what young Mr. Long knew about his specialty. Nothing, Huey replied. Terriberry pressed the issue. "What would you do in a case involving admiralty law?" Huey handled this one easily. "I'd associate Mr. Terriberry with me," he said, "and divide the fee with him." The committee had no hesitation in passing him. Almost immediately, on May 15, 1915, he appeared before the supreme court and was formally admitted to the bar. He was a full-fledged lawyer at the age of twenty-one.[8]

Within a few days after he was admitted, Huey was back in Winnfield, ready and eager to offer his legal knowledge to clients and courts. It seemed that he would have no trouble getting business. Huey began to practice in conditions that most young lawyers would have envied. He became a junior partner to Julius and thus shared Julius's considerable practice and office and library; and he and Rose, and also Julius, lived in the Long home and thus were able to cut down on living expenses. But this apparently ideal arrangement lasted only a few months. Then it blew up in bitter controversy. Julius and Huey dissolved their partnership, Huey moved out of Julius's office, and Huey and Rose moved out of the Long home and into a small apartment in a neighbor's house. Huey never presented his side of the quarrel, but Julius had no hesitancy in giving his. As Julius told it later, Huey did all kinds of

[8] Charles J. Rivet; Long: *Every Man a King*, pp. 16–17; Frost, article in New Orleans *States*, August 28, 1927; Charles E. Dunbar; George H. Maines, article in Flint *News-Advertiser*, September 20, 1955. Long, in his autobiography and in his statements to Frost and Maines, said that he also took an examination before the supreme court. Ordinarily a candidate who had passed the bar committee appeared before the court only to be ceremonially admitted. If the justices did administer a second test, it would have been but a perfunctory one.

strange things—he wanted to defend in criminal cases that Julius, as district attorney, was prosecuting, and he tried to take over Julius's private clients. Running through Julius's complaints was the usual note that the younger brother was not properly deferential, was not, Julius was really saying, properly inferior. That was the nub of it. Huey irritated all the older lawyers in Winnfield with his brash confidence, and he could not for long be junior to Julius or anyone else. The specific incident that broke up the partnership revealed much about the relationship of the partners. Julius wrote a brief for a case and showed it to Huey. Huey read it hastily, said it was not worth a damn, and tore it up.[9]

Now that he was on his own, Huey had to set up his own office, and he had little money to do it with. He negotiated for one on the second floor of the Bank of Winnfield, of which his Uncle George was still president, but backed out when he found that the rent was ten dollars a month. He finally took an anteroom to an office in the building at four dollars a month and persuaded the bank to trust him for the first month's payment. Into the small room, only eight by ten feet, he moved what few belongings he had or could buy on credit —three law books, two straight-backed chairs, a small supply of stationery and legal forms, and a desk. The desk was a large dry-goods box that he got from a local store. Its bare appearance so distressed Rose that she finally made curtains to drape its sides. The only illumination in the room was supplied by a kerosene lamp. Optimistically, Huey ordered additional equipment—law books from a firm in New Orleans, a new typewriter, a typewriter table, and a filing cabinet. He bought all of these items on credit, agreeing to pay thirty dollars each month and confident that he could. He hung his sign outside the door and waited for the clients to come in.[1]

Some came, but they were few in number and brought small cases that returned small fees. On the income he earned as a lawyer, Huey could barely support himself and his wife, let alone meet the payments on his purchases of office supplies. He met the crisis by becoming a salesman again. Securing the sales agency in north Louisiana for the Never Fail kerosene home oil can, he hit the road for several months in the latter part of 1915. The Never Fail can

[9] Bozeman, in *Winn Parish Enterprise*, October 3, 1957; Julius T. Long: "What I Know About My Brother," *Real America*, II (September 1933), 35; Julius T. Long to W. D. Robinson, June 2, 1933, in W. D. Robinson Papers, Southern Historical Collection, University of North Carolina Library, Chapel Hill; confidential communication; R. W. Oglesby.

[1] Bozeman, in *Winn Parrish Enterprise*, October 17, 1957; R. W. Oglesby; Long: *Every Man a King*, pp. 18, 23; Frost, article in New Orleans *States*, August 28, 1927.

held five gallons of oil and came with a small hand pump that made it easy for the user to fill a lamp. In an age when most people in rural areas still used oil lamps, it sold readily. Huey disposed of the cans to stores on a commission basis, and he finally developed such a business that he could not handle all of it alone. He sublet the trade in the small towns to his brother Earl and kept the larger and more lucrative centers for himself.

His company, understandably eager to facilitate his travel to these cities, offered to advance him money to buy a car. Huey took them up on the offer, although he did not know how to drive. In Shreveport he purchased a Model-T Ford roadster, which with the aid of a Negro boy he drove to the home of his brother-in-law, Dave McConnell. He asked McConnell to give him driving lessons. McConnell explained the complicated pedal arrangement that characterized the cars of that era, and under McConnell's eye, Huey drove the car out in the country at a good clip. Near a small town Huey stopped to admire his vehicle. An acquaintance who chanced by remarked that the bumper was so placed that it would soon damage the radiator. McConnell was startled to hear his pupil ask: "What is the radiator?" After having this item identified, Huey turned the car back to Shreveport. Confident that he had mastered the art of driving, he stepped up the speed. But he forgot to release the low-gear pedal and thus overheated the motor and then stalled it. He could not understand what he had done wrong and was completely mystified by McConnell's technical explanation.

After a few more lessons Huey felt that he knew enough to take the car alone on his trips around north Louisiana. The crude dirt roads he had to use presented all kinds of dangers to drivers. In wet weather they were impassable for long stretches, and travelers who got stuck had to pay some farmer to pull them out with his team. From more experienced travelers Huey learned to carry a bottle of bootleg whisky in the car—a farmer was much more likely to get his horses out if he was promised a drink as an additional reward. But Huey never learned to drive well. He was too nervous and erratic and too certain that he could make a car do anything he desired, much as he thought he could do with people.[2]

During Huey's absences on the road, Rose kept the law office open and reported to him on what clients had come in. There were still very few of them, and Huey was easily able to take care of their cases during his interludes in Winnfield. The cases were the typical

[2] Bozeman, in *Winn Parish Enterprise*, October 17, 24, 1957, December 18, 1958; David B. McConnell.

ones of a young, small-town Southern lawyer. Several concerned Negro divorce cases. In one of them, Frank Moss, described in Winn-field parlance as a "balloon-head nigger," asked Huey to procure two divorces—one for himself and one for his common-law wife, whom he wanted to marry legally! Huey dutifully procured the separations, charging twenty dollars for the man's and nothing for the woman's. Moss was convinced that he had got a terrific bargain, and the Negro population concluded that Huey was the lawyer to employ in such cases. In the Moss case Huey used another Negro man as an "accessory," the third party, and he continued to use the same man in other divorce cases that came to him. One day when he appeared in court with his accessory, the judge abruptly stopped the proceedings and administered a notable judicial rebuke—he said he was acquainted with the runner and knew he was no lady's man, and warned Huey that if he ever brought him into a case again, no divorce would be granted.

Some cases Huey took because no other lawyer in Winnfield would take them—either they seemed impossible to win or they would return too small a fee. Typical was one brought to him by John Stoehr, a local baker. Stoehr had ordered a certain brand of flour from a Shreveport company, which sent him another brand. He used six sacks of it, and finding that it produced poor bread he sent the balance back and refused to pay for what he had used. Although other Winnfield lawyers thought his case was hopeless, Huey took it and fought it all the way up to the state supreme court. The high tribunal held that a merchant had the right to test a product and was not liable for the part tested if it was inferior. Stoehr, who throughout had contended that he was standing for a principle, thus escaped having to pay a twenty-three dollar bill. He paid a twenty-five dollar fee to Huey, who must have incurred far greater costs in prosecuting the case. Huey assumed financial losses in other cases. In one he represented a woman who was sued for back rent. He lost the case, and later the woman's sewing machine was sold at auction to satisfy the judgment. Huey bought it for eight dollars and returned it to her.[3]

In some cases Huey pioneered in a new area of law—that govern-ing workmen's compensation cases. In 1914 Louisiana had enacted a comprehensive statute governing compensation for industrial in-juries. With the legalities of the subject defined for the first time, compensation cases began to flood the courts, and aspiring young

[3] R. W. Oglesby; Frost, article in New Orleans *States*, August 28, 1927; Long: *Every Man a King*, pp. 29–30; Kenneth Watts.

lawyers like Huey found it profitable to become compensation experts. Under the Louisiana law, as subsequently amended, five thousand dollars was the maximum that could be awarded. The lawyer who won an injury case was entitled to claim one third of the settlement as his fee, but often he was satisfied to take a fourth. Most judgments were under a thousand, and the average was five hundred dollars. The lawyer who lost received nothing, of course, and, because his client was always a poor man, had to bear the costs of the case. Nothing in the law stipulated that the lawyer had to prove negligence on the part of the employer. He had only to convince the jury that his client had suffered a grievous injury and hence deserved compensation. The amount was fixed by the judge. Because of the ambiguity of the law in this respect, employers and compensation lawyers preferred to come to a settlement outside court.

Huey picked up what may have been his first personal-damage case on one of his selling trips in the last part of 1915. On some of these jaunts he took Harley Bozeman with him, who was then representing a patent medicine concern, and Bozeman shared the automobile expenses with Huey. One December day they pulled into the little sawmill town of Wyatt, which lived in the economic shadow of the Wyatt Lumber Company. While they were soliciting orders at the commissary of the company, somebody came in from the mill and said that a Negro worker had just been killed. Immediately Huey realized the possibility of a damage suit. He asked Bozeman to go over to the Negro quarters and tell the relatives of the dead man that Lawyer Long was in town and could help them get some money. (He hoped that the Negroes would think Lawyer Long was the better-known Julius.) Bozeman asked why he did not go himself. Huey replied that it was unethical for a lawyer to solicit business. In the quarters Bozeman found two brothers of the worker and told them about Huey's offer. Grieving and helpless, they needed no persuasion. "Take us to Lawyer Long right quick," one of them begged. "Us ain't got no money to even bury our brother."

They signed a contract making Huey their counsel. And Huey immediately marched into the manager's office and demanded for his clients a thousand dollars damages and burial costs. The manager reacted with pained fury. He declared the demand outrageous and said he would fight it through every court in the state. Huey retorted that the company's negligence had cost a human life. The two continued to shout and wrangle for four hours, although both men knew they were going through a prescribed act; they were really probing for the monetary figure at which they could settle. In the end they agreed that it would be fair if the company paid in cash three hundred dollars and the burial expenses. For his services Huey charged the Negroes seventy-five dollars. To Bozeman he said: "For doing a good ambulance chasing job, your part of the car expense for the rest of the week won't be anything."[4]

Huey did not say whether he thought three hundred dollars was adequate compensation for a human life. Nor did he express any regret at the Negro's death nor any sympathy for the grief of his brothers or their pathetic economic plight. In his reasoning, they should have been thankful that he was on the scene. They probably would have received nothing if he had not been there; they were lucky to get, with his help, even a little. There was no conscious racism in this attitude, although at this stage of Huey's development he had something of the Southern white view that a Negro life was not as valuable as a white one. A compensation lawyer had to be two people simultaneously. On the one hand, he was the defender of the poor who stood up bravely to the heartless corporations. On the other, he was the realistic lawyer who settled for what he could get, which by law was limited, and then took a part of it for himself. If his action in the first area awakened his humanitarian instincts, that in the second stunted those instincts and left him a more cynical person. Necessarily, compensation lawyers had to develop a hard protective outer shell, had to affect an apparent flippancy about maimed bodies. Otherwise they could not have represented their clients—or lived with themselves. Huey, even when he was out of the business, could not talk about it except jokingly. Back when he was a damage-suit lawyer, he once recalled, the courts went by a sound principle: "that a widow was entitled to less damages for a dead husband than for an injured one, because when he was dead she didn't have to support him."[5]

Huey did so well with his oil-can business that he was soon able to retire most of his outstanding financial obligations. Freed of worry that his office equipment might be confiscated, he resumed early in 1916 the practice of law on practically a full-time basis. But, as before, few clients came to him, and those that did brought the same kind of small cases, which returned unrewarding fees. It was what he later called "a little chip and whet-stone practice." And it

[4] Will Harvey Todd; F. Leonard Hargrove; Robert Brothers; Charles W. Pipkin: "Social Legislation," in W. T. Couch, ed.: *Culture in the South* (Chapel Hill, 1935), pp. 652–3; Bozeman, in *Winn Parish Enterprise*, October 17, 1957.
[5] Long, quoted in press dispatch, n.d. [probably 1929], in Lucille May Grace Scrapbook, Louisiana State University Library; Russell B. Long.

would continue to be until he could get the kind of case that every young lawyer needs and prays for, one that will enable him to win a spectacular triumph by a display of natural shrewdness, one that will immediately stamp him as being so clever that clients will flock to secure his services.

Forced to subsist on a reduced income, Huey got into financial trouble again. He had established a modest checking account at the bank, and one day he wrote a check that he knew would slightly overdraw his balance. To him the action was perfectly proper. He would cover the overdraft, as the bank must realize, and furthermore, the bank was Uncle George's, in the family. Soon afterward he went to the bank to deposit enough money to make up for the deficiency. He was met by an officer of the bank, possibly Uncle George himself, who roughly informed him that there was no overdraft, because the bank had refused to honor the check, and also that the bank was getting very impatient with Huey's failure to pay his office rent. Taken aback and resentful, Huey muttered: "Now I understand you." The officer concluded his lecture with a threat: "Well, if you understand that, then understand that we expect that office rent paid, and that may keep you here a while longer than you will be if things go like they are now. I looked that office over and there ain't anything to move." Huey left the bank in a fury. Within a few days he would have an opportunity to make another call on the bank, one he liked much better.[6]

Shortly after the interview a widow named Martha DeLoach came to his office. She wanted to sue the Bank of Winnfield, but no lawyer in town would take her case. Her story was a pathetic one. Years back she had deposited some insurance money in a bank that had since been absorbed by Uncle George's institution. An official of the first bank had taken some of her money for his own use. When his act was detected, he paid Mrs. DeLoach part of her money and gave her a note for the remainder, $276. Then he fled the state. She thought the Bank of Winnfield should be liable for the balance, but the bank thought otherwise. So did all the lawyers whom she had consulted before going to Huey. They told her that in accepting the offender's note she had released any claim upon the bank and that, in addition, the second bank could not be held responsible for the sins of the first. Although her case did rest on a somewhat dubious basis, the lawyers' reaction sprang from their reluctance to challenge the powerful bank and the leading attorneys who represented

[6] Long: *Every Man a King*, pp. 22–3.

it. This consideration did not influence Huey, who had no reputation to lose and who could make one by defeating the bank that had just humiliated him. He told Mrs. DeLoach that he would take the case.

It was with immense satisfaction that he filed the suit—and informed the bank of his action. But when the case came to trial, the bank's lawyers sprang a surprise that nearly ended the hearing before it started. They blandly observed to the judge that the attorney for the plaintiff would have to post bond to cover the costs of the case. Huey had forgotten this technicality, and he was staggered when the judge, agreeing with the suggestion, set the bond at one hundred dollars. Neither he nor Mrs. DeLoach had anything like that sum. Hastily he asked for and won an adjournment. He spent the rest of the day and part of the night going around town trying to persuade someone to put up the money. On every hand he met refusal. Nobody wanted to risk such an amount in a doubtful fight against the bank. Near midnight he saw a light burning in Senator Harper's office, and desperate and almost ready to give up, Huey went in. He found the senator at his desk, reading a history of the world. Although he was aware that Harper was a director of the bank, he also knew that the old man had a natural sympathy for the underdog, so he asked for help. Harper reacted as Huey thought he would. The woman deserved a hearing, the senator exclaimed. He could not properly ask anybody to sign the bond, he went on, but he would lend Huey part of the required sum in cash, say seventy-five dollars. Huey could post the cash and get a waiver on the balance until the costs exceeded that amount.

The news that the bank had forced the widow to put up a cost bond inflamed the community. Huey bore down hard on this point all during the trial. He denounced in unsparing terms the greed of the bank's president, Uncle George, and its vice-president, B. W. Bailey. He charged that since the big bank had bought the assets of the other, it was therefore responsible for its liabilities, even to the humblest citizen. Remembering that Mrs. DeLoach had a number of small children, he commanded her: "Get all those kids down there for the jury to see." The children sat in the courtroom day after day, directly in front of the jury, all of them raggedly dressed, probably because of the widow's poverty but possibly by Huey's design. As the trial continued, public sentiment against the bank mounted to new bitterness. Finally Vice-President Bailey called Harley Bozeman to his office and begged him to ask Huey to stop attacking the bank's officials. Plaintively Bailey said that he could not understand Huey's personal animus—he and Uncle George were the best friends Huey's family had. When Bozeman relayed this conversation to Huey, the crusading young lawyer smiled tolerantly and said that he had no personal feeling against the bank's officers. But he recalled his low status when he had started to practice law. "I was the littlest of the least here in Winnfield," he went on. "Uncle George, Mr. Bailey, and the bank were the biggest people and thing." By taking out after the bank, he had lifted himself up to a level with the big people. "You go back and tell Uncle George and Mr. Bailey that they should feel complimented," he told Bozeman—"that Huey Long don't take out after topwaters but after the big fish." He was revealing a technique, here used by him for the first time, that he would employ later again and again in his rise to political power—if you want to attract popular attention and support, denounce the biggest, closest target at hand.[7]

It was Huey's use of this technique, more than any display of legal skill, that enabled him to win the DeLoach case. The court held that the widow was entitled to her $276 plus five per cent interest to run from the date of judgment. Despite the small amount of money involved, the suit made Huey as a lawyer. This was the kind of case he had been waiting for, one that would mark him as the smartest lawyer around. That was the way most people in the parish viewed him after the DeLoach case. "I cleaned hell out of them in that suit," he later recalled, "and after that I had all the law business I could handle." Now the clients came in ever larger numbers, and he won more and more cases. He saw to it that his victories were well publicized. A little earlier, to enlarge his income, he had become the Winnfield correspondent of several daily papers in Shreveport and other north Louisiana cities. Suddenly most of the news from Winnfield told of legal triumphs scored by a certain young lawyer. The name of Huey P. Long was beginning to be known outside Winn parish.[8]

Many of the clients now coming to Huey were landowners who were involved in disputes with lumber companies over timber rights.

[7] Ibid., pp. 23–5; Frost, article in New Orleans *States*, August 28, 1927; O. B. Thompson; Harley B. Bozeman; Bozeman, in *Winn Parish Enterprise*, November 7, 1957.
[8] The decision is filed in a bound volume entitled Judicial Proceedings, Fifth Judicial District, Winn parish, in clerk of court records, parish courthouse, Winnfield: *DeLoach* v. *Bank of Winnfield*, Civil Suits Book B, Suit 3194; Deutsch: "Prelude to a Heterocrat," *Saturday Evening Post*, September 7, 1935, p. 85; Kenneth Watts; Harley B. Bozeman; Bozeman, in *Winn Parish Enterprise*, September 18, 1958.

The subject of timber titles was a burning one in the upland parishes at that time, and the litigation growing out of it offered almost unlimited opportunities to an adept lawyer. The situation bordered on the chaotic. As the forest reserves dwindled, the lumber companies had rushed to buy up every available tract of timbered land. Sometimes they dealt fairly with the owners, sometimes they cheated them, and sometimes they took possession of land without securing a clear title. Whatever they did, they did in hot haste, and they brought down endless lawsuits on themselves. Most of the suits stemmed from the peculiar Louisiana law requiring the transmission of property to several heirs. As a result of its operation, the ownership of a typical piece of land, or the timber rights on it, was very likely to be vested in a number of people. A company might, for instance, buy a tract from a husband whose wife had died. Immediately her heirs would appear and claim their equity in the land. A lawyer for a plaintiff in a land-title case had to have special qualities—an instinct to recognize when he had a suable case, an ability to grasp the one point that would win the case, and a willingness to gamble that he would get a fee.

This kind of litigation was made to order for Huey, and for a time he specialized in land-title work. He won most of his cases. His fees from these victories enabled him to enlarge his office space in the bank, increase his law library, and acquire the other possessions that were the mark of a successful lawyer. Sometimes he took his fee in timber or land, either because the client had nothing else to offer or because the potential value of the timber or land was greater than a cash fee. He sold the timber at the best market price. The land he held on to, renting some of it out and selling other parts over the years. Just how much land he owned altogether is impossible to determine. But as late as 1935, when he was in the Senate, he admitted that he still held three farms.[9]

Of Huey's various title cases, the one most rewarding financially and most revealing of his technique was popularly known as the Urania case. It featured all the ingredients that were rapidly becoming typical of the suits that Long brought—the evil big corporation, the wronged humble client, and the idealistic but sharp young lawyer. The corporation was the Urania Lumber Company, one of the biggest in the state, headed by former state senator Henry Hardtner,

[9] Long: *Every Man a King*, pp. 29–31; Maines, article in Flint *News-Advertiser*, September 27, 1955; Bozeman, in *Winn Parish Enterprise*, November 7, 1957; Long, quoted in *American Progress*, May 1935.

of Alexandria, who had three main ambitions: to acquire timber-
lands, wield political power, and develop scientific forestry practices.
The plaintiff was Mrs. Hattie D. Wheelus, who brought suit in her
name and her husband's. The Wheeluses claimed that they owned
all of the timber on parts of two sections on which Urania claimed
that it had one half undivided ownership, signed over to it by Mrs.
Wheelus. The plaintiff asserted that she had not signed any transfer
or, cryptically, that if she had, it had been obtained by fraud. Huey
won the case by convincing the court that one of her complaints had
to be true. He thereby earned the undying enmity of Hardtner, who
protested that Huey's presentation had been unscrupulous. The real
reasons for Hardtner's animosity went deeper. Huey had thwarted
one of his ambitions, to grasp land, and threatened another, to retain power. The lumber magnate dimly sensed, as did others of his
class, that this brash young lawyer represented some kind of threat
to their position.[1]

For his fee Huey received part of the property claimed by the
Wheeluses, 160 acres of richly timbered land. He was an elated man
after the settlement. He told Harley Bozeman as the two of them left
his law office on a Sunday night: "That 160 acres of land I got . . . is
the biggest fee I have collected since I hung out my shingle. The
timber on it is worth at least $1,500." He babbled on about his
success as he and Bozeman walked down the street. At one point
they came to a temporary open-air Baptist tabernacle, which the
congregation was using until a permanent structure could be built.
They could hear the preacher asking for donations, starting at twenty-
five dollars and coming steadily down as he evoked no response.
Suddenly Huey darted into the church. Standing in the center aisle,
he shouted: "Brother, what you taking up a collection for?" The
pastor, astonished both at Huey's unexpected appearance in church
and his manner in asking the question, said that the collection was
for the building fund. Huey strode down the aisle, pulling out his
checkbook and fountain pen as he went, and quickly wrote a check.
Returning to the entrance, he grabbed Bozeman and said brusquely:
"Let's go." Outside he admitted with embarrassment that he had
contributed $150, a tenth of his Wheelus fee.[2] Personally sympathetic
to anybody in want, he was capable of doing a generous act on

[1] *Wheelus* v. *Urania Lumber Company*, in Fifth District Judicial Proceedings,
Civil Suits, Book B, Suit 3264, and Conveyance Records, Book X, p. 528; Harley
B. Bozeman.
[2] Harley B. Bozeman.

impulse. But on this occasion he possibly was responding to a feeling of contrition—expiating for the sin of having taken a large material reward for an action about which he had some doubts.

In the Urania case Huey had been pitted against some of the best-known corporation lawyers in the state, and the outcome caused his own reputation to soar to new levels. His intimates differ as to what attention he expected to accrue to him as a result of his success and what kind of career he expected to follow. Bozeman was convinced that Huey thought the corporations would now recognize his ability and come running to him to secure him as their counsel. At this time Huey would rather have been a prosperous corporation lawyer than anything else, Bozeman thought. When the corporations held back, Huey decided in 1918 to run for a seat on the Railroad Commission, from which regulative agency he could strike at the companies that had ignored him. But according to another intimate, the corporations did try to employ him: two oil companies, for instance, offered him large yearly retainers to become their counsel. He turned them down, saying that he could not receive that much money and still represent the interests of the people. Huey himself gave tacit support to the latter interpretation by claiming in his autobiography that in all his cases he had represented "the small man—the underdog" and that he had never taken a case against a poor man. The second part of the statement was true; the first false. He did, after the Urania case, represent corporate interests in some cases. But he did it only on rare occasions, and it seems unlikely that he ever seriously desired to be a corporation lawyer. His only real ambition was to get into politics, and he knew better than to saddle himself with the handicap of being known as the attorney of the rich. He could safely accept a case from a corporation now and then, but he could not afford to be hired on a regular retainer basis.[3] He would give up the practice of law in Winnfield in 1918 and become a "city" lawyer. But in his new location he would continue to represent the same kind of clients—the "small men and the underdogs."

[3] Harley B. Bozeman; Maines, article in Flint *News-Advertiser*, September 27, 1955; Long: *Every Man a King*, p. 37. Long's entry into politics as a member of the Railroad Commission, which very soon afterward became the Public Service Commission, is treated in Chapter VI.

# CHAPTER 5

# *I Won a Very Good Lawsuit*

I N NOVEMBER 1918, after his election to the Railroad Commission, Huey moved his residence and his law practice to Shreveport, the metropolis of northwestern Louisiana. His duties on the Commission, which required among others the supervision of public carriers in twenty-eight northern parishes, dictated that he locate in a larger and more accessible place than Winnfield. But considerations of his law career also influenced him to make the shift—in an urban center he ought to be able to expand his practice. This possibility was urged on him by one of his closest friends, O. B. Thompson, an independent oil and sawmill operator who had previously employed Huey as counsel in various cases. Thompson, a large, rugged, and dominating man, had come to have a warm admiration for Huey and to think of the young lawyer as his protégé. Now he told Huey that he would assist him with the expenses involved in moving to Shreveport and renting an office. With Thompson's help, Huey secured a front office on the third floor of the Merchant's Building, an exceptionally good spot. Huey himself found for his family a small house, on the west end of town, that rented at a reasonable price.[1] That family was growing. A daughter, Rose, had been born in Winnfield in April 1917, and a son, Russell B., was born in Shreveport the month the Longs moved there. With more mouths to feed, Huey had an additional incentive to increase his law business.

Also urging Huey to make the move to Shreveport had been Julius Long. The brothers had had a reconciliation in 1918, and

[1] O. B. Thompson.

Julius supported Huey in the Railroad Commission race. Soon after
that Julius's own political fortunes dipped badly. Having been district attorney for eight years, he ventured to run for district judge and
was defeated. Out of a job and recently married, he decided to return to the practice of law full time. In December 1920 he too came
to Shreveport, and he and Huey formed a partnership, both of them
occupying Huey's office. This partnership did not last much longer
than the previous one. Almost immediately the two fell into the old
pattern—bitter quarrels, violent recriminations, and long periods
when they did not speak to each other. Finally, in August 1921,
Huey served Julius with a written notice to vacate the office. But
then, according to Julius, Huey noticed that there was a vacant
office on the same floor, and fearing that Julius would take it and
steal his clients, he asked Julius to re-form the partnership. Whatever the truth, they signed a new agreement. Its terms indicated the
nature of the disagreements between them. Each bound himself to so
behave as to indicate to clients that the other was an equal partner,
to refrain from personal disagreement in the presence of clients, and
to hold up and preserve the reputation of the other. Each was to
have his private office, which the other was not to enter except by
invitation or by announcement. If these were intended to be restrictions on Huey, they were as ineffective as they might have been
expected to be. Within a few days of their signing, there was another
terrible scene, and the partnership was dissolved again, this time
finally. According to one source, Huey literally kicked Julius out of
the office.[2]

For a time after the breakup Huey worked alone. As a new
lawyer in a strange town, he had to work hard to build up a practice.
He appeared in his office every day at five in the morning and remained there into the night. "I must stay here and sit on the lid,"
he wrote to a friend. The strain of the long hours eventually told on
him. He who as a politician would be considered tireless by his
associates had now to confess to a great weariness. "I am now literally
worn out," he wrote to another friend. "I cannot take the leisure
which some few months ago I thought I could take." But he stuck it
out, and soon he had the satisfaction of seeing his practice grow.
After he became established, he returned to the partnership arrangement and enjoyed again the advantage that its division of labor gave.
Among the lawyers who were joined with him at various times were
J. B. Crow, Philip H. Mecom, George T. McSween, Robert J.

[2] Julius T. Long: "What I Know About My Brother," *Real America*, II (September 1933), 35–7; Lewis Gottlieb; confidential communication.

O'Neal, and Harvey Fields. They were all good lawyers, and each one would later carve out a solid legal reputation. But while they practiced with Huey, every one of them was literally as well as formally a junior partner. It could not be any other way with him.[3]

Huey also entered into what might be called a long-distance partnership with a lawyer in Prescott, Arkansas, by the name of William Denman. The purpose of this unusual arrangement was to enlarge his practice in compensation cases, the field of law that specially interested him and that for a time offered him his principal business. He was located in an ideal spot for a compensation lawyer. Shreveport, standing near the Arkansas–Louisiana border, was in the center of the oil and lumber enterprises of both states. Workers in these industries suffered injuries almost every day. Which state an injured man sued in for compensation was a matter of some importance to him and his lawyer, and to the company concerned. In Arkansas the lawyer for the plaintiff had to prove negligence on the part of the employer, but there was no limit on the amount of money that could be awarded. In Louisiana he did not have to prove negligence and hence could win more easily, but there was a maximum limit to the possible financial award. The difference in the laws of the two states influenced the course of both parties to an injury. For instance, a Louisiana industrialist might own a plant in Arkansas. If one of his employees there was hurt, he would rush the man to a Shreveport hospital so that the resulting suit would be brought in Louisiana. Or, if a laborer resident in Arkansas but employed in Louisiana was injured at work, his lawyer would, if he thought he could demonstrate negligence, seek to try the case in Arkansas. Huey's association with Denman enabled him to bring more suits in that state than otherwise would have been possible. "Denman would get the cases," one Long associate recalled. "Huey would win them."[4]

But necessarily, because of his location, Huey had to try the majority of his cases in Louisiana. As most of them were compensation cases, the fee he could charge if he won was limited by law to

[3] Huey P. Long to George J. Soper, February 22, 1921; to Leland H. Moss, September 8, 1921; and to T. J. Maloney, September 25, 1921, in Huey P. Long Papers, Private Law Cases File, Department of Archives and Manuscripts, Louisiana State University Library, Baton Rouge (hereafter cited as Long Papers, Law File). This collection, apparently the only body of Long manuscripts extant, consists of two sections, of which the Law File is one. The other consists of correspondence dealing with Long's tenure on the Public Service Commission; it will be cited hereafter as Long Papers, Public Service Commission File. On Long's partnerships, see Harvey G. Fields: *A True History of the Life, Works, Assassination and Death of Huey P. Long* (Silver Spring, Md., 1944), p. 19.

[4] Robert Brothers; Frank Hood; F. Leonard Hargrove.

one third of the amount awarded. In other damage cases, however, such as injuries resulting from railroad or automobile collisions, he could claim up to one half of the settlement. But if he lost a damage suit, he, or his client if the latter could afford it, had to pay all the costs. Nearly always Huey found that he had to bear the costs of a lost suit himself. After one such case he had to tell his witnesses that he could not at the moment reimburse them for their expenses. "I lost several hundred dollars trying to help Mr. Sermons out," he explained to one witness. He went on to describe the economic problem of the compensation lawyer: "I represent these poor people and do the best I can. There isn't any actual money that will amount to very much, if I win them all." He frequently warned clients that even if victorious they could expect only a modest settlement. "I am afraid we will never get anything," he frankly told one plaintiff, "but I want to pluck along and get anything that I can."[5]

Plucking along, he usually got but little for his clients and hence for himself. In one typical suit, he represented an oil worker whose foot had been injured by a drill pipe that fell from a derrick. Claiming that the man had been permanently disabled, Huey sued the employer for eight thousand dollars, and then settled out of court for three hundred, of which a third went to him as a fee. In another, he represented a woman who had been hurt in an automobile collision with a laundry truck. He sued the laundry company for five thousand dollars, but adjusted the claim out of court for two hundred dollars, of which he received half as a fee. In still another, he took the case of a man who had been hit in an automobile by a railroad handcar at a crossing. This man gave his suit to Huey with complete confidence, writing to a friend: "Oh if a man ever was in trouble it me. Getting so I cant hardly walk. Mr. Meek the company would do nothing for me so I am suing them. Turned the case over to Hughy P. Long and McSween. Old Hughy said they couldnt get out of it said he would make them come across so now." But Old Hughy was able to secure a judgment of only five hundred dollars, and half of this went as his fee.[6]

It may be speculated that Huey settled suits like the above because he realized that in each he had a weak case—he compromised because only by so doing could he get anything for his clients. It is

[5] Long to H. McCormick, January 12, 1926; to J. H. Drewitt, April 9, 1926; and A. B. T. Simonds, February 23, 1927, in Long Papers, Law File.

[6] *Smith* v. *Scott, Singer* v. *Excelsior Steam Laundry Company, McCormick* v. *Kansas City Southern Railroad Company*, cases and correspondence, ibid.; J. H. McCormick to Gordon Meek, December 7, 1925, ibid.

possible too that he suspected that some of his clients were over-stating the extent of their injuries. He acted quite differently when he had a strong case that excited his sympathies. Thus he pushed relentlessly the suit of a worker who had been injured in an iron works plant at Shreveport, and he won for the man a judgment of $2,868. He took the case of an injured oil worker and fought the suit from 1924 to 1931, finishing it when he was governor, all to get the man an award of $4,000 (his fee here was over $1,300).[7] He won, indeed, most of the cases he had any chance of winning. In the opinion of friends and foes alike, he was one of the ablest compensation and personal-injury lawyers in his area. A corporation attorney who did not like him nonetheless recalled: "I opposed Huey in lots of cases. There was little law on either side in them. You got your doctors and witnesses down there and tried to convince the jury. Huey would ask 'Is this a leg or arm case?' and then he'd go to bat. He had no deep knowledge of the law. But he could listen to five or six suggestions and pick out the one that would win a case." One of his partners said the same thing about his ability to cut to the center of a damage case. He recounted that once the firm had taken the case of a little girl whose arm had been broken when a piece of plaster fell on her in a building. While two of the partners were debating how much to sue for, Huey came in. He listened to the discussion a while and then exclaimed: "I'm sure she's got swimming in the head too. Let me prepare that petition. Nobody can beat me at drawing up a petition." He drew one claiming thirty thousand dollars and eventually settled the case for ten thousand dollars.[8]

Huey took many compensation cases because for a time they were the only kind he could get. But he continued to take them after he had become established and could have refused them. Undoubtedly, he relished the role of prosecutor for the poor, which was a good part for an aspiring politician. He liked having clients write him such expressions as the following from an injured worker: "Have always been told that you were always the undermans friend so I feel confident you will give this your emediate attention. And make the Judge come across." But beyond reasons of personal satisfaction, he remained a compensation lawyer because of that streak of impulsive generosity in his nature that made him do such things as give part of his Urania fee to the church. He could not resist the sight of

<hr>

[7] *McCorley* v. *Union Iron Works, Simonds* v. *Austin Oil Company*, cases and correspondence, ibid.; Long to Simonds, January 29, 1931, and Simonds to Long, February 2, 1931, ibid.

[8] F. Leonard Hargrove; Robert J. O'Neal.

somebody in want. Once he and a friend passed on the street a poor woman and her ragged brood of children. He went on a few steps and then stopped. "That breaks my heart," he muttered. He went back and gave all the change in his pocket to the woman. At a conference in his office he became so affected by a client's recital of poverty that he broke down and wept before his partners, and then directed them to fight the case twice as hard for half the fee.[9]

These displays of tenderness were almost always acts of the moment. But in one case he spread a deed of kindness over a period of several years. A Mrs. Jennie K. Bankston asked him to handle the equity of her two stepsons in the estate of her husband, their father. He did so, and because of Mrs. Bankston's relationship to the boys, one twenty-one and the other seventeen, the court appointed Huey as the disburser of the funds. The older boy, Wyatt, soon became ill of tuberculosis and went to a sanitarium in San Angelo, Texas. Huey watched over Wyatt like a father. He wrote the boy regularly, all the letters filled with advice and encouragement—rest and eat good and you will get well, and when you are recovered I'll help you get a job. He persuaded the stepmother and the other brother to let him pay to Wyatt the balance of the estate fund. One day he had to tell Mrs. Bankston that all the money had been paid out. He made an interesting admission: "Over and above that, I have given Wyatt quite a little of my own money." This soft side of his nature was visible to but a few people and would have been unbelievable to the many who knew him only as the ruthless ruler of politics.[1] It is unbelievable to many even today.

IN THE TEN YEARS THAT Huey practiced law in Shreveport he rarely had a big case, that is, one in which he represented a large economic interest and which would have returned him a large fee if he had won it. Local corporations and businessmen did not seek out his services, even after he had established a reputation as an able lawyer. They did merely not come to him, they actually shunned him. The reasons for his ostracism lay partly with the town and partly with him. Shreveport was an ultraconservative community, and its power structure was determined to keep the situation unchanged. The regents of the city would resent any individual who challenged their

[9] Curt Sheets to Long, August 16, 1926, in Long Papers, Law File: Jess Nugent; Fields: *Long*, p.15.
[1] Bankston Succession and Tutorship, documents and correspondence, in Long Papers, Law File; Long to Mrs. J. K. Bankston, April 6, 1928, ibid.

power or derided their comfortable ideals, and if they could, they would suppress such a rebel. Huey disturbed them by his brash and breezy manner, his blatant championship of workers' rights, and his violent attacks on corporate greed. Their acidly expressed disapproval did not faze Huey in the slightest. He never tried to conciliate the power elite or compromise with them. On the contrary, he seemed to delight in deviling them; he hurled every insult with obvious relish. "He made his enemies in Shreveport," admitted a man who liked him. "The old or first families fought him. They resented him." Said a representative of these families: "I would never have liked him regardless of his ideas. I would never have asked him to my house. He didn't associate with the nice people."

On several occasions the sense of outrage felt by conservative Shreveporters boiled over into attempted or actual violence on his person. The assailant in the most sensational of these episodes was Randall Moore, an official of the Commercial National Bank, the largest financial institution in the city. Infuriated by a recent Long attack on the bank, Moore jammed Huey up against a building on Market Street, pulled a knife, and muttered: "I ought to cut your goddamned throat." Huey must have known that Moore had previously cut several people. He later explained to a reporter how he had escaped possible serious injury: "What would you do if a man had a knife on you and dared you to say something? I didn't say nothing."

In another incident Huey was the aggressor. Dolph Frantz, editor of the Shreveport *Journal*, had printed statements charging that on a recent trip to Baton Rouge Long had got drunk and had disgraced himself. Stung by the accusation, Huey threatened a libel suit. One day a friend told him on the street that the *Journal* had repeated the story. At that moment Frantz came out of his office. Huey started across the street at him, calling: "I'm tired of your lies." The two men clinched and fell rolling in the gutter, and when bystanders separated them Frantz was bleeding around the mouth. Huey went to the police station and offered to give himself up. He would stand any charge Frantz chose to bring (the editor would bring none), he announced, if he could stop the lies in the newspaper.[2]

[2] Overton Brooks; confidential communication; Robert J. O'Neal; Frank J. Peterman; Rupert Peyton; New Orleans *States*, October 10, 1921. Many of my newspaper citations were taken from the Huey P. Long Scrapbooks, a huge collection of 57 volumes in the Louisiana State University Library, Baton Rouge. Hereafter the Long Scrapbook and other scrapbooks will not be cited by name unless a clipping from them is unidentified.

The only corporation that ever employed Huey as its lawyer was not a Shreveport or even a Louisiana company, but an out-of-state concern, the Consolidated-Progressive Oil Corporation, which had its headquarters in Hoboken, New Jersey. Consolidated was a relatively young, small company that was trying to break into the developing and potentially rich oil territory of northwestern Louisiana. It claimed that in the Homer field in Claiborne parish it owned leaseholds and mineral rights that had been fraudulently transferred by a former president to other companies. In attempting to assert its claims, the company became involved in a series of suits that extended over seven years. The directors engaged Huey with the thought that in prosecuting suits in Louisiana courts they would do better with a Louisiana lawyer than with an outsider. Huey first came to their attention under odd circumstances: in 1920 he represented an official of the company, Thomas A. Nevins, in a suit against the company. Nevins had sold part of the Homer field for the company and claimed that he was not paid his share of the proceeds, or $35,000. Huey took the case on a contingent fee; he was to receive twenty-three per cent of the settlement, or $7,000, if Nevins recovered the full amount. He began the suit in the district court of Caddo parish, where he won the judgment, but Consolidated appealed to the state supreme court. Before the latter body could act, the case was settled by agreement between the parties. The amount of the settlement is not known, and hence Huey's share of it cannot be determined. He probably consented to a modest fee since by then he was representing Consolidated in still another suit.[3]

Consolidated, among its other troubles, was going through the throes of a reorganization fight. A new president, Edward F. McDermott, and a new board of directors, of whom Nevins was one, was trying to oust the old board. The new board proposed to move aggressively to recover the Claiborne leases, and, probably at Nevins's suggestion, it employed Huey to press its claims. Huey agreed to work for a small cash retainer and a large contingent fee, one tenth of the value of the disputed holdings, which were estimated to run into the millions. But before the new board could do anything, it had to assert its authority in the company, and it asked Huey to handle the

[3] *Nevins* v. *Consolidated-Progressive Oil Corporation*, documents and correspondence, in Long Papers, Law File. Long to Nevins, August 4 and 20, 1920, Long to J. F. Minturn, September 12, 1921, L. H. Moss to Abraham Levitan, February 6, 1922, ibid. I am indebted to attorney F. Leonard Hargrove of Shreveport for aid in analyzing this case and for supplying citations.

proceedings against the old board. Huey accepted both assignments enthusiastically. He went to New York to confer with the board, wrote a statement of intent for McDermott to read to the board, and in correspondence with his clients used freely the word "we"—we have the bunch whipped, we should soon be in control—quite as if he were a principal stockholder.

He had assumed from the start that he would direct completely the strategy of the suits, and he was infuriated when he discovered that McDermott and another director, Charles C. Gates, had entered into negotiations with the old board, looking to a compromise. "Their method of negotiating," he wrote to another director, "adjourning, renegotiating, awaiting the arrival of a guest, dinners, tete a tetes, etc., would frustrate any kind of plan." Any organization built around such men, he went on, was as useless as "a fur-lined pajama in Brazil." He became so disgusted at one point that he addressed a blanket condemnation to all the directors. Their actions past and present constituted "one continuous and added disgust," he told them. They were like "an elephant who must be pulled through the snow." He ended: "I am thoroughly through with you."[4]

Huey did not carry out his threat to quit, however, and when the squabble within the company was finally settled, he prepared to represent it in suits against its outside enemies. The first of these was the Paramount Petroleum Company, a locally owned concern. Consolidated had transferred to Paramount rights in one half of its claimed holdings in Claiborne parish. Paramount had furnished a bond to pay, but had not paid and had placed a mortgage on the transferred property. Huey sued to throw Paramount into receivership and to force the sureties (guarantors) of the bond to honor its amount. He started the case in 1921. It dragged on for years, the attorneys for Paramount and the sureties using every trick to delay its course. Not until 1926 was Huey able to secure a judgment. Then Paramount alone, not the sureties, was directed to return $29,566 to Consolidated. The victory brought little financial reward to Consolidated or its lawyer, but Huey was not too disappointed by the outcome. Paramount was broke—had, in fact, been broke for years.

[4] *Consolidated-Progressive Oil Corporation* v. *O'Toole* [of the board], documents and correspondence, in Long Papers, Law File. Statement by E. F. McDermott to board of directors, April 17, 1920; Long to C. C. Gates, April 26, June 22, 1920; Long to T. A. Nevins, August 20, 1920; Long to G. J. Soper, December 23, 1920; indenture between Long and Consolidated-Progressive Oil Corporation, July 5, 1921, Long to Consolidated-Progressive Oil Corporation, August 7, 1921, ibid.

Knowing this, Huey had predicted that winning a judgment against it would be "very much like finding the treasure of a Central American republic after the president had left for Spain."[5]

The suit against Paramount was only a preliminary skirmish against a minor, though irritating, foe. Next Huey and Consolidated moved against their major enemy, the corporate interest that stood between them and incredible wealth. It was no ordinary antagonist they proposed to sue—the Standard Oil Company of Louisiana, a subsidiary of the parent corporation and the industrial giant of the state. Consolidated contended that the former president, who had signed away so many of its holdings in Claiborne parish, had fraudulently transferred a valuable lease to another party who had then transferred the tract to Standard. Huey recited these facts in the suit he brought against Standard in 1921. He asked for damages of nine million dollars for three million barrels of oil produced from the lease and for return of the lease. On the eve of the trial he was in a mood of savage confidence. "I will put the fear of hell in their heart, if such the Standard has," he exclaimed. Although he had a personal and a political grudge against the company, he had a real pecuniary incentive to win the suit. His contingent fee would be one tenth of the demanded judgment.

The case got under way in the district court of Claiborne parish. Standard, represented by some of the ablest lawyers in the state, claimed that Consolidated had no cause of action, and the court sustained the plea. Huey immediately appealed to the state supreme court, which overruled the no-action exception and remanded the case back to the district court for trial. But now Huey, for some reason, was not eager to try the case. He failed to push it, and a delay of five years ensued. It is probable that he "lost" his witnesses, that is, that some of them, perhaps hoping to make a compromise with Standard, would not testify as they had said they would. At the same time, Standard, which had originally sought to delay the proceedings, suddenly became anxious to secure a decision and in 1927 began pressing for a trial. Desperately, Huey filed with the district court motions for a continuance, seven of them in all. The motions revealed both his anxiety and his adeptness. One was based on the illness of a Consolidated official who was a necessary witness. Another was based on Huey's own influenza. A third was based on the

[5] *Consolidated-Progressive Oil Corporation* v. *Paramount Petroleum Company*, documents and correspondence; Long to Consolidated-Progressive Oil Corporation, September 12 and 21, 1921, April 14, 1923, ibid.; Philip H. Mecom. For aid in analyzing this case, I am again indebted to F. Leonard Hargrove.

great flood of 1927 and inconveniences resulting therefrom. Six of
the motions were granted, but the seventh and last was overruled. The
case was then dismissed as "non-suit" because of the failure of the
plaintiff's lawyer to prosecute his case.[6]

Huey's fees from all the cases he fought for Consolidated probably amounted to only a few thousand dollars. That he had not done
any better was no reflection on his capacities as a lawyer. On the
contrary, he had demonstrated high legal skills in every suit he
brought. The fault lay with the company and the cases it gave him.
Consolidated was essentially a gambling enterprise—that is, it was
gambling that it could secure possession of oil leases without which it
was nothing—and any suit in its name was also a gamble. Huey
knew this when he agreed to work for the company. He took its
cases, as doubtful as they were, because he too was willing to gamble
for a large reward. But in each of them, and notably in the Standard
suit, he exhibited a certain unsureness of touch that revealed his
inner reservations. He proceeded quite differently in another set of
cases that he tried and won at the same time that he was fighting
fruitlessly for Consolidated. For winning these other cases, which
became famous in Louisiana judicial history as the Bernstein cases,
he received the only big fee of his legal career.

Ernest R. Bernstein was the first vice-president of the Commercial National Bank. In his official capacity he approved loans to
several companies, one of them an oil concern, in which he had a
partial interest. Later the oil company and some of the others ran
into economic difficulties and were unable to meet their obligations
to the bank. Bernstein had done nothing dishonest or even reckless.
Most Shreveport banking officials owned stock in industrial companies, and every one of them was accustomed to making loans to
oil companies, even though oil was the most speculative of enterprises. Nevertheless, the bank's president and some of its other officers
resolved to use the episode of the loans as a weapon to oust Bernstein.
First, they persuaded the federal controller of currency to issue an
opinion that Bernstein had acted improperly. Armed with this document, they induced Bernstein to sign an agreement guaranteeing that
he would make good the loan to the oil company, which was now in
receivership, up to seventy thousand dollars of the hundred thousand
dollars due. Still not satisfied, they prepared a pamphlet detailing

[6] *Consolidated-Progressive Oil Corporation* v. *Standard Oil of Louisiana*, 158
Louisiana 982, 105 Southern 36 (1925); Long to G. J. Soper, February 22, 1921, in
Long Papers, Law File. Attorney William H. Shaw of Homer, Claiborne parish,
kindly surveyed for me the pleadings and the evidence in the case.

Bernstein's conduct and circulated a thousand copies of it throughout
Louisiana and other states. In this last move they had gone too far.
They had damaged Bernstein's reputation as a businessman and
hence had given him cause to sue for libel—if he could find a lawyer
who would sue the bank.

Securing a lawyer was a real problem for Bernstein. He wanted to
sue, but it seemed for a time that he would not be able to get anyone
to represent him. None of the older, established lawyers in Shreveport
would take on the powerful bank, which was the center of credit in
the community, or compete with the outstanding attorneys of the
three firms who were retained by it. Bernstein was one of the few
businessmen who had maintained friendly relations with Huey; and
finally, rebuffed everywhere else, he went to Long's office. In a de-
spondent mood, he said that he would give up if Huey would not
represent him and that maybe he should quit anyway. Huey responded
excitedly, saying that they would fight, and win. Already he was exhibiting a proprietary interest in the case. On August 8, 1922, he
filed in the district court of Caddo parish a suit against the Commercial National Bank. He asked for damages of five hundred thousand
dollars for defamation of his client's character and for the cancella-
tion of Bernstein's guaranty of seventy thousand dollars, which he
alleged in the petition to have been illegally obtained.[7]

Immediately the bank and the receiver for the oil company struck
back with two countersuits against Bernstein, each of them claiming
damages amounting to several hundred thousand dollars. The three
cases were tried concurrently for the next four years, with Huey
prosecuting in one and defending in the other two.[8] But it was the
first case, Bernstein's suit against the bank, which was the important
one. On its outcome great results hung—a huge financial award, the
rehabilitation of Bernstein's good name, and the making of a famous
legal name for Bernstein's lawyer. In addition, the decision would
influence the disposition of the other suits. Huey realized what the
case meant to him, and he worked as he never had before. Although

[7] *Bernstein* v. *Commercial National Bank*, 153 Louisiana 653, 96 Southern 506
(1923). In the petition filed with the suit Long included the salient facts in Bernstein's
relations with the bank. This petition was an exceptionally well-drawn document and
made expert use of the chronology of events. I am indebted to attorney Nina Nichols
Pugh of Baton Rouge for her help in analyzing this case and for supplying several
citations. Shreveport *Journal*, February 26, 1923; O. B. Thompson; Overton Brooks;
John St. Paul, Jr.; A. M. Wallace.

[8] *Commercial National Bank* v. *Bernstein*, 161 Louisiana 38, 108 Southern 117
(1926); *Smalley* v. *Bernstein*, 165 Louisiana 1, 115 Southern 347 (1927), *cert. denied*,
277 United States 599 (1928); Huey P. Long: *Every Man a King* (New Orleans,
1933), pp. 78–9.

he employed another lawyer to assist him as junior counsel, Robert A. Hunter, a fine legal scholar, he prepared most of the supporting documentary material himself and conducted practically all of the hearings. He drafted his brief with special care, laboring on it at home to get away from interruptions at the office. When the children proved too distracting, he said to Rose: "I've got to win this case," and packed up and took a room at a hotel for two months. At one stage he wrote complainingly to Bernstein: "I am just wondering how much wear and tear, toil, worry and turmoil I can endure."[9]

At the first hearing the attorneys for the bank moved to dismiss the case on a technical exception, that the suit as drawn made an improper joinder of parties. The court sustained the exception. Huey thereupon appealed to the supreme court, which overruled the exception and returned the case to the district court. Forced to try the case on the merits, the district court rendered a judgment against Bernstein. Huey appealed the decision to the state supreme court. At this second hearing Huey won the essential part of his suit. The court held that Bernstein had been defamed, although it awarded him only five thousand dollars damages and ordered his guaranty of the oil loan canceled. In the other two suits Huey was also successful, making a satisfactory out-of-court settlement that saved Bernstein almost two hundred thousand dollars in one and obtaining dismissal in the other. All in all, it was a moment of sweet triumph for him, and he openly gloated over his victory. "I have just won a very good lawsuit up here that has torn this town, so far as concerns its financial circles, from center to circumference," he informed a friend. "It seemed no one thought Bernstein was going to beat the Commercial Bank and its several millionaire allies, but we did."[1]

The Bernstein case became a part of the Long legend. The story has it that Huey received a fee of eighty thousand dollars. With this money, he was able to run for governor in 1928 and win, and so his whole political career sprang from this one lawsuit. So goes the tale. Like some others that are told about him, it contains some exaggeration. In his legal files there is a lengthy correspondence between him and Bernstein concerning his fee, but it is impossible to determine from it just how much money he received. Only one thing is certain —almost from the beginning of the case Huey feared that he would

[9] Rose Long McFarland; Robert A. Hunter; Long to E. R. Bernstein, December 30, 1924, in Long Papers, Law File.

[1] Shreveport *Journal*, February 26, 1923; Long: *Every Man a King*, pp. 78–9; Long to F. E. Jones, January 8, 1926, in Long Papers, Law File (*Ashcraft* v. *Louisiana Central Lumber Company* folders); New Orleans *States*, October 31, 1927.

not get enough and began to press Bernstein for more. Midway through the suit he wrote a curious letter casting up for Bernstein the benefits he was going to win for his client and the torment he was going through to win them. "Read this letter twice, and see if you can guess what I have in mind," he exhorted. "I don't know myself."[2]

If he did not know what was in his mind, neither did Bernstein know what was in his. The two men had, as their correspondence reveals, a hopelessly confused understanding about their financial arrangements. A large part of the trouble was that Bernstein had pledged to pay Huey, and Hunter, a fee for each of the three cases, plus fifty per cent of whatever money Huey was able to save for his client in settlements with the bank. They could never agree on how much money Huey had saved for Bernstein. A minor complication was that in 1924 Bernstein had advanced Huey a political contribution of forty-six hundred dollars. Each of them juggled this sum around in the negotiations, adding it or subtracting it as his individual advantage indicated. Huey admitted receiving from Bernstein a total of fifty-three thousand dollars, not including the contribution, but argued that out of this he had had to pay Hunter's fee and other expenses. He claimed to have spent twelve thousand dollars of his own money for additional expenses. Bernstein contended that he had paid Huey a total of sixty-six thousand dollars, including the contribution, Hunter's fee, costs, and fees for other cases. Balancing off the conflicting claims as best as possible, it would seem a fair estimate that Huey came out of the affair with forty thousand dollars clear.[3]

Even if the reward was only half of what it was reputed to be, forty thousand dollars was nonetheless a large fee for that period, and Huey was suddenly wealthier than he had ever been or, probably, had ever hoped to be. At first he did not know what to do with the money. Rose had a suggestion. "We ought to have a home of our own," she said. Somewhat to her surprise, he readily agreed. He bought a lot on Forrest Avenue, in the best residential section, and fell to planning the house with an almost compulsive enthusiasm. It could not be a veneer house, he declared, because people would say that he was like the house, showy on the outside, nothing on the inside. He finally decided on a Spanish-type structure of white brick. Throughout the construction period he displayed a feverish impatience to get

[2] Long to Bernstein, December 30, 1924, in Long Papers, Law File.
[3] Bernstein to Long, January 13, 1925, receipt signed by Long on reception of $29,500, January 28, 1926, Long to Bernstein, April 30, 1927, Bernstein to Long, [no day or month], 1927, ibid.

into the house. On the night before the family was scheduled to move in, he could wait no longer. He borrowed a pallet and slept on the floor by himself. As a final touch, he had installed over the front door a balcony of black wrought iron. Entwined in the iron design was a monogram. But the letters were not HPL. He thought that as the Commercial National Bank had really built the house, albeit unwillingly, he should record his appreciation. Standing out in bold relief were the letters CNB.[4]

THE BERNSTEIN SUIT WAS Huey's last important case. After that he was too deeply immersed in politics to give much attention to the law. If he had elected to make the law his career, he could have been one of the great lawyers of his time. By the almost unanimous testimony of colleagues and opponents, he had all the qualities that are associated with a lawyer of distinction: a personality that attracted clients and instilled confidence in juries, an ability to arrive at the heart of a matter and present a case with brevity, effective verbal expression, a peculiarly retentive mind, and a capacity to work. His associate in the Bernstein case thought that his greatest gift was his power to make a case come alive. "He knew that the facts outside the court must be brought into the courtroom," said this man. "The court must see the case as it exists outside. He was a stickler for facts in the order of their happening. It is rare for a young lawyer to know the importance of chronology." A similar evaluation came from one of his partners: "He could reason with judge and jury and bring it down to where you couldn't get around it." Perhaps the finest tribute to Huey's legal ability was paid by Chief Justice William Howard Taft of the United States Supreme Court. After Long had argued a case before the highest tribunal while public service commissioner Taft said that he had seldom seem a lawyer with a greater legal mind or a better capacity to argue a legal point.[5]

From now on that mind and that capacity to argue would be devoted wholly to the great art of politics.

[4] Rose McConnell Long; Lucille Long Hunt; Long: *Every Man a King*, pp. 86–7.

[5] John P. Frank: *Lincoln as a Lawyer* (Urbana, 1961), pp. 97–8; Robert A. Hunter; Robert J. O'Neal; John H. McSween; A. M. Wallace; David Blackshear; Karl E. Mundt.

# The Sport of Kings

A NY NUMBER OF PEOPLE can tell you confidently how it all
began. "I am the man," they say, "who launched Huey Long
on his political career." One will boast that he was the first to glimpse
the greatness in Huey—that he had to reveal to the young Long the
truth about himself. Another told Huey what office to run for first,
and another financed and guided the first campaign. "And so," all
their stories end, "if it had not been for me . . . ," Long would never
have gone into politics or would have been defeated on his initial try
and returned to obscurity.

All of these people are sincere in their conviction that they
planted the idea of a political career in Huey's mind, and there is
some basis for their convictions. The facts are accurate: Some of
them did suggest that he run first for a particular office, and all of
them worked for him and advised with him in his first campaign.
But they see the scene from a reversed focus, and so they draw the
wrong conclusion. The chief actor in the play was not following their
directions, although he may have let each of them think this. Like all
great politicians, Huey Long was never—not even in his early years
—the tool of any man. He was not used by these people; he used
them. And had they not been there, he would have used others to
help him toward the goal that he had marked out for himself.

All his surviving sisters testify that he had a consciousness of
mission. "Huey felt he was a man of destiny who was put here for a
purpose," one of them recalls. They are not sure, however, as to
when he began to talk about that purpose, or how long it took for him
to see it clearly. At family gatherings he would admit that he had

political ambitions, but he insisted that these were only local: he wanted to "fix up" Winnfield and maybe later the parish. Even as he ran on in this vein, however, he would frequently let slip larger visions, which encompassed the whole state. On occasion he betrayed a quality always found in men who feel they have been born to lead —an arrogance that induces a scorn for possible rivals and even for the people who are to be led. Thus he once announced: "They think I'm so smart. Maybe I'm not. Maybe it's that there are a lot of dumb people in the world."[1]

Huey's somewhat guarded references to his future plans in family conversations may have resulted from a fear that his strong-minded brothers and sisters would ridicule him if he was too specific. But he spoke without reserve to the one person he knew who would not sneer, Rose McConnell. To her he revealed all his dreams, and her testimony establishes beyond a doubt that he dreamed of greatness even as a youth. When she first met him, in his salesman days, he would write frequent letters on any pretext to United States senators. Naturally intrigued, she asked him why he did it. "I want to let them know I'm here," he explained. "I'm going to be there myself some-day." If this answer surprised her, she was shocked when a little later he listed for her the offices he intended to occupy in progression— first, he would win a secondary state office; next, he would be elected governor; third, he would go to the Senate; and finally and inevitably, he would become President. "It almost gave you the cold chills to hear him tell about it," said Mrs. Long, shivering slightly even as she looked back from a perspective of half a century. "He was measuring it all."[2]

He was measuring it, certainly. But it would be a mistake to make too much of this calculation, to conclude from it, as some would, that he was a deviate from the normal political pattern, a native proto-type of certain European leaders of his century. It does not follow that because he planned and predicted his future, that because he talked about his destiny, he saw himself as a projection of mystic and mechanistic historical forces. He was no Hitler or Mussolini, respond-ing to voices that whispered of a call to duty and greatness, a holy purpose and a course that had to be followed to a predetermined and glorious end. He was too American and too Southern ever to see himself in such a role. Huey Long certainly intended to go up and to go up high, but he was going to ascend in an American context, in the milieu of parties and politics. And he was going to employ the

[1] Clara Long Knott; Charlotte Long Davis; Lucille Long Hunt.
[2] Rose McConnell Long.

traditional methods of the politician—cajolery, compromise, organization, and, when it was necessary, the slick deal. He felt he had great powers, but even if he had not, he would have gone into politics; he was a natural, an instinctive, politician, and his entrance into politics was, literally, a compulsive act. He was fascinated with it for itself—it was an art and also a science, a game for high stakes, a constant contest in a great arena. Most of all, he was fascinated with its possibilities for building power. Like all masters of the art of politics, he delighted in playing with the "blocks" that make up a power structure, arranging the blocks to suit his purpose—and piling them ever higher. Even if such a man has no ideals to put into practice, he may find politics so exciting and exhilarating that merely to be in it is satisfaction enough. Long had his ideals, but he also loved politics for its own sake. Once when he was at the crest of his career, on the eve of one of his many conflicts, he exclaimed happily to a friend as he plunged into the fray: "This is the sport of kings."[3]

HUEY HAD BEEN DABBLING around the edges of politics ever since he was in high school. But until he became a lawyer, he had played at the game only in sporadic interludes, and nearly always he had acted under the direction of somebody else, such as his father or Julius. What may be described as his formal entrance into full-time politics did not come until after he had established himself in the law. The timing was not fortuitous but deliberate. His principal reason for studying law had been to use the legal profession as a base for political operations. To an aspiring politician, the law offered several obvious advantages. It provided a measure of economic security and a haven to return to in case of reverse. It educated a man in the art of public speaking and supplied him a forum from which to speak. It enabled him to help large numbers of people and thereby later garner their grateful votes. Perhaps most important of all, in the course of his work a lawyer became familiar with issues that were currently being debated in political circles and considered in legislative halls.

Thus it was his experience with compensation law that prompted Huey to make his first foray into politics. Characteristically, he intervened in a fairly sensational way and on a state rather than a local issue.

[3] Richard W. Leche.

In the course of his work as a compensation lawyer he had frequently denounced the Louisiana employers' liability law for the meager payments it allowed to injured workers, but these statements were scarcely heard beyond Winn parish. Then in the spring of 1916 he went to Senator Harper, who was a member of the senate committee on capital and labor and sympathetic to the working class, and showed the old man some amendments he had drafted to the law. His proposals advocated raising the maximum amount allowable in injury cases and requiring companies to pay damage assessments in a lump sum instead of installments. Harper readily agreed to present them to the committee, but it probably did not occur to him that he could use the young lawyer's help in Baton Rouge. Huey accompanied him, nonetheless, probably having invited himself.

Huey had never seen a legislature in session before, and the sight of this one filled his idealistic young mind with disgust. The members seemed afraid of some mysterious power, he recalled; they kowtowed before it and guarded their talk as if fearing they "would slip on something" if they ventured too far. Around the capital he met an older man named Faust, whom he did not otherwise identify, who revealed to him what the hidden power was—it was the great business interests and particularly the Standard Oil Company. But the people could change the situation, Huey argued. Yes, agreed Faust, but they could not be aroused. A leader who tried to stir them would be hired over by the interests, Faust said. "Or," he concluded, smiling at Huey, "they will snuff you out if they can."

Huey's description of the legislature was reasonably accurate. But it is improbable that he was as shocked by the spectacle as he claimed. Coming from realistic Winn parish and having heard politics discussed all his life, he certainly knew who was running the state. The account of the interview with Faust seems contrived, designed to portray Huey as an innocent reformer, and the meeting itself may well have been fictitious. There is no reason, however, to doubt his version of his experience with the senate committee that considered his amendments at an evening session. He was denied permission to speak and was ridiculed when he tried to get the floor. Once when he arose, the chairman asked him whom he represented. "Several thousand common laborers," Huey answered. Were they paying him anything? the chairman pressed. No, snapped Huey. "They seem to have good sense," the chairman observed, to loud laughter. Other members of the committee wanted to know why a twenty-two-year-old lawyer who had just begun to practice thought he was competent to advise the legislature on such a weighty issue. Finally, toward midnight, somebody moved that the committee adjourn without taking any action, a procedure tantamount to rejecting the amendments.

Huey had taken all that he could. Without asking for recognition, he got up from his seat at the foot of the table and began to speak. Later he thought well enough of his remarks to reproduce them in his autobiography. His rendition was probably accurate for the most part, although it bears some evidence of having been polished up. His opening sentences revealed that his protestations of political innocence had been nothing but a pretense. "For twenty years has the Louisiana Legislature been dominated by the henchmen and attorneys of the interests," he cried. "Those seeking reforms have from necessity bowed their heads in regret and shame when witnessing the victories of these corrupting influences at this capitol." And now these same influences had the brazen audacity to deny to a laborer's family a fair compensation for a grievous injury or a lost life. And to make it worse, they claimed that they were acting in the name of justice. "What a subterfuge!" Huey declared. It was like an infidel invoking God or an anarchist calling on the government for protection.

These were strange, strong words to fling at a legislative committee. Huey was charging that his hearers—and a majority of the legislators—were purchased tools of the corporations. The committee members were outraged and immediately proceeded to express their feelings by voting down the amendments.

At first consideration, it might seem that Huey was employing the poorest of strategies, that he was needlessly arousing antagonisms and hurting his cause. Actually, he was following an extremely shrewd course for one in his situation—a political unknown battling for labor legislation against powerful foes. On the purely personal level, he had advertised his name in a way that was certain to cause admiring talk all over rural Louisiana: Say, did you hear how that young Long fellow from Winnfield told off the big boys down in Baton Rouge? For his proposed legislation, he had struck a peculiarly effective blow. By the sheer enormity of his accusation, he had made it difficult for the legislature to reject the amendments. If the lawmakers turned them down, they would seem to be bowing to the will of the interest he had described. If they passed the amendments, they would seem to be acting not out of virtue but out of fear of a public sentiment that he had called into being. Whatever the outcome, Huey Long was sure to emerge with large credit.

He was fairly certain of the outcome. From the beginning of the fight he had sensed that there was strong though latent popular support for reform of the compensation law. His dramatic confrontation with the committee had been designed to activate this sentiment, to cause it to bring pressure on the legislature. His plan worked. Soon insistent demands arose that the legislature at least consider whether the law needed changing. Harper was easily able to bring the most important of the amendments to a vote on the senate floor and to pass them. They were readily acceded to by the lower house and thus became law. Huey, in later statewide campaigns, never failed to remind labor that he was the author of what came to be known gratefully in union circles as the Harper Amendments. Uncharacteristically, however, he did not claim that he was responsible for their passage.

He was properly modest in this instance because he understood the social forces that had made his success possible—and because he respected those forces. Louisiana was at the time experiencing some of the impact of the "progressive" movement that was affecting the whole country and both major parties. On the national level, progressives advocated placing certain restraints on business, restraints that were supposed to curb the evils of bigness. In state legislatures, they championed legislation that would provide certain benefits and protections for working people, legislation intended to soften the harsher aspects of industrial capitalism. Progressivism appealed particularly to middle-class reformers, for it stressed that enlightened men must cultivate a social conscience and that an enlightened society must extend social benefits to its workers.

Although the progressive movement naturally exerted its greatest influence in industrial states, it also appeared in rural states, including some in the South, like Louisiana, that were just beginning to feel the impulse of industry. In Louisiana the principal effect of progressivism was to arouse a new social consciousness in some groups —publishers, editors, educators, clergymen, and others. Suddenly many people realized that industry could bring evils along with its benefits, and they voiced demands that the legislature act to mitigate the worst evils. As an example of the potency of this opinion, in the same year that Huey wrote the Harper Amendments, another legislator asked him to draft a bill making it a criminal offense for an employer to retain defective and hence dangerous machinery in his plant, and this bill was duly enacted as the Jordan Safety Appliance Act. Thus when Huey proposed higher compensation rates, he was not fighting a lone battle but was only giving a push to a movement already under way. But he had pushed strongly and with a clever technique that nobody else on his side would have conceived. He did not pause to analyze whether he was a middle-class reformer or a rural progressive who knew what was good for industry. His motivation was simple. He had an instinctive sympathy for the poor and a sure sense of what would be a vote-getting issue. In the course of the episode he must have taken note of the growing though unorganized sentiment for reform, and he must have noticed how easy it was to outwit the stuffy opponents of change. No one, apparently, had thought to throw an obvious charge at him—that by bringing about an increase in compensation payments he was enlarging his own capacity to collect bigger fees.[4]

It had been a spectacular political debut for Huey, and he was grateful to the man who made it possible, Senator Harper. He had a genuine regard for the old solon who had lent him money when he went to Tulane and come to his aid in the DeLoach case. He had to respect too the way Harper had pulled himself up in the world. As a youth Harper had come to Winnfield from the country and had worked as a carpenter. Often he made only seventy-five cents a day, but he saved his money and eventually had enough to start a general merchandise store and to become a cotton buyer. He was also able to indulge a taste for reading. He bought books, acquiring over the course of the years a fair-sized library, and as he read and meditated, he developed a set of distinctly unconventional ideas. He was vociferously against war, the Bible, Wall Street, bankers, corsets and high heels for women, intoxicating liquors, strict discipline in prisons, the microbe theory, algebra, and any new notion about education. The list of things he favored was shorter and included socialism, practical education, and limitations on wealth. He was exceedingly critical of clergymen and was probably an atheist. Like some other rural radicals of the time, he was convinced that most of the big international bankers were Jews and were working together to further the power of world Jewry. His study of their machinations led him to correspond with Henry Klein of New York City, a Jew who had become a Christian, and who had written pamphlets denouncing bankers, the Standard Oil Company, and Jews in general. Klein apprised Harper of even wider ramifications of the Jewish menace. The Zionists, working through the governing Sanhedrin of the Jews, were plotting nothing

[4] Huey P. Long: *Every Man a King* (New Orleans, 1933), pp. 25–8; Maines, article in Flint *News-Advertiser*, September 22, 1955; Long, quoted in New Orleans *Times-Picayune*, December 19, 1923; Terrence J. Darsey, president of Louisiana Longshoremen's Union, quoted in Long circular, 1928, in my possession.

less than the takeover of the United States and other great countries. To prove the charge, Klein supplied Harper with a copy of a document detailing the plan, the Protocols of Zion, which later scholarship would expose as fraudulent but which seemed genuine enough to Harper. He gave free voice to all his ideas, and it was a mark of the unorthodoxy of Winn voters that they would elect such a man to represent them in the legislature.[5]

Some recorders of the Long story have concluded that Harper was young Huey's political mentor and that the senator's economic notions formed the basis of Long's subsequent economic philosophy. The supposition stems from the known intimacy of the two men and from an assumption that the older one must have been the dominant partner. Although the conjecture has a certain plausibility about it, it is, like many that have been made about Long, erroneous. Contemporaries who knew both men well state emphatically that Harper had very little influence on Huey. If influence was exerted, they imply, Huey exerted it. This is apparent even without their testimony. It simply was not in Huey's nature to follow anybody out of blind admiration or to borrow ideas blindly. He was too calculating to do either. He could admire Harper's independence and courage, and he could agree with some of the senator's ideas, such as placing limitations on wealth. But he was too realistic to commit himself further. He could see that the breadth of Harper's intellectual interests was a weakness in a politician—the old man embraced too many ideas, so many that some of them had to be eccentric. It was all right to talk about limiting wealth, for example, but to advocate socialism was something else. It was fine to condemn Wall Street bankers, but to denounce Jewish bankers was another thing. If only for his ideas about Jews, Huey would have looked on Harper with condescension. He had no strong prejudices of any kind himself, but if he had had, he would have concealed them—a politician was downright foolish if he alienated any group of voters.[6]

Still, he felt an obligation to Harper, and he seized an early opportunity to repay it. The senator had been an outspoken opponent of America's entrance into the World War. He muted his sentiments

[5] S. J. Harper Scrapbook, in possession of Maud H. Harper, formerly of Winnfield; Maud H. Harper; Harry Gamble. Miss Harper kindly loaned me her father's scrapbook, which contains, in addition to clippings, a number of letters written by Harper or to him.

[6] Carleton Beals: *The Story of Huey P. Long* (Philadelphia, 1935), p. 37; Julius T. Long; Harry Gamble.

somewhat after the war was declared, but then he demanded that it be financed by conscripting wealth. Specifically he advocated that the government issue legal tender certificates instead of bonds; it should emulate the Civil War example of "our Grand Old Ex-president Abraham Lincoln," he said, using brave words for a Southern politician. At first he confined his remarks to conversations and correspondence, but inevitably he grew bolder. He published a pamphlet detailing his views. Entitled *The Issues of the Day—Free Speech—Financial Slavery*, it denounced bankers and war profiteers, charged that the war was being waged not for democracy but for Wall Street, and called for a conscription of wealth. A minority of the people already owned most of the national wealth, the pamphlet claimed, and they would own all of it before this war was ended. Harper followed up this blast by announcing early in 1918 that he would be a candidate for Congress. He had gone too far. Popular support of the war was as intense and hysterical in Louisiana as in other parts of the country, and public officials were just as ready to crush dissent. A federal grand jury in Alexandria promptly indicted Harper on the absurd charge that he had violated the Espionage Act.

Huey volunteered to serve as the senator's counsel. His first step, after arranging bail for Harper, was to issue a statement to the press denouncing the indictment as political persecution of a man whose only crime had been to oppose the war profiteers. Then, having himself made the case a political one, he demanded an early hearing to take advantage of the atmosphere he had created. At the trial in Shreveport Huey associated his more experienced brother Julius with him as co-counsel. While Julius handled the preliminary motions, Huey circulated among the prospective jurymen, all of whom, he had discovered, were being shadowed by government agents. He picked out those whom he thought were unfriendly to his case and ostentatiously bought them drinks and engaged them in whispered conversations. When the jurors were called, the government asked each one who had been seen with Huey if he had talked about the case. Each one answered truthfully that he had not. But the skeptical government attorneys excused them and thus exhausted all but one of their peremptory challenges. At this point a recess was called, and Huey was fearful that what he later called his "prank" had been discovered. But when the court reconvened, the presiding judge merely read a statement reprimanding Huey for his remarks to the press. Huey and Julius were eventually able to win an acquittal for their client, although not necessarily because of any skill on their part or of Huey's sharp work with the jury. The government simply had a shaky case.

Huey had been quite right to label the prosecution as political and to fight it on political grounds.[7]

His motives in defending Harper can only be conjectured. A facile conclusion would be that he merely jumped at another chance to put himself in the limelight. This analysis, however, assumes that Huey would deliberately embrace an unpopular cause. In this case, he might have advertised his name, but he could not have helped his political fortunes and might have injured them. Another easy explanation would be that he simply liked Harper and thought his friend was the victim of an injustice. This was true enough, but Huey hardly ever acted out of pure sentiment or simple motives, and he did not so act now. Governing everything that he did in this episode was a cynical doubt as to what the war was for—he did not believe that it was a crusade to make the world safe for democracy. This conviction was his real reason for helping Harper, who had the same suspicion.

These doubts about the rectitude of the war were also his justification, or so he would claim later, for avoiding military service. He asked the Winn parish draft board to exempt him from the draft on the grounds that he had a wife and child to support and did not have much income. (A second child, a son, Russell B., would be born early in November 1918, just before the war ended.) The board responded by placing him in Class IV, the category for men with dependents. There was nothing unusual in this classification; many men similarly situated were thus exempted. But he tried to make himself doubly safe by applying for an additional deferment, claiming that since he was a notary public he should be placed also in Class V, which was reserved for state officials. This request the board refused.[8]

In later years friends and some members of his family would offer excuses for him—he had dependents, he was contributing to the support of a sick sister in the West, and he had two brothers-in-law who went into the service. They would also claim that he helped the war effort by speaking at Liberty Bond rallies. The last defense was not very creditable to Huey. If he advocated the buying of bonds,

[7] Harper to Congressman James B. Aswell, April 19, 1917, in Harper Scrapbook; Long: *Every Man a King*, pp. 33–6 (includes Long's statement in New Orleans *Times-Picayune*, February 22, 1918); Maines, articles in Flint *News-Advertiser*, September 27, 1955; Harry Gamble.

[8] Statement of W. T. Heflin, chairman of the Winn draft board, in *Louisiana Progress*, September 4, 1930; statement on Long's draft record, in Robinson Papers; R. G. 163: Records of the Selective Service System (1917–19): Draft Registration cards of Local Boards, in Federal Records Center, East Point, Georgia. The Center made available to me a copy of Long's registration card.

he must have pictured the war as a righteous endeavor, and therefore said what he believed to be a lie.[9] But nothing about his behavior during the war is very creditable to him. He seems to have realized this himself. He was always a little uncomfortable at later charges that he had been a draft dodger. But he met every criticism with boldness. "I did not go into that war," he proclaimed in the Senate. "I was within the draft age. I could have gone, except for my dependents. I did not go because I did not want to go, aside from that fact. . . . I did not go because I was not mad at anybody over there, for another reason. I did not go because it was not the first time in history that the sons of America had volunteered themselves as cannon fodder under the misguided apprehension that it was going to be a fight for humanity," when in reality they had been used to centralize "the wealth of the United States and of the world in the hands of a few." Curiously, the attack on his war record came in the late twenties and early thirties. It was a time when such an accusation helped rather than hurt his career. Then a man who had realized the "phoniness" of the World War was thought to be a smart one, indeed.[1]

Huey's skepticism about the nature of the war was a direct result of his continuing study of a subject that had interested him for years —maldistribution of wealth. If a few rich men dominated the economy, he seemed to reason, then they must be running the government and directing everything that it did. Early in 1918 he expressed his ideas in a letter to the principal newspapers of the state. In this document he cited figures to prove that two per cent of the people owned seventy per cent of the wealth. And every decade this concentration of wealth was increasing, he wrote. Its most unfortunate effect was that the ordinary man could no longer provide an education for his children. "What do you think of such a game of life, so brutally and cruelly unfair, with the dice so loaded that the child of today must enter it with only fourteen chances out of a thousand in his favor of getting a college education . . . ?" he asked.

His statistics came from an editorial in a 1916 issue of the *Saturday Evening Post*, summarizing a report from the federal Com-

[9] Lucille Long Hunt; David B. McConnell; Julius T. Long: "What I Know About My Brother," *Real America*, II (September 1933), 40, 56. Julius conceded that Huey had participated in Liberty Bond drives but charged that the younger brother had painted the war as a just one and had spoken on a number of platforms with an alleged war hero who turned out to be an imposter and a crook.

[1] Long, quoted in Earle J. Christenberry, ed.: *Speeches by the Late Huey P. Long* (n.p., n.d.), unpaginated, speech of March 13, 1933; hereafter cited as Christenberry, ed.: *Speeches by Long*. See also Long, quoted in *American Progress*, August 24, 1933, May 10, 1935.

mission on Industrial Relations, and years later, when he was in the Senate, he congratulated the magazine for having helped to start him on his movement to redistribute wealth. This was, of course, only an impish dig at the conservative *Post*. He had not drawn his idea that wealth must be shared from the *Post* or from any one person or source. It was a product of several influences—his Winn parish heritage, the Populist and Socialist conversations of his elders, and his own wide reading. It is impossible to determine which of these forces played upon him first or with greatest impact. But it is possible to isolate the time when he first became impressed by the danger of concentrated wealth. It was when he was introduced to the Louisiana law of forced heirship, during his student days at Tulane. And it was from the Louisiana law that he derived his first notion of how to deal with the problem of concentrated wealth. He revealed it in 1922 in a letter he wrote to Senator Albert J. Beveridge of Indiana. Ostensibly, he wrote to say that he had just finished reading the scholarly Beveridge's four-volume life of John Marshall and liked the work, but his real purpose was to urge on the senator a plan to break up fortunes. The nation should adopt the Louisiana law that forced a decedent to divide his property equally among his children; trust funds should not be allowed to run for more than ten years. "This will mean that the snow ball disintegrates each generation, instead of growing as it rolls," he argued. If something like this were not done, there would be a social revolt, he concluded; and when a revolt like that began, it could not be ended. A great deal of speculation has been wasted trying to determine just where Long got his idea of sharing the wealth. What is important is that he had it at an early date and, moreover, that he had a plan for doing it.[2]

Huey's critical views of corporate wealth were not entirely abstract. He had been involved in an episode during the war that gave him a close look into business practices, cost him some money, and left him with an abiding hatred for one large company. In 1927 a new oil discovery was made in Caddo parish, in what became known as the Pine Island extension of the Caddo field. A number of small oil companies were hastily formed and rushed in to exploit the field. One of these firms was the Banks Oil Company, which was organized by Huey's sawmill friend, O. B. Thompson, and a group of Winnfield men. Another friend, Oscar K. Allen, locally called O.K., was the

[2] Long: *Every Man a King*, pp. 37–9; Long, quoted in *American Progress*, June, 1935; Long to Albert J. Beveridge, October 15, 1922, in Beveridge Papers, Division of Manuscripts, Library of Congress, Washington, D.C. For calling my attention to the last item, I am grateful to Richard Lowitt and John Braeman.

company's secretary-treasurer. Huey was retained as its lawyer, and he either bought some stock valued at $1,050 or accepted it as his fee.

The Banks Company and the other independent producers made money during the war. Although the Pine Island oil was, in a phrase of the industry, of low gravity, and hence not of the highest grade, it was serviceable as fuel oil, and the government was buying large quantities of crude oil for the U.S. Navy and the navies of its allies. The independents sold their oil to the Standard Oil Company of Louisiana, which transported it to market over its pipelines, the only available cheap outlet. The arrangement was profitable for all parties, as shown by an offer Huey made to sell his modest thousand-dollar interest to Standard for twelve thousand dollars. Standard's president was willing to pay eighty-five hundred dollars at the time, but Huey, dazzled by dreams of future wealth, refused to sell at that price. Then suddenly the bottom fell out for him and for everybody. The war ended in November 1918, and the government canceled its orders for fuel oil. Standard responded by curtailing its purchases of Pine Island crude and reducing the price. Stock in the Banks and other independent companies plummeted to forty cents on the dollar and less. The independents were ruined; with no more demand for low-grade oil, they could not sell their product anywhere, even though Standard offered to pipe it out for them.

O. B. Thompson went to New York City to sell the Banks Company for any figure he could get. He took Huey with him to draw up the papers. After the transaction was concluded, they remained in the city to enjoy its pleasures. One day while the two were in their hotel room, a man came in with some diamonds wrapped in a handkerchief and offered to sell one. Huey was immediately fascinated. He picked out one the size of a thumbnail and asked its price. The man said he would let it go for a thousand dollars. Thompson cautioned that they should have it appraised. He took it to a jeweler, who valued it at eight thousand dollars. Huey bought the stone, although he must have known that there was something odd and possibly illegal about the whole deal. He had it set in a ring, which he wore proudly and ostentatiously. It was his first precious material possession, and it seemed to have special importance to him.

The Pine Island episode left independent producers furious at Standard. They screamed that the big company was deliberately trying to freeze out the small concerns. As proof of their suspicion, they charged that Standard was at the same time transporting large quantities of Mexican crude to its Baton Rouge refinery. Standard retorted that the Mexican oil had value because of its asphalt base.

Loudly leading the attack of the independents was Huey. At a meeting in Shreveport between the Pine Island producers and officials of Standard he shouted at the spokesman of the corporation: "You've done this before and got by with it, but this time, go do it and see when you hear the last of it." He was true to his word. Standard never heard the last of it. He pursued the company mercilessly throughout his whole career. Sometimes he liked to give the impression that he was acting out of revenge, that he was only paying back those who had defrauded a poor "country yap." Undoubtedly there was a measure of personal vengeance in his course—nobody made Huey Long look silly without suffering the consequences. But essentially he struck at Standard with calculated political motives. It was a perfect target for a politician. And he would strike at it with political weapons.[3]

HUEY RAN FOR HIS FIRST political office in 1918. The stories of how he happened to run are legion, and they all have the same theme—an innocent Huey made a very casual decision on the advice of friends. The most frequent version has a group of men sitting around a Winnfield store talking politics. One of them says: Huey, you're ambitious, why don't you run for railroad commissioner? Huey asks what the office is. Somebody hunts up a book that contains a copy of the state constitution, and they discover that the commissioner from the third, or northern, district represents twenty-eight parishes and that each of the three commissioners for the state is elected for a term of six years and receives a salary of three thousand dollars a year. Huey says: That sounds like a pretty good office to run for—I'll do it. Harley Bozeman gives an account that is more complicated but has the same motif. According to Bozeman, Huey, flushed by his recent legal triumphs, had announced in 1916 that he was going to run for district attorney against Julius. Bozeman tried to talk him out of it, pointing out that he could not beat Julius. This argument did

[3] Bozeman, in *Winn Parish Enterprise*, January 9, 1958, February 7, 1963; T. O. Harris: *The Kingfish: Huey P. Long, Dictator* (New Orleans, 1938), pp. 21–3; John L. Loos: *Oil on Stream!* (Baton Rouge, 1959), pp. 85–6; Georgia Sweet Gibb and Evelyn H. Knowlton: *The Resurgent Years: History of Standard Oil Company (New Jersey) 1911–1927* (New York, 1956), p. 464; O. B. Thompson; Long: *Every Man a King*, pp. 41–3; Long, quoted in New Orleans *States*, September 22, 1923; David B. McConnell; Shelby Kidd; F. Leonard Hargrove.

not move Huey. Bozeman then suggested that Huey wait two years and run for railroad commissioner. "What the hell is that job?" Huey asked. Bozeman answered that he did not know much about it, but that in some Southern states men had used it as a stepping stone to the governorship. Immediately Huey was intrigued. He went to his office, looked up what the constitution had to say about the job, and then and there resolved to try for it. Huey himself later lent some support to this tale of his casual entrance into politics by saying that he decided to run for railroad commissioner because there was no age minimum prescribed for the office, so at twenty-four he was eligible.[4]

This story has the defect of so many told about Long, the same defect that appears in stories told about other power artists in history. It is too pat, too simple, and it overlooks the fact that the hero may have had something to do with determining the course of events. It ignores, too, another fact of politics, that the great politician, who is always sure of himself, may do as Abraham Lincoln did so expertly—let it appear that he is being managed when, in reality, he is doing exactly what he wants to do. It is highly probable that this is what Huey was doing in this episode. His threat to run against Julius may have been intended only to force the latter to support him in a later race. He had been saying for years that he would run for some state office before he tried for the governorship, and he could hardly have considered a district attorneyship as an adequate first step. He undoubtedly did consult with friends about what office he should run for, and it is very likely that one or more of them suggested the Railroad Commission. That agency was such an ideal spot for an ambitious politician that anybody with political sense would have seen its possibilities.

The Commission had been created in the constitution of 1898. It was empowered by the constitution and subsequent legislative acts to regulate the practices and rates of railroads, steamboats and other vessels, sleeping cars, telephone and telegraph companies, and pipelines. Despite its seemingly spacious authority, the Commission had been for the most part an almost moribund body. The men who had been elected to it, dignified political has-beens or political hacks looking for a soft place, had not tried to use its powers. But a dynamic young member could turn the Commission into a dynamic agency.

[4] Richard W. Leche, quoting O. K. Allen; Rupert S. Whitley; Harry Gamble; Bozeman, in *Winn Parish Enterprise*, October 31, 1957; Long: *Every Man a King*, p. 39.

He could, by enforcing the laws on utility corporations, make a state-wide name for himself. Huey saw all these possibilities. He told O. B. Thompson that he was going to run for the office and win it and go on from there to the governorship. Speaking of the incumbent, he said confidently: "I can beat that old man."[5]

The Honorable Burk A. Bridges, as he like to be called, was in his middle fifties, hardly an old man. But he seemed old. He was a resident of Homer, in Claiborne parish, a town that prided itself on retaining the ante-bellum graces. He epitomized those graces, perhaps with some calculation. About six feet in height, handsome, dignified in manner, always impeccably dressed, he looked like an artist's drawing of an old-time Southern politician. He had been elected to the Railroad Commission in 1912, and he expected to be re-elected in 1918 and to retain the office as long as he wanted it. Although he was blind to current social issues, as were most Louisiana politicians, he was no easy opponent. In his younger years he had been a travel-ing salesman for a large wholesale dry goods company and had formed enduring friendships with most of the important and influen-tial merchants in his district. Moreover, he had close contacts with the so-called "courthouse gang" or "ring" in almost every one of the twenty-eight parishes—the sheriff, the clerk of court, the assessor, and other officials, who could always turn out a vote. In an election in which relatively few people voted, as had always been the case in a Railroad Commission contest, the support of the courthouse gang could be decisive. The Honorable Burk, even though he faced three other opponents besides Huey, felt little worry. He did not bother to make much of a campaign.[6]

Bridges might indeed have won—if this had been an ordinary campaign. But Huey turned it into something quite out of the ordi-nary. He began his own campaign a long time before the summer, the traditional time for electioneering. First, he put together a list of all the local officials in the third district—police jurors, justices of the peace, and constables—and also of the defeated candidates for these offices. Probably as early as 1916 he had begun corresponding with these men and sending them copies of his public remarks. He assumed that Bridges would rely on his courthouse alliances and

[5] *Twentieth Annual Report of the Railroad Commission of Louisiana* (Baton Rouge, 1919), pp. 9–10; O. B. Thompson.

[6] Harley B. Bozeman; Rupert Peyton. The mere fact that there were five candi-dates in the race suggests that the office could not have been as obscure as Huey's friends think it was.

would visit only the larger towns. Huey's purpose in contacting so many local leaders was to build up an organization in the smaller towns and rural areas, where few people voted except in a statewide election. He was still selling his Never Fail oil cans, and on his trips around the district he would call on many of the men he had corresponded with. He also had a file of addresses of his customers, and these too he bombarded with letters. Thus long before he formally announced a candidacy, Huey had laid the basis of an effective organization.[7]

Only a few people appreciated what he was doing. Someone in Winnfield said that Huey had only three men in his organization—O. B. Thompson, Bozeman, and O. K. Allen, who was now the assessor of Winn parish. The slighting reference was to what might be called his central or headquarters organization. Actually, it contained a number of people. The whole Long family swung in behind Huey, carrying with them the many Long connections all over Winn parish. Julius gave support and advice and fancied himself as a campaign manager. Brother Earl paid Huey's filing fee of $125 and traveled over the whole district soliciting votes. An important member of the staff was Mrs. Long. Huey set up his personal headquarters at her mother's house in Shreveport. While Huey was out campaigning, Rose sat behind a desk and mailed out Long literature and answered letters. Every day Huey would send back a batch of new names to be added to the mailing list. Rose finally had to hire children in the neighborhood to fold the documents and put them into envelopes, and she herself lugged them to the post office in a bulging suitcase. Most of the documents were circulars, printed one-sheet items extolling Huey Long and attacking his opponents. The political circular was a familiar campaign device in Winn parish. Huey had first used circulars in Oklahoma and had been impressed with their potential. Now, typically, he took an idea developed by someone else and made it enormously more effective by extending it—or, really, by giving it system. Before the campaign was over, he had almost literally plastered the third district with his circulars. They stood forth from trees, fences, walls of buildings—any place that would support them.[8]

These display circulars were put up by Huey himself. He was able

[7] Bozeman, in Winn Parish Enterprise, October 31, 1957; Hermann B. Deutsch: "Prelude to a Heterocrat," Saturday Evening Post, CCVII (September 7, 1935), 86.

[8] Harley B. Bozeman; Matt Milam, Sr.; Julius T. Long; Frank Odom; Rose McConnell Long; Frost, article in New Orleans States, August 28, 1927; Long: Every Man a King, pp. 39–40; Deutsch: "Prelude to a Heterocrat," Saturday Evening Post, September 7, 1935, p. 86; Lucille Long Hunt.

to distribute them widely because he campaigned in an automobile, a form of transportation that he was one of the first Louisiana politicians to use. At the beginning of the summer he borrowed money and bought a second-hand Overland 90. He and his brother-in-law Dave McConnell crammed the car with circulars, took hammers and tacks, and crisscrossed the district in it. Whenever they saw a likely place for a circular, they stopped and nailed one up.

The automobile enabled Huey to get around extensively and quickly, but it was costly to use. Also expensive were the circulars he was having printed in increasing numbers. At a critical point in the campaign Huey found that his slender funds were running out. He drove into Winnfield and went to the office of O. K. Allen. He told Allen that unless he could lay his hands on some money, he would have to get out of the race. Allen, obeying one of the first rules of political friendship, without question went to the bank, signed a note for five hundred dollars, and handed the sum to Huey in cash.[9]

Huey's use of an automobile violated one of the most respected rules of Louisiana politicians: Never campaign in a car among country people; they will resent it as a pretense of superiority and vote against you. Huey knew that the rule existed only in the politicians' minds. From his observation of Vardaman and Jeff Davis during his days as a traveling salesman, he had learned that the masses were more likely to follow one of their own if that man showed that in some ways he was better than they. "That young Long fellow, now, he's a smart one, he drives a car." Just as boldly, Huey disregarded other maxims. He did not as yet know much about correct dress, and he appeared before the voters in any apparel that pleased his fancy. His clothes were sloppy and ill-fitting—usually he wore a suit of clashing colors—but they expressed his concept of expensive elegance. Again he was trying to play the role of the superior leader, the wool-hat boy who dressed better than his followers.

One of his techniques was so unorthodox that it seemed suicidal. In the rural areas he deliberately did a lot of his campaigning at night. He would chug up to a farmhouse at a late hour, often after the family had retired, and call the husband out. "I'm Huey Long," he would say, "and I'm running for the Railroad Commission and I'd like your support." The farmer was not offended but flattered—he thought he must be a pretty important man to have a politician call on him at such an hour. Probably Huey remembered from his salesman experi-

[9] David B. McConnell; O. B. Thompson; Trent James; Long: *Every Man a King*, p. 40.

ence that lonesome farm families like to receive a late visitor. Huey's antics led one editor to write that it might be a good idea to elect a crazy man to office; he might start something.[1]

Far from being crazy, Huey was conducting as imaginative a campaign as Louisiana had ever seen. He also did a lot of conventional electioneering. In addition to visiting countless farm homes, he drove to practically every town and village in the district. On arriving in a town he would walk its streets, talking to any group of people he met, or any individual. Usually he would simply announce his name, say he was running for railroad commissioner, and ask for support. Sometimes he would stop at a Baptist church and ask to sing in the choir. Moving tirelessly from place to place, he talked to hundreds of people who had never seen Bridges—or any politician other than a local one. His efforts brought results. One man, offering to help him, said: "I don't know why I shouldn't. I know you, and I don't know the other fellow." Another, trying to recall later why he had decided to vote for Huey, said simply: "I just naturally went with him." A local leader had no doubts as to his reasons: "I liked the way Huey moved, so I told him I was going to do my best to get him elected because we sure needed somebody there." If Huey did not already know the value of personal contacts from his days as a salesman, he learned in this campaign that for a politician they were vital.[2]

He also won many votes by promising that if elected he would force the railroads to extend their services or their lines. It was a pledge of this kind that enabled him to sweep the vote of a hamlet known as Shooter's Station. Its people had a burning grievance—a train called the Cannonball did not stop there on its way to larger towns. When Huey spoke at Shooter's, he timed his remarks so that they would be interrupted by the Cannonball, roaring through town with a great whistle. When the noise subsided, he looked up with an expression of surprise and said: "Folks, do you mean to tell me the Cannonball don't stop at Shooter's Station? Well, you elect me and that'll be changed."

Some of his commitments he honored. Others he forgot about. One of the latter was to an old man who controlled forty votes and who was angry at a railroad for not putting a station on his property. Huey walked to his house on a hot day and, asking for a drink of water complained about the distance he had had to trudge from the

---

[1] D. J. Anders; Ira Gleason; Mrs. Gaston Porterie; David Blackshear; David B. McConnell; Long: *Every Man a King*, pp. 40-1; Mason Spencer.

[2] R. S. Copeland; D. J. Anders; Clara Long Knott; W. Harry Talbot; W. M. Hallack; Ira Gleason.

nearest station. Taking the bait, the old man burst into an explanation of the injustice that had been done him. Huey, feigning shocked indignation, promised to get the station moved to his property. Later someone asked Huey if he had moved it. "Why no," Huey answered, "the old bastard wasn't entitled to it to start with." By Huey's standards it was not immoral to break a promise given to somebody who was so stupid or so greedy as to ask an unreasonable favor.[3]

The effectiveness of Huey's campaign was apparent in the results of the first Democratic primary election. Bridges ran first, but Huey was a close second, only two thousand votes behind. The other three candidates divided a small vote. Bridges did not have a majority of the total vote, however, and hence would have to stand in a second primary against Huey. He could have withdrawn, and Huey would have won by default, but he decided to stay in. Bridges must have realized that he faced defeat. He had carried every courthouse town but three, of which Winnfield was one, but he had trailed Huey in the smaller towns and in the country. He was not likely to increase his vote very much, whereas Huey stood to pick up most of the supporters of the defeated candidates. Although the odds were against him, Bridges made a good race. In the second primary, held in November 1918, Huey squeezed through to victory by a margin of only 635 votes. As there was no Republican candidate, Huey was declared elected, to assume his office on the expiration of Bridges's term in December. He had just turned twenty-five.[4]

HUEY ATTENDED HIS FIRST meeting of the Railroad Commission in January. There he met his colleagues. He could not have been very impressed by what he saw. Shelby Taylor, the commissioner from the second district and the chairman, was a Baton Rouge lawyer. Heavily built and paunchy, with a moon-shaped face, he had been on the Commission since 1908. There was something about him that suggested a lack of resolution; people said that he talked a better game than he played. John T. Michel, of the first district, a New Orleans man, had held his office since 1912. He was a ward leader in the organization that ruled New Orleans, the Old Regulars. With machine support he had four times been elected secretary of state, and once he had tried unsuccessfully for the governorship. Short, dumpy, and inarticulate, he was a model of the type of mediocre professional

[3] Will Harvey Todd; D. J. Anders; Edmund E. Talbot; Harry Gamble.
[4] Long: *Every Man a King*, p. 41; Bozeman, in *Winn Parish Enterprise*, October 3, 1957.

politician that had long dominated the Commission. At this meeting Huey also met the Commission's secretary, Henry Jastremski, who would shortly become his ardent ally and agent. He may have met its counsel, W. M. Barrow, from the attorney general's office.[5]

Almost immediately the whole state became aware that there was a new presence on the Commission. Although the agency usually met in Baton Rouge, it sometimes convened in other cities. The February meeting was scheduled for Shreveport, and to this gathering Huey summoned representatives of the independent oil producers of the area. These men denounced Standard Oil and the pipeline companies for freezing them out of Pine Island. After the session Huey prepared a statement summarizing the grievances of the independents. It charged that Louisiana oil was being wasted while Standard Oil was importing large quantities of Mexican crude oil. This statement Huey took with him to the March meeting of the Commission in Baton Rouge. He also took copies of a resolution recommending that the legislature enact a law strengthening the Commission's power to regulate the pipelines, a law that would declare the companies to be public utilities and thus give Huey and his colleagues a firmer control over them. He said nothing publicly about his plan and did not disclose it even to Taylor and Michel. He meant to spring it suddenly on the Commission, secure favorable action, and then force the governor, Ruffin G. Pleasant, to call a special session of the legislature.

At the March meeting Huey waited until the Commission finished its public business and went into executive session. Then he presented his report and asked for its adoption. Michel seemed willing to follow Huey's lead. But Taylor hesitated, as well he might. In Baton Rouge stood Standard's huge refinery, reputed to be the largest in the world, and the company was a growing power in the little city, socially and politically as well as economically. Huey later related how he swung Taylor to his side. While Taylor read over the document, Huey happened to look out of the window of their meeting room in the capitol. The building was situated on a bluff overlooking the Mississippi, and an oil tanker was steaming up the river. "Look at that, Shelby," Huey cried. "There is a ship coming up the river loaded with Mexican crude to go in the tanks where they will not let us put our oil." Taylor took one look and signed, and so did Michel. The incident may well have occurred, but Huey's account of it is suspiciously dramatic. More probably, Taylor and Michel simply yielded to the arguments of a stronger man. That night Huey had the signed report officially certified and gave out copies to the newspapers. He was not taking any chances on letting his associates back out on him. Besides, by reporting it himself he would receive the major attention in the newspaper accounts.

Huey's forebodings about the backbone of his colleagues were well founded. The press reports brought lawyers and lobbyists of Standard swarming before the Commission when it met the following day. Taylor was obviously ill at ease and irritated. Finally he asked Secretary Jastremski for the report he had signed. "I will tear it up," he said. Huey heard him and intervened to say that the report was official and could not be recalled. Taylor subsided. But although the decision stood, Huey failed to accomplish his purpose. Governor Pleasant, a dignified and conservative representative of the old regime who would become one of Huey's bitterest enemies, stubbornly refused to call the legislature into session to consider a pipeline law.[6]

Probably Huey was pleased to have the matter end that way, for the moment. He did not want a pipeline law, not just yet. The Standard Oil issue was too good to drop. It offered infinite possibilities to a rising politician. It could be made the central question in the gubernatorial election of 1920. That election would occur in the first month of the year, but already, in the summer of 1919, prospective candidates were in the field, and the campaign was warming up with the weather. On July 4 the town of Hot Wells, a resort in the central part of the state, announced a great political rally and invited the candidates to appear. Four of them accepted. Most of the state's political leaders flocked to Hot Wells to see how the orators conducted themselves and perhaps to get a line on what deals were being made. A large crowd was on hand. Three of the speakers denounced the Old Regular machine or, as it was known in the country areas, the New Orleans Ring. Candidates who had no hopes of securing the Ring's support always went through the motions of damning it. The fourth speaker, who nourished hopes of Ring support, denounced other things. The speeches were dull, and the crowd was getting bored.

Then the chairman introduced an added speaker, who was neither on the program nor a candidate for governor, but who had asked to

[6] *Third Annual Report of the Public Service Commission of Louisiana* (Baton Rouge, 1934), pp. 29–34; Long: *Every Man a King*, pp. 43–6; Loos: *Oil on Stream!,* p. 86; Minute Book of the Railroad Commission and Public Service Commission of Louisiana, I, entries of February 18, March 25, 1919; hereafter cited as Minute Book, I, Louisiana Public Service Commission. The last item is a summary running account of the Commission's actions. This record of Huey's tenure on the agency is in two bound volumes in the office of the Louisiana Public Service Commission in the state capitol.

appear because he wanted to say something about what was happening in Louisiana. Huey stood up. He looked rustic and awkward and young, no match for the experienced politicians who had preceded him. He began to speak. Pausing only momentarily to fling a gibe at the Ring, he launched into his main theme, a denunciation of Standard Oil and Governor Pleasant and all their works. Standard was an "octopus," and its officials were among "the nation's most notorious and leading criminals." Pleasant was an agent of the octopus and had done its bidding when he refused to call a special session. Huey shouted out, addressing the absent governor: "It will take you forty years and forty barfly appointees to live this down!" The crowd was galvanized. This was no ordinary speech, no stale rehashing of rings and personalities. Huey had introduced into the campaign a new issue —really a whole new kind of politics. After the meeting nobody said anything about the speeches of the candidates. All the talk was of Huey. "Say, who the hell is he?" was a common question. Those who did not know were about to be enlightened.[7]

---

[7] Long: *Every Man a King*, pp. 46–7; Hermann B. Deutsch: "The Kingdom of the Kingfish," in New Orleans *Item*, July 20, 1939. This series of articles by Deutsch forms one of the best journalistic commentaries on Long.

# CHAPTER 7

# *The Fight Is Just Beginning*

**T**HE FOUR GUBERNATORIAL CANDIDATES who had offered themselves to the voters at Hot Wells found reason to withdraw
from the race before the end of the summer of 1919. Two other
aspirants, who had not appeared at the rally, also discovered that
they had other matters to attend to and eliminated themselves.

Louisianians noted appreciatively that the campaign was getting
off to a normal start. Such a sudden and fearsome decimation of
political hopefuls was a familiar feature of elections. At the beginning of a contest a large number of candidates would "announce"
for the chief office, but few remained in the running. The majority
were unable to make the necessary "deals"—to secure pledges of adequate financial aid or to round up sufficient organizational support
—and eventually they "pulled down." Nearly always a withdrawing
candidate would endorse one of the two or three men who felt strong
enough to stay in, extracting from him a promise of a favor in return
for some presumably deliverable vote. The surviving candidates would
then battle it out in the Democratic primary.

Solemnly repeated every four years, the performance seemed
haphazard, often irrational, and sometimes downright unreal. Actually, it had a measure of logic in it, for it was the only way the
existing political structure could operate. Louisiana was a state without a state machine and hence without the good and the evil such an
organization could provide, the ordered efficiency and the iron control. In this politically conscious state there were local organizations,
to be sure; Louisiana was full of them. Every parish had its court-

house ring, usually headed by the sheriff, and its rival "out" ring, which was trying to get in. The sheriff was an unusually powerful official, and in most parishes he functioned as the local boss, deciding what candidates the ring would support and delivering a specified vote on election day. That vote might come from only a fraction of the total number of eligible voters—those who for one reason or another were devoted to the sheriff—but it was a certain vote. One veteran sheriff was asked to explain why a holder of the office was so influential. He answered simply: "His duties are not defined by law or confined by law." He meant that a Louisiana sheriff to a considerable degree combined in himself the essential powers of government. He could detain or punish or release or favor. Thus, although he was technically an enforcer of law, he was in reality, because of his latitude in interpreting the application of law, also its maker and its judge.[1]

The political power of the sheriffs was particularly evident in a gubernatorial campaign. The first move of a candidate for governor was to line up as many sheriffs as he could. If he could secure the support of a sizable number of courthouse rings, he could approach the biggest ring of all, the New Orleans Old Regular machine, and ask for its support. He could say to the city bosses: See the strength that I have in the country; if you will go with me, I can be elected. A candidate with a strong country following and with an Old Regular endorsement was almost certain to win. Conversely, a candidate running against Old Regular opposition, even though he had country support, would probably lose. Of the four governors between 1900 and 1916, only one was elected without the support of the New Orleans Ring. The secret of the Ring's power was simple: it controlled the largest block of votes in the state. Over a fifth of Louisiana's population was concentrated in the metropolitan area, and the Old Regulars, as efficient an urban machine as any in the nation, could turn out an obedient majority of the city's voters in any election. This ability to deliver a vote was the greatest pride of the head boss, Martin Behrman, heavy-set, round-faced, with a thick toothbrush mustache his most distinguishing feature; he had been mayor of New Orleans so long that some people thought he had inherited the job. Behrman liked to boast that even as late as the night before an election he could send down the word and swing twenty-five thousand votes to any candidate. (Although Behrman violated a political rule by bragging in that way, he was a man of competence and a ready wit. He is

[1] Milton Coverdale.

reported to have said: "You can make prostitution illegal in Louisiana, but you can't make it unpopular.")

But although the city machine could almost ensure the victory of a country candidate, it could not elect one of its own men. It had once tried, putting up Michel of the Railroad Commission, and had failed. Normally it sought to make a deal with one of the strong country aspirants. In return for its support, it asked for state legislation favorable to the city and for control of state patronage in New Orleans. If its candidate won, he and the machine usually preserved their alliance for the duration of his term. But because no governor was able to create anything like a statewide organization, and was not immediately eligible to succeed himself, the arrangement fell apart at the end of four years—and the process started all over again.[2]

In 1919 the Old Regulars, after much stalling and negotiating, finally decided to back Frank P. Stubbs of Monroe. Stubbs had recently returned from France as colonel of the First Louisiana Infantry and had the aura of a war hero. In addition, he was supposed to have strong support in the northern part of the state. Florid and gray-haired, Stubbs was a dignified figure but not a very good public speaker. His advisers did not think that his oratorical deficiencies would hurt him; nor did they worry that the voters would resent his being the head of a firm of corporation lawyers in his home town. With the kind of support that he had, he did not need any special abilities to win. It was the news of the Ring's endorsement of Stubbs that caused six of the candidates to withdraw. The odds in his favor seemed so overwhelming that they saw no other recourse. Only one candidate remained to oppose him.

That candidate was, however, a very special figure in state politics, the most compelling personality to appear in the first twenty years of the century. Louisianians did not always agree with John M. Parker, but they could not ignore him, and they felt a perverse pride in him even when they disagreed with him or when he violated some of the most respected tenets of Louisiana and Southern politics. His most flagrant violation was deserting the Democratic party in 1912 to follow Theodore Roosevelt into the national Progressive party. He followed this heresy by running for governor in 1916 as a Progressive, opposing and losing to the Democratic nominee, Ruffin Pleasant, who

[2] L. Vaughan Howard: *Civil Service Development in Louisiana* (New Orleans, 1956), p. 35; George M. Reynolds: *Machine Politics in New Orleans, 1897–1926* (New York, 1936), pp. 197–8; Perry H. Howard: *Political Tendencies in Louisiana, 1812–1952* (Baton Rouge, 1957), pp. 111–12, 116–18; confidential communication; Hermann B. Deutsch.

had Ring support. Although Parker had not joined the Republicans, he had supported a Republican, Roosevelt, and was thus tainted by association with a party that was anathema in the South; furthermore, he had espoused some Progressive reforms and hence was viewed in conservative circles as a somewhat visionary radical. Such behavior would have ruined most Democratic politicians, but Parker had such impeccable social credentials that he was able to rebel against the party and then return to it as a leader. "He was one of them," said one man in explaining the anomaly. "He was a plantation owner." Parker was one of the wealthiest men in the state, a reputed million-aire. He owned and operated a cotton factorage business in New Orleans that was one of the largest in the South and also a plantation in the lovely, rolling country north of Baton Rouge known as the Felicianas. When he was not conducting his business in the city, he could be found at the plantation hunting or fishing. Although people thought of him as a planter type, he was just as much the urban-business type. Thus he united in himself two of the most important economic interests of the modern South. Perhaps the planter legend clung to him because of his appearance. Of average height, he had piercing eyes and iron-gray hair and mustache. He chewed tobacco and customarily in summer wore a white linen suit. In sum, he looked like the typical old-fashioned Southern gentleman and politician.[3]

His platform, however, was hardly a traditional Southern declaration. He promised to destroy the New Orleans Ring; to overhaul the existing tax structure with the view of forcing corporations to carry their fair share of the tax burden; to protect the independent oil producers against the large operators (presumably by strengthening the law regulating pipelines); to bring cheap natural gas to the homes and industries of New Orleans; to extend the state highway system; to increase the appropriation to Louisiana State University and particularly to build up the agricultural college; and to call a constitutional convention to rewrite the crazy quilt of the existing fundamental law. In its call for the state to exercise greater authority over the economy, and in its stress on reform, the platform reflected the influence of Parker's association with Progressivism. It was primarily an expression of the personal faith of the candidate. Certainly it did not represent the beliefs of many of his backers.[4]

[3] James P. O'Connor; Hermann B. Deutsch; William Wiegand; Baton Rouge *State-Times*, May 19, 1924.

[4] P. H. Howard: *Political Tendencies*, p. 121; Spencer Phillips: "Administration of Governor Parker" (unpublished M.A. thesis, Louisiana State University, 1933), pp. 23–4.

The Parker camp housed a strange mixture of political bedfellows. Prominent among the organizations supporting him was the Good Government League, which Parker himself had formed in 1912 and which was a collection of patrician and business leaders devoted to honest government, largely centered in New Orleans. Also plugging for the reformer was a rebellious offshoot of the Old Regulars, the Orleans Democratic Association, which was quite as devoted to spoils politics as the parent machine that it hoped to supplant. If its support of Parker seemed somewhat incongruous, so also did the conduct of Governor Pleasant, who had been elected with Ring support but who now broke with Behrman and spoke at Parker meetings. Pleasant did more than speak. In New Orleans he fired hundreds of state employees who were Ring henchmen, replacing them with men pledged to Parker. Another former beneficiary of the Ring also turned on it and endorsed Parker: this was Jared Y. Sanders, who had one of the biggest political names in the state. J. Y., as he was universally known, had been lieutenant governor, governor, and congressman. He had accepted Ring support in his race for governor in 1908 and had recently sought it again in a bid for a Senate seat but had been rebuffed. Now it appeared to him that the Old Regulars were "the Prussians of Louisiana politics" and "the Hun that is ever thundering at our gates." A large and rather ponderous man and a spellbinding orator, Sanders had been born in the plantation parish of St. Mary in south Louisiana and now lived in nearby Hammond. He was a thorough conservative and had little sympathy with Parker's reforms; he also disliked the candidate personally. He was moved by no other reason than his own wounded pride. Even more opposed to reform was another Parker supporter, Lee E. Thomas, the conservative mayor of Shreveport. The coalition was a perfect example of the absence of order in Louisiana politics. The most incongruous member in it was the crusading young railroad commissioner from the third district.[5]

Huey decided to support Parker because he understood that the candidate would if elected back a bill to regulate pipelines more effectively. Later Huey claimed that he met Parker in a Shreveport hotel room and extracted a pipeline pledge in return for an endorsement. As Huey told it, Parker readily gave the pledge, saying that Standard Oil had once skinned him out of a patent. "I felt that this created a community of interest between us, as I had been skinned by the Stand-

---

[5] Charles E. Dunbar; Hermann B. Deutsch: "The Kingdom of the Kingfish," in New Orleans *Item*, July 23, 1939; copy of Sanders' speech in Jared Y. Sanders and Family Papers, Department of Archives and Manuscripts, Louisiana State University Library.

ard," Huey recalled. Another version of the meeting has it that Huey asked for a commitment and that Parker characteristically snapped: "Neither to you nor to any other living man will I make any pledge or promise of any kind to secure support." Actually, Huey had no need to ask for a pledge. Parker had already announced his platform and had indicated that he favored some kind of pipeline measure. Huey probably sought the confrontation to satisfy himself about Parker's sincerity, and Parker was quite ready to convince him, for he very much needed Huey's support. In 1916 he had run well only in the southern parishes, and if he was going to win this time, he had to break into the north. In the latter area he had strength in the plantation belts along the Mississippi River and in the Red River Valley, but little in the hill parishes, where Huey had his greatest following.[6]

In deciding to go for Parker, Huey was gambling his own political fortunes. If Parker lost, Huey's reputation as a rising man would suffer. But if Parker won, Huey could claim that he had elected him, and the Long name would take on added potency. Huey was fully aware of these possibilities. He threw everything that he could command into an effort to carry north Louisiana for Parker, even contributing twenty-two hundred dollars of his own money for expenses, a large sum for one in his circumstances. For an organization, he used the informal machine he had created in his race for railroad commissioner. He was also able, in some way, to absorb the organization that Julius had formed to win the district attorneyship of Winn and Jackson parishes and that Julius wanted to put behind Stubbs. "He took my crowd to Parker," Julius complained. "He took my leaders away from me."

To bring the Parker cause to the voters, Huey relied on the same methods that he had employed so successfully in his own behalf two years before. He had thousands of circulars printed and distributed, and he embarked on a whirlwind stump tour, speaking at least once daily for seventy days and going to remote places where no other campaigner had ever appeared. In his speeches he voiced his own interpretation of what the Parker movement represented and of what Parker would do as governor. There was one overriding reason why Parker should be elected, Huey explained: Parker was hostile to the large oil interests and would get a pipeline bill through the legislature. Huey even detailed what the provisions of the bill would be—it would

[6] Long, quoted in New Orleans *Times-Picayune*, November 5, 1921; Huey P. Long: *Every Man a King* (New Orleans, 1933), pp. 47–8; Hermann B. Deutsch: "Kingdom of the Kingfish," in New Orleans *Item*, July 23, 1939.

declare the lines to be common carriers and would divorce them from the oil producers and especially from Standard Oil. His emphasis was markedly different from the note struck by other Parker orators and, for that matter, by the candidate, all of whom talked mainly about destroying the wicked Ring.

Huey himself used the Ring issue against Stubbs on occasion. Although Stubbs had accepted the support of the city machine, he liked to denounce urban sin and vice in speeches to moralistic north Louisiana audiences. Somebody told Huey that Stubbs's most prominent supporters in New Orleans were frequenters of the town's night spots and that he ought to use against Stubbs the scriptural passage: "Ephraim is joined to his idols; let him alone." According to Julius Long, Huey was much struck by the aptness of the quotation and said to an aide: "Go over to Hirsch and Lehman's store and buy me the best damned Bible they've got." He could not resist such an opportunity to taunt the Ring, but for the most part he hammered away at the pipeline question. It was evident that his aim was to commit the Parker administration to support a pipeline law, and Parker could hardly have been pleased with the position his north Louisiana lieutenant was putting him in.[7]

But Parker had to admit that Huey's support had some value. The January primary disclosed a victory for the reform candidate. He ran unexpectedly well in New Orleans, trailing there by only five thousand votes, carried most of the southern parishes by a substantial vote, and topped Stubbs in most of the northern parishes by a narrow margin. Although he had shown strength in every section, each of his leaders immediately claimed credit for the victory: each said that without the vote he had rolled up, Parker would have been defeated. The loudest claim came from Huey. Actually, neither he nor any single person was responsible for the outcome. The Parker vote was primarily a popular revulsion against the kind of politics the voters were accustomed to. But Huey could rightly affirm that he had played as large a part as anybody in determining the result. With his stress on economic issues, he had injected a fresh and more realistic kind of politics into the campaign, and he had undoubtedly rallied his large personal following to Parker. Parker's greatest gains over his 1916 vote were in the north and in the farmer parishes, and without this accretion he might have been forced into a second primary. Huey

---

[7] Long, quoted in New Orleans *States*, September 2, 1923; Julius T. Long; Long: *Every Man a King*, p. 48; John L. Loos: *Oil on Stream!* (Baton Rouge, 1959), pp. 86–7; Julius T. Long: "What I Know About My Brother," *Real America*, II (September 1933), 56.

had every reason to think that he would have some influence with the incoming administration.[8]

THERE ARE OBSERVERS of the Louisiana political scene who contend that John M. Parker was the greatest governor of his century. "Parker broke the pattern of controlled governors and governors who did nothing," said one of these, himself a former chief executive. He meant that Parker was the first governor in modern times who was not obligated to some organization and the first one who realized the need for social change and did something to bring it about. The favorable evaluations of Parker are in part valid, but they ignore a whole vital area of the Parker story and obscure the real import of his administration. Only within a very narrow definition of success was Parker a successful governor. Judged in a larger context, he was a failure, a prime example of the tragedy of the progressive reformer limited by his own vision. His most serious error, say some commentators, was that he did not destroy the New Orleans Ring and build his own organization. Although he was able to secure Behrman's defeat for mayor in 1920, the Ring soon regained its power. In 1924 it elected its candidate for governor over the opposition of Parker, who had lost most of his influence, and in the following year it returned Behrman to his mayoralty seat.

The usual defense of Parker's omission is that he was too high-minded to be a good politician. He would not create a ring to destroy another. It is true that Parker professed scorn for machine politics. "Politics and pie are the same thing," he liked to say. Yet on occasion he employed the crassest kind of political pressure. He consistently denied the state patronage in New Orleans, an estimated seven thousand jobs, to the Old Regulars, and in the mayoralty campaign of 1920 he deliberately padded the payrolls of the Dock Board, which employed some three thousand men, with anti-Behrman employees, leading Behrman to complain that the wharves were so full of workers that cargoes could not be loaded or unloaded. Parker permitted, at least in some areas of state government, the continuation of one of the most flagrant practices of Louisiana politics, the levying of financial assessments on employees during campaigns.

It was not a reluctance to use political means that caused Parker's troubles as governor. It was that he did not use them with enough frequency and ruthlessness. There was a limitation in him that always

[8] P. H. Howard: *Political Tendencies*, p. 119.

rose up to restrict his actions. He could carry the war to his enemies —up to a point, but he could not cross the Rubicon to conquer them. He lacked, perhaps, the will to wield power and was hardly ever the master of a situation.[9]

Parker's indecision also colored his approach to the social and economic problems he had said he was going to solve. A highly intelligent man, better educated than most politicians, Parker was sensitive to the problems of the industrial age, and he sincerely wanted to do something to alleviate them. But he was never quite sure how far he should go to get rid of an evil. Most of the time he did not go nearly far enough. This was a weakness shared by most progressive reformers. As members of the middle class, they saw the need for change and pushed it to a certain point but drew back from making the change really effective. With Parker, it was his aristocratic associations that held him back. If he pressed his reforms too hard, he would hurt his friends financially and, worse, offend them socially. Politicians like Parker prepare the way for revolutionary change. They improve conditions somewhat, enough to arouse desires for more change but not enough to satisfy existing needs. They sow the seed, but bolder men have to do the harvesting.

Parker's psychology shaped, and flawed, all of his legislative program. He supported amendments to the compensation act increasing payments for injury and disability, but the increases were slight and did not satisfy the demands of labor. He sponsored a law creating a state highway commission and appropriating money for road construction and became known as the "gravel roads" governor, but he did nothing to meet the crying need for hard-surfaced roads. He enlarged the appropriation to the state university, giving it the income from a dedicated tax, and he provided state money to purchase a new and more spacious campus. He liked to be called the father of LSU, but he envisioned that the maximum enrollment would never be more than three thousand. Interested in conservation of natural resources, as any progressive should be, he talked bravely about the necessity of regu-

[9] Sam H. Jones; Phillips: "Administration of Governor Parker," pp. 150–7; P. H. Howard: *Political Tendencies,* pp. 122–3; Baton Rouge *State-Times,* May 19, 1924; L. V. Howard: *Civil Service . . . in Louisiana,* pp. 32–3; Charles E. Dunbar; *Hearings Before the Special Committee on Investigation of Campaign Expenditures,* 72 Cong., 2 sess. (Washington, 1933), Pt. I, 456–7, 459, testimony of Abraham Shushan. The last item is a report of a Senate inquiry into the 1932 election of John H. Overton to the United States Senate. For various reasons the investigators decided to delve into events long preceding the election, and the testimony is a storehouse of information on Louisiana politics over a period of years. It will hereafter be cited as *Overton Hearing,* I.

lating the natural-gas industry and preventing the gas waste in the manufacture of carbon black. Carbon black was made by burning natural gas in such a way that the carbon was recovered in solid form but the heating value was lost. But when the gas industry objected to his proposed bill and employed J. Y. Sanders as its spokesman, Parker gave way and accepted an ineffective substitute measure, offering as an excuse that it was the only bill he could get.[1]

The governor gave a typical display of his limitations when he came to redeem his pledge to get a pipeline bill enacted. In Huey's apt words: "He appeared to desire only such legislation as was agreed to in compromise on all sides." There were several sides, and each had its own idea as to what kind of bill should be passed. Huey had drawn up a measure that he wanted the independent producers, who had formed a loose association, to sponsor. But for some reason the independents would not accept Huey's bill. Instead, they endorsed one drafted by a Shreveport pipeline lawyer. Possibly some of them thought that Huey's bill was too drastic and could not be passed. Huey believed that many of the independents had been suborned by Standard Oil, which had gained their favor by purchasing their holdings. The big oil and pipeline companies preferred no bill at all but were resigned to the passage of some kind of legislation.

Huey, in a letter to Parker, explained why he thought the independents' bill was "worthless" and why his own would be effective. He argued that although the former broadened the existing definition of a common carrier, it would not prevent the big oil companies from destroying the small producers by an embargo, as the big ones had done at Pine Island. The only remedy, which his bill provided, was to declare the pipelines to be common carriers or "merely a facility of transportation," which could not discriminate in their purchases. In other words, pipelines would have to be divorced from producing concerns, and his favorite enemy, Standard Oil, would lose one of its largest properties. "Now I propose to be on hand when the Legislature meets," Huey warned Parker. He would have his bill ready but would not bring it forward if the independents could agree on a good bill. But if a satisfactory measure was not offered, he would have his own introduced and would try to fight it through to passage. Although he regretted that Parker had not seen fit to call him into a personal conference, he asserted that he still had faith in the honesty of the

[1] Phillips: "Administration of Governor Parker," pp. 49–51, 78, 100–1; confidential communication; Parker to A. V. Coco, April 8, 1922, O. C. Dawkins to Parker, April 4, 1924, in Governor's Correspondence, Department of Archives and Manuscripts, Louisiana State University Library.

candidate he had supported. But perhaps Parker did not care to do the right thing. In that case, Huey ended, vaguely but menacingly: "I am able to take care of the ordinary emergency which may arise so far as I am concerned."[2]

When the legislature met, the independents' bill was introduced. It extended the definition of a common carrier pipeline. A line would become a common carrier if it transported any oil belonging to or produced by any company other than the one owning the line, and since all oil companies at one time or another found it necessary to buy oil from other producers, all pipelines thus came under the regulation of the law. Although the bill did not go as far as Huey wished, he supported it, and it passed the lower house by a narrow margin. The big oil companies had fought the bill every step of the way, and at this juncture they appealed to Parker to call a conference to see if a compromise satisfactory to all sides could not be worked out. The independents, either because they had been bought off, as Huey had affirmed, or because they had no hope of passing their present bill in the senate, readily agreed to a meeting. Only one of the interested parties dissented. Huey went to the Railroad Commission office and typed out on a mimeograph stencil a statement denouncing the proposed conference, ran off copies himself, and laid a copy on the desk of every legislator and of the governor. The document, a variation of his circulars, charged that the Standard Oil lobby was "about to make itself a part of the legislative machinery of Louisiana." It also observed, hitting at an unmistakable target, that whether the Ring or the reformers sat in the seats of government, the same "plunderbunding politicians" determined the fate of legislation.

Huey refused to participate officially in the conference, held in the anteroom of the governor's office on July 2, 1920. He was present as a spectator, however, and made some biting remarks about independents who had sold out. Immediately the meeting broke out in an uproar. Parker and representatives of the big oil companies demanded to know whether Huey had meant to reflect on them in his circular. Huey denied that he had had anyone present in mind, but he stuck to his general indictment that something peculiar was going on. Finally Parker quieted the session down and asked if there was not some way the bill could be changed to satisfy all sides. After hours of discussion the conferees agreed on a softened definition of what constituted a common carrier. A pipeline would not automatically become a

2 Long: *Every Man a King*, p. 49; Long to Parker, April 21, 1920, in John M. Parker Papers, Southern Historical Collection, University of North Carolina Library, Chapel Hill.

common carrier if it transported oil from a producer other than its owner. But it could be adjudged by the courts to be a common carrier if it carried the oil of other producers on anything like a regular schedule. Both the independents and the oil companies pledged support for the compromise, and it easily passed the legislature. Only Huey refused to accept the result. He broke openly with Parker and from then on fought the administration at every turn. In rejecting a settlement that represented a consensus, he was not acting as a normal or pragmatic politician. A mixture of reasons influenced his decision. In part his reaction was narrowly personal: anger at Parker for going back on a pledge, hatred of Standard Oil, and a burning desire to humiliate the company. More important, however, was the realization that he had laid hold of a good political issue. He was going to keep it alive until he got the most out of it. But mixed with his baser motives was an element of sound economics. He was right in contending that no really effective regulation of pipelines would be possible unless they were separated from the owning oil companies.[3]

If Huey had not broken with Parker on the pipeline measure, he would have had to do it later over the issue of the severance tax. A severance tax is one exacted from companies or individuals engaged in severing natural resources from the soil or water. In the twenties the practice was to base the amount of the tax on the quantity of the resources extracted or on the value of such resources when severed, and in Louisiana, a state rich with oil, natural gas, lumber, salt, sulphur, and other reserves, a severance tax could be a source of large and constant revenues. There was a severance-tax law on the books, but its provisions were so loose and its enforcement so difficult that the state realized almost no income from it. In his campaign Parker had said nothing specific about changing the law, but he had promised to see that the tax structure was so revised as to make industry bear a more equitable share of the burden. He had also pledged that he would provide funds to build up the state university and would do so without adding a cent to property taxes. Opponents had asked how he hoped to accomplish this miracle.

After he was elected but before he was actually inaugurated, Parker revealed his plan. He was going to get the legislature to pass a more realistic severance-tax bill—one that would produce a revenue. If disclosing his purpose before he had the power to enforce it betrayed his impracticality, his next action attested to his idealistic belief in the essential goodness of men, typical of the progressives. He called

[3] Deutsch: "Kingdom of the Kingfish," in New Orleans *Item*, July 25, 1939; Loos: *Oil on Stream!*, p. 87; Long: *Every Man a King*, pp. 49–50.

a series of conferences with representatives and attorneys of the very interests that would have to endure any tax increase, and asked them to agree on a bill that he could submit to the legislature. The governor-elect suggested that the tax should be based on the value of the resource severed and that a rate of two and a half or even three per cent would be fair. Grandly he lectured the tough-minded men before him on their civic duty: They were drawing a "golden harvest" from Louisiana, and, naturally, they would be willing to return a small part of it in taxes to support the state's educational and other institutions. Their replies shocked him. They admitted no obligation to the state and no desire to contribute to its well-being. Especially adamant were the representatives of the Standard Oil Company and other oil concerns. If they were forced to, they would assent to a tax of one per cent or perhaps one and a half, they said, but nothing higher. Impressed by this unexpected opposition, Parker characteristically offered a compromise. He would agree to two per cent, but he would go no lower and would recommend this rate to the legislature whether the industries liked it or not.

Now the businessmen were taken back. If the governor was determined to press for a severance-tax law, he could probably get one enacted, and it might be the wise move to go along with him and try to make the measure as palatable as possible. The lumber interests executives called on the governor-elect and said they would accept the two per cent rate. At some point in the discussion the question was raised as to whether the tax, once voted, would be increased. Parker pledged that it would remain the same during his administration.

The word spread fast that the solid front of the industries had been broken. An hour after the lumber people left Parker's office, another group called, officials and represenatives of the Standard Oil Company. They too offered to accept the two per cent rate. But they were even more worried than the previous visitors that the rate might be juggled up. Parker confidently reassured them. He said he would make with them a "gentleman's agreement"—after all, everyone present was a gentleman—if they would not attack the legality of the law in the courts he would pledge that the tax would not be raised during his administration. The oil men were still not satisfied. One of their attorneys said that tax laws generally had a joker or two in them and asked who would write the bill. Parker, basking in the glow of his success and the company of fellow aristocrats, gave a fantastic reply. "You gentlemen can write it," he said. His callers must have found it hard to believe their ears, but they eagerly accepted the offer. The severance-tax law of 1920 was drafted in the legal department of the Standard Oil Company, with assistance from lawyers of other affected industries. As enacted, it was a "license" law that levied a temporary license tax on industries engaged in severing natural resources. Otherwise it would have had to be cast in the form of a constitutional amendment, and as Parker had promised to call a constitutional convention, it was thought better to let that body frame a permanent severance-tax act. Parker later attempted to give excuses for his action. He claimed that he had spoken "jokingly" when he told the Standard attorneys they could write the law. He had had their measure inspected by other lawyers, he said, and certainly he had to do something to get money for the state. His defense was not very convincing. If he had spoken in jest, why did he permit the Standard lawyers to proceed to frame the law? Huey Long and others like him failed to see any humor in the spectacle of a corporation drafting a law to tax itself.[4]

The "gentleman's agreement" followed Parker like an evil specter for the rest of his administration. He had looked forward with anticipation to the meeting of the constitutional convention, which was to convene in Baton Rouge early in 1921. This body would reduce Louisiana's patchwork constitution to a compact document, a result that Parker believed would be the greatest monument to his governorship. But when the convention met, it spent most of its time wrangling over the severance tax. There was a strong sentiment among the delegates to raise the tax to three per cent and to embody this rate in the constitution. Behind the drive for an increase were men and interests with entirely different motives. Many members had the same philosophy as Huey, who was not a delegate but could count friends among those who were: they thought the corporations should bear a greater share of the tax burden. Strongly allied with them were conservatives from the oil parishes who hoped to enact a provision that part of the tax be diverted to the parish where the tax was collected. Former governor Pleasant went so far as to propose that one per cent of the tax be allocated to the oil parishes, which would have been a windfall for Caddo, his own parish. When he encountered opposition, Pleasant denounced the oil trust in such radical terms that a report went the rounds that he was getting his inspiration from Huey Long.

[4] Parker, quoted in New Orleans *Item*, November 23, 1921; Phillips: "Administration of Governor Parker," pp. 46–7; Deutsch: "Kingdom of the Kingfish," in New Orleans *Item*, July 25, 1939; Leslie Moses: "The Growth of Severance Taxation in Louisiana and Its Relation to the Oil and Gas Industry," *Tulane Law Review*, XVII (1943), 607; T. N. Farris: *Severance Taxation in Louisiana* (University, La., 1938), Pt. I, pp. 10–13.

The oil companies and the other affected industries were opposed to an increase, but they hesitated to state their stand openly, and at first it seemed that the supporters of the three per cent rate would have little trouble in imposing their will. But suddenly Parker intervened in the deliberations of the convention. He secured permission to appear before its taxation committee, and he sternly told the members that an upward revision would constitute "a breach of faith" on the part of the state. It would be dishonorable, his somewhat astounded auditors learned, because it would violate the gentleman's agreement, which, although it was verbal, had the binding effect of a contract. This was a new and unusual theory of democratic government, that the word of one man, even if he was a governor and a gentleman, could commit other men to observe an agreement, could prevent even a state convention, fresh from the sovereign people with a mandate, from acting. But as dubious as Parker's doctrine was, it had the effect of throwing the convention into confusion. Some delegates who had been inclined to favor the three per cent rate now hesitated to cross the governor. Many continued to support it and expressed anger at Parker's assumption that he could limit their action. It soon became·evident that an increase of some kind would be enacted, and it was just as evident that it would have to represent a compromise satisfactory to a number of parties —the governor, the industries, the oil parishes, and the proponents of the tax. From the convention, committees and knots of leaders sallied forth to sound out Parker on what he would accept. One of these meetings, held on the steps of the governor's mansion, became notorious as the "front porch" conference. At it Parker did something all too characteristic of him. Those present had suggested that a rate of two and a half per cent, with the half going to the parishes, might be an acceptable solution. Parker said that he might go along with it —but that first he would have to check with someone. He telephoned the treasurer of Standard Oil and invited him to join the group, and when that official arrived, the governor asked him if the proposal would be agreeable to the big company.

Reluctantly, Parker concluded that he would have to submit to a breach in the gentleman's agreement. But he was determined to exercise some influence over the nature of the settlement, and to that end he asked the convention for permission to address it. In an effective speech, he reviewed the history of his compact with the industries, stressed the importance of the revenue from the severance tax to the state, and cautioned against diverting too much of it to the parishes. He urged that the tax be left at its present level. But he emphasized that whatever was done, the convention should not place a set, inflexible rate in the constitution, and future rates should be left to the discretion of future legislatures. There was so much wisdom in the last admonition that the convention followed it. As finally enacted, the severance-tax provision authorized the legislature to levy a tax based on either the value or the quantity of the resource extracted. A portion of the taxes collected would be returned to the parishes where the severance was made, although the allocated amount was smaller than these parishes desired. As a concession to the industries, the tax was declared to be a "lieu" levy, that is, one in lieu of other taxes that might be laid on machinery and various productive facilities and on rising land values resulting from the discovery under the land of resources. Every party to the controversy got something, and everyone seemed satisfied.[5]

Parker was pleased with his partial success in controlling the outcome of the severance-tax fight. Beyond the settlement of this issue, he could take pride in the larger accomplishment of having led the state to revise at last its whole fundamental law. The result was desirable, but he could hardly claim that the new constitution was the progressive kind of document he had said was needed. Sacred to progressives everywhere as a device to limit wealth was the income tax, and progressives in the convention had attempted to authorize the state to exercise such a levy. They met ignominious defeat. Conservative opponents almost succeeded in placing an absolute prohibition of an income tax in the constitution, but they relented to permit enactment of a provision so meaningless that future legislatures could not implement it. Progressives and other advocates of change proposed that the convention go on record as favoring a bond issue to construct roads and bridges. Conservatives countered that highways should be built on a pay-as-you-go principle. Supporting such a plan, J. Y. Sanders urged that automobile and truck licenses be raised from five dollars to fifteen and twenty-five dollars respectively and that a tax of one cent a gallon be placed on gasoline. This program, the former governor proclaimed dramatically, would provide all the funds that the highway commission could expend sensibly in any one year and would enable the state to build a complete system of gravel roads without incurring a dollar of debt. His proposal, which appealed

[5] Farris: *Severance Taxation*, Pt. I, pp. 13–17; Phillips: "Administration of Governor Parker," pp. 86–8; Deutsch: "Kingdom of the Kingfish," in New Orleans *Item*, July 28, 1939; A. K. Gordon, treasurer of the Standard Oil Company, quoted in New Orleans *Item*, November 4, 1921; Moses: "Growth of Severance Taxation," *Tulane Law Review*, XXVII, 608–10.

strongly to the thinking of fiscal conservatives, was made a part of the constitution. Among the few progressive features of the document was an article changing the name of the Railroad Commission to the more appropriate title of Public Service Commission and widening somewhat its regulatory powers.[6]

The commissioner from the third district of the newly named agency had followed events in the convention with close and calculating interest. He sensed immediately that to a politician on the way up the severance-tax settlement offered glittering possibilities. It did not take much perception to realize that Parker and the ruling class had blundered badly. Huey had more than ordinary perception, and he prided himself on his ability to recognize a break and to take advantage of it. "It ain't enough to get the breaks," he liked to say. "You gotta know how to use 'em." Therefore, he determined to turn the abundant evidence of Parker's dealings with the oil companies to the governor's hurt and to the furtherance of his own ambitions. He soon found an opportunity to execute his purpose. The convention, before adjourning, had issued a call for a special session of the legislature to meet in September 1921 so that it could enact enabling legislation to implement some of the new constitutional mandates. When the session convened, the severance-tax controversy inevitably flared up anew. Proponents of a higher levy, arguing that the constitution authorized flexibility, proposed that the rate be raised to three per cent. Again they ran into opposition from Parker, who contended that the gentleman's agreement ran to the end of his administration and could not be disturbed. In the light of his recent speech to the convention, his reasoning was not very convincing. He himself seemed to realize that he was on untenable ground, and eventually, after tempers on both sides had boiled over, he persuaded himself that he could accept the increase without impairing his honor.[7]

But the big fireworks of the session were not provided by the severance-tax fight, the outcome of which was predictable, but by Huey, who was not. One morning soon after the legislature convened, every member of both houses found on his desk another mimeographed circular signed by Huey. It charged flatly that the Standard Oil Company was running the Parker administration. As proof of his accusation, Huey cited the facts that the governor had repudiated

---

[6] Phillips: "Administration of Governor Parker," p. 86; Deutsch: "Kingdom of the Kingfish," in New Orleans *Item*, July 28, 1939; *Twenty-third Annual Report of the Railroad Commission of Louisiana* (Baton Rouge, 1922), p. 15.

[7] Mildred Adams: "Huey the Great," *Forum*, LXXXIX (February 1933), 72–3; editorials in New Orleans *States*, November 12 and 13, 1921; Phillips: "Administration of Governor Parker," p. 112; Long: *Every Man a King*, pp. 63, 64, 65.

his pledge to support an effective pipeline bill and had permitted the Standard attorneys to write the severance-tax law. And Standard's power was growing, he went on. Heretofore an "invisible empire," it was now so bold as to admit that it controlled the state. At its demand Parker had appointed the son of its chief counsel, Hunter C. Leake, as superintendent of the state Charity Hospital in New Orleans. What was much more shameful, Parker had submitted the proposed severance-tax bill to the parent New York office of Standard for approval. Were the legislators such "fallen chattels," Huey asked, that they would stand by and see their laws written at 26 Broadway? Before the surprised targets of his attack could arouse themselves to make effective reply, Huey distributed to the legislators two more circulars of similar tenor. All three documents he typed out in the Public Service Commission's office and ran off on office equipment.[8]

The reaction to Huey's first circular was one of stunned incredulity. His accusations were so enormous that most people found it difficult to comprehend that they had been made—it was impossible that the whole government of the state had been corrupted by Standard Oil. It so happened that shortly before this Huey had stated at a Commission hearing and to the newspapers that Shelby Taylor had repudiated a pledge to him to deny a rate increase to the Cumberland Telephone and Telegraph Company. He implied that both Taylor and Michel had received favors from the company and that he could have had some himself if he had wanted to be bought, and this almost simultaneous blast at a second giant corporation added to the pervading mood of disbelief. But the shock effect wore off shortly, and first of all with the men of the power structure. Huey had actually made the terrible charge, they realized, and with realization came determination that he must be punished. A storm of denunciation broke upon Huey, who was prepared for it and, indeed, wanted it to come.

It began in the house of representatives. There the discussion centered on Huey's statements that his associates on the Public Service Commission had come under the influence of the telephone company. The reasoning of house leaders seemed to be that as the Commission was an official agency, a criticism of its integrity had to be reviewed by the legislature, another official body. The logic here was a bit fuzzy, and members indirectly admitted this in their speeches. They wanted to eliminate Huey from the Commission, but they could not decide how they could proceed against him legally. One proposal

[8] Long: *Every Man a King*, pp. 57–8; Deutsch: "Kingdom of the Kingfish," in New Orleans *Item*, July 30, 1939.

was to have him bound over to a sanity commission for examination. Another was to try him for contempt of the house and jail him if guilty. A north Louisiana member, wiser than his colleagues, said that he had known "the immortal Huey since he had molasses in his beard and cockleburrs in his hair" and that the upstart simply wanted attention and should be ignored. The real cause of all the confusion was the knowledge that no action could be taken against Huey alone. His charges implicated Taylor and Michel, and if the house wanted to discipline Huey it would first have to establish that the other two commissioners were innocent. The frustrated members finally acknowledged their dilemma and voted a resolution directing the house, sitting as a committee of the whole, to investigate the Commission's handling of the phone-rate case. Supporters of this maneuver hoped that a formal hearing would uncover evidence that would justify bringing impeachment charges against Huey.

The news that the house was going to investigate and possibly impeach Commissioner Long created a sensation. Then, immediately after the house had acted, an even more dramatic development hit the front pages of the newspapers. Governor Parker announced that he had sworn out two affidavits charging Huey with criminal libel. If Long's charges against him were true, he was unfit to be governor, Parker declared. But if the charges were false, Long should be dismissed from office and put in jail. Huey had gone to Shreveport to tend to some law business, and he learned of the governor's action from the sheriff of Caddo parish, who was required to execute the affidavits. This official made only a technical arrest, serving the writs and telling Huey to go to Baton Rouge and make bond. Huey returned to the capital on October 3. He was in a cocky mood when he appeared to arrange bond. He pulled five thousand dollars in cash out of his pocket and said: "I figured you boys might be short of ready money down here."[9]

This large sum had been supplied to him, according to rumor, by one of his attorneys, James G. Palmer, of Shreveport. Palmer had ambitions to run for governor in 1924, and, supposedly, he had offered to represent Huey without fee if Long would support him. Huey also engaged Robert R. Reid, of Amite, in south Louisiana, as a paid attorney, apparently thinking that in a case with political overtones he should have geographical representation in his counsel. Immediately Huey rewarded his lawyers in a strange way. His third child, a son, had just been born, and he named the boy after both of

---

[9] Deutsch: "Kingdom of the Kingfish," in New Orleans *Item*, July 30, 1939; Long: *Every Man a King*, pp. 58–9.

them: Palmer Reid Long. Still another member of the defense staff was Julius Long, who, even though he and Huey had recently dissolved their partnership, volunteered to serve without remuneration. With this battery of able lawyers representing him, Huey could look forward to the trial with confidence. It would be almost two weeks before he was arraigned, however, and a month before the case would be called. In the meantime he had to endure the ordeal of the legislative inquiry into his charges against his colleagues on the Commission.[1]

That hearing began on October 5 in the house chamber, with the senate in attendance and a packed crowd in the galleries. It was an uproarious and at times unruly session, setting, in the opinion of an observant reporter, a new high for the number of times the word "liar" was used in direct discourse on the legislative floor. Huey was asked to state what evidence he had to justify his charges. In a reply that was somewhat rambling—probably deliberately so, to obscure the fact that he had no very good legal evidence—Huey said that Shelby Taylor had promised to oppose a telephone-rate increase and then inexplicably had switched and that James C. Henriques, Sr., attorney for the telephone company, had told Huey that a good deal of legal work could be thrown his way if he was cooperative. While Huey was testifying, both Taylor and Henriques jumped up several times and shouted "liar," and both of them repeated the epithet in almost every sentence of their own testimony. Once when Huey attempted to question Henriques about one of his statements, the lawyer snapped: "I don't even want to talk to such a liar as you are."

Huey, when he was not testifying or examining other witnesses, stood against a wall at the rear of the chamber discussing strategy with house members who were adherents of his. These were men who admired his opposition to corporate influence or had a grievance against the Parker administration or had decided to attach themselves to his rising star. Huey, by his own later admission, instructed them to do everything that they could to confuse the proceedings. At one point he told one of them to get up and propose that all three commissioners be required to resign and stand for re-election. Another supporter immediately stated that he was authorized to say that Long would accept this arrangement. Some legislators caught at the suggestion—it seemed to promise an easy out from the situation that they still were not sure how to handle. One alert member saw the

[1] T. O. Harris: *The Kingfish: Huey P. Long, Dictator* (New Orleans, 1938), p. 24; Julius T. Long: "What I Know About My Brother," *Real America*, II (September 1933), 35–6.

trap that had been set for them. In his haste to expose it, however, he confessed the futility of any device that might be adopted to remove Huey from the Commission. "But Long's the only one of the bunch that would be re-elected," he blurted out. His recognition of the hard facts of the case seemed to convince even the managers of the hearing that they were running a farce. After a second tumultuous session they ended the spectacle and merely asked the committee of the whole to vote a resolution recommending impeachment of all three commissioners. Although the resolution was passed, the house itself took no action on it. No testimony had been adduced that would justify impeaching Huey, and nobody in the Parker administration wanted to do anything that would endanger the position of Taylor. The resolution was, as everyone knew, no more than a device of the legislature to save face. Conservative Louisianians could only wait for the libel trial and hope that the court would put in his place the man who had so outrageously defied them.[2]

When Huey had been arraigned in mid-October, his attorneys had asked dismissal of the case on the ground that the statements in his circulars referred to the Parker administration and not to the governor personally. Judge Harney F. Brunot denied the demurrer and set the trial for November 3. Although Palmer and Reid had indicated that they expected to present a strictly technical defense, their client insisted that they must regard the case as a political one. When one of his lawyers urged him to "play a safe situation," which probably meant only that Huey should keep his mouth shut until after the trial, Long answered, in a letter that sounded exactly like one of his circulars, that it was too late for him to play it safe. His efforts to destroy control of the state by the Standard Oil Company and its allied corporate interests were now at a crucial stage, he said. He had to go on: "Too much depends upon my standing my ground, continuing the fight and maintaining the position heretofore taken."

The trial, featuring the governor, a public service commissioner, and an array of lesser though important officials, gripped the attention of the whole state. Parker, who was represented by two luminaries of the Baton Rouge bar, John Fred Odom and Charles F. Holcombe, testified for six hours and called Huey a liar at least once

[2] Deutsch: "Kingdom of the Kingfish," in New Orleans *Item*, July 31, 1939; Long: *Every Man a King*, pp. 59–60; Adams: "Huey the Great," *Forum*, February 1933, pp. 72–3. Long, in later comments on this episode, gave the impression that he had narrowly escaped removal. But in a letter written at the time to one of his oil clients he revealed that he had no doubts but that the impeachment attempt would fail. Long to Consolidated-Progressive Oil Corporation, October 25, 1921, in Long Papers, Law File.

every hour. Without seeming to realize what he was doing, Parker confirmed the accuracy of Huey's charges. He said that he had permitted the Standard Oil lawyers to write the severance-tax law, and that he had discussed with representatives of Standard and other corporations the propriety of raising the tax rate. He could make such a damaging admission because he could see nothing wrong in what he had done.

Huey was on the stand for most of one day and displayed great mental agility in his testimony. When Parker's lawyers asked him if he would repeat his charges under oath, he countered with a proposal that Parker sue him on the record in civil court. He would resign from the Commission if Parker got a judgment; but if Parker did not win, he would have to resign the governorship. Asked to explain what he had meant by charging that the once invisible empire of the corporation had become visible under Parker, he simply referred to the governor's testimony about the severance tax. His circular had been a political and not a personal attack, he argued. "I ain't interested in saving Governor Parker's personal soul," he said jeeringly. "I've been trying to do something for the people of the state."

The taking of testimony was completed in a few days, and on November 8 Brunot announced his verdict. The judge found Huey guilty on both counts. On the first charge Brunot sentenced Huey to thirty days in the parish prison but suspended the penalty; on the second he fined Long one dollar or, in default of payment, to serve one hour in the prison. In explaining his decision, Brunot said that Huey was guilty of libel but only in a technical sense. The purpose of the mild sentence was to prevent a repetition of the offense without inflicting too harsh a sentence. Addressing himself directly to Long, the judge intoned solemnly: "Yours is an impulsive nature, given to ill-considered and at times indiscreet utterances." Huey startled the large crowd that had come to hear the verdict by saying he would not pay the fine. Thereupon Palmer reached in his pocket and pulled out a dollar and laid it before Brunot. Huey, smiling broadly, walked out of the courtroom. He and his friends considered the verdict a victory for him. Parker and his friends were equally convinced that it was a vindication for Parker.[3]

The two protagonists in the case and their supporters would argue

[3] Long: *Every Man a King*, pp. 61–3; Deutsch: "Kingdom of the Kingfish," in New Orleans *Item*, July 31, 1939; Curtis Hodges: "The Politics of Huey P. Long" (unpublished M.A. thesis, Louisiana State University, 1940), pp. 30–1; New Orleans *States*, November 6, 1921; Shreveport *Journal*, November 9; Shreveport *Times*, November 9.

for years to come over the meaning of the verdict. Huey at times took the line that the Standard Oil Company had exerted pressure on the court. Brunot had yielded to it in that he handed down a verdict of guilty, but he had been afraid to impose harsh punishment on the champion of the people. At other times Huey absolved Brunot of any complicity. The judge had fined Huey only because he thought he should save face for Parker and had actually paid fifty cents of the penalty himself. Parker's friends, for their part, claimed that the light sentence was a result of the governor's intercession with the court. He had brought the suit only to vindicate himself, and he had requested Brunot to deal lightly with the offender. If Parker did suggest the nature of the sentence to the judge, he acted improperly. Being the kind of man that he was, he undoubtedly did not do it. The probable explanation of the mild sentence is that Parker had a poor case to begin with and weakened it still more by his own testimony. Brunot must have realized, as Parker must have also, that a heavy sentence was almost certain to be overturned on appeal by the supreme court. That tribunal was famous for its reluctance to impose heavy penalties in libel suits.[4]

Actually, at the conclusion of the trial Huey was enraged at Brunot. The decision confirmed one of his most deeply held beliefs, that the state's judiciary was filled with men who would do the bidding of the corporations. It was a situation that he had already started to reform. The only way to do it, he had decided, was to secure the election of men who agreed with his philosophy to the supreme court, which could always reverse decisions of the lower courts. To that end, he had recently managed the victorious campaign of John R. Land for elevation to the court from the northern district. Now, as a result of the trial, he set his sights on a new objective. A justice from one of the southern districts was scheduled to retire in 1922, and it was common knowledge that Brunot expected to run for the seat. Huey made no secret of his intentions to intervene in that election. On the night of the day he had been found guilty, he ate supper with Reid in a capital restaurant. Throughout the meal he conducted a loud conversation with his counsel that was audible to lurking reporters. "You are going to run for the Supreme Court against Brunot," he commanded over and over. J. Y. Sanders ambled by the table and said something to Huey. The remark prompted Huey to an outburst

that was heard all over the room. "Brunot will never go to the supreme bench," he announced. Reid did run against Brunot and
defeated him. Brunot would eventually be a member of the court,
but in order to hold his seat he had to transfer his allegiance to Huey.[5]

A few days after the trial Huey issued an exultant statement to
the press. He had proved what he had set out to prove, he declared.
Now the people knew that the big corporations had been running
Louisiana. He had checked their march to power by exposing them,
but they had been only halted and would try again. The state would
not be free until they were brought under the control of the greater
power of the people. He was going to see to it that that control was
created. "The fight is just beginning," he promised grimly.

He spoke with confidence and certainty, almost with exaltation.
He knew now that what he had been doing for three years and more
—his emotional denunciations of corporations and sober economic
dissection of them, his speeches and circulars, his tricks and antics
—was at last reaching and influencing the people. The masses of
Louisiana were stirring, sluggishly, gropingly, falteringly, but they
were stirring: the trappers and fishermen of the bayous, the Cajun
farmers of the south and the redneck farmers of the hill parishes, the
sharecroppers and tenants everywhere, and the laborers in the towns
and the small businessmen in the villages. For generations they had
been sunk in poverty or ignorance, resigned to the drabness of their
lives, even to the realization that their rulers did not fear them. Now
suddenly a champion had appeared to them, one who promised to
lead them to a better life, one who, even if he did nothing else, would
give them vicariously the exciting satisfaction of insulting the great
ones who ignored them. The great ones did not ignore Huey Long.
They were afraid of him; they had tried to remove him from office
and silence him by a lawsuit. He was a man for the masses to follow.

A local south Louisiana politician tried to explain the situation
to a New Orleans reporter. There was a new force, mysterious and
vaguely menacing, loose in the politics of the state, he thought. An
awful illogic seemed to have gripped the people. "They don't know
Huey Long," he said. "They never saw him and would not know him
if he stepped off the train at our station. But, they know him in name
and you can't make them believe he is not their defender."[6]

[5] Long to Consolidated-Progressive Oil Corporation, September 1, 1921, in Long
Papers, Law File; New Orleans *States*, October 4, 1922.
[6] New Orleans *States*, November 11 and 14, 1921.

# CHAPTER 8

# *We Are Forcing*
# *Them Back*

OR THE POLITICAL REPORTERS in Baton Rouge the twenty-sixth
of February 1921 was an unusually dull Saturday. The constitutional convention was going to convene on the following Tuesday,
and pending its meeting other political activities seemed to have come
to a stop. In the capitol the Public Service Commission had just concluded a three-day hearing on an application of the Cumberland
Telephone and Telegraph Company for an increase in rates, but this
event had not produced any important or interesting news. The sessions had been quiet and routine; the testimony of the witnesses had
been statistical and boring; and only two members of the Commission, Chairman Taylor and John T. Michel, had been present. The
hearing had come to a close about four in the afternoon, and Taylor
and Michel had retired to their offices. Now the Commission, following its normal procedures, would, with the aid of its staff, study the
evidence and within a few days issue its decision or, if it desired more
information, announce a continuation of the hearing. This was obviously going to be one of those weekends when no big news broke,
and many of the reporters from out of town, most of whom represented New Orleans papers, decided to go home. Some of the New
Orleans correspondents took the same late-afternoon train that carried
the lawyer who had presented the city's case against a rate increase
and his accountant adviser.

Left almost alone in the capitol press gallery was a reporter for
the New Orleans *Item*. This man had been instructed by his editor to
remain in Baton Rouge to cover the constitutional convention. He

wandered through the corridors, partly because he had nothing else
to do, partly because his journalist's instinct told him that he might
run onto something. As he passed the door of the Public Service Commission's office, he heard typewriters clicking busily. Instantly he
surmised that the opinion on the phone-rate increase was being
written. Knocking on the door, he brought out Wylie M. Barrow, the
Commission's counsel. "All I want to know," he said to Barrow, "is
whether the request for an increase has been granted. I can get the
exact wording later." Barrow thought a moment and then said: "Yes,
it's been granted, but the opinion won't be ready to give out until
about midnight." The elated reporter rushed out and wired the information to his editor. That evening the *Item* headlined exclusive
news: the Cumberland Company had received an increase in rates
that averaged twenty per cent. The paper hit the streets shortly after
the city's attorney and his accountant arrived at the railway station.
These men were profoundly shocked. Not only had a case supposedly
under advisement been decided, but apparently the text of the order
had been written immediately after the hearing had ended.

Emotions other than shock spread over the state the next day as
the *Item*'s scoop became general knowledge. The official text of the
decision was given out around midnight, as Barrow had promised,
and it appeared in the Sunday morning editions of many newspapers.
The officials of a number of municipalities that had sent representatives to the hearing to protest the rate increase expressed suspicion
and bitter anger. The order would permit the company to gouge its
customers, they charged; and the odd circumstances of its issuance
indicated that the Commission had acted without proper deliberation
and obviously at corporate dictation. But these outcries seemed like
gentle reprimands in comparison with the blast that issued from
Shreveport, from the commissioner for the third district. That Saturday night an enterprising reporter had roused Huey from sleep and
informed him of the decision. Huey unhesitatingly characterized it
as the "most humiliating document" ever signed by a majority of the
agency. Later he issued a formal statement. He was not surprised that
Michel had signed the opinion, he said, because the New Orleans
man was a political tool of James C. Henriques, Sr., one of the company's attorneys, and had favored granting the company's request
from the moment it was made. The company had tried to enlist his
own support, Huey went on. Twice it had offered to throw profitable
legal business his way if he would vote right, but he had stood firm
against a rate increase. Taylor had also opposed an increase and had

assured Huey he would vote against it. Huey said that he did not know what had caused the chairman to switch. He did not have to offer a conjecture. The implication of his remarks was unmistakable —Taylor had succumbed to the offers that Huey had refused. The indignant Taylor replied with words that he was to repeat many times in the weeks ahead: "Huey Long is a liar."[1]

Huey ended his statement by promising to continue the fight against the higher rates. He meant what he said. During the next two years he kept the Cumberland case constantly before the Commission —and before the public. Some observers of the Louisiana political scene think that it was his efforts in this case more than in any other that made his name known throughout the state and put him in a strong position from which to run for governor. There can be no doubt that his battle against the company helped his career. Cumberland served approximately sixty-six thousand customers, and any politician who took up the cause of that many people was certain to win their gratitude, whether he won or lost the fight. Huey was fully aware of the possibilities in the situation when he intervened in it. But his motives were not completely political. They were, rather, as was generally true with him and is usually true with men of his type, a mixture of self-interest and idealism. He gave his attention and energy also to a host of small cases that did not always win him notices, and although the cumulative effect of his efforts in these may have built up his public image, he acted as he did because something in him made him believe in certain principles, because he had a private image of what Huey Long should do.

In one of its reports the Public Service Commission explained how the rapidly changing nature of a modern economy could influence the concept of state regulation. Its forebear, the Railroad Commission, had functioned in a relatively simple society and had been able to perform its job by exercising a minimum of authority. But as the state had become more industrial and urban, it became obvious that the Commission would have to enlarge the scope of its regulation. The need for a stronger agency had been recognized by the constitutional convention of 1921, which transformed the older, narrower body into the Public Service Commission. The new agency had immediately "set about toward a reformation of many perplexing problems thrust upon it." It had been forced by circumstances to "delve into questions and phases of regulation of a far greater importance

---

[1] Hermann B. Deutsch: "Kingdom of the Kingfish," in New Orleans *Item*, July 27, 1939; Shreveport *Times*, February 27, 1921.

and of a wider variety" than could have been anticipated by men of only one generation before.[2]

The cases that came before the Commission after 1921 were assuredly of a wide variety. Most of them were brought by municipalities that wanted the Commission to force a railroad or some other utility to lower its rates or institute a service or improve an existing service. The issues involved were usually simple and could be resolved by an easy, rule-of-thumb procedure. But sometimes a case presented a very subtle economic problem, and in such a controversy members of the Commission had to have, or procure, a good deal of technical knowledge, and follow the most advanced regulatory principles. Thus on one occasion the agency ordered the Baton Rouge Electric Company to reduce its rates but suspended part of the reduction on condition that the company enlarge its facilities to meet the needs of a growing town. The corporation readily agreed to the settlement, probably because it wished to prevent further investigation of its finances. But then it asked for an increase in rates on the lines it was going to build! To Shelby Taylor, the economic reasoning of his home town's largest utility—that it should be rewarded for something it had not done—did not seem at all odd. But to Long, who was then chairman, the request was the essence of bad economics and a piece of corporate effrontery as well. In the precise language he could use when he wanted to, he read Taylor a lesson in regulatory procedure. No commission in the country would "authorize a rate for something that is not even in existence," he snapped, and the Louisiana Commission was not going to violate this sound principle to gratify a corporation that assumed it could bargain as to whether it would obey an order.[3]

The cases brought by the municipalities might have offered variety, but most of them were, on the face of it, of little importance, affecting neither the over-all economy of the state nor its developing pattern of regulation. But the impression of triviality was deceptive. The mass of little cases, by their very number, had the effect of transforming the economy, and for the same reason they enlarged immeasurably the regulatory scope of the Commission. Moreover, they had real meaning for the people in the communities concerned and

[2] *Second Annual Report of the Public Service Commission of Louisiana* (Baton Rouge, 1923), n.p. In the publications of the Commission the summary report of the past year's activities usually appeared without pagination; the pagination began with the list of orders issued.

[3] *Louisiana Public Service Commission, Third Annual Report*, Appendix B, pp. 39–40; Long to Taylor, March 22, 1924, in Long Papers, Public Service Commission File.

hence had great political importance. This fact was readily apparent to Commissioner Long. More than any other member of the agency, he gave attention to these routine cases and especially to those that came from the smaller towns. Indeed, it was in this area that he thought the Commission could perform its most valuable and lasting work. "Now, we have been given jurisdiction over all the little cities' rates," he once wrote Secretary Jastremski, "and that ought to be impressed upon these people, so that they will understand we have to fight battles for every city."

The files of the Commission are crammed with documents attesting that he did fight these battles. He forced one railroad company to build a new depot at Monroe, after personally taking the Commission members there to inspect the existing and inadequate structure, and he made another company erect shelters outside the station in Ruston. The most minute complaint could engage his interest. "I am informed," he wrote one railroad company, "that the cistern at Bordelonville is either out of fix or else that none is there, and that one is needed very much. Will you please look into the matter and advise me." To a man who had filed a charge that the boarding platforms at the hamlets of Bayou Sara and Plattenburg were too low came a prompt and assuring reply: Commissioner Long had ordered the companies to raise them.[4]

Huey did not, however, respond with automatic favor to every request. A complaint with no merit he would reject without hesitation. His course in one such case revealed that he had not only courage but also a philosophy of regulation. His home town of Winnfield petitioned the Commission to order the railroads serving it to build a union depot. Huey put the suit on the docket but deliberately delayed consideration of it so that it never came to a vote. The only explanation he offered for his action was so cryptic as to defy analysis, but it hinted at a fundamental motive. Although he did not care to admit it on this occasion, he was showing his respect for a regulatory principle that he espoused in other cases—that local interests have to be subordinated to the general interest. Certainly he introduced this concept, which was followed by the most advanced commissions in the country, to the Louisiana Commission, and he enforced it

[4] Long to Henry Jastremski, January 28, 1924, in Public Service Commission Files, File No. 3, in office of the Louisiana Public Service Commission, state capitol, Baton Rouge, hereafter cited as Public Service Commission File 3; *Fourth Annual Report of the Public Service Commission of Louisiana* (Baton Rouge, 1925), pp. 57–8; Ruston *Daily Leader*, October 20, 1922; Long to Louisiana Railway and Navigation Company, July 8, 1924, and to J. W. A. Richardson, July 27, in Long Papers, Public Service Commission File.

more consistently than any of his colleagues. As he wrote in another case: "We are going to have to compel in each instance and each locality to subordinate itself to this Commission, and to the general State welfare." Winnfield would have to get along without a union station.[5]

Long introduced other concepts to the Commission. He was the first member, and for a time the only member, who understood that a representative on a modern regulatory board was not just another officeholder; he was someone who held great power to influence delicate economic situations, and if he intervened in these situations ignorantly he could do great mischief. Therefore he had to work at his job, know something about economics and regulatory practices in other states, study the facts of a case and find out the law that applied to it. Huey worked hard on every case that rose above routine importance. "He informed himself," admitted a contemporary who was generally critical of him. "He probably knew more on that Commission than the railroad lawyers who appeared before the Commission about what had been done . . . and what the authority was."

Huey also informed himself about the activities of other state commissions, and the knowledge that he gained prompted him to introduce several procedural reforms to the Louisiana Commission. One was fundamental in nature. Before Huey came to dominate the agency, one-man hearings had been its policy, even for important cases. A member who had an interest in a particular case would call a hearing, summon witnesses, and, after listening to as much evidence as he cared to, prepare an order and get his two associates to sign it. When Huey became chairman, he stopped this practice. To permit one man to determine the outcome of a complicated case was bad administrative policy, he instructed his colleagues; furthermore, the courts were disinclined to accept evidence presented to only one member. His colleagues naturally wanted to continue the single sessions, and Huey had to overrule them. "Except in the most formal matters," he told a protesting member, "we are going to have to discontinue one-man hearings."[6]

He could adhere to the most correct and technical rules of procedure, and he could conduct himself at hearings with the most solemn decorum, but when a mischievous mood seized him or when

[5] Long to Henry Jastremski, July 8, 1924, in Long Papers, Public Service Commission File; Long to Jastremski, August 11, 1924, and to Shelby Taylor and Francis Williams, October 18, in Public Service Commission File 3.

[6] Harry Gamble; Long to Francis Williams, May 26, 1924, and to Henry Jastremski, May 26, 1924, in Long Papers, Public Service Commission File; Long to Jastremski, September 30, 1924, in Public Service Commission File 3.

he wished to disconcert his opponents, he could also commit outrageous rudenesses or act with unscrupulous cunning. Once the Commission scheduled a hearing at Shreveport to consider, among other
items, a request from the Texas and Pacific Railroad that it be permitted to eliminate a branch service. Although the case was of no
great moment, Huey had determined that the request must be denied.
Shortly before the hearing, while on a visit to New Orleans, he met
on the street Charles Dunbar, once his teacher at Tulane, one of the
best-known lawyers in the state, and one of a number of attorneys
retained by the railroad. In the course of the conversation Huey remarked that the Commission was having a meeting at Shreveport next
week at which some cases involving interesting legal points were to
be heard—and he suggested to Dunbar that he attend. Dunbar agreed.
At the hearing, which drew a large crowd, Chairman Long decreed
that the railroad case would be considered first. Then he announced,
to Dunbar's astonishment: "The Texas and Pacific has sent as its
counsel an eminent attorney and a member of the faculty of Tulane
University. That shows their interest in this case, but we will win."
At another hearing the venerable Edward T. Merrick, counsel for the
Illinois Central Railroad, who had been on Huey's examining committee, was just getting into his argument when he was interrupted
by a yell from the chairman. "Damn it, sit down," Huey ordered.
Later he apologized to Merrick. "I have to impress these people,"
he said.[7]

He could decide cases strictly on their merits, and he could act
for reasons of principle alone, but he could also conduct persecu-
tions that were primarily expressions of his personal animosities. An
example of his vindictiveness was his treatment of the Louisiana
Railway and Navigation Company, a concern that was having financial difficulties and consequently was not maintaining its equipment
and service. Huey harried the company constantly and mercilessly,
threatening again and again to hale it before the Commission. "You
haven't a decent coach on the railroad that I have seen," he wrote in
a typical denunciation. "To us it seems that Providence has indeed
been with the passengers who ride your road. Why more people have
not been killed is not only due to the slow schedules which you have
maintained, which is too fast at that, but to the most fortunate of
circumstances." "It looks as if you were dodging again," he charged
in one letter, and he ended another with a warning that the company
had to do something "seriously, scientifically and quickly." The L R

[7] Richard Foster.

and N was undoubtedly a poor railroad, and many of Huey's complaints against it were justified. But he pursued it with a zest that suggests a personal motive. He was, it is true, paying off an old score. The president of the company was the same William Edenborn who had once, according to Huey, tried to defraud Winnfield with a deceptive promise to build it a railroad.[8]

He could be savage when he let his feelings rule him, but he was more likely to be benign. He gratified dozens of requests for help from ordinary individuals. Indeed, it was almost impossible for him to reject a plea from someone in trouble. He had an instinctive and impulsive sympathy for anybody who was deprived of something, and he liked the feeling of power that came to him when he could help such a person.

This side of his character became known all over the state, and people who had grievances unerringly headed to Commissioner Long for redress. For instance, an oil man who had moved to Shreveport found that the telephone company would not install a phone in his home. He did not like Huey's politics and had made no secret of his opinion. But he knew where to go to get action. He sought out Huey in his law office—which was also the Commission office for the third district[9]—and explained his plight: he had a wife and an infant son, he was on the road a lot, and he needed a phone at home. Huey asked no questions. He called the telephone company and said he wanted the oilman to get his phone. When a week passed without the installation of the phone, the petitioner returned to Huey's office. "This time," this individual related, "he got on the phone and he was very emphatic and direct and profane. The phone came almost immediately." In another case, an independent logger in Sabine parish learned that the Kansas City Southern Railroad would not haul for him and other small producers. He called Huey. Huey told him to have his wood ready to go immediately: "I'll have a fast freight pick up your logs tonight and I'll tell 'em to spot your stuff." The man

[8] Long to Louisiana Railway and Navigation Company, May 8, 12, and 22, 1924, and to William Edenborn, May 27, 1924, in Long Papers, Public Service Commission File.

[9] Huey was entitled to receive $250 a month for expenses necessary to carrying out the duties of his position. He was expected to maintain an office for the transaction of Commission business, and for convenience, he established the Commission office in his law office, for which he paid $130 a month rent. He soon found that it was almost impossible to segregate his official expenses from his legal expenses. He therefore informed Secretary Jastremski that he would bear all the telephone, light, and water charges himself; Long to Henry Jastremski, April 30, 1924, in Public Service Commission File 3.

did not quite believe Huey, but he put his logs out and they were picked up. The logger's wife, however, was shocked at Huey's action. She said that a man who would do such things was a dictator. Her husband answered in words that would become a refrain in Louisiana in the years ahead: "What's the difference? He gets things done."[1]

Huey's activities in small cases won him favorable attention around the state. Hardly a month passed that the newspapers did not chronicle another victory won for the people by the energetic young commissioner from the northern district. Typical headlines proclaimed: "Long to Fine Rails That Don't Give Service," "Long Wins Rate Fight For Sugar," "Long Answers Farmers' Plea." The story under the last heading featured a counterplea from Huey. He was glad to fight the battles of the people, he said, but those who were always asking him to redouble his efforts should do something to assist him. Using rural terminology he said: "Let them go out and help to get the turkeys themselves. I am not the only man in the state who is being paid to do something for the people."[2]

Some of this newspaper publicity was the voluntary expression of editors who appreciated something that Huey had done to help their communities. Thus Charles Manship of the influential Baton Rouge *State-Times* was "delighted" that Huey had stood by the capital city in a controversy with the Missouri Pacific Railroad, and he sent the commissioner word that he was going to "play him up." Some of it was legitimate reporting of news: Huey made headlines because he had done something important or interesting. But a lot of it was contrived publicity, the kind of stuff that later and more cynical generations would classify as press agentry, and it was contrived by Huey himself. He regularly wrote articles extolling his activities and mailed them to the principal newspapers. He described a typical effusion for Secretary Jastremski: "I am sending you a copy of the article that I have sent to the Times-Picayune, the Item, and the Daily States and the Shreveport Times. Make up some copies and send them out as bulletins. Send me a few of them so I may be able to answer inquiries." Sometimes he would personally deliver his productions to newspaper rooms and accompany them with a gift designed to impress the reporters. One veteran journalist recalled that during the Cumberland controversy Huey appeared frequently in the office of a Shreveport paper: "He would bring these long statements on foolscap and without

---

[1] Confidential communication; William J. Dodd.

[2] Headlines from news stories in New Orleans *States*, September 15, 1922, November 7, 1924, Shreveport *Times*, October 2, 1924.

saying anything would bring the manuscript in and lay it down on the city editor's desk and weight it down with a half-gallon fruit jar of homemade moonshine."[3]

The publicity Huey received in the small, routine cases added to his reputation. If he had done no more than fight these cases, he still would have won a name as an able and devoted public servant. He would not, however, have become a state figure of compelling importance whose name was a household word. That status he attained by his actions in a number of big cases that involved him in controversies with the biggest corporations in the state. The first of these was the Cumberland telephone case.

The Cumberland case opened with the company's first appearance before the Commission in 1920. In September of that year the company applied for increases in its telephone rates averaging twenty-five per cent. Such a large increment was easily justified, the application stated: the company needed capital to expand services and it was entitled to a return on its investment of eight per cent. The application quoted abundant figures on what the profit rate of a utility should be, but it offered almost no data on Cumberland's own costs or economic structure, and it did not specify how the proposed increase would affect individual exchanges. It was evident that the company expected to get what it wanted and that it did not feel compelled to explain technical economic details to the commissioners, who would not understand them anyway. The suggested schedule of rates had been submitted to the Commission's counsel, Wylie M. Barrow, before it was revealed to Chairman Taylor. The Commission called a hearing on the application in Baton Rouge on October 15.

Commissioner Long was not interested in hearing any evidence that the company might present at the hearing. He was going to vote against any increase in rates as a matter of principle—and of politics. But he was not sure that he could persuade his colleagues to turn down the application. He knew from Michel's past conduct that the New Orleans man would vote with the big corporation. His only hope was to get Taylor on his side. On the morning of the day of the hearing he called on Taylor in the latter's office. What, Huey asked innocently, did the chairman know about this case? The chairman roared that he knew nothing, which was exactly the response that Huey wanted to evoke. His purpose was to goad Taylor into a rage against the company. "Well," said Huey, "you and I are the majority

---

[3] Henry Jastremski to Long, May 27, 1924, and Long to Jastremski, December 20, 1924, in Public Service Commission File 3; Paul Flowers.

of the commission. You're the chairman, and if these people are going to tell anybody anything, I think you would have been the first man they would have seen." Taylor's anger mounted as he listened to Huey's words, and soon he found himself agreeing that at the hearing that afternoon they would vote to delay consideration of the application.

Huey continued to use his nettling tactics at the hearing. The officials of the company walked into the room headed by their counsel, Hunt Chipley, who had, in Huey's words, the bearing of an English duke. Chipley was smoking a cigarette in an ornate holder, and Huey whispered to Taylor: "Look at that pompous guy with that decorated cigarette holder—looks like he has taken charge now." If the Cumberland representatives had expected a friendly reception, they were abruptly disappointed. They were barraged by hostile questions from Taylor and Long. Why had they bypassed the chairman? Why hadn't they submitted adequate and specific supporting data to justify their request? Whenever Chipley tried to present his case, he was interrupted by more questions. The classic query came from Huey, now sprawled back in his chair. "What I want to know," he drawled, "is just how much this is going to cost a subscriber in Winnfield, for instance." The stormy session ended when Huey moved that as the company had not properly explained its position, the hearing be continued on a date in December.

At the December meeting the company presented for the first time some supporting data. But by that time a number of municipalities had been alerted to the threat of a rate increase at their exchanges, and they sent representatives to the hearing to protest. The conflicting testimony consumed three days. Then the Commission took the case under advisement: it would study the evidence and announce its decision. But while the commissioners deliberated, a new party entered the controversy. The city council of New Orleans, whose citizens would bear the brunt of the proposed increase, filed a request that the case be reopened. The application stressed that the city's attorney had engaged an expert utilities accountant who would offer important evidence. The Commission agreed to hear the New Orleans representatives on February 24, 1921.[4]

Huey did not bother to attend the February session. He could cast his vote against the rate increase in writing, and as Taylor had

[4] Huey P. Long: *Every Man a King* (New Orleans, 1933), pp. 52–5; Deutsch: "Kingdom of the Kingfish," in New Orleans *Item*, July 27, 1939; *Louisiana Public Service Commission, First Annual Report*, pp. 19–20; Paul Maloney.

promised to vote no also, or so Huey always claimed, there was no need for him to go to Baton Rouge. At least, that was the excuse he offered for skipping one of the most important meetings the Commission ever held. Quite possibly he did not think that he had the votes to deny Cumberland's application. However, it seems strange that he would not take the time to judge a case in which he was vitally interested. Did he know that it was going to come out in another way —and did he perhaps want it to?

The February meeting was the one at which the Commission issued its decision within a few hours after the hearing ended, the general tenor of which was scooped by the *Item*. The official text of the decision, when it was released, explained why Taylor and Michel had felt impelled to grant the company almost the full amount of the requested increase. The language was defensive throughout, and the logic was, in some parts, dubious. There could be no criticism of the assumption that the company should be allowed to charge a rate that returned it a fair profit on the value of its property: basing rates on the value of investments was a common practice with state and national commissions. Not so valid, however, was the conclusion that Cumberland was entitled to a return of eight per cent because that was the level of the prevailing interest rate. This reasoning was not very convincing to ordinary people, who were enduring the pinch of declining incomes in the recession that followed the war. The decision admitted that it was unfortunate that telephone rates had to be raised when prices of farm production and wages were falling. But it jovially exhorted users to remember that they had enjoyed prosperity during the war, when the company had received no increase in rates. The most curious feature of the decision was its refusal to concede that Cumberland's connection with two larger companies had any influence on its own activities or any relationship to its economic position.

No such reticence marked the written dissenting opinion of Commissioner Long. In vigorous language he stressed that ninety-four per cent of the stock of Cumberland was owned by the Bell Telephone System, which was completely owned by the American Telephone and Telegraph Company. Moreover, A T & T owned ninety-seven per cent of the stock of the Western Electric Company, which furnished Cumberland with all its equipment. All of these concerns were really one, Long contended, and the Commission should have taken this fact into account. "Under these conditions," he concluded, "it is not proper to impose an added burden upon a public struggling under recent economic reverses. I, therefore, record my vote against any raise in rates."[5]

The February order threw the state into an angry uproar. Municipalities denounced the Commission for allowing the company such a drastic increase in rates. Progressive reformers claimed that the speed with which the order was issued was the result of corrupt corporate influence. Whipping up the excitement and really leading it was Huey. His charges that Cumberland had tried to secure his own support and had indeed won Taylor over by improper means seemed to confirm all the seething rumors. The popular reaction finally assumed such proportions that the Commission felt compelled to schedule a meeting to hear arguments for a rehearing of the case. This session, which was held in late March, was marked by the turmoil that was coming to be characteristic of Cumberland hearings. A large crowd attended —officials of most of the cities, delegates from the constitutional convention, which was then in session, and ordinary but interested citizens—and practically every one of them wanted to tell the Commission emphatically and loudly that the case should be reopened. One of the speakers was W. F. Brown, a local official from a southern parish. He referred to the hurried issuance of the decision. Taylor retorted that the case had been under consideration for months. Huey, who sat looking at the ceiling, drawled: "Why that decision was written before the testimony was closed." Taylor labeled this charge a lie and then turned to Brown and said that he would not tolerate any more personal remarks. "That's all right," Brown returned. "I cover all the ground I stand on." "So do I," growled Taylor. Huey, still looking at the ceiling, said suggestively: "Leave the personalities for later, Mr. Brown." The moment the hearing adjourned, Brown rushed over to the rostrum and struck Taylor twice in the face heavily. Spectators separated the two, and Brown was placed under technical arrest for assault. The next day Huey arranged for his release on payment of a small fine.

Two weeks after the hearing the Commission issued a new order. Signed by Taylor and Michel, it stated that since many requests for a rehearing had been received and since the February order had not been based on full information the Commission would continue to examine the case. But pending the outcome of these proceedings, the rate increase granted in February would stand. Huey filed a written opinion stating merely that he voted for a rehearing. He thought that

[5] *Louisiana Public Service Commission, First Annual Report*, pp. 24, 28–31.

during the rehearing the pre-February rates should be restored, but he knew that he could not bring his associates to agree with him.[6]

Nor could he influence them to alter their stand in the months after the March meeting. At periodic intervals the Commission heard protests against the rate increase, received additional statistical material, and entered on its records that it was investigating the case. But it took no action. Huey moved at one session to suspend the rate increase while the inquiry was in progress, but he could not get a second. He was a frustrated minority of the Commission, and there was every propect that in important cases like the one involving Cumberland he would be a permanent minority. Then an event happened that held out the promise of a change. John T. Michel died in November 1921. Governor Parker toyed with the idea of appointing a man of his own to fill out Michel's term. But he was persuaded that he was required by law to call an election, and he scheduled the contest for March.[7]

The first, or southern, district comprised Orleans parish and several adjoining parishes. The bulk of its population, and hence its vote, was concentrated in New Orleans, and the city was usually able to elect the commissioner. Or, in actual practice, the commissioner was usually the candidate supported by the Old Regular machine, which customarily awarded the position to one of its lesser luminaries. But in the first years of the Parker administration the machine was not operating with its customary efficiency. Martin Behrman, its perennial mayor, had been defeated in 1920 by a candidate backed by the governor and a newly formed rival organization, the Orleans Democratic Association. Deprived of state and city patronage, the machine was experiencing lean days. It would sweep back into power in 1925, but in 1922 it could not turn out its normal heavy vote for a candidate.

The machine candidate for commissioner was Stuart A. Seelye. He was opposed by four other aspirants. Three of them were men who had no chance to win and knew it; they were in the race, as were men like them in every city contest, for personal enjoyment. But the fourth was a formidable rival. Francis Williams had backing that was organized. The Orleans Democratic Association, an uneasy alliance of dissident Old Regulars and Parker reformers, was on the point of breaking up. One of its leaders, John P. Sullivan, merged the

[6] Ibid., p. 52; Deutsch: "Kingdom of the Kingfish," in New Orleans *Item*, July 27, 1939; Paul Maloney.

[7] Minute Book, Louisiana Public Service Commission, July 26, 1921; Shreveport *Journal*, November 22, 1921; New Orleans *States*, November 25.

remnants of it with a new organization that he called the New Regulars, and this faction supported Williams. Sullivan nourished visions of becoming the boss of the city. He had the looks to play the part. A gigantic figure of a man—he was six feet four and weighed 260 pounds—he had in his youth been a cadet at West Point. At the academy he reportedly had had twenty-seven fights in one month because he refused to submit to hazing and was finally flunked out because he could not pass mathematics. He wore expensive silk shirts and tailor-made suits, and he was always seen smoking a cigar. The cigars were also tailor-made, especially for him, and cost ninety cents each. Sullivan believed that electing Williams could be his first step in taking over the city.

He had acted shrewdly in deciding to place the prestige of his faction behind Williams's candidacy. Williams, a big, blond man with curly reddish hair, was an attractive figure. He was a fiery stump orator and a master of vituperative language. Words came easily to him, sometimes too easily. He was prone to be carried away by his own eloquence and say things that damaged his cause and that of anyone he was supporting. He saw himself as an urban progressive, a spokesman of labor and the lower middle class. His devotion to progressive ideals was real, but he was also intensely ambitious. He and his younger brother Augustus, nicknamed Gus, dreamed that someday they might become the ruling power in New Orleans. The Williams boys, as they were known, were quite ready to work toward their goal by affiliating with Sullivan. They were equally ready, if the occasion offered, to strike out on their own.

Huey watched the first district race with avid interest. He did not, however, attempt to intervene in it. He had no organization in the city, and even if he had wanted to support one of the candidates, he could have done no more than offer a verbal endorsement. But it was not in his interest to endorse a candidate. His only hope of controlling the Commission was to form an alliance with whichever candidate was victorious, and he could not risk backing a possible loser. He must have known, however, that Williams stood closer to him in beliefs than did the other aspirants, and he must have been gratified when the results of the March election disclosed that the big blond led the field. Williams did not have a majority, however, and ordinarily a second primary would have been necessary to determine the winner. But the Old Regular bosses knew that they had polled all the votes they could for Seelye and that in a second primary he was certain to be defeated. They therefore pulled their man down, thus conceding the victory to Williams. Shortly after the election

Huey went to New Orleans, ostensibly on law business, but probably mainly to meet Williams. They were introduced in the supreme court room. "Here's your new partner on the Public Service Commission, Huey," said the man who brought them together. Huey looked Williams over and said: "Well, you got to be against the corporations if you expect to be with me." "How the hell do you know anybody wants to be with you?" snarled Williams.[8]

The exchange was not nearly so hostile as it seemed. Beneath the tough words two strong men were testing each other, measuring whether they could join forces and on what terms. Huey and Williams had every reason to strike a bargain. Huey needed an ally on the Commission, and if he intended to run for governor, he would have to have with him a New Orleans leader who commanded organized support. Williams would be unable to do anything on the Commission unless he had an ally, and as an ambitious city politician he could see the advantage of affiliating with a rising state figure who might become governor. Both men believed that as a matter of good principle and good politics the Commission should more vigorously regulate the activities of the big corporations. They soon reached a working agreement. The existence of the compact was revealed when Williams attended his first meeting of the Commission on April 28.

The official journal of the Commission tersely records the sequence of remarkable events at that meeting. Hardly had Shelby Taylor called the session to order when Williams moved that Huey P. Long be made chairman. The journal continues: "The motion was seconded by Commissioner Long and carried." Williams next moved that the Cumberland Telephone and Telegraph Company be directed to be present at a hearing in New Orleans on May 2 to show cause why the rate increase previously granted should not be held in abeyance pending a rehearing. The motion was seconded by Long and carried. It was evident that a new majority had taken over the Commission.[9]

Four days later the Cumberland rehearing opened in the council chamber at the New Orleans city hall. An array of distinguished lawyers was present to represent both sides. For the company there appeared Hunt Chipley, James C. Henriques, Sr., and J. Blanc Monroe, a dignified member of the city bar. The Commission was represented by its counsel, Wylie Barrow, and attorney general A. V.

[8] George M. Reynolds: *Machine Politics in New Orleans, 1897–1926* (New York, 1936), pp. 216–17; Hermann B. Deutsch; Clayton Coleman; Deutsch: "Kingdom of the Kingfish," in New Orleans *Item*, August 1, 1939.

[9] Minute Book, Louisiana Public Service Commission, April 28, 1922.

Coco. The city council, which had previously intervened in the case, sent its attorney, Ivy Kittredge, to speak for its interest. None of the lawyers, however, was given much opportunity to participate. From the first raucous moment it was apparent that the new chairman and his ally were going to run the hearing according to their own peculiar concepts of correct procedure.

The session had barely come to order when Blanc Monroe arose and said he wished to offer a motion. Monroe produced a campaign card put out by Williams on which the candidate stated that if elected he would vote to reduce the phone rates. Williams had prejudged the case and therefore should recuse himself, Monroe declared, and began to read his motion. He was stopped by a command from the chairman. "Don't read the motion," Huey shouted. "We will not allow the motion to be read this time nor will we entertain it." Monroe bristled. "I want the record to show," he said, "that the motion to recuse has never been read to this body, and that the chairman of the Commission, without consulting any of its members . . ." Again he was interrupted by the chairman, who this time addressed himself to the stenographer who was taking down the proceedings. "Let nothing be shown on the record except what I say will be shown on the record," Huey instructed. He thought a minute and then dictated his own concept of what should appear: "The motion is overruled, with Mr. Williams concurring." The significance of what was happening escaped Monroe. He did not understand that for Cumberland—and all other big corporations in Louisiana—one era of regulation had just passed and that another was about to begin. He tried again. "I am going to have the record show . . ." he began. "You are going to jail if you infringe upon the Commission's procedure another minute," Huey roared. "If you want to settle this issue, I'll send for the sheriff right now." Under threat of a contempt citation, Monroe subsided, and the Commission went about the taking of evidence on the rate increase. It heard witnesses that day and the next and then announced that it had taken the case under advisement.[1]

This meant, it turned out, that Long took the record back to Shreveport and drafted an opinion and an order. When he finished, he called the Commission into special session on May 13. At this meeting Huey moved that the rehearing should continue and that pending a final decision, all telephone rate increases allowed on or

[1] Long: *Every Man a King*, pp. 66–7; Deutsch: "Kingdom of the Kingfish," in New Orleans *Item*, August 1, 1939; New Orleans *Item*, May 2, 1922. The conversation as reported in these three sources differs in detail. The account reproduced in the text is a composite of the three versions.

after February 26, 1921, were suspended. The motion was seconded by Williams and carried by a vote of two to one. A concluding hearing was scheduled in June. But this meeting would not be held. Cumberland went immediately before federal judge Rufus E. Foster of the eastern district court of Louisiana and asked for an injunction forbidding the Commission from enforcing its order. Foster granted the injunction. Now the Commission, if it wished to sustain its order, would have to appeal the injunction and fight the case through the federal courts. At Huey's suggestion, he was named to represent the Commission as chief counsel.[2]

The legal maneuvers that now occurred rivaled in confusion and color the previous hearings of the Commission. Huey appealed the injunction to a three-judge court, of which Foster was a member, on the grounds that under the federal judicial code a single district judge could not enjoin a state board. This panel agreed with his argument and voided the injunction by a vote of two to one. But the company appealed this decision and asked Foster to reinstate his order pending the outcome. Huey represented the Commission before Foster. While making his plea, he took off his coat and rolled up his shirt sleeves. "Judge Foster cannot revive a dead body," he proclaimed confidently. But Foster tried to; he reissued his original order. The company's lawyers were jubilant at their apparent victory. "Long is making a political football of the telephone company," said Monroe. Henriques chimed in: "He wants to kick himself into the office of governor of Louisiana." Huey was outraged at Foster's action. "I felt that if he were right," he said, "the state of Louisiana has largely lost its right to exist as a free sovereignty." But he was not disheartened. He was prepared to carry the fight to the Supreme Court itself if he had to. As a first move, he filed an application to dissolve Foster's order.[3]

The Supreme Court agreed to entertain the application, and Huey, Williams, and Barrow went to Washington to present the Commission's case. The company was represented by Henriques, who stressed in his argument that the rates before the increase had been confiscatory. But the issue at stake was not substantive but procedural —not whether the rates were fair but whether one judge could continue an injunction denied by two others. Foster's order clearly was contrary to the judicial code, and the Court had no choice but to so

[2] Minute Book, Louisiana Public Service Commission, May 13 and 19, 1922; *Louisiana Public Service Commission, Second Annual Report*, p. 48; Long: *Every Man a King*, pp. 67–8.

[3] *Cumberland Tel. & Tel. Co.* v. *Louisiana Public Serv. Comm'n*, Fed. 215 (E.D. La., 1922); New Orleans *Item*, July 26 and 27, 1922; New Orleans *Times-Picayune*, July 27 and 28, 1922.

rule. On November 20 it voided the injunction and returned the case to the original three-judge district panel. Now it was Huey's turn to be jubilant. "We are gradually forcing them back to where they belong," he announced, "and we are going to get a fair deal for the people of Louisiana."[4]

How fair the deal would be was now going to be determined by the Commission. The district panel, when it received the Supreme Court ruling, remanded the case to the Commission, and Huey called a final hearing for January 11, 1923. In the interim before the meeting, strong public pressure was brought to bear on both the Commission and the company to effect a compromise. It came from municipalities and civic organizations that were weary of the long struggle and wanted some kind of stable rate structure. Huey knew that he would have to take this sentiment into account. He recognized the presence of a classic crisis for a popular leader. Such a leader can arouse his followers only to a certain pitch; when they tire of the cause, he must abandon it, getting off with as many concessions as he can. Huey was in a mood to compromise when he called the hearing to order on January 11.

The company too was in a conciliatory mood. It presented a revised set of rates that it hoped would be acceptable. The city attorney of New Orleans presented a counter, and lower, scale. Then Hunt Chipley, no longer looking so ducal, begged that the Commission arrive at some compromise. "The representatives of the people," as the Commission's journal styled the members, took the matter under advisement. Two days later two of the representatives, Long and Williams (Taylor was absent), announced their decision. The Commission would allow rate increases that averaged fifty per cent of the company's original twenty per cent boost. But the company was to return to its consumers one hundred per cent of all increases levied between May 13, 1922, and January 13, 1923—that is, all of the twenty per cent increase levied after the Commission's May order holding the increase in abeyance. And the company was to make the refund by actual payment, by checks, and not by reducing current or accruing bills to consumers. Moreover, the Company was to proceed immediately with the construction program that it had outlined to the Commission and to use every means to improve and expand its services—or the Commission would reopen the case. Huey explained the proposed order to the company's lawyers. He was particularly in-

[4] *Cumberland Tel. & Tel. Co.* v. *Louisiana Public Serv. Comm'n, Motion granted,* 260 U.S. 698 (1922), *rendered,* 260 U.S. 212 (1922), *injunction denied,* 260 U.S. 759 (1923).

sistent that Cumberland agree to pay the refund. "Rejection will mean that we will fight you to the bitter end," he warned. "There will be no compromise from this Commission other than the order which we have presented this day." The company accepted the decision within two days.[5]

The sum that the Cumberland was forced to refund added up to $440,000. It had to distribute this amount on an exact basis of cost to over eighty thousand people (the number of customers had expanded each year). The expense of carrying out this operation cannot be calculated. One of the company's top officials recalled with a sigh: "And the work and the cost to get those checks out, to find the names and figure out how much each one should get. Some had changed their addresses or even their phone companies [exchanges]." Nor was the refund the only exaction that the Commission levied on the Cumberland. The company was required to bear the costs of litigation incurred by the Commission, ten thousand dollars, and to pay the Commission another ten thousand dollars to defray the expenses of verifying documents submitted by the company. Since Long and Counsel Barrow had represented the Commission, they were entitled to the attorney's fees. Huey's share was reputed to be ten thousand dollars, but he could have received this sum only if Barrow was reimbursed out of the second fund or was not paid at all. Huey did, however, collect a substantial fee. What he did with the money is a matter of some mystery. He claimed later that he gave it to a sanitarium in the West where his ill sister was confined. He probably did turn all or part of it over to some charity agency. He was capable of acts of impulsive generosity, but in this instance it is more likely that he was moved by political reasons. He could not risk the charge that he had profited personally from the case.[6]

The state press rang with praise of Huey for his handling of the Cumberland case. Even newspapers that did not like him admitted that he had been responsible for the settlement. Long had, said one journal, "brought a new point of view into public utility practice in Louisiana, and galvanized the Commission." Another said: "The victory is not one of self-interest but of public trust. It is a victory of a public representative for the people." Some who praised him then would later try to belittle his accomplishment. They would say that he had acted solely for his own political advantage, that he had denied

[5] Minute Book, Louisiana Public Service Commission, January 11 and 13, April 4, 1923; *Louisiana Public Commission, Third Annual Report*, pp. 3–6; New Orleans *States*, January 13 and 25, 1923.
[6] Perry Craddock; confidential communication.

Cumberland a twenty per cent increase but had granted it a ten per cent raise, that he had posed as a defender of the people and then sold them out. The critics had something of a point. But they missed the import of the whole affair. Huey had acted the part of a typical pragmatic American politician. He had made his play for a principle and then he had made a compromise.[7]

Every man or woman who received a refund check from Cumberland remembered gratefully who had gotten them that check. If any of them were ever disposed to forget it, Huey gave them no opportunity. Few speeches he made in the next five years did not refer to the telephone case and to how he had saved the people thousands of dollars in refunds and future lower rates. The use of phones was expanding from year to year, and so the total number of people who felt an obligation to Huey grew far beyond the approximately eighty thousand who had received refund checks. Nor were the users of phones the only ones who became Long adulators. The poor masses who did not have phones were exhilarated by the way Huey handled the case, by his explosive exchanges with the company's attorneys, by his bullying statements to those men. Louisiana had found a man who was not afraid of the big boys, who knew how to make them toe the line—a man who ought to be governor. Huey intensified this image of himself when, immediately after the conclusion of the telephone case, he took on another big corporation, one that was bigger than Cumberland, in fact, the biggest economic aggregation in the state. He challenged the Standard Oil Company of Louisiana.

It was inevitable that sooner or later Huey would attempt to use the Commission as a weapon against Standard Oil. Forceful influences edged him toward a confrontation. He nourished a deep personal hatred of the corporation, born of the Pine Island debacle, and a desire to humiliate it. He believed that as a matter of principle many of its activities should be brought under state regulation. And finally —and at the moment this was a ruling consideration with him—he knew that if he attacked the gigantic corporation, he would increase immeasurably his reputation as a crusader for the people and his

[7] Editorials in Baton Rouge *State-Times*, November 23, 1922, New Orleans *Item*, May 17, December 21, 1922, January 19, 1923, New Orleans *States*, December 1, 1922, January 18, 1923, Shreveport *Times*, November 1, 1922, January 16, 1923, reprinted in *American Progress*, August 23, 1934. Long behaved exactly the same way in cases involving two other corporations, the Shreveport Railway Company and the Southwestern Gas and Electric Company. The issue in both cases concerned what rates the companies could charge. On both occasions Huey at first denied the increase requested by the companies, thus asserting the power of the Commission over them, but later allowed a moderate concession.

chances to be elected governor. He had not been able to move while he was a minority of one on the Commission. But once Francis Williams became a member, and he and Huey made their bargain, and Huey was elected chairman, the situation took a new and, for Standard Oil, an ominous turn. Any reasonably well-informed observer could predict what would happen next—Long would open on Standard and employ the strategy of investigating its pipeline department. Pipelines were a special concern of his, as he had shown by his efforts to get the Parker administration to pass a bill regulating them. That bill had declared the lines to be common carriers and under the jurisdiction of the Commission. He could therefore aggravate the pipeline issue, and through it he could reach his real objective, the parent company.

The attack was not long in coming. On December 5, 1922, Long and Williams signed an order directing Secretary Jastremski to issue a citation addressed to the Standard Oil Company and to all common-carrier pipelines in the state. The order required the various companies to show cause why they should not be adjudged common carriers and why a scale of rates should not be prescribed for the transportation of oil in Louisiana. It further required Standard to show cause why it should not be prohibited from owning or operating oil wells or other holdings of a company engaged in the transportation of oil, and why it should not be compelled to divest itself of such ownership and forbidden to discriminate in transporting oil in which it had an interest. All parties named in the citation were commanded to appear at a hearing on a date to be set later by the Commission.[8]

At the time the order was being prepared, officials of Standard of Louisiana were, by a curious coincidence, in New York, discussing with officials of Standard of New Jersey plans to organize the pipeline department of the Louisiana company as a separate corporation. The Louisiana company had recently extended its pipeline operations into Arkansas and thus was now subject to regulation by the Interstate Commerce Commission. The officials of the owning Jersey company

---

[8] Case 197, *Louisiana Public Service Commission* v. *Standard Oil Company of Louisiana*, order of December 5, 1922, in records of Louisiana Public Service Commission, state capitol, Baton Rouge, hereafter cited as Case 197; John L. Loos: *Oil on Stream!* (Baton Rouge, 1959), p. 88. These two sources form the basis of the above account in the text. Case 197—this was the number given the case in the Commission's system of listing—is a collection of documents that gives a full history of the episode: orders, testimony, briefs, and court decisions. Documents cited from it will be identified by their nature or date of issuance. Professor Loos's history of the pipeline company contains an excellent summary of the case, drawn from records of Standard Oil and the Commission and from court records.

did not want the national agency looking into the books of its Louisiana affiliate. Neither did the officials of the Louisiana company, but they were more alarmed by the probability that Huey Long might want to look at the books. If the pipeline department was cut loose, neither commission could demand to see the records of the present concern. The decision at the New York conference was to proceed with the separation. But while the Louisiana representatives were on the way home, they read in a newspaper of the Commission's order. They realized at once that the reorganization plan would have to be speeded up. Early in January 1923 the Louisiana company announced that it had divested itself of its pipeline properties by creating the Standard Pipe Line Company.[9]

Three days later the Commission issued an announcement of its own. It was summoning a hearing in New Orleans in early February, and all companies cited in its previous order were directed to attend. As the Standard Pipe Line Company had been organized as a common carrier, it was present at the February meeting in the person of its attorney, Thomas M. Milling. His appearance added a note of drama to the proceedings that was not appreciated by the spectators. He was of the Winnfield Millings, the family that in Long eyes had once defrauded the Long family in a land deal, and hence to every Long he was an enemy. Also present were attorneys of Standard Oil and of other pipeline companies. The Standard lawyers informed the Commission that they did not consider their client subject to its jurisdiction—it had sold its pipeline properties to the Standard Pipe Line Company and therefore was no longer engaged in transporting oil from any point to another in Louisiana. Huey listened calmly to this news and then directed that the new company be made a party to the proceedings. But he denied Standard's contention that it was not subject to the Commission's control. He also denied approval of a proposed scale of rates which the Standard Pipe Line submitted. The Commission would prescribe its own scale later, he said coldly. Both of his rulings were supported by Williams, who obviously did not understand the technical points at issue and was content to let the chairman run the hearing as he saw fit.[1]

The pipeline companies anxiously waited for the Commission's schedule of rates to be published. But during the next two months no order issued from the agency's office. Presumably its staff was gathering evidence on which to base a realistic scale. Finally, on April 14, the order appeared. It was a curious and puzzling docu-

[9] Loos: *Oil on Stream!*, pp. 88–9.
[1] Ibid., pp. 89–90; Case 197, Commission proceedings of February 7–8, 1923.

ment. It prescribed no rates or rules for the regulation of common-carrier pipelines. Instead, it was a historical review of the activities of the Standard Oil Company in Louisiana and an economic analysis of the power of the company over independent producers. The historical section, to no one's surprise, emphasized the "freeze out" of the independents at Pine Island. After reciting the various evils committed by Standard the report summarized: "We can only describe it as an institution which has profited with every development, but which has never developed; as an industry for capitalizing the efforts of others, but which never hazards its own fortune; as an enterprise which has discouraged and paralyzed the independent chance-taking capitalist, small farmer, and independent oil operator through their constant financial attacks and destruction to property." The economic analysis declared that Standard of Louisiana was owned almost completely by Standard of Jersey and that any effective regulation of such a concern would have to be a combined national–state process. "The oil industry in all its phases, for the protection of the American public, must be recognized as a public necessity and should be subject to all regulations . . . ," the report concluded. It was not difficult to guess the author of the report, nor his purpose in writing it. He was aiming at bigger game than the pipeline company.[2]

That purpose was more fully revealed in the next move of the Commission. Late in April it directed officials of the Standard Pipe Line Company to appear before it on May 4 in New Orleans and present data on the volume of oil it transported in intra- and inter-state commerce and to disclose certain information relating to its expenses. Presumably the Commission was now going to proceed with the business outlined in its original citation—gathering evidence on which to base a rate schedule. But other orders, signed by Long and Williams, were simultaneously issued from the Commission office. These commanded officers of Standard to appear at the same meeting, instructed Standard to permit its books to be inspected by auditors selected by the Commission, and required the company to show cause why its Baton Rouge refinery should not be adjudged a public utility, subject to the Commission's regulation. The Commission, to make sure that it would get the books, issued a subpoena for them.[3]

The pipeline company, having acknowledged itself to be a common carrier, had no choice but to comply with the summons. But the

[2] *Louisiana Public Service Commission, Third Annual Report*, pp. 29–35. Taylor joined Long and Williams in signing the order.
[3] Case 197, Commission orders of April 25 and 28, 1923; Loos: *Oil on Stream!*, pp. 91–2; New Orleans *States*, April 27, 1923.

officials of Standard were determined not to obey it. They realized that the crisis was upon them at last. If the Commission, which in their eyes was Huey Long, could make them produce their records, then Huey Long could enforce on the company almost any kind of regulatory rule that he dreamed up. Attorneys of Standard went immediately before Judge Brunot's district court in Baton Rouge and asked for an interlocutory (intermediate) decree restraining the Commission from taking any action to declare Standard a public utility, attempting to exercise any action to declare Standard a public utility, or attempting to exercise any jurisdiction over its personnel or records. Although the petition employed legal language and rested its argument on legal grounds, it stressed one point above all others, and this point was not completely legal in nature. The chairman of the Commission, the petition charged, had a personal grudge against the company, and had prejudged the case and was going to hold the company guilty regardless of the evidence. In fact, the petition ended heatedly, the chairman had publicly boasted at a hotel in Shreveport that he was going to put the officers of Standard Oil in jail for contempt.[4]

When Huey heard that Standard would refuse to surrender its books, he professed not to be disturbed. He told the press that the Commission at its hearing would compel the company to produce the records. "The power of the state will not be sacrificed this time," he promised. "Friday morning will tell the story. The Standard Oil Company shall not rule this state." But on May 1 he learned that Standard had gone before Brunot's court and that the judge had issued the injunction asked for by the company. If the injunction stood, the Commission would be powerless to do anything except prescribe rates for the pipeline company. Two days later, the day before the date of the hearing, Huey applied to the supreme court for a mandamus forbidding Brunot to enforce the injunction. His application was supported by a twenty-eight-page brief, which he had had to whip up in four hours. It was, considering the time he had to write it, a remarkable document, showing great familiarity with state and national regulatory practices and citing a number of cases to uphold its points. Huey contended that the injunction was illegal because Standard's lawyers had not given, as required by law, a five-day notice that they intended to apply for an order, but had gone immediately before the district court. Moreover, he argued, a district court could not enjoin a state regulative agency from using powers granted it by the consti-

---

[4] Case 197, Standard Oil petition of May 1, 1923.

tution. If a lower court could enjoin a state agency from gathering information on which to base action, then state regulation would become but "an idle function." The supreme court was not convinced by Huey's reasoning. He seemed to be saying that he wanted only to secure data to establish rates, whereas, as everbody knew, he had threatened to declare Standard to be a public utility. The court denied the application on the same day that it was filed.[5]

Therefore, at the hearing on the following day the Commission had to restrict itself to prescribing rates for the pipeline company. Huey explained the situation in a dignified opening statement. Brunot's injunction was illegal, he said. The Commission could, if it wished, proceed to disregard it, with no fear of contempt penalties. But the Commission was such an important body in the life of the state that it should not do anything that even seemed to show disrespect for the law. It would move to have the dissolution dissolved, and anticipating success, it would schedule tentatively a hearing on the status of Standard for May 17. In the meantime, it would hear evidence from the pipeline company relating to rates. The session was short and quiet, and Huey adjourned it with an announcement that the Commission would soon issue an order establishing a scale of rates for the company.[6]

What he meant by "soon," the company discovered to its surprise, was the very next day. On May 5 the Commission published a detailed order regulating the practices and rates of the pipeline company. A critical newspaper exclaimed that it was "the most sensational and drastic order ever issued by the Long Commission." It first estimated the value of the company's properties and the amount of its operating costs as a basis on which to fix a fair return, and in the company's view it estimated everything too low. It then prescribed a set of rates that reduced substantially the present schedule being charged by the company, a scale that in the company's eyes was ruinous. The officers of the company, when they recovered from their shock, promptly went before Judge Brunot's court and asked for an intermediate injunction forbidding the Commission from enforcing the order. They also asked that on final trial of the matter the court establish the rates that they had submitted to the Commission. The language of the petition betrayed that it was drawn by the same legal hand that had drafted the earlier petition of the Standard Oil Company. Huey P. Long, the document recited, was an "avowed enemy,

[5] Shreveport *Times*, May 1, 1923; Case 197, brief by Long of May 3, 1923; Loos: *Oil on Stream!*, p. 92.
[6] Case 197, Commission proceedings of May 4, 1923.

personally biased and prejudiced," and he had a personal interest in compelling the company to abide by his rules. The obliging Brunot immediately granted the injunction, thus adding one more count to the list he would some day have to ask Huey to forgive. A final hearing was fixed for May 23.[7]

On the eve of the hearing Huey issued a statement to the press. He was apparently resigned to the knowledge that Brunot would make the injunction final, and for the first time in the case he betrayed signs of anger. Standard Oil and the state officials controlled by it were using every means to cripple the Commission, he declared. The agency did not have the money to pay the costs of fighting constant legal battles, he went on, and he had had to put up some of his own money. He ended with a threat that he evidently meant to execute some time in the future: "We are going to see that the throats of every one of these double-decking politicians is cut from ear to ear." His war on Standard was beginning to touch the raw nerves of conservative Louisiana. Mounting denunciations reverberated across the state. The loudest came from Baton Rouge, where Standard had its refinery. There the *State-Times*, whose owner had just a few months before wanted to play Huey up for his action in the Cumberland case, now dismissed him as "demagogic" and "outrageous."[8]

Brunot, acting as Huey had expected he would, enjoined the Commission from enforcing its rate order. Huey made no effort to reverse the order by appealing it to a higher court. He thus left the pipeline company free to fix its own rates but placed it in the position of operating without Commission approval. Apparently he was content to permit this anomalous condition to continue for a while. He then turned his attention to Standard. On the day that Brunot forbade the Commission to interfere with the pipeline company's rates, May 30, Long, in a dramatic counterstroke, appealed to the supreme court to reverse the judge's order of May 1 forbidding the Commission to declare Standard a public utility or to exercise jurisdiction over its personnel or books. This time he won a partial success. The high court, by a vote of four to one, modified Brunot's order to permit the Commission to examine Standard's books insofar as anything in them pertained to the operations of the Standard Pipe Line Company. But the court also declared that the Commission had clearly exceeded its authority in attempting to classify Standard itself as a public utility. Huey hailed the decision as a complete victory. For the first time

---

[7] Loos: *Oil on Stream!*, pp. 92–5; *Louisiana Public Service Commission, Third Annual Report*, pp. 41–5; Case 197, Standard Pipe Line petition of May 14, 1923.

[8] Shreveport *Times*, May 23, 1922; Baton Rouge *State-Times*, May, 26, 1922.

Standard had been brought to terms, he claimed. Actually, he had achieved very little. He could inspect only a part of the company's records, and he had failed to have it adjudged as a utility. He made no attempt to exercise his right to look at the books. By the time the matter was settled, the summer of 1923 had arrived. Candidates for the governorship were preparing to hit the campaign trail, and Huey was getting ready to announce. He could take care of Standard Oil later.[9]

IN COMPARISON WITH THE Cumberland case the Standard episode was dull. There had been no tumultuous hearings marked by shouting contests between Huey and lawyers for the opposition, no bullying of witnesses by the Commission's chairman, and, until the last, no exciting newspaper headlines. Throughout, Huey had been calm, detached, scientific, the informed chairman who was watching out for the public interest. He had been resolute, but he had never really pressed any of his views very hard. The impression that comes out of the records of the case is that he did not expect to accomplish very much—that he did not believe he would be able to have Standard declared a utility or to get into its books—that, perhaps, at this time he did not care particularly whether he won the case. He did what he did because it completed the image that he had been building of Huey Long, champion of the people, the man who knew how to handle the big corporations. In the minds of his followers he had defeated another of the big ones. Hadn't he made it get rid of its pipeline company? Couldn't he have examined its books if he wanted to? And if he hadn't done everything he had said he was going to, why, just wait till he gets elected governor and see what happens. The Standard issue, coming to a climax on the eve of the gubernatorial campaign, put him in the race with a head start.

He had made the play deliberately and had executed it flawlessly, and he was satisfied with himself. He would have been embarrassed if matters had turned out otherwise, if he had been able to put Standard under the iron regulation that he threatened. Everything he did on the Commission points to the conclusion that he preferred compromise victories over the corporations, that he liked settlements which were practical, partial, and political. "We are gradually forcing them back," he had said when he sensed success in the Cumberland case. It was the word "gradually" that was the key to the sentence.

[9] Loos: *Oil on Stream!*, pp. 95–7; New Orleans *Item*, June 4, 1923.

# CHAPTER 9

# *Blood on the Moon*

**H**UEY FELT NO SCRUPLES in telling people how he was going to run his campaign in 1923. "I'm going to run for governor and I'll tell you how I'm going to win," he said to one man. "In every parish there is a boss, usually the sheriff. He has forty per cent of the votes, forty per cent are opposed to him, and twenty per cent are in-betweens. I'm going into every parish and cuss out the boss. That gives me forty per cent of the votes to begin with, and I'll hoss trade 'em out of the in-betweens."

How he executed his technique is still remembered in Louisiana, and by its victims with bitterness even yet. The son of J. Y. Sanders recalled: "He would go into a community that was strange to him. He went to Hammond where my father lived, and he knew that my father wasn't supporting him. He would get up on the stump and attack Sanders. He would go to the hotel and those who didn't like Sanders would come around and talk to him. That was the nucleus of his organization right there. He did that all over the state and attacked the biggest figures opposed to him. He went to Alexandria and jumped on George Bolton, a big financial fellow. It was blasphemy to attack Bolton in Alexandria. Well, he knew that Bolton wasn't ever going to support him. He wanted to get to the anti-Bolton vote."

In a country parish the boss might be a plantation owner, and then Huey would give the attack an economic emphasis. He would say: "Now, Mr. Gilbert, I don't want your vote. There is no reason why you should vote for me. You are a rich man. You own all the land around here. You have all these poor devils working for you. . . .

I'm trying to help these poor fellows that you are giving a raw deal. I want the vote of these peapickers that have come here to hear me talk." Over and over he shouted his message, in every speech, in every parish: "I don't want the bosses. I want the people on my side. There's going to be a new day in Louisiana."[1]

A new day it would be if Huey, or any candidate who said the things he was saying, could carry a Louisiana election. The barriers in his way seemed insuperable. Indeed, to some people it seemed a colossal impudence that he was even running. To run for governor then, explained a later Long leader, "You had either to be endorsed by the sugar barons, the banks, or the railroads. Without them putting their hands on you and anointing you, you were beyond the pale. The idea of you running in this state without them being your boss was unheard of. . . . He was the first man . . . who dared to run for governor without having the anointment of the big, big trusts, who, incidentally, were lined up with the political machines."[2] The power structure described by this leader was real and even more complex than he described it. Its origins went far back in the history of the state.

EVERY SOUTHERN STATE had a tradition of government by an elite. The membership of the elite has been characterized by various phrases—an upper-class or upper-income group, an alliance of planters and businessmen, a ruling hierarchy, oligarchy, or caste. Southerners sometimes summed it up by saying that they lived under a government of gentlemen. Like all concepts of its kind, the tradition had both exaggerations and omissions, but it had more reality than most traditions. It was particularly real in Louisiana, where rule by an elite was an institution of long standing. It dated from at least the 1830's when a coalition of planters and merchants appeared that dominated politics until the coming of the Civil War. After the war and after Reconstruction a similar combination would appear and would rule unchallenged for half a century. But during Reconstruction a sensational break in the chain of control occurred.[3]

Reconstruction brought into power in Louisiana, and in other Southern states, a whole new collection of interests—alien professional politicians, "carpetbaggers" from the North; natives of varying

[1] Rupert Peyton; J. Y. Sanders, Jr.; Russell B. Long; Waldo H. Dugas.

[2] James P. O'Connor.

[3] Roger A. Shugg: *Origins of Class Struggle in Louisiana* (Baton Rouge, 1939), pp. 121–56, chapter entitled "Government by Gentlemen."

social status and integrity who for one reason or another were willing to cooperate with the victors; corruptionists, both imported and indigenous; and the Negro masses, ignorant but aspiring, pliable yet compelling notice by their very numbers, and, above all, terribly poor and eager to improve their lot. The economic condition of the Negroes is, in fact, one of the keys to an understanding of the nature of Reconstruction. For the first time in Southern history poor men exercised an influential voice in government. They used their influence to secure legislation that foreshadowed the later welfare state.

Reconstruction might have been government for and of poor men, but it was not government by poor men. Negroes held various offices in every state. But they did not usually occupy the big and therefore important offices, and hardly ever did they determine policy. The actual powers of government remained in the hands of white leaders, Northern or Southern men who dominated the Republican party leadership. Some of these whites exhibited a rare understanding of the requirements of power—they were imaginative, daring, and often unscrupulous. And one of them displayed qualities that revealed he had a touch of genius. He was Henry Clay Warmoth, carpetbag governor of Louisiana. Tall, handsome, magnetic, Warmoth fascinated people even while he alarmed them. An uneasy associate described him as "a man full of resources . . . such a man as would rise to power in any great civil disturbance, embodying in himself the elements of revolution, and delighting in the exercise of his natural gifts in the midst of political excitement."

Coming into office in a revolutionary situation and therefore having an insecure power basis, Warmoth pressured the legislature to enact a series of laws that invested him with imperial authority. He could appoint, and remove, local registrars of voters, tax collectors, and assessors. He could fill all vacancies in local offices, including the potent parish police juries. He could appoint the board of police commissioners in New Orleans, which determined the selection of all police personnel. He could name constables for every parish except Orleans and adjoining Jefferson and St. Bernard, which were subject to a body called the Metropolitan Police, itself accountable to the governor. He controlled all appointments to the militia. He could order the arrest of persons anywhere in the state and direct local enforcement officers to execute his warrant and authorize officers in one parish to aid those in another. He appointed the board of public works, the board of registration, which supervised all elections, and the returning board, which passed on the validity of election results. These were his official powers, and he augmented them with unofficial techniques that were almost as effective. He would storm into the chambers of the legislature to lobby for his bills, shouting commands at his followers and promising rewards to those who voted right and penalties for those who voted wrong. He required appointees to important positions to sign undated resignations, thus reserving to himself the power to remove them by a stroke of the pen.[4]

Huey Long had been fascinated with Warmoth from the time he first heard of the old governor, which was in his high-school class in Louisiana history. Apparently he read a great deal about Warmoth in the years after he left high school and about the Reconstruction period generally. Although Warmoth lived until 1931 and resided in New Orleans, Huey never tried to meet him. Huey may have thought that it was risky politics to fraternize with a man who had been a carpetbagger, who in the Southern mythology of Reconstruction had been a force for evil. But he never hesitated to express his respect for Warmoth. "Warmoth possibly knows almost as much about present Louisiana politics as I do," he said to one associate. Huey's admiration for Warmoth was professional, the esteem of one power artist for another. When he became governor himself, Huey secured the enactment of laws that gave him the same control over local government and election machinery that Warmoth had had, and he employed the same devices to pass his laws that Warmoth had found so effective.[5]

It was a part of Warmoth's genius that he instinctively understood that the politics of his adopted state was peculiar, differing subtly from the art as practiced in any other state. Warmoth appreciated the difference and flourished, whereas the average outside operator would not even have survived. Louisiana politics was speculative, devious, personal, exuberant, and highly professional. The objective was to win, and in no other state were the devices employed to win —stratagems, deals, oratory—so studied and admired by the populace. It had been like this in the ante-bellum era, it was like this in Warmoth's time, and it would be like this in the future. This professionalism has always amazed visiting observers. An impressed twentieth-century critic wrote: "Louisiana politics is of an intensity

[4] *Congressional Globe,* 42 Cong. 3 Sess., Appendix, 200; Shugg: *Origins of Class Struggle,* pp. 224–5, 227; Ben B. Taylor, Jr.: "A Study of the Appointive and Removal Powers of the Governor of Louisiana" (unpublished M.A. thesis, Louisiana State University, 1935), pp. 70–1, 77–8, 89–90.

[5] Harley B. Bozeman; Bozeman, in *Winn Parish Enterprise,* September 24, 1964; Eugene Stanley. The late Mr. Stanley, a participant in the politics of Huey's time and later an observer of the political scene, was one of the first to notice the resemblance between Warmoth's program and Long's.

and complexity that are matched, in my experience, only in the Republic of Lebanon." He decided that the state as a whole, but especially its southern section, was a part of the Hellenistic-Mediterranean littoral, and in a memorable phrase he called it the westernmost of the Arab states. Its people had a tolerance of corruption not found anywhere else in America, he concluded. Other observers have noted this particular psychology, but they have ascribed it to the state's Latin-French background. Some have gone so far as to suggest that Louisiana is not really an American state but a "banana republic," a Latin enclave of immorality set down in a country of Anglo-Saxon righteousness. Whatever the explanation, it is undeniable that Louisianians have always had a non-American attitude toward corruption. They have accepted it as a necessary part of political life, and they have even admired it when it is executed with style and, above all, with a jest. What is more remarkable, and what is most offensive to moralists, they have frankly admitted that corruption exists. In 1939 Gallup pollsters asked a sample group in the state if they thought elections in recent years had been honestly conducted. Twenty-five per cent answered "Yes," fifteen per cent ventured no opinion, but sixty per cent chorused "No." This raw realism could shock even as seasoned and cynical an operator as Warmoth. A reporter once asked the governor if it was true that the state government was permeated with dishonesty. Warmoth's answer reflected anguish: "Why, damn it, everybody is demoralized down here. Corruption is the fashion."[6]

Warmoth and the Republicans and the Negroes and the alien forces they all represented fell from power with the end of Reconstruction, and a combination of native politicians resumed control of the state. It was a combination almost identical with the one that had ruled before the war, a hierarchy of planters and merchants and professional politicians. Such a group dominated every Southern state in the years between the 1870's and the turn of the century. But after 1900 new elements sought and won admittance to the inner circle. As the South entered the industrial age, manufacturing interests became important forces, and in Louisiana these interests were more numerous than in other states and larger and more powerful and

[6] Shugg: *Origins of Class Struggle*, pp. 150–1; Gilbert L. Dupre: *Political Reminiscences, 1876–1892* (Baton Rouge, n.d.), p. 145; A. J. Liebling: "The Great State," *New Yorker*, XXXVI (May 28, 1960), 48 (June 11, 1960), 100; George Gallup and Saul Forbes Rae: *The Pulse of Democracy* (New York, 1940), p. 156; New Orleans *Picayune*, February 25, 1872.

more politically conscious. The state experienced a substantial economic expansion in the first third of the century. The value of its industrial products increased from $121 million to $685 million, its railroad mileage doubled, the number of its corporations rose from 468 to over 1,000, and the size of its laboring force grew from 42,000 to 87,000. This forward surge placed Louisiana in the front rank of Southern industrial states. The leading industries in 1930 were, in the order of the value of their products, oil refining, sugar refining, lumber and timber products, rice cleaning and polishing, cottonseed oil and cakes, paper, and alcohol. Smaller than these enterprises but expanding were the manufacture of bags, planing mills, machine shops and foundries, and coffee roasting. Not a part of the industrial complex but allied with it and representing almost as much wealth were shipping and financial interests, centered in New Orleans, and the railroads and gas and electrical and telephone utilities.[7]

The same span of years witnessed a similar development of the state's human resources. The population almost doubled, going from 1,381,000 persons in 1900 to 2,101,000 by 1930. That of New Orleans rose from 287,000 to 458,000. The increase in the metropolis was, in part, the result of a drift of people there from the country parishes. The same shift occurred in other parts of the state and swelled the population of the towns and cities. In 1900, 73 per cent of the population had lived in rural areas and 21 per cent in urban, but by 1930 the rural figure had decreased to 60.3 per cent and the urban had risen to 39.7 per cent. Louisiana was apparently moving into the modern industrial and urban age, and the statistics seemed to tell a story of glittering progress. But the data of economic expansion told only a partial story. Other evidence presented a different picture, of a state mired in mass poverty, ranking near the bottom in all the indexes that measured wealth, and afflicted with a social system that was almost primitive in comparison with commonwealths in other sections. Louisiana ranked thirty-ninth in average gross income, with a figure of $1,270; forty-third in the value of farm property; forty-fourth in the number of farms with piped water; forty-fifth in the number of farms with electric lights; and forty-seventh in the number of farms with electric motors. Nor was the growth of its industries quite as impressive as it seemed. The annual value of its

[7] George M. Reynolds: *Machine Politics in New Orleans, 1897–1926* (New York, 1936), pp. 41–8; Stanley W. Preston: "Survey of Louisiana Manufacturing, 1929–1939," *Louisiana Business Bulletin,* VIII (1946), 30; Rudolph Heberle: *The Labor Force in Louisiana* (Baton Rouge, 1948), pp. 3, 64.

manufactured goods, $685 million, was almost $300 million less than that of Wisconsin, a midwestern state of modest manufacturing status. Louisiana could report in 1930 no individual with a taxable income over $1 million, only one with an income of over $500,000, seven over $250,000, and 43 over $100,000. (The figures for Wisconsin in these categories were 4, 12, 33, and 171, respectively.) Louisiana's eighty-seven thousand wage earners numbered less than two per cent of the total population, and the vast majority of them were unorganized and hence unable to act effectively to better their condition or to influence elections. The most shocking example of the state's backwardness was in education. Among the forty-eight states Louisiana stood next to the last in literacy. Almost fourteen per cent of its population over ten years of age was classified as illiterate, and sixteen per cent of its adult population. Whites as well as Negroes were victims of the lack of educational facilities. Over fourteen per cent of the rural white males had not completed a single year's schooling, and four out of ten farm men had not finished the fourth grade.[8]

One reason why educational and other services were poor or nonexistent was that the state was poor, unable to finance a broad program of social benefits. But they were poor for the additional reason that the ruling hierarchy was little interested in using what resources the state had available to provide services and was even less interested in employing the power of the state to create new resources so that more services could be supported. The hierarchy was smug, satisfied with things as they were, devoted to the protection of privilege. Its leaders were gentlemen in frock coats, string ties, and wide hats, and they gave the state a kind of government like themselves—dignified, usually honest, though sometimes discreetly corrupt, and backward-looking. It might be described as "government by goatee." A woman who was a member of the caste described its psychology frankly: "We were secure. We were the old families. We had what we wanted. We didn't bother anybody. All we wanted was to keep it." Huey Long once attempted to analyze the strength of the hierarchy for his Senate colleagues. He did not need to exaggerate. "There was a State," he said, "lying under the domination of the great white angels of feudal democracy. The feudal State of America was the State of Louisiana.

[8] Reynolds: *Machine Politics*, pp. 39–40; V. O. Key, Jr.: *Southern Politics* (New York, 1949), p. 160; Howard W. Odum: *Southern Regions of the United States* (Chapel Hill, 1936), material drawn from charts and maps, *passim*; E. H. (Lige) Williams (early Louisiana labor leader).

That is the way it had been run and had been allowed to be run, and nobody dared gainsay any of them because the political organizations were so entrenched that no one tried to change it."[9]

The Louisiana hierarchy was indeed strongly entrenched. It was, in fact, stronger and more effective than any similar group in any other Southern state. Its power rested on a wider base than existed in other states. In the Louisiana organization there were elements not usually found in the economy or politics of the South. The planter interests, notably those representing cotton, were present in most states, but the sugar growers were peculiar to Louisiana. The mercantile, financial, and utility interests in Louisiana could be duplicated in other states, but here they were more prominent because they were concentrated in New Orleans, the region's largest city. But what really set the Louisiana hierarchy apart was the fact that it included so many industrial interests, interests of greater variety and wealth than those operating elsewhere. The lumber industry, for example, was much more aggressive in building political influence than in any other state. The sugar refiners were also a militant interest. But towering above all Louisiana's industries in size and political consciousness was the Standard Oil Company, the biggest economic aggregation in the state and the only really big corporation in the South.[1]

Also present in the Louisiana hierarchy, and investing it with another aspect of uniqueness, was the only genuine big-city machine in the South, the Old Regular organization in New Orleans. Formed soon after the Civil War and perfected by Martin Behrman, the machine was as efficient an organization as could be found in any city. Its success was due in no small part to the simplicity of its organization. The governing agency consisted of seventeen men, the leaders of the seventeen wards of the city, of whom the mayor was one. These leaders determined what candidates the machine would nominate or support and what stand the Orleans delegation in the legislature should take on issues. An appendage of the Old Regulars and sometimes confused with them in name was the Choctaw Club, with twenty-one hundred members, whose principal function was to hand out baskets to the poor at Christmas and take care of hardship cases. The Choctaws were the second level of workers in the machine. Each member paid a yearly assessment of twelve dollars, which gave the machine a permanent chest of twenty-four thousand dollars, and the club building was the headquarters of the Old Regular organization.

[9] Confidential communication; *American Progress*, February 8, 1934.
[1] Key: *Southern Politics*, pp. 159–60.

The seventeen ward leaders were members of the club, and the two organizations were so much one that the interchangeability of names was justified.[2]

An Old Regular mayor who came after Behrman once blandly told a United States Senate investigative committee that the machine's principal reason for existence was to engage in "philanthropic and political uplift." The monumental falsehood of the words convulsed Louisianians in the hearing room.

Everybody who followed politics—that is, every adult citizen in the state—knew that the Old Regulars existed for one purpose, to win elections, and most people had a fairly accurate picture of how the machine went about it. It controlled the registration office and padded the rolls generously, with the names of dead people, imaginary people, and people who had moved elsewhere. It paid the poll taxes of large numbers of indigents and voted them in blocs. It virtually controlled the selection of commissioners, who could often determine the outcome of an election in a close ward.

Commissioners policed the polls, challenged the voters who were expected to vote wrong, and made sure that their people voted right. By law a voter could be assisted by a commissioner, and a commissioner would insist on going in the booth with a man who had promised to sell his vote. If the commissioner came out with a pencil over his ear, it signified that the citizen had observed his bargain, and a watcher paid him off.

Commissioners were chosen in various ways. Every candidate for office was allowed so many commissioners. The machine put up "dummy" candidates, a practice also used in other places in the state. A dummy had his filing fee paid by his sponsor, and he was expected to withdraw on the last day for pulling down. But he retained the right to name commissioners, who were, of course, picked by the machine. A certain number of commissioners were chosen by lot. Drawings were held at courtrooms over the city, usually with a little girl drawing a number of slips from a box. Choctaw officials placed the names in the box, and they would crimp the slips bearing the names of their men and stand them up, leaving the others lying flat. Naturally the drawer, especially if a child, would pick up the crimped pieces. A onetime member of the organization, recounting its varied

[2] *Hearings Before the Special Committee on Investigation of Campaign Expenditures*, 72 Cong., 2 Sess. (Washington, 1934), Pt. II, pp. 1955, 1959, 2001; this is the second volume of hearings on the election of Senator Overton and is hereafter cited as *Overton Hearing*, II. The material on the organization of the Old Regulars is taken from statements by officials of the organization.

stratagems, concluded admiringly: "The Old Regulars were used to buying out and trading out and swapping out."[3]

But the machine's most effective weapon in an election was the police force. Or so its opponents charged. "The way the Old Regulars used to use the police force was terrific," one man recalled. "The police force down here could win an election. It was really rough. If you didn't vote right they would arrest you, and they would have nine witnesses that you were doing something." An Old Regular police chief, when asked if the charge of police influence was true, denied it, but in somewhat ambiguous language: "That is not true, not true. Not any more than in any other political organization. I wouldn't say the police organization pressured people. Maybe the Old Regulars did. What they used to do was start these fights in the early morning. Say if you were working as a commissioner at the polls and the polls opened at six, you had to be there at five-thirty. Somebody might get in a fight in the street and didn't get there at five-thirty." At this point he laughed appreciatively and went on: "There might have been an occasional case where a policeman might have bothered somebody but not often, a rare occasion. Of course, any political organization is going to have that."[4]

The Old Regular organization might command a mass vote and it might hand out baskets to the poor at Christmas, but not even its friendliest critics ever contended that it represented the aspirations of the poor masses. It was one of the most business-oriented machines in the country. Behrman and later leaders maintained extremely close relations with the city's utility, financial, and manufacturing interests, and the organization acted consistently to protect corporate privilege. It opposed state regulation of utilities and municipal ownership of utilities. The city's electric rate was among the highest in the nation, and its direct tax on business property was among the lowest. The city government showed no interest in bringing in available, cheap, natural gas, preferring to let its citizens pay steep rates on artificial gas. The Orleans delegation in the legislature, under Old Regular control, voted against all labor proposals, even measures abolishing child labor or setting minimum work hours for women and children.[5]

The conservative character of the machine made it more palatable to patrician leaders in the state. These men, who were scions of old

---

[3] Clem H. Sehrt; Eugene Stanley; Lantz Womack; W. Harry Talbot; confidential communication.

[4] Confidential communications.

[5] Robert W. Williams, Jr.: "Martin Behrman and New Orleans Civil Development, 1904–1920," *Louisiana History*, II (1961), 396–7; Reynolds: *Machine Politics*, pp. 139, 144–5; Harnett T. Kane: *Louisiana Hayride* (New York, 1941), pp. 32–3.

families or who preached ideals of honest government, might decry the methods of the organization, but they could work with it because it stood for the same economic principles that they did. They could accept it for the further reason that it was effective—it could deliver a vote that the patrician leaders needed. The Old Regulars were an integral part of the hierarchy, and a big reason for its sustained success. The Louisiana hierarchy enjoyed a longer period of power than similar groups in other states. In other states rebels rose to challenge their rulers, to voice the aspirations of the masses. They were the men known in Southern history as the demagogues, and the hierarchy had to face them down or absorb them. No demagogue appeared to disturb the serenity of the Louisiana scene. No rebel dared to defy the state's rulers—until 1924.[6]

HUEY STARTED MAKING noises like a candidate as early as the latter part of 1922. Every time he came to New Orleans on Public Service Commission business, which was often, he permitted himself to be interviewed, and in these sessions he spoke grandly but vaguely of the support he had throughout the state. He would announce at a later time, he said—if he should decide to run. In one of these interviews he touched briefly on a subject that very obviously was worrying him. A reporter asked where he stood on the Ku Klux Klan. The hooded order was suddenly emerging as an issue in the campaign. The Louisiana Klan was part of a national society that had been founded in 1915 and that after 1920 enlarged its membership sensationally in the South and the Middle West. In those rural regions the Klan's call for a return to its own peculiar brand of Americanism—extolling the older and simpler virtues and damning Catholics, aliens, Negroes, and radicals—appealed to people who felt frustrated by the complexities of the modern age. The Klan in Louisiana counted its greatest numbers and influence in the northern parishes, and in 1922 an event in one of these parishes focused public attention on the growing power of the organization. There two opponents of the Klan disappeared, and later their murdered bodies were found in a lake. Civic leaders denounced the Klan as a lawless society, and Governor Parker asked the legislature to enact an antimasking law. A bill was introduced but was stalled, probably by covert Klan opposition.

---

[6] Again the reader's attention is directed to a peculiarity of the Louisiana election system. A gubernatorial primary election was held in January of every fourth even-numbered year, but practically all the campaigning was done in the last four or five months of the preceding year. Thus, students of Louisiana history speak of the election of 1924, but the campaign they are talking about occurred in 1923.

Parker's attorney general then announced that an antimasking law of 1872 aimed at the Klan of Reconstruction times was still effective. But sentiment for a modern measure continued to mount, and the whole question of the Klan was clearly going to become an issue in the campaign.

It was an issue that most politicians would have liked to avoid, for whatever stand a candidate took, he was going to alienate some voters. A candidate from south, and Catholic, Louisiana could play it one of two ways. He could denounce the Klan fiercely and hope that the Catholic vote would put him in the second primary. Or he could denounce the Klan moderately and hope that he would get a substantial part of the Catholic vote and pick up some of the Klan vote as a lesser enemy. But for a candidate from north Louisiana, like Huey, the Klan issue was pure dynamite. If he condemned the order, he lost votes in the area where he was strongest. But if he did not condemn it, he would run badly in the more populous south and would lose in the first primary. Huey betrayed his uneasiness at the implications of the Klan issue in his press interviews. When the reporters tried to get him to state a position, he cut them off. The Klan issue was a false one, he snapped. The real issue was Standard Oil and corporate domination of the state. "We have had invisible government in Louisiana since 1879," he said, and this was the kind of secret control the people should be thinking about.[7]

Huey continued to talk like a candidate during the first months of 1923. He boasted to reporters that support for him was increasing all over the state and that he would run as the head of the "Long ticket," that is, with a slate of candidates for the lesser offices who were committed to him. His trips to New Orleans grew more frequent, and observers guessed that he was trying to line up organizational support in the city. It was thought that because of his connection with the Williams brothers he would receive the endorsement of John Sullivan's New Regulars, and one rumor stated that Francis Williams would be Huey's running mate for lieutenant governor. Other country candidates were also in New Orleans soliciting support. One was James G. Palmer of Shreveport, who had been Huey's lawyer in the Parker libel case. Palmer was turned down by both the Old and the New Regulars, presumably because he was supposed to be a former Klansman. Thereupon he withdrew from the race. Political gossips whispered an additional reason for his pulling down—Huey had repudiated a promise to support him. According to this story, Huey

[7] New Orleans *States*, November 26, 1922; Leo Glenn Douthit: "The Governorship of Huey Long" (unpublished M.A. thesis, Tulane University, 1947), p. 25.

pledged during the libel case to campaign for Palmer and then under-cut his benefactor by announcing himself. The supposition may have had some basis of truth. Huey possibly did make some kind of com-mitment to Palmer. But the Shreveport lawyer was never a serious candidate and was out of the contest before Huey was formally in it.[8]

Indeed, it seemed shortly that Huey himself was not going to be a candidate. In May, after holding two meetings in New Orleans with people who were supposed to be supporting him, he announced that he was withdrawing from the race. He gave as his reason that he had to devote all his energy and time to prosecuting the Public Service Commission's case against the Standard Oil Company. The political pundits of the press corps speculated that Huey's reason was not the real one. They decided, on the basis of information leaked by attend-ants at Huey's meetings, that the Williams boys had demanded that Huey sign a statement denouncing the Klan, that Huey had refused, and that he had thus lost the only organized support he had in New Orleans. Huey declined to comment on these speculations. Talking with reporters, he affected a philosophic mood. "I would advise the young man to keep away from seeking political office," he said. "To some a political career may seem a bed of roses, but there are lots of thorns." The smart dopesters surmised that he would soon be back in the race.[9]

Huey and his urban associates probably did discuss the Klan issue, and it is quite possible that he was pressed to make some kind of commitment. Politicians from a city as heavily Catholic as New Orleans would naturally prefer that the candidate they supported be anti-Klan. On the other hand, politicians as experienced as the Wil-liams brothers certainly knew that if Huey issued too strong a denun-ciation of the Klan, he would hurt his chances, and it seems unlikely that they would have insisted that he sign such a statement. Huey probably withdrew because the Williamses admitted at the May meetings that they could not persuade the New Regulars to endorse him. Without some organized support in the city Huey had no chance at all. So he withdrew, undoubtedly with the intention of re-entering later—if the New Regulars could be induced to support him or, more probably, if the Williams boys could be brought to revolt against their faction and form their own organization.

[8] New Orleans *Item*, March 18, 1923; Shreveport *Journal*, March 23, 1923; New Orleans *Times-Picayune*, April 29; Marshall Ballard, article in New Orleans *Item*, February 3, 1924; T. O. Harris: *The Kingfish: Huey P. Long, Dictator* (New Orleans, 1938), pp. 24–5.

[9] New Orleans *Times-Picayune*, May 13, 1923; New Orleans *Item*, May 13 and June 17, 1923; New Orleans *Times-Picayune*, May 20, 1923.

At the moment neither New Orleans machine was in a position to endorse a candidate. Not all the possible aspirants had yet announced their intentions, and until they all were in the field, the city leaders would hold off. This was the proclaimed policy of Martin Behrman of the Old Regulars, who was preparing to run for mayor again, and his deputy, Paul Maloney, and John P. Sullivan of the New Regulars. When all the candidates had been announced, the city leaders could determine which one seemed to have the largest country following and was disposed to make the best deal with their faction. There was never any chance that the Old Regulars would go for Huey. Behrman hoped to avoid an election fought on the Klan issue, and he suspected that any candidate from north Louisiana would be tainted with intolerance. Even more compelling with him was his conviction that Huey was a radical enemy of business. Sullivan disliked Long for much the same reasons.[1]

As the summer opened, the candidates and their backers finally emerged. Former governors Sanders and Pleasant, after surveying the possibilities, decided to throw their influence behind Henry L. Fuqua, general manager of the state penitentiary at Angola. Fuqua, who had been president of a Baton Rouge hardware company, had been appointed to the position at Angola by Pleasant and reappointed by Parker. Heavily built and paunchy, with a pudgy face and sparse hair, he was not a particularly dynamic figure or a very impressive public speaker. But he had an affable and friendly manner that stood him well in individual contacts, and he looked like a solid, safe small-town businessman who could be depended on to do nothing rash. He was a Protestant but from south Louisiana. He was known to favor some kind of antimasking law, but he did not denounce the Klan violently and was expected to pick up votes in the north, even from Klan adherents. Backed by powerful country leaders, he was a formidable candidate.[2]

Although Fuqua held an important office in the Parker administration, he was not the candidate of the governor. Parker had his own hand-picked candidate, his lieutenant governor, Hewitt Bouanchaud of Pointe Coupee parish, a French, southern parish. A representative of an old parish family, Bouanchaud was short, spare, and swarthy. A successful lawyer, he spoke French fluently and, what was rare in a south Louisiana Frenchman, English without an accent. He

[1] Clipping, n.d., probably New Orleans *Times-Picayune*, May 1923, in John H. Overton Scrapbooks, in possession of Mrs. John H. Overton, Alexandria, Louisiana.
[2] Sketch of Fuqua's career in New Orleans *States*, August 19, 1923; Hermann B. Deutsch.

was an attractive figure but an unlikely candidate. Although he was amiable in personal intercourse, publicly he gave an impression of stiffness and restraint. John P. Sullivan once dismissed him as "a cold drink of water." But what made him next to impossible was that he was a Catholic. It was practically an unwritten law of Louisiana politics that a Catholic should not run for governor. A Catholic candidate was almost certain to lose the northern parishes, and he would alienate enough Protestant votes in the southern parishes to ensure his defeat. It was true that on occasion in the distant past a Catholic had won the governorship, and it was conceivable that an especially appealing Catholic leader might be elected in the future. But it was impossible that a Catholic could win in a year when the state was convulsed by the Klan–religious issue. Why Parker ever put Bouanchaud in the race is hard to explain. Personal loyalty to his lieutenant governor probably had something to do with it. So also did Parker's own ego. He wanted to demonstrate that he could choose his successor and elect him over any opposition, whether it was Sanders or Pleasant or the Old Regulars, who were certain to oppose a candidate backed by Parker. But above personal reasons, Parker had, characteristically, an idealistic reason. He was obsessed with the notion that one candidate had to be an anti-Klan man. Bouanchaud was willing to denounce the Klan and advocate legislation to control it, and hence he fitted Parker's specifications. Only a politician of Parker's impracticality and integrity could have placed such a candidate on such a platform.[3]

For a time it seemed that Bouanchaud would have to face the competition of a candidate from his own area of strength, the southern parishes. Still another aspirant offered himself—Dudley Guilbeau of St. Landry parish. Guilbeau was a short, dumpy man who spoke English with a marked French accent and who had the looks and manner of a typical south Louisiana country politician. His appeal was strictly local, and when he failed to draw any organizational support, he withdrew, endorsed Bouanchaud, and became the latter's campaign manager. Guilbeau was a Catholic and bitterly anti-Klan, and his presence in the Bouanchaud camp influenced the candidate to emphasize the Klan issue to the neglect of all others.[4]

Throughout the summer months the candidates and their principal backers were busy lining up the support of sheriffs and courthouse rings and negotiating for an endorsement from one of the New Orleans factions. The city machines did not formally reveal their

[3] New Orleans *Item*, January 6 and 24, 1924; Hermann B. Deutsch.
[4] Hermann B. Deutsch; New Orleans *Times-Picayune*, October 4, 1923.

choices until September, after all the candidates had announced, but by late summer it was known how they would go. The Old Regulars, obviously on the comeback—they would later elect Behrman mayor —settled on Fuqua. Behrman was impressed by the Baton Rouge man's country support; he thought that Fuqua was a relatively tolerant Protestant who was anti-Klan but not so violently so that he would turn the campaign into a religious fight, and he was certain that Bouanchaud had no chance. And even if Behrman had been disposed to favor Bouanchaud, he would have been reluctant to join forces with Parker. The New Regulars, after some hesitation, endorsed Bouanchaud. Sullivan did not like the Frenchman and thought that he was a weak candidate. But after the Choctaws came out for Fuqua, the New Regulars had no choice but to line up behind Bouanchaud. Their fumbling approach to the situation indicated that Sullivan did not have a very tight control over his leaders.[5]

The New Regulars were having other internal problems. In June they had lost a part of their organization. A number of leaders seceded and announced the formation of a new faction, the Independent Regulars. The Independent chiefs were the Williams boys, John St. Paul, Jr., scion of an aristocratic Creole family and son of a supreme court justice; Thomas I. O'Connor, superintendent of the courthouse building; and Richard Dowling, judge of a criminal district court. Political forecasters immediately guessed that the new machine had been formed to support Huey and that the recently withdrawn candidate would soon return to the race. The expected announcement was not long in coming. On August 17 Huey checked in at the Monteleone Hotel in New Orleans and met the press. He revealed that he would formally announce on August 30, his birthday, when he would be thirty years old and eligible for the office. He also made a statement that showed what he hoped would be the issue of the campaign. "The Standard Oil Company and other predatory corporations will not be permitted to rule Louisiana," he said.[6]

By late August it was evident that the race was going to be among three candidates, Fuqua, Bouanchaud, and Long. Guilbeau had not yet withdrawn, but he shortly would. Of the three candidates, Fuqua had the strongest organized support. He had the Old Regulars, who were certain to roll out a big vote for him in New Orleans, powerful state leaders like Sanders and Pleasant, and more sheriffs and courthouse rings than any other candidate. He was expected to garner the

[5] Reynolds: *Machine Politics*, pp. 218–19; New Orleans *Times-Picayune*, September 4, 1923; Marshall Ballard, article in New Orleans *Item*, February 3, 1924.
[6] New Orleans *Times-Picayune*, June 6 and August 17, 1923.

moderate anti-Klan vote, the people who would be satisfied with regulatory legislation, and also the moderate Klan vote, those Klansmen who thought that they could live with an antimasking law and who preferred something like this to the more stringent measures Bouanchaud might be able to enact. Bouanchaud had the New Regulars, who probably would not carry New Orleans but who could send him out of it with a respectable vote, a number of sheriffs in the southern parishes, and Governor Parker, who presumably could command some votes in the north. Bouanchaud could rely on receiving the extreme anti-Klan vote, those people in the south, Catholic or otherwise, who wanted the Klan denounced and who demanded legislation outlawing it.

Long had the least organized support. He had some sheriffs—a September survey revealed seven for him, fourteen for Fuqua, and ten for Bouanchaud—and some local officials. He also had some local "out" leaders who hoped to overthrow the "in" courthouse crowd by attaching themselves to Huey. His country backers could be found in every part of the state, but he had nothing resembling a country parish organization. Those officials who supported him did so because they liked him personally or what he stood for or because they hoped to rise with him. He had a large personal following, people who admired him for fighting the corporations, but whether substantial numbers of them would vote depended almost completely on the intensity of their devotion. It was thought at the beginning of the campaign that Huey would have the extreme Klan vote, but this surmise had no more basis than an assumption that the Klan parishes would support a north Louisianian. Only in New Orleans did Huey have a semblance of an organization, and it was little more than a semblance. Seasoned observers did not think that the Williamses and their Independent Regulars could turn out many votes for Huey. Huey did not think so either, but he thought that he did not need many votes in New Orleans. He told the Williamses: "Give me a handful of city votes—no more than 15,000, and I'm as good as elected. Just wait and see what I'll do in the country."[7]

A week before Huey was to announce his entry, the state was flooded with Long circulars. Lacking much newspaper support, Huey

[7] Hermann B. Deutsch: "Kingdom of the Kingfish," in New Orleans *Item,* August 2 and 3, 1939; article on sources of strength of the candidates, in New Orleans *Times-Picayune,* September 30, 1923, and articles by Marshall Ballard, New Orleans *Item,* December 22, 1922, January 9, 1924; Shirley G. Wimberly; Charles Frampton; Paul Maloney. The Old and New Regulars had organizations in the parishes and towns surrounding New Orleans and their influence extended somewhat beyond the city.

was going to employ right at the beginning the use of circulars, which had stood him in such good stead in his race for the Public Service Commission. The circulars were sent through the mails. An estimated hundred thousand envelopes, each containing four to five circulars, were mailed, reaching an audience of over four hundred thousand. The documents contained reprints of newspaper editorials praising Long for his fight against the Cumberland Telephone Company. It was the state's introduction to the system of campaigning with circulars, and the conservative press reacted with nervous irritability. The New Orleans *Item* said that it was a pity a young man of Huey's "indomitable impudence and occasional industry" was blighted with a streak of demagoguery, and it styled the candidate "The Prince of Piffle."[8]

On August 30 Huey attended a small birthday party in his honor at the office of Gus Williams in New Orleans. His friends presented him with a platinum-mounted, jeweled elk's tooth. In accepting it, he stressed that the Elks was the only fraternal order of which he was a member. He then handed out to reporters, who had been invited, a typed statement announcing his candidacy. It was a remarkable document—abounding in long and awkward sentences and polysyllabic words. The opening sentences read: "This state shows every need for a constructive administration, devoted to the protection and expansion of labor and capital, industry and agriculture, all working toward the efficiency of our courts, public schools, freedom in religious beliefs, and reduction in taxation and burdens of government, and toward liberating our state and our institutions from the ever growing modern tendency of monopoly and concentration of power. Our present state government has descended into one of deplorable, misunderstood orgy, of frequent corporate dictations, mingled with bewildering cataclysms of various criminations and recriminations amongst the personal satellites of the governor and the beneficiaries of the immense public plunder which he has dispensed." As an example of the plunder, the statement charged in a typical sentence that the department of conservation had spent huge sums on "a horde of useless patronage."

This composite of pompous nonsense was not Huey's way of speaking. Either somebody else had written the statement for him, or, if he wrote it, he had been convinced by some adviser that as a candidate he must utter dignified platitudes. It occasioned a good deal of ridicule. The *Picayune*, in an editorial entitled "Boom! Boom!,"

[8] New Orleans *Item*, August 30, 1923, and New Orleans *Times-Picayune*, August 31, 1923; Douthit: "Governorship of Long," p. 28; Huey P. Long: *Every Man a King* (New Orleans, 1933), pp. 71–3.

chortled: "There is a warlike spirit in the polysyllabic Huey and blood is on the moon that shines so fair these August nights of 1923. Why not? Huey, who is thirty this August 30, 1923, was twenty-three in April, 1917! The spirit of the times contaged him finally."⁹

Two days later Huey opened his campaign in a speech at Shreveport's city hall. If he delivered the version of the speech that was printed, he must have bored the audience with his recital of facts and figures. He probably used only selected portions. In large part an announcement of his platform, the speech was intended for newspaper reproduction and circulation as a pamphlet. He came out for a road construction program ("We continue to wade in the mud where we had expected asphalt"), increased state support for public schools, free textbooks (supplied by the state) for school children, improvement and enlargement of the court system, and state warehouses and cold-storage depositories to enable farmers to hold their products pending a good market. Although state services were to be increased, taxes would be lowered by eliminating extravagance. He approved the right of labor to organize, and he condemned the use of injunctions in labor disputes, corporate influence on government, and concentrated wealth (the "bloated plutocracy" of two per cent owned sixty-five per cent of the wealth). He denounced Governor Parker for moving LSU from its old campus ("these buildings for which we hold dear memories") and for building an expensive new agricultural college to teach fancy ways of farming. He vowed opposition to any form of supergovernment, whether it was capital, labor, or the Klan. "I am not," he said, "a member of any secret order of any kind or character, nor have I ever been. I have never been requested to join nor have I applied for membership in any of them." It was not the best speech he was capable of giving, but for what it was intended to be, it sufficed. He had said what he stood for—an increased role for the state government in the economy—and if he decided to denounce in his own style the things he had said he was against, blood might indeed appear on the moon.¹

⁹ New Orleans *Times-Picayune*, August 31, 1923; Deutsch: "Kingdom of the Kingfish," in New Orleans *Item*, August 2, 1939.

¹ New Orleans *States*, September 1, 1923; *Speech and Platform of Huey P. Long* (pamphlet, n.p., n.d.), in Long Scrapbooks, I. Of the issues raised by Long in his speech, one of the most popular would be the promise of free textbooks. Where Huey got the idea or why he proposed it is not certain, although several neighboring states supplied free books, and Huey could easily have known of their practice. Harley B. Bozeman, in *Winn Parish Enterprise*, April 17, 1958, claimed that he and a cousin of Huey's thought up the free-books issue to aid the campaign of a candidate in Winn parish who was running for the legislature. They sent copies of their plan to Huey, who was out on the stump, and Huey adopted it. But as Huey had previously

As he entered the campaign, Huey at the age of thirty looked very much as he did the rest of his life. He was about five feet eleven in height and weighed around 160 pounds; in later years he would have to fight a tendency to put on weight. His features were a cartoonist's delight—exaggerated, comic, and yet impressive. The nose was fleshy, almost bulbous, and tilted up impudently. The face was full, inclining to jowliness, the mouth wide, and the chin cut by a deep cleft or a dimple that gave him when smiling a pixylike mien. His hair was reddish-brown and unruly, and one curling forelock dipped down across his forehead. His eyes were brown, and in personal conversation he had a habit of thrusting his head forward and staring intently at his listener. Some part of him was always in motion. He waved his hands, hunched his shoulders, rocked on his heels, or scratched at a leg. The same nervous energy pervaded his "walking." No one who describes him ever says that Huey walked. The usual expression is something like: "Huey came running up." As he walked, or ran, he threw out his legs to the side in an odd movement. A man who knew him well and studied him closely thus described his gait: "He walked like a sidling pony, sort of paced, like a jake-leg nigger." If he was walking with a group, he scurried ahead of the pack.[2]

He still had not developed much taste in choosing clothes. His customary attire in the campaign was a gray suit, a black bow tie, and white shoes and socks. His trousers and shoes did not meet, and to one man who saw him he looked like "a dressed-up country boy." But Huey thought that he dressed in high style, and using the same psychology that he had in his Public Service Commission race, he deliberately sought to impress on his followers that he was their leader by displaying his splendor. The diamond that he had bought in New York glittered from a ring, and somehow he had acquired another stone that sparkled from his shirt front. His appearance might have offended the sensibilities of people of the better class, but now and then a member of it would see him and sense that behind the bizarre exterior was a distinctly uncommon man. "I was a young lawyer," one of them recalled of that time, "and when Huey Long walked into

discussed free books in his Shreveport speech, though only in passing, Mr. Bozeman is clearly mistaken, at least as to time. It is possible that Huey did not realize initially what a good issue he had hit on and was impressed with the fact by popular reaction and the urging of friends like Bozeman.

[2] David B. McConnell; Jess Nugent; Lucille Long Hunt; Mason Spencer; William Wiegand; Hermann B. Deutsch: "Paradox in Pajamas," *Saturday Evening Post,* CCVIII (October 5, 1935), 14; Kane: *Louisiana Hayride,* p. 40; Mildred Adams: "Huey the Great," *Forum,* LXXXIX (February 1933), 71; Forrest Davis: *Huey Long: A Candid Biography* (New York, 1935), pp. 25–6.

the court building at Royal and Conti, the whole building would sort of catch on fire."[3]

It took a lot of money to finance a gubernatorial campaign. A candidate had to travel all over the state to speak, appearing in every important center at least once; he had to pay the expenses of other speakers; he had to bear the costs of newspaper advertising and other printed materials; and he had to reward his workers and commissioners. Fuqua and Bouanchaud were well supplied with money. They received initial contributions from the organizations and leaders supporting them. In addition, as the campaign progressed, they were given large sums by rich individuals who admired them or who hoped to secure something in return. Thus Bouanchaud secured donations from wealthy men even in north Louisiana, and Fuqua had important backers in the oil industry. In comparison, Huey had a very modest campaign chest. He got some money from members of his family, who thought that he was trying for the office too soon but who supported him, and from Winnfield friends like O. K. Allen and H. B. Bozeman. He received many small, voluntary contributions from followers and workers. Leaders of the Independent Regulars put up what they could; for example, John St. Paul, Jr., advanced two thousand dollars. But Huey also had some big backers. His friend and client, Ernest Bernstein, provided forty-six hundred dollars. Swords Lee of Alexandria, a distant cousin who was a wealthy lumberman and a Klan leader, contributed and raised several thousand dollars. William K. Henderson of Shreveport, operator of a large foundry and machine shop and owner of a pioneer radio station, raised ten thousand dollars and gave Huey a good deal of free publicity over the air. Julius Long later claimed that the Southwestern Gas Company of Shreveport presented Huey with ten thousand dollars in return for a rate concession, but Huey denied the charge. Some of these men supported Huey because they honestly admired him. Others hoped to control him if elected or to get something out of him. They did not, however, feel entirely comfortable in their association with a man with such a reputation for radicalism. "Huey is not as bad as a lot of them say," Will Henderson said in a curious defense, "and not all they say of him is true."[4]

[3] New Orleans *Times-Picayune*, September 21, 1923, account of meeting at Franklinton; Henry D. Larcade; Deutsch: "Paradox in Pajamas," *Saturday Evening Post*, October 5, 1935, p. 36; Lester Lautenschlaeger.

[4] Clara Long Knott; Long to Frank Odom, December 26, 1923, acknowledging a contribution of twenty-five dollars (letter in possession of Frank Odom, Baton Rouge); John St. Paul, Jr.; Long to Bernstein, December 30, 1924, in Long Papers, Law File; New Orleans *Item*, September 4, 1923, and Marshall Ballard, article, ibid.,

Although Huey did not have as much money as his two rivals, he had more than has been suspected and certainly enough to run a respectable campaign. It would take money to wage the kind of campaign he planned. He intended to speak in every town and to plaster the state with his circulars. Some of the circulars were mailed from his home or law office in Shreveport, but he put up many of them himself. He bought a car, a Hupmobile, and asked his brother-in-law, Dave McConnell, to accompany him as a driver and helper. With McConnell doing most of the driving, they crisscrossed the state, the car filled with circulars and posters. When they came to a town, they would ask the owners of stores and shops for permission to place posters in windows. Huey liked to line windows in barber shops with posters, on the theory that customers would have to sit and look at his picture and would remember him. He and McConnell were always permitted to hang their materials, but if they happened to return to a town a few days later they frequently found that the posters had been torn down. This happened most often in south Louisiana, and Huey blamed the Old Regulars or other Fuqua adherents. He also discovered that his posters were being removed from buildings and trees along the road. So he resorted to the device of gluing the posters on windows, and on the road he would drive close to a tall tree, climb on top of the car, and with a long hammer put a poster up above the reach of any hands.[5]

At every town he visited, Huey made a speech, and he appeared twice in some places. McConnell estimated that Huey held 120 meetings. On an average day Huey would speak at several towns, put up posters and distribute circulars, confer with local leaders, and shake hands with dozens of people. He would stay up till one or two o'clock in the morning and rise before dawn to drive to the next town. One day in New Orleans he toured the industrial plants, shook hands with a thousand workers, made several speeches, and ended his activities by going into a newspaper office and, to prove to the employees that he had once been a printer's devil, setting some type. He spoke outside, standing on the street, or inside, usually in a courthouse. Before appearing in a town to speak, he would advertise his coming by having his local leaders hand out dodgers announcing the time and place. Sometimes he had no leaders, and on such an occasion the crowd would be small. He addressed audiences of less than a hundred, of

December 9, 1923; Harvey G. Fields: *A True History of the Life, Works, Assassination and Death of Huey P. Long* (Silver Spring, Md., 1944), p. 27; *Overton Hearing,* I, 953.

[5] David B. McConnell; Long: *Every Man a King,* pp. 73–5; Vernon Parenton.

more than a hundred, and in the larger cities, of several thousand. Sometimes Mrs. Long accompanied him and mingled with the crowd to get their reaction and report it to him.[6]

At this stage of his career Huey had some things to learn about the art of public speaking. He tended to gesticulate too much, distracting his hearers by slicing the air with his arms. He had a good voice, resonant and clear, but when he became excited, he raised it too high, so that it sounded raucous. Some of his platform habits that offended urban audiences captivated his country hearers. He would pace up and down with what a New Orleans reporter called a "panther tread." As he talked on, he would rumple his hair, take off his coat and his tie, and loosen his collar and shirt. A woman who saw him at a meeting later said to one of his supporters: "I liked your friend, but I was worried. I didn't know what he was going to take off next."[7] His strenuous actions on the platform, repeated several times a day and day after day, finally told on him—even though he had such extraordinary energy. His voice became hoarse, and at several meetings it was inaudible toward the end of his speech. In the last phase of the campaign he resorted to the radio. In January he broadcast over station WCAG in New Orleans. The station's owner said there were eight thousand sets in the city, and if only half of them were tuned in, with five listeners each, Huey would reach an audience of twenty thousand. Huey thus became one of the first politicians in Louisiana to utilize the new medium. He grasped immediately its capacity to reach large numbers and would use it increasingly in the future.[8]

Right from the start, Huey's speeches were attacks. He attacked the local bosses in whatever parish he was in, the state bosses, such as Parker, Sanders, and Pleasant, the New Orleans machines, the

---

[6] David B. McConnell; New Orleans *States*, December 19, 1923; Waldo H. Dugas; W. V. Larcade; Ernest Clements; New Orleans *Item*, February 16, 1936. It is conjectured that when Huey addressed crowds of two to four thousand persons, as he did in New Orleans, he used a microphone or some other amplifying mechanism. He would employ such devices in his campaign four years later.

[7] New Orleans *Times-Picayune*, September 21, 1923; Arthur Marvin Shaw: "The First Time I Saw Huey," *Southwest Review*, XXXV (1950), 60–1; Mrs. Gaston Porterie. Dr. Shaw described Huey as a wooden and uninspiring speaker who did not know what issues would move his audience. Because Shaw was an academic observer, his description is often cited as an accurate analysis of Huey's early speech habits. It is, however, sharply at variance with the recollections of others and with contemporary accounts. Possibly Shaw saw Huey when the latter was having a poor day. Or, more probably, Shaw was influenced by Robert Penn Warren's novel, *All the King's Men* (New York, 1946). Shaw's depiction of Huey Long is suspiciously similar to Warren's description of Willie Stark in his first campaign.

[8] New Orleans *Item*, November 12, 1923; New Orleans *States*, January 4, 1924.

New Orleans press, and the corporations. The outraged victims invariably fell into his trap. They replied in such shrill, violent language that many people thought Huey's charges must be true. The exchanges gave Huey more publicity and contributed to the image he had created of an idealistic young reformer beset by powerful and greedy foes. As an initial target, he picked on Standard Oil. He charged that the company had made a deal with the Sultan of Turkey to import Turkish oil to Louisiana refineries. Why, he demanded to know, was Standard favoring "the Crescent over the children of Moses," and why did it prefer to help a foreign ruler at the expense of the poor and the needy of Louisiana? The answer was obvious—the company was an arrogant corporate power. It was, in fact, so arrogant that it thought it could defeat him. Its vice-president, C. K. Clarke, was sending emissaries all over the state to instruct businessmen that Standard forbade them to support Huey Long.[9] Just as arrogant was the New Orleans press, the lying big city newspapers. Their corporate owners told them what lies to print, Huey revealed. The *Item* was owned by Wall Street interests, and the *Picayune* was controlled by New York bankers and by Esmond Phelps of New Orleans, attorney for the Western Union Telegraph Company and the Texas and Pacific Railroad. The special butt of Huey's gibes was the *Item*, which pilloried him mercilessly, and its clever political editor, Marshall Ballard, who could write things that got under Huey's skin. "There is as much honor in the New Orleans *Item* as there is in the heel of a flea," Huey once cried, and he characterized Ballard as the "Imperial Wizard of Pen-pushers."[1]

The principal theme of Huey's attacks was that his two opponents and everybody opposed to him were in reality working together, that the whole crowd was controlled by the same corporate interests. Fuqua and Bouanchaud had both been put into the race by Parker —they were the "Parker Gold Dust Twins." Behrman and Sullivan, the supposed enemies, were both henchmen of Wall Street: "If Behrman took a dose of laudanum, Sullivan would get sleepy in ten minutes." The same families had run the state for years—Sanders, Pleasant, Fuqua, Bouanchaud, and others: they just swapped power from administration to administration.[2] These sallies were only a sophisticated version of his high popalorum and low popahirum illus-

[9] New Orleans *States*, September 4, 1923; New Orleans *Times-Picayune*, September 6, 1923.

[1] New Orleans *Item*, September 19 and December 19, 1923.

[2] New Orleans *Item*, October 29, 1923; Shreveport *Times*, December 3, 1923; New Orleans *Times-Picayune*, December 19 and 21, 1923.

tration, but he thought the technique was so effective that at a high point in the campaign he planned to demolish his opponents with it. The three candidates had been invited to appear at a huge rally on Armistice Day at Lafayette Square in New Orleans. With Fuqua and Bouanchaud seated on the platform with him, Huey was going to tell this story: A man who owned some guineas was annoyed by their constant cackling. He determined to produce a new and quieter type. Taking two guinea eggs, he placed one under a turkey and one under a blue hen. He expected that when hatched, one would be a cross between a turkey and a guinea, and the other, between a hen and a guinea and that the resulting products would not cackle. But when the eggs broke, both disclosed guineas. Huey was going to conclude by pointing at his rivals, both products of the nest of John M. Parker, one hatched by Behrman and one by Sullivan, and both cackling like Parker. But Fuqua and Bouanchaud, probably not wanting to confront Long, did not appear, sending their regrets at the last minute. Huey told his story anyway to the crowd of four thousand, but without his targets there it lost something of its effect.[3]

The effrontery of Huey's attacks threw his opponents off balance. Clarke of Standard Oil sputtered that Huey's "vaporings are usually of as much moment as the braying of an ass or the yelping of a locoed coyote." Former governor Pleasant, exhausting his arsenal of abuse, declared that Huey was "a pompous, inflated, chesty, loose-mouthed, rattle-trap" who had "a demagogical and Bolshevistic tendency." The Bolshevik had blackmailed the Southwestern Gas Company into giving him a contribution, Pleasant charged. Moreover, Huey had come dangerously close to treason during the World War; his "tortuous tongue" had "giggled fast and hissed so loud" that the secret service had placed him under watch.[4] Denunciations almost as venomous came from the conservative press. Most papers took the line that he was a radical demogogue and unprincipled liar. Not in the last twenty years, said the *Picayune*, had a candidate appeared whose public utterances were "so shot through with gross error, so irresponsibly perversive of the public record, so careless of truth generally." The *Item* more wisely employed the weapon of ridicule. Its cartoonist, Trist Wood, who was something of a genius, consistently portrayed Huey in a jester costume, the Prince of Piffle, accompanied by two insipid little girls, Fanny and Gussie, representing the Williams brothers. Huey, who could appreciate ability in an opponent, ad-

---

[3] New Orleans *Times-Picayune*, November 12 and 13, 1923; Long: *Every Man a King*, pp. 75–7.

[4] New Orleans *Times-Picayune*, September 8, 22, 23, and 27, 1923.

mired the cartoons. He decided that if he ever had a newspaper of his own, he would hire Trist to work for him.[5]

Although the emphasis in Huey's speeches was on whom he was against, he also discussed what he was for. He was for making the corporations obey the laws and pay their share of the taxes ("and when I am governor I will make them do it"). He was for free text-books. ("They are changing text books in Louisiana every year. They are costing our parents millions.") He was for "better schools, better institutions of every kind." He was for bringing natural gas to New Orleans, and he was for a fair deal for labor. ("I come from the common people and I am a friend of labor.") He was going to improve state services and at the same time reduce taxes. He would accomplish this feat by cutting out fraud and eliminating useless employees: while institutions were suffering for money, the state hired fifty-three "coon chasers" to harass poor men during the hunting season. Even as hostile a critic as the *Item* had to concede that Huey was the only one of the three candidates who talked about economic issues and offered a positive program.[6]

Huey had to endure some embarrassing moments in the campaign. He had to face small crowds and apathetic or restless ones, and at some of his meetings in New Orleans he had to deal with hecklers or booers. These sessions degenerated into shouting contests. Thus at his Armistic Day appearance he paid tribute to the men of the American Legion for overthrowing Prussianism. Before he could continue, some people in the audience began to chant: "Where were you then?" Huey should have ignored them, but he lost his head. "Well, I can take care of any one of you, anyway," he yelled. One of his supporters on the platform jumped up and added his threat: "And if he can't there's plenty here that can."[7]

But the worst episode occurred in September, when Huey was scheduled to make his first appearance in New Orleans at the Athenaeum building. Three nights before the meeting a motorcycle

[5] Baton Rouge *Morning News*, September 6, 1923; Baton Rouge *State-Times*, September 1, 7, and 8, 1923; New Orleans *Times-Picayune*, September 19, 1923; New Orleans *Item*, September 20, 1923; confidential communication. Some of the reporting of Huey's meetings in the New Orleans papers were hardly models of objectivity. Typical *Picayune* headlines were "Long Finds Crowd Cool"; "Mansfield Audience Hears His Usual Line of Invective, His Speech Was Along the Usual Lines"; issues of October 22 and November 20, 1923.

[6] New Orleans *States*, September 19 and December 17, 1923; New Orleans *Times-Picayune*, October 29 and 31, December 19, 1923; Shreveport *Times*, December 3, 1923; New Orleans *Item*, November 26, 1923.

[7] New Orleans *Times-Picayune*, November 12, 1923; New Orleans *Item*, November 12, 1923.

patrolman, Oliver Barrios, was on duty on the Shell Road leading from the west end of the city, which was then the red-light district. He spotted a car roaring down the road at a speed far above the limit and gave chase. On overhauling the car, he found in it two men, the driver and Gus Williams. Gus hastily explained that the car was his, that the driver was his chauffeur, and that they were racing to fill an engagement. If Barrios would not arrest the chauffeur, Gus would appear at court in the morning and pay his fine. But Barrios knew his duty. He took both men to the nearest precinct station and booked the chauffeur for speeding. Gus gave the driver's name as Harold Swan. The next morning Gus appeared in traffic court as Swan's attorney and paid the fine. There the matter might have ended. But by coincidence Barrios was one of the officers assigned to handle traffic in front of the Athenaeum at the rally. He had heard a great deal about Huey and was eager to see him. As the candidate and his party approached the door, Barrios asked another officer which one was Long. The colleague pointed to Huey. "No, not that one," Barrios snorted. "I know him. That's Harold Swan, Gus Williams' chauffeur. I ought to know. I arrested him the other night."

The news Barrios dropped spread rapidly to the reporters. It was too juicy an item to keep from the public. They immediately sought out Gus Williams. Gus insisted that the arrested man had been Harold Swan and added some details about the incident. He had been "partaking" of a fish dinner at the Moulin Rouge restaurant when he suddenly remembered that he had an engagement with his wife. As his own car was laid up, he borrowed Huey's. But Huey had not been at the Moulin Rouge, Gus emphasized. Other guests at the restaurant that night, however, recalled that Huey had been there with Gus and had consumed a lot of liquor and had bounced around from table to table inviting people to attend his inaugural ball in May. The city papers had a field day with the episode. They suggested that since Gus had said Long was not at the restaurant, Huey's astral body must have greeted the diners. The cartoonists began to portray Huey as always being followed by a fish. Trist Wood created a new creature —a bird with a long neck and Huey's face—whose ancestry was a combination of Swan and Long and was therefore a Swong. A hilarious poem in the *Item* concluded:

> That demon chauffeur, Who was he?
> On this the public disagree;
> Some give his name as "Harold Long."
> And others say 'twas "Huey Swong."

Huey was deeply resentful of the way the newspapers played up the story, and he made the mistake of betraying his feelings. Questioned by reporters for his version, he snapped: "Go to Hell! I have only that answer for all questions by newspapers." Actually, although he felt he had been humiliated, he was probably helped more than hurt by the incident. People in the French-Catholic southern parishes savored good food and drink and fun, and they could appreciate a politician who liked the same things. Even in the puritanical northern parishes, men would admire, though secretly, Huey's escapade. After all, he had done only what they would like to do: Doggone it, did you hear how ole Huey's been kicking up his heels down in the city?[8]

Huey's rural followers of the north could understand his deviation from the moral code. But they could not understand his position on one of the important issues of the campaign, an issue that, as the canvass progressed, tended to take precedence over all others. Nor were people in other parts of the state satisfied with Huey's stand on this question. This was the Klan issue, the one that Huey had foreseen at the start would give him trouble. Try as he might, he could not surmount it, and his efforts to avoid it cost him an undeterminable number of votes.

Commentators on the election commonly say that Huey was caught in the middle on the Klan issue. The statement is misleading in that it implies Huey was a moderate standing between two extremes, Klan and anti-Klan. Both the other candidates were anti-Klan. Bouanchaud was violently and vociferously anti; he discussed no other issue and charged Fuqua with having Klan support. Fuqua was temperately anti; he mostly delivered platitudes and denied that he was the Klan candidate. Both of them endorsed at the start of the campaign legislation forbidding the wearing of masks on public highways and other properties and requiring secret organizations to file lists of their membership. The Klan candidate at first was supposed to be Huey, who was from the Klan country of the north. In fact, it was charged then, and later, that he was a member of the organization. He was not, although somebody, perhaps his backer Swords Lee, may have made him an honorary member of the Alexandria klavern. The supposition that Huey would get the Klan vote merely because he was from the north had a questionable basis. The Klan membership of that area was extremely conservative, and some of its

---

[8] Deutsch: "Kingdom of the Kingfish," in New Orleans *Item*, August 3, 1939; New Orleans *Item*, September 21 and 25, 1923; New Orleans *Times-Picayune*, September 21 and 25, 1923. The newspaper accounts say that the car, a new Buick, was Huey's. If the identification was accurate, Huey must have acquired another car.

*Huey Long on left with his sister Lucille and his brother Earl*

Courtesy of Hurley B. Bozeman

*Huey and Rose McConnell Long at the time of their marriage*

*The Long family home in Winnfield, built in 1907 by Huey's father*

Mrs. Drew Nelson Hays in Louisiana:
Sketches of Historical Homes and Sights

The cover of an LSU song sheet, music written by Huey Long in collaboration with bandmaster Castro Carazo

A typical Long speaking schedule. Such handbills outlined his appearances during a campaign

*With retiring governor O. H. Simpson, May 1928*

*(opposite) Long making his inaugural address as governor of Louisiana*

## Dropping the Pilot

*The Young Kaiser Sends His Iron Chancellor Over the Side*

*Chase, in the New Orleans Item*

When Long dismissed his autocratic backer, Colonel Ewing, a New Orleans cartoonist likened it to Wilhelm II's dropping of Bismarck

*(opposite) Long with the commander of the German cruiser* Emden *and Commodore Ernest Lee Jahncke at the time of the Green Pajamas episode*

*Long before an LSU football train*

*Office of Information Services, Louisiana State University*

The governor and some LSU campus queens

(opposite) August 29, 1932. Clad in a cotton nightshirt, on a cotton mattress with cotton sheets and blankets, Long signs the No-Crop Bill forbidding cotton planting during the coming year

Huey on the gridiron before a game between LSU and Arkansas

*Reviewing the Louisiana National Guard*

*(opposite) The Kingfish descending the steps of a parish courthouse in a Louisiana country town*

*A gathering of Long's enemies as drawn by Trist Wood, a young cartoonist Long hired from the New Orleans* Item *to work for* Louisiana Progress

The nation's cartoonists had a field day after Huey's encounter in the washroom at Sands Point

Louisiana state senate impeachment hearings. On Long's left, John Overton and Lewis Morgan, two of his eight lawyers; on his right, Representative Perrault of the House Board of Managers, who conducted the investigation of Long's alleged election rigging

leaders were wealthy oil men who detested Huey for his attacks on business. Whether a leader or an average member, a Klansman was likely to regard Huey as a wild radical. He probably would not have secured much of a Klan vote even if he had made some gesture to the organization.[9]

Huey offered no gesture. And he made but a faint and reluctant gesture to the anti-Klan vote. In his early speeches he again said only that he was opposed to any form of supergovernment. He doubted that any additional legislation was needed. An existing law (the one of 1872) forbade the wearing of masks, and it was ineffective. "Why have two of them?" he asked. Subjected to great pressure from the newspapers to declare his position, and probably also from some of his supporters, he finally announced that he would support anti-masking and antisecrecy legislation.[1] But after delivering this affirmation, he dropped the issue and hardly discussed it during the rest of the campaign. "They say the state is seething in the throes of a religious war but I refuse to become embroiled," he said. "I am interested in too many things that have to do with the lives, happiness and conveniences of our people, with the problems of education, roads, levees and equally important matters." Fuqua and Bouanchaud had no issue but Klan and anti-Klan, he charged, and the only difference between them was that Bouanchaud wanted to hang the Klansmen before the election and Fuqua wanted them to vote for him first and then hang them. Huey was caught in the middle of the Klan fight only in the sense that he tried to avoid the issue. As the candidate with the least organized support, he felt that he could not afford to take a stand. If he was anti, he lost votes in his own north; if he was pro, he lost the populous south. But expediency alone did not determine his action. Above any reasons of the moment, Huey thought that any issue of religion or race was an artificial one in politics. It sidetracked consideration of more important issues and interfered with the main business of politics. "I have never stepped aside to denounce a Klansman or anti-Klansman," he said later. He did not mean that he had no objections to intolerance. As a matter of fact, he detested the Klan,

[9] Jess Nugent; David B. McConnell; Rupert Peyton. The number of Klan members and hence Klan voters in the state has been estimated, without very much evidence, at fifty thousand. It was probably closer to twenty-five thousand. See the careful estimate in Kenneth Harrell: "The Ku Klux Klan in Louisiana, 1920–1930" (unpublished Ph.D. dissertation, Louisiana State University, 1966).

[1] New Orleans *Times-Picayune*, September 5, 1923, quoted in Douthit: "Governorship of Long," pp. 29–30; New Orleans *Item*, September 6, 7, 11, and 12, 1923; New Orleans *Times-Picayune*, September 11 and 13, 1923; New Orleans *States*, September 19, 1923.

but primarily he regarded it as a nuisance, a hindrance to his plans. To him the only issues that mattered were ones of economics—and power.[2]

But he could not escape the Klan question. Just when he thought he had, a member of his family brought him back to it. Late in the campaign Dr. George Long reappeared in Louisiana and joined Huey's caravan in Bossier parish in the northwest. George had just resigned from the Oklahoma legislature—had been forced to resign, it was reputed, because he had accepted money to secure pardons for two men convicted of election frauds. George was a known Klansman and had run for the Oklahoma legislature as a Klan candidate. Immediately the Louisiana press speculated that he had returned to help Huey by using his influence with local Klan leaders. Huey issued a defensive statement in which he said he had evidence that George was innocent of the charges against him, that George had merely ridden from town to town with him, and that he could not be held responsible for what societies his brother belonged to. Huey was willing to let George accompany him in Klan country. But when "Shan" attempted to follow him to south Louisiana, Huey had had enough. "You get the hell back to Oklahoma," he ordered.[3]

Then, a few days before the election, copies of a document purporting to show that Huey was a member of the Klan began to circulate in north Louisiana. The document was a reproduction of a membership certificate, and Huey's name appeared on it in indelible pencil, although on a certificate the name was supposed to be engrossed. Almost immediately an advertisement in an Alexandria newspaper labeled the document as a forgery. The ad was inserted by Fuqua supporters who were obviously Klansmen. The signers pointed out the inconsistency in the form of the name and swore that state and national Klan records showed that Huey was not and never had been a member. All loyal Klansmen should repudiate Long, the perpetrator of the forgery, and vote for Fuqua, the ad concluded. Although some people thought that Huey had put out the false documents, the conclusion of most observers was that the Fuqua people were responsible for them. The appearance of the certificates, followed by evidence presented by Fuqua supporters that they were

[2] New Orleans *Times-Picayune*, December 16 and 21, 1923; New Orleans *Item*, December 21, 1923; Long, circular, 1934, in Richard W. Leche Scrapbooks, Department of Archives and Manuscripts, Louisiana State University.

[3] New Orleans *Times-Picayune*, December 1, 1923; New Orleans *Item*, December 6 and 11, 1923; David B. McConnell.

fraudulent, was calculated to injure Huey with Klansmen, and the late release of the documents gave him no time to counteract the effect. The incident lost him an estimated five thousand votes. The Klan leaders had determined to throw their vote to Fuqua, who was only moderately anti and preferable to Bouanchaud and who had a generally conservative outlook that coincided with theirs. O. B. Thompson, Huey's friend and a charter Klan member, attended a special meeting in Shreveport on the eve of the election. There, over Thompson's opposition, the decision was made—the word was to be passed down to vote for Fuqua and not to vote for Huey.[4]

As election day approached, the political prophets of the press began to issue their forecasts. Marshall Ballard of the *Item* said in late December that Huey ought to get out of the race while he could. The "quaint fakir" would not get more than twenty-five hundred votes in New Orleans, Ballard observed happily, and would carry only six small parishes. A *Picayune* prediction of January, based on a sample poll, showed Huey running somewhat better but offered no cause for alarm. Bouanchaud would lead with seventy-seven thousand votes, Fuqua would follow with sixty-three thousand votes, and Long would trail badly with forty-nine thousand votes. A revised *Item* estimate of the same month gave Bouanchaud ninety-five thousand and Fuqua ninety-two thousand and put Long way back with fifty-three thousand.[5]

After these comforting assurances, the results of the election on January 15 came as a real shock to conservative Louisiana. Bouanchaud, with 84,162 votes, led the field. Right behind him was Fuqua with 81,382 votes. And close behind Fuqua was Huey, with the unexpected total of 73,985. Since no candidate had a majority, the first two, Bouanchaud and Fuqua, would have to face each other in a second primary in February. But at the moment nobody gave much thought to the runoff; Fuqua, who would pick up most of Long's north Louisiana following, was obviously going to win it. It was the magnitude of the Long vote that fixed the attention of politicians and commentators and aristocrats. How had Huey done it? What had gone wrong? What did it mean?

[4] New Orleans *Times-Picayune*, January 13 and 14, 1924; New Orleans *Item*, January 13 and 17, March 24, 1924; O. B. Thompson. The Fuqua advertisement appeared in the Alexandria *Town Talk* on January 11 and was reproduced in the *Picayune*.

[5] New Orleans *Item*, December 23, 1923, January 6, 1924; New Orleans *Times-Picayune*, January 13, 1924.

Marshall Ballard assured his readers that there was no cause for worry—Huey's demagoguery had simply appealed to "the lazy, the violent, and the vicious" and to good people who did not know him. But as more was learned about the distribution of the vote, it became apparent that there was reason for alarm. Bouanchaud had a majority in twenty-two parishes and a plurality in one, all of them in the south. Fuqua had a majority in only six parishes and a plurality in seven. He owed his finish to his showing in the cities, especially in New Orleans, where the Old Regulars counted thirty-three thousand votes for him, substantially more than the twenty-three thousand the New Regulars turned out for Bouanchaud. But Huey had rolled up a majority in twenty-one parishes and captured a plurality in seven. Even more than the scope of his strength, its source frightened conservatives. He had carried every parish but three in north and central Louisiana and three parishes in the southeast. Every one of them was a small-farmer, poor parish. For the first time the masses of Louisiana had rallied behind a leader, and it was terrifyingly evident that they realized their power and that they liked the sensation.[6]

Immediately after the election Huey offered an analysis of his defeat. The rain had cost him the governorship, he said. On the night before and on the day of the election it had rained over the whole state, and many of his country supporters had not been able to get to the polls. In time the story of the rain took on the proportions of a myth, created and fostered by Huey. He elaborated on it in his autobiography. He said that he knew he was defeated on the afternoon of the election. Somebody told him that the first returns had just come in: "It's the Clay box. Sixty-one votes cast there and you got sixty of them." "I'm beat," Huey had himself replying. "There should have been a hundred for me and one against me. Forty per cent of my country vote is lost in that box. It will be that great in the others." This was sheer fabrication. There was some shrinkage in his vote because of the rain, but it was not decisive. As several observers pointed out at the time, Huey lost because he did not get enough of a proportion of the votes in New Orleans and in the populous southwestern parishes. In New Orleans he picked up only twelve thousand votes, and as a hostile critic admitted, this figure was primarily a personal tribute. The Independent Regulars had done practically nothing for him; Francis Williams had lost even his own ward to the

[6] Allen P. Sindler: *Huey Long's Louisiana: State Politics, 1920–1952* (Baltimore, 1956), p. 49; Perry H. Howard: *Political Tendencies in Louisiana, 1812–1952* (Baton Rouge, 1957), pp. 124–5; New Orleans *Item*, January 20, 1924.

Choctaws. Huey understood quite well the real reasons for his defeat and set out immediately to remedy the situation.[7]

Huey did not congratulate or endorse either Fuqua or Bouanchaud. Instead, he issued a statement of his future intentions. "We have only begun to fight," he promised. "Some day our people will call the roll again." Everybody knew that he would be back in 1928. He started running, in fact, the day after the election. "We will march forward [next] time organized . . . ," he threatened. Some conservatives saw the handwriting on the wall. An Alexandria road contractor who had supported Fuqua prepared to go over to Huey. "We can't raise enough money to beat him again!" he said.[8]

[7] New Orleans *Item*, January 19 and 26, 1924; New Orleans *States*, January 16, 1924; Long: *Every Man a King*, p. 77; Rose McConnell Long.

[8] New Orleans *Item*, January 19, 1924; Orlean Thomas.

# CHAPTER 10

# I Am a Candidate

EVEN BEFORE THE RETURNS of the January primary were complete, Long leaders all over the state announced that if there was to be a runoff they would support Fuqua. Diverse motives promoted their choice. Some of them acted for religious reasons; they were ardent Protestants and would oppose Bouanchaud or any Catholic candidate. Those from north Louisiana were influenced not only by religious considerations but also by their traditional aversion to a south Louisianian's holding the governorship. Still others were disgusted by Bouanchaud's refusal to discuss any question but the Klan and his failure to state a position on any economic issue. Many may have sensed that the realignment of factions following the election would inevitably produce a Fuqua victory and hastened to put themselves on the right side. Political observers, noting the rush of Longites to the Fuqua camp, predicted that in a second primary the Baton Rouge hardware merchant would win handily. Some of Bouanchaud's advisers foresaw the same result, and they urged him to withdraw gracefully. But Bouanchaud, either thinking he had a chance or manifesting the stubborness the French are capable of, announced that he was staying in.[1]

Most of Huey's leaders who joined Fuqua acted without consulting him, and their independence demonstrates that at this stage of his career he had very little control over his organization. Shortly after the election he had presided over a caucus of his supporters in New

[1] New Orleans *Times-Picayune*, January 17, 19, 20, and 27, 1924.

Orleans, at which they voted to oppose a second primary and to take no part in one if held. But after Bouanchaud announced that he was remaining in, Huey could not restrain his people from taking sides. The majority of them followed the first acceders to Fuqua, but a few endorsed Bouanchaud. The Williams-Independent Regulars, as if determined to back a loser, threw their support to the Frenchman. Their action must have confirmed Huey's suspicion that the Williams brothers were not very astute. He also was beginning to suspect that they would be a frail reliance in the city in the future. Some of his associates had criticized the Williamses for the small vote they had turned out for him, and Huey, although he publicly defended them, was approaching the point where he would welcome a break.

Huey himself refused to endorse either candidate. They both were from the Parker household, he said, and whichever one was elected would be controlled by Parker. He recalled that when Parker had tried to put him off the Public Service Commission, they had assisted the conspiracy. "I have never forgotten," Huey said, "nor do I propose to forget." He remained aloof even when Bouanchaud bid for his support by adopting his plank that promised free textbooks, and he offered no comment on the result when Fuqua won decisively in the February runoff.[2] His stance of lofty neutrality was taken deliberately and was extremely shrewd politics. He had not aided the victor, yet he had not hurt the loser. He had not left any deep scars, and supporters of both candidates had no reason to feel animosity toward him. If something should go wrong in the Fuqua administration, he would be the natural rallying point for the opposition.

The conservatives who were frightened by Huey's showing in the election of January were cheered by an event that occurred in the summer. It seemed to show that the upstart demagogue was not so strong after all, that the right people still ruled, that nothing had really changed. The Democratic state convention was scheduled to meet in June in Baton Rouge to select delegates to the national convention. A method of choosing the delegates had been developed over the years and had been practiced for so long that it had acquired a quasi-legal status. Before the convention, elected by a few "interested" voters, the governor met with the state leaders and the New Orleans bosses and agreed on a slate; they then presented it to the convention, which accepted it, adjourned, and went home. That the delegates would be chosen in the traditional way this time was the natural

[2] New Orleans *States*, January 25, 1924; New Orleans *Times-Picayune*, January 31, February 1, 8, and 12, 1924.

assumption of Governor Fuqua and his most powerful backer and most frequent adviser, J. Y. Sanders. Some time before the convention they conferred with Martin Behrman and made out a slate of twenty delegates, sixteen of whom represented geographical districts and four of whom were delegates at large. But a problem arose over the choice of the at-large delegates. It was customary to name the United States senators as two of these, and if the rule had been followed, Joseph E. Ransdell and Edwin S. Broussard would have been given places. But Ransdell was to come up for reelection in September, and Sanders was preparing to run against him. J. Y. conceived the notion that it would redound to his advantage if he was named an at-large delegate and Ransdell was denied a seat, so in the conferences he insisted that both senators be excluded, and he carried his demand. It was agreed that the delegates at large would be Fuqua, Sanders, Behrman, and Lee E. Thomas, mayor of Shreveport.

Inevitably, news of the decision leaked out to the press. It was symptomatic of a new pattern of political thought developing in the state that many people expressed criticism of the way the delegates had been selected. Some pertinent questions were raised. Why should three men arrogate to themselves the power to choose the state's representatives? And by what right had they nominated themselves?

The loudest objection came from Shreveport. Huey Long denounced the secret meetings as a mockery of democracy and the slate of delegates as a fraud. Sanders had been defeated when he ran for the Senate in 1920 and Behrman when he ran for mayor in the next year, yet now they assumed that they should represent the people who had repudiated them. Why should the "rejects" have these places? asked Huey, overlooking the fact that he had just been rejected himself. He was going to the convention as a delegate from Caddo parish, and he announced that he was contacting other delegates to ask them to oppose the Fuqua-Sanders-Behrman slate and support a plan of his to name a new slate.[3]

On the night of the fifth of June, 716 delegates crowded into the Community Club pavilion in the capital city. The atmosphere was tense with anticipation. At eight o'clock Martin Behrman, who had been named by the state Democratic committee as temporary chairman, entered the building, an impressive figure in a snowy white suit. Excited comments ran through the hall as he and J. Y. Sanders were observed to embrace: maybe the city machine was going to support

---

[3] Leo Glenn Douthit: "The Governorship of Huey Long" (unpublished M.A. thesis, Tulane University, 1947), pp. 34–6; Hermann B. Deutsch: "Kingdom of the Kingfish," in New Orleans *Item*, August 4, 1939.

J. Y.'s bid for the senatorship. (Sanders apparently had forgotten that the Old Regulars were the Huns at the gate.)

Behrman called the meeting to order and was elected permanent chairman. Quickly he announced that, hearing no objection, he would name Sanders as chairman of the resolutions committee. Just as quickly Sanders moved that no resolutions be debated or voted or even read to the convention until they had been passed on by his committee. A stentorian voice from the rear of the hall interrupted the smooth flow of the proceedings: "I object." It came from Huey, who rose from his seat and began to speak. Or rather, it was conjectured that he was speaking. He could be seen to move his lips and hands, but nothing he said was heard. The instant he stood up, a roar of boos and imprecations shook the building and continued for several minutes. Behrman pounded his gavel on a marble-topped table until he broke the marble. Finally he quieted the bedlam sufficiently to announce that he was ruling Huey out of order, and Sanders's motion passed. Now a loud protest broke out from Huey's forces, obviously in a minority but determined to be vocal. Huey, on his feet again, demanded a roll-call vote on Sanders's motion. Behrman ruled against him, and Huey appealed the order. A New Orleans delegate moved that the appeal be tabled. A Long supporter shouted: "Don't run the steamroller too fast over us." The calling of the roll on the motion to table consumed twenty-five minutes and was conducted in a continuous uproar. Most of the delegates did not know what they were voting on and simply followed the directions of their leaders. Finally the result was announced—536 votes to table and 180 votes against. Huey had lost the first round.

The resolutions committee then left the building to prepare its report. While it was out, the delegates milled around restively or wandered outside for a breath of air. At ten o'clock the committee returned. Sanders mounted the rostrum and presented a few short resolutions that stated the party's position on vital state and national issues. They praised Thomas Jefferson and Woodrow Wilson, Democratic leaders who had supported the sovereignty of the states against the encroaching central government; demanded a system of permanent flood control on the Mississippi River and its tributaries, to be financed by the federal government; pledged cooperation with Governor Fuqua; and endorsed the slate of delegates chosen in the secret conferences. One change was proposed in the make-up of the at-large delegates. Former governor Pleasant was to be substituted for Lee E. Thomas, who was a personal enemy of Huey's and who presumably was being dropped as a concession to Long.

Some delegates thought they could amend the resolutions, not yet realizing the iron control that Behrman and Sanders were determined to exercise over the convention. A delegate from south Louisiana moved that the delegation propose in the national convention a plank denouncing the Klan. As if a signal had been given, an uproar instantly filled the hall. A motion was made to table the amendment, and after a noisy, confused voice vote it was declared defeated. Another delegate came to the rostrum and tried to present a resolution putting the party on record as favoring repeal of the Eighteenth (Prohibition) Amendment. Behrman shoved him off the platform while the delegates stomped and cheered. "It was a wild, riotous night," wrote one reporter, adding that the assemblage was about as turbulent as a mob could be without committing actual physical violence. Finally Huey was seen approaching the platform, and pandemonium really broke loose. He had to stand at the rostrum five mintues before he could gain the attention of the crowd. But when he got it, he held it. He was the only speaker of the evening who commanded absolute silence. Looking directly at Behrman, he denounced the "bosses and bosslets," "the clicksters and ringers" who were "contaminating" democratic government in the state. He offered a resolution to double the number of the at-large delegation to eight, with each member having half a vote. His plan would permit rejects like Behrman and Sanders to retain their places, he said, while opening up seats to men who represented the people.

Huey's resolution had no chance. A move to table it was approved by a voice vote, and he was denied the privilege of a roll call. On this typical last note, the convention adjourned. Apparently Huey had suffered a resounding defeat. He had failed to carry a single one of his points, and he seemed to have slipped in prestige and influence. But the impression of failure was deceptive. He had been howled down and forced down in as thoroughly bossed a convention as Louisiana had ever seen. And this fact about the convention was understood all over the state. It could hardly have been misunderstood after the display of naked power put on by Behrman and Sanders. Only those who wanted to be deluded could believe that this had been a democratic meeting. Nor was the spectacle of the screaming mob, many of them representatives of the "better" class, calculated to inspire respect for the decisions that had been arrived at. But all of this did not matter to most conservatives. What did matter was that Huey Long had been defeated and that the menace he embodied would now disappear. "Huey P. Long and his supporters were swept aside like chaff before the wind," gloated the *Picayune*. Marshall Ballard wrote for the *Item* another obituary: Huey P. Long is finished. There would eventually be a lengthy list of such statements.[4]

Huey stormed out of the convention and into another contest. His term as public service commissioner would expire in September, and he had to spend most of the remainder of the summer campaigning for re-election. It was vital to his future plans that he hold his seat, for if he could not carry his own northern district, he obviously could not hope to run for governor in 1928. At first it seemed that he would have to face two opponents, state senator Walter L. Bagwell from Oak Grove, in the northeastern plantation belt, and Judge William C. Barnette of Shreveport. But Barnette, who was the more formidable of the pair, shortly withdrew from the race. Political gossip whispered that he had been pulled out by the Klan, whose leaders wanted Huey to have a clear field. The simple truth was that Barnette realized that he had no chance and got out while he could. Bagwell remained in, encouraged by a promise from Fuqua that the administration would throw its full support behind him.[5]

In the same September election a United States Senate seat was also at stake. The incumbent was dignified, goateed Joseph E. Ransdell of Lake Providence, in the northeastern delta. Born in 1858 on a plantation, he had been educated at an eastern college, had practiced law, had served in the House of Representatives, and was elected to the Senate in 1912. In the upper chamber he attracted some attention by specializing in flood-control legislation and by advocating an amendment to the Constitution prohibiting a divorced person from remarrying.[6] His only distinction was his Senate seat, and he desperately wanted to hang on to it. Just as anxious to grasp it was J. Y. Sanders, who wanted to crown his career with election to the Senate. Sanders was so eager that he brought himself to pay a pilgrimage to New Orleans to beg Behrman for Old Regular support. Behrman refused him. The machine had promised Ransdell some time ago not to oppose him, the boss said. Besides, Ransdell was a Catholic, and should he be defeated by a Protestant just after the election of a Protestant governor, the state would be polarized on religious lines.

[4] New Orleans *Times-Picayune*, June 7, 1924; New Orleans *Item*, June 6, 1924.

[5] Adras Laborde: *A National Southerner: Ransdell of Louisiana* (New York, 1951), pp. 107–9; Henry Jastremski to Long, August 1, 1924, in Public Service Commission File 3; Douthit: "Governorship of Long," p. 36.

[6] Sketch of Ransdell drawn from contemporary newspapers and Laborde: *Ransdell of Louisiana, passim*.

If Sanders would wait until 1926, Behrman concluded, the organization would support him against Ed Broussard. Sanders was bitterly disappointed, but he had to abide by the decision.[7]

As soon as it was known that Sanders would withdraw, another hopeful announced, one who had been waiting in the wings. The new candidate was Lee E. Thomas. The Shreveport mayor, who was completely bald and had big ears and very wide jaws, and who was known as "Wet Jug," was a member of the Sanders–Fuqua clique.[8] The governor agreed to support him, and so did Sanders. Thomas could not count on much help from the Old Regulars—the machine was going to stay out of this contest—but with the backing of two of the state's most powerful leaders he seemed to offer a real threat to Ransdell. Any anxiety that the senator may have felt was quickly dissipated. On the eve of the campaign he received a dramatic and unexpected accession of strength. Huey Long announced that he was supporting Ransdell and would campaign for him in north Louisiana. Huey meant what he said. He spoke for Ransdell and with him, and feeling assured of his own victory, he devoted more space in his speeches to praising the senator than he did to pushing himself.[9]

There have been some strange alliances in Louisiana politics, but none more incongruous than this one. The senator was a patrician and had all the prejudices of his class against a man of Huey's social status. He was extreme conservative, a "planter statesman," and he must have viewed Huey's economic notions as the rankest heresies. He was a part of the "establishment" that Huey was fighting, and if he did not have the support of the Old Regulars, he certainly did not have their opposition. Yet he could accept Huey's support—for the simple reason that he needed it. Huey's reasons for offering it were not so apparent. Some observers thought that Huey was moved solely by hatred of Thomas. It was true that he and "Wet Jug" were enemies, but their enmity was what might be described as a professional relationship. Each respected the other's ability with words and enjoyed their exchanges and worked hard to score a success. Thus during the campaign Huey decided to emphasize that Thomas had lived off the

---

[7] Harry Gamble; Jared Y. Sanders, Sr.: "The Senatorial Campaign of 1926," *Tangipahoa Parish News*, October 28, 1926. Mr. Sanders wrote for this newspaper a series of articles describing his career from 1924 to 1926; it will hereafter be cited as Sanders: "Campaign of 1926." Mr. Gamble accompanied Sanders on the visit to Behrman.

[8] Hermann B. Deutsch.

[9] Huey P. Long: *Every Man a King* (New Orleans, 1933), p. 79; Douthit: "Governorship of Long," p. 36.

public during his entire adult life, and he developed a story to drive home the point.

In Winn parish, outdoor religious revivals were popular in the summer, he would begin, and parents would bring their small children to these meetings. Sometimes a baby would become restless during the services and start to cry, whereupon its mother, prepared for such a crisis, would place a sweetened rag in its mouth, and the baby would suck the rag and go off to sleep. This primitive pacifier was known as a "sugartit," Huey would say, and then came his conclusion: "But, ladies and gentlemen, at birth the sugar 'tit' of the State of Louisiana landed in L. E. Thomas's mouth. It's been there ever since. He's worn out a dozen of them. Now he's grabbing for more."

Thomas came right back with a story of his own. A man was passing through hell and was shown by the devil a large iron box, securely locked. The vistor proposed that they open it and see what it contained. "Oh, no," the devil said hastily. "That's Huey Long in there. We can't let him out. He'd take charge of hell if we did."[1]

Huey could attack Thomas with real relish, but he did not intervene in the senatorial campaign to gratify any personal animosity. He acted with cold calculation and with thoughts of 1928 uppermost in his mind. He wanted to attach Ransdell to his camp.

The accession could mean much to Huey. The senator was a figure of importance if only because of his office, and he had a following in the northeastern parishes. By supporting him now, Huey could command his allegiance four years hence. Moreover, Ransdell was the most prominent Catholic layman in the state and was extremely popular with his fellow religionists. By coming to his aid, Huey could erase any impression among Catholics that he had intolerant, Klan-like prejudices. He took particular care to see that his support of the senator was well publicized in the southern parishes.[2]

In dealing with his own opponent, Huey was relaxed, condescending, and mischievous. He knew that he would win an easy victory, and in his speeches he seemed to be toying with Bagwell. He enjoyed especially the occasions when he and Bagwell came together in the same town and spoke from the same platform. One of these encounters he described in a letter to a friend: "Brother Bagwell and I met in Cloutierville, down in the woods. . . . The crowd was 175% Long and about 80% Ransdell. Bagwell . . . threw just enough mud to put

[1] Long: *Every Man a King*, pp. 80–1.
[2] Long to Henry Jastremski, July 7, 1924, in Public Service Commission File 3.

the crowd on its tip-toes. He looked like 30¢ when I got through with him, and got up and left without shaking hands with a man." Sometimes he turned his talent for ridicule on Bagwell. The senator, a tall man with a long neck and small head, was what was known as a "flashy" dresser. He wore expensive clothes and liked to sport a vest of a different color from his coat and trousers. His trademark was a high, stiff standing collar, adorned with a colorful cravat. Huey would point at him and say: "You all ever take a good look at the fancy vests and cravats and high standing collars that Senator Bagwell wears? He wears the highest standing collar I ever saw. It is so high that every time the senator spits he has to tiptoe to spit over it."

Perhaps one reason Huey always faced Bagwell with confidence was that he knew exactly what the other man was going to say. An associate of Huey's who later broke with him claimed that Bagwell had a secretary who needed money and got it by selling copies of his employer's correspondence to Long. Quite possibly Huey did buy some information, but if he did, it was only to amuse himself. He had no need to resort to any kind of undercover action. The results of the September election disclosed an unprecedented triumph for him. He carried every one of the twenty-eight parishes in his district and piled up forty-five thousand votes, as against only eighty-six hundred votes for Bagwell, or 83.9 per cent of the total. It was an impressive success by any measurement, but it took on even greater proportions when compared with Ransdell's victory over Thomas. The man Huey had backed won handily, but his vote in the whole state was slightly less than Huey's in one part. Although Huey had not been able to deliver his full following to Ransdell, he could say with some justice that he had returned the senator to Washington. As conservatives surveyed the outcome, their summer rejoicings seemed like hideous mockeries. Huey Long was not finished at all. He was stronger than ever and more dangerous.[3]

Huey knew he was stronger than he had been. In 1928 he could rely on having his own north almost solidly behind him. But he knew too that this was not enough. If he was going to win the governorship, he would have to enlarge his power base in the south, would have to build alliances with leaders and organizations in that section who could deliver him a vote. He had taken a first step in this direction

[3] Long to Jastremski, August 18, 1924, ibid.; W. D. Robinson to Julius Long, June 8, 1933, in Robinson Papers; Harley B. Bozeman; Allen P. Sindler: *Huey Long's Louisiana: State Politics, 1920–1952* (Baltimore, 1956), p. 50; Deutsch: "Kingdom of the Kingfish," in New Orleans *Item*, August 3, 1939; New Orleans *Times-Picayune*, September 18, 1924.

when he supported Ransdell and removed any stigma of the Klan that might be attached to him. Now he took another and a more important step. With the prestige of his recent victory fresh in the politicians' minds, he intervened in the New Orleans mayoralty campaign. That campaign was warming up in the last months of 1924, although the election would not occur until February of the next year. It had started slowly and with every indication that it would not be much of a contest. Everybody knew that Behrman would run as the Old Regular candidate—a man who had been four times mayor until he was defeated by the Parker-backed Andrew McShane in 1920, who had fought his way back and had so rejuvenated the machine that now he was thought to be unbeatable. Francis Williams announced that he would oppose the boss, but nobody, except perhaps Gus, believed Francis had a chance. The only support he could muster would be the "good government" reformers, who could not deliver much of a vote, and Sullivan's New Regulars, who were in a state of decline after going down with Bouanchaud.

But a dramatic event changed the picture completely. The Old Regular caucus met to select a candidate and, for the first time in its history, split. Another leader challenged Behrman for the endorsement, Paul Maloney, who had been the only machine man to be returned to the city council in the McShane sweep of 1920. Maloney, short, florid, whose pleasant manner masked a determined will and an astute political brain, had been the organization's representative in the city government for four years, and now he thought that he deserved the chance to be its candidate. The caucus rejected him and endorsed Behrman, whereupon Maloney led his followers out and announced that he would run anyway. There were now, in effect, two Old Regular aspirants in the field, and the campaign took on new life. It was at this point that Huey interjected himself into the situation.

One day early in December an *Item* headline noted alarmingly: "Huey Long Is In Town." Huey registered at the St. Charles Hotel and immediately went into a secret huddle with his city friends. The political reporters, although they could get no information as to what was being discussed, guessed that Huey was advising Williams to withdraw and the Williams faction to support Maloney. They read the signs correctly. Shortly Francis announced that he was pulling out and that he would back Maloney. This was interesting news, but it did not promise to help Maloney very much—the Williamses could not bring him any great strength. But other news followed fast. Huey had made only a first move, and it soon appeared that he had much larger ones in mind. He paid other visits to New Orleans and was observed talking with various individuals. One of them was John Sullivan, who still nourished hopes of becoming a state power and who had been impressed by Huey's recent show of country strength. What he and Long talked about or what promises they exchanged was not known. But soon Sullivan announced that the New Regulars would support Maloney.

Huey was also seen talking with Robert Ewing, publisher of the New Orleans *States*, the Shreveport *Times*, and two papers in Monroe, and this development really set political tongues wagging. Colonel Ewing, as he was called, was definitely a personality. Imperious in manner, his bristling white moustache making him look like an angry schnauzer, he was accustomed to getting whatever he wanted. What he wanted now was influence—in the city government and, more so, in the state government; he wanted to be able to call in a governor and tell him what to do. He had been searching for a rising country politician who would like to be advised. What he and Huey talked about or what understanding they reached was not known. But shortly Ewing announced that the *States* would support Maloney.

The Old Regulars observed these meetings with alarm, and adopting a rare tone of outraged civic righteousness, they denounced them as dirty politics. The purpose of all the maneuvers was not to elect Maloney, Choctaw spokesmen charged, but to make Huey Long governor in 1928.

The same suspicion was voiced by the New Orleans press, which was torn between a desire to oppose the machine and a compulsion to destroy Huey. With most of the papers, hatred of Huey won out over reform. The combinations being formed were bad, the *Picayune* pontificated. The "sane and safe citizens" of New Orleans did not want to see Long in the governor's chair.

In the February election Maloney came within an eyelash of scoring an upset. He might have won if Andrew McShane, the reform incumbent who had disappointed the reformers, had not entered the race at the last minute. McShane polled only some four thousand votes, but presumably he drew them from Maloney. The election was so close, with Behrman leading narrowly, that these four thousand votes might have swung the balance. As neither candidate had a majority, it seemed that a second primary would have to be held. But none was. One of Sullivan's ward leaders extracted from the Old Regulars a promise of a material reward and then announced that if there was a runoff, he would support Behrman. Maloney, disheartened by this defection, withdrew, and Behrman won his fifth term without opposition. The result was disappointing to Huey, but looking beyond it to the future, he had every reason to be immensely satisfied with what he had accomplished. He had brought into his camp important accessions—Maloney, an able ward leader with a personal following, Sullivan and the New Regulars, and Ewing, the owner of an influential New Orleans newspaper. With these men committed to him, he should be able to secure a respectable percentage of the New Orleans vote in 1928. Now he had only to form an alliance in the southwestern parishes and he would be in.[4]

AFTER HIS TRIUMPHANT RE-ELECTION to the Public Service Commission, it might be expected that Huey, his dominance over the agency more assured than ever, would have enlarged and intensified its regulatory activities. Nothing of the sort happened. The Commission was in the next few years a relatively passive body. It initiated only a small number of important suits, and its name and labors rarely appeared in newspaper headlines. In part, this apparent inertness was the inevitable aftermath of the vigorous regulation exercised by the Commission in the preceding four years—it had established a pattern that the corporations had had to accept and now there was less work for it to do. But essentially the Commission entered on a quiet period because its chairman showed little interest in its work and made little effort to enforce its powers. Huey had transformed it into an effective, modern agency—and thereby had rendered a service to the state— but he had also used it to advance himself politically. Now he could not see that the Commission, or its cases, could help him any more. He attended comparatively few meetings after 1924, and when he did take hold of a case, he did so primarily because it would further his gubernatorial hopes.

One such case vitally concerned the welfare of New Orleans. It became known in Commission parlance as the Galveston rate case. It began when the national Interstate Commerce Commission promulgated an order permitting a reduction in rail rates on certain products—wheat and oil notably—moving to the port of Galveston. The New Orleans exporting interests and business and civic groups immediately lodged a sharp protest—Galveston did not have the

[4] New Orleans *Item*, December 9, 1924, January 19 and 27, 1925; New Orleans *Times-Picayune*, February 16, 1925; William Wiegand; Hermann B. Deutsch; Paul Maloney; Deutsch: "Kingdom of the Kingfish," in New Orleans *Item*, August 6, 1939; Douthit: "Governorship of Long," p. 37. Behrman died within a year after his election. In a special election, Arthur J. O'Keefe, an Old Regular, was elected without opposition, and the next election was scheduled four years hence.

facilities to handle the increased trade that would come to it as a result of the order, they claimed, whereas New Orleans had ample elevators and wharves. The protest was loud, but it did not seem to reach Washington. Something more had to be done; someone in an official capacity would have to go to Washington and personally present the city's case to the ICC. The savior was not long in coming. "Huey Long Opens Official Assault," proclaimed a *Picayune* headline, followed by the statement "Huey Long announced he would leave for Washington in a few days to press the fight against the order."

Huey, on hearing of the order, had called the Commission into session and dictated that it issue a protest and appoint him as its lawyer to present the protest. He then petitioned the ICC to reopen the case and suspend the order, and he went to Washington to use his persuasive powers directly. He was completely successful, but only after much hard work: "changing the members of the commission over is like pulling eye-teeth," he confided to a friend. The ICC agreed to suspend its order, which meant that the shipping rates to Galveston reverted to their former level.

Huey had saved New Orleans from a blow that could have damaged its economy severely, and he thought that the city's leaders would be grateful to him. He soon found that many of them were not. Some critics complained that as chairman of the Commission he should have been informed as to what the ICC was doing and should have acted to protest the order before it was issued. Others said that he did know of the preparation of the order but had permitted it to be published so that he could get it revoked and claim the political credit. Huey's motives in intervening in the case were clearly political—he hoped that his action would bring important New Orleans business interests to his side. But the criticisms of him were unfair. It is hardly likely that, as busy as he was with state politics, he could have known everything that was happening in the bureaucratic recesses of Washington.

When he returned to Louisiana, he encountered a dramatic demonstration of what New Orleans thought of him. The lavish Roosevelt Hotel was being opened, and to celebrate the event the business leaders sponsored a testimonial banquet to which twelve hundred leading citizens were invited. A businessman who had come to admire Huey, William P. Dillon, insisted that an invitation be extended to the man who had just won the Galveston rate case. Against his own judgment Huey attended the banquet. He was not seated at the head table, and he did not expect to be called on to speak. But after a number of speeches had been made, the chairman called on Huey. As Huey stood up, a large portion of the audience burst into boos. He sat down without attempting to say anything. He was both infuriated and saddened by the episode. It had been planned to embarrass him, he wrote Dillon. He added resignedly: "The commercial interests of that city owe me a debt which I never expect them to realize."[5]

Another case that Huey figured in had, in the beginning, only the most tenuous connection with the Commission. Huey dragged the Commission into it because he wanted to give official status to what was really a political issue. The case is known in Louisiana history as the Watson-Williams bridge or the Lake Pontchartrain bridge case. From its inception to its end, it was an extremely complicated suit, bristling with technical legal and economic points, and its detail is likely to become wearying. But the episode was an important one in Huey's career—it gave him one more weapon to use in his crusade to overthrow the rule of the hierarchy—and nothing illustrates more perfectly the restricted thinking of the men he was seeking to overthrow.

The case grew out of the peculiar geographical situation of New Orleans. The city is almost completely surrounded by water, and with the coming of the automobile it acutely needed to secure easy road access to the east and the west. Bridges were of first priority, and it was obvious that the state, with its larger financial resources, would have to build them. It was also obvious that, as the use of the automobile increased, the state would have to construct other bridges across the rivers and bayous that laced Louisiana. Therefore, the kind of bridges decided on for New Orleans might determine the nature of all later bridges. Would they be operated as free public facilities or as toll bridges? Or would the state turn over to private interests the job of building the bridges and let these interests charge tolls?

In 1918 the state apparently laid down a policy. A law that was cast in the form of a constitutional amendment authorized the construction of a free bridge across Lake Pontchartrain to the north of New Orleans, giving the city a shorter route to the Mississippi Gulf Coast. No action was taken by subsequent legislatures to implement

[5] New Orleans *Times-Picayune*, August 21 and September 11, 1925; Deutsch: "Kingdom of the Kingfish," in New Orleans *Item*, August 7, 1939; Long to William P. Dillon, February 3, 1926 (letter in possession of William P. Dillon, New Orleans); William P. Dillon. Huey's expenses that he submitted to the Commission for his Washington trip were remarkably small, as was true of all his official trips. His total bill for transportation, hotel accommodations, and meals was only $154.44; document in Long Papers, Public Service Commission File.

the law. Only a limited amount of money was available for highway construction under the pay-as-you-go principle that the state was operating on, and all of this was being put into roads; at that time there was no strong pressure from New Orleans for a bridge. But about the time the Fuqua administration took office, the situation had changed. New Orleans, growing industrially and commercially, and increasingly conscious that in the modern age it needed good transportation by land as well as by water, demanded a bridge to the east and brought all the influence it could marshal on the state government to provide a bridge, whatever kind. The 1924 legislature was persuaded to enact a law authorizing the Highway Commission to contract with private firms to erect toll bridges. By an interesting coincidence two private-interest groups immediately appeared on the scene, each offering to build a toll bridge over Lake Pontchartrain. One was known as the Watson-Williams Syndicate, from the names of two of its chief backers, Eli T. Watson and George Williams. This group had the foresight to employ as its legal representative the firm headed by former governor Sanders. The other group was equally prescient in choosing its legal counsel, although it was never organized tightly enough to acquire a name. It retained the law firm headed by former governor Pleasant. The groups proposed to utilize two different routes. Both would, of course, start from the south shore of Pontchartrain. The Sanders combination would build from the eastern side of the city northeasterly to Slidell. The Pleasant aggregation would build from the "west end" of the city proper northerly to Mandeville. Still a third route was available, but this was the one that the constitutional amendment had marked out for the state. It crossed two small arms of the lake, the Chef Menteur and the Rigolets, which meant that two bridges would have to be built. Roughly, this route paralleled the Sanders route to the south.

As the state did not have enough money to build any bridge, and as the Fuqua administration obviously was not going to raise taxes to get the money, the proponents of the bridge had to consider that a toll span might have to be accepted. If a private concern was going to construct the bridge, it would have to secure permission from the state. That permission now became the prize sought by the two competing syndicates, and Sanders and Pleasant, once allies, were turned into enemies as they fought for their clients. Of the two competing routes, many interests in New Orleans favored the Pleasant artery because it would connect with the most populous part of the city. But the Sanders route had its adherents, and, more important than local support, Sanders had the ear of the governor. The smart dopesters predicted that Fuqua would decide to award the franchise to the Sanders group. Up to a point the struggle was conducted quietly, in offices in Baton Rouge and New Orleans. There was no secret about what was going on, but neither was there much advertisement of it and the public seemed uninterested. No voice was raised to say that there was anything wrong with the undercover negotiations or the very concept of a toll bridge, or that the public had an interest in the outcome.

That is, no one protested until the chairman of the Public Service Commission decided to raise his objections. On New Year's Day, 1925, Huey issued a blistering statement that broke the bridge deal into the open. The Fuqua administration, dominated by J. Y. Sanders, was planning to award an exclusive franchise to the Watson-Williams gang, he charged. But those who were plotting this behind doors were not going to get away with it. Neither the governor acting alone nor the governor acting through the Highway Commission had the legal power to grant the franchise. This power was vested solely in the Public Service Commission. Let the schemers know that they are acting at their peril, he cried: "This state is not going to be bartered away nor subsidized just because a bunch of lobbyists happen to be in control just at this time." He followed this statement with others that were even more personal and accusatory. Was there a state worse cursed by an exploiter than Louisiana was by Sanders? Was the conscience of the state dead, that it would permit the payment of a large sum of money to J. Y. just to get a bridge when a free bridge was already authorized? Were the people going to let themselves be despoiled "out of multiplied millions and millions of their money and property"?[6]

Huey had found another issue that would help to move him along the path to the governorship. First of all, he won additional support in New Orleans, which was badly divided on the issue of the bridge. Some groups favored the Sanders route; others, like the influential Louisiana Motor League, preferred the Pleasant route; still others were willing to wait for the state to build a free bridge. By opposing the Sanders route Huey secured the gratitude of the last two factions. At the same time he advised his friends in the city to help both Sanders and Pleasant. "Help Pleasant to show up Sanders; then help Sanders to show up Pleasant," he suggested. Puzzled by this proposed strategy, which Machiavelli would have recognized and admired, the

[6] New Orleans *Times-Picayune*, January 2, 1925; New Orleans *States*, July 4, 1925; Baton Rouge *State-Times*, December 4, 1925; Long: *Every Man a King*, pp. 88–9; J. Y. Sanders, Jr.

friends asked where they would "land." "We'll land against them both," Huey answered, "in time for a free bridge owned by the State. In the meantime, let's help them cut each other to the ground, if we can."[7]

The second advantage that Huey gained by his action was even more important. He attracted to his following additional voters all over the state. Once again the people saw him in the great role he had created—the courageous young reformer battling the forces of corporate greed. And this time he had played the scene in a particularly dramatic way. He had exposed a powerful syndicate that was grabbing for a monopoly, and he had revealed that two of the state's most powerful leaders, Sanders and Fuqua, were its willing and perhaps corrupt tools. In the popular mind there was but one conclusion to all this—others might fail them, but Huey Long could always be depended on to watch over the interests of the people.

For Huey the bridge issue was a politician's dream. He could be idealistic and at the same time practical. On principle he was opposed to a toll bridge and a monopoly, and by standing on principle he could make votes. And as an extra dividend, he could amuse himself by sticking pins in Sanders and other conservative leaders. His charges that J. Y. was acting for personal gain were believed by many people, although the indictment was unjust. Huey knew that it was unjust, and Sanders knew that Huey did not believe it. The former governor thought that he understood Huey's psychology. "He has no resentment and bears no malice," Sanders said of his tormentor, "and no matter how bitter he may seem when denouncing you the party denounced may always know that he is play-acting; he means it not; it is for effect."[8]

It was for effect, but Sanders misunderstood the purpose behind it. Huey enjoyed attacking the sacred figures of the hierarchy, but he did not do it merely for personal pleasure. Nor did he do it because, as some thought, he had a streak of vindictiveness or jealousy in him. He attacked the promoters of the toll bridge in personal terms because that strategy gave the best promise of defeating them, of putting down the philosophy of government that they represented. He did denounce the philosophy, but it was easier and more effective to charge that the spokesman of conservatism had ulterior motives.

The frankest exponent of the conservative view was Sanders. Over and over J. Y. explained his reasons for supporting the toll

[7] Long: *Every Man a King*, p. 89.
[8] J. Y. Sanders: "Campaign of 1926," in *Tangipahoa Parish News*, December 2, 1926.

bridge, completely conscious that his motives were good and honest, utterly unconscious that he spoke for an age that was passing. The state could not, out of current revenues, build free bridges, Sanders insisted. It could get enough money only by diverting funds from the road-construction program, thus wrecking "our splendid Pay-As-You-Go plan," or by borrowing it, and, as he said: "I have had all my life a holy horror of interest." How much better it would be to let private interests risk their capital to build this bridge and others that might be required—"these costly structures." And how much more logical it was that such bridges should be paid for, not by the taxpayers, but by those who used them—"principally tourists and pleasure seekers" and people who could afford to pay tolls to take a short cut. Apparently it never occurred to the old aristocrat that people who could not afford to pay the charges might also like to tour and seek pleasure and enjoy the convenience of a short route.[9]

Before Huey could arouse public opinion by his assaults on the proposed toll bridge, the Highway Commission awarded a franchise to build it to the Watson-Williams group. The commission met with representatives of the syndicate in late February 1925 and arrived at what was described in the press as an informal agreement. Although the terms were not immediately announced, they were fairly well understood and were reported in the newspapers. The syndicate was to construct a bridge at an estimated cost of five and a half million dollars. It would have a monopoly on vehicular traffic over the bridge for twenty years and could charge a system of graduated tolls based on usage of the span. At the end of twenty years the state could take possession of the bridge by paying the syndicate the cost of its investment.[1]

Up to this time Huey had conducted his opposition to the bridge on a political level. That is, he had denounced the project and its promoters, but he had done no more than denounce. Now that an agency of the government had in an official action awarded a fran-

[9] Ibid., issues of February 3 and 24, 1927; Sanders, speech of June 11, 1926, to Fourteenth Ward Civic League of New Orleans, MS in Sanders Family Papers; Sanders to C. B. Sherrouse, July 9, 1926, ibid. The amount of toll a user of the bridge would have to pay was a subject of dispute between Huey and Sanders. Huey claimed that to recover its investment the syndicate would have to charge $3.60 for a one-way trip. Sanders retorted that the toll would be no more than $2.60 and probably would be $1.30. But he was basing this estimate on the assumption that the minimum number of cars crossing the bridge annually would be three hundred thousand and the maximum number five hundred thousand. If the number of users dipped below the minimum, the toll would have to be raised.

[1] New Orleans *Times-Picayune*, February 27, 1925; Long: *Every Man a King*, pp. 88–90.

chise, however, he could act officially. He could try to revoke the franchise. But in order to act he would have to bring the Public Service Commission into the controversy, to establish that the question of the bridge was Commission business. This was easy for him. He convoked a meeting of the Commission in May and presented it with a resolution, ready to be adopted. The resolution stated that since the Highway Commission had authorized the syndicate to fix tolls, it was really fixing them itself; but that the power to set rates for a public utility was vested solely in the Public Service Commission, which regarded the bridge as a utility; and that therefore Huey P. Long was directed in behalf of the Commission to initiate such legal proceedings as were necessary to annul the bridge contract. Huey filed a suit and took it to the supreme court. That body refused to negate the contract, which was probably what he expected it to do, but it did rule that the state could still erect a free bridge at the point specified in the amendment of 1918, though at none other.[2]

Although he was unable to induce the court to act, Huey had so publicized the issue of the bridge that public opinion was at last aroused. The legislature, then in the last phase of its session before adjourning for the summer, felt constrained to consider the controversy. Against administration opposition, a bill was introduced providing for the construction of free bridges at the Chef Menteur-Rigolets route to be financed by money diverted from highway funds. Because the proposal would delay highway progress, it was not very appealing to advocates of a free bridge, and the toll-bridge interests had little trouble in persuading the legislature to agree on a compromise bill. This measure approved the franchise granted by the Highway Commission but modified it in that the state could purchase the bridge at any time and operate it as a toll bridge until its costs were met. Thus assured of official sanction, the syndicate, now reorganized as the Pontchartrain Bridge Company, proceeded to advertise its bonds for sale throughout the country, making no mention, however, of the fact that the state could build free bridges paralleling its route. Huey, still seeking ways to harass the company and asserting that he wanted to warn possible investors that they would be buying doubtful bonds, drafted another order for the Commission to issue. This one declared the bridge to be a public utility and directed the company to halt construction until the Commission had approved its plans and rates. The company promptly secured an injunction for-

[2] Minute Book, Louisiana Public Service Commission, II, May 25, 1925; Long: *Every Man a King*, pp. 89–90; *La. Pub. Serv. Comm.* v. *La. Highway Comm.* 159 La. 932, 106 So. 385 (1925).

bidding enforcement of the order, and when Huey appealed to the supreme court, that tribunal ruled that the Commission could take no jurisdiction until the bridge was built. Again assured that the state supported it, and now apparently impregnable, the company went ahead with its sale of bonds and shortly started construction. Huey professed no alarm at the turn of events. "Go build the bridge," he grimly told its promoters, "and before you finish it I will be elected governor and will have free bridges right beside it. You are building the most expensive buzzard roost in the United States."[3]

At the height of the bridge controversy Huey and his ally Francis Williams came to a parting of the ways. It was inevitable that sooner or later the two would break. They were ambitious men, and they had joined forces only to further their own aspirations. Each had tried to use the other—Huey hoping to use Francis to get votes in New Orleans, Francis hoping to use Huey to ride into power in Baton Rouge. Each had some cause to be disappointed in the results of the alliance, but Huey had more cause. The Williams faction had been of little help to him in 1924 and obviously would be of less help in the future. After Huey had made his arrangements with Maloney, Sullivan, and Ewing, he did not need the Williamses any longer, and he was looking for an opportunity to break with them. Francis was aware of the change in Huey's feelings, and being by temperament emotional and sensitive, he became angrily aggressive. If his colleague was cooling toward him, Francis would anticipate the outcome by breaking first. He waited only for a favorable issue. He judged that he had found one in the Galveston rate case. As Francis saw the case, he had done all the hard preliminary work, and now Huey, who had entered it at the last moment, was getting the headlines. He issued a public statement blistering Long and extolling himself. Without any trouble, he discovered other cases in which Huey was undercutting him. Francis had been trying to get the Commission to order the railroads using New Orleans to build a union station. Now it appeared that Huey was attempting to scuttle the project because he did not want Williams to have the credit for it. Francis informed the public of this villainy. By the end of 1925 it was open knowledge that he and Huey had broken.

Huey was well satisfied to see the split develop and to have it

---

[3] Deutsch: "Kingdom of the Kingfish," in New Orleans *Item*, August 7, 1939; Long: *Every Man a King*, pp. 91–2; Minute Book, Louisiana Public Service Commission II, October 5, 1926; *Sixth Annual Report of the Louisiana Public Service Commission* (Baton Rouge, 1927), pp. 101–2; *N. O. Pontchartrain Bridge Co. v. La. Pub. Serv. Comm.* 162 La. 874, 111 So. 265 (1927).

come as it did—Francis had made the overt move and seemed to be the aggressor. He did not deign to answer many of the bitter statements that Francis published, and when he did reply, he spoke in tones of pained sorrow: he regretted that his esteemed former associate had let himself be led into making such wild charges in such intemperate language. But even as he affected this attitude of detachment, he was working feverishly to forestall a threat to his position that was posed by William's defection. If Francis should form an alliance with Shelby Taylor, Huey would become a minority on the Commission and lose his chairmanship. Quickly Huey made his own agreement with Taylor, and the two men who not so long ago had been denouncing each other as scoundrels now acted together as a smooth new majority.

The strength of their union was revealed in a dramatic way at a Commission meeting in New Orleans. At this session Gus Williams, angered by something that Taylor said to his brother, suddenly rose and interrupted the proceedings. In the words of the official journal Gus used "loud, boisterous, vociferous and profane language" and "brandishing a clenched fist," shouted at Taylor: "I'll fix you and I'll fix the Chairman of the Commission too, if necessary." The chairman calmly "admonished" Gus that he must cease his disorder and take his seat. Gus uttered some more profanity but finally subsided. Thereupon the Commission by a two-to-one vote, with Francis Williams voting no, adjudged Gus guilty of contempt and sentenced him to serve twenty-four hours in the parish prison and to pay a fine of ten dollars.[4]

The ease with which Long and Taylor formed their alliance illustrates one of the strangest aspects of Louisiana politics, one that has always puzzled outside observers who do not understand the conditions that produce it. Louisiana politicians were and are much like feudal barons. They operate as rulers of geographical principalities or personal followings, independently, calculatingly, and sometimes irresponsibly or petulantly. Two barons may seem to be friends and allies, and then suddenly, because one or the other senses an advantage to be gained or is seized by a whim, they break and become enemies. Conversely, two barons may seem to be political and per-

[4] Deutsch: "Kingdom of the Kingfish," in New Orleans *Item*, August 7, 1939; Shreveport *Journal*, September 10, 1925; New Orleans *States*, September 11, 1925; New Orleans *Times-Picayune*, September 11, 1925; Long to William C. Dufour and John St. Paul, Jr., October 18, 1926, and Francis Williams to Long, March 8, in Long Papers, Public Service Commission File; Minute Book, Louisiana Public Service Commission, II, February 3 and 4, 1926.

sonal enemies, and just as suddenly and for similar reasons, they will come together as allies. Over a stretch of years the pattern can become bewilderingly complex, as leaders break, ally, and rebreak, in an endless chain of combinations. The process is peculiar to Louisiana, a product of the state's exaggerated devotion to professional politics. It appeared in striking form in the next campaign that Huey entered, the senatorial contest of 1926.

United States Senator Edwin S. Broussard was up for re-election in 1926. He came of a family that long had been powerful in the populous southwestern French parishes, the area that made up the third congressional district. His brother Robert had held the Senate seat before him and had been something of an idol to the Frenchmen before death cut short his career. His followers, with familial affection, called him "Coozan Bob." He was swarthy, friendly, and eloquent. Edwin was a somewhat faint carbon copy of Bob, not as swarthy or friendly or eloquent, but still a Broussard and worthy of succeeding to Bob's place and of being called "Coozan Ed." Ordinarily Broussard would have had little fear of not being re-elected. It was a standing rule of Louisiana politics, nearly always observed, that one of the senators should be from the north and one from the south. As the north was already represented by Ransdell, it could hardly put forward a candidate for the other seat. Another south Louisianian might challenge for the Democratic nomination, but unless he was a particularly strong candidate, he would have no chance. The French third-district parishes would vote almost solidly for Broussard, and as the vote in a senatorial election was usually light, their support alone could conceivably sweep him to victory. But the situation was not normal in 1926. An opponent from the south was challenging Broussard, and he was a rival of great stature and strength. J. Y. Sanders, although he was a Protestant, was popular in the southern parishes and was certain to cut into Broussard's vote in his home ground. Moreover, because Sanders was a Protestant, he could expect to poll a heavy vote in north Louisiana against the Catholic Broussard. "Coozan Ed" knew that he would need all the support he could muster to win.[5]

Support for one candidate or the other developed quickly once the campaign got under way. In each camp there were some unexpected recruits, some individuals who logically should have been in the other camp, and some former enemies who were obviously uncomfortable in their association. The strongest single force behind

[5] Hermann B. Deutsch; J. Y. Sanders, Jr.

Sanders was the Old Regulars, who remembered Behrman's pledge of 1924 to support J. Y. and who now, although the boss was dead, felt constrained to honor his commitment. But the machine leaders worked for their candidate with a noticeable lack of enthusiasm. They did not like his stand on an issue that was rising in importance in Louisiana and the nation—the question of whether or not the Eighteenth, or Prohibition, Amendment should be repealed: Sanders was an avowed "dry," a supporter of retention. The Old Regulars, for once executing the wishes of their constituents, were "wets," champions of repeal. The irony of the situation was that Broussard was the wettest wet in the state. He advocated not only repeal of the amendment but also passage of legislation to permit the manufacture and sale of light wines and beer pending repeal, and the Old Regulars could have supported him with fervor.

Another strong organizational presence in the Sanders camp was the Fuqua administration. The governor personally endorsed Sanders and attempted, or so it was charged, to place behind him all the vote-getting resources of such patronage-rich agencies as the Highway Commission and the Department of Conservation. With the Old Regulars and the administration supporting him, Sanders had a distinct advantage to begin with. But this was countered when other organizations announced for his opponent. John Sullivan took the New Regulars into the Broussard camp. Paul Maloney, after some hesitation, led his Old Regular faction to Broussard, thereby causing Sanders to charge that Maloney had broken a promise to support him. Sanders was bitter at the defection of others whom he had counted on to help him. The New Orleans *Times-Picayune*, the city's most influential and conservative newspaper, which had supported Sanders in his previous campaigns, came out for Broussard and attacked Sanders as a tool of corporate interests. "The venom and the spleen and the hatred that the management of this paper had for me dripped and drooled for many months," Sanders recited. He ascribed a crass motive to the paper: its directors owned land in the vicinity of the rival bridge. Another deserter was Ruffin Pleasant, attorney of the rival bridge group, who once had been J. Y.'s close ally and who had held with him equal rank as a spokesman of conservative ideals. Now Pleasant was supporting Broussard. Sanders had a ready explanation for his former colleague's perfidy. When Pleasant had lost out in the bridge deal, "he went mad with hatred."[6]

The spectacle of the honest, decent people falling out and flinging

---

[6] Douthit: "Governorship of Long," pp. 37–8; Sanders: "Campaign of 1926," in *Tangipahoa Parish News*, November 4, 11, 18, and 25, 1926.

charges of corruption at one another added one more note of confusion to the campaign. A crowning note was added when the last important leader to declare himself revealed his preference. Huey Long announced that he was for Broussard and would campaign all over the state for the Frenchman. There had been a great deal of speculation as to which candidate Huey would endorse. Some observers thought that he would have to come out for Sanders, despite their enmity, because of the issue of prohibition. The people of the northern parishes, the area of Huey's greatest strength, were strong upholders of prohibition (and equally strong consumers of illegal whisky), and it was thought that he would not dare go for Broussard. Actually, Huey had decided at an early date which candidate he wanted to support. If he could make the deal, he would support Broussard. The deal was that Broussard must support him in 1928.

Huey's aim since 1924 had been to build up new bases of strength in the south. He had formed promising alliances in New Orleans. Now if he could win the allegiance of a southwestern leader and pick up the heavy country vote of the French parishes, he should be a sure thing. The bait that he could hold out to Broussard was the delivery of the Long vote in the north. He and Broussard needed each other, but they had to engage in sustained negotiation, some of it conducted by intermediaries, before each was satisfied that the other would abide by an agreement. The announcement that the alliance had been concluded was greeted with some disbelief. It just did not seem possible. Huey Long the radical was lined up with the *Picayune* and Pleasant—and was welcomed by his new associates![7]

Huey entered the campaign in characteristic style—loudly, dramatically, and on the offensive. He embarked on a stump tour that eventually took him all over the state, and in every speech he devoted most of his time to attacking Sanders. The charges he flung at the former governor were numerous and sensational. Sanders said later that if there was anything Huey didn't say against him, it was an oversight. Among the sins ascribed to J. Y., the following were major ones: he was the paid spokesman of the toll-bridge and gas and carbon-black interests; he dominated the Fuqua administration and had used his influence to keep cheap natural gas from coming to

[7] John St. Paul, Jr.; Deutsch: "Kingdom of the Kingfish," in New Orleans *Item*, August 7, 1939. Huey and Broussard, after they had become enemies, presented different versions of their negotiations. Broussard said that he refused to support Huey in 1928 and that Huey left the campaign but was persuaded to come back by Ewing. Huey admitted that he left the campaign but claimed that he returned at the request of Broussard leaders. The statement of neither man rings completely true. *Congressional Record*, 72 Cong. 2 Sess., pp. 2817–18.

New Orleans; he controlled the hiring and firing of personnel in the highway and conservation departments and had built up in them a huge machine of jobholders; he had once persuaded the legislature to divert a fund intended for the deaf and dumb asylum to the conservation, or "coonservation," department to employ more "coon watchers"; and on other occasions he had used state money and patronage to manipulate votes in the legislature. Some commentators have suggested that Huey used so many personal attacks because he had to avoid discussing prohibition; he could not risk alienating his northern supporters by identifying himself with Broussard's wetness. The supposition has some basis in fact, but the liquor question had only a slight influence in determining Huey's strategy. He attacked because he believed that attack was the best weapon—a campaign was like a battle and the general, or politician, who took the offensive held the initiative.

Sanders observed the mounting barrage of charges at first with anger and then with resignation. He attempted to deny them and was able to demonstrate that some of them were inaccurate. But he soon discovered that denials with fruitless. His factual rejoinders were not nearly as interesting to the voters as Huey's lurid accusations. Moreover, by the time he had nailed one story as false, Huey had started another that had to be met. Sanders was being placed in a position that to a politician is fatal—he was always on the defensive, always responding to moves of his opponent and never moving on his own. Sanders gave it up. But although he resented the attacks, J. Y., himself a spellbinder and assaulter of considerable talent, also admired the artistry of Huey's effort. The sheer effrontery of it evoked a reluctant respect. "When it comes to arousing prejudice and passion," he wrote of Huey, "when it comes to ranting and raving, when it comes to vituperation and vilification, when it comes to denunciation and demagoguery, there is one who stands out by himself alone. He has many imitators but no equals."[8]

Huey and Broussard stumped the French third district together. The purpose of this arrangement was to show Huey to the French voters in company with Coozan Ed. Broussard spoke in French, the only language many of his hearers understood, and Huey spoke in what the *Picayune* admiringly called "unmistakable 'dynamite' English." The Frenchmen went wild about Huey, partly because he was appearing with their idol, partly because he was a friendly,

---

[8] Douthit: "Governorship of Long," pp. 38–9; Deutsch: "Kingdom of the Kingfish," in New Orleans *Item*, August 7, 1939; Sanders: "Campaign of 1926," in *Tangipahoa Parish News*, December 2, 1926.

humorous type who understood that a man had to take a drink now and then or flirt with the girls—just the kind of politician Frenchmen should like. They hailed him as Huey Polycarp Long, an adopted son of the district, and vowed to remember him in 1928.

After covering the south, Huey and Broussard moved on to the north. Here the purpose was to show Broussard to the redneck hill farmers in the company of Huey. The senator had never had to campaign in this area and was virtually unknown to the voters. Huey took charge of the meetings and introduced Broussard. He never presented the candidate as the leading wet of the state but as his friend, the man who was standing with him against the toll-bridge outrage and the Sanders gang.[9]

At one meeting in the north the most sensational episode of the campaign occurred. In his speeches in south Louisiana Huey had repeatedly attacked the Department of Conservation for employing large numbers of useless agents, the "coon watchers." As an example of this corrupt extravagance, he had cited Robert L. Prophit of Monroe, an agent who was also a member of the legislature. Prophit, a small, fiery man, thought he had some excuse for holding two jobs: he had lost a leg as the result of an accident when a boy and had to use a cane. He learned of Huey's references to him from newspaper clippings sent to him by Old Regular leaders in New Orleans. He was naturally angered, and when his informants suggested a way that he could retaliate, he readily agreed to their plan. Huey was scheduled to speak in the Monroe area. Prophit should appear at one of the meetings and physically assault Huey, the New Orleans schemers advised. As Huey was known to be a coward (this impression was already abroad), he would run, and his flight from a disabled man would stamp him for what he was and ruin him with his rural followers.

Prophit decided to make his move when Huey spoke in Columbia, a small town that was the parish seat of an adjoining parish. He went to Columbia and announced his intention to the sheriff, who was anti-Long (this official very shortly became one of Huey's staunchest supporters). Then he waited in front of the courthouse for Huey to appear. Soon Huey drove into town, accompanied by Broussard. A large crowd had assembled, and Huey, after greeting friends, crossed the street to reach his rostrum, the courthouse steps. At the gate of the yard he encountered Prophit and said: "Hello, Bob." As Prophit relates it, at this point he hit Huey with his fist.

---

[9] Deutsch: "Kingdom of the Kingfish," in New Orleans *Item*, August 7, 1939; Douthit: "Governorship of Long," pp. 38–9.

Huey started to run, and Prophit swung at him with his cane but missed and broke the stick on the iron gate. He chased Huey down the sidewalk until friends of Huey stopped him by forming a circle around him. Huey, seeing that his assailant was restrained, returned to the courthouse, swinging a wild blow as he went by; he missed Prophit by two feet. A deputy sheriff now appeared and took Prophit to the sheriff's office, where he was held until Huey's meeting concluded. (Prophit was later arrested, tried for assault, and fined.) Admirers of Huey who saw the attack had a different version of what happened. A number of them signed a statement charging that Prophit came on Long from behind and struck him on the head with the cane. The statement added that the citizens were preparing to handle Prophit in "a ready way" when Huey asked that no harm be done to him.

The exact facts of the case are unclear, but there is no doubt about the result. Prophit, when asked if the incident hurt Huey, answered emphatically: "No. Those people didn't care. Huey could do anything. Those New Orleans people thought it would hurt him, but it didn't." Huey removed any impression of humiliation by treating the affair humorously, a technique that he would later repeat in similar episodes. Speaking in Monroe right after the attack, he held up half of Prophit's cane that he had somehow acquired and said: "I had no trouble finding a conservation agent in Columbia."[1]

The election in September was so close that for a time the result was in doubt. When the last votes were counted, Broussard had squeezed through to victory by a scant thirty-four hundred votes. Huey immediately proclaimed that he had won the victory for Broussard, that if he had not swung his northern following to the senator, Sanders would have triumphed. There was some basis for Huey's claim, although he was able to turn out for Broussard only a fraction of the vote he himself had received in 1924. But Broussard accepted Huey's analysis of the outcome, and the two men continued in alliance. Broussard's Frenchmen could be depended on to support Huey Polycarp in 1928.[2]

[1] Robert L. Prophit; statement of September 9, 1926, signed by approximately fifteen names, in Huey P. Long Papers, Emory University Library, Atlanta, Ga., hereafter cited as Long Papers, Emory.

[2] Sindler: *Huey Long's Louisiana*, pp. 50–1. Professor Sindler points out that whereas in a number of northern parishes Huey had received seventy per cent of the vote in 1924, Broussard received only forty per cent in 1926, and he concludes, therefore, that Long's support was not very important. This view overlooks the fact that if Long had not supported Broussard, the latter would have received a smaller percentage than forty and in a close election would have been defeated.

It soon became evident that other politicians believed that Huey had determined the outcome of the election and was the rising power in state politics. Early in October Governor Fuqua died, and the lieutenant governor, Oramel H. Simpson, succeeded to the office. Simpson, short and dumpy, had been secretary of the senate for twenty undistinguished years before he was elevated to the state's second office. Now he had the first place and wanted to hang on to it. He hastened to support what had become the popular side of the bridge controversy. He announced that the state would proceed to build the authorized free bridge at the Chef Menteur-Rigolets route. Removing the Fuqua-appointed members of the Highway Commission, he appointed a new commission, which immediately let contracts to begin the construction of supporting piers. Some of Huey's critics chuckled—the new governor had stolen Huey's clothes while he was swimming, they said. But Huey expressed lofty unconcern. "I will lay all my plans on the front porch," he said, "and I will never holler 'Stop Thief' when they make their get-away if they want them." He could afford to appear detached. He knew that the people would never give Simpson credit for the free bridge.[3]

When Huey campaigned for Broussard, he also solicited votes for another candidate. Shelby Taylor was up for re-election to the Public Service Commission from the second district, and Huey was supporting him. Huey did not like Taylor personally, and although he had effected a reconciliation with him, he would have preferred another colleague to work with. He had no recourse, however, but to go for Taylor. The latter faced an opponent who was backed by Francis Williams—Dudley J. LeBlanc of Lafayette, in the heart of the French country—and if LeBlanc won, Huey would be a minority on the Commission and would lose his chairmanship. LeBlanc was a redoubtable foe. Ebullient and witty, he was a clever stump speaker, a political salesman of rare persuasive power. Moreover, he was a Frenchman and could address country French audiences in their own language, and he was certain to poll a heavy vote in the French parishes. Huey did his best for Taylor, but he must have known that it would not be enough. He did not as yet have enough pull in the southern parishes to defeat a native son. The September election confirmed his fears. LeBlanc led Taylor and two minor opponents, and although he did not have a majority, he was so close to it that Taylor refused to enter a second primary. LeBlanc an-

[3] Long: *Every Man a King*, pp. 92–3; Deutsch: "Kingdom of the Kingfish," in New Orleans *Item*, August 3 and 9, 1939.

nounced that the result was a mandate to him—his people wanted him to vote to remove Long as chairman.[4]

The advertised blow was not long in falling. LeBlanc took his seat at the next regular meeting of the Commission on December 3. Huey, knowing what would happen, did not bother to attend. The scene that ensued was an exact reproduction of the procedure by which Huey earlier had removed Taylor. LeBlanc moved that the Commission be reorganized and nominated Williams as chairman. The motion was seconded by Williams and carried unanimously. Williams then took the chair and announced that during his tenure the position would not be used, as it had been in the past, to further the "selfish political ambitions of any member" or as "an instrument of personal or political revenge." It was immediately evident that other understandings had been reached. On the very next day the attorney of the Standard Pipe Line Company appeared before the Commission and asked it to annul Huey's order of May 5, 1923, that had set rates the company considered confiscatory. (This was the order that Huey had been enjoined by court action from enforcing but that still was on the books.) The company also asked that a new set of rates, which it suggested, be prescribed by the Commission. Within two weeks the new majority, without holding a hearing, acceded to the company's requests. The May order was annulled, and the rate schedule proposed by the company was accepted. In announcing its decision, the Commission even used much of the same language contained in the company's petition. Huey's long struggle against Standard had apparently ended in failure.[5]

Huey rarely attended a meeting after the reorganization. He took the position that it would be no use for him to appear. Williams and LeBlanc would do what they wanted to do, and would favor the corporations, whether or not he was present. On one occasion Williams and LeBlanc invited him through Secretary Jastremski to come to a meeting where an issue that he had special knowledge of was to be discussed. Huey fired back a hot reply to the secretary: "Let Francis Williams and Dudley LeBlanc write their own letters to me and sign them. I recognize no message sent by them

[4] Sindler: *Huey Long's Louisiana*, p. 51; Deutsch: "Kingdom of the Kingfish," in New Orleans *Item*, August 7, 1939; LeBlanc, quoted in unidentified clipping, December 2, 1926, in Arthur Provost Scrapbook, in possession of Arthur Provost, New Iberia, La.

[5] Long: *Every Man a King*, pp. 84–5; John L. Loos: *Oil on Stream!* (Baton Rouge, 1959), pp. 97–9; Minute Book, Louisiana Public Service Commission, II, December 3, 1926; *Louisiana Public Service Commission, Sixth Annual Report*, pp. 133–5.

through you. If either of them wish to concede their incompetency to fill the position to which they elected themselves let them put it in writing and sign it and not make such a confession through you. Wire them to this effect."

The two other members soon discovered that they would need Huey's help to conduct the business of the Commission. He had so completely dominated the agency that he alone knew the background and the relevant facts of many cases that Williams and LeBlanc had to consider. Moreover, he had acted as the Commission's attorney in cases that got into the courts, and some of these suits were now pending and demanded attention. Williams and LeBlanc did not have the technical knowledge or the competency to handle the cases, and they had to ask Huey to take them over. He watched their squirming with amused scorn. To a request from Williams that he represent the Commission, Huey answered that Francis and Dudley must defend the agency themselves. "I am not saying that you are competent to do it," he wrote. "I am simply accepting the fact that you have elected yourselves to do it, and I will not interfere, but will rather defer to your demonstrations, despite the fact that they have heretofore been disappointing."[6]

It was not pride or pique that kept Huey away from the meetings, but lack of interest. Even when he was chairman, he had attended only a few sessions. In fact, he had not really been interested in the Commission or its work since 1924. After that year he directed all his thought and effort to the attainment of one goal, the governorship, the next step on the ladder that long ago he had said he would climb. A reporter asked him after the Broussard campaign if a rumor that he might run for a lesser office was true. Huey answered with an emphatic no. "I am now," he said, "and have been for the past three years—in fact, ever since the last election day rain—a candidate for governor in the next election."[7]

[6] Long to Henry Jastremski, December 16, 1926 (telegram), January 13, 1927, Francis Williams to Long, January 19, 1927, Long to Williams, January 29, 1927, in Long Papers, Public Service Commission File.
[7] New Orleans *States*, October 17, 1926.

# CHAPTER 11

# *In the Radiance of the Future*

SEASONED POLITICAL OBSERVERS could not recall a gubernatorial campaign ever getting off to such an early start. In February 1927, with the election a full eleven months away, the political pot was already bubbling with rumors of things to come. Customarily a campaign did not open until the late spring or early summer. At that time the various hopefuls would put out their feelers, attempt to make their deals, and publish their tentative announcements. The serious campaigning would not begin until the fall, when the candidates who had survived the first round of elimination embarked on their stump-speaking tours. But in 1927 it was evident that the pattern was going to be different.

In February pudgy Arthur O'Keefe, Behrman's successor as mayor of New Orleans and titular head of the Old Regulars, felt called upon to state what the policy of his organization would be in the coming campaign. The machine would "let the country pick the candidate," the mayor said, and would endorse the aspirant most favored in the parishes. Such a statement of purpose—"we'll keep our hands off till we make the deal"—had regularly issued from whoever was chief of the Old Regulars in every campaign, but never before had it come so early.

Political observers immediately surmised what had prompted the mayor to make his declaration. In this campaign candidates for the chief office were appearing long before the customary time for them to announce. In fact, two "name" contenders were already in the field, and although they had not formally declared themselves, they were openly running. Governor Oramel H. Simpson had been an avowed candidate almost from the day he succeeded Fuqua in the fall of 1926. If this seemed an unusually long period to sustain a race, it paled to nothing in comparison with the feat of the other candidate. Huey P. Long had been running since he nominated himself the day after the 1924 election.[1]

Both of these early runners were obviously developing strength, but neither was acceptable to the powerful Old Regular organization, and this was the message that Mayor O'Keefe was trying to signal to the state's politicians. He was saying, in effect, bring forward a candidate that we in the city can support, one who has a chance of beating Long and Simpson.

By its very nature, the machine had to reject Huey. Its conservative leaders viewed him as a wild radical who should be crushed before he became dangerous. But even if they could have accommodated themselves to his economic ideas, they would still have opposed him, because they recognized his political type—he had to lead, and he would subordinate any group that went with him, even the most potent of machines, to his own personal power.

No such profound reason dictated the machine's veto of Simpson's candidacy. Nothing in what was known of the governor's economic thinking disturbed the Old Regular chiefs. Simpson had, in fact, no clearly articulated philosophy of the role of the state in the economy, and the few ideas that he had expressed on the subject indicated a basic conservatism. True, he had aligned himself with the force supporting a free state bridge and had thereby offended the machine, which was allied with the Watson-Williams syndicate, but this was not put down against him as an indication of radicalism but was regarded indulgently as a bid for votes.

Nor did the Choctaw leaders have any fears that as governor he would be too dominating. On the contrary, there was every evidence that he would be the most understanding and pliable of chief executives. His long service as secretary of the senate had left him with what might be called a "caretaker" psychology; he instinctively operated to please all the elements in a power structure, giving highest priority to the most powerful.

It was simple politics that caused the Old Regulars to repudiate Simpson. They did not think he could be elected. He did not have the standing or stature to qualify as a candidate. Born in one of the southern parishes, he had spent most of his adult life in New Orleans and knew hardly any people in the rest of the state. He had

[1] Hermann B. Deutsch: "Kingdom of the Kingfish," in New Orleans *Item*, August 8, 1939.

what passed for an organization, but it had been hastily formed and was restricted to the south. He had no personal magnetism and was a poor speaker. One positive attribute he did have, but it was an additional handicap—he was said to be a heavy drinker. Louisianians more than most people tolerated drinking by their politicians, but even they were shocked by tales of the governor's addiction. All in all, he did not impress the Old Regulars as a strong candidate. He was certainly not the man to accomplish what was rapidly becoming a principal objective with them—defeating Huey Long. Expectantly they studied the situation in the state and waited for a candidate to appear.[2]

For a time no one came forward who could attract organized support or stir popular interest with his own personality or an exciting issue. Mayor Lee Thomas of Shreveport was openly declaring himself, but he had almost no following, and his only issue was denouncing Long. Some evidence indicates that the Old Regulars asked state senator Henry Hardtner of Alexandria to make the race. Hardtner, whose district included Winn parish, was immensely wealthy from lumber and oil holdings and was thought able to finance his own campaign. Moreover, he had an incentive to run, in that he hated Huey, who had soundly beaten him in an important lawsuit (the Wheelus-Urania Lumber Company case) and had outraged him by attacking big business while on the Public Service Commission. In fact, it was reported that Hardtner had once threatened to leave the state unless Huey was removed from the Commission. But now he showed no desire to take on Huey. Declining the offer of the Old Regulars, he is said to have told them that the man they should back was the Congressman from the northeastern district, a resident of Ruston, Riley J. Wilson, who was known to his constituents as Riley Joe. Wilson would be a strong candidate, Hardtner urged, adding that he would be willing to make a generous financial contribution to help Wilson's campaign. Quite possibly Hardtner, as well as others, did press Wilson on the machine. But the city bosses were not going to take anyone up simply because influential leaders recommended him. They had to be convinced that Wilson had a chance, and to have a chance he had to have an issue. Suddenly, in the spring, one was literally thrown in his lap.

This lack of an issue was one big reason why more candidates had not entered the race. The Klan question that had dominated the campaign of 1924 was dead, killed by the antimasking legisla-

<hr>

[2] Confidential communication; sketch of Simpson drawn from Louisiana newspapers of 1927.

tion enacted by the Fuqua administration. The Klan had accepted the law, believing that it could live with it, and the public believed it would bring the downfall of the hooded order. Actually, the Klan had been weakened, but not because of the law; rather, and this was an experience duplicated in other states, its venture into politics had caused inner dissensions and a decline in membership. Although most of the politicians had reason to be glad that this issue had been eliminated, Huey had particular reason to rejoice. He could now concentrate on the economic issues that mattered most to him and that, to the surprise of the state's bosses, apparently mattered to the voters. He had, and this was what dismayed potential rivals, appropriated these issues to himself—free bridges, free textbooks, an expanded program of road construction, improved educational and institutional services, and opposition to machine and corporate rule. A candidate who took up the same planks would seem to be only aping Huey and would not profit by the action. A candidate who hoped to oppose Huey with any chance of success would have to raise a new issue, one with enough drama to catch the public's interest.

Such an issue seemed to develop in the spring, and it pushed Wilson immediately into the gubernatorial picture. It arose out of one of the worst natural disasters ever to strike Louisiana. The Mississippi, rolling down with its crest at an unusually high level, suddenly broke through the protecting levees and flooded nearly two million acres of land in Louisiana and other states and left 750,000 people homeless. The water covered the land for two months, and so vivid was the disaster to the people that for years to come it would be recalled simply as "the great flood of 1927." Published accounts of the suffering of people in the submerged area aroused nationwide sympathy. Relief trains bearing provisions were dispatched from Chicago and other cities, and from Washington came Secretary of Commerce Herbert Hoover to make a personal inspection for President Calvin Coolidge. As knowledge of the severity of the disaster spread, demands arose from the Mississippi Valley states for a more effective system of flood controls. The sheer extent of the inundation pointed up an obvious fact—a flood in the Valley was a problem for the whole nation, and to be effective, a control system would have to be constructed by the federal government. It was now evident that levees alone were not enough; spillways, bypasses, and reservoirs would be needed. A bill providing for these features was introduced in Congress by an Illinois representative. It was passed, although it was opposed by some who thought that the Val-

HUEY LONG / 248

ley states should bear part of the cost. Playing a prominent role in getting the bill through was the chairman of the House committee on flood control, who happened to be Riley Joe Wilson. He had been in the House for fourteen years and by the workings of the seniority system had risen to be chairman of the committee. In all his years of service he had achieved no particular distinction and in the normal course of events would have continued to be what he was, a useful but ordinary congressman. But now he seemed to stand forth in a new light, as an expert on flood control and a champion of Louisiana's welfare, the hero of the hour—and to the Old Regulars and the conservative hierarchy he appeared to be the man they had been looking for, the candidate with a fresh issue, the savior who could rescue them from Huey Long. Quickly the decision was reached and the plans were made—the state's rulers would back Riley Joe.[3]

Now that the lines were drawn, the tempo of the campaign picked up. Simpson officially declared his candidacy on July 5. He would state his platform and take the stump later, the governor said. He first had to see to it that the victims of the flood were cared for, and to that end he had summoned the legislature to meet in a special session in August to provide relief. Simpson's announcement did not stir very much public interest. It had been expected and had somewhat of an anticlimactic effect; furthermore, in the popular estimation he had slipped badly in strength now that it was known that the city-state organization would put a candidate in the field. The leaders of the hierarchy had called for a convention to take place in Alexandria on July 11, and it was on this gathering that public attention was focused.

The Alexandria meeting was a large, enthusiastic, and apparently successful one. Some two thousand delegates and supporters streamed into the little city and filled the high-school auditorium where the sessions were held. The New Orleans delegates arrived on a special train, each member sporting a large badge proclaiming: "It won't be Long." The keynote speaker announced that the meeting had been called to settle on a candidate to oppose Huey P. Long. The crowd chanted: "It won't be Long now." Other speakers instructed the delegates that they should unanimously endorse that sterling statesman who was fighting Louisiana's battle for flood control, Riley Joe Wilson. The delegates immediately endorsed Riley Joe Wilson and passed resolutions approving his efforts for

[3] Harley B. Bozeman; Bozeman, in *Winn Parish Enterprise*, January 22, 1959; Deutsch: "Kingdom of the Kingfish," in New Orleans *Item*, August 8, 1939.

flood control. A few days later J. Y. Sanders announced that he would support the choice of the convention. Coincidentally, J. Y. filed a petition in federal court to halt construction of the piers for the free Chef-Rigolets bridge, a project that by every indication had immense popular support. The chiefs of the hierarchy were rallying to the standard in characteristic fashion.[4]

Probably none of the chiefs realized that their convention had been a failure—that it had revealed serious weaknesses in their organization and that it had been inexpertly managed. A number of parishes had not been represented by delegations, and of the total number of delegates a disproportionately large fraction had come from one parish, Orleans. The enthusiasm of the delegates was obviously artificial, most of it whipped up by the noisy city representatives. Popular reaction to the proceedings was largely hostile. People wondered why the delegates, if they were so interested in flood control, had spent their main efforts in whooping it up against Huey Long. But what most repelled the voters was the full, painful evidence that this was a "bossed" convention. The bosses had summoned the convention, they had dictated to it the candidate, and then they had dismissed it. The democratic ritual had been openly affronted. The most interested—and the most delighted—observer of the meeting was Huey. He measured its effect perfectly. When a reporter asked for his reaction, he chortled: "That was a great convention. Give 'em rope." In a more intimate vein he wrote to a friend: "They held their Alexandria conference, but it has become a stench in the nostrils of the good people and gained us thousands of votes. Their effort to put out a band-box candidate, hand-picked by a set of plunder-bunders, has been of remarkable benefit for me."[5]

Riley Joe was not exactly the passive, pliable man that Huey described. He would not go to the hierarchy and ask for instructions nor repeat speeches that its leaders put into his mouth. He did not need its instruction, for he already believed in its ideals and voiced them with sincere conviction. Like Huey, he had been born in Winn parish, but he had been brought up in poverty, as an orphan. He had managed to attain an education, even to get in a year or so of college; he had taught school; and he had studied law and been ad-

[4] Leo Glenn Douthit: "The Governorship of Huey Long" (unpublished M.A. thesis, Tulane University, 1947), pp. 39–42; Shreveport *Daily Caucasian*, July 9, 1927; Huey P. Long: *Every Man a King* (New Orleans, 1933), p. 97.

[5] Lake Charles *American Press*, July 9, 1927; Long to Frank Odom, July 11, 1927 (letter in possession of Mr. Odom of Baton Rouge).

mitted to the bar. Moving about in the northern parishes, he went into politics wherever he lived. He had been a member of the legislature, a district attorney, and a judge. Settling down in Ruston in Lincoln parish, he had been elected to the House in 1914 and had held his seat ever since.

Of medium height, he had a stocky build and rugged features. His face and rough hands revealed the hard outdoor labor he had done in his youth. Or so pointed out his supporters, who tried hard, too hard, to depict him as a son of the poor. Why, they said, he had had to go without shoes as a boy.

He had come from the poor, but by his own efforts he had pulled himself above them. He was a recognizable type, the self-made man, who thought that all poor men were capable of rising as he had, by their own labors and without the intervention of state aid. The conservatives could have found no more dedicated spokesman for their views. In his speeches he stressed flood control, because that was supposed to be his particular issue, but he spoke with more conviction when he discussed restricting the role of government, economy in government, and the virtues of low taxes. He thought Huey's program to pave roads was preposterous—it would cost too much money. He opposed Huey's proposal to issue free textbooks because it would necessitate raising taxes; he would, however, provide books for the children of very poor parents if it could be done without "embarrassing" the recipients.[6] He was a perfect target for Huey, who took an impish delight in puncturing him. Two of Huey's quips became classics in Louisiana politics. Of Wilson's claim to be an expert on flood control, Huey observed: "The 'Honorable Riley of Ruston' they tell you is running for governor on his flood record, and I say that record is 14 feet of higher water this year than ever before, one foot for each one of his 14 years in Congress." And referring to the claim of Wilson's supporters that their candidate had gone barefoot as a boy, Huey rejoined: "I can go Mr. Wilson one better; I was born barefoot."[7]

Simpson had to wait until the special legislative session ended in August before he could announce his platform. When he did, it turned out to have few differences from Wilson's. Simpson admitted

[6] New Orleans *Morning Tribune*, August 11, 1927; Shreveport *Times*, August 20, 1927; Harrisonburg *News*, September 17, 1927; Slidell *Sun*, October 27, 1927; Rupert Peyton.

[7] Shreveport *Times*, September 11 and 17, 1927; Lafayette *Advertiser*, November 3, 1927.

the necessity for some change, for some kind of enlarged role for the state in economic matters, but he veiled his statements in such obscure language that he could have retreated from them if he had had to. He was in favor of free schoolbooks but only if the money to provide them could be secured without raising taxes: it should come from a tax on some nonproductive activity, like racetracks.[8] His principal lieutenants, however, made no secret of their conservatism or their belief that their leader was a conservative. His running mate, for lieutenant governor, Dr. Benjamin Pavy of St. Landry parish, declared that Simpson represented the "conservative element," as opposed to a candidate who stood for "radicalism and demagogism." Lee Thomas, possibly the most confirmed conservative in the state, endorsed Simpson; earlier he had said that the election of a "destructive and bolshevistic type" of candidate would be worse than the floods. To prevent the election of such a candidate the people should vote for the "safe and sane" Simpson, the Simpson leaders chorused. There was no doubt as to which candidate they were warning the voters to repudiate. They became more explicit as the campaign progressed. One of them, a rising young New Orleans politician, Richard W. Leche, referred to Long in a speech as "a patent medicine man with a cure for all ills, who will promise anything, but who is without a real constructive thought." Leche added witheringly: "Anybody can talk destruction." Both the Simpson and the Wilson people finally came to talk about nothing but the danger of Russian Communism as represented by Huey Long taking over the state. "Louisiana Must Not Let Bolshevism In" ran the headline of an editorial in a Shreveport paper. The writer admitted that Huey was brilliant—but so also had been Marx, Trotsky, and Lenin.[9]

Huey formally announced his candidacy on July 17. He would state his platform later, he said—at his opening rally, which would be held in Alexandria in the same auditorium used by the Wilson conclave. He was in a relaxed and confident mood as he talked about his plans, as if he knew that the victory was going to be his. The mood never left him during the campaign. He believed that even if he was defeated, the principles that he stood for and that he had awakened the people to strive for would win. Again and again,

[8] Douthit: "Governorship of Long," pp. 42–3; New Orleans *Times-Picayune*, December 5, 1927.

[9] Douthit: "Governorship of Long," pp. 39, 43; New Orleans *Times-Picayune*, November 14, 1927; Shreveport *Daily Caucasian*, December 8, 1927.

in speech after speech, he proclaimed his certainty in the ultimate triumph. "He who falls in this fight," he cried, "falls in the radiance of the future."[1]

His faith that the people were finally aroused was based on his own intuitive understanding of the popular mind, and it was well founded. But he was not going to rely on faith alone. In this campaign he would have, for the first time, an adequate amount of money to spend. He may have had, in fact, the largest fund of the three candidates. Just how large it was cannot be determined, but his public-relations representative later estimated it to have been over ninety thousand dollars. This man made his appraisal after he had broken with Huey and was trying to destroy him, so he was hardly an objective witness. He listed as substantial contributors several gamblers who may or may not have provided funds. On the other hand, he did not know about the contributions of other individuals who gave as much as he put the gamblers down for. It would seem a safe guess that Huey had a chest of well over a hundred thousand dollars, a huge sum for that time.[2]

The money came from a variety of sources. Some of it was contributed by individuals who wanted to stand in with the winner, politicians who hoped to be rewarded with an appointment, or businessmen who aspired to influence the course of legislation. A substantial part of it was advanced by men in the road business, contractors and cement and gravel dealers, who saw obvious possibilities in Huey's program to build surfaced roads. A donor with an equally obvious incentive was "Mike" Moss, of the Union Indemnity Company of New Orleans, which did a large bonding business with the state. Some of the contributors had mixed motives. They were friends or members of his family who admired or liked him or who were attracted by some part of his program. At the same time they hoped to get something in return for their support, an office or a law perhaps, but more important, they wanted to be a part of his entourage, to sit in the inner councils of the new power. Swords Lee, his cousin-contractor, handed over thirty thousand dollars. Will Henderson provided money, free radio time, and amplifiers for Huey's larger meetings. Earl Long, who had been making good money as a salesman for a shoe-polish company, put up ten thousand

[1] New Orleans *States*, August 26, 1927. Long either borrowed such flights of language from his reading or, as he apparently did in this case, composed them himself.

[2] Undated and unsigned memorandum, obviously by W. D. Robinson, in Robinson Papers.

dollars. Earl went all out for Huey in this campaign, but later he would charge, and Julius would back him up, that a public-utility company gave Huey at least ten thousand dollars in cash on the promise of expected favors. Possibly such a contribution was made, but the story told by Earl and Julius does not ring quite true. They spoke in a moment of bitter anger with Huey, and they disagreed on so many details that they have to be doubted.[3]

The largest contributor was a newcomer to the Long circle. Robert S. Maestri was reputed to be one of the wealthiest men in New Orleans and perhaps its biggest property owner. Of Italian ancestry, swarthy, impassive Maestri was the son of a poultry peddler who acquired enough money to buy a furniture store on the edge of the city's red-light district. Young Bob had no more than a third-grade education, but he was extremely shrewd, and upon taking over the store he built it into one of the town's largest retail outlets. He bought other property in the red-light district and, according to his critics, profited by selling beds and other items to the houses of prostitution. If a house was raided, he reclaimed the beds and resold them, thus instituting a process that was called "the original model of perpetual motion." Maestri denied that the bulk of his holdings was centered in the district and also denied that he held large interests in gambling houses in parishes adjoining Orleans. But whatever the sources of his wealth may have been, they were plentiful. He was rich, he was only in his early forties, and he was ambitious for other things besides money—notably power. Since he knew that he himself could not grasp it, he was looking for a greater man to seize it and then allot a part of it to him. At some time that cannot be determined, probably early in 1927, he settled on Huey. Just as he needed Huey, the rising politician, so Huey needed Maestri, the rich man who wanted to put his money on the line. How they came together is not certain—John P. Sullivan may have been the intermediary— nor are the terms of their compact known. But Maestri agreed to provide a large sum of money—probably close to forty thousand dollars.

He would give other and larger sums in the years ahead, whenever Huey asked for them. Huey knew that when he was in a financial pinch, he could go to Maestri and say: "Bob, I need fifty thousand dollars," and get it without a question. Hardly ever were

[3] Jess Nugent; Long: *Every Man a King,* p. 136; Harvey G. Fields: *A True History of the Life, Works, Assassination and Death of Huey P. Long* (Silver Spring, Md., 1944), p. 27; Harley B. Bozeman; Frank Odom; Paul B. Habans; *Overton Hearing,* I, 817–18, 841, 953–4.

these "loans" repaid. Maestri once ruefully remarked that the un-redeemed pledges reposed among his "souvenirs." He did not expect to be paid back, although on one occasion he consented to accept Huey's house in Shreveport as a surety. Sometimes he compensated himself by placing an odd bet: he would wager, say ten thousand dollars, at odds of one to five, that the governor would not honor his obligation. He generally found a taker, and when he collected, Huey would laugh and say: "You're paid back, ain't you?" Maestri did not care whether or not he was repaid in money: his recompense was something that was much more important to him. Not only did he hold an appointive office, but better than that, he was a member of the Long retinue; he sat in the inner council, very close to Huey. He gave unswerving loyalty to Huey and to the Long program. It is doubtful, however, that he ever understood Huey's social objectives or the methods that Huey as a politician had to use to win his objectives. Ignorant of the theory of democracy and as taciturn as an Indian, he did not appreciate the necessity for a dialogue between a leader and the people. He never ceased to be amazed that Huey felt called on to explain issues to the voters. "Huey and his explaining," he would say, and shake his head.[4]

Every contribution to Huey's fund was, as far as can be determined, in the form of cash. And every expenditure was in cash. Huey was not, if he could help it, going to leave any documentary evidence for his enemies to seize on. But there were problems involved in handling such large sums of cash. The money had to be kept somewhere; and when Huey, campaigning over the state, needed a certain amount, he had to have some reliable person he could telephone to bring it to him. Apparently he put part of his fund in a safety vault in a Shreveport bank. He entrusted another part of it to an individual who now appeared for the first time as an important member of the Long group, and who from this time on would assume increasingly greater prominence. This was Alice Lee Grosjean, who officially was Huey's secretary. Slight but well-proportioned, pretty, and intelligent, she had had only two years of secretarial experience before she caught on with Huey in 1923 at

[4] Harnett T. Kane: *Louisiana Hayride* (New York, 1941), p. 241; Hamilton Basso: "The Death and Legacy of Huey Long," *New Republic*, LXXXV (January 1, 1936), 216; Fields: *Long*, p. 68; *Overton Hearing*, I, 382–3, 392; Charles Frampton; Richard W. Leche. Maestri's aversion to extended speech became a tradition in Louisiana. It was perfectly illustrated when years hence as mayor of New Orleans he served as host to President Franklin D. Roosevelt when the latter visited the city. During a luncheon at Antoine's the mayor addressed but one remark to the President: "How do you like them ersters?"

the age of eighteen. In his first race for governor she proved to be an adept worker, and after it she gradually took on a larger role. She became Huey's confidante to whom he turned for advice and comfort in moments of reverse and for praise in times of triumph. Close associates of his have said that he trusted her completely, which is not quite accurate. He was too cynical ever to place his full faith in any person, but as much of it as he could give, he gave Miss Grosjean. In 1927 he let her hold a large portion of his money. She carried it in bills hidden in her bosom. In Shreveport she would await a telephone call from Huey telling her where to meet him. After handing over to him the amount he needed, she would return to Shreveport, where she probably replenished her cache from Huey's vault funds.[5]

Huey faced the campaign with confidence, because he had money and also because he now had an organization. It was an organization that he had built up himself in the three years since the last election, and it showed that it was not only hastily constructed but also completely a one-man machine. Indeed, on the state level it hardly deserved to be called a machine. Rather, it was a loose alliance of leaders presided over by Huey. These leaders were men who had an obligation to Huey, who hoped to ride into power with him, or who had no other place to go. Among them were some big names. Senator Edwin Broussard, although he did not take an active part in the campaign, honored his commitment made two years earlier and let it be known to his followers in the southwestern parishes that he favored Huey. Also redeeming a commitment was Senator Joseph Ransdell, who obviously felt uncomfortable in the Long camp. Ransdell endorsed Huey through his brother, F. X. Ransdell, denying defensively that Long was a radical.

Another "name" figure in the state group was John H. Overton of Alexandria, a recent recruit to the Long cause. No pledge of the past had brought Overton in; rather, he wanted a stake in the future. Overton was an unusual figure in Louisiana politics and in some ways a pathetic one. Although he was a man of ability, he had never achieved his ambitions. He believed he could grace a high office, governor or United States senator, and he had tried repeatedly to get the state's leaders to support him for one or the other of these offices and every time had failed. On the surface he seemed to have all the qualities that would ensure success. He was a skilled lawyer, a gentleman and an aristocrat who sympathized with the aspirations

[5] Unidentified clipping in Grace Scrapbook; confidential communications; W. D. Robinson to Julius Long, June 1, 1933, in Robinson Papers.

of the masses, and a politician of reputed absolute probity. Of average height and heavily built, he was a spellbinding stump orator, and he had personal contacts all over the state. His admirers have a ready explanation for his failure: he was too fine a man to be a good politician. "Overton stood aloof from the massy side of politics," said one of them. It would be more accurate to say that he lacked some of the qualities necessary to a politician. Most serious, he had a fatal fault in communication. He could dazzle audiences with his oratory, but could not persuade them that he loved them and wanted to help them. Overton came to realize his shortcoming. If he was going to achieve his ambition, he would have to ally himself with a "massy" leader. He decided to go with Huey, and friends of his insist that he did this without asking Huey for a promise of any kind. This is probably accurate, but only in a literal sense. Overton did not ask for a specific office, and Huey did not offer him one. But politicians dealing in such a situation do not ordinarily discuss specifics; they do not have to. Both Huey and Overton understood what was required of them and their need for each other. Huey wanted Overton and went out of his way to get him. Overton could bring to the Long cause some valuable assets—respectability, social standing, a reputation for idealism and honesty. He deserved a reward and would get it—at the proper time.[6]

An important part of the state organization, though operating largely on its own, was the New Orleans faction. It too was a recent creation, and like the state coalition it exhibited some qualities that were the result of its origin—a certain incoherence, a lack of central purpose or direction. Huey had forged it in the Broussard campaign of 1926, and at that time it had included three elements he thought would be helpful to him in his own campaign: Colonel Robert Ewing and his influential *States*, John P. Sullivan and his New Regulars, and Paul Maloney and his dissident Old Regulars. Huey understood he had pledges of support from all three men, but it soon developed that they did not feel they were bound to him. Ewing and Sullivan hemmed and hawed and refused to make a public pronouncement of their choice. Either they had fears that Huey would not follow their direction and held out for a promise of some kind, or they could not agree as to which of them would dominate him. Huey had to negotiate further with them before he secured their endorsements. Maloney was even more difficult. He too held back from announcing a decision and then finally came out for Simpson, becoming, in fact, the governor's campaign manager in New Orleans.

Even with the loss of Maloney, Huey had high hopes of what his city organization could do for him. He knew it could not carry the metropolis, but he thought it should be able to turn out a substantial vote, large enough when combined with his country vote to sweep him to victory in the first primary. He was overlooking or refusing to recognize the structural weakness of the organization. Presumably it was to be directed by Sullivan, the professional politician, but the division of authority between him and Ewing, the amateur, was not clearly drawn. Also trying to exercise influence was Maestri, who naturally was interested in how the campaign was to be run in his own city. And competing with Maestri was another wealthy Italian-American, Nicholas Carbajal, who had put up ten thousand dollars for the campaign chest. Carbajal had thought he would be the Long leader in the city, but he found himself being pushed into the background by Sullivan and Maestri. He presided dutifully over the state headquarters in the Pere Marquette building, but he was resentful and likely to act on his own.[7]

Originally, Huey's campaign headquarters were to have been in Covington, a small town in another parish, near New Orleans. Huey had designated as his state manager a prominent citizen of the town, Harvey Ellis, a scion of an old and aristocratic family. Ellis's position was largely titular—what central direction was exercised came from Huey—but his name at the head of the organization invested it with respectability. He had hardly taken up his duties, however, when he resigned, publicly and with a blast at Huey. He did not like Sullivan and felt that the city campaign manager ignored him. In his public letter to Huey he charged that Sullivan was affiliated with gambling and other vice interests and said his support should not have been accepted. Huey replied in a public letter that was a masterpiece of equivocation. He did not deny the charges against Sullivan but observed in a sanctimonious tone that he himself had never bet on a

---

[7] Long: *Every Man a King*, pp. 94, 96–7; Deutsch: "Kingdom of the Kingfish," in New Orleans *Item*, August 9, 1939; Paul Maloney; confidential communication; Fields: *Long*, p. 68; Shreveport *Times*, June 12, 1927. Long's account of the formation of his city organization does not seem to me to be in strict accord with the facts. It does not mention his conversations with Ewing and Sullivan in 1926 and it implies that he was doubtful about accepting Sullivan's support. Actually he wanted both men. With Ewing behind him, he had the support of one of the three most widely circulated papers in the city, the *States*. The *Times-Picayune* went for Simpson, and the *Item* endorsed Wilson, as did the *Morning Tribune*, which on Sunday appeared as the *Item-Tribune*.

horse or dog race in his life. He seemed to be saying that if bad men wanted to support him he could safely let them because he could control them. He named a new manager, whose position was also titular, Sheriff Charles L. Pecot of St. Mary's parish in the south.[8]

It was significant that in choosing his so-called managers Huey in each case picked a man from a rural parish. He did this because in the country parishes he had a real organization, one that he was relying on to furnish the bulk of his votes. Its effectiveness was attested to later by an Old Regular leader who himself was something of an expert organizer: "Well, he had a wonderful country organization when he was elected Governor, the best I have ever seen in my political experience."[9] The country organization of 1927 was the basis or the prototype of what later would be called "the Long machine." It was a true machine, but it is hard to describe; and when its structure is outlined it does not seem to fit the common concept of what a machine is. The word "machine" conjures up certain pictures: a boss who sits in a central headquarters and issues orders down through a neat chain of command, sub-bosses who execute the orders through blocs of workers who in turn supervise blocs of voters, and the whole held together by some mechanistic power. Conceivably there have been machines like this, certainly in urban centers, but it is doubtful that many such organizations ever existed in many states, especially in any rural state, as Louisiana was in the 1920's.

What makes the Long machine so hard to describe is, paradoxically, its apparent simplicity. Structurally it was no more than a combination of sheriffs and courthouse rings and local leaders. Some of the "rings," an undeterminable number, but a minority, had gone with Huey in 1924. Since that election more and more of them, from all over the state, had drifted into his camp. Probably by 1927 a majority of these powerful groups were aligned with him. They had not come over because their chiefs agreed with Huey's program or admired him personally, although in some cases these were their motives, nor had they come because the chiefs had negotiated with Huey as equals and secured some kind of promise from him. They came without any negotiation and with no promises and as subordinates. They had to come. They were responding to one of the most impelling rules of politics—self-preservation, the desire to survive and to be with the winner. Some of these men, when asked

---

[8] Shreveport *Times*, June 12, 1927; James T. Burns.

[9] T. Semmes Walmsley, mayor of New Orleans, quoted in *Overton Hearing*, II, 1977–8.

to explain their action, cannot or will not do so. The usual response is: "We just naturally went with him." Others, franker or more perceptive, see the reason—the leaders were only obeying the clear, demanding will of their people. "They fell in line," said an official of Allen, a poor small-farmer parish. "The people were for him."

The people were for him because he had held up to them the hope of a better life and because now, at last, they were convinced, by him, that they could have it. "He taught them to think," said a leader of the French parish of Lafourche. "He educated them to him." In some French parishes—Lafourche and Terrebonne, for example—the sentiment for Huey was so strong that the sheriffs and courthouse crowds declared for him even before the campaign began. Soon after it started, the rings in most of the southwestern parishes came out for Huey. This was Senator Broussard's home territory, and it has been supposed that the various machines were only repaying Huey for his support of Coozan Ed in 1926. Some of them may have been moved by a sense of obligation, but the majority acted for cold political reasons. Their leaders measured the sentiments of their people, calculated the probable outcome in the state, and then decided to cooperate with the inevitable. Lafayette parish is a case in point. The twelve ring chiefs in this populous area were exceptionally able and completely professional. They had a rule that they would ballot on a candidate and all would support the choice of the majority. In 1927, when Huey was in the city of Lafayette on a campaign visit, they met and voted overwhelmingly to support him, inviting him then to come to the meeting to hear their decision. He had not asked for their endorsement and gave them no promises. Following the conference, however, nearly every elected and appointed official in the parish signed a resolution affirming support of Huey. Not even Senator Broussard had ever commanded such a united outpouring of approval.[1]

In some parishes Huey had the support of the richest and most powerful men of the area. They might or might not be connected

[1] Confidential communications; Ernest Clements; Harvey Peltier; Numa F. Montet; Montet to Long, April 15, 1927, in Long Papers, Law File; Wilson J. Peck; Edgar G. Mouton; A. Wilmot Dalferes; Waldo A. Dugas; Shreveport *Times*, August 18, 1927; Lafayette *Advertiser*, November 3, 1927. Although the parish examples cited above were in south Louisiana, the psychology of local leaders in the north, Huey's home ground, and in central and western Louisiana was the same and often even more pronounced: C. J. Downs (Rapides); C. C. Barham (Lincoln); R. S. Copeland (Vernon). Mr. Copeland provided a rundown on the financing of a campaign in a parish. He put up all the money spent in Vernon, $3,150; a newspaper publisher in Leesville printed all of Huey's advertisements and other material free; and the local leaders distributed Huey's circulars at their own expense.

with the courthouse crowd. If they were with it, they dominated it. If they were outside it, they overshadowed it. This situation was most likely to exist in the French parishes, where the masses had a tradition of voting at the direction of the local "great man," the "grand seigneur" or lord. These seigneurs had something of the psychology of a benevolent despot. They were men of wealth who led poor men, and they had paternalistic feelings toward those under them. They wanted to help their followers, to uplift them economically and educationally. They enjoyed the sensation when those who had been helped thanked them—and pledged their undying allegiance. Such men would naturally be attracted to Huey. A vigorous governor who expanded state services could do much for them. He could give them roads, schools, and patronage to dispense, and they would be more powerful and would seem even more benevolent. Huey, for his part, needed the seigneurs. They could bring to him large blocs of votes and the prestige of their names. He went out to get them. He played on their sense of responsibility and on their vanity with flattery. In the words of one who was secured, he sold them "a bill of goods." His sales talk, as reproduced by this man, went something like this: "If you stick by me, I can do this for the people. The people will be better not only in your community but in the state as a whole. I'm proud of this state. But I need people like you to help me. Without people like you I can't do any good."

With such an approach Huey drew to his side the powerful Fisher family of Jefferson, a coastal parish adjoining Orleans. The Fishers operated a variety of enterprises related to the economy of the area—furs, fishing, canning. Isidore Fisher was the head of the clan, assisted by his son and lieutenant, Joseph. Isidore's brother, Jules, was a state senator and president of the Fisher Shrimp Company, whose sales markets reached to Latin America. Through their network of enterprises the family dealt with a host of common folk —fishermen, trappers, cannery workers—and they commanded the allegiance of these people, not only in Jefferson but in other coastal parishes as well. They liked Huey and much of his program, realized his appeal to their people, and saw him as the power of the future; and together with the Jefferson courthouse ring they went all out to elect him.[2]

In the nearby parish of Assumption a similar yet somewhat different power arrangement existed. The courthouse crowd was

[2] Joseph Fisher.

loosely organized and exercised little influence. Control of the parish's politics, and also of a good part of its economy, rested with two men, Clay Dugas and Clarence Savoie. Dugas was the manager of a plantation, Belle Rose, that was owned by out-of-state land-lords. He was a man of moderate economic circumstances, but he had immense personal prestige with the French people. He was their friend and protector and political mentor: "Nonc," or Uncle, Clay, and when Nonc Clay said to vote for a certain man because he was a good man and also because he might do something for Nonc Clay, they were very likely to do it. He wanted to raise his people from poverty, and he liked Huey's program of free school-books and surfaced roads (he saw also that better roads would make it easier for poor people to vote), and he would probably have sup-ported Huey for ideological reasons alone. Huey wanted to secure him and, to make sure that he would, promised him the directorship of the state penitentiary at Angola, an institution badly in need of reform. Savoie, in contrast to Dugas, was a man of great wealth. He owned a string of plantations and employed on them a large number of workers to whom he was a kindly, paternalistic boss. He needed nothing from Huey. He already had money, and though, like Dugas, he enjoyed the feeling of helping people, he could already do so. Yet he joined Huey and remained a Long man, even assisting to pass laws that he disapproved of and that ran counter to his eco-nomic interests. Huey got him and held him with flattery, and Savoie was fascinated by Huey and by the power apparatus that Huey built. Like Maestri, the son of the Italian peddler, this planter was intoxicated by the knowledge that he was a part of the apparatus, one of its leaders, able to walk into the governor's office any time he wanted to.

All over the state Huey had supporters like the Fishers or Savoie. In Madison parish there was J. B. ("Jeff") Snyder, judge, feudal overlord, patron of authors, "king of the river"; in Ouachita, Print M. Atkins, wealthy and respected banker; in Iberville, Calvin K. Schwing, state senator and owner of rich lumber and oil lands; in East Baton Rouge, Justin C. Daspit and Elmo Badley, scions of old and aristocratic families. The Long movement might represent the aspirations of the common people, but in 1927 many of its leaders were of the upper classes.[3]

[3] C. J. (Bobbie) Dugas; Felix Dugas; Leon LeSueur; Donaldsonville *Chief,* De-cember 17, 1927, January 7, 1928; Roland B. Howell; Mrs. Theo Terzia; Shreveport *Times,* June 12, 1927; New Orleans *States,* October 12, 1927. Nothing in the above

Over three thousand people crowded into the auditorium of Bolton high school at Alexandria on the night of August 3 to hear Huey deliver his opening address of the campaign. Another five thousand assembled on the lawn in front of the school, or so a friendly newspaper estimated. The papers customarily exaggerated the size of the audiences at meetings of candidates they favored, but in this case the figure was probably not far wrong. Huey's speech was carried to the people in the building and beyond it by amplifiers borrowed from a radio station, and the novelty of the device alone was calculated to attract listeners.

Above the platform stretched banners proclaiming the Long slogan: Every Man a King, But No One Wears a Crown.[4] John H. Overton presided and introduced the dignitaries on the platform, among whom were John P. Sullivan and Swords Lee, and the candidate, who was also the speaker of the evening. Huey gave the same kind of speech that he had given in launching his campaign four years before, the kind that every candidate had to deliver as an opener—a lengthy, factual, and not very inspiring address that was in reality a recital of his platform. He observed the ritual of denouncing the New Orleans Ring ("I have always fought that regime") and stigmatized former governor Sanders as the evil force behind the state ring (J. Y. had replaced Parker as the directing genius). He wanted to make Louisiana into "a progressive, educated and modern commonwealth." He promised free textbooks, free bridges, surfaced roads ("practically every public road" should be surfaced), improved state hospitals and other institutions, natural gas for New Orleans and other cities, state warehouses to aid farmers in marketing their crops, vocational training for the deaf, dumb, and blind, and an expanded court system. He strongly implied that the state should supply financial assistance to local school

---

portrait of Long leaders is intended to deny that some of them were actuated by crass motives. They hoped to get patronage or state contracts or some easy money, and some of them later collected. They would have expected such rewards, however, from any candidate they chose to support. The point to be made is that, while still hopeful of rewards, they went for Huey for other reasons; they were not calling the tune.

[4] Long took this slogan from a speech by the Democratic leader of an earlier generation, William Jennings Bryan, which he quoted as: "Behold a Republic! whose every man is a King, but no one wears a crown"; Long: *Every Man a King*, p. 297 n. He rendered Bryan's words somewhat freely, although he did not distort their sense. For the speech, see Wayne D. Williams: *William Jennings Bryan: A Study in Political Vindication* (New York, 1923), p. 35. I am indebted to Professor Paolo Coletta for help in determining this question.

units (every boy and girl should be able to live at home and have access to an education) and to students of poor families who wished to attend higher institutions. He denied that he was hostile to corporations. He had opposed only the evil ones, but he thought that all the big ones should bear a higher and fairer burden of taxation.

There was little that was new in what he said. He had advocated most of these proposals four years before and had been preaching them ever since. He did inject one new note, however. He announced that he was running at the head of a "ticket," with a slate of supporting candidates. One of these appeared on the platform, Paul N. Cyr, candidate for lieutenant governor, a dentist of Jeanerette in the southwest who spoke French fluently and was expected to appeal to the French voters. Other Long candidates were H. B. Conner of Baton Rouge for state treasurer, Columbus Reid of a southern parish—whose father had represented Huey in the Parker libel case —for attorney general, and John S. Patten of a northern parish for superintendent of education. It was a bobtailed ticket—he had no candidates for secretary of state, state auditor, register of lands, and commissioner of agriculture—but it was more complete than a Louisiana ticket had ever been. A candidate for governor would usually associate with himself an aspirant for the second office, a man from a different section who could bring him votes, but he would leave the lesser offices to whoever wanted to scramble for them, to the so-called independents. To conservatives Huey's departure from tradition seemed like an unprincipled bid for votes.

It was Overton rather than Huey who carried off the oratorical honors of the meeting. In his opening remarks Overton, who had a talent for satire, drew a vivid picture of the meeting of the Wilson delegates in the same building a month earlier. They had come together, he said, because the word had been passed that "an heir-apparent and a Crown Prince was going to be born to rule over the State of Louisiana for the next four years." And so the loyal nobles of the reigning dynasty had assembled. "The Lords and Dukes and the Earls took leave in their Lincoln limousines, in their Rolls Royce automobiles, and in their Pullman palace cars, and went down to Alexandria to witness the birth of the Royal Crown Prince and Heir-Apparent to the throne of the State of Louisiana. And lo and behold, on the day of their arrival the political stork arrived, and lo and behold, was born the Imperial Crown Prince, Riley, of Ruston!" Huey was convulsed as he listened to the description, and later he said to Overton: "Think yourself up another speech, John.

I'm going to use yours." He quoted parts of it in almost every speech he made during the campaign.[5]

Before he ever entered on the campaign, Huey had planned every detail of how he would conduct it. He saw no reason to alter any of his familiar techniques. But now, with more money at his disposal, he was able to enlarge and improve them. Thus in 1927 he relied again on his circulars to carry his message to the people, but he published a greater volume of them than he ever had before. A careful estimate concludes that in the last four months of the year he prepared broadsides dealing with a dozen different issues and distributed more than a million copies of them. One circular contained statistical evidence on the high cost of schoolbooks in Louisiana and a comparison with the cost in Texas, where the state provided the books; another reproduced a letter from New Orleans business interests thanking him for his services to the city in the Galveston rate case; and a third proclaimed that the Old Regular-controlled city government had failed to develop the port of New Orleans.

Huey wrote the copy for every circular himself, scrawling it out in longhand or dictating it to a secretary. Sometimes he personally delivered the copy to the concern that printed them, the Franklin Printing Company of New Orleans. The Franklin Company had first done some printing for Huey in 1923, and after that date it did all of his big jobs. Huey liked and trusted the president, Joseph B. David, who worshipped Huey. David even worked without compensation, confident that Huey would pay up when he could. No detail of the printing escaped Huey's attention. He selected the quality of the paper on which the circulars were printed. Mindful of the sanitary practices of his rural constituents, he instructed David: "Don't use any of that damn smooth stuff. Use some that they can use on their backsides after they get through reading it." The printed circulars were delivered to the Long headquarters in New Orleans and from there mailed out over the state. Typically, a consignment would be sent to the Long leaders in every parish; they, in turn, were expected to distribute them in any way they chose, as long as it was effective.

The state organization distributed some circulars directly. Huey employed a number of "advertising trucks" that, with their sides emblazoned with pictures of Huey, went into towns and villages carrying circulars, posters, and other materials. The trucks, an-

[5] *Speeches of Huey P. Long, John H. Overton, Paul N. Cyr Delivered at Alexandria* (pamphlet, New Orleans, n.d., probably 1927), *passim*; Shreveport *Times*, August 4, 1927; New Orleans *States*, August 4, 1927; Long: *Every Man a King*, 97–9; Douthit: "Governorship of Long," pp. 40–1; Seymour Weiss; Roland B. Howell; Mrs. John H. Overton.

other of Huey's innovations in Louisiana politics, were under the direction of Earl Long and Frank Odom of Baton Rouge, both veteran salesmen who were expert at putting out display advertising.[6]

In 1923 Huey had had to distribute his literature and tack up his posters himself. Now he could entrust this work to members of his organization and save his main energies for stumping the state. He knew the vital importance of a stump tour, knew that, in fact, a successful one could determine the outcome of a statewide election. The voters of Louisiana prized oratory as an art, judged it with a professional interest, and evaluated a candidate almost solely by how he handled himself on the platform. They wanted to hear the candidates, and they also wanted to see them, to shake their hands, to exchange a greeting with them. Huey knew also that he faced two rivals who were poor speakers and colorless personalities and that in contrast with them he would show to brilliant advantage. So he decided to present himself to as many people as he could reach; he wanted to reach, if possible, every voter, to conduct a tour such as the state had never seen, one so extensive and intensive that it would tax even his powers of energy. It was a prodigious goal he set for himself, but he came close to accomplishing it. For fast transportation he traveled in an automobile, doing some of the driving himself, entrusting some of it to Dave McConnell or one of his numerous cousins, Otho Long. On some days he made as many as nine speeches, beginning at nine-thirty in the morning, riding and speaking all day, and ending with an address at eight o'clock at night. To the amazement of those who tried to follow him, he did not break under his labors but, rather, seemed to thrive on them. "I am feeling fine," he assured an associate in a tone of almost manic elation. "Just making three and four speeches a day. Conferring and organizing is simply wonderful work. I am in fine shape today. I can knock 'em dead for the next ten or fifteen days. I never felt as well in my lifetime." At the end of the campaign he estimated—and his figures were not far wrong—that he had traveled fifteen thousand miles by automobile, made six hundred speeches, and addressed a total of three hundred thousand people.[7]

Huey's speaking habits were much the same as they had been

[6] Burton H. Hotaling: "Huey Pierce Long as Journalist and Propagandist," *Journalism Quarterly*, XX (1943), 22; Long, circular on free books, in my possession; circulars on Galveston case and New Orleans port, in Leche Scrapbooks; Joseph B. David; Bozeman, in *Winn Parish Enterprise*, December 18, 1958.

[7] Shreveport *Times*, December 14, 1927; Long to W. D. Robinson, October 10, 1927, in Robinson Papers; New Orleans *States*, January 5, 1928.

in his previous campaigns. His voice was reasonably deep, resonant, and vibrant, and it could reach to the edges of a large audience without strain. Inside a building he could talk for an hour or more to crowds of fifteen hundred or two thousand people. His outside rallies drew throngs of thirty-five hundred or four thousand people, and on these occasions he used amplifiers when he could procure them. He had apparently curbed an earlier fault of raising his voice shrilly when making a point. By the standards of professional speech judges, he still made too many motions while speaking. But his rural audiences expected an orator to move, and his contortions added to his effectiveness. A man who traveled with him in 1927 thus describes him on the platform: "He had a mannerism of always being in motion. He had a freewheeling body. Head, hair, arms, shoulders—everything would move in a different direction, and he kept the people looking at him, even two hours at a stretch in the hot sun." He used no notes or any written aids while speaking, relying on his memory to supply him with whatever facts, figures, or names he required. He usually gave the same speech in each town, varying it only with local references. Wherever he was speaking, in city, town, or hamlet, he projected the same appealing image—the young, idealistic reformer who wanted to move the state forward. A reporter who heard him in a village on Bayou Teche remembered the scene vividly: "It was late fall, but the long bayou summer had lingered and the evening was hot and still. There were patches of perspiration on the blue shirts of the fishermen and the women stirred the air with slow palmetto fans. Huey, his shirt plastered to his back with sweat, was speaking from the rear seat of a Ford. . . ." As the reporter listened to the speaker attacking the big corporations and promising a better life for the poor, he was as impressed as the audience: "I thought that here was a young and forceful radical it would be well to support." He reflected how refreshing Huey appeared beside the Old Regular chiefs and especially in contrast to Mayor O'Keefe, who had on one occasion refused a request by a delegation of women to build a proposed municipal entertainment center in the shape of a Greek theater. There weren't enough Greeks in New Orleans to support such a theater, the mayor explained.[8]

Huey's speeches were reported with reasonable accuracy and fullness in the press, even in papers that were opposed to him, which included practically all the urban dailies. The coverage was more the

[8] Paul Flowers; Shreveport *Times*, September 11, 1927; Leon Gary; David B. McConnell; Hamilton Basso: "Huey Long and His Background," *Harper's Magazine*, CLXX (May 1935), 663–4.

result of activity by Huey and his aides than of objectivity on the part of the papers. Huey had a skeleton public-relations staff. In charge of it was a professional newspaper man, W. D. Robinson, who had also worked with him in 1923. Robinson spent most of the time at central headquarters in New Orleans, apparently handling publicity for the city's papers. Reports to the smaller city and the country papers were sent out daily by men traveling with Huey, such as Harley Bozeman, or by a local leader in the area where Huey was campaigning. Sometimes at the end of a long day Huey would sit down in a hotel room, type out a summary of his speech himself and hand it to an assistant with instruction to get copies to the press.[9]

The Huey Long who appeared before audiences in 1927 was not the gangling young hick of 1924. He had filled out in face and figure, probably weighing 175 pounds, and he seemed more mature and sophisticated. He had also learned something about how to dress. Gone were the ill-fitting clothes, the flashy trimmings that had made him appear "country." Newspaper photographs of him on the platform usually show him wearing a conservative double-breasted suit. On occasion he sported the costume that later became his trademark, a white linen suit. He had always flouted the rule that a politician must not dress better than his followers, but now, in more conventional and expensive attire, he was setting himself even higher above the one-gallus boys. He did it deliberately, knowing that his supporters did not care how splendidly their leader dressed. And in case they should be resentful, he perpetrated enough crudities to reassure them of his loyalties. For instance, during the campaign a wealthy family in Lafayette gave a large luncheon in his honor. The dining room sparkled with china and silver. Huey came in, glanced around contemptuously, and swept his place setting to the floor. "Give me a knife and fork," he bellowed. "I don't know how to handle all this cutlery." The action might seem wantonly brutal, but it was coldly calculated. He knew that the story would go out all over the parish and that the people who used only one knife and one fork, the majority, would roar with laughter and vote for the hero.[1]

When Huey violated an established political rule, he did so knowing that the rule had no validity and that he would gain by the

---

[9] Otho Long; publicity release by J. L. Bujol of East Baton Rouge parish, January 2, 1928, typed copy in my possession. Robinson's activities are referred to but not detailed in the Robinson Papers.

[1] Deutsch: "Prelude to a Heterocrat," *Saturday Evening Post*, CCVII (September 7, 1935), 86; John St. Paul, Jr.

violation. He was nearly always right. But in 1927 he came dangerously close to infringing an important rule. He had been drinking for years, probably since his earliest traveling salesman days. The habit took increasing command over him and was most likely to grip him in times of excitement, like a campaign. Liquor had an immediate and unfortunate impact on him. It either stimulated him to words or acts of rashness, or it knocked him out. Intensely nervous as he was, a few drinks affected him. Before at least one meeting in the campaign his aides had to work hard to sober him up sufficiently to appear on the platform. Characteristically he attempted to brush off criticism with impudence, by bragging about his addiction. To a friend who remarked that he did not drink, Huey replied: "I do, but no more than Riley Joe and not as much as Simpson. I have to drink some to get votes in south Louisiana." He told one audience that his enemies were even charging that he was allied with the distilling interests and then shouted boldly: "I want every man in this crowd who ever took a drink of whisky to vote for me." It was the best strategy he could have used. If old Huey was admitting he drank, the popular reasoning ran, he couldn't be hitting it too hard. He carried it off this time, but a weakness in him had been disclosed, one that unless curbed could cause him trouble in the future.[2]

In his first speeches of the campaign Huey relied on his favorite weapon, the personal attack. He paid relatively little attention to Wilson and Simpson, whom he dismissed as figureheads, concentrating his fire on the forces behind them. His two rivals might claim that they were opposed to one another, he said, but in reality they were running as a team and were controlled by one man. That man was J. Y. Sanders, who also controlled the city and state machine and the big corporations. Wilson and Simpson were like waiters serving food in different camps, said Huey, employing a version of his favorite metaphor, but they got the food from the same kitchen and J. Y. was the cook. In fact, Huey elaborated, friends of Sanders had come to him and said that J. Y. would pull Wilson and Simpson out of the race—if Huey promised that as governor he would favor Sanders's toll bridge and carbon-black clients.[3]

Huey pointed to other sinister figures and groups in the organizations of his opponents. Holding a high place in the Wilson crowd,

[2] Otho Long; Robert J. O'Neal; Douthit: "Governorship of Long," p. 45.

[3] New Orleans *Morning Tribune*, August 26, 1927; New Orleans *States*, August 26, 1927; New Orleans *Times-Picayune*, November 16, 1927.

which claimed to represent the forces of morality, was Andrew Querbes, a Shreveport bank president. Yet this now-respected man had begun his career as an operator of a Negro saloon and dive, Huey sneered, making a rare appeal to race prejudice. Also supporting the moral Wilson were the employees of the "coonservation" department, the horde of "coon watchers," who held jobs under Simpson but obeyed the mandate of their permanent masters in the state machine to vote for Riley Joe. Huey disclosed that the department had hired a doctor in Shreveport at $250 a month just to see that no "coons" got loose on the streets. This man had complained that he could not watch for "coons" at night, so the department put his son on the payroll at $150 a month to guard the city during the hours of darkness.

For his main target in the Simpson camp, Huey singled out Lee E. Thomas. He did not concentrate on the Shreveport mayor to weaken his influence, because Thomas had little outside his own parish, nor did he do it out of personal malice, although he enjoyed nothing more than puncturing Thomas. It was, rather, that the mayor was such a perfect symbol of conservative politics. Just as Sanders was a convenient symbol of the old aristocracy, so Thomas epitomized the perennial officeholder of the old regime. Huey was merciless in exposing him: "You take a yearling and when he gets twelve or fourteen months old he gets ashamed of himself and weans himself automatically. You take the pig, even the hog is ashamed of himself and weans himself when he gets to be a good sized shoat. But you take a pie eater and trough feeder like L. E. Thomas who has been sucking the pap for thirty-five years. You cannot wean him at all." Thomas retaliated with a charge that Huey had accepted a campaign contribution from a gas company under corrupt circumstances. Huey denied the charge and then told another story to illustrate the character of his accuser. A Chinaman, a Fiji Islander, and Thomas made a bet as to who could stay longest in a room with a polecat. The Chinaman stuck it out for ten minutes and the Fiji Islander for fifteen. "Thomas's time came. He went in and stayed five minutes, and the pole cat ran out." This remark and others like it were too much for Thomas: he sued Huey for slander. The suit was dismissed on a technicality; the enraged mayor had forgotten to include in his bill of information that he was a man "of good repute."[4]

[4] *Address of Huey P. Long at Shreveport* (pamphlet, Shreveport, n.d., probably 1927), *passim;* Long: *Every Man a King,* pp. 100–1; Douthit: "Governorship of Long," pp. 45–6.

Thomas's anger was not just an expression of the feelings of one man. It was a reflection of the feelings of many men and of a new mood that was infusing Louisiana politics. Ordinarily in a campaign politicians did not take too seriously the charges of other politicians. It was assumed that some accusations would be hurled around: after all, the personal attack was one of the oldest of political strategies. But it was also assumed that the attacks would be kept within certain restraints, within the bounds of understood rules. Huey ignored the rules. Where others stopped at a recognized limit, he could ruin a reputation. "He would plow right through you to his goal," said one of his supporters. "He didn't care if the dirt covered you."[5] His victims reacted with primitive rage. For the first time in the modern history of Louisiana, people tried to commit acts of violence on a gubernatorial candidate.

At a meeting in New Orleans, Huey shared the platform with his running mate, Paul Cyr. "Doc," as everybody called him, was a remarkable physical specimen, the grandson of a professional Canadian strong woman, an ox of a man who loved to fight. Huey, in the course of his speech, attacked a man who was in the audience. The object of the tirade suddenly rose and started toward the platform. Huey turned to Cyr and said: "You handle that fellow." Cyr jumped from the platform and held the man back—and all the time Huey continued his attack. After that Huey wanted Cyr with him at every meeting.[6]

Just before a meeting in Minden a man with a criminal record, recently jailed for cutting tires, was released from prison. He was freed to break up Huey's meeting, or so Huey's friends would later charge. Whatever the facts, he stood up when Huey began to speak and yelled: "Hold on, you sonofabitch." He got no further. A state highway patrolman whose home was in Minden had been detailed to direct traffic at the rally. He was Louis Jones, a short but compact and muscular man. Jones seemed to be just another policeman, but actually he was a man of lethal instincts, as deadly as a rattler. Hardly had the heckler got the words out of his mouth when Jones slugged him. As Jones related the episode: "I cut his eyebrow so it fell down over his eye. I really whipped the hell out of him. I went down on top of him." As Jones went down, he felt somebody pull his gun out of the holster. It was his brother, who had seen another man slash at Jones's belt with a knife. The brother waved the gun and ordered everybody to stand back, and Louis Jones marched

[5] Confidential communication.
[6] Leon Gary.

his victim off to jail. Huey stood on the platform watching the fracas and at its conclusion cried: "That's what I call enforcing the law." He would not forget "Louie" Jones.[7]

But these and other clashes seemed dull and inconsequential in comparison with an encounter that occurred in New Orleans. This one was staged in the lobby of the plush Roosevelt Hotel and featured as participants none other than Huey himself and J. Y. Sanders. The two happened to run into each other outside a dining room. The old governor was in an ugly mood. He had been brooding over Huey's charge that he had offered to pull Wilson and Simpson out of the race. Just a year before, in the Broussard campaign, he had brushed off Huey's accusations with regal scorn. But now he felt like other conservative citizens—he had had enough, and he thought the time had come to stop the fellow. He had resolved that if he saw Huey he would charge him with being a liar. Suddenly the liar was right in front of him. Sanders stepped forward and told Huey that he wanted to ask him a question. Both J. Y. and Huey in relating the episode later agreed as to what followed immediately. Huey said that in a conversation with Sanders he wanted witnesses present and then ran out to the main lobby. Sanders followed him. From this point their accounts differ dramatically.

Sanders's account stated that Huey returned with another man. Sanders told Huey that his charges were lies. Thereupon the other man grabbed him, and Huey hit "at" him and then ran down the lobby toward an elevator. J. Y. broke free from the man and followed Huey. He caught Long in the elevator and hit him once or twice before others separated them.

Long's account related that he collected several witnesses and returned to meet Sanders. The former governor called him a liar, and Huey hit him. Thereupon his friends, fearing that he might injure J. Y., hustled him to the elevator. But Sanders followed them and renewed the fight. "It was in the elevator that I gave him a good beating," Huey said. "It took four men tugging at my legs to get me off Sanders." As proof that he had won the victory, Huey waved a cuff that he had torn from J. Y.'s sleeve with the cuff button gleaming from it.

The New Orleans reporters, whose stories formed the basis of press accounts of the affair, awarded the victory to Sanders. They stressed that Huey had fled ignominiously down the lobby pursued by J. Y. One of them suggested mockingly that a return bout should be scheduled at the Fair Grounds race track, where Huey could

[7] Louis A. Jones.

show his speed to better advantage. Mockery of Huey was the key-note of the stories, and the suspicion is inescapable that the writers were interested only in presenting acts that put him in a bad light. For example, they ignored the fact that he moved fast in any situation. Sanders himself testified to this peculiarity in describing how Huey proceeded to the lobby to get witnesses, when he certainly was not fleeing: Huey "ran out," J. Y. said. The reporters juggled other circumstances. Huey had been whipped by a much older man, they crowed. Sanders was older than Huey, but he was also much heavier. Actually, there was no victor. Both contestants were poorly conditioned and could not have fought very long or hurt each other seriously. This aspect of the struggle was apparently noticeable only to an interested female bystander. She said she could not see much of Huey. His head was visible occasionally, but most of the time it was lost in J. Y.'s stomach.[8]

It is entirely probable that Huey did leave the scene of the fight. He had avoided physical encounters since boyhood. At that time and all through his life he would fight only when he could not back away or when he saw some advantage to be gained by fighting. A normal masculine emotion never appeared in him—that occasional red rage which makes a man want to fling himself at the throat of another man. He seemed, in fact, to have an aversion to any kind of close contact with men. Many who knew him have said he had the limpest handshake they ever felt. It was as though he thought that people wanted to come near him so that they could harm him. Often during the campaign, while staying at a hotel, he would get out of bed and listen and then tell whoever was rooming with him that he could hear somebody prowling in the hall outside the door. In this campaign year he revealed the first symptoms of what would soon become a phobia with him—that he was in constant danger of physical attack and had to have protection against it.[9]

As the campaign progressed, Huey gradually tapered off in his personal attacks and began to concentrate on issues. The new emphasis was not the result of a fear of reprisal. It was a deliberately adopted and clever strategy that he would have employed had there been no assaults on him. He had attacked at first because his follow-ers expected him to and because he wanted to put his opponents on the defensive. But he sensed that in this campaign he had to do more

[8] New Orleans *Times-Picayune*, November 16, 1927; Shreveport *Times*, November 17, 1927; New Orleans *Item*, November 16, 1927.
[9] Leon Gary.

than attack, that whole blocs of additional voters were wavering toward him, but that these other voters had to be convinced that he was for something as well as against something. So a new Huey Long appeared on the platform, a positive, reasoning Huey who discussed issues and proposed programs and soared into lofty flights of rhetoric.

He talked about many things—roads, bridges, schools, hospitals, honest government. But mostly he talked about free schoolbooks to be provided by the state. He had introduced this proposal four years before but had not emphasized it. Since then he had found out more about the existing situation in regard to books and had come to realize what a burning issue he had aroused. The procedure for choosing and distributing textbooks was a complicated one. The state Department of Education chose the books that could be used. At periodic intervals it published an "approved list," which might only repeat the last list or might include many new selections. Publishers whose books were on the list maintained in New Orleans a central distributing agency, the F. F. Hansell Book Company, which was commonly referred to as the "state depository." Hansell bought books from the publishers on consignment and shipped them out on consignment to "local depositories." These latter were stores, usually drugstores, in the towns and villages, which had agreed for a commission to handle the books in their localities. When a school term started, parents would come in to the local depository and buy the books their children had to have.[1]

The system was by its nature expensive. Added to the publishers' price were the commissions of Hansell and the local depositories. Huey calculated, and he had the evidence to support his estimate, that the average cost per child was $5.99. Thus a parent with four or five children would have to pay out each year $25 or $30, a sum that would strain the resources of a small farmer or sharecropper. He would not have to pay this amount, of course, if the books could be handed down in the family from child to child. But, said Huey, the state department, in collusion with the publishers or distributors, changed the books all the time. To illustrate his point, he would come on the platform with a box of textbooks that had been discarded. He had two other boxes in his car that he could not bring up, he would say. Then he would stack as many as thirty books on a chair and discuss each one. Here was a hygiene book that had been used last year, but it had been eliminated and next year the child

[1] John M. Foote; J. W. Brouillette.

would have to purchase "some other hygiene" that was no different. And here was a speller devised by James Aswell, a Louisiana educator, that had been tossed out. "And there ain't been six words inserted in the dictionary since Aswell wrote that speller. Here are three stories of Louisiana history, and they've done changed them all three."

The state could provide the books at a nominal cost, Huey contended. He cited the example of Texas, which furnished free books at an average cost of ninety cents per pupil. His reasoning drew expressions of amused scorn from conservative opponents. The most redoubtable of these was T. H. Harris, one of the most powerful politicians in the state and superintendent of education since 1908, in whose home Huey had stayed when as a high-school youth he had attended the rally at Louisiana State University. Harris and other critics charged that it was misleading to cite merely the cost of distribution of the books. Where, they asked, was the state going to get the huge sum that would be required for the initial purchase of the books? Huey answered with a formula that he must have known was unrealistic—he would get the money by eliminating useless jobs in the state departments.[2]

In some speeches Huey ignored specific issues. He spoke instead of his aspirations for the masses of Louisiana, of his dreams to lift them to a better life. He voiced his ideals in especially moving words at the little town of St. Martinsville in the French country, where the legend of Evangeline still lived. He thought so well of his remarks that he incorporated them in his autobiography. They have been much admired and quoted as an eloquent expression of the spirit of liberal Southern reform. Standing under the famous oak, he said:

And it is here, under this oak where Evangeline waited for her lover, Gabriel, who never came. This oak is an immortal spot, made so by Longfellow's poem, but Evangeline is not the only one who has waited here in disappointment. Where are the schools that you have waited for your children to have, that have never come? Where are the roads and the highways that you send your money to build, that are no nearer now than ever before? Where are the institutions to care for the sick and the disabled? Evangeline wept bitter tears in her disappointment, but it lasted through only one lifetime. Your tears in this country,

[2] *Address of Long at Shreveport*, pp. 10–13; Port Allen *Observer*, September 2, 1927; Baton Rouge *State-Times*, September 14, 1927; Monroe *News-Star*, September 15, 1927; Long, circular on free books, in my possession.

around this oak, have lasted for generations. Give me the chance to dry the tears of those who still weep here!

Some critics have cast doubt on the authenticity of the speech. They have suggested that Huey made up the statement later for publication in his autobiography. But newspaper accounts reveal that he said something very similar. They also disclose that he added a sentence he did not see fit to reproduce. He ended: "But if you wait here too long an agent from the 'coonservation' department will touch you on the shoulder and tell you you are casting for minnows illegally."[3]

On the eve of the January election Huey was supremely confident. He assured a friend that he was certain to land in the second primary and might even win in the first. His prediction would have amused the Wilson camp. For weeks the conservative press had been comforting its readers with predictions that Huey would run a poor third. Ballard's *Item* asserted that he would receive fewer votes than in 1924 and stated flatly, again, that Huey Long was on the way out. What made the Wilsonites so cocky was their faith that the Old Regulars would roll out an exceptionally large vote for Riley Joe. Simpson was also expected to amass a good vote in the city, and it was thought that the combined Wilson-Simpson vote would far outweigh Long's country majority and rule out the possibility of a second primary. Wilson had left the campaign to attend to his flood-control duties in Washington, where he awaited notification of his victory.[4]

On election night it seemed that the bright hopes of all the enemies of Huey Long had come to pass. The New Orleans vote, which came in first, disclosed a Wilson sweep. Riley Joe had piled up 38,244 votes. Far behind was Simpson with 22,324 and still farther back was Huey with 17,819. Even with the Ewing–Sullivan faction behind him, Huey had polled only five thousand more votes than he had in 1924 and trailed Wilson by almost twenty-one thousand.[5] The Old Regular leaders and Wilson exchanged exultant congratulatory telegrams, and bottles were uncorked for a celebration at the

[3] Long: *Every Man a King*, p. 99; New Orleans *States*, November 4, 1927.

[4] Long to William P. Dillon, January 12, 1928 (letter in possession of Mr. Dillon of New Orleans); New Orleans *Item*, November 26, 1927.

[5] Long, in *Every Man a King*, pp. 102, 119, said that he received a smaller percentage of the city vote than he had in 1924. This was written, however, after he had broken with Ewing and Sullivan and wanted to discredit their importance. Actually, his city vote had increased from eighteen per cent of the total to twenty-three per cent. He had, of course, expected to do much better.

Choctaw Club. Everybody agreed that no matter what Huey did in the country, he could not overtake Wilson's city lead or match the Wilson–Simpson total. There would not be a second primary.[6]

The country vote did not begin to come in till later at night and the next morning. Election day had been pleasant and clear, and a heavy turnout of rural voters was to be expected. The Wilson leaders were not surprised, therefore, when the returns from the northern parishes showed Huey with a large majority. These were the parishes he had carried four years before when he had been defeated. But then the returns from the French southern parishes started to arrive. The city politicians could not believe what they saw. Huey was sweeping the south as he had the north. In some of the French parishes his vote was sixty to seventy per cent of the total. By noon of the day after the election he had pulled virtually even with Wilson and at its end had forged ahead. By the next day he had drawn twenty thousand votes ahead of Wilson, and by nightfall it was evident that his lead could go over forty thousand. The final figures held no comfort for conservative Louisianians, only confirming the disaster: Long, 126,842; Wilson, 81,747; Simpson, 80,326. Huey had carried six of the eight congressional districts and forty-seven of the sixty-four parishes. He did not have a majority of the popular vote, but he had a bigger lead than any previous gubernatorial candidate' had ever amassed, and he would be almost impossible to beat in a second primary. Some conservatives refused to admit the reality of what had happened. "Longism suffers a defeat in the first primary by a clear majority," firmly trumpeted one New Orleans paper.[7]

Only a miracle could keep Huey from the governorship now, the kind of miracle that hardly ever occurs in politics. Too many contingencies would have to be combined. Simpson and his leaders and big backers would have to believe that Wilson had a chance and would have to endorse him. The Wilson leaders would have to be convinced that Simpson could deliver the bulk of his vote to their man. Finally, a large sum of money would have to be raised to finance another campaign, and to get this money the Wilson people

[6] New Orleans *Item*, January 18, 1928; Deutsch: "Kingdom of the Kingfish," in New Orleans *Item*, August 9, 1939; Douthit: "Governorship of Long," p. 46.

[7] Allen P. Sindler: *Huey Long's Louisiana: State Politics, 1920–1952* (Baltimore, 1956), p. 55; P. H. Howard: *Political Tendencies in Louisiana, 1812–1952* (Baton Rouge, 1957), pp. 124–6; Deutsch: "Kingdom of the Kingfish," in New Orleans *Item*, August 9, 1939; Douthit: "Governorship of Long," pp. 46–7; New Orleans *Morning Tribune*, January 20, 1928.

would have to persuade contributors that a man who had finished a poor second in the first primary would somehow be able to do better in the second. The impossibity of overcoming these realities was all too apparent to the forces that would have to form an anti-Long coalition. They began to crumble almost immediately.

First to break up was the Simpson faction. Its disintegration was largely a natural process. The leaders were professional politicians who had been attached to Simpson by the loosest of loyalties, a desire to go with a winner. Now it was obvious that he was not going to win, and they wanted to join themselves to the candidate who clearly *was* going to win, Huey. Simpson himself made no effort to control his people, to sway them to Wilson. He had been embittered by the attacks made on him by some of the newspapers supporting Wilson, and now he withdrew into seclusion. Left without a leader, his followers wavered, wanting to be plucked, and Huey, noting their condition, moved quickly.

Huey was in New Orleans the day after the election. He set up headquarters in the Roosevelt Hotel and went to work. First, he arranged a meeting with Paul Maloney, the most powerful of the Simpson leaders. He asked Maloney to endorse him if there was a runoff. Maloney liked Huey personally, had considered supporting him before deciding to go for Simpson, and now saw the direction of the political wind. He readily acceded to Huey's request and said that he would call a meeting of his leaders and ask them to ratify his decision. Huey was delighted. "What can I do for you?" he asked. Maloney answered that he wanted nothing. "Well," Huey said, "I'll do anything for Simpson." "I'll ask him," Maloney promised.[8]

Maloney's organization met on the night of January 20, a Friday, and unanimously endorsed Huey. That morning the *Times-Picayune,* Simpson's principal journalistic supporter, had told Wilson in an editorial that he had no chance and advised him to withdraw. The news of these two developments threw the Old Regulars and the Wilson headquarters into deepest gloom. With the promise of Maloney's support Huey's chances were immeasurably increased, and with the *Picayune*'s threatened defection Wilson's chances had sunk even lower. All of Saturday and on into Sunday the Wilson leaders engaged in agonizing appraisals. Rumors from the conference room said that the Old Regulars had offered to go into a second primary if the Wilson people in the country would promise to put up

[8] Harry Gamble; Paul Maloney; Paul B. Habans.

a campaign chest of $150,000. Efforts to raise the money had elicited pledges of only $52,000. One Choctaw leader was reported to have said that it would take $500,000 to create even the possibility of a Wilson victory. All during the meetings men were leaving the Wilson headquarters, some of them going back to their homes in the country, some of them drifting hopefully over to Huey's headquarters.

On Saturday afternoon Huey called three of his old Winnfield friends to come down to New Orleans—O. K. Allen, who had just defeated Henry Hardtner for a senate seat, Harley B. Bozeman, who had run for the house and faced a possible opponent in the second primary, and O. B. Thompson. The three arrived by train early Sunday morning and went to Huey's hotel suite. They found him in pajamas, sitting up in bed. He told them that before the end of the day they would all find "the end of the rainbow," that the Wilson people were about ready to throw in the sponge. Turning to Bozeman, he said that when the Wilsonites conceded, Bozeman's opponent would withdraw and he would be the representative from Winn. As the day wore on, the suite began filling up with visitors— politicians, businessmen, reporters. Huey whispered to his three friends to stick around and observe how "big time" politics was played. Emissaries from the Wilson and Simpson camps kept coming in. Huey talked with them, but always at his elbow were John P. Sullivan and Colonel Ewing. Finally, in the afternoon, the news that all of them had been waiting for came—it was announced that the Old Regulars had decided not to back Wilson in a second primary and that Riley Joe had withdrawn from the race. Soon newspaper extras hit the streets, and newsboys could be heard screaming: "Huey Long elected governor."[9]

When Maloney asked Simpson if he wanted an office in the incoming administration, the governor snapped that he would not take anything from Long. Simpson was still in his withdrawn mood, crushed by his defeat and bitter at everyone who had helped to bring it about. Soon he came out of it and evinced a desire to cooperate with Huey. Huey, eager to strike at the Pontchartrain toll bridge before he became governor, asked Simpson to begin the operation of free ferries parallel to the span. Simpson obligingly issued an order instituting the ferries. Later he accepted a minor position in the Long administration and thus remained in politics, but at the edges of power, a rather pathetic figure whose abilities were not great enough to accomplish his ambitions.[1]

As Huey basked in the glow of his victory, he also reflected that it had been an incomplete one. Even in the great sweep of his vote, he had carried into office with him only two members of his ticket, Paul Cyr as lieutenant governor and H. B. Conner as state treasurer. His hold on the legislature promised to be tenuous. Of the one hundred members of the house of representatives, only eighteen had been elected as Long candidates, and of the thirty-nine senators only nine were announced Long men. And he soon realized that he could not even depend on all those who had supported him. The way the realization was brought to him shocked him, as hardened as he was to the realities of politics. He told an associate that a man had come to him and offered him a retainer of $250,000 if he would permit the toll bridge to be completed and to operate without competition. "And it was my city campaign manager that made the proposition," he exploded. "But no goddamn measly $250,000 can buy Huey Long."[2]

[1] Paul Maloney; Long: *Every Man a King*, p. 105. Some of Simpson's associates thought that Simpson's seclusion was caused by a prolonged drunk that he went on after the election; confidential communication.

[2] Long: *Every Man a King*, p. 107; T. O. Harris: *The Kingfish: Huey P. Long, Dictator* (New Orleans, 1938), pp. 33–4; confidential communication.

# CHAPTER 12

# *Fry Me a Steak*

T HE REACTION OF CONSERVATIVE LOUISIANA to Huey's election
was predictable, the classic Southern response to the elevation
of a demagogue. The radical was going to be governor. There was
no way to keep him out of the office, but his course could easily be
influenced and controlled. The hierarchy would absorb him and thus
render him harmless. The first move in the process was to show him
social attention, to demonstrate to him that, after all, gentlemen
liked him and wanted to help him in the difficult job ahead. Huey,
elected in January, would not assume office until May, but the conservatives decided to act immediately. They found an occasion for
their purpose ready at hand. Some of Huey's leaders in New Orleans
were planning a dinner to honor him in February. The elite of the
city announced that they were supporting the dinner, that they
wanted to pay their respects to the incoming governor. They took
the affair over, in fact.

Over eight hundred persons attended the dinner, held in the Tip
Top Inn of the Roosevelt Hotel. Colonel Robert Ewing, inflated with
the certainty that he would be the power behind the Long regime,
presided. The list of speakers was long and distinguished. Every one
of them lauded the new governor and emphasized that his administration would be marked by harmony. The president of one of the
city's largest banks offered Huey the cooperation of the business
interests. Chief Justice Charles O'Niell, not very tactfully comparing
those present to the contestants in the World War, hailed the banquet as the "signing of another armistice." Federal Judge Rufus E.
Foster, who not so long before had handed down injunctions re-

straining Huey's activities on the Public Service Commission, now spoke with friendly condescension. "I have not always agreed with what this young man said and did," Foster said, "and I have sometimes considered him as a bad boy making faces at authority. But I think he has grown up." At the conclusion of the tributes a large chest full of silver dinnerware was presented to Huey and his wife.

The guest of honor obviously was not taken in by the syrupy words. He seemed bored if not embarrassed by the flow of praise. Nevertheless, when he responded, he spoke with propriety and modesty. "I go into the Governor's office as your servant," he promised, "in no sense of the word as the master of the people or of any set of people." In general terms he outlined what he hoped to accomplish, although he knew that most of those in the audience would object to large parts of his program: improved education facilities, an attack on illiteracy, better care of the unfortunate, and fairer laws for labor. He pledged specific benefits for New Orleans—state aid for roads and bridges, state help to restore the port to its former great position, and the bringing of natural gas to the city. He carried his audience with him as he spoke, and when he sat down, they shook the room with applause. They did not like him or trust him, but they were Louisianians, and they responded instinctively to skilled oratory.[1]

If the conservatives thought they had charmed Huey into docility, they were speedily disabused. A few days after the banquet the Democratic state central committee met in New Orleans to arrange for the calling of a state convention that would select delegates to the national party convention. The procedure was hallowed by custom. The committee would issue the call and lay down rules as to how the delegates would be chosen—so many from each congressional district, so many at large. The governor and the state and city bosses would agree on a slate of delegates and put them up, and the few voters who were interested would elect the representatives and endorse the slate. By precedent the various factions within the party were allowed delegates in proportion to their strength, a principle that assured the Old Regulars of always having a sizable representation.

It was a method of selection that would give Huey but little control over the convention or its choice of delegates. His organization, so personal in nature, could turn out a big vote for its leader, but it was not tight enough to elect the representatives to the convention

[1] New Orleans *Item*, February 15, 1928; New Orleans *Morning Tribune*, February 16, 1928; Harry Gamble.

that he might endorse. He faced two probabilities, both unpleasant. First, the convention would be under no control, and its activities would degenerate into mere "horse-trading." Or, worse, it would fall under the control of his enemies. In either eventuality his position would be weakened at the very beginning of his administration. He would stand revealed as a governor who could not influence even the selection of his party's national delegation. The legislature would be encouraged to rebel against him before he could ever organize it.

Impressed with the dangers posed by the situation, Huey began studying the methods by which past conventions had been chosen. Helping him in the research was Harvey G. Fields, an able north Louisiana lawyer and a rising power in the Long organization. To their surprise, they discovered that the state constitution recognized but did not require the selection of delegates by a convention; the statutes merely stipulated how the method should function if it was used. Instantly Huey made his decision; the central committee had the authority to dispense with the convention, to decide that delegates to the national convention could be chosen by another method. It could, in fact, name the delegates itself. The latter was the procedure that Huey determined would be employed. Through the promise of jobs he could control a majority of the committee.

He had rounded up his majority when the committee met on February 18. Hardly had the meeting come to order when one of his supporters offered a resolution stating that the committee should select the national delegates. It passed quickly and by a decisive vote. Almost as quickly, another resolution naming a slate of delegates was accepted. On it there was not a single representative of the Old Regulars and none of Huey's prominent opponents. Colonel Ewing was designated as national committeeman, and Huey was made one of the delegates at large.

The news of the committee's action threw the opposition into a sputtering, helpless rage. Anguished comments came from Mayor O'Keefe and the Old Regular chiefs and from old leaders like J. Y. Sanders and Ruffin Pleasant, who had dominated the delegations in the past. Huey observed their response with amused contempt. "No music ever sounded one-half so refreshing as the whines and groans of the pie-eating politicians," he said. "They say that they were steamrollered. I think that is true. The only reason that the roller didn't pass over more of them was because there were no more in the way."

The reaction of the conservatives was in large part an expression of shock. They did not realize as yet that they were dealing with a man who was not going to be limited by existing rules, who, if the rules stood in his way, would make up his own. They eventually recovered sufficiently to convoke a rump convention that selected a protesting delegation headed by Sanders and Pleasant. Both delegations set out for the Democratic convention in Houston in June, Huey remaining behind because the legislature was in session. But he maintained close contact with his group through Fields, who acted as its chairman.

The Long delegation traveled by train, boarding at New Orleans. The train already had aboard a number of delegations from the Eastern states, and shortly a member of one of these sought Fields out. He said that he was Franklin D. Roosevelt of New York and that he was managing the campaign of his state's governor, Alfred E. Smith, for the presidential nomination. Roosevelt said that if the Long delegation would pledge to vote for Smith, he would see to it that New York supported its bid for admission. Fields, after reaching Houston, telephoned Huey to tell him about the proposed deal and advised accepting it. Smith was certain to get the nomination, he urged, and it would be smart for Louisiana to stand in with the nominee and the possible President. "Damn a President," Huey snapped. "I don't care about that. I just want the Huey Long delegation seated. You tell 'em to vote for Smith."

The two Louisiana delegations presented their cases to the credentials committee, which readily voted to seat Huey's group. The Long delegation had official status, whereas the protesters were really self-elected. Moreover, the powerful Smith forces favored Huey's representatives, as Roosevelt had promised they would. The Long delegation, after it was seated, observed the bargain and supported the New York governor, who won the nomination.[2]

The convention coup should have apprised conservatives that Huey was going to be unlike any governor they had known. They could have read the warning in another of his actions. In his speech at the testimonial dinner he had said that he was going to bring natural gas to New Orleans, thereby repeating a pledge that he had made in the campaign. It was a promise that was applauded, although his hearers did not expect him to do anything to carry it out. Gubernatorial candidates had for years been promising to bring

[2] Leo Glenn Douthit: "The Governorship of Huey Long" (unpublished M.A. thesis, Tulane University, 1947), pp. 50–1; Harvey G. Fields: *A True History of the Life, Works, Assassination and Death of Huey P. Long* (Silver Spring, Md., 1944), pp. 33–4; T. O. Harris: *The Kingfish: Huey P. Long, Dictator* (New Orleans, 1938), pp. 35–6; New Orleans *Times-Picayune*, February 25, 1928; Harvey G. Fields.

cheap natural gas to heat the homes of the city, but those who had been elected had heretofore always found reasons not to redeem their pledge.

To governors Parker and Fuqua the reasons had seemed formidable enough. They were rooted in the close relationship between the city government—that is, the Old Regular machine—and the city's business interests, particularly its largest public utility. One company furnished practically all urban services—New Orleans Public Service Incorporated (NOPSI), which in turn was owned largely by the Electric Bond and Share Company of New York City. NOPSI provided all gas and electricity for the city and also operated the streetcar system. In 1921 it had been forced to accept a revised franchise which stipulated that the city could buy its properties at a specified valuation and operate them as a municipal project, but there was little danger that the Ring-dominated city government would attempt such a "socialistic" move, and in 1928 the company felt secure. It charged rates on its enterprises that returned earnings of seven and a half per cent.

The gas that NOPSI provided was artificial gas, which it dispensed at the high rate of $1.35 per thousand cubic feet. For a long time artificial gas had been the only fuel available. Natural gas was abundantly present in the northeastern gas fields, but the cost of transporting it to other areas was prohibitive. Then the development of industry in south Louisiana created a demand for cheap fuel, and private companies began to construct pipelines southward from the fields, and cities in the path of the lines seized the opportunity to provide natural gas to domestic consumers. By 1927 the lines had almost reached New Orleans, and several individuals offered to organize companies to bring gas into the city. But NOPSI, whose consent to any arrangement was necessary, blocked every effort. Neither would it agree to bring the gas in itself. The company contended that it could not transport gas from the northern fields and distribute it without suffering a loss. Furthermore, the warm climate of New Orleans would discourage consumers from using gas consistently, company spokesmen blandly explained. The city government accepted their arguments and exerted no pressure on the company to act.[3]

[3] New Orleans *Item*, August 15, December 29 and 31, 1927; New Orleans *Times-Picayune*, November 20, December 30 and 31, 1927; New Orleans *States*, November 20 and 28 (editorial), December 28, 1927, March 10, 1928; New Orleans *Morning Tribune*, December 30, 1927; George Coad, article in *The New York Times*, March 18, 1928; Hermann B. Deutsch: "Kingdom of the Kingfish," in New Orleans *Item*, August 11, 1939.

There were pressures from other sources, however. The city press was divided on the issue, and some of the papers leveled a running barrage of criticism at NOPSI and the city council. Consumers naturally desired anything that would lower their fuel bills, but this sentiment in favor of natural gas was unorganized, and by itself would have been insufficient to persuade the council and the company to move. But suddenly it received a recruit, a formidable one who threatened to exert a great deal of pressure. Governor-elect Long, spending much of his time before his inauguration in the city, issued a string of statements affirming his determination to provide natural gas. "We are going to secure natural gas for New Orleans," he said in one interview. "It is plain to me that New Orleans is being fought from within. Those who have been elected to protect and serve the people have failed in their duties for the past many years." In another statement he uttered a warning: "I hope that natural gas can be brought to New Orleans peacefully. But if the gentlemen who are banded to keep it from coming here want a rough-house, they want to remember that I can stand more rough-house than they ever saw."[4]

The reaction of the city's rulers to Huey's promises and threats was one of lordly disdain. Only one Old Regular chief deigned to comment—T. Semmes Walmsley, who was commissioner of finance in the city council and who had been tapped by the organization as Mayor O'Keefe's successor. "It is impossible to hasten this development," Walmsley said. "It must be undertaken in a sane, orderly and scientific manner and we certainly do not propose to use any 'half-baked' methods." In short, they did not propose to do anything.[5]

Huey could not act until he took over the governorship, but he was willing to bide his time. He knew that he had grasped a potent issue. By manipulating it correctly he could build up his strength; at one stroke he could attack the city machine and the predatory monopoly and intensify his image as the idealistic champion of the people. The conservatives, as though bent on their own destruction, were presenting him with an issue. With natural gas at the very back door of New Orleans, they were going to deny it to the people. It was an issue that no politician of good sense and good principle would ignore.

[4] New Orleans *Item*, January 23 and February 15, 1928; New Orleans *States*, February 19, 1928; New Orleans *Times-Picayune*, March 16, 1928.
[5] New Orleans *Morning Tribune*, January 24, 1928; New Orleans *Item*, March 16, 1928.

Huey was inaugurated on May 21. It was a gala day—the inaugural parade in the morning and the ceremonies at noon on the capitol grounds, concerts in the afternoon, a reception for the governor and his wife at eight thirty in the evening, and finally the inaugural ball beginning at nine thirty. The printed program of events stipulated, properly for a governor of the common people, that no invitation was needed for any function. All day the little city of Baton Rouge rang with music from various units that had been invited or whose sponsors wanted to impress the governor—the Louisiana State University Band, the "New Regular Democratic" Band of John Sullivan's organization, the Rotary Boys Band of Lafayette, the Standard Oil Refinery Band, and something called "Sou De Generes's Augmented Orchestra of Baton Rouge." Over fifteen thousand visitors poured into the city, the largest crowd ever to attend an inauguration. An honored guest was Mayor William Hale Thompson, "Big Bill," of Chicago, who had become friendly with Huey because both of them were interested in flood control. Big Bill and Huey were the only speakers at the inaugural ceremony.

Huey relished every minute of the long day. As he rode in the parade, he almost flung himself out of the car in his eagerness to return the cheers of the crowd. "It seemed as if over half of his body was through the window of the car," one observer recalled, "and he was waving both of his arms."[6]

Huey's mood was inspired not only by the applause of the onlookers; he had an even more auspicious reason to exult. The legislature had opened its session a week before the inauguration, and during that week Huey had succeeded in organizing it, in placing followers of his in key positions. Organization was a goal he had been working toward since the election. He had had to overcome obstacles that would have discouraged a lesser man, for no governor in recent times had gone into office with as few pledged supporters as Huey had. Of the state officials elected in January, only two were

---

[6] *Inaugural Ceremonies of Governor Huey P. Long* . . . (pamphlet, Baton Rouge, 1928); Bozeman, in *Winn Enterprise*, June 4, 1959; Carleton Beals: *The Story of Huey P. Long* (Philadelphia, 1935), p. 86; W. C. Alford; Mrs. J. Polk Morris, Jr. One author has offered another explanation of Thompson's presence—Richard Briley, III: *Death of the Kingfish* (Dallas, 1960), *passim*. Briley speculates that Al Capone was with Thompson and had come because of a prior agreement with Huey permitting the Capone gang to take over gambling in Louisiana. Mr. Briley's account seems to me to be without foundation. It is based mainly on the later gossip of certain north Louisiana politicians who had been dropped by Huey. Neutral observers in a position to know state emphatically that there is nothing to the story.

members of his ticket: Lieutenant Governor Cyr and State Treasurer H. B. Conner, although Fred Grace, registrar of state lands, came over almost immediately. The others were anti-Long or neutral: Secretary of State James Bailey, Attorney General Percy Saint, Superintendent of Education T. H. Harris, Commissioner of Agriculture Harry D. Wilson, and State Auditor L. B. Baynard. In the senate and the house of representatives only a minority in each chamber had run as Long adherents. On the other hand, only a minority were strongly anti-Long. The majority of the members were uncommitted, watching to see what the new governor would propose, waiting to be persuaded, by one means or another, to support him. It was to this middle group that Huey directed his efforts.

He and his lieutenants labored behind the scenes for months. He had numerous helpers, so many, in fact, that they tended to get in one another's way and in his. Colonel Ewing and Sullivan naturally expected to exercise a determining voice in every decision, as did Swords Lee and other big financial backers. The veteran south Louisiana politicians who had climbed on to Huey's bandwagon felt that they knew much more about organizing a legislature than the governor-elect, and they forced their advice and assistance on him.

Huey listened to all of them graciously and said he was grateful to have their advice. He could not afford at this stage to turn away anyone who offered to help him. Moreover, some of these men had something to offer—they knew the political ropes, they had valuable contacts, they could line up votes. He used them, but he did not take them into his full confidence. He chose for his closest advisers men from Winn parish, old cronies whom he seemed to feel he could trust. He summoned these men to confer with him at his office in Shreveport immediately after the election, and he took them with him when he went to Baton Rouge early in May. The principal figures in the Winn group were O. K. Allen and Harley Bozeman. Allen was going into the senate and had asked Huey to appoint him chairman of the influential Highway Commission when the time was right. Bozeman had been elected to the house and had told Huey he wanted to be chairman of the important appropriations committee. Another member, although he did not sit in policy conferences, was George Wallace, a Winnfield lawyer. Wallace had one of the best legal minds in the state, but a weakness for alcohol had hindered his career. Huey attached him to advise on constitutional questions and to draft administration bills.

Huey gave Allen and Bozeman a list of members of the legislature categorized according to possible affiliation—pledged, doubtful, anti-Long. He instructed them to cover the state and line up all those who were open to a Long affiliation. Allen and Bozeman spent most of their time between January and May traveling, talking to legislators and local leaders who could influence legislators. By the time the legislature was to meet they were certain that they had secured the promises of a majority of the members. But the lieutenants had had to make some promises themselves. "They all didn't come for free," Bozeman recalled.[7]

The first business of the legislature was to elect presiding officers in both houses. Traditionally the governor had a strong voice in determining who these officials would be. Sometimes the various Democratic factions would put forward competing candidates, hoping that the governor would favor their man in return for their votes. But these contests were always fought out in the secrecy of a caucus. Not since the end of Reconstruction had one of them been brought to the floor of the senate or the house. But now the Old Regulars and the most conservative of the country members decided to oppose Huey's choices. This was dangerous strategy, for if they failed, they would reveal their lack of strength.

For president pro tem of the senate the Long forces had settled on a swarthy, paunchy little Frenchman from a southern parish, Philip H. Gilbert (pronounced Jil-bear). Gilbert had held the office in the preceding administration; he was popular with his colleagues; and he had the support of Lieutenant Governor Cyr. He won an easy victory over his opponent by a vote of twenty-seven to ten, assuring Huey of an experienced legislator to watch over his interests in the senate.

In the house Huey faced a more difficult situation. For speaker he had intended to back a veteran legislator who had come over to his side, but the man had not been re-elected. Of the remaining Long members with experience no one met two standards Huey thought were vital—the speaker had to be a man of above-average ability and he had to be someone whom Huey could trust absolutely. Ruefully Huey decided that he would have to put forward a freshman member. The man he settled on was John B. Fournet, a young lawyer of Jennings, in the southwest. Huey had met Fournet only in the recent campaign and then casually, but the Frenchman had

---

[7] Bozeman, in *Winn Parish Enterprise*, April 23 and 30, 1959; Harley B. Bozeman; confidential communications; Fred Blanche.

impressed him, and subsequent inquiry satisfied him that Fournet could fill the job. He telephoned Fournet to come to Shreveport immediately. Fournet, on being ushered into Huey's office, was astounded when Huey introduced him to people present as the next speaker. "And that was all the conversation we had about it," Fournet affirmed. Huey did not ask for any promises and gave none himself.

Against Fournet the opposition put up a respected north Louisiana legislator who had previously been speaker. Although the larger membership of the house made it harder to control than the senate, the Long lines held, and Fournet won by a vote of seventy-two to twenty-seven. The opposition in both houses stood exposed as a minority.

The new speaker was tall, strongly built, with a round face and bland expression. Like Huey, he had a penchant for flashy gems and wore a ring set with an extraordinarily large diamond. He would have much to learn before he became an efficient presiding officer, but he had a good mind and a ready wit that served him in good stead in emergencies. On one occasion a drunk member waved an almost emptied bottle of whisky at the chair and shouted "Point of order." Fournet looked at the bottle and drawled: "The pint is well taken."

With the installation of Gilbert and Fournet, Huey had taken a long first step toward organizing the legislature. That body's rules provided that the president of the senate and the speaker appoint the committees of each house, but in practice this authority was seldom exercised. The various factions designated which legislators they would like to have on which committee, and the two officials staffed the committees accordingly, allotting most of the places to members of the majority faction (which was nearly always the governor's), but also including representatives of all the other groups. Some committees were composed of members who had a special interest in their work. Thus the twenty-member house committee on city affairs of New Orleans was made up of representatives from that city, which meant, in practice, Old Regulars. The customary method of appointing committee members would have given Huey himself little voice—so he ignored it. He personally dictated to Gilbert and Fournet the name of every member of every committee. He gave some places to followers of Simpson who had swung over to him and some to uncommitted members whom he was in the process of swinging over, and for form's sake he gave a few to the Old Regulars and the conservatives. But the majority of the places, and the choice chairmanships, went to men who were pledged Longites. As a crowning insult to the opposition, he allotted only two seats on the New Orleans city affairs committee to Old Regulars, and he filled thirteen places on it with men from country parishes. The city machine responded angrily, but Huey answered only that he liked to hear the "whines and groans of the old, plundering element."[8]

Huey had been able to exercise this initial control of the legislature because he could offer jobs to people who would go with him. A Louisiana governor has more jobs at his disposal than executives in many other states, including some that in other states are filled by local authorities. A certain number of these are always vacant when a new governor comes in, and previous governors had used them in much the same way that Huey was using them now. But Huey was not satisfied merely to hand out available jobs. He knew that the program he was going to offer to the legislature would arouse determined opposition. To carry it through he would need to have at his disposal every reward he could lay his hands on. Indeed, he decided, he would have to have control of the major share of the state patronage. Accordingly, in the months after his inauguration he moved to take over the various boards and agencies that administered the state's business, every one of which provided a number of juicy jobs. Previous governors had attempted to exercise some influence over these boards, but none had aspired to the absolute control that Huey reached for—nor had they acted with such ruthless skill.

The first agency to fall to him was the Highway Commission, the personnel of which was by law subject to gubernatorial appointment. Allen was named chairman, and later Bozeman was made a member. Executing Huey's instructions, Allen left the technical employees, the engineers and draftsmen, undisturbed in their jobs, but a number of lower-ranking jobholders were replaced with Long men. Next Huey moved on the Orleans parish Levee Board, an agency that oversaw the upkeep of the dikes protecting the city and that had one of the largest employment rolls in the state. But here he ran into a legal restriction. The nine members of the board served fixed terms and could not be removed at the pleasure of a governor. Huey solved the difficulty by a simple expedient—he had

[8] Bozeman, in *Winn Parish Enterprise*, May 14, 1959; John B. Fournet; Douthit: "Governorship of Long," pp. 51–2; Harris: *The Kingfish*, pp. 36–7; Hermann B. Deutsch; Deutsch: "Kingdom of the Kingfish," in New Orleans *Item*, August 10, 1939; New Orleans *Times-Picayune*, May 20, 1928.

the legislature pass a law changing the board to a five-member body.[9] To the new board he named four men who were pledged to him or to John Sullivan. Joseph Haspel, president of the old board, was retained but was smothered by the Long majority.

Flushed with these easy successes, Huey turned to two other patronage-rich agencies—the Board of Health and the Conservation Commission. Their heads, Dr. Oscar Dowling and Dr. Valentine K. Irion, respectively, had held their jobs so long they had come to think of them as their private possessions. Dowling had outlasted five administrations, and Irion had defied an attempt by Simpson to remove him. Huey believed, with a good deal of justice, that both of them were essentially politicians and that they ran their departments on a political basis. In his campaign he had denounced the Conservation, or "coonservation," Commission for hiring large numbers of useless employees, and now he repeated the accusation, charging also that Dowling was wasting half a million dollars every year. He demanded that the two chairmen resign, but they spurned him. If he was going to oust them, he would have to resort to the extreme method he had used against the Levee Board.

In the end, however, Huey found another way to get rid of the two men. A search of the statutes regulating the composition of the boards disclosed that the constitution stipulated no fixed terms for the chairmen and members. The terms had been set by legislative enactment, and Dowling and Irion had four years to go on theirs. Huey determined that since a previous legislature had decided on one term, this one could change the term. He forced through the legislature bills concluding the terms of Dowling and Irion in 1928 instead of 1932. He then named Dr. Joseph A. O'Hara, one of his New Orleans leaders, to Dowling's place. Dowling charged that the act authorizing his removal was unconstitutional, that the legislature could not reduce the term of an office during the tenure of an incumbent. Fortified by an opinion from Attorney General Saint that his position was legal, Dowling refused to yield the office. Huey responded by having the legislature pass a law giving the governor authority to file "intrusion-in-office" suits against recalcitrant jobholders without the approval of the attorney general. The suit

[9] To avoid excessive documentation, the hundreds of laws enacted by successive legislatures and referred to in this study will not be cited to official sources. They may be found in *Acts of Louisiana*, 1928–1935, where they are listed by number, and in *Journal of the Proceedings of the House of Representatives* and *Journal of the Proceedings of the Senate*, 1928–1935. The *Journals* contain no record of debates. The Louisiana newspapers of the time reported legislative proceedings and acts with a fullness not found in later years.

brought against Dowling was fought by both parties right up to the supreme court and not decided until January 1929. Then the high tribunal ruled that as the constitution did not fix the term of his office, the legislature could change it.

It took even longer to oust Irion. The conservation chairman had also refused to yield his office to the successor appointed by Huey, Bob Maestri. An intrusion suit filed against Irion consumed over a year in the courts. The supreme court finally ruled, in November 1929, that Maestri was entitled to the office, but even then Irion held on, asking the supreme court to grant him an appeal to the federal courts. Huey was furious at this latest delay. "If I can't get him out any other way," he said, "I'll get a corkscrew and screw him out." He told the adjutant general of the National Guard to assemble a company in New Orleans, where Irion had his office, and to eject the chairman by force if necessary. Only the refusal of the supreme court to grant Irion an appeal saved him from the humiliation of a physical removal.[1]

At the same time that he started his assaults on the state boards, Huey moved to take over the board of administrators of one of the largest institutions operated by the state—Charity Hospital in New Orleans, which was maintained for indigent patients and which was the most extensive hospital of its kind in the South. It was governed by a nine-man board, of which the governor was an ex-officio member. By a law of 1890 the members served four-year terms that overlapped, which ensured that a new governor could make only two appointments on taking office and could not make more than four during his administration. Ostensibly the law was designed to remove Charity Hospital from political control, but it had not had that effect. An ambitious governor could eventually gain a majority on the board, and most previous governors had exercised some influence over it and over the hospital personnel.

Under the existing arrangement Huey would not be able to muster a majority on the board until 1930. He was too impatient to wait that long. He had a bill introduced in the legislature that would have reorganized the board immediately. But he could not jam it through. Some legislators sincerely thought that Charity Hospital should not

[1] Douthit: "Governorship of Long," pp. 55–7, 102; Norman Lant; Harley B. Bozeman; Deutsch: "Kingdom of the Kingfish," in New Orleans *Item*, August 13, 1939; L. Vaughan Howard: *Civil Service Development in Louisiana* (New Orleans, 1956), pp. 37, 39; Ben B. Taylor, Jr.: "A Study of the Appointive and Removal Powers of the Governor of Louisiana" (unpublished M.A. thesis, Louisiana State University, 1935), pp. 132–3; Ira Gleason; Shreveport *Journal*, November 28, 1929; New Orleans *Morning Tribune*, December 3, 1929.

be subjected to political interference; others responded to the considerable pressure the board was able to exert on the politicians. Refusing to admit defeat, Huey turned his attention to the board itself, and what he found delighted him. Two of the members were serving without legal sanction. Their terms had expired under Simpson, and the governor had not reappointed them. Declaring them removed, Huey filled their places and also appointed the two members he was authorized to name. With his own vote he now had a majority.

Only one day after he secured control, Huey called a meeting of the board in his suite at the Roosevelt Hotel. He informed the members that they were present for the purpose of selecting a new superintendent at Charity to replace Dr. William W. Leake, who had held the position since 1921. Huey also told them that he was nominating a successor, Dr. Arthur Vidrine, a young surgeon of Ville Platte, a small city in the southern part of the state. Vidrine was confirmed by a majority vote.

Critics of Huey then and later charged that he removed Leake for personal and political reasons. Leake was the son of Hunter Leake, a Standard Oil attorney who had fought Huey in a number of Public Service Commission cases. So, the critics reasoned, the relationship must have been the cause of the removal. Huey doubtless did enjoy ejecting the son of a Standard Oil official, but vengeance was not his motive. He simply wanted to have a man of his own in charge of Charity. Moreover, he had not appointed a political hack. Vidrine was a doctor of stature. He had graduated from the Tulane University medical school with a brilliant record and had been awarded a Rhodes scholarship. After two years of study in London, Paris, and Vienna, he had returned home and served for a time as junior intern at Charity before settling at Ville Platte. He was remarkably successful, and at the time of his appointment his income was reputedly twenty-five thousand dollars a year.[2]

Gradually Huey extended his control to other agencies. He met a rebuff now and then when he asked the legislature to reorganize a board, but by the end of the year he had acquired some degree of influence over most of the boards. In everything he did, his only objective seemed to be political—to build a machine and personal power. He required many appointees, including every member of

[2] Deutsch: "Kingdom of the Kingfish," in New Orleans *Item*, August 10 and 13, 1939; Stella O'Conner: "The Charity Hospital of New Orleans," *Louisiana Historical Quarterly*, XXXI (1948), 87–8; Dr. Cecil O. Lorio; New Orleans *States*, January 4, 1931.

the Levee Board, to sign undated resignations. He could thus remove anyone who had agreed to the arrangement by merely filling
in a date and writing his acceptance. His reasons for demanding
the resignations were complex and went beyond a crass desire to
grasp control. He asked them of some people because he had reason
to doubt their competence or honesty; if he found that he was wrong,
he returned the resignations. Sometimes he required every member
of a newly appointed board to sign resignations because he was not
sure of one man; the resignations of the men he trusted were then
secretly returned. Again, he sometimes had to appoint to a board a
man he did not like because one of his allies, like Sullivan, insisted
on it; he then made all the members sign resignations so that in
good time he could get rid of the distasteful one. One associate who
thought that Huey was wrong in demanding the resignations later
admitted that he had been right. Earl Long, when he became governor, found that often his appointees spurned even a reasonable request. "Huey was right," Earl reflected. "You have to have that
control."[3]

It was control of the large administrative agencies that mattered
most to Huey at this stage. The patronage that they, in turn, controlled was important, but even more important to Huey was his
program as a whole, which would be jeopardized if it was entrusted
to boards composed of his enemies, men who were unsympathetic
to his ideals. Actually, Huey could have justified his policy by an
eminently respectable philosophy of government. The boards in
Louisiana, as in all other states, were adjuncts of the governor's
office, and the governor was thus ultimately responsible for their
success or failure. Therefore, he could well argue that he should
have control over them.[4]

Huey never admitted that he was aware of this philosophy of
patronage. He always explained his appointments as examples of
unmitigated politics, as though he took a perverse delight in placing
himself in the worst possible light. It is clear, however, that he was
following a philosophy of some kind. He was not nearly so crass

[3] *Overton Hearing*, I, 907; *Official Journal of the Proceedings of the House of Representatives and the Senate of Louisiana*, 5th Extraordinary Session, 1929 (2 vols.; Baton Rouge, 1929), I, 415–17, 420–1, 426, 429. The latter source contains the testimony of witnesses in the impeachment proceedings against Governor Long; it will hereafter be cited as *Impeachment Proceedings*, I or II. The quotation from Earl Long came to me from a source that prefers to remain confidential.
[4] The question of whether the governor should control the boards has been a constant one in Louisiana politics. Practically every governor since Huey has insisted on control, and some of them have acted as boldly as he did.

as he affected to be. Thus, he did not sweep out so many jobholders as he could have: according to the estimate of one observer, in the first two years of his administration not more than a third of the state employees were Long people. Again, although he exercised a strong control over the policies of the boards and some control over their patronage policies, he did not try to politicalize their whole structure. "He never asked me to do anything I couldn't do," one official affirmed. "I mean anything dishonest. Oh, he might say, 'So and so is one of our friends. Don't be too rough on him.' But that was all."

Some officials and departments he did not interfere with at all. He instinctively understood one of the indispensable requirements of modern administration, one that no other Louisiana governor of modern times has fully grasped: some functions of government are so technical in nature that they must be operated by experts who are relatively free of control. If mere ward heelers were awarded these jobs they would botch them and criticism would fall on the governor and his organization. Huey retained in office some men from previous administrations who knew their jobs, and he appointed some men solely because he thought that they had the capacity to learn their jobs. Often he sent for these men and asked them to accept an appointment. Many of them told him frankly that they had voted against him and might do so again. They also said that they would have to have virtual freedom from political control. Huey agreed to the condition, although he did not like to be told that he had to grant it. He preferred not to give a guarantee in words but to have it understood. Then he could agree with criticism of an official but could continue to support him. He demurred to one man who insisted on having a guarantee but then said: "Look, I know what you're doing. If you hear that I called you a sonofabitch, well, that's all I can do about it." This man, who served for years without any interference, concluded that Huey had a definite philosophy of patronage: "He was smart that way. He knew where to fit men into positions—nonelastic men."[5]

As Huey's first legislature got down to work, he had little time to philosophize. Although he had mustered a majority in organizing the houses, he could not be certain of retaining it on key bills. Moreover, he would need more than a simple majority if he was going to enact his program. The Louisiana constitution, one of the longest and most unwieldy in the nation, required that some measures, such

[5] Harley B. Bozeman; W. A. Cooper; Bozeman in *Winn Parish Enterprise*, June 11, 1959; Harold Moise; Raymond H. Fleming; Louis F. Guerre; Charles J. Rivet.

as bond issues, be framed in the form of constitutional amendments. To pass amendments Huey would have to command a two-thirds majority—and then he would have to campaign to persuade the voters to ratify the amendments.

Patronage was one of the weapons Huey used to maintain a majority. He put some legislators on the big boards and awarded others easy jobs as attorneys or enforcement officers in some agency. In some cases, as with Allen and Bozeman, he was rewarding a trusted follower, but more often he was trying to draw new followers to him. Previous governors had used the same practice, but not on this scale, and for the first time the term "double dipper" became common in the Louisiana vocabulary. How many legislators held jobs cannot be determined accurately, but in 1930 sixteen lawmakers had to resign state jobs when the supreme court held that a member of the legislature could not simultaneously occupy another position. In the preceding two years the number was probably greater.[6]

Huey also employed patronage as a threat. Legislators who refused to vote with him were told that unless they "got right," relatives of theirs on the state payroll would be removed. If they ignored the warning, the threat was carried out. "He knew everything about you and how to get at you," recalled a senator whose father-in-law was one such victim. A representative thought that Huey resorted to even more ruthless methods. "Huey's great talent was to get men on his side," this man recalled. "There were men in the legislature that went over to him that I never thought would go. He bought them or got something on them." He may well have bought some men, in one fashion or another. There were legislators who could be purchased and for a modest price and who as a matter of course were usually bought by someone. But when Huey sought to buy or intimidate men, he chose those who he knew would submit to him. He treated with respect men who told him that they would support him on some issues but that because of their principles or the sentiments of their constituents they would have to oppose him on others. He said to one member who spoke to him thus; "Go ahead, and when you can support me, tell me." This man added, in recalling the scene: "We were friends from then on."[7]

[6] Harley B. Bozeman; John Kingston Fineran: *The Career of a Tin Pot Napoleon* (New Orleans, 1932), pp. 112–13; F. Raymond Daniell, article in *The New York Times,* reprinted in New Orleans *Item,* July 23, 1939. At that time legislators were paid ten dollars a day during a session and were quite willing to increase their income.

[7] Donald Labbe; Cecil Morgan; Norman Bauer; Fred Blanche; Allen J. Ellender.

On the day after his inauguration Huey went to the capitol to deliver his first message to the legislature, meeting in joint session. The capitol was a small, quaint building set on a low hill overlooking the Mississippi River. A turreted Gothic structure, it had been throughout its history the butt of ridicule of many observers, the cruelest gibes coming from Mark Twain, but it had a lovely interior and because of its association with the past was reverenced by old Louisianians. It had almost none of the facilities to speed legislation that were becoming popular in more progressive states. In neither chamber were there microphones or speaking devices, and members had to shout to make themselves heard above the hubbub of conversation on the floor. Only the house had a voting machine, and it was a primitive instrument, operated by unreliable wet batteries.

Huey faced the assembled lawmakers in the house chamber. To the disappointment of some members, and particularly of those in the opposition, he did not reveal in detail the legislation he was going to propose. Not until a few days later, when his floor leaders introduced the administration bills, did the exact nature of his program become known. The most important measures provided for bringing natural gas to New Orleans, for free schoolbooks supplied by the state, for a bond issue to hasten highway construction, and for increasing the severance tax on oil and other extractive products.[8]

The character of his floor leaders was probably what prompted Huey to conceal the details of his legislation until the last minute. Necessarily he had had to choose as leaders men of little or no legislative experience. Nearly all of the men most firmly committed to him, men that he knew he could trust, were newly elected members. The veterans who knew the complexities of parliamentary maneuvering, of how to steer a bill to passage, were either in the opposition or standing aloof. Sometimes he made someone a floor leader to keep him from joining the opposition. Members in the house who emerged as his leaders were Bozeman, heading the important appropriations committee; J. E. McClanahan, who as a sheriff had stood by just two years before when Bob Prophit assaulted Huey in Columbia; Allen J. Ellender, who had been elected on the Simpson ticket but whose southern parish had gone overwhelmingly for Long; and Lorris M. Wimberly and Smith Hoffpauir, young members in their twenties who would soon make their reputations. In the senate the veteran Gilbert gave guidance to a

8 New Orleans *Item*, May 23, 1928.

coterie of varying abilities: Oscar K. Allen, the Winn dependable; James L. Anderson, a fiery Baptist preacher; Harvey Peltier, a shrewd Frenchman; and William C. Boone, brilliant but erratic both as a lawmaker and a lawyer. Many of these men eventually would prove that they had real capacity, but in 1929 they were amateurs, just beginning to learn the ways of leadership.[9]

They might have learned more rapidly if Huey had given them a freer hand. But on crucial bills, he insisted on acting as his own floor leader. He would storm into either chamber and rush up and down the aisles barking out commands to his followers—Move for passage or rejection; Vote aye or nay. On a voice vote, he would sometimes himself answer for one of his adherents, bellowing the vote he wanted the man to cast. His antics pained his supporters, although they were not so much concerned about the proprieties as about being exposed openly as his henchmen. Some of them begged him to stay off the floor. He refused. "I'd rather violate every one of the damn conventions and see my bills passed, than sit back in my office, all nice and proper, and watch 'em die," he said. But it was not only concern for his bills that drove him into the chambers. He confessed the real reason to a representative who suggested that he summon members to his office: "I can't stay out. I just got to be there." There was a compulsion in him to place himself in the center of a scene of strife and excitement—and to try to dominate it.[1]

Arrayed against Huey's inexperienced leaders and waiting to sabotage his program was an adept conservative faction. They were a minority in both houses, but they were a cohesive minority, mustering a consistent twenty-seven votes in the house, and it was possible that their ability and knowledge of parliamentary devices would enable them to sidetrack Huey's bills. The house group was the more militant and the better organized and, because it was out to explode Huey's legislation, was known as the "Dynamite Squad." Its leaders were Cecil Morgan and Harney Bogan of Caddo parish, Mason Spencer of Madison, Norman Bauer of St. Mary, George K. Perrault of St. Landry, and J. Y. Sanders, Jr., of East Baton Rouge. They held nightly meetings in young Sanders's law office to discuss strategy. These dedicated men were members of the aristocracy, but they were tied in with the machine that had recently ruled the state, and they were friendly with the Old Regulars. They were

[9] John B. Fournet; Allen J. Ellender; W. V. Larcade.

[1] Deutsch: "Paradox in Pajamas," *Saturday Evening Post*, CCVIII (October 5, 1935), 36; Harrison Jordan; Lester Lautenschlaeger.

politicians but in some ways not typical ones. An excessive devotion to principle was their most marked quality. Surviving members of the faction were very frank in stating what principles impelled them to oppose Huey.

A representative: "People like me were not so much opposed to his measures as to his overbearing ways, his denunciations of you. . . . We resented being told we had to be with him."

A representative explaining his vote against the bond issue for highway construction: "My views were that if that bond issue was passed, Huey Long would use the money to corrupt the people of Louisiana."

A representative who had opposed the bond issue for the same reason but would have done so even if he had thought Huey was honest: "I thought it was too much debt. The two worst things that ever happened are universal suffrage and universal education."

A senator explaining why he voted against the bill to provide free schoolbooks: "I was elected with the support of powerful, wealthy people, and they were against it. . . . Later I could see Huey was right about some of his bills."

A representative: "The conservatives were blind to the times. They could have stopped Huey easily by giving the people a few things."

A senator: "That was the mistake of the opposition. They opposed everything he was for."[2]

They opposed everything he was for and often, it seemed, merely because he was for it. A neutral member once asked the leaders of the Dynamite Squad if they did not think that Huey could do one thing that was right, even if accidentally. One of the members said no: "If he did it, it would just have to be wrong.[3]

The legislature had hardly settled down to work before rumors circulated that Huey would demand that it act to bring natural gas to New Orleans. The stories elicited only amused scorn from the city's rulers: no governor could do anything to force his will on the metropolis. "The government of New Orleans is still in the hands of the people of New Orleans," said the *Item*, overlooking some embarrassing facts to make such a statement. "It will remain there when oblivion envelops Mr. Long." Huey, blithely unaware of his dark fate, continued to say that the gas would be brought in. He even stipulated what rate the public service company could charge—ninety cents per thousand cubic feet, plus a meter charge of twenty-five cents a month. The city government would accept this, he said. The city council and NOPSI ignored him: let him make his harmless noises as previous governors had made theirs.[4]

The conservatives still did not realize that this governor was not going to be satisfied by the sound of his own voice. They began to get an inkling, however, in early June. A Long lieutenant introduced three measures in the senate: one was a constitutional amendment authorizing the city government of New Orleans to issue up to fifty million dollars in bonds to purchase the properties of NOPSI. The other two were enabling acts to the amendment, permitting the city either to operate utilities or to sell or lease them to private interests. The senator who introduced the measures was swarthy Joachim O. Fernandez of New Orleans, who had been elected as an anti-Long candidate but who had immediately switched over to Huey's side. Fernandez was a typical product of the city's politics, marvelously adept at sniffing the political winds. He was known as "Bathtub Joe" because he got rid of unwelcome callers with the excuse that he was taking a bath.[5]

The Fernandez bills went through the senate at breakneck speed. In the space of a week they were introduced, reported out of committee, and enacted. They then were sent to the house, where, at Huey's direction, they were stalled in the judiciary committee. He held them up so that he could study the reactions of the parties to the controversy. Those reactions were interesting. The city council suddenly decided that it wanted to provide its people with natural gas. It further stated piously that Huey's basic rate of ninety cents was too high. The council, therefore, favored the Fernandez bills as a lever to force NOPSI to bring its own rates down. The corporation also became a sudden convert to the cause of natural gas. It insisted, however, that it would have to charge $1.15 per thousand cubic feet plus a monthly meter charge of fifty cents. Neither party, it seemed, was going to consider Huey's original proposal to fix the rates at ninety cents. Their complacency was short-lived. Huey announced that he was calling a conference at the Roosevelt Hotel of the city council, officials of NOPSI, and representatives of the parent Electric Bond and Share Company. He was

[4] New Orleans *Times-Picayune*, May 24 and 27, 1928; New Orleans *Item*, May 27, 1928.

[5] Hermann B. Deutsch; Deutsch: "Kingdom of the Kingfish," in New Orleans *Item*, August 11, 1939; Douthit: "Governorship of Long," p. 60.

going to explain the facts of the situation to those present, he said.[6]

It was a conference in name only. The governor took immediate charge and did all the talking. He told his listeners that but one course of action was open to them—accepting his rate proposal. As they listened in sullen astonishment, he outlined what would happen if they tried another course. If the company refused his terms and the city accepted them, he would put the Fernandez bills through the legislature. If the city refused his terms and the company accepted them, he would kill the bills, thus leaving the city no weapon against the company. If both parties declined his terms, he would obtain passage of a bill creating a state gas commission with power to grant franchises in any city.

Both city and company were appalled. The conservative city council had supported the Fernandez bills only so it could pose as the champion of lower rates. The company had opposed the bills out of shortsighted selfishness. Now there was the threat of public ownership, which was equally repugnant to both of them.

Huey told them the hard facts. "A deck has fifty-two cards," he said, "and in Baton Rouge I hold all fifty-two of them and can shuffle and deal as I please." Taking out his watch, he said that he was going to Baton Rouge and that he wanted an answer by the next day. Back in Baton Rouge he relented slightly, extending the deadline by two days.[7]

An immediate answer came from the company: it rejected Huey's proposal. The council, however, after a last frantic attempt to influence the legislature had failed, voted to give in. Mayor O'Keefe wired Huey that the city would consent to the rate of ninety cents. Huey accepted the surrender but announced that as the company had not yielded, the house judiciary committee would hold its scheduled hearing on the Fernandez bills. Actually, Huey himself did not want to see the bills passed nor public ownership set up, but unless the company also submitted, he might have to call his own bluff. Time was needed to allow public sentiment to build up against the company. On the day before the house committee was to meet, therefore, he demanded that the city council embody the ninety-cent rate in a formal ordinance. If it did not, he said, he would not permit the committee to meet.

[6] New Orleans *States*, June 23, 1928; New Orleans *Times-Picayune*, June 25, 1928; New Orleans *Morning Tribune*, June 25, 1928.

[7] New Orleans *Times-Picayune*, June 26, 1928; New Orleans *Morning Tribune*, June 26, 1928.

Despite the governor's threat, the council sent a representative to the meeting, Commissioner Walmsley, who bore an official statement to the effect that the city had agreed to Huey's terms but did not want to bind itself by an ordinance. Walmsley handed the statement to Huey while the committee was assembling. Huey strode up and down the room in a feigned rage. "In that case there'll be no committee meeting," he stormed. The chairman of the committee was Gilbert Dupre, a courtly, conservative old gentleman from one of the French parishes. Totally deaf, he did not at first hear Huey's statement. Somebody wrote the import of it on a pad and handed it to him. Trembling with fury, he rapped his gavel and said: "This meeting will come to order." Huey walked over to the Long members, a majority, and whispered to them. Each of them rose and left the room, leaving the committee without a quorum. Cries of protest came from the New Orleans representatives and others present. Huey slapped his chest. "Blame it all on me! Me! Huey Long!" he shouted. He repeated that New Orleans would have to enact an ordinance, and then he walked out himself.[8]

On the next day the council, now standing in surrender, passed a motion adopting Huey's rate and sent a certified copy to Baton Rouge by special messenger. Huey refused to accept it. He had to have an ordinance, he said. Then suddenly, on July 7, came the news he had been waiting for. The company had yielded. It notified the city that it would accept the rate of ninety cents. Two days later the house judiciary committee killed the Fernandez bills.

Huey had won his fight. And New Orleans had its natural gas. But if Huey had expected that he would garner much gratitude for his efforts, he was disappointed, just as he had been after the Galveston rate case. The city officials and most of the press denounced him as a tool of the company! At its dictate, it was charged, he had forced a rate that was too high: his ninety cents, plus the meter charge of twenty-five cents, made a monthly rate of $1.15 per thousand cubic feet, which was little less than the rate of $1.35 then in effect. The critics overlooked the fact that the saving to the consumer was actually forty cents a month, since natural gas was' more efficient than artificial gas and thus the consumer would need less of it. They overlooked too that if Huey had not intervened in the controversy, the coming of natural gas would have been delayed for years. The city officials who condemned Huey had not acted until he had made

---

[8] Deutsch: "Kingdom of the Kingfish," in New Orleans *Item*, August 11, 1939; New Orleans *Morning Tribune*, July 4, 1928; *Impeachment Proceedings*, I, 574–5.

them. "Huey held their feet to the fire," said a member of the council as he recalled the episode.[9]

He had had to act with almost brutal directness. If he had used gentler methods, he would not have been able to achieve his purpose. As it was, he had succeeded dramatically where previous governors had failed. And he had achieved even more than his immediate victory. He had taught his opponents where the power was, and had given the other measures on his legislative program a big boost toward passage.

One of the most popular issues that Huey had raised in the campaign was the promise of an expanded system of roads. Some associates—and some opponents—think this issue elected him. Certainly the people of Louisiana were eager, pathetically so, for better highways. They knew that people in other states enjoyed the use of surfaced roads, whereas they had very few. The estimates of the number of miles of improved roads in the state in 1928 differ, but the most optimistic assessment makes it 296 miles of concrete roads, 35 miles of asphalt roads, and 5,728 miles of gravel roads. A publication of the Long administration, however, put the total figure for hard-surfaced roads lower:. 109 miles of "high type" (concrete) roads and 154 miles of "low type" (asphalt and similar coverings) roads. An official memorandum of the present Highway Commission gives an even lower figure: 31 miles of concrete roads completed and 20 miles under construction, 65 miles of asphalt roads competed and 4 miles under construction.[1]

Whatever the exact figures, they were pitifully low for a state in the modern era. Louisiana was, in a phrase of the time that became a permanent part of the state's vocabulary, "in the mud." It was in the mud because the old ruling class had insisted on following a roads policy that made extensive or quick construction impossible. The question of a comprehensive policy first arose in the constitutional convention of 1921. Before that date demands for surfaced roads had been few, and construction had been sparse and sporadic.

[9] New Orleans *Times-Picayune*, July 8, 1928; New Orleans *States*, July 8, 1928; Deutsch: "Kingdom of the Kingfish," in New Orleans *Item*, August 11, 1939; Paul B. Habans. Huey's procedure in the affair was reminiscent of his Public Service technique, a fierce denunciation of a corporation, followed by a fair settlement. His defense of the $1.15 rate was that it was necessary to assure NOPSI of a fair return. It was still a good deal lower than the $1.65 the company had originally demanded.

[1] Allen P. Sindler: *Huey Long's Louisiana: State Politics, 1920–1952* (Baltimore, 1956), p. 103; *American Progress*, December 28, 1933; memorandum furnished to me by the Highway Commission, January 29, 1957.

The state had been able to meet the costs out of current revenues. But by 1921 the demand for roads had assumed a new form. It was not limited to roads enthusiasts or interested communities. Rather, it was a public demand, and the delegates had to consider it and to act upon it. Specifically, they had to decide how the state should finance a roads program.

Some delegates argued that bonds would have to be issued. But this proposal immediately met the fierce resistance of the conservatives, led by J. Y. Sanders, Sr. No state bonds had ever been sold for highway purposes, the conservatives argued, and none should ever be. Let Louisiana continue to finance its highways on the same sound fiscal principle it had always used—paying for them as it built, out of revenues from license and gasoline taxes. The conservatives won, and a provision was written into the constitution stipulating that all construction was to be paid for from current taxes. This was equivalent to a prohibition on the issuance of bonds, and its effect was to limit severely the mileage that could be laid down in any one year. But it was impossible for the Highway Commission to keep its contracts within the constitutional restriction: because of rising or unforeseen costs and because the commission was usually graft-ridden, expenses always outran income. When Huey took over, he found overdrawn bank accounts and also an unsecured contractual debt of five million dollars.[2]

It was obvious to anyone who took the trouble to think about it that the existing policy would never permit Louisiana to build an adequate highway system. The revenues from taxes were simply not large enough to construct many roads. Yet no governor had tried to change the policy. None of them since 1921 had wanted to change it. To do so would mean selling bonds—putting the state into debt —and such a break with the past would arouse the wrath of the ruling class. Moreover, there were troublesome technical difficulties that would have to be surmounted. A bond issue could not be authorized by simple legislative enactment. It would have to be embodied in a constitutional amendment, which would have to receive the approval of two thirds of the members of both legislative houses and would then have to be ratified by the voters. The governors before Huey, even if they had wanted to change the policy, would have flinched before the difficulties.

It was not in Huey's nature to flinch. Obstacles were likely only

[2] William D. Ross: *Financing Highway Improvements in Louisiana* (Baton Rouge, 1955), pp. 41–5.

to excite him to more audacious action. But in dealing with this matter of roads he moved with cunning caution. He was determined to give the people roads, the roads that they wanted, the roads that would enlist them as grateful followers of Huey Long. He knew that there was only one way to get the money that would be required—through a bond issue. But he knew also that he could move too fast on the bond issue; by demanding too much too soon he would arouse opposition and wreck his plans for the future. So he decided to ask the legislature to authorize a comparatively small issue, thirty million dollars. This sum was certain to be accepted. With it he could not build many roads, but enough to show the people what good roads were, enough to give them a taste for more.

There is no evidence that Huey understood the concept that later would be called deficit financing—that the economy of an area would be improved if its government borrowed money and spent it, and that government had an obligation to do so. When he proposed bonds as a means to finance roads, he was probably thinking in purely pragmatic terms: there was an immediate need for roads and the only immediate way the state could finance them was to sell bonds. It is possible, however, that he intuitively grasped the implications of the spending theory. He was not content with forcing the legislature to authorize bonds for roads but also persuaded it to approve an issue to build bridges—there were only three major bridges in the state system—and another issue to improve the shores of Lake Pontchartrain with a sea wall. Nor would he stop here. He would continue to borrow, and in the years ahead bonds more than taxes would finance the Long program. But he would always couple with his spending a sense of fiscal responsibility. He never instituted a bond issue that was not secured by a tax. Thus as a companion to the bond issue financing highways, he insisted that the legislature enact a constitutional amendment raising the gasoline tax from two cents a gallon to four cents. One cent of the tax was to go into a fund to retire the bonds, and three cents was dedicated to the general highway fund.[3]

If the bond issue for roads had required only a majority vote, Huey would have had little trouble getting it through the legislature. His control of the chambers was such that he could force passage of most bills simply by backing them, and this measure had behind it

[3] Ibid., pp. 45–6, 50–1; Sindler: *Huey Longs' Louisiana*, p. 59; Huey P. Long: *Every Man a King* (New Orleans, 1933), p. 108; Douthit: "Governorship of Long," pp. 52–3.

the added impetus of popular support. But he had to use all his powers of persuasion and pressure to round up the two-thirds majority in both houses. He finally secured commitments from sixty-five of the sixty-seven members he needed in the house. He thought he had the promises of two additional members, but these men absented themselves when the vote was about to be taken. Huey's patience snapped at this point. He found out where the men were hiding and had them brought to the floor of the house by state policemen.[4]

Huey had to work equally hard to secure the passage of the companion measure to the bond issue, the amendment increasing the tax on gasoline. Opponents claimed that the taxpayers could not bear such a financial burden and charged that the money would be spent to create useless jobs on the Highway Commission. Some members who voted for the amendment privately hoped that the voters would reject it. The opposition continued, growing still louder after the legislature adjourned. Critics centered their fire on the absence of any safeguard in the amendment to ensure that the money would be expended on highways. They charged that the governor might even use the fund as a campaign chest. As this was exactly what Louisianians would expect any governor to do, the charge was telling and threatened to defeat ratification of the amendment. Huey realized that some dramatic action on his part was necessary to save it. He announced that he would set up his own safeguard. If the voters approved the two amendments, he promised, he would appoint an advisory board of eleven prominent citizens to oversee the expenditure of highway funds. No disbursement of money from the bond issue and contracts payable out of it would be made without the approval of this board. He mentioned some men that he would name to the board, leading businessmen who had been opposed to him.

This unexpected concession threw his foes into confusion. The Old Regulars sought to counter with what they thought was a clever move. They demanded that the governor summon a special session of the legislature and have the advisory board written into the amendment. Huey countered, even more cleverly. He agreed to call the legislature if the Old Regulars would pledge to support the amendments in the November election. Hastily the city chiefs backed away from their own proposal. Huey emerged from the episode with new strength. He seemed to be a reasonable and honest leader,

---

[4] W. C. Pegues. In *Every Man a King*, pp. 110–11, Huey gave a polite version of this episode.

but his opponents appeared as inflexible conservatives and political opportunists.[5]

Even more popular than roads as a campaign issue had been Huey's promise to have the state provide free schoolbooks. He would provide them, he had said, without imposing additional direct taxes. Conservative opponents dismissed this issue as nothing but demagoguery. Where would Huey get the money? He had said he was going to furnish books to all children, in parochial and private schools as well as in public. Did he not know that there were state and federal prohibitions on the use of public funds to aid religious institutions? Also looking doubtfully at the free-books proposal were the educational leaders. Superintendent of Education T. H. Harris, who had been elected over Huey's opposition, had denounced Huey's idea in the campaign. Harris feared that Huey would get the money for the books by taking it from the already limited funds allocated to the schools.

Huey and Harris met after the election and concluded an alliance. Harris hoped to persuade the governor to support his favorite reform plan—the creation of a state equalizing fund that would place schools in the poor parishes on a par with those in wealthier areas. Huey wanted Harris, who commanded great influence in the state and also in the teachers' lobby, to throw his weight behind a free-books law. Harris said he would like to go along—if the money was not taken from the school fund. Huey assured him that he would find new tax sources.

A few days after he took office, Huey read to the superintendent a draft of a free-books act that he was going to send to the legislature. It was a short and simple document that Huey had originally written on the back of a piece of cardboard he had taken out of a freshly laundered shirt. It stated that books would be distributed free to "the schoolchildren" of Louisiana and that the money to provide them would come out of the severance tax on natural resources. Harris was aghast. The act would provide books to children in elementary and secondary schools regardless of whether they were public or private. Most of the private schools were operated by the Catholic church, he protested, and the state was prohibited from aiding religious institutions. Huey dismissed the objection. The state was not providing books to *schools*, he pointed out, but to *children*. It would use the schools merely as distribution centers. He

[5] New Orleans *Morning Tribune*, August 23, 1928; New Orleans *Times-Picayune*, August 23 and September 21, 1928; Deutsch: "Kingdom of the Kingfish," in New Orleans *Item*, August 13, 1939; Douthit: "Governorship of Long," pp. 62–4.

was obviously elated at his brilliant legal stratagem. "I am a better lawyer than you are," he exclaimed, "and books for children attending private schools go in the act." Huey's argument that the act was legal was convincing to the legislature. It was passed by large majorities in both houses and with almost no debate. An appropriation of $750,000 a year was voted for two years to provide the books.[6]

To provide the money, Huey proposed to the legislature a fundamental change in the severance tax. It was one of a number of reforms he intended to bring about in the existing tax system, which needed reforming. Louisiana was known as a state that levied remarkably few taxes—an ad valorem tax on local property, an inheritance tax, an occupational license tax, and a severance tax. These various taxes brought in only a modest revenue, not enough to support the kind of program Huey envisioned. The most lucrative one, the property tax, bore more heavily on the taxpayer of average or below-average means than on the wealthy. One senator who studied it was so impressed by its inequities that he swung over to Huey's side, although he had been elected as an opposition candidate. "It was wrong," he recalled with emotion, even after many years. "It fell on the poor man, his land, his horses, his furniture." Huey sent two career officials from the Tax Commission to every Southern state to examine its rates. His theory of taxation, as one of these men explained it, was to "cover everything in sight," to "throw out a network of taxes with low rates to catch everything." "Never overlook anything in taxes," he liked to say.[7]

The existing severance-tax law, enacted under Governor Parker, based levies on natural resources on their market value when extracted. Huey proposed that the levies be based on quantity—so much per barrel of oil, per thousand feet of lumber, per ton of sulphur. A quantity tax was calculated to produce more revenue, which was why Huey advocated it, but his enemies charged that he had a different reason, a personal one. A shift from a value to a quantity basis would not change materially the amount of taxes paid by most of the extractive industries. It would, however, place a heavier burden on the oil and gas industries, and representatives of these interests charged that Huey was trying to pay off his score against the Standard Oil Company. Particularly incensed were the

[6] T. H. Harris: *The Memoirs of T. H. Harris* (Baton Rouge, 1963), pp. 125–6, 159; Sindler: *Huey Long's Louisiana*, pp. 58–9; Seymour Weiss; Guy C. Mitchell: "The Growth of State Control of Public Education in Louisiana" (unpublished Ph.D. dissertation, University of Michigan, 1942), pp. 440–1, 443.

[7] H. Lester Hughes; W. A. Cooper.

oil operators of north Louisiana. The bill that Huey's lieutenants introduced provided for a sliding scale based on the gravity of the quantity of oil, the scale ranging from four cents a barrel on oil of low gravity to eleven cents on that of high gravity. The gravity of oil produced in north Louisiana was uniform throughout the area, whereas in the south the gravity varied widely. They were being discriminated against, the northern operators cried. They threatened that if the tax was passed, they would contest it in the courts.[8]

Just how the proposed rates would strike harder at Standard Oil than at any other company was not explained. Actually, the loudest protests did not come from the biggest company but from small operators and from the Ohio Oil Company, which had extensive holdings in the north. Huey, however, chose to give credence to the charge that he was engaged in a personal vendetta. He appeared before the house committee that was considering the severance-tax bill and asked for its passage. In an emotion-packed speech of half an hour he recounted how he had been cheated out of a two million-dollar lease by Standard at Pine Island. But now, he gloated, he was going to make the company pay much more than two million. In a quick shift of themes, he recalled the poverty of his youth. Free books would have meant much to a family like the Longs, he said. He could remember many a cold winter day when he and his brothers and sisters had had to walk to school shoeless. The large crowd of spectators listened enraptured, cheering his every statement. In the audience was the wife of former governor Ruffin G. Pleasant, who had held a legal job with the state until Huey ejected him from it. Mrs. Pleasant, a doughty old aristocrat, finally could stand no more. She rose and reminded Huey that he was infringing on the function of the legislature. Didn't he know, she asked, that the state constitution provided for three separate branches of government? "Yes, I know that," Huey answered sweetly, "and I have removed your husband from one of those departments."

He delighted in a performance such as this. Nothing pleased him quite as much as an opportunity to attack Standard Oil, to paint it as the evil enemy of progress and himself as the young champion who had risen from poverty to conquer it. But his actions were not entirely based on juvenile malice; there was shrewd calculation, smart politics, in what he did. If he was going to put through

---

[8] T. N. Farris: *Severance Taxation in Louisiana* (University, La., 1938), Pt. II, pp. 12–13, 14–15, 18, 48–52; Leslie Moses: "The Growth of Severance Taxation in Louisiana and Its Relation to the Oil and Gas Industry," *Tulane Law Review,* XVII (1943), 611.

his program, he had to be able to personify to the public the forces that were opposing him. The big oil company was a natural, obvious enemy. His strategy was justified when the severance tax passed both houses by substantial majorities.[9]

Huey proposed one other major tax bill—a levy of four cents a pound on the manufacture of carbon black. The tax was required to provide money for hospitals and other charitable state institutions, he claimed. The manufacturers of carbon black, whose plants were located near the gas fields in northeastern Louisiana, had endured wide criticism for years. State fiscal officials complained that the industry made huge profits but returned no taxes to the government. Conservationists complained that in its manufacturing process natural gas was burned wastefully. Yet the manufacturers had been able to fight off all attempts to regulate or tax them. They now mustered a powerful lobby in Baton Rouge to oppose Huey's bill. Some of the lobbyists hinted that if the bill was passed, the industry would leave the state. Huey denied this, but added scornfully: "In the opinion of most of the people of the State if the tax will drive the carbon interest out . . . it would do considerable good." He made no strong effort, however, to force passage of the bill. He had known that he would encounter stubborn resistance, and he had probably put in the four cents as a "trading" figure. In the end he agreed with the industry to compromise the levy at a half a cent a pound. It was nonetheless a triumph that he had succeeded in imposing any tax.[1]

Huey could look back on many triumphs as the legislative session closed. He had carried most of the measures that he had proposed, and his setbacks had been few and minor. No governor in recent times had enacted so comprehensive a program, had exerted such influence over the legislature, or had extended so much control over the various state agencies. He was in an exultant mood as he prepared to campaign for ratification of his amendments.

Then abruptly an unforeseen development threatened to undo much of what he had accomplished and dissipate the aura of success that enveloped him. The schools were almost ready to open for the fall session, and all over the state parents were looking forward to free schoolbooks. The books had been ordered, but with the severance tax as yet uncollected, there was no money on hand to pay

[9] New Orleans *Morning Tribune*, June 20, 1928; New Orleans *States*, July 28, 1928; *Overton Hearing*, II, 2324–5.
[1] Farris: *Severance Taxation*, Pt. I, pp. 16–17; Douthit: "Governorship of Long," pp. 52–3; New Orleans *States*, June 1, 1928.

for them. In ordinary circumstances the situation could have been handled easily. The state normally found itself without funds for certain purposes at this time of the year. The traditional procedure was for the governor to call a meeting of the Board of Liquidation, an appointive body that he controlled, and ask for permission to borrow whatever sum was required from the New Orleans clearing house, which represented the city's banks. The board had always given permission, and as the requested loan was secured by the collection of incoming taxes, the banks had always cooperated. But this time there were complications. Parties opposed to the free-books law had instituted a suit denying its legality, and the Ohio Oil Company had entered a suit challenging the legality of the severance tax.

When Huey went to New Orleans to appear before the bankers, he found himself facing some embarrassed men. They finally told him, after much hemming and hawing, that they did not think Board of Liquidation loans were any longer legal. Their refusal struck him with dismay. But in a moment he recovered his audacity. Rising, he said that he would be guided by their decision. Board of Liquidation loans were illegal—but the state already owed almost a million dollars in such loans and if they were illegal, the state was not going to repay them. He waited, but none of the bankers spoke. He walked slowly from the room, but no one came after him.

He went to a nearby restaurant and sat down at a table. He was sure that his bluff had not worked. When a waiter came up, he ordered a sandwich. At this moment one of the bankers entered. "Governor," he said, "Let's stop this talk where it is. We voted to make you the loan."

"When can I have it?" Huey asked. "Right now," assured the banker. Huey's exultant mood returned. Just then the waiter came with the sandwich. "Take back the sandwich," Huey commanded. "Fry me a steak."[2]

[2] Long: *Every Man a King*, pp. 112–14; Seymour Weiss; Allen J. Ellender.

# CHAPTER 13

# *Kingfish of the Lodge*

L OUISIANA PROVIDED AN official residence for its governors, "the executive mansion," as everybody in Baton Rouge called it. Built before the Civil War, its architecture was typical of Southern tastes of that era: outside, square white pillars supported broad galleries; inside, wide halls connected high-ceilinged rooms.[1] It was situated three blocks from the capitol in a neighborhood of large homes, some of them more pretentious than the so-called mansion, and all of them inhabited by the "old families" who ruled Baton Rouge society and who looked with suspicious eyes on newcomers. They accepted or rejected governors—or Standard Oil magnates— on their own terms, ignoring with icy politeness those who did not meet their tests. None of these people came to call on the new governor. They had not liked Huey before he was elected, liked him less on closer acquaintance—and increasingly less as that acquaintance grew. He was "common." They could never ignore him, but they could isolate themselves from him.

Huey was not, however, lonely in the mansion. His leaders and friends from the far corners of the state flocked into Baton Rouge and filled the house. Some of them, at his invitation, even stayed there. At night they would sit around the dining-room table and argue politics or listen to the radio.

At one of these gatherings Huey acquired a significant nickname. He and his cronies liked to listen to the popular radio show "Amos 'n' Andy," and according to Huey, he began calling one of his followers "Brother Crawford," the name of a lodge brother

[1] New Orleans *Item*, April 5, 1924.

in the Mystic Knights of the Sea, to which Amos and Andy belonged. In return, said Huey, "Brother Crawford" dubbed him "Kingfish," the leader of the lodge, and the name stuck.

Stories differ, however, as to when the name originated, and how. A reporter who was close to Huey claimed that the governor christened himself. According to his account, the leaders were arguing some point in Huey's presence when he shouted them down, bellowing, "Shut up, you sonsofbitches, shut up! This is the Kingfish, talking!"

Whatever its origin, the name tickled Huey. He liked its connotation of homespun majesty and frequently applied it to himself. He used it most often when calling somebody on the phone. "This is the Kingfish," he would say. In Louisiana no further identification was needed.[2]

Noticeably absent from the lodge meetings at the mansion were members of the Long family, the Kingfish's brothers and sisters. They did not appear, Julius Long explained, because Huey did not want them there—in fact, he had let them know that they would not be welcome. His conduct toward his closest kin was "insulting and contemptible," Julius charged. Nor, according to Julius, was this the least or last of Huey's slights to his family. Huey refused to invite his father to the mansion during the entire time that he was governor. The old man was now reduced to living with various relatives, and Julius and Earl bore the main burden of his support. Julius suggested to Huey that the burden could be eased if "Papa" was given a room at the mansion, but Huey spurned the request. Huey contributed almost nothing to the support of the father, Julius complained, and also did very little to help the sick sister in the West. It was Julius's conclusion that Huey had no sense of family.[3]

[2] Davis: *Long*, p. 28; Harley B. Bozeman; Deutsch, "Kingdom of the Kingfish," in New Orleans *Item*, August 23, 1939. Deutsch has the scene occurring in New Orleans in 1930. In reproducing Huey's statement, Deutsch used blanks to indicate an expletive. I have assumed that Huey uttered his favorite term of endearment or condemnation.

[3] Forrest Davis: *Huey Long, A Candid Biography* (New York, 1935), p. 145; Julius Long: "What I Know About My Brother," *Real America*, II (September, 1933), 34–7; Walter Davenport: "Catching up with Huey," *Collier's*, XCII (June 1, 1933), 12–13. Julius's version of Old Hu's situation is somewhat at variance with the facts. The old man remarried in 1921 and was living at Dry Prong in 1931 when his wife sued for a divorce on grounds of desertion; New Orleans *Times-Picayune*, July 7, 1931. Julius, when he proposed that their father be given a room at the mansion, was either incredibly naïve or was trying to make Huey look selfish. It would have been political dynamite for Huey to put his father up at state expense. Julius made the request in a letter, and the tone of the letter suggests that he expected and wanted a refusal.

The analysis of Huey's older brother was not wide of the mark. Huey did not have normal familial feelings. He was not close to his family, and he even disliked some members of it. A friend once told Huey that he had come back from another state because he wanted to live near his family. "I'd like to get as far away from my damn kinfolks as I could," Huey observed. He frequently commented publicly on his low opinion of his relatives. "This state's full of sapsucker, hillbilly and Cajun relatives of mine," he announced on one occasion, "and there ain't enough dignity in the bunch to keep a chigger still long enough to brush his hair."[4]

These deprecations brought from his enemies scornful disbelief. Huey talked like this only to deceive the public, they charged; he was really strongly attached to all his family. As proof, they pointed to the large number of Long "connections" that he had rewarded with state jobs. Just how many he had appointed became a political issue. One estimate placed the number at at least sixty, and a list issued by an anti-Long organization named twenty-four "family" employees, whose annual salaries totaled almost seventy-six thousand dollars. The estimate of sixty was a wild guess. The documented list was accurate on the surface, but misleading. It included Huey, with his annual salary of seventy-five hundred dollars, as an "employee." It cited his sister Olive, who had been on the faculty of one of the state colleges when he was elected, in the same category with recipients of patronage. Moreover, it contained the names of some individuals who were only remotely connected with Long, who were, in Huey's words, "ninth cousins, the in-laws and cousins of in-laws." With some justice, Huey observed that any politician could be similarly smeared with the charge that his relatives were feeding from the public trough. He suggested that his critics investigate the roster of the state penitentiary—they would probably find that some of his kin were being supported there.[5]

Huey's defense was plausible enough, but, like the criticism of him, it omitted some pertinent facts. He was, after all, guilty of nepotism, probably to a greater degree than any previous governor. But he had what seemed to him legitimate reasons for appointing those relatives that he did. The reasons were, in most cases, more political than personal. He gave jobs to some because they had

[4] David Blackshear; unidentified clipping, n. d., in Persac Scrapbook.
[5] Will Irwin: "The Empire of the Kingfish," *Liberty*, XII (April 6, 1935), 14–16; L. Vaughan Howard: *Civil Service Development in Louisiana* (New Orleans, 1956), pp. 40–1; memorandum of employees, September 26, 1929, in Robinson Papers; New Orleans *Times-Picayune*, September 28, 1929.

helped him in the campaign and, like other workers, deserved a reward. He selected others because he judged that he could trust them or believed that they had special abilities for particular positions. Only a few did he appoint for personal reasons. And, although this is pure conjecture, he did not necessarily name even these because he liked them. Rather, he placed them because he experienced a pleasant sensation of superiority when he saw them working for Huey Long, who was now undeniably the head Long, because now he could browbeat them and make them take it. Thus one kinsman, a "cousin," had to endure for years a routine that Huey developed. "Look at old ——" Huey would say in this man's presence. "He's the best employee in the whole state. He does his work better than anybody we got." Somebody always asked the cue question: "What does he do, Huey?" "Not a goddamn thing," Huey would explode with malicious glee.[6]

It is significant that practically all of these relatives were in comparatively minor jobs. Not one was put where he could influence the making of policy or challenge Huey's primacy. Indeed, not one was placed where Huey would see him very often. Clearly this was the way Huey wanted it. After he became governor he drew more and more away from his family, and Winnfield. In the four years of his governorship he made only one trip back to his hometown, and that was in 1932, when he made a fleeting visit to have his picture taken as he started on a campaign.

Only one member of his immediate family remained at all close to Huey. This was his younger brother Earl, who had been his close companion during childhood. Earl had helped Huey in both campaigns for the governorship, and Huey rewarded him with a position that was one of the most lucrative of the state jobs, though not an influential one. Earl became attorney for the inheritance-tax collector in New Orleans at a salary of over fourteen thousand dollars a year. "That was a plum he gave me," Earl recalled. It was a plum with a string attached, however. Huey insisted that as a condition of getting the job Earl was to assume the financial support of their father and their sick sister.[7]

Earl's duties were so light that they took very little time. He was in Baton Rouge more than he was in New Orleans, and when he was in the capital, he was generally closeted with Huey. "Earl bothers me more than anybody," Huey confided to an associate. "He will bring up a thousand things, but I always listen because I

[6] Confidential communications.
[7] Earl K. Long; Harley B. Bozeman.

can use one of them." Huey found that in fact he had many uses for Earl himself. He employed Earl as a contact man with legislators and with Long leaders in the state and as an organizer of Long machines in the parishes. Surviving politicians testify admiringly to Earl's skill in handling the assignments Huey gave him. "Earl was better at conniving than Huey," they say, meaning that Earl was more adept in dealing with individuals. Huey frequently praised Earl's peculiar talents. "You give Earl a few dollars," Huey once said, "and turn him loose on the road and he will make more contacts and better contacts than any ten men with a barrel of money." But although Huey found Earl useful, he did not completely trust him, according to some witnesses. "You have to watch Earl," he warned a friend: "If you live long enough, he'll double-cross you. He'd double-cross Jesus Christ if he was down here on earth."[8]

Earl Long would survive Huey by many years and would become something of a legend himself, and some would even say that he was a greater politician than Huey. But associates who knew both men intimately universally agree that Huey was so far the superior that there is no comparison. "It's like comparing a university graduate and a grade schooler," one of them said. Earl was a superb politician, they concede, but he did not have the ability or the ambition to operate above the state level. But Huey was a "national" politician. "Huey looked a long way down the road but Earl's vision was limited," said one leader. The more perceptive of these associates emphasize another difference: Earl was the more loved by the people, was closer to them. They hasten to explain that this is additional evidence of Earl's inferiority. "Earl was like us," they say. Earl was a leader, but he was not the great leader who stood above the people, who awed them with his superiority. "They loved Earl but feared Huey," said one man. Another suggested that this difference between the two was reflected in their methods. "Huey drove 'em to water," he said; "Earl had to lead 'em."[9]

Huey's other brothers and his sisters were not the only members of his family who did not appear at the mansion. Even more conspicuous by their absence were Mrs. Long and his three children. They had attended the inauguration and had moved into the mansion. But shortly thereafter Rose suddenly returned to their home in Shreveport with the children. According to some Long associates,

[8] David B. McConnell; Wilson J. Peck; Edgar G. Mouton; Fred Blanche; John B. Fournet; Louis A. Jones; E. J. Bourg; confidential communication.
[9] James T. Burns; William Cleveland; Fred Blanche; Robert Angelle; Sam H. Jones; E. J. Bourg; Lantz Womack.

she left because Huey had installed his pretty young secretary, Alice Lee Grosjean, in the mansion and was openly carrying on an affair with her. As these sources relate it, Rose threatened to institute a suit for divorce. "I belong down there, and my children," she stated flatly. "I won't start a suit if he brings me down there." When her word was relayed to Huey, he promised to move Miss Grosjean to a more circumspect location.[1]

Twenty-two-year-old Alice Lee had been an object of public curiosity from the moment she arrived in Baton Rouge with Huey. It was known that she had been Huey's secretary and political assistant and that she would assume a similar position in the Long administration. Gossip whispered that she was more than a secretary. Indeed, there had been a good deal of speculation about her relationship with Huey almost from the time she went to work for him. She was married to James Terrell, whom she had eloped with when she was only fifteen, but she obviously cared little for him and now saw him less and less. Then, in 1928, she and Terrell agreed to a separation and a divorce. This development, coming as Huey prepared to take her to the capital, naturally added fuel to the speculation. Colonel Ewing and other associates advised Huey not to name her as his secretary, that the appointment would cause gossip even if there was no foundation for it.[2]

The gossip grew and would continue for the rest of Huey's life and for years after his death. Whether it had any basis in fact is difficult to determine. Affairs of love, legal or illegal, are rarely attended by witnesses. The testimony of people who knew the alleged principals well is contradictory. There are those who affirm that Huey kept Alice Lee near him only because she was extremely efficient in any job and because he could trust her. These same people deny other stories about Huey—that he chased after other women besides Alice Lee. "They say he ran around with women," said a man who traveled with him for years. "I can tell you I never saw anything of it and as close as I was I would have known."[3]

There are other witnesses, equally close to Huey, who are certain that Alice Lee was his mistress. "Huey was fooling around with her," said one of them. These people say also that Huey pursued

[1] Confidential communications. According to another confidential source, Huey housed Miss Grosjean in the mansion only to have ready access to her secretarial services and installed an aunt of hers in the same room.

[2] Article in *Every Week Magazine*, November 30, 1930; Marquis Childs, article in St. Louis *Post-Dispatch*, Sunday magazine section, March 31, 1931; W. D. Robinson to Julius Long, June 1, 1933, in Robinson Papers.

[3] Raymond H. Fleming; Mrs. Clarence Pierson; Murphy Roden.

other women. He was subject to sudden, violent sexual impulses, they think. When one of these impulses struck him, he acted, even if he was in a public place. One informant related that on a train trip Huey was invited to the car of a man he met and that later he attacked his host's daughter. When his companions reproached him, he said: "You gotta try, don't you?"[4]

It is difficult for the historian to render a verdict on the question. Most of the evidence on either side is supposition, and although all of it is based on close observation, it is not firm enough to sustain an unqualified conclusion. The historian may, however, do some supposing himself. Huey Long was a great politician, and it often has been noted that such men have stronger physical appetites than the average man, that they are, in the words of one analyst, "of a large and vigorous animal nature." But such men are likely to indulge their desires—for food, liquor, women, or whatever—only sporadically. With them one passion transcends all others—the love of politics—and this they pursue with almost undivided energy. Huey was clearly such a "political animal." Probably the most accurate summation of his relations with women was given by a rural leader who was one of his shrewdest lieutenants. "Huey had no time for women," this man said, "no time to sleep."[5]

Huey was oppressed by time. He often remarked to Rose that time frightened him; he feared he would not have enough of it to accomplish all his goals. He begrudged giving much of it even to his family. "I can't live a normal family life," he once confessed to Rose. She was tragically aware that he spoke the truth. She and the children moved back into the mansion after Miss Grosjean left, but they stayed only a short time before returning to Shreveport. Thereafter she was seen in Baton Rouge only at intervals and for brief periods, usually at mansion soirees or political occasions. Huey himself was seen less at the mansion. He engaged a suite at the Heidelberg Hotel, the capital's largest, and another at the Roosevelt Hotel in New Orleans, and in these public houses he ate and slept and lived a public existence.

It was the way he lived that drove Rose away from him, or at any rate that was a larger cause than jealousy or suspicions about his relationships with other women. On those occasions when he spared some time to his family he could be a solicitous husband and

---

[4] The above is based on the testimony of four witnesses, who naturally insisted on remaining anonymous.

[5] Henry Taylor: *The Statesman* (Mentor edn.; New York, 1958), 140; Trent James.

a devoted father. A guest at the mansion recalled a Christmas day when Huey got down on the floor with the children and played with the electric trains they had received. He liked to take the boys to bed with him and read aloud to them from a book that he thought would improve their minds; a late visitor once found him reading them a history of the French Revolution. He also liked to get the boys aside and talk to them about the benefits of "right living," giving the kind of admonitory lecture all fathers think they should give. He enjoyed being with the children, but because he was tense and nervous, he sometimes found the noise of their play intolerable. Then he would "blow up," and storm at them in sudden, frightening fury. Only Rose could calm him when he was so aroused. She would speak to him quietly, and he would immediately subside. "She had the Indian sign on him," said one admiring observer.[6]

The occasions when Huey relaxed with his family were few. He was too intense to relax easily, and he did not enjoy any form of recreation that would have helped him to do so. Rose "adored" playing bridge, but Huey, who had in his youth gambled whenever he could, now refused to play any kind of cards. Almost any pastime that he and Rose attempted would end up, frustratingly for her, as a political event. Thus after a dinner in the home of a New Orleans socialite, the host drew Rose aside and revealed the purpose behind the dinner—he wanted Rose to influence Huey to endorse him for United States senator. Sometimes they went for automobile drives on Sunday, but Huey looked at nothing except the state projects he had initiated, the roads and bridges, and talked about nothing except the rate of progress on them. On one of these trips a group of children recognized Huey and cheered him. He pained Rose deeply by saying: "This makes it all worthwhile."[7]

Huey's inability to relax was apparent in everything he did. "He could never relax, even when eating," an associate recalled. "Sometimes he wouldn't even touch his meal, because he was too busy phoning or talking." When he did eat, he bolted the food in great gulps so that he could finish and get on with something important. His tastes in food were those of a rural Southerner. He liked "plain food"—potlikker, a concoction peculiar to the South that he would later make famous, turnip greens, corn bread, sweet potatoes, and hot biscuits. As governor, living in a more urban environment, he

---

[6] Rose McConnell Long; Rose Long McFarland; W. E. Butler; Edmund E. Talbot; Mrs. Clarence Pierson; J. Cleveland Fruge.

[7] Rose McConnell Long; interview with Mrs. Long, in New Orleans *Item-Tribune*, October 30, 1932.

developed a liking for somewhat more sophisticated items, for steaks and fried oysters. But he never learned to like the exotic French foods of New Orleans. Once while eating at one of the city's famed restaurants he showed obvious displeasure with his dinner. The owner hastened over to the table. "What's this wood I'm eating?" Huey demanded. "That's not wood, it's a bay leaf," said the owner, shocked as only a Frenchman could be in the circumstances. "You are not supposed to eat it. It is for seasoning." Huey pushed his plate away in disgust. "It's too hot," he said.[8]

But usually Huey consumed whatever food was put before him, almost literally not seeing or tasting it, merely because it was there. Indeed, he would on occasion eat any food that was near him. "In some ways he didn't act like a normal human being," said an associate. "He would reach over and take your meal and eat it." Sometimes he would bustle into a luncheon conference with friends or foes, sit down and begin talking and, while he talked, reach out and collect the chop of one diner, the potatoes of another, and so on until he had assembled a meal. Occasionally he would enter an eating place alone, spot an acquaintance already eating, join him, and raid his plate; or on the way in he would snatch a tray of food away from a passing waiter and proceed to a table. Usually he did not realize that he was acting rudely, did not, indeed, realize what he was doing —he had something on his mind that he had to talk about and in a very real sense did not know that he was eating while he talked. But sometimes he perpetrated these vulgarities deliberately. Significantly, the worst ones were directed toward aristocrats, to humiliate these proud men who had scorned him but now had to submit to him. If they had to sit while he commandeered their food, they would know who the power in Louisiana was, know that he could if he wished take other things from them.[9]

Reluctant to take time for his family, unable to eat normally or to relax in any social situation, Huey even begrudged giving time to sleep. He usually slept only four hours out of every twenty-four, but sometimes even then he only dozed, letting his mind play on problems that were bothering him. Some of his best ideas came to him late at night, he said, so he placed a pencil and tablet by his bed before retiring, and when a solution came to him, he turned on the light and wrote it down. He liked a big bed and eventually had

[8] M. J. Kavanaugh; Rose McConnell Long; Sidney Bowman; Castro Carazo; J. C. Broussard.

[9] Robert J. O'Neal; Richard W. Leche; Richard Foster; Mason Spencer; John P. Brashears; Shelby Kidd.

one seven feet long built for him and installed in a special suite at the capitol. He would not allow pillows on his bed. Sleeping on pillows, he believed, was harmful to the natural curves of the body and could even make people humpbacked. "When they made a place to sleep," he liked to say, "they didn't invent no pillows."[1]

Conservative Louisianians looked with wonder and disgust on the people in the Kingfish's "lodge," the associates who gathered at the mansion and followed Huey around. Accustomed to dignified governors who had surrounded themselves with staid associates, the conservatives could not understand this new governor, who collected such strange followers. Easily the oddest members of the Long entourage, and the ones most shocking to old-line citizens, were those who were referred to as "the guards." These were the bodyguards that Huey had employed, and they went everywhere with him.

Huey's apprehension that he was in physical danger, displayed during the campaign, assumed the proportions of a psychosis after he became governor. Before he was elected, he had seemed to think that enemies were lying in wait to beat him up; he still thought so, but now he began to fear assassination. A caller at the mansion one night was amazed to see the governor carefully pull down every shade and asked the reason. "I'm a cinch to get shot," Huey answered. He told one man that Chicago gangsters were out to get him. He was probably spoofing on this occasion, but he genuinely feared that his enemies in Louisiana would try to eliminate him. He took to carrying a small revolver when he went among a crowd.[2]

It was not in Huey's nature to protect himself, however. Nor, if he was in the danger he imagined, could he do so efficiently. He needed other eyes to watch over him and other bodies to shield him. Thinking that one man could protect him, he first employed as a bodyguard a hulking former prize fighter, Harry "Battling" Bozeman. Bozeman was officially an employee of the Highway Commission, but his commission job was a front. His actual duty was to accompany Huey everywhere and not let anybody "hurt" his employer. Or so Bozeman interpreted Huey's instructions. As Bozeman told it, Huey said that he had enemies in the legislature and out who might try to "jump" him, and if they did, Bozeman was to "pull them off." That Huey intended Bozeman to have such a relatively passive role is unlikely. The "Battler" probably understood but dimly what Huey said to him. Being slow-moving and dull-witted,

[1] W. M. Hallack; Theophile Landry; Louis F. Guerre; Joseph Cawthorn; Charles Frampton; William T. Burton; John St. Paul, Jr.; Raymond H. Fleming.
[2] Herve Racevitch; *Impeachment Proceedings*, I, 358, 447–8.

he was not alert enough to be a good guard. In addition, he was too amiable; he did not have the lethal instinct of the born guard, that readiness to do whatever he had to do to protect his boss. He was not, in fact, really devoted to Huey, and when Huey realized this last weakness, he let Bozeman go.[3]

In Bozeman's place there soon appeared another, very different, kind of man. Joe Messina was a dark, squat Italian who hung around the Heidelberg Hotel in Baton Rouge. He claimed to be a tailor and did repair work on the clothes of guests, but he also performed any menial tasks that the management asked him to do. In his spare moments he acted as a self-appointed house detective. He had served in the World War as an army truck driver and reportedly had suffered severe "shell shock." People whispered that his mental faculties had been impaired. He himself admitted that since the war he had not required much sleep, "in the daytime or at night either."

Messina met Huey at the hotel, presumably when Huey took a suite there, and naturally was attentive to the governor. He apparently conceived an immediate, doglike devotion to Long. Huey, for his part, found the odd fellow amusing. He offered Messina a position as his personal attendant and assistant. Joe snapped at the opportunity. Thereafter he went everywhere with Huey, literally lived with him. He performed varied functions, such as looking after Huey's clothes and waiting on his employer at the table. Asked once under oath what he did for the governor, he provided an admirable summary: "Anything that he may ask me to do, that comes to hand that he wants done." Some Long associates characterize him as having been merely a valet, but one of his assignments was clearly to protect Huey. He was given a commission on the Highway Patrol, authorizing him to check delinquent licenses on automobiles, and although he seldom worked at this job, the commission gave him an official status and took care of his salary. Moreover, as a policeman he was entitled to carry arms. He equipped himself with a bulky pearl-handled revolver and wore it ostentatiously on his hip. Huey liked to brag to interviewers that Messina was a dead shot, but the truth seems to be that Joe had little skill with a gun, and there is no record that he ever used his revolver in Huey's defense. In an emergency he relied on his fists or a blackjack. He had some of the qualities of the ideal guard. Although unintelligent, he could act quickly enough in a crisis, and he would slug with joyful passion

---

[3] J. Y. Sanders, Jr.; *Impeachment Proceedings*, I, 804, Bozeman's testimony. Harry Bozeman was not related to Huey's friend Harley Bozeman.

any man who seemed about to threaten Huey. He was also loyal. He would have laid down his life for Huey's.

Huey gradually took on other guards, until finally he was surrounded by a retinue of protectors wherever he went. One of the accessions was Paul Voitier, a former preliminary prize fighter. Another member of the entourage was a little fellow who was a protégé of Bob Maestri's, Jim Moran, an Italian. More a cook than a guard, he served up Italian repasts when Huey decided to have a party at the mansion or in his hotel suite. Messina, Voitier, and Moran were typical of the men Huey tended to choose as guards. He did not pick men who had particular qualifications for the job, who were known to be good shots or who had experience in security work. His basis of selection was personal—he employed men whom he liked, whom he thought he would like to have around him.

Huey's only efficient guards were selected for him by officials in the Highway Patrol or its adjunct, the Bureau of Criminal Identification. These functionaries, realizing his compulsion to be guarded, assigned men of theirs to do the job, men who had some qualifications—Murphy Roden, who acted as the governor's chauffeur but was really a security guard, Louie Jones, who had slugged Huey's heckler at Minden, George McQuiston, Goldman Grant, and others. Huey liked all of them and swaggered behind their protection. Once he and Louie Jones were in the coffee shop of the Heidelberg Hotel when a man at a nearby table began to curse Huey loudly. Motioning to Jones to come with him, Huey headed for his vilifier. The man jumped up as they approached, but before he could do anything, Jones swung and knocked him unconscious. Later in his suite at the hotel, Huey begged Jones: "Don't say anything about it. He thinks I hit him."[4]

HUEY'S FIRST LEGISLATURE had adjourned in July. His political labors did not end with the session, however. The road-bond and gasoline-tax amendments would be voted on in November, and he had to campaign for their ratification. He spent a good part of the hot summer months touring the state, asking for support.

[4] *Impeachment Proceedings*, I, 470–1, 477, Messina's testimony; *Overton Hearing*, I, 1015–18, Messina's testimony; Hermann B. Deutsch: "Paradox in Pajamas," *Saturday Evening Post*, CCVIII (October 5, 1935), 38; Theophile Landry; Westbrook Pegler, column in New York *World-Telegram*, August 18, 1935; E. P. Roy; Louis F. Guerre; John DeArmond; Jerome Beatty: "You Can't Laugh Him Off," *American Magazine*, CXV (January 1933), 115; W. S. Foshee; Otho Long; Murphy Roden; M. J. Kavanaugh; Louis A. Jones.

But even as he stumped for the amendments, he had to turn to face a fire in his rear, to fend off conservative efforts to sabotage his laws providing for free schoolbooks and the severance tax. He had thought that the last obstacle in the way of the operation of the free-books act had been removed when he obtained the emergency loan from New Orleans banks. But suddenly the school boards of two parishes, Caddo and Bossier, instituted legal action to prevent the books from being distributed. A third suit was started by influential citizens of Caddo. The Caddo board went even further. Just before the fall term was to open, it gave notice that it would not accept or distribute the books. The parents of Caddo would not take charity, the board said, but would buy books for their children as they always had. Caddo, with its chief city, Shreveport, was the most conservative area in the state, and Bossier, adjacent to Caddo, was almost as unyielding. The officials and citizens of the two parishes who brought the suits alleged that they were acting for legal-religious reasons—they were trying to prevent the unconstitutional allocation of aid to Catholic schools. Religious considerations undoubtedly were in their minds, for the people that they represented were almost entirely Protestant and fiercely anti-Catholic, but in Caddo opposition was based equally on political grounds. The rulers of the parish did not think that the state should give anything to people. Any kind of state welfare was socialism, and this particular act of socialism was doubly odious because it was being perpetrated by their former detested fellow townsman, Huey Long.[5]

The plaintiffs won a preliminary order prohibiting the State Board of Education from distributing the books. But the board, acting on behalf of the state, appealed to the district court in Baton Rouge. The judge of this court, although strongly anti-Long, held that the law was constitutional, that the books were not being given to religious schools but to children. The complaining citizens then took the case to the supreme court. That tribunal upheld the ruling of the district court. The suing parties then appealed to the Supreme Court of the United States. Pending a decision from the federal court, the state felt safe in proceeding to distribute the books.

Huey took no direct part in the litigation, although he must have champed to act as the state's attorney. At one stage he did act vigorously to ensure that a justice friendly to him, and to the school-

[5] T. H. Harris: *Memoirs of T. H. Harris* (Baton Rouge, 1963), p. 159; *Impeachment Proceedings*, I, 667, testimony of a member of the Caddo board; Guy C. Mitchell: "The State Control of Public Education in Louisiana" (unpublished Ph.D. dissertation, University of Michigan, 1942), pp. 441–3.

books law, would remain on the supreme court. The term of office of Judge John Land was about to expire. Land represented the northern judicial district, which included Shreveport, and he faced an opponent who was strongly supported by the conservative interests. Huey felt that he had to support Land; he could not afford to lose a single vote on the court. He went to Shreveport and personally took charge of Land's campaign. Largely because of Huey's efforts, the judge, although beaten in Shreveport, was re-elected by a substantial majority.[6]

Instigated simultaneously with the suits challenging the legality of the schoolbooks law was another suit that if successful would have destroyed the financial base of the law and thus would have prevented its operation. The Ohio Oil Company filed a suit to enjoin the collection of the severance tax, whose proceeds were dedicated to the books fund, alleging that the state, by the tax, was depriving it of equal protection as guaranteed by the Fourteenth Amendment —the tax was based on the gravity of the oil, thus favoring producers in south Louisiana, and hence was discriminatory. Because of the nature of the legal question raised by the company, the case originated in the federal district court at Shreveport. Important results rode on its outcome. If the company won it, the books fund would be left without a continuing revenue. Even worse, in the long run, the taxing power of the state would be seriously circumscribed. Huey realized these dangers, but he naturally assumed that Attorney General Saint would adequately defend the state's interest. On the day before the case was to be heard, however, he learned from Saint that no case whatever had been prepared. Huey ascribed this strange inaction to Saint's political enmity and economic conservatism, although the attorney general may have held back because he did not understand the technicalities of the case. Severance-tax law was a special area that not every lawyer could handle. Huey, with his long experience in oil matters, was a master of it. Now he brought his knowledge into immediate play. Telling Saint that he would take charge of the case, he borrowed one of Saint's staff to assist him and worked up his pleadings in a few hours. He boarded the night train for Shreveport and appeared in court the next day to represent the state. His defense of the tax was simple—a state was entitled to some latitude in fixing taxes, and a difference based on gravity was not discriminatory. The court found his argument convincing and ruled

---

[6] T. H. Harris: *Memoirs*, pp. 159–60; Huey P. Long: *Every Man a King* (New Orleans, 1933), pp. 115–17; *Impeachment Proceedings*, I, 581–2, circular published by Long supporting Judge Land.

for the state. The company thereupon appealed the decision to the U.S. Supreme Court. But while the case was making its way upward, the state was able to collect the severance tax.[7]

Heartened by these initial legal successes, Huey turned with fresh vigor to arousing support for his amendments. He soon discovered that he did not have to worry; public sentiment was obviously running in their favor. The Old Regulars and the conservatives went through the motions of denouncing the measures, but recognizing defeat, they did not try to organize any effective opposition. Consequently, as the fall months wore on, Huey devoted less attention to the amendments in his speeches and more to another issue that would also be voted on on November 6—the choice of a President of the United States.

Normally a presidential election aroused little interest in Louisiana because the Democratic candidate was expected to carry this Deep South state easily against only a token Republican vote. The Republicans did not waste money or time campaigning, and neither did the Democrats, although a Louisiana governor might perfunctorily speak some favorable words about his party's standard bearers, merely to put himself on record. But in 1928 the campaign was not normal. The Democratic candidate was Alfred E. Smith, the man the Louisiana delegation had supported at the Houston convention. His nomination caused violent resentment in the traditionally Democratic South. Smith represented too many things that the South disliked—he was a product of the urban civilization of New York, he had been affiliated with the Tammany Hall machine, he was a "wet," in favor of repeal of Prohibition, and, worst of all, he was a Catholic. To many Southerners he seemed much more "alien" than his Republican opponent, the popular Herbert Hoover. For the first time since Reconstruction, threats of revolt against the Democratic party sounded in the South. They were loudest in the upper South, but they were heard in the lower South also and in Louisiana.

The situation in Louisiana was somewhat different from that in any other Southern state. In the other states the population was predominantly Protestant, and established Democratic leaders in them could safely endorse Hoover or remain neutral. But a politician who followed either of these courses in Louisiana ran the risk of offending the numerous Catholic voters. On the other hand, if he stayed

---

[7] Long: *Every Man a King*, pp. 116–17; Leslie Moses: "The Growth of Severance Taxation in Louisiana and Its Relation to The Oil and Gas Industry," *Tulane Law Review*, XVII (1943), 611.

loyal and supported Smith, he might antagonize the Protestants of the northern parishes. The perils of the alternative were apparent to Huey, but he did not hesitate. He would go with the nominee of his party.

Political considerations played a part in his decision. At this stage of his career he could not afford to bolt. As a recently elected governor and a young man on the way up, he could not let himself be branded a maverick, a politician who took his party allegiance lightly. He could gain nothing and lose much by bolting. The Democrats would probably carry Louisiana despite the rumblings of revolt, and in this result he would be a leader repudiated by his own people. Even if the Republicans took the state and the election, he could expect little attention and few rewards from a Republican President. Naturally, these contingencies were in Huey's mind. But other factors, not strictly political, weighed equally and perhaps more with him. He reacted with disgust and anger to the attacks made on Smith because of his religion. Huey himself had no religion, in the usual meaning of the term. He never went to church, and although he accepted the existence of God, he probably never thought of that Being except in odd moments and never with any spiritual contemplation. But neither did he have any religious prejudice. He would not have refused to associate with a man because of his religion, and he would not repudiate a candidate because of his religion. He would consistently denounce religion in politics as an artificial issue. He could have supported Smith and ignored the religious question. But he chose to meet it head on. "I have no patience with two-bit ministers who are injecting religion into this campaign," he proclaimed, "and we are going to find out if this is a free country and whether right or bigotry is the stronger."

These were courageous words for a Southern politician to utter in 1928. They were also undiplomatic ones. Such a frank recognition of the presence of prejudice in the campaign, such a biting denunciation of the Protestant ministry, was certain to arouse resentment. Huey realized that he was treading on dangerous ground and sought to protect himself by raising another issue. Ironically, while condemning one form of prejudice he appealed to another, racial prejudice. It was for him a rare departure. In his climb to power he had hardly ever resorted to beating the "nigger" issue, the favorite distraction of Southern demagogues of the time. This abstention has frequently drawn admiring comments from historians, who have said that it made him unique among Dixie politicians. The praise is deserved, but Huey did, more frequently than has been supposed, indulge in race baiting. He never did it very well, however, and obviously did not enjoy doing it when he felt, as he did now, that he had to.

He was at his worst in a speech at Alexandria. In a rambling discourse he lauded the Democratic party for having made Louisiana a white man's country, extolled Tammany Hall for having opposed Reconstruction, denounced Hoover for being a Quaker and opposed to war, and charged the Republican candidate with favoring integration. If party lines were broken in the South, "negro domination or social equality" would come immediately, he concluded. While he was ranting, a Negro woman walked on to the platform and kissed an American flag that had been placed there. The chairman indignantly ordered her to leave. It was later explained that the woman was "mentally deranged."[8]

The defeat of Smith in the November election could not have been much of a disappointment to Huey. The Democratic candidate carried Louisiana while losing several traditionally Democratic Southern states, and Huey took on added stature as a result. More important to him was the fate of his amendments. The amendments were approved by an overwhelming majority, even in New Orleans. The road-bond measure, which the Old Regulars had opposed, carried all but two of the seventeen wards in the city and failed in those two by a total of only eight votes.[9]

The massive vote for the amendments, which must have surprised even Huey, sent his political stock soaring to a new high. With this evidence of popular support for his measures before them, his enemies, even the Old Regulars, were impressed. Huey realized that the opposition was in a state of shock, but he knew too that it would soon wear off. He moved quickly to exploit his victory. He announced he would call a special session of the legislature to meet on December 10. The session would last only six days, he said, and its sole business would be to enact enabling legislation to collect the gasoline tax and begin construction of roads. Later he broadened the list to include other items, at the request of legislators with various pet measures. But he did not oblige them until he exacted their promise to support his program. One of the most urgent requests came from Shreveport and Caddo parish, and he seized on it

[8] Leo Glenn Douthit: "The Governorship of Huey Long" (unpublished M.A. thesis, Tulane University, 1949), p. 61; New Orleans *Times-Picayune*, September 15, 1928; Alexandria *Town Talk*, October 18, 1928.

[9] New Orleans *Times-Picayune*, November 20, 1928; Hermann B. Deutsch: "Kingdom of the Kingfish," in New Orleans *Item*, August 13, 1939.

as an opportunity to bend to his will those who were the most bitter
and unyielding of his opponents.

The federal government was selecting a site for an extensive
army air base, and Shreveport had emerged as the leading contender
for the rich prize. One of the conditions set by the government
was the availability of a tract of land adequate for the base, which
the chosen city would donate to the army. Such a tract was available
near Shreveport, eighty acres in size and only a few miles from the
city, but it lay in the adjoining parish of Bossier. If the city was
going to acquire it, it would have to secure permission from the legislature to exercise its authority outside the boundaries of Caddo.
The whole state was behind Shreveport's bid. The federal government was expected to spend at least five million dollars to build the
base; several thousand officers would be stationed in Shreveport; and
although the installation would benefit most directly the economy
of the immediate area, other sections also would ultimately be affected. Consequently, a bill introduced in the regular legislative
session in May to help Shreveport's application encountered no opposition. It authorized cities to acquire land "within or without" their
parishes and donate it to the federal government. The bill was duly
passed and signed by the governor. But by some accident, when the
bill was enrolled or recorded the words "or without" were omitted.
The error was not discovered until after the legislature adjourned.
Shreveport was aghast: it might lose the base after all.[1]

The city had appointed a committee of business leaders and
legal experts to direct its effort, and to these men Huey's call for a
special session seemed providential. The governor could save Shreveport simply by including in his call legislation to correct the defect
in the original bill. Members of the committee contacted Huey by
telegrams, letters, and telephone calls, asking him to add the air
base to the subjects the legislature could act on. To their shock and
surprise he refused. Shreveport had not treated him right, he told
them, and it was not going to get the base. Indeed, he informed one
man, if the people of Caddo wanted anything, he would see that
they did not get it. The dismayed committeemen did not know where
to turn. But their chairman, John D. Ewing, the son of Colonel
Ewing and editor of the colonel's Shreveport paper, had a suggestion. His father was close to Huey and could influence him, young
Ewing said. He proposed asking the colonel to arrange a conference
in his New Orleans office with the governor and a representative of

[1] Douthit: "Governorship of Long," p. 65; *Impeachment Proceedings*, I, 651.

the committee. Colonel Ewing was eager to help, and a committee member journeyed to New Orleans to attend the conference.

The meeting was a stormy one. Huey opened it by charging that the Shreveport leaders had slighted him by not inviting him to banquets for representatives of the army and that young Ewing had denied him adequate publicity in the Shreveport paper. He then presented a four-point ultimatum to the city. One, its chamber of commerce would have to apologize in a newspaper advertisement for the way the town had treated him; two, hereafter the city and the Ewing newspaper would have to show him more respect; three, the Caddo school board would have to withdraw its suit against the free-books law and agree to distribute the books; and four, the Caddo delegation in the legislature would have to announce that it was going to support the governor's program in the special session. When these demands were met, he would include the desired corrective legislation in his call. Colonel Ewing indignantly refused to let the first two points be transmitted. The other two points the representative of the committee consented to take back to Shreveport.

The ultimatum threw the committee into a rage. They unanimously agreed that they would not present the ultimatum to either the school board or the legislative delegation. But immediately after they took their stand, the awaited word from Washington finally arrived—Shreveport had been chosen as the site for the base. Now it was more vital than ever that clarifying legislation should be included in the governor's call. In desperation, the committeemen persuaded Will Henderson to phone Huey and plead for the city. Henderson, a friend of Huey's and a contributor to his campaign, was met with a flat rejection. By now the issue had become public knowledge, and from all over the state came entreaties to Huey to relent. He refused them. Caddo parish had spurned the free books, he said. "People so well off don't need an airport," he sneered. When he issued his call on December 8, the air base was not included in the subjects to be acted on.

The Shreveport conservatives, who epitomized in extreme degree the psychology of conservatives of their class throughout the state, still did not realize the nature of the man they faced. In the past the conservatives had been able to get what they wanted from a governor by appealing to his sense of fairness or by threatening him with hierarchic displeasure. Neither approach worked with Huey. He seemed to have no concept of fairness and to welcome conservative displeasure. But the Shreveporters decided to make one more effort. On the day after the session opened, Senator Pike Hall of Caddo induced twenty-seven other senators to sign a petition asking the governor to include the matter of the air base in a supplemental call. All of the signers had consistently opposed Huey's major measures in the regular session. To their move Huey made no open response, but secretly he conferred with one of them, V. V. Whittington, who represented Bossier and Webster parishes. Whittington had been elected with the support of the conservative planters who dominated his district, and he himself was conservative by inclination. He was a reasonable man, however, and had thought some of Huey's bills were good; except for the pressure of his backers he would have voted for them. Now he heard Huey offer a proposal that appealed to his instinct for moderation. Huey had a petition of his own that he wanted Whittington to circulate among the twenty-eight opposition senators. It urged the Caddo school board to distribute the books but stipulated that it could do so without prejudicing its lawsuit. The board could accede to this request without losing face, Huey explained, and he could then include the air-base legislation in a supplemental call.

Whittington saw the point and agreed to handle the petition. Pike Hall angrily refused to sign it, but twenty-five conservative senators affixed their names. The moment the petition was completed, Huey wired it to the president of the Shreveport chamber of commerce. The city's leaders capitulated immediately. They talked to officials of the school board, the board hastily met and adopted a resolution pledging to distribute the books, and word of its action was wired to the governor. Huey immediately issued a supplemental call adding the air base to the business before the legislature.[2]

Some time after the corrective act was passed and the air base was a reality, Huey was asked how he had forced Caddo to accept the free books. "They said they were coerced," he said. "I didn't coerce them." He contemplated for a moment and then shouted: "I stomped them into distributing the books." The remark has fascinated writers ever since and is quoted frequently, always to demonstrate that Huey had a brutal nature and was proud of it. He had been arrogant, inflexible, imperious—had shown, in fact, the characteristics of a dictator. Actually, as even a casual analysis will

[2] *Impeachment Proceedings*, I, 651–2, 656–7, 661; New Orleans *Times-Picayune*, December 10, 1928; Douthit: "Governorship of Long," pp. 65–6; V. V. Whittington; Deutsch: "Kingdom of the Kingfish," in New Orleans *Item*, August 14, 1939.

reveal, these accusations are not justified. He was not savage or extreme, and he did not "trample" the people of Caddo. All that he did, really, was to force the school board to distribute the books as provided by law. He was not nearly as extremist or unyielding as the Caddo leaders. It was he, not they, who initiated a compromise. And in the compromise he gave his opponents a face-saving out. Throughout the episode his actions were those of a typically pragmatic American politician, one who liked to appear more terrible, and more powerful, than he actually was. His fierce threats were only strategy, designed to frighten his foes. His avowed ruthlessness—"I stomped"—was a boast rather than an accurate statement.[3]

The special session went off without a hitch or a hint of opposition. The administration's bills were introduced, referred to committees and quickly approved, brought back to the floor, and enacted with almost no debate. The gasoline-tax bill and the enabling legislation for the bond issue to build roads received the support of the Old Regulars and most of the rural conservatives. Legislators who had opposed these measures in the regular session arose to announce that they would now vote to carry out the will of the people as expressed in the recent election. Although the solons were in session for six days, the whole legislative process was transacted in only three.[4]

Now that the enabling legislation for the roads program had been passed, Huey was anxious to get construction started. One day he went to the office of the Highway Commission and took a map of the state and drew lines on it. The first roads were to follow these lines, he said. The engineers and technicians in the office were incredulous. Huey's road system was a patchwork pattern. There were only a few lines, representing proposed miles of paving, in each parish. In most parishes the lines led into and out of the principal town and then stopped. Huey, delighted at the engineers' reaction, explained his purpose. He was deliberately going to bestrew the state with samplings of good highways to give the people a taste for more. Inevitably they would demand that the links be connected, and then more, and bigger, bond issues would have to be passed and more roads would be built. For some of his close associates he sketched another map that showed the final system he envisioned, one with modern highways spanning the whole state. He

[3] New Orleans *Times-Picayune*, April 24, 1929.

[4] Ibid., December 11, 13, 14, and 15, 1928; Baton Rouge *State-Times*, December 12, 1928; Deutsch: "Kingdom of the Kingfish," in New Orleans *Item*, August 14, 1939; Douthit: "Governorship of Long," pp. 67–8.

vowed that these roads, good roads, would be built at a cost of only fifteen thousand dollars a mile.[5]

He knew that he could not do all he wanted without expert help. He needed at his side more engineers, draftsmen, and inspectors than were then employed in the Highway Commission. More would have to be found, but Louisiana colleges did not turn out many engineers or draftsmen. Most of those presently working at the Highway Commission had come from out of state, and Huey decided that further imports would be needed. He sent O. K. Allen to examine the highway organization of the state of North Carolina, which had a large construction program under way. Allen reported that North Carolina's chief engineer, Leslie R. Ames, was a first-rate man. Hire him, ordered Huey. When told that Ames was making six thousand a year in North Carolina, Huey offered him thirteen thousand dollars, the highest salary of any Louisiana state official. Huey pirated other men from North Carolina, twenty-one in all. He hired a maintenance engineer from Oklahoma and a purchasing agent from Missouri. Louisiana had never seen such an influx of foreign employees. Many Louisianians felt the jobs should rightfully go to natives of the state. This reaction was not surprising. That the natives might not be able to handle the jobs was not considered. Huey was introducing a modern concept, the use of experts in government. It was new to the state, and strange to all classes, including the aristocracy, whose supposedly cosmopolitan members were its severest critics.[6]

AS THE FIRST YEAR of his governorship ended, Huey could look back at a record of rare accomplishment. He had put through the major items of his legislative program, he had demonstrated in the amendments' victory that the people approved his program, and he had held together and strengthened his political organization. His conservative opponents, as if awed by his success, had subsided. He seemed to be strong, secure, and prepared to go on to new heights. But where, the prognosticators wondered, would he go? He had already secured the enactment of the major part of his program. Besides, a governor had little power to influence legislation after his first two years in office; by that time he had handed out the awards at his

[5] Norman Lant; Seymour Weiss; Charles Frampton; Long: *Every Man a King*, p. 201; W. C. Pegues.

[6] Jess Nugent; Norman Lant; Deutsch: "Kingdom of the Kingfish," in New Orleans *Item*, August 15, 1939; *Impeachment Proceedings*, I, 43.

disposal and had to be content to let the legislature follow its own lead. Perhaps Huey now would relax his efforts and serve out the remainder of his term quietly. Perhaps now the state would return to the repose that had characterized previous administrations.

The state still had much to learn about its governor. It was not in Huey's nature to be silent and unnoticed. And it was not in his plan to allow Louisiana to lapse into its former placidity. He opened the year of 1929 with controversy. As a starter, he announced that he would no longer live in the executive mansion.

He was not really living there at the time. He ate and slept in the Heidelberg Hotel and went to the mansion only occasionally. Because of the absence of his family, he did not need it, but he liked to pretend that he had left the mansion solely because it was not fit to live in. The house was full of "damn rats," he told one interviewer. "There were too many clocks in the place," he added. "They kept me awake. You know how it is. I tried to make 'em all strike together. Then the rats would get into 'em and I'd lie awake listening to 'em." This statement was largely fabrication, but Huey's basic complaint was justified. He had evidence that the house was unfit for habitation. The legislature had voted funds to repair the structure, and in October 1928 Huey had set a crew of carpenters to work. But the laborers soon notified him that the building was so infested with termites that repairs would be useless. Huey reported this information to the Board of Liquidation, the state lending agency, and asked for permission to tear the mansion down. The board was receptive to the idea but properly decided that it should have an expert opinion. Accordingly, it requested the building inspector of Baton Rouge to look at the house. That official reported that the building did have termites, although the situation was not as serious as the governor had claimed. "The structure is in a generally dilapidated condition and would need to be completely reconditioned," he concluded.[7]

Just what "completely reconditioned" meant, and how much the process would cost, eluded the board. It tried over a period of several months to find an answer but with no success. Experts in termite extermination offered to' apply their treatment to the mansion, but they admitted that they could not guarantee saving the whole building. And even if the termites were destroyed, there remained the problems of a leaking roof, damaged interiors, and weakened

[7] Adams: "Huey the Great," *Forum*, LXXXIX (February 1933), 73; *Impeachment Proceedings*, I, 544, 567–9, 723; Baton Rouge *Morning Advocate*, October 27, 1928.

walls. Huey did not press the issue further during the remainder of the year not did he bring the question before the legislature at his special session in December. He sensed that a bill to replace the old house would meet defeat. But after the session adjourned, he renewed his pressure on the Board of Liquidation. He appeared before the agency in January and requested permission to borrow $150,000 to construct a new mansion on the site of the present one. The board granted the authorization by a unanimous vote, with the proviso that the governor was to secure legislative approval for the loan by a mail poll.[8]

There was wide criticism of the way Huey had proceeded. Perhaps a new executive mansion was needed, conservatives said, but the question was so important that it should be decided by the legislature in open session, not by a board that was controlled by the governor. This legal objection was simply an excuse, since the conservatives did not want a new mansion. To condone building one would be to recognize that change had to come in Louisiana. The old mansion was a symbol to them, a reminder of a comfortable past, a fortress against an uncertain future. Besides, a house that had been good enough for aristocratic governors ought to be good enough for a creature like Huey Long. Huey replied that the objectors reminded him of an old man who kept a boardinghouse. When a guest complained that the towel beside the wash basin was dirty, the old man said: "People have been wiping on that towel for a month without complaining; I don't see what's the matter with you."

Curiously, the conservatives could not believe that Huey would actually destroy the mansion; he would not dare. But he did destroy it, and in a particularly ruthless way, one that he must have chosen to humiliate his critics. He phoned the warden of the state penitentiary and instructed him to send a gang of convicts to the capitol. Just how many came is uncertain—estimates run from thirty to a hundred—but there were enough to make a public show. Huey personally led them from the capitol to the mansion and gave them orders to tear it down. The job was done fast. The upper classes were horrified—the old house that had harbored great governors was gone and great traditions were gone with it, torn down by jailbirds![9]

[8] *Impeachment Proceedings*, I, 310–12, 544; New Orleans *Times-Picayune*, January 26, 1929.

[9] E. J. Bourg; *Impeachment Proceedings*, I, 482; New Orleans *States*, March 18, 1929; Long: *Every Man a King*, pp. 223–5.

Huey derived a good deal of sardonic pleasure from the demolition, but he had not ordered it out of simple malevolence. In anything that he did, there was a cool purpose, even when he seemed wildly angry or vengeful. There was design in every move he made in the mansion episode. He had not started the controversy because he could not live in the old house: creature comforts were not that important to him. A new mansion was a symbol to him, just as the old one was to conservatives. A modern structure would be a token of the modern era that Louisiana was about to enter, that she was going to enter even if she was unwilling, because Huey Long, if he had to, would jerk her into it forcibly. His apparently wanton destruction of the old mansion was his way of impressing his enemies that he would be ruthless in moving to his goals, was perhaps intended to stun them into a state of acquiescence.

This planned ruthlessness was a technique that he would employ increasingly from now on. He had been ruthless in impressing his power on his foes. Now he would impress it on his friends. He set out to rivet an absolute control over his own organization: to bend its leaders to him or to break them. He would truly be the Kingfish of his lodge. He began by taking on his lieutenant governor, Paul Cyr.

Cyr had been a difficult member of the Long organization from the first. He would have been difficult in any organization. Imperious, ambitious, and emotional, he could not discipline himself to work under direction or in cooperation with others. He lacked, in short, some of the necessary qualities of a politician. His attitude toward Huey was superior and paternal. He frequently lectured Huey on the latter's behavior, especially toward women. He also presumed to advise Huey on political matters. He had been loyal to Huey during the regular session of 1928, but thereafter he was seen in frequent conference with Old Regular leaders. He several times suggestively asked Huey who would be the administration's next candidate for governor.

It was almost inevitable that he and Huey would come to a break. Both of them wanted it and were looking for a pretext. They found one, not in an issue of policy, but in a gruesome murder that became famous in Louisiana annals of crime as the Dreher-LeBoeuf case.[1]

The facts of the case are difficult to reconstruct. They rest on newspaper accounts, which were wildly sensational, and on courtroom

---

[1] Leon Gary; confidential communication; Long: *Every Man a King*, p. 126.

testimony, which was contradictory. The principals were James Le-
Boeuf, an electrician in Morgan City, a small town near the Gulf
coast; his attractive wife, Ada; Dr. Thomas Dreher, a wealthy physician of a good family; and the doctor's guide in that trapping and
fishing country, Jim Beadle. Ada and Dr. Dreher, according to town
gossip, started a torrid love affair. Then, in July 1927, LeBoeuf suddenly disappeared, after having been seen paddling in a pirogue
with Ada on a nearby lake. A short time later some frog hunters
out on the lake at night saw a body on the surface and hauled it
in. It had risen in spite of being weighted with heavy pieces of angle
iron. It was the body of LeBoeuf, and he had been shot to death.

Suspicion naturally pointed at Mrs. LeBoeuf and Dr. Dreher, and
they and the guide Beadle were arrested and held for presentation
to the grand jury. Then and later the three told changing and contradictory stories. But to the trial jury that finally heard the case
at the parish seat of Franklin, the facts admitted of but one conclusion: murder. The jury held that Dreher and Ada were guilty
of murder in the first degree, a finding that automatically carried
with it the sentence of death by hanging. Beadle was found to be an
accessory and was sentenced by the judge to life imprisonment.

The trial received full and lurid treatment in the state press.
Sensational murders were especially prized in the Roaring Twenties.
A particularly good one gave a state a kind of distinction, and this
was Louisiana's best. Louisianians gleefully modified a current
popular song to give it a local setting and to make Ada its heroine:
"Pirogue-paddling mama, don't you angle-iron me."[2]

Dr. Dreher and Ada appealed the decision of the trial court to
the supreme court. The high tribunal ruled soon after Huey became
governor, affirming the conviction by a vote of five to one. The dis-
senter was Chief Justice Charles O'Niel, who was from St. Mary
parish, where the crime had occurred. O'Niel, who knew the prominent Dreher family socially, manifested an unusual interest in the
case. He had even attended the trial at Franklin, although he must
have known that he later would have to hear an appeal from it.

Dreher and Mrs. LeBoeuf still did not give up hope. They appealed to the Board of Pardons for clemency, asking that the sentence be commuted to life imprisonment. Public sentiment, at first
hostile to them, was now turning in their favor. Newspapers that
had previously played up the gory details of the murder were whip-

---

[2] Unidentified clipping, International Feature story, in Long Scrapbook, XX;
Deutsch, column in New Orleans *Times-Picayune*, January 17, 1963; Long: *Every
Man a King*, pp. 126–8.

ping up opinion to demand mercy for the pair. Some people who supported the demand had honest doubts about the guilt of the accused; they argued that the circumstantial nature of the evidence did not justify a death sentence. But with the majority, maudlin sympathy was the ruling emotion. The doctor and his alleged paramour suddenly became romantic figures, devoted lovers who were the victims of local jealousy and malice. The most ridiculous contention of the advocates of clemency was that Ada should not be executed because she was a white woman. No white woman had ever been hanged in Louisiana, and if one were, the Southern code of chivalry would be violated, even though the woman was guilty of murder. The movement for mercy was strong, but without a prominent leader, it lacked direction and force. Then suddenly a leader appeared: when Dreher and Ada applied to the Board of Pardons for clemency, Paul Cyr, a member of the board in his capacity as lieutenant governor, became their champion. The other members were the attorney general, Percy Saint, and the trial judge. The board could not itself commute the sentence of the applicants, but it could recommend commutation to the governor, and hardly ever had a governor refused to follow the board's advice. Saint and the judge voted to let the original sentence stand. Cyr, however, voted to substitute life imprisonment for death.

Personal reasons may have had some influence on Cyr's decision to enter the controversy. Like O'Niell, he was from the same section of the state as the accused pair, and he knew them and their families well; friendship for Dreher may have been a factor, or a desire to save two constituents. But the intensity with which he pushed the issue, his insistence on publicizing his every move, suggest that his impelling motive was personal. He seems to have judged hastily that the existing public excitement about the case would endure, that he could exploit it and thus publicize himself and become a stronger contender for the governorship.

Great pressure was now brought on Huey to overrule the Board, but he refused. He signed the death warrants. But as the execution would have fallen during the Christmas holidays, he granted a reprieve until after the new year.

The fixing of an actual date for the execution stirred popular feeling to a fever pitch. The politicians studied the outcry with interest. Some of those who were most bitterly opposed to Huey saw in it a possible opportunity to damage him—Huey Long the radical was also the governor who would let a white woman be hanged. One of those who sensed the opportunity and who came over to advocate clemency was Attorney General Saint. It was announced that he and Cyr, a majority of the Board of Pardons, had decided to grant Dreher and Mrs. LeBoeuf another hearing. At this session Cyr and Saint voted to recommend commutation, whereas the trial judge dissented violently.

Now Huey had to deal with an entirely different situation. If he permitted the execution to proceed, he would be defying the will of the Board of Pardons. He spent several sleepless days and nights trying to decide what to do. He could easily have bowed to the board and to public opinion and commuted the sentence. But he could find no grounds in the evidence to justify commutation. Moreover, he had to consider the political implications the case was assuming. If he commuted, he would seem to be yielding to pressures, would seem to be yielding particularly to Cyr. He would have no control over Cyr in the future and might even lose his hold on his whole organization. He could break with Cyr now, on a good issue. He announced that he was rejecting the recommendation of the board and that the executions would take place. "This was a cold-blooded murder," he said, "and the law should be allowed to take its course." His stand evoked applause from some of his severest critics, moving even the *Times-Picayune*. "We honor him for the courage he displays," the paper said.

Huey's announcement enraged Cyr. The lieutenant governor issued a statement charging that Huey had "double-crossed" him. He claimed that he had asked the governor to leave the state for a short time so that he, as acting governor, could commute the death sentences. Understanding that Huey had agreed, Cyr had driven the 130 miles from his home in Jeanerette to Baton Rouge only to learn that Huey refused to leave. Cyr could not understand why Huey objected to such an arrangement—the governor had only to cross over into Mississippi for a few hours and everything could be fixed up. He did not seem to realize that Huey would be put in an impossible position, that of shirking his duty, or that he himself would be placed in a bad light. Cyr, in fact, was fast losing any perspective he might ever have had on the controversy. When a rumor came to him that Huey had been kidnapped and taken out of the state, he said he hoped that the report was true. "I'd not only settle the LeBoeuf-Dreher case," he declared, "but I would pardon the kidnappers."

The execution date was set for January 5. It seemed now that nothing could save the accused pair. But their supporters had one more move to make. Chief Justice O'Niell again manifested his curious interest in the case. He issued a writ directing the sheriff of St. Mary parish not to carry out the order for execution. O'Niell was one of the most colorful and unusual judges in Louisiana's judicial history. He was slight, had a ruddy complexion—caused by heavy drinking, some people said—and a shock of unruly white hair. One of his legs was impaired, and he walked with a noticeable limp. He had sat on the court since 1909, an arrant conservative and quite capable of acting in an unjudicial manner. His interest in the case was political as well as personal—he was a bitter anti-Longite. His issuance of the stay writ raised an important legal question: could one member of the court overrule and negate the previous decision of the tribunal? Huey thought not and said O'Niell was a "crooked-legged sonofabitch." But he had no choice but to reprieve Dreher and Ada until the full court spoke. It ruled a few days later and de-clared O'Niell's order null. Huey then set the execution for Febru-ary 1. He warned the sheriff of St. Mary that if he had to, he would call out the militia to enforce his order. The sheriff promised to carry out the execution and did.[3]

The break between Huey and Cyr was complete and lasting. Thereafter they never exchanged a friendly word. Cyr's hatred for Huey grew into a consuming passion. Once when the governor paused beside him in the senate, the muscular Cyr was heard to growl: "I wish I could get that sonofabitch in the woods with me. Only one of us would come out."[4] Although Huey could hardly have avoided the quarrel, he had made a dangerous enemy. Cyr, as pre-siding officer of the senate, was in a position to obstruct Huey's legislative program and would soon do so.

As if not satisfied to eliminate just one rival in his organization, Huey simultaneously broke with two others, Colonel Ewing and John Sullivan. He made this move with much more deliberation than he had displayed in the Cyr case. Whereas he had been con-tent to let the lieutenant governor institute a rupture, he himself precipitated hostilities with Ewing and Sullivan. Later he would ad-vance elaborate explanations to justify his action. The trouble lay almost entirely with Sullivan, he said. Sullivan was not the kind of man he wanted in his organization. The city leader was known to be connected with gambling interests, casinos and race tracks, and

[3] New Orleans *Times-Picayune*, December 16, 1928, January 3, 4, 6, 8, and 12, 1929; New Orleans *Item*, January 11, 1929; Seymour Weiss; Herve Racevitch; Long: *Every Man a King*, pp. 128–31; Douthit: "Governorship of Long," pp. 69–71; Deutsch: "Kingdom of the Kingfish," in New Orleans *Item*, August 15, 1939; Rose McConnell Long; David B. McConnell; Hermann B. Deutsch.

[4] John Nuckolls.

the underworld. Sullivan was also corrupt: he had tried to bribe Huey to let the Williams–Watson bridge monopoly continue and he had informed Huey that a construction company he was associated with was going to milk all the money out of the road fund. Huey had told Ewing of Sullivan's villainies and had said they must separate from him. The colonel had seemed to agree but had then still clung to Sullivan.[5]

Some of Huey's charges were true. Sullivan was connected with gambling interests, as were a number of prominent men in New Orleans. Gambling was one of the city's principal industries and had been since a time no living man remembered. Sullivan's association with it was quite open and had been known to Huey when he accepted the boss's support in the gubernatorial campaign, so his belated claim that he was shocked was a virtuous pretense. Huey would not have objected to circumspect connections with gambling activities. Nor could he have believed that Sullivan's interests in themselves detracted from his political effectiveness; some of the city's ablest politicians had similar interests. But Huey did have a legitimate complaint about Sullivan's effectiveness. The boss's New Regulars and Ewing's newspaper had not delivered much of a vote to Huey in 1928. And it did not seem likely that the Sullivan–Ewing combine would do any better in the future. Huey was going to need a strong city organization for contests to come, and he did not have one. Yet the two leaders of his city machine made greater demands upon him than any of his other associates. Sullivan pressed continuously for patronage and for financial awards. Ewing assumed that he was a kind of prime minister, who would determine every important decision the young governor made. These were the reasons Huey forced a break with them. He could not control them, indeed had to struggle to prevent them from dominating him, and he could safely dispense with them. He took to making fun of them in private conversations, applying derisive nicknames that soon became public. He called Sullivan, because of his attendance at horse races, "Bang Tail." Colonel Ewing, with his walrus mustache and imperious, barking manner, he labeled "Colonel Bow Wow." It was only a question of time until the break came.[6]

The issue precipitating the break was, as in the Cyr case, apparently unrelated to political policy. In the summer of 1928 civic organizations in New Orleans appealed to the governor to crack down on gambling in the city and in the adjoining parishes of St. Ber-

[5] Long: *Every Man a King*, pp. 119–21; confidential communication.
[6] Confidential communication.

nard and Jefferson, where large and lavish houses of chance were operated openly. Huey responded with a statement directing the officials of St. Bernard and Jefferson to halt the gambling and warning the city government to enforce the laws against gamblers. "We are not going to stand for open lawlessness in the New Orleans area during the four years I am governor," he announced. His exhortation went largely unheeded, since governors were expected to make such virtuous statements but were also expected not to act upon them. Consequently, the houses in St. Bernard were unprepared for what happened in August. A detachment of the national guard descended on them, wrecked or burned their equipment, and confiscated their money. "Let this be a warning to all gamblers in the New Orleans area," Huey proclaimed. A short time later, in early November, a group of guardsmen raided the establishments in Jefferson parish and gave them the same treatment.[7]

Huey employed a technique in the raids that was new to law enforcement in the state. He did not go to a judge and ask for search warrants, and he did not utilize ordinary police personnel. Instead, he summoned secretly the man whom he had appointed adjutant general of the national guard, Raymond H. Fleming. General Fleming was tall, capable, and single-mindedly devoted to the organization he headed—and to his commander in chief. Huey explained his purpose to Fleming, which was, in Fleming's words, "to cut out the wide-open gambling." He gave Fleming written orders: the general was to mobilize enough militiamen to do the job—to raid the gambling places, to confiscate and destroy their equipment, and to seize all money found and deposit it with the state treasurer. Fleming carried out his assignment faithfully: He assembled several hundred guardsmen for each raid without word of their gathering leaking out. Determined that no one could charge that his men had personally appropriated any of the seized money, the general took extraordinary precautions. When a raid took place, guardsmen carried a locked safe into the establishment. As the commanding officer went from table to table or from game to game, he insisted that all money be counted by a patron or an employee of the house. The cash was then placed in the safe, and the manager was given an itemized, signed statement of the amount that was being taken.[8]

[7] New Orleans *Times-Picayune*, August 12, September 17 and 18, November 12 and 13, 1928; Douthit: "Governorship of Long," pp. 66–7; Deutsch: "Kingdom of the Kingfish," in New Orleans *Item*, August 14, 1939.

[8] Raymond H. Fleming; *Impeachment Proceedings*, I, 487–9, 493–5, 545–6, 549, 555.

The raids received commendation from civic and religious groups, but they also aroused a storm of criticism. Some of the criticism was to be expected; it came from the gamblers and from patrons who had been held temporarily and searched. Most of it, however, emanated from persons who had not been affected by the raids, from respectable people who presumably disapproved of gambling. They were also, by a remarkable coincidence, political enemies of Huey's. If the governor was so opposed to gambling, they asked, why did he send the guardsmen only into St. Bernard and Jefferson? Why did he not also hit New Orleans? Was it because he wanted to make a reputation for morality by a few sensational raids? Or was he trying to penalize places that Sullivan might be connected with? (General Fleming, when asked to explain the immunity of New Orleans, said that gambling there was small and "hid away.") The conservatives also professed horror at the crude way the raids were conducted. The guardsmen had burst into establishments with guns drawn and had forced patrons to hold up their hands and back against a wall. In some places women patrons had been held and searched for money—searched by women brought in for that purpose, it was true, but nonetheless searched. What seemed to anger the conservatives most was that Huey had used militia, that he had sent soldiers into private establishments without search warrants and without issuing a proclamation of martial law. This was tyranny, they cried. Attorney General Saint officially declared the raids illegal because the governor had not proceeded in accordance with the law. Huey calmly responded: "We have paid no attention to, and will pay no attention to any opinion of the Attorney General protecting the gambling interests."[9]

Colonel Ewing in particular was furious. He managed to confine himself to private expressions, but he was especially incensed by the stories that women had been searched. The colonel had a strong streak of old-fashioned Southern chivalry in him, and any report of an indignity to any kind of woman made him livid. Now he sputtered disapproval of Huey, not pausing to reflect that some female frequenters of gambling houses might be of questionable character. He did not realize that he had other motives—subconscious and more compelling—for his anger. The governor that he had made had launched the raids without securing his advice and permission. Indeed, the young man seemed to think that he could do whatever he wanted to without first coming to his prime minister.

[9] Raymond H. Fleming; New Orleans *Times-Picayune*, November 18 and 19, 1929; Douthit: "Governorship of Long," p. 67.

Soon the colonel noted other disturbing signs of independence. The governor refused to cooperate with the Shreveport air-base committee before the December special session, even though Ewing's son was chairman of the committee. Worse, Huey insultingly addressed young John D. as "Squirt." Then came the Dreher–LeBoeuf case. Ewing's papers, the New Orleans *States* and the Shreveport *Times*, led the press in their strident demands for clemency—and also initiated the shrill denunciations of Huey for letting a white woman be executed. The papers let loose another blast when Huey secured from the Board of Liquidation authority to borrow money to build a new mansion, echoing the conservative argument that what had been good enough in the past should suffice for the present day. Next Ewing arrogantly presumed to tell Huey to reform his organization. The New and Old Regulars should be merged, the colonel publicly proposed. Huey replied that he would never join with the corrupt Ring. Ewing acidly observed that the governor seemed to have delusions of grandeur. The break was almost complete.

Huey seemed determined to bring it about. In early February he sent the national guard swooping down again into St. Bernard and Jefferson. Two raids, on a larger scale than the previous ones, gutted the biggest establishments in the parishes. According to press reports, ten thousand dollars in cash was seized, and twenty thousand dollars worth of equipment destroyed. Again patrons, including women, were searched. Ewing's *States* published an interview with one of the women. She declared indignantly that she was merely a patron and had been subjected to indecent treatment. The next day another paper identified her as the wife of a gambler and printed a picture of her that it said had been secured from police files. Huey pounced on the exposé. He suggested that Ewing ought to stop trying to shield "murderers [Mrs. LeBoeuf] and habitues of the rogues' gallery." Ewing was infuriated, his anger accentuated by the knowledge that he had been caught in an inaccuracy. In a blistering editorial that dodged the issue, he called Huey a "cheap libeler of men whose shoes he is not fit to tie." He hurled a countercharge: while the raids were being conducted, the governor who claimed to be so virtuous had been attending an immoral party at a French Quarter "studio."

Huey now had Ewing and Sullivan exactly where he wanted them. He announced that if Ewing wanted to take the word of underworld characters as to what was going on—well, that was to be expected. As for the colonel's colleague, John Sullivan—well, apparently Sullivan was the kind of man Ewing preferred to associate with. But Huey was finished with both of them. The ax fell quickly. The two members of the three-man Levee Board who had been appointed at Sullivan's solicitation suddenly learned, from newspaper reporters, that they had "resigned." When they expressed mystification, somebody reminded them that they had signed undated resignations. "Hell," said one, "I didn't know they were using that." Other officeholders who were Sullivan or Ewing men also "resigned" or were discharged outright. Sullivan himself was removed as a member of the board of election supervisors and replaced with a Long follower. The New Regulars announced that they were disbanding and would join the Old Regulars and fight Huey Long to the death. Big John, burning with hatred for Huey, consented to accept a position as a mere Old Regular co-leader in one ward, the better to carry on his warfare with the man who had destroyed him.[1]

HUEY WAS IN A STRANGE MOOD after he crushed Cyr, Ewing, and Sullivan. He had experienced periods of high elation after previous victories, but the elation he showed now was of a different quality. It had about it something savage and frenzied; it was almost manic. He exhibited it when a delegation from Caddo parish came down to see him in February to request some financial aid for roads. To the astonishment of the visitors, he launched into a bitter tirade against Caddo. The parish would not get anything out of him until it humbled itself, he shouted. He concluded with a threat: "I will teach you to get off the sidewalk, take off your hat, and bow down damn low when Governor Long comes to town." He was revealing the effect that the possession of power was beginning to have on him. He thought that he was invincible. His perception, his sense of reality, was temporarily blunted.[2]

Suddenly an event occurred that should have jarred him. His severance-tax law had successfully passed its test before the lower federal courts. But when it came up before the Supreme Court, it hit a snag. The Court took cognizance of the fact that under Louisiana law corporations or individuals paying taxes erroneously could

[1] Deutsch: "Kingdom of the Kingfish," in New Orleans *Item*, August 15, 1939; Paul B. Habans; New Orleans *Times-Picayune*, February 9, 10, 14, 17, 20, and 22, 1929; Douthit: "Governorship of Long," pp. 72–3; *Impeachment Proceedings*, I, 425–6.

[2] *Impeachment Proceedings*, I, 219.

not recover them without the consent of the state. Therefore, it issued an interlocutory decree holding the issue in abeyance. Practically, this meant that the oil companies could ignore the increased levy and pay the former, lower, rate until the case was settled. The Court's action posed a crisis for the free-schoolbooks law, which was supported by the severance tax. The state had borrowed heavily in anticipation of tax collections, and now the expected revenue was denied. Obviously the state would have to do something to meet the emergency. The governor was reassuring. He announced on March 14 that he would call a special session of the legislature to enact legislation correcting the law objected to by the Court. He would also ask for changes in the inheritance laws and the paving laws affecting New Orleans, he said. "One or two other matters may be included," he added mysteriously. He explained that the session would last only five or six days. The legislature would proceed as it had in December. Each house would agree by a two-thirds vote to suspend the rules: thus bills could be introduced, passed to the third reading immediately, and enacted.[3]

The Kingfish had been going from one triumph to another, treading the peaks. Now in the session that was about to meet he would encounter sudden and frightening defeat. He would enter a dark valley that seemed to lead to political oblivion.

[3] New Orleans *Times-Picayune*, March 14 and 15, 1929; Long: *Every Man a King*, p. 122; Deutsch: "Kingdom of the Kingfish," in New Orleans *Item*, August 15, 1939.

# CHAPTER 14

# *Bloody Monday—*
# *and Impeachment*

O N MARCH 16, two days after he revealed his plan for a special session, Huey issued his call to the legislators. They were to assemble on March 18 for a session of six days. The call listed the subjects on which they could legislate. Included were the items he had previously mentioned: a law to enable corporations and individuals paying taxes erroneously to recover them by lawsuit or other means and revision of the inheritance and paving laws. Also in the call were the "one or two other matters." Only one of them dealt with a major issue. But this issue was of such great and peculiar consequence that its inclusion changed completely the purpose of the session. By introducing it, Huey shattered overnight the amity that had recently prevailed in state politics. He demanded legislation imposing an occupational license tax, or manufacturers' tax, of five cents a barrel on the refining of oil. He claimed that the money was needed to support education and to care for such unfortunates as the blind, deaf, and insane. "I am hoping that the oil trusts will not make any opposition to this form of license, as they have done to progressive measures before," he said provocatively.[1]

Up to now he had angered conservatives and at times had alarmed them. But he had so far done nothing that really struck at the bases of their power. They did not like the roads program or

---

[1] New Orleans *Times-Picayune*, March 16, 1929; Shreveport *Journal*, March 16, 1929; Leo Glenn Douthit: "The Governorship of Huey Long" (unpublished M.A. thesis, Tulane University, 1949), p. 75; Hermann B. Deutsch: "Kingdom of the Kingfish," in New Orleans *Item*, August 15, 1939; Huey P. Long: *Every Man a King* (New Orleans, 1933), pp. 122–3.

the free books, but they could live with these innovations. They could accept even the severance tax, distasteful as it was, because it was only an extension of an existing tax. But the oil tax was something else—new and frightening. The oil industry was the largest one in the state, and businessmen generally felt they had a vested interest in the industry's continuing development and prosperity. Even persons in ordinary circumstances and with no connection with the oil business were likely to react with alarm to an attack upon it. A particular object of respect was the Standard Oil Company. Its operations were centered in Baton Rouge, where its huge refinery employed eight thousand persons, who in turn supported eighteen thousand others, but its activities and influence encompassed the whole state. The proposed tax would hit Standard hard. It might even force the closing of the Baton Rouge plant, spokesmen of the company indicated. The Baton Rouge *State-Times* rushed into print with a double-column, front-page editorial detailing the ruin that threatened the town and begging the legislature to defeat the tax. Even some of Huey's closest associates were appalled by his proposal. Harley Bozeman and other leaders pleaded with him to abandon the tax. But he refused. He would put it through over all opposition, he said.[2]

Bozeman was sure then and later that Huey's motive in demanding the tax was personal enmity toward Standard Oil, that he was seeking revenge for what the company had done to him in the past. Many others have advanced the same analysis. Such an interpretation is faulty, although Huey may well have pretended that he was acting for personal reasons. What his real reasons were he never frankly stated. A passage in his autobiography implies that he hoped to use an oil-tax bill for trading purposes—to threaten the oil companies with its passage unless they withdrew their opposition to the severance tax. But it is more probable that he actually thought he could force a tax bill through the legislature. Exhilarated by the exercise of power, made confident by his easy control of the December session, he anticipated no serious opposition in this session. He misjudged completely the depth of the reaction he had aroused and the determination of the men who were directing that reaction.[3]

He got his first intimation that something was wrong when the

[2] Baton Rouge *State-Times*, March 18, 1929; New Orleans *Item*, March 18, 1929; Harley B. Bozeman; T. O. Harris: *The Kingfish: Huey P. Long, Dictator* (New Orleans, 1938), pp. 51–2.

[3] Long: *Every Man a King*, pp. 122–3.

legislature convened on March 18, a Monday. When his leaders in both houses offered resolutions to suspend the rules, the resolutions failed to secure the two-thirds majority necessary for passage. In the house the administration could muster only forty votes for suspension, as compared with thirty-six votes against. The Kingfish was surprised, but he could not believe that the legislature had broken away from his control. Hurriedly he moved to mobilize pressure on the solons. At his suggestion, Superintendent of Education Harris called a meeting in Baton Rouge of local superintendents throughout the state. This gathering announced that since the oil tax would benefit education, all school people should support it. Coincidentally a tick-eradication conference was meeting in the capital city. The eradicationists were dedicated to securing a state law requiring the compulsory dipping of farm animals. Huey, in response to farmer opinion, had prevented passage of such a law in the 1928 regular session. But now he unabashedly offered a deal to the conference. He would include a tick-eradication bill in a supplemental call if the eradication people would agree to support his oil tax. He would even divert part of the proceeds from the tax to eradication purposes. They spurned him.

Huey suddenly realized that he was not going to be able to command a two-thirds majority. He would have to revise his strategy. Reflecting that in a long session he would not have to suspend the rules, he decided to issue a call for a new session. He summoned it to meet immediately, on March 20. It was to remain in session not more than eighteen days and thus would have to end its deliberations by midnight on April 6. The new call listed as subjects permissible for action those in the former call, including the oil tax, but added numerous items, some of them of a minor nature, such as one to enact legislation enabling the Highway Commission to take over a road in Claiborne parish. By including these local matters Huey hoped to pick up votes from legislators in the areas concerned. He looked with confidence to the coming session. In eighteen days he could pass his oil tax and other bills by a simple majority.[4]

The new session convened on Wednesday night. The administration leaders in the house introduced the oil-tax bill, but it was immediately evident that the bill was going to have rough going. In fact, it was clear that any measure favored by the governor would

---

[4] New Orleans *Times-Picayune*, March 18, 20, and 21, 1929; Baton Rouge *State-Times*, March 18, 1929; Shreveport *Journal*, March 19, 1929; Douthit: "Governorship of Long," pp. 76–7; *Impeachment Proceedings*, I, 3–4, for the call.

be in difficulty. When Huey appeared on the floor of the house to lobby for the tax bill, an opposition member asked that the rule barring unauthorized visitors be invoked. The house voted to apply it by a thunderous majority, and Huey left hastily, just ahead of the sergeant at arms. Then J. Y. Sanders, Jr., "Little J. Y.," who as a representative was aptly upholding the philosophy of his father, rose to present a resolution. He referred to press reports that Huey had offered to the tick-eradication conference part of the proceeds from the oil tax. Members of the legislature reportedly were in the group to which the governor spoke, Sanders continued, and if this was true, then the governor was guilty of bribery, of violating the provision of the state constitution that prohibited the offer of a consideration to a member of the legislature to influence his vote. "The very foundation of our democracy is threatened when support of any measure is offered or sought through the promise of reward," Sanders cried. His resolution asked condemnation of any such attempt even if made by the governor. It passed overwhelmingly and on the next day was concurred in by the senate.

Other condemnatory resolutions were adopted by the house on Thursday. One denounced the governor for appointing members of the legislature to positions in the various departments and bureaus. The purpose of these appointments was to place the legislature under "obligations" to the governor and was "subversive" of popular government, the resolution declared. Another paid eloquent tribute to the great oil industry that had done so much for Louisiana and exhorted the governor not to strike his "terrible blow" at it.[5]

Thursday was a day of sensations. Lieutenant Governor Cyr asked permission to address the senate. In an emotion-packed speech, Cyr charged that the governor had permitted valuable state oil lands to be leased to a Texas company. Cyr stopped just short of accusing Huey of profiting personally by the deal, but he minced no words in asserting that the state had been defrauded. Cyr became visibly more excited as he continued, and his excitement communicated itself to the senators and the galleries. He shouted that the governor had turned into a tyrant. In a conclusion that brought his hearers to their feet applauding, he solemnly called on God to forgive him for having supported Huey Long. Neither Cyr nor the applauders seemed to realize that his accusation was monstrously illogical—he had said that Huey Long, the man who was

[5] *Impeachment Proceedings*, I, 6, 9–10; New Orleans *Morning Tribune*, March 21, 1929; Baton Rouge *Morning Advocate*, March 22, 1929.

trying to destroy the oil industry, was in collusion with an oil company.[6]

While tongues were still wagging at the Cyr blast, another bombshell exploded. The Baton Rouge *State-Times* hit the streets with a front-page editorial that aroused the anti-Long people to a fury. The *State-Times* was one of two papers published in the capital city, the other being the *Morning Advocate*. Both were owned by Charles Manship, they had the same editorial line, and they were always referred to as "the Manship papers." Traditionally the papers did not take a decided position on political issues, but Huey's introduction of the oil tax had drawn them out of their neutrality. They struck at Huey with everything they had. Their editorials, like all the protests in Baton Rouge, had a hysterical note—a "grass will grow in the streets if this tax is enacted" theme—but they were still effective. They stung Huey, and he made the mistake of letting his feelings be known. On the night of March 20 he encountered in the capitol C. P. Liter, managing editor of the *State-Times*. While they were talking, Huey suddenly interjected: "By the way, I want you to tell Manship for me that I want him to lay off me." Liter asked what he meant. Huey replied that the editorials were getting too strong. He repeated his warning: "Tell Manship that if he don't lay off me I am going to have to publish a list of the names of the people who are fighting me who have relatives in the insane asylum." He did not have to tell Liter that he knew Charlie Manship's brother Douglas was in the East Louisiana Hospital for mental patients at Jackson. Later Huey met Manship himself. "Did you get the message I sent you?" he queried. When Manship said that he had not, Huey growled: "Well, I sent you one by Liter." Manship returned to his office and asked Liter what the message was. Reluctantly Liter told him. The publisher realized that he would have to meet the issue head-on.

The title of Thursday's editorial blazed in the center of the front page: "This, Gentlemen, Is the Way Your Governor Fights." The

---

[6] Baton Rouge *Morning Advocate*, March 22, 1929; New Orleans *Times-Picayune*, March 25, 1929; Leon Gary; statement by Julien St. Gilbert defending the leases, unidentified clipping, in Grace Scrapbook; Douthit: "Governorship of Long," p. 79. The lands in question had been leased to a Louisiana company in earlier administrations. Under Huey the leases were transferred to a Texas company. It is difficult to assess the validity of Cyr's charge. As with so many cases involving oil, the historian can only suggest possiblities. The state could profitably have retained the lands and developed them but at its own expense. Or the state could profitably have leased them to a private company that would develop them at its expense and return royalties to the state.

gentlemen to whom the editorial was addressed were, as the text developed, the members of the legislature. Manship summarized for the gentlemen Huey's conversations with Liter and himself. He admitted that his brother was undergoing mental treatment. He said that he did not think it was necessary to comment on the low tactics the governor had indulged in. "I might say, however," he added, "that my brother Douglas, whom Governor Long has brought in the discussion, is about the same age as the Governor. He was in France in 1918, wearing the uniform of a United States soldier, while Governor Long was campaigning for office."[7]

By Friday it was obvious that the legislature was not going to pass the oil-tax bill. Legislators who had gone down the line with Huey in previous sessions announced that they would vote against the measure. The most prominent deserter was William H. Bennett, one of his house floor leaders. Indeed, on this day it developed that Huey no longer commanded a majority vote even on other issues. By a vote of seventeen to fifteen the senate voted to create a committee to investigate the governor's claim that the hospitals and other institutions were suffering for want of money. Huey knew that he was beaten. He issued a supplemental call stating that the legislature could enact any kind of revenue-raising measure for the support of the schools and institutions that it chose to, an admission that he was willing to abandon the oil tax. But his surrender did not satisfy his enemies. They demanded that the tax bill, which had been stalled in a house committee, be brought out and voted down. The Kingfish realized that if this happened, he would have lost all control of the legislature, and other humiliating defeats would follow. That Friday night, as the legislature took its customary weekend recess, he caucused with his leaders. They decided that they would have to adjourn the legislature sine die and thus end the session. They would attempt it on Monday night, when the solons returned. The plan was to adjourn first the house, where a majority for adjournment was assured. Then the senate would be informed of the house's action, and not anything Paul Cyr could do would stop the upper chamber from following suit.[8]

Before he had given up on the oil-tax bill, Huey had made some radio speeches asking for its passage. In one of them he violently

[7] *Impeachment Proceedings*, I, 129–31; Baton Rouge *State-Times*, March 21, 1929.

[8] New Orleans *Times-Picayune*, March 23 and 24, 1929; *Impeachment Proceedings*, I, 39–40, for the call; Douthit: "Governorship of Long," pp. 79–80; Deutsch: "Kingdom of the Kingfish," in New Orleans *Item*, August 16, 1939; Allen J. Ellender.

attacked the Standard Oil Company for lobbying against the bill. He became specific as to how the lobbying was being conducted. "Oh! you know what I mean," he cried, "all you financial agents, you henchmen of the Standard Oil Company who are listening to me. You know what I mean that you are using money in the city of Baton Rouge today, and the members of legislature know what I mean when I say that you are using money in an effort to defeat the will of the people." This language was not just the extravagant rhetoric of a politician who was in a corner. Huey knew whereof he spoke.[9]

Many members of the legislature who opposed the oil tax acted out of principle, believing it to be bad economics or bad public policy. Some of them, it is true, arrived at their conclusions for reasons that might not seem very idealistic—the state must not tax the big corporations because the corporations were important to the state and if taxed might leave the state. Nonetheless, they were activated by their concept of principle. They might appear to be serving the interests of business, but they were not acting under command or pressure; they believed in the ideals of a business-dominated economy. The Standard Oil Company and the other oil companies valued their support. But Standard was not going to sit back and rely on these men of principle to defeat the tax bill. There were too many other legislators who operated on more practical levels, and Standard moved to reach these men, in ways appropriate to them.

The man who directed Standard's compaign was Daniel R. Weller, the president of the Louisiana company. Weller took a suite at the Heidelberg Hotel for the duration of the session. But Weller did not think that he should deal with legislators himself, partly because he was not good at it, partly because he did not wish to bring criticism on the company. He needed an agent, and he knew the man he wanted. One night he placed a telephone call to a town in the northeastern corner of the state. He was trying to get in touch with a man who will here be referred to as "Jim." Jim was the dominant political figure in this area and was widely known throughout the state. Charming, friendly, and persuasive, he was famous for his ability to manipulate people. He had been a Long supporter but was opposed to the oil tax. Weller knew that Jim was at his fishing camp some forty miles from town. The president talked to a younger associate of Jim's and asked him to bring Jim in to a tele-

[9] *Impeachment Proceedings*, I, 87.

phone. Jim was the only man who could stop the tax bill, Weller emphasized.

The associate drove out to the camp that night and returned with Jim. When Jim called Weller, he learned what the president wanted him to do. Jim must come down to Baton Rouge and take charge of the drive against the tax bill, Weller said. As the associate related the story, Jim agreed to come if Weller "would go all out to help him." Weller quickly assented. Jim said: "Reserve me a whole floor of the Heidelberg Hotel."

Jim took his associate with him to Baton Rouge. Because he still considered himself a friend of Huey's, Jim told the governor what he was going to do. Then he went to work. To his floor of the hotel the associate brought legislators and people from over the state who could exert pressure on the legislators. Jim used whatever methods of persuasion he had to: they were usually blunt. The associate summarized them: "By the time Jim got through paying 'em off things were pretty hot." Surviving members of the legislature remember Jim's activities. "The money he spent was terrific," said one. "You could pick up $15,000 or $20,000 any evening then."

When it was obvious that the oil-tax bill had no chance, Jim prepared to return home. By that time some of Huey's enemies were talking about bringing impeachment charges against him. They broached their plans to Jim. He said: "If you are going to impeach him, do it right now. If you wait, he is so smart he will think up something to beat you." He had small faith that the impeachers would follow his advice. "They are going to fool around and lose him," he said to his associate, and departed.[1]

The legislators who were talking about impeachment were the dedicated conservatives who made up the Dynamite Squad. The idea was not new with them. They had discussed for months the possibility of bringing charges against Huey and had appointed a committee of four of their members to collect incriminating information. Leading the opposition to Huey in the session, they caucused every night in the law office of J. Y. Sanders, Jr., to determine their strategy for the following day. At these meetings they also debated whether to try to impeach Huey now or to wait for the regular session. They had not reached a conclusion when they heard rumors of Huey's plan to adjourn the session on Monday night. Adjournment

---

[1] This account is based on the recollections of three men who were on the scene. Two of them do not want their names used, and I have deleted the name of the third. Other surviving legislators who were asked about the incident smiled knowingly but refused to say anything.

would wreck all of their plans. It would mean that the oil tax would not be brought up and voted down, and they were determined to have the bill formally defeated, partly because they wanted to humiliate Huey and weaken his power, mostly because they thought it was imperative for the legislature to go on record as condemning an occupational tax. They realized that Huey could command a majority for adjournment in the house and that if the house adjourned, the senate would have to end its session. In desperation, they cast about for an issue that would enable them to hold the house in session.

At one of the caucuses Harney Bogan, a representative from Caddo, remarked that Battling Bozeman, Huey's former bodyguard, had told him that the governor was planning to have J. Y. Sanders murdered. The other members at first thought that the story was too fantastic to deserve consideration. But Bogan said that the Battler was willing to make an affidavit. Bogan offered to get the affidavit. He brought it in to the caucus on Monday afternoon. It was a long, rambling, and bitter document. After relating that Huey had fired him, Bozeman stated that some time before the session the governor had called him to the executive mansion. At this meeting, Huey, who had been drinking, revealed to Bozeman that he was going to call a special session. "Little J. Y." would oppose all his measures, the governor went on, and therefore would have to be killed. Bozeman was to do the job. "I mean for you to kill the sonofabitch," Bozeman had Huey say; "leave him in the ditch where nobody will know how or when he got there. I'm the Governor of this state and if you were to be found out I would give you a full pardon and many gold dollars." Bozeman had himself replying that he was no gangster and indignantly refusing the proposal. The caucus members did not know how to evaluate the document. Sanders was convinced then, and for the rest of his life, that Huey actually said in essence what Bozeman reported. But J. Y. also thought that Huey was drunk and did not mean for Bozeman to act on his words. Mason Spencer, another member, did not believe any part of Bozeman's tale. "But what a wonderful witness he made," Spencer exclaimed admiringly as he recalled the incident. The caucus finally decided that the affidavit had some credibility, at least enough to justify their using it. If they revealed its contents, they could perhaps hold the house in session. Cecil Morgan of Caddo, an adept lawyer, was designated to present it to the house on Monday night.[2]

[2] J. Y. Sanders, Jr.; Cecil Morgan; Mason Spencer; *Impeachment Proceedings*, I, 29–32, for the affidavit; Norman Bauer.

Both chambers convened in an atmosphere of charged emotion and expectancy. Just as word of Huey's plan to adjourn the house had leaked to the conservatives, so an intimation that the opposition would attempt some spectacular move to prevent adjournment had reached Huey's people. In the house all but three of the one hundred members were in attendance, although not all of them answered to the opening roll call. Huey had instructed his followers carefully. As soon as the house was in session, after the prayer and approval of the journal, J. Cleveland Fruge, a Long leader, was to move adjournment sine die. Speaker Fournet was to recognize nobody but Fruge and put the motion. As Huey had fifty or so members pledged to vote for adjournment, the thing would be over in a matter of minutes. Fournet was then to name a chairman of a committee to notify the senate that the house stood ready to adjourn. This chairman had already been designated in a caucus of Long supporters and was told to get to the senate quickly.

After the opening formalities the clerk of the house, Martian Hamley, called the roll. The instant it was concluded, Fruge rose to make his motion. But before he could utter a word, Morgan jumped to his feet and began talking from his desk. Morgan had Bozeman's affidavit in his hand, and he waved the paper as he spoke. "Bozeman charges that Governor Long offered him money and immunity if he would assassinate Representative J. Y. Sanders," Morgan cried. At this moment Fruge shouted his motion to adjourn. Fournet recognized Fruge. But Morgan continued to talk. He demanded the creation of a committee to investigate Bozeman's charges. Fournet ordered Morgan to take his seat. The Caddo representative stood his ground and continued to talk. "Put Mr. Morgan in his seat," Fournet snapped to the sergeant at arms. As this official started toward Morgan, he was pushed aside by members of the Dynamite Squad. Morgan, his face white with emotion, then started down the center aisle toward the podium. By this time the house was in an uproar. Fruge was yelling for his motion to be put to a vote. Members of both factions were shouting and milling around the floor. When Morgan reached the podium, he resumed his speech. Ten or more of his friends had followed him and now stood around him with their arms locked to prevent the sergeant at arms from getting at him. Suddenly Fournet called for the vote. The lights on the voting machine flashed on. They showed sixty-seven yeas, in green, and only thirteen nays, in red. Fournet declared the motion passed, threw down his gavel, and left the chamber. Then pandemonium broke loose.

All over the floor men rose from their seats, and many of them pushed toward the podium, some in their haste climbing over the intervening desks. One word rang about above the bedlam—*No, No.* The protestors were trying to inform somebody—just whom they were not sure—that the vote was wrong. Members who had voted against adjournment had seen the green light flash beside their names—their nays had been counted as yeas. Naturally they assumed that the vote had been faked, that the voting machine had been rigged, that the Long forces had in desperation resorted to an illegal move. They were not going to let them get by with it.

Lavinius Williams, an anti-Long representative from New Orleans, ran to the steps leading to the speaker's chair. "The house will come to order," he shouted. At this moment Fournet, who had gone to his office, returned and took his seat on the dais. All around it stood angry, yelling men. Into the mass charged Clinton Sayes, a bald-headed, hot-tempered member from Avoyelles parish. Sayes had run across the tops of desks to get to the front. His purpose was to mount the dais and from its eminence inform the chamber of the fraud that had been committed. When he saw Fournet already there, his fury increased. He started up the steps, and, according to Fournet, yelled out that he was going to remove the speaker physically. By this time several Long legislators had forced their way through the crowd and taken position in front of Fournet. One of them was Lorris Wimberly, a floor leader. Another was Lester Lautenschlaeger of New Orleans, a former Tulane football star, who had been chairman of the committee to notify the senate of the house's action and who had returned to find this scene of confusion. As Sayes started up, he pushed at Wimberly and other people on the steps. Wimberly struck back. He had a small diamond ring on his hand, and the blow caused a few drops of blood to appear on Sayes's forehead. Or so the Long people say in describing this episode. The antis say that Sayes was hit by somebody wearing brass knuckles and that the blood gushed forth in a stream. One Longite has still another version: he swears that he saw Sayes stand on a desk where he was struck by a blade from a ceiling electric fan. Whatever the facts may be, blood was undeniably drawn, enough of it to give a name to this wild night. Thereafter in Louisiana it was always referred to as "Bloody Monday."

The wounding of Sayes was like a signal. In an instant fights broke out among the members congregated before the podium and in small groups all over the floor. Longs and anti-Longs slugged at each other and threw inkwells and paste pots in every direction,

while the sergeant at arms and his assistants charged into the bat-
tlers and tried to separate them. Finally a measure of order was
restored. Several antis went up to Fournet and asked him to put a
motion appealing his ruling that the house had adjourned. "The
house is not in session," Fournet growled, "and there is no motion to be put." One of the antis then jumped up on the press table.
He was Mason Spencer, chairman of the Dynamite Squad, a hulking, paunchy man with a stentorian voice. He bellowed for attention, or as one member put it, gave a "hog call": "Let us be sane.
Let there be silence, and let the house be polled by oral roll call on
the appeal from Speaker Fournet's ruling that the house is adjourned
without date." As if by magic, the house fell silent. Spencer sensed
that he had established an ascendancy, realized too the sudden opportunity that had come to his side. He announced that he would poll
the house himself on the motion. In measured tones he called the
name of each member. A great roar went up when he announced the
result: only nine votes to sustain Fournet's ruling and seventy-nine to
override it. Still pressing his advantage, Spencer declared magnanimously that he had no wish to be temporary speaker—he had assumed both the title and the position—and nominated another anti,
George J. Ginsberg, to preside. Ginsberg was chosen by a loud voice
vote. On taking the chair he announced that he thought the house
should not attempt to transact any more business but should adjourn
until eleven o'clock the following morning. A motion to that effect
was offered and passed with a roar of yeas. Members and spectators
rushed from the chamber to find out what was happening in the
senate.

While these convulsions had been rending the house, the senate
had been proceeding in relative calm. Immediately after convening, it adopted a resolution by Senator Charles Holcombe of Baton
Rouge condemning the principle of occupational taxes. The vote
was an ominous indication of an anti-Long majority. Then Philip
Gilbert, the Long leader, offered a motion to adjourn. While the
senate debated the motion, the chairman of the house notification
committee arrived with word that the other chamber had adjourned.
This news gave impetus to the adjournment movement. But soon
different information came in, brought by persons who rushed over
from the other chamber: the house had not adjourned but was still
in session, and, finally, the house had adjourned only until the next
morning. Now the antis were encouraged, and at this critical moment Lieutenant Governor Cyr did his part. He ruled Gilbert's
motion out of order. Gilbert appealed the decision, but it was upheld

by a vote of nineteen to seventeen. The senate then voted to adjourn until eleven o'clock the following morning. Huey's bold bid to send the legislature home had failed. His opponents were in an exultant mood. One of them, Senator Charles Huson, expressed their feeling in a speech on the floor. "We have turned from demagoguery to decency and decorum, and I am proud of this legislature," he trumpeted. "Louisiana has come back into its own and in the future no governor will be able to impose on the legislature of our state."[3]

Not until later that night, when tempers had cooled, did the participants in the house scene realize what had touched off the brawl. The explanation was simple. Nobody had rigged the voting machine and attempted a fraud. The fault lay with the machine and with the inability of the people who operated it to control its technical deficiencies. One of the first mechanical devices of its kind to be used in a state legislature anywhere, it was a good machine for its time. But it registered votes in a slow, cumbersome fashion. A legislator sitting at his desk pushed a button to indicate his vote: one push for yea, two for nay, three for not-voting. The vote of each member was registered inside a booth, where a photostatic camera recorded three successive copies of a roll call, one for the speaker, one for the clerk of the house, and one for the official journal. The votes also flashed on a board outside the booth and on dials on the desks of the speaker and clerk Hamley. These dials were something like the speedometer needle on an automobile: they registered an approximate though not a precise total. On a close vote the speaker depended on the clerk to hand him a slip showing the exact figures. During the time that the vote was being taken, the machine automatically locked itself and remained locked until the photostatic copies of the vote were made. It then cleared itself for the next vote. The process took some time.

Time was the one thing that the tense men on both sides would not allow the machine that night. The first vote taken was the roll call to record those present. Then Fruge rose and Morgan began to speak. Shortly, probably within a minute or so, Fournet had put Fruge's motion to a vote and directed Hamley to turn the key. But the machine had not had time to clear from the initial roll call. Thus the votes that the members saw flashed on the board were still re-

[3] J. Cleveland Fruge; Cecil Morgan; J. Y. Sanders, Jr.; W. C. Pegues; Norman Bauer; John B. Fournet; Lester Lautenschlaeger; George J. Ginsberg; unidentified clipping, news story by George Vandervoort, probably in New Orleans *Times-Picayune*, March 26, 1929, in Grace Scrapbook; New Orleans *Morning Tribune*, March 26, 1929; *Impeachment Proceedings*, I, 26–7.

cording essentially the answer to the roll call. The sixty-seven green, or yea, votes represented members present. Presumably the thirteen red, or nay, votes were those of members who for some reason had recorded themselves as not voting or who were off the floor and had asked colleagues to push their buttons. It is possible that one or two of them were new votes that registered on the incompletely cleared machine. A few members on both sides realized immediately what had happened. Some Longites yelled at Fournet that the machine was jammed. Those antis who suspected the truth chose to remain quiet, to take advantage of the opportunity offered them to discredit the Long side. Fournet attested at the time and later that he and Hamley both thought the vote was genuine and that he announced it in good faith. Anti legislators in recalling the scene now absolve the speaker of any intent to commit fraud. But they think that he must have known that the large majority for adjournment was a mistake and that he tried to capitalize on the mechanical accident. The probable truth is that Fournet was so rattled by the turn of events that he did not know what he was doing. He did the worst possible thing in walking out. He should have stayed in the chair, declared the vote void, and ordered a new vote. The Long majority would have held and voted adjournment, and the legislature would have gone home.[4]

The members of the Dynamite Squad sat up all that night in Sanders's office. They decided that this was the time to start impeachment proceedings. Their committee of four that had been gathering evidence was instructed to prepare charges for presentation the next morning. Stenographers were brought in to type copies of the indictment. The members also decided that they would move for open hearings so that the people could hear and judge the nature of their evidence. As a matter of strategy, they determined to have the house consider the charges in committee of the whole. Proceeding in this way, the chamber could name a chairman other than the speaker and lay down whatever rules it chose concerning the reception of evidence. After considering a charge, the house would then revert to its usual character and vote on the charge. The caucus drafted nineteen charges of misconduct against Huey and then wearily broke up.[5]

[4] Deutsch: "Kingdom of the Kingfish," in New Orleans *Item*, August 17, 1939; Deutsch, column in New Orleans *Item*, March 16, 1959; John B. Fournet; *Impeachment Proceedings*, I, 27–8; Mason Spencer.

[5] J. Y. Sanders, Jr.; Cecil Morgan.

The house convened on the following morning in a quiet but tense mood. Speaker Fournet took the podium and apologized for anything he had done to cause the previous day's disturbance. He explained that he had been confused by the noise and had not understood the "mechanical difficulty" in the machine. A Long leader next offered a resolution to adjourn. It received only thirty-nine votes, an indication that Huey's support was shrinking fast. Then the Dynamite Squad took over. Cecil Morgan presented a resolution asking for an investigation of Battling Bozeman's charge that the governor had offered him a bribe to kill Sanders. Morgan followed this with two more resolutions. They stated that the governor had used $6,000 of state money to entertain a national conference of governors in New Orleans and $10,965 of state money to repair the capitol and mansion but had made no accounting of these sums. The resolutions directed the chief executive to give the house within twenty-four hours an itemized statement of how the moneys had been spent. The house could not act immediately on the resolutions—they had to lie over—but it was obvious that they would be passed. They caused a sensation, but a bigger one was yet to come. The Dynamiters' committee of four announced that it had a resolution to present.

The resolution was read in solemn tones by one of the committee members. It came to the point immediately: "Whereas, Huey P. Long, Governor of the State of Louisiana, has been guilty of high crimes and misdemeanors in office, incompetency, corruption, favoritism, oppression in office, gross misconduct," be it resolved that Huey P. Long be impeached "for said offences" and tried before the senate. The resolution then proceeded to list the nineteen charges agreed on by the Dynamiters in caucus. The charges accused Huey of using his appointing powers to influence the judiciary and of boasting of his control over the judges; of attempting to bribe legislators to support his legislation; of requiring undated resignations of appointees; of having through controlled boards misused state funds; of contracting illegal state loans; of removing school officials for political purposes and intimidating teachers; of illegally using the militia to pillage private property; of trying to force parish-governing bodies to follow his dictation to get legislation they wanted; of carrying concealed weapons on his person; of using abusive language to officials and private citizens; of engaging in immoral behavior at a New Orleans night spot; of usurping the powers of the legislature and its committees; of forcing the state penitentiary to construct a refrigerating plant without asking for bids; of attempting to intimidate Charles Manship; of destroying the executive mansion; of destroying and disposing of property and furniture in the mansion, the capitol, and state offices; of illegally paroling a convict; of intruding on the legislature and interfering with its conduct of business; and of trying to employ Bozeman to kill Sanders.[6]

For conservative Louisiana the Tuesday after Bloody Monday was a day of rejoicing. First had come the news that the legislature had defied the governor's attempt to adjourn it. "Crooked Game of Long Is Blocked," crowed a headline in Ewing's *States*, typical of newspaper reaction. Manship's *State-Times* exulted that the state had not been so stirred since the days of carpetbag rule. The people felt that Long was trying to "crush Louisiana's industries and the happiness of her people," the paper declared, engaging in Baton Rouge's characteristic tendency to confuse the welfare of Standard Oil Company with that of the state as a whole. The capital city gave itself over to merrymaking. Happy crowds surged past the building that housed Sanders's office, where the Dynamite Squad was meeting. "Baton Rouge has seen the day it had been waiting for," a newspaper correspondent wrote. Many individuals in the throng volunteered to reporters why they were elated. They all stressed the note struck by the *State-Times*: Louisiana was returning to greatness, as she had done in Reconstruction when she freed herself of carpetbag domination. None of the commentators seemed to remember that Huey was a native Louisianian or that Standard Oil was a "foreign" corporation.[7]

While the excitement over the legislature's stand was still bubbling, the news of the impeachment move broke, creating an even greater sensation. Now it appeared that the legislature not only would defy the tyrant but would also remove him from office. Simultaneously with the offering of impeachment in the house, public announcements blazoned that there would be a mass meeting in Baton Rouge that night to protest against "the attack on the prosperity and credit" of the state embodied in "radical legislation" proposed by Governor Long. Special invitations were extended to members of the legislature, who were assured of reserved seats. The swiftness with which the meeting was organized and the fact that its sponsors were from all sections of the state suggest that it had been planned some time before. The Dynamite Squad was spearheading

[6] *Impeachment Proceedings*, I, 27–8, 32–3.

[7] New Orleans *States*, March 26, 1929; Baton Rouge *State-Times*, March 26, 1929; New Orleans *Item*, March 26, 1929.

the impeachment effort, but its members had quite evidently been in frequent consultation with other conservative leaders.[8]

The mass meeting, held at the Community Club pavilion, was an enthusiastic affair, attended by some six thousand people, according to the estimate of friendly journalists. Music was furnished by the Standard Oil band. Its members did not wear their customary uniforms, but the name "Stanacola Band" was plainly visible on the drum. Delegations from all parts of the state were present, the largest and noisiest one coming from New Orleans and consisting mostly of Old Regulars. The speakers were many and fiery. Some were men who had consistently opposed Huey, but others had supported him in his previous campaigns and up to the time he proposed the oil tax. Denunciation of the tax was the theme of the speeches and the resolutions adopted at the conclusion of the meeting. The lead resolution charged that Huey had instigated the tax to satisfy "a personal grudge." It then proceeded to state the economic philosophy of its conservative sponsors: "That we condemn as being vicious, dangerous and utterly without merit, any and all systems of taxation" that ". . . seek to impose tax burdens upon industries" in Louisiana. Because Governor Long had tried to impose such burdens, the meeting resolved, the legislature should act immediately on the impeachment indictment brought against him.[9]

The sponsors of the meeting had handed Huey a shining weapon to use against them. They had said, flatly and frankly, that the governor should be impeached because he had tried to place a tax on Standard Oil. It was a position that seemed logical to many conservatives at the time and later. "Of course," said a surviving member of the Dynamite Squad, "the truth is, the Standard Oil business was what brought the impeachment on." But even if the conservatives thought that the tax constituted grounds for impeachment, they were foolish to admit it. They were casting themselves as defenders of corporate privilege. Furthermore, they were contending that Huey's advocacy of the tax was an impeachable offense as defined by the Louisiana constitution.[1]

That constitution included as grounds for impeachment more offenses than were commonly included in state charters. An elected or appointed official could be impeached for "high crimes and mis-

[8] *Impeachment Proceedings*, I, 38.

[9] New Orleans *Times-Picayune*, March 27, 1929; New Orleans *States*, March 27, 1929; F. Raymond Daniell: "The Gentleman from Louisiana," *Current History*, XLI (November 1934), 175; Long: *Every Man a King*, pp. 139–41.

[1] New Orleans *States*, April 30, 1929; Norman Bauer.

demeanors in office," a catch-all that appeared in most state constitutions and also in the U.S. Constitution, for "incompetency,"
which would be difficult to demonstrate, for corruption, favoritism,
or extortion in office, for gross misconduct or "habitual drunken-
ness." Some of the charges brought against Huey would, if proved,
obviously justify removal: that he had influenced the judiciary, offered bribes to legislators, improperly used state moneys. Others
were borderline cases: that he had attempted to intimidate officials and teachers. Many were clearly outside the prescribed list and
were absurd: that he had used abusive language to citizens, carried
concealed weapons, and fondled a New Orleans nightclub "strip-
per." "Some of the charges were just thrown in for scenery," conceded one surviving advocate of impeachment. But others insist that
all the charges were impeachable. "You can impeach for whatever
you want to impeach for," Cecil Morgan explained, "for any act
not consistent with the duty of the office. It is not like a criminal or
civil court." More blunt was Mason Spencer. "You can impeach for
anything," he stated. "A misdemeanor can be anything. Impeachment is a political move." Back in Reconstruction times Thaddeus
Stevens had used almost identical words in defending the attempt of
the Radical Republicans to remove President Andrew Johnson because his political ideas were opposed to those of the legislative
majority.[2]

The impeachers were confident that they had a strong case. They
were also confident that they had created an organization effective
enough to carry their case to victory. They had devised it in part
before they decided to move for impeachment, and they completed
it immediately after they made their decision. Their headquarters
were in Sanders's office. Here the Dynamite Squad and other conservative leaders met daily to formulate strategy. In an adjacent office
were installed lawyers, researchers, and typists. The last two groups
were paid workers. Some of the lawyers were also retained, but
others, like Esmond Phelps and Edward Rightor, leading figures of
the New Orleans bar, volunteered their services. After the leaders
decided what charge would be presented on a particular day, the
researchers supplied them with supporting data, and the lawyers
provided them with legal citations and precedents. Those members
of the Dynamite Squad who were lawyers were to present the
charges, each man taking one or more that interested him. Morgan

[2] *Impeachment Proceedings*, II, 223; Norman Bauer; Cecil Morgan; Mason
Spencer; J. Y. Sanders, Jr.

was to act as general floor leader, to call the witnesses and conduct the examination of them. Ready and assured, the impeachers acted quickly. On Wednesday Spencer moved that the house appoint a subcommittee to formulate rules and procedures to conduct the impeachment, and the chamber voted to receive the report of the committee on Monday, April 1.[3]

Not prepared with a ready-made case, not supported by an eager staff, and certainly not assured was Huey. The events of Bloody Monday shocked him, and the move to impeach, following immediately, shook him to the core. For a day or so he apparently was in a state of mental paralysis. Julius Long, who came condescendingly down from Shreveport to offer aid, later said that he found Huey lying on a bed sobbing and tearing at his clothes convulsively. Julius feared that Huey might commit suicide. The older brother was always a prejudiced witness where Huey was concerned, and he exaggerated Huey's condition. But beyond question Huey was in a dark mood—depressed, defenseless, ready to give up. "They've got me," he confided to two country supporters who called on him at his hotel suite. He had good reason to be downcast. He stood at a crossroads in his career. Phenomenally successful in his first year in office and seemingly certain to go on to greater feats, in his second year he suddenly faced the prospect of political death. Such an abrupt shift in fortune could not but induce a kind of melancholia. But he rallied quickly from his somber mood and began to strike back.[4]

He took up as his first weapon—almost instinctively, as though he knew he could rely on it above all others—the circular. On March 28 he published the first of a series of circulars on the impeachment issue, a series that would flood the state. Its title screamed its content: The Same Fight Again! The Standard Oil Company vs. Huey P. Long. The opening sentences drew the line on which he was going to stand: "I had rather go down to a thousand impeachments than to admit that I am the governor of the State that does not dare to call the Standard Oil Company to account so that we can educate our children and care for [the] destitute, sick, and afflicted. If this State is still to be ruled by the power of the money of this corporation, I am too weak for its governor." He had proposed that this corporation pay a fair tax to support the poor and unfortunate, whose "pleas for help are like a phantom in the dark," and because

[3] Cecil Morgan; Mason Spencer; *Impeachment Proceedings*, I, 50, 63.

[4] Julius T. Long; Harry Gamble; W. V. Larcade; J. Cleveland Fruge; Deutsch: "Kingdom of the Kingfish," in New Orleans *Item*, August 17, 1939.

he had dared to do this it was making another, and a supreme, effort to destroy him. The company was pouring out huge sums of money to carry out its purpose, Huey charged. It had even invaded the legislature and bought up a number of lawmakers. Huey followed this circular with others. They all sounded the same note. This was a fight pitting Standard Oil and its paid henchmen against Huey Long, the champion of the people. If the people wanted to continue to receive free schoolbooks, good roads, better hospitals, they must rally to their leader.[5]

Huey wrote the copy for every circular, and most of them appeared with his name at the bottom. When he finished one, the copy was rushed to Joe David's Franklin Printing Company in New Orleans, where David, alerted that a new composition was on the way, had his presses ready to roll. During the impeachment crisis, April–May, the various editions of circulars printed totaled nine hundred thousand copies. To distribute this mass of material was a herculean job. Huey had previously used the mails to disseminate his documents, but after he became governor he worked out a more efficient system, one that in his autobiography he coyly called "hand to hand distribution." When a batch of circulars was ready to go, a number of unmarked trucks and automobiles would appear in front of the Franklin plant. They were state vehicles, most of them belonging to the state police: Policemen out of uniform would pick up bundles of circulars, each bundle marked with the name of a parish leader to whom it was to be delivered. The circulars would reach the leaders that night or the next morning. These leaders had been told by telephone that the material was coming, and they, in turn, had told their precinct captains to be ready. A parish leader got his circulars to the captains by various methods. He might hire people to deliver them or direct state employees or the state policemen in his district to do the work. The captains saw to it that the circulars reached their people, thus completing the distribution process. The system functioned with astonishing rapidity. Huey claimed that a circular printed on one day would be on the porch of practically every home in the state by the next morning, and he was not indulging in much exaggeration.[6]

[5] Circular, "The Same Fight Again," in my possession; Long: *Every Man a King*, pp. 147–8, 150–3.

[6] Joseph David; Burton H. Hotaling: "Huey Pierce Long as Journalist and Propagandist," *Journalism Quarterly*, XX (1943), 22–3; Seymour Weiss; Harvey Peltier; D. J. Anders; J. Maxime Roy; George Stagg.

At the same time that he launched his circular campaign, Huey laid plans to call a huge mass meeting of his supporters in Baton Rouge. He had been impressed by the publicity his opponents had received after their conclave and was determined to outdo them. His meeting was held on April 4, in the same Community Club where the conservatives had gathered. The crowd overflowed the pavilion, but the many who had to stand outside heard the proceedings easily over loudspeakers. Huey said that most of those who attended were farmers and laborers who had come to the capital to demonstrate their support for their leader. His enemies said that the crowd was made up of state employees who were there under orders. Both groups were indeed present. John Overton gave the opening address. At his oratorical best, Overton drew a vivid picture of Huey, the popular champion, now backed to the wall by his enemies. "As I see him there now," he concluded, "with his rapier flashing, fencing off the enemies to the left, to the front and to the right, when this smoke of battle shall have cleared, as in the beginning, I will be standing or lying by the side of Huey P. Long." Huey followed with a speech that lasted two hours. He recounted his efforts over the years to help the masses and described the opposition he had aroused from Standard Oil and other corporations. And now, just when he was at the point of succeeding, his enemies had combined to strike him down. "The buzzards have returned," he roared. "They want to gloat and gulp at the expense of the poor and afflicted." He ended near midnight, quoting "Invictus," the poem that had so impressed him in his boyhood:

> I am the master of my fate;
> I am the captain of my soul.

The meeting adopted resolutions demanding that the house "reject and cast out" all articles of impeachment against the governor.[7]

Huey's sudden offensive shook somewhat the confidence of the impeachers. They were most worried by his charge that Standard Oil had influenced members of the legislature: this was the kind of accusation that the realistic Louisiana voters were likely to believe. They decided on what they thought was a cunning move to call his hand. Both houses passed resolutions demanding that the governor

---

[7] Long: *Every Man a King*, pp. 148–50; hostile story by Rupert Peyton and A. P. dispatch, both in Shreveport *Journal*, April 5, 1929; *Impeachment Proceedings*, II, 74–5.

furnish the names of those legislators who had been "bought or bribed" and the names of the Standard agents who had done the buying. Huey replied that his knowledge was hearsay—he knew only what had been told to him in confidence by legislators. But the legislature could easily elicit this information, he said. If it would appoint a committee to investigate the matter, he would give the committee the names of men who could testify directly. The solons hastily dropped the issue: an investigation could prove embarrassing to many of them.[8]

The kind of campaign Huey was waging required huge sums of money to sustain it. He estimated that the circulars alone would cost forty thousand dollars. He did not have anything like that amount when he began his fight. He spoke of his need for money one night at a meeting of his friends in his hotel suite. "If I had enough money, I could whip that bunch," he said. Taciturn Bob Maestri growled out a question: "How much do you need?" Huey named a figure that associates remember as ranging from thirty to forty thousand dollars. "Send Earl down to New Orleans for it to-morrow," said Maestri, as casually as if he was handing a dollar to a needy acquaintance. Later Huey received contributions from other sources, notably from road contractors who had an obvious motive for keeping a highway-minded governor in office. But Maestri's donation, coming when Huey needed it most, was decisive. Huey never forgot Maestri's loyalty. Maestri provided him with "the implements of warfare," he said gratefully.[9]

As Huey expanded his campaign, he built up a staff to assist him in running it. Matching the retinue of the impeachers, he had his own lawyers, lieutenants, and clerical workers. Among the lawyers, John Overton was the biggest name and the unofficial director of Huey's legal case. Overton had been in his hometown of Alexandria when news of the impeachment broke. According to Mrs. Overton, he came home from his office and said: "Pack a suitcase. I'm going to Baton Rouge to see if these charges are true. If they are, I will break with him. If they are not, I will stand by him." He went to the capital and saw Huey and was convinced that the charges were false. He agreed to defend Huey and made his speech at the Com-

[8] *Impeachment Proceedings*, I, 63, 68; II, 35–6, 41.

[9] O. B. Thompson; Harley B. Bozeman; Leander H. Perez; Harvey Peltier; Orlean Thomas; Long: *Every Man a King*, pp. 146–8. Swords Lee, who had contributed liberally to Huey's causes in the past, was no longer present to help him; he died shortly before the impeachment proceedings began.

munity Club in which he said that he would be found standing or lying by Huey's side. But some people close to Long hoot at this story. They say that Overton refused to go to Huey's aid until he was promised money by somebody in the Long organization. In the scornful words of one, he demanded five thousand to lie by Huey's side.[1]

Another lawyer working for Huey, and probably the best legal mind in the group, was Leander H. Perez of Plaquemines parish on the Gulf Coast. Perez was a young man and a secondary figure in the political organization of his parish, which was allied with Huey's state organization. Plaquemines and adjoining St. Bernard parish nearly always voted for the same candidates in a state contest, casting an almost unanimous vote for the aspirants designated by parish leaders. These leaders were not politicians in the ordinary sense of the word. They were more like *caudillos* in a Latin country. They might on occasion cajole, but usually they issued genial orders. Perez in later years would become the boss of the two parishes and would be called their dictator. He went with Huey during the impeachment because his organization was with Huey and because he judged that Huey was going to be the power in Louisiana for a long time. He was ruthless, realistic, and extremely intelligent, and he performed a larger role than legal counsel. Under Huey's supervision, he acted as general strategist for the Long forces. Almost every day Huey's house followers caucused in the Heidelberg Hotel —some thirty or more of them—and at these meetings Perez presided and outlined moves that could be made at the next session.[2]

More important than Perez as an executor of strategy was Earl Long. Whereas Perez spoke to people in groups, Earl dealt with them as individuals, in whispered corner conferences in the capitol or in covert conversations behind hotel doors. This was the kind of negotiating in which he excelled, in which he was better than Huey. Earl devoted his persuasive powers to members of the legislature, convincing men inclined to Huey to remain loyal, inducing undecided men to come over to the Long side. As an example of his efforts, he asked a north Louisiana businessman to come down to Baton Rouge to put pressure on a senator. When the man demurred because of the length of the trip, Earl sent an airplane to get him. Earl also acted as a go-between with legislators, carrying messages from Huey to particular members and taking back to Huey their

[1] Mrs. John H. Overton; *Overton Hearing*, II, 1224; confidential communications.
[2] Leander H. Perez; J. Cleveland Fruge; Waldo H. Dugas.

reactions to events. The younger brother was tireless in Huey's defense. He worked all day and most of every night. "Earl never slept in the impeachment," a legislator recalled admiringly.[3]

Most of Huey's old cronies stayed loyal to him during the impeachment crisis. O. K. Allen, for example, was always at Huey's side and urging aggressive resistance. But some of his friends left him. They thought he had gone too far with the oil tax and in his grasp for power, or they judged that he was finished and hastened to shift their allegiance. These partings were accomplished in bitter and angry scenes. The most tragic one was with Harley Bozeman, Huey's boyhood friend. Bozeman, chairman of the house appropriations committee and chairman of the Tax Commission, was an influential figure in the Long organization. But he had become increasingly dissatisfied with his position. He was too peppery and independent to accept Huey's dictation, and he had known Huey too long to be awed by him. Moreover, he was irritated that Huey seemed to rely for advice on certain New Orleans leaders instead of his Winn parish friends. He had opposed the oil tax, and now he was convinced that Huey could not escape impeachment and should resign the governorship. He decided to take it on himself to suggest resignation. Late one night he went to Huey's hotel room. Huey had just come out of the bathroom and was dressing. Bozeman made his plea and, according to Huey, added: "You ought to be willing to save your friends." The Kingfish was sitting on the edge of the bed paring his toenails. He listened to Bozeman with mounting fury. He could discharge a man and take him back, but he could not forgive anyone who gave up on him. He pointed to a piece of nail on the floor and said: "Bozeman, I wouldn't give the value of that toenail for a sonofabitch like you." Ironically, Bozeman shortly would have to take the course he had recommended to Huey. He would be forced to resign from the Tax Commission.[4]

On April 1 the house convened and heard the report of the subcommittee on rules and procedures. That body, dominated by the impeachers, recommended that the charges against Huey be considered in committee of the whole and that that committee have "complete and plenary power" to investigate the official conduct of

[3] H. Lester Hughes; Ernest Clements; Leonard Spinks; John Doles; Harrison Jordan; Waldo H. Dugas.

[4] *Overton Hearing,* I, 917–18; confidential communication. Mr. Bozeman denies every part of this story, but a witness corroborates it. In the Overton investigation Huey and Bozeman exchanged loud opinions as to its accuracy, and a conscientious secretary recorded their charges in an all-too-proper form. Huey: "You are a lying scoundrel." Bozeman: "You are another one."

the governor. The report laid over to the next day for a vote. When it came up, Long leaders raised objections to the legality of the proposed procedure. A few days earlier a Longite had made a point of order that impeachment was illegal because it was not included in the governor's call and because it could not be consummated within the time limit set by the call, which stipulated that the session was to end on April 6. His motion was ruled out of order, but more would be heard on the issue later. Now, on Tuesday, the Long people offered a new objection. They had discovered a law of 1855 bearing on impeachment that prescribed a different and more cumbersome process than the one being considered. Their motion to adopt this process was decisively defeated, and even more decisively the report of the committee was approved. The impeachers would be able to conduct the investigation as they had planned, naming one of their men to preside over the committee of the whole and making their own rules.[5]

Now that the way was cleared, the house proceeded immediately to take testimony. It would listen to witnesses almost every day until April 25. A large crowd of spectators overflowed the galleries at each session. Some of them were senators who came over to get a preview of the evidence they would vote on later. One person in the galleries attracted more attention than the others. Mrs. Long sat quietly day after day. Huey had asked her to come down from Shreveport and attend. He suggested that she buy two or three new dresses and that she wear a white dress when she first appeared. Rose heard a prominent Baton Rouge woman say: "Doesn't Mrs. Long have cheek, wearing white when she should have on black."[6]

The hearings drew crowds because they were a good show. The testimony was on occasion technical or dull and sometimes repetitious, but usually it was excitingly personal, spicy and even scandalous, and fascinating in its intimate revelations. The whole procedure had about it an air of high drama, the suspense of a state trial involving a great public figure. And commingled satisfyingly with the drama were moments of rare and unforgettable comedy.

The house first took evidence on the Manship charge. On this count only two witnesses were heard, Liter and Manship. Then the inquisitors moved to the charge that Huey had attempted to bribe members of the legislature. A representative who was a planter testified that the governor had offered to help him get a bank loan if he would vote with the administration. According to this man, the

[5] *Impeachment Proceedings*, I, 51, 71, 85.
[6] Rose McConnell Long.

Kingfish had boasted that he controlled the banks through the state examiners. A senator affirmed that Huey had hinted he could throw some appointments to him. A representative who had voted against an administration bill related that he was called to the governor's office, where Huey asked him what he would like to have. "I want a job," said the representative, who was obviously a man who went to the point immediately. Huey awarded him a modest position with the Highway Commission, but he voted against the oil tax nonetheless.[7]

The highlight of the bribery testimony concerned William H. Bennett, a representative from a parish just north of Baton Rouge. Bennett had been elected to the house in 1928 as an anti-Long candidate. Soon after the regular session of that year opened, he went over to Huey's side and became a Long floor leader. Now several politicians from Bennett's parish but from a faction opposed to him described a visit they had made to the governor after the session. The delegation had requested some favors, and after their business was transacted, had fallen into a general conversation with Huey. He was in a high good humor and a mood to boast. In the course of the talk Bennett's name came up. Huey leaned back in his chair and laughed. "I suppose you folks have heard that Bennett is with me now," he said. "He belongs to me now. I bought him and paid for him." One of the visitors asked if Huey meant his words literally. "Yes," Huey replied, "I bought him and paid for him like you would a load of potatoes." His hearers did not take him too seriously. They evaluated the statement for what it obviously was— a political brag uttered partly in jest.

Bennett was inclined to take the same view of the matter when he heard the testimony. He thought, however, that he should place his version of the story on record and asked the privilege of being heard as a witness. What he related reflected no serious discredit on either him or Huey. On the eve of the 1928 session Huey had asked him to support such administration measures as he could. He had agreed to go along with the bulk of Huey's program, had voted for most of Huey's bills, and had steered some of them to passage. Toward the end of the session he had called on Huey and reminded the governor of his support. He went on to say that his children lived in Baton Rouge, that he might want to move there, and that therefore he would like to have a state job. Huey, expressing deep gratitude, assigned him a good job with the Highway Commission.

[7] *Impeachment Proceedings*, I, 96, 114, 115, 232.

Bennett said he did not believe that Huey had made the slurring reference to potatoes, and he exhibited a statement from the governor that denied the story. But by the next day Bennett had second thoughts. He decided on the basis of additional evidence that Huey actually had said it. In an emotional speech to the house he labeled the remark a "contemptible and dirty libel" and resigned his highway post. The episode became one of the Long legends. It grew with retelling over the years until Huey was recalled as having said that he had bought any number of legislators like sacks of potatoes.[8]

The impeachers concluded that they had better back away from any inquiries about bribery. The evidence that they had uncovered was not really very damaging to Huey. He had clearly offered jobs and favors in return for votes, but it was straining logic to label what he had done as bribery. And if it was bribery, then practically every recent governor had been guilty in varying degree of the practice. Moreover, the impeachers had come to realize that there was danger in pushing the bribery investigation too far. They might inadvertently reveal that one or more of their own faction had accepted some kind of favor from Huey. They were also having sobering thoughts about opening up the matter of Huey's alleged influence over the judiciary. Such a line of inquiry could possibly embarrass some judges and besmirch the whole judicial branch. Hastily the house adopted a resolution offered by Cecil Morgan affirming that all the judges if summoned would swear that they had never been influenced by the governor.[9]

The inquisitors turned to a safer charge that promised to be more rewarding: Huey's alleged mishandling of state funds to entertain the national conference of governors in New Orleans in 1928. The coming of the conference to the Crescent City had stirred the pride of Louisianians, who felt the state must entertain the distinguished visitors properly. This view made sense to Huey, and he asked the Board of Liquidation for authority to borrow six thousand dollars to fete the governors. The authority was granted, the conference duly met and was a great success, and natives glowed at the compliments paid to the state by the visitors. But the impeachers had heard stories about the expenditure of the state money that aroused their suspicions. Rumors said that in no state office was there an accounting of how the money had been spent. Perhaps all of it had not been expended on the conference. Maybe Huey had appropri-

[8] Ibid., 107–9, 111, 120–1, 124–7, 165–6.
[9] Ibid., 149–50.

ated part of it for himself. The impeachers decided to sniff up this likely trail, and they summoned as witnesses a battery of state officials and New Orleans hotel functionaries.

They elicited certain facts with no difficulty. When the six thousand dollars came from the banks, it had been deposited in the state treasurer's account in a Baton Rouge bank. Shortly Miss Grosjean appeared with a check signed by the governor and asked for the sum in cash, in twenty-dollar bills, and departed. From this point on the interrogators ran into a stone wall of secrecy. They could not discover what had happened to Miss Grosjean's bills. The conference had been held in the Roosevelt Hotel, and the hotel's auditor volunteered that the state had paid the hotel thirty-five hundred dollars, in cash, for its expenses in connection with the meeting. He knew of no other expenditures, and apparently no one else knew of any. What then had been done with the remaining twenty-five hundred dollars? The impeachers were determined to find out, and they summoned a man who should know, Seymour Weiss, associate manager of the Roosevelt and a rapidly raising power in the Long organization.[1]

Weiss had been born in Abbeville, a small town in southwestern Louisiana, the son of a Jewish merchant. His father evidently had been very poor, for the boy's formal education ended after the third grade. On reaching young manhood, Weiss moved to the Alexandria area and worked in various lowly occupations. In 1925 he went to New Orleans and took a job as clerk in a shoe store for twenty-five dollars a week. From this humble place he transferred to the Roosevelt Hotel, where he became manager of the barber shop. Thereafter his rise was rapid. He became press agent and assistant manager of the hotel in 1927 and associate director in the following year. A few years later he would become general manager, president, and principal owner. There was good reason for his ascent. He was extremely intelligent, and he had a definite "presence" that was an asset in a hotelman. Of above-average height, he had a slender build and an erect bearing. He had acquired elegant manners, and he dressed in the latest and most expensive style. He liked to be surrounded by luxury: in his office the rugs were usually thick and the cigar lighters unusually large. He first met Huey in 1928 in the governorship race, when Huey established his personal headquarters in the hotel. "I learned to love and admire him," Weiss recalled. He was understating his feelings. He worshipped Huey. Huey,

[1] Ibid., 154, 156, 157–8, 168, 185.

in turn, appreciated Weiss's loyalty and intelligence and his obvious ability for organization. Weiss became one of Huey's most trusted advisers, the receiver of all moneys paid into the Long political fund. The friendship between him and Huey never wavered.[2]

When Weiss appeared on the stand, he was polite, bland—and uncommunicative. He readily volunteered that the total expenses of the conference had run up to sixty-two hundred dollars. The hotel bill had been thirty-five hundred, and Huey had paid him this sum in cash. Huey had asked what other expenses had been incurred and had paid all the other bills, also in cash. The impeachers demanded an account of these remaining expenses. Mr. Weiss could not say for certain. There had been various forms of "entertainments" over a period of four or five days, and they had been quite costly. He could not divulge the nature of the entertainments. He had simply followed the governor's instructions to do anything for the visitors that "they wanted me to do for them." The wrath of the anti-Longs mounted as they heard Weiss again and again refuse to answer their questions. "There is an insect here from New Orleans," old Judge Dupre sputtered. "He is a contemptible specimen of manhood, who has set himself up here as a smoke screen to protect the governor." Weiss was indeed protecting the governor, and the visiting governors as well. Most of the unaccounted money had been spent to buy illegal liquor for the executives and also to furnish other diversions for which New Orleans was famous. Huey could hardly admit that state money had been used for such purposes, and the governors did not want it known that they had been, in Weiss's later words, "on a big drunken spree." The legislators who were probing so hard for evidence of fraud must have known that the money had gone for liquor. The carryings-on at the conference were public knowledge.[3]

Somewhat baffled by the intricacies of Long financing but convinced that they had got hold of a good issue, the impeachers turned to allied charges. In the 1928 session Huey had asked the legislature to provide him with an automobile. The conservatives had succeeded in defeating the request. To some of them Huey said smilingly: "You damn suckers wouldn't give me $10,000 for a car but

[2] Article on Weiss, in *Town Talk*, a hotel trade magazine, December 15, 1963; article by David Zinman, in Baton Rouge *Morning Advocate*, August 5, 1963; confidential communications; New Orleans *Times-Picayune*, December 15, 1934; article by Clark Newlon, in Seattle *Star*, January, 1935; Seymour Weiss.

[3] *Impeachment Proceedings*, I, 188, 195; Shreveport *Journal*, April 17, 1929; Seymour Weiss.

I will get the car just the same." Soon after this he was seen driving a sporty red Buick. On one of the doors was painted: "Not State Property, Executive Department." He negotiated for the purchase of the car the day after Miss Grosjean had cashed the six-thousand-dollar check for the governors' conference, and the coincidence had aroused suspicion in Cecil Morgan. Morgan was sure Huey had purchased the car with state money, and he conducted a private investigation that convinced him he was correct. Now he insisted that officials of the Buick agency in Baton Rouge be called to testify. They described in detail their dealings with Huey. He had traded in a car of his own and had paid thirteen hundred for the Buick. How, Morgan purred, did he pay the sum? In cash, answered an agency representative. And in what form was the cash? In twenty-dollar bills. The impeachers burst into smiles. They felt that they had proved their charge. Possibly Huey had done just what they were accusing him of. But the lawyers among them must have known that the unsupported circumstantial evidence they were relying on would have had little weight in any court.[4]

Elated now, the impeachers delved into other Long expenditures. They had uncovered in their private investigations stories that Huey had played fast and loose with money allotted to him by the legislature to maintain his office, but they needed official substantiation to make a charge. To get it they summoned before the house W. N. McFarland, the supervisor of public accounts. How, they asked him, had the governor administered the various funds at his disposal? McFarland unfolded a fascinating but, to the impeachers, a frustrating analysis. Huey had originally kept three separate bank accounts, he explained. One was for office expenses, one was for traveling expenses, and one was for mansion expenses. But how had he expended the funds? the inquisitors pressed. That was hard to say, McFarland answered. Within a few months after assuming office the governor had combined the three accounts into one. One could not say with certainty what fund a particular check was drawn on, McFarland complained. But he could identify some payments that were made before the accounts were combined. Huey had purchased a law library from a publishing company and had written a check for eleven hundred dollars on the mansion fund. He had also drawn traveling money from the same fund and had paid Joe Messina two hundred dollars from it. Again the impeachers felt they had scored. And so they had, although not quite as

[4] *Impeachment Proceedings*, I, 170–2, 180.

heavily as they thought. Huey had what he considered good reasons for raiding the mansion fund. Since the mansion could not be efficiently maintained, it was ridiculous to throw away money on it. Furthermore, he was going to build a new mansion. His defense was plausible, but it rested on shaky moral and legal grounds. He had no right to spend funds granted for one purpose for another one. To characterize his action in the mildest terms possible, he showed a reckless disdain for sound financial procedures. His purchase of the law books was inexcusable and, although the sum was small, was close to being an impeachable offense. Although he might plead that the governor needed a law library, he obviously regarded the books as his private possession. They were stored in a Highway Commission room until he could move them to his office.[5]

Spectator interest in the bribery and corruption charges was keen, and the crowds at these hearings were large and attentive. But the sessions that drew the largest throngs were those that exposed alleged acts of personal misconduct by Huey, and these were the sessions that produced the most vivid moments of the investigation. One avenue of inquiry in this area was especially inviting to the impeachers—the abusive and vulgar language Huey was supposed to have directed at citizens and officials in conversation. If they could prove this charge, they would damage Huey seriously, for Southerners, more than most Americans, expected their officials to behave with decorum. The impeachers had no difficulty in finding witnesses who could testify on this count; the state was rife with people who had been denounced by Huey. They summoned first a woman who had been a telephone operator at the Highway Commission office but had been discharged. She explained why she had lost her job. One day a call came from Shreveport for Chairman Allen. Soon after she connected Allen, Huey cut in on his phone. She confessed that she remained on the circuit to hear the conversation. Huey realized that she was there and barked at Allen to go out and "fire that blankety-blank woman." She volunteered that she had often heard Huey curse employees of the commission, but she primly refused to repeat his language. She did not reveal why she had eavesdropped on conversations, and she did not say, if she knew, that Huey had pegged her as a spy for the opposition.[6]

Hardly had she left the stand when a group of citizens from

[5] Ibid., 466–7, 470. After Huey's death his family sold his law library to the state. The fine collection is housed today in the capitol. The books he bought in 1928 form the nucleus of the collection.

[6] *Impeachment Proceedings*, I, 782–6, 790–1.

Caddo parish appeared. These were some of the men who had come to Baton Rouge in February to ask Huey for more consideration for Caddo in the awarding of roads and who had been told that if they expected anything, they would have to bow down low. They wanted to inform the legislature that the Kingfish had insulted and reviled them, and they went into detail as to what he had said. H. H. Huckaby, a prominent Caddo planter and merchant, said that the governor had denounced in violent terms his enemies in Shreveport, some of the town's most prominent men. Huckaby hesitated; he would like to be excused from repeating Huey's words, he said, because there were ladies in the audience. The impeachers leaned forward expectantly. The member conducting the examination stated that the witness must repeat the exact words—the legislature wanted the whole truth. Thus pressed, Huckaby reproduced Huey's diatribe, and it was dutifully printed in the official record of the impeachment: "There is that goddamned nigger loving Andrew Querbes; there is that goddamned Randall sonofabitch Moore, 'and he mentioned something concerning Mr. Sidney Herold—' and that goddamned shitass Ewing."

As Huckaby concluded, horrified gasps arose all over the chamber. Women in the gallery blushed, and the impeachers looked sick. They had gotten more than they bargained for and thereby hurt their cause. Huey might have uttered the terrible words, but he had said them in private. It was his enemies who had flaunted them before the public and in doing so had offended Southern standards of taste. The Longites sensed the reaction of the audience. They saw a chance to shut off further testimony on this line. Two of them jumped to their feet. Were Southern gentlemen going to permit this kind of language to be used in the presence of ladies? they demanded. The gentlemen of the legislature were not. Each member of the Caddo delegation who testified after Huckaby was told that he would be allowed simply to stipulate that the governor had said what Mr. Huckaby had said he said.[7]

Hopefully the impeachers turned to another alleged act of improper behavior by the governor—his participation in a wild party at a New Orleans night spot. Huey's presence at this affair had been revealed by Colonel Ewing when he and Huey were breaking, and the impeachers thought the story was worth pursuing. The principal witness was Alfred D. Danziger, a New Orleans hotelman. Danziger was a personal and political friend of Huey's, although he

---

[7] *Impeachment Proceedings*, I, 217–18, 222–3, 224, 226, 230; Harrison Jordan.

had opposed the governor's oil tax. He related that on a night in February he had invited Huey to a birthday party at the Jung Hotel. After the dinner he suggested that Huey go with him to a "studio" that he maintained in the French Quarter, where he sometimes had paid entertainers perform for his guests. On this night the entertainers consisted of a piano player and six girls. The girls did several dances, including a hula. One of the inquisitors asked to "what extent" the girls were clothed. Danziger seemed astonished that anyone should have to ask. "In the conventional or I should say unconventional costume that they ordinarily use," he explained. He recalled seeing Huey with a glass in his hand but did not think that the governor had more than one drink. He also remembered that one of the girls had tried to sit on Huey's lap but that he had pushed her away. The governor left after a half hour or so, Danziger concluded. His testimony did not please the impeachers. They had hoped for something intimate and scandalous, and they tried to get it from one of the entertainers, Helen Clifford. She had made an affidavit that Huey had acted indecently, but on the stand she was painfully cautious. She said that Huey had been "very frisky" that night. How had he been frisky? Well, he had danced by himself with a glass in his hand. He had wanted to dance with the girls. He had sat down by a guest and had admired and stroked her hair. He had pulled Miss Clifford on to his lap when she went over to sing to him, but she had left freely when she finished the song. Her story was not very convincing, and it was completely discredited when her husband, from whom she was separated, testified that she had been offered a job to make her affidavit. The impeachers had drawn a big blank.[8]

The last witness to testify was Battling Bozeman. By the logic of the impeachers' case he should have appeared first. He was the key figure of the investigation. After all, he had set the whole train of events in motion. He had revealed Huey's desire to have Sanders assassinated, and, presumably, it was because of his act that the legislature had remained in session and instigated impeachment. But now he was an ignored and a pathetic figure. The impeachers no longer took his story seriously, if indeed they ever had. They had to allow him to repeat it, but they obviously wanted to be done with him. He stressed that he had been without employment since Huey fired him and said with transparent purpose that he would like to get some work. He was asked what he was doing now. "At this particular time whatever work I am doing I do it around the house," he said. "I may fix up a little flower bed for my wife or something like that. I planted a few butterbeans, but they did not come up." The Battler wanted to be sure that the legislators were fully informed as to his activities. "I have not planted any potatoes yet, though," he added.[9]

Out of the mass of testimony, the impeachers selected eight charges to bring against the governor. Of the original nineteen indictments, some were dropped because of insufficient evidence. Others, such as the one that Huey had used the militia to pillage private property, were defeated when brought to a vote. The eight charges that stood were as follows: (1) Huey had attempted to intimidate Manship; (2) he had tried to bribe members of the legislature; (3) he had taken money appropriated for the governors' conference and had not accounted for it (this included the alleged purchase of an automobile with state money); (4) he had illegally interfered with the state colony and training school and had removed one of its officials; (5) he had spent money appropriated for the repair and maintenance of the mansion for other purposes; (6) he had purchased with state money a private law library; (7) he had permitted a construction company to build defective culverts and had paid the company for the work; (8) he had—this was a catch-all —forced appointees to sign undated resignations, insulted citizens, discharged a college president, appointed a corrupt parole officer, and demonstrated that he was incompetent and temperamentally unfit for his office.[1]

The House processed the charges slowly. The Manship charge was presented to the senate on April 6. The second charge was presented on April 11, the next five on April 25, and the eighth on April 26. The impeachers realized that they were courting danger by not moving faster. They were giving Huey time to organize his resistance, and they might bore the public if they spun the investigation out too long. They were able to process the Manship charge quickly because few witnesses were involved. Moreover, they made a special effort to put it before the senate by April 6, the day named in Huey's call as the terminal date of the session. They knew that the Longites were saying the legislature could not act on anything after that day. They did not accept this argument, contending that no call could limit the constitutional power to impeach, but still they thought it wise to meet the terminal date in part. If a charge

[9] Ibid., 814.
[1] Ibid., 274, 294, 356–9, 732–6, 763–72, 854, 871.

was presented to the senate on that date and if the upper chamber resolved itself into a court, then the Long objection would be repudiated.

On April 6 one of the impeachment leaders, George Perrault, from St. Landry parish, moved that the house vote to impeach the governor on the Manship charge. "Such a character should, and you know it in your heart of hearts, be eliminated by the proper legal action of any further right to continue to cast disgrace on our fair State," Perrault thundered. The Longites sprang into immediate action. Allen Ellender, now one of Huey's most trusted leaders, conceded that the governor's threat to Manship might constitute blackmail. But Huey had uttered the threat as a private individual and not in his capacity as governor, Ellender argued, and therefore was not guilty of committing an official and impeachable crime. His words stirred the antis to angry scorn. How could the governor act unofficially in political matters? they demanded. Judge Dupre, who delighted in characterizing Huey as the epitome of vulgarity, dismissed the Long argument as "heifer manure." Suddenly a Long representative arose and requested the privilege of making a formal address. He was George Delesdernier, a cadaverous, eccentric man from Plaquemines parish. He proceeded to deliver what has been called the most ridiculous speech in the history of Louisiana.

"Bear with me in patience while I say what I have to say," Delesdernier began. "The title of my speech will be 'The Cross of Wood and with Shackles of Paper.' Nineteen hundred years ago there was a cross of wood erected and a Divine Creature of that time was nailed to the cross." This Divine Creature had been relieving the poor and afflicted, the speaker continued, and he had aroused the opposition of the mighty. "He was surrounded by a committee of twelve. There was a traitor in the ranks. Charges were referred before a judge . . . and they took this Divine Creature and crucified him. . . . Today we have a creature among us who is relieving the sick and the destitute. . . ." At this point the conservatives, who had listened with amusement, realized the drift of Delesdernier's remarks. There were shouted objections that he was being sacrilegious. "We don't want him to compare the governor with Jesus Christ," one member cried. "I did not mention Jesus Christ," Delesdernier said reasonably. The presiding officer cautioned him to confine his remarks to the subject at hand. "Today there is a creature relieving the sick and the blind, aiding the lame and the halt, and trying to drive illiteracy from the state," the orator resumed, "and he is being shackled with paper to a cross. The cross was manufactured—one of the uprights—out of a saintly piece; the horizontal part of the cross is from the beams of the moon; and this divine creature is being shackled—I mean this creature of today—is being shackled with paper." Again there were loud and angry objections. Delesdernier declaimed: "Take my life but give me my character," and fell onto the floor in a faint. He lay there until the vote was taken and then was carried away by friends.[2]

The house voted to impeach on the Manship charge by a margin of eighteen votes—fifty-eight votes for and forty votes against. But in voting one charge, the house also had impeached Huey of various crimes and misdemeanors, of which one, the Manship charge, was exhibited. Other articles would be offered in due course. The Manship count simply put the general process in motion. Then the house elected nine of its members to serve as managers of the case to be presented to the senate. Members of the Dynamite Squad dominated the board of managers, and one of them, Mason Spencer, was chosen as its chairman. The managers repaired immediately to the senate to announce the house's action. Spencer solemnly proclaimed: "The House of Representatives, acting for themselves and in the name of all the people of Louisiana, have ordered the impeachment of Huey P. Long, Governor of Louisiana." In the name of the house, he demanded that the said Huey P. Long "be put to answer the charges" that would be filed against him. The managers then withdrew to permit the senate to organize itself to consider the charges.[3]

The process of impeachment in Louisiana followed the same practice as that in other states. If the lower house preferred charges against an official, the upper chamber had to resolve itself into a court to try the charges. The chief justice presided over the trial sessions. If the senate voted by a two-thirds majority that one, or more, of the charges was proved, the guilty official would be removed.

The senate transformed itself into a court within a matter of minutes after the managers withdrew. Although it would obviously have to sit after April 6, not a single Long senator raised an objec-

[2] Ibid., 274, 278–9, 281, 291–2.

[3] Ibid., I, 294, 296; II, 99–101. The vote on the first charge was an accurate indicator of the strength of the Long and anti-Long factions. The division on the remaining charges was roughly the same. On most of the charges, the votes for impeachment totaled in the high fifties. On a few, they went down to fifty. The votes against impeachment averaged forty, occasionally rose a little above that figure, and on occasion dipped to thirty-nine.

tion to the legality of the procedure. The senate then named a committee to escort Chief Justice O'Niell to the chair. The peppery jurist, expecting that his presence would be required, had come up from New Orleans and had gone into immediate conference with the managers in Cyr's office. Upon arriving in the chamber, O'Niell took the oath as presiding officer. He next administered the oath to the thirty-six senators, or judges, then present. Now that the senate had become a court, the managers returned. Spencer presented the Manship charge, whereupon the managers withdrew again. The senate appointed a committee to draw up rules of procedure to govern its conduct during the trial. Then it adjourned until April 11. By an odd coincidence, this would be the date on which the managers would present the second charge. The impeachers in the two chambers were obviously working in close concert.[4]

That night Chief Justice O'Niell reeled up to a member of the Dynamite Squad in the lobby of the Heidelberg Hotel. He was, in the words of the conservative leader, "staggering drunk." He complained that people were saying he was prejudiced against Huey and should therefore recuse himself from presiding over the senate. He could not understand why they were talking so. "Don't they think that I'll give the thieving sonofabitch a fair trial?" he asked.[5]

[4] Ibid., II, 101–2, 105; confidential communication, as to O'Niell's meeting with the managers.
[5] Confidential communication. Similar words have been attributed to other judges in similar situations. But another witness independently related the above story.

# CHAPTER 15

# *The Round Robins*

T HE ATMOSPHERE IN THE HOUSE when impeachment was voted crackled with tension. Members of both factions were edgy, suspicious of trickery, and belligerent. J. E. McClanahan, a Long leader, became involved in an altercation with an anti seated near him. McClanahan shouted: "I'm tired of being insulted by that rat." The anti yelled: "I want to change my seat. I don't want to sit beside him."[1]

The tension had built up day by day. The formal voting of impeachment had the effect of a declaration of war, and the legislature came to resemble a battlefield. Men armed themselves and warily eyed acquaintances and even friends of long standing who were now in the opposing faction. One Dynamite Squad leader recalled that he sat at his desk in the house for weeks with a pistol on his hip. The Dynamiters believed that Huey had called in a number of gunmen to intimidate them, and they were extremely cautious, always eating together and never going out singly at night. There is no evidence that Huey had employed any thugs, but the bodyguards he had previously collected were always with him, obviously armed and eager. One night a legislative employee who was staying at a boardinghouse saw a guard open a suitcase, take out two pistols, put them in his coat pockets, and calmly walk out. Probably most of those men in either faction who carried arms were thinking defensively—they were preparing for an attack if one came. But there were some who advocated violence and who, presumably, were ready to resort to it. Thus, a New Orleans businessman who was

[1] Shreveport *Journal*, April 7, 1929.

fiercely conservative issued a circular discussing the best method of eliminating Huey. Hanging, shooting, or knifing would be too good for the "cowardly coyote," the writer decided. He concluded: "Perhaps it were best to nail him by the ears to a blackjack post, strip him stark naked, and have him thoroughly horsewhipped by a blue-gum nigger."[2]

Inevitably these pent-up emotions had to erupt in some kind of clash. The encounter, when it came, was a stellar attraction. One night in a capitol corridor Harney Bogan, a Dynamiter, met Bob Maestri, and the two fell into conversation. While they were talking, Earl Long came by. Earl was enraged when he saw Maestri in company with this enemy of his brother's. Why, he asked Maestri, was he talking to that sonofabitch? Bogan thereupon hit Earl, and they clinched and rolled on the floor. Earl fought, as he always did, with savage abandon. According to Bogan, Earl bit him on several parts of the face and neck, scratched him, and jabbed a finger in his mouth and tried to tear his cheek off. Bogan was so worried about his wounds that he took an injection of "antilockjaw" serum. According to Earl, Bogan's lip had accidentally found its way between his teeth, and he had naturally taken advantage of an opportunity. But he did brag after the fight: "I just tore Harney Bogan to pieces."[3]

Huey was in his hotel room when the fight occurred. Someone came in and told him about it. He jumped from his chair with an expectant expression. "I bet Earl bit him, didn't he?" he asked. "Earl always bites." Impulsively he suggested to one of his senatorial followers, William C. Boone, that they walk to the capitol, only a block away: he had to go to the scene and be part of the excitement. As he and Boone neared the gates to the capitol grounds, they saw a crowd of several hundred men milling in front of the building. It was plainly an angry crowd, and it became angrier when it saw Huey. These were anti-Long men who had heard about the fight and who were enraged; they were capable of meting revenge to any Long. Boone drew a penknife from his pocket and covered it with a handkerchief to give the impression that he had a larger weapon. He kept saying: "Governor, let's get out of here," and finally drew Huey away. Boone was convinced that many of the men in the yard carried pistols and that Huey would have been shot if they had remained.[4]

[2] George J. Ginsberg; Cecil Morgan; John Nuckolls; document signed by Oscar A. Whilden, April 23, 1929, in Huey P. Long Papers, Duke University Library, Durham, North Carolina, hereafter cited as Long Papers, Duke.

[3] New Orleans *Times-Picayune*, April 27, 1929; William C. Boone.

[4] Mason Spencer; William C. Boone.

The drama of the impeachment riveted public attention to the legislative halls—to the debates, the hearings, the trial. It was natural and right that this should be so. This was, after all, a spectacle that a democratic people should follow and one in which they could take pride. One of the fundamental processes of democracy was on exhibit—the right of a legislature to remove an executive whom it judged to be tyrannical or evil. The representatives of the people in the lower house had impeached this executive of high crimes, and the representatives of the people in the upper house were going to weigh the evidence and arrive at a judicious opinion. So it seemed on the surface and so in part it was. But it was also something else. Under the surface men and forces were at work that the public never saw. Almost from the moment impeachment was decided on, both sides entered into a struggle to control votes in the legislature. At first the effort was centered in the house, where the contending factions strove to secure votes for or against impeachment. After impeachment was voted, the battle shifted to the senate. Here it became more intense, for now the stakes were higher—the contest was for votes that would determine whether the governor was convicted or acquitted. Both sides employed methods of persuasion that had nothing to do with evidence or reason and that would shock theoretical students of democracy.

Huey charged during the impeachment that his opponents were trying to buy votes to convict him. The Standard Oil Company alone had brought enough money into Baton Rouge "to burn a wet mule," he said. He repeated the charge many times later, elaborating on it and supplying supporting detail. Nine members of the senate were offered from a thousand dollars up to vote for his conviction. Three senators were offered $250,000 for their votes as a package. Some senators were told that they could have anything: "the sky was the limit." Huey did not identify specifically who made the various offers. He rang in the names of the Standard and the Watson–Williams bridge operators, but usually he referred simply to "the opposition."[5]

His charges have received scant attention in the works about him or the impeachment. Most writers do not mention them, and those who do dismiss them as fantastic or the vaporings of a politician. Practically all of the commentators assume, however, that Huey used various forms of pressure to influence legislators. This is a familiar

[5] Carleton Beals: *The Story of Huey P. Long* (Philadelphia, 1935), pp. 141–2; *Overton Hearing*, I, 62; Huey P. Long: *Every Man a King* (New Orleans, 1933), p. 166; *Congressional Record*, 72 Cong. 2 Sess., p 2812.

phenomenon in most writing about American political history, and it has often resulted in obscuring the truth. It obviously demands explanation, as applied to Huey or to other leaders like him. One reason for the rejection of his charges, one may surmise, was that they were so enormous. What he said was simply incredible: no one would have spent such huge sums to buy votes. But the real reason for the repudiation went deeper. Those who write about Long, like other chroniclers of the American scene, have been unknowing victims of the genteel tradition. They saw that Huey's opponents were gentlemen, and from their observation they predicated a mode of conduct. Cultured, gentle people do not do evil or corrupt things— therefore the Louisiana conservatives could not have done anything immoral. Huey, on the other hand, was not a gentleman. He was a crass popular leader who had bad table manners. A politician of his type might have some sound ideas, but he would be careless in the methods he selected to achieve his goals. Ergo, the stories told by anti-Longs that Huey had improperly influenced legislators must be true.

Actually, as the evidence makes clear beyond a doubt, both sides engaged in some practices that violated the code of pure conduct as prescribed in the civics books. The antis did their share of influencing. "We had to swap and trade to get enough votes for each charge," Mason Spencer conceded. He and other surviving antis would not detail what swapping they did, possibly out of a reluctance to name names, more probably because the incidents had become hazy in their memories. But some episodes were recalled, sharp in their focus on the behind-the-scenes maneuvering and revealing in the way they depict the realities of politics. One concerned the handicap that the impeachers carried in Paul Cyr, who would succeed to the governorship if Huey was convicted. The antagonism and distrust that he engendered was so strong that it drove wavering legislators into the Long camp. "We could have traded as good as Huey if we had had a man who was trusted," Spencer said. "We'd bring delegations to see Cyr and they'd walk out. Take my word, Cyr saved Huey Long. I told three senators we'd impeach Cyr if they'd vote to impeach Huey." The antis could hardly have dared to impeach Cyr. But they could have lifted the onus of him somewhat if they could have arranged to have a good man available to succeed him if anything should happen to him during his incumbency or as a candidate in 1932. To that end, they approached Senator Philip H. Gilbert, the president of the upper chamber and one of its most well-liked and respected members. If Gilbert came over to their side, several other senators were certain to follow him. They offered Gilbert any reward he might want, including the governorship. Gilbert had a strong measure of idealism in him, and he was stubbornly loyal to Huey. He turned the offer down. "We were shaken when Phil Gilbert left us," Spencer confessed.[6]

An interesting and unusual example of conservative pressure was related by Lester Lautenschlaeger, the representative who had been designated to notify the senate of the house adjournment on Bloody Monday. Lautenschlaeger had been elected with the support of John Sullivan and was originally listed as a Long supporter. After Sullivan and Huey broke, "Lesty" followed a somewhat independent course. He liked Huey personally and voted for some administration measures but opposed others. He had connections in the upper social reaches of New Orleans and was the backfield coach of the football team at his alma mater, Tulane University, where he had previously starred. One morning at four o'clock he heard a knock on the door of his hotel room. He got out of bed and admitted Huey. "Lester," Huey said, "I haven't any time. My nose is bloody, and I have to have yes or no in a hurry. If you vote with me, anything you want the rest of your life in politics, if I win, you can have." Lester said that he could not promise to vote yes or no on any charge; he would have to hear the evidence. Huey said: "Shake, no hard feelings, but we are finished politically," and departed. Later in the morning Lautenschlaeger went down to the hotel lobby. He encountered Esmond Phelps, aristocratic and wealthy New Orleans lawyer and chairman of the Tulane board of administrators. "Lester," said Phelps, "I haven't got much time. I want to know yes or no now. Your friends at Tulane are counting on you to be against Huey on all these charges."

Lester replied essentially as he had to Huey. Phelps snapped: "Unless we can count on you now your position at Tulane is at stake." About an hour later Lautenschlaeger received a telegram from the athletic director at Tulane terminating his coaching services. Only the threat of the other coaches to resign caused him to be reinstated.[7]

There is also evidence to support Huey's charge that money was offered for votes to convict him. Surviving members of the Dynamite Squad deny emphatically that any of them proffered money, and their evident sincerity carries conviction. They also say that they know of no money that was handed out by anyone, and they prob-

[6] Mason Spencer; Hermann B. Deutsch; Long: *Every Man a King*, p. 168.
[7] Lester Lautenschlaeger.

ably were not aware that any was. But it is obvious that they were not fully informed as to what was going on. Some people on the side of impeachment definitely tried to buy votes. The number of legislators who were approached or the number who succumbed cannot be accurately established. One source estimated that there were twenty legislators who could have been purchased by either side. "Until impeachment I never knew how low humanity could sink," he said. Neither is it possible to identify the individuals who attempted the buying. Surviving legislators and politicians have been reluctant to discuss the subject, even though they acknowledge that money was passed around. Those who have talked most freely have been Long men, and although they have a motive for besmirching the opposition, they have preserved a certain discretion in their revelations, as if embarrassed to be too frank. Yes, money was offered for votes, "a lot of it." Who did the offering? Here the answers become vague: "they," "the other side." One former legislator did say that he saw several Old Regular leaders in a hotel room in Baton Rouge "with rolls of money" that they offered for votes. A Baton Rouge businessman stated that he was asked to contribute to a fund to "get" Huey. The fund was administered and paid out by prominent conservatives. This man put up a thousand dollars, and he understood that the total amount collected ran well into five figures.[8]

Two former legislators related fairly specific examples of attempted buying. Representative Joe Fisher of Jefferson parish described the efforts of the antis to secure Senator Jules Fisher, Joe's uncle, who was a Longite. They offered him patronage and favors for Jefferson, "power unheard of." Jules wavered but remained firm when Joe threatened to rally the trappers and fishermen against him if he deserted Huey. Then the antis tried to get Jules through Joe. They offered Joe forty thousand dollars, in thousand-dollar bills, to influence his uncle. Joe laughed at them. Senator William C. Boone affirmed that an anti leader in his parish offered him twenty-five thousand dollars to vote for Huey's conviction. He refused it. Later the man returned and upped the amount to fifty thousand dollars. "I said I'd kill him if he did it again," Boone stated. Boone believed that this individual was acting for the impeachers in the house.[9]

[8] J. Y. Sanders, Jr.; George J. Ginsberg; Mason Spencer; Cecil Morgan; Leander H. Perez; Joseph Fisher; confidential communications.

[9] Joseph Fisher; Fisher, quoted in Baton Rouge *State-Times*, April 23, 1935; William C. Boone.

While the impeachers were plying their arts, Huey was exerting his own forms of pressure. He did not have much money to offer for votes, and apparently he paid out money on only one occasion. But he could employ various political weapons. One that was particularly effective with doubtful legislators was to demonstrate to them that he had enormous support in their home districts. He called forth this support by various methods. One day a man who had just started a typewriter agency in Baton Rouge received a phone call from Earl Long. Earl asked him how many machines he had available. The owner said that he thought he could assemble thirty-five. Earl ordered the man to take them immediately to the governor's office. The machines were duly delivered, and magically a person appeared to operate each one. Huey also appeared. He strode up and down the room dictating telegrams to be sent to persons all over the state, to hundreds of people. The recipients were asked to wire or write their senator and representative to vote against impeachment. The agency man was impressed with the speed and efficiency with which the job was conducted. And he was astounded that Huey had no list of names with him. The governor carried the names and addresses in his prodigious memory.[1]

Huey did not stop at directing distant people to write or wire their legislators. Sometimes he ordered a local leader to bring a large delegation to the legislature. "Bring the boys to Baton Rouge," a typical telegram from him would read. The "boys" would call on their legislators and parade through the legislative halls cheering for the Kingfish. But more frequently Huey relied on the local leaders themselves to apply pressure to particular solons. Thus he asked two leaders from a southwestern district represented by two senators to come to Baton Rouge. He feared that he was losing the senators, Henry D. Larcade and Homer Barousse, and he wanted his leaders to talk to them. "Henry wasn't right at first," related one of the leaders, a sheriff. "Canan [the other leader] had to nurse him along. They almost pulled Henry away. You could always put the finger on Barousse because he stayed with the ins." One sheriff of a southern parish made periodic trips to Baton Rouge to check on the conduct of his legislators. "The people down there are pretty solid for Long," he warned a representative. "You better stick with him."[2]

When Huey brought popular pressure to bear on legislators, he was employing a traditional technique that could not be justly

---

[1] L. P. Bahan.
[2] Rollo C. Lawrence; W. V. Larcade; Sidney Marchand.

criticized. But he resorted to other techniques that were, like those of the impeachers, open to question. By tendering material rewards to a number of legislators, he tried to secure their votes. A legislator would be told that if he voted right he would receive, say, a surfaced road in his parish. Huey also offered jobs. A senator recounted a conversation that was revealing of Huey's approach. The governor first remarked that the impeachment was a crime. Then, without asking for a commitment he said: "I guess you know I am holding that registrars of voters position open down in New Orleans, and I am satisfied that you can have it." He tried to get to some senators by promising to support them for higher elective offices. Senator Whittington related an effort, a vain one, that was made to sway him. One night Earl Long and O. K. Allen came to his hotel room at eleven o'clock and stayed until four in the morning. They were authorized to offer large inducements. "I could have anything but the governorship," Whittington stated: "Congressman, state treasurer, or the handling of the state insurance, which would have meant $50,000 a year."[3]

In one "influence" case, the most celebrated one of the impeachment, Huey and his opponents came into direct competition—they were trying to secure the same man. The episode illustrates as nothing else does the nature of the undercover struggle for votes. Huey wrote a discreet and not completely frank account of it in his autobiography. His version relates that while he was on a speaking tour in his own defense, he noticed a newspaper statement by a senator committed to him. The senator had declared that he was not irrevocably bound to the governor. Huey next heard that the senator was going to make, or had made, a surreptitious trip to Shreveport. Immediately Huey went to the senator's home and demanded an explanation. The senator evasively said that he was going to Shreveport to see a sick friend. The friend happened to be a wealthy man who was a deadly enemy of Huey's. Huey then said that he was having a meeting in Shreveport on the following night and the senator could join him on the platform. But on that night the senator did not appear. Huey, his suspicions now aroused, charged at the meeting that certain men in Shreveport were calling senators to the town to pay them to vote for his conviction. Huey then went to Monroe to speak, and here he heard that the senator had gone to Baton Rouge. He decided that he should get to the capital himself and fast. After his speech he drove all night and entered Baton

3 Robert Brothers; Harry Gilbert; *Impeachment Proceedings,* I, 688–9; J. Y. Sanders, Jr.; Donald Labbe; V. V. Whittington.

HUEY LONG / 392

Rouge at dawn. He went to the senator's hotel room and demanded admittance. The senator finally explained the mystery. He had been negotiating with people on the impeaching side for money in return for his vote. In order to draw these people on, he had pretended to break with Huey. He was going to bring the money to Huey and thus expose the corrupt nature of the impeachers. In fact, he confided, he was to go to New Orleans that day to collect his reward from "Big John"—this was Sullivan. Huey told him to go. But first Huey prepared an affidavit for him to sign stating the facts he had just related. When the senator returned with the money, the affidavit would be made public. The senator came back that night, but empty-handed. Somebody had tipped Sullivan off about his meeting with Huey, and Sullivan had refused to pay.[4]

Huey did not name the senator. But he is easily identified as James L. Anderson, of a north-central district. Anderson, in addition to being a senator, was a Baptist minister and was usually called "Preacher" or "Preach." He was supposed to have an immoderate appetite for strong whisky and loose women. Huey's account of Anderson's eccentric activities was, up to a point, accurate. Anderson did criticize Huey publicly, but it was because the governor had removed an official over his wishes. Anderson did refuse to speak at the Shreveport meeting. But at that meeting Huey was more specific than he said he was in his book. He charged that a wealthy lumberman-banker had been trying to get *a* senator to come to Shreveport to receive his payoff. Everybody knew that he was referring to Anderson. In fact, the senator hotly and publicly denied the accusation and repeated the excuse about a sick friend.[5] This was an excuse and nothing else. Anderson was undoubtedly engaged in some kind of negotiations with both sides. He was not acting as a come-on for Huey. Huey's account of "Preach" Anderson acting as a smooth espionage agent defies belief. Huey concocted his story to cover up for Anderson, who eventually decided to remain a Long supporter and to cover up some things he did himself.

Long associates related a fuller and franker story. They were confused as to some details and occasionally vague about the chronological sequence of events, but they were specific about the main facts, and their recollections combine to make a connected and credible narrative. They agree that at some stage in the episode—they are not sure when—Huey "framed" Anderson. They hasten to

[4] Long: *Every Man a King*, pp. 163–6.
[5] Shreveport *Journal*, April 20, 1929; New Orleans *Times-Picayune*, April 23 and 24, 1929.

explain their use of frame: Huey employed a necessary and legitimate political device. Anderson had been committed to Huey, but he had gone over, or was about to go over, to the opposition. He had been "bought," the Long people think. Huey had to bring him back and bind him to stay, and he could not be choosy about the method. The method decided on was drastic and effective. One night the sensual senator received an invitation from a woman, supposedly one of uncertain virtue, to have a drink in her room in a Baton Rouge hotel. He went. After he entered, the door was locked from the outside. A Negro porter gave the key to some Long men who shortly opened the door and burst in on the pair. One Long leader said to Huey: "You ought to pension that little nigger." The episode probably took place before Anderson went to Shreveport to see his "sick friend." He had been brought back, but he was capable of leaving again.

When Huey found that Anderson had been to Shreveport, the Long people continue, he had the senator brought to him. A violent scene ensued, with the two principals almost coming to blows. Huey cursed Anderson roundly and accused him of treachery. Anderson denied the charge. But he intimated that he could have something from the other side if he wanted it and indicated that he thought Huey should promise him something. He also mentioned that he owed his friend in Shreveport some money. Huey handed him enough cash to repay the loan—it may have been as little as a thousand dollars—and said he was saving a good job in the Highway Commission for Anderson. It was after this interview, presumably, that Anderson agreed to make the effort to entice somebody on the other side to pay him money. Every Long leader who recounted the affair justified Huey's conduct. "They bought him," one said, "and we bought him back." Another said that the struggle to control legislators was like a war: "I don't believe in killing people, but in war I think you have to kill people."[6]

While the scramble for votes was going on, the house was grinding slowly through the process of examining witnesses. During this interim the senate had little to do. It met infrequently and briefly, to receive a charge from the house, when one came through, or to transact routine business. But at one of these apparently unimportant sessions an issue was raised that would in due course determine the outcome of the impeachment. On April 15 Philip Gilbert offered a resolution stating that no charges presented to the house after

6 Confidential communication; William C. Boone; Mason Spencer; Trent James; Otho Long; Orlean Thomas; O. B. Thompson; John B. Fournet.

midnight on April 6 should be received, considered, or acted on. Gilbert explained why he was making his motion. The governor had stipulated in his call that the session was to end on that date. Therefore, when the house convened after April 6, it was a spontaneous body; it had no official standing and could take no official action. The only charge the senate could receive was the Manship charge. Gilbert was modifying somewhat an objection raised earlier, but not prominently, by the Longites—that the house could not act on impeachment because that subject was not included in the call and the house could not sit after April 6. The resolution admitted, without so stating, that the house could impeach, but only if it processed a charge within the time limit fixed in the call. When put to a vote, the resolution was defeated by a margin of twenty-three to fifteen. Nobody on the impeaching side attached much significance to Gilbert's move. It was merely another delaying maneuver on the part of the Longites, and it had failed. But the vote should have galvanized the impeachers into instant and furious action. Fifteen senators had declared that they would consider any charge brought after April 6 to be illegal. The total membership of the senate was thirty-nine. To convict Huey, twenty-six votes, two thirds of the total, would be required. A vote of fourteen for acquittal would save him. The vote on the Gilbert resolution revealed that Huey had one more senator than he needed.[7]

Two days later Huey held a press conference. He announced that he was going to embark on a speaking tour in his defense. He would cover all parts of the state, he said, and in some cities he would speak over the radio. He seemed gay and assured. In the course of the meeting he let slip the reason for his mood. "I have fourteen senators who will stand by me regardless," he said. He did not reveal, then, why he had one less than the number who had supported the Gilbert resolution.[8]

Huey found himself greeted by large and responsive crowds wherever he spoke. The masses, it was obvious, did not approve of

[7] *Impeachment Proceedings*, II, 120–1. The issues of whether the legislature could impeach if impeachment had not been included in the call or whether it could legally act after April 6 excited much legal comment at the time and later. The best opinion is that impeachment is a constitutional process, not a legislative process, and that the power of impeachment cannot be limited. Therefore, the legislature could consider impeachment and could continue its action after April 6. See Newman F. Baker: "Some Legal Aspects of Impeachment in Louisiana," *Southwestern Political and Social Science Quarterly*, X (1930), 359–87.

[8] Baton Rouge *State-Times*, April 18 and 19, 1929.

the goings on in Baton Rouge. They did not believe the charges that had been brought against their leader, and they came out in droves to demonstrate to him their trust. Huey sensed the friendship of the crowds and exploited it. At the conclusion of every speech he would call for those in the audience who thought he should be impeached to stand up. Naturally nobody rose. Even if any antis were present, they would hardly have dared to show themselves. Then Huey would ask for those who thought he should not be impeached to stand. The whole crowd would come to its feet.[9]

In his speeches Huey hit out vigorously at his opponents. "They may put me out," he roared, "but damn them, they will have to fight." He identified the people who were trying to put him out. The principal villains were—as his rural auditors were not surprised to hear—the agents of the Standard Oil Company. The company had defeated the oil tax by buying thirty representatives and now owned these men, Huey charged. It had purchased one representative, W. H. Cutrer, who, like Senator Anderson, was a Baptist minister, "so cheap that they felt like they were stealing him." Huey attacked other legislators who were impeachers, attempting to incite the people of their districts to evict them from office. In Lafayette he charged that Senator Donald Labbe had accepted an automobile from Standard Oil to vote for conviction. "You can watch Senator Labbe or you can recall him," he shouted. "I'd a sight rather see you recall him." In Opelousas, the hometown of Judge Dupre, he hinted that the old aristocrat was not as pure as he seemed. Referring to the judge's affliction, he said: "Deafness sometimes passes for honesty." Dupre struck back angrily. "No gentleman refers to another's infirmity," he snapped. Then, completely unconscious of any inconsistency, he observed that the governor was crazy: "He will end either in the insane asylum or the penitentiary."

Only rarely did Huey refer to the charges that had been leveled at him or offer a defense against them. He preferred to attack. When he did notice a charge, he discussed it jeeringly. "They say I tried to get that numbskull J. Y. Sanders, Jr., killed," he said in one speech. "Why if J. Y. Sanders, Sr., had died twenty years ago I wouldn't be governor. If J. Y. Sanders, Jr., lives twenty more years I may be President of the United States. A Sanders is what I need to assure my political future." This was his way of stating a fundamental

[9] Jess Nugent.

truth about Louisiana politics. He was saying that the conservatives could be depended on to accomplish their own destruction by opposing needed changes.[1]

When Huey said that he had fourteen senators who would stand by him, he was not idly boasting. He had fourteen, and shortly he had fifteen, committed to stand with him to the last. Moreover, he had their names signed to a document stating that they would remain with him. This document was probably signed some time soon after the vote on the Gilbert resolution, between April 15 and 17. In Louisiana political annals it would become famous, or in the minds of some, infamous, as the Round Robin. It is not generally realized, however, that there were two Round Robins. A second one was prepared a month later, and when people talk about "the" Round Robin it is to the second one that they refer. Some of the men closest to Huey, men who had a great deal to do with the issuance of the documents, do not know, or have forgotten, that there were two of them. Even the surviving signers are hazy on the matter. They recall that there were two Robins, but they are uncertain as to how they differed or when they were concocted. Only Leander H. Perez, of Huey's legal staff, could reconstruct the episode with relative clarity.[2]

The text of the first Round Robin does not exist, and its content has to be surmised. Huey quoted a brief portion of it in his autobiography. This excerpt stated that the signing senators would not vote to convict Huey on any charges heretofore filed or that might be filed. They were taking this stand because of the "legal irregularities and circumstances" surrounding the impeachment procedure. This language meant, presumably, that the house, in bringing impeachment, had not adhered to certain technical legal requirements. It also meant, again presumably, that the house and the senate could not sit legally after April 6. But the document contained other objections to impeachment, as is evident from hints in Huey's account and from the recollections of one of the signers. It declared that the charges that had been filed, the Manship and bribery charges, and the ones that might be filed, whose nature could be deduced from the nineteen-point indictment, were defective and

[1] New Orleans *Times-Picayune*, April 20, 21, 22, and 24, 1929; unidentified clipping, April 23, 1929, in Grace Scrapbook; Donald Labbe; Waldo H. Dugas.

[2] The failure to recognize the existence of two documents is all the stranger because Huey specifically stated in his autobiography that there were two; Long: *Every Man a King*, pp. 160, 169. The surviving signers with whom I talked were William C. Boone, H. Lester Hughes, and Henry D. Larcade.

hence invalid. They were invalid because they did not deal with impeachable offences. Huey compared this section to a demurrer in a court—a plea that a client, even if guilty, cannot be tried on a defective charge.[3]

The language in the document was primarily the work of Representative Allen J. Ellender, who did the drafting at Huey's request. Huey looked the text over and made a few changes.[4] Once the document was in hand, Huey placed telephone calls to a number of Longite senators asking them to come to Baton Rouge. One by one Huey received them in his hotel suite and asked them to affix their signatures to the Round Robin. In his autobiography he said that he relied solely on legal arguments to persuade them. He undoubtedly did use legal reasoning, but primarily to convince the senators that they would be standing on unassailable legal ground if they stood with him. But he resorted to other arguments as well, that to some of the senators were more compelling—offers, even if only hinted at, of patronage, roads, and other favors. He had need to be persuasive. Some senators were under great pressure in their home districts to vote for conviction. In Opelousas, the home of Henry D. Larcade, printed notices were appearing: "If Henry Larcade votes to acquit he will be tarred and feathered if he returns to Opelousas." Still Huey was able to secure the signatures of thirteen senators. If he could get one more, he was saved. A fourteenth senator, Fred Oser of New Orleans, was known to be driving to Baton Rouge. Huey, with a few friends around him, settled down to keep an anxious vigil.

The hours passed, but Oser did not come. Disquieting rumors came to Huey's room that Oser had gone over to the opposition. But finally, around midnight, the senator arrived. He had been delayed by car trouble, he said. Huey pressed him to sign the Round Robin, emphasizing that his signature was all that was needed to block impeachment. Oser expressed reluctance to add his name. He said that he was against impeachment but doubted the propriety of promising his verdict before he heard the evidence. He and Huey argued the issue into the small hours of the morning. At last Oser said that he could not decide without consulting his law partner in

[3] Long: *Every Man a King*, pp. 160–2; Henry D. Larcade.

[4] Allen J. Ellender; George M. Wallace. Both these witnesses affirmed that Ellender prepared the document, but Ellender could recall only one Round Robin, and he was obviously referring to the second one. His confusion is probably explained by the fact that he wrote the first one and that the second, which in part resembled the first, followed his draft.

New Orleans, Hugh Wilkinson. Huey was not going to let him get away with that one. Picking up the phone, Huey called Wilkinson and asked him to come up to Baton Rouge. There was an important matter he was discussing with Fred Oser, he said. The lawyer drove to the capital immediately. When he arrived, he took Oser off for a conference. They returned shortly and announced their decision: Oser would sign. A collective sigh of relief went up from Huey and his friends in the room. Somebody asked Huey if he wouldn't like to get some breakfast. The Kingfish stood up and stretched. "This is the first time I've been able to eat breakfast in months," he said.[5]

The little drama with Oser was not nearly so crucial as it seemed. Later that same day Huey persuaded another senator, T. A. McConnell, to sign the Round Robin. He now had one more vote than he needed. He also secured from two additional senators their promise to vote against impeachment. These men refused to sign the Round Robin but pledged their votes if they should be required. Huey could now sit back and observe the impeachers with amusement as they solemnly pushed their case through the house. But he took care not to reveal the reason for his confidence. He kept the existence of the Robin a close secret. The document reposed for a short time in the bosom of Miss Grosjean and was then transferred to the safety of a bank box in a Baton Rouge bank.[6]

The names on the Round Robin were not affixed in any order of senority or any other system. The senators signed, in whatever order they happened to enter Huey's room and were persuaded. Probably the first seven to sign, and in the following order, were Philip H. Gilbert, Hugo Dore, William C. Boone, Benjamin H. Ducros, Thomas C. Wingate, Homer Barousse, and Henry D. Larcade. The order in which the remaining eight signed cannot be determined with exactness. They were Jules C. Fisher, F. E. Delahoussaye (called "Barrel Head" because it was said he had to have a reward where he could get it immediately), E. B. Robinson, H. Lester Hughes, Robert B. Knott (whose brother was married to Huey's sister Clara), James L. Anderson, Fred Oser, and T. A. McConnell. These fifteen were the same senators who had voted for the Gilbert resolution. The Round Robin was in a sense only a private affirmation of a position previously and publicly stated. Still it was a brilliant coup. Some of the men who had voted for the Gilbert resolution

[5] Long: *Every Man a King*, pp. 160–2; Henry D. Larcade; Paul Maloney; Hugh Wilkinson.

[6] H. Lester Hughes; Henry D. Larcade; Leander H. Perez; Frank Odom; Leonard Spinks; Frank J. Peterman.

might have wavered and deserted Huey. But they could hardly leave him once they had signed their names to a manifesto pledging to stay with him.[7]

Later, when the Round Robin had become a legend of Louisiana politics and was acclaimed as the great strategic stroke of the impeachment, various individuals associated with Huey would assert that they had conceived it and had suggested it to him. Julius Long insisted that it was his idea. But Julius took the credit for every accomplishment of Huey's. Moreover, he related at different times accounts that were contradictory in parts and that did not square with known facts. His statements have to be doubted. Some friends of Earl Long claimed that he was the originator. Earl labored valiantly for Huey and sat in on the strategy conferences of the Long forces. But no evidence indicates that he did anything except execute Huey's orders. He was not a creator of strategy.[8]

Just who did conceive the Round Robin may never be known. When men who were among Huey's closest advisers are asked to name the author, they present conflicting answers. Some think that it was one of the signing senators, maybe Hugo Dore. Senator Boone was certain that he himself had hit on the idea and had told Preacher Anderson to propose it to Huey. Boone took no great credit, however, saying that the Robin was only a statement of what had already been voted in the Gilbert resolution. Paul Maloney, Huey's New Orleans leader, equally certain that the originator was former Governor Simpson, related a detailed story to support his assertion. Simpson, longtime clerk of the senate, was considered the greatest parliamentarian in the state, and Maloney, who had come up to Baton Rouge to help Huey fight the impeachment, suggested that Simpson be asked for advice on strategy. "Lord, you know Simpson could help me," Huey said. "Do you think you could get him to help me?" Maloney said that he would try. He found Simpson re-

---

[7] The surmise as to the first seven signers is based on the recollection of Henry D. Larcade, who recalled the order more clearly than any other survivor. My conclusion as to when it was signed is based on the following facts: On April 17 Huey said that he had fourteen senators who would stand by him. On that same day he showed Senator Fernandez a document that he said contained the names of "a bunch of senators" (*Impeachment Proceedings*, I, 689). As there were fifteen signers, the last one must have signed later that day or the next day. Also, one of the signers, Senator Boone, was positive that the document was prepared after a decisive vote in the senate. He thought that this vote came on May 15, but he was obviously talking about the Gilbert resolution. It is possible, of course, that the Robin was signed before the vote on Gilbert's motion.

[8] Julius T. Long; Harris: *The Kingfish*, p. 73; Lucille Long Hunt; Harley B. Bozeman; confidential communications.

luctant to assist the man who had supplanted him, but finally he agreed to give the matter thought. A short time later he handed Maloney a document. It was the statement that became the Round Robin, said Maloney, who rushed with it to Huey. The story is plausible, because Simpson had a mind capable of producing such a stratagem. But another man with an equally ingenious mind and as close to Huey as Maloney, Leander Perez, denied Simpson's authorship. "It wasn't Julius or Dore or Simpson," Perez declared. "Do you want me to say it was me? I couldn't honestly say whether it was me or Huey. We were talking one day, and the idea came to one of us." Huey's mind was superior to that of any of the people about him, and he was more likely than any of them to have thought of the Round Robin.[9]

ON APRIL 26 MASON SPENCER, acting for the house managers, presented to the senate the eighth charge and announced that with it the house was concluding its indictment of Huey P. Long. The senate took note that it was now in possession of all the charges and on the following day ordered that a summons be served on the governor to appear to answer the charges on May 14.[1]

The opening date of the trial was held off to enable the lawyers on both sides to prepare their cases and to allow time to ready the small senate chamber to accommodate the coming spectacle. A battery of carpenters was turned loose in the chamber, and they transformed it in a short time. Desks for the opposing lawyers were set up at the front of the room. Along either side of the chamber were rows of desks for reporters, who were coming in from all over the country, and for telegraph operators for the press services. At the rear of the room bleacher-like seats were erected for 120 spectators. Tickets were required for admission, a restriction that did not cause much popular resentment, for persons who could not get in could follow the trial in the newspapers. It would last, according to press predictions, for six weeks. Louisianians settled back to enjoy a good, protracted show.[2]

Every space in the chamber was filled when the trial opened. A

[9] Confidential communication; William C. Boone; Paul Maloney; Leander H. Perez. The strategy of the Round Robin was one that was familiar to Louisiana lawyers, particularly to those in criminal practice. A lawyer defending a client in a tight case would try to place on the jury a man, or several men, committed to vote for acquittal. Such a man was called a "sinker."

[1] *Impeachment Proceedings*, II, 155.

[2] Shreveport *Journal*, May 14, 1929.

hum of conversation from senators and spectators filled the room. It did not cease when the house managers came in and took their seats. But the crowd calmed when Huey entered, followed by eight lawyers, Overton and Perez at their head. The Kingfish was dressed in a white suit with black tie, and, as if flouting the solemnity of the occasion, he carried a cigar in one hand. As he walked down the aisle, he paused to shake hands with several senators. Soon Chief Justice O'Niell mounted the rostrum. Glancing at the assemblage, he proclaimed that the senate of Louisiana sitting as a court of impeachment was in session to hear charges proffered against Huey P. Long. Huey rose and said: "I am ready, if your honor please."[3]

Huey's lawyers, as the representatives of the accused, had the right to make the argument, or, in legal terminology, to file a demurrer, a claim that the plea of the plaintiff was defective. John Overton led off for the defense. He offered a demurrer to charges two through eight and a separate exception to the first, or Manship, charge. It was to the more general demurrer that he devoted his argument. The seven charges after the first were illegal and of no effect, the speaker contended. They were illegal because impeachment was not one of the subjects included in the governor's call and because they were adopted after April 6. Turning to the Manship exception, Overton went over the facts in the episode in detail, laying the groundwork for later treatment by Perez, but stating the essence of the Long position: Huey had not committed the alleged act in an official capacity, and therefore the offense was not an impeachable one. George Perrault replied for the house managers. He emphasized that one charge had been voted and presented before the eight and that in any case, no time restriction could apply to the house acting in its judicial capacity. The opposing arguments had consumed much time, and the senators wanted time to consider them. A motion to recess until the following morning was quickly passed.[4]

On that next morning the first order of business was to vote on the demurrer to charges two through eight. A number of senators asked leave to explain why they had decided to vote as they would. Delos R. Johnson, who was an anti, though not a bitter one, stated that he was impressed with the argument that the house could not sit after April 6 and would therefore vote to sustain the demurrer.

[3] *Impeachment Proceedings*, II, 201, 203, 209; unidentified clipping, May 15, 1929, in Grace Scrapbook. In addition to Overton and Perez, Huey was represented by Louis L. Morgan, Allen J. Ellender, Harvey Peltier, George M. Wallace, Caleb C. Weber, and Dudley Guilbeau.
[4] *Impeachment Proceedings*, II, 203–9, 211–33.

Two other senators of independent views expressed agreement with him. Finally a vote was called for. The tally disclosed nineteen votes to sustain and twenty against. It seemed to be a victory for the impeachers. The senate had declared that impeachment proceedings were legal; therefore, the charges had been brought legally and would be heard. Actually, the ballot should have signaled defeat to the impeachers, should have told them that they could not hope to attain a two-thirds majority on any charge. By a margin of only one vote the Long forces had failed to throw out seven of the charges. Nineteen senators, the Round Robineers and four others, had voted their conviction that the impeachment proceeding was illegal.[5]

Following the vote, Perez took up the exception to the Manship charge. In an able argument he stressed that the information Huey had threatened to divulge about Douglas Manship was fact: Douglas was undergoing mental treatment in a state institution. Moreover, the information was already public knowledge, because the names of people in state institutions were available to any taxpayer. Even if the governor had committed an indiscretion, he had done it in a personal capacity, in a private matter between him and Charles Manship, and not in his official capacity. George Ginsberg refuted for the managers, contending that Huey had made the threat to influence Manship to call off his editorial attacks and that by attempting to influence Manship he was somehow trying to influence the legislature. It was a laborious argument and not very convincing. The Manship charge was perhaps the weakest of the eight presented. It had been filed first only because it could be processed quickly and because the impeachers had been eager to get one charge on the record by April 6. But on this charge would come the first real test of the trial. The Overton demurrer had been concerned with procedure, but the Perez demurrer was substantive, challenging the content of a charge. The vote dismayed the impeachers: twenty-one votes to sustain the demurrer, or to dismiss the charge, eighteen against sustaining. On the ballot three senators who had voted to uphold the Overton demurrer went over to the anti side. One senator who had voted with the Long forces before remained steadfast. But five who had voted against the Overton demurrer joined the Longites. In their switch there was a significance greater than their numbers—an indication of how some senators were reacting to the various pressures of the impeachment. One of the recruits was Whittington, the moderate conservative, who felt that impeachment could not succeed and should be called off before it tore the state apart. One was Labbe of Lafayette parish, who was beginning to feel the popular resentments aroused against him by Huey's speech in Lafayette. And one was a man who had been promised a road in his district in return for his vote.[6]

After the vote the senate recessed until the following morning. Then the arguments on the second, or bribery, charge would begin. The Dynamite Squad must have gathered in gloom that night. But at Huey's hotel suite the Long people met in jubilation. The only charge that they admitted was legal had been thrown out. In their view the remaining charges could not be acted on. Therefore, they decided on a change in strategy. The Round Robin was brought from its bank box. A new one was prepared, one that Huey described as a "condensed" version of the first. The same fifteen senators signed it, although not in the same order as on the original. Then the first document was destroyed. Philip Gilbert was designated to present the second Round Robin to the senate the next day.[7]

The minute the senate went into session on May 16, Gilbert rose. "Mr. Chief Justice," he said, "on behalf of myself and fourteen other senators, I desire at this time to file a motion and ask the secretary to read it." He handed the Round Robin to the secretary and said: "Mr. Secretary, I wish you would read the motion and read the names of the senators attached thereto." Slowly the secretary read the document. It recited certain facts: on April 6 the senate had resolved itself into a court of impeachment and received the Manship charge; on May 15 the senate had sustained a demurrer to this charge; on that same day nineteen members had voted for a demurrer declaring that all the charges were illegal and hence null. Therefore the fifteen senators whose names were signed to the motion, consituting more than a third of the senate, desired to announce that on account of the "unconstitutionality and invalidity" of the charges they would not vote "to convict thereon." As further proceedings would be useless, the fifteen moved that the senate as a court now adjourn sine die. The conservatives listened to the reading in stunned disbelief. They had heard rumors that such a document would be presented to the senate, but they did not dream that as many senators would sign it as had. Their incredulity is amazing.

[6] Ibid., 244–64; V. V. Whittington; Donald Labbe; confidential communication.
[7] Leander H. Perez; Long: *Every Man a King*, p. 169.

They had not looked at the plain facts—at the repeated votes that demonstrated Huey had at least fifteen senators committed to go with him to the last.[8]

The antis shortly recovered from their shock. Delos Johnson, who had voted to rule out the charges brought after April 6 but had supported the Manship charge, sprang to his feet. "Mr. Chief Justice," he cried, "in view of the extraordinary nature of the document filed . . . on which appears the purported signatures of fifteen senators, I move that the Chief Justice, as each name is called, propound to the fifteen senators the question if the document contains their personal and general signature, and if the declaration in that document are their fixed position and decision in this matter." Johnson paused a moment and then said: "And I would add, regardless of the testimony that may be submitted."

O'Niell ordered that Johnson's question be put to the fifteen signers. As their names were called, each rose and affirmed that his signature was genuine and that he stood by the declaration. Every one of them emphasized that he would not vote to convict because all the charges after the Manship charge had been brought after April 6 and hence were illegal. Not one said that he would refuse to convict regardless of the evidence. In their view, they did not have to address themselves to Johnson's query: the evidence on the seven illegal charges did not matter. But Johnson's question, although perhaps not so designed, was a deadly trap for the fifteen, and it enmeshed them in history. Because it had been asked, it would be assumed that it had been answered. And since the Robineers said they would not vote to convict, it would be further assumed that they must have said they did not care about the evidence. Their response is thus stigmatized in practically everything that has been written about Huey or the impeachment. Thus another Long legend was born, with even less factual basis than most of the others. It had, however, a certain truth to it. The Robineers undoubtedly would have voted to acquit no matter what the evidence. Their position deserves criticism and has received a great deal. But then the impeachers should also be criticized. They would have convicted Huey, if not regardless of the evidence, on some very flimsy evidence and on some very doubtful charges. "It would not have been a trial," an independent legislator commented; "it would have been a travesty."[9]

After the last of the Robineers concluded his statement, the

[8] *Impeachment Proceedings*, II, 265–6; J. Y. Sanders, Jr.
[9] *Impeachment Proceedings*, II, 266–8; Harrison Jordan.

senate sat for some minutes in an odd silence. The impeachers did not seem to know what to do next. Finally somebody moved a recess until noon. Most of the senators who had not signed the Round Robin retired to the secretary's room for a conference. They returned when the session reconvened and announced that they wished to place a statement in the record. The statement deplored the action of the fifteen signers and argued that it was to the interest of the governor to have the charges tried. But, it ended, "in view of the situation, further action would be vain and useless." The conservatives were admitting defeat. When a motion to adjourn sine die was offered, they made no opposition.[1]

When Gilbert offered the Round Robin resolution, Huey left the senate chamber and went to his office. Soon a happy crowd of supporters burst in to tell him that the senate had adjourned. Rose embraced and kissed him. He responded with a characteristically political remark: "Well, you are still the first lady of the state." Yes, she answered, she was, but now she wanted to telephone the good news to the children in Shreveport. As she went to the phone, the men in the room, legislators and leaders, pushed forward to Huey's desk. They congratulated him and reminded him of their services during the crisis. He thanked them all but made a special reference to Gilbert. "There's a man," he said, "who refused to vote against me to make himself lieutenant governor." Some people handed slips of paper to him and asked for an autograph. He wrote on each piece: "Huey P. Long, governor of Louisiana by the grace of the people." Joe Messina, grinning broadly, leaned against the door. A reporter asked him if he was feeling happy now. "I never did feel no other way," Joe replied.

The next day the capitol began to return to normal. Porters picked up the trash left by visitors in the halls and on the lawn. Carpenters removed from the senate the special desks and chairs installed for the spectacle that had been expected to last six weeks. Workers in various state offices, who had been taking time off to follow the trial, reluctantly returned to their duties. There was a general exodus of politicians from the city. The impeachers departed in gloom and silence. But Huey's people left in shouting joy. Huey personally led one party out. He took the Robineers and some of his advisers to Grand Isle, a resort spot off the Gulf Coast, for a big celebration. Lobster, crab, and other delicacies were served, and

---

[1] *Impeachment Proceedings*, II, 269–70; T. O. Harris: *The Kingfish: Huey P. Long, Dictator* (New Orleans, 1938), pp. 71–2.

everybody, including Huey, got drunk. One important member of his circle was not at the party. Rose, her role played, had gone back to Shreveport.[2]

Huey never forgot that the signers of the Round Robin had saved him in his hour of danger. Any break that came between him and one of them was initiated by the senator. A legislator related a typical episode that happened years after the impeachment, when O. K. Allen was governor and Huey was a U.S. senator. This legislator happened to be in an anteroom to Allen's office while Huey was conferring with the governor. Also sitting there was one of the signers, now advanced in years and out of office. He had come to beg the governor for a job and had had to wait for several hours. Finally the secretary went in to Allen's office and said that so-and-so was out there and wanted a job. The legislator heard Allen say: "I just don't have any jobs to give him." Then Huey cut in: "Who did you say it was?" Allen repeated the name. "That's one of my old friends who signed the Round Robin to keep them from impeaching me," Huey said. "What do you mean, you haven't got a job?" "But I don't have any job or anything that he can do," Allen expostulated. "Well, find one for him," the Kingfish snapped.[3]

Huey showed his gratitude to the Robineers and to other supporters immediately after the trial. Every man who had stood firm received something. Gilbert was appointed a district judge and retired from active politics. Preacher Anderson was named chief enforcement officer of the Highway Commission. Representative McClanahan became warden of the state penitentiary. Speaker Fournet and several Robineers received positions as legal counsel to various state agencies. Still others were rewarded with jobs in these bureaus.[4]

Huey saw nothing wrong in taking care of these men. They were his men, and although now he was rewarding them specifically for standing by him in the impeachment, he would have given them similar awards in time for their general service. Still, he sometimes became irritated with them. Whenever one of them pressed for a

[2] Shreveport *Journal*, May 17, 1929; New Orleans *Morning Tribune*, May 17, 1929; three unidentified clippings, May 16 and 17, 1929, in Grace Scrapbook; Otho Long.

[3] W. C. Pegues; Harvey Peltier.

[4] New Orleans *Times-Picayune*, May 22, 1929; Harris: *The Kingfish*, p. 74; John Kingston Fineran: *The Career of a Tin Pot Napoleon* (New Orleans, 1932), pp. 98–100. Former Governor Simpson was given a job as supervisor of assessments in New Orleans. The reward indicates that he had rendered important help of some kind.

favor, he always emphasized that he had signed the Round Robin. One senator who was especially importunate called Huey one night at the Roosevelt Hotel. He asked for something, something more, that Huey was reluctant to grant. Huey would say, whenever the senator paused: "You're a hog." Finally he yielded. But he snarled a last gibe into the phone: "The only difference between you and a hog is that a hog jerks when it pisses."[5]

Just as Huey remembered who had been his friends in the crisis, he also remembered his most inveterate enemies. These men he never forgave, and he never gave up trying to drive them out of politics. He attempted to remove some legislators immediately. He had a double motive for defeating the antis who were members of the legislature. Although the attempt to impeach had been turned back, the charges still stood, not having been tried, and technically they could be renewed by a hostile legislature. Somebody reminded Huey of this possibility. "I'll just have to grow me a new crop of legislators," he replied.[6]

His first move was to have recall elections instigated against at least nine legislators. The Louisiana recall law, a relatively recent one, followed the model of other states, stipulating that a special election had to be held if a certain percentage of the voters in an official's district signed a petition demanding that he be recalled. In the districts of the nine legislators, Long leaders fanned out to secure the necessary number of signatures. Some of these leaders were not fully familiar with the law, which contained some unusual features designed to prevent fraud. For example, if a man could not write his name, two witnesses had to attest to his signature. The leaders, in ignorance or by intent or simply because they were in a hurry, signed up some names illegally. Their carelessness was public knowledge, and it inspired the threatened legislators, who were outraged by the recalls, to counteraction. In a number of districts they brought suits to enjoin the registrar of voters from certifying the names on the petitions. In Bossier parish conservative Representative Clark Hughes, whose recall had been petitioned, made such a challenge and the judge, after scanning the list, agreed and threw out over half the names, thus voiding the petition. Moreover, he had two Long leaders, Ira Gleason and George Beckcom, jailed for intent to commit a fraud. They were soon free on bail and were never brought to trial. In later years both of them were willing to

[5] Confidential communication.
[6] Hermann B. Deutsch: "Kingdom of the Kingfish," in New Orleans *Item*, August 21, 1939.

admit that in their haste they had permitted some illegal names to get on their petition, but they insisted that the antis had also resorted to questionable methods. Gleason, a businessman with varied interests, related that he was subjected to severe economic pressure —he was told that if he did not cease his recall activities, the banks would refuse him credit and the wholesale houses would refuse to sell to him.

By bringing these lawsuits the conservatives were able to prevent most of the recall elections from being held. In the few districts where elections did take place, Huey campaigned vigorously for the defeat of the incumbent. Thus for nine days he stumped one parish, where a representative named Bacon was up for recall. "Keep home the Bacon," he exhorted the voters. But the voters sent the Bacon back to Baton Rouge by a large majority. Huey suffered similar reverses in other elections. He succeeded in recalling only one legislator and only by a paper-thin margin. He failed because the legislators he tried to unseat were from strong anti-Long districts. Also, as he soon found out, the voters did not like to be inconvenienced by having to participate in a special election. So he dropped his plans for more recalls. He would wait for the regular elections to defeat his enemies. With some of them he had to wait a long time, but his patience was vast. One that he marked for oblivion was George J. Ginsberg, a leader of the house impeachment forces. He attacked Ginsberg constantly and bitterly. In one speech he referred to his foe as George Jackass Ginsberg. The next day somebody had a bale of hay delivered to Ginsberg's law office. Huey finally brought about Ginsberg's defeat in 1932, spending a large sum of money to do it. "He really unloaded on me," recalled Ginsberg, who had to retire from politics.[7]

Not satisfied to strike solely at his more prominent opponents, Huey extended his vengeance to antis all down the line. He shook up the entire state patronage, ruthlessly discharging even minor officeholders who were adherents of Sullivan or Ewing or who had ranged themselves on the side of the impeachers. Into the places of the departed he put firm Long men. The purge eliminated a number of his New Orleans leaders and wrecked such organization as he had in the city. Seeking to build a new organization there, he created the Louisiana Democratic Association, modeled on the Old Regulars, with seventeen ward leaders. With it he hoped to defeat the Old

[7] Ibid., August 21, 1939; Fineran: *Tin Pot Napoleon*, pp. 100–1; Ira Gleason; George E. Beckcom, Seymour Weiss; George J. Ginsberg. Ginsberg also said that Huey, through the state bank examiner, forced the closing of his Alexandria bank.

Regulars. From now on, he would give increasing attention to the manipulation of patronage and the management of organization.[8]

Just as the impeachment was about to collapse, a member of the Northeastern progressive hierarchy who had been touring the country dropped off in New Orleans. He properly paid his respects to former governor Parker, a former progressive, and met various friends of Parker's. But the highlight of the visit for him was a meeting with Huey. He described his impressions in a letter to an older progressive leader: "Even met the new young Governor Long, who they were all agin, but whom I thought was a dandy—and thought then that he would win out—has personality, plus lots of courage." The Easterner noted with interest that the "best people" denounced Huey but that they admitted the reason for their enmity —"at bottom it was his opposition to the oil, lumber, and cotton interests because of a 'severance' tax."[9]

The correspondent was writing in the language affected by professional progressives—liberal young politicians were always "dandies" or "bricks." And he was evaluating Huey in a characteristic progressive context. Huey was the idealistic young governor who had been beset by powerful foes but had triumphed over them because he was virtuous. He would now go on to achieve greater legislative reforms. But he would continue to be virtuous, and if by chance he should stumble and fall, it would be only because he was too good, and sometimes such a man was defeated by men who were not virtuous.

Some people who knew Huey intimately agree that he was an idealistic reformer—up to 1929. Before that year, they say, he was open and frank, devoted to democratic ideals and committed to achieving his ends by democratic means. But the ordeal of the impeachment changed him. One of his sisters, who was a particularly sensitive observer, described the change. "Before impeachment Huey took everybody into his confidence. After it he didn't talk so much. He knew that he had to be prepared then. He didn't put his cards on the table as he used to. It was his crossroads. It did something to him." A country leader offered a similar assessment. The impeachment made Huey realize that "average political tactics were inadequate to cope with his opposition," this man said; "After the impeachment he knew he had to fight with every weapon. There was

[8] *Overton Hearing*, I, 41, 1188–9.

[9] Harry A. Slattery to Gifford Pinchot, May 25, 1929, in Harry A. Slattery Papers, Duke University Library, Durham, North Carolina. For calling my attention to this letter, I am indebted to Richard Lowitt.

nothing vicious about him till then. He was reasonable, humane, kind. But impeachment did something to him. It made him vicious. After that he fought his enemies with everything he had." This leader quoted a remark of Huey's after the impeachment: "I wish we could have good decent government without all the fighting it takes to get it. You have to risk something to get the right kind of government."[1]

For every Long intimate who says that impeachment changed Huey, there are a dozen who say it did not. "He was always ruthless," said one man. "He always intended to move along the road he had mapped out for himself."[2] Those who think the impeachment did not change Huey are probably right. But their opinion needs some modification: the experience affected him but did not alter him appreciably. He had ideals before the impeachment and continued to cherish them, but he had never had any illusion that reform in Louisiana could be accomplished by appeals to principle and reason alone. He said, more than once, that he wished he could achieve his ends by means other than those he felt he had to use, but these expressions were no more than a wistful longing for something that he knew was impossible. He had always realized the intensity of the conservatives' opposition to change. What the impeachment did was impress on him the lengths to which the conservatives would go to destroy anyone who proposed change. It sharpened a determination that he probably already had to destroy the conservatives, or, more specifically, their bases of power. The impeachment hardened him only in the sense that it gave him a greater awareness of the dangers he faced. He would try to see to it that his enemies could never again place him in danger. But had there been no impeachment he would have followed much the same course that he did. He had chosen his way long before 1929, the way of the artist in the use of power—the way of the great politician.

The works about him say that his was the way of the demagogue. Some writers concede that he was a great demagogue, and hence a very dangerous one, but still a demagogue, one of those swaggering blusterers, those base fellows who have throughout history deceived the masses with turbulent rhetoric, cynical promises, and clownish tricks. He was, in fact, an example of the worst form of the genre: he was a Southern demagogue, from the region that produced the most and the cheapest demagogues.

Those who apply the label of demagogue to Huey or to other

[1] Clara Long Knott; Leonard Spinks.
[2] Confidential communication.

politicians hardly ever trouble to invest the term with any precise definition. It was coined by the ancient Greeks, who were sorely afflicted by rabble-rousing orators and who described them scornfully. The demagogue, said Euripides, was "base-born," "a man of loose tongue, intemperate, trusting to tumult, leading the populace to mischief with empty words." For the Greeks the term had actuality. In a small city-state like Athens a fiery speaker could easily whip a street-corner crowd into a frenzy with his words, could with the crowd at his back perhaps force the portals of power. Obviously such a scene could not occur in a much larger context, especially in a country as extensive and varied as the United States. But although the original concept of the demagogue has little validity for the American scene, the term has survived and is one of the most frequently used words in the national political vocabulary. It is usually applied in a special and subjective context: a demagogue is someone who arouses the people against the established order, and in this sense it has been applied to many American leaders. A perceptive journalist, reflecting on this fact, concluded that "wherever a man in public life was called a demagogue, there was something good about him. . . . And . . . since the plutagogues could not fasten any crime on him they fell back on the all-sufficient charge that he was a demagogue."[3]

Demagogues, or men who have been called demagogues, have appeared in all parts of America and throughout its history. But one section has produced an inordinate number of them, perhaps more than all other sections of the country together: the South, and specifically that South that came into being after the Civil War. It was by no accident or whim of history that this newer South was a breeding ground of demagogues. There were forces within this unique region that inevitably generated dissent. Indeed, it might be said that this was a region that required dissent, that demanded men who would challenge its established order. The South was the poorest part of the country. Even its fabled upper classes were only modestly wealthy in comparison with the top groups in most other sections. Its masses existed on the lowest scale of living in the nation, in grinding poverty and in dull, lonely, rural isolation. Its conservative hierarchies showed almost no realization that the region had any problems. They were content to rule, to keep the succession to office closed except to their own members, consenting to change

---

[3] Richard H. Rovere: *Senator Joe McCarthy* (New York, 1959), pp. 45–6, for a discussion of the origin of the term; *The Autobiography of Lincoln Steffens* (New York, 1931), p. 474.

only when they could not resist it. It was against the hierarchies and their conservatism and their pretension that the demagogues rebelled.

The demagogues of Dixie conform in many ways to the classic definition of the term. They were not "base-born"—most of them were of middle-class origin—but they were loud, flashy, and, if they had to be to impress their followers, crude. They employed a violent rhetoric and uttered extravagant promises—they would hurl the great ones from power and usher in a decent life for the people. Some of them won office—because the people desired a better life and thought the demagogues might conceivably bring it about, or because the people were simply tired of the sterile rule of the hierarchies and wanted a change, any kind of change; and also because the demagogues were immensely entertaining and offered the people at least a release from the frustration of their daily lives. The demagogues forced their way into the seats hitherto reserved for members of the hierarchy and grasped the powers of office. But then—after the tumult and the shouting died—nothing much happened. The average demagogic leader did not enact the program he had promised, did not create that better life he had held out to his followers. At the most he pushed through a few mild reforms and subsided into inaction. The career of one of them is typical of all of them, that of Benjamin Tillman, "Pitchfork Ben," of South Carolina, who aroused the farmers of his state to make him governor. "These men," summarized one commentator, "he led within sight of the promised land and there he left them. But he could not have carried them further. As if realizing this they stood around uncertainly in the glare of the light for a moment, as a new stratum of politicians filtered through them and occupied the places of power. And then they went back to their farming."[4]

The demagogues failed for a variety of reasons. A few of them did not mean the grand promises they uttered. They were interested in position rather than progress, and once ensconced in office they forgot their pledges. Others did mean what they said but had only a vague notion as to how they should proceed. They did not understand the nature of a modern state and hence could offer no concrete program to cope with its problems. After a few bumbling attempts at reforms, they gave up and turned to the more satisfying

[4] W. J. Cash: *The Mind of the South* (Garden City, N.Y., 1954), pp. 252–6; Gerald W. Johnson: "Live Demagogue, or Dead Gentleman?" *Virginia Quarterly Review*, XII (1936), 13; Rupert B. Vance: "Rebels and Agrarians All: Studies in One-Party Politics," *Southern Review*, IV (1938), 33–4, quoting Phillips Russell.

pastime of criticizing "niggers" and Yankees who, as everybody knew, were the real causes of the South's troubles. Some of the demagogues did have a program or the semblance of one, but they were able to get little if any of it enacted into law. They failed as surely as did their lesser fellows, and for a reason that was fundamental to the frustration of all the demagogues—their own nature. These apparent rebels were not really very rebellious. They liked the feel of power, and most of them wanted to lift up the masses, but they could not bring themselves to do what they had to do to retain power and put through reform. They would not deal ruthlessly with their conservative opposition. Some of them, it is true, built their own machines to counter the already organized conservatives. But they did no more, and it was only a question of time before the conservative machine overthrew them and ended their tenure. They never conceived of the possibility of overwhelming the established machine and replacing it with one of their own. They did not have the imagination or, more probably, the will to act daringly.

Huey Long was called a demagogue at every stage of his career. Being a remarkably introspective politician, he gave some thought to whether he deserved the label, and in so doing he was led to wonder about the loose way the term was used. In one statement he seemed to admit that it applied to him. Referring to his program, he said: "I shall have to admit it is a demagogy, because in the old Greek parlance that meant the language which was acceptable to the majority. That is not meant as a derogatory term, and I do not take it as such, because when I advocated free school books in Louisiana that was called demagoguery; when I advocated free bridges instead of toll bridges it was called demagoguery; when I advocated paved highways instead of dirt roads that likewise was called demagoguery." But in another statement issued at about the same time he seemed to deny that he was a demagogue. He pointed out that the term was never used with much precision. Then he went on: "There are all kinds of demagogues. Some deceive the people in the interests of the lords and masters of creation, the Rockefellers and the Morgans. Some of them deceive the people in their own interest. I would describe a demagogue as a politician who don't keep his promises." On that basis, he said, he was not a demagogue, for he had kept every promise he had made to the people.[5]

A few commentators have admitted that Huey was in some ways a departure from the pattern of the Southern demagogue. W.

[5] *American Progress*, July 1935; Forrest Davis: *Huey Long, A Candid Biography* (New York, 1935), p. 38.

J. Cash noted that Huey did not resort to the usual demagogic appeals, such as "nigger" baiting, but addressed himself to economic issues. Cash also perceived that Huey showed rare artistry in using power, that he was the first Southern popular leader to set himself, not just to bring the opposing machine to terms, but to destroy it. Gerald W. Johnson rendered an even higher tribute. He said that Huey was the first Southern politician since the great Virginians of the eighteenth century to have an original idea, the first to extend the boundaries of political thought by challenging the accepted faith. Huey's contribution, said Johnson, was to inject some realism into Southern politics: he made Southerners think that the problems of their time were something very different from the problems of the Civil War and Reconstruction era. V. O. Key conceded that Huey had a program and enacted it and brought to his work "a streak of genius." But Cash and Johnson found serious shortcomings in Huey. Cash thought that Huey never came really to grips with the economic problems of the common Southerner, tenantry and share-cropping. Johnson distrusted Huey's integrity and condemned his methods as "detestable." Both of them essentially viewed Huey as simply a greater demagogue. Key broke Huey out of the demagogue pattern, but then left him, as though he thought such a remarkable deviate could not be classified.[6]

Huey himself liked to pretend that he was too different to be classified. On one occasion, in his hotel suite in New Orleans, while he dozed on a bed, a group of visiting reporters fell to analyzing his personality. He finally roused himself and ended the discussion. "Oh, hell," he said, "say that I'm *sui generis* and let it go at that."[7] He was different from all other Southern politicians of his time and from most contemporary politicians anywhere in the nation. But he was not unique and he does not defy classification.

A term that does classify leaders of Huey's type has been suggested by Eric Hoffer—the mass leader. The mass leader is a man who sets a popular movement in motion. "He articulates and justifies the resentment dammed up in the souls of the frustrated. He kindles the vision of a breathtaking future." He does not hesitate to "harness man's hungers and fears to weld a following and make it zealous unto death in the service of a holy cause." The mass leader must have certain qualities, suggests Hoffer, and he lists as the most

[6] Cash: *Mind of the South*, pp. 286–9; Johnson: "Live Demagogue, or Dead Gentleman?" *Virginia Quarterly Review*, XII, 9–11; V. O. Key, Jr.: *Southern Politics* (New York, 1949), p. 157.

[7] Davis: *Long*, pp. 21–2.

important ones audacity, an iron will, faith in himself and his cause and his destiny, a recognition that the innermost craving of a following is for "communion" or a sense of collectivity, unbounded brazenness, which enables the leader to disregard consistency, and a capacity for hatred, without which he may be deflected from his goals. Hoffer names several examples of the mass leader: Hitler, Mussolini, Stalin, and also Lincoln, Gandhi, Franklin D. Roosevelt. But he makes an important distinction between his leaders. There are "bad" mass leaders and "good" ones. The good leaders, the Lincolns, the Gandhis, will harness man's hungers and fears to a cause. But they do not attempt to use the frustration of man to build a brave new world. They have too much faith in humanity to use man in such a fashion.[8]

It is immediately apparent that some additions can be made to Hoffer's list of necessary qualities. For one, the mass leader has to have immense physical vitality, a capacity to labor in his cause hour after hour, day after day, without flagging—a quality prominent in, for one example, Theodore Roosevelt. An awed Henry Adams wrote of T. R.: "Power, when wielded by abnormal energy, is the most serious of facts and all his friends knew that his restless and combative energy was more than abnormal. . . . He was pure act."[9]

It is also evident that some modification has to be made of Hoffer's qualities when applied to American leaders. This is especially true of the capacity to hate, which has also been stressed by Crane Brinton. Hoffer and Brinton note its importance to European leaders who in their rise to power have had to resort to extreme methods, have had on occasion to eliminate rivals. Politicians in a stable democratic society do not have to employ such methods, and the capacity to hate is not for them a necessary attribute. Indeed, if they possess it in too great a degree they may be handicapped; they will be led into needless quarrels. The democratic politician, as an astute Englishman pointed out long ago, should not quarrel except deliberately, when he cannot avoid being embroiled—and then he should conduct the quarrel with a cool head. The technique was entirely familiar to Huey Long, who knew its value instinctively. Many people, especially his enemies, think that he was filled with hatred, that he was vindictive, spiteful. He hated many of the things that conservatives stood for and he did hate some men. But he hardly ever acted out of hatred. He could seem vindictive, he could

[8] Eric Hoffer: *The True Believer* (New York, 1951), pp. 111–14, 147–8.
[9] Henry Adams: *The Education of Henry Adams* (New York, 1931), p. 417.

seem beside himself with rage, he could seem to destroy an enemy in passion—but in every case he was actually calculating, cool, and detached, and always his motives were political rather than personal. If he eliminated a man, it was only because that man stood in the way of one of his objectives or had become unnecessary to his plans. "I don't know of a single case where Huey took after an individual or kept after him just for the sake of harming him," said one intimate. "The minute a man ceased to be a threat, Huey lost interest in him."[1]

The mass leader in a democratic society may, however, find it advantageous to appear to be vindictive. For then he will be feared, and as Machiavelli advised his prince, it is sometimes better to be feared than to be loved. There is no evidence that Huey had ever read the great Florentine. But he often employed techniques recommended by Machiavelli, knowing them, it would seem, by some kind of instinct. He realized the value of being feared: people were likely to give way to a leader who could, if he willed, punish them. Hence his efforts to create an image of a Huey who could hate—his boasting of his power, his crude threats against his enemies, his violent attacks on them. Many of his threats he never executed. Indeed, taking another page from Machiavelli, and showing another quality desirable in a mass leader, he deliberately preserved some of his enemies, as symbols of the continuing evil he fought against, as "devil-tokens" to keep his followers united in the holy cause. There can be no doubt that he really cherished his favorite target, the Standard Oil Company. "Corporations are the finest political enemies in the world," he once explained appreciatively. He cherished too his political enemies, the Sanderses and the Old Regulars, for, as he often said, without them there would be no Long. The day would come when he would break the power of the Old Regulars, but he gave them up with some reluctance. An associate asked him why he did not remove the then mayor of New Orleans, Semmes Walmsley. "No," Huey answered, "that would be bad psychology. You always leave a figurehead for your boys to fight against. If you don't, they start fighting against themselves. Walmsley is a perfect target for us to fight. He's impotent and can't do us any harm."[2]

Huey had most of the qualities of the mass leader. He had audacity, an iron will, faith in himself and his cause, and brazenness. He

[1] Crane Brinton: *The Anatomy of Revolution* (New York, 1957), p. 153; Henry Taylor: *The Statesman* (New York, 1958), p. 77; Joseph Fisher; Robert D. Jones; Waldo H. Dugas; Richard W. Leche.
[2] Richard W. Leche; Charles Frampton.

had also in marked degree the capacity to arouse a sense of communion in his followers. He could excite an audience with his words.
He could, indeed, communicate a sense of excitement to a crowd
merely by appearing before it. One person who heard him said that
he had a "kindlin' power." It is a gift that has been possessed by
such diverse leaders as Adolph Hitler and Franklin Roosevelt. Men
who have it are said to be "charismatic." They are immediately recognized by the masses as a leader. The charismatic politician may be
folksy and friendly in manner, and he may employ a broad and
quizzical humor and even clown a bit. But to the masses he is still
the leader, remote and revered, a mysterious figure who has an
inner power that can only be ascribed, not described.[3]

Huey never used a written manuscript, or even notes, in his
speeches in Louisiana, and he rarely used prepared material in an
address anywhere. He relied entirely on his mind and his memory.
Yet he never rambled, and his speeches followed a logical plan of
organization that was obviously the result of prior planning. He
could tailor a speech to an audience. Before an urban or university
group, he would appear suave and sophisticated and would speak
in correct and cultured language. But before a rural crowd he was a
completely different man. "Watch me vaudeville 'em," he would say
to associates before he rose. He would begin by telling jokes or
stories. "I figure that the most of the people would rather laugh
than weep," he once explained. "I like to cut around the opposition
with a joke." Then he would advance a number of themes, searching
for one that would move the audience. Thus he once had to address
a largely unfriendly crowd in Baton Rouge. "He fumbled for about
fifteen minutes, trying out various appeals, feeling out the audience,"
a hearer recounted. "Then he got one and he knew he had it, and I
never saw an audience change so."

Once he had an audience in hand, he held it in rapt, almost
mesmerized, attention. "I couldn't believe people could be so spell-
bound by a man," said a state policeman who accompanied him to
many meetings. Some of them might later decide that he had been
wrong, but while he was speaking, everything he said seemed true
and beautiful. A Long country leader related an episode showing
that Huey could charm a man even against his will. This leader,
presiding at a meeting in his hometown where Huey spoke, noticed
in the crowd a man who bitterly hated Huey. Shortly he saw that
the man had left, and next day he asked him why. "I left because I

[3] Alvin W. Gouldner, ed.: *Studies in Leadership* (New York, 1950), pp. 62, 402.

was afraid," the man explained. "That guy was convincing me. I had to get out."

Sometimes Huey persuaded by resorting to dramatic actions on the platform. It is easy to dismiss these performances as the tricks of a demagogue; they would have been, if practiced by a lesser man. But in his mind they were legitimate devices: he had to be dramatic to drive home his message to an illiterate and submerged electorate. He gave a typical display of his technique at a meeting in a small north Louisiana town. It was right after the onset of the grim depression in 1929. He spoke out of doors to an immense audience made up mostly of farmers and their families, who had come miles to hear him. Poor before the depression, these people were now even poorer, and they stood around uncertainly, hoping that the man on the platform could tell them what had gone wrong in America, hoping that maybe he could show them a way out of their despair. Huey rose and looked over the crowd. "How many of you wear silk socks?" he shot out. Not a man raised his hand. "How many of you wear cotton socks?" Huey next asked. A great show of hands went up. Huey bent over and pulled up a pants leg to display a cotton sock. Then he gave them the clincher: "How many of you have holes in your socks?" Again there was a forest of hands. Huey took off one of his shoes—and sticking out of the sock was his big toe. The crowd exploded in applause. This man was theirs.

He was theirs, but he was not like them or of them. Always he was the remote great leader, to be revered and followed because he could save them, but not to be approached too closely, not to be treated too familiarly. The crowds who came to hear him speak would assemble early, waiting for him to appear. He would wait until the last moment and then walk slowly through them to the platform. "It was weird to watch the people," an associate recalled. "They would reach out to touch him as he passed." They would touch his sleeve, lightly, almost religiously. Some people would follow him from meeting to meeting, hearing the same speech over and over, just to touch him again, as though they derived some special kind of grace from this laying on of hands. A state policeman assigned to guard him said: "That was our problem, to get him away from the people."[4]

It is sometimes said, by reputable historians who like to think that the course of history is foreordained, that Huey Long was an inevitable product of conditions in Louisiana. Those conditions de-

[4] Harvey Peltier; Richard Foster; Davis: *Long*, p. 29; Fred Blanche; George Stagg; Robert D. Jones; Margaret F. Newberry; Ernest Clements; M. J. Kavanaugh.

manded reform, these writers say, and therefore Huey Long the reformer appeared. If it had not been he, it would have been some-body else. This thesis obscures the greatness of Huey and other mass leaders. It springs from a desire to deny the leadership principle or the role of the great man in history. Obviously, conditions in Louisiana were ripe for reform and a mass movement. Huey could not have conjured his movement or his following out of a void. Sooner or later a reform leader would have appeared. But that leader could have been a very mild reformer who would have satisfied popular desires for change with relatively little change, or he could have been a charlatan who would have propitiated the people with mere rhetoric. He did not have to be a Huey Long. But it was Huey Long who appeared, a man of great power, with the capacity within him to bring about large and even revolutionary change, and to do much good—or evil.[5]

[5] By way of analogy, although not to suggest that the analogy is exact, it can be said that the situation in Germany after World War I demanded that a leader arise who would relieve the frustrations of the German people. But that leader did not have to be an Adolf Hitler.

# CHAPTER 16

# *We Propose to Go Faster*

O NE OF THE MEN who deserted Huey during the impeachment was the high-salaried highway engineer he had imported from North Carolina, L. R. Ames. Ames had put together a good organization in the technical section of the Highway Commission and had rendered valuable service in launching the limited construction program allowed by the bond issue of 1928, but he became increasingly unhappy in his position. Having negotiated directly with Huey for the job, he had understood that he would have complete authority in it, particularly in selecting personnel. He soon found, however, that such was not the case: the head of the commission, O. K. Allen, insisted on supervising Ames's department and exercising a voice in the hiring of technical assistants. Ames chafed under this authority and finally decided to resign. He confided his resentment to some of Huey's enemies and during the impeachment was especially friendly with Paul Cyr. Huey probably would have discharged him if he had not resigned. A mutual friend tried to reconcile Ames and the governor before a final rupture occurred. Huey was willing to keep Ames if the engineer would promise political loyalty. Ames said that he would like to stay but would have to talk the matter over with his wife. "Goodbye," Huey snorted, "just forget it."[1]

This reaction was typical of his attitude toward subordinates after the impeachment. He wanted none around him who had any doubts as to where their allegiance lay. He began a campaign to

[1] Norman Lant; unidentified clipping, May 27, 1929, in Grace Scrapbook; Shreveport *Journal*, May 27, 1929; Jess Nugent.

force from the state boards men who either had not stood by him in the recent crisis or might not do so in the future. He moved immediately on the agencies that controlled the largest number of state jobs. The president of the Orleans Levee Board, a Simpson appointee who had been allowed to remain at the price of signing an undated resignation, suddenly announced that the press of his business duties made it necessary for him to resign. The Long majority on the board promptly named as president a member who had been appointed by Huey, a man who was coming up fast in the Long organization. Abraham Shushan was the principal owner and manager of a lucrative dry-goods company in the city. One reason for its prosperity was that it consistently managed to bid lower than its competitors on large orders from state institutions. Abe Shushan, of Jewish stock, was short, stout, and moon-faced, and his black hair had the sheen of patent leather. He was obsequious to those above him and painfully so to Huey. But he was steadfastly loyal to his chief and contributed generously to campaign funds. Out of regard for Huey, he often carried for long periods the bills due him by the state, waiting even until after competing companies had been paid.[2]

Another patronage-laden agency was the Orleans Dock Board, on which Huey needed one more Long man to give him a dependable majority. He used a complicated maneuver to gain control, trying first to force the president of the board to resign. He charged that this man, a cotton shipper, was sending out cotton through the rival port of Houston, and he demanded his resignation. The president, however, dismissed the charge and stood his ground. But suddenly another member announced his resignation, explaining that he was resigning because Huey had offered to make him president and he did not care to become involved in a controversy between the governor and the incumbent! What pressure or inducement Huey had used is not known. But when he filled the place with a Long stalwart, he at last had taken control of every important board.[3]

While Huey was moving to strengthen his base of power, some of his enemies were organizing to destroy him. They were the most

[2] New Orleans *Item*, May 27, 1929; Hermann B. Deutsch: "Kingdom of the Kingfish," in New Orleans *Item*, August 21, 1939; *Overton Hearing*, I, 435, 457; Charles L. Dufour; Hermann B. Deutsch.

[3] New Orleans *Times-Picayune*, August 27, September 3, October 10, 19, and 20, 1929; Hermann B. Deutsch: "Kingdom of the Kingfish," in New Orleans *Item*, August 21, 1939; Leo Glenn Douthit: "The Governorship of Huey Long" (unpublished M.A. thesis, Tulane University, 1949), pp. 100–1; L. Vaughan Howard: *Civil Service Development in Louisiana* (New Orleans, 1956), pp. 38–9.

sincere and idealistic of his opponents and hence the most inept and least dangerous ones. They exhibited to the full their lack of political understanding at their first meeting in June in New Orleans. First of all, the city was not a good place in which to launch a movement to overthrow a leader who was popular in rural areas. Country people were likely to regard a meeting held there as a conspiracy of urban slicksters and millionaires. Secondly, the sponsors did not trouble to hide the fact that this was an assemblage of "fat cats." Colonel Ewing's *States*, an enthusiastic supporter of the movement, described the 250 men present as the "most representative gathering of citizens" in Louisiana in a decade. Actually, the "citizens" were aged conservative politicians who did not know that their era had passed, businessmen, and corporation lawyers. They voted to call their organization the Constitutional League and elected former governor Parker as its president. The name and the choice of a leader revealed their concept of strategy. They were going to fight for "the constitution of Louisiana" and for honest government, and they were going to expose corruption and save the state from Huey Long and restore it to gentlemen like John Parker. Although they talked only about political reform, they betrayed that they were not oblivious to such mundane matters as money. When contributions to further the League's work were requested, the businessmen in the meeting subscribed a hundred thousand dollars in less than fifteen minutes. Many people must have wondered if the contributors, at least, were not more concerned with their own economic interests than with Huey's politics. Soon after the League was formed, Huey expressed those ideas in a way that displeased conservatives. He refused to mobilize the militia in a strike by street-railway employees in New Orleans that caused much disorder. "I will not call out the militia to shoot down union men," he proclaimed.[4]

The men who directed the League's activities, Parker and others, were, it turned out, concerned with political reform alone. They set a staff to digging into state records for evidence of wrongdoing, and these investigators came up with several bits of information that impressed the League leaders: money was being spent wastefully by the Highway Commission, various relatives of the governor held state jobs, and a number of Long legislators occupied positions in the executive departments. The League publicized all its findings but decided to concentrate its fire on the legislators.

[4] New Orleans *States*, June 11, 1929; New Orleans *Times-Picayune*, June 11 and 26, 1929; Douthit: "Governorship of Long," pp. 97–8; Bogalusa *News*, July 9, 1929.

These men were obviously under Huey's influence, the League charged, and his practice of awarding job's to legislators was a particularly nefarious example of his manipulative skills. Accordingly, the League filed a lawsuit to oust the "double dippers." The supreme court, which finally pronounced on the case, sustained the League's complaint, holding that the practice of awarding state jobs to legislators violated political morality and the principle of the separation of powers and ordering the holders to resign either from their positions or from their legislative seats. Some sixteen legislators who were or had been Long supporters had to give up their extra-legislative posts. One of them was Senator Boone, who had been quarreling with Huey over patronage in his district and who used the decision as an excuse to break with the governor. The court's action had a comic aftereffect not foreseen by the League. It was discovered that eight Old Regular legislators were holding positions with the New Orleans government, and these men also had to resign their jobs. In spite of this the League affected to think that it had won a great triumph, although actually the mass of voters regarded its campaign with indifference. It had not uncovered any big cases of corruption, and its exposé of legislators did not particularly shock the public: after all, legislators had held executive jobs in previous administrations. Huey watched the League's efforts with amusement, and when he deigned to comment on the organization, he referred to it as "the League of Notions."[5]

But some people were not amused by the League's activities. A group of industrial and banking leaders, comprising some of the richest and most influential men in the state, had concluded that the recent and current political turmoil was holding back industrial development. A large chemical company was considering building a plant in Louisiana but was fearful that it might be subjected to an occupational tax. These businessmen decided that the state needed a period of repose, and they proposed to bring it about by appealing to the governor. On July 18 they addressed a public letter to Huey requesting his help in ending the "political disturbances" agitating the state. They asked the governor to pledge that he would not seek to enact an occupational tax during his administration and that he would cease his recall efforts against certain legislators. The list of eight signers was headed by the name of Harvey Couch, and there was obvious design in Couch's prominence. One of the South's

[5] New Orleans *Times-Picayune*, September 7 and 28, 1929, January 30, February 4 and 7, 1930; L. V. Howard: *Civil Service in Louisiana*, p. 40; Douthit: "Governorship of Long," pp. 104–6.

leading businessmen, he was the president of the Louisiana Power and Light Company and the Louisiana and Arkansas Railroad Company. More important, he was an old Winnfield boy. Although he had been born in Arkansas, he had spent his youth in Winnfield and had started his career there. He and Huey had early contracted a friendship, which they managed to maintain despite sharp differences on political matters. Couch and his fellow signers stated that if Long would agree to a truce, they would use their influence not only to discourage attempts to renew impeachment proceedings but also to marshal support for Huey's legislative program.

Huey answered the appeal within two days, also in a public letter. But the tenor of his reply indicated that in the interim some private face-to-face negotiating had been going on. He said that he would try to halt the recall proceedings and would pledge that an occupational tax would not be enacted during his administration. But he was doing this, he stipulated, because of an understanding that the business interests would cooperate in surveying the needs of the state institutions and would support his legislative program for more roads and better schools. Appearing simultaneously with Huey's letter was an announcement by the Standard Oil Company that it would not oppose in court the severance tax, which provided for the free schoolbooks, and that it was about to build an addition to its Baton Rouge refinery. The next day the chemical company revealed that it would locate its plant in Louisiana. In the light of these developments the criticisms of the Constitutional League seemed carping and its campaign appeared to be a petulant effort at revenge.[6]

The businessmen who had arranged the truce had not inquired very closely into the nature of the legislative program they promised to support. They had assumed that it would be a continuation of Huey's existing program: somewhat more money would be spent for roads and schools. They soon learned, however, that the governor had ambitious new plans that he was going to recommend to the legislature at the regular session in May 1930, plans that went beyond anything he had previously advanced. Huey outlined these plans in speeches and public statements during the remaining months of 1929 and the first months of 1930. He struck the same

[6] Bozeman, in *Winn Parish Enterprise*, May 30 and November 14, 1957, for a sketch of Couch's career; New Orleans *Times-Picayune*, July 19 and 21, 1929; T. O. Harris: *The Kingfish: Huey P. Long, Dictator* (New Orleans, 1938), p. 79; Deutsch: "Kingdom of the Kingfish," in New Orleans *Item*, August 21, 1939; Douthit: "Governorship of Long," pp. 99–100.

theme over and over: Louisiana had been progressing under his administration but it would have to increase its rate of economic growth. "We propose to go faster," he announced.

First of all, he would recommend legislation to restore New Orleans to its position as a great port and put it on the way to becoming a great city. The state should subscribe money to retire the port's debts, contracted under previous governors, and to improve the public docks; the state should also enlarge the road system in and around the city and construct a free bridge across the Mississippi to facilitate the flow of transportation. Although this legislation would benefit New Orleans most directly, it would ultimately affect the whole state, which would thrive as its largest city grew wealthier. But he was also going to recommend other legislation that would directly help all parts of the state—a bond issue to provide money to construct three thousand miles of surfaced roads and a number of bridges over the larger rivers. He would ask for another bond issue to build a new capitol, a project that would aid Baton Rouge. He admitted that the program would cost a great deal of money, probably a hundred million dollars, and that virtually all of that amount would have to be raised by selling bonds. But existing taxes were sufficient to underwrite the bonds, he insisted; thus part of the gasoline tax could be bonded to take care of the highway costs. And even if the state debt did increase, he contended, it was imperative that Louisiana embark now on a public-improvements program. The stock market had crashed in October, and the prosperity of the 1920's was fading fast before the onset of the great depression. His program would provide jobs and cushion the impact of the collapse. His new business backers gulped at the scope of the projects, but they saw the force of his argument and decided to go along with him. A group of civic leaders in New Orleans, summoned by him to a meeting, readily agreed to appoint a Commercial Affairs Committee to survey the needs of the city and the state.[7]

Huey's call to the civic leaders for help was also signed by the newly elected mayor of New Orleans, T. Semmes Walmsley. Walmsley, the Old Regular candidate, had won the office in January 1930, defeating Francis Williams of the Public Service Commission, who ran ostensibly as an independent. Huey took no open part in the campaign, which occupied the city during the last months of 1929. He had tried to persuade his friend Paul Maloney to enter the

[7] New Orleans *Times-Picayune*, December 3 and 18, 1929, January 7, 1930; *Louisiana Progress*, March 27, 1930.

race, but Maloney had declined. Huey then announced that he would not choose between Walmsley and Williams, that neither of them deserved his support. His precinct leaders of the Louisiana Democratic Association could advise their followers to vote as they pleased, he said; as for himself, he was busy with his plans for public improvements.

Political observers surmised that he was keeping his hands off because he hoped to pick up some support from the Choctaw legislative delegation for his bills at the May session. They also doubted that he was completely neutral. Reportedly, on the night before the election he sent word to his leaders to show a good vote for Walmsley in some wards so that he could make a claim on Walmsley in event of an Old Regular victory. The leaders had to catch some voters on the way to the polls to transmit the new instructions. Walmsley won by a narrow margin, some nine thousand votes. Too late, Huey realized that he could have determined the result. Through state patronage he controlled at least five thousand votes in the city, and a shift of this many votes would have changed the outcome.

Huey had rejected suggestions by Bob Maestri and his brother Earl that he endorse Williams. He gave as his reason that Williams could not win. But it is more probable that he could not bring himself to support his former friend, who was now one of his fiercest critics. The enmity between the two was deeply personal. Williams had attacked Huey in unmeasured terms, and Huey never referred to Williams by any other name than Frans-Ass. But Williams's showing in the election could not but impress Long the politician. Huey made a secret overture to Williams—if Francis wished to contest a second primary the Long organization would support him. Williams hesitated over the offer. He was not sure that he could win, even with Huey's aid, and he was not sure that he should ally himself with the Kingfish. He consulted his city manager, Harry Gamble, a dedicated conservative. Gamble persuaded him that he could not accept the support of the man he had denounced and that he should withdraw. "I may have given the wrong advice on this one," Gamble conceded years later.[8]

With no Republican opposition, Walmsley became mayor. He was also the recognized head of the Old Regular organization. As

[8] New Orleans *Times-Picayune*, August 23, October 26, November 23 and 24, 1929; Paul Maloney; Deutsch, article in New Orleans *Item-Tribune*, December 31, 1933; Deutsch: "Kingdom of the Kingfish," in New Orleans *Item*, August 21, 1939; Harry Gamble.

mayor and leader, he was a different type from Behrman the ward politician, whose mantle he had inherited. A scion of a good New Orleans family and educated at Tulane University, he had the manner of a gentleman. Entering politics as a young man, he had risen fast in the Choctaw hierarchy and had been commissioner of finance in the city council before becoming mayor. He would hold his new office for several years and would be a figure of importance in state politics. But he was not a good politician. Men who were among his closest associates admit that he was not very smart. Said one: "Walmsley never got beyond being fourteen years old. He couldn't say no. In one campaign we had $100,000 to spend, and he spent $140,000." Another one called attention to a more serious shortcoming. "Walmsley wouldn't keep his word, which is the first rule of politics," he said. "He would break it without reason. You had to get everything in writing." These faults were not yet apparent in 1930 when he and Huey met and struck up an alliance. Huey must have disliked him instinctively. Walmsley, six feet two inches tall, bony and baldish, must have looked on Huey as a crude redneck. Later Huey, reflecting on Walmsley's appearance, would derisively refer to him as "Turkey Head."[9]

THE KINGFISH GLOWED with enthusiasm when he discussed any of his projects. But he waxed almost lyrical when he described the new capitol that he was going to build. The present little castlelike edifice was outmoded, he said, and he was going to give the state a building worthy of Louisiana's place in the modern era. Sometimes he appeared to consider the capitol a private venture under the management of Huey Long. In truth, it was almost that. He was determined to build a capitol, as he had been to build a new mansion, and he proceeded much as he had in the mansion episode, launching the project on his own initiative and creating conditions that made its completion almost inevitable. In January 1930 he appeared before the Board of Liquidation and requested, and received, funds to employ an architect to draw plans for the new building. He then employed a New Orleans architect. When the plans were completed, he revealed them with great fanfare. The building would be built like a skyscraper, he announced, twenty-four stories high, large enough to accommodate all the various departments of the govern-

[9] *Overton Hearing,* II, 1954-5, for a sketch of Walmsley's career; confidential communications.

ment. It would have a steel frame and a limestone exterior and probably would cost only a little more than a million dollars. He also divulged that he had selected the site for the building, on the old Louisiana State University campus, which had become vacant after the school was moved to its new campus. Somebody asked him what disposition he would make of the old capitol. "Turn it over to some collector of antiques," he said happily.[1]

The need for a new capitol was so obvious that most Louisianians approved of Huey's proposal. Only diehard conservatives opposed it—but they admitted the desirability of having a new building, so they had to offer curious arguments. Huey was holding forth the capitol as bait to get the votes of the East Baton Rouge legislative delegation, they charged, just as he was dangling other bait before other cities to get the votes of their legislators. It appeared that the critics were saying that all the baits should be rejected and that no city should get anything. It turned out that they were not saying this at all. The Baton Rouge *State-Times* explained their position in a long editorial, which stated that Louisiana, and Baton Rouge, should have a new capitol, and New Orleans should have an improved port, and Shreveport should have a new bridge. These projects were good, but they must come in "an orderly and proper way," and be initiated and planned by the legislature. Huey Long should have no part in them—and, the editorial almost admitted, no part of the credit for them.[2]

While Huey was acting to get construction started on one new state building, he was superintending the completion of work on another one, the executive mansion. He was anxious to have the mansion ready for occupancy before the legislature met in May, so that he could point to it as another achievement of his administration. Consequently, he spent a good deal of time at the site, spurring the foremen and workers on to greater efforts. He even went to the building late at night, accompanied by some friend he had aroused from bed, and grabbing a flashlight from an astonished watchman, he would go over the structure inch by inch to assure himself that all the specifications were being followed. With his stimulus the work proceeded rapidly, and the mansion was ready by early May.[3]

Meanwhile, Huey had continued to live in hotels. He had one

[1] New Orleans *Times-Picayune*, January 18 and February 18, 1930; Shreveport *Journal*, January 27, 1930.

[2] Baton Rouge *State-Times*, February 27, 1930; Shreveport *Journal*, May 19, 1930.

[3] H. Lester Hughes; New Orleans *Times-Picayune*, May 7, 1930.

suite at the Heidelberg in Baton Rouge and another at Seymour Weiss's Roosevelt in New Orleans. When the legislature was not in session, he stayed at the Roosevelt, going up to Baton Rouge only when he had to attend to some official matter. He was in New Orleans almost constantly during the first months of 1930, and while there he was the central figure in some escapades that attracted attention throughout the country.

In February social circles in the city buzzed with excitement at the news of the coming visit of a former President. Calvin Coolidge and his wife, on a leisurely rail trip from Florida to California, were going to stop off for a few days in New Orleans, and naturally they were going to stay at the Roosevelt. They were installed in the hotel's best suite, which was almost large enough to accommodate the reporters who thronged in after them. Close behind the reporters came Governor Long, who said he merely wanted to pay his respects. But when Huey spotted the journalists present, he could not resist taking over the scene. Was there anything he could do for the distinguished guests? he loudly asked. "About all I've got is some ducks and geese. I'll be glad to send you some up." Coolidge gravely said that the hotel would provide ample fare, and then, to keep the conversation going, inquired what town in Louisiana the governor was from. "Winnfield, way out in the sticks," Huey bubbled. "I'm a hillbilly, more or less, like yourself." Dropping this subject, the former President asked how the governor got along with the two Louisiana senators. Huey assumed a mock judicious air. He didn't know how he stood with them, he said finally. He then revealed a fact of Louisiana politics to Coolidge: "One of our troubles down here is you just can't tell how long you're going to be friendly." He bustled out shortly, leaving a puzzled New England pair to cogitate on the vagaries of Southern politics.

The final event of the Coolidge visit was a large formal banquet. Huey, who had had to go up to Baton Rouge, rushed in, thirty minutes late, to take his assigned seat next to the elegantly dressed Mrs. Coolidge. He was wearing a brown suit and a pale blue shirt. Throughout the evening he was observed to be carrying on an animated conversation with her. A New Orleans aristocrat in evening clothes watching the pair was moved to remark: "If Winn parish could only see Huey now." Before the Coolidges left, photographers asked to snap their picture with Huey. As the trio lined up, Huey quipped: "It's a picture of past and future Presidents." Later he told reporters that he had asked Coolidge what condition the White House was in. "You see," he explained, "every time I move into a house I have to tear it down. Mr. Coolidge told me the White House was not in very good shape. I guess I will have to go up there and tear it down and build another one."[4]

The press accounts of Huey's reception of the Coolidges aroused amused snickers from people in other states. Many readers relished his impudence to the solemn visitors. But almost immediately he involved himself in an episode that evoked quite different reactions, horrifying some observers but stirring others to raucous laughter. Early in March, at the height of the carnival season, the German cruiser *Emden*, on a goodwill tour to the United States, docked at New Orleans. Its commander, proud and punctilious Lothar von Arnauld de la Perière, thought that as one of his first duties he should pay a courtesy call on the governor of Louisiana. He asked the German consul in New Orleans, Rolf L. Jaegar, where he would find him. Jaegar, a pompous, fussy man, said that Governor Long was in New Orleans, at the Roosevelt Hotel, and he said he would make arrangements for the captain to meet Huey. Jaegar phoned Seymour Weiss and announced that the German commander and the consul would like to pay their respects to the governor. Weiss consulted Huey, who professed pleasure with the proposed visit. Weiss suggested to the Germans that they come on a Sunday morning.

On the appointed day von Arnauld and Jaegar arrived at Weiss's office. The commander was in dress uniform, glittering with gold braid and medals, and the consul wore correct formal attire. They were pleased to see that Weiss was also properly gotten up. Huey had made the hotel executive a colonel in the militia, and Weiss, delighting in the title and the rank, exhibited both whenever possible. For this occasion he had donned his own uniform, which, though not as splendid as the commander's, was nevertheless adequately flashy. With a number of reporters following, Colonel Weiss conducted the visitors to the gubernatorial suite. Huey walked out from the bedroom, where he had been listening to a radio sermon. He was wearing green pajamas, a red and blue lounging robe, and blue bedroom slippers and, in the words of one of the reporters, looked like "an explosion in a paint factory." He apologized for his costume, saying that he had worked all night and had not had time to dress. He and the commander chatted amiably about New

Orleans and the carnival season, and shortly the Germans took their departure. Von Arnauld seemed to enjoy the conversation.

Jaegar, however, had been on edge from the moment he had seen the governor and had taken little part in the interview. About half an hour after it ended, he burst into Weiss's office, his face red with anger. "My country has been insulted," he shouted, "and I demand an apology." The colonel, taken aback, inquired as to the nature of the insult. The consul sputtered his complaints—Huey had received the commander in pajamas; he had insulted the German government and would have to apologize. Weiss finally calmed Jaegar, and told him to wait while he talked to the governor about it. Going to Huey's suite, Weiss said: "You played hell. We're going to have an international incident here." He repeated the consul's words and demand for an apology. "Tell him to go jump in the lake," Huey said cheerfully. "I'm not apologizing for anything." Weiss returned to his office and told the consul that Huey had apologized for his attire when the party entered and would not again. But, he added, he personally would like to make amends and would try to persuade the governor to make some kind of gesture. The consul, somewhat mollified, said that the honor of his government would be satisfied if the governor paid an official visit to the *Emden.*

Weiss relayed the message. "Huey," he said, "let's do this thing right. Let's take some of the members of your staff that have uniforms and you put on a swallowtail coat and striped pants and we'll go down and see this guy. We'll take the *Hugh McCloskey* [the Dock Board launch] and we'll go right down to the ship." Huey began to see possibilities of publicity in the expedition. But, he asked: "Where are we going to get those kind of clothes?" Weiss answered that he had them and would send them to Huey's room. The colonel arranged for the call to be made on the following morning.

On Monday Huey appeared at the door of Weiss's office, wearing the swallowtail coat, the striped trousers, spats—and a red necktie! "Jesus Christ," Weiss said, "you can't go down there like that." Huey asked why not. Weiss, without a word, went to his closet, took out a gray tie, and handed it to him. Just before the party took off, it was discovered that nobody had thought to provide Huey with a stovepipe hat. Alfred Danziger offered to lend his gray fedora, and Huey carried it in his hand. Boarding the *Hugh McCloskey,* the group steamed down to the German ship. Von Arnauld received them cordially and on the governor's departure ordered the firing of a twenty-one gun salute. The commander volunteered to reporters that he thought Governor Long was "a very interesting, intelligent and unusual person."[5]

Another foreign visitor was also in New Orleans for Mardi Gras at the time of the incident—the Countess de Topar Lakopolanki of Poland. She issued a statement defending Huey's choice of pajamas as an official costume. She said that Benito Mussolini, the dictator of Italy, and Primo de Rivera, the former dictator of Spain, had often received even royalty while wearing "intimate garments." Although Huey could not have liked being compared to these two despots, he expressed delight with the countess's statement. Noting that she had cited precedents of royalty, he said that perhaps everybody should "go back to the common starting point, maybe to old Uncle Noah, to find out what there is in this garb complication anyway." But he admitted anxiety about one aspect of the incident. He was ruined in Winn parish now that the people there knew he slept in pajamas, he said.[6]

The pajamas affair excited wide comment in the national and foreign press. Naturally people wondered why Huey had behaved in such a fashion. Louisiana conservatives had no doubts as to the reason: their crude governor did not know any better. He sometimes received important visitors in his underwear, they said, and he had once received a Baton Rouge delegation without even the underwear. A remark supposedly made by Huey to Weiss was quoted as proof of his social ignorance. When Weiss said that Huey should apologize to the Germans, Huey answered: "Apologize! What for? I treated them like home folks." Huey may or may not have said it. If he did, he was joking. He had not been brought up in a society in which people welcomed guests, even close friends, in sleeping clothes.

More objective observers were ready to concede that Huey realized he was violating protocol and had done so deliberately, as a publicity stunt—although they did not explain how the publicity would help him. The episode did, of course, amuse his country followers: they relished the spectacle of their hero embarrassing the dignified Germans. But he did not need to rally his people with a crude display. He did have, however, a reason for what he did. It

[5] New Orleans *Times-Picayune*, March 4, 1930; Baton Rouge *Morning Advocate*, March 5, 1930; Shreveport *Journal*, March 7, 1930; Seymour Weiss; Carleton Beals: *The Story of Huey P. Long* (Philadelphia, 1935), pp. 174–6. Long, in *Every Man a King*, pp. 193–9, reproduced the *Picayune's* somewhat satiric account without comment.

[6] New Orleans *Times-Picayune*, March 10, 1930; Beals: *Long*, p. 176.

was a very subtle one and has escaped the notice of all writers. He frequently received people when he was in informal dress, and he liked to receive them in private surroundings—if he could so arrange it, in his bedroom. He conceived of these meetings as a kind of regal ceremony, a symbol of his power. If Huey Long could receive people in any kind of dress and in any place he chose then people would know how great he was. One journalist witnessed a typical Long audience in Huey's bedchamber in the new mansion. The Kingfish, dressed in a golfing outfit, with his collar unbuttoned and his belt unbuckled, lay on a huge bed with an orange bedspread. People entered the room in a constant stream, one by one approaching the figure on the bed to ask a favor. He graciously granted some their wish and brusquely dismissed others. The reporter thoughtfully observed that the scene was very much like a "levee of state" in the age of Louis XIV.[7]

Huey's social activities became somewhat more sedate after he moved into the new mansion in May. He may have felt that he should conduct himself with more decorum now that he had a permanent official residence. A more probable reason is that there was someone in the mansion who could exert some influence on him, his wife. Rose had moved in, bringing the children with her, and she tried to keep Huey at home as much as she could. Although she went back to Shreveport at frequent intervals, she stayed in Baton Rouge for longer periods than she had before. She was usually present at the large social affairs at the mansion. At the opening reception she looked charming in an ecru lace evening dress with green accessories. Huey appeared in a white linen suit and spent much of his time listening to the music, which was provided by the Louisiana State University cadet band.[8]

Huey often asked the LSU band to come to the mansion to play concerts or serenades. He was not content merely to listen to it, however. He also attempted to instruct its members. On one occasion he spent a good part of the evening lecturing on how the bassoons should be brought out and the movements arranged. Then he said that he would accompany the band on his jew's-harp. Unable to find it, he said resignedly that Mrs. Long always threw away his harps. He retrieved one two days later and gave an informal concert to callers at the mansion, rendering a somewhat varied reper-

[7] Beals: *Long*, pp. 176–7; Baton Rouge *Morning Advocate*, March 5, 1929; Marquis Childs, in St. Louis *Post-Dispatch*, Sunday magazine section, March 22, 1931.

[8] Baton Rouge *Morning Advocate*, May 28, 1930.

toire—"Turkey in the Straw," "Cotton-Eyed Joe," "The Kingdom Is Coming," and "I Can, I Will, I Do Believe." "The jew's harp is stroked from the cheek outward," he pontificated. "It should be done with a forward movement. A jew's harp carries naturally without artificial addition, the music of the soul to the world."[9]

He liked to deliver these little lectures and to give the impression that he knew a great deal about music. He managed, in fact, to establish a reputation as a good amateur musician, a man who could play various instruments, sing well, and even compose pieces. Actually he had very little knowledge of the subject, and anyone who did know music could easily deceive him. Once at a cadet concert he asked for a bassoon solo. The student who played the bassoon told his fellows that he was too nervous to play properly, so a cadet behind him leaned forward and played the request on a tenor saxophone. Huey delightedly exclaimed that it was the best bassoon solo he had ever heard. Huey's musical deficiencies were summarized by an artist who knew him intimately: "He had no technical knowledge of music; he couldn't tell one note from another. He did not play the piano or any instrument. He couldn't. He had no voice for singing." A singer who had known Huey from youth and who became a nationally known entertainer confirmed that Huey had no voice. This man, reflecting on Huey's rural Baptist background, described it as "a sing all day and dinner on the grounds voice."[1]

Huey's knowledge of music might have been feigned, but his love for it was real. The same artist who dismissed his musical pretensions thought this affection was "inherent" with him. "Music was a release for him," this man explained. "It was the soft, tender part of him. He liked music that was soft." He liked to be surrounded by music. He had pianos installed wherever he spent much time—in his hotel suites, at the mansion, and, later, in an apartment he had set up in the capitol. When he could get someone to play for him, he would sit on the bench or on the floor and listen with rapt attention. He also liked to have musicians around him on every possible occasion, and he did not care if they were white or black. He knew some of the Negro jazz artists in New Orleans and, by their firm testimony, treated them with respect and without prejudice. He had a special arrangement with a Negro band in the city headed by Manuel Manetta, who went by the name of "Professor." Somebody at the hotel would tell a member of the band when Huey was

[9] Baton Rouge *State-Times*, May 22, 1931; Baton Rouge *Morning Advocate*, May 24, 1931.
[1] Lewellyn B. Williams; Castro Carazo; Gene Austin.

expected, and the band would meet him at the railroad station and pipe him up the street to the Roosevelt and into his suite. As recalled by Manetta, the summons went: "Get the band, get the band. Huey's comin' in tonight." At the station, "He come off the train, man, we'd be by the depot. Man, there was like bodyguard fellows with him. And, man, he come marching down. . . . March all the way from the station to the Roosevelt." Manetta was asked who led the procession. "Oh yeah," he answered as if the question needed no answer, "he was grand marshal."[2]

In 1930 Huey met a man who became his musical companion and colleague. Castro Carazo was then the orchestra director at the Roosevelt Hotel. Born in Costa Rica, Carazo had had a varied career. He had studied music in his native land and at the Spanish Royal Conservatory in Barcelona. Returning to Costa Rica, he toured with various opera companies before becoming music director of the Saenger Amusement Company, which sent him to New Orleans. He remained in New Orleans for nine years, took American citizenship, and then, after a brief return to Costa Rica, accepted the position at the Roosevelt.[3]

Huey frequently danced in the Roosevelt's Blue Room or one of the other rooms where Carazo directed the orchestra. Carazo had, of course, noticed him, but the two had not met. One day Carazo was rehearsing the orchestra in the dining room, which was closed for the occasion. Suddenly Huey came in through the kitchen door and sat down and listened. Finally he said: "Can I direct them, Castro?" Taking over, he got through a couple of pieces—but only because the members had been rehearsed. It was the beginning of an enduring friendship. Thereafter Huey spent countless hours with Carazo, listening to the artist play or discussing music with him. Carazo became thoroughly familiar with Huey's tastes, which ran to simple, sentimental music. His favorite composers were Victor Herbert and Sigmund Romberg, and his favorite songs were "Harvest Moon," "Smoke Gets in Your Eyes," and "Look Down that Lonesome Road." "He loved 'Harvest Moon,' " Carazo recalled. "When he was dancing in the Blue Room and I'd play it, he was in heaven. He would look dreamy and blissful and look at me as if to say thank you and dance with his eyes half closed." Later Huey would see to it that

[2] Castro Carazo; "Fats" Pichon; Manuel Manetta. I had a short interview with Mr. Manetta in the back room of a New Orleans night spot. Later William Russell and Richard Allen of the Archive of New Orleans Jazz, Tulane University, New Orleans, furnished me with a copy of their longer interview with him.

[3] Baton Rouge *State-Times*, April 7, 1935; Castro Carazo.

Carazo was appointed as band director at Louisiana State University, and he and Carazo would collaborate in writing songs, with the artist doing the music and Huey the words. In all their years of association, Carazo said, Huey never discussed politics with him. But sometimes he would say: "Castro, when I'm elected President, I'm going to make you director of the Marine Band."[4]

When Rose was in the mansion or with Huey at social functions, she tried to control some of his habits that she thought were offensive to others or bad for him. He had chewed tobacco as a boy and youth, but gave it up at her request after they were married. He then turned to cigars, however, and nearly always had one in his mouth, usually unlit. However, there was one habit of Huey's that Rose was unable to control—his drinking. He still drank too much and under the influence of liquor became loud or arrogant. He would fill a glass almost full of whisky or half full of whisky and half of wine and empty it at a gulp. One drink would stimulate him, two would make him drunk, and a half pint would set him off on a roaring drunk or cause him to pass out. But he generally recovered from the effects of a debauch quickly. Indeed, sometimes while he was apparently sleeping off a drunk, an idea for a political move would come to him, and he would rouse himself and write it down or awaken an associate to make a copy. He told one intimate: "I've been under the influence of liquor more nights of my adult life than I've been sober, and out of this have come some of the most brilliant ideas of my career."[5]

Huey did not worry that drinking would affect his health. But at the time he moved into the mansion, he was mildly anxious about his growing weight. When he was elected governor, he weighed approximately 175 pounds. But in the following two years he took little exercise and ate richer foods than he ever had before, and his weight increased to two hundred. He tried to take some of it off while he was living in New Orleans. He enrolled in a physical education course at an exclusive private gymnasium. The experiment was not, however, very successful. He performed some of the exercises but only sporadically, when it pleased him to do so. Much of the time he simply clowned. When he was issued his togs, he insisted that his name be stamped across the front of the sweatshirt, the seat of the trunks, and the toes of the shoes. At the exercising sessions he

[4] Castro Carazo; Gene Austin.
[5] Baton Rouge *Morning Advocate*, May 24, 1931; Shirley G. Wimberly; Richard Foster; Charles Frampton; William T. Burton; Henry D. Larcade; Murphy Roden.

put on such a show that as many as fifty people would come in off the street to watch him.[6]

After moving into the mansion, Huey continued his efforts to reduce. He purchased various gymnasium appliances, a rowing machine, a medicine ball, and other items, and had them installed in one of the rooms. How much he used them is questionable. Sometimes he collected his bodyguards or other associates and went to a camp owned by his cousin Jess Nugent at Maringouin, near Baton Rouge. Here he relaxed for days at a stretch and for exercise sawed wood—with a guard at the other end of the crosscut saw. One of the guards said that after they had sawed seven or eight pieces, Huey would fall to talking. He also took up golf, and this was the form of exercise that he engaged in more than any other. He played in both New Orleans and Baton Rouge. In New Orleans his score was consistently 115, but at Baton Rouge he always did much better, thanks to the cooperation of two Negro boys, "Coal Oil" and "Cornfield," whom he engaged to retrieve his badly hit balls and place them in a favorable position. His opponents in Baton Rouge were mystified by his success there, but Coal Oil and Cornfield remained discreet. By playing golf and by doing whatever other exercise he could force himself to do, Huey brought his weight down somewhat, but from this time on his figure was noticeably pudgy.[7]

Huey developed this weight problem because he liked the rich foods that were spread before him in hotels or at banquets. If his country followers could have seen him at some of these affairs, they would have said that Huey was "eatin' high on the hawg." They would not have minded that he was, but they would have been bewildered. For at the very time that he was savoring the fleshpots, Huey was launching a campaign to publicize one of the simplest and most beloved dishes of Southern rural people, potlikker. Potlikker is the juice that remains in a pot after certain vegetables and their greens are boiled. Huey began to extol the concoction in 1930, and in the following year he talked so much about it that he received national attention. Potlikker was good for gall-bladder trouble or almost any other human ailment and would help women trim down their figures, he proclaimed. He revealed to the public his own recipe for preparing it. Mocking his critics, he called his creation

[6] Baton Rouge *State-Times*, January 17, 1931; Irwin F. Poche.
[7] Baton Rouge *Morning Advocate*, January 8, 1931; Baton Rouge *State-Times*, January 17; Louis F. Guerre; Louis A. Jones; Theophile Landry; New Orleans *States*, March 8, 1931; Richard W. Leche.

"potlikker a le dictator" and described it as "the noblest dish the mind of man has yet conceived." Take some turnips, cut up into pieces, and some turnip greens, he advised, and place in a pot with a half pound of salt fat pork, for seasoning, on the top; add water and boil until the vegetables are tender; then remove and place the pot-likker in a bowl and the greens and pork in a dish. Next came the eating, which had to be done in a certain way or the food could not be appreciated. There should be plenty of "cornpone"—patties made of corn meal, hot water and salt—"cooked in a greasy skillet" until "hard enough to knock down a yearling." The diner must hold the cornpone in the left hand and a soup spoon in the right, take a sip of the soup, and then dunk the cornpone in the juice and bite off a piece. The real potlikker devotee always dunked, Huey insisted; he never committed the crudity of crumbling the pone in the soup.

Huey's description of the ceremonial consumption of potlikker delighted newspaper men all over the country. In the first grim years of the depression they welcomed any item that promised relief from the drab daily record of lengthening unemployment. Julian Harris, the witty and cultured editor of the influential Atlanta *Constitution*, devoted a lead editorial to Huey's recipe. The governor of Louisiana might know how to prepare potlikker, Harris said, but he certainly did not know how to eat it: anybody who appreciated this delectable dish crumbled the cornpone. Huey, matching Harris's mock serious-ness, fired off a telegram to the editor, defending his recipe. Harris retaliated with a charge that Huey crumbled in private. Huey replied in a letter addressed to Harris as the editor of the Potlikker and Cornpone Department. He had been resentful at first, he said, but had concluded that Harris was honest at heart, though "ignorant of the finer arts of the subject." But, continued Huey, Harris had gone beyond the limits of respectable journalism with the charge that he crumbled privately. He had merely crumbled before a few friends to demonstrate the faults of the technique.

The dunking-versus-crumbling controversy ballooned into na-tional proportions. People all over the country lined up on one side or the other or pronounced on the merits of potlikker as a food, showing a familiarity with it that must have surprised Southerners. Dr. W. A. Evans, who wrote a widely syndicated newspaper column, "Health Hints," said that he did not like Huey Long but for once Long was right: potlikker was a good food, rich in vitamins. Emily Post, the arbiter of taste, was asked her opinion on the relative merits of dunking and crumbling, but she refused to take a stand. Governor Franklin D. Roosevelt of New York, forging to the front as a Democratic presidential possibility, rushed uninvited into the argument. Roosevelt, who had a farm in Georgia and considered himself an adopted son of the state, wrote a public letter to Julian Harris, whom he addressed, copying Huey's salutation, as editor of the Potlikker and Cornpone Department. He was "deeply stirred by the great controversy," Roosevelt said, and was gratified that the North was at last learning about this fine Southern dish. He suggested referring the dunking–crumbling issue to the platform committee of the 1932 Democratic national convention. But he did not mind stating his own preference. "I must admit that I crumble mine," said Roosevelt.[8]

Eventually the potlikker craze died away, but from the episode Huey had reaped a bountiful crop of publicity. He appeared in the national press as a likeable fellow, a little comic perhaps, but kindly, interested in people's welfare, and extremely entertaining. He said later that he introduced his recipe to persuade the people of Louisiana to help themselves in the depression by raising gardens. Such a purpose was probably an afterthought. More likely, he started the potlikker issue on impulse, just to be saying something. When it aroused national attention, he realized the publicity value and kept it going, but essentially he was only amusing himself. He confessed as much to Harris, with whom he became very friendly. The controversy was, Huey said, the "only delightful pastime" he had had since becoming governor.[9]

A CASUAL OBSERVER might have concluded in the first months of 1930 that Huey was doing nothing but engaging in social activities. Actually, he was working as hard as he ever had. Behind the scenes he was laboring to line up support for the public-improvements program he was going to propose to the May session of the legislature. He was particularly anxious to secure the active backing of his new business friends for the program, and he spent much time in New Orleans discussing it with the recently created Commercial

[8] Deutsch, in New Orleans *Morning Tribune*, May 16, 1930; Huey P. Long: *Every Man a King* (New Orleans, 1933), pp. 264–5; unidentified clipping, probably February 28, 1930, in Grace Scrapbook; Long to Julian Harris, February 16 and March 3, 1931, in Long Papers, Emory University; Baton Rouge *Morning Advocate*, February 17 and 19, March 26, 1931 (for Evans's column); Baton Rouge *State-Times*, February 17, 1931; New Orleans *States*, February 18 and March 1, 1931; Elliott Roosevelt, ed.: *F. D. R.: His Personal Letters, 1947–1950* (New York, 1947–50), III (*1928–1945*), 176–7.

[9] *Congressional Record*, 74 Cong., 1 Sess., p. 3445, March 12, 1935; Long to Julian Harris, May 7, 1931, in Long Papers, Emory University.

Affairs Committee. These meetings were not entirely free of discord. The committee was disposed to favor the large bond issues that would be required to finance the highway and port programs. But some of the members objected that such huge sums should not be expended without proper supervision. The leading objectors were the publishers of the three principal New Orleans newspapers, who persuaded the committee to demand that the governor allow the appointment of an advisory committee to oversee the administration of the highway fund, the largest of the proposed bond issues. Huey readily agreed to the suggestion: he could see advantages in having available a board of distinguished citizens who probably would not scrutinize very closely the activities of the Highway Commission. He appointed the advisory committee from a panel of names submitted by the publishers and promised to give it legal status by including it in the bond amendment.

The publishers then persuaded the Commercial Affairs Committee to demand another concession. As the Dock Board would be given increased money to spend on port improvements, its personnel must be depoliticized. The governor would have to agree to appoint a new board, composed of men recommended to him by the city's business leaders. The Kingfish had had enough. He rejected the proposal to reconstitute the Dock Board. He also announced that the highway advisory committee would not be given constitutional status. The committee could continue to exist, but he would determine its function. His enemies pounced on his statement, charging that this was the same old Huey, who was determined to exercise complete power over money and patronage. Thoughts of power were never absent from Huey's mind, and they were present when he repudiated the committee's proposals. But he could easily have justified his course as sound governmental policy. The Highway Commission and the Dock Board were arms of the executive branch of the state government, and as governor he was responsible for what they did. He had every right to claim undivided authority over them.[1]

The squabble over safeguarding the expenditure of the bond funds revealed that the alliance between Huey and the businessmen was wearing a little thin. The business leaders did not entirely trust Huey and wanted to impose restrictions on him, reasonable to them but not applicable to the world of politics. Huey had no intention

[1] Lengthy editorial summaries of this controversy appear in the New Orleans *Times-Picayune, States,* and *Item* of March 11, 1930. See also Deutsch: "Kingdom of the Kingfish," in New Orleans *Item,* August 22, 1939.

of being restricted, and although he valued the support of the businessmen, he regarded them only as convenient allies. He might make concessions to them, but he expected them to cooperate with him largely on his terms. He showed how little respect he had for business opinion immediately after the funds fight. The Dock Board, whose policies had been an issue in the fight, employed a number of part-time attorneys. One of these was a New Orleans man, Arthur B. Hammond, who was a brother-in-law of Esmond Phelps, a *Times-Picayune* mogul and a leader in the drive to impose restraints on Huey's handling of bond funds. Huey discovered that Hammond was also a part-time lawyer for the Levee Board. Striking a pose of offended civic righteousness, he directed that "double-dipping" Hammond be discharged from both posts. He cited as justification for his action that state law forbade an individual to draw two official salaries. This was correct, although there was some question as to whether Hammond's retainer fees were salaries. But the *Picayune* had in the past bitingly attacked Huey for permitting his henchmen to hold dual jobs. Now he could say that he had adopted the paper's views. He had not, of course, been suddenly converted to political purity. Rather, he had chosen the Hammond episode to display his power nakedly, to show the New Orleans business community what he could do if he wanted to. Whether he made his point is doubtful; the immediate result was to create for himself an unrelenting enemy. Hammond's redoubtable wife, Hilda Phelps, swore vengeance on the man who had humiliated her husband. She shortly organized the Louisiana Women's Association, composed of other aristocratic women, all of them dedicated to removing the tyrant Long from public life.[2]

Political observers, studying Huey's projected public improvements, noticed a strange omission in the program—bridge construction. The man who owed his rise in part to his championship of free bridges had apparently dropped this issue. However, the observers were missing something: Huey had pushed as vigorous a bridge program as he could with his resources, which were slender. The legislature had in 1928 authorized a bond issue to construct bridges, but the amendment had been faultily drawn, and since its validity was doubtful, the state had been unable to dispose of any of the bonds. Consequently, the Highway Commission had to draw on its current revenue to build bridges. Even thus hampered, it achieved respectable results. The Chef and Rigolets bridges were completed,

[2] *Louisiana Progress*, April 3, 1930; Forrest Davis: *Huey Long*, pp. 127–8; Hilda Phelps Hammond: *Let Freedom Ring* (New York, 1936), pp. 44–5.

providing at last a toll-free route from New Orleans to the Gulf Coast and forcing the Watson–Williams Syndicate to go into receivership. Unable to build other bridges, the Highway Commission, at Huey's direction, entered into negotiations with the companies that operated ferry boats over the principal streams. These companies charged set fees, so much for an automobile, so much for the passengers in it. The state agreed to pay the operators a generous sum each month to run the ferries free.[3]

The reason Huey had not included a bridge proposal in his program was shortly explained. In February 1930 he announced that he had a plan to provide the state with eight new steel and concrete bridges within a relatively short time. Only a few details of a financial nature remained to be worked out, he said. He disclosed these details at a meeting of his highway advisory committee. He had been negotiating with a private concern, the Nashville Bridge Company, to build the eight bridges at a cost of something over six million dollars, a million less than the cost estimated by the Highway Commission's engineers. To protect its investment, the company would be allowed to charge tolls that would give it a return of six per cent. Everything above six per cent would go into a sinking fund to enable the state eventually to purchase the bridges. By the terms of the contract the state could, in fact, buy the bridges whenever it was financially able to do so—hence, Huey explained, the interests of the public were well protected, and the state would get needed bridges without waiting for the voting of another bond issue. But the advisory board expressed reluctance to approve the proposal. After deliberation, it stated that it had no jurisdiction in this case: the governor and the Highway Commission would have to make the decision.[4]

Huey had resolved the mystery of how he would build bridges, but in doing so he had created a greater mystery. Why was the great opponent of toll bridges sponsoring a plan to construct eight of them? Back of his action was a tangled story of complicated motives. He and other participants offered public explanations later, but their combined account is not clear, and it is impossible today to determine exactly what happened. Only the chronology of events is simple. Sometime in 1929 Huey had called in a representative of

[3] Unidentified clipping, February 1930, in Long Scrapbooks, XI; New Orleans *Times-Picayune*, June 9, 1930; Norman Lant. The *Picayune* in its story gave all the credit for the Chef–Rigolets bridges to Governor Simpson. The Watson–Williams bridge was purchased by the state in 1938 and made a free bridge.

[4] Unidentified clipping, February 13, 1930, in Grace Scrapbook; New Orleans *Times-Picayune*, February 28, 1930.

the Nashville Bridge Company and broached the plan to him. The representative had readily agreed to it. In the course of the conversation either he or Huey mentioned that the company would need a lawyer to handle legal matters, and Huey remarked that John Overton was an excellent one. Apparently Huey specified that Overton not be told that he had suggested him. Overton, unaware of Huey's part in the affair, gladly accepted the employment, studied the plan, decided that it would be beneficial for the state, and in complete innocence proposed it to Huey. He was gratified to find that the governor seemed "much interested." Or so he and Huey related under oath.

But Earl Long, also speaking under oath, gave an entirely different account. According to Earl, Overton himself instigated the bridge deal. Overton did it to get money, Earl said. He quoted O. K. Allen, chairman of the Highway Commission, as saying that Overton hoped to receive as his fee two hundred thousand dollars. Earl also quoted Huey as saying that Overton was "money mad." When Earl made this charge, he was estranged from Huey and was eager to damage his brother and everyone associated with him, but his story is supported by others who were in a position to know what happened. As they tell it, Huey was trying to pay off his obligation to Overton, but the engineers in the Highway Commission got wind of the scheme and determined to stop it. They knew that if it went through, any prospect of federal aid for Louisiana bridges would be closed off, for the federal government had a firm policy of not participating in the construction of toll bridges. The engineers conveyed their feeling to Chairman Allen and enlisted him on their side.

Beyond question the engineers went to Allen, and undoubtedly they alarmed him by warning about the loss of federal aid. But he was already disposed to oppose the bridge deal, because he too disapproved of toll spans on principle. Moreover, he foresaw a hostile public reaction to Huey's plan—Huey had committed himself and his followers to free bridges. If the governor should now support this program, he would repudiate his principle and seriously damage the Long movement. Allen decided that he would have to stop the bridge deal. It was not characteristic of him to be so resolute. He is universally considered to have been a weak man, the most unheroic figure in the Long group, and he was pliable, especially to Huey's influence. But he had a stubborn streak and a fair measure of integrity, and when he made up his mind about something, he would fight. He fought now. He discussed the bridge plan with the other two members of the commission and found that they were as doubtful about it as he was. At his suggestion they joined him in a written statement to the governor declaring that they would not approve the plan. Huey attempted to sway them, and at one meeting he and Allen roundly cursed each other. But then, probably to the surprise of Allen and his colleagues, Huey gave way. He allowed the commission to announce that the plan for toll bridges had been scrapped. According to one source, the news so enraged Overton that he threw his hat on the floor and stamped on it. He did not feel compensated when the Nashville Bridge Company paid him five thousand dollars for his expenses. He did not know that Huey had given the company the money to pay over to him. Huey later explained how he got the money: he simply asked some of his "friends" for it.[5]

Although Huey's course in the affair seems tortuous, his motives were probably quite simple. It is inconceivable that he contrived such a complex scheme merely to enable Overton to get some money. If Overton had demanded remuneration, which is not proved, he did not have the power to force Huey to pay him. And if Huey had felt constrained to pay up, he could easily have collected more than five thousand dollars from private sources. The bridge scheme undoubtedly originated in Huey's always present desire to achieve quick results. He wanted to get on with the building of bridges, he did not have the money to build them, and so he negotiated the contract with the Nashville Bridge Company. "We were in a hurry," he said later, as though he thought that his urgency entitled him to take whatever action he saw fit.[6] He brought Overton into the deal as an afterthought. The company had to have a lawyer, the lawyer's fee would be handsome, and it might as well go to a Long supporter. Overton was understandably enraged when Allen blocked the plan. It was Allen who emerged from the episode with the greatest credit. He upheld a principle that Huey should have sustained, and he convinced Huey of the political dangers in the deal. Huey's rather easy submission to Allen and the other members of the Highway Commission is to be explained as a sudden realization on his part of these dangers. The really strange aspect of the affair is that he had to be made to realize them. He had again betrayed the fact that when he was in an exuberant mood, he could misjudge a situation as readily as an ordinary politician.

He had reason to feel exuberant in the weeks immediately

[5] *Overton Hearing*, I, 620–1, 624–5, 798, 802, 876–9, 883–4, 910–11, 936–43, 1086–9; confidential communications; Shreveport *Journal*, April 15, 1930.
[6] *Overton Hearing*, I, 878–9.

preceding the meeting of the legislature. As one triumph after another came his way, their combined effect was enough to make
him feel invincible. In April the Supreme Court of the United
States handed down decisions upholding two important Long laws
that had been in litigation for a year. One decision rejected the
complaint of certain citizens of Caddo parish that the free-schoolbooks law was unconstitutional. The Court held, as Huey had predicted
it would, that the law did not violate the provision against state
aid to religious institutions: the books were being given to children, not to schools. The other decision ruled against the suit of
the Ohio Oil Company that the severance tax was discriminatory
because it permitted the state to base the levy on the gravity of the
oil. The state was only exercising a reasonable latitude, the Court
stated. Its finding meant that the chief source of revenue for the
schoolbooks was safe from attack. While Huey was still savoring
this success, the Louisiana Police Jurors' Association met in its annual convention and voted by a decisive majority to support the
road-bond amendment and the other items in the governor's improvements program. Huey naturally was pleased that he had the
approval of this influential organization, but he was positively delighted that the Orleans delegation, headed by Mayor Walmsley,
had voted to support the program. Although Walmsley shortly
hedged his position by stating that he favored adequate safeguards
over the expenditure of the bond funds, Huey had grounds for
thinking that the Old Regular legislators would be with him in the
approaching session.[7]

The legislature convened on May 11. If Huey had nourished
hopes that his patient wooing of conservative opinion had had any
effect, he was rudely disappointed. In the house the opposition
moved immediately to unseat Fournet as speaker. Conservative
representatives arose to recall Fournet's conduct in the Bloody Monday fracas and to charge that he had made other unfair rulings. It
was obvious that the move had been long planned and was well
organized, for powerful figures circulated in the lobby urging Fournet's removal: John M. Parker, J. Y. Sanders, Sr., Lieutenant Governor Cyr, and from New Orleans, Esmond Phelps of the *Picayune*
and publisher James Thomson of the *Item*. The reason for this
concerted effort soon became apparent. Conservatives boasted that
if it succeeded, the next step would be to revive impeachment.
But Huey was also on hand lobbying, and he mobilized enough sup-

[3] Shreveport *Journal*, April 15 and 29, 1930; New Orleans *Item*, April 15, 1930;
New Orleans *Times-Picayune*, April 18, 1930.

port to save Fournet. The resolution to remove him received forty-four votes, but fifty-five were cast against it.

Simultaneously the opposition attempted to organize the senate. Its presiding officer, Cyr, was already with them, but they wanted to put one of their men into the office of president pro tem, made vacant by the retirement of Philip Gilbert to accept a judgeship. The Long forces turned back this move but only by supporting a senator who had not been a consistent Longite during the impeachment, Alvin O. King of Lake Charles, in southwestern Louisiana. King defeated the anti candidate by a vote of twenty-two to fifteen. The voting totals in both chambers portended ill for Huey's program. He had an undoubted majority, but he would need a two-thirds majority to enact his road-bond amendment and the legislation for some of his other public improvements.[8]

On the day after the houses were organized, Huey addressed them in joint session. Speaking from notes, a departure from his usual style, he outlined the administration's program. He referred to the debt of the port of New Orleans and said that the state should help to retire it and should also act to improve the port's facilities. But mostly he talked about roads. He revealed that his leaders would introduce a constitutional amendment authorizing the sale of sixty-eight million dollars in bonds, the money to be used to construct three thousand miles of surfaced roads. Careful, as always, to follow sound financial practice, he recommended that the legislature dedicate two cents of the current four-cent gasoline tax to secure the bonds. The amendment to provide good roads would be the only measure that the administration would back, he said, deceiving nobody. The conservative press described his proposals with that calm balance that it reserved for the Kingfish. The *Picayune* charged that the governor was well on his way to accomplishing "his dream of absolute dictatorship," and a city correspondent analyzed the road bill when it was introduced as "sheer broth of dementia" and a piece of "executive hysteria."[9]

Huey's leaders introduced a number of other measures during the first two weeks of the session, including an amendment providing for the sale of five million dollars in bonds to build a new capitol—Huey's estimated cost of the structure had risen dramatic-

[8] Baton Rouge *Morning Advocate*, May 11, 1930; Shreveport *Journal*, May 12, 1930; Baton Rouge *State-Times*, May 12, 1930; *Louisiana Progress*, May 15, 1930.
[9] Shreveport *Journal*, May 13, 1930; New Orleans *Times-Picayune*, May 13, 1930; Deutsch, in New Orleans *Morning Tribune*, May 20, 1930.

ally—and legislation to improve the New Orleans port. Although this was the program that Huey had been talking about for months, the conservatives greeted it as though it was a new and particularly shameful display of demagoguery. By holding forth several pieces of legislation, the governor was trying to buy support for the road bill, they cried, but he would find that some people were not for sale. Their analysis was not entirely correct, but they were basically right—he would not be able to placate his opposition. The Baton Rouge legislative delegation announced that capitol or no capitol they were going to vote against the road amendment. They had been expected to oppose it, and their stand did not materially affect the prospects of the measure. The delegation that everybody was watching was the big New Orleans group: which way would it decide to go? The answer was not long in coming. The Old Regular ward leaders caucused at the Choctaw Club and with Mayor Walmsley in the chair voted to oppose all the bond amendments. Immediately a majority of the city delegation announced that they would obey the ruling of the caucus. This development caught Huey completely by surprise. He had counted on some Old Regular support. Deprived of it, he would be hard put to secure the two-thirds majority he needed to pass his amendments.[1]

Huey's surprise shortly became anger. He had thought he had an understanding with Walmsley to support the amendments—as he probably had—and now the mayor had run out on him. He struck back savagely, at the city itself rather than at its leaders. He aimed his blow at the most vulnerable part, the city's peculiar system of finance. New Orleans operated largely on borrowed money for the first half of each year: it negotiated bank loans and redeemed them by taxes collected during the second half. Walmsley's administration had borrowed sums greatly in excess of the taxes it could expect to collect, Huey announced, naming as his source for this information the state bank examiner, J. S. Brock, who was disturbed by the situation. It had worried him too, he said, and he had decided to take remedial action. But as Brock had revealed the information around the first of March, it had taken Huey a rather long time to become disturbed. Cynical observers noted that he had not been seriously agitated until the Old Regulars voted to oppose his program.

His first move was to exert state pressure on the New Orleans banks. At his direction, Brock instructed these institutions that they

[1] Baton Rouge *State-Times*, May 19, 1930; Shreveport *Journal*, May 19, 1930; New Orleans *Times-Picayune*, June 1, 1930; *Louisiana Progress*, May 22, 1930.

must call in and reduce the loans they had made to the city to a figure commensurate with the expected tax revenue. Since he and Brock claimed that the Walmsley administration had borrowed five million dollars in excess of this revenue, this curtailment would leave the city with virtually no income. Next Huey demanded that the state supervisor of public accounts be allowed to audit the city's books. The council tartly refused its permission, observing that the books were open to any citizen of the city but not to outsiders. Huey then induced one of his local supporters who was a public accountant to ask to look at the books. The council could hardly deny the "citizen" access to the records, but it ejected him after one day on the ground that he was compiling information for political purposes. Huey retaliated with another display of state power. By law the Tax Commission received the tax books of municipalities and reviewed their assessments. Huey directed the commission to hold up New Orleans's tax book, without which the city could not make out any tax bills and hence could not collect any taxes. The council had to secure a court order to compel the return of the book.[2]

At the height of the controversy Huey called a public meeting of his supporters in New Orleans, announcing that he wanted to explain the city's financial straits to its citizens. A large and enthusiastic crowd turned out to hear him. Friendly sources estimated that fifteen thousand persons were present; the city press put the figure lower but admitted that eight thousand persons were there. Huey did review the financial crisis but only briefly. He devoted his remarks to attacking his enemies—Colonel "Bow Wow" Ewing, "Old Dr. *Times-Picayune*, the widow woman of the press," and "Turkey Head" Walmsley. The crowd, revealing evidence of prior coaching, chanted when Walmsley was mentioned: "Impeach him! Impeach him, governor." Huey then passed on to Esmond Phelps and charged that Phelps had placed his brother-in-law, Arthur Hammond, in two state jobs to save himself the expense of supporting him. "I take full responsibility for cutting Hammond away from teat number one and teat number two," Huey roared. "Esmond Phelps never spent a dime for a shoe shine in his life," he went on. "He uses Shinola and if he has none rubs his shoes on his pants' legs." (The dignified Phelps never recovered from the effect of this sally. He was known thereafter as "Shinola" Phelps.) Huey con-

[2] New Orleans *Times-Picayune*, June 1, 2, 6, and 8, 1930; *Louisiana Progress*, June 12, 1930; Deutsch: "Kingdom of the Kingfish," in New Orleans *Item*, August 22 and 23, 1939.

cluded with an exhortation: "Let's have a free people and fear no newspaper. To hell with them all."[3]

This speech, which apparently disregarded cynically the issues of the controversy, infuriated the conservatives. Walmsley exploded trying to find epithets to characterize the governor: Huey was "an insane man," "an anarchist," "a liar," and "a brute." Colonel Ewing declared that Huey's harassment of New Orleans was worse than anything the carpetbaggers had attempted during Reconstruction. But recalling the "valiant heroes" who had driven out the carpetbaggers, the colonel predicted that their descendants would know how to deal with the "little chineapin-headed misfit now in the governor's chair." The Baton Rouge *State-Times* also recalled the parallel of Reconstruction. New Orleans had not lain down then before "alien soldiers," the paper said, and it would not yield now to the "little sniveling demagogue" from Winn parish. And, as it turned out, the city did not have to yield. The council was able to negotiate a loan from New York banks that enabled it to meet expenses until taxes were collected. Conservatives rejoiced at the victory. But those of them who had just been invoking the spirit of Reconstruction failed to notice an irony of the triumph: New Orleans had saved herself by begging "alien" Northern bankers for aid.[4]

While the controversy was swirling to an end, Huey's road-bond amendment, his most important piece of legislation, cleared a committee hearing and came before the house of representatives. As evidence of its priority, two floor leaders had it in charge. One was Allen Ellender, now the top Long leader. The other, to the astonishment of observers, was William H. ("Sack of Potatoes") Bennett, who was now back with Huey. But they seemed strangely reluctant to move the measure along—appeared, in fact, to be deliberately stalling its progress. The explanation was quite simple: Huey needed time to line up the two-thirds majority required to pass the amendment. He did not permit his leaders to bring it to a vote until mid-June. Then it was revealed that his efforts had failed. Only thirty-two votes were cast against the amendment, but the sixty for it were seven short of the needed majority.[5]

[3] Shreveport *Times*, June 9, 1930; *Louisiana Progress*, June 12, 1930.
[4] Shreveport *Times*, June 9, 1930; Ewing, quoted in *Time*, June 16, 1930; Baton Rouge *State-Times*, quoted in Webster Smith: *The Kingfish* (New York, 1933), pp. 191–2.
[5] New Orleans *Times-Picayune*, June 18, 1930.

Huey must have known that he did not have enough votes to pass the amendment and probably allowed the test simply to demonstrate the large support behind the measure. Before the vote was taken, however, he had prepared a shrewd countermove. On June 11, the last day on which bills could be introduced, one of his leaders tossed into the house hopper a bill providing for the calling of a constitutional convention. The legislature could convoke a convention by a simple majority, and Huey unquestionably commanded a majority in both houses. He was thus presenting the conservatives with a choice between two defeats. The convention would certainly enact the road-bond measure. It could do so by adopting it as a constitutional amendment, which would then be submitted to the people, or it could embody the amendment in an entirely new constitution. Although Huey said that the convention would deal only with the road issue, the conservatives did not believe him. They pointed to a proviso in the bill as introduced that stated that no new constitution could be written unless it was submitted to a popular vote. This dangerous man was really planning to change the whole governmental structure of the state, they charged. "Don't Trust Him," blared the title of an editorial in Ewing's *States*. Huey had counted on such reactions. Now he offered his alternative plan to the conservatives. They could easily remove the threat of a convention, he said, by permitting the legislature to adopt the road amendment and send it on to the people.[6]

The strategy was a brilliant expression of Machiavellian theory, but its application was difficult. Time was running against Huey. The bill to call the convention, "the con-con bill" as it became known, had been introduced so late that it was far down on the calendar, reposing behind two hundred other bills. The opposition in the house, realizing that the measure would pass if brought to a vote, resolved to hold up the progress of every bill ahead of it. They resorted to every delaying tactic they could think of, debating endlessly even minor measures. Hoping to demonstrate that public opinion was on their side, the conservative leaders called a mass meeting of their supporters in Baton Rouge on June 18. Huey promptly announced that he would hold a rival meeting on the same night. The Baton Rouge *State-Times* urged the capital's citizens to attend the opposition gathering and not that of Long, who had "tried to destroy this city."[7]

[6] *Louisiana Progress*, June 19, 1930; New Orleans *States*, June 24, 1930.
[7] New Orleans *Times-Picayune*, June 16, 1930; Baton Rouge *State-Times*, June 18, 1930.

Thousands of people poured into Baton Rouge on the appointed day. Over two thousand antis came from New Orleans alone, riding a special train of twenty-eight cars bearing the name "Walmsley Special." Also from New Orleans came two trains of Longites, who were, according to the conservative press, jobholders who had been ordered to attend the Long meeting. Whenever members of the two factions met on the streets, fights broke out. The crowd at the anti meeting was estimated to number between four thousand and six thousand persons. It heard several speakers denounce Huey and his program. Mayor Walmsley denied that he had made a deal with the governor to support the road amendment. Former Governor Parker charged that graft was rampant in the Long administration and demanded that Huey be put in the state penitentiary or a lunatic asylum.

Even hostile newspapers admitted that the crowd at Huey's meeting was large, numbering perhaps seven thousand persons. Huey told reporters that there were thirty thousand persons present, and a Long leader, as though determined to outdo his chief in arithmetic, announced that a hundred thousand people had assembled. Huey gave the main address. He said that the constitutional convention plan was the only way to get the road-bond amendment before the people and asked his listeners to bring pressure on their legislators to vote for the con-con bill. In violent language he denounced the men at the rival meeting. They were "till-tempting thieves," "guttersnipes," and "galley rats." "For them to hold such a meeting is like sending a safe blower into a prayer meeting to tell them what the Bible says," he roared. "Why if you put J. Y. Sanders, Ruffin G. Pleasant, and John M. Parker into a room with a pole cat, the pole cat would walk out."[8]

Three days after the meeting, on Saturday, June 21, the Long forces made a desperate effort to push the convention bill up on the house calendar. As the representatives assembled for the usual short session before the weekend adjournment, Huey suddenly appeared and went from desk to desk talking to his followers. Then Ellender rose and moved that the rules be changed to permit the bill to be considered out of its regular order on Monday. Such a change could be made by a simple majority instead of a two-thirds vote, he argued. Speaker Fournet ruled that the motion was admissible. Instantly the house exploded in an uproar reminiscent of Bloody Monday. "By your ruling last year that the house had adjourned you

[8] New Orleans *Times-Picayune*, June 19, 1930; Baton Rouge *State-Times*, June 19, 1930; *Louisiana Progress*, June 26, 1930.

stamped yourself as a fool," one conservative called out. "By your ruling today . . . you branded yourself as a knave." Another one appealed the ruling and demanded that the chamber be cleared of unauthorized visitors. Huey hastily departed. In the debate that followed, one angry anti after another denounced Ellender's motion as an outrageous violation of the rules. Ellender listened calmly and finally walked to the dais. He said that he was gratified to learn that the opposition respected the rules. A filibuster was not a part of the rules, he continued, and apparently the opposition was going to cease its delaying tactics. On that understanding he was withdrawing his motion and allowing the house to adjourn. But he had made his meaning clear. If the antis would not agree to let the con-con bill come up out of order on the following week, he would reoffer his motion and pass it. Faced by certain defeat, the opposition capitulated. The bill was brought to a vote on June 25 and passed by a vote of fifty-six to forty-two. Its passage evoked shrill pleas from the conservative press—now only the senate could save the state.[9]

There was strong reason to think that the senate could do so. The Long majority in the upper chamber was smaller than in the house. And whereas in the house the Longites had the help of a friendly presiding officer, in the senate they would have to deal with the hostile Cyr—and with little time to overcome him. By law the term of a regular session was fixed at sixty days, and thus this session would have to end on July 10. Unless the Long leaders could shake the bill out of the ordinary legislative process, they would fail. They tried repeatedly to free it by moving to suspend the rules and bring the bill up out of order, but they could not muster the twenty votes required to make the change. Cyr consistently refused to recognize Long senators, although he permitted one anti senator to hold the floor for days, drinking pop and discoursing on how the governor had persecuted him in his parish. Huey finally told his leaders to give up the fight. "I am licked," he admitted. The legislature adjourned without having enacted a single revenue bill.[1]

It had enacted hardly any important legislation. One measure that did get through was a tick-eradication law, providing for compulsory dipping of farm animals. In the past Huey had usually

[9] New Orleans *Times-Picayune*, June 22, 1930; Baton Rouge *State-Times*, June 21, 1930; Shreveport *Journal*, June 21, 1930; Allen J. Ellender; Deutsch: "Kingdom of the Kingfish," in New Orleans *Item*, August 22, 1939.

[1] New Orleans *Times-Picayune*, July 1, 8, and 9, 1930; Baton Rouge *State-Times*, July 4, 1930; *Louisiana Progress*, July 17, 1930; Henry D. Larcade; Deutsch: "Kingdom of the Kingfish," in New Orleans *Item*, August 22, 1939.

opposed such a law, because many farmers were against it, although in 1928 he had offered to support one in return for eradicationist backing for his tax program. He had no particular feelings on the issue, but a strong sentiment for a law had developed in the session, spurred on by some of his own leaders. He had to take account of it. Therefore he announced that he would sign the law if passed, but veto an appropriation to enforce it. An admirer exclaimed ecstatically: "And so Louisiana has shown itself as having a governor who never forgets his obligation to the little man . . . and at the same time who pleases the citizens of towns by bringing about a result that is desired by all."[2]

The legislature had passed a number of appropriation bills. Some of these Huey promptly and zestfully vetoed. By one veto he cut off the funds of the Public Service Commission: Francis Williams was going to have a lean year. By another he deprived Paul Cyr of money for traveling expenses and for expenses incurred while acting as governor. "He ain't going nowhere, so he don't need traveling expenses," Huey explained, "and he ain't going to act as governor for a holy minute, so he won't need either of those items." Observers wondered why he was in such high spirits. They soon learned the reason. On July 15 he announced that he was filing as a candidate for the United States Senate against Joseph Ransdell. His issue would be his program for good roads. "Should a majority of the people approve of my candidacy," he said, "then no member of the legislature can have the slightest ground upon which to stand and say that the people do not favor the good roads program. . . . In effect, my election will mean that the legislature will submit my plan to the people, or those who refuse to accede to the publicly expressed stand of the voters will be signing their own political death warrant."[3]

[2] Harvey Peltier; *Louisiana Progress*, July 3, 1930.
[3] Deutsch: "Kingdom of the Kingfish," in New Orleans *Item*, August 23, 1939; *Louisiana Progress*, July 17, 1930.

# CHAPTER 17

# *Beating the Feather Duster*

ONE DAY IN 1933 Arthur Krock, the Washington correspondent of *The New York Times*, met Huey Long coming out of the Senate. Huey stopped Krock and said that he could not understand the paper's treatment of him: it opposed him editorially but carried lengthy accounts of his speeches. "Why do you print what I say?" he demanded. "We have this foolish idea that the news columns should be honest," Krock explained, "and, since you make news, we print it." The Kingfish seemed dumbfounded. "Goddamn it! I wouldn't run a newspaper that way if I owned one," he said.[1]

All of his life Huey had an absorbing interest in media and methods that influenced public opinion. As a boy learning the printing trade, he had studied the workings of a small-town newspaper. He had also noticed the Winn parish device of the political circular, and when he first ran for office he had used the circular as a principal weapon. He issued circulars in his gubernatorial campaigns, and after becoming governor he relied on them to bring his views before the people. He always insisted on writing the copy of every circular himself. He would scrawl one out on several sheets of tablet paper and hand it to a secretary to be typed. He told one secretary his concept of effective political language. "Always write everything so a six-year-old child can understand it," he said.[2]

During the first two years of his governorship he avoided reporters and seemed indifferent to newspaper publicity. But his atti-

---

[1] Arthur Krock, memoir in Columbia University, Oral History Project.
[2] Joseph David; Louis A. Jones; Ollie Hicks Sheffield.

tude was only a reaction to the notice he got. The papers in all the
cities and larger towns, and in some of the smaller towns as well,
were bitterly opposed to him. He felt, with some justification, that
they were not going to give him fair treatment in their columns even
if he cooperated with their reporters. Consequently, he often refused
to see Louisiana reporters or, if he did see them, to tell them anything. United Press, discovering that their local men could not get to
the governor, resorted to telephoning him from Dallas, Kansas
City, or even New York. To their surprise, they found that he would
talk freely and would answer all their questions.[3]

To only one Louisiana newspaper would Huey give out any
news, and he did it through what must surely be one of the most
curious arrangements in the history of journalism. One day soon
after becoming governor, while in New Orleans, he called the city
editor of the *Item*. The reporters sitting around the city room could
hear his loud, distinctive voice over the receiver. "I'm getting damn
tired of these reporters following me all the time," he rasped. "Have
you got one man over there that's got any sense at all that I can talk
with and I'll clear everything with this one man." The editor glanced
over his reporters, letting his eye linger meaningfully on Charles
Frampton. Yes, he said, he had such a man. "Put that sonofabitch
on the phone," Huey roared. "Chick" Frampton, amused and yet
angry, picked up the instrument and said: "Now look. Before we go
any further, I don't want you to use that kind of language to me."
"You'll do," Huey chortled, "come on over here." He and Frampton
hit it off from the start. Frampton was allowed to go into Huey's
room or office at any time, day or night, the only reporter so privileged. When Huey wanted to release an important story, he told
Frampton first. "He never asked me to slant the news in his behalf,"
the reporter said. "He told me that he realized all the newspapers
were against him, including mine, and that he knew that the paper
would change my story when I handed it in, but that all he asked
was that I give them the facts."[4]

Early in the spring of 1930 Huey decided that he would have to
establish his own newspaper. Only in a paper that he controlled
could he present his views on public issues as fully as he thought
they should be presented and only in such a paper would his activities be reported with an objectivity he would define. In starting a

[3] Tom Mahoney.
[4] Charles Frampton. A sample study of Frampton's dispatches confirms that he
did not color them in Huey's favor, nor does his paper seem to have altered them
in any significant way.

newspaper, he was following an example set by other mass leaders. In Wisconsin, "Fighting Bob" LaFollette had his *LaFollette's Progressive*; in Mississippi, Theodore Bilbo had his *Free Lance*; in Texas, James, "Jim," Ferguson his *Ferguson Forum*; in Oklahoma, William, "Alfalfa Bill," Murray his *Blue Valley Farmer*. Huey's paper, a weekly, was *The Louisiana Progress*. In the first issue, which appeared on March 26, an editorial announced its policy. The paper believed that Louisiana would progress if "it buries the fossils, runs out grafters, runs over obstructionists, exposes liars, keeps its ears and eyes open, its tongue ready with opinion; its hands ready with the ballot." Above all the paper believed that the state had to have "forceful, effective, courageous leadership." It left no doubt as to who was meant: a front-page cartoon showed Governor Long handing out schoolbooks to eager children. Curiously, the front page carried an incorrect date line, March 27, although the remaining seven pages were correctly dated March 26.[5]

The confusion in dates probably resulted from the haste with which the first issue was launched. Once Huey had decided to start a paper, he wanted it immediately. To organize the venture he engaged James E. Edmonds, who formerly had been managing editor of the *Times-Picayune* and the *Item* and who now headed a public relations firm in New Orleans. Edmonds negotiated the necessary contracts, selected a staff, oversaw the production of the first two issues, and then retired. He chose as editor John D. Klorer, a tall, balding young man who had previously been night editor of the *Picayune,* and as assistant editors two former *Item* reporters, George French and Morley Cassidy. These three, with the help of a few writers, constituted the entire working staff. In a special category from the other staffers was a man who had been chosen by Huey himself. Huey had long admired the cartoons of Trist Wood, the *Item* artist who sketched politicians with bitterly satiric lines. Huey had been one of his special targets, but he admired the cartoonist's technique. He had often said that he wished Wood could work for him, and now he had his chance. He hired Wood away from the *Item* by offering to double his salary. At least one cartoon by "Trist" appeared in every issue of the *Progress*. A typical Trist cartoon contained a large number of people but always a dominating figure. If it was not Huey in a heroic role, it was one of his enemies depicted in cruel caricature—the *Picayune*, a tall, thin man with horn-rimmed glasses, "Dr. Times-Picayune"; Colonel Ewing, his mustache bristling, looking very much like Kaiser Bill; George Perrault, a rotund anti leader whose immense hips almost filled the cartoon. Huey and Trist collaborated on the cartoons, and frequently the idea for one was Huey's. By the standards of other cartoonists Trist's drawings were too crowded with people; a reader had to study them to get the point. But the people who were going to look at them had time to study. In lonely farmhouses all over Louisiana followers of Huey pored over the cartoons and laughed at Trist's routing of their hero's enemies.[6]

Naturally his enemies were curious as to who owned the *Progress* and who was financing it. A search of the public records disclosed that the publisher of the paper was the Louisiana Progress Publishing Company. The officials of the company were listed as Bernard Cuniffe, a New Orleans assessor and Long leader, B. R. Harrell, a state officeholder, and Robert Brothers of New Orleans. They were obviously acting as fronts for someone else, and the inclusion of Brothers among them left no doubt as to who it was. Bob Brothers was as close to Huey as anybody. Dapper in manner and something of a dandy in dress, he could always be distinguished in the group around Huey by his turned-up hat brim. He was by Huey's side at every opportunity. Although usually described as a mere hanger-on in the Long circle, he was more than that. He was intelligent and clever, adept at meeting people and gifted with a rare ability to pick up information. Huey used him to do things that an official associate could not or would not do. Brothers did them because he completely and honestly adored Huey. Some Long leaders resented him, and once one of them said to Huey: "Why do you put up with that sonofabitch?" The Kingfish caught the questioner by the lapels of his coat. "Listen," he growled, "he's my sonofabitch, ain't he?"[7]

The articles of incorporation revealed that the three officers had subscribed eight thousand dollars in stock to launch the venture. Obviously, this trifling sum was not sufficient to operate a paper of the proposed scope of the *Progress*. Stories in the conservative press charged that state employees had been forced to contribute twenty per cent of their salaries for one month to provide an initial fund. The accusation was broadly accurate. Some employees were "asked" to contribute a specified part of their salaries at first and, possibly,

---

[6] Burton H. Hotaling: "Huey Pierce Long as Journalist and Propagandist," *Journalism Quarterly*, XX (1943), 24; New Orleans *Times-Picayune*, March 27, 1930; Hermann B. Deutsch; Joseph David; Huey P. Long: *Every Man a King* (New Orleans, 1933), p. 188; George M. Wallace.

[7] New Orleans *Times-Picayune*, March 29, 1930; A. P. White; W. A. Cooper.

later. Others were requested to take out subscriptions for a varying
number of people, the number running from two to twenty, according to the employee's salary. From these sources enough money was
raised to provide some two thousand dollars weekly for early
production costs and for the payroll. But before long, income from
another source made the paper practically self-supporting—it began to carry an impressive number of advertisements.[8]

The first issue had carried no ads, and not until the fifth issue
did any appear. Then there were only two of them, one extolling the
qualities of "Pa-Poose" root beer and the other listing a real estate
firm operated by one of Huey's backers, and together they did not
take up a column of space. But thereafter the number of ads steadily
increased, and within a few months the advertising linage accounted for forty per cent of the space of an issue. Some of the ads
merely listed the name and address of a business firm, and these
were obviously placed by men who thought that it was smart to
stand in well with the state government. But many were conventional display notices of the kind that could be seen in any newspaper. They were placed by businessmen who very evidently believed
that an ad in the widely circulated *Progress* would increase sales.
To accommodate these eager patrons, the paper had to add an advertising department and a force of traveling salesmen.[9]

The first readers of the paper received it free. These were people
who were on Huey's mailing list for circulars. He had begun compiling this list when he ran for the Railroad Commission in 1918,
and he had added to it every year thereafter. At the time he became
governor, it contained at least ten thousand names, and by 1930 it
had, by Huey's estimate, forty thousand names.[1] The latter figure
is probably accurate, because the circulation figure of the *Progress*
within a few months reached a total of between forty thousand and
fifty thousand and remained at that level. Obviously, the people who

[8] New Orleans *Times-Picayune*, March 27, 1930; Hotaling: "Long as Journalist,"
*Journalism Quarterly*, XX, 25.

[9] Elsie B. Stallsworth, "A Survey of the Louisiana *Progresses* of the 1930's" (unpublished M.A. thesis, Louisiana State University, 1948), p. 60; Hotaling: "Long as
Journalist," *Journalism Quarterly*, XX, 24–6. My account of the *Progress* is based
on these two careful studies and my own examination of the complete file of the
paper in the William B. Wisdom Collection, Howard-Tilton Memorial Library,
Tulane University, New Orleans. Unless otherwise noted, immediately succeeding
statements are cited from Stallsworth or Hotaling or from the paper itself.

[1] *Overton Hearing*, I, 224. Only once did the *Progress* list its circulation in the
official manual of the newspaper world, giving a figure of forty-seven thousand;
N. W. Ayer *Directory of Newspapers and Periodicals* (Philadelphia, 1932), p. 379.

had been receiving the circulars responded to Huey's appeal to support the paper and sent in their two dollars for a year's subscription. The circulation figure has to be conjectured from varying totals cited by the paper. On occasion it boasted of reaching 125,000 a week. The last figure was probably attained and even eclipsed, but only when Huey decided that he had to broadcast a particular message and had copies mailed out wholesale. Strangely enough, for the mailing system the paper was entered as second-class material at the post office in another state, at Meridian, Mississippi. Presumably to avert the possibility of libel suits, it was indeed printed in that city, on the presses of the Meridian *Star*.[2]

The first issue displayed a conventional makeup—plain block type, eight columns, and three-line indented headlines, with a banner head only over the main story. But by the time the second issue appeared, a week later, the format had been enlivened. This issue and subsequent ones featured double-banner heads on the first page and single ones on the inside pages. The block type was succeeded by a more ornate one. Between "Louisiana" and "Progress" in the title a map of the state was inserted, and under the title was blazoned: "The People's Defense." Shortly an even more flamboyant alteration was made: front-page headlines were printed in red ink. This transition to sensational makeup was completed in December, when the paper became a tabloid.

From the start the *Progress* strove to make itself seem like a conventional paper, a journal that the average family could enjoy. It carried a column on the movies by "Patsy the Hollywood Stenographer," articles on the latest Paris styles, a Bible column, a stock-market commentary, and a column for troubled lovers by Virginia Vance, "Counsel for the Lovelorn." It also contained a full sports page. But even with these features it remained a political newspaper devoted to furthering the interests of Huey P. Long. The news columns emphasized the utterances and activities of Huey or his lieutenants and legislative doings and measures. Issues frequently displayed a front-page editorial by Huey, and this feature was probably more popular with readers than anything else. Its political character was reflected in its changing format. In December 1930 the weekly became a monthly. In June 1931 it returned to a weekly basis for a short time, then appeared at irregular intervals, and ceased publication in January 1932. Its existence as a monthly

[2] John Bosworth, column in Meridian *Star*, September 24, 1961.

coincided with periods when political activity in the state was slack
or when Huey felt unusually secure. But in the first months of its life
it was aggressive, spirited, and exceedingly vocal. It was going to
help elect Huey Long to the U.S. Senate.

RUMORS THAT HUEY would run for the Senate against Ransdell
sprang up in the spring of 1930. He was coy when reporters pressed
him as to whether they were true. The election in September was a
long time off, he said, and even if he was disposed to run, it was
too early to announce. But, he added: "Even my enemies know
that all I have to do to get that job is have my name put on the
ticket."[3]
    Shortly he became more definite. He would probably be a candi-
date, he said, but he wanted to satisfy himself that if elected he
could serve out his term as governor. "I am practically sure I'm going to run," he said, "but I won't if I have to let that good friend
of mine, the lieutenant governor, get the office. I love him too much
to impose the duties of governor on him." Cyr would, of course,
inherit the governorship if Huey stepped out, and it was this fact that
was giving Huey pause. As governor Cyr could sweep the patronage rolls of Long people, create his own machine, and supplant
Huey as the real power in the state even if Huey was senator.
Huey's problem was one of time and law. Ransdell's term expired
in March 1931, but Huey's did not end until May 1932. If Huey
won the senatorial election and resigned as governor, Cyr would
have fourteen months to work his will. But if Huey won and did not
resign, he would be in violation of a provision in the Louisiana constitution prohibiting a person from holding a federal and a state
office of profit simultaneously. As a further complication, if he did
not assume his seat until May 1932, he would lay himself open to
the charge that he was depriving the state of its full representation.[4]
    Huey did not betray any such worries when at last he announced
his candidacy. In mid-July, immediately after the legislature adjourned, he went to Shreveport by airplane to register that city as
his legal domicile. He explained to reporters that he wanted to avoid
any technical question as to where he was from. He would run
against Ransdell, he announced, but if elected, he would finish his
term as governor. "Paul Cyr will never be governor of this state

[3] Baton Rouge *State-Times*, April 1, 1930; New Orleans *Times-Picayune*, April 2, 1930.
    [4] Shreveport *Journal*, April 14, 1930; New Orleans *Times-Picayune*, May 5, 1930.

for one minute," he said, using an expression that was becoming a favorite with him. He airily dismissed anticipated objections to his course. As he would not draw any salary as senator-elect, he would not be violating the prohibition of holding a state and a federal office of profit. He derided the idea that by delaying to take his seat he would diminish Louisiana's representation in the Senate. He pointed out that a newly elected senator would not take the seat until December 1931, and then Congress would adjourn until January. As he would take his seat in May, he would miss only a short session. "I will have to stay out of the Senate four months," he asserted, "leaving the place just as vacant for that four months as it has been for the last thirty-two years."[5]

Huey's announcement outraged conservative Louisianians. "He wouldn't dare . . ." was their reaction. The *Picayune* contemplated wrathfully the spectacle of the distinguished Ransdell being forced to compete with "the eccentric whose fantastic and flagrant performances as governor have earned him national reputation as a freak." Judge Dupre said that Huey's presumption in opposing a "gentleman" like Ransdell showed that the governor had a "malformed or diseased mind."[6]

The conservatives would not have understood all of Huey's reasons for running even if he had explained them frankly. They sneered at the one that he did offer—that if he ran and won his victory would demonstrate that the people wanted his program, which had just been sabotaged in the legislature. Yet there was a large measure of truth in what he said. He could make the election into a referendum on roads and bridges, and a victory would most certainly force another legislature to enact his program. He was, actually, following a normal course for a progressive governor. In many a state a liberal executive, similarly frustrated, had felt constrained to run for the Senate merely to strengthen his hold on his own bailiwick.

Another reason for his candidacy Huey could not reveal. The conservatives suspected it—his ambition—but they could not have grasped the enormity of his design. When he was a mere youth, he had shocked Rose McConnell by telling her that he had planned his career—he would be a secondary state official, governor, senator, and President. Now, with calculation and deliberation, he was about to rise to the third of these steps. Why he chose to make his move at

[5] Baton Rouge *State-Times*, July 16 and 17, 1930; Shreveport *Journal*, July 17, 1930; New Orleans *Times-Picayune*, July 18, 1930.
[6] New Orleans *Times-Picayune*, July 23 and 25, 1930.

this time is open to conjecture. If the legislature had cooperated with him, he might have waited until 1932 and contested against Senator Broussard, but he would probably have acted when he did in any case. A victory in 1930 would put him in an incomparably strong position two years later. As governor–senator, he could select his successor—he could not succeed himself—and probably elect a candidate over Broussard. And overshadowing all these motives was the urge of his own personality: He could never wait or hold back— he had to rush on, to greater scenes, to wider power, to his destiny.

The *Progress* announced Huey's candidacy with spectacular headlines: his rural followers could have reasonably supposed that this was the big story in the news capitals of the world. The paper also featured a cruel cartoon of his opponent. Drawn by Trist, it depicted Ransdell as a bald, goateed, silly-looking old man. Captions reinforced the artist's message: "Louisiana's World Famous Archaeological Exhibit in Washington, D. C."; "Hailed by his admirers as a genuine cross between Rip Van Winkle and Old King Tut." Out of the Senator's mouth were coming words labeled as his "brightest remarks": "Well, well!"; "Dear me!"[7]

Malicious as the cartoon was, it brilliantly exposed Ransdell's weakness. The senator was one of the most ineffective members of Congress, practically a cipher in Washington's political community. He had identified himself with only two issues. He supported public health legislation but mainly with vague speeches. He posed as a champion of flood control in the Mississippi Valley but insisted on the discredited system of "levees only" and opposed such newer concepts as reservoirs. He did not really live in the modern world but in the simpler age of the last century. Uncomprehending of the new economic issues that were agitating the nation and his state, he thought it was sufficient answer to them to eulogize the plain old virtues. One of his favorite lectures was "The Home": "Home, where we were taught to love, honor, and obey our parents and all lawful superiors; home, where we received our first idea of government, a little state in which our fond parents were the rulers and we, the children, were willing subjects; home, the greatest protection from anarchy, the strongest defense against socialism. . . ."[8]

The onetime alliance between Ransdell and Huey had broken up before 1930. The conservative senator and the progressive governor were far apart in their philosophies, and they had joined only

[7] *Louisiana Progress*, July 24, 1930.
[8] Adras Laborde: *A National Southerner: Ransdell of Louisiana* (New York, 1951), p. 51.

because for a time they needed each other's help. Ransdell had not come to Huey's support during the impeachment crisis—Senator Broussard had also remained coldly aloof—and later Ransdell had publicly endorsed the Constitutional League.[9]

Ransdell must have expected that Huey would oppose his bid for re-election, but he probably thought the governor would be content to offer a token resistance, supporting a rival candidate. If he was shocked when Huey himself entered the race, he gave no sign of anxiety. After all, he had reason to believe that he would win easily. He had behind him the prestige of his name and his long service, which gave him seniority on committees. He had the support of the conservative organization in the state and the Old Regular machine in New Orleans. He had also ample campaign funds. Huey charged that the Ransdell campaign chest totaled more than a million dollars, and although this was an exaggeration, the senator still had more money than Huey. Perhaps most important of all, Ransdell had behind him the tradition of "the system," Louisiana's historic way of selecting a senator. A senator was considered to be an emissary of the state in Washington and his office an award from the state. The ruling machine handed out the awards, assigning them on the basis of service, age, and geographical origin. Thus the two senators were likely to be veteran politicians, and always one was from north Louisiana and one from south Louisiana. Once chosen, a senator could hold his place virtually for as long as he wished. Hardly ever had an incumbent been denied re-election. Even as powerful a leader as J. Y. Sanders, Sr., had been unable to break the system when he rebelled against it in 1926.[1]

The senator radiated confidence when he opened his campaign on July 31 at his hometown of Lake Providence. As he rose to speak, a delegation of local housewives presented him with a huge feather duster. Their leader informed him that it was offered as a symbol of clean government and his own clean record. Accepting it, Ransdell responded characteristically: "I feel greatly honored that the women should turn over to me this almost sacred emblem of cleanliness in the home. The feather duster has been used by wives, mothers, and grandmothers for centuries past to clean the sanctuaries of their homes, and the fact that you fine women should entrust it to me for the purpose of carrying on your good work by helping to clean up

[9] Long: *Every Man a King*, pp. 139, 211.
[1] New Orleans *Times-Picayune*, July 21, 1930; Shreveport *Journal*, July 26, 1930. Huey's charges as to the amount of the Ransdell fund are in *American Progress*, February 8, 1934, and *Congressional Record*, 73 Cong., 2 Sess., p. 1556.

Louisiana politics, touches me deeply." The state's politics needed cleaning up, he went on, for the present governor was as corrupt as the carpetbaggers of Reconstruction. He then launched into his prepared remarks. He spoke almost entirely of national issues, stressing his work for flood control and emphasizing the value to the state of his seniority. Nothing in the speech indicated that he was aware of the depression, whose shadows were lengthening over the country, or of the obvious desire of the people of Louisiana for a state government that acted to improve their lot.[2]

The good housewives of Lake Providence had been unwise in choosing their symbol for their candidate, for the feather duster suggested the Senator's physical trademark, his goatee. Huey saw the similarity at once and seized on it. Throughout the campaign he hardly ever referred to his opponent except as "Old Feather Duster" Ransdell. It was a telling form of ridicule, and its effect did not end with the campaign. For the rest of his life Ransdell had to live with the name.

Huey did not open his campaign until August 2, only a little more than a month before the primary election. He spoke at St. Martinsville, under the Evangeline oak, where in the gubernatorial race he had asked the poor of Louisiana to give him a chance to dry their tears. Now he spoke in a different vein. He denounced the Old Regulars as a crooked machine and Ransdell as a tool of Wall Street. An opposition newspaper stigmatized the speech as a "vituperative, vicious attack." Observers wondered why Huey had delayed his stumping to such a late date and why he seemed so relaxed and confident.[3]

The Kingfish was confident, and with reason. He embarked on the campaign with a better organization than he had had in any previous contest. His state managers were his two top legislative floor leaders, Harvey Peltier of the senate and Allen J. Ellender of the house. Huey picked them partly because they were astute operators but mainly because they were legislators. As he explained to Peltier: "This campaign will have to do with what happened at the last session of the legislature. That's going to be the issue." He meant, of course, that the legislature had wrecked his program, and now he would put forward as managers members who could explain to the voters how the wrecking had been done.

[2] New Orleans *Times-Picayune*, August 1, 1930; Baton Rouge *Morning Advocate*, August 1, 1930; *Louisiana Progress*, August 14, 1930; Laborde: *Ransdell of Louisiana*, pp. 188–9.
[3] Baton Rouge *Morning Advocate*, August 3, 1930.

His New Orleans campaign he entrusted largely to the leaders of his recently formed Louisiana Democratic Association, Bob Maestri and Dr. Joseph O'Hara. Coordinating their efforts was Paul Maloney, the former Old Regular chief who had moved openly into the Long camp. Maloney was popular in the "uptown" section of the city, the "American" and well-to-do side of Canal Street, where Huey had always run poorly. Overlooking no possibility to garner votes, Huey asked Maloney at a conference in the city to run for Congress, arguing that his name would swing voters to the Long senatorial cause. Maloney expressed strong reluctance and left the meeting. But as he emerged on the street, he heard a newsboy shouting a recent development: "Maloney a candidate for Congress." He went to his office and found a crowd of his supporters waiting to congratulate him on his decision to run. As Maloney recalled his feelings: "That's where I got converted."[4]

The organization that Huey's managers directed under his supervision consisted of the state employees, practically all of them working for boards that he controlled, and his country leaders, sheriffs, and other officeholders or men who were for him merely because they admired him. Of the various boards, the Dock Board was the most blatantly open in its support of the Long candidacy. Huey had just appointed to it his friend Seymour Weiss, and according to the opposition press, Weiss's function was to weed out employees who were not pro-Long and to organize the vast body of workers to vote for Huey. Employees of all the boards were asked to contribute ten per cent of their salary, probably for two months, to the Long campaign chest. The amount collected was over fifty thousand dollars, estimated the opposition press, which also charged that Huey extorted funds from highway and other contractors doing business with the state. But Huey affirmed that he had at his disposal only thirty thousand dollars, and he was probably speaking the truth. He neglected to add a vital fact—he could have raised more money if he needed it; he did not think that he needed much to defeat Ransdell.[5]

He had enough money to operate his customary kind of campaign. Even though he now had his own newspaper, he continued to rely on circulars. Each edition of them bore the unmistakable stamp of Huey's authorship. One, asking the voters to elect Huey to show their support for his road and bridge program, bore the title: "Who

[4] Harvey Peltier; Allen J. Ellender; Paul Maloney.
[5] New Orleans *Times-Picayune*, April 2, July 16, and August 8, 1930; *Congressional Record*, 74 Cong., 1 Sess., p. 15057.

Should Rule, the People or the Old New Orleans Ring and Their Lying Newspapers?" Another charged that Ransdell had entered into a corrupt arrangement with one Samuel Zemurray, a New Orleans fruit importer (in Huey's words, "a banana peddler") who had interests in Central America: Zemurray had given a nephew of Ransdell a job, and the senator had induced the War Department to dispatch troops to Central America to protect the Zemurray holdings. A third, directed to the voters of New Orleans, listed the results of Ransdell's long years of officeholding:

1. We lost the United States Mint.
2. We lost the Federal Reserve Bank.
3. The United States Navy Yards in New Orleans were closed down.
4. The United States Army abandoned the Military post at Jackson Barracks.
5. We lost a station on the Transcontinental Air Mail Route.

WE HAVE NOT YET LOST THE POST OFFICE.

Over two million of these and other circulars were distributed during the campaign. In addition, extra copies of the *Progress* were printed almost every week and sent without charge to people throughout the state.[6]

The reason for Huey's slowness in opening his stumping tour was soon apparent. As in previous campaigns, he intended to speak all over the state and reach with his voice every possible voter. But he had devised a way to do it that would enable him to escape the physically exhausting tours that previously had compelled him to appear in almost every town. He had had constructed a sound truck, its equipment capable of carrying his words to a huge audience without any strain on his part. It was, he boasted, the first such truck to be used in an American campaign. With this vehicle, Huey could cover the state leisurely, speaking only in the parish seats and larger towns and delivering only three or four speeches a day but reaching a large number of voters. Huge crowds turned out to hear him, attracted as much by the novelty of the truck as by himself. Customarily, the truck would precede Huey into a town and cruise up and

[6] Circular, "Who Should Rule?" in Long Scrapbooks, XI; circular, "Why the Zemurray Millions Support the Ring," in Long: *Every Man a King*, pp. 213–19, and Long in *Louisiana Progress*, August 28, 1930; circular, "Landmarks of Senator Ransdell's Progress," in Leche Scrapbooks; Hotaling: "Long as Journalist," *Journalism Quarterly*, XX, 22.

down the streets, blaring the news that Governor Long would arrive at such an hour. Huey followed in a car. His driver in the campaign was Murphy Roden of the state police, who had become one of the favorite guards. Also in the car was faithful Joe Messina.[7]

Huey emphasized the same theme in all his speeches—the sabotage of his road and bridge program by the legislature. If the people did not want this program, if they believed that the state should be ruled by a few men, they should vote for Ransdell. "But," he thundered, "if you believe that Louisiana is to be ruled by the people, that the poor man is as good as the rich man, that the people have a right to pass on issues themselves; if you believe that this is a state where every man is king but no man wears a crown, then I want you to vote for Huey Long for the United States Senate. That is the platform I am running on." He was reducing the issue to an even simpler basis than he indicated. He was saying, in effect: You have only two choices, voting for Huey Long or against him.[8]

He also struck at Ransdell, but in a light and jesting fashion, as though he scorned dealing seriously with such a nonentity. He gave a typical demonstration of this technique in a small town in the northwestern part of the state. He arrived early, just as the sun was coming up, but virtually the entire population of a thousand people was awaiting him, and a thousand more people from the surrounding country were present. The first of the cotton had come into town, and Huey mounted a bale outside a warehouse. Holding a Bible in one hand, he looked out over the crowd for several minutes. Then suddenly he shot out: "Is there a single person here who can tell me the name of your United States Senator, my opponent?" By some indefinable method he had cast an immediate spell over his hearers. A businessman in the audience who prided himself on his presence of mind recalled that momentarily he could not think of Ransdell's name. Huey looked at the perplexed faces for a moment and then spoke. "Well, I'll tell you," he said. "It's Old Feather Duster Ransdell. But when I get to Washington, you'll know the name of your Senator."[9]

In some of his speeches he ignored Ransdell and even his own program and talked only of himself, chatting, as it were, with his hearers about what a rare person this Huey Long was. He frequently

[7] Long: *Every Man a King*, pp. 219–20; *Overton Hearing*, I, 235, II, 1195; *Louisiana Progress*, August 21, 1930, for a typical schedule of a speaking day; Murphy Roden.

[8] *Louisiana Progress*, August 7, 1930.

[9] Ibid., August 28, 1930; John Doles.

described to delighted rural audiences his social escapades in New Orleans and the sense of outrage they had evoked in the aristocracy. He solemnly confessed that in receiving the commander of the *Emden* in pajamas he had committed a breach of international "eat-a-calf." He promised a French audience in southern Louisiana that he would behave even more badly in the future. His hearers whooped as he unblushingly explained: "I have too much Cajun blood in me to be dignified."[1]

As the campaign continued, the opposition press criticized Huey heavily for discussing only local issues. He was running for a national office: where did he stand on national questions? The complaint had enough validity to force Huey to consider it. In some speeches he attempted to deal with what he thought were the main issues before Congress. They were, as he defined them, flood control, farm relief, foreign affairs, and labor. On flood control, he favored reservoirs and opposed relying solely on levees. On farm relief, he supported the export debenture plan, an arrangement whereby the federal government would compensate farmers for marketing surplus crops abroad at a loss. He also advocated an "absolute" protective tariff on foreign farm goods and particularly one on sugar that competed with the Louisiana product. On foreign policy, his only issue seemed to be that the United States should not send troops to Latin America to protect the interests of Sam Zemurray. On labor, he stood on the right of workers to organize and opposed the practice of the "yellow-dog contract," whereby a man had to sign an agreement not to engage in union activities. Ransdell favored the yellow-dog contract, Huey noted. He obviously was not conversant with these issues, however, and just as obviously his audiences were not interested in them. As if realizing this, he soon returned to his theme of roads and bridges.[2]

The labor issue, however, became one of the burning questions of the campaign. Ransdell had a record of voting against labor, and the state Federation of Labor endorsed Huey and attacked the senator bitterly. It concentrated its fire on one act of Ransdell's—he had voted to confirm the appointment to the Supreme Court of a jurist known to favor the yellow-dog contract. William Green, the president of the American Federation of Labor, commended the stand of the state group and gave it his official approval. Huey welcomed the support of labor and joined in the criticism of Ransdell.

[1] New Orleans *Times-Picayune*, August 31, 1930.
[2] Bogalusa *News*, August 8, 1930; *Louisiana Progress*, August 7 and 28, 1930.

The senator might well have ignored the matter—he was not going to get the small labor vote in any case—but he chose to meet the challenge by raising another issue, the stock Southern one, of race. He disclosed that he had supported the judge because he had been opposed by the National Association for the Advancement of Colored People. Racial, not antilabor, considerations had influenced him. Therefore it followed that Huey in assailing him must also be influenced by racial reasons. Obviously, said the senator, Huey was wittingly or unwittingly working with certain Negro leaders who were plotting to make colored people equal to whites.

That Ransdell should level such a charge revealed that he was either inept or desperate. An accusation of racial collaboration was one of the riskiest strategies in Southern politics, a two-edged weapon that could easily be turned on its wielder. It was a rare officeholder who had not at one time or another had to deal with Negroes, even if only in a very formal fashion, and a written record of these doings usually existed. Ransdell was inviting retaliation, and it came quickly. The *Progress* dug up and printed a letter that Ransdell had written in 1922 to a Negro Republican boss in New Orleans. Ransdell had merely asked this man to endorse the application of another Negro for a minor federal job. But, the *Progress* emphasized, the senator had seen fit to address the Negro as "Dear Mr.," as though he were a "schoolmate and buddie." If Ransdell was going to "take his hat off" to a Negro boss, he should have done it to get the job for a white man. The paper passed on to its readers the conclusion to be drawn from the episode: "Go to the polls and vote for the right of labor and for white supremacy—that means a vote against Joseph E. Ransdell."[3]

The appearance of the race issue was an unmistakable indicator that the campaign had taken an especially ugly turn. At the beginning of the contest the *Progress* had declared that Huey would not resort to criticism of his enemies but would discuss issues. Then, with a fine disregard for logic or consistency, the paper predicted that his speeches would be a welcome contrast to "the tawdry howls of his senile, asinine, scurrilous" foes.[4]

Huey observed in part the pledge offered for him by his newspaper. He criticized Ransdell in nearly every speech, but he did so in a jocular fashion, poking fun at his opponent rather than attacking

[3] Baton Rouge *State-Times*, August 20, 1930; *Louisiana Progress*, August 21 and September 4, 1930.
[4] *Louisiana Progress*, August 7, 1930.

him. He was relatively mild even when he referred to his old enemies, the men of the New Orleans Ring or the conservative chiefs in the state. And he did discuss issues. But the conservatives fulfilled the prediction of the *Progress*. They attacked Huey from the start and in violent and vicious language. They were affronted that he had dared to offer himself for a position that had been reserved for gentlemen, but this alone would not have aroused them to the fury that they exhibited. They seemed to sense that this was the last chance to stop him in his onward march. Their remarks about him rank high in the literature of American political abuse.

Colonel Ewing's newspaper compared the governor with the worst ruler New Orleans had ever known, General Benjamin F. Butler, who had commanded the occupation forces during the Civil War and whose name had been a synonym for evil ever since. "The people of New Orleans have more reason for voting against Huey Long than they would have had for voting against Ben Butler," the *States* fulminated. "Bad as Ben Butler's government of New Orleans was, there is not in all his record any attempt for anarchy and the destruction of orderly, civilized government, such as Long has undertaken."[5]

Former Governor Pleasant denounced Long as "an ultra-Socialist" whose views went beyond "Marx, Lenin, and Trotsky." John Sullivan declared that Jesse James, the most infamous outlaw in American history, was superior to Huey. "Jesse James was a gentleman compared with Long," Sullivan cried, "because Jesse James at least wore a mask. Long has the face of a clown, the heart of a petty larceny burglar, and the disposition of a tyrant." Frank J. Looney, a Shreveport conservative, stigmatized Huey as "a degenerate in mind and morals." Former Governor Parker said Long was "a creature devoid of every element of honor and decency."[6]

Mrs. Ruffin Pleasant easily demonstrated that she could outdo her husband in vituperation. Long was "common beyond words," she stated. "He has not only common ways, but a common, sordid, dirty soul." His face betrayed that he had the qualities of the lower animals: "the greed and coarseness of the swine, the cunning of the fox, the venom of the snake, the cruel cowardice of the skulking hyena."[7]

The conservative attack came to a strange climax at a Ransdell

[5] Clipping, New Orleans *States* [no day and month date], 1930, in Grace Scrapbook.

[6] New Orleans *Times-Picayune*, August 22, 23, and 24, 1930; Baton Rouge *State-Times*, September 4, 1930.

[7] Shreveport *Journal*, August 26, 1930.

rally in Alexandria. The main speaker was Roland B. Howell, a member of an aristocratic south Louisiana family and a fiery orator. Tall and erect, Howell had served in the First World War and later had been state commander of the American Legion. Major Howell, as he was generally called, had some of the same progressive ideas that Huey had, but his personal antipathy to the governor was so violent that he could not associate himself with the Long movement. In his speech he drew the issue in the campaign as between "decency and degradation." Then he paused and seemed to look into the world of the hereafter. "But now, comrades," he went on, "hearken to my voice, once again follow me. Listen to the command of our comrades speaking from the bivouac of the dead." He paused again. "I am giving the message . . ." he intoned. The reception was apparently unusually good that night, for the message came through immediately. The dead spoke clearly and with amazing detail through the voice of Howell: they directed their comrades not to vote for Huey Long, "a notorious liar, a slinking coward, and a self-acclaimed slacker."[8]

Thus far the campaign had lacked a frequent feature of Louisiana contests: some spectacular episode that usually occurred a few days before an election and affected the results dramatically. But one was indeed to come in this race, and in lurid drama it would eclipse any similar incident of the past. On September 1—the election fell on September 9—a man named Sam Irby called at the Ransdell headquarters in New Orleans and offered to provide proof of widespread graft in the Highway Commission. The Ransdell people received him with interest. They knew who Irby was. He had worked for the commission for almost two years, having been given a job when Huey became governor, and had recently been discharged, although he claimed to have resigned. Not only were the Ransdell workers interested in the valuable information Irby might possess, but they were also intrigued by his peculiar relationship with Huey. He was a member of the governor's "unofficial" family. His wife was an aunt of Alice Lee Grosjean, who had at one time lived with the Irbys and who was frequently seen with them, and Huey, in Baton Rouge. Moreover, Irby was known to be extremely close to Alice Lee's former husband, Jimmie Terrell, who now lived in Arkansas but often came to Louisiana. Irby could well know about goings-on much more damaging to Huey than corruption in the Highway Commission. Even if he did not, he was a convenient weapon with

[8] New Orleans *Morning Tribune*, September 4, 1930.

which to strike at Huey—a onetime Longite who now realized what a rascal the governor was.

After listening to Irby, the Ransdell leaders advised him to lay his proof before the district court in Baton Rouge, where the alleged graft had been committed. They must also have told him how to go about doing it, for upon leaving them he went to the New Orleans branch office of the attorney general's department. There he told his story to the assistant in charge. This minion of Percy Saint's immediately sniffed the political possibilities in a lawsuit brought in the closing days of the campaign and whisked Irby up to Baton Rouge. In the capital Irby held a long private conference with district judge George K. Favrot, a strong anti-Longite. When he came out, he offered to reveal to the reporters awaiting him what he had told the judge, but they sensibly refused to receive information that might become a judicial record. Irby then returned to New Orleans. But hardly had he arrived than he announced that he was flying to Shreveport to file a slander suit against Huey and O. K. Allen. They had told his wife that he had got drunk in the Heidelberg Hotel and beaten up two women, he said, and he was going to sue them for fifty thousand dollars in damages. On reaching Shreveport he was joined by Terrell. Irby stated to reporters that he would institute his suit right after the election, and then he and Terrell went into seclusion in a hotel room.

A few hours later Irby telephoned the city police headquarters and said that some men were trying to take him out of the room. He thought that they were state policemen. He also opened a window and shouted for help. Naturally the news of these strange events soon spread around town, and the local reporters picked it up. They converged first on the police headquarters and later on the hotel, but they could find out nothing. The chief of police said that his men had not seen any state officers around the hotel. The hotel's personnel said that Irby and Terrell had checked out early on September 4, a Thursday, but they knew nothing more. Irby and Terrell did not turn up in Baton Rouge or New Orleans or anywhere. They had simply disappeared.[9]

Huey knew, of course, about Irby's appearance at the Ransdell headquarters and the threatened lawsuit, but he was not particularly disturbed. Charges of graft in the Highway Commission were made practically every year, and a new one was not going to command

---

[9] Deutsch: "Kingdom of the Kingfish," in New Orleans *Item*, August 24, 1939; Shreveport *Journal*, September 4, 1930; David B. McConnell.

much attention. As for the slander suit, it was so patently ridiculous
that it could be laughed off. But when Huey heard that Irby and
Terrell were together in Shreveport, he was dismayed. Irby drank
heavily, and when he was intoxicated he was likely to talk and act
recklessly, especially if he was prompted by somebody with him.
What worried Huey was that some of his enemies in Shreveport or
Terrell might egg on Irby to say something about his relationship
with Alice Lee Grosjean. Such a charge exploded so late in the
campaign could have serious repercussions. Soon Huey learned
that his fears were justified. Miss Grosjean relayed word to him that
Irby and her former husband were drunk in their room and that
her uncle was threatening to expose her as Huey's mistress. Huey
called a conference of some of his advisers to consider how to stop
Irby from talking.

At the meeting various plans were discussed. One man proposed
that Irby be taken to some out-of-the-way place and held until after
the election. Earl Long said: "Let's take the sonofabitch and kill
him." A participant recalled Huey's reaction to the suggestion: "He
wheeled Earl around and I never kicked a nigger in the ass like he
did Earl." Huey shouted at his brother: "Get out of here! I don't
want to be United States Senator or anything else if I have to murder
anybody." Finally Huey determined what he should do. Irby and
Terrell would have to be removed from Shreveport and put where
they could have no contact with the press or the judicial officials
of Orleans or East Baton Rouge parishes. But the removal would
have to have an appearance of legality. Huey decided that Irby and
Terrell would be "arrested." The district attorney of Jefferson parish,
which adjoined Orleans and was the stronghold of the Fisher family,
obligingly signed a writ charging the two men with possessing certain
state documents. They were to be brought to Jefferson so that the
parish officials could question them about the nature of the documents.[1]

The men that Irby heard outside his door were indeed state
policemen. Six of them came to the hotel, headed by Dave McConnell,
Huey's brother-in-law, who knew both Irby and Terrell well. McConnell and two others went to Irby's room and knocked. Irby shouted
that he was armed and would shoot the first man to enter. McConnell
answered: "I'm your friend. I'm trying to help you." It was at this
point that Irby telephoned the city police and opened a window and
cried for help. Two city policemen arrived, but meekly departed

[1] Louis A. Jones; Joseph Fisher; David B. McConnell.

when McConnell explained to them that he was merely taking Irby to the parish jail. He then went into the room. Irby and Terrell, who were drunk, suddenly became abject. McConnell said that Alice Lee's father was out looking for Irby and that he would remove Sam to a place of safety. "Let's go," Irby exclaimed. The two men were taken downstairs and placed in separate cars. Irby was driven to a town on the Gulf coast. Here a boat was waiting, and also Representative Joe Fisher of Jefferson. Fisher took Irby to a camp on Grand Isle. Terrell was taken to a hideout nearby on Barataria Bay.[2]

The abduction was too sensational to remain a secret long. The Shreveport papers soon ferreted out the details of what had happened at the hotel and printed accounts that were widely copied by other journals. The whole state blazed with curiosity: where were the missing men? Especially eager to find out was Attorney General Saint's assistant in New Orleans. He would have no evidence to prove graft in the Highway Commission if his prime witness, Irby, could not be produced. He therefore went into the federal court of Judge Wayne Borah and asked for a writ charging Huey, the Jefferson district attorney, and the six policemen with abduction. Borah granted the request and directed the federal marshal to serve the writ on the governor, who was then at the Roosevelt Hotel.

As the marshal entered Huey's suite, there slipped in behind him an *Item* reporter, William Wiegand, who had heard that the summons would be served. In the crowd of Long retainers milling around in the room, Wiegand remained unobserved until the marshal left. Then Huey spotted him and demanded to know who he was. Wiegand identified himself. Thereupon Huey broke into a violent denunciation of the *Item*, pacing up and down and waving his arms as he spoke. He came up to Wiegand finally and said: "As for you, you're a sonofabitch." Enraged, Wiegand struck at him, the blow landing glancingly on the mouth. Two bodyguards quickly grabbed the reporter by the arms. The incident seemed to throw Huey into a frenzy. "Search him for weapons," he ordered. When it was discovered that Wiegand was unarmed, Huey became calmer. "Young man," he said, "you have done a terrible thing. You have struck the governor of Louisiana." Wiegand said that he thought the governor had said a pretty terrible thing. Suddenly Huey hit Wiegand in the eye. "Now we're even," he said with satisfaction, and then apologized for using the epithet.[3]

[2] David B. McConnell; Joseph Fisher; Shreveport *Journal*, September 5, 1930.

[3] Shreveport *Journal*, September 6 and 7, 1930; Baton Rouge *State-Times*, September 8, 1930; William Wiegand.

Borah's writ directed that Huey and the others named with him appear in court on September 10, the day after the election, to answer the charge of abduction. Huey had realized that eventually he was going to have to produce Irby and Terrell and had intended to release them after the election. But now he had a sudden inspiration. He would bring Irby forth before the election, and the hearing, and do it in such a way as to turn the episode on his enemies and make votes for himself. Quickly he laid his plan. He prepared a short statement and handed it to Dave McConnell, telling him to go to Grand Isle and get Irby to sign it. According to McConnell, he found Irby fishing and drinking; Sam signed the document without reading it. Next, Huey sent word to Joe Fisher to take Irby to Jefferson parish; a small plane would be provided for the purpose. When Huey sent further word, Fisher was to put Irby in an automobile and with the utmost secrecy bring him to Huey's suite at the Roosevelt. At the same time Huey tipped off reporters that a big news story would break on Sunday night, September 7, and that it would be revealed over the radio.[4]

Every part of the plan went off on schedule. Fisher, when he received the message from Huey, loaded Irby into a car and drove into New Orleans. Because the city police would pick up Irby on sight, to turn him over to Borah's court, Fisher maneuvered through back streets and to the Roosevelt by a side entrance. He hustled Irby up to Huey's suite on a freight elevator. In the room were Huey and some of his leaders and bodyguards. Only two reporters were present, although the corridor outside the room was filled with a clamoring crowd of them. Also in the room was a microphone. The Kingfish stepped up to it and announced that it had been installed to enable Mr. Sam Irby to broadcast a message to the people of Louisiana. He presented Mr. Irby.

Irby obviously had been coached as to his part in the scene. As Huey held before him the statement that he had signed, Irby read it. The opening words must have amazed the radio audience. "This is Sam Irby talking to you, ladies and gentlemen," Irby read. "I am Sam Irby that is supposed to have been kidnapped. There never was a more complete lie told on Governor Huey P. Long in his lifetime." Irby went on to reveal that he had not gone to Shreveport to expose any wrongdoing on the governor's part but to entrap the governor's enemies. His "play" had succeeded. Somebody had placed twenty-five hundred dollars under his pillow; he implied that it had

[4] David B. McConnell; Joseph Fisher.

been put there by Cecil Morgan and Harney Bogan. He was not sure why he had been given this "good Ransdell money," but once he had it, he sent word to those who were in with him on the plot. He and they then arranged for an apparent kidnapping to take place. He had had a pleasant time camping on Grand Isle, and now all that he asked was for the governor to protect him from the New Orleans Ring police.

The minute Irby finished reading, Fisher and several other men grabbed him and rushed him to the freight elevator. Reporters who tried to stop them were elbowed aside. Once outside, Fisher and Irby jumped into Joe's car and sped off for Jefferson parish. City police cars followed, but Fisher lost them and got over the parish line.

As Irby left the room, the radio audience heard Huey say: "And now he's gone out into the wide, wide world. Watch him go. Sam, if anything happens, phone back here and tell me about it." Then Huey could be heard telling the two reporters present that they had a scoop and that he would pay them a thousand dollars if their stories made the front page. They apparently offered no answer, for next a loud, sardonic laugh came over the air. "Ha! Ha! Ha!" Huey jeered.[5]

He had a right to laugh. He had had to deal with an unexpected and potentially ugly episode that could have damaged him. But he had handled it in such a way that it had redounded to his advantage. The public could gather several impressions from Irby's broadcast, each favorable to Huey: Irby had been working with Huey; Irby had been put up to something by Huey's enemies but had been caught at it and had come over to Huey; or Irby was a monumental liar and must have been lying when he said he could expose Huey. The conservatives who had played up Irby as a crusader for honesty suddenly looked rather foolish.

Huey obviously now had nothing to fear from Irby. The man seemed completely under Huey's control. So also, it was soon revealed, was Terrell, who was released from Barataria on the night of the election. Both men appeared at Borah's hearing on September 11. Irby testified for himself and Terrell. He insisted that they had been on a fishing trip at their own expense and that they wanted the charge of abduction dropped. This was at complete variance with his claim in the broadcast that he had arranged an abduction. But

[5] New Orleans *Times-Picayune*, September 8, 1930; Baton Rouge *State-Times*, September 8, 1930; *Louisiana Progress*, September 11, 1930; David B. McConnell; Joseph Fisher; Charles Frampton.

the court had to accept his sworn statement, and it destroyed the case against Huey. Borah had to dismiss the writ.[6]

The Irby episode survived the years and became a fixture in the Long story. It was remembered mainly because two years later Irby wrote a book, *Kidnapped by the Kingfish*, which recounted in lurid detail the brutalities that the author had suffered at the hands of Huey Long's hirelings.[7] Historians and other writers have been somewhat skeptical of parts of it but have accepted its account as basically accurate. It seemed to confirm their concept of Long's character, to demonstrate their suspicion that he was a brutal dictator.

Irby was living at Laurel, Mississippi, when he decided to write his book. As he confessed in it, he had fallen on hard days since 1930. After the election he asked Huey for a job, and Huey helped him to get one with a corporation. He lost this job and another that he secured. He believed that in each case Huey had been responsible for his discharge. Finally he prepared to file a lawsuit against Huey. But in New Orleans he was arrested, placed in a strait jacket, and then confined in an insane asylum. When he was released, his wife announced that she was leaving him. She accepted a state job, obviously given to her by Huey for turning against her husband.[8]

Irby, when he began to write the book, found that he had trouble composing it. Because he needed help and because he wanted to have it published in Louisiana, he entered into correspondence with an anti-Long leader in New Orleans, Shirley Wimberly, who would before very long transfer his allegiance to Huey and become a Long leader. Wimberly agreed to revise the manuscript and arrange for its publication. He apparently mentioned the book to another anti, Joseph J. Fineran, and may have asked Fineran to take over the task for him. Whatever the case, Fineran was immediately excited at the prospect. He wrote to Irby and offered to help prepare the book and get it published. Irby welcomed this new ally and agreed to divide the net profits equally with him.[9]

The two men then plunged into the job of preparing the book. Irby would draft a chapter or two and send the copy to Fineran. Fineran would suggest revisions and return the manuscript to Irby.

[6] New Orleans *Times-Picayune*, September 11, 1930; Hermann B. Deutsch: "Kingdom of the Kingfish," in New Orleans *Item*, August 24, 1939.

[7] Sam Irby: *Kidnapped by the Kingfish* (New Orleans, 1932), *passim*.

[8] Ibid., pp. 70–88.

[9] Fineran to Irby, July 24, 1932, and Irby to Fineran, August 19, 1932, in Sam Irby Papers, Duke University Library, Durham, North Carolina.

From the beginning they had divergent ideas as to what kind of book it should be. Irby wanted to turn out a work that would sell, and he insisted that the relationship between Huey and Miss Grosjean be emphasized. "Expand on the love matters," he instructed in one letter. But Fineran wanted to produce a book that could be used as a political weapon against Huey in the state campaign of 1932. Therefore he advised playing down the sex angle and giving the greater space to the kidnapping. "There is also a disposition among those who will furnish money to tone down on the Grosjean material," he told Irby. The two also disagreed as to the facts of the episode. Fineran in one of his revisions stated that Irby was manacled to a tree on Grand Isle and beaten by his captors. Irby sharply corrected his colleague. He had not been beaten at all and had been hit only once, when he tried to escape. Usually Irby was not so objective. Pressed by Fineran to supply details of the scene at the broadcast, he remembered that there were fifty "gunmen" in the room and that some of them "menaced" him with pistols while he was reading his statement. But he admitted that he did not think Huey would have let him be killed.[1]

The book as it appeared in final form was more Fineran's than Irby's. Printed as a paperback, it contained only eighty-eight pages. Over thirty of them were a dull recital of Huey's political career. Only brief mention was made of Miss Grosjean's relationship with Huey. The bulk of the book was devoted to the kidnapping. Here Fineran went beyond anything that Irby had told him. He related that Irby had been manacled to a tree on Grand Isle, devoured by mosquitoes, starved, and threatened with death. His captors were "gangsters," and they had forced him to broadcast at the Roosevelt by holding guns to his back.[2]

Two of the "gangsters," Dave McConnell and Joe Fisher, recalled the episode with calm clarity. They affirmed that Irby had not been mistreated in any way and that he had not resented his "captivity." On the contrary, they said, he seemed to enjoy it. He had some money on him—possibly given to him by Huey's enemies or by Huey himself—and he bet a large part of it that Huey would win the election. On election day he told Fisher that he wanted to vote for Huey, and Joe magnanimously offered to let Irby cast his ballot in Jefferson parish. The picture of Irby that emerges from the recol-

[1] Fineran to Irby, August 21, 23, and 25, 1932, and Irby to Fineran, n.d., probably August 23 and 24, ibid.
[2] Irby: *Kidnapped by the Kingfish*, pp. 6, 45–68.

lèctions of McConnell and Fisher is credible. He was an unstable and unpredictable man who created a situation that could have hurt others. Because he was inept and weak, he was the one who was hurt.[3]

As the day of the primary neared, tension mounted throughout the state. Both sides realized that this was a decisive contest, that the outcome could determine the direction Louisiana would take—whether the state would continue along the path blazed by Huey or return to the old conservative way. Both sides put forth their best efforts, which were often their most unscrupulous ones.

The center of the struggle was New Orleans, which Ransdell would have to carry by a substantial majority if he was to overcome Huey's expected country lead. The Old Regular organization mobilized its resources to roll out the required vote for the senator. The city police permitted Ring henchmen to harass Long meetings and arrested some of Huey's workers on flimsy charges. In an effort to protect his people Huey dispatched a large force of state policemen to the city on the eve of the election. The city police chief, George Reyer, promptly clapped a hundred of these men in jail on the grounds that they were disturbing the peace. A rumor spread that a large force of state troopers would raid the jail and attempt to free their colleagues. The city authorities, alarmed at the prospect of bloodshed, approached Huey with a deal—they would release the prisoners if Huey would take them out of the city. He agreed to do so but sent some additional policemen back on election day.[4]

A short time before the primary the Old Regulars decided to enter eleven "dummy" candidates for minor offices, men who would later be withdrawn but who before that time would have the privilege of naming election commissioners. Ward leader Ulric Burke was instructed to file papers for the dummies shortly before midnight on the last day for making nominations. Word of this move leaked out to Allen Ellender, who determined to checkmate it. Ellender prepared papers for twenty-three Long dummies but held them secret. On the final filing day he telephoned Burke, whom he knew well, and suggested that they play pool that night. Burke readily agreed, and the two men spent a pleasant evening together. But just before midnight Ellender turned on Burke and said that he had heard about the Old Regular dummies. Burke smugly acknowledged that the story was true. "I'm glad you told me," Ellender said blandly and

[3] David B. McConnell; Joseph Fisher.
[4] *Louisiana Progress*, September 11, 1930; Harvey Peltier; *Overton Hearing*, I, 1102–3, 1105.

pulled out of a pocket his list of candidates. Burke was aghast and hurriedly departed. The next day Ellender received a message to come to Walmsley's office. He was greeted by a querulous mayor, who demanded to know what he was up to. "All I want is equal representation," Ellender answered. "If you withdraw the dummies I will too." Walmsley realized that unless he yielded, the Longites might end up with more commissioners than the Old Regulars. He and Ellender agreed to apportion the number of commissioners equally in each ward. Huey would get a more honest count in the city than he had ever had before.[5]

Ordinarily in Louisiana a senatorial primary attracted fewer voters than a gubernatorial contest. Many people simply were not interested in national issues, and others stayed at home because they thought it was useless to vote when the state's rulers had already decided who the winner would be. But on September 9 almost as many voters turned out as had in 1928. It was a mark of the popular interest that Huey had stirred with his plea to vote approval of his program —and himself.

It was apparent as early as the night of the election that Huey was the victor. He amassed in the country approximately the same number of votes as he had in the 1928 election, 110,000 votes, far surpassing Ransdell's country total of 68,000 votes. The Ransdell people confidently waited for the big Orleans parish vote to come in. Ransdell did carry the parish, but only by some 4,000 votes, 43,000 votes to almost 39,000 votes for Huey. Huey had more than doubled his Orleans vote of 1928, and in his sweep had elected two Long men to Congress, Paul Maloney and Bathtub Joe Fernandez. His Orleans vote was the result, in part, of the alertness of his commissioners and the efficiency of his local leaders. But primarily it was a testimonial to him. Large numbers of the city's citizens had broken away from the Ring and from tradition and had voted for a man who promised a program for Louisiana.[6]

The total vote in the state was 149,640 for Huey and 111,451 for Ransdell. Huey had a clear majority, and there would be no second primary. And as there was no Republican candidate, there would be no general election. Huey P. Long was a United States senator. But until he should decide to take his seat in Washington, he was also governor of Louisiana. He had just turned thirty-seven years of age.

---

[5] *Overton Hearing*, I, 138–9, 227, 275–6; Allen J. Ellender.

[6] Allen P. Sindler: *Huey Long's Louisiana: State Politics, 1920–1952* (Baltimore, 1956), pp. 71–3; New Orleans *Times-Picayune*, September 10, 1930.

THE OUTCOME OF THE election stunned the conservatives. They had been reluctant to believe that the people would choose such a person as Huey for the high office of senator. But the people had spoken and in thundering terms—they approved of Governor Long, and they wanted his program put into operation. This large endorsement effected the collapse of the opposition. On the day after the election the Constitutional League announced that it was disbanding. The disappearance of this ineffective group was of no particular significance. But of great moment was another piece of news—the very effective Old Regular organization was capitulating and coming over to the governor.

The Choctaw chiefs had been amazed by Huey's vote in the city, and they could not understand what had gone wrong. Some of the ward leaders could have enlightened them, for leaders in the labor wards had not been able to hold their followers in line for Ransdell. Huey's personal popularity and the appeal of his program had proved more potent than loyalty to the machine. One ward leader had been so impressed by Huey's showing that he had considered taking his organization independently into the Long camp.

This stirring in the lower ranks would not in itself have greatly influenced Mayor Walmsley, who was singularly obtuse to popular opinion. To him the election signified only that a demagogue had gained an unaccountable triumph; the city organization could safely ignore the result and continue to fight the demagogue. If any of the ward leaders urged a different course on Walmsley, he did not heed them. But other people did urge him, and they were people to whom he always listened, the banking and business leaders of the city. These men impressed some hard facts on the mayor. As a result of the election, Huey would have control of the legislature. He would be in a position to help the city solve its worst problems—the streets needed paving and repairing, and the debt of the port had to be retired. And, the bankers emphasized meaningfully, the municipal debt of three and a half million dollars, which the banks held, had to be refinanced. The spokesman of the businessmen was Rudolph Hecht, president of the Hibernia Bank and one of the pillars of the community. Hecht and Huey had met in 1928 or possibly earlier and, although they disagreed on political issues, had become friends and social intimates. Hecht pressed Walmsley to meet with Huey and try to come to an accommodation. The banker said he was certain Huey was prepared to offer generous terms.

Subjected to such pressure, Walmsley agreed to see Huey. He was told by Hecht that he would have to go to the governor's suite at

the Roosevelt Hotel. Huey, who had known of Hecht's negotiation
and may, indeed, have instigated it, chose the meeting place. There
was a proper symbolism in his selection. He was the victor, and
Walmsley, the defeated, would have to come to him to sue for peace.
But as Hecht had predicted, he was disposed to be a generous victor.
He would gain strength by being magnanimous. As soon as he could,
he meant to call a special session of the legislature and place before
it his public-improvements program. That program was certain to
pass if he had the support of the large Orleans delegation, most of
them Old Regulars. He was willing to make it easy for the machine
to surrender.

At the end of the meeting the participants released a statement
detailing the agreement they had reached, very much as though they
represented warring nations that had concluded a peace treaty. The
statement revealed that shortly the governor would convene the
legislature in special session. At the session the Orleans delegation
would support a seventy-five million-dollar bond issue for roads and
bridges, an increase in the gasoline tax of from four to five cents, a
bond issue for a new capitol, and a resolution withdrawing the impeachment charges, which, not having been voted on, could still be
revived. Huey, for his part, pledged that seven million dollars of the
road and bridge bond issue would be set aside to construct a free
bridge over the Mississippi at New Orleans, that an annual appropriation of seven hundred thousand dollars would be provided to pave
and repair the city's streets, that one half of the additional one cent
on the gasoline tax would be dedicated to retire the debt of the port,
the other half going to the public schools, and that the state would
participate in a plan to refinance the city's debt.[7]

The concessions to New Orleans, and all the provisions of the
pact, were Huey's. Walmsley was in no position to bargain. Huey
could have given much less and still forced the Old Regulars to
support him. The agreement reveals a side of him that has not been
appreciated. For all his increasing ruthlessness and grasping of power,
he was still capable of acting like a normal, pragmatic politician, of
seeking a reasonable compromise with his opponents. It is doubtful,
however, that he expected this compromise to last very long. He did
not trust Walmsley and believed that sooner or later the mayor would
find reason to back out of the alliance. He himself weakened its basis

[7] William Bisso, fourteenth ward Old Regular leader; New Orleans *Times-
Picayune*, September 14, 1930; Baton Rouge *Morning Advocate*, September 14, 1930;
*Louisiana Progress*, January 12, 1931; T. O. Harris: *The Kingfish: Huey P. Long,
Dictator* (New Orleans, 1938), pp. 90–1; *Overton Hearing*, II, 1974–5.

by constantly reminding the Old Regulars that he was the dominant partner. To a Choctaw leader who ventured to remonstrate that the machine had some rights, he snapped: "You've got no rights. You're a captured province."[8]

But at the moment harmony seemed to rule the Louisiana political scene, and the New Orleans businessmen who had helped to bring about the truce decided to celebrate it with a great "peace" gathering. They tendered the governor a public banquet at which he and his onetime enemies would express their esteem for one another. The affair, held at the Roosevelt Hotel, attracted more than six hundred people. Speaker after speaker arose to laud the honored guest. He was able, energetic, brilliant, a "genius." He was the best governor the state had ever had, and he would be the best U.S. senator it had ever had. A burst of applause shook the room as Walmsley came to the podium. "I am glad to be here tonight," the mayor began. He too paid lavish tribute to the governor, that generous man who had in the hour of Choctaw defeat "stretched to us the hand of friendship." Walmsley continued, not realizing how much he was admitting: "You would have thought that he was the mayor of New Orleans, if you had seen the indefatigable way he took hold of the problems of New Orleans and worked to solve those problems."

The Kingfish acknowledged the eulogies briefly and modestly but indicated that he was not deceived by them. He related a story of a man in Winn parish who had died, leaving behind him a wife and a mother-in-law. At the funeral the preacher recounted at length the virtues of the deceased. The mother-in-law, at each tribute, would rise from her seat, peer into the casket, and then sit down. But after an especially fulsome passage she remained standing. The minister asked compassionately if there was anything the neighbors could do to relieve her grief. She answered: "I just want to stand here, parson, to be sure that that man you're talking about was my son-in-law."[9]

HUEY CALLED THE LEGISLATURE to meet in special session on September 16. His proclamation listed as subjects for legislation the measures laid down in the pact with Walmsley and one additional item: an appropriation to construct a modern airport for New

[8] Seymour Weiss; Shirley G. Wimberly.

[9] New Orleans *Item*, September 18, 1930; New Orleans *Times-Picayune*, September 19, 1930; *Louisiana Progress*, September 18, 1930; Long: *Every Man a King*, pp. 227–35.

Orleans. A predictable amendment authorizing a bond issue to build a
new capitol was also included, but for the first time the amount of
the issue was disclosed: five million dollars. Huey opened the session
by addressing both houses. He asked for support of his public-
improvements program. Because of the depression, he emphasized,
the costs of labor and materials were low. Now was the time to build,
and in building, the state would also help the unemployed and mitigate the effect of the depression. "Let us forget our political differences," he urged, "and provide prosperity for the people who are
looking to us to help the condition of the state."[1]

The legislature that heard him was virtually the same body that
just two months earlier had bottled up his program. But now it was
in a chastened mood. Fresh in the minds of the members were the
results of the recent election, and not many of them would dare to
cast themselves as opposers of progress and the will of the people.
There would be no delays or filibusters in this session. The house,
which received most of the major bills, voted to suspend the rules
and refer the measures immediately to committees. The bills came
out of the committees after hearings that consumed only one or two
days and were reported on the floor. There the Long and Old Regulars factions, functioning smoothly together, passed them quickly.
Only twelve votes were registered against the bond issue for roads,
ten against the increase in the gasoline tax, and twenty against a
resolution to quash the impeachment charges. On reaching the
senate the bills went through the same routine and were enacted by
large majorities. The legislature had convened on a Monday, and
by the following Monday it had completed its work and was ready
to adjourn.[2]

Only on the proposed bond issue for a capitol did the conservatives
try to put up a fight, offering at least vocal opposition. Their spokesman in the house was Judge Dupre, who insisted that the present
building was adequate and that a new one would be an extravagance.
Huey decided to have some fun with the old man. It so happened
that rain fell heavily during the session, and as the roof of the house
chamber was in poor condition, water frequently leaked in on the
members. Huey, according to good evidence, had a hole made in
the ceiling above Dupre's desk. Then, during an especially heavy
rain, he walked innocently into the chamber. Dupre had just moved

[1] New Orleans *Morning Tribune*, September 16, 1930; New Orleans *Times-
Picayune*, September 17, 1930; *Louisiana Progress*, September 18, 1930.
[2] Baton Rouge *State-Times*, September 18 and 20, 1930; *Louisiana Progress*,
September 18, 1930.

his chair to escape the drip. When he saw Huey, he stood up and, shaking with rage, demanded that the governor have the roof repaired. Huey seized the writing pad that the judge always kept by him and scribbled on it: "Are you in favor of the new capitol?" "Hell, no!" Dupre shouted. Huey pushed the judge's chair under the cascade and grabbed the pad again. "Die, damn it, in the faith," he wrote.[3]

Huey gave hardly a thought to the conservative opposition to the capitol measure. But he was midly concerned at some resistance that developed within his own family, from his brother Earl. Earl later testified as to his reasons for fighting the project—a new capitol was not needed, and some of Huey's cronies were going to get rake-offs on the costs. Earl professed even to dislike the proposed architectural design of the building, which Huey had decreed would be a skyscraper. Earl said it would look like a farm silo. Huey undoubtedly suspected what Earl's real reasons were. The younger brother was feeling his political oats. His ambition was to run for a high state office in 1932, and he thought, strangely, that he would further his chances if he demonstrated that he could defeat one of Huey's measures and thereby show his independence of Huey.

Huey knew that Earl was intriguing against the capitol amendment, but he did not regard his brother's efforts as seriously as he should have. He overlooked the fact that Earl was a Long and might have some of his own talent for manipulating people. On the day the house was to vote on the amendment, Huey strolled onto the floor to observe another victory. But as the votes flashed on the board, he saw to his dismay that the yea total fell short of a two-thirds majority. Hastily he signaled to Speaker Fournet to hold up announcement of the vote. Then he went up to several followers of his who had voted nay and asked them to change their votes. To his surprise they declined, smiling at him knowingly as they did so. He finally found out what was at the bottom of their actions. Earl had told them that the governor really wanted the capitol measure defeated and would make a last-minute plea for it only in order to seem sincere. By using some emphatic language Huey convinced them that he was in earnest, and enough of them shifted their votes to pass the measure. In recalling the scene a legislator said appreciatively: "Huey had to run around unchanging Earl."[4]

At the end of the session Huey issued a public statement con-

[3] Baton Rouge *State-Times*, September 18, 1930; Long: *Every Man a King*, p. 239; E. J. Oakes; Frank Odom; E. J. Bourg; J. Y. Sanders, Jr.

[4] *Overton Hearing*, I, 795; Long: *Every Man a King*, pp. 238–9; Mason Spencer.

gratulating the legislature and the state, and also himself, on the enactment of the Long program. "Louisiana's plan and forward step, if followed immediately by all other states, will solve all problems of unemployment and depression for two years to come," he rhapsodized. He predicted that the people of the state would ratify the bond issue for roads and the other amendments in the November election. His prophecy proved to be dazzlingly correct. In November the voters approved all the amendments by majorities of twenty and thirty to one.[5]

Anticipating that the road amendment would be ratified, Huey had previously called in the bureau heads and engineers of the Highway Commission and told them to prepare plans for an extensive construction program. As soon as money was available from bond sales, the work would begin, he promised. Some contracts were let immediately, and during the closing months of the year approximately fifty miles of concrete roads were built or under construction.[6]

Huey had hoped to build the roads at a cost of fifteen thousand dollars a mile. He soon found that that figure was unrealistically low and would have to be upped. But he was determined to keep costs down—lower costs meant more roads—and he constantly bedeviled his engineers to make economies without sacrificing quality. The average cost of his best concrete roads turned out to be around twenty-six thousand dollars a mile, although some were constructed for less. The Louisiana average compared favorably with that in other states, even though in many parts of the state soft soil posed special problems, making roads in those areas cost more than the national average. One reason for the moderate costs was that Huey ordered the engineers to dispense whenever they could with roadbeds or backdrains: slabs of concrete were simply laid on the ground. In adopting this procedure he was thinking of economy but also of speed. He wanted the roads built quickly, and they were. By mid-1931 Louisiana had constructed over two thousand miles of surfaced roads of all types and was employing over eight thousand men in highway projects, a record better than that of any other state currently engaged in building programs.[7]

[5] *Louisiana Progress*, September 25, 1930; Baton Rouge *Morning Advocate*, November 5, 1930.

[6] Norman Lant; Warren Taylor.

[7] W. C. Pegues; Warren Taylor; Jess Nugent; Forrest Davis: *Huey Long, A Candid Biography* (New York, 1935), pp. 26–7; *Louisiana Progress*, April, 1931; news story by Charles Frampton, in New Orleans *Item-Tribune*, October 4, 1931.

Huey had allowed to be written into the road-bond amendment a provision setting up an advisory board to supervise the awarding of contracts. Previously he had opposed setting up such an agency on a constitutional basis, but now, knowing that its creation would gain votes for the measure, he accepted it. The membership was to consist of seven elected state officials, the governor, lieutenant governor, and others, a representative selected by the police juries, and eleven citizens appointed by the governor. As the citizen members Huey named prominent businessmen, some of them political enemies of his. All contracts had to be submitted to the board, and if it disapproved of one, the contract could not be let. The board performed its duties conscientiously, although the members did not always understand fully the technical details of the contracts. The citizen representatives, busy men, tended to approve whatever was put before them unless it was palpably improper. On the whole the board found little to object to, and its relations with the governor were friendly if not cordial. Huey would not have minded if it had spotted a corrupt contract. He once explained that he had appointed the surprising number of his opponents to the board specifically to prevent graft: "My enemies kept my own crowd straight and, of course, I kept control of where the roads were to be built—and all I wanted was the roads."[8]

He could not afford to permit blatant graft in his roads program. The roads were a vital part of his political program, and corruption in their construction would endanger his larger objectives. He did allow, however, a certain amount of petty grafting, of the kind that was common in the politics of Louisiana and many other states. For example, he hit on the idea that the state should buy cement in large quantities from manufacturers and resell it to contractors. The purchases were made from selected cement companies. Sometimes a company got a contract because its Louisiana representatives were supporters of his. But some companies won awards by paying money into the Long campaign coffers. Again, the state bought large consignments of shell, which was supplied by local dealers. One of these was Representative Joe Fisher, who had sold to the state on bid under previous governors. According to Fisher, Huey put the purchasing on a new basis. He called in the shell dealers and said to them: "I don't want the state to be overcharged for shells. But the

[8] Long: *Every Man a King*, pp. 239–40; *American Progress*, May 1935; Norman Lant; St. Louis *Post-Dispatch*, September 11, 1935.

state wants to give you a fair price. You boys get together and pick out your districts and try to get your share of the business in that district." Fisher conceded: "Now that might not sound so good to the public but there was nothing crooked about it." He insisted that the price was fair to both parties and that the system was "fixed" only in that it ensured that Huey's friends would get a fair share of the state's business.[9]

AFTER THE LABORS of the senatorial campaign and the special session Huey had time to relax. Confident that the amendments would receive overwhelming ratification, he did little stumping for them and during the last months of 1930 made few speeches on any subject. In one of these appearances he confessed that he wished he could assume his Senate seat. "I look forward to going to the United States Senate," he said, "so that I may enter upon a new field of endeavor, and with the hope that I may solve the economic problem that is nationwide and worldwide." But for the time, the nation and the world would have to get along without his help. He reiterated that he would not permit Paul Cyr to become governor: not even for "one split second," he now stipulated. His determination to deny Cyr the office had become a fixation. He refused an invitation to attend the dedication of a new Mississippi River bridge connecting Louisiana and Mississippi at Vicksburg—because the program provided that he would have to cross the bridge and stand on Mississippi soil for a few minutes. Soon after this episode he was invited to appear at a flood-control meeting in St. Louis. He mentioned at a board of liquidation meeting at which Cyr was present that he would go if it were not for the lieutenant governor. Cyr suggested that they could go together. "Fine," Huey responded. "And I think it would be best if we bunked together. We don't want to get out of each other's sight." But in the end he called the trip off, perhaps fearing that Cyr would made a sudden dash back to the state.[1]

In this slack period only one piece of political news made the headlines, but it set tongues wagging all over the state. Early in October Secretary of State James J. Bailey, an anti-Longite, suddenly died of a heart attack. To serve out his unexpired term the Kingfish appointed Alice Lee Grosjean. His action, taken suddenly, caught

9 Seymour Weiss; Fred Dent; Joseph Fisher.
1 *Louisiana Progress*, October 23, 1930; Shreveport *Journal*, November 6, 1930; Pensacola *Journal*, November 15, 1930.

the capitol reporters by surprise. As if not believing that he had actually named his young assistant to one of the most important offices in the state, they sought out the new secretary for confirmation. Yes, it was true, she said, and she was "thrilled" at the prospect of the job. Would she run for election to it in 1932? the reporters pressed. No, she expected to go to Washington with Governor Long as his secretary, she answered. "I prefer my politics from the sidelines," she added archly.[2]

Another story, just as sensational in its way as the Grosjean appointment, broke in December. Loyola University, a Catholic institution in New Orleans, announced that in February it would award to Governor Long an honorary degree, doctor of laws.[3] Most Louisianians were amused: Huey in cap and gown in the rarefied halls of Academe should be a sight to see. But the conservatives were aghast. They decided that he must have engaged in some clever machination to persuade a respectable university to extend him this recognition.

Every contemporary and later writer who dealt with Huey accepted the conservative interpretation, and in time the incident of the Loyola degree became another myth in the Long story. Somehow Huey had "connived" to get Loyola to grant him the degree. As is the case with other episodes in his career, he himself was partially responsible for creating the myth. He introduced an element of confusion into the record that helped cloud the truth.

The most common version is that Huey desperately wanted an honorary degree from some university and preferably from Tulane. But he thought that to receive one, he would have to present a thesis, and he began to think about a possible subject. At the same time George Wallace, the Winnfield lawyer whom he had brought to Baton Rouge to draft laws, was working on a compilation of the various constitutions of Louisiana. Wallace suggested that Huey appropriate his project and use it as a thesis. Huey snapped at the offer and assigned several young lawyers to assist Wallace in completing the book. It appeared in print in March 1930, as a state publication, under the title *Constitutions of the State of Louisiana*. Huey P. Long was named on the title page as "compiler." The work related each section of the latest constitution, the one of 1921, to corresponding articles in earlier constitutions. Legal authorities hailed it as an invaluable reference and showered praise on the supposed

[2] Unidentified clipping, October 9, 1930, in Grace Scrapbook.
[3] New Orleans *Item-Tribune*, December 28, 1930.

author. The officials of Loyola, deceived as everybody else was, decided to award this scholarly governor an honorary degree.[4]

At the time of publication Huey claimed full authorship of the book. He said that he had worked on it in spare moments since becoming governor. Later, when word of Wallace's part had got around, he became more cautious. In his autobiography he admitted that he had had assistance from some "members" of his administration. But he still insisted that he had conceived the project and directed it. And, he claimed, Loyola had seen fit to accept the work as a thesis for the degree of doctor of law.[5]

Both in the usual version of the affair and in Huey's account there are some partial truths. Wallace was certainly the author or the principal author of the book, although Huey, with his deep interest in the law, may have suggested the idea for it or may have had a minor part in its preparation.[6] Just why Huey appropriated the work is not clear. It is unlikely that he did so for the purpose of securing an honorary degree. If he desired a degree, which is possible, he did not have to present a thesis to get it. A university may award an honorary degree to anyone it chooses and for any reason, good or bad, that it decides on. If it wishes to pretend that the recipient has produced something scholarly, it can easily find an example. Thus Loyola could have cited some of Huey's law briefs as proof of authorship. Huey may not have known how simple the process could be. Wanting a degree, he may have thought that he had to present a scholarly work and thus have seized on Wallace's project. But it is also possible that he was moved by as simple a motive as personal vanity: he wanted to see his name on a book. He would "produce" two more books later, and with both of them he displayed an inordinate pride of authorship.

Loyola presented the degree on February 2 at a ceremony attended by justices of the supreme court and other dignitaries. The citation mentioned that the recipient had recently compiled a legal manual, a "vade mecum," but only incidentally. It dwelt largely on his accomplishments in the political world. He was a shining example of the American democratic leader, "a true son of Columbia." On the Public Service Commission he had labored to bring about

[4] Huey P. Long, comp.: *Constitutions of the State of Louisiana* (Baton Rouge, 1930); New Orleans *Times-Picayune*, March 23, 1930; Hotaling: "Long as Journalist," *Journalism Quarterly*, XX, 24. One thousand copies of the book were printed and distributed to libraries and lawyers in the state.

[5] Unidentified clipping, March 22, 1930, in Grace Scrapbook; Long: *Every Man a King*, p. 271.

[6] Confidential communications.

effective regulation of common carriers. As governor he had worked "unceasingly" for the good of his state. His crowning achievement was the great system of highways now being constructed, a system that would rival Italy's renowned Via Appia, known as "the Queen of Long Ways." Tucked in the middle of the citation, not emphasized, was a reference to another accomplishment of the honoree— he had "opened wide the gates of Education by his stand on free textbooks." Here, almost in passing, the real reason for the award was revealed. Loyola, the leading Catholic institution of the state, was recording its regard, and the regard of all Catholics in the state, for the governor who had made it possible for Catholic children to receive free schoolbooks. Undoubtedly, Loyola would have bestowed the degree if Huey had not compiled his manual. Its only influence was to furnish the university a convenient reason for acting.[7]

At the time Huey received the degree, he was engaged in his potlikker controversy. He began to sign some of his humorous pronouncements on the issue: "Huey P. Long, LL.D., Governor and Senator-Elect." He could not have sought the honor very vigorously, for although he was pleased with it, he was obviously not overwhelmed by it. It was vastly more important that he was governor and senator and the power in Louisiana.

[7] Long: *Every Man a King*, pp. 271–4.

# CHAPTER 18

# *I've Got a University*

**T**HAT FREDERICK THE GREAT was "the greatest sonofabitch who ever lived," Senator Huey Long volunteered to some Washington reporters one day in 1935. He then related an episode in the life of the Prussian ruler. Frederick had decided to seize the Austrian capital of Vienna. His ministers were horrified. They told him that he could not take the city, for if he did he would shock world opinion. But "Old Fred" was not deterred. "The hell I can't," he said. "My soldiers will take Vienna and my professors at Heidelberg will explain the reasons why." The Kingfish of Louisiana paused to observe the effect of his story. "Hell," he chortled, "I've got a university down in Louisiana that cost me $15,000,000, that can tell you why I do like I do."[1]

Just south of Baton Rouge the campus of Louisiana State University nestled under the shade of tall magnolia and live-oak trees. Everybody called it "the new campus," to distinguish it from the downtown campus that the school had previously occupied and from which it had removed in 1925. Governor Parker had made it possible for the university to acquire the new site, on the extensive grounds of a plantation. He had also done the school another service that ultimately was even more important. By inducing the legislature to dedicate a portion of the severance tax to LSU, he had provided the institution with a fixed revenue, larger than it had ever had. Buttressed by this support, LSU experienced a modest expansion after 1925. The number of students enrolled and of faculty members

---

[1] *Time*, April 1, 1935, pp. 15–17. The magazine employed a blank space to indicate an expletive. I have assumed that Huey used his usual one.

employed increased somewhat, and buildings began to rise on the flat expanse of fields.

This was rapid progress—judged by the measuring standards of conservative Louisiana; but judged by more realistic standards and in comparison with developments in many other states, it was coming at a pitifully slow pace. In 1928 LSU had an enrollment of only eighteen hundred students, ranking eighty-eighth in size among American universities. The faculty numbered but 168, and although a few of its members were scholars of reputation, the general level was undistinguished. The operating budget was a mere eight hundred thousand dollars. In the rating of schools maintained by the inter-collegiate Association of State Universities, LSU was on the "C" list, or third-rate.[2]

The school's lowly status was the result of years of inadequate financial support by the state. But the skimpy budget was only an immediate cause, an expression of something fundamental in the Louisiana, and Southern, view of education. Louisianians had an attitude toward education that can only be described as resigned. They had a kind of pride in their university and state colleges and lower schools. But at the same time they knew these institutions were not very good, and they did not think much could be done to improve them. Louisianians were victims of the psychological retrogression into which the South lapsed after the Civil War: the South was poor, and in certain areas, such as education, Southerners simply had to be content with second or third best. Educational reformers in the state had striven against this passivity, but their efforts had been all but useless. The attitude was not going to change until a leader appeared who would challenge the concepts underlying it, who would inspire the people to believe that they *could* have a first-rate university and a first-rate educational system—and who would do whatever was necessary to make their vision a reality.

Huey displayed only a cursory interest in LSU during the first two years of his governorship. He permitted its appropriation from the state to be increased in 1929, but only slightly. When he discussed his far-ranging plans for Louisiana, he did not mention the university. He did not attend any of its functions, such as the gradua-

[2] Don Wharton: "Louisiana State University," *Scribner's Magazine*, CII (September 1937), 33–4, 38; *American Progress*, December 14, 1933, July 1935. The data cited above is based upon the preceding sources but mainly upon material from the university's files supplied to me by the administration. It is difficult to compute the budget with any exactness, as the financial records of the university for this period are deficient and incomplete.

tion exercises, to which as governor he was invited, and apparently he did not even visit the campus. He seemed anxious to avoid giving the impression that he meant to interfere with the operation of the institution. Sharp in his mind was a recollection of how he had burned his fingers by dragging LSU into the campaign of 1924. Seeking an issue, he had attacked the administration and had promised to discharge a number of deans and professors. Popular reaction to his proposal was so hostile that he had hastily dropped it, and in the campaign of 1928 he had referred to the university only in general and complimentary terms. He might yet include LSU in his plans, but just then he was inclined to go cautiously in any dealings he had with it.

He did not intervene actively in university affairs until 1930, and then only because an administrative crisis there forced him to. In the first month of the year it became public knowledge that the president of LSU, Thomas W. Atkinson, would soon have to resign; he had recently suffered a heart attack, and was in such bad health that frequently he could not appear at his office. There was avid speculation both in the university and throughout the state as to who his successor would be. This was not surprising, since choosing a president of LSU was almost a public act. The choice was made by a public body, the board of supervisors, the governing agency of the university. The members of the board were appointed by the governor for fixed terms, each governor having a number of appointments. The terms of a majority of the members overlapped a gubernatorial election by two years, and hence an incoming governor could not name any new members until midway in his term. Thus Huey on becoming governor found a board appointed by previous executives. He had made no move to take it over, as he had done with the political boards, apparently being content to wait his turn to make appointments.

Atkinson had been chosen to be president in peculiar circumstances, and these now threatened to complicate the selection of a successor. In 1926, when the position had fallen vacant, the board had offered it to Colonel Campbell B. Hodges, a professional soldier and a native of Louisiana who was the commandant of the Military Academy at West Point. Hodges was interested but could not persuade the army to release him prior to the end of his service. The board, hoping that the army would change its position and free him, decided to appoint an acting president. Their choice fell on Atkinson, a veteran teacher and administrator at LSU. He served two years as acting president, and then the board, despairing of getting Hodges, named him president. When he became ill and talk of a possible successor sprang up, members of the board naturally recalled their offer to Hodges. Some of them suggested to Huey, probably in the latter part of 1929, that the colonel might now be available.

The members who made the suggestion had the most altruistic of motives. By their standards Hodges was an ideal choice. He was a Louisianian (by tradition the president had to be an "insider"), he had a good military record, and having been commandant of West Point, he must know something about education. Their reasoning might have puzzled educators at Harvard or Yale, but the notion of a soldier-president seemed sensible to many Louisianians and even to many administrators at the university. LSU was almost a military school. It had been established as a military academy on the eve of the Civil War, and after it became a university, it retained strong vestiges of its origin. Its ROTC unit and program was one of the largest of any in the country's universities. Some of its graduates had entered military service and attained high positions. Alumni and admirers liked to refer to it fondly as "the Old War Skule." Campbell Hodges would fit perfectly into this environment. In pushing him for the presidency, the board members were accurately reflecting the educational ideals of Louisiana.

They were, however, overlooking or disregarding something more important—the realities of Louisiana politics. Hodges was a scion of an aristocratic planter family of north Louisiana, one that ruled the politics of its area. The Hodgeses were extremely conservative, and a brother of the colonel's was one of Huey's bitterest foes. In Huey's view every Hodges was a political enemy, and when the board members suggested Campbell as president, his reaction was no more than might have been expected: he saw a cunning move to elevate an opponent to the highest educational job in the state. Emphatically (and probably profanely), he vetoed the suggestion. If LSU was going to get a new president, that man should be a civilian, not a soldier, he said. According to rumor, he was grooming such a candidate, Superintendent of Education Harris—but only because he wished to destroy the powerful Harris. He would make Harris president and then unseat him after he had elected a Longite to the office of superintendent. The rumor had a partial basis in fact. Huey did discuss the presidency with Harris, but probably without any ulterior motive. Harris said, however, that he had no desire to change jobs.[3]

[3] New Orleans *Morning Tribune*, January 4, 1930; Long: *Every Man a King*, pp. 184–6; T. H. Harris: *The Memoirs of T. H. Harris* (Baton Rouge, 1963), p. 168.

If the board members who proposed Hodges had deliberately sought to focus Huey's attention on LSU, they could not have chosen a more effective means. He suddenly saw the university in a new light—as an instrument that his enemies wished to control. Perhaps even now they controlled it and would try to use it against him. He began to wonder whether the school was as free of politics as it claimed to be and should be. An incident that occurred during the presidential crisis increased his doubts.

One of the most colorful students on the campus in the fall of 1929 was a brash young man named Kemble K. Kennedy. K.K., as he was known, was an orphan who had come to LSU from Union parish, a Long stronghold. He himself was an ardent Longite and had campaigned for Huey in his parish and at LSU. He had also pushed his own political fortunes, running for president of the law school and winning the election handily. Immediately he revealed that he had an unusually expansive view of his office. In December he led a delegation of fifty law students to Huey's office to inform the governor that the school was not being operated efficiently and was retrogressing rapidly. He laid the blame on its dean, Robert Lee Tullis, and boldly suggested that Tullis should be relegated to an emeritus status. Huey must have listened to this proposal with sympathy, for the dean, a salty character, was an outspoken critic of Longism in all of its manifestations. But he merely remarked that perhaps Tullis had outlived his usefulness and said that he would refer the protest to the board of supervisors.[4]

The administrative officials at LSU must have been angered at Kennedy's obvious disregard of their authority, and shortly they received additional and more sensational evidence of his concept of student freedom. Among the events that marked the end of the school term in June was the appearance of a student magazine of humor called the *Whangdoodle*. Modeled on similar journals of the time in other colleges, it featured anecdotes and lampoons of students and faculty members and satiric comments on developments of the past year. Produced anonymously by a student group, it delighted undergraduates and mildly amused administrators and professors.

The issue of 1930 appeared on June 1. Readers who snatched it up could scarcely believe their eyes: the corny jokes and heavy lampoons were gone, replaced with anecdotes of the kind commonly classified as "dirty stories." Even more startling, the magazine carried juicy bits of gossip about faculty members. The most sensational item

[4] Baton Rouge *Morning Advocate*, December 10, 1929; Shreveport *Journal*, December 11, 1929.

concerned the wife of a certain professor who regularly received a lover from the town when her husband was absent in the classroom. Except for the students, nobody was amused at this issue. The faculty was enraged and demanded with a united voice that the perpetrators be identified and punished. President Atkinson hired a detective to discover the guilty parties. This man was able to establish the facts easily—the magazine had been put out by members of a fraternity, Theta Nu Epsilon, a social group that seemed to be assuming the character of a Long political organization. The guiding spirit of the group and the probable editor was K. K. Kennedy.

The identification of Kennedy as the principal culprit came approximately a week before he was to receive his law degree. But Atkinson, demonstrating why he was sometimes referred to as "Guts," promptly expelled the almost-lawyer. Simultaneously, the district attorney of East Baton Rouge parish, John Fred Odom, a vociferous anti-Long, had K. K. arrested and bound over for trial on the charge of complicity in producing the *Whangdoodle*. At this point, according to newspaper gossip, Huey suddenly intervened in the situation. Reportedly, he demanded of Atkinson that Kennedy be reinstated and granted his degree, and he threatened the university and the president with dire punishment if his will was defied. It is doubtful that he was this dramatic. He did intercede for Kennedy. He thought that denying the boy a degree was unduly severe, and he wondered why of the various guilty students only a supporter of his had been singled out for punishment. But he gave way readily when Atkinson refused to rescind his edict. Apparently Huey had not read the offending issue, but when Atkinson showed it to him, he said that he could not condone such scurrilous stuff. The president announced: "Governor Long now understands my position and approves of it."[5]

Kennedy's trial came up in November. He did not deny his part in putting out the *Whangdoodle*, but pleaded that he was taking the onus for others. He was found guilty of criminal libel and sentenced to serve one year in the parish prison. Immediately petitions for a reprieve, originating in a Long parish, were sent to the governor's office, and reporters sought out Huey to ask his reactions. "I'd like to see the whole fifty or sixty that were in on getting out these sheets have about thirty or sixty days each in jail, and then they would all learn the lesson they need," he said. It was wrong to punish Kennedy alone: "All of them were as mean as the dickens or they couldn't

[5] Baton Rouge *State-Times*, June 2, 1930; New Orleans *Times-Picayune*, June 5, 6, and 7, 1930; Shreveport *Journal*, June 6, 1930; Joseph Cawthorn; Hermann B. Deutsch: "Kingdom of the Kingfish," in New Orleans *Item*, August 23, 1939.

have been in it." To no one's surprise Kennedy received a gubernatorial reprieve after spending only one week in prison. The governor's office explained that the prisoner had recently suffered a fractured arm in an automobile accident and needed medical attention. K. K. exclaimed: "Thank God," adding that he would resume his law studies.[6]

Sometime in November, before the Kennedy trial had ended, Huey decided that he needed to know more about the operation of the university. He suspected that the board of supervisors and possibly the administration were encouraging anti-Longism. He had also begun to think that the people who were running LSU were bound too much by antiquated educational traditions. Characteristically, he determined to find out what he wanted to know by the most direct method.

THE STUDENT WHO WAS President Atkinson's secretary looked up from her desk to see who entered her office. Startled, she recognized the governor. Huey had taken to carrying a gold-headed cane when he appeared in public, and now he tapped it loudly on the floor and asked to see the president. The secretary answered that Atkinson was at home, ill. Huey said he would talk to the business manager. The girl explained that this man's office was in a nearby building but that she would run over to get him. Shortly she returned and reported that the business manager was absent too, checking on a matter on the old campus. Huey was secretly enjoying the situation but affected to be angry. Pounding his cane on the table, he roared: "This is a hell of a note. Is there anybody out here I can talk to?" The secretary, now reduced to tears, suddenly remembered that the office of the newly appointed dean of men, Fred C. Frey, was in the same building. She ran to Frey's office and begged him to come and see the governor.

Huey was still rapping the table when Frey entered. He looked Frey up and down and said he had not come to talk to a "damn kid." Frey, a young sociologist of engaging manner, remarked that he was two years older than the governor. Huey laughed and suggested that they go into the president's office, where he sat down in Atkinson's chair and put his feet on the desk. Grinning at Frey, he said: "How do you think I would look as president of this damn outfit?" Just great, Frey answered, and waited for the governor to explain his

[6] Baton Rouge *Morning Advocate*, November 18, 1930; Baton Rouge *State-Times*, November 20, 1930.

visit. It came out immediately. Huey instructed Frey to send for F. T., "Pops," Guilbeau, who directed the band, was the grounds keeper, and held several other jobs as well. "I'm going to fire the sonofabitch," Huey announced. "I want a band." Frey protested that if the governor interfered with the hiring and firing of personnel LSU would get in trouble with the accrediting associations. Any action of that kind must be done by the president, he emphasized. But, said Huey, the president was sick. "I'll get me a new president," he said. Frey then turned to another argument. He pointed out that the band was part of the ROTC unit and that any political interference with it might attract unfavorable attention from the federal government. Perhaps, he suggested, the governor should confer with the recently named commandant of cadets, Major Troy H. Middleton.

Middleton was an unusual commandant. Although a professional soldier, he was not a graduate of West Point. He had had extensive civilian experience and was an expert at getting along with all kinds of people. The army had taken account of his background and tact in assigning him to LSU. "They've got a governor down there . . . ," he had been told. When Huey confronted him, he brought these skills to bear. In effect, he repeated Frey's arguments: in any matter regarding personnel the governor would have to act through the president. He added that he was sure Guilbeau would be happy to be relieved of one of his jobs. Huey was beginning to get the point —he should not fire a man himself but should try to persuade the president to do it for him. He insisted, however, that he was going to have a real band at LSU, a big one. The present band num- bered only twenty-eight pieces. "Hell," he said, "I had a band of twelve pieces in my campaign that made more noise than yours does." He told Middleton that the band should be increased to at least a hundred and twenty-five pieces and that it must have a new director. He would find the necessary money, he said.

A few days later he turned up in Middleton's office with a man. "Here's your band director," he said, introducing A. W. Wickboldt, a former army musician whom someone had told him about. Middle- ton inquired if Atkinson knew about the arrangement. "To hell with him," Huey said. "You and I are going to have us a real band." After Huey left, Middleton decided that he should inform the president of what was happening. Atkinson was surprised, not by the news that the governor had selected a director, but by the size of the band envisioned by Huey. He told Middleton to go ahead with the plans, but to restrict the band to seventy-five pieces. Soon after this Huey called Middleton to ask how the band was developing. Middleton repeated Atkinson's dictum as to size. Over the phone came a loud explosion of profanity. "I told you he has nothing to do with it," Huey bellowed. He ordered the major to create a band of the size that he had directed, and hung up.[7]

When compared with Huey Long's major projects, the LSU band seems ludicrously unimportant. Even as part of an overall plan for a great LSU, the time and attention that Huey gave to the band seems out of all proportion—the ultimate quality of the university was not going to be determined by the size of its band. But the issue of a large versus a small band was a symbol of two conflicting philosophies of education and progress, represented, respectively, by Huey and by the LSU administration. Huey's expansive plans for the state as a whole included expansive plans for LSU, and his ambitions were boundless. The administration obviously did not share his vision of a Louisiana greater than her sister states in education, as in all other aspects. Technically, the governor had no business deciding on the size of the band or selecting a director; these were the business of the LSU administration. But if Huey had not intervened, the band would have continued to be small—inadequate for his purposes. He would enlarge and improve the university in other, more important areas, but any program had to begin somewhere—and a consummate politician would instinctively begin with something impressive, something that was also simple—something that anyone with eyes to see or ears to hear could understand. Huey began by enlarging the band.

During the November of the Kennedy trial President Atkinson resigned. In continuing bad health, he did not feel able to cope with the duties of his office and the pressures placed on him by a vigorous and interfering governor. Almost immediately the board of supervisors chose a new president. The election of this man has become another one of the Long legends. The usual version is that Huey decided to "hire himself" a pliable educational hack. He asked various cronies to suggest a likely candidate. One of them—a stationery salesman, according to one account—said that James Monroe Smith was a possibility. "Who the hell is he?" Huey is said to have asked. He was told that Smith was dean of the college of education at Southwestern Louisiana Institute, a small state college in Lafayette. "Bring him over," Huey snapped. Smith came to Baton Rouge and had a brief interview with the governor, at the end of which Huey informed him that he had the job. Huey then called a meeting of the board of supervisors and ordered it to ratify his choice. And so LSU got a

[7] Fred C. Frey; Troy H. Middleton.

new president, elected, the popular version implies, by a method unprecedented in its history.[8]

Actually, the mechanics of the selection were completely in accord with the LSU tradition. Presidents of the institution have nearly always been designated instantaneously and have been men who were already on the staff or were Louisianians. Only twice has a search been conducted for a president and an "outsider" chosen—just prior to the Civil War, when William Tecumseh Sherman was picked to head the military academy that later became LSU, and in the 1940's, when the faculty for the first and last time achieved a voice in the selection. Smith's technical qualifications for the job were as good as those of most men who have filled it. Forty-two years of age, he had spent all of his adult life in education. He had been a country schoolteacher and principal, he had attended LSU, he had been a professor and dean at Southwestern, and along the way he had managed to secure a Ph.D. in educational administration from Columbia University.

In only one respect did the process of selection differ from the pattern. Huey did exercise more influence in it than was usual for a governor, but exactly how he did so is difficult to establish. It is certain that he was determined to get a man who would think in large terms—that is, one who would think as he did and who would cooperate with him. It is also certain that he was not going to permit an opponent, a Campbell Hodges, to get the post: the president did not have to be a Longite, but he could not be an anti-Longite. And Huey was in a position to enforce his will on the board of supervisors. The terms of a number of members had recently expired, and he had filled their places with followers of his. But even if he had not had these added votes, the board, so soon after his triumph in the senatorial election, would not have dared to defy him.

What is not clear is how he went about finding the kind of man he wanted or how he happened to settle on Smith. Certainly he did not proceed in the informal and haphazard way that has been reported. He did ask a number of people for recommendations. Some of these were politicians, but others were educators. The man who suggested Smith probably was George Everett, a member of the board of supervisors who operated a stationery and office-supply store in Baton Rouge, the "stationery salesman" of one of the popular accounts. Everett had met Smith through selling supplies to Southwestern and had been impressed with him. But other people also

---

[8] Harnett T. Kane: *Louisiana Hayride* (New York, 1941), pp. 213–15; Wharton: "Louisiana State University," *Scribner's*, September 1937, p. 36.

proposed Smith or spoke favorably of him when queried by Huey. According to one source, Huey expressed doubt about Smith's qualifications and was convinced only after he had himself interviewed Smith at length. He may have swung over when he learned that Smith was from Winn parish.[9]

Tradition has it that Smith came to the interview clad in a shabby suit and that he presented a generally dowdy appearance. Huey handed him a large bill and said: "God damn you, go out and buy a new suit. At least try to look like a president." But this story is dubious; it is told also of several other men whom Huey had elevated. If Smith was nondescript at the beginning, he changed quickly. People who were students during his administration remember him as a somewhat impressive figure. Of above average height and heavy-set, he was friendly and even effusive in manner—"democratic," thought the students, with whom he was extremely popular.[1]

If some people had doubted that Smith was big enough for the job, they were quickly disabused. He was an excellent administrator, imaginative and bold in devising new educational policies. Administrators who served under him and under presidents before and after him rank him as one of the best executives, if not the best one, of the modern period. Not the least of his talents was that he knew how to handle Huey, a skill he had to exercise frequently. Huey, now that he had a cooperative president, was bursting with ideas of how to improve the university. He would appear suddenly in Smith's office on the campus or summon Smith to his own office and excitedly reveal a project he had just thought of. Smith patiently heard out every proposal. He knew Huey was willing to pour out huge sums of money to develop LSU—not always having fixed opinions as to how they should be spent. Smith accordingly tried to get as much as he could for educational aspects of the university—new buildings, increases in faculty salaries, and the like. But when he found that Huey wanted to spend a large sum on an extracurricular activity such as a larger band, he went along. He would take the unimportant to get the important. He might argue an issue on occasion, but if Huey exploded and issued a command, he obeyed it. "He took his orders running," one observer commiseratingly recalled.[2]

Huey exploded at Smith often. In dealing with all official subordinates, he was blunt and could be harsh. He was especially rough on a man who he judged would take an affront. He had measured

[9] Bozeman, in *Winn Parish Enterprise*, February 4, 1960; Fred C. Frey.
[1] Confidential communications; W. E. Butler.
[2] Troy H. Middleton; Fred C. Frey; confidential communications.

Smith, just as the president had measured him. He saw that this genial servant would submit to much to get what he wanted, and he callously exploited the relationship. The stories of his maltreatment of Smith are legion: some of them legend, some of them true. The true ones tend to miss an important point: although Huey sometimes called Smith down merely to indulge his own meanness, other times he acted for the president's protection.

Thus on one occasion he had to intervene to save Smith from a situation created by Mrs. Smith. Thelma Smith did not make the transition from obscurity to prominence as gracefully as her husband did. She was immensely impressed by her position as first lady of the university and was determined to use it to make herself one of the social figures of the town. She gave large and elegant parties at the president's home, and Baton Rouge and the state buzzed with gossip about the nature of these affairs—male guests clad in tuxedos and female guests in evening gowns, tables laden with delectable and exotic foods, waiters hovering everywhere, the hostess moving among the crowd obviously unconcerned with how much it all cost. The ordinary citizen who read accounts of the soirees was incredulous. If LSU had a president who would countenance such luxury, was it the school for poor boys and girls that Huey was talking about?

Shortly Thelma gave the gossip mill more grist. A retired army officer in Baton Rouge started a riding club. Thelma joined it and became its social sponsor. The newspapers ran stories of her riding skill and described the expensive thoroughbred horse she had purchased and the outfits she wore on her rides. Some coeds joined the club, and one of them was thrown from her horse and badly injured. The news went out over the state: girl student, member of Mrs. Smith's riding club, hurt. Huey was out campaigning when the story broke. He had had enough of Thelma's nonsense. He sent a succinct telegram to Smith: "SELL THEM PLUGS." The peremptory tone distressed Smith. He rushed to George Everett's office and showed the telegram to the member of the board of supervisors. "Why show it to me?" Everett asked. "I don't know whether I'm on the board or off. He fires me every other day. But I know what you're going to do—sell them plugs."[3]

LSU students of 1930 and 1931 could easily have gotten the impression that Governor Long was on the campus every day. Huey came frequently, whenever he could wring a spare moment from his political schedule. Sometimes he came to check on the new band.

[3] Byrne M. Womack; Fred C. Frey; Troy H. Middleton; Kane: *Louisiana Hayride*, p. 226.

The band practiced once a week, and he often appeared at these sessions. He would sit with Director Wickboldt and for a time listen quietly, but then he would intervene. "Try 'Harvest Moon' again, a little softer," he would direct. Nearly always he ended by actually directing the musicians. He supervised every detail of the band's development. He helped design the uniform of the members, a flamboyant pattern that featured LSU's colors of purple and gold. He announced that he meant to enlarge the band still more and that he had decided on what pieces would be added: "bassoon, oboe, and piccolo players." His earlier allegiance to the cornets and brasses had been shifted to the reeds, he explained. He selected the drum majors and insisted that they must be the tallest boys that could be found. His unofficial agents scoured the state and went even into neighboring states to get such boys. Huey equipped them with huge shakos that made them look gigantic.

This was his band, and he was enormously proud of it. He exhibited it on all possible occasions—with himself at the head, striding between the drum majors, waving a baton. He loved to lead it in parades, at football games, and at ceremonial occasions. Once he led it through the streets of New Orleans in the pomp of Mardi Gras. At a traffic light some policemen, not recognizing him, ordered the marchers to stop. Huey raised his baton imperiously. "Stand back," he roared. "This is the Kingfish."[4]

The band was the first object at LSU to enlist his affection, and he would always be interested in it. But soon after his initial visit to the campus he turned his restless attention to another student activity, one that attracted him even more than the band. Huey became a football fan, the most ardent and vociferous one in Louisiana.

One day in late November 1930, shortly before the traditional game with Tulane, the LSU football squad, known as the Tigers, noticed that two visitors had come on to the practice field—one of them was Governor Long. Coach Russell, "Russ," Cohen collected them into a group to receive the governor. Huey introduced his companion: he had brought Dr. Smith to meet the team. Cohen snapped to attention, held his cap over his chest, and said: "Boys, this is your new president." The new president, however, went unnoticed after his presentation. Huey told Cohen he would like to watch the team practice. Wandering around the field, he studied a player who was practicing kicks for extra points after touchdowns. Suddenly he stripped off his coat and said: "Let me try that." When

[4] John T. Hood; Lewellyn B. Williams; Alton E. Broussard; Fred Digby; Lawrence M. Jones; Baton Rouge *State-Times*, May 22, 1931, February 9, 1932.

he received the ball on the snap, he lunged forward mightily—and saw the ball roll a few inches on the ground. He tried it once more but with the same result. "I guess I'm a little off today," he remarked.

Putting on his coat, he told Cohen that he would like to talk to the team. Cohen blew his whistle and directed the players to gather round the governor. Huey asked them how LSU was going to do against archrival Tulane in the last game of the season. Pretty good, one of the coaches answered, but Tulane had a great halfback named Zimmerman. Huey was immediately struck with an idea. "What's the matter with us getting him for that game?" he asked. "I'll give his dad a job with the state and get him up here and we'll put the boy in at LSU." There was an embarrassed silence, and then someone explained that it was against the rules of college football to pirate a player. Huey was dumfounded: "That's a hell of a rule," he complained. But in a moment he brightened. Maybe, he suggested, LSU could run the ball back for a touchdown when it received the first kick. Somebody asked how he knew LSU would receive. "Well," he said, "we kicked off in last year's game, so it's our turn to receive." Another strained silence ensued. One of the coaches finally volunteered that a flip of a coin determined who would kick off in a game. Huey showed great interest in this information. He was obviously going to be involved in football at LSU.[5]

His amused audience did not realize how deep this interest was or how it would influence the athletic fortunes of LSU—or their own immediate futures. Huey tried to give an inkling of his intentions to one of the coaches shortly after this visit. "I don't fool around with losers," he said. "LSU can't have a losing team because that'll mean I'm associated with a loser."[6]

LSU in recent years had not had a losing team, but its performance had not been impressive. Its record during the 1920's when interest in football had first blossomed at the school and in the state, had been mediocre. Hoping to better the situation, the administration in 1928 brought in a new, young coach, Russ Cohen, who had been a star at Vanderbilt and was then an assistant coach at Alabama. Cohen had not fulfilled the expectations promised by his reputation. In his first year LSU won six games, lost two, and tied one. In 1929 the record was six wins and three losses. In 1930, up until the Tulane game, LSU had won six and lost three. Although the over-all record showed more victories than defeats, most of the victories had been over small colleges. Against schools in LSU's class, Cohen had won

[5] Oliver P. Carriere; W. E. Butler; Sidney Bowman; Harry Rabenhorst.
[6] Oliver P. Carriere.

seven games, lost eight, and tied one. Most disappointing of all, he had done poorly against Tulane. In 1928 the two rivals played to a scoreless tie, but the next year Tulane crushed LSU 21 to 0. And in 1930 Tulane was favored to win by an even larger score.[7]

In part, Cohen was the victim of circumstances. The administration did not encourage him to recruit players, and although some boys appeared at LSU who developed into stars, his squads lacked depth. But his material was better than his record would suggest. Players and coaches who were associated with him say unanimously that he was not a good coach. He knew the game and could teach techniques, but he could not reach into a boy's heart to inspire him to an extra effort. "He couldn't get close to the boys," one player recalled. "His pep talks were like a record. He couldn't get you up." He astonished one squad by telling them that he did not want to see them smiling, that smiling indicated a lack of desire to win. The players were nervous in his presence, especially at the important half-time sessions.[8]

Huey quickly decided that Cohen could not build the kind of team that would bring honor to LSU and Huey Long—and having decided he acted. Just before the Tulane game he told Cohen his contract would be terminated as soon as the game was over. President Smith and the board of supervisors were apparently to be informed of the action later. Cohen was in a savage but dejected mood when he took his team to New Orleans for the game. His assistants and the sports reporters were also angry. They thought Huey could have waited until after the game to announce the discharge. These men were in Cohen's hotel room on the morning of the game discussing the matter when Huey suddenly walked in. He suggested that something to eat and drink be ordered up. One of the coaches said bitterly: "You got the money to pay for it?" Unabashed by his hostile reception, Huey said he was going to sit on the LSU side during the game.[9]

That afternoon the twenty-five thousand people at the Tulane stadium saw two shows, and they were torn as to which one to watch —the game or the governor. Huey arrived at the stadium early, sporting a huge LSU badge of purple and gold. He went immediately to the Tiger dressing room, and when the team ran out onto the field,

[7] The compilation of games is based on material supplied by the LSU Athletic Department.
[8] Lewis Gottlieb; Oliver P. Carriere; Sidney Bowman; W. E. Butler; Harry Rabenhorst.
[9] Fred Digby; Oliver P. Carriere.

he was with them. Ignoring the governor's box on the Tulane side, he raced to the LSU bench. Reporters asked him what he had told the players. He had thought of nothing better than the hoary exhortation "Get out there and fight." During the first half he ran up and down the sideline following the plays. When Tulane threatened to score, he sank on the ground as if in prayer and chanted: "Hold 'em, Tigers." At half time he started for the dressing room again. Two of his cohorts reminded him that he was supposed to pose for a shot by Paramount News. "To hell with 'em" he snapped. "I'm running my team." As the second half began, he returned to the LSU bench. At the end of the third quarter Tulane led 12 to 7. Huey got up and started for the Tulane side. "I've done my damndest," he said resignedly. The Tulane stands rose and booed him as he crossed the field to his box.

Late in the fourth quarter Huey must have wished he had stayed on the LSU side. LSU moved the ball close to the Tulane goal line and seemed on the point of scoring when the game ended. The Tiger fans were jubilant—their team had won a moral victory.[1]

In the LSU dressing room after the game, pandemonium reigned. Players, coaches, and reporters shouted with joy. One reporter grabbed Huey by the lapels of his coat and shook him. "Are you going to fire that man after a game like that?" he demanded. Other reporters and the coaches shouted the same question. Finally Huey made himself heard above the tumult. "Cohen will stay as coach, that's official," he yelled. He added, still speaking officially for the university: "We plan to brave up the athletic department with some new material. The new administration will give some athletic help." A few days later Cohen was awarded a new contract that raised his salary to seventy-five hundred dollars, probably the highest in the South. Curiously, the contract was signed not at LSU but at the governor's mansion. Although Dr. Smith was present at the ceremony, he remained in the background. Huey presided over the meeting. He announced that Cohen would have a free hand in running the team.[2]

Huey acted immediately to enable the administration to carry out his pledge. He made money available to increase the athletic department's budget. A graduate manager, really an athletic director, was appointed to schedule games, and the coaching staff was en-

[1] Frost, in New Orleans *States*, November 28, 1930; Harry Rabenhorst; W. E. Butler; Fred Digby; Oliver P. Carriere.

[2] Fred Digby; Oliver P. Carriere; New Orleans *Morning Tribune*, November 28 and December 2, 1930; unidentified clipping, n.d., in Grace Scrapbook.

larged. And, for the first time, a systematic program to recruit promising high-school players was established. Huey took a direct hand in this. Once he read of a player in Arizona who could run unusually fast. He told the director to drive out and bring the boy back. The boy could run, but soon after he arrived, it was found that he had tuberculosis and he had to be returned to his home. On another occasion Huey personally interviewed a much-sought-after Shreveport star who was not sure what college he should attend. The boy said that he might go to Centenary College, a Methodist institution in his home town. Huey snorted contemptuosuly. "All they got there is old Sexton, who teaches the Bible," he said. "I know a hell of a lot more about the Bible than he does. You come to LSU and I'll teach you the Bible." His argument was surely unique in the annals of American education, and it worked.[3]

For the football boys, "his boys," Huey would do almost anything. They were the object of his constant and affectionate attention. One year three stars were injured in the first game. Huey heard they were being treated at the school infirmary. Immediately he invited them to move into the mansion to recuperate. "I'm a better doctor than those doctors at LSU," he told one of them. His idea of doctoring was to feed them twice a day with steaks, turnip greens, cornbread, and pineapple upside-down cake. When a boy had finished a steak, Huey put another one on his plate, so the players soon learned to eat the first helping very slowly. They naturally gained in strength, but the treatment had its dangers. A fullback put on fifty pounds and in the Tulane game collapsed after five plays.

Huey was equally solicitous of the boys during games. At the half-time intermission he would head for the dressing room to help the trainers repair any damages that might have been suffered. He would sponge the faces of perspiring players and hold towels packed with ice to their necks, all the time exhorting them to get back in there and fight. He insisted on doctoring injured players himself, often prescribing remedies from Winn parish folklore. At one game an end complained he had a boil between his legs. Huey said he knew just the thing to cure it. Ordering various ingredients sent in, he concocted a dosage whose base was epsom salts and made the boy drink it. During the second half the player became violently nauseated and vomited continuously. The other players would not permit him to line up in the huddle but made him stand at a distance. His unorthodox position confused the opposing team, and

[3] Fred Digby; Harry Rabenhorst; Sidney Bowman; Lewis Gottlieb.

the incident caused some observers to believe that Huey invented the formation of "the lonesome end."[4]

One of his pledges made at the rehiring of Cohen—to let the coach have a free hand—Huey forgot almost immediately. He probably meant it at the time, but it was not in his nature to stay aloof from any activity that interested him. He was determined to have good football developed at LSU, and he could not resist telling Cohen and the other coaches and the players how to do it. Thus during the season of 1931 he appeared at practice sessions with diagrams of plays that he wanted Cohen to test and then use. Some of them he had taken from articles in sporting magazines or from the sports pages of newspapers. Some he begged from acquaintances who knew something about the game. He even persuaded an assistant coach at Tulane to provide a few, promising solemnly that they would not be used against Tulane. Some he designed himself, and these were highly unorthodox and generally so intricate that they were not practical. The coaches received the plays with thanks, tried them in his presence, and then usually forgot them. Huey apparently thought that some of them were used, for he was still so ignorant of the game that he could not follow plays.[5]

Cohen was irritated by Huey's attempts to influence strategy, but as they were harmless, he could put up with them. Other forms of gubernatorial interference were harder to tolerate. Huey insisted that he should have a voice in directing the team on the field. Thus before one game Cohen was telling the squad that he would signal which plays to run by holding his hat in certain positions. Huey interrupted: "And when I grab the coach around the neck," he said, "that means a forward pass." During the game Huey grabbed Cohen so often that the players could not see the hat signals, and the disgusted coach got a stiff neck that lasted for days.[6]

Particularly hard for Cohen to take was Huey's insistence on addressing the team before a game and during half time. The coach should have forced a showdown on this issue, threatening to resign if Huey did not stop the practice. But he weakly permitted Huey to take over, and Huey characteristically pushed his advantage. According to standard football theory, Huey's talks should have been worthless to the players and possibly bad for them. They should have been listening to a technician instead of to a rank amateur. But men who played under Cohen state emphatically that Huey's appearances

[4] Sidney Bowman; W. E. Butler.
[5] W. E. Butler; Lester Lautenschlaeger; Harry Rabenhorst; Sidney Bowman.
[6] Lawrence M. Jones.

helped. He unloosened the boys after Cohen had put them in a nervous or gloomy mood. One man recalled a scene before the Mississippi State game of 1931. In the dressing room Cohen was making one of his wooden speeches, and the players were getting restless. Suddenly they heard a voice bellowing outside the door: "Here comes the best damn football player in America." In burst Huey, wearing a purple sweater with a huge L emblazoned on it and swinging a cane. "They ain't got a thing," he announced. "You ought to beat them 40 to 0." The players broke out laughing and relaxed immediately. They won the game 31 to 0.

He had probably planned every detail of his entrance, clowning deliberately to ease the boys' tension. He employed a similar technique before the Arkansas game. This game was played in Shreveport, and the teams stayed in the same hotel. On the night before the game Cohen called a conference of his squad in a hotel room. He had caught a glimpse of the Arkansas players, and he was appalled by their size. Walking up and down, he kept muttering that Arkansas was big, big. The players were plainly getting edgy. Huey abruptly intervened. "There's nothing to worry about," he said. "Joe Messina just scouted them in the lobby. They're not too tough. Messina says so." The sheer absurdity of Messina's acting as a scout convulsed the boys. Immediately they felt more confident, and although they lost the game, they held their favored opponents to a close score.[7]

Huey had hoped that the season of 1931 would signal a dramatic upturn in LSU's fortunes. At first it seemed that he would have his wish. The Tigers lost the first game but won the next four. Then, in November, came a game that Huey desperately wanted to win. It was an intersectional game, the first one LSU had played; it was with an opponent of national reputation, the U.S. Military Academy; and it was to take place at West Point. Huey had started planning for the trip back in July. LSU needed advertising and here was a chance to get it, he excitedly announced. The state should send a large delegation to West Point to support the team—no less than three thousand citizens and students. And, he continued, he had arranged with the railroads to take them, in five special trains and at a cost of only $150 a person. He would go himself, in a special car; all the high state officials would go; and Lieutenant Governor Cyr would go—but in a special car of his own. A story in the *Progress* outlined the proposed route to West Point. It was somewhat indirect, via the following places with stopovers in each: St. Louis, Cleveland, Niagara

Falls, and New York City, where the fans would see a Broadway play, chosen by Huey. The purpose of the stopovers, it was explained, was to permit the band to parade in the Northern cities. Exhorting readers to sign up for the elaborate eight-day trip, the *Progress* redundantly assured them that all details had been foreseen "by Governor Huey P. Long."[8]

The magnificence of the project caught the popular imagination: Louisiana was going "big-time" at last. Significantly, nobody doubted but that Huey would bring it off; the state was finally growing up to him. Especially excited were the students at LSU. Huey had said that three thousand people would make the trip. There were twenty-eight hundred students at LSU, so he was obviously intending to take all of them, and, moreover, pay their passage. Huey probably had no such intention, although he did hope that many students would be able to make the journey at their own expense. Whatever he had planned, however, he shortly had to dash their expectations. In September he appeared on the campus and asked Dr. Smith to call a meeting of the student body. Classes were hastily suspended, and the excited youngsters gathered to hear the governor. Sadly Huey told them that the West Point junket had been canceled—only the football squad and the band would make the trip. He himself would not be able to go, because Cyr had refused to accompany him. The students listened with mounting anger, and later they sent a petition to the lieutenant governor, begging him to go with Huey. But Cyr refused them, and Huey had to remain at home.[9]

Perhaps it was better for him that he did not go. His ego would have suffered some hard blows. In New York his band paraded up Broadway, but in the hubbub of the big city it attracted little attention. At West Point his team fell before the Army, 20 to 0. None of his hopes for the trip had materialized, and his dream of a sensational winning season had been dimmed. LSU came up to the Tulane game with a record of five victories and three losses. Only a triumph over the traditional rival could save the season.[1]

The Tulane game was played in New Orleans, and the large crowd was gratifyingly responsive to everything that went on on the

[8] Baton Rouge *Morning Advocate*, July 28, 1931; New Orleans *States*, August 16, 1931; *Louisiana Progress*, August 18, 1931.

[9] Baton Rouge *State-Times*, September 29, 1931; Shreveport *Times*, October 2, 1931; W. E. Butler. Mr. Butler thinks that Huey had intended to take the students but was unable to persuade the railroads to offer a low enough rate.

[1] Baton Rouge *State-Times*, November 5 and 7, 1931; New Orleans *Times-Picayune*, November 8, 1931; W. E. Butler; Fred Digby; John T. Hood; Sidney Bowman.

field, especially to the artistry of the unofficial leader of the band and the antics of the unofficial head coach. But the result of the game was a grievous disappointment to Huey. Tulane crushed the Tigers by a score of 34 to 7. After the game Huey announced that Cohen had been fired. LSU was buying up his contract, which had a year to run. A search for a new coach would begin immediately, and the choice would fall on a "name" coach, a man of national reputation.[2]

Huey's antics at LSU have fascinated all observers. They have wondered why a governor would want to lead a band or give a pep talk to a football team. Some have put it down to a juvenile quality in the adult Huey. He had never been an undergraduate or enjoyed the delights of college life, they say, and he was only recreating an existence that he had always longed for. When he strutted at the head of the band, he was young Huey Long from Winnfield who had become a campus figure at LSU. Others have thought that Huey's interest in LSU was sinister, that he viewed the school as a personal plaything, a glittering toy that he could toss around for his amusement. Some people who watched him at the time, including football players, decided he had political motives. One former athlete recalled that Huey frequently talked with the boys about politics and urged them to become interested in it. "He was thinking of the future in all this," this man said. "He was getting people who would be for him when he'd follow the ball up and down the field and wave to students." An astute Washington journalist cited another possible reason for Huey's actions. He pointed out that Huey was the only politician to get generous and continuing publicity in a section of the newspaper customarily denied to politicians, the sports pages.[3]

These various speculations may be accurate. Perhaps Huey was trying to recreate a youthful dream or win the allegiance of future voters. But the speculators have been so dazzled by his campus escapades that they have ignored other things he did at LSU. Hardly anyone has considered that Huey might have been seriously interested in education or in building up the university—or that he might have exploited such activities as football or the band to get public support for more serious endeavors—a technique that countless college administrators have resorted to.

In late December 1930 Huey made an announcement that startled educational and medical circles: LSU was shortly going to

[2] Fred Digby; Oliver P. Carriere; Sidney Bowman.
[3] Sidney Bowman; "Unofficial Observer" [John E. Carter]: *American Messiahs* (New York, 1935), p. 15, hereafter cited as Carter: *American Messiahs*.

establish a medical school in New Orleans. He explained briefly why such a school was needed. The only medical school in the state, at Tulane University, was so crowded it had to refuse many qualified applicants. The creation of a second institution would enable these and other young men to secure a medical education and would provide Louisiana with more doctors. There was ample money available to establish a medical school, he said, without revealing where it would come from. His confidence mystified even people in his administration who handled financial matters. But nobody seemed puzzled by another aspect of the announcement. It was the governor—not the president of the university—who revealed this dramatic expansion of LSU's facilities. The state was becoming accustomed to the way the Kingfish did things.[4]

Greater oddities followed. On January 3 the LSU board of supervisors and the governing board of Charity Hospital, the state hospital in New Orleans, met in joint session—at Huey's suite in the Roosevelt Hotel. With the governor presiding, the boards agreed to create a medical school, and they completed the entire transaction in two hours. Huey promised he had the money to erect the necessary buildings and operate the school. He suggested that Dr. Arthur Vidrine, the superintendent of Charity, could act also as dean of the new school. Dr. Smith promptly nominated Vidrine, and the appointment was confirmed. At the end of the meeting Huey proclaimed: "Our act has done more to prolong life and help medical education than anything I've seen in my lifetime." An incredulous state official looked at Huey with admiration. "Governor," he said, "they tell me Rome wasn't built in a day. You've got it all over Rome."[5]

More conservative people were not so impressed. The precipitate creation of the school suggested an absence of proper planning, another impulsive action of Huey Long's. The impression was wrong. Huey had acted only after long deliberation and careful planning. He had been concerned about medical conditions in the state almost from the time he became governor, specifically about the lack of care for poor people and even for people in the middle-income group. Seeking a reason for this, he was logically led to study the facilities for medical education, and he had become convinced of one fact—a major reason for the inadequate medical care was

[4] New Orleans *Times-Picayune*, December 21, 1930; Baton Rouge *Morning Advocate*, December 23, 1930; Shreveport *Journal*, December 23, 1930.
[5] Frost, in New Orleans *States*, January 4, 1931; unidentified clipping, January 4, 1931, in Grace Scrapbook.

that Louisiana did not have enough doctors. Tulane could not provide them; it was already overcrowded, and even if it was enlarged, its high tuition fees would exclude boys from any except well-to-do families. Therefore, it was obvious that another medical school was needed, and the state would have to establish it. Before he even broached his plan, Huey collected as much information as he could about medical education. Once he discussed his idea in general terms with a doctor who was also a member of the Tulane faculty, who recalled: "I was utterly astonished by his knowledge of medical history and what was needed to make a good medical school."[6]

Huey's opponents, and other people as well, could not understand why he had to create a new medical school when Tulane was already operating one. The consensus was that he must be once again gratifying his grudge against Tulane for refusing to grant him an honorary degree. By building a competing school he would lower Tulane's prestige, and this would irritate his aristocratic enemies on its governing board. The critics did not see the absurdity of their analysis—they were assuming that Huey brooded constantly over the slight Tulane had supposedly given him, and that he was going to construct an expensive medical school merely to spite Tulane.[7]

Actually, he did not envision the LSU school as a competitor of Tulane's but simply as an additional medical center that was badly needed. But if Tulane chose to be sensitive about his school, he was not going to worry and was, in fact, prepared to relish Tulane's discomfort. A *Picayune* editor, concerned by the mere announcement of the new school, telephoned to protest that Tulane would suffer. Huey snapped back: "Raise all the hell you want to, print what you want to. But we're going to have that medical school and every qualified poor boy can go."[8]

If people were impressed at the swift creation of the school, they were amazed at its rapid construction. The architects presented their plan for the buildings in January, the contracts were let in March, construction started in April, and in October classes began. In the meantime, Dean Vidrine had gathered an able faculty. One of the members was Dr. Aristide Agramonte, famous for his work with yellow fever in Cuba, who headed the department of tropical medicine. The school opened with only 109 students. But this figure

[6] Joseph Cawthorn; Dr. Abraham Mickal; Dr. Isidore Cohn.
[7] Kane: *Louisiana Hayride*, p. 216, is an example of this interpretation of Long's motive.
[8] Joseph Cawthorn.

doubled in the following year and grew every year after that, and by 1935 there were over nine hundred students. During the same years the enrollment at Tulane increased slightly but steadily each year. The development of the two schools amply confirmed Huey's conviction that Louisiana needed more doctors.[9]

Simultaneously with the founding of the LSU school, an incident occurred that seemed to demonstrate that Huey was indeed acting out of spite against Tulane. The Tulane faculty had long used the facilities of Charity Hospital as a vital classroom laboratory—the large number of patients offered a continuing supply of clinical examples for them and their students to study. By permission of Charity's governing board, most of the Tulane professors were "visiting doctors" at Charity and had full access to it; the care of five hundred patients in the hospital (in hospital language, the use of five hundred beds) was allocated to, or available to, Tulane professors and their students. The total number of available "beds," or patients, was seventeen hundred at this time. The LSU faculty and students would, of course, also have the use of the hospital. The resolution creating the new school stipulated that Tulane would continue to have hospital privileges; the LSU administrators promised there would be no interference with the rights of other institutions. "There are enough beds in Charity Hospital for three or four medical schools," Dean Vidrine observed, with some exaggeration.

One of the visiting professors from Tulane was the head of the department of surgery, the well-known surgeon Alton Ochsner. Dr. Ochsner, one of the most distinguished doctors in the South, was bitterly anti-Long. He was convinced that Huey was "politicalizing" the hospital and had expressed this opinion in a letter to a friend in Baltimore. A copy of this letter came into Huey's hands, and almost immediately thereafter the board of Charity announced that Ochsner had been deprived of his visiting privileges, obviously at Huey's direction. This savage retribution is usually interpreted as another example of Long's vendetta against Tulane. Actually, it was an expression of something much more sinister—his concept of administration. He tended to think, and the tendency would grow, that anything he created or supported was his personal possession and that the people in it owed their position to him. He would never have interfered with the technical operation of Charity Hospital. But since he had improved and enlarged its facilities, and was going to

[9] Wharton: "Louisiana State University," *Scribner's*, September 1937, pp. 37–8; *Louisiana Progress*, February, 1931; data on enrollment from files at Louisiana State University.

do more, it was his hospital. He would not permit anybody connected with it to criticize or oppose him.

The ban against Ochsner continued for two years, eventually coming to the attention of the accreditation committee of the Association of Southern Universities, which passed on the admission of new schools. An "A" rating from this committee was vital to a medical school, for without it the graduates might not be accepted for advanced work in other schools or be recognized by state medical associations. The committee viewed the prohibition on Ochsner as evidence that Huey was also interfering with the LSU medical school. It also had doubts about the qualifications of one LSU faculty member, the head of the department of surgery. This man was an able doctor, but he was young and had no reputation. Consequently, the committee refused to grant LSU the A rating.

This action shocked and angered Huey. His fine school into which he was pouring money was threatened in its very existence—and for a reason that to him was incomprehensible. But he realized that in the accrediting committee he had met a power that he had to come to terms with. Seeking advice, he was told that LSU would receive accreditation if it could employ as head of its department of surgery Dr. Urban Maes, a New Orleans doctor of distinguished reputation. Huey seized on the suggestion. Ignoring Dean Vidrine, he went to Maes and offered him the job. Maes said he would accept it on two conditions: the ban on Ochsner must be lifted, and there must be no political interference in the school or the hospital. Huey quickly agreed to both demands. He kept his pledge, and shortly LSU received the desired A rating.[1]

The Ochsner incident created another Long myth. It is widely believed in Louisiana, and has been frequently stated in Long literature, that Huey had the entire Tulane medical faculty and all of the students banned from Charity Hospital. Some Tulane doctors did indeed experience difficulty in securing hospital rights: their applications were delayed and sometimes rejected. But this was because the quota of patients allotted to visiting doctors was full, although occasionally the claim that no beds were available may have been an excuse to exclude an openly anti-Long doctor. There was no sweeping ban against the group as a whole, as shown by a letter from Huey

[1] George M. Wallace, who drafted the resolution creating the LSU medical school; Frost, in New Orleans *States*, January 4, 1931; unidentified clipping, probably January 4, 1931, in Grace Scrapbook; Stella O'Conner: "The Charity Hospital of New Orleans" *Louisiana Historical Quarterly*, XXXI (1948), 90; Isidore Cohn and Hermann B. Deutsch: *Rudolph Matas* (New York, 1960), pp. 386-7; Dr. Isidore Cohn.

himself to the hospital governing board requesting visiting privileges for a Tulane professor. In the letter he complained that anything he did in regard to Charity was interpreted as being political. He admitted that on occasion he might have had political considerations in mind. But, he ended, by using political power he had built the hospital into a great institution.[2]

SOMETIME LATE IN 1930 Huey suggested to President Smith that LSU should enlarge its physical plant on the Baton Rouge campus. "Go ahead with your buildings," he urged. "Get your architects and start on what you need." Smith expressed satisfaction but cautiously asked where the money would come from. "That will be part of my job," Huey replied. "You have got to dare a bit if you build this school. Start ahead. Let the people see what we propose, and we will find a way to do it." Still dubious, but encouraged, Smith began. Plans for a huge construction program were drawn, but held in abeyance until Huey could make the money available.

Huey had a plan for financing the program, a very ingenious one, but he did not reveal it until the meeting in New Orleans at which the medical school was created. Then he sprang it on those present, and on the public, with obvious delight. He led up to it by describing the great new capitol then being built on the site of the old campus. But suddenly he said: "We are going to need more ground for the new capitol than we expected, and we will purchase it from the university for $350,000." This sum would be used to build the medical school. But, he went on, the university would still own much acreage in the neighborhood of the capitol, and the state would wish to purchase sections of it from time to time on which to erect needed office buildings. From these sales LSU would probably realize three million dollars, thus assuring it a financial reservoir for years in the future.

One sale occurred almost immediately thereafter. Huey "discovered" that the Highway Commission needed new offices and other space in the vicinity of the capitol. He "suggested" to the LSU board of supervisors that it should oblige the commission by selling twenty-two acres of land and a few buildings. The commission would be glad to pay $1,800,000 for the facility, he remarked casually. The board quickly agreed to sell. Huey then had the legal document drawn that was necessary to authorize the transfer. He

[2] Long to Board of Administrators, Charity Hospital, July 15, 1933, in behalf of Dr. Isidore Cohn, copy furnished me by Dr. Cohn.

summoned to the mansion to sign the document two members of the three-man commission. One of the members expressed doubt that it was legal for one state agency to buy property from another. He said that he would sign the resolution only if Huey signed it first. "Is that what you want?" Huey shouted. "Hand me that resolution." Across it he wrote: "Approved by Huey P. Long, Governor of Louisiana."[3]

When the transaction was made public, other people also thought that it was illegal. Conservatives conceded that it may have helped LSU, but they condemned Huey's headlong haste. Some of the critics charged that in effect he had stolen $1,800,000 of the state's money. Huey dismissed the accusation contemptuously. His enemies were not giving him enough credit, he said; they were not including in their figure the $350,000 for the medical school. "I want to confess the whole sin, if I have done anything wrong," he said. The more he thought about the matter, the more he realized that he had hit on exactly the right defense. Soon he took to calling himself "the official thief" for LSU.[4]

Assured of ample financial support, LSU embarked on its building program. Construction proceeded at a rapid pace. Within a year there sprang up on the campus a music and dramatic arts building that housed a music school with more equipment than any in the South (reputedly eighty grand pianos), a fine arts building, extensive dormitories for girls, a gymnasium, an enlarged football stadium, and a student center, the Huey P. Long Field House. This was only a beginning. Huey continued to divert money to LSU for still more construction, a total of over nine million dollars within the next few years, so that by 1935 LSU could boast of having the finest and largest physical plant in the South.[5]

Attached to the Huey P. Long Field House was an outdoor swimming pool. The idea for a pool came from Major Middleton, the ROTC commandant, who proposed it to George Everett of the board of supervisors. Together Middleton and Everett worked out a plan for a pool that would cost seventy-five thousand dollars. Everett took the plan to Huey and explained that it was Middleton's.

[3] Long: *Every Man a King*, pp. 247–9; unidentified clipping, January 4, 1931, in Grace Scrapbook; Frost, in New Orleans *States*, January 4, 1931; Baton Rouge *State-Times*, April 21, 1931; Jess Nugent.

[4] *American Progress*, December 14, 1933.

[5] Baton Rouge *State-Times*, June 8, 1931; *American Progress*, December 14, 1933; Long, in radio address, July 19, 1935, in Christenberry, ed.: *Speeches by Long*; Kane: *Louisiana Hayride*, p. 221.

Huey sniffed. "Hell," he said, "he don't know nothing about pools, but I do." Quickly he sketched a design for one that would cost half a million dollars and directed that it be built adjacent to the Field House. One day while the pool was being constructed, Huey appeared in Middleton's office. "Major," he said, "let's go over and see that swimmin' hole of yours." As he walked along the edge of the project, he asked if this was the longest pool in the country. Middleton said he thought the one at the United States Naval Academy was a little longer. Huey turned to the construction foreman. "Put ten more feet on this pool," he ordered. When completed the pool was 180 feet long and 48 feet wide—and in Louisiana was believed to be not only the largest in the country but the largest in the world.[6]

At the same time that he was putting money into the construction program, Huey was seeing to it that the state allotted additional support to LSU for operating expenses. The appropriation to the university was raised to almost one million dollars in 1931 and was increased each year thereafter, reaching by 1935 a total of approximately $2,870,000. As the money came pouring in, the administration was able to improve existing education programs and start ambitious new ones. Thus, although LSU had had a graduate school, it had granted only the master's degree. But in 1931 it was announced that henceforth LSU would offer the degree of doctor of philosophy. The announcement was made simultaneously by President Smith and Governor Long.

As the school widened the scope of its services, it enlarged the size of its teaching staff. New faculty members were added every year, and from the total of 168 employed when Huey became governor, the figure grew to 245 by 1935 (or to 394, if the medical faculty is included). The improvement was qualitative as well as quantitative. Many of the new professors were brought in from Northern schools and were already scholars of some reputation. The LSU faculty for the first time attracted national attention, and Louisianians glowed with pride. "The psychological effect was tremendous," an administrator recalled. "We were no longer a little college stuck off down here but a first-class school or on the way to it." The accrediting association now rated LSU as an A instead of a C institution.

But what most impressed the people of the state was the increase

[6] Troy H. Middleton; Baton Rouge *State-Times*, April 4, 1932.

in student enrollment. The number of students shot up each year until by 1935 the total reached approximately forty-three hundred, and with the medical school included, fifty-two hundred. From eighty-eighth in size among the country's universities LSU rose to twentieth and among state universities to eleventh. This rapid growth was in part a result of LSU's new reputation, but largely it was a reflection of economic conditions. LSU charged practically no tuition and provided a generous number of scholarships to needy students. It was well on the way to achieving the goal Huey had set for it—to make its facilities available to every poor boy and girl in the state.[7]

Huey avidly followed the various educational developments at LSU. Frequently he appeared at campus meetings to discuss the progress being made and promise his continued support. "We are going to make this school as complete a school as we can," he vowed in one address. In another he said: "Whatever else we need we are going to have." But his academic interests rarely extended beyond general university policies. Contrary to a widely held belief, he did not often interfere with details or dictate academic appointments. Only occasionally did he ask Dr. Smith to name somebody to the business staff or to a graduate assistantship. In fact, longtime LSU administrators contend that during Huey's administration less political pressure was exerted for appointments than in most previous or later administrations. He did not concern himself with what was taught in the classroom. This was not because he understood the concept of academic freedom and respected it, but because he did not think that the exercise of academic freedom could possibly affect him. He laid only one restriction on professors at LSU—they could not publicly criticize Huey Long. Academic freedom did not include the privilege of denouncing the man responsible for the splendor that was LSU.[8]

The splendor was real, though not as great as Huey imagined—a magnificent plant, ample financial support, an alert faculty that was being steadily augmented and improved, and, most important of all, a growing pride in LSU by people connected with it and by the public, a conviction on everybody's part that it would continue to

[7] Data on appropriations, size of staff and student enrollment computed from files at Louisiana State University; Baton Rouge *Morning-Advocate*, July 28, 1931; Fred C. Frey; Troy H. Middleton; Wharton: "Louisiana State University," *Scribner's*, September 1937, p. 33.

[8] Baton Rouge *State-Times*, May 22 and June 8, 1931; Fred C. Frey; Troy H. Middleton; confidential communications.

progress. If Huey, contemplating what he had accomplished for the school in a few years, sometimes exaggerated the effect, he could be pardoned. And he did exaggerate on occasion: once he ranked the great universities of the country Harvard, Yale, Johns Hopkins —and right behind them, Louisiana State University.[9]

Huey's interest in education did not stop with LSU. He was concerned with the whole educational structure of the state—with the problems of the elementary and secondary schools and, to a lesser degree, the state colleges. And whereas he did not turn his attention to LSU until he had been in the governor's chair for two years, he had given immediate heed to conditions at lower levels.

In devising plans to improve these conditions, he had the support of a powerful ally, Superintendent of Education Harris. A dynamic and dominating man, Harris believed that the public-school system would not make appreciable progress until control of it was shifted from local school boards to the state, and specifically to his office. Presently control rested with the localities, because they provided by far the greater share of the financial support of the schools. Of the total amount spent on public schools in the state, local districts furnished seventy-five per cent, and the state only twenty-five per cent. Harris had repeatedly advocated that the state should take over the burden of support—collecting the required amount by taxation and then funneling the money back to the localities—in return for state control over curriculums, teacher certification, and other matters. But during his long tenure in office he had never been able to persuade a governor to back his program— until 1928.[1]

Huey immediately grasped all the implications of Harris's plan. It would not only aid the school system but would also bring greater state control over the system, and state control over local governments generally was one of Huey's goals. He also understood that the most efficient way to advance control was to use the power to tax; in time he would centralize the collection of most taxes in the hands of the state. In using the technique to extend control to education, he risked increasing the power of the already powerful Harris. But he was confident that if a clash of wills should occur, he could handle Harris.

[9] Long, radio address of July 19, 1935, in Christenberry, ed.: *Speeches by Long*.
[1] Guy C. Mitchell: "The Growth of State Control of Public Education in Louisiana" (unpublished Ph.D. dissertation, University of Michigan, 1942), pp. 342–3, 357–8, 501.

Having decided on his policy, Huey acted, as usual, promptly and forcefully. In 1928 he personally drafted a tax law that he hoped would enable the state to take over a greater share of the support of the schools. It provided for a tax on malt syrups, the proceeds to go into a fund to equalize facilities in poor parishes with those in rich ones. That is, the state would pay some money from the fund to all parishes but more money to the poorer ones. The equalization fund was Harris's idea and obviously a device to increase state control. The revenue from this tax, however, was inadequate to the purpose, and in 1930 Huey proposed to Harris a more far-reaching scheme. He said he was going to have the legislature enact an additional one-cent tax on gasoline and that one half of the proceeds would be dedicated to the schools for an equalization fund. Harris pressed him to allot the entire amount to the schools. "If I did," Huey answered, "you'd want two cents. When you can get a bushel you want a barrel. No, half a cent is all I can do right now." Harris quickly retreated.

With the creation of an ample equalization fund, the state began to exercise greater control over the local school authorities. It insisted, for example, that it would not pay out money to schools unless their teachers met certification requirements, proving they had advanced training. As a result many teachers went back to college or resigned their jobs. Within two years the state department of education could report that ninety-two per cent of the teachers had received two years or more of professional education beyond high school. The state also demanded that parishes drawing benefits from the fund establish a minimum salary scale for their teachers, higher than the existing one, and lengthen the school year.

Huey was not content to stop with the creation of the equalization fund. Between 1932 and 1934 he secured the enactment of additional legislation that shifted to the state the responsibility for collecting most of the taxes to support education. As a result of his efforts, the state pledged to pay into the school fund a minimum of ten million dollars a year, twice the amount of state support in 1928, and by 1935 it was bearing sixty per cent of the total cost of public education.[2]

The various tax laws did not produce quite the result Huey had hoped for. Enacted as the spreading depression was drying up sources of wealth all over the country, they brought in less revenue than he had expected. Indeed, in 1932–3, when the income from

[2] Ibid., pp. 348, 350–3, 354, 362–5, 390–1, 513; T. H. Harris: *Memoirs*, pp. 126–30; Harris, in John Klorer, ed.: *New Louisiana* (New Orleans, 1936), p. 166.

all taxes collected in the state fell drastically, they returned very little, and in 1933 the amount of money contributed by the state to education dropped below the level of 1928. Temporarily the salaries of teachers had to be reduced and the length of the school year shortened. In 1934 the economic stituation improved somewhat, and the state was able to increase its contribution to the schools. In 1935 it was paying almost the ten million-dollar minimum that Huey had promised. His laws did not have the effect that he had envisioned until years later, after his death. By dedicating the proceeds of certain taxes to education, he had made it certain that education would have an assured income. These taxes would soon provide the schools with a minimum of twenty million a year, a figure that exceeded, perhaps, even his expectations.[3]

As though obsessed with a determination to lift up the educational condition of the state overnight, Huey turned his attention to a problem beyond the view of the schools—to the appalling illiteracy rate among adults, both white and Negro. This was a problem the state would have to attack by a new method of instruction, he decided. Working with Harris, he devised a plan to set up throughout the state a number of night schools that would offer illiterates the rudiments of an education. He diverted enough tax money to launch the program, and the Rosenwald Foundation, impressed by his purpose, agreed to add to its support. The classes met three times a week for approximately a year and were conducted in school buildings, churches, and even private homes. They were taught by white and Negro teachers who were recruited by Harris's office and paid extra compensation for their work. Over a hundred thousand adults, most of them Negroes, attended the classes and on completion of the course were certified as being literate. The effect of the program was reflected in the census table of 1930. The illiteracy rate for whites, ten per cent in 1920, was reduced to seven per cent, and the rate for Negroes from thirty-eight per cent to twenty-three per cent.[4]

[3] *American Progress*, November 1935, for a table of state appropriations to schools from 1921 to 1935; Allen P. Sindler: *Huey Long's Louisiana: State Politics, 1920–1952* (Baltimore, 1956), p. 104; Oliver Carlson: "Huey Long at Home," in New York *Post*, May 9, 1935, hereafter cited as Carlson, in New York *Post*; John Blair: "Huey Long—Words and Deeds," in *Student Outlook*, III (April 1935), 8–9. The commentators cited and others, overlooking the effect of the depression or fastening their attention on one bad year in it, have assumed that during the Long period education in Louisiana did not go forward and probably went backward.

[4] *Louisiana Progress*, March 27 and September 25, 1930; Baton Rouge *State-Times*, June 4, 1931; T. H. Harris, in Klorer, ed.: *New Louisiana*, pp. 165–6.

Huey was immensely proud of the experiment and described it on frequent occasions. Once, in a remarkably sensitive and intro-spective way, he discussed his reasons for starting it. He admitted that political considerations had not been entirely absent from his mind, but his statement revealed that he regarded the social implica-tions of illiteracy as being more important that the political ones. "We started them to school," he said. "They learned to read. They learned to work simple arithmetic problems. Now some of our plantation owners can't figure the poor devils out of everything at the close of each year. They can find the name Huey P. Long on the ballot. They put a cross beside it—that's part of what is the matter with me and Louisiana."[5] He meant that both he and the state suf-fered from this kind of voting, even when the vote went to him.

The public-school fund also supported the state colleges, in-stitutions with small enrollments, most of them offering a specialized training such as teacher education. As the state increased its con-tribution to the fund, the colleges received as their share larger appropriations. How much each one got was determined by the State Board of Education, which was the governing body of the colleges. Its method of allotment was of little concern to Huey. He did not have for the colleges that fierce possessiveness and pride he had for LSU. He was willing to help them go ahead, but he would not make the all-out effort for them that he would for the university.

But although standing aloof from them personally, he inter-fered frequently and often improperly in their operation. His inter-ventions were directed almost entirely at the top administrative personnel. He was determined that the presidents should not be anti-Long men and preferably should be Long adherents. Thus in his first year in the governorship he forced the Board of Education to discharge a president, a veteran educator who was suspected of anti activities—but then, as if he thought the man would understand that he had to be fired, offered him a desk job in the Department of Education. He continued to influence the board's choice of execu-tives, and eventually all the presidents were men who owed their places to him and were subservient to him.

Possibly, if the Board of Education or the presidents had re-sisted his domination, he would have backed down. But encounter-ing little resistance, he rode roughshod over the yielders. He treated the presidents with harsh contempt. One of them once expelled a

[5] *American Progress*, March 15, 1934.

student whose father was a supporter of Huey's. Huey telephoned
the president to say that the student must not be expelled. The
president protested. "The State Board of Education is my boss," he
said. "Who the hell do you think is the boss of the State Board of
Education?" Huey snapped.[6]

[6] *Impeachment Proceedings*, I, 341–52, 383–97; Mitchell: "Growth of State
Control of Education," pp. 417–18; William J. Dodd.

# CHAPTER 19

# *Completing Our Great Program*

ONE MAJOR QUESTION occupied the attention of Louisiana political observers during the early months of 1931. Would the alliance that Huey and the Old Regulars had formed after the senatorial election continue in the coming regular legislative session and in the gubernatorial campaign that would get underway later in the year? There seemed to be evidence that it would. In March Huey came to New Orleans and conferred with Mayor Walmsley. Immediately rumors sprang up that the Old Regulars and Huey's Louisiana Democratic Association were going to formally merge. But when reporters asked Walmsley if the reports were true, he denied them angrily. "No one could merge with Huey Long in anything," he said. "There can't be any divided authority, because he will be the whole show or none." Huey also denied that there was a possibility of a merger. "Nobody can give me the Ring," he barked. "I won't have it."[1]

The exchange revealed what was holding the two factions apart: they could not agree on a division of authority and patronage. But they had a compelling reason to try to reach an agreement—each needed the other's strength—and Huey and Walmsley held further conferences. They had achieved at least a working pact when the legislature met in May, for their groups voted together on most bills during the session, which was an uneventful one, because the gover-

[1] New Orleans *Times-Picayune*, March 10, 1931; Baton Rouge *State-Times*, March 10, 1931.

nor advocated no particularly controversial legislation. Moreover, the Old Regulars on the State Democratic Committee supported Huey's choice for the post of national committeeman, made vacant by the recent death of Colonel Ewing. The new committeeman, elected unanimously, was Governor Long.[2]

The Old Regulars held back from endorsing Huey's choice for another office. He wanted them to announce that they would support his candidate for governor, who, according to rumor, would be Oscar K. Allen. Walmsley and his chiefs did not object to Allen. They were willing to support him and, if he was elected, his program—in return for his support of measures important to the city. What they balked at was the price Huey demanded for the privilege of the alliance, that he be allowed to name the legislative candidates for the coming election in a number of the city's wards. To the Choctaws, this went beyond merger: Huey meant to absorb them. They balked, but in the end they had to give way. Huey held too many cards for them; because of his power over the legislature he could cut off the financial benefits that had been awarded to New Orleans in the recent special session.

Their surrender was announced on July 2 after a four-day conference between Huey and Walmsley at the Roosevelt Hotel. Although the two principals did not issue a statement detailing what they had agreed on, the terms of their pact were common knowledge and appeared in the press. The Old Regulars promised to support Allen or whomever Huey designated as his candidate for governor. They also agreed to let the governor name eight of the candidates for the house from the city's seventeen wards, and three of the candidates for the senate from the seven senatorial districts of the city. Not generally known was Huey's only substantial concession to the machine: he pledged to give it a free hand in the city election in 1934. Walmsley understandably did not want to discuss the negotiations with reporters. "It's too hot to talk politics," he snapped. The Kingfish, however, was jubilant, and obviously not inclined to be a generous or tactful victor. He chortled that if the Old Regulars had refused to ally with him, they would have been "exterminated" by their own people.[3]

[2] New Orleans *Morning Tribune*, June 2, 1931; New Orleans *Times-Picayune*, June 3, 1931.

[3] Baton Rouge *State-Times*, July 3, 1931; unidentified clipping, July 3, 1931, in Grace Scrapbook; Eugene Stanley; Hermann B. Deutsch: "Kingdom of the Kingfish," in New Orleans *Item*, August 25, 1939.

HUEY HAD DECIDED who his gubernatorial candidate would be before he met with Walmsley. He had determined, in fact, to run a complete "Long ticket," putting up a man for each of the nine major state offices and, in consultation with his leaders, had settled on a slate of candidates. The identity of these men was known to the press, which published the names, but Huey withheld an official announcement until the conclusion of his agreement with the Old Regulars. Then he revealed what everybody had suspected—that the Long standard-bearer would be Allen.[4]

Only a few intimates knew that Huey had decided to support Allen after an agonizing appraisal of O. K.'s fitness to be his successor. He did not doubt Allen's loyalty to him, but he feared his friend's character was not strong enough to withstand the contending pressures he would face in the office. Even after settling on Allen, he still had misgivings, and finally decided to pull O. K. out and put up instead John B. Fournet, the speaker of the house. Or so Fournet thought, and still thinks. But another associate says that Huey did not make the offer to Fournet seriously. He was merely trying to protect Allen from the importunities of favor-seekers, to whom O. K. was making rash promises; by seeming to remove Allen from the race, he would remove him from the temptations to which he was vulnerable. Later, when he judged he could do so safely, he switched back to Allen—and placated Fournet by offering him the lieutenant governorship. Huey's maneuverings were so complicated it is difficult to establish the truth about them. But probably his first choice was always Allen. O. K. was an ideal successor, as one leader pointed out to Huey. "He'll do anything you want," this man said. "Nobody else will. You can be in Washington and still run things down here."[5]

However sincere (or insincere) Huey may have been when he discussed the governorship with Fournet, he was in deadly earnest when he offered him the second place on the ticket. He begged Fournet to accept it so he could rule out another aspirant—his brother Earl. Earl was demanding the lieutenant governorship as a reward for his faithful service, and he was being vociferously backed by his sisters and Julius, who thought that from the office he could vault into the governorship in 1936. One of the sisters later conceded that perhaps the family had erred in pushing Earl. "We had growing pains," she said. "We were a little premature." Earl be-

[4] Shreveport *Journal*, June 22, 1931; New Orleans *Times-Picayune*, July 3, 1931.
[5] John B. Fournet; Allen J. Ellender; O. B. Thompson.

lieved that he had also the support of Allen, in which he may have been right. If such was the case, O. K. was demonstrating the ineptitude that Huey suspected: the two top candidates could not both be from Winn parish. Earl also failed to understand this elementary truth, thus revealing that at this stage of his career he still had much to learn about politics. Huey had another reason to look unfavorably on Earl's ambition. He knew that he dared not leave Earl behind in a position of power while he himself went to Washington. Earl as lieutenant governor would dominate Allen: the wrong Long would be running the state.

Earl approached Huey in a confident mood, not dreaming his brother would withstand the family's wishes. He was shocked to meet with a blunt refusal. Earl's candidacy would be "too much Long mixed up" in the campaign, Huey said. Earl then said he would run as an independent and asked Huey not to put up a candidate against him. Huey replied that the administration would have its own candidate, and shortly thereafter he told Earl that the choice had fallen on Fournet. Earl immediately realized the real reason for his rejection and angrily told Huey so. It was not the possibility of "too much Long" in state politics that was worrying the Kingfish, Earl said: it was that there might not be "enough Huey Long."[6]

Two candidates for governor had announced before the Allen–Fournet ticket was revealed. First in the field was Dudley J. LeBlanc of the Public Service Commission. That agency, so active under Huey's chairmanship, had become almost moribund under his governorship. He was responsible for its fallen state. Two of its three members were among his most unrelenting enemies, Chairman Francis Williams and LeBlanc, and they smothered the voice of the Long member, Harvey Fields. Huey was not going to let this body get any credit for its regulative activities. In a ruthless display of power, and with utter disregard for the public interest, he vetoed the legislative appropriations to the Commission in 1928 and 1930. It was, however, still able to function. The salaries of the members were fixed in the constitution and hence were not subject to gubernatorial veto. Moreover, it had a source of revenue in addition to its appropriation from a special "supervisory" tax that it collected from corporations under its jurisdiction. But this tax was paid into a fund that could be disbursed only by the Board of Liquidation, and

[6] John B. Fournet; Lucille Long Hunt; Clara Long Knott; Earl K. Long, quoted in New Orleans *States-Item*, September 5, 1960; *Overton Hearing*, I, 867.

in 1930 Huey directed the board to withhold even this money. The work of the Commission virtually came to a stop.[7]

LeBlanc had not entered the race because of an idealistic desire to restore the Commission's status or even because of personal anger at Huey for hamstringing it. He seemed, in fact, to have no logical reason to run. Certainly he had no chance of winning. The only organized support he had was that of Williams's weak New Orleans faction. Nor did he have wide popular appeal. He was a clever and humorous speaker, but as a Frenchman and a Catholic he would seem alien and dangerous to the people of the northern parishes. He could expect to pile up a fair vote in the French parishes, and probably he hoped that if there was a second primary, he could offer to swing his vote to one of the front runners in return for some promise. It was a technique he would employ in later elections.

Close on the heels of LeBlanc's announcement came the entrance of Paul Cyr. The lieutenant governor revealed his candidacy in a statement of some five thousand words that contained far more criticism of Huey than praise of himself. Cyr won the immediate support of Senator Edwin Broussard, who urged the voters to unite against the "dictator" Long. A third anti-Long candidate entered the lists after Allen announced, George S. Guion, a member of an aristocratic south Louisiana family and a respected New Orleans lawyer but a man with small political reputation.

Huey hardly deigned to comment on the opposition candidates. He had no time for politics, he said; he was too busy carrying to completion his public-improvements projects, "our great program," and he would not be able to take part in the campaign until at least October. He did profess surprise at Cyr's candidacy. He said he had understood that Paul would run for an office to which he had some hope of being elected, for the school board or for justice of the peace in his home town of Jeanerette.[8]

Huey was not, of course, so occupied with the "great program" that he could not give attention to other matters. In fact, in August he neglected the state program for several weeks as he turned his energy to solving a problem that Louisiana shared with all the

[7] Williams to Long, March 9 and June 1, 1931, in Long Papers, Public Service Commission File; Deutsch: "Kingdom of the Kingfish," in New Orleans *Item*, August 25, 1939.

[8] Shreveport *Journal*, June 26, 1931; New Orleans *States*, June 28, 1931; Baton Rouge *State-Times*, July 3, 1931; Baton Rouge *Morning Advocate*, July 26, 1931; Huey P. Long: *Every Man a King* (New Orleans, 1933), pp. 254–8; Walter Hamlin; Hermann B. Deutsch.

Southern states—the steadily falling price of cotton. In 1931 it had dropped to a new low, and planters and farmers were crying for help, cotton being the basic product of the section's economy. Agricultural experts were certain they knew the reason for the depressed prices—the supply of cotton exceeded the demand—but none of them seemed to know how to get rid of the surplus. The Department of Agriculture suggested that the cotton farmers might voluntarily reduce their acreage, a proposal that received the scorn it deserved: the public and the farmers themselves recognized that voluntary reduction would not receive the cooperation required to make it work. Then a group of planters in north Louisiana came up with a more drastic plan and got their congressman to present it to Huey for his consideration. It was boldly simple: Louisiana and the other cotton-growing states should enact legislation forbidding the planting of cotton in 1932.

The daring of the idea appealed to Huey. He studied the plan— for twenty-four hours, he claimed—and announced he would support it. He sent telegrams to the governors and other officials of the seven cotton states inviting them to meet with him in New Orleans to discuss ways to implement the plan. The Southern governors could save the farmers if they had "the courage to act now and decisively," he argued. They would have to back legislation in their states prohibiting the raising of "a single bale" of cotton during 1932. If they would do this, the surplus would be consumed and prices would rise. "Louisiana will pass this law if other states will join us," he promised, speaking with an assurance that the other governors must have envied.[9]

The governors, it was immediately evident, were cool toward Huey's plan. They responded to his call in noncommittal terms, and only two of them, the governors of Arkansas and South Carolina, accepted the invitation to the conference. The other five sent representatives or regrets. Consequently, the meeting that convened in the Roosevelt Hotel on August 21 was not the authoritative body Huey had hoped for. Still, it was an "official" gathering, and the delegates at Huey's urging approved a resolution recommending the moratorium to their states. But they attached to the resolution a proviso stating that the plan would not go into effect until enacting legislation had been adopted by states producing three fourths of the total cotton supply. The proviso was in reality aimed at only one state, Texas, which produced more than a fourth of the crop. Governor

[9] New Orleans *Times-Picayune*, August 17, 18, and 19, 1931; Baton Rouge *State-Times*, August 17, 18, and 19, 1931; *Louisiana Progress*, September 10, 1931.

Ross Sterling of Texas, on being informed of the conference's action, indicated that his state had no intention of passing the first prohibitory law. "It's Governor Long's baby," Sterling said, "let him wash it first." "We'll be glad to wash the baby first," Huey responded. He dashed up to Baton Rouge and summoned the Louisiana legislature into special session for six days to consider one law—a measure declaring a moratorium on planting cotton. Political wits immediately dubbed this meeting "the wash the baby session."[1]

Huey, clad in a white cotton suit, addressed the legislators on opening night and urged them to enact the plan into law. He did not need to urge. Public sentiment overwhelmingly supported the principle of prohibition, and all factions in the legislature favored some kind of measure. Actually, the strongest supporters of a drastic law were not the Longites but antis from the cotton parishes, who represented planter interests. It was, in fact, antis who introduced the bill to implement the plan, and the measure embodied as much of their thinking as of Huey's. Adequately drastic, it prohibited the planting, gathering, and ginning of cotton in the state during 1932, although the governor was authorized to suspend the operation of the law if states producing three fourths of the crop did not enact similar legislation. Huey had probably drafted the act, and certainly the preamble, which recited the legal justification for the measure: it was a bill prohibiting the planting of cotton and providing for the extermination of the Mexican boll weevil, "*Anthonomus grandis*, Bohemian."

Introduced in the house, the bill won unanimous approval and was immediately sent to the senate. The upper chamber acted on it as soon as it legally could and ratified it unanimously. It was near midnight when final passage came, but the act was rushed to the mansion for Huey to sign. The Kingfish received the bill in his bedroom, wearing a cotton nightshirt he had bought for the ceremony. After being photographed signing the bill he said: "Now I can take this damned thing off," and climbed back into his customary silk pajamas. Before retiring he instructed O. K. Allen to charter a plane and take a copy of the act to Governor Sterling.[2]

Allen flew to Austin, only to learn that Sterling had left the capital for Houston. Not to be frustrated, O. K. went on to Houston

[1] New Orleans *Times-Picayune*, August 22, 23, and 24, 1931; Baton Rouge *State-Times*, August 24, 1931.

[2] Baton Rouge *State-Times*, August 26 and 27, 1931; New Orleans *Morning Tribune*, August 26, 1931; *Louisiana Progress*, September 10, 1931, for text of the law; *Time*, October 3, 1932.

and caught Sterling in the airport. Handing the act to the Texas governor, he said: "Here is Governor Long's baby, all washed, powdered, and wrapped in a cotton dress." Sterling did not seem pleased to have the baby thrown back to him. He said that most of his legislators were opposed to the Long plan and that he doubted he would call a session to consider it. But, it soon developed, some legislators were interested in the plan, and so were some of the cotton planters. Sterling reluctantly had to call the legislature into session. On convening, the solons invited Huey to address them. Huey, excited at the prospect of reaching a new audience, prepared to travel to Austin by plane, a form of transportation he ordinarily feared to use. But again he ran into the problem of Paul Cyr, whom he asked to promise in writing that he would not act as governor during the trip. But Cyr refused. Huey had to be content with addressing by radio a meeting of moratorium supporters in Texas.

He would not have influenced many members in the Texas legislature if he had addressed it. He was proposing something that frightened the average politician—bold, even revolutionary action. Thus, although the Texas legislators were obviously intrigued by his plan, they could not bring themselves to vote for it. Instead, they adopted a law imposing a limited acreage reduction on cotton producers. Without Texas' cooperation the moratorium was dead. But it was dead anyway. Every cotton state but South Carolina rejected the Long plan and decided for acreage reduction. Reduction was a meaningless gesture that did not touch the problem of the surplus; every governor who advocated it knew that it would be useless. Huey alone among the Southern executives had shown vision and courage, and as he contemplated the collapse of his great design, he must have reflected that the South was urgently in need of leadership—specifically, that it required an expansion of the influence of Huey Long.[3]

He was, in fact, moving to extend his influence before his cotton plan failed. Neighboring Mississippi was in the throes of a gubernatorial campaign during the summer of 1931, and Huey was mixing in it, trying to hide his part but finally coming into the open. It was not his first intervention in Mississippi affairs. He had shown an almost proprietary interest in the state ever since assuming the governorship, probably because he hoped to dominate the man who simultaneously became governor in Mississippi, Theodore Bilbo. The two governors had much to draw them together—both were

[3] Baton Rouge *Morning Advocate*, August 29, 1931; Baton Rouge *State-Times*, September 3, 15, and 16, 1931; New Orleans *Times-Picayune*, September 6, 9, 10, and 17, 1931; Shreveport *Journal*, September 9 and 17, 1931.

mass leaders and supporters of reform—but Huey as the younger man on the way up expected to be the controlling partner. The peppery Bilbo, however, refused to be influenced, and although he and Huey began on an amiable basis, their friendship soon dissolved into exchanges of insults. Huey took delight in comparing Louisiana's road-construction program with Mississippi's lesser one, and he said pointedly that the other state should elect a governor whom it could back all the way down the line.[4]

Bilbo, like Huey, could not succeed himself. But, unlike Huey, he did not have the power, in the more open politics of Mississippi, to designate an heir. Two candidates were competing in 1931 who had in effect nominated themselves. They were the heads of personal factions that for this election had allied with other personal factions: Sennett "Mike" Conner and Hugh White. Between them there was no marked ideological difference. Both were conservative, but White was more consistently and loudly conservative than his rival. Conner was more flexible, more receptive to new issues. He had met Huey, and the two had liked each other. And now, although he had not asked for it, he was going to get Huey's support. He would obviously make the kind of governor that Mississippi, and Huey Long, should have.

As a first assist to Conner, Huey dispatched to Mississippi two of his ablest lieutenants, Bob Brothers and Frank Odom, who were to help the candidate build up his local organizations. Simultaneously the Kingfish placed telephone calls to a number of local leaders and urged them to line up with Conner. Inevitably his activities became known and were revealed in the press. It was reported that he was having printed three hundred thousand circulars asking support of Conner. Then it was charged that Seymour Weiss had gone to Jackson to direct the Conner headquarters. White raged at this outside interference, and one of his leaders said grimly: "It is no longer a question of White and Conner. It is a question of Huey Long." Conner won easily in the election, and Huey thought he had secured a grateful ally.[5]

As THE LOUISIANA gubernatorial campaign got under way, men who were still uncommitted hastened to line up with one candidate or another. There were, as in all Louisiana contests, some strange shiftings of loyalty. Easily the most sensational example was the an-

[4] A. Wigfall Green: *The Man Bilbo* (Baton Rouge, 1963), p. 80.
[5] New Orleans *Times-Picayune*, August 11, 13, 14, and 26, 1931; Frank Odom.

nouncement by the New Orleans *Item*, perhaps the bitterest of the anti-Long papers, that it would support Allen and the Long ticket. The announcement was made by the publisher, James Thomson, who in making his decision had overruled the objections of his political editor, Marshall Ballard, whose acid pen had scorched Huey for years. Thomson, a crusading reform publisher, had previously viewed Huey as an enemy of good government who had to be destroyed. But Huey's cotton-moratorium plan had caught Thomson's fancy, and suddenly Huey appeared in a new light—as a progressive, reforming governor. The *Item* backed the Long plan to the last, and then Thomson decided to continue to cooperate with Huey. Huey, for his part, was delighted with this unexpected accession to his ranks. He passed down the word that he thought state employees might like to subscribe to the *Item*, and that the state would make it easy for them to do so by deducting the amount of the subscription from their salaries.

Another strange recruit shortly turned up in the Long camp, one whose conversion seemed even more startling than Thomson's. Old Judge Dupre revealed he was going to support Allen. The story behind his decision was tragic. The judge had intended to stand for re-election to his seat in the house, which he had held for years without any serious opposition. In his native St. Landry parish, election to an office depended on the endorsement of the ruling families, who were strongly anti-Long and who previously had looked on Dupre with high favor. But now he learned that he was to be opposed by a member of one of the great families, who was his own son-in-law, Octave Pavy, and who was running with the support of Huey. Reportedly the Pavys had lined up with Huey in return for a promise from him of a state road through their land. Dupre faced certain defeat, and rather than suffer it, he withdrew. He also faced the prospect of being without an income, for his legislative salary was his principal means of livelihood. Desperate and humiliated, he had to ask the governor whom he had denounced so fiercely for a job. Huey gave him a position as a columnist on the staff of the *Louisiana Progress*. In his articles the judge took a firm pro-Long line.[6]

With the election scheduled for January, the candidates did not begin to campaign actively until autumn. It was immediately evident that the anti aspirants were going to make Huey the issue, that they were running against him rather than Allen. Indeed, more

[6] Hermann B. Deutsch; *Overton Hearing*, I, 392–3; New Orleans *Item-Tribune*, October 11, 1931; Isom Guillory; J. Cleveland Fruge.

irrelevant issues would be raised in this campaign than were usual even for a Louisiana contest, and few elections in the state's history have seen such bitter vituperation hurled from the stump.

LeBlanc, although he sometimes advocated that the state should provide pensions to needy old people, devoted his main effort to attacking Huey and praising himself. He presented as his principal qualification to be governor that he had served in the army during the First World War and was a member of the American Legion, never failing to contrast his record with that of the "cowardly slacker" Long. "I now call upon those buddies who fought with me in the trenches for fourteen long months to go to the polls and vote for me," he cried. Guion did not resort to personal slurs, but he stressed the theme of honest government and charged the Long administration with corruption. If he lacked the talent to deal out abuse, his supporters more than made up for his deficiency. One of the bitterest of them was Cyr, who, seeing that he had no chance, withdrew and endorsed Guion. In one speech Cyr brought Huey's eating manners into the campaign. They were horrible, he shouted: "I want to tell you that he belongs to the hog family and the piney woods razor-back type at that."

But the most vituperative member of Guion's group was his candidate for lieutenant governor. Earl Long, after announcing as an independent, decided he could help himself by allying with a gubernatorial aspirant and joined with Guion. Earl stumped with Julius, and the pair of them exposed every dereliction of Huey's they could conjure up—and also every piece of soiled linen in the Long family. Earl related that all his life he had had to protect Huey from physical assaults—and now the "big-bellied coward" was ungratefully opposing his bid for office. Julius sounded but one theme in his speeches: I, with some help from Earl, made Huey Long; I educated him and set him up as a lawyer; Earl and I elected him to the Public Service Commission; Earl saved him during the impeachment crisis. In fact, Julius seemed to think that the issue of the campaign was Huey's refusal to be guided by his advice. Huey's sisters, campaigning for Earl, contributed to the family barrage against Huey. One of them, Lucille, went so far as to liken his rejection of Earl to the treachery of Judas Iscariot.[7]

As the campaign began, Huey was in a relaxed mood, seemingly

[7] Carleton Beals: *The Story of Huey P. Long* (Philadelphia, 1935), pp. 220–2; John Kingston Fineran: *The Career of a Tin Pot Napoleon* (New Orleans, 1932), pp. 165–6; Baton Rouge *State-Times*, November 20, 1931; New Orleans *Morning Tribune*, November 27; Shreveport *Journal*, January 8, 1932.

certain of victory for his slate of candidates, which he had labeled
the "Complete the Work Ticket." He had reason to be confident. In
early November the Old Regulars, fulfilling their pact with him,
endorsed Allen and the whole Long ticket. Allen and his running
mates were assured of an overwhelming majority in New Orleans.
O. K. could concentrate his campaigning in the country. It was announced that he would open his campaign on Thanksgiving day.
The announcement was made by Huey, and observers immediately
deduced that the candidate would play a decidedly secondary role
in the campaign.[8]

As it turned out, Allen played almost no part at all. Huey and
O. K. toured together and spoke from the same platform. But Huey
always gave the longer speech, and when Allen finally got to talk,
Huey, sitting behind him, interrupted frequently to suggest different
themes to develop. For his own themes Huey chose any topic he
fancied, whether or not it was related to the campaign. Thus in one
speech he disclosed that he intended to elect John Overton as the
next U.S. senator from Louisiana. In another he declared that he
was champing to enter the Senate himself. In fact, he confessed, he
had been looking toward Washington so "religiously" that he felt
like Moses gazing out over the Promised Land.[9]

But he also discussed serious issues—the public-improvements
program that he had inaugurated and that Allen would now take
over—and asked the voters to return a friendly legislature so that
Allen could complete the "great program." Dwelling on the benefits
it would bring the state, he asserted that he had no wish to discuss
personalities. In particular, he was not going to reply to the attacks
being made on him by Earl and Julius. "I will be a better brother to
them than they are to me," he said. He explained why he was not
supporting Earl. "I have three brothers, five sisters, five thousand
cousins, and three or four uncles," he said. "When I run a family
ticket I'm going to run a full ticket and not a half of one." He almost kept his word not to attack his brothers. But he could not resist relating to audiences an incident that he said had occurred in his
boyhood. He would begin the story by describing a social gathering
popular with rural Protestants—an "all-day singing" at the church,
with "dinner on the grounds." At such a meeting in Winnfield, he
would continue, the mothers had laid their babies on a pallet under
a tree during the dinner. As they were clearing the table, a violent

[8] New Orleans *Times-Picayune*, October 5, November 5 and 6, 1931; unidentified clipping, in Grace Scrapbook.

[9] New Orleans *Times-Picayune*, December 1, 7, and 9, 1931.

storm suddenly broke. Each mother hastily collected her child. But there was one baby that nobody would claim, an ugly, squalling brat. Mrs. Long, unwilling to see the child abandoned, had taken it home and adopted it. "That was Earl," Huey would conclude as his hearers exploded with laughter.[1]

Toward only one of the opposing candidates did Huey show personal animosity, Dudley LeBlanc. He attacked LeBlanc with a ferocity that was rare even for him. No worry that "Dud" was a formidable candidate drove him on: he knew as well as anyone that the Frenchman would poll but a negligible vote. His immediate purpose was to discredit LeBlanc and prevent his re-election to the Public Service Commission the following year. But beyond that, he intended to drive from political life this man who had defied him and denounced him. He subjected LeBlanc to a running fire of ridicule. Had Dud really volunteered and fought in France? No, he had been drafted and had been in uniform only four months and in a camp in America. How did one pronounce that queer French name of LeBlanc? Why, you do it by "trying to grunt like a hog and changing your mind when you're halfway through."[2]

Huey did not stop at ridicule. He had acquired some information he thought would ruin LeBlanc, and although it had no conceivable relationship to any issue in the campaign, he proceeded to use it. LeBlanc was the secretary-treasurer, really the director, of an organization named the Thibodaux Benevolent Association. It was primarily a mutual-aid burial society. When a member died, the other members were assessed sixty-five cents, of which fifty cents went to the heirs of the deceased and fifteen cents to the officers of the association, who arranged the burial and paid the costs. The members were, naturally, of the very poorest class; most of them, and some of the officers, were Negroes. Huey suspected that the group was predominantly Negro, but he needed proof. He planted an agent in the headquarters, and this man stole and turned over to him a number of assessment cards. With malicious glee Huey announced that he had proof LeBlanc was working intimately with "niggers." "LeBlanc ain't got time to be governor," he chortled, "because he's got to go back and be secretary-treasurer of that nigger lodge."

He was not satisfied to smear LeBlanc with the charge of being

[1] New Orleans *Item-Tribune*, November 27, 1931; New Orleans *Times-Picayune*, December 1, 1931; Woody N. Miley; confidential communications.
[2] Beals: *Long*, pp. 220–2.

a "nigger lover." His real purpose was to destroy Dud's business. Invading the districts which contained most of the association's Negro members, he described LeBlanc's method of burying a person. "He charges for a coffin and he charges $7.50 for a shroud," he cried. "I am informed that the nigger is laid out, and after the mourners had left, LeBlanc takes the body into a backroom, takes off the shroud, nails them up into a pine box, and buries them at a total cost of $3.67 and ½ cents." LeBlanc's Negro clients, horrified that perhaps the shrouds were being used again and again, left him in droves.[3]

The returns of the election on January 19 disclosed a smashing triumph for Huey's ticket. Allen swept Orleans parish with a vote of almost 70,000, overwhelmed his rivals in the country parishes, and amassed a total of approximately 215,000 votes. LeBlanc, with 110,000 votes, was a poor second, and Guion, with only 54,000, a dismal third. Earl Long did somewhat better than Guion but finished third among the contenders for the lieutenant governorship. So great was the magnitude of the victory that every one of the eight candidates for the lesser state offices running with Allen or endorsed by him also was elected. The Long candidates had, in fact, carried fifty-four of the state's sixty-four parishes, a feat of organization unexampled in Louisiana politics.[4]

Amazed political observers were immediately struck by the strength of the vote for Allen in one parish, St. Bernard. This French parish had previously attracted wide and not altogether favorable attention for its voting behavior in the 1930 senatorial election. At that time its dominant faction, headed by the sheriff, Dr. L. A. Mereaux, had delivered 3,979 votes to Huey—whereas Ransdell had received only 9 votes, and in four of the parish's seven wards had not polled a single vote. Critics immediately charged that the return had been doctored, and not just because of the size of the Long vote. According to United States census figures, the total population of voting age, white and black, was but 4,051 persons, and since the Negroes could not vote, the white voting population numbered only 2,510 persons. Where, cynics asked, had the extra

<hr/>

[3] *Benevolent News*, organ of the association, June, 1931, copy in Long Scrapbooks, XIII; *Louisiana Progress*, August 18, 1931; New Orleans *Times-Picayune*, December 1 and 6, 1931; Charles Frampton; Arthur Provost.

[4] Allen P. Sindler: *Huey Long's Louisiana: State Politics 1920–1952* (Baltimore, 1956), p. 78; New Orleans *States*, January 20, 1932; New Orleans *Times-Picayune*, January 20, 1932; Shreveport *Journal*, January 26, 1932.

votes come from? Huey attempted to answer by saying, with some justice, that many of the people lived on "houseboats" so deep in the marshes that the census takers never found them.

St Bernard had not liked the criticism it had been subjected to, and in 1932 it struck back at those who had been sneering. Curiously, its reaction was that it would show the critics what the parish could deliver in the way of a vote when aroused. St. Bernard cast 3,152 votes for Allen and for every member of his ticket—and not a single vote for any opposition candidate. But the vote had not been "fixed," and the voters were not, by their standards, acting corruptly or in response to corrupt influences. They were simply voting as their leader asked them to, following his guidance, which was the way their ancestors had been voting since the Civil War. Actually, the parish leaders could accurately compute the vote weeks before the election. Thus during the campaign Huey had met Sheriff Mereaux in New Orleans and asked how many votes the opposition would get. About two, Mereaux answered. When on election night the unanimous return from St. Bernard came in, Huey said to Mereaux: "Doc, what the hell happened to those two fellows?" "They changed their minds at the last minute," Mereaux replied.[5]

ALLEN WOULD NOT TAKE office until May. If Huey observed his promise to keep Paul Cyr out of the governorship, which he repeated at the beginning of the campaign, he would have to wait until Allen was inaugurated before he could assume his senatorial seat. But during the campaign an episode occurred that altered completely the legal situation in which Huey felt he was entangled. In a moment of extreme anger, Cyr committed one of the rashest moves of his reckless career.

Early in October he appeared in Shreveport, accompanied by a local attorney, and announced he was going to file a suit in the district court of Long's home parish to have Long declared a senator. The basis of the suit would be that when Huey had forwarded to Washington his certificate of election over Ransdell, he had thereby vacated the governorship. But Cyr was not content to await the outcome of the suit. Going before the clerk of the court, he had himself sworn in as governor, issued a statement proclaiming that he was in fact governor, and then departed for Jeanerette.

[5] *Overton Hearing*, I, 16–18, 21, 833–4, 872; Theophile Landry.

Huey was in New Orleans when the news of Cyr's move broke. Reacting quickly, he telephoned to state police headquarters in Baton Rouge to throw a guard around the mansion and prevent Cyr from entering it. Then he put a pistol in his pocket and announced to Chick Frampton, his favorite reporter, that they were driving to the capital. Frampton was surprised, because Huey rarely drove himself after becoming governor. The reporter never forgot that trip. Huey pushed the car up to a speed of over ninety miles an hour and several times came close to crashing. When they reached Baton Rouge, they found policemen strung around the mansion and a company of national guardsmen protecting the capital. Surprised to see the militiamen, Huey asked: "What's all this about?" Told that General Fleming had summoned them, Huey said that they would not be needed and should be dismissed. He learned that Cyr had not as yet come to Baton Rouge. But the lieutenant governor was expected, and according to rumor he was recruiting a private army to take possession of the state government. Huey ordered that strong detachments of state policemen be placed around the mansion and the capitol and machine guns mounted at all possible points of entry.[6]

Louisianians watched the drama being enacted at Baton Rouge with rapt but amused attention. Nobody but a few anti-Long diehards believed that Cyr had a chance to become governor, and most people thought that his way of grasping at the office was incredibly comic. It was, indeed, so diverting that others decided to play at being governor. In Shreveport an unemployed bill collector named Walter Aldrich appeared before a notary public and took the oath as governor. "Governor" Aldrich then issued a statement announcing he was going to file suits to oust Long and Cyr from the office they were illegally holding. Almost simultaneously in other towns throughout the state men went to notaries and had themselves sworn in as governor, dozens probably engaging in the farce. The spectacle was played up in the national press and caught the popular fancy. Suddenly, in cities across the country, dozens of men appeared before public officials and demanded to be sworn in as governor of Louisiana.[7]

---

[6] Baton Rouge *State-Times*, October 2 and 14, 1931; Charles Frampton; New Orleans *Morning Tribune*, October 14, 1931; New Orleans *Times-Picayune*, October 15, 1931; W. E. Butler.

[7] Baton Rouge *State-Times*, October 14, 1931; Shreveport *Journal*, October 15, 1931; Hermann B. Deutsch.

Huey probably relished the mass swearings-in, knowing they would make Cyr seem ridiculous. But he was most interested in the legal situation created by Cyr's action, for he had immediately detected that his enemy had made a false move. He announced that the office of lieutenant governor was now vacant: Cyr had abandoned it when he took the oath as governor. Therefore he was summoning to Baton Rouge from Lake Charles the man next in line for the second office, Alvin O. King, president of the senate. King duly arrived and was sworn in as lieutenant governor, thereby setting off a new craze in the state—now men clamored to become lieutenant governor. Then Huey revealed he was filing a countersuit against Cyr, claiming that inasmuch as the lieutenant governor had acquiesced for months in the office he held, he had no cause for action. The combined suits were heard at Shreveport in November, and although Huey was represented by a battery of lawyers, he argued his own case. He stressed that the courts could not remove a governor and that the qualifications of a senator were to be decided by the Senate. The court accepted his reasoning, dismissing Cyr's suit as having no basis for redress. Cyr appealed to the supreme court, which considered the appeal in December. Huey, taking time off from campaigning, again argued his case. The court reserved its opinion until after the January election.[8]

Two days after the election the high tribunal, by a vote of four to three, dismissed Cyr's suit. The decision seemed to have no effect on Cyr. He was like a man in a trance, lost to reality. Leaving Jeanerette, he drove to Baton Rouge and for the second time took the oath as governor. Then he announced that he was setting up his "seat of government" at a room in the Heidelberg Hotel. From this "capitol" he issued a proclamation reciting that Alvin O. King, "at the head of insurrectionary forces," had seized control of the state government and warning all good citizens not to have any dealings with the rebel regime. But he made no attempt to enter the mansion or the capitol, which were still heavily guarded. He was convinced that Huey would not hesitate to arrest him if given an excuse and feared that worse might happen to him. According to an associate, armed men followed them in a car from Jeanerette to Baton Rouge and other armed men shadowed them constantly in the hotel.

Huey observed Cyr's pretensions with scorn. His rival had no claim in law to be governor and obviously would not dare to try to

---

[8] Baton Rouge *State-Times*, October 14, November 11 and 18, December 5, 1931; Shreveport *Journal*, October 15, 1931; New Orleans *Morning Tribune*, November 1, 1931.

seize the office by force. He could at long last take his Senate seat, leaving King to succeed him as governor. However, he could not afford to give Cyr the slightest chance to make a countermove. Without any advance notice, he, with a select group of associates, boarded a train in New Orleans for Washington on the night of January 23. He arrived in Washington on January 25 and was sworn in as senator that day. By prearrangement a telephone wire to Baton Rouge was kept open, and the minute Huey took the oath, Seymour Weiss relayed the news to the executive mansion, where King was waiting. In another minute King took the oath as governor. Cyr was furious when he discovered he had been circumvented. He announced that he would file an ouster suit against King and issued more proclamations from his seat of government. But now he had to move his capitol. Huey phoned the proprietor of the Heidelberg and suggested that Cyr should be made to leave. Brusquely the owner told Cyr to take his government elsewhere. Cyr transferred to the shabby Louisian Hotel and put forth a last and pathetic proclamation. "I call upon the people to say if they wish me to step aside," he said. "Call me at my hotel. My offices are open day and night." Nobody called. People were getting bored with Cyr, and besides, the carnival season was coming on, and it promised to be much more interesting than the fulminations of a defeated and embittered politician.[9]

Fighting lawsuits with Cyr was not the only activity that diverted Huey's attention from the gubernatorial campaign. He also had to take time off to deal with a banking crisis that threatened to cause a collapse of the state's financial institutions. One day in December, as he was about to leave the Roosevelt Hotel on a stumping tour, he was met in his suite by the presidents of all the banks in New Orleans. They had dire news for him, of the nature that governors in most states were receiving in those depression years. A large bank in Jackson, Mississippi, unable to meet the demands of its depositors, was about to close; and the government of Mississippi, hoping to prevent a panic, was going to declare a bank moratorium. Once that was done, Mississippi banks and citizens would withdraw their considerable deposits from banks in New Orleans and other Louisiana cities and precipitate a run on all the banks in

[9] Baton Rouge *State-Times*, January 22 and 29, February 5, 1932; Crowley *Daily Signal*, January 26, 1932; Baton Rouge *Morning Advocate*, January 26, 1932; New Orleans *States*, February 1, 1932; T. O. Harris: *The Kingfish: Huey P. Long, Dictator* (New Orleans, 1938), pp. 100–2; Leon Gary; Seymour Weiss; Jess Nugent; Huey P. Long: *Every Man a King* (New Orleans, 1933), p. 288.

the state. The presidents, some of them near hysteria, demanded that Huey proclaim a moratorium in Louisiana.

He looked at them with undisguised disgust and cursed roundly. "Have you insane men done anything about this yet?" he finally asked. They admitted that they could not think of anything to do, and some of them, irritated by the governor's manner, began leaving. "Oh, no, you ain't," the Kingfish shouted. "You crazy men ain't going nowheres. When a man goes crazy, regardless of how big he is, he's got to be protected from doing harm to himself and others." Turning to Joe Messina, he ordered the guard to stand by the door and not to let anyone go out or use the phones without his permission.

Going into his bedroom, he tried to think of someone who could help him. The only name that came to him was that of a New York City banker who had recently visited the state on business and who had come to the mansion to pay his respects. He grabbed a phone and called this man. "I asked him," he related later, "if he cared anything about the gold standard or the silver standard or any other kind of a damn standard." If the banker did care, he would have to act fast to avert a crisis that might spread throughout the South. The New Yorker was impressed and promised that he would call the head of the National Credit Corporation and that this federal official would in turn call Huey.

While he waited for the call to come through, he kept the bankers under surveillance by Messina. At the lunch hour he told Seymour Weiss to send some food up to the suite. "Seymour said he would help Joe Messina hold up the gold standard," Huey chuckled later. Finally the federal official telephoned and, when Huey explained the situation, agreed to release a hundred million dollars to shore up the threatened Southern banks. None of the banks in Louisiana were in trouble, Huey snapped. It was those in Mississippi that needed help, and the official should get down there fast, without stopping to bathe or shave, because the "bath might cost this country too damn much." The official acted on Huey's advice and arrived in time to avert a moratorium in Mississippi.[1]

Huey had to use similar drastic methods to prevent a bank in his own state from closing. One Friday night in New Orleans he learned that a bank in Lafayette was faced with a run that might force it to liquidate. Summoning Seymour Weiss, he said that they

[1] Hermann B. Deutsch: "Paradox in Pajamas," *Saturday Evening Post*, October 5, 1935, p. 38.

were going to drive to Lafayette that night. They reached Lafayette at seven o'clock in the morning and went directly to the bank. There a haggard president informed them that customers were already forming to demand a return of their deposits. There was nothing to worry about, Huey said. Seating himself in the president's office, he told Weiss to stand at the cashier's desk and to send the first customer in to him.

This man soon appeared, waving a check for $18,000 and confident that he, at least, would get his money. Entering the office, he was startled to see Governor Long behind the desk. Huey was waving a check himself. "The state of Louisiana has got $265,000 in this bank," he explained genially, "and here's the state's check for it. There ain't but about that much cash in the bank, and I was here before you were. You insist on drawing out your $18,000, and I'll insist on drawing out the state's $265,000—and I get first draw, so there'll be nothing left to pay you. You agree to leave yours in, and I'll leave the state's in, and nobody'll be hurt. I'm staying right here till closing time at noon, in case anybody else wants to draw out." The staggered customer had no choice but to agree to leave his money in. So also did every depositor who entered after him. The bank closed at noon still solvent, and over the weekend Huey was able to bring in enough money from other banks to keep it going.[2]

He saved this bank and others that were similarly threatened by a simple but effective expedient. He informed banks that were relatively prosperous and secure that they were going to lend a specified amount of money to the endangered institution. Any bank president so notified complied immediately. He knew that if he refused, a state bank examiner would call the next day and demand to see his books—and would certainly find something wrong. Bankers might have resented this kind of pressure, but they had to admit that it saved Louisiana from the debacle that was beginning to engulf the banks in other states. In the country as a whole some forty-eight hundred banks failed between the onset of the depression in 1929 and 1932. But in Louisiana only seven banks collapsed, and most of these were small or weak institutions. Huey never tired of boasting that Louisiana had fewer bank failures than any state in the country.[3]

[2] Ibid.; Seymour Weiss; Richard W. Leche; Long: *Every Man a King*, pp. 242–4.
[3] *Cong. Record*, 73 Cong., 1st Sess., p. 5269; Hermann B. Deutsch; George Coad, in *The New York Times*, January 22, 1933.

HUEY COULD POINT to many accomplishments during his almost four years as governor. And because he was proud of what he had done and because he wanted the people to realize what he had done for them, he pointed frequently, compiling and publicizing records of his achievements. As the most important ones, he listed the construction of roads and bridges, an increase in the facilities of the charity hospitals in New Orleans and Shreveport, the improvement and humanizing of services in state hospitals for victims of mental disorders and epilepsy, the expansion of Louisiana State University and the creation of its medical school, the founding of night schools for illiterates, the furnishing of free books to school children, the enlargement of the port of New Orleans, the bringing of natural gas to New Orleans, the construction of one of the largest airports in the country at New Orleans, and the erection of the new capitol.[4]

Once Huey discussed with a visiting journalist the impact of his program on Louisiana. He said that the conservatives would tell the correspondent about the evils of the Long regime and would say that "Longism" had to be destroyed. Just let them try to destroy it, he declared. They would have to blow up the roads and the buildings and snatch the schoolbooks from the hands of the children. "Then you'll be rid of Longism in this state, and not till then," he concluded grimly.[5]

Some of his accomplishments he stressed more than others. He properly placed the greatest emphasis on the road construction program, which was the largest in the South and which compared favorably with the programs of states with more abundant resources. In the four years of his governorship the state had built 1,583 miles of concrete roads, 718 miles of asphalt roads, and 2,816 miles of gravel roads. It had also constructed 111 bridges, many of them major structures spanning the bigger streams. As a mark of the scope of the program, in 1931 the expenditures for roads and bridges accounted for sixty-six per cent of the state's total spending. But the money spent on roads employed a large number of men who otherwise would have been thrown on public relief. In fact, Louisiana employed more men on road work than any other state in the country, 22,200 men in 1931 as compared to 20,597 for New York and 18,960 for Pennsylvania. Of the total number of men working on

[4] Long: *Every Man a King*, pp. 280–84; Forrest Davis: *Huey Long, A Candid Biography* (New York, 1935), pp. 148–9; Long circular, "Answering Ten Months of Lies," in my possession; *Time*, October 3, 1932; *Literary Digest*, September 8, 1934.
[5] Davis: *Long*, p. 170.

highway projects in all states, ten per cent were employed in Louisiana alone.[6]

After the road program, Huey placed his efforts to improve the state hospitals. As his prime example, he pointed to Charity Hospital in New Orleans, which had increased the number of patients it could handle daily from sixteen hundred to thirty eight hundred and had reduced its death rate by thirty per cent. He also drew attention to the humanizing of services at the institutions for the insane, where such practices as the strait-jacketing and chaining of inmates had been abolished. Moreover, at these places the state had for the first time introduced dental care, and at one of them, according to Huey, dentists had had to extract seventeen hundred rotted and abscessed teeth from the inmates. His critics could not deny his claim that the hospitals had been enlarged and bettered. But they charged that he was exercising political influence on their operation and specifically on Charity Hospital, where Long associates who were not poor received free treatment. "Charity à la Kingfish," said a *Picayune* editorial deprecating the practice. The charge was substantially accurate. But it did not cite the fact that the practice was not new: persons with political influence had always been able to get into the hospital. What was new, and hence very apparent, was that now more of them got in—because there were more beds.[7]

In his zeal to reform the facilities maintained by the state Huey was led to tackle the institution that was the most difficult of all to improve—the state penitentiary at Angola. The problem of Angola has confronted every governor of modern times, and it has baffled nearly every one of them. The only state prison, Angola houses a large number of inmates—there were probably two thousand during Huey's governorship—and is costly to maintain. Public opinion, and hence the legislature, has been reluctant to vote money to support convicts on anything but a subsistence level, and Angola has generally been operated as a primitive and sometimes brutal place of detention for criminals who are expected to remain criminals after their release.

Huey, on becoming governor, did not show any special interest

[6] *Louisiana Progress*, July 15 and November 10, 1931; *American Progress*, December 28, 1933; memorandum, January 29, 1957, furnished me by the Louisiana Department of Highways.

[7] Long: *Every Man a King*, 280–1; circular, "Answering Ten Months of Lies"; New Orleans *Times-Picayune*, August 6 and 11, 1932; Stella O'Conner: "The Charity Hospital of New Orleans," *Louisiana Historical Quarterly*, XXXI (1948), 89–90; Dr. Isidore Cohn.

in Angola. He appointed to the top administrative posts the same kind of men named by most previous governors, political followers who needed jobs. But within the next two years he became impressed by the fact that the prison's expenses exceeded its appropriation and that it was falling ever heavier in debt. He wondered why Angola, which owned acres of rice land and could command abundant free labor, should not be able to itself produce many of the goods consumed by its inmates, why, in fact, it should not become self-supporting. Then in 1930 a senate investigative committee disclosed gross inefficiency in the prison's management. Consequently, in the following year Huey decided to appoint as general manager a man who had some qualifications for the position. He offered it to the business manager of Louisiana State University, Robert L. Himes, who had handled the school's finances so efficiently that he had acquired the nickname of "Tighty." Huey asked Himes if the thought he could run Angola. Tighty said he could if the governor would keep his hands off. "You are appointed," Huey said, "and there will be no interference from me or any other politician."

Himes took over at Angola with his usual efficiency. Improving practices inaugurated by previous managers, he set the prisoners to planting vegetable gardens, tending herds of cattle, and growing cotton. The garden products were consumed in the dining hall; the cattle when slaughtered furnished beef, and their hides were tanned and made by the inmates into shoes; and the cotton was turned on convict-operated machines into uniforms and bed sheets and pillowcases. By these economies Himes temporarily put the penitentiary on a self-supporting basis, although he was not able to keep it so. He cut expenses further by an expedient that later penology would have approved. Many of the inmates had been sent there for minor crimes: thus, ten Negroes who had killed a yearling steer worth four dollars had been sentenced to terms of two years each. If they served their full term, each, like any prisoner, would on release be entitled to receive a suit of clothes and ten dollars for transportation money. Himes thought, and Huey agreed with him, that the sentences for small offenders were too harsh and, moreover, that it was costing the state too much to release such prisoners. So Tighty, with Huey's support, reprieved a large number of them before their sentences were up and thus escaped having to give them any compensation.

But saving money was not Himes's only concern. Although he had had no training or experience in prison administration, he knew, probably because of his university background, that a penitentiary should be more than a place of detention, that it should attempt to train and reform criminals so that when released they might become law-abiding citizens. Accordingly, he inaugurated the first prisoner-rehabilitation program in Louisiana history. Some of the harsher punishments that had been prevalent were abolished, although whippings were retained, and inmates were awarded certain privileges in return for good conduct. Entering prisoners were given medical checkups, and a system of regular medical care was introduced. Classes to teach illiterates were established, and vocational training was made available to prisoners who demonstrated special aptitudes. Himes was widely applauded for his work, even by conservatives. Only one person expressed dissatisfaction—Abe Shushan, who complained that Tighty's economies were cutting down on the amounts of supplies he sold to Angola. "I'm going to get Huey to fire that bastard," Abe vowed. But Himes was not fired. He held on to his position through the Allen administration and continued to run the prison as he pleased. Huey kept his word that there would be no interference from any source.[8]

Shushan could take solace for any business he had lost in the knowledge that the new airport the state was building for New Orleans would be named for him. He had been the foremost advocate of state aid for the facility, and Huey had said it should be called Shushan Airport. When completed on the edge of Lake Ponchartrain, it would contain six runways, each a mile long, and could accommodate both land planes and hydroplanes. By the standards of the time it was a huge and lavish terminal, and Louisianians glowed with pride when they contemplated it. Out-of-state visitors praised it, and nationally syndicated columnist Arthur Brisbane characterized it as incomparably the finest airport in the country. Another well-known journalist, Paul Y. Anderson, was inclined to agree, although he insisted that the place was both "impressive and funny." It was funny because Shushan had put his name on every possible part of the terminal building—on the front and outside walls, on the roof and the floor, and even on the door knobs and plumbing fixtures. Somebody asked Shushan why he had scattered his name about so.

[8] Baton Rouge *State-Times*, April 18, 1931; T. H. Harris: *The Memoirs of T. T. Harris* (Baton Rouge, 1963), pp. 64–5; *Overton Hearing*, II, 1210–11; confidential communication. In this section on Angola, I have benefited from suggestions by Mark T. Carleton, a graduate student at Stanford University, who is preparing a dissertation entitled "The Political History of the Louisiana State Penitentiaries, 1835–1968."

Abe explained frankly: "We may lose out sometime, and they may change the name of Shushan Airport—but it'll cost 'em $60,000 at the least, and I doubt whether they could do it for $100,000."[9]

As the physical monuments to the Long regime—the roads, bridges, hospitals, and schools—rose higher and multiplied in number, even Huey's bitterest critics had to concede that progress was being made. But, they argued, it was coming at too great a financial cost. Huey Long had spent more money in four years than governors Pleasant, Parker, Fuqua, and Simpson had in twelve years. The state was staggering under a load of burdensome taxes, and because of extravagance and graft the cost of government in Louisiana was the highest in the country.[1]

These criticisms of Long, like so many others from the conservatives, were not based on facts. The critics were misrepresenting the facts, or, more probably, were so blinded by emotion that they could not see them. Thus the charge that the per capita cost of government in Louisiana was the highest in the country was based on a comparison of the cost of all governmental units in Louisiana—state, parish, and municipal—with the cost of the state government alone in other states. Louisiana's total per capita cost of $41.97 was contrasted with New York's $19.02 for the state only; but the total cost in New York was $94.17. Actually, Louisiana's costs were low in relation to those of other states. Of the twenty-four states that kept records on combined costs, Louisiana was third from the lowest, bettered only by Virginia and Oklahoma, neither of which supported such an extensive road, educational, or welfare program.[2]

Also erroneous was the opinion that the Long regime had imposed a drastic tax load on the state. It is true that the revenues from taxes rose during Huey's governorship, but they went up only moderately. In 1928 the state collected in taxes approximately twenty-two million dollars; in 1929, twenty-six million dollars; and in 1930 and 1931, twenty-seven million dollars. The percentage increase, as a careful study shows, was lower than the national average during these years, a rise of 2.2 per cent in Louisiana as compared to an average increase of 4.7 per cent in all other states.[3]

[9] Brisbane, in *American Progress*, December 7, 1933; Anderson, in St. Louis *Post-Dispatch*, February 3, 1935.

[1] Shreveport *Journal*, July 27, 1932; *Time*, October 3, 1932.

[2] F. Raymond Daniell: "The Gentleman from Louisiana," *Current History*, XLI (November 1934), 176; Davis: *Long*, pp. 240–2.

[3] Ansel Miree Sharp: "A Study of the Counter-Cyclical Aspects of Total Government Fiscal Policy" (unpublished Ph.D. dissertation, Louisiana State University, 1956), pp. 158, 160–2, 171–2.

The impression that taxes had been raised sharply arose because the Long administration threw out a network of levies, some of which were new ones. But most of these were taxes that caught the corporations or the well-to-do classes—such as the severance tax on natural resources, the tax on carbon black, and sales taxes on such items as tobacco or malt. The state did continue to collect a property tax that hit the average citizen, but it reduced the assessment by twenty per cent and hence the amount collected. The tax on gasoline was raised, but the increase was not passed on to the ordinary consumer in the form of higher prices. Gas prices were, in fact, lower in Louisiana than in neighboring states where the tax was less. Huey once explained why the gas companies had not upped the price. "They know that I know how much it costs them to refine and distribute gasoline," the Kingfish said, "and that if they jacked up the price I'd be on 'em with some compensating taxes."[4]

For only one of their criticisms of Huey's fiscal policy did the conservatives have a factual basis. They were quite right when they said that state spending had increased during his administration. It had, in fact, increased probably more they knew. In 1928 the total amount of money spent by the state was almost twenty-nine million dollars. In 1929 the figure rose to over thirty-five million and in 1930 to almost forty-seven million. But in 1931 the total jumped to a staggering sum of well over eighty-three million dollars. The magnitude of the increase becomes more dramatic when presented in percentages. State spending increased 189 per cent between 1929 and 1931. Even more startling was the increase in these years of net spending, the amount expended above revenue, which rose 912 per cent. Indeed, the increase in net spending by Louisiana alone constituted twenty-six per cent of the increase in total net spending by all states.

Most of the increased expenditures went to build roads, with smaller amounts going to improve or expand educational and health facilities. Or, put another way, the money was spent on public works whose construction required the employment of large numbers of workers. The national government, seeking to combat the depression, would later spend large sums of money on public works, and since the 1930's it has been universally accepted that this is the kind of spending a government should engage in during a depression. Huey, who had never read much economics and who at the time he became governor did not know the newer economic theories that stressed the

[4] Christenberry, ed.: *Speeches of Long*, speech of February 21, 1935; Davis: *Long*, pp. 240–2.

benefits of government spending, had—driven on by his great ambitions—applied a modern theory.

And he had used modern methods to raise the money for his projects. The state government had borrowed the money it required, just as the national government was then borrowing money and as all American governments have borrowed ever since the depression decade. Thus in 1931, when the state's spending rose to a new height, over seventy-four million dollars in bonds was sold, and this sum constituted sixty-eight per cent of the state's total revenue for that year. There were so many bond issues that the conservatives could not always keep track of them. They charged that Huey had increased the state debt from $11,000,000 to $125,000,000, but the actual increase was probably somewhat higher. Succeeding generations would have to pay the debt—most of the bond issues ran for twenty years—but the generation of the 1930's saw only that the roads and the other improvements were there for them to use. They were not going to forget who had built them.[5]

HUEY WENT TO WASHINGTON accompanied by a large Louisiana entourage. Traveling with him in a private car were Rose, Seymour Weiss, Mayor Walmsley, Governor-elect Allen, and other cronies and followers. On arriving in the capital the party checked in at the Mayflower Hotel, where Huey had booked a suite. His associates had come to see him sworn in as senator, after which they would return home.[6]

On January 25 Huey went to the Senate to take the oath. He met the leader of the Democratic minority, Senator Joseph T. Robinson of Arkansas, who conducted him to the lounging room, where he was to wait until he was escorted to the vice-president's chair to be sworn in. Senate tradition stipulated that a new senator should be escorted by the other senator from his state. But Huey had reason to doubt that Senator Broussard would do him this honor. The two men were now avowed political enemies, and Broussard had intimated to reporters, who had printed his remarks, that he might not walk up with his colleague. While Huey sat alone in the lounging room, Broussard entered. He and Huey immediately became embroiled

[5] Sharp: "Aspects of Fiscal Policy," pp. 182–3, 201–4, 207–8, 223–4, 300, 304. Louisiana's spending dropped drastically after 1931 and the completion of the road program.
[6] Baton Rouge *State-Times*, January 23, 1932; New Orleans *Times-Picayune*, January 27, 1932; Seymour Weiss; Jess Nugent.

in an angry, petty exchange. Huey said that he, and not Broussard, would decide who would introduce him. "I won't introduce you unless you ask me to," Broussard snapped. "Don't hold your breath until I do, Edwin," Huey replied. Soon after Broussard stomped out, Robinson returned, and Huey told him of the conversation. Robinson said that he would escort Huey himself. This was what Huey wanted and why he had baited Broussard. He would attract more attention if he broke a Senate tradition at the outset. Reporters noted that he flouted another tradition when he went up the Senate aisle with Robinson. He carried a lighted cigar, which he placed in an ashtray on Robinson's desk before he took the oath.[7]

On the morning of January 25, before he went to the Senate, Huey had received reporters in his suite. He was clad only in violent pink pajamas and was smoking a cigar. He gave the visitors his impressions of various men who were possible candidates for the Democratic presidential nomination. He listed as strong contenders Speaker of the House John N. Garner of Texas, Senator Byron "Pat" Harrison of Mississippi, and Senator Robinson. He ruled out Governor Franklin D. Roosevelt of New York as a probable loser to President Herbert Hoover, who would be the Republican candidate. One of the reporters asked how their host should be addressed, as governor or senator? Huey leaned back in his chair and puffed at his cigar. "They call me Kingfish down there," he said.[8]

[7] Long: *Every Man a King*, pp. 286–7; New Orleans *States*, January 25 and 26, 1932.
[8] Shreveport *Journal*, January 25, 1932.

# CHAPTER 20

# We Always Have a Wild Man

**H**UEY SEEMED TO ENJOY his first day in the Senate. After being sworn in, he went around the chamber greeting other senators warmly. He put his arm around several senior colleagues and told them Louisiana anecdotes, singling out for special notice George W. Norris of Nebraska and William E. Borah of Idaho, veteran progressive Republican senators. His listeners usually responded with appreciative laughter. Within an hour he had met every member who was on the floor. As he ambled about the chamber, he kept two pages busy bringing him the latest issues of Eastern newspapers or taking messages to his followers from Louisiana who were admiring his performance from the gallery. Reporters asked if he had expressed any preferences for his committee appointments. No, he replied judiciously, "I am going to look on and inform myself about matters here first."

When the session settled down to business, he followed the debate closely. The principal measure under consideration was a bill creating a government agency to be known as the Reconstruction Finance Corporation, which would lend money to distressed business concerns. Senator Hugo Black of Alabama offered a series of amendments designed to limit the salaries of officials of corporations that were to receive loans from the RFC. The amendments were supported by the "progressive bloc"—the band of Democratic and Republican senators who thought that not only President Hoover but also the Senate leadership was being too tender about regulating big business. The progressives resented particularly the attitude of the Democratic leader, Robinson. The number of Democratic senators was almost equal to that of the Republicans, and the Democrats and the progressive Republicans together were a majority. Robinson, however, usually held his followers to a conservative line. Huey had been expected to align himself with the progressive bloc, and now he was seen to confer with Black. Several times he appeared to be on the verge of speaking but managed to restrain himself. He voted for all the amendments, but they were defeated by decisive margins.[1]

He made his first remarks on the following day, January 26, on a bill dealing with deportation of alien seamen, speaking briefly of his knowledge of sailors coming into New Orleans. On the twenty-seventh he joined in the debate on the nomination of a businessman to the Federal Trade Commission, rising to say that he would vote against confirming any appointment that would put a representative of a given industry into an agency regulating that industry. At the conclusion of the session he arranged to secure leave from the Senate, went to his hotel, and that night, without notifying his office, left for New Orleans by train. Reporters caught him at Charlotte, North Carolina, and asked him why he had departed so suddenly. He said that he had to move his family out of the executive mansion and into a new home in New Orleans.[2]

It was not generally known in New Orleans that he owned a house there, and when he arrived in the city reporters met him to ask about this unexpected news. He revealed that he had recently acquired a large residence on Audubon Avenue, near Tulane University, in which he would install Rose and the children. He did not disclose the unusual circumstances through which he had come into possession of the house, although the story soon became common knowledge in New Orleans. The house had belonged to a man named Schwartz who had lost it, along with practically all his possessions, at one of the city's gaming clubs. According to one version, Huey called Schwartz up and said that he was taking over the house and that the club would cancel part of Schwartz's debt. The truth, however, seems to be that Schwartz, needing money to recoup his losses, sold the house to Bob Maestri, who assumed a mortgage of forty thousand dollars and transferred the house and the debt to Huey, who was to repay Maestri in installments.

Huey told the reporters why he was shifting his residence from Shreveport. He was setting up a law business in New Orleans—he

[1] New Orleans *Morning Tribune*, January 26, 1932; *Congressional Record*, 72 Cong., 1 Sess., pp. 2641–5.
[2] *Congressional Record*, 72 Cong., 1 Sess., pp. 2728, 2785, 2792; Baton Rouge *State-Times*, January 28, 1932.

and a lawyer named Hugh Wilkinson had set up a partnership—and he expected to spend two thirds of his time in Louisiana practicing law. He was making New Orleans his home and his legal head-quarters because the city was easy to reach from Washington.[3]

The reasons that Huey gave for leaving the Senate so abruptly did not ring quite true. Although he naturally would be interested in seeing the house he had bought, he did not have to supervise the move into it personally; or, if he did, he could have waited until he had spent a somewhat longer time in Washington. Some of his friends thought that he had returned simply because he was homesick, that he wanted to see Louisiana people. But simple homesickness would not explain his statement that he expected to spend most of his time practicing law in New Orleans. Quite possibly he was speaking sin-cerely: he may have been seriously considering a return to the legal profession. He had not liked his brief taste of national politics and said so frankly. Queried as to his opinion of President Hoover, he answered: "For the miserable party he represents, he is about as good as any other." But, he said, the Democrats in the Senate were no better than Hoover. They cowered before the President like "a whipped rooster"; they were afflicted with "political paralysis" and were afraid to bring up "real" issues.[4]

Huey returned to the Senate on February 25. But he remained only a few days, taking a minor part in the debates in progress, and then on March 1 asked for leave and went back to Louisiana for two weeks. He would request other leaves later and during this ses-sion would be absent eighty-one days and present but fifty-six days. He did not seem to be interested in the work of the committees to which he was appointed—naval affairs, manufactures and inter-oceanic canals, and commerce—and rarely attended their meetings.[5]

He was restive because his colleagues, and particularly those who were Democrats, showed little desire to deal with the problem that he considered fundamental—the concentration of wealth in the country. He decided that the "real" issue would never be considered unless he forced it on the Senate. In March he seized the floor twice and injected the subject of concentrated wealth into debates on other subjects. What was the cause of the depression? he asked in one

[3] New Orleans *States*, February 1 and 21. 1932; Charles Frampton; Richard Foster; Earle J. Christenberry; Hugh Wilkinson.

[4] Jess Nugent; New Orleans *Morning Tribune*, February 5, 1932; New Orleans *States*, February 7, 1932.

[5] *Congressional Record*, 72 Cong., 1 Sess., pp. 3498, 4776-7, 5019, 6451-2, 9107; M. S. Cushman: "Huey Long's First Session in the United States Senate," *Proceedings of the West Virginia Academy of Science*, XI (1937), 131.

speech, and answered: "There is but one reason; it is because a handful of men in the United States own all the money in this country." In a longer address he cited statistics to prove that wealth was maldistributed, using as his source an article in the *Saturday Evening Post* that he remembered having read in 1916. It was even more concentrated now, he cried, and yet comfortable conservatives complained that communism was making progress. "Certainly we are facing communism in America," he boldly declared. "The country has been going toward communism ever since the wealth of this country began to get into the hands of a few people." And the threat of communism would grow stronger, he continued, unless the government acted to curb concentrated wealth by imposing higher income and inheritance taxes or, better still, had the vision and courage to follow the Biblical injunction to tax profits.[6]

On April 4 he returned to this theme in a major address, which he entitled "The Doom of America's Dream." The Senate was considering a message from the President on the necessity of economizing on the costs of government and balancing the budget. Huey contemptuously ignored the message and the remarks of his colleagues on it. If this Congress did not enact legislation to provide for a redistribution of wealth, he warned, there would be no need to worry about a deficit. The country would face a much larger and more dangerous problem—the threat of revolution. "You want to enforce the law, you want to balance the budget?" he asked acidly. "I tell you that if in any country I live in, despite every physical and intellectual effort I could put forth, I should see my children starving and my wife starving, its laws against robbing and against stealing . . . would not amount to any more to me than they would to any other man, when it came to facing the time of starvation." The wealthy classes were complaining that the effort of the progressives to secure higher income and inheritance taxes was a "soak the rich" campaign. "It is no campaign to soak the rich," he cried. "It is a campaign to save the rich. It is a campaign the success of which they will wish for when it is too late."

How, he asked at the climax of his speech, could senators be concerned with a balanced budget when they saw what was happening to the old dream of America as a land of free men? "This great and grand dream of America that all men are created free and equal, endowed with the inalienable right of life and liberty and the pursuit of happiness," he thundered, "this great dream of America, this great

[6] *Congressional Record*, 72 Cong., 1 Sess., pp. 6451-2, 6538-45, speeches of March 18 and 21, 1932.

light, and this great hope, have almost gone out of sight in this day and time, and everybody knows it; and there is a mere candle flicker here and yonder to take the place of what the great dream of America was supposed to be."[7]

Huey's speech excited the attention of the Washington correspondents of the national press. One of them described Huey's delivery: the Kingfish frequently ran his hands through his hair, swung his fists, and bobbed his body like former heavyweight champion Jack Dempsey weaving in the ring. This man also noted that Huey had piled books, pamphlets, and other documents on his desk and consulted them as he spoke. In his previous speeches Huey had listed as authorities for his doctrine only the Bible and the *Saturday Evening Post*, but he now cited a variety of sources, including philosopher John Dewey, Samuel Gompers, president of the American Federation of Labor, and Wallace B. Donham, economist and dean of Harvard's school of business administration.

These names were not merely window-dressing. Huey had become aware, if only from listening to other senators, that his knowledge of the economic issues he was discussing was sketchy, and he had determined to remedy this deficiency. He consulted a journalist acquaintance, probably Raymond Daniell of *The New York Times*, asking for the titles of some recent books on economic matters. The reporter named five or six volumes, and Huey bought and read them before he gave his speech. One impressed him particularly, *The Epic of America*, by James Truslow Adams, a popular historical work. He scribbled notes on the margins of his copy, and it was from this book that he took the phrase "the American dream." Hereafter he would do more research for his speeches, sending a member of his staff to various governmental departments to collect materials and using the services of departmental analysts.[8]

The remarkable content of "The Doom of America's Dream" impressed the correspondents even more than Huey's free-wheeling delivery. They marveled at his sheer radicalism, his bold proposal to redistribute wealth by taxation, his apparent justification of violence if necessary to avert want his calm but ominous prediction that the country faced revolution. A veteran observer wrote: "No such stirring plea for the impoverished masses has been made in the Senate for years." Huey went beyond all the other progressives, this

[7] Ibid., 7333–78.
[8] Frank R. Kent, in Baltimore *Sun*, reprinted in Bogalusa *News*, April 15, 1932; Carter: *American Messiahs* (New York, 1935), pp. 18–19; Deutsch, column in New Orleans *States*, February 25, 1959; Mary B. Walle; Earle J. Christenberry.

man concluded, and made even Senator Norris look like a reactionary. A columnist described the speech as a hodgepodge of facts but said that its cumulative effect was startling—"strong, bitter, merciless, and inflaming." He warned conservatives not to make the mistake of dismissing the senator from Louisiana as just another demagogue. Another columnist asserted that in Long the Senate had a type it had never had, a genuine proletarian. Huey "could spot" the Eastern urban radicals "a Karl Marx and a couple of Kropotkins" and still knock them off, this writer predicted.[9]

Even more amazed than the press corps were Huey's Senate colleagues. They had expected him to be a troublesome influence in their calm deliberations—but were confident that they could suppress him. The Senate had developed a technique to handle obstreperous newcomers. A conservative senator explained: "We always have a wild man. We let him blow off steam—and then tame him." The senior members were outwardly confident that they would be able to control Huey, wild though he seemed to be, but now a few of them must have begun to harbor secret doubts. The Senate, like Louisiana earlier, would have much to learn.[1]

Huey's speech established him as a leading member of the progressive bloc in the Senate. His closest associates in the group were Northern Republicans, Norris, Borah, and Robert M. LaFollette of Wisconsin. He respected Norris above every other senator and was seen frequently conferring with him. Norris, in turn, was fond of Huey, and reporters speculated that the two had a father-son relationship, with Norris acting the part of adviser on questions of Senate deportment. They were a study in contrasts as they stood together on the floor, Norris, dignified, white-haired, always dressed in somber attire, and Huey, bouncy and, as the warmer months came on, clad in a white suit, with a pink necktie, and sporting an orange handkerchief in his breast pocket.[2]

Of the Democratic progressives, Huey most admired and trusted Burton K. Wheeler of Montana. But his relationship with most Democratic senators was a formal one, and he was not a member of the inner Democratic circle of the Senate. Interestingly, Huey had few friends among the Southern Democrats, who because of their

[9] Kent, in Baltimore *Sun*, reprinted in Bogalusa *News*, April 15, 1932; Henry Suydam, April 5, 1932, and Lemuel F. Parton, May 3, 1932, clippings in Long Scrapbooks, XVII.

[1] Will Irwin: "The Empire of the Kingfish," *Liberty*, XII (April 6, 1935), 14–16.

[2] Burton K. Wheeler: *Yankee from the West* (New York, 1962), p. 282; Fred Blanche; New Orleans *Item*, July 11, 1932.

seniority held high-ranking committee positions. In turn, most of his Southern colleagues disliked him and made no secret of their feelings. They gave as their reason that he was a demagogue and a clown, but what they really resented was his politics. The great majority of them were conservatives, differing hardly at all from most Republicans, and they viewed Huey as a dangerous radical who was not in the Southern tradition. Huey, for his part, detested the Southerners as men playing the Republican game. He developed a special antipathy for Joe Robinson, his leader, who denounced the Republicans in his speeches and then usually voted with them. Other Democratic senators shared Long's feeling, but some of them for a different reason. The massive Arkansan was one of the most autocratic leaders in the Senate's history. Arrogant and imperious, he held no caucuses and issued orders through his lieutenants. The orders were always obeyed. He controlled the appointments of Democrats to committees, and he was a master of debate, cutting down with a biting barb anybody who showed a hint of resistance. Many Democrats resented him, but none had dared to take him on.[3]

Huey decided to throw down a challenge to Robinson and to do it in a particularly dramatic way—not over a matter of routine legislation but over the kind of leadership the senator was imposing on the Democratic party. That leadership, he believed, if continued, would destroy the party. In addition to this honest conviction, he had another reason to attack Robinson, a highly personal one. He had not come to the Senate to be just another member. He was Huey Long, who was going to be a national leader and some day, President. He viewed the Senate primarily as a forum from which he could advertise Huey Long to the country. The most immediate way to secure attention was to attack the biggest Democrat in the Senate. It was the same technique he had used early in his career, when he had aimed at the Standard Oil Company, the New Orleans Ring, Governor Parker, and other big targets.

On April 29 he called up a resolution he had introduced a few days earlier instructing the finance committee to "reform" the revenue bill then under consideration so as to provide higher tax rates on the rich. In discussing rates heretofore he had been general as to what they should be. Now, for the first time, he proposed a specific plan. His resolution stipulated that no person should receive an annual income in excess of one million dollars and that no person

[3] Wheeler: *Yankee from the West*, pp. 282, 284; Robert S. Allen, article in *Real Detective*, February 1933, clipping in Long Scrapbooks, XVII; Joseph Alsop, column in Baton Rouge *Morning Advocate*, March 10, 1959.

*Taking the oath as United States senator, 1932*

THE REAL ISSUE IN WASHINGTON

PATRIOTISM vs COMMUNISM

MAY 5 - 1932

*Soon after he entered Congress, Long was shown in a newspaper cartoon as a radical preaching alien doctrines while Joe Robinson was depicted as a defender of Americanism*

*Celebrating victory of James P. O'Connor, Jr., in election to the Public Service Commission. L to R, Louisiana Supreme Court Justice Faurnet, O'Connor, Long, Governor O. K. Allen*

*(opposite) Speaking before the Democratic National Convention in 1932, defending the seating of his group of delegates*

*Campaigning with Hattie Caraway in Arkansas, 1932*

*The Veto Protest parade during the soldiers' bonus fight*

*With Governor O. K. Allen*

*Long with wife and daughter, Rose*

*With son, Russell*

*Long's body lying in state in the state capitol, Baton Rouge, La.*

*(opposite) Long in 1935 outside United States Senate Office Building*

*Newspaper cartoon after Long's assassination*

should receive during his or her lifetime gifts, inheritances, or other bequests of more than five million dollars.

Speaking in support of his resolution, Huey said little about the mechanics of his plan, of how the amounts received by individuals would be determined or of how the cumulative collections would decrease the concentration of wealth. Instead, he launched into an attack on the Democratic leadership in the Senate and the House for sponsoring a sales tax in the revenue bill. The Democrats had a majority in the House and with the progressives controlled the Senate, he said, and this might be their last chance to do something to redistribute wealth, for the Republicans could well win in the November election. "All we can do is to get what we have now," he cried. But the Democratic leadership, dominated by the same big banking interests that ruled the Republicans, was afraid to offend the rich. As Huey continued, his face darkened with feigned rage, and he screamed out his words. He threatened that if the Democrats nominated a presidential candidate advocating the ideas of Robinson, he would vote for a Farmer-Labor candidate or a Republican candidate, if either of them stood for cutting down swollen fortunes "as God Almighty demanded and ordained." Then came his clincher, his formal repudiation of Robinson's leadership: "I send to the desk, Mr. President, my resignation from every committee . . . that has been given to me by the Democratic leadership since I have been here." He went on more calmly: "The people of this country want relief, and they do not have to eat a whole side of beef to tell when it is tainted. They have bitten off the hoof of this situation in the United States. They know. We have given them no place to go." He ended by repeating his conviction that the country faced revolution.

Robinson had listened to the tirade with cold but mounting anger. Here was a Democrat who not only was defying him but was contemptuously throwing back to him the awards he used to maintain discipline, the committee appointments. He jumped to his feet the instant that Huey sat down. Resorting to heavy sarcasm, he said that if Long was as good as he obviously thought he was, then Long should be the Democratic leader. It was easy to arouse class hatred, he went on, but it was something else to devise remedies for the problems afflicting the country. As for Huey's resignation from the committees, it was a "comic-opera performance" not worthy of "the great actor from Louisiana."

Huey was delighted that he had provoked Robinson into an outburst of passion. He now became a model of the reasonable senator.

He would not make a test of strength between Robinson and himself in the Senate, he said—but he might sometime in Arkansas. He asked for a roll-call vote on his resolution but failed to secure one. The resolution was defeated on a voice vote. But he was well satisfied with what he had accomplished. He had cut himself loose from the Democratic leadership, and he had trumpeted the name of Huey Long to all parts of the country—the champion of the poor and the unemployed and the enemy of the rich.[4]

Having found an inviting target in Robinson, Huey prepared to hurl more darts. On May 12 he rose at his desk, brandishing a copy of the Chicago *Tribune*, an extremist Republican newspaper that was perhaps the bitterest journalistic critic of progressivism in the country. He exhibited to his colleagues a cartoon in color on the front page, depicting Robinson carrying an American flag and Huey Long, "new Senate radical," carrying a red flag. Affecting a tone of injured indignation, he complained that the cartoon did not do justice to his friend, the great minority leader. For one thing, it did not show any stars on the flag he was bearing.

But, Huey announced dramatically, he would supply the stars himself, forty-three of them, stars that should be in a flag carried by Joe Robinson. He then produced the legal directory of Little Rock, Robinson's home town, and read off the names of the clients of Robinson's law firm, forty-three corporations—oil, utility, and chain-store companies—some of them among the largest corporations in the South and the country. If he accepted the leadership of Robinson, he cried, he would be following the lead of a corporation attorney. "It may, Mr. President, be communism for me not to accept that as being a proper sphere and location for my activities," he said sarcastically. He had never bowed to the will of the corporations, he shouted, and he was not going to bow to these interests in the Senate of the United States. If the leadership wanted to discipline him, let them try it. "The only way they can read me out of the Democratic party is to beat me down in the state of Louisiana," he roared, "and that has been tried one or two times and can be tried again whenever they see fit."

Abruptly dropping Robinson as though disdaining to give him any more attention, he charged that the Democratic and Republican parties were both controlled by two big New York bankers. Bernard M. Baruch was running the Democrats, even though he was "the twin-bed mate of Hooverism," and Eugene Meyer, recently ap-

[4] *Congressional Record*, 72 Cong., 1 Sess., pp. 9202, 9213–14; Genevieve Forbes Herrick, in New Orleans *Times-Picayune*, May 2, 1932.

pointed to head the Reconstruction Finance Corporation, was running the Republicans. Thus Hooverism controlled the Senate, "spouting through the two foghorns, Baruch on the one hand and Meyer on the other, Robinson on the left and somebody else on the right." Why, he said, the Republicans and Democrats reminded him of the patent medicines he had known in his salesman days: there was no more difference between them than between "high popalorum" and "low popahirum."

At one stage in his remarks Huey was forced to take his seat when a senator complained that he was violating the rule not to reflect on another member: he was implying that Robinson's corporate connection had influenced his votes. Allowed to continue but cautioned to observe the rule, he jumped up and said impudently: "I want now to disclaim that I have the slightest motive of saying, or that in my heart I believe, that such a man could to the slightest degree be influenced in any vote which he casts in this body by the fact that that association might mean hundreds of thousands and millions of dollars in the way of lucrative fees." The Senate could not restrain an appreciative laugh.[5]

Robinson had not been present when Huey began his speech. He came in later and sat at his desk, his face red with anger. But he made no attempt to reply. Significantly, no Democratic senator rose to defend him. The Democratic liberals were delighted with Huey's attack. None of them had known of Robinson's corporate clients because none of them had taken the trouble to dig up the facts. The Democratic conservatives, in an election year, hesitated to range themselves on the side of a man who had been exposed as a corporation attorney. The only senator who tried to defend Robinson was a Republican, David A. Reed of Pennsylvania, one of the most conservative members of the body.[6]

Huey continued to fire away at the pending revenue bill. He supported amendments to it, offered by progressive senators, to raise the surtaxes in the higher brackets, and he offered an amendment of his own to fix the rates at sixty-three per cent on incomes of one million dollars or above and sixty-five per cent on those of two million dollars or more. In one speech in favor of the higher rates he rambled for three hours, ridiculing the Senate's methods of procedure, denouncing sales taxes, telling "nigger" stories, and quoting poetry: the finance committee in reporting the bill had followed the

[5] *Congressional Record*, 72 Cong., 1 Sess., pp. 10062–8.
[6] Tom Connally: *My Name Is Tom Connally* (New York, 1954), pp. 166–7; Scripps-Howard dispatch, in Buffalo *Times*, May 14, 1932.

orders of the secretary of the treasury; "theirs not to reason why, theirs but to do and die." He was, as he confessed, conducting a mild filibuster to prevent the Treasury from getting to undecided senators. "I am feeling the urge to talk," he said. "I am becoming convinced by my own logic that it is necessary to talk a long time on this matter."

As he talked, he disregarded the rule that a senator should stand by his desk when addressing the Senate. He wandered into the center aisle, flinging his arms wildly and almost hitting a conservative colleague on the nose. Outraged Senate veterans told reporters that they could not recall such a scene ever before. Many senators were irritated by the performance, but in spite of themselves they had to laugh at Huey's sallies. His amendment and the amendments of other progressives were voted down by solid majorities. But again he had made known to the country that Huey Long was the advocate of the poor against the rich—and furthermore, that he was a tremendously interesting and colorful senator.[7]

Huey's votes on other amendments to the revenue bill should have interested those commentators who had pegged him as a radical. Senators from various states offered amendments raising the tariff duties on various products coming into the country from abroad—oil and lumber, which were Louisiana products, and coal and copper. Huey voted for every increase and spoke at length in support of a pro-tariff policy. When other Democrats protested that high tariffs were contrary to Democratic tradition, he read from the record to demonstrate that the protestors had in the past voted to increase the duties on products produced in their own states. One of the senators thus exposed, Walter George of Georgia, cried angrily that the senator from Louisiana was "utterly lacking in the sensibilities which usually characterized the intercourse between men in this body." Another senator, Millard Tydings of Maryland, said that Long had no concept of how courtesy was defined.

Unabashed, Huey defended his stand. He was particularly interested in protecting oil and especially Louisiana's oil. He contended that there were many small operators in the oil industry and that these men would be hurt if cheap foreign oil was permitted to enter the country. Moreover, the foreign oil would reduce the revenue from oil taxes and thus deprive of revenue LSU, "that great institution." What he said about the oil industry was true enough, but it was not the whole story. A tariff on oil would benefit also the

[7] *Congressional Record*, 72 Cong., 1 Sess., pp. 10294–10309, 10390–7, 10400, May 16 and 17, 1932; Baton Rouge *State-Times*, May 17, 1932.

large oil corporations and especially the Standard Oil Company, which supposedly he wanted to destroy. When a corporate interest in his own state was threatened, the great radical responded like any other senator.[8]

In late May Huey secured leave and returned to New Orleans. Arriving at the railroad station with a golf bag thrown over his shoulder, he was met by his son Russell, who embraced him. To reporters who inquired the reason for his presence he answered: "I just saw that I couldn't do any good in Washington and decided to come home. All I want is a rest." His real reason became apparent the next day. Governor Allen came down from Baton Rouge and the two men went into conference. Two days later Huey went to Baton Rouge. The Kingfish had come back to see if his governor was performing satisfactorily and to check on the status of the administration program in the legislature.[9]

SOME OBSERVERS THOUGHT that Allen would be a successful governor. Handsome, silver-haired, dignified, he looked the part. Raised in the same kind of environment in Winn parish as Huey had been, he had risen as Huey had, though in not so spectacular a fashion. He had been a country schoolteacher, a sawmill laborer and operator, and a businessman. Entering politics, he had held various local offices and supposedly knew the problems of parish governments. Elected to the senate in 1928, he had been a Long floor leader and then chairman of the Highway Commission and thus had had experience in two branches of the state government. Mild and modest in manner, he impressed people at first acquaintance, though not always thereafter.[1]

Actually, he lacked many of the qualities that even the ordinary politician has to have. He did not have the knack of remembering people, their names and associations, and therefore he could not say to them the flattering things they liked to hear from a leader. His clumsiness in dealing with people became, in fact, proverbial in Louisiana. According to one of the stories told about him, he was once moving through a courthouse square before a rally, shaking hands with people, when he met a boy whom he vaguely recog-

[8] *Congressional Record*, 72 Cong., 1 Sess., pp. 10549–55, 10782, 1080–12, 10898, 11009.

[9] New Orleans *Item*, May 27, 1932.

[1] Sketches of Allen's career, in New Orleans *States*, September 11, 1935, and Baton Rouge *State-Times*, September 11, 1935.

nized. "How's your father?" he inquired. "Dead," the boy answered. "Too bad," Allen muttered. Continuing to move around, he came on the boy again. "How's your father?" he asked. "He's still dead," the boy said.[2]

His greatest shortcoming was a weakness of character, an amiability and desire to oblige that made him susceptible to the influence of stronger personalities. One of these was his wife, Florence. Huey, reflecting on her control, once said that Oscar's trouble was that he had twenty-five rooms in the mansion and should have only one. "The next man I elect governor has got to be unhappily married," the Kingfish sighed. Allen's penchant for following the direction of others became legend. Earl Long said that once when the governor was sitting in his office signing official documents, a leaf blew in the window onto his desk. Allen signed the leaf, Earl said sarcastically.[3]

Huey was aware of this proclivity of Allen's. Fearful of possible consequences, he tried to prevent the worst effects by using the only method he could think of—dominating Allen himself, crudely and even brutally. He bullied and abused the governor, often in the presence of others. "Huey used to cuss him unmercifully," an associate recalled. "But he thought that he had to do it to keep Oscar in line." In caucus deliberations, if Allen dared to intervene, Huey would shout: "Oscar, you sonofabitch, shut up!" Allen once asked Huey not to curse him publicly. "Oscar asked me not to call him a grayheaded old sonofabitch in public again," said Huey, and he had promised not to, adding: "But, Oscar, I don't consider eighteen or twenty people gathered in an informal group to be the public." Earl Long charged Huey to his face with directing every activity of Allen's life. "I don't think Allen went to the picture show, talked to his wife or let his children change their clothes unless you told him all about it," Earl said.[4]

On occasion Huey pretended that he had no influence over Allen, when he did not want to grant a request or reveal information. Then he would say that Allen would not let him do something or tell him anything. "I can't move Oscar," he would say blandly. "Oscar is adamant." Once reporters asked him if there was going to be a special session of the legislature. "As far as I know," he an-

[2] B. W. Bradford.

[3] Mason Spencer; confidential communication.

[4] Richard W. Leche; Arthur Provost; Mason Spencer; Scoville Walker; W. C. Pegues; *Time*, October 3, 1932; *Overton Hearing*, I, 840.

swered, "Oscar hasn't made up his mind about if he'll call one any time soon. Leastaways he never said a word to me about it." "When are you going to make up his mind so he can tell you?" a reporter inquired. "He'd near about kill you if he heard you say that," Huey grinned, "and his wife would finish the job."[5]

Huey could control Allen when he was with him, but there were long periods when he could not be in Baton Rouge. Before Allen took over the governorship, Huey had realized he would have to have a man of his own in Allen's office, someone who could watch over and advise Oscar and report to Washington if anything went wrong. After consulting with some of his associates, he chose for the position a young New Orleans attorney, Richard W. Leche, who had formerly belonged to the Simpson organization but who had come over to the Long camp after 1928 and also had recently managed Allen's campaign in the city.

He informed Leche of his decision in typical fashion. As related by the tall, burly lawyer, at two o'clock one morning he was wakened by the ringing of the telephone. It was Huey calling from the Roosevelt Hotel. "That was a peculiar habit Huey had," Leche recalled resignedly. "He always called you between two and four in the morning." Huey said he wanted to talk to Leche. The lawyer asked if it couldn't wait till later in the day. Huey said it had to be right away. So Leche drove to the hotel and found Huey in his suite, propped up in bed but as wide awake and alert as if he was just beginning the day.

Huey first made some general remarks and then observed: "You know, Oscar Allen is a pretty good fellow." Leche, sensing that Huey was going to ask him to do something, agreed. "You know Oscar is not a lawyer," Huey continued, "and the governorship of this state is essentially a lawyer's job. Too many legal angles for Oscar. Oscar needs somebody up there who knows law." Leche asked him to come to the point. Huey finally came out with it—he wanted Leche to become Allen's secretary: "You know Oscar. I need somebody in that office." Leche protested that he had a good law business and that some of his clients were corporations Huey had denounced. That was all right, Huey assured, he liked to have corporations for enemies. "I'll double your corporate business," he promised. Leche accepted the job.[6]

[5] Mason Spencer; Hermann B. Deutsch: *The Huey Long Murder Case* (New York, 1963), pp. 54–5.
[6] Confidential communications; Richard W. Leche.

The May session of the legislature convened in the new capitol. Work on the building had proceeded rapidly after the contract had been let in December 1930. The contract went to a Washington, D. C., firm whose bid of $2,394,000 was considerably less than the sum provided in the amendment authorizing the structure. The remaining money was spent equipping the building with bronze doors and statuary and landscaping the grounds. Attracting wide attention were the spacious chambers of the two houses. Each contained a voting machine, the latest and best type available, and a microphone beneath the presiding officer's dais from which speakers could easily address their colleagues. At Huey's suggestion, the microphones were connected to the governor's office, so that the chief executive could follow the debates and, if he wished, speak to the houses from his desk. Also in the governor's office was a voting machine that reproduced the tallies of the other machines and apprised the governor if any of his adherents were straying from the fold. Soaring like a skyscraper and exhibiting the most modern technological devices to be found in any capitol, the handsome building was a fitting symbol of the new Louisiana that had come into being since 1928.[7]

When the legislators had gathered, few of them had any inkling as to what program the administration would propose. No word had come out of the governor's office during the weeks preceding the session, when Huey was putting on his show in Washington. But now the word came abruptly. The solons had hardly settled in their seats for the opening night meeting when Long floor leaders in the house introduced four revenue bills imposing new taxes on tobacco, soft drinks, electricity, insurance premiums, and other items, and a corporation franchise tax. The bills were referred immediately to the committee on ways and means, and shortly before midnight the house, and then the senate, adjourned. That night Huey arrived from New Orleans and was seen conferring with various legislators.

The ways and means committee convened early the next morning. Waiting in the hearing room were lobbyists of the industries that would bear the new taxes. Immediately after the chairman rapped for order, the Kingfish strode in and took over the meeting. "Where are these bills?" he barked. Someone said they had not as yet been brought up from the enrolling clerk's room. Huey ordered George Wallace to get the bills. Then, turning to the committee and

[7] Baton Rouge *State-Times*, December 10, 1930, May 12 and 16, 1932; Crowley *Daily Signal*, April 14, 1932; Norman Lant; E. J. Bourg.

the crowd, he explained that he had been invited to attend by the chairman. "I was asked to explain some of the provisions of the bills," he said blandly. The lobbyist of the New Orleans chamber of commerce stated that his organization would like the opportunity to present evidence showing that some of the taxes were ill-advised. "The Assassination of Commerce didn't amount to much during my administration and ain't going to amount to even that much now," Huey answered. It took a moment for the lobbyists to realize that he was saying there were to be no hearings. The chairman moved to report the bills favorably to the house, and the top-heavy Long majority on the committee sustained him. When protests rose in the house and in the press that this speedy procedure was unprecedented, Huey announced from Governor Allen's office that there would be plenty of time to hold hearings after the bills passed the house and came before the senate finance committee.

The committee's action had a precedent, but only one. In the Mississippi River flood crisis of 1927 Governor Simpson, seeking quick passage of his relief measures, had devised a stratagem to put a bill through the legislature in five days. Ordinarily a bill had to be read on three separate days in each house and placed in printed form on the desks of legislators forty-eight hours before it was voted on. Simpson telescoped the process. First, the legislature had to agree by a two-thirds majority to suspend the rules. Then a bill could be introduced in the house before midnight on the opening day, Sunday, read, and referred to a committee. Just after midnight, or later on the next morning, the committee could report it favorably back to the house. It would be read again—the clerk could merely mumble the title—and be considered, and on Tuesday, the third day, be read and enacted. Rushed immediately to the senate, it could be read there and referred to a committee, read again and considered on Wednesday, and read and passed finally on Thursday. Actually, if everything went off without a hitch, a bill could be enacted and signed by the governor a few minutes after the fourth midnight. Yet it would have had three readings in each house!

Huey had been in Baton Rouge during the 1927 session and had observed with interest Simpson's technique. He either remembered it or had it recalled to him by George Wallace, for he employed it in this session to jam through the four revenue bills. His followers and the Old Regulars constituted a two-thirds majority and easily suspended the rules in each chamber. The bills passed the lower house by large margins, the opposition being able to muster only thirty to thirty-five votes against them. The conservatives, recognizing the hopelessness of the struggle, gave up when the bills went to the senate. Huey went to the hearing of the senate finance committee to defend the measures, only to find that no lobbyists were present. Where were the indignant taxpayers? he asked in mock anger. "It's the damndest outrage I ever heard," he fumed. "Here I sat up all night working up a set speech and there's no audience." The senate dutifully enacted the revenue bills. They were expected to bring in an annual yield of five million dollars, money that was needed to sustain the educational and roads program that Huey had inaugurated.[8]

With the administration's key measures successfully behind them, the legislators concerned themselves with routine matters for the duration of the session. Only some physical encounters enlivened the dullness of the political front. One of the lesser bills before the legislature was a measure to regulate companies that sold burial insurance. It seemed to be a harmless bill and was not labeled as an administration measure. Actually, it was directed at Dudley LeBlanc's company, and it was in the charge of a newly appointed Long floor leader, Octave Pavy, Judge Dupre's successor. Dud came to Baton Rouge to lobby against the bill. He was accompanied by Francis Williams and also by Joseph Boudreaux, who acted as a kind of bodyguard to the French leader. Boudreaux had a reputation as a tough: fifteen charges of physical assault had been filed against him, and he had once beaten up Bob Brothers so badly that Bob had had to go to a hospital.

One night Boudreaux went with LeBlanc and Williams to the capitol. While he was there—this was Boudreaux's later story—he learned that LeBlanc's chauffeur had been taken out of the building by Joe Messina at the point of a gun. Going to look for the driver, he encountered Messina, who grabbed his arm and told him that he would have to leave too. He was hustled out to the steps and suddenly "the lights went out." He claimed that Louie Jones had come up behind him and clubbed him with the butt end of a pistol, fracturing his skull. Jones, recalling the incident years later, readily admitted that he had hit Boudreaux. But according to Jones, Boudreaux had accosted Huey in the capitol and said: "I'm going to black both your eyes before you go back to the Senate." Thereupon

[8] Baton Rouge *State-Times*, May 31, 1932; New Orleans *Item*, May 31 and June 7, 1932; Hermann B. Deutsch: "Kingdom of the Kingfish," in New Orleans *Item*, August 8 and 28, 1939; Deutsch: *Long Murder Case*, pp. 53–4.

Jones had rushed Boudreaux outside, where the latter pulled a pistol. "I beat him to it with mine," Jones said, "and knocked hell out of him." Jones was indicted by the East Baton Rouge authorities for assault and sentenced to six months in jail. Governor Allen reprieved him after he had served only two months.[9]

Shortly after the Boudreaux episode a nasty incident involving Mrs. Ruffin Pleasant occurred. Mrs. Pleasant came to the capitol and marched into Alice Lee Grosjean's office, where she demanded to see certain records concerning LSU. While she was arguing with the clerk, Huey came in. According to Mrs. Pleasant, he ordered that she be ejected. "I can't have a drunken, cursing woman in the capitol," he said. Thereupon a state policeman seized her by the arm, while Huey "booed" her. Huey then said that she could stay but would have to leave if she cursed. He left himself, but soon another policeman came in and told Mrs. Pleasant to get out. This man told reporters that she had a pistol in her handbag and was acting as though she was insane. Huey suspected that Mrs. Pleasant was armed. He feared, in fact, that she was one of those who might try to assassinate him.[1]

HUEY HAD USED THE Simpson technique to enact his bills because it promised quick results, and he was always in a hurry. But at this particular time he had a special reason to desire speed. The Democratic national convention was to meet in Chicago on June 27, and he wanted to have all controversial measures out of the way before he left the state. As the national committeeman of Louisiana, he would head his state's delegation, and as the Kingfish, he would control its vote. He was going to use his power to try to secure the Presidential nomination for a progressive. If the Democrats put up a progressive and elected him, the Democrats in Congress might feel constrained to do something to redistribute wealth.

The Louisiana delegation to the convention had been chosen in February. It had been appointed by the method Huey had devised in 1928: the state central committee named the delegates, which meant that he named them. The few conservatives on the committee protested that the delegates should be chosen by a convention, but

[9] *Overton Hearing,* I, 1004-5; Louis A. Jones; New Orleans *Times-Picayune,* November 24, 1932; Baton Rouge *State-Times,* November 25, 1932; Lafayette *Daily Advertiser,* November 29, 1932.

[1] Shreveport *Journal,* June 16, 1932; Louis A. Jones.

they were smothered by the Long–Old Regular majority. The same majority dominated the delegation, although some anti-Longs, such as Senator Broussard, were picked as a matter of form. The delegation would vote as a unit, but it was not instructed in advance to vote for any one candidate. It was thought that most of its members favored John N. Garner of Texas, the speaker of the house.[2]

The delegation was uninstructed because Huey had not as yet decided whom it should be instructed for. The leading candidates were Governor Roosevelt of New York, Garner, and Alfred E. Smith, who had been the party's standard-bearer in 1928. Roosevelt had a larger number of delegates pledged to him than did any other aspirant. In addition to these leaders, there were a number of favorite-son candidates, governors or senators, each holding the vote of his own state. As the front-runner was Roosevelt, the strategy of the other candidates was to effect a combination against him. By an ancient rule of the party, the nominee had to secure a two-thirds majority of the total number of delegates, and if Roosevelt's rivals could throw the convention into a deadlock, one of them might capture the prize.

Before he went to Washington, Huey probably had favored Garner or one of the Southern senators, Robinson or Pat Harrison of Mississippi. He did not know Roosevelt and had, for some reason, gotten it in his mind that the New Yorker could not be elected. But early in his days in the Senate, he decided that he could not support any of the Southern contenders; he had only to study the rulings of Garner or listen to Robinson or Harrison to know that they were as conservative as Hoover. He finally repudiated the Southerners openly, stating sarcastically that Robinson ought to run with Hoover for the vice-presidency. As for the Democrats, he said, if they had any sense, they would nominate progressive Republican Senator Norris.[3]

Slowly Huey began to turn toward Roosevelt as the only Democratic aspirant who showed any inclination to progressivism. Urging him to come out for the governor was his friend Burton Wheeler. Huey finally said: "Well, if Norris will tell me he's for him, I'll be for him." Norris assured him that he was going to support Roosevelt. Huey thereupon suggested that it would be particularly effective if he should announce for Roosevelt and say that he was acting on Norris's advice. Norris agreed to this plan. A little later Huey saw

---

[2] New Orleans *Item-Tribune*, February 14, 1932.

[3] Shreveport *Journal*, January 25, 1932; Baton Rouge *State-Times*, April 30, 1932.

Wheeler and said: "I didn't like your sonofabitch but I'll be for him."

Huey was about to leave for one of his visits to New Orleans when he came to his decision. He told Norris that he would get off the train in Atlanta—Georgia was a Roosevelt stronghold—and announce for Roosevelt. To ensure that he would receive the maximum publicity, he telephoned an Atlanta newspaperman whom he knew to meet him when his train passed through the city. He would have an important statement to make, he said.

The statement was that the Louisiana delegation would vote for Roosevelt. He emphasized that in deciding for Roosevelt he was following Norris's advice. If the Democrats hoped to win, he went on, they would have to attract the support of Norris and the Republican progressives. They would have to nominate a progressive candidate, and Roosevelt was a progressive. The candidate had recently made a speech in which he indicated—the indication was vague—that he favored the redistribution of wealth, that is, the Long plan. As Huey had foreseen, his way of announcing his shift to Roosevelt secured wide press notice.[4]

The conservatives had been fuming ever since the delegation to the convention had been chosen. Not only had it been selected in a manner that they thought was illegal, it also did not include any of them. Now, in June, they decided to fight back by sending a contesting delegation to Chicago. Conservative members of the state central committee and some parish committee chairmen called a convention to meet in Shreveport. It was announced that one representative from each parish would attend and that therefore the convention would meet the requirements of law and that its delegation would have more standing than the one chosen by the central committee.

Because the conservatives had to act hastily, they were not able to secure the presence of a representative from every parish. But most of the parishes were represented, and the convention confidently assumed that it spoke for the Democratic party of Louisiana. It elected a national committeeman to replace Huey, John D., "Squirt," Ewing, and a national committeewoman to replace the individual selected by the central committee. It also picked a delegation to go to Chicago. The delegation was headed by ex-governor

⁴ Wheeler: *Yankee from the West*, 285; Huey P. Long: *Every Man a King* (New Orleans, 1933), pp. 298, 300–3; New Orleans *Times-Picayune*, May 5, 1932; *Congressional Record*, 72 Cong., 2 Sess., speech by Long, December 6, 1932. Wheeler, in quoting Long, used a blank to indicate an expletive.

Sanders, and ex-governors Parker and Pleasant and other figures
out of the past were members. Huey scornfully referred to it as the
delegation of "the exes."[5]

He did not think the national convention would seat the protesters—the convention of 1928 had turned down a similar delegation, and the one of 1932 would probably follow precedent. But he
could not be sure. The factions of the contending candidates for the
nomination were so numerous and the party so disorganized that
anything might happen. He decided he should be prepared for the
eventuality that his delegation might be refused recognition.

He was in Baton Rouge when the Shreveport convention met,
and he summoned Bob Brothers to the governor's office. To his
henchman he announced that a third faction of the state party was
about to come into existence, the Unterrified Democrats. "The Unterrified Democrats of Louisiana are going to have a convention to-
morrow," he said, "and you're their leader. They will meet in the
capitol. I have the banners made and a band hired. March into the
capitol and take over."

He explained his plan more specifically. Brothers was to lead the
new party—a sufficient number of state employees to make up a
respectable parade would be turned out—into the house of representatives. There he was to announce that the house was sitting as a
convention of the Unterrified Democrats. The members would think
it a huge joke, but, being amused, they would go through with the
act. Brothers would then have the house select delegates to the national convention, delegates who would be chosen in a meeting in
which every parish was represented. Everything had been prepared, Huey assured Bob: four members of the central committee
had signed a call for the "convention," and certain members of the
house would cooperate in the farce. Huey even designated the candidates that the Unterrified Democrats would be pledged to, and
managed to do it without laughing: Senator Jules Fisher of Jefferson parish and Representative George Delesdernier, who had made
the speech during the impeachment that likened Huey to Christ.

On the following morning Brothers led a shouting line of followers down the main street of Baton Rouge to the capitol. Many of
them carried banners that, because the name lent itself to Democratic alliteration, advertised the candidacy of Delesdernier: "Democracy Demands Delesdernier" and "Delesdernier, Democracy's Darling." Led by a band blaring forth spirited music, the procession

[5] Baton Rouge *Morning Advocate*, June 4, 1932; New Orleans *Times-Picayune*,
June 10, 15, and 16, 1932.

straggled into the house chamber. By prearrangement Representative Pat McGrath of New Orleans, one of the house "characters," was in the chair. Among his other distinctive features, he weighed over three hundred pounds. Once when an anti succeeded in inserting in the house record a *Picayune* editorial characterizing Huey as a demagogue, Pat hoisted himself to his feet and said indignantly: "I think that the worst demigod in the state is the *Times-Picayune* itself." Now he said he would entertain a motion to recess. This was agreed to, and McGrath then nominated Brothers as chairman of the house in recess. The members crowded expectantly toward the rostrum.

Brothers rose and announced that the convention of the Unterrified Democrats was in session. He said that its business was to elect a delegation to the national convention pledged to Fisher and Delesdernier and to choose a national committeeman and a national committeewoman. Huey had neglected to give him a list of the delegates, so he had to make one up on the spur of the moment, scribbling the names on an envelope. Calling up a Long member, he told this man that he was chairman of the nominating committee and, handing him the envelope, told him to read his report. Brothers then asked all in favor of the report to say aye. A thunderous silence followed. "Hearing no response, it is so ordered," he cried.

He next proceeded to designate the faction's choices for national committeeman and committeewoman. For the former post he named McGrath, and for the latter the only woman he could think of at the moment who was not opposed to Huey, Dorothy Dix of New Orleans, who conducted a syndicated column for the lovelorn. He asked for a second. Again there was silence. "Hearing none, I declare them nominated," he said. At this point Huey, who was observing the spectacle from the rear of the chamber, exclaimed delightedly: "The sonofabitch is trying to imitate me." To end the convention, Brothers called on Delesdernier to address the delegates. The vice-presidential candidate proclaimed that his principal plank was to bring gin fizz, a drink peculiar to New Orleans, to the attention of the nation.[6]

Huey would send the Brothers delegation to Chicago. He instructed Brothers that the group should demand recognition from the credentials committee and that its spokesman, a member who was a lawyer, should emphasize that it was opposed to the Long

[6] Robert Brothers; New Orleans *Times-Picayune*, June 16 and 17, 1932; New Orleans *States*, June 16 and 17, 1932; Westbrook Pegler, column in New York *World-Telegraph*, August 18, 1935, for McGrath's defense of Huey.

faction and also to the conservative faction. If by mischance the Long delegation was not seated, Huey intended to put forward the Unterrified Democrats as the true representatives of Louisiana. He apparently thought he could pull off this arrangement. Either he was in one of his abnormally elated moods, when his judgment was bad, or, more likely, he still had things to learn about national politics. A stunt that amused Louisianians would seem to people elsewhere merely crude clowning.

Huey and his delegation arrived in Chicago a week before the convention was to convene. He was met at the train station by four members of the Louisiana state police who had gone on ahead of him and who at his request had been made honorary members of the Chicago police office, which entitled them to carry arms. One of them had the mission of shadowing Mrs. Pleasant, who came in with the conservative delegation. He was to leap into action if she decided to take a shot at Huey in a hotel or on the convention floor.[7]

Also on hand to meet the senator were a number of reporters. They hurled questions at him. The little National Farmer-Labor party had recently offered to nominate him for President, but he had declined the honor. Was he then a candidate for the Democratic nomination? the reporters asked. No, he said, he was for Roosevelt all the way. Would he accept the vice-presidential nomination? a reporter queried. The Kingfish turned angrily on the questioner. "Huey Long ain't vice to anybody or anything," he snapped.[8]

Other politicians had also arrived in Chicago early. The managers for the various candidates were there, canvassing the situation, buttonholing leaders who could deliver votes, and planning strategy. Easily the most prominent among them was James A. Farley of New York, who was directing Roosevelt's campaign. Big Jim was particularly anxious that delegations pledged to Roosevelt should vote by the unit rule, which would give their full strength to his man. He had wired the chairman of each delegation asking what procedure it would follow. He was intrigued by Huey's answering wire. "We vote as a unit on everything," the Kingfish said.[9]

[7] Louis A. Jones.

[8] Crowley, in Louisiana *Daily Signal*, June 18, 1932; Baton Rouge *State-Times*, June 18, 1932; Donald R. McCoy: *Angry Voices: Left of Center Politics in the New Deal Era* (Lawrence, Kan., 1958), p. 12; Frank Odom; Carleton Beals: *The Story of Huey P. Long* (Philadelphia, 1935), pp. 238–9.

[9] James A. Farley: *Behind the Ballots* (New York, 1938), p. 112.

Farley invited Huey to attend a strategy meeting of sixty-five Roosevelt leaders on June 24, and had occasion to regret he had done so. The meeting had barely got under way when Huey rose and moved that the Roosevelt forces commit themselves to work for the abolition of the two-thirds rule. Farley was horrified at this unexpected development. For himself, he would have been happy if the rule was discarded. But not all the delegations supporting Roosevelt disliked the rule; those from the South, in fact, prized it because it gave their section a veto over nominations. Moreover, if the Roosevelt people moved to abolish the rule and failed, they would expose their weakness. Farley tried to stall off action, suggesting that Huey's motion lay over, but he made the mistake of allowing discussion of it. Huey asked for permission to second his own motion. Taking off his coat, he delivered a speech that in Farley's words took the hardened politicians present "by storm." At its end they voted enthusiastically to support abolition of the two-thirds rule.

Farley, fearful of possible repercussions, made no effort to push the resolution, and indeed, persuaded the rules committee to drop the issue. The incident caused some of his associates to doubt that the Roosevelt forces should support the seating of the Long delegation, which was led by this wild man. But Farley and other leaders realized that they had no choice but to go for Huey's group. Huey was committed to Roosevelt, and the legal claim of his delegation was undeniably superior to that of the conservative delegation.[1]

In addition to the Louisiana delegations, there were also contesting delegations from Minnesota and the territory of Puerto Rico. In each case, the issue was broadly similar: one group was pledged to Roosevelt and one was opposed to him or uncommitted. Who would decide which of the delegations would be seated? The national committee, controlled by supporters of Al Smith, had issued an edict that a subcommittee appointed by it would pass on the disputes. Huey knew that before such a court his delegation would be rejected. He knew too that the national committee could not arrogate this power to itself. Calmly he declared that he would refuse to appear before any subcommittee. He would present his case only to the full national committee or to the credentials committee. The legal Minnesota and Puerto Rico delegations agreed with him, he said. The national committee hastily backed down. It announced

---

[1] Ibid., pp. 116–17, 124–5; Frank Freidel: *Franklin D. Roosevelt: The Triumph* (New York, 1956), p. 299; Arthur M. Schlesinger, Jr.: *The Crisis of the Old Order, 1919–1933* (New York, 1957), p. 299; Lela Stiles: *The Man Behind Roosevelt* (Cleveland, 1954), p. 171.

that the question of the contesting delegations would be decided by the credentials committee.[2]

Huey faced the coming fight with confidence. He knew that the Roosevelt forces had a majority on the credentials committee, and he believed that if the contest was carried to the floor of the convention, Farley could rally a majority to vote for his delegation. Besides, he was picking up allies by his own efforts. The Tennessee delegation was pledged to vote its full strength for him. He had approached the man who controlled the delegation, Edward Crump, Mister Ed, the boss of Memphis, saying: "I'm Huey Long. I did you a favor once." He reminded Crump that when he was a young traveling salesman headquartered in Memphis, he had mixed in an election brawl in Crump's behalf and for his intervention had been arrested. Crump, a great local politician, remembered the episode and acknowledged the obligation. Using a Memphis expression meaning to support to the last, Mister Ed said: "I'll go to the bridge for you, boy."[3]

The credentials committee heard the Louisiana case first. Former Governor Sanders represented his delegation and delivered what a listener called "a magnolia-and-molasses speech" in the old Southern tradition. Then the spokesman of the Unterrified Democrats, Ferdnand Mouton, appeared. Acting on Huey's instructions, he launched into a rambling, clowning address in which he attacked both "the Kingfish crowd" and "the ex-fish crowd." The committee members were not deceived. They knew he was a front for Huey, and they were angered that he would use the hearing as a forum for buffoonery. Huey himself spoke for his delegation. Although he presented evidence to show that his group had been chosen legally, he devoted most of his remarks to coarse abuse of members of the Sanders faction, who, he said, had been handpicked by a "bossed" convention. Some of the Roosevelt members on the committee were disgusted at his exhibition, but they voted with their majority to recommend that his delegation be seated. The majority voted to recommend also that the Roosevelt delegations from Minnesota and Puerto Rico be seated. The anti-Roosevelt members promptly filed a minority report advocating the seating of the Sanders group and the protestors from Minnesota and Puerto Rico.

[2] Long: *Every Man a King*, pp. 307–11; New Orleans *Times-Picayune*, June 23, 1932; New Orleans *States*, June 23, 1932.
[3] Manuscript reminiscence of Marvin Pope, Crump's secretary, copy furnished to me by Professor William D. Miller, Crump's biographer; Allan Michie and Frank Phylick: *Dixie Demagogues* (New York, 1939), pp. 251–2.

Now the fight would go to the floor of the convention. There, according to rumor, the case for the Sanders delegation would be championed by, among others, John W. Davis, who had been the party's presidential candidate in 1924 and was now for Smith and who was possibly the most distinguished constitutional lawyer in the country. The Roosevelt leaders were worried. The Louisiana case was the key to all the disputed delegations: the way it was decided would decide the other cases also. If Huey spoke for his delegation and acted as he had before the credentials committee, he would repel the mass of delegates and cause his defeat, and deal the Roosevelt cause irreparable damage. Senate friends of Huey's and lieutenants of Roosevelt came to the Kingfish and begged him not to clown or engage in vituperation when he presented his case. The proceedings of the convention were to be broadcast by radio, and he would be addressing the whole country. Huey grinned and answered that he knew what he had to do.[4]

The atmosphere in the convention hall was strained as the debate on the Louisiana contest began, and it became tenser as the argument continued. The galleries were packed with Smith supporters who howled approval of those who spoke against the Long delegation and disapproval of those who spoke for it. The delegates themselves were in a restive and noisy mood and continually interrupted the speakers. None of the speakers was able to command full attention. When Huey, clad in a white suit, finally came to the rostrum, a round of booing broke out. Leaning toward the microphone, he cried: "Don't applaud me! Don't applaud me! My time is limited, and I don't want applause!" He knew that they were booing him, but he shrewdly guessed that radio listeners in Louisiana, hearing the noise, would take his word that they were applauding him.[5]

Then he began to talk, and slowly the delegates and the galleries quieted and listened. This was not the Huey Long they had expected to ridicule—the clown, the Southern demagogue. This was a lawyer talking about law—logically, calmly, almost coldly. This Huey Long did not have to fear comparison even with John W. Davis. He had on a table behind him a pile of lawbooks that he had had sent up from Louisiana, and frequently he would pause and

[4] Baton Rouge *State-Times*, June 25, 26, and 27, 1932; Wheeler: *Yankee from the West*, pp. 285–6; Edward J. Flynn: *You're the Boss* (New York, 1947), pp. 95–6; Arthur F. Mullen: *Western Democrat* (New York, 1940), p. 264; Alben W. Barkley: *That Reminds Me* (New York, 1954), p. 160; Freidel: *Roosevelt: The Triumph*, pp. 301–2.

[5] Wheeler: *Yankee from the West*, p. 286.

ask an assistant to hand him one of the books. He would open it, obviously to a marked page, and without reading would quote from it, sometimes several paragraphs. He explained carefully the Louisiana law governing the method of selecting delegates, emphasizing that it permitted but did not require that they be chosen by a convention. His delegation had been designated by a method that was completely legal, he insisted. Moreover, it was a delegation that represented the *living* Democratic party of Louisiana. "Who is our delegation?" he cried. He answered the question impressively: "The eight Congressmen, the two United States Senators, the governor and the retiring governor [this was Alvin King], and the mayor of New Orleans." Was the convention going to refuse to admit these men? he demanded. He had the audience with him now, and he was cheered when he made a point and applauded roundly when he finished.[6]

The convention then proceeded to vote on the reports of the credentials committee, the majority motion favoring the Long delegation and the minority resolution recommending the Sanders delegation. The vote was 638 to 514 to seat Huey's group. By a larger vote the convention admitted the Roosevelt delegations from Minnesota and Puerto Rico. The Roosevelt leaders breathed easier. A dangerous crisis for their candidate had been averted. They could claim some credit for the victory, saying that their forces had contributed the needed votes. But Huey could also claim a share of the victory. He could have ruined the Roosevelt cause, but, instead, he had saved it and in the process had achieved a great personal triumph. Will Rogers, whose humorous but shrewd comments captivated millions of newspaper readers, summed up the feelings of most people at the convention: "By golly, he made a good speech today. He won his own game." Huey probably appreciated more the comment of another observer. Clarence Darrow, Chicago's famed criminal lawyer, went up to Huey at the conclusion of the speech and said it was one of the greatest summaries of fact and evidence he had ever heard.[7]

Huey was something of a convention hero after his speech, and the Roosevelt leaders treated him with new respect. He obviously had some kind of ability, although they were not sure exactly what

---

[6] Chicago *Tribune*, June 29, 1932; Arthur Brisbane, Claude G. Bowers, columns in Chicago *American*, June 29, 1932; Leander H. Perez; Paul Maloney; John Dyer; Robert Brothers.

[7] Rogers, columns in Chicago *American*, June 29 and 30, 1932; Robert Brothers; Frank Odom.

it was, and influence in some quarters, in those strange Southern states with their peculiar politics; and he could be used, if he was kept under tight rein. They found that they had need to use him at a critical moment in the balloting for the nomination. Roosevelt took an early lead and held it for three roll calls. But he was far short of the two-thirds majority he had to have, and his total did not advance appreciably. The coalition of candidates against him showed no indication that it would crumble. Instead, on the third ballot, which was held during an all-night session, it was the Roosevelt forces that seemed about to disintegrate. The dismaying news came to Farley's headquarters that Arkansas and Mississippi, which had been voting for Roosevelt under the unit rule, were threatening to break away, that on this ballot or the next one they would scatter their votes, giving some to Garner and some to favorite-son candidates. Arkansas was especially crucial, because it voted so early in the roll call. If this Roosevelt delegation wavered, a stampede away from the New Yorker might well start. The Roosevelt leaders, in desperation, turned to Huey. They begged him to hold the two restive delegations in line.

He grabbed at the assignment. He stormed out on the floor and into the midst of the Mississippi delegation. He shook his fist in the face of Senator Pat Harrison, who was an arrant conservative and cool to Roosevelt, and shouted: "If you break the unit rule, you sonofabitch, I'll go into Mississippi and break you." When he went into the Arkansas delegation, he threatened Joe Robinson with the same fate. All during that night session, his face dripping with sweat and his pongee suit wilting about him, he dashed back and forth between the two delegations and also used his persuasive powers on other Southern delegations that showed evidence of weakening. Arkansas and Mississippi remained in line on the third ballot and also on the fourth, when Garner swung his strength to Roosevelt, receiving as compensation the vice-presidential nomination. It was over at last. But it was the third ballot that had been the crucial test. If the Kingfish had not held the Southern states for Roosevelt, the result could well have been different, as a few Roosevelt leaders were ready to concede.[8]

[8] Flynn: *You're the Boss*, pp. 100–1; Wheeler: *Yankee from the West*, pp. 286–7; Thomas L. Stokes: *Chip Off My Shoulder* (Princeton, 1940), pp. 321–2; Long, quoted in *American Progress*, February 1 and April 1935; Murphy Roden; Freidel: *Roosevelt: The Triumph*, p. 306; Schlesinger: *Crisis of the Old Order*, p. 307; Arthur Mullen, Roosevelt leader, quoted in New Orleans *Item-Tribune*, July 17, 1932. Flynn, in quoting Huey's threat to Harrison, used a blank to indicate an expletive.

Huey did not claim that he had nominated Roosevelt. But he did insist that he had had an important part in bringing about the nomination, and he was proud of it and satisfied that he had supported the right man. The candidate was a progressive, and if elected he would influence the party to follow a progressive line and take the advice of wild men like Huey Long. Huey was going to do what he could to elect Roosevelt, but first he had to turn his attention to campaigns nearer to home.

# CHAPTER 21

# *A Circus Hitched to a Tornado*

LATE ONE NIGHT IN JULY 1932, the telephone rang in the New Orleans home of Joe David, the printer. When David answered, Huey's excited voice volleyed from the receiver: Hurry up and get your crew together and meet me at the shop. "Huey," David said wearily, "what election are we going to print tonight? There is no election on." "We're going to invade Arkansas," Huey bellowed. "I want you to do some printing for me for Hattie Caraway." David made the arrangements, agreeable enough but puzzled. As he waited for Huey to arrive with the copy, he wondered just who Hattie Caraway was.[1]

Hattie Caraway was the junior United States senator from Arkansas and the first woman ever elected to the Senate. She had won her seat in the aftermath of an odd political situation. Her husband was Senator Thaddeus Caraway, a colorful but not particularly able man, who had died suddenly in November 1931 with more than a year of his term still to serve. In the view of the ruling Arkansas politicians, he had timed his death inconveniently: he had not taken account of the state law regulating senatorial tenure. That law stipulated that if an incumbent died with a certain part of his term still to serve, the governor could fill the place by appointment. But if he died before the time fixed in law, his successor had to be chosen in an election. If Caraway had died three days later than he did, the governor could have appointed a replacement and, as a gracious gesture, would probably have named the late senator's widow. But

[1] Joseph B. David.

now an election was obligatory, and gracious gestures were impractical. The leading politicians of the state cast covetous eyes on the
seat, but they could not agree as to which of them should inherit it.
Their ambitions threatened to embroil the state in a bitter struggle.

After some preliminary maneuvering they decided that the prize
was not worth a fight, since the winner would hold the seat for only
a short time. The decision might as well be put off until the regular
election of 1932. By then they might be able to compose their
differences and agree on a successor, or one of them might develop
such strength that he could not be denied. But in the meantime the
seat had to be warmed by someone. Let the empty distinction go to
Mrs. Caraway. The state central committee could easily declare her
to be the Democratic nominee, and in Arkansas this was tantamount
to election. And so it had been done. Mrs. Caraway had become a
senator without having to lift a finger in her own behalf, without
having to make a single speech in her campaign. She would, of
course, the politicians thought, understand why she had been chosen
and at the expiration of her term gracefully retire.[2]

Hattie Caraway was one of the most inconspicuous members of
the Senate. A mousy little woman, she sat quietly at her desk and
made no long speeches and few short remarks. She was sitting there
when the new young senator from Louisiana was sworn in in January 1932, and was assigned a seat next to her. She got up and shook
hands with him and, as she said later, "treated him like a human
being in the general to-do about him." Huey at first paid her little
attention. But soon he began to notice the way she voted. To his
surprise, she supported most of the measures sponsored by progressive members. But what really impressed him was that she dared to
stand with the small group that voted for his bill to limit incomes to
one million dollars a year. This apparently drab woman had courage
and vision. She was a very different kind of senator from her colleague, Joe Robinson, and from most of the other Southern Democrats. He cultivated Mrs. Caraway and became her friend and
adviser.[3]

Back in Arkansas the political leaders scarcely noticed Mrs.
Caraway's voting record. It could not possibly matter. Such issues as

[2] Hermann B. Deutsch: "Hattie and Huey," *Saturday Evening Post*, CC (October 15, 1932), 6–7, 88–90, 92. Mr. Deutsch accompanied Hattie and Huey in the
1932 campaign, and his article is the fullest extant description of it. My account is
based on his article unless otherwise indicated.

[3] Clipping, September 10, 1932, in Persac Scrapbook, interview with Mrs.
Caraway.

the concentration of wealth and the schedules of income taxes could not possibly matter to Arkansas. Besides, a politician did not rise because he took a stand on issues, but because in an election he had the right people behind him (local leaders who could turn out votes and rich supporters who could supply him with campaign funds) and because he knew what to say in a campaign—recall the past, the "wah" of the 1860's and the grasping Yankees who ever since it had oppressed the South, and perhaps allude to the ever-present "nigger" menace. That was what the voters wanted to hear, not unfamiliar discussions of economic questions. That was the way the leaders were planning to campaign in 1932, when Mrs. Caraway's term expired and one of them would succeed to her seat.

They still had not been able to agree as to which of their number should be the successor, and in the summer, as the time for campaigning approached, six candidates announced for the office and began to line up support. Four of them were among the most prominent men in the state—a former governor, a former national commander of the American Legion, a justice of the supreme court who had also served a term in the Senate, and the present Democratic national committeeman. It would be a battle of giants, political observers predicted gleefully.

The observers almost ignored an unexpected development: Mrs. Caraway also filed her name. They sneered at her chances. She had no organization and no rich backers. Besides, she was a woman, and Southerners did not like women to enter politics, although it was acceptable for one to succeed briefly to her late husband's place. The observers predicted that Mrs. Caraway would finish a poor last, that out of a total vote of 250,000 she would be lucky to get 3,000 votes, from dedicated feminists and devoted followers of her husband.

And, as if determined to add to her other handicaps, she had come into the campaign late. Here it was mid-July; the other candidates had been speaking for weeks, and she had barely started and made few speeches when she did. But, the pundits speculated, she probably would not undertake a serious campaign, and, indeed, could not, since she had no powerful or eloquent friends who would organize and finance her campaign or appear with her and speak for her.

But then, as July waned, it was announced that Mrs. Caraway would campaign. Arkansans were surprised, partly at the news, more so at the way the announcement was issued. Although it mentioned that Mrs. Caraway was the candidate, it gave far more emphasis to another personality who was about to enter the campaign. Huey Long was coming to Arkansas to stump for his friend Hattie, and the announcement was made, not in Arkansas, but in Louisiana. Huey would open at Magnolia, in the southern part of the state, on August 1, a Monday, and would speak every day that week.

Arkansas politicians greeted the announcement with disdain. But they could not repress snickers at Huey's speaking schedule. The election fell on August 9. What did this Kingfish fellow think that he could accomplish in six days for the weakest candidate in the race?[4]

Huey's decision to support Mrs. Caraway had been taken suddenly. When he learned that she was thinking of entering the race, he had advised against it. "You haven't a chance to win," he said. She agreed but said she would go down fighting. On the morning after this conference Huey came to her office. "Mrs. Caraway," he said, "I'm going to come into your campaign." She expressed gratification but said that he must not use the campaign as an excuse to jump on Robinson. He said that he wouldn't. Then he told her to give him a statement that she had been attending to her duties in the Senate but that now she was going back to Arkansas to look after her own affairs. He would read the statement in the Senate and make a speech extolling her record. Later he would join her in Arkansas and enter her campaign.[5]

He read her statement the next day and recounted her votes on important measures. Mrs. Caraway had consistently voted on the side of the common people, he cried. "We have had in this body entirely too much representation from some of the Southern states that has not been in accord with the will and the varied interests of the people," he said, looking at Joe Robinson. Still looking at Robinson, he said that senators who called themselves progressives ought to help this little woman in her hour of need.[6]

He always called Mrs. Caraway "the little woman" when he talked about her plight. This led some of his friends to believe that Huey had decided to support her because he felt sorry for her. He had a sentimental and chivalric streak, they believed, and Mrs. Caraway had touched it. They were partly right. He was sentimental or, rather, thought he was, which was almost the same thing, be-

[4] Baton Rouge *State-Times*, July 15, 1932; New Orleans *Morning Tribune*, July 18; New Orleans *Item*, July 20, 1932.

[5] Clipping, September 10, 1932, in Persac Scrapbook.

[6] *Congressional Record*, 72 Cong., 1 Sess., p. 15192, speech of July 13, 1932.

cause conceiving of himself as being so he occasionally did impulsive, generous things. There were times when he may have honestly believed that he had gone to Mrs. Caraway's aid because she was a woman in distress, but usually he admitted his real motive. When he went back to Louisiana to inform his leaders that he was going to support her, he had to fight down objections from some of them. He was taking on a hopeless task, they said. He brushed their arguments aside. "I can elect her," he said, "and it will help my prestige." He was moving with his customary calculation. If he could elect Mrs. Caraway, he would take a long step on the road that he had marked out for himself; he would demonstrate that the influence of Huey Long was not confined to Louisiana but that it could be extended to other Southern states and possibly even to other parts of the country. And as part of the triumph he would give a big scare to Joe Robinson.[7]

Before daybreak on the morning of August 1 a motor caravan left Shreveport, headed for the Arkansas line. Leading it was a big black car in which sat Huey, with a bodyguard from the state police.[8]

Behind the car lumbered seven trucks. Two of them were sound trucks, improved models of the type Huey had used in his senatorial campaign two years earlier. Each was equipped with four amplifier horns, two projecting on either side. The interior of each was equipped with loudspeaker panels, an attachment for playing phonograph records, and folding chairs, a folding table, and a pitcher and glasses. The roof of each was slatted and could be easily reached from a portable stairway. Thus if no platform was available in a town, the table, the chairs, and the pitcher and glasses could be carried to the roof, and Huey could ascend to a serviceable platform. He had a reason for bringing two sound trucks. On this whirlwind tour he was going to speak five or six times a day in as many towns. While he was speaking from one truck in one town, the second vehicle would speed to the next town where he was scheduled to speak. There its attendants would play music and attract and hold a crowd until he arrived.

Of the other trucks, a small one also preceded Huey into a town. Its crew picked out a site for the meeting, distributed handbills, and helped the crew of the sound truck wire into the town's electric system or, if this was impractical, to start the batteries in the sound

[7] Harvey Peltier; Seymour Weiss.

[8] Baton Rouge *State-Times*, August 1, 1932; Shreveport *Journal*, August 1, 1932; New Orleans *Morning Tribune*, August 2, 1932; Murphy Roden; Louis A. Jones; Theophile Landry.

truck. The four remaining trucks were loaded with an estimated two tons of literature—posters and handbills but predominantly circulars: reprints of Huey's speech eulogizing Mrs. Caraway, his speech "The Doom of America's Dream," and others. The Arkansans who read these documents were going to learn much more about Huey than they did about Hattie.

As the cavalcade rolled into Arkansas and toward Magnolia, people came out of every farmhouse and stood at the side of the road, and people lined the streets of every village. They did not only stand and look in curiosity—they also waved and cheered and cried encouragement. An amazed reporter wrote that the procession became a continuous reception. Huey arrived at Magnolia at nine o'clock. The dusty square was jammed with people, most of them farmers who had driven into town and who had been standing patiently for hours. They had heard that this man who was to address them had a plan to help the people, and they were here to hear him explain it.[9]

When Huey rose to speak, he held a Bible in his hands. "We're all here to pull a lot of potbellied politicians off a little woman's neck," he began. Then he launched into his speech. He would give the same speech over and over that week. Many of those who came to hear him at other towns must have already read long excerpts from it in the newspapers. But still they came to hear him say it in person. It struck a new theme in Arkansas and Southern politics. The theme was stated in one paragraph:

"We have more food in this country . . . than we could eat up in two years if we never plowed another furrow or fattened another shote—and yet people are hungry and starving. We have more cotton and wool and leather than we could wear out in two years if we never raised another boll of cotton, sheared another sheep, or tanned another hide—and yet people are ragged and naked. We have more houses than ever before in this country's history and more of them are unoccupied than ever before—and yet people are homeless."

Why was the country in such a condition? Because wealth had become concentrated. Why, 540 men on Wall Street made every year a million dollars, more than all the farmers in the country combined. "And you people wonder why your belly's flat up against your backbone!" Furthermore, these men on Wall Street controlled

[9] New Orleans *Item*, August 1 and 2, 1932.

the Congress of the United States, told it what laws to pass and not to pass. They exercised their control through the Democratic and the Republican leaders in both houses. They were like men running a restaurant. "They've got a set of Republican waiters on one side and a set of Democratic waiters on the other side, but no matter which set of waiters brings you the dish, the legislative grub is all prepared in the same Wall Street kitchen." (Huey was keeping his promise to Mrs. Caraway not to attack Robinson by name, but his reference was unmistakable.)

Could anything be done to save the country from its perilous condition? Yes, one simple action would restore prosperity. Huey held up his Bible. It's all in here, he proclaimed. The Lord had pointed the way: a country had to redistribute its wealth to the people every fifty years. "The trouble is," he said, "we've got too many men running things in this country that think they're smarter than the Lord."

He recounted his efforts to have the Lord's law enacted by Congress. He had proposed to limit incomes to a million dollars a year, "one measly, lousy, slivery million dollars." "Why," he exclaimed, "it was awful! That meant that if one of those birds stepped under an electric fan in the summertime to cool off, he wouldn't be getting but about four dollars a minute while he was doing it. That meant that if he went to bathe and shave, he wouldn't be but about five hundred dollars richer by the time he got his clothes back on."

Who had supported him in his efforts? Only a small number of senators, but that number would grow as the issue became clearer. One senator, however, had given him consistent support—Mrs. Caraway. That "brave little woman" had defied the big men of Wall Street, had stood by the people, and now the "big men politicians" of her own state had "their feet on her neck." They would take them off before he left Arkansas, he vowed.[1]

That first crowd, in Magnolia, had followed the speech with rapt attention, laughing at his commiseration with the rich man who had to live on a million dollars a year, cheering at his praise of Mrs. Caraway, and roaring full-throated approval of his demand that wealth be redistributed. A Magnolia politician who observed the reactions decided that he should warn the state's rulers of this new and dangerous force in the campaign. He sent a telegram to a

[1] My reproduction of this speech combines material from Mr. Deutsch's article and accounts in the New Orleans *Item*, August 1 and 2, 1932.

friend in Little Rock, the capital: "A cyclone just went through here and is headed your way. Very few trees left standing and even these are badly scarred up."

As soon as he could get away from the crowd, Huey headed for El Dorado, forty miles away, where his second sound truck had set up operations and where he was scheduled to speak at eleven o'clock. On leaving El Dorado, he sped thirty-one miles to Camden, where he spoke at two-thirty. Then he dashed twenty-nine miles to Fordyce and addressed a meeting at four-thirty, and finally drove to Pine Bluff, where he spoke to a night rally at eight o'clock.[2] He had made five speeches in one day and through his sound truck had reached thousands of people. He would maintain this schedule for five more days. Mrs. Caraway had been apprehensive when he had said that he would come into Arkansas for such a short time. He had tried to reassure her. "We can make that campaign in one week," he said. "That's all we need." Now she understood why he had been so confident.

She was beginning to be confident herself, even to think she could help the campaign. She had spoken briefly at Huey's first meetings, but her remarks were awkward and had not been well received. She improved rapidly, however, and was soon drawing applause. Huey, amused but pleased at the change in her, told her she had learned to speak by studying his techniques.

She was being educated politically, and so were many other Arkansans. As Huey roared across the state, observers exclaimed at the efficiency and organization that marked every aspect of his campaign—at the almost military precision with which the caravan moved from town to town, at the clocklike regularity with which the meetings opened, and at the amplifiers which enabled him to reach the farthest limits of the audience.

The observers noticed too the men who assisted him at meetings. They were young men, state policemen out of uniform or other officeholders, chosen by Huey to accompany him on campaigns. He had trained them to meet any emergency.[3] They displayed their varied skills now. Sometimes when Huey was speaking, an infant's wail would be heard in the crowd. Huey would stop and motion with a finger. One of his men instantly appeared below the platform. Huey would hand him a glass of water, and the man would dash into the

[2] Murphy Roden, the driver of Huey's car, stated that he customarily drove at seventy to eighty miles an hour on roads that were mostly gravel. In one week he blew six sets of tires.

[3] Theophile Landry; Louis A. Jones.

crowd, take the baby out of its mother's lap, give it a drink of water, and hand it back. If the child continued to cry, he would reach into his pocket and hand it a piece of candy or an "all-day sucker." While this little act was going on, Huey would lecture the audience on child care. "Ninety-nine times out of a hundred, when a baby cries, it's only thirsty and if you give it a drink of water it goes right back to sleep," he would pontificate. "That's a good thing to know when you're not so fixed that you can hire nurses to take care of your children like the rich people do."

Arksansans had never seen a campaign like it. It was like "a circus hitched to a tornado," one bewildered observer said. The crowds grew larger every day, and candidates for lesser offices began to follow Huey's caravan so that they could distribute their literature to his audiences.[4] At Little Rock a crowd estimated between twenty-five thousand and thirty-five thousand persons turned out, the largest meeting of any kind that had ever been held in the state. Mrs. Caraway's opponents, the "big men politicians," observed the continuing triumph with helpless rage. One of them finally recovered sufficiently to charge that Huey had no business interfering in the politics of Arkansas. The Kingfish barely deigned to notice the criticism. "I heard where one of Mrs. Caraway's opponents is hollering already," he said. "I ain't going to call his name because I wouldn't give him that much advertising in this big a crowd; and besides my parents taught me not to speak ill of the dead, even if they're only politically dead."

Huey wound up his campaign on Saturday at Texarkana. He had intended to drive back to Shreveport that night. But before he could leave, a delegation from the eastern counties along the Mississippi River, which had not been included in his itinerary, waited on him. These men informed him that their people were demanding to hear the speech that had Arkansas ablaze. They asked him if he would remain in the state over the weekend and on Monday, the day before the election, speak in their area. Huey readily agreed to their request. He drove to Little Rock and went to a hotel to rest.

There the reporters covering the campaign sought him out to ask about his revised schedule. One of them, observing that the next day was Sunday, inquired where the senator would attend church. Huey seemed amazed at the question. "Me go to church?" he said. "Why I haven't been to a church in so many years I don't know when." "But you're always quoting the Bible . . . ," the puzzled reporter

4 New Orleans *Item*, August 3, 1932.

began. Huey snapped him off. "Bible's the greatest book ever written," he said, "but I sure don't need anybody I can buy for six bits and a chew of tobacco to explain it to me. When I need preachers I buy 'em cheap."[5]

On Monday Huey swept through the river counties, speaking to large audiences in six towns. On that day he could look back on his tour with justifiable pride. In seven days of campaigning he had delivered thirty-nine speeches, traveled twenty-one hundred miles, and addressed approximately two hundred thousand persons. No other American politician had ever waged such a campaign.[6]

He was exhausted at the conclusion of his last speech on Monday and did not want to endure the rigors of a return to Louisiana by automobile. One of his guards drove him to Memphis and put him on a train to New Orleans, and it was in New Orleans that he heard the result of the Arkansas election the next night. The outcome was evident from the earliest returns—it was going to be a Caraway landslide. Mrs. Caraway carried sixty-one of the seventy-five counties in the state, and her popular vote equalled the total vote of her six opponents. She was the first woman to be elected to a full six-year term in the Senate.[7]

It was immediately conceded that Hattie Caraway had been elected by Huey Long. He had accomplished a miracle: he had taken up a candidate who didn't have a chance and had somehow put her over. He had influence that nobody had dreamed of and was a man to be respected and even feared, for he might even repeat his feat in some Northern states, those where the effect of the depression had struck hard. Suddenly Huey was not a comic demagogue but a leader who represented a strange force that might be the way of the future.

So it seemed, and so it partially was. Huey had achieved a stunning success in Arkansas, but not quite a miracle. If he had not entered the campaign, Mrs. Caraway would not have been elected, but she would have run better than the observers predicted. She had a bedrock support that a progressive candidate in some other Southern states would not have had. But then Arkansas was not a typically Southern state. It had a predominantly small-farmer econ-

[5] Hermann B. Deutsch: *The Huey Long Murder Case* (New York, 1963), pp. 24–5.

[6] New Orleans *Times-Picayune*, August 11, 1932.

[7] Murphy Roden; Louis A. Jones; Stuart Towns: "A Louisiana Medicine Show: The Kingfish Elects an Arkansas Senator," *Arkansas Historical Quarterly*, XXV (1946), 117–27.

omy, and its farmers, pinched hard by the depression, were in a restive mood. They remembered that Thad Caraway had been at least a vocal champion of farm interests, and they knew that his widow had supported farm-relief measures in the Senate. Many of them would have voted for Mrs. Caraway in any case, which would have put her, probably, around the midpoint or even above it in the final standing of the candidates. What Huey had done—and it was a considerable feat—was to arouse into a full fury this resentment vaguely felt by the farmers, to weld it, really, into a genuine class protest. The task was made easier for him because there was no one strong, organized faction to oppose him; the petty Arkansas chiefs had no chance against the Long efficiency, and they fell almost without a struggle. It did not follow that Huey could carry the day so easily in other Southern states.[8]

HUEY HAD ASSURED HIS Arkansas audiences that senatorial support for his proposal to limit incomes was increasing. Recently Oklahoma and Missouri had elected senators who favored redistributing wealth, and in September a new senator from Louisiana would replace Edwin Broussard, adding another vote to the bloc that stood for the people. "Broussard's been one of Wall Street's own," Huey roared. "Watch us clean that bird's plow for him next month." He returned from Arkansas and plunged almost immediately into the Louisiana senatorial campaign.[9]

Shortly before he left for Arkansas, he had selected the candidate his organization would run against Broussard—John H. Overton. Some of his leaders suggested that he should remain at home and help in this campaign. Huey answered that he had promised to help Mrs. Caraway, but that he would be back in time to elect Overton. He had pledged to reward this faithful follower with an office, and he would fulfill his pledge.[1]

Overton had been pressing for a reward since 1928, and after he came to Huey's aid during the impeachment, he became much more importunate. Huey appreciated his services and liked Overton personally. Moreover, the Kingfish regarded Overton as a valuable po-

[8] Mrs. Caraway carried twenty-nine of the thirty-one counties in which she and Huey campaigned. But she took thirty-two of the forty-four in which they did not campaign. In this latter group she was undoubtedly helped by Huey's well-publicized support, but she obviously had her own following.
[9] Hermann B. Deutsch: "Huey Long—the Last Phase," *Saturday Evening Post*, CCVIII (October 12, 1935), 87.
[1] *Overton Hearing*, II, 1192–3.

litical asset: he was the aristocrat who gave a certain tone to the Long movement. Huey's problem was to find an office important enough to gratify Overton's ambitions but not too taxing for his somewhat limited talents. "Overton knows less about politics and more about law and government than any other man I ever knew," Huey once said. He recognized that Overton would be happy only in an office that would give scope for oratory.[2]

Such an office had become available in 1931. In that year the incumbent Congressman in Overton's district died suddenly, and when Overton expressed a desire to fill the unexpired term, Huey supported him. Overton won, but he was not satisfied being a mere Congressman. He demanded immediately of Huey that he be named the Long candidate for governor, the recognition that eventually went to O. K. Allen. Huey bluntly refused him and told him why. "If you ever take this governor's office you will die in one year; you will worry yourself to death," Huey said. "You will imagine somebody is going to accuse you of something—one newspaper article and you will think the Tower of Babel is going to fall on you, and I have just decided to tell you, you aren't the man to go in there." But, Huey continued, several people had suggested to him (he had probably told them to do so) that Overton should run for the Senate in 1932, and he was willing to support Overton for this office. Overton jumped at the offer.[3]

Huey set up an organization to operate Overton's campaign just before he left for Arkansas. At his "suggestion" the Louisiana Democratic Association named as Overton's managers Harvey Peltier and Allen Ellender, who had acted in the same capacity for the Kingfish in 1930. Overton was not present at the meeting at which they were chosen and, indeed, was not asked if they were satisfactory to him. He was asked later if he had been consulted in any way in the selection of his managers. "I was consulted in this way," he explained. "I was advised that they had been selected." Neither was he consulted about any other aspect of his organization. "The man who knew the least about the campaign was Overton," recalled a Long leader who knew a great deal about it.[4]

This leader was Seymour Weiss, designated by Huey to handle the financing of the campaign. Weiss had at his disposal ample money—some of it exacted by himself or Huey from individuals or

[2] Robert Brothers; Louis A. Jones; *Overton Hearing*, II, 2331.
[3] *Overton Hearing*, II, 812, 1189; Robert Brothers.
[4] *Overton Hearing*, I, 91; Seymour Weiss.

companies that saw a reason to contribute, some of it deducted from the salaries of state employees. All of it was paid in cash and was delivered to Weiss at the Roosevelt Hotel and placed by him in his private safe. "I didn't have any bank accounts," he said frankly. He was equally candid about disbursements. "I paid cash for everything," he said. "I didn't draw any checks." If a local Long candidate or worker needed money, he went to the Roosevelt and asked Weiss for a specified sum. If the request seemed reasonable, Weiss handed over the money in an envelope. "Nobody had any idea what the campaign cost," Weiss stated, insisting that he was not certain himself.[5]

Huey needed a large fund in this campaign, for he was actually waging several other campaigns as a part of this one. In addition to running Overton against Broussard, he was supporting a candidate for the Public Service Commission against Dudley LeBlanc— Wade O. Martin—and he desperately wanted to win this contest, for Martin's election would give the Long forces a majority on the Commission. He was also backing seven of the eight incumbent congressmen, and some of these men faced strong opposition. He had to give Martin and his other candidates money to conduct their campaigns locally—Martin received probably twelve thousand dollars—and he also assisted them directly from his central campaign headquarters. Thus he issued a deluge of circulars, most of them urging the election of Overton but some of them calling for the election of the lesser candidates. At least 1,400,000 circulars are known to have been distributed, and the number was probably much larger.

Their distribution was placed in the hands of Louie Jones, who was now assistant superintendent of the highway patrol, and Jones carried out the assignment with the same brisk efficiency he had demonstrated in physical encounters. He transported the documents from town to town in trucks and cars belonging to the Highway Commission and commandeered employees of the commission as drivers. To meet his expenses—for gas, oil, replaced tires—he drew cash from Weiss. He scrupulously kept a record of his expenditures, but, like Weiss, he had unconventional notions of bookkeeping. Sometimes when he had to employ young local boys to hand out circulars in a town, he charged their pay as "repairs" on the trucks.[6]

[5] Seymour Weiss; *Overton Hearing*, II, 1494, 1506, 2115–16.
[6] *Overton Hearing*, I, 174, 179; II, 1495–6, 2632–3, 2637–8; Louis A. Jones.

Huey also needed money to pay the filing fees for the numerous dummy candidates he entered in this election. He had used dummies before, but never on such a large scale. Long-sponsored candidates for minor offices literally sprouted out of the ground in the French parishes in which Broussard and LeBlanc were strong. The anti-Long forces raged hopelessly: they knew they did not have the money or the organization to enter a corresponding number of dummies. But they did attempt to fight back by resorting to court action. Judge Benjamin F. Pavy, whose jurisdiction included his native St. Landry and adjoining Evangeline parish, enjoined the Democratic committee in each parish from certifying the names of the commissioners submitted by the dummies. (Whatever reason the powerful Pavy family had had to ally with Huey had now disappeared.) The antis hardly had time to savor his order when Attorney General Gaston Porterie instructed the committees to certify the names anyway. The Evangeline committee did so, whereupon Pavy committed five of them to jail for disobeying his injunction. But they did not go, since Governor Allen issued telegraphic reprieves suspending their sentences until after the election. A conservative attempt to have the state supreme court rule on the use of dummies failed when the high tribunal held by a vote of four to three that it had no authority to interfere with the actions of parish committees.[7]

Huey had an obvious reason for entering numerous dummies in these southern country parishes: the election was expected to be close in them, and he wanted Long commissioners on hand to watch over his interests. But he also filed a large number of dummy candidates in New Orleans, ostensibly to protect Overton's interest—so many that Overton ended with 1,119 commissioners in the city to only 61 for Broussard. Why he did this is not clear. It was conceded even by the bitterest anti-Longites that Overton would sweep New Orleans. The Old Regulars had endorsed him after some hesitation—Walmsley had dallied with the idea of running himself—and the combined power of the Ring and Huey's organization was unbeatable. Moreover, Huey had no local candidates who faced serious opposition. It has been suggested that he entered the dummies to guarantee a large vote to Overton, but this explanation does not make sense. It is much more probable that he was trying to build up his city organization for the day when he would

[7] Hermann B. Deutsch: "Kingdom of the Kingfish," in New Orleans *Item*, August 29, 1939;· *Overton Hearing*, I, 17–20, 29–31.

break with the Old Regulars and would have to rely on his own forces during an election.[8]

The campaign had started while Huey was in Arkansas. He rested a few days and then joined Overton's party in the northern part of the state. Traveling with Overton were Governor Allen, Lieutenant Governor Fournet, and other, lesser dignitaries. Overton had been delivering the main address at each rally, regaling the crowd with his old-fashioned oratory, and Allen had followed with a shorter speech. Huey altered their procedure drastically.

He presided at every meeting and introduced Overton and Allen. They would, he said, speak briefly: he usually allotted the candidate ten minutes and the governor five minutes. Cutting them off on schedule, he then arose and talked himself for as long as he wished. But he did not always allow the other two to have their full time, interrupting them to criticize their delivery or to suggest themes to discuss. At one meeting Overton was hoarse and began by asking the audience to bear with him. He had laryngitis, he explained. Huey, sitting behind him, kicked him. "Laryngitis, hell," the Kingfish shouted, "you got a sore throat." He later rebuked Overton for having committed an indiscretion. "What do you mean, giving a sore throat such a fancy name?" he asked. "They might think it's something catching. You could lose the election."[9]

Huey drove himself hard after joining the campaign, because with the election falling on September 13, he had but a short time in which to reach the voters. Nor could he reach as many of them as he had hoped to or as easily. His sound trucks needed repairs after the Arkansas trip and were not available when he started to campaign. After making thirteen speeches in three days, he had to confess to reporters that his own throat was sore. But, he said, cheerfully, "I usually stay hoarse until I make about twenty-five speeches and after that it clears up."[1]

In his speeches he discussed but one issue—the plight the country was in because its wealth was concentrated. And he made but one appeal to his audiences: elect Overton and give us this additional vote that we need in the Senate to bring about the decentralization of wealth. He was projecting an important national issue into the campaign, but he evoked no response from Broussard and other conservatives. In an ironic turnabout, the conservatives,

[8] *Overton Hearing,* II, 1957, 1973.
[9] Robert Brothers; *Overton Hearing,* I, 796.
[1] New Orleans *Times-Picayune,* August 23, 1932.

who in 1930 had criticized Huey for ignoring national issues, now
ignored them themselves. They discussed only state problems, and
these they resolved into one overriding issue: Huey Long and his
power. Huey Long had, it appeared, placed all three branches of
the state government under his control, had, in the words of one
conservative orator, enfolded in his "slimy clutches" even the supreme court. Huey hardly deigned to reply to these attacks. He
could afford to be magnanimous because he was practically certain
that Overton and his other candidates would be elected. Nothing
could prevent a Long sweep unless an incident embarrassing to
himself or to one of his associates should break late in the campaign.[2]

A man who could have created such an incident was traveling
with the campaign caravan. Louie Jones had picked up a Baptist
preacher in Farmerville, in the extreme northern part of Louisiana,
and had enlisted him as an Overton worker. It was Louie's idea to
use the preacher to open and close meetings with a prayer, and for
a time the experiment seemed effective. The minister was eloquent,
and never more so than at a small-town rally in the southern part of
the state in the closing days of the campaign. After the meeting
the members of the party piled into cars to drive to New Orleans.

Otho Long, one of Huey's numerous cousins, pushed into the car
where the preacher sat with Jones. He pulled out a bottle of whisky
and said: "Parson, you'll have to excuse me, but I got to have a
drink." The parson grabbed the bottle from Otho's hands. "Goddamn
you, Otho," he shouted, "have you been holding out on me?" Jones
reported the parson's remarks to Huey. "Put him on the train to
Farmerville tonight," the Kingfish commanded.[3]

THE ELECTION ON SEPTEMBER 13 passed quietly in all parts of the
state. Calm prevailed even in New Orleans, which usually witnessed
violence or at least the threat of it. The Broussard leaders in the city,
apprehensive that the police would harass their supporters and that
the Long–Old Regular workers might try to steal some ballot boxes,
had asked that an arbitration committee be appointed to handle
complaints of irregularities. Huey and Walmsley, speaking for their
side, readily agreed to the proposal, and a committee representing

[2] New Orleans *Item*, August 23 and 26, 1932; Baton Rouge *State-Times*, August
27, 1932; New Orleans *Times-Picayune*, August 29, 1932; New Orleans *Morning
Tribune*, August 29 and September 3, 1932.
[3] Louis A. Jones.

both sides had been named. It reported that few complaints had been received and that the election had apparently been conducted fairly.[4]

Overton, as had been expected, swept New Orleans, his vote there being approximately twice that of Broussard's. He also carried most of the country parishes, and in the final tally he led Broussard by the comfortable margin of 181,464 votes to 124,935 votes. In only one area did he fail to roll up a large majority—in the French parishes of the southwest, where the personal popularity of Broussard and LeBlanc resisted even the magic of Huey's endorsement. These parishes comprised part of the district in which Martin was running for the Public Service Commission, and Huey was barely able to elect his candidate over LeBlanc.[5]

Two French parishes, however, remained faithfully in line, returning their normal, almost unanimous Long vote—St. Bernard and Plaquemines. The conservatives charged that the vote in both parishes had been doctored, and Earl Long would later lend support to their suspicions. Earl stated under oath that on election night, after the polls had closed, he saw Huey going over the tally sheets from these two parishes with his leaders in the Roosevelt suite. Earl did not say that Huey had altered the sheets, but he implied that his brother would have done so if it had been necessary. This story was absurd, as Earl must have known. Huey did not need to worry about the results in these parishes. If he was at all anxious, it was because he feared that the returns would be so overwhelmingly pro-Long that they would arouse criticism. Sometime that night he telephoned Sheriff Mereaux of St. Bernard to ask how many votes Overton had received. Mereaux replied that he did not know as yet. "We are still voting," he said. Huey was horrified. "We have already won," he shouted. "For God's sake, stop counting."[6]

After the election the Long forces held a victory banquet at the Roosevelt Hotel. At its conclusion Huey announced that he was resigning as president of the Louisiana Democratic Association, and that his friend Bob Maestri would succeed him. "I'm leaving state politics for good," he continued. "I've done all I can for Louisiana. Now I want to help the rest of the country." Nobody in the room believed that he meant to leave the state to anyone else's control. Indeed, he repudiated his statement in almost the next breath:

[4] *Overton Hearing*, I, 1100–3, 1106–7; II, 2035.
[5] Allen P. Sindler: *Huey Long's Louisiana: State Politics, 1920–1952* (Baltimore, 1956), p. 82; Baton Rouge *State-Times*, September 16, 1932.
[6] *Overton Hearing*, I, 829–31; confidential communication.

He would retain his interest in state politics until "every one of our dadgum maligners" was driven out of office. One of those maligners was Francis Williams, he said, and Williams would be deposed as chairman of the Public Service Commission just as soon as Wade Martin took his seat on the Commission.[7]

Huey's announcement did not deceive Louisianians, but it impressed others. *Time* ran his picture on the cover of an October issue and hailed him as an emerging national figure. If Franklin Roosevelt was elected President, the "Incredible Kingfish" would probably be the Southern Democrat closest to the White House during the next four years.[8]

A PHONE RANG in the busy Roosevelt headquarters that Jim Farley had set up in New York City soon after the Democratic convention. The secretary who answered it asked who was calling. Huey Long, said the voice on the other end, and Huey Long wanted an appointment to see Farley. Certainly, the secretary said, and where could Senator Long be reached? "I'm at the Waldorf-Astoria," the Kingfish answered, "in rooms 1220, 1222, 1224, 1226, 1228 and 1230." He went over to headquarters shortly and informed Farley that he wanted to campaign for Roosevelt—and that he had his own campaign strategy. He proposed that the national committee provide him with a special train equipped with loudspeakers in which he would crisscross the entire country, speaking in every state. Farley listened, aghast. Not only would the project involve tremendous costs, but if Huey stumped in such grand fashion he would overshadow the presidential candidate. But Farley knew that if he rejected the plan out of hand he would offend Huey and possibly lose his support. He diplomatically said that he would take up the idea with his advisers and inform Huey shortly of his decision.

A few days later he asked Huey to come back to headquarters. Soothingly he explained that he and his advisers had had to modify Huey's plan. They certainly wanted the Kingfish to campaign for Roosevelt, but a substitute speaking schedule had been worked out for him that would send him into just a few states. These states, although Farley did not say so, were believed to be safe for Roosevelt or hopelessly lost to him. Therefore Huey could not harm Roosevelt's cause in them. Farley and the other men at headquarters still tended

[7] Baton Rouge *State-Times*, September 16, 1932; Thibodaux *Sentinel*, September 17, 1932.
[8] *Time*, October 3, 1932.

to underrate Huey, to regard him, in Farley's words, as "somewhat of a freak."

Huey recognized that he was being given a big run-around. Jumping to his feet, he strode around the room and then charged to Farley's desk and pounded on it. "I hate to tell you, Jim, but you're gonna get licked," he said. "Hoover is going back into the White House. . . . I tried to save you, but if you don't want to be saved, it's all right with me." He intimated that perhaps he should not campaign at all. He was so committed to the proposition that wealth must be decentralized that he would be worthless discussing other issues. His implied threat to desert Roosevelt alarmed the party leaders. He might be a clown, but as he had demonstrated at the Chicago convention, he had a certain influence and was not to be scorned. Farley urged him to fulfill the speaking tour devised for him, and Roosevelt wrote him a flattering letter asking for his help. Huey finally agreed to campaign.[9]

Roosevelt followed with another form of flattery. He invited Huey to visit him at his Hyde Park home and discuss the campaign. Huey accepted eagerly. He had never met Roosevelt, although they had been in Chicago at almost the same time in June. Roosevelt had flown there to deliver his acceptance speech to the convention, but Huey had departed for Louisiana shortly before the candidate arrived. Now Huey would have an opportunity to measure face to face the man he was supporting—but for some reason did not entirely trust.

Huey went first to New York City, where he conferred with representatives of Farley, and then on to Hyde Park, arriving on a Sunday morning, October 9. He was informed that Roosevelt had just returned from church and had first to receive some other callers. The governor would see Senator Long at lunch. Huey dallied on the front steps, chatting with newsmen. He said that he might take the stump but not in the South, which was safe for Roosevelt. While he was waiting, Mrs. Roosevelt arrived in an automobile. Huey introduced himself, and after she entered the house, he told the reporters that she bore a striking resemblance to the beautiful Mrs. Coolidge. He was as capable as any Southerner of exaggerated politeness.[1]

Shortly Huey went into the house himself. The members of the

[9] James A. Farley: *Behind the Ballots* (New York, 1938), pp. 170–1; Frank Freidel: *Franklin D. Roosevelt: The Triumph* (New York, 1956), p. 331; Baton Rouge *State-Times*, September 16, 1932.
[1] Washington *Star*, October 10, 1932.

Roosevelt household were amazed at his attire for the occasion—a loud suit, an orchid shirt, and a pink necktie. Although he had learned something about how to dress since becoming governor, his taste still ran to the flamboyant. And this outfit was garish even for him. He had probably chosen it deliberately to shock the aristocratic Roosevelts, perhaps even to insult them, to let them know that Huey Long would not conform to their standards.

Roosevelt himself showed no sign of irritation. He indicated that Huey was to sit at his right, and during the meal the two men engaged in an animated but obviously private discussion. The other people at the table tried to talk among themselves, but their conversation tendered to taper off into long silences. During one of these lulls the governor's mother, Sara Delano Roosevelt, whispered audibly: "Who is that *awful* man sitting on my son's right?" The others hastily began to converse loudly, hoping that Huey had not heard her. He did not turn from his colloquy with Roosevelt, although he probably caught the remark. He later gave a friend his impression of Roosevelt as derived from this first meeting: "I like him. He's not a strong man, but he means well. But by God, I feel sorry for him. He's got even more sonsofbitches in his family than I got in mine."[2]

What Huey and Roosevelt talked about—and agreed or disagreed on—was never fully revealed. Huey undoubtedly pressed on Roosevelt his plan to decentralize wealth, and Roosevelt probably endorsed the principle of the plan but only in general terms. Huey said later that he had asked only one pledge from Roosevelt, that in appointing his cabinet he name to the Treasury and Justice departments men who would be acceptable to the progressives.[3]

Huey went from Hyde Park to Washington and prepared to embark on the speaking tour that Farley had mapped out for him—in North and South Dakota, Nebraska, and Kansas. He telephoned Louie Jones and directed that the sound and other trucks be brought to Bismarck, North Dakota, where he was to open. He also phoned

[2] Grace Tully: *F.D.R., My Boss* (New York, 1949), pp. 323–4; Arthur M. Schlesinger, Jr.: *The Crisis of the Old Order, 1919–1933* (New York, 1957), p. 418; Lewis Gottlieb. Two of Huey's sisters, Charlotte Long Davis and Lucille Long Hunt, related a different version of the Hyde Park incident. In their account, based on recollections of what Huey told them, Sara Roosevelt cried: "Frankie, you're not going to let Huey Long tell you what to do, are you?" One of Huey's intimates, George Maines, had still another version, in which Huey cursed and threatened Roosevelt. But Mr. Maines thought that the meeting occurred before the Chicago convention, and this would have been before Huey had met Roosevelt.

[3] *Congressional Record*, 73 Cong., 1 Sess., pp. 4261–2, speech of May 26, 1933.

Seymour Weiss, asking the hotelman to join him in Bismarck to schedule his meetings. Jones wondered if Huey had enough money to finance what was obviously going to be a costly tour. He was reassured when he reached Bismarck. One of the small trucks was in poor condition, and when he told Huey about it, Huey gave him a check on a New York bank to buy a new truck. It was the only time Jones saw him use anything but cash.[4]

Huey had money, but he had not received it from the national committee. He had to bear the entire expense of the tour himself. The money came from his customary Louisiana sources, for a total of sixty-nine thousand dollars. As this was more than he required for his trip, he contributed a share of it to the national committee to be used in the national campaign. He explained later why he had been so generous. He had been called on in New York by "a little bit of a low-ceiling fellow that wore glasses" who had asked him for help, and he thought that he should aid states not so fortunate as Louisiana.[5]

On his tour Huey addressed large and enthusiastic crowds in every town. At Fargo, North Dakota, for example, the crowd overflowed the auditorium, and hundreds of people stood in the street outside, listening to his voice over his sound truck's amplifiers that had been attached in the building. In the depressed farm states of the plains his emphasis on the need to redistribute wealth struck a responsive chord. But it was the speaker rather than the speech that attracted the crowds; his shrewd humor and colorful language appealed as strongly to the farmers of the West as to those of Louisiana and Arkansas. As he continued on his triumphal way, five Democratic state chairmen of the region wired Farley a message: "If you have any doubtful state, send Huey Long to it." Farley was astounded at the reaction to Huey. After the election he decided that he should have sent Huey into Pennsylvania, that if the Kingfish had campaigned in the coal mining districts, he would have carried the state for the Democrats. "We never again underrated him," Farley admitted.[6]

When Roosevelt was elected in November, Huey could feel that he had played some part of the victory and could look forward to

[4] Louis A. Jones; Seymour Weiss.

[5] *Congressional Record*, 73 Cong., 2 Sess., p. 6106, speech of April 5, 1934; George E. Sokolsky: "Huey Long," *Atlantic Monthly*, CLVI (November 1935), 529–30.

[6] Baton Rouge *State-Times*, October 20, 1932; New Orleans *Morning Tribune*, October 24, 1932; New Orleans *Times-Picayune*, October 26, 1932; Farley: *Behind the Ballots*, p. 171.

March 1933, when Roosevelt would take office. Surely the incoming administration would recognize the influence of the man who, in addition to helping elect a President, had by his own efforts elected two senators.

ONE OF THOSE SENATORS, however, John Overton, faced the possibility of not being allowed to take his seat in March. Almost immediately after the September primary the man he had defeated, Edwin Broussard, laid a formal complaint before the Senate special committee on campaign expenditures, charging that Overton's victory had been accomplished by fraudulent means. The Long organization had filed so many dummy candidates that it had secured "absolute control of the election machinery," and as a result he had not received a fair vote, Broussard said. He asked that a committee be appointed to investigate the returns from all parishes where dummies had been used and to impound the boxes in New Orleans and its adjoining parishes, where the number of dummies had been especially flagrant. Remembering that the committee was a special body created to check on undue campaign expenditures, Broussard suggested that it should also investigate the huge sums of money spent by the Long organization.[7]

The tradition of the Senate dictated that a request for an investigation by a defeated but still incumbent member had to be accepted, even though the subsequent inquiry might be only perfunctory. But Broussard's request was received with unusual warmth. The committee immediately sent investigators to Louisiana to collect evidence bearing on Broussard's charges, and its chairman, Republican Robert B. Howell of Nebraska, announced that a subcommittee of two senators would soon go to New Orleans to conduct a preliminary inquiry. The committee's alacrity suggests that it was actuated by more than consideration for Broussard—that its Republican majority, and some of its Democratic members, sensed an opportunity to discredit Huey Long.

The investigators in Louisiana talked to representatives of the Long and anti-Long factions and took sworn statements from Overton and his campaign managers, Peltier and Ellender, as to how much money had been expended in Overton's behalf. Overton stated that he had received no contributions personally from any source and that he had expended out of his own pocket only four or five

[7] Overton Hearing, I, 3.

hundred dollars. He had been informed that the Louisiana Democratic Association had received contributions and disbursed them to help him and other candidates, but he did not know how much had been received or spent. The investigators tried to secure this information from Peltier and Ellender. The managers supplied a list given them by Weiss of men who had contributed to Overton's campaign fund a total sum of slightly more than thirteen thousand dollars. They had spent this money, and they thought that more money had possibly been spent by someone else in the Long organization, but they were not sure by whom or how much. This was about the extent of the information that the investigators were able to present to the subcommittee before it came to New Orleans.[8]

The subcommittee opened its hearing on October 5, just a few days before Huey was to go to Hyde Park to meet Roosevelt and only two weeks before he was scheduled to embark on his speaking tour for the Democratic ticket. Howell had cannily sent two Democratic senators to open the inquiry into the election of a Democratic senator —Tom Connally of Texas, who acted as chairman, and Sam G. Bratton of New Mexico. Connally, from his Senate acquaintance with Huey, had come to detest the Kingfish, and he had a holier-than-thou attitude toward Louisiana politics. He was to write later that when he was in the state he felt as if he was "wallowing in mud."[9]

Connally called the hearing to order in a room in the post office building that had been made available by the federal government. Present were Broussard and his attorney Edward Rightor, Overton, Huey, and Burt W. Henry, chairman of the Honest Election League. The league was an organization of rich New Orleanians which had announced that its purpose was to bring about honest elections in the state. Formed during the recent senatorial campaign, it had as a first step toward its goal supported Broussard. Now Henry asked for permission to file a brief supporting Broussard's complaint and to act as lawyer for the league. Permission was granted. Connally then asked Huey if he was appearing as Overton's lawyer. "Yes, sir," Huey answered, "for him and with him."[1]

Rightor, as Broussard's attorney, led off for the complainants. A dignified and somewhat pretentious man, he was a member of the New Orleans social elite and a dedicated anti-Longite. He had also a strong personal dislike for Huey, who had fixed on him the nickname of "Whistle Britches": according to one account, because his

[8] Ibid., I, 7–8.
[9] Tom Connally: *My Name Is Tom Connally* (New York, 1954), p. 167.
[1] *Overton Hearing*, I, 1–2, 9–10, 12–14, 54.

legs came so close together as he walked that the pants gave off a swishing sound; but according to a more accepted story because he was subject to flatulence.[2]

He startled the committee somewhat by stating that Broussard was not asking to be declared the victor in the recent primary election. He did not claim to be the nominee, and neither this committee nor any legislative or judicial body in Louisiana could certify him to be the nominee. The complainants simply wished the committee to find that Overton had been elected by fraudulent means, which would mean that he would be refused his seat by the Senate and that a new election would have to be called. Rightor conceded that he did not have evidence to prove fraud. But it was "general knowledge" that fraud had been practiced: the Long organization had entered dummy candidates and spent large sums of money. It was for the committee with its investigative resources to prove the charges brought by Broussard and "prominent citizens." Henry, following Rightor, resorted to an even more interesting line of reasoning. "When you bring out the use of dummy candidates," he argued, "you don't need any other evidence. They could be used for only one purpose, to practice fraud in the election."[3]

Rightor and Henry took two days to present their allegations. Huey was allowed on both days to rebut the charges. He did so in lengthy and sometimes rambling statements. He admitted that the Long organization had collected money for the campaign. The money had been contributed by various individuals, and probably all of them had been asked to contribute. "Nobody ever comes to you voluntarily and hands you campaign contributions," he said. "This matter of getting election money is hard business." Senator Bratton was curious about the method used to account for the contributions. "Did you have a central office . . . ," he began. "We had a central office for paying it," Huey cut him off.

As to the use of dummy candidates, Huey dismissed the subject as irrelevant. Dummies had been used in elections in Louisiana before he ever entered politics and by his enemies against him in previous elections, he said, naming examples. "Cain has cried for the blood of Abel and he has got it on his own hands by this record," he shouted. Moreover, there was no evidence that the use of dummies had resulted in fraud or influenced the returns. To prove his point, he cited the fact that there had been no dummy candidates in twenty-nine parishes in north Louisiana and yet in these parishes

[2] Confidential communications.
[3] *Overton Hearing*, I, 38, 52, 55.

Overton had received a better vote than in a number of southern parishes where dummies had been put up. This was specious reasoning designed to becloud the issue. North Louisiana was a Long stronghold, and there he had not needed extra commissioners. But his reasoning was sharp and telling when he reminded the committee that in New Orleans an arbitration committee had attested to the fairness of the election in the city. Representatives of Broussard had sat on the committee and had signed its decision.[4]

After hearing the opposing arguments, the subcommittee announced that it would report its findings to the special committee. If the parent body decided that the evidence of fraud was sufficient to justify a full-scale investigation, it would come to New Orleans itself.

The committee sat on the matter during the remainder of 1932. Although it gave no inkling of its intention, it was known to have sent additional investigators to Louisiana and to be studying the reports sent back by them. Then, early in 1933, the committee announced that chairman Howell and another member would soon open hearings in New Orleans; it had received sufficient evidence of fraud in the Louisiana election to justify an investigation.

The members of the committee were probably impressed by the evidence given to them by the investigators. But there is reason to believe that they were at least equally impressed by other information supplied by their sleuths. These men had talked almost entirely with anti-Long leaders, and the antis apparently had insinuated the idea that the investigation of the election should be a pretext for a broader inquiry—one that would delve into every aspect of the Long regime and expose the evil nature of its leader. The antis emphasized that whatever the form of the investigation, the committee would have to employ as its counsel a lawyer capable of dealing with Huey, who would continue to represent Overton. They may even have suggested the man the committee should engage, Samuel T. Ansell, a skilled legal performer who had at one time been judge advocate general of the army and was known to possess a dominating courtroom presence. At any rate, Ansell was named as counsel, and the antis gleefully predicted that he would "out-Huey Huey."[5]

The committee held its first session on February 3, 1933, in the room in the post office building where the subcommittee had met earlier. Howell (who, said a reporter present, looked like a stern

[4] Ibid., I, 19–20, 22–3, 27, 42, 57.
[5] Confidential communication.

college president) and his colleague, Robert Carey of Wyoming, presented counsel Ansell. Huey announced that he would represent Overton. Over three hundred people had crowded into the room, and a reporter observed that when one person moved, they all moved. The spectators had come expecting to see a good show, and as the hearing unfolded over a span of two weeks, they were not disappointed.[6]

The session was barely under way when Ansell and Huey clashed. Ansell had a number of documents he wanted to put into the record, and he started to read them. Huey interrupted to say that from the time counsel was taking, he must need a job. "Not half as bad as you do. You have always had one, brother," Ansell retorted. "I can be elected but you can not," Huey came back. "I have not run for office yet," Ansell countered, "nor shall I run for office under your circumstances." Ansell clearly had the better of the exchange, and emboldened, he essayed a stroke of the polished irony for which he was noted. "Senator Long," he asked, "is it offensive to refer to you, as the newspapers do, as the Kingfish of Louisiana?" This was exactly the kind of question not to ask in Louisiana, as the laughter of the crowd should have told him. Huey solemnly supplied his correct title. "I claim to be the Kingfish of the lodge," he said. "Of this lodge?" Ansell asked, incredulous that Huey would admit the scope of his power. "Of this lodge," Huey repeated. Huey obviously enjoyed these exchanges with Ansell, even when he did not win. After one of them he tilted back in his chair and drawled: "Then proceed, son, proceed."[7]

The hearing would see other confrontations between Ansell and Huey, and some between Ansell and certain Long leaders that reached the level of drama. It would also witness episodes that were unforgettably comic. One day Joseph Boudreaux was testifying—he was the man who had been slugged by Louie Jones—and he charged that armed bodyguards of Huey's were in the room for the purpose of intimidating witnesses. Asked by Ansell to identify them, he pointed to Joe Messina and a man named Wheaton Stillson. Ansell seemed beside himself with anger. He demanded that Messina and Stillson be sworn and examined. Messina admitted that he was armed; Stillson said that he had been armed at previous meet-

[6] Frost, in Baton Rouge *State-Times*, February 3, 1933; Deutsch, in New Orleans *Times-Picayune*, February 3, 1933; F. E. Hebert, in New Orleans *States*, February 11, 1933.
[7] *Overton Hearing*, I, 85, 138; Deutsch, in New Orleans *Times-Picayune*, February 3, 1933.

ings but that on being informed that the committee might object, he had "disarmed" himself. Huey intervened to say that both men had commissions from the state that permitted them to bear arms. But chairman Howell overruled him. Nobody could come armed into the "presence of the United States Senate," he intoned.

Howell was apparently willing to excuse the two men with a reprimand. Messina was obviously guilty of nothing but ignorance, and Stillson was guilty of nothing at all. And neither had had any connection with the Overton campaign. But Ansell insisted that he should examine them: he sensed in their appearance an opportunity to discredit the Long regime. He began with Messina. What was Messina's job with the state? Messina answered that he was with the state police and that he patrolled highways. And how many days had Messina attended the hearing? Practically every day since it had started, Joe said. Ansell pounced: When then did the witness do his patrolling? Messina was flustered, but he explained that he worked all night and attended this interesting "free meeting" all day.

Somewhat baffled, but convinced that he was proving a form of corruption, Ansell turned to Stillson. And what did Mr. Stillson do for the state? Stillson answered easily that he was a "roving" inspector for the Dock Board and, when he was needed, acted as a guard for Senator Long. Ansell wondered that Stillson could perform such varied duties. Stillson enlightened the counsel. "I am," he said, "rather versatile and ambidextrous, as it were." Ansell was puzzled. "Ambidextrous?" he queried. Yes, the witness replied. Ansell finally understood. "Use a gun with both hands?" he asked. "When I have to," Stillson said.[8]

The most hilarious moments of the hearing occurred when a number of dummy candidates appeared, to explain why they had decided to run. Their reasons were, it appeared, quite simple. They had been asked to run by someone in the Long organization, and they had acceded. They assumed that someone had paid their filing fee. Later they were asked by someone to withdraw, and they had done so. Some of the dummies had announced as candidates for the House of Representatives, and to them Ansell gave particular attention, probing as to their background and knowledge of government. He asked one man what he did for a living. The aspirant for national office said that he cut grass for the Dock Board. He was eager to explain how he cut the grass; with "a big long blade with a handle; a long handle." Ansell asked another man if he kept up with national affairs. Yes, the witness answered, "generally" through the newspapers. Who then was the speaker of the house? The dummy did not know, but on being asked who was President, he said, with an air of having special knowledge: "Hoover."[9]

The dummies shriveled under Ansell's relentless questioning. Only one of them stood up to him. Charles Suer identified himself as a painter for the Dock Board. He volunteered that when he was not painting, he operated a small restaurant and acted as a salesman for the New Orleans Laboratory. Asked to explain the imposing title of the latter organization, he said that it exterminated "insects, ants, roaches, and mosquitoes, and all like that." Queried as to how much education he had, he said that he could not remember the name of the school in New Orleans that he had attended, but that he had gone up to the third grade. Anticipating another easy triumph, Ansell moved in on him.

What had given Mr. Suer the idea that he should run for Congress? Why, Mr. Suer answered, he had just thought he was qualified. And, Ansell pursued, he had also thought that he could convince other people that he was qualified? The witness assumed a judicious mien. "No, sir," he said. "I couldn't convince anybody, because the facts are I never spoke to anybody about my being a candidate." Ansell was flabbergasted. Nobody? he asked, as if he had not heard right. Not a soul, Mr. Suer said, not even his wife. But surely Mr. Suer must have announced his candidacy in the newspapers or on posters? No, Mr. Suer had not. Ansell fell into the trap. "Well," he demanded, "how in the world did you expect to be elected to Congress, eh?" The witness paused and seemed to meditate, as the spectators leaned forward expectantly. "That is the chance you take," he said.[1]

Ansell could easily demonstrate that the dummies had not been serious candidates. He could also show that they had been entered to secure more commissioners for Overton. In fact, this purpose was admitted by Long leaders who testified. But, try as he might, he could not prove that the extra commissioners had influenced the result of the election. They undoubtedly had exercised an influence in some precincts, but their methods were necessarily subtle and could not easily be identified. Moreover, it was clear that whatever influence they had exerted was small. The Long leaders who admitted that they had filed dummies to get more commissioners stated that

[9] Ibid., I, 566, 554-5, 630, 638.
[1] Ibid., I, 587-91, 594.

they wished they had not done so—Overton would have won by the same majority without the dummies. Apparently in frustration, Ansell charged at one stage that because manager Peltier predicted the result of the election, he must have had advance information as to what the vote would be, and he must have gotten it from the commissioners.[2]

But perhaps the counsel was not as frustrated as he seemed. It quickly became apparent that he and the committee were using the election as a springboard from which to investigate Huey Long and the Long organization. The inquiry developed, in fact, into a gigantic "fishing" project that plumbed Huey's political career, even back to the days when he had run for the Public Service Commission. Men who had been his associates when he became governor but had broken with him were invited to appear and testify as to his iniquities. Julius and Earl Long took the stand and related, among other things, that in his 1928 campaign for governor Huey had accepted financial contributions from public utility companies. ("That is a goddamn lie," Huey screamed at one point during Earl's recital.)[3]

Huey was irritated at the irrelevance of the testimony, but sometimes he could not help being amused by its absurd range. When one witness charged that the state government corruptly overpaid dealers for cement to build roads, Huey interrupted the testimony. "Why not try us on the price of eggs?" he cried. "Why not try us on the price of calico? What has that got to do with the Overton seat in the United States Senate? Why not try us on whether the hens laid more eggs in June than they did in January?" When it came his turn to present witnesses, he promised that he would not introduce any testimony to contradict what had been said about his "family raising"—this was right after Julius and Earl had appeared—or any testimony to contradict what had been said about his campaigns in 1918, 1924, and 1928. He would introduce only testimony contradicting what had been said about the Overton–Broussard campaign, and there was so little of that that he could refute it in two or three hours. In a more savage vein, he issued a circular denouncing the committee as a "Kangaroo Court."[4]

The committee did try to find out how Overton's campaign had been financed, and if it sometimes wandered from that issue to the intriguing subject of Long financing in general, its interest was un-

[2] Ibid., I, 208–9, 243, 686–7.
[3] Ibid., I, 817–18, 835, 841, 953–4, for the testimony of Earl and Julius.
[4] Ibid., I, 683, 1096; II, 1231–2.

derstandable. For instance, the committee seemed to be fascinated by the collection of the deducts. The chief witness on this subject was Dr. Joseph O'Hara, who had succeeded Maestri as head of the Louisiana Democratic Association. Dr. O'Hara readily explained that the employees of the state in the city contributed ten per cent of their monthly salary to the association's campaign chest. The committee understood that: but were the workers forced to contribute? Oh, no, said O'Hara, they "had to pay that ten per cent voluntarily."[5]

The committee began its effort by asking Peltier and Ellender to relate from what sources they had secured the money to run Overton's campaign. The managers stated that Senator Long and Seymour Weiss had raised the money, that the money had been kept at the Roosevelt Hotel, and that they had drawn from the fund when they needed to. As far as they knew, no record of contributions or expenditures had been kept, although Weiss had given them a list of men who had donated to the fund, which they had turned over to the committee.[6]

Not satisfied with their explanation, the committee summoned Bob Maestri. Surely he could supply more explicit information—he had been president of the Louisiana Democratic Association and was high in the Long council. The visitors from Washington did not know Mr. Maestri. He testified for four hours, revealing nothing pertinent but introducing into the record a mass of detail that left the committee bewildered. For example, he related that during the Allen campaign he had been asked by Weiss to contribute eight thousand dollars to the Louisiana Democratic Association. But, he hastened to explain, this money was not to be used for campaign purposes; it was intended for the use of the New Orleans Welfare Committee. Maestri then digressed to describe at length what this committee was. The civic leaders of New Orleans, who had been raising private funds to support the large number of people on relief, had asked Governor Long and Mayor Walmsley for help. Huey and Walmsley had agreed to ask city and state employees in New Orleans to contribute every month five per cent of their salaries to a relief fund. The money received was administered by the Welfare Committee, composed of distinguished citizens, and Mr. Maestri had desired to aid this worthy organization.

Ansell handed the witness a list of contributors to Allen's campaign fund. It seemed, the counsel said, that Weiss had included Maestri's eight thousand dollars on the list. Yes, Maestri agreed,

[5] Ibid., I, 419–20, 428.
[6] Ibid., I, 155, 160, 165, 235–6, 258–9, 263.

that apparently was the case. Had Weiss then asked for the money for campaign purposes? "No; for the relief fund to be put in the expenses of the campaign," Maestri said maddeningly. The committee gave up on Mr. Maestri. It had but one confused impression from his testimony: that very probably contributions to Overton's campaign fund had been mixed in with contributions to the relief fund, and that the two types of contribution could not possibly be segregated.[7]

But the committee decided to make one more effort. As all the Long financial trails seemed to lead to Weiss, the committee summoned him to the stand. He testified on three separate days, appearing first on February 7. On this day he was asked if he had kept any records of receipts and disbursements. He said that he had given Peltier and Ellender a record of contributions, which they had turned over to the committee. He had made up the record from "memorandums" on his desk. Where were the memorandums now? He had destroyed them. Did he have any other records? No, he had not. Ansell exploded, saying that since no records were available, he would demand that the witness state the names of "each and every bank" in New Orleans in which he had any money on account during 1932. Huey instructed the witness not to answer the question and asked Howell for a recess. He and the committee and Ansell conferred briefly, and when the hearing was resumed, Ansell asked a different question. The reason for shutting off the line of inquiry about the banks was not disclosed until later.[8]

Weiss returned to the stand on February 9. This time Ansell pressed him on his inability to produce a record of contributions and expenditures. He asked him if there was any "particular" reason why Weiss had failed to keep a record. "Well, there are a couple of reasons," the witness answered. "First, I did not want to, and second, it was too much trouble." Again Ansell exploded. Addressing the committee, he demanded a greater latitude in examining Weiss and other Long witnesses. He could not be bound by rules of "legal materiality," because he was dealing with a deliberate, "evil design" to prevent the committee from discovering how much money had been spent in the Overton campaign, and everyone knew who was directing that design. His charge stung Huey to an angry reply, and Ansell finally invited Huey to step outside and settle matters. "I will walk out with you and whip hell out of you," Huey snarled.

[7] Ibid., I, 340, 355–6, 367–9.
[8] Ibid., I, 308–9, 315; *Congressional Record*, 72 Cong., 2 Sess., pp. 4658–75, speech by Long, February 21, 1933.

"Would you walk alone or with a lot of armed guards?" Ansell sneered.[9]

Ansell had obviously won his demand for a free hand when Weiss resumed testifying on February 17. Now he asked the question Weiss had not had to answer on February 7: in what New Orleans banks did Weiss have accounts in 1932? Weiss's answer was brief: "None of your business." Ansell repeated the question, again and again, and Weiss returned the same answer. When Howell admonished him, Weiss said that he had put no political funds in any banks. He had accounts in various banks, but they were his accounts and he saw no reason why he should reveal his private business to the committee.[1]

While the grilling was going on, Huey went down the hall to the office of the assistant United States attorney, Edmund E. Talbot. Slapping down on Talbot's desk a volume of Supreme Court reports, he opened it to a case involving a witness before a congressional committee who had refused to answer certain questions on the ground that they were irrelevant. He had been cited for contempt, but the Supreme Court had held that he was within his rights. "Ain't that the law, Ed?" Huey demanded. Talbot, puzzled that Huey should ask his opinion, said: "You're a lawyer. You know that's the law in that particular case." Returning to the hearing room, Huey waited for an opportune moment. Interrupting the questioning of Weiss, he announced that he had secured a ruling from the assistant United States attorney that the witness did not have to answer irrelevant questions about his bank accounts! The committee was thunderstruck and summoned Talbot to ask why he had intervened in the hearing. The embarrassed lawyer had to explain that he thought he was ruling on a general principle.[2]

The uncommunicative Weiss was finally excused. As he left the stand, Huey said that he had been tempted to ask the witness certain questions but had restrained himself. "For the love I have for this country and for this community I cannot afford to ask the questions," he said. The committee knew what his reasons were, for he had disclosed them privately to the committee on February 7.[3]

February 7 had fallen on a Tuesday. On the preceding weekend New Orleans had been faced with one of the worst financial crises

[9] *Overton Hearing*, I, 472, 677, 681.
[1] Ibid., I, 1048–9, 1051–2, 1057.
[2] Ibid., I, 1053–4; Edmund E. Talbot.
[3] *Overton Hearing*, I, 1060.

in its history, one that could have brought about the closure of its major banks and probably of many of the banks in the state. The situation broke suddenly. On February 2 a member of the House of Representatives delivered a speech in which he leveled grave charges at Huey's friend Rudolph Hecht, who was president of the Hibernia Bank of New Orleans and also chairman of the regional advisory board of the Reconstruction Finance Corporation. The congressman claimed that Hecht had exerted his influence with the RFC to obtain a loan for a bonding company in New Orleans in which he owned an interest; the company had almost immediately failed, and, he continued, the money had been used to pay a loan owed by the company to the Hibernia Bank. (Hecht probably had employed his influence to help the company but had not expected it to fail.)

On February 3, a Friday, the congressman's speech was front-page news in every city in the country—except New Orleans. Realizing the effect the charges would have—if Hecht had engineered such a deal, his own bank must be shaky—the city's press had killed the story. But inevitably word of the speech spread around town—some people received out-of-town newspapers, and many people listened to the radio—and soon rumors began to spread: A large corporation had withdrawn its funds from the Hibernia, and Eastern depositers had decided that they had better get their money out. By late afternoon a run on the Hibernia was on. It was halted only when the bank locked its doors at closing time.

Huey, occupied at the hearing, did not hear about the situation until he returned to his home that night. Then a frantic bank president phoned to inform him and ask for his help. Huey responded by first apprising the committee of the crisis and winning its assent to postpone the hearing to Monday. Then he went to his suite at the Roosevelt Hotel and summoned the banking leaders of the city. He also phoned Governor Allen to get to New Orleans as fast as he could and to bring the great seal of Louisiana used to attest proclamations. He explained to the bankers that he had a plan to save the Hibernia. He would call Washington and demand that the Reconstruction Finance Corporation and the Federal Reserve System transfer twenty million dollars in cash to the threatened bank. He was confident that the money would be forthcoming. But the transfer could not possibly be completed before Monday, and since the next day was Saturday, February 4, the Hibernia would have to open and the run would continue. He had to have a pretext to have Allen proclaim a holiday on which banks and other institutions would be closed. Had anything happened in American history on February 4? he asked the bankers.

None of them could think of an event. In desperation, Huey phoned people in the city who might know—librarians, teachers, newspaper publishers and editors—and put them to work. The amount of historical research done in New Orleans that night must have set a record. The city librarian was roused from bed, but after hours of reading he had to report that he could discover nothing. Other diggers into the past announced the same result—February 4 apparently was the most unmemorable day in the history of the nation. But then a publisher phoned to say that his wife had found in the World Almanac that on February 3, 1917, President Woodrow Wilson had severed diplomatic relations with Germany. Huey decided the event would do. He turned to Allen, who had arrived with the seal, and said: "It took them two nights at least to do a job like that. Oscar, make it for the nights of February third and fourth."

He dictated the proclamation that appeared in the newspapers on Saturday morning: "Whereas . . . Woodrow Wilson . . . severed . . . Whereas, more than sixteen years have intervened . . . Now, therefore, I Oscar Kelly Allen . . . do hereby ordain." The morning papers had agreed to hold their presses until the proclamation was ready. But the *Picayune* hit the streets with an early edition that disclosed some details of what had happened at the conference, although those attending it had sworn themselves to secrecy. Huey decided that a *Picayune* executive who had been present in his capacity as a bank director had leaked the news. In a towering rage, he gave an interesting display of his concept of his role in Louisiana's government. He—not Governor Allen—summoned General Fleming, and ordered the militia commander to seize control of the *Picayune* office. Only a promise by the paper to recall the edition prevented Fleming from becoming for a time an editor and publisher.

The holiday averted a run on the Hibernia on Saturday. But Huey still had to persuade the national government to speed twenty million dollars to New Orleans by Monday. Without having slept on Friday, he was on the phone for most of Saturday and Saturday night and into Sunday. The government was willing to transfer money but haggled over the amount and did not agree to the sum that Huey demanded until Sunday afternoon.

On Monday morning the Hibernia and other banks opened early. The papers had announced that the government had placed money in the Hibernia, and there was no run on the bank. Huey showed up early in the lobby and deposited twelve thousand dollars. He explained to a group of customers who gathered: "It is money I borrowed on my life insurance, and I just want everybody to know that I can't think of a safer place to put the money than right here." A few days later he revealed that the state government would deposit several hundred thousand dollars in the Hibernia.

It was on the following day that Ansell asked Weiss to state in what banks in the city he had accounts. When Huey asked for a recess, he explained to the committee that Weiss would have to say that he had accounts only in a few banks. He stressed that this revelation by a Long leader and prominent businessman would be taken by the public as an indication of a lack of confidence in other banks and would precipitate another crisis. For the same reason he would not let Weiss answer Ansell's question on February 17. He was right to be cautious. The banks of Louisiana, like those in other states, were in a precarious condition; indeed, within a month practically every bank in the country would have to close. It was not a time for anyone to make an unguarded statement. But Huey was purposely exaggerating the effect of a statement by Weiss, which would hardly have caused a financial collapse in Louisiana. He had another reason for sealing Weiss's lips. That reason may have been sinister, but it was probably quite simple. Like Weiss, he felt that his methods of raising and spending campaign money were none of the committee's business.[4]

The hearing ran until February 17, and the committee left New Orleans without announcing a decision as to Overton's status. But chairman Howell declared in a letter to a colleague that he thought Overton should be asked to stand aside for a time: the committee had not as yet elicited the full facts and would have to investigate further. Interestingly, the reasons that Howell advanced for continuing the investigation had nothing to do with Overton. "The facts that we have elicited," he said, "indicate bad conditions in Louisiana, and should we not complete our investigation conditions will tend to become worse than those that have been obtaining." The committee would eventually resume its investigation, but under an-

[4] New Orleans *Item-Tribune*, February 5, 1933; New Orleans *Item*, February 8, 1933; New Orleans *Times-Picayune*, February 8, 1933; *Time*, February 17, 1933; Seymour Weiss; Richard Foster; Charles Frampton; Raymond H. Fleming; Hermann B. Deutsch; Webster Smith: *The Kingfish* (New York, 1933), pp. 282–4; *Congressional Record*, 72 Cong., 2 Sess., pp. 4658–75, speech by Long, February 21, 1933.

other chairman. Howell had become ill toward the end of the investigation, and died in Washington in March. Some anti-Longites in Louisiana were convinced that he had been murdered. He must have sought medical attention in New Orleans, and since Huey Long controlled the hospitals and laboratories in Louisiana, a henchman of his had somehow administered a germ to Howell![5]

[5] Robert B. Howell to George W. Norris, February 3, 1933, in George W. Norris Papers, Division of Manuscripts, Library of Congress, Washington, D.C.; C. F. Hyde to Byron P. Harrison and Theodore Bilbo, February 18, 1935, in Robinson Papers.

# CHAPTER 22

# *He Lied to Me*

**H**UEY LOOKED FORWARD to the session of Congress that would open on December 5, 1932. True, it would be a "lame duck" session, containing many members who had been defeated for re-election, and it would have to function under the leadership of a lame-duck President. But surely Hoover and the conservative Republicans would recognize that the election in November was a mandate for reform and would permit some progressive legislation to be enacted. And even if the President and his followers proved obdurate, the Democrats would realize that President-elect Roosevelt desired a progressive program and would use their large vote in both houses to push through some appropriate measures.

Huey's optimism was raised when just before he left for Washington he received an invitation from Roosevelt to stop off at the latter's winter home at Warm Springs, Georgia. He thought the President-elect was seeking his advice because he was a progressive: Roosevelt might even want to discuss a plan to redistribute wealth. Actually, Roosevelt was receiving at Warm Springs a stream of Democratic leaders of all shades of opinion. He questioned each one about the program the incoming administration should follow, listened politely—and did not commit himself. Huey was disappointed after his interview with his leader. "When I talk to him, he says 'Fine! Fine! Fine!'" the Kingfish said. "But Joe Robinson goes to see him the next day and again he says 'Fine! Fine! Fine!' Maybe he says 'Fine!' to everybody."[1]

[1] Baton Rouge *State-Times*, November 30, 1932; Arthur M. Schlesinger, Jr.: *The Crisis of the Old Order, 1919–1933* (New York, 1957), p. 452.

Disturbed, Huey went on to Washington, and there he decided he would serve notice on Roosevelt that the progressives expected him to act with them. On December 6, the second day of the session, he rose to discuss, ostensibly, Hoover's recommendation that Congress should enact a sales tax. Instead, he talked about what kind of program Roosevelt should recommend to the Democrats. He took pains to say that he was not undertaking, and would not undertake, to frustrate the President-elect in any way. But he was equally careful to emphasize that the legislation required to carry out the Democratic platform would have to be largely "formulated, planned, executed" by members of Congress. Some senators were saying that Roosevelt would not cooperate in carrying out the platform, but the senator from Louisiana denied this charge. Roosevelt surely understood that he had been nominated and elected on a single issue: "that he might carry out the one great fundamental, necessary principle of the decentralization of wealth." Roosevelt must also understand that the kind of legislation needed would not be instigated by the present Democratic leadership of the Senate. Happily that leadership would probably soon be changed. But if it was not changed, the progressives should unite behind Senator Norris to force through legislation that would accomplish their most urgent goals: limiting working hours, so that every laborer could have a job; placing the agricultural surplus under the "control and ownership" of the government, so that farm supplies could be regulated; and inflating the currency, so that prices of commodities would go up.[2]

After flinging this ultimatum at Roosevelt, Huey remained relatively quiet during the rest of December. But in January he renewed his attack on the conservative Democratic leadership of the Senate. The occasion for this onslaught was a banking bill introduced by one of the most conservative of the Democratic senators—diminutive, caustic Carter Glass of Virginia. Glass was the financial expert of the Democrats, and although this title was largely self-bestowed, it was widely acknowledged. He had long been convinced that the banking system needed reform, and as the depression worsened and the system showed increasing signs of strain, his concern heightened to urgency. The Glass bill proposed important changes in existing arrangements: commercial and investment banking were to be separated (to lessen opportunities for speculation), the Federal Reserve Board would be given greater authority over national banks,

[2] *Congressional Record*, 72 Cong., 2 Sess., pp. 54–9.

and national banks would be placed on a parity with state banks in branch operations.

As the bill imposed somewhat greater governmental regulation on the banks, some bankers opposed it, but the financial community as a whole, and especially the powerful Eastern group, was willing to go along with the bill; for all its regulatory features, it would enhance the position of the largest banks in branch operations in the states. The bill was, indeed, acceptable to most conservatives. Some Republican senators opposed it, but their motive was political—by stalling action on the banking situation they hoped to force the incoming Democratic administration to call a special session of Congress. Joe Robinson and other Democrats endorsed the bill, giving it practically the status of a party measure. It was expected to pass without difficulty.

Glass brought the bill before the Senate on January 5. Immediately it was evident that the progressives of both parties were going to oppose it and that Huey Long was their captain. He led off by proposing an amendment to prohibit a national bank from establishing a branch bank anywhere except in the town where it was already located. "We shall have to say, right here and now," he declared, "that the hand of imperial finance shall not go farther in its strangulation of the American people and that the hand of imperialistic banking control shall be decentralized instead of centralized in America." But, he continued, he objected to more than the branch-banking provision of the bill. The measure was basically defective because nothing in it provided for the decentralization of wealth: it did not embody the promise of the Democratic platform. Still determined to commit the President-elect, he said that if Roosevelt was President, he would have to veto this iniquitous measure.[3]

The debate on the introduction of the bill was brief. But on January 10 the measure became the main business before the Senate. As the session came to order, Huey astonished his colleagues by demanding that the journal of the previous day be read, a formality always dispensed with in the interest of saving time. Then, when the Glass bill was called up, he took the floor and held it for four and a half hours. He had two Bibles on his desk—"Two Bibles is never too many," he told reporters—and he quoted from them liberally as he spoke. "Go to now, ye rich men, weep and howl for your miseries that shall come upon you," he intoned. "You do not hear that read in the pulpit today," he continued. "If you do, the man will not be

[3] Ibid., 1330–5.

in the pulpit very long." Then he launched into a sermon on the concentration of wealth and the necessity of following the Lord's command to redistribute it. The Congress should stop fooling around with bills that would not help the country and should enact legislation raising income and inheritance taxes and inflating the currency, he shouted. He discussed the Glass bill only in passing references. At the end of the long session it dawned on senators that Huey was conducting a filibuster.[4]

He resumed his speech immediately on the next day, and although he sometimes referred to the Glass bill, he lectured primarily on the evils of concentrated wealth. At one stage, seeking a momentary rest, he sent to the chair a document to be read by the clerk. Glass was on his feet at once. He said that he was sure the Senate would prefer to hear the "mellifluous voice" of the senator from Louisiana rather than the voice of the clerk. The objection was sustained, but this form of Senate hazing did not disturb Huey. He said that he was flattered at the compliment to his "vocal strains" and would be happy to read the resolution. He read it very slowly, pausing at each comma and coming to a full stop at each period. Frequently he would look up innocently and ask: "Am I going too fast?" Glass exploded that the Senate was being prevented from legislating and demanded that it break the filibuster by sitting in longer sessions.[5]

The Senate resorted to evening sessions, but the filibuster went on. Huey dominated it, seizing the floor day after day. When he showed signs of tiring, which was rarely, Elmer Thomas of Oklahoma, an inflationist, came to his assistance. Huey proclaimed that he and Thomas would hold the Senate in session until it was ready to consider measures to decentralize wealth and increase the amount of currency. He used every opportunity to consume time. On the seventh day of the filibuster the Senate received a message from Hoover vetoing the bill to grant independence to the Philippines, a measure for which Huey had voted. He was recognized to discuss the message but launched into another speech on the Glass bill. Glass finally seemed to abandon hope. A reporter observed the little Virginian sitting dejectedly at his desk and felt sorry for him. Glass believed that the bill was necessary for the country, the reporter

[4] Ibid., 1451–64; Baton Rouge *Morning Advocate*, January 11, 1933; New Orleans *Item*, January 11, 1933; Baton Rouge *State-Times*, January 11, 1933.

[5] *Congressional Record*, 72 Cong., 2 Sess., pp. 1573–81, speech of January 11, 1933; clipping, January 11, 1933, in Long Scrapbooks, XIX; Baton Rouge *State-Times*, January 12, 1933.

He Lied to Me / 6 2 3

wrote, but Huey had him entrapped in words. Another commentator, humorist Will Rogers, predicted that the filibuster would not be broken. "Imagine ninety-five Senators trying to outtalk Huey Long," Rogers said. "They can't get him warmed up." Rogers thought that Huey was getting so close to the truth in his criticisms of the bill that Wall Street was on the verge of calling him "a menace."[6]

Joe Robinson, outraged at what some people were calling the "Long spectacle," induced twenty-nine Democratic senators to sign a petition asking for cloture on the bank bill. Some senators of both parties were willing to support Robinson's move but others were reluctant to depart from the senate's tradition of unlimited debate. Hence when the cloture proposal was brought up on January 19, it failed, but by a margin of only one vote. Huey naturally opposed cloture, but he indicated that he might agree to limit the time each senator could speak on the bill and amendments to it. His conciliatory gesture was not prompted by a sudden compassion for a helpless Senate. He realized that if the filibuster was prolonged, cloture would probably be invoked—hence he preferred to offer a concession, and thus appear as a victor rather than wait for a reverse. And he could claim one victory. He had forced the adoption of an amendment to the bill that restricted national banks from establishing branches except in states permitting such branches, of which there were only nine.[7]

A motion to limit debate was finally agreed to. But even this did not stop the flow of talk. Opponents of the bill offered so many amendments that discussion of them took up almost another week. Huey proposed several himself. He knew that they would be defeated, but by introducing them he could expound on any economic issue that he chose. In one discussion he endorsed an idea just beginning to attract notice, that the government should guarantee bank deposits, becoming one of the first senators to approve this proposal.[8]

On January 25, three weeks after the Glass bill had been introduced, the Senate finally voted on it. Huey voiced a last, brief plea for its defeat. "We have dressed it up and crippled it up," he

[6] *Congressional Record*, 72 Cong., 2 Sess., pp. 1624–36, 1835–51, debates of January 12, 14, and 16, 1933; clipping, January 12, 1933, in Long Scrapbooks, XIX; Rogers, in Baton Rouge *State-Times*, January 14, 1933, and New Orleans *Times-Picayune*, January 16, 1933.

[7] *Congressional Record*, 72 Cong., 2 Sess., pp. 2005, 2007, 2144–5, debates of January 18 and 19, 1933.

[8] Ibid., pp. 2208, 2264–6, 2272–82, 2283, 2293–4, 2392–8, 2493–5, debates of January 21, 23, 24, and 25, 1933.

said. "We have taken off the right leg of the corpse and its right arm and chiseled into its lungs," and now the "carcass" should be taken out and buried. Unmoved by this clinical obituary, his colleagues passed the bill by a substantial majority. But it did not become law. Roosevelt, impressed by the opposition to it and unsure of what kind of banking legislation to support, passed word to the Democratic majority in the House to bury the bill.[9]

The spectacle of Huey subjecting the Senate to his will for so long angered conservatives inside the chamber and out. Typical of the critical comment of his conduct was a lead editorial in *The New York Times*: "No argument moves him. Appeals to reason he despises. Like a slavedriver, he cracks his whip over the backs of the leaders of the Senate. How long will the Senate lie down under his insults?" The Senate was not quite supine, but in the opinion of the Washington correspondents it did not know how to cope with Huey. One columnist noted that the Kingfish had the qualities of the born filibusterer: needling interruptions did not irritate him and make him lose his head; the nastier the digs thrown at him, the more jovial he became. Another journalist observed that the Senate had thought it could haze Huey into submission. Instead, he had been hazing it ever since he arrived.[1]

Shortly after the filibuster ended, Huey asked the Senate for leave, since he had to go to Louisiana to take part in the Overton hearing that was to open early in February. He did not return to the Senate until late in the month, and he had barely resumed his seat when he created a sensation. He demanded the floor to discuss the Overton investigation, and in the course of his remarks he unloosed a savage attack on Ansell, whom he labeled as "a scoundrel and a thief and a rascal and a crook." As proof of his charges, he cited that during the World War Ansell, then in the adjutant general's office, had conspired to free from prison a notorious draft dodger, presumably in order to split with the man a sum of gold he had hidden away. The Senate listened to the diatribe with amazement, and finally a member rose to object that he had rarely heard anybody so abused. Was Senator Long speaking under his privilege of congressional immunity? Carried away by his own oratory, Huey answered rashly: "I do not claim any privilege from this scoundrel anywhere on earth under God's living sun." Was Long then inviting

[9] Ibid., pp. 2508, 2517.

[1] *The New York Times*, January 17, 1933; Herbert Plummer, in Baton Rouge *State-Times*, January 23, 1933; Rodney Dutcher, in Baton Rouge *Morning Advocate*, January 27, 1933.

Ansell to test the truth of the charges in the courts? the senator asked. Huey suddenly realized that he was being led into a trap. "I invite him to sue me in any court of competent jurisdiction," he qualified. He did not define such a court, but it was obvious that he meant one in Louisiana.

Ansell took Huey's words at their face value and filed a slander suit for five hundred thousand dollars in the federal court in the District of Columbia. The court dismissed the suit on the ground that a member of Congress could not waive his immunity. But Huey had printed excerpts from his speech in a circular, and Ansell brought a second suit based on the circular. The court accepted this complaint, holding that when a member of Congress published speeches at his own expense, he lost his immunity. This suit would drag through the courts for months, a minor but irritating threat that Huey had to fight off.[2]

While the filibuster against the Glass bill was at its height, President-elect Roosevelt came to Washington at Hoover's request to discuss the relation of the dollar to the international monetary situation. Various Democratic leaders viewed the visit as an opportunity to discuss their problems with Roosevelt and sought him out at his suite at the Mayflower Hotel. Among those asking for an appointment was Huey. He arrived for the meeting thirty minutes late and told reporters congregated in the hall: "I'm going to ask him did you mean it, or didn't you mean it?" Then he pounded loudly on the door of the suite and entered.

He came out shortly, smiling. "He is the same old Frank," he shouted. "He is all wool and a yard wide." Roosevelt knew even more about the Bible than he did, he continued, inferring that the President-elect had answered his question by endorsing the Long plan to decentralize wealth. The reporters, thinking of Huey's attacks on the Senate Democratic leadership, asked if Roosevelt was going to crack down on him. "He don't want to crack down on me," the Kingfish bubbled. "He told me 'Huey, you're going to do just as I tell you,' and that is just what I'm a-going to do."[3]

Huey seemed to be professing complete loyalty to Roosevelt. And he was speaking sincerely, though within the context of what he thought his relationship to Roosevelt would be when the latter became President. His concept of that relationship was peculiar. He was perfectly willing to recognize Roosevelt as his leader—in a

[2] *Congressional Record*, 72 Cong., 2 Sess., pp. 4658–75; New Orleans *Times-Picayune*, March 2, 1933; New York *Evening Post*, May 13, 1933.

[3] New Orleans *Times-Picayune*, January 20, 1933.

titular capacity. He did not think Roosevelt had the wish or the will to be anything but a token leader. Thus when Roosevelt, smiling pleasantly, had said that he was the boss, Huey readily agreed that this was so. But he could not believe that this urbane and apparently soft man would actually lead. After all, he had just said, or so Huey believed, that he would support the Long plan to decentralize wealth. He would doubtless follow the Long line on other issues. Huey felt he would be able to work with this President, as a partner, with the identity of the senior partner being recognized.

Huey was convinced that the partnership of Long and Roosevelt was necessary to save the country from the awful catastrophe toward which it was drifting—the collapse of its capitalistic economy followed by a revolution, perhaps communist in nature. He told a Senate colleague: "A mob is coming here in six months to hang the other ninety-five of you damned scoundrels and I'm undecided whether to stick here with you or go out and lead them." He repeated the remark to another senator, the dour Cordell Hull of Tennessee, who retorted: "Let the mob hang the ninety-five of us, and then, if you want to do complete justice, go out and commit suicide yourself."[4]

Roosevelt thought that he had cajoled Huey into temporary submissiveness and that probably he would be able to make the Kingfish into a supporter of the administration. But some of Roosevelt's advisers doubted this, and they also wondered whether he was worth saving: he was not the kind of man the administration should have in its ranks. One of them was horrified by a scene Huey precipitated a day or so before Roosevelt was inaugurated on March 4, 1933. The adviser was entertaining a small group in his hotel room when Huey suddenly burst in. Seizing an apple from a table, Huey bit into it, and then walked up to a man known to be close to Roosevelt and, tapping his shirt front with the apple, said: "I don't like you and your goddamned banker friends." This was only Huey's way of attracting attention, but to the Roosevelt people it indicated a crude irresponsibility, characteristic of the senator who had refused to accept any committee assignments.[5]

Those who thought that Huey would shirk his senatorial duties failed to notice that he had changed his tune about committees and had applied for assignments to them. In the session beginning in

[4] Gladys Baker, interview with Long, in Birmingham News-Age-Herald, February 19, 1933. Huey roared with laughter when he quoted Hull's remark.
[5] Raymond Moley: Twenty-Seven Masters of Politics (New York, 1949), pp. 227–8; Lela Stiles: The Man Behind Roosevelt (Cleveland, 1954), pp. 236–7.

March he would serve on the committees on the judiciary, interstate commerce, and interoceanic affairs, and on the first, one of the most important agencies of the Senate, he would labor so diligently as to win high praise from his colleagues. His willingness to take on committee work indicates that at the beginning of the Roosevelt administration he had some intention of behaving like a conventional senator.[6]

Roosevelt assumed office just as the banking situation exploded, when all over the country banks that had been barely holding on began to close. The President, seeking to avert a complete financial collapse and displaying a boldness that must have astonished Huey, issued a proclamation closing all banks until midnight on Thursday, March 9, the day Congress was scheduled to convene, when the administration would introduce legislation to deal with the crisis.

During the next few days the administration's leaders and financial advisers, working with feverish haste, hammered together a bill that authorized the Treasury to reopen the banks that met certain safeguards. Known as the Emergency Banking Act, it was introduced in both houses almost simultaneously and was expected to pass almost without opposition. But to the surprise of the administration, opposition did develop in the Senate. There Huey proposed an amendment empowering the President to declare state banks members of the Federal Reserve System, entitled to receive the benefits of the measure. In an angry speech he charged that the act as drafted would permit only Federal Reserve banks to open. He wanted to save the "little county seat banks" and the small depositors who had invested everything they had in these institutions, he said. Turning on Carter Glass, who was championing the bill, he charged that the Virginian wanted to open only 5,100 banks and keep 14,900 others closed. The gibe stung Glass, and banging his fist on his desk, he cried: "Be more civil." Huey's amendment had no chance, being shouted down in a voice vote. He then joined with the majority to pass the bill.[7]

But he had not given up the fight for the small banks. Two days later he reoffered his amendment. Again he emphasized that it was ridiculous and dangerous to reopen only ten per cent of the banks. The ninety per cent that were not protected by the government would never be able to open, and the ten per cent that were pro-

[6] New Orleans *Item*, December 9, 1932; *Congressional Record*, 73 Cong., I Sess., pp. 1714, 4958, April 14 and June 5, 1933.

[7] *Congressional Record*, 73 Cong., I Sess., pp. 52–67; New Orleans *Morning Tribune*, March 10, 1933.

tected would soon have to close. When the government reopened the banks under the terms of the emergency act, America would experience the "blackest day" in her history, he predicted. Several senators expressed approval of the amendment, and it was evident that support for it was gathering. Senators had had time to think about the bill that had been rushed through so hastily, and now they were becoming convinced that it did not provide adequate safeguards for the state banks. They were strengthened in their conviction when an administration leader revealed that a clause similar to the Long amendment had been in the original White House draft of the bill but had been deleted. The amendment was referred to the committee on banking and currency, an action that indicated it would receive serious consideration.[8]

One senator remained unimpressed by Huey's argument, Carter Glass, who had endured several Long barbs during the debate. At its conclusion Glass started to leave the chamber with Joe Robinson, now the majority leader. Stopping suddenly, Glass said: "I'm tired of having him try to make a personal issue of this discussion." He whirled on Huey and rasped out: "You damn sonofabitch." Huey called Glass the same name and leaped forward. Before the two men could grapple, Robinson hustled Glass out of the chamber and two other senators quieted Huey. Shortly afterward Huey got into a taxi and went to the White House to see Roosevelt. Emerging from the conference, he announced ambiguously that the government would be "all right" if it could get away from the influence of the big bankers.[9]

That Huey had influence with the administration soon became evident. Robinson himself introduced a bill embodying the essence of Huey's amendment to the banking bill: it authorized the Reconstruction Finance Corporation and Federal Reserve banks to make loans to state banks that needed help. Moreover, before the bill was introduced, it had been read to Huey from the White House by telephone to secure his approval. Eventually enacted, it provided a necessary prop to the smaller banks and was a sensible financial reform. Although it did not bear Huey's name, it was his bill, the first piece of legislation that he was responsible for.[1]

As though encouraged by this minor success to think that he could accomplish something larger, he prepared and introduced three

[8] *Congressional Record*, 73 Cong., 1 Sess., pp. 187–90, debate of March 11, 1933.
[9] New Orleans *Times-Picayune*, March 12, 1933.
[1] *Congressional Record*, 73 Cong., 1 Sess., pp. 335, 421–4, 431–3, 711–21, debates of March 14, 15, and 22, 1933.

bills that contained his latest thinking on the problem of concentrated wealth. He called them collectively "the Long plan" for the "Redistribution of Wealth." The first bill imposed a capital levy on fortunes beginning at one million dollars. If a man had over a million dollars, he would be required to give one per cent of it to the government; if he had over two million dollars, he would be required to give two per cent of it to the government; and the rates would rise progressively until a man with over a hundred million dollars would have to give everything above that amount to the government. The second bill raised income-tax rates so that an individual could not earn more than a million dollars in any one year. The third bill increased inheritance-tax rates so that an individual could not inherit more than five million dollars.[2]

Immediately after introducing his bills, Huey did something so unorthodox for a senator that it attracted wide and astonished attention: he bought time from the National Broadcasting Company to speak in support of the bills over all the company's radio stations. Politicians were just beginning to realize the importance of radio as a medium of mass communication and were experimenting cautiously with the use of it. Roosevelt had employed it effectively during the campaign and would use it even more persuasively as President to explain his policies to the country. But Huey was the first politician to attempt to reach a national audience. Senators and lesser leaders had confined their radio speaking to their own constituencies. By contracting for a national hook-up, Huey was in effect placing himself on a level with the President. He too had a program for the nation, and he would plead for it and ask the public to bring pressure on the Senate to pass it, and on the President to accept it.

The radio was a familiar device to him. He had used it to campaign and to explain his policies to Louisianians. On those occasions he had usually spoken from a New Orleans station with a large listening audience, engaging it for incredibly long broadcasts, in which he alternated his remarks with musical selections from a band. Thus in one campaign he began his fourth hour of speaking at midnight. In these marathon efforts he would pause at intervals and say: "This is Huey P. Long speaking to you. Ring up your friends and tell them to tune in on WDSU if you want to know what is going on around here." As long as he talked, people listened. In downtown New Orleans people would sit or stand on the sidewalks,

[2] Ibid., pp. 124–5, 275–6, speeches of March 10 and 13, 1933.

sometimes taking up a whole block, listening to Huey's voice blaring from a radio in a barroom, until one o'clock in the morning.[3]

He would employ the radio frequently during his senatorial career, more so than any politician except the President, and radio editors and technicians would rate him as one of its most expert users. They noted that, unlike most speakers, he did not turn away from the microphone and that he seemed to know every shade of inflection and emphasis of voice. He never read from a manuscript but relied on a few notes scribbled on foolscap. He would sometimes stack some books in front of him—he nearly always had a Bible—but he rarely referred to them. The observers thought, correctly, that he ad-libbed a great deal.[4]

He did not ad-lib when he spoke in defense of his bills on March 17. In a brief and fact-loaded speech, he explained the bills and why their passage was imperative: unless wealth was redistributed, a revolution would rend the country. To justify his argument that this concentration of wealth was a menace to the well-being of any country he quoted a number of authorities—the Bible, Oliver Goldsmith, Lord Bacon, Daniel Webster—but he cited one person more frequently than all others—Roosevelt. The President had pledged himself in his campaign speeches and inaugural address to decentralize wealth, Huey claimed. Roosevelt would have to have "much help" to carry out his pledges: "We must be patient and not expect too much too quickly." The people could help Roosevelt by letting the Senate know that they supported the Long plan.[5]

The speech impressed many people who did not expect such a cogent and careful address from the Kingfish of Louisiana. Huey was fully aware that he was regarded in some circles as a comic figure. But he did not think that such a reputation was harmful to a politician, or at least to him. Shortly after he had delivered his radio speech, he discussed his image with a reporter. "When the time comes," he said, "I'm going to knock this idea that I'm a clown or a monster into a cocked hat. Just give me a week in each state." He did not say when the time would come or what he would do in each state. But the meaning was obvious, and it carried ominous implications for Roosevelt.[6]

He spelled out further implications in a Senate speech in April.

---

[3] Francis Burns; Castro Carazo; Baton Rouge *Morning Advocate*, September 6, 1935.

[4] Charles J. Gilchrest, in Chicago *Daily News*, January 19, 1935.

[5] Radio address of March 17, 1933, copy in my possession.

[6] New Orleans *Item*, March 26, 1933.

What was the program of the administration as so far developed? he asked. As he saw it, it was to close half the banks, deflate the currency, and offer an economy-in-government bill that would cut out benefits to veterans of World War I. And now to cap it all the administration was proposing a "gracious and glorious bill" to plant trees. (The trees were to serve as windbreakers and thus check soil erosion, and the planting of them was to furnish employment.) This bill was known as the "sapling bill," but it should be called the "sapsucker's bill," charged Huey, and he paid his respects to the saplings: "I will eat every one of them that comes up in my state," he bellowed. "We are not going to have any planted there." The economic system was in worse shape than when Roosevelt came in, he continued, and the same old conservative gang was in control. He was not falling out with the President, he emphasized, but somebody ought to tell Roosevelt that he was not carrying out his campaign promises. As for himself, he would oppose the administration when he thought it was wrong, regardless of the consequences. "So as far as I am concerned in voting," he said, "they can take my patronage and go . . . I will be unchanged."[7]

He found immediate cause to oppose the administration. Its farm bill, the Agricultural Adjustment Act, cleared the House in April and came before the Senate. Based on the principle that the government should pay farmers to limit production, the bill had gone through the House without encountering much difficulty. But in the Senate it ran into fierce resistance from the inflationists, led by Huey, Burton Wheeler, and Elmer Thomas. These men were not opposed to the farm bill as such; they simply thought that it would be a useless measure unless it provided for raising farm prices by inflating the currency. Huey favored issuing more silver currency, whereas others in the group advocated printing paper money or devaluing the gold content of the dollar. Although not in absolute agreement, they acted together in supporting inflationary amendments—Huey offered a silver amendment—and held up the farm bill for twelve days. Fearing that they would succeed in putting a mandatory inflation clause in the bill, Roosevelt agreed to accept an amendment authorizing him to inflate with silver, paper, or a devalued dollar. Huey claimed, with some exaggeration, that the President had "swallowed our demand, hook, line, and sinker." He and his allies then allowed the bill to pass.[8]

[7] *Congressional Record*, 73 Cong., 1 Sess., pp. 1477–8, speech of April 11, 1933.
[8] Ibid., pp. 1568, 1741–2, 1817–20, 2211–12, 2457–60, 2531, 2562, debates of April 12, 14, 17, 21, 27, and 28, 1933.

Huey apparently thought that many of the colleagues with whom he had been operating victoriously would support his bills to redistribute wealth, for he called the bills up on May 12, lumping them together as an amendment to the pending revenue bill. Springing another Long innovation on the Senate, he had prepared and mounted a number of charts showing the continuing concentration of wealth in the country, and as he explained the bills, he pointed in schoolmaster fashion to data on the charts. His speech was largely a rehash of things he had said before, but in one section he struck a new and significant theme. He demonstrated on his charts that the middle-income group was being gradually squeezed out; a few members of it worked themselves up into the "plutocracy of one per cent" that owned most of the wealth, but most of them sank back into the "general class," the ninety-nine per cent of the people that owned very little of the wealth. "There is no middle class," he proclaimed.

As Huey continued his discussion, Borah interrupted with a question: the Long plan would take money from the rich, but how would the money collected be redistributed to the people? The answer was simple, Huey said. For one thing, the mass of people would be relieved of having to pay taxes to support the government. For another, the money gathered in would be spent for various government purposes: for rivers and harbors, national defense, veterans' pensions, roads, schools; and gradually it would "filter out" to the masses. "In fact," he said grandly, "there is no such thing as public money spent that does not inure to the population almost as a whole." His answer was too simple. What he said was in part true. But he had had to dodge the question, for the Long plan as then developed did not contain an arrangement to redistribute wealth. It was simply a scheme to tax wealth.

Toward the end of the speech Huey alluded to his differences with Roosevelt. He said that some senators might feel that he should have discussed his bills with Roosevelt. "I have not done so," he said. "I have taken our great President at his word. That he says nothing now for [redistribution of wealth] does not detract from what he has said. I have come here to help him carry out his promises to the people."

Before the vote was taken on the bills, a progressive Republican senator suggested to Huey that the vote for them would be larger if the capital-levy proposal was deleted. Huey thereupon withdrew this measure, leaving only the income- and inheritance-tax bills for consideration. They went down to apparently overwhelming defeat:

there were only fourteen votes for them and fifty votes against them. Four senators were announced as paired for the bills, so that the division was really eighteen to fifty-four. The eighteen were comprised of the most progressive Democrats and Republicans in the Senate. Only four Southerners, besides Huey, were numbered among them: Mrs. Caraway; Overton, who had been admitted although his election was still being investigated; a senator from North Carolina; and a senator from Florida. The rejection of the bills was not, however, as emphatic as it seemed. Twenty-four senators had failed to record a vote either way. It is probable that many of them wished to vote for the bills but for various reasons—fear of disapproval from the administration or from powerful supporters—dared not do so.[9]

Huey had not expected to pass his bills on the first attempt. But he had thought that he would get a larger vote than he did, one that would encourage further efforts, and he was bitter at the President for not supporting the bills, for even, as he believed, covertly opposing them. In late May he expressed his feelings in a speech entitled "Our Constant Rulers." His pretext was a resolution proposing an investigation of the banking house of J. P. Morgan, but what he discussed was the Morgan influence on the administration. Roosevelt was filling the Treasury Department with appointees from the Morgan company, he charged. And he was doing this after he had promised in his inaugural address to "drive the money changers from the temple." "We face the humiliating fact that . . . instead of being out of the temple, they not only inject themselves in the temple but they sit in the seats of the mighty and pass judgment on the balance of us who waged that fight to deliver this country back to the American people," he cried. By appointing such men, the administration was nullifying its efforts to regulate business. "We can enact all the laws we wish to regulate the conduct of the financiers, the bloated masters of fortune and power," he warned, "but it does not make any difference what kind of law we write on the books so long as we make them the masters of the law."[1]

He followed this blast with an attack on the administration for its attitude toward the banking bill then moving through Congress. This measure bore the title of the Glass-Steagall Act and was essentially the same measure that Glass had offered in January and that Huey had filibustered against. It now contained the amendment Huey had fought for, restricting the power of national banks to establish branches. Observers wondered whether he would accept the

[9] Ibid., pp. 3319–24, 3328–9.
[1] Ibid., pp. 4259–63, speech of May 26, 1933.

revised bill or oppose it. They were sure that whatever position he took, he would help determine the bill's fate. A Washington newspaper predicted: "The Morgans, the Rockefellers, and the Louisiana Kingfish will dominate consideration of the banking reform bill."[2]

Huey made his position known early. He would accept the bill, but only if it contained a provision that he and other progressives had advocated at the last session: government insurance of deposits in all banks, national and state. Popular support for guaranteed deposits was strong, and such a clause was inserted in the bill. Roosevelt was cool to the idea, however, and in the final stages of the bill's evolution it was rumored that he had ordered his leaders to modify the guaranty clause: state banks could not share in the benefits of the bill unless they became Federal Reserve banks. Huey divulged this news in the Senate and denounced the President's intervention. Roosevelt was acting under the influence of the Morgan tools in the Treasury Department, he charged. He was, however, still willing to credit Roosevelt with good intentions. "I wish the President would take my advice just one time," he said wistfully. Roosevelt was not moved by Huey's advice, but he had to yield to the pressure aroused by Huey and the progressives. The bill as finally enacted guaranteed the deposits in all banks. Huey had played a large role in putting through yet another important banking reform.[3]

In June, the last month of the session, the administration brought before Congress the most controversial piece of legislation it had yet offered, the National Recovery Act. This was a bold and imaginative effort to cope with the related problems of falling prices and wages and cutthroat competition in industry. It was made up of two "titles," or sections, the first part authorizing industries to write, subject to government approval, codes of fair conduct that prescribed wages and hours of labor and also prices and production quotas; to permit them to do these things, the bill suspended the antitrust laws. Section two empowered the government to set up a public works program.

The second section excited no opposition except from extreme conservatives. But the first section aroused violent controversy among men of all shades of opinion. To some, the proposed relation between government and industry seemed to resemble the "corporate state" arrangment in Italy and smacked of fascism. To others, the relaxing of the antitrust laws threatened a return to monopoly. The

[2] Clipping, May 20, 1933, in Grace Scrapbook.
[3] *Congressional Record*, 73 Cong., 1 Sess., pp. 4839–44, 5085, speeches of June 2, 6, 1933.

progressives were divided on the section. Urban progressives generally favored it, regarding it as a step toward intelligent economic planning. Rural progressives mostly opposed it, as a sellout to big business.

Huey was one of the progressives who fought the bill. His reasons for opposing it, as he explained them in debate, differed somewhat from those of his rural fellows. Although he expressed a fear that the measure would encourage monopoly, he was more emphatic in his conviction that it would give the government too much power over the economy. "Every fault of socialism is found in this bill, without one of its virtues," he said. "Every crime of a monarchy is in here, without one of the things that would give it credit. . . . It is a combination of every evil that can possibly be imagined, worse than anything proposed under the Soviet, because in this thing we go into the realms of the imaginary and the unknown." The President had previously asked Congress to delegate wide authority to him and now he was requesting still greater powers. Some would doubtless accede to his demand, but as for Huey Long: "I am not going to indulge in any more blind voting. I have cast my last blind vote."

It soon became evident, however, that a majority of the Democratic senators would vote blind: the bill was obviously going to pass. Huey admitted defeat in bitter words. "The Democratic party dies tonight," he said. "We will bury it." Curiously, he would cast a partially blind vote himself. When the vote was taken on the bill, he voted nay. Then, reflecting on the desirability of the public works section, he queried Vice-President Garner: "How should a vote be cast when a Senator is half against and half in favor of a bill?" Garner answered acidly that he presumed the senator would have to cut himself in two. Huey, amid jeering laughter, then changed his vote to yea.

He subsequently performed another switch. There were minor differences between the Senate and House versions of the bill, and these had to be ironed out in a conference report. Huey voted against accepting the report, which was equivalent to voting against the bill. Other progressive senators followed a similarly inconsistent course. They were not being opportunists, but rather, on this intricate measure, which was filled with far-reaching innovations, they were torn by conflicting feelings.[4]

Huey hurled yet one more attack on the administration before

[4] Ibid., pp. 5174–84, 5238–53, 5307–8, 5424, 5608, 5601, debates of June 7, 8, 9, 10, and 13, 1933.

Congress finally adjourned. Throughout the session he had fought constantly for the payment of a bonus and other benefits to veterans, winning recognition as the leader of the "veterans' lobby." But he had been blocked in all his efforts by the President's opposition: Roosevelt contended that in this time of stringency the government could not afford to hand out lucrative payments to veterans. Toward the end of the session Huey and other bonus senators decided to make one more attempt to carry their way. An amendment limiting cuts in benefits to veterans was tacked onto an appropriation bill for "independent offices" under the President. When it seemed likely that the amendment would pass, administration Senate leaders announced that the President would veto the whole bill. Huey was infuriated by this threat of executive pressure. He exhorted the Senate to take up the challenge. "I am going to vote to override the veto," he shouted. But he could not move his colleagues to oppose the President's will. He had to concede defeat again, and again he used bitter words. "I will not participate in the Democratic victory tonight," he said. He had joined in many Democratic victories, but they had been over "monopolies" and "giants of finance." He concluded: "I do not care for my share in a victory that means that the poor and the downtrodden, the blind, the helpless, the orphaned, the bleeding, the wounded, the hungry, and the distressed will be the victims."[5]

One day late in June, as the session was about to end, Roosevelt told Jim Farley, now postmaster general, to ask Huey to come to the White House for a conference. It was going to be a showdown meeting, the President said. He had not responded to Huey's fierce attacks on him, but now he was going to show his resentment in action. He had decided to deny the federal patronage in Louisiana to Huey and was going to tell the Kingfish so. Farley arranged a morning appointment for two days later.

Huey came to the meeting dressed in a summer suit and wearing a straw hat. He took a chair opposite the President, and the two men began to discuss their differences. The conversation was amiable, but Farley was angered to see that Huey did not remove his hat except to occasionally tap Roosevelt's knee with it. Farley thought that Huey was pulling the stunt deliberately to test Roosevelt's mettle. (This may have been the case, but it was more probably an oversight on Huey's part, for midway in the interview he took his hat off.) Huey argued that he was entitled to be con-

[5] Ibid., 6106–10, 6130.

sulted in the distribution of patronage because he had backed Roosevelt at the Chicago convention and because he had supported the President's program better than many other senators. Roosevelt blandly reiterated that he was interested only in seeing that good men were appointed to office. When the meeting ended, Huey and Farley left together. Outside the office Huey said, according to Farley: "What the hell is the use of coming down to see this fellow? I can't win any decision over him." Huey undoubtedly said something like this, but Farley misunderstood the remark. He thought that Huey was admitting Roosevelt's political skill. What Huey was trying to say was that he could not get a straight answer out of Roosevelt.[6]

Huey did not seem concerned at his loss of patronage. Telling his secretary that the issue was unimportant, he instructed him to go to Farley's office and get the Louisiana patronage list and tear it up in front of the postmaster general. Finding Farley out, the secretary compromised by destroying the list in the presence of Farley's secretary. Huey expressed the same lack of concern to reporters who pressed him for a statement critical of Roosevelt. He would not fall out with Roosevelt over patronage, he declared. "I understand the rules of war in politics," he said. "No one has practiced them more." After all, the President was doing only what he had done when he was governor of Louisiana. "I contend Mr. Roosevelt is adopting more of the Huey Long policy every day," he observed jocularly.[7]

He also refused to criticize Roosevelt for not following a more progressive course. The President had done some good things and would have done more if he had not been influenced by conservative advisers, Huey contended. Roosevelt was still for the decentralization of wealth. "The trouble is," Huey said, "Roosevelt hasn't taken all of my ideas; just part of them. I'm about one hundred yards ahead of him. We're on the same road, but I'm here and he's there."[8]

Huey still thought that he and Roosevelt could be partners. He told a friend that they both had the same end in view: he "shouted" for the decentralization of wealth while Roosevelt worked for it in a "cultured way." He refused to believe that the administration had broken with him. Why should it? He had voted for most of its bills, and on a rating based on his votes alone, he would have to be classified as an administration supporter. He had, in fact, one of the most

[6] James A. Farley: *Behind the Ballots* (New York, 1938), pp. 240–2.

[7] Earle J. Christenberry; New Orleans *Times-Picayune*, July 27, 1933; New Orleans *Morning Tribune*, July 28, 1933; Shreveport *Journal*, July 29, 1933.

[8] New Orleans *Times-Picayune*, August 23, 1933.

liberal voting records of any senator. A columnist of a labor journal estimated that at least eighty per cent of Long's votes had been on the progressive side, and a writer in a leftist magazine ranked Huey among eight senators who had voted consistently in "the public interest."[9]

Believing that Roosevelt valued his support, Huey did not take the denial of patronage seriously. The President had imposed the ban in a moment of personal pique and would soon lift it. But as the summer months of 1933 wore into autumn, the ban was not eased. Instead, it was tightened. In awarding jobs in Louisiana, the administration consulted only anti-Long leaders—John Sullivan, Edward Rightor, and John M. Parker—and appointed antis almost exclusively to the jobs. Moreover, government officials leveled a barrage of criticism at the state administration, implying that it could not be trusted to handle federal funds, and the government named someone from outside the state to direct unemployment relief, Louisiana being the only state to be thus stigmatized.[1]

As Huey watched these developments, he became increasingly angered. He was not greatly concerned about the practical effect of his loss of the patronage: the number of federal jobs involved was relatively small, and the number of state jobs at his disposal was more than sufficient to enable him to sustain his power. But it was humiliating to him that his enemies should control the patronage and then boast about it. It would encourage them to continue their opposition to him and could in the long run weaken his position. Most irritating of all, the ban advertised that Huey Long was not in the confidence of the administration, that he was not one of those who was consulted about national policy and who influenced that policy. This was the kind of affront that the Kingfish could not endure. Sooner or later his patience was certain to snap.

The snap, when it came, was heard throughout the country. In October Secretary of the Interior Harold L. Ickes, who also administered the public works program, criticized Louisiana for using only half of the money allotted to her for highway construction. Such reluctance on the part of a state to take federal money was unexampled, and Ickes hinted that there must be some sinister reason for the refusal. The reason lay with Huey, and although it was not exactly sinister, it was not very much to his credit. He had prevented the state from accepting the money because it would be

---

[9] Harvey G. Fields; Raymond Lonergan, in *Labor*, June 27, 1930; Robert Morris: "Senate Batting Averages," *Plain Talk*, IX (September 1933), 10–11.

[1] New Orleans *Times-Picayune*, October 20, 1933.

spent under the supervision of his enemies. In replying to Ickes Huey had, however, a different explanation. At a press conference in New Orleans he charged that the men the administration had appointed to office in Louisiana were of questionable character and were likely to steal the money. He made no effort to hide his anger at the President and the latter's advisers. "And while you are at it," he told the reporters in closing, "pay them my further respects up there in Washington. Tell them they can go to hell."[2]

He was telling them to go to hell with their patronage, but he was really repudiating Roosevelt's leadership. He was not ready as yet to declare open war on the President. He would still mildly commend Roosevelt on occasion, and he would continue to vote for some of the administration's bills. But he could no longer be ranked as an administration supporter.

Huey explained his reason for breaking with Roosevelt to several of his Louisiana leaders, some of whom protested his action as unwise. These men, in recalling their conversations with him, quoted him in remarkably similar language, the essence of which was: "He lied to me." They were uncertain, however, as to what Huey said Roosevelt had lied about. Some of them thought he was referring to the President's notorious reluctance to confront a situation squarely, to return an honest answer if that answer had to be negative. Huey was certainly aware of this trait in Roosevelt, for he once spoke of it to a presidential adviser. "I go to that office intending to give that fellow a lecture which he needs," he said. "Then after a while I find myself leaving without speaking my piece. He's hard to talk to." But he was thinking of more than this amiable weakness when he charged Roosevelt with lying. He meant that the President had violated his promise, made personally to Huey, to decentralize wealth. Huey could have forgiven Roosevelt for going back on a campaign pledge, since he understood that a politician had to engage occasionally in public lying. But it was contrary to his code to repudiate a commitment made to an associate, and he never trusted Roosevelt again.[3]

Roosevelt, who was responsible for initiating the break, did not explain his reasons for acting, although he hinted at them to various associates. As reproduced by these men, they are not very revealing.

[2] Baton Rouge *State-Times*, October 9, 1933; Turner Catledge, in *The New York Times*, October 8, 1933, quoted in *American Progress*, October 12, 1933.

[3] Seymour Weiss; Jess Nugent; O. B. Thompson; Charles Frampton; Clem H. Sehrt; Gene Austin; Fred Blanche; Richard W. Leche; Frank Odom; Moley: *Twenty-Seven Masters of Politics*, p. 228.

Thus it has been suggested that the President was moved by dislike of Huey's crudities and of demagoguery and despotism in Louisiana. But Roosevelt tolerated other politicians who were crude and demagogic and conciliated other bosses who held quite as much power as Huey had in 1933. The President would not have broken off relations for these reasons alone.

One presidential intimate has advanced another explanation. He relates that one day soon after the Chicago convention Roosevelt, at a meeting of his advisers, fell to discussing Huey and said: "It's all very well for us to laugh over Huey. But actually we have to remember all the time that he really is one of the two most dangerous men in the country." Roosevelt identified the other dangerous man as General Douglas MacArthur and went on to describe what could happen in the country if the crisis of the depression was not met. The people would become impatient with the democratic process and would demand a strong man to save them. An upheaval of some kind, possibly a violent one, would occur, led either from the left by Long or from the right by MacArthur. If Roosevelt said this, he was engaging in some fanciful forecasting. Huey had done nothing up to 1932, at least, to indicate that he was an antidemocrat. And as he and Roosevelt had not at that time met, Roosevelt could not have formed his judgment from personal knowledge. True, Roosevelt would later decide that Huey was a dangerous man, but it has to be doubted that he broke with Huey because he saw him in this role in 1933. If this was his reason, he chose a peculiarly prosaic way to destroy a revolutionary, by cutting off his patronage.[4]

It was Roosevelt's choice of method that revealed the real reason for the break: two great politicians had come into inevitable conflict. Each was so constituted that he had to dominate other and lesser men. Neither could yield to the other without submerging himself and dimming his destiny. And instinctively each recognized the other's greatness, and feared it.

A CAMPAIGN to destroy Huey with adverse newspaper publicity was organized in 1933. Or so charged correspondents of left-wing journals, who admired the stand that the Louisiana senator had taken in the recent session of Congress. According to these men, a powerful business interest—they all but said it was the banking house of J. P. Morgan—had employed a famous public relations

[4] Moley: *Twenty-Seven Masters of Politics*, p. 229; Rexford G. Tugwell: *The Democratic Roosevelt* (New York, 1957), pp. 348–51.

firm at a fee in excess of twenty-five thousand dollars to handle the campaign and the firm was busily preparing copy for newspapers and press associations smearing the Kingfish. It was one of the "most ferocious" assaults on a politician in American history, one writer claimed.[5]

Huey was certainly getting a bad press in 1933, and some of the stories may have been inspired by his enemies. But the treatment of him by the press was largely spontaneous. He was attacked because he had established himself as a radical, and most of the urban newspapers were strongly conservative. They meted out practically the same criticism to the much milder Roosevelt. But whereas Roosevelt was irritated at the attitude of the press, Huey was not, although on occasion he pretended to be. He thought that any publicity calling attention to him was good, preferring to be attacked to being ignored, and he judged that the onslaughts of the "big city" papers would only strengthen the image of him as a champion of the small people. Besides, he now had means of his own to secure favorable public notice—men in his service who did nothing else but create news about him.

One of these was a press agent whom he had employed soon after he entered the Senate, an able man named George H. Maines. Maines came to the position after a strange train of events. Originally a reporter for the chain of newspapers controlled by William Randolph Hearst, he had been sent by Hearst to Louisiana to check on what kind of politician the new young senator from that state was. Thinking that he could secure information more easily if not known to be a reporter, Maines went south in the guise of a public relations man for the touring show of Gene Austin, a Broadway singing star from Louisiana, who was a friend of Huey's. Maines soon concluded that Huey had done much good for Louisiana, and he wanted to publicize his accomplishment. But first he thought that he should inform the senator of his true identity. Going to Huey's suite at the Roosevelt Hotel, he was met with suspicion and then with hostility. Huey thought he was an investigator for the Senate committee delving into the Overton election and cursed him, and Joe Messina had to be restrained from slugging him.

Shouting "Goddammit, I'm a friendly reporter," Maines left angrily and sent Huey a telegram stating his purpose. He was then invited to meet Huey, and he explained that he wanted to help the senator and could do it by securing favorable publicity in the

[5] Lonergan, in *Labor*, June 27, 1933; Morris A. Bealle: "Kingfishophobia," *Plain Talk*, X (January 1934), 8.

Hearst papers. Huey was impressed by the argument but more so by Maines and his evident wide contacts in the journalistic world. He shortly hired the reporter away from Hearst to write for him and about him.[6]

Another maker of Long publicity was George R. Allen, a Washington newspaperman and public relations agent. Allen apparently worked for Huey only on special assignments, although some of them occupied him for weeks at a time. He did research for Maines or for others on Huey's staff, tried to influence editors to publish material favorable to Huey, and wrote favorable material himself. He provided an interesting example of his writing technique in a letter to Huey. He had persuaded a press-association syndicate to accept a pro-Long article, he said. But the association insisted that it would have also to run an anti-Long article. Therefore he was going to write the anti-article himself! "In the first article I will give the opposition their day," he said, "and in the second I will knock it into a cocked hat."[7]

Huey's use of press agents shows how clearly he perceived the value of publicity and how resourceful he was at getting it: he planned and directed a larger and more successful publicity apparatus than any other senator. But he wanted an even more extensive coverage than his agents secured for him. He therefore established his own newspaper, the *American Progress*, which began publication in August 1933. In name and makeup it was similar to his *Louisiana Progress*, which had ceased publication early in 1932, but whereas he had founded the previous paper to influence Louisianians, he was more ambitious for the new journal: its prospectus announced that it would feature national news designed for a national audience. As a bait to readers, the subscription price was set at only fifty cents a year, although this was shortly raised to a dollar, when the paper expanded in size. As a further inducement, it was promised that Senator Long would write an article for every issue discussing the most important question before the country—the need to redistribute wealth.[8]

The announcement that Huey would contribute articles was a tip-

[6] George H. Maines.

[7] George R. Allen to Earle J. Christenberry, July 16, 1933, and to Long, August 15 and 16, 1933, in John McGuire Collection. Mr. McGuire, of New Orleans, owns a collection of papers consisting of letters from or to Long, most of them dealing with Long's relations with the press; he kindly made this material available to me.

[8] Long, form letter announcing establishment of the paper, July 1, 1933, in Long Papers, Duke University; printed prospectus of the paper, undated, copy in my possession; *American Progress*, August 24, 1933.

off as to the character of the *Progress*: it was primarily an organ of opinion, a journal devoted to expounding the ideas of its founder, either through his own articles or through articles and speeches by men with similar ideas. It was not really a newspaper in the traditional sense of the word. It carried stories that were written and set like news stories, but the "news" was inevitably old, because early in 1934 the weekly became a monthly. Moreover, although Huey had set out to create a paper that would interest people all over the country, most of the stories dealt with Louisiana affairs, which primarily interested Louisianians. Because the paper contained so many articles designed to form opinion, its tone was serious and often heavy. Even Huey's articles did not give it life. He was not at his best in these effusions. Obviously written in haste, they were usually lamentations over Roosevelt's failure to support redistribution of wealth and were frequently only rehashes of Huey's Senate speeches.[9]

The parochial character that the paper usually exhibited reflected the background of the staff Huey had chosen. It was the same group that had edited the *Louisiana Progress*—John Klorer and his assistants. They were good newspaper men, but their press experience had been limited to Louisiana, and they had a provincial outlook. Moreover, they had to prepare their copy for the paper in New Orleans. Huey had hoped to establish the editorial office in Washington, but he was not able to do so, probably because of the expense involved. The *Progress* office consisted of four rooms in the office of the Christenberry Reporting Company, a concern that specialized in stenographic work and whose president, Earle J. Christenberry, held the world's speed record as a typist. Christenberry had met Huey late in 1932, and Huey, looking for a good secretary to take charge of his Washington office, had offered this expert the job. Officially Huey could pay Christenberry only thirty-nine hundred dollars a year, the sum allotted to a senator for a secretary, but he augmented this salary generously with money from his private sources.[1]

It was revenue from these sources, "deduct" money and contri-

[9] Burton H. Hotaling: "Huey Pierce Long as Journalist and Propagandist," *Journalism Quarterly*, XX (1943), 26; Elsie B. Stallsworth: "A Survey of the Louisiana *Progresses* of the 1930's" (unpublished M.A. thesis, Louisiana State University, 1948), pp. 67–8; Long, articles in *American Progress*, August 24, September 24, 31, October 12, 19, 26, November 2, 16, 1933. My account of the *Progress* is based on the two works cited and my examination of the complete file of the paper in the Wisdom Collection, Tulane University.

[1] New Orleans *Morning Tribune*, November 12, 1932; Earle J. Christenberry.

butions from political supporters, that enabled Huey to finance the expensive *Progress*. It was printed in Meridian, Mississippi, as its Louisiana predecessor had been (and for the same reason—to avoid libel suits), and the printing bill for each issue ran to more than six thousand dollars. Another steady expense was salaries. The paper itself was always in the red. It took in little advertising, to give itself the guise of being independent, and thus deprived itself of a potent source of income. Nor did it derive much income from its subscribers. The number of copies circulated rose steadily and in 1935 reached a total of 375,000 copies. But it is not certain that all of them went to paying subscribers. Probably only some hundred thousand persons actually subscribed, the other copies being sent free to people on Huey's mailing list. Although Huey must have been disappointed at the reception of the paper, he continued to support it, believing that it would ultimately help him accomplish his great design.[2]

Huey tried to supervise the content of the *Progress*. Before an issue appeared, he would telephone Klorer and ask him to read out the headlines and first sentences of the lead stories. If he did not like what he heard, he would make revisions and instruct Klorer to use them. But his political duties kept him so busy that he could give only sporadic attention to the paper. He had to entrust it to the staff, and other publicity about himself to his agents. He was not satisfied with their efforts, for he was always convinced that he could do a better job than anybody else, especially about himself. In the autumn of 1933 he created what he thought was his finest production to date: he published his autobiography.

The idea of writing an account of his life occurred to Huey in 1932, and he worked on it at intervals during that year and the following year, in Baton Rouge and in New Orleans. He dictated the material to a secretary—or, actually, to several secretaries, female employees of the state who were called in to take dictation when he could snatch the time to talk. "He did it without notes," one of these women stated. "He would stand up and perform each incident." It is true that he related the story largely out of his mind, but he also did some haphazard research. As he described an incident, he would sometimes decide that he should verify the date of it. Then he would

[2] Earle J. Christenberry; Hotaling: "Long as Journalist," *Journalism Quarterly*, XX, 26; Stallsworth: "The Louisiana Progresses," p. 85. The paper was ostensibly the property of the American Progress Publishing Company, whose small amount of stock was owned by Christenberry.

ask state senator Harvey Peltier to help him. Peltier, as he recalled these occasions, could not restrain his awe of Huey's memory. "Harvey," Huey would say, "if you will go to the *Times-Picayune* for February 2, 1932, on the second page, in such and such a column you will find such and such a story." The story was invariably where Huey said it was.

Huey had begun the book without a title in mind, and he still did not have one when he finished it. He and Peltier discussed the problem for days, but neither could hit on one. Finally, one night, while they were lying in their beds at Huey's room at the Heidelberg Hotel, Peltier had an inspiration. What was that slogan that Huey had used in his campaign for governor in 1928 and quoted frequently in his speeches on redistributing wealth? he asked. Wasn't it "Every man a king?" Huey stood up in his bed. "By God, that's it," he cried.[3]

Now that the book was titled, Huey had to find a publisher. He turned this problem over to George Allen, who went to New York City to talk with various firms. Allen discovered that the publishers were reluctant to take the work. With some difficulty he persuaded one company, J. J. Little and Ives, to sign a contract, and then he had to promise that Huey would advance the company the sum of seven thousand dollars. Little and Ives prepared the plates for the book, but before it was printed the company suddenly announced that it was canceling the contract: its lawyers had warned that the book contained libelous matter. In this crisis Allen had to act fast. He induced a small firm in New York to print the text and a bindery in New Jersey to assemble and bind it. But even then the crisis was not over, for the book had to bear the imprint of a publishing company. In New Orleans the National Book Company was hastily organized, incorporated by Christenberry, Bob Maestri, and Abe Shushan, and in October 1933 *Every Man a King* was published.[4]

Huey followed Allen's negotiations with interest and also gave him a number of explicit instructions. He insisted that the book be wrapped in a gold jacket featuring a picture of the state capitol and himself. He also gave minute directions as to how the illustrations in the book itself should be arranged. To achieve economy of space,

[3] Mary B. Walle; Harvey Peltier.
[4] Earle J. Christenberry; Baton Rouge *State-Times*, October 21, 1933. A mass of documents in the McGuire Collection tell fully the story of the printing of the book. See particularly J. J. Little and Ives Company to Long, August 31, 1933. Allen to Long, August 31, September 21 and 30, October 24, 1933, Long to National Bank of Commerce of New Orleans, September 13, 1933, Long to Allen, September 13 and 18, 1933.

they should appear on both sides of a sheet, he said, but no picture was to be placed on the reverse side of his photograph. He was willing to go to considerable expense to get the kind of book he wanted, but he was appalled by the rapacity of the New York publishers. "Be careful with those people up there," he warned Allen. "They seem to be a cagy set. I have never seen anything like it." Not many people so impressed the Kingfish.[5]

It was a relatively simple matter for the National Book Company to publish the book, but selling it was something else. The company simply did not have the salesmen or the contacts with sales outlets to market the volume. Christenberry and Allen did what they could, writing to bookstores and sometimes traveling to particular cities to talk to dealers and to set up displays in stores. But results were disappointing, even though the price of the book was set, at Huey's insistence, at only a dollar. Probably only twenty thousand copies were disposed of through sales, out of a first printing of fifty thousand copies. But still the book achieved a wide distribution, for Huey gave away copies lavishly, sending them to people on his mailing list. The number given away is conjectural, being based on guesses at the size of subsequent printings, but according to a reliable estimate it ran to seventy thousand copies.[6]

In New Orleans there was an organized attempt to prevent the book from being sold. There Hilda Phelps Hammond, who had sworn revenge on Huey for removing her husband from his state job, rallied her followers, now known as the Women's Committee of Louisiana, to bring pressure on stores handling the book. The ladies telephoned the stores and demanded that the work be withdrawn from sale. If it was not, they threatened, they would cancel their charge accounts. The stores were not frightened.[7]

Reviewers gave the book a varied reception. In progressive newspapers it was generally praised as the product of a liberal politician who had accurately portrayed his struggle against the corporations. Writers in conservative journals denounced it as a demagogic work by a demagogue. Intellectual reviewers condescendingly dismissed both the book and its author. One, a Columbia University history professor, admitted that Huey had done some good in Louisi-

[5] Long to Allen, September 12, 1933, and Allen to Long, September 30, 1933, in McGuire Collection.

[6] Earle J. Christenberry; Robert Brothers; Frank Odom; Hotaling: "Long as Journalist," *Journalism Quarterly,* XX, 27. Hotaling estimates that one hundred thousand copies were printed.

[7] Baton Rouge *State-Times,* October 23, 1933.

ana, but labeled him as one of "our cheaper politicians, a most dangerous type."[8]

It was really a fairly good book, being written in a sprightly style and hence interesting, and, on many phases of Huey's career, was remarkably informative. It was not always completely frank, displaying in this respect a common shortcoming of autobiographies. And like most autobiographies, it did not reveal much about the inner nature of the author, about what kind of man he was. From the point of view of literary artistry, it had a shortcoming—it was incomplete. Approximately 285 of its 343 pages were devoted to Huey's life before he became a senator. The hero of the story had arrived on his great stage, but he had not as yet taken over the play. He was only beginning to reveal his part. The author was obviously going to write another installment.

[8] Excerpts from various reviews, in *American Progress*, November 30, 1933; Allan Nevins, in *Saturday Review of Literature*, X (December 9, 1933), 324.

# CHAPTER 23

## *Polecats Everywhere*

ONE DAY IN LATE AUGUST 1933 word spread through the New York City press corps that Huey Long was in town, at the Hotel New Yorker. Immediately a number of reporters went to his suite to seek an interview.

They found the Kingfish in an amiable and expansive mood, willing to answer most questions and even to volunteer information. He was in the city, he said, to raise money for his proposed *American Progress*—although he did not say what sources he expected to tap—and, he continued, he had just had a motion picture made for distribution in Louisiana showing the great progress accomplished in the state under the Long–Allen regimes. Queried about his relations with Roosevelt, he said that he still backed the President, even though the latter had lagged in supporting redistribution of wealth. Having got onto his favorite issue, he inevitably digressed to discuss the Book that upheld his position. "You never see anybody getting into trouble that lives up to the Bible," he intoned. "By the way, where the hell is that Bible I had anyway?" The reporters tried to bring him back to a more secular subject. Hadn't Huey got drunk in his room on the previous night and had a fight with some friends? they asked. The Kingfish brusquely shut off this line of inquiry. "No polecat questions," he said.[1]

A few days later Huey took a suburban train to Long Island and went to the home of a friend, Gene Buck, a nationally famous composer of popular songs, who had written such hits as "Mother

---

[1] New Orleans *Times-Picayune*, August 23, 1933.

Is Her Name" and "Tulip Time." He and Huey had met during one of the senator's trips to New York—Huey had probably sought the meeting—and had been drawn to each other by their mutual love of music. After that, Huey spent much of his time with Buck whenever he was in New York. Buck was currently the president of the American Society of Composers, Authors and Publishers, and he had invited Huey to join a group that he was taking to a charity show and ball sponsored by the society at the Sands Point Bath and Country Club. At Buck's home Huey met the other people making up the party: Mrs. Buck, Edward P. Mulrooney, former police commissioner of New York City, and his wife and daughter, and Alford J. Williams, onetime flier in the navy, and now an oil business executive, and Mrs. Williams. The group decided to have drinks before going to the club, and someone asked Huey what was in a sazerac cocktail, a drink indigenous to New Orleans. Huey volunteered to mix up a batch of sazeracs and downed several glasses himself. Finally Buck, warning that it was late, hustled the party off to nearby Sands Point.

On arriving, they found that the floor show had started, and they went immediately to their table. Shortly a young man approached and asked Huey if he would come to meet a young lady who, he said, was a granddaughter of a former governor of Louisiana. Huey said that he would talk with her later. After dinner he went to the other table and did not return to his own party for some time. When he did, at about eleven o'clock, he asked Buck where the men's washroom was and disappeared again. He was absent for over half an hour. When he reappeared, he was holding a napkin to his forehead, with which he was trying to stem a flow of blood from a cut above one eye. "Gene," he said, "let's get out of here. I'm on the spot."[2]

Buck was mystified, but he realized that he should get Huey out of the club, if for no other reason than to prevent unpleasant publicity. As he had sent his own car home, he asked Jack Curley, a wrestling promoter, to drive him and Huey to his house. Huey might require the services of a doctor, he explained to Curley. In the the car Huey was able to stanch the bleeding, and when they reached Buck's residence, he said that he did not need a doctor. He asked Buck to call a cab to take him back to New York. Before he left, he

---

[2] George H. Maines; Maines, article in *Zit's Theatrical Newspaper*, September 1, 1934, and "Framing the Kingfish," in *Plain Talk*, XII (July 1936), 40–3. Maines was not at Sands Point but received an account of the episode from Buck. His version is slanted in Huey's favor, but the main outline of events is probably correct.

told Buck and Curley an astonishing tale of being attacked in the washroom by gangsters.[3]

Some of the people at the club had seen Huey come out of the washroom holding the napkin over his eye, and the word soon spread that apparently someone had hit the senator. The news spread farther during the next few days, as those who had been present retold the story to friends and acquaintances, and inevitably it grew in the telling. Reporters from the New York papers shortly flocked to Sands Point and questioned guests and employees of the club and persons in the neighborhood. Coincidentally, Huey, who had gone into seclusion at his hotel, had to make a public appearance. He had agreed to speak at a veterans' convention in Milwaukee, and when he reached there, he did indeed have a wound of some kind over one eye. The New York papers chose this moment to break their story, and it immediately became front-page news in papers all over the country. The usual heading on the stories was: "Who Hit Huey?"

These stories provided full, if not always consistent, accounts of Huey's behavior before he went to the washroom. Various unidentified witnesses affirmed that he had dismissed the bartender at the club and mixed drinks for the guests (this bit probably grew out of his making sazeracs at Buck's home); that he had dragged a young woman he had not been introduced to onto the dance floor and forced her to dance with him; that he had gone from table to table grabbing asparagus from the diners' plates and eating it; and that he had approached a lady of statuesque proportions and taken away her plate, saying: "I'll eat this for you. You're too fat anyway." These "witnesses" offered confident theories as to what had happened in the washroom: (1) the escort of one of the girls Huey had insulted followed him and hit him; (2) his hands were buttery from grabbing asparagus and he wiped them on the coat of a man, who thereupon hit him; or (3) a local police chief, present in his official capacity, and some other men were rebuking him for his conduct when the chief became angered and struck him.

And some reporters picked up still another theory, the most titillating of all, and this one came to be accepted as the most probable. The papers at first only hinted at it: there was a rather vague statement that Huey had come up behind a man and done "something" the man had to resent. Some publications soon frankly explained that the man was using the urinal, and that Huey had tried

[3] Boston *Post*, August 30, 1933; New Orleans *Times-Picayune*, September 1, 1933.

to see if he could urinate between the man's legs. He succeeded only in drenching the man. The victim, who had promptly retaliated with a vigorous blow, had been wearing a dress suit, and this circumstance moved Will Rogers to offer his own explanation: "Huey didn't recognize him in the disguise," Rogers chuckled. "Dress suits are only used in Louisiana to encase dead politicians."

The hitter was variously identified: "a young man," a New York architect, the police chief, or—most frequently—Al Williams, the former aviator. These men all denied any part in the affair, but none of them appeared to resent the charges. Rather, each denial implied that credit rather than blame was involved, leaving the impression that any one of them might deserve the honor that, for the record, he disavowed.[4]

Huey at first would not talk about the incident. But finally he gave several, and somewhat differing, accounts to various reporters. In one he said simply: "A member of the house of Morgan slipped up behind and hit me with a blackjack." In another account he supplied more detail: while he was standing at the basin in the washroom, he had suddenly been slugged from behind. Turning, he saw three or four men coming at him. One of them lashed at his head with a knife, but he ducked, so the knife only grazed his forehead. Breaking away from his assailants, he made for the door. But blocking it was another villain, who stood with his legs outspread. "I stumbled low through him," the Kingfish said, and thus escaped. In still another version, he said that he had been set upon by a number of men, who had struck him twenty times before he could escape. When he had come to New York on this trip, he said, he had been warned by friends not to venture outside his hotel. "I realize that I have powerful enemies," he said cryptically.[5]

The truth of what happened in the washroom was and still is uncertain. Even Huey's closest associates, when asked to recall the episode, could not, or would not, throw any light on it. Probably Huey, to avoid their reproaches, told them nothing. He seems to have discussed the affair with only one of his friends, whose recollection of Huey's explanation is simple and logical: "He was always kind of

[4] New Orleans *Times-Picayune*, August 29, 31, September 1, 1933, Washington *Times*, August 29, 1933; New Orleans *Morning Tribune*, August 29, 1933; George H. Maines. Mr. Maines stated that Williams had not left his table during the evening, but that when the episode made front pages, he agreed, at the suggestion of his public relations man, to appear as the hitter, and that to give this claim credence, he had his right hand bandaged.

[5] New Orleans *Times-Picayune*, August 29, 1933; New York *World-Telegram*, August 29, 1933, quoted in New Orleans *Item*, August 30, 1933.

sloppy, and that night he had been drinking. He went to the rest room and to the urinal. That aviator, Williams, was standing next to him. It was an accident. He just swung it too far and hit the fellow's shoe, and he socked him."[6]

The glee with which the press celebrated the battle of Sands Point was understandable. The story was legitimate news: it was not every day that a United States senator was beaten up in a washroom. But the ardor with which some papers publicized the episode made it clear that to them it was more than a straight news story. These were conservative journals, who seized the opportunity to ridicule and perhaps thus to destroy the politician who had emerged as the leader of the American left.

Leading the conservative pack was *Collier's Weekly*, which had a special reason to attack Huey. During the recent session of Congress, while a committee was investigating the influence of the Morgan banking house in the financial community, he had appeared before it, asking for permission to cross-examine a Morgan executive. He had drawn from this man an admission that he was a director of the publishing company that controlled *Collier's*.

The next day Huey had risen in the Senate and, after recounting his success before the committee, had introduced into the record excerpts from two articles about him in the magazine, one published in 1930 and the other in 1933. Those from the earlier article praised Huey highly, whereas those from the later piece smeared him unmercifully. The reason for the abrupt reversal was obvious, Huey said. He had been a shining young governor in 1930, but when he arrived in the Senate and began to attack the big banks, he became a cheap and dangerous politician. His analysis was perhaps too simple, but to say the least, he had demonstrated that the editorial opinion at *Collier's* was remarkably mercurial.[7]

Now the magazine struck back. One of its editors, acting, he claimed, on a whim, suggested to a New York paper that he would like to start a fund to strike a medal to the "unknown Hero" who had hit Huey. The paper obligingly ran a notice of the idea, which was immediately taken up by papers and radio stations throughout the country. Contributions to the fund poured in to *Collier's*, more than enough finally to make the proposed medal. A cartoonist for the

---

[6] Murphy Roden.

[7] Philadelphia *Record*, June 10, 1933; *Congressional Record*, 73 Cong., 1 Sess., pp. 5541–2, speech of June 10, 1933. The two articles, by Walter Davenport, were "Yes, Your Excellency," in issue of December 13, 1930, p. 22 *passim*, and "Catching Up with Huey," in issue of June 1, 1933, p. 12 *passim*.

magazine volunteered to prepare its design: in the form of a toilet seat, it showed Huey, with a fishlike head, being struck by a fist. A Princeton professor retained as a consultant by *Collier's* composed a Latin inscription for it, which translated read: "In public acclaim for a deed done in private." The perpetrators of the stunt had intended to present the medal to the owner of the fist, but the hero refused to identify himself. Somewhat puzzled as to what to do with it, they finally turned it over to the American Numismatic Society.[8]

The medal project backfired on its sponsors. A Washington, D. C., paper not friendly to Huey said that the "medal mountebanks" had succeeded only in impressing on the public "the conspicuous absence of ordinary brains and breeding in the idle rich." And this was a widespread reaction. Huey, however, was irritated by the incident and tried to counteract it. He prepared a circular in the form of a letter to gangster Al Capone, then languishing in a federal prison, in which he suggested to Capone a way to get out. Let Capone inform *Collier's* that it was he who had arranged for Senator Long to be beat up at Sands Point, and the house of Morgan would effect his release![9]

Huey need not have been bothered by the medal publicity or the campaign of the conservative newspapers to ridicule him into oblivion. Neither damaged him seriously, although they would have ruined an ordinary politician. Such a man would have issued solemn denials which would not have been believed. Huey chose exactly the right defense: he told a monumental falsehood. Hardly anyone believed that he had been beaten up by gangsters sent to Sands Point by the Morgans, but the story was so magnificently conceived that people laughed admiringly and overlooked his indiscretion.

JUST AS THE Sands Point story broke, Huey arrived in Milwaukee to address the national convention of the Veterans of Foreign Wars. The New Orleans chapter of the organization, in recognition of his efforts to secure financial benefits for veterans, had enrolled him as an honorary member, and the national officers, also grateful, had invited him to the convention.

[8] Owen P. White: *The Autobiography of a Durable Sinner* (New York, 1942), pp. 270–1; clipping, New York *World-Telegram*, n.d., in my possession.

[9] Washington *Herald* and other papers, quoted in *American Progress*, September 14 and 28, 1933; circular, "J. P. Morgan and Company Points Way for Capone's Release," in my possession. This document had the largest circulation of any of Huey's circulars, 1,225,000 copies; Burton H. Hotaling: "Huey Pierce Long as Journalist and Propagandist," *Journalism Quarterly*, XX (1943), 22.

When Huey reached Milwaukee he was edgy and belligerently sensitive about the cut above his eye. Seeing photographers in front of the platform, he exclaimed that he would not permit any pictures. As sergeants-at-arms rushed the photographers out of the hall, many of the veterans jumped up, shouting their approval. When quiet was restored, Huey turned his attention to the reporters present. Nobody should believe anything in the newspapers, he bellowed. Reporters were like "polecats"—"skunks in the woods." He had driven the polecats from Louisiana, and here they had turned up in Milwaukee. Again the convention was thrown into a turmoil, as delegates surged into the aisles and threatened the reporters. But Huey did not demand that the correspondents be removed—he was not going to forgo the publicity they could give him—and eventually he launched into his speech, a plea for the redistribution of wealth and a resounding attack on the Roosevelt administration, Wall Street, and the house of Morgan, who were other polecats trying to destroy Huey Long.[1]

THE POLECATS SEEMED indeed to be everywhere in 1933, attacking Huey from every direction. That year there was apparently a dramatic downturn in his prestige and power, so much so that many observers predicted his political demise. The fiercest onslaughts came in Louisiana.

In the November 1932 general election in Louisiana the voters had been asked to pass on other questions in addition to the choice of a President. The recent legislature had enacted fifteen amendments to the constitution, and they were up for ratification. Most of them dealt with matters that were trivial but that under the peculiar Louisiana practice had to be presented to the voters. Two of them, however, were of importance—they authorized bond issues to cover Board of Liquidation debts and to enable New Orleans to purchase a ferry—and they were vigorously opposed by anti-Longites. They were supported just as ardently by the allied Long and Old Regular organizations.

When the votes on the amendments were announced—it naturally took some time to tabulate them—it was disclosed that all fifteen of them had been approved. Although the two bond amendments had been defeated in the country parishes, the heavy vote they received in New Orleans, a margin of approximately ten to one,

[1] New Orleans *Times-Picayune*, August 30, 1933; Baton Rouge *State-Times*, August 30, 1933; *American Progress*, August 31, 1933.

had enabled them to carry. The vote in the city for all the amendments was of similar proportions, much larger than the Long–Walmsley machine had been expected to deliver, and this development stirred the suspicions of officers of the Honest Election League and other conservatives. An unofficial investigation revealed some interesting facts. In sixteen precincts the vote for the fifteen amendments was unanimous; in twenty-eight other precincts identical numbers of votes were recorded for the amendments and against them; and in fifteen additional precincts less than ten votes were cast against any of the amendments. In the fifty-nine precincts surveyed, the total vote for the amendments was 18,481 and the vote against them was only 423. The conservatives were elated at the evidence. They saw in it an opportunity to prove that they were crusaders for honesty and that the Long regime had engineered fraud in the election. They petitioned the district attorney of Orleans parish, Eugene Stanley, to take action to expose the fraud.

Stanley was something of a political oddity. Not of the Old Regulars and yet not strongly against them, he had been elected with independent support. He chose now an independent course. He obtained a court order directing that four ballot boxes from the precincts under suspicion be turned over to the parish grand jury on the ground that they contained evidence necessary for an investigation into charges of fraudulent returns. The order was issued on November 23.

On the next day, before the boxes were delivered, Stanley was summoned from the grand jury room to take a telephone call from Baton Rouge. It was from the state's attorney general, Gaston Porterie, who asked Stanley to call off the investigation. Porterie explained that if fraud was uncovered, the legality of the bond issues might come under question. Stanley replied that this eventuality was unlikely because the amendments had been officially promulgated. But Porterie still pressed his request, and when Stanley refused to grant it, the attorney general said that as the state's legal officer he could supplant a district attorney in the prosecution of a case (this was permitted by the constitution if the state's interest was concerned) and that he would take over the conduct of this case. He came to New Orleans on November 29 and was closeted with the grand jury. Emerging from the session, he announced that the jurors had adjourned without taking any action on the disputed returns, and the foreman of the jury, when questioned by reporters, said only: "We had a nice lunch, and it is a very nice day."

If Porterie thought he had blocked the investigation, he was soon disillusioned, since his intervention in fact strengthened the demand for an inquiry. Conservatives reasoned that the attorney general had entered the case because he, or whoever was directing him, feared the result of an investigation, and in their minds there was no doubt that Huey Long was doing the directing. Other groups joined the Honest Election League in demanding that the inquiry be resumed—the Louisiana Bar Association, the New Orleans Bar Association, and the Young Men's Business Club of New Orleans. They requested specifically that Porterie retire from the case and turn it back to Stanley.

The attorney general refused to step out, but he did meet again on two occasions with the grand jury. At one of these sessions the four boxes were brought into the jury room but were not opened, and at the other session the boxes were opened but immediately resealed. The jurors finally informed Judge A. D. Henriques, who was presiding over this session of the civil criminal court, that they were adjourning without taking any action. Porterie told the court that he would like to make a statement. The judge cut him off acidly: "Under the law there are only three things a grand jury can do. They can find a true bill, they can find a no-true bill, or they can pretermit. Is there any other legal information I can give you?" Outraged conservatives charged that Porterie had brought improper influence upon the jury, and the state bar association asked its ethics committee to inquire into the attorney general's fitness to be a member of the association. Meanwhile, early in 1933, the bonds Porterie had said would be endangered were sold, and this alleged reason for stopping the investigation no longer had validity.

Coincidentally, a new judge, Frank T. Echezabal, assumed jurisdiction of the civil criminal court. He was known as a "tough" judge and an anti-Long, and when he empaneled a new grand jury and advised it to investigate the charges of vote frauds, conservatives gleefully predicted that quick results would follow. The jury dutifully met, Porterie met with it, and then on May 17, 1933, the jurors came before Judge Echezabal to announce their finding— they wished to present a verbal no-true bill, that is, to present no charges. The judge was furious. He refused to accept the bill, declaring that any recommendation of the jury had to be cast in written form, and he instructed the jurors to continue the investigation and to be thorough, by which he meant that they should open the ballot boxes and inspect the ballots. Also angered by this unexpected outcome was the Louisiana Bar Association, whose executive committee expelled Porterie from its membership on the ground that by his action in the case he had violated legal ethics.

The grand jury seemed to think that the judge's instructions for it to be thorough meant for it to be deliberate. It did not meet again until June 30. Then an assistant of Porterie's appeared before it and presented an indictment of every election official in New Orleans in the November election, and the four ballot boxes were brought into the jury room. The jurors did not open the boxes, and after some discussion decided by a vote of nine to three to return a no-true bill. Since Echezabal was on vacation, the verdict was delivered to another judge of the same court, Alexander O'Donnell. In presenting the bill, the jury impudently observed that it had received no co-operation from Stanley. The district attorney was present and jumped to his feet. "That's quite true," he cried. "I wouldn't lay the case of a Negro charged with stealing chickens before this grand jury." O'Donnell coldly rejected the no-true bill and ordered the jurors from the room. He then directed the criminal sheriff of Orleans parish, a John Sullivan supporter, to take custody of the ballot boxes. As Sullivan had been ejected from the Old Regular hierarchy at Huey's demand, the boxes were in the care of a man opposed to both Long and Walmsley.[2]

O'Donnell was loudly applauded by conservatives for his action, and perhaps influenced by this approval—of humble origin, he was, according to Longites, eager for social recognition—he intervened further in the dispute. On July 25 he ordered an open court inquiry into the vote on the amendments in all precincts and appointed Stanley to conduct the inquiry, with no interference from Porterie. Five days later, on July 30, Senator Long, fresh from his jousts with the Roosevelt administration, arrived in New Orleans and went to the Roosevelt Hotel, where he conferred with Governor Allen and other state officials who had rushed down from Baton Rouge that morning. Simultaneously two companies of national guardsmen were assembled at Jackson Barracks, near the city.

The next day Allen issued a proclamation imposing "partial martial law" in New Orleans. He explained that he was acting in response to a petition from eleven of the twelve grand jurors, who had complained that they had been ejected from O'Donnell's court and had requested protection for their deliberations. The conservatives

[2] *Overton Hearing*, II, 2710, 2726–8, 2736–7, 2740; New Orleans *Times-Picayune*, November 30, 1932; Hermann B. Deutsch: "Kingdom of the Kingfish," in New Orleans *Item*, August 29 and 30, 1939.

promptly charged that Huey Long was now trying to intimidate the courts. O'Donnell and Stanley proclaimed that they would not be intimidated, and on August 1 the judge summoned the grand jury to witness the opening of the ballot boxes. Militia soldiers stood outside the jury room as the recounting of the votes began. But that night Allen, as suddenly as he had invoked martial law, revoked it. Order was being maintained by the civil authorities, he explained lamely.[3]

While the recounting proceeded in O'Donnell's court, Judge Echezabal returned from his vacation. His first official act was to discharge the grand jury and to order a new one empaneled. The import of this move was obvious: if any evidence of fraud were to be found, the conservatives would not entrust it to a jury that was, as they claimed, under Long influence. They contended that the recount was disclosing such evidence, pointing as proof to various discrepancies in the tabulations. Thus, in one precinct 332 votes had been tallied for the amendments and 3 votes against them; the recount revised the figures to 350 votes for and 27 votes against. In another box 400 votes had been counted for the amendments and 11 votes against them; the revision changed the totals to 350 votes for and 30 votes against.

In some boxes the corrected vote cut the margin for the amendments more drastically. Interestingly, the most glaring difference in a box was discovered in the one in Mayor Walmsley's precinct, where 177 votes for the amendments had been counted, to 68 votes against them. The recount shifted this aggregate to 59 votes for and 154 votes against the amendments. In the city as a whole, the vote for the measures was reduced by approximately eighteen thousand votes, leaving them still approved by a comfortable majority. Longites contended, with some plausibility, that the recount had disclosed not fraud but careless counting by the election commissioners in some precincts. These harried officials had counted the votes on the first few amendments and found an overwhelming vote for them, and they had then recorded the same vote for the remaining amendments. Huey himself said that he was surprised that the majority for the amendments had been cut as little as it was, since the ballot boxes had been in the custody of a sheriff controlled by John Sullivan. He promised that he would protect any commissioners who were prosecuted as a result of the recount.

The prosecutions were not long in coming. As the recount de-

[3] New Orleans *Times-Picayune*, July 31 and August 1, 1933.

veloped discrepancies in various precincts, Stanley brought charges
of fraud against the commissioners who had presided over them.
By September 1, when the recount was completed, the district attorney had indicted 512 officials. Three of them were brought to
trial in October and in December were convicted and sentenced to
prison. But they did not serve their sentences. Early in 1934 a special
session of the legislature enacted a law amending the existing law
on election fraud to the effect that a fraud had to be proved to have
been committed "willfully." As it was manifestly impossible to prove
that the remaining commissioners had deliberately engaged in fraud,
the prosecutions were dropped, and Governor Allen pardoned the
three officials who had been found guilty. Huey had kept his promise
to protect the commissioners.[4]

The battle of the ballot boxes was an apparently minor but revealing episode in the Long story. Ostensibly it had begun as a dispute
between the state government and certain judicial officials in New
Orleans. Huey did not appear as an actor until the closing scenes,
but obviously he had directed from the first the moves to block the
investigation, such as Porterie's sudden intervention and the repeated refusal of the grand jury to open the boxes.

Huey's motives for acting as he did are puzzling. He would not
have suffered seriously from the investigation, and the amendments
could not conceivably have been affected. They had been passed
and promulgated, and the worst that an inquiry could have done
would have been to cut down their majority somewhat. The argument that the bond issues would be endangered by the investigation
was fallacious, as shown by the efforts to shut it off after the bonds
were sold. If the early investigation had disclosed discrepancies in
the vote, Huey could have explained them, as he did later, as the
result of hasty counting. Or, although he would have strained his alliance with the Old Regulars, he could have said that many of the
commissioners had been chosen by the city organization and that
it was these officials who had allowed whatever fraud was committed.

His motives were no puzzle to his enemies, however. They
charged that in his brutal bid for more power, he had called out the
national guard to intimidate the courts. Their reasoning was naïve.
If the militia was summoned to awe the judiciary the maneuver was

[4] Baton Rouge *State-Times*, August 2 and 25, 1933; New Orleans *Times-Picayune*,
August 4, 8, December 7, 1933; *Overton Hearing*, II, 2728; Deutsch: "Kingdom of
the Kingfish," in New Orleans *Item*, August 30, 1939; Huey P. Long: *Every Man a
King*, pp. 328–32.

feebly conceived and executed—two companies of soldiers were sent to stand outside the grand jury room and then were almost immediately recalled. The use of the guardsmen was, as the conservatives contended, improper. But this was not the move of a power-mad dictator. Rather, it was the response of a politician who was off balance and not acting with his normal perception.

Throughout 1933 Huey alternated between moods of abnormal elation and depression. Early in the year he was elated—he had challenged the President himself and believed that he would win his battle with Roosevelt and go on to the goal he had set for himself. Then had come unexpected reverses—the denial of federal patronage, the consequent strengthening of the anti-Long forces in Louisiana, the episode at Sands Point and the ensuing vicious press campaign. His enemies were powerful and apparently would stop at nothing. Fires broke out twice in his house in New Orleans under such mysterious circumstances that he concluded they were the work of incendiaries, and his daughter Rose received an anonymous kidnapping threat.[5]

These incidents plunged Huey into an abnormal depression. He was suspicious, fearful, and dangerous. He saw the ballot-box investigation as another attempt to destroy him—which in part it was—and he struck back savagely. He did not act like a democratic politician or even a smart one. He betrayed that in either extreme of emotion he could lose sight of reality.

He revealed in other actions that he was laboring under strain. In the late summer and fall of 1933 he flooded the state with circulars that attacked his enemies with unusual venom. One of these struck the theme that during a flood the animals of the woods, the polecats, the skunks, and others, sought safety on high ground, where they lay peaceably together until the danger passed. Such a flood was now rising in Louisiana, "the waters of public opinion," and the animals were flocking to safety, the whole lot of conservatives who had opposed a fair deal for the people of Louisiana. They were named in a bitter article and also were pictured in grotesque feral forms in a Trist cartoon: Parker, Sanders, Sullivan, and others. To some of them Huey applied the damaging nicknames that he had previously bestowed: "Shinola" Phelps, "Squirt" Ewing. He added two new enemies to his list and also supplied them with titles. One was Leonard Nicholson of the *Times-Picayune* hierarchy, who had heavy, dark cheeks and presumably because of this feature was

[5] Rose McConnell Long; Rose Long McFarland; Washington *Star*, September 23, 1933.

labeled "Liverwurst." The other was Alvin Howard, also of the *Picayune* group, who had black, closely curled hair: he was named "Kinky." There was no doubt that this name insinuated that Howard was part Negro. Huey was, in a rare display for him, resorting to the ugly weapon of racial prejudice.[6]

IN 1932 THE LEGISLATURE had created the Tax Reform Commission, an agency to study the state's fiscal system and to make recommendations for improving it. The commission examined at length the existing tax structure and the machinery of the state government. It did not turn in its report until the summer of 1933. The report recommended a complete readjustment of the tax structure, which would include imposing some new taxes, the dedication of much of the money from these new levies to the schools and road program, and, in the interest of economy, the abolition of certain state jobs. To offset the burden that the taxes would place on the average citizen, the commission proposed that the state property tax be eased by allowing a two thousand-dollar homestead exemption to homeowners. Because the schools urgently needed aid, the commission suggested that a special session of the legislature be called to enact its plan into law.

The report was officially addressed to Governor Allen, but this was only a formality, since everyone knew it would ultimately go to Senator Long, who would decide what would be done with it and then tell Allen to do it. Senator Long, when he saw the document, had mixed reactions. He liked the recommendation for additional taxes, which would help to support the always expanding public-improvements program that he had set in motion, and which would also help the people employed in the program. But he objected strongly to the proposal to eliminate a number of state jobs, which would lessen the patronage at his disposal. He tried to induce the commission to abandon this suggestion, and after some heated discussion with the members he won his way.

The amended report said nothing about the need for economy in government. It recommended seven new taxes: on incomes, oil produced or marketed in Louisiana (the rate was higher on oil brought in from other states), natural gas, tobacco, liquor, lubricating oil (Huey soon backed off from this levy), and public utilities receipts. The report also approved a two thousand-dollar homestead

---

[6] "Answering Ten Months of Lies"; Baton Rouge *State-Times*, August 5, 1933.

exemption. Huey made the report public in October 1933 and said that he would immediately embark on a speaking tour of the state to arouse public support for the proposed taxes.[7]

He began his tour in the southern parishes, opening at Donaldsonville, where a large crowd had assembled at the annual South Louisiana Fair. This was Long territory, and ordinarily Huey would have had a friendly reception. But now he found an audience that was cold and withdrawn and at times even hostile. He was booed when he asked for support of the new taxes and again when he attacked Roosevelt. At the height of one of the interruptions a heckler yelled: "What about that Long Island affair?" Huey let the question anger him. "Come down out of that grandstand," he screamed, "and I'll man to man it with you." It was the worst possible response. The crowd could see that he did not mean to back up his challenge, since a protective line of state policemen stood in front of the speaker's platform.[8]

He encountered much the same reception when he moved on to other towns in the southern section. The crowds came out to hear him, and although they sometimes booed or heckled, they generally listened attentively. In fact, they listened too well, as though they were turning his message over and over and were not being convinced by it, as though they were refusing to be convinced. Their reaction was understandable. Huey was taking a line that was certain to be unpopular with many of his people. In a Southern state, he was attacking a Democratic President and, moreover, a President who in his first year of office was becoming a beloved figure, because, having entered office during a depression, he had set himself to fight that depression and apparently was succeeding. But Huey was criticizing this good man, contending that his efforts to aid the people were futile, and he was thereby endangering the chances of Louisiana to secure its share of federal aid. And on top of this he was asking the people of Louisiana to vote additional taxes on themselves, as though he thought the state itself should combat the depression.

The hostile demonstrations of the crowds were usually spontaneous and were expressed in booing or some other form of verbal disapproval. But sometimes they were premeditated—fomented before a meeting by conservative antis who detested Roosevelt but were

[7] Hermann B. Deutsch: "Kingdom of the Kingfish," in New Orleans *Item*, September 3, 1939; T. O. Harris: *The Kingfish: Huey P. Long, Dictator* (New Orleans, 1938), pp. 143–6; *American Progress*, October 19, 1933.
[8] New Orleans *Times-Picayune*, October 10, 1933.

willing to exploit the popular affection for him to damage Huey—and these displays were often violent. For example, a visitor in the office of a lawyer in a small town near Hammond saw there a large basket piled with eggs. The visitor inquired if the lawyer was also in the poultry business. "Hell, no," the attorney answered. "Those eggs are for Huey Long." He explained that he had gotten them at the advice of a newspaper in Hammond, which had urged that Huey be egged when he spoke there. As it turned out, so many citizens made known their intention to follow the paper's advice that Huey had to cancel the meeting.[9]

The exhibitions of violence became even more frequent when Huey invaded north Louisiana. While he was speaking at Monroe, two men repeatedly arose and shouted interruptions, one calling the senator a liar. They were finally escorted from the meeting by state policemen. When similar incidents occurred at other towns, Huey charged that "hoodlums and bandits" were being sent by his opponents to break up his meetings. "I am proud of my enemies," he cried defiantly.[1]

At Monroe and other towns Huey attacked in virulent personal terms an anti leader from Minden, in Webster parish in the northwest, Harmon Drew. He promised that he would repeat his words when he spoke in Minden, even if Drew was present. His threat enraged Drew and his friends in Webster parish and also other anti leaders in neighboring parishes, who decided that the time had come to close the mouth of this demagogue who attacked gentlemen. They resolved to stop Huey from making his speech about Drew—no matter what method they had to use. One of them recalled the emotion-charged conference: "At that time there were men all over the state who believed that Huey had to be killed, that to kill him would be a moral act. The word went out for armed men to come to Minden that night. A score or more from Webster and other parishes came. This was the plan. Drew was to take a seat in the front row. If Huey attacked him, Drew would reply. If the guards made for Drew, all hell was to break loose. Each man in the plot had a guard to shoot, and several were assigned to shoot Huey."[2]

One of the plotters, however, had qualms: too many people were likely to be killed. He revealed the plan to a friend of Huey's,

[9] W. D. Robinson to Louis Howe, October 23, 1933, in Robinson Papers.

[1] New Orleans *Morning Tribune*, November 9, 1933; Baton Rouge *State-Times*, November 9, 1933; Baton Rouge *Morning Advocate*, November 9, 1933.

[2] Rupert Peyton; A. M. Wallace.

who passed the message on to Colonel E. P. Roy, head of the state
police and in charge of security arrangements for Huey during the
stump tour. Roy received the news just as Huey was preparing to
drive to Minden to speak. Getting into the car with the senator, Roy
explained the plot. He begged Huey to cancel the meeting and go on
to Shreveport. Huey insisted that he was going to talk, and talk
about Drew. But Roy persisted, stressing that a number of people
would lose their lives if Huey stuck to his purpose. Huey finally
agreed to a compromise: he would speak at Minden but he would
not mention Drew.

The meeting at Minden was scheduled in the courthouse square,
and the space was packed with people when Huey and his party,
most of them state policemen and bodyguards, arrived. In front of
the speaker's platform stood men with revolvers or pistols clearly
bulging in their coats, Drew's supporters. As Huey mounted the
platform, Drew himself appeared and paced back and forth menacingly. Louie Jones, back in his home town, went up to Drew and
said: "If you put a foot on the platform, I'll kill you." Other guards
stationed themselves before the platform and shifting their guns on
their hips, looked meaningfully at the Drew adherents. "We had
everybody covered," Murphy Roden recalled.

Huey spoke briefly, without mentioning Drew, and then, escorted
by policemen, went to his car and drove to Shreveport. The moment
he left the platform, Drew ascended it and spoke to those of the
crowd that remained. He boasted that Huey had not had the nerve
to denounce him to his face. It was an ungracious remark. Huey
had shown physical courage in speaking before armed men who were
looking for an excuse to kill him. And he had demonstrated some
moral courage—he had been willing to curb his remarks to save
lives.[3]

Huey ended his tour at Alexandria. Here too he spoke outside,
in front of the city hall, and here again he found that his enemies
had prepared a reception for him. He had hardly launched into his
speech when a barrage of rotten eggs, overripe fruit, and homemade
stinkbombs struck the platform. They came from open windows in
a nearby bank building, and several state troopers dashed to the
door, intending to enter and find the culprits. They found the way
barred by the city's chief of police, Clint O'Malley, and a number of
city policemen. Mr. O'Malley blandly explained that the bank was

[3] E. P. Roy; Louis A. Jones; Murphy Roden; Theophile Landry; Baton Rouge
State-Times, November 11, 1933.

private property and that he was present to prevent an illegal entry. He did not seem to think his duty compelled him to prevent the egg throwers from using it as a base.

The hecklers, knowing that they were secure, hurled their missiles throughout Huey's speech, which lasted for two hours. Huey was not struck, largely because of the dexterity of his guards, who stationed themselves in front of the platform and caught in their hands eggs that were aimed at the speaker. But other people on the platform were hit. One was an old man who had been invited to sit near Huey. An egg splattered on his shoulder. He calmly took a long knife out of his pocket and with the blade removed the stain, muttering angrily: "If I could catch the dirty little rat that threw this, I'd scrape his ass just like I'm scraping this off." At the conclusion of the meeting Huey was escorted to his hotel by a hundred supporters, who feared that he would be attacked if he were unattended.[4]

If Huey seemed to be laboring under unusual strain in 1933, if he sometimes seemed impatient with democratic procedures, he was not unique. Some of his pious enemies also showed signs of irrational impatience late in that year.

In June 1933 an unexpected vacancy was created in the Louisiana congressional delegation. Bolivar Kemp, representative from the sixth district, died suddenly, with eighteen months of his term yet to serve. Kemp had had Huey's support when he was elected to his seat in 1930 and re-elected in 1932, although he had not affiliated with the Long faction and had not followed a consistent Long line. He could afford to be independent, for the district he represented, in which Baton Rouge lay, was a center of resistance to the Long movement. Huey usually lost it in elections, and when he carried it he did so by the narrowest of margins.

According to Louisiana law, when a congressman died in office, the governor set a date for a special election. The district Democratic executive committee then arranged for a primary election to select a nominee, the primary having to come thirty days before the general election specified in the governor's call. But this procedure was not put in motion after Kemp's death. Governor Allen did not call an election, and consequently the district committee, on which Long men were a majority, could not fix a primary date. When criticism of the governor mounted, a spokesman explained that Allen

[4] New Orleans *Times-Picayune*, November 11, 1933; *American Progress*, November 16, 1933; Theophile Landry; H. Lester Hughes; M. J. Kavanaugh.

was delaying action in the hope that some other election would develop that could be coupled with the sixth-district contest, thus relieving the state of the expense of two elections.[5]

The explanation was a clumsy prevarication that fooled no one. The real reason for the failure of the governor to act was too apparent—Huey would not let the governor call an election because one held at this time would probably result in the choice of an anti-Long candidate. Five candidates had expressed an interest in running, but only two of them were of front-rank stature: Mrs. Bolivar Kemp, who as the widow of the late congressman was expected to have Long's support, and state senator J. Y. Sanders, Jr., who because of his name and record was endorsed by most of the anti-Long leaders in the district.

These anti leaders resolved to bring pressure on Allen to force him to call an election. In November they presented the governor with a petition signed by ten thousand voters of the district demanding that an election date be set. Allen ignored the request. Then the anti leaders made a sensational move. They announced that they were summoning a mass meeting in Baton Rouge on November 28 to "select" a congressman. The meeting would authorize a "citizens' election," a general election, and would set up machinery to hold the contest. For a group of private citizens to presume to represent the mass of the citizenry and call an election was clearly illegal. But J. Y. Sanders, in recalling the maneuver, contended that it was morally defensible. "We figured that under the law we had no right to call a primary," he said. "That right was vested in the government. But the sovereign people could call a general election."[6]

The proposed election might be illegal, but it posed a worrisome threat to Huey. The candidate chosen in it, who would certainly be Sanders, could make a plausible case when he presented his credentials to the House of Representatives: he had had to be elected illegally because the governor would not allow a legal election. And the House, encouraged by Roosevelt to do anything that would hurt Senator Long, would probably seat him. Contemplating this possibility, Huey moved quickly.

On November 27, the day before the scheduled citizens' meeting in Baton Rouge, Allen called a general election to be held on De-

[5] Deutsch: "Kingdom of the Kingfish," in New Orleans *Item*, September 1, 1939; *American Progress*, January 11, 1934.

[6] New Orleans *Times-Picayune*, November 15, 1933; Baton Rouge *State-Times*, November 20, 1933; J. Y. Sanders, Jr.

cember 5. On the same day the Long majority on the Democratic district committee, without giving notice to the other members, convened in New Orleans, outside the district, and announced that because of the early date set for the election by the governor, there was not time to hold a primary. It therefore certified Mrs. Kemp as the Democratic nominee. In justification of its action, the committee stated that it had received petitions signed by twenty-five thousand voters of the district requesting it to designate Mrs. Kemp to succeed her husband and that it considered these documents to represent the wishes of the people.[7]

This sudden development surprised and enraged the antis, who, interestingly, denounced it as being illegal. But they were not going to let it stop their plan. At their meeting in Baton Rouge on the following day they set the date for the citizens' election on December 27 and established electoral machinery. They were careful to observe every formality of an official election. Ballots, on which all five candidates were invited to place their names, would be printed and distributed to the clerks of court of every parish in the district, and to these officials would also go lists of the qualified voters in each parish. The expense of preparing this paraphernalia was considerable, but wealthy men in the anti group were willing to bear it.[8]

While arranging to hold their election, the men at the meeting discussed ways to prevent the one called by Allen from taking place. Some of them argued that the other election would deprive the people of the district of a free choice and should be stopped by force. The time had come to resort to "shotgun government," these men said. But others advised that redress should first be sought in the courts, and their views prevailed. A group of the leaders went before anti Judge George K. Favrot of Baton Rouge and obtained a temporary injunction prohibiting the secretary of state from printing ballots bearing the name of Mrs. Kemp or any other person as the Democratic nominee. Now Huey was checkmated, the antis thought. A hearing on whether the injunction should be made permanent could not possibly be held in time to permit the ballots to be printed before December 5, election day, and consequently the election would have to be called off. But the antis had another surprise waiting for them. The secretary of state revealed that the ballots list-

---

[7] New Orleans *Times-Picayune*, November 28, 1933; *American Progress*, November 30, 1933.

[8] Baton Rouge *State-Times*, November 28, 1933; *American Progress*, December 14, 1933; J. Y. Sanders, Jr.

ing Mrs. Kemp as the nominee had already been printed and distributed to the parish clerks of court—before Allen had called the election and the district committee had met in New Orleans.

This disclosure aroused a storm of protest in the sixth district. Even people who were not anti-Long were angered at this latest Long coup, which seemed to display a bold and cynical disregard of the democratic process. Indignant citizens or officials in nine of the district's twelve parishes brought suits in the district courts to enjoin the distribution of the ballots and won favorable decisions. One judge, whose jurisdiction included three parishes, swore in a hundred special deputies to enforce his injunction and authorized each one to appoint other deputies, ending with a thousand men under his control, who hastened to arm themselves with shotguns and pistols. Men in other parishes who were not deputized also armed themselves and formed organizations that came to be called by general consent "shotgun clubs." A spokesman for one of these groups said grimly: "It is likely our club will fill a long-felt need."

The deputies and members of the clubs proceeded to enforce the injunctions with methods unique in judicial annals. They went into courthouses or homes of parish clerks, forcing an entrance if resisted, took out the ballots and other election materials, and publicly burned them. When the state attempted to send in additional ballots in trucks escorted by state police, the armed men shot up the trucks and forced them to turn back. They threatened that if the state sent militia into the district on election day, they would shoot the militia.

No militia appeared on December 5, although it was rumored that Huey had mobilized a sizable force in New Orleans. Only a few precincts were open in a few of the parishes, and whereas there were between thirty and forty thousand voters in the district, only five thousand persons turned out to vote—for the only candidate they could vote for, Mrs. Kemp.[9]

On the day after the election Mrs. Kemp expressed regret at the small vote and doubt that she should claim her seat. She thought another election should be held, and Governor Allen intimated that he would call one in the spring of 1934. The Long forces obviously hoped that by offering this concession they could persuade the antis

[9] New Orleans *Times-Picayune*, December 2, 4, and 5, 1933; Baton Rouge *Morning Advocate*, December 3, 1933; Baton Rouge *State-Times*, December 4, 5, and 6, 1933; New York *Sun*, December 21, 1933; Deutsch: "Kingdom of the Kingfish," in New Orleans *Item*, September 1, 1939; Hodding Carter: "Kingfish to Crawfish," *New Republic*, LXXVII (January 24, 1934), 303–4.

not to hold their election on December 27. But the antis, elated at the fiasco of the Allen election, were not to be persuaded. They gave full voice to their feelings at a rally in Baton Rouge on the night before the election. One speaker taunted Huey for being afraid to use force in the sixth district and said that the Kingfish should now be known as the Crawfish. Another one, Judge Favrot, who saw no impropriety in appearing with men on whose side he had recently ruled, denounced the Long regime as worse than that of the carpetbaggers of Reconstruction. The meeting came to a rousing close when a little girl sang a song written for the occasion by a local woman: "Huey Doesn't Live Here Any More."[1]

At the election on December 27 committees of citizens presided over the ballot boxes, which were set up in most of the district's precincts. Since the other candidates had declined to list their names, only that of Sanders appeared on the ballot, and he received all of the 19,500 votes that were cast. He and Mrs. Kemp left at once for Washington to present their claims, but the House of Representatives, after hearing a report from its elections committee, ruled that neither applicant was entitled to admittance, since both elections had been illegal.[2]

The judgment between pot and kettle is not an easy one. The two elections were illegal, but Huey had called his first. The antis had called their election only in retaliation. On the other hand, Huey had shown at the last more restraint than his opponents. When he realized what a storm he had aroused, he drew back. He refused to use force, either to ensure that the election on December 5 would come off or that the one on December 27 would not come off. It was the antis who used force and seemed to welcome the use of it and then twitted Huey for being afraid to counter violence with violence. Neither side had strengthened the practice of democracy in Louisiana. They would weaken it even more in another campaign that got underway late in 1933.

The New Orleans mayoralty and municipal election would not occur until January 1934, but by the fall of 1933 the first maneuvers were getting underway. It was known that one of the candidates for mayor would be the incumbent, Semmes Walmsley, backed by the Old Regular organization. Another sure candidate would be the man defeated by Walmsley in 1930, Francis Williams, backed by the

---

[1] New Orleans *Times-Picayune*, December 27, 1933.

[2] Baton Rouge *State-Times*, December 27, 1933; January 21, 1934; New Orleans *Times-Picayune*, December 28, 1933; New Orleans *Morning Tribune*, January 30, 1934.

Williams brothers' organization. Other candidates were talking about running, but they were minor politicians backed by small, personal organizations just recently formed. Of the probable candidates, only Walmsley had a large organization, and he was the choice of observers to win the election, who could envision only one development that would threaten his chances—if the other large organization in the city, Huey's Louisiana Democratic Association, should decide to break with the Old Regulars and put forward a candidate of its own.

Rumors that Huey and the Old Regulars were at the point of a break recurred at intervals during the year. Walmsley had voiced warm approval of Roosevelt and as head of the city government had applied for various federal aid projects, and his attitude was known to have angered Huey. Walmsley did not deny the rumors, but Huey felt called upon to notice them. Would there be a break between his forces and the city organization? There could not be one because there had never been a merger. What line would his faction take in the city campaign? It would do what "is best for our people." His organization did not need the Old Regulars to carry the city, and it would not act with the "lice and rats," the Louisiana agents of the national administration, who were marauding the state.[3]

Observers decided that Huey was toying with the idea of putting a ticket in the field, and they were correct. He tried first to induce an Old Regular member of the city council to run as his candidate, and when this man refused to desert the machine, he turned to Paul Maloney and then to Joe O'Hara, the head of the Louisiana Democratic Association. Both of these men were reluctant to make the race. They and other leaders pointed out the difficulties to Huey. Organizing a campaign would require a large amount of money and a tremendous effort, and the effort would probably fail: Walmsley was too strong. In fact, to put a Long candidate in the race would ensure Walmsley's election, for this candidate and Williams would divide the anti-Ring vote. Huey was finally convinced and resigned himself to the situation. If he wished to retain an influence in the city, he would have to make a deal with Walmsley or with Williams.[4]

Even if he had not despised Williams personally, Huey had more reason to deal with Walmsley. He and the Old Regulars had

[3] Circular, "The Course of the City Campaign," September 13, 1933, in Long Scrapbooks, XVI.

[4] New Orleans *Item*, October 29, 1933; Paul Maloney; Seymour Weiss.

been working together to their mutual profit, and a continuation of the association promised more rewards for each party. Walmsley was aware of these benefits and was therefore likely to accede to what demands Huey made as his price for a renewal of the alliance. Reasoning thus, Huey sent word to Walmsley that he would like to discuss the possibility of forming a coalition city ticket.

Walmsley was willing to negotiate, and he and Huey met secretly several times in December. The mayor was shocked at Huey's idea of a coalition ticket. Huey demanded that he should name two of the five members of the commission council, and also the criminal sheriff, the civil sheriff, and the district attorney. "He wants everything," Walmsley complained. Huey wanted what he could get, but it quickly became evident that he had put forward his demands as bargaining points. He retreated from them when Walmsley objected, and finally said that he would be satisfied if he could designate the candidate for district attorney. In view of the support that he could bring to the Old Regular ticket, he was showing great moderation in asking the right to name only one candidate. But on this right he insisted, giving the Old Regulars until December 19 to agree to his terms.

He had cause to be adamant about the choice for district attorney. For this office the Old Regulars wanted to endorse Eugene Stanley, the incumbent, who was then engaged in prosecuting the Long commissioners in the cases arising from the amendment election and was thereby winning plaudits from all anti-Longs. His nomination would be a slap in the face to Huey, and that Walmsley should try to engineer it showed that the mayor was seeking to bring about a break. Walmsley, indeed, admitted that this was his intention. "We are going to have a new deal," he said grimly on December 19, the day Huey had set as his deadline. That night the Choctaw caucus voted by a margin of twelve to five to reject Huey's demand and to choose their own ticket in every office. Coincidentally, Choctaw Chief of Police George Reyer withdrew the police detail that had been guarding Huey's home since fires had broken out there, and city police arrested seven state employees for distributing Long circulars without a license.[5]

The Choctaw caucus had, as expected, endorsed Walmsley for mayor, and as Francis Williams had already announced, the voters

[5] Baton Rouge *State-Times*, December 20, 1933; New Orleans *Times-Picayune*, December 20 and 21, 1933; New York *Sun*, December 21, 1933; *American Progress*, December 28, 1933; Eugene Stanley; Deutsch: "Kingdom of the Kingfish," in New Orleans *Item*, September 3, 1939.

of the city were left to choose between these two candidates. Huey thought he should explain to his followers what his stand on the candidates was. In a long statement issued on December 20 he declared that his organization would remain neutral. "We will not be aligned with either the Walmsley or the Williams crowd," he said. He admitted that he had considered putting out a third ticket but had decided not to because his slate would have to go into a second primary to win. "Nothing deserves such effort on our part," he said. "To capture City Hall now would be like Napoleon capturing Moscow, and we probably would be ruined by our new possession." The statement brought relief to his city leaders: he was going to abide by their advice and not intervene in the campaign.[6]

Their satisfaction lasted but a few hours. On the following day Huey informed them that he was putting together a city ticket. He was excited and exuberant. He had persuaded a man to run who was certain to win, he said: John Klorer, Sr., the father of the man who edited the *American Progress*, and a distinguished engineer and respected citizen. He was going to persuade men of similar stature to run with Klorer, he explained. Turning to one of his leaders, he said reproachfully: "You almost made me sell my birthright."[7]

Because he was fielding his ticket late, Huey had to form it hastily. Still, when he was finished, he had a slate that compared in ability, if not in political experience, with the two rival tickets. Klorer had held appointive engineering jobs with the state and the city but had held only one elective office and that, a long time before, in 1920, when he had won a seat on the commission council on the reform ticket of Andrew McShane. He was the most unpolitical candidate to run since McShane.[8]

Of Huey's four candidates for the commission council (the mayor was the fifth member), two were of sufficient reputation to attract voters: Alfred Danziger, of the business community, and Dr. George F. Roeling, the present coroner, who had been elected as an Old Regular but who had left the organization. The other two candidates were good enough men but were relatively unknown, one a lumberman and the other a labor union official. Huey also offered candidates for the ten executive offices of the city, criminal sheriff, civil sheriff, coroner, and others. Only two of them were politicians

[6] New Orleans *Times-Picayune*, December 21, 1933; *American Progress*, December 21, 1933.

[7] Seymour Weiss.

[8] Paul B. Habans; James P. O'Connor; Richard W. Leche; *American Progress*, December 28, 1933.

of standing, and their positions had been such that their appearance on the ticket caused surprise. Nick Carbajal, endorsed for state tax collector, had once been a rising figure in the Long organization but, having been shunted aside, had joined the Williams faction and denounced Huey unsparingly. But the candidate for district attorney was even more remarkable—Gus Williams, thought to be Huey's unrelenting enemy, was now running against his brother's ticket and taking part of the Williams organization into Huey's camp.[9]

Whether Huey offered Gus any inducement to come over is not known. The two men engaged in what an observer called some "highly spiced dialogue," which ended with Gus's saying: "You don't like me and I despise you, but I'll run on your goddamn ticket." Gus, an ambitious man, probably wanted nothing more than a nomination to some office by some faction, so he was able to make one of those abrupt switches of allegiance then frequent in Louisiana politics. There were other curious migrations in the election. Francis Williams, who in 1930 had denounced Stanley as being unfit to be district attorney, now offered Stanley the nomination for the office on his ticket, and Stanley accepted, thus running as the candidate of two factions, each of which contended that the other was corrupt. The reformers of the Honest Election League, who had long condemned the Old Regulars for having a crooked machine and who had considered the Williams organization as only a minor version of the Old Regulars, hastened to declare their support for either Walmsley or Williams. None of them endorsed Klorer, who once had been hailed as a reform hero. "The horns replaced the halo," a Long leader recalled bitterly.[1]

The campaign did not warm up until January, but once it got under way it generated enough heat to satisfy even jaded New Orleans. Observers could not recall a contest in which the rallies had been so numerous, the crowds so large and enthusiastic, and the speeches so abusive and profane that the newspapers were forced to reproduce large sections of them in dashes.

Huey carried the oratorical burden for the Klorer ticket, speaking on the radio hour after hour for days at a stretch. He seemed to be tireless, but also feverishly excited. He did odd things, such as cutting off his speeches sometimes to croon songs he had made up (his favorite was "Anti-Long, little bogey"). He presented to the

[9] Baton Rouge *State-Times*, December 23, 1933; *American Progress*, December 28, 1933; New Orleans *Times-Picayune*, December 29, 1933.

[1] Hermann B. Deutsch; Clem H. Sehrt; New Orleans *Item-Tribune*, December 31, 1933; Richard W. Leche.

radio audience one-act plays in which the heroes were always shining young Longites and the villains corrupt Choctaws. In all of his radio programs he lashed out savagely at his enemies, especially Walmsley, gibing the mayor to a challenge. "I hereby call on him to meet me any place, anytime," Walmsley said. "If I can't catch him here, I'll follow him to Washington."[2]

Late at night on January 16, a week before the election, two Old Regular leaders coming from a rally dropped in at Choctaw headquarters. No one was there, but they discovered a bottle of whisky and had settled down to have a drink when the telephone rang. An excited voice announced that Huey was at the office of the municipal registrar of voters, scratching names off the registration lists. The leaders forgot their drinks. They phoned Chief of Police Reyer to send some men to the registrar's office immediately and then set out for it themselves.

The Choctaws had been worried about the voting lists ever since the break with Huey. The lists were, as provided by law, in the custody of the registrar, who was a state appointee, usually one acceptable to the machine and likely to do its bidding. But the present holder of the office, C. S. Barnes, was a loyal Longite who would probably do Huey's bidding, who might purge the rolls of Old Regular voters and of fraudulent voters. Seeking to tie his hands, the Choctaws had secured a court order restraining him from removing any names until a list of qualified voters was prepared seven days before the election. But now he apparently was drawing up a list, and without proper supervision.

The two Choctaw leaders forced their way into the registrar's office, where they found Barnes and a group of men, some of whom were armed, busily scratching names off the lists. Huey was not present. ("I always thought he was close by, maybe riding around the block," one of the Choctaws said.) Instead of telling the Choctaws to get out, Long's men began to explain what they were doing, but in the midst of the explanations the police arrived and placed Barnes and his helpers under arrest. They were charged by District Attorney Stanley with defacing the registration books and were jailed for ten hours before a lawyer sent by Huey got them released on bond.

The Choctaws now had to prevent the lists from being returned to Barnes. Going before an Old Regular judge, they obtained an order turning the lists over to the civil sheriff of Orleans

[2] Chicago *Tribune*, January 18, 1934; Philadelphia *Inquirer*, January 21, 1934; *The New York Times*, January 23, 1934.

parish, who was directed to put them in a place of safety until election day. The sheriff had an inspiration: he placed them in the parish prison in the tier of cells reserved for criminals who were awaiting execution.[3]

The seizure of the books touched off an uproar. Governor Allen charged that the city government meant to seize other state records and ordered General Fleming to take charge of all state offices in New Orleans and to mobilize as many men as he needed to guard the offices. Fleming summoned only twenty-four guardsmen, but it was rumored that he would have a much larger force under his command on election day. The city government threatened that if the militia appeared then, it would swear in ten thousand special police. A possible clash of arms was averted when on the eve of the election the Long and Walmsley factions agreed to submit all complaints to an arbitration committee of seven citizens.[4]

The election on January 23 went off in relative quiet. The results were known early and disclosed an Old Regular victory. Walmsley and his ticket led the field, with some forty-eight thousand votes. Klorer was second, with thirty-two thousand votes, and close behind was Williams, with twenty-eight thousand. Without a majority, Walmsley faced the possibility of a second primary. Whether one would occur depended on Williams, who was besought by emissaries from Huey to declare that he would support Klorer. Williams said emphatically and profanely that he would never endorse a man backed by Huey Long. Huey thus had no choice but to withdraw Klorer.[5]

Conservatives in Louisiana and throughout the nation rejoiced at the outcome. Huey had suffered another reverse, they crowed, and the "Long empire" was crumbling.

[3] Confidential communications; Philadelphia *Inquirer*, January 21, 1934; Deutsch: "Kingdom of the Kingfish," in New Orleans *Item*, September 3, 1939.

[4] New Orleans *Times-Picayune*, January 19, 1934; Baton Rouge *State-Times*, January 20, 1934; *The New York Times*, January 23, 1934.

[5] *The New York Times*, January 26, 1934; New York *Herald-Tribune*, January 28, 1934; Joseph Fisher; Shirley G. Wimberly. Actually, Huey's ticket had not done badly. It pulled twenty-nine per cent of the vote, which was his normal strength in the city. He had not lost in his strength, but his enemies had gained in theirs.

# CHAPTER 24

# *Share Our Wealth*

WASHINGTON SOCIETY was wryly amused at the latest action of the Louisiana Kingfish: he had asked that his name be withdrawn from the *Washington Social Register*. In his letter to the sponsor of the publication he had been rather diverting. He said that he had been grievously disappointed in capital society. He had tried to "train" members of the "elite" in the art of eating potlikker, but to no avail. Their taste was not "sufficiently cultured" to enable them to appreciate this delectable concoction, and those few who did take to it insisted on crumbling their corn pone instead of dunking it. Moreover, Washingtonians were naïve socially. They thought they were doing something new when they drank soup out of bowls with handles on them. But he had drunk soup out of a "plate" when he was a boy, and without any handles on the plate, either. Finally, he was worried that people of distinction who had not been admitted to the book were wondering how he had got in. "My conscience has begun to hurt, my nights are near sleepless," he claimed, "and in such shattered embraces as Morpheus now and then accords, my dreams envisage phantoms of the deserving excluded, who seem as though they were trying to lisp: 'How could you.' "[1]

In asking that his name be removed from the book, Huey was having some fun at the expense of capital society and was also making one of his gestures to show that he scorned the rich. He could make this gesture easily, for he was not giving up anything he prized. He had never really been "in" Washington society. Indeed,

[1] Baton Rouge *Morning Advocate*, December 16, 1933; *American Progress*, December 21, 1933.

in Washington, he did not have much of a social life of any kind, any more than he had had one in Baton Rouge.

When Huey came to Washington in 1932 to assume his seat, he had taken rooms at the Mayflower Hotel for himself and Mrs. Long. Rose stayed but a few days, however, and then returned to New Orleans. Huey continued to live at the Mayflower until March 1934, when he moved to the Broadmoor Hotel, where he took a three-room kitchenette apartment. The change was not made to accommodate Mrs. Long, for she remained in Louisiana, coming to Washington only infrequently on brief visits. Rather, Huey needed larger quarters to house the various men who lived with him. Some of them were temporary though long-term lodgers, Louisiana cronies, like Bob Brothers, who had a political problem to discuss or who simply liked being with him and who came up and stayed for days or even weeks at a stretch. But three men lived with him permanently. They were bodyguards, and during his waking hours two of them sat outside the door and admitted callers, while the other stood behind Huey until the callers left.[2]

These guards were members of the Louisiana state police, two of them from the highway patrol and one from the bureau of criminal identification: George McQuiston, Murphy Roden, and Theophile Landry. They had been "assigned" by the state government at state expense to protect the person of the state's senior senator. They protected him almost everywhere he went, even to the Senate, where they sat in the gallery. They went armed, carrying plainly bulging pistols under their coats. They divested themselves of the weapons only in the Senate, which had a rule prohibiting the carrying of firearms. Once they forgot the rule and appeared in the gallery with their guns. Joe Robinson, tipped off as to their presence, arose and demanded that the guards of his colleague from Louisiana be searched. They ran to Huey's office and got rid of the guns and then returned and virtuously asked to be inspected.

On some occasions, when Huey appeared out of doors in places where people were congregated, such as a golf course, one of them, usually McQuiston, bore an additional weapon. He carried it in a paper package, which was broken at the bottom to give access to the trigger, and only the barrel end and the butt showed. It was thought by most observers to be a submachine gun, but it was really a sawed-off shotgun with a massive revolver-like butt. McQuiston consented to show it to one reporter and laconically described its

[2] Washington *Post*, March 8, 1934; *Time*, April 1, 1935, pp. 15–17; Eleanor Patterson, in New Orleans *Item-Tribune*, February 16, 1939.

merits. "Very effective at close range," he grunted. "Kill a man at seventy-five yards."[3]

Huey was rarely seen at social functions in Washington homes, but his absence was not entirely of his own doing. His reputation for crudity was partially responsible for his exclusion, but there was a more important reason. He had few intimate friends among his Senate colleagues, men who knew him well enough to ask him to meet their families. The home of Burton Wheeler was the only one that he visited with any frequency. But he declined some of the invitations that he did receive. The truth was that he did not feel comfortable in a private home, because he could not take his bodyguards in with him.

He was seen most often, night after night, in Washington night clubs, where he could take the guards. He would arrive at a club late, usually after midnight, have some drinks and watch the show, and then go on to another spot, sometimes not finishing his tour until just before dawn. The clubs came to expect him and put on special shows for him, and according to Washington gossip, the Kingfish frequently joined the entertainers and put on his own kind of show.[4]

But early in 1934 Huey suddenly dropped his playboy routine. He still went to the clubs occasionally, and when he did, generally comported himself quietly. This change in his behavior astonished capital observers, but not as much as another piece of news—he had decided to quit drinking. His announcement of this resolve surprised also his friends, many of whom had begged him to give up the habit but had not believed he would. He not only gave it up but, like most reformed drinkers, he wanted other people to give it up and bored them with moralizing lectures on why they should. "A man is a fool to drink," he pontificated to one reporter, and to another he said, "My boy, never drink and never smoke." He had also simultaneously quit smoking, claiming that the cigars to which he had been addicted gave him hay fever.[5]

Not satisfied to curb his vices, he attempted to discipline other appetites, especially that for rich foods. He had given this yearning

[3] Theophile Landry; Carter: *American Messiahs* (New York, 1935), pp. 7–8; J. Y. Sanders, Jr.; Paul Y. Anderson, in St. Louis *Post-Dispatch*, February 10, 1935.

[4] *Time*, April 1, 1935, pp. 15–17; New Orleans *Item*, September 11, 1935; Murphy Roden.

[5] W. C. Pegues; Theophile Landry; Paul Maloney; Clayton Coleman; Associated Press dispatch, November 18, 1934, in Long Scrapbooks, XVII; Associated Press dispatch, September 9, 1935, in Persac Scrapbook.

full play during his first two years in the Senate, eating gargantuan meals in restaurants or his apartment, where he often concocted for visitors some Louisiana dish for which he claimed to have a special recipe. He achieved, in fact, something of a reputation as an epicurean, and at private dinner parties he had consented to attend he often was asked by the hostess to make one of his specialties. An awed guest at one of these affairs saw him mix a salad dressing and thought that his ideas of the cooking art were as grandiose as his concepts of politics and finance: he used a whole pound of Roquefort cheese in one stirring.[6]

Stuffing himself as he did, he gained weight, going up finally to over two hundred pounds. Then he decided he would have to reduce. First, he laid out a regime of exercise, and for a change stuck to it. Several days a week he played golf at the Congressional Country Club, usually appearing with his guards shortly after daybreak. On other days he sawed and chopped wood, going with a guard to a camp in Virginia that he rented or, when he was in Louisiana, to the camp of a friend near Baton Rouge. Second, and harder for him to do, he cut out the rich foods that he loved and held himself on a rigorous diet. He ate only two meals a day and on every Wednesday subsisted on liquids alone. The results were gratifying. His weight went down to one hundred and seventy-five pounds, and he was so elated that he proclaimed he was giving up even potlikker.[7]

Huey was obviously trying to create a new public image of himself—to erase the impression of the drunken playboy of Sands Point and replace it with one of a sober and sedate statesman who was presidential timber. He had yet another, a perfecting, touch to add to his reformation. Late in 1934 he announced in Baton Rouge that he was going to take his wife away on a honeymoon. "Mrs. Long and I never had a honeymoon, and we're going to have one now," he explained. "I'm fulfilling a promise I made." Reporters asked where he and his bride would go. "I'm going so damn far it will take a ten dollar postage stamp to reach me," he said grandly, somewhere "out West." Cynical observers decided that the proposed journey was a publicity stunt: Huey was attempting to convince the

[6] Virgilia Stephens: "Salad à la Kingfish," in Washington *Herald*, clipping, n.d., in Overton Scrapbooks; John J. O'Connor.

[7] International News dispatch, August 22, 1934, in Long Scrapbooks, XXIX; Theophile Landry; Paul Maloney; Des Moines *Register*, April 28, 1935; New Orleans *Item*, September 11, 1935.

voters that he had a normal and happy home life. Their suspicions were soon confirmed. Huey took Rose only to Hot Springs, in southern Arkansas; two bodyguards went along; he issued a stream of political statements from their retreat; and he stayed but a short time before rushing back to Washington, without Rose.[8]

The tourists who thronged to Washington would be asked by the guides who had them in charge to make a "must" list of things they wanted to see. The most frequently requested itinerary read: "White House, Monument, Capitol—and the Kingfish." The visitors wanted to hear Huey speak. They might disagree with what he said, but they had to see him in action. Before he had come to the Senate, only one member could fill the galleries, Borah. Huey not only filled them, but, as one correspondent wrote wonderingly, "he caused them to overflow, piling up long lines of people in the corridors." He never disappointed his audience. The show was always good.[9]

It was good because he was usually attacking somebody, the President or the Democratic leadership. He delighted in starting a fight. Often he would say to his secretary, Earle Christenberry: "Things are awfully quiet around here. What have you got in your files that we can liven them up with?" Then he would rush onto the floor and announce that he had just confirmed a charge against Joe Robinson or some other prominent Democrat.[1]

Robinson was his favorite target, but receiving almost as much attention were the majority leader's assistants, Pat Harrison of Mississippi and Kenneth McKellar of Tennessee. Huey once explained why he goaded McKellar, whom he liked personally. "I can't resist it," he said. "Mac gets mad so quickly. . . . I have to have a little fun with him now and then." Once before roaring galleries he flicked McKellar with humorous barbs and gradually reduced the Tennessean to a state of sputtering wrath. Finally the presiding officer threatened to clear the galleries if the laughter did not cease. Alben W. Barkley of Kentucky, thinking to rescue McKellar, asked the chair not to be too hard on the spectators, saying: "When the people go to a circus, they ought to be allowed to laugh at the monkey." Huey was on his feet instantly, exuding indignation. "Mistuh President," he bellowed. "I resent that unwarranted remark on the

[8] New York *Sun*, November 19, 1934; Baltimore *News-Post*, November 23, 1934; New Orleans *Times-Picayune*, November 23, 1934; Westbrook Pegler, in New York *World-Telegram*, January 3, 1935.

[9] Michael Liston, in Washington *Post*, clipping, n.d., in Persac Scrapbook.

[1] Earle J. Christenberry.

part of the Senator from Kentucky, directed toward my good friend, the Senator from Tennessee."[2]

This quickness of wit was one of the qualities that made him so effective in debate and absolutely unmanageable by the leadership. He had other qualities, as some of the ablest parliamentarians of the Senate acknowledged. Wheeler said Huey's mind was so brilliant that he could discourse endlessly on any issue without preparation. Borah declared that Huey was the only man he had ever known who could argue from a wrong premise to a right conclusion. A Southern senator summed up many opinions when he said that Huey simply could think faster on his feet than any of his colleagues.[3]

Few senators cared to take Huey on in debate. A Democratic member once explained why. "Frankly, we are afraid of him," he said. "He is unscrupulous beyond belief. He might say anything about me, something entirely untrue, but it would ruin me in my state. . . . It's like challenging a buzz saw. He will go the limit. It is safer for me and the rest of us to leave him alone."[4]

A senator who once did challenge Huey was Alben Barkley, himself known as a wit and master debater. He denounced Huey with great effect and then took his seat with an air of satisfaction. Huey rose to reply, apparently bowed with sorrow. He said he always wanted to have the good opinion of the famous senator from Kentucky and now that he realized he did not have this opinion he would go grieving, into his grave. It reminded him of a farmer, a God-fearing man, down in Louisiana, he went on. One day this farmer was plowing and stopped at the end of a row to inspect his plow. As he was bending over it, a pet goat that he had trusted ran at him and gored him mortally. His shrieks of agony brought his wife to the scene, and he cried out that he was dying. "But you never was afraid of dyin'," she said. "You're a religious man. You know you're going to Heaven. Why do you carry on this way about dyin'?" He answered: "Honey, I don't mind dyin', but I do hate to face my Maker on the horns of a vicious goat."[5]

In 1934 a man was elected to the Senate who would, administration leaders hoped, take Huey on—Theodore Bilbo from Mississippi. In running for the seat, Bilbo was making a comeback, and

[2] St. Louis *Post Dispatch*, September 11, 1935; Alben W. Barkley: *That Reminds Me* (New York, 1954), p. 161.

[3] George E. Sokolsky: "Huey Long," *Atlantic Monthly*, CLVI (November 1935), 532; Burton K. Wheeler: *Yankee from the West* (New York, 1962), pp. 282–3; Clem H. Sehrt; article by Felix Belair, Jr., clipping, n.d., n.p., in Persac Scrapbook.

[4] John Bantry, in Boston *Post*, March 10, 1935.

[5] Arthur Krock, memoir in Columbia University Oral History Project.

Huey, willing to put aside their past differences, had offered to support him, but on condition that Bilbo publicly endorse the Long program to redistribute wealth. Bilbo had refused to commit himself, and after being elected had issued several statements critical of Huey. When he took his seat, Pat Harrison and other Roosevelt stalwarts egged him on to attack Long, and he promised that he would. But although he studied Huey closely in debate, he did not challenge him. When the confrontation between the two men finally came, it occurred in a Washington night spot. The encounter became known when the following day Bilbo appeared in the Senate with a black eye and Huey was a bandaged left hand. Questioned by reporters, Bilbo at first said that he had at last "met up" with Huey but later changed his story to say that he had been in an automobile accident. Huey, grinning and displaying his hand, said that he had a touch of "athlete's foot."[6]

HUEY'S ENEMIES IN Louisiana seemed determined to give him no quarter. Throughout 1933 they kept up a constant public demand that the Senate special committee on campaign expenditures resume its investigation of the Overton election, even though Overton had been seated by the Senate. They claimed that they had uncovered new evidence to prove that the Long regime was corrupt and had tampered with the election, and they insisted that the committee come to New Orleans to hear their evidence and declare Overton's seat void.[7]

But they were not satisfied just to oust Overton. They further demanded that the Senate expel Huey himself. Former Governor Parker and others formally petitioned Vice-President Garner to appoint a committee to investigate Huey's fitness to be a senator, charging that the Kingfish was "personally dishonest, corrupt, and immoral." In a covering letter to Garner, Parker advanced another reason that Huey should be removed from public life. He said that psychiatrists had told him Huey was a "dangerous paranoiac." Solemnly the old conservative advised how to deal with the madman: "The Senate should have him examined by experts and to save certain trouble and probable killing have him permanently incarcerated in the criminal insane asylum in Washington."[8]

[6] Carter: *American Messiahs*, p. 184; Bilbo to W. D. Robinson, February 11 and 26, 1935, in Robinson Papers; Baton Rouge *Morning Advocate*, February 22, 1935.

[7] Raymond Lonergan, in *Labor*, December 19, 1933.

[8] Copy of the petition, April 11, 1933, in Long Scrapbooks, XVI; Parker to Garner, April 11, 1933, in Parker Papers.

The Senate special committee was reluctant to reopen the Overton investigation. Its hesitation was in part influenced by Senate tradition: Overton was now the incumbent, and to throw him out would be a nasty business, of the kind senators did not like to engage in. But tradition alone would not have restrained the committee. Another and a more valid reason supported its reluctance. The members who had participated in the previous inquiry had been disgusted at the poor showing of the anti-Long complainants—having assured the committee that they could expose the Long regime, they had produced no evidence but only allegations. The members did not wish to get their fingers burned again, especially if Huey was tending the fire. But the demands from Louisiana for an investigation were too loud to deny. Tom Connally, who was now the chairman, announced that he would send a subcommittee of two to New Orleans in November and that he would come himself as soon as he cleared up some Senate business.

The subcommittee, chairmaned by Marvel M. Logan of Kentucky, opened the hearing on November 13 in a room of the federal building. So large was the crowd that attempted to get in and so great was the public interest in the inquiry that on the following day Logan consented to shift the proceedings to the auditorium of the Scottish Rite Cathedral and to permit the sessions to be broadcast.

Present at the first meeting as participants were many of the same people who had played parts in the previous hearing: Overton, Huey, Broussard and his attorney, Rightor, and Burt Henry of the Honest Election League. Missing was Ansell, who had decided that the committee did not mean to undertake a serious inquiry and had resigned as counsel. Huey was also resigning as counsel, it was immediately revealed. Overton arose and announced that he would represent himself. Huey had formerly represented him for a good reason, Overton continued: previously, the committee had obviously been interested in investigating Senator Long and not the election that it was supposed to investigate, and Huey had had to have an opportunity to defend himself. But, Overton concluded, it was hoped that this committee would restrict its inquiry to its assignment.[9]

Rightor and Henry then presented prepared statements reciting the case of the complainants. A crooked and dictatorial political

[9] *Overton Hearing*, II, 1133, 1136. Huey undoubtedly retired at Overton's request. Overton, relying on the committee to conduct a restricted investigation, wanted to get Huey out of the case so the issue of Longism could be kept out of the investigation.

machine controlled Louisiana, and if the committee would call the right witnesses and search out the right documents, it would expose this machine, which had, among its other sins, stolen the election under investigation. At the conclusion of the statements Senator Logan exploded, saying that this was more of the same: the complainants were still expecting the committee to prove their case. Angrily he told Rightor and Henry that they had not put forward "one line of evidence" but only "vague charges." The committee was not interested in the Long machine or the political iniquities of Senator Long, he lectured. It was concerned solely with discovering whether fraud had been committed in the primary election of 1932 and whether Overton had had knowledge of this fraud. Rightor rose with an incredulous look on his face. Did the complainants have to prove that Overton had known about the fraud? he asked. Of course, Logan snapped, for if Overton had had no knowledge he could not be held responsible for the fraud. Logan then directed that the first witness be called.

This was Seymour Weiss, who would, the committee hoped, disclose more information on the financing of the Overton campaign than he had in his previous appearances. But before the members could question Weiss, the committee's chief investigator, John G. Holland, leaped to his feet. Holland was a Louisianian and a bitter anti-Long, and he had a grievance he was determined to air. He shouted that the Democrats on the committee would not ask any searching questions of Weiss, the man who was "responsible, along . . . with the rat from Louisiana [Huey] for sending Senator Howell to his grave." The Democratic members did not want a real investigation, Holland charged. "Senator Connally is so yellow he didn't even have the guts to come here today," the investigator yelled. Logan sat stunned as the outburst continued but recovered sufficiently to say that he thought Holland was crazy and should be fired.

When Weiss finally testified, he proved to be somewhat more communicative than he had been previously. He explained that he had been reticent about discussing his bank accounts earlier because he had known that the banking situation in New Orleans was delicate and he had feared harassment by federal Treasury agents who had been checking his income. Moreover, he had raised all the funds expended in the campaign in cash, just as he had previously testified. The committee seemed satisfied with his answers, but a member of the audience was not. Hilda Phelps Hammond rose from her seat and addressed Logan. The senator was surprised that a spectator should presume to intervene but politely asked: "Did you have something?"

Mrs. Hammond answered by shouting that the witness had answered the questions so quickly that he must have known what he would be asked. Weiss's testimony was "a disgrace" to the United States flag, she concluded with confusing irrelevance.[1]

The proceedings on the first day set a pattern that would prevail throughout the hearing. The antis had quickly realized that the committee was not going to conduct the "fishing" kind of inquiry that they wanted: it was going to stick to the primary election, and it was going to demand specific evidence. Knowing that they would come off badly in such an inquiry, the antis then set out to disrupt the sessions and so turn the investigation into a farce. On the second day Rightor rose and said he had a statement to make that represented the opinion of Broussard and of the people of the state. The statement was pithy: "We have lost all confidence in this committee," and Broussard was therefore withdrawing from the case. Logan testily replied that Rightor was trying to block the investigation. Rightor asked if Logan wished him to amplify the statement. "No, sir," Logan cried. "My desire is for you to get away and stay away." Immediately following this exchange, Francis Williams stood up in the audience and, as supporters who clustered around him shouted approval, demanded the right to testify from the floor. Logan finally had to call on the federal marshal to make Williams sit down.

On the third day Connally arrived and on assuming the chair referred to Holland's statement that the committee was afraid to conduct a real investigation. Denying the charge, Connally declared that the only people who were afraid of an inquiry were "the cowards who are slipping around here in Louisiana." Thereupon an indignant anti, a spectator, bellowed a challenge to the chairman to step outside. On the fourth day Connally and a colleague arrived at the auditorium but found such a large crowd packed in front of it that they could not make their way to the door. Somebody advised them to go around to the side of the building, where there was a fire escape. Painfully ascending this stairway, they climbed through an open window into a washroom, from which they entered the hearing room. As they emerged, they were greeted from the audience by mocking cries of "Sands Point" and "Don't get socked."[2]

The committee refused to be daunted by the impediments

[1] *Overton Hearing*, II, 1172, 1174-7, 1181, 1186.

[2] Ibid., II, 1232-5, 1251-2; article, "Vox Populi in Louisiana," in New York *Herald-Tribune*, quoted in New Orleans *Times-Picayune*, December 9, 1933; Tom Connally: *My Name Is Tom Connally* (New York, 1954), pp. 167-8.

thrown in its way or even by the embarrassing fact that the principal complainants had withdrawn from the case. It continued the investigation for three weeks, hearing witnesses whom it summoned or who offered to appear and furnish special knowledge. It listened to long discussions of the deducts and the dummies and other aspects of the election. A mass of evidence was added to the record, but most of it only amplified what had previously been testified to. When the committee finally went back to Washington to frame its report, it knew little more than when it came.[3]

Chairman Connally presented the report to the Senate in January 1934. It was a curious document. The committee found that the device of the dummy candidates and the practice of enforced deduct contributions were conducive to fraud and that fraud had probably occurred in the election. But the investigation had not been able to establish that the fraud had influenced the outcome of the election. Moreover, no evidence indicated that Overton was aware of the fraud. The Senate, somewhat puzzled as to what to conclude from the report, referred it to the committee on elections. This agency advised that as there was insufficient evidence to show that Overton had been elected fraudulently, he was entitled to retain his seat, and its recommendation was finally accepted by the Senate. Connally concurred in the decision but observed bitterly: "I advise anyone who thinks he knows something about politics to go down in Louisiana and take a postgraduate course."[4]

The senators, however, did not have to go to Louisiana to be educated, for Louisianians had come to the Senate to tutor them personally. They were led by John Parker and other conservatives.

Parker's petition demanding an investigation of Huey's fitness to be a senator, along with supporting documents, had been referred by Vice-President Garner to the elections committee, which made the materials "privileged," or confidential. But almost immediately summaries of the charges appeared in the press. Huey was naturally incensed at this disclosure of information he had not been able to see himself, and he requested the Senate to refer the petition to the judiciary committee, of which he was a member, with instructions to determine if the documents were privileged and if the Senate had a right to receive them. His strategy was evident: he wanted to prevent his enemies from prematurely publicizing the charges and

[3] Overton Hearing, II, 1510, 1886–9, 2227–9, 2330, for sample testimony.
[4] Congressional Record, 73 Cong., 2 Sess., pp. 1552–64, debate of January 30, 1934; Deutsch: "Kingdom of the Kingfish," in New Orleans Item, August 31, 1939; clipping from Time, January 30, 1934, in Long Scrapbooks, XIX.

by transferring the case to the judiciary committee he hoped to control an investigation if one was decided on.

He was only partially successful in his design. The judiciary committee referred the petition to a subcommittee, which sat on it during the remainder of the year but finally reported in January 1934. The report advised that the Senate had a right to receive the petition and the supporting material. These documents were, however, privileged, and the allegations in them could not be published except by a Senate committee or a senator performing some duty in relation to the petition. If the judiciary committee chose to consider the documents, it should do so in secret session.[5]

Huey was bitter that even a preliminary investigation should be contemplated. He explained his feelings to his colleagues in a speech recounting his political career and the constant opposition that he had had to meet. "I never held a public office in my life during which I was not under some kind of threat of removal or impeachment from the day I went into politics until the present day," he said. "I have never held one, and I do not expect to hold one." He seemed wistful but also grim as he continued: "I have tried for about sixteen years to have it some other way, and it has never been any other way, so now I have stopped trying to have it any other way." It was a revealing statement. He was saying that he had had to be ruthless because his enemies were ruthless, and that henceforth he would be even more ruthless.[6]

When the judiciary committee came to consider the Parker petition, it was astonished at the flimsiness of the charges: they had little to do with political misconduct; they were sensationally personal, accusing Huey of immorality and dishonesty; and they were not supported by any specific evidence. The committee hastily backed away from the dispute. Labeling the charges as "scurrilous and defamatory," it advised the Senate that they should not have been received. Huey's enemies seemed to have been turned back in their latest move against him.[7]

[5] Memorandum by Senator William H. King, chairman of the subcommittee, January 8, 1934, in Norris Papers.

[6] *American Progress*, February 8, 1934.

[7] *Senate Report*, No. 499, 73 Cong., 2 Sess.; New Orleans *Times-Picayune*, March 19 and 21, 1934; New Orleans *States*, March 19, 1934; New Orleans *Item*, March 19, 1934. Because the committee ruled that the charges should not be acted on, the documents supporting them were not released and are still under restriction in the National Archives. The nature of the charges can be surmised from materials in the Robinson Papers. For helpful advice on this episode, I am indebted to Professor Matthew Schott.

But they would not admit defeat. Parker and his associates next turned to the elections committee, notifying this agency that they had information which proved both Huey and Overton were unfit to be senators and demanding an investigation of the two. And now the male conservatives were joined by redoubtable female auxiliaries—Hilda Phelps Hammond, representing her women's committee, and Mrs. Ruffin Pleasant, representing herself. Mrs. Hammond had gone so far as to employ her own counsel, two lawyers who had recently formed a firm, Sam Ansell and John Holland, who had also resigned his position with the Connally committee. The money to pay the attorneys had been supplied by her associates on her committee, and they had raised it by offering at public auction prized heirlooms from their homes—antique furniture, Oriental rugs, pieces of china, and gold and silver ornaments. The array of treasures from the past was almost too much for a Northern reporter, who gushed that the "delicate mahogany escritoires, inlaid with mother-of-pearl, silently told the story of many a love letter written on them by daughters of Dixie in crinolines."[8]

Mrs. Pleasant submitted to the committee a separate complaint, a document that Mrs. Phelps, who seemed to resent any feminine rivals, characterized as "a hodgepodge." It was rather a representation of the curious way Louisiana conservatives sometimes reasoned. The former governor's wife exhorted that the Senate had to investigate the "depraved and dangerous creature" who was using it as a "sounding board for his Bolshevistic utterances." For if the Senate did not oust him, then the decent citizens of the state would have to resort to the methods they had employed to drive out the carpetbaggers. As she had penned this threat, she apparently reflected that some of the senators she was addressing were Northerners; so she added that she had heard her father, who had been a Confederate general, say that the "best element" in the North had not approved of the carpetbaggers. She cited further reasons why the Kingfish should be removed as a senator: as governor he had increased taxes and the state debt and involved the state penitentiary in debt, and he was hypocritical in quoting the Bible.[9]

The elections committee felt that it had to give the complainants a hearing, and it asked them, and Huey, to appear on May 29, 1934. Parker denounced Huey in an angry statement and demanded that he be given an opportunity to prove the charges that he had previ-

[8] Rodney Dutcher, in Tuscaloosa *News*, May 14, 1934; Chicago *Tribune*, June 14, 1934.

[9] Undated memorandum by Mrs. Pleasant, in Norris Papers.

ously submitted to the judiciary committee. Mrs. Phelps, accompanied by her counsel, presented a set of written charges. Then Mrs. Pleasant jumped to her feet. "The Senate will not have to eject Long from his seat," she shouted shrilly. "He will be attended to by others as soon as he gets rid of his bodyguards and machine guns." She then recounted for the committee the set-to she had had with Huey in Alice Lee Grosjean's office. "I put my finger as close to his red-clubbed nose as I could and shook it just as hard as I could," she sputtered, as senators and spectators roared with laughter. Huey too seemed to be amused, but suddenly he turned on Mrs. Pleasant. Hadn't she once tried to have her husband arrested in Shreveport? he asked. She advanced toward him and screamed: "Unspeakable coward." He regarded her coolly for a moment and then sprang another question. Hadn't she once been treated for a mental disorder? She broke into hysterical sobs. Yes, she admitted, she had been treated in an institution in Asheville, North Carolina, for a "general rundown condition," but the doctors there had finally pronounced her mental condition to be excellent.[1]

The committee received the charges of the complainants, but it was not impressed with them. They were too much like the accusations that the judiciary committee had thrown out—personal and unsupported. Moreover, with Congress scheduled to adjourn in June, there was little time to undertake an investigation. The committee therefore stalled until the closing days of the session. Then it requested the Senate to discharge it from the duty of investigating the charges, and to do so without debate. Huey's enemies had lost another round.[2]

Other Louisiana politicians appeared before the Senate in 1934. They were men who came to urge Senate confirmation of anti-Longites who had been appointed to federal positions in Louisiana by the President and to exhort the Senate to ignore Huey Long's opposition to approval of these appointees.

That they would meet Huey's opposition was certain, for every one of them was an anti-Longite, recommended by the Louisianians to whom Roosevelt had handed the federal patronage—Parker, John Sullivan, and a few others. The administration's attitude toward recommendations was revealed in a scene that occurred in the

[1] Hilda Phelps Hammond: *Let Freedom Ring* (New York, 1936), pp. 178–80; John Herrick, in Chicago *Tribune*, May 30, 1934.

[2] New Orleans *Times-Picayune*, June 20, 1934. As was the case with the charges laid before the judiciary committee, those submitted to the elections committee, not being acted on, were not made public.

anterooms of the offices of the Democratic National Committee. A crowd of job seekers were presenting their credentials, and one man said he was from Louisiana and had a letter recommending him. A committee aide glanced at the letter and brusquely rejected the applicant, and then addressed the crowd: "If you want a job here, you must bring an endorsement from any Democratic Senator or Congressman—except Huey Long."[3]

Two appointees who were antis were seeking Senate confirmation early in 1934. One of them was trying for the second time. Rene Viosca, of New Orleans, had in the previous year been named as United States attorney for the eastern district of Louisiana, but his confirmation had been blocked by Huey, who, invoking one of the most respected of Senate traditions, said that Viosca was personally objectionable to him. Roosevelt thereupon withdrew Viosca's name but gave the latter a recess appointment. The President, determined to override Huey's opposition, had resubmitted Viosca's name. Huey announced that he would still fight the appointment, and for other reasons than a personal objection—Viosca had at one time represented the Watson–Williams bridge syndicate and presently was being sponsored by Sullivan.[4]

The other seeker of Senate approval was Daniel D. Moore, one-time managing editor of the *Picayune*, who had been appointed collector of internal revenue for Louisiana. Huey announced that he would also oppose Moore's confirmation and explained his reasons to the Senate. Moore was personally objectionable to him and objectionable to organized labor, having as a *Picayune* executive refused to negotiate with a printers' union. But worse, he was controlled by Sullivan, the "gambling king" who was allied with any number of questionable individuals, the most notorious of whom was E. R. Bradley. Bradley was known as a Kentucky sportsman and racetrack owner, but Huey identified him as a gambler who operated "dives" in Florida and New Orleans. And his partner in running these places was Sullivan, the man who had been chosen by Roosevelt to pass on patronage in Louisiana. Huey demanded that he be given the opportunity to prove his charges against Moore before the Senate finance committee.[5]

[3] Drew Pearson and Robert S. Allen, in New York *Daily Mirror*, August 5, 1934.
[4] New Orleans *Times-Picayune*, February 15, 1934; New Orleans *Item-Tribune*, February 21, 1934.
[5] *Congressional Record*, 73 Cong., 2 Sess., pp. 3899–901, 5234–52, speeches of March 7 and 23, 1934. A Florida newspaper supported Huey's charge against Bradley,

Present at the committee's hearing were Huey, Sullivan, Bradley, and Moore and his attorney, "Whistle Britches" Rightor, who, though just come from denouncing machine politicians to the Connally committee, unofficially represented Sullivan. Such an assembly of enemies was certain to produce an explosion. It came when Huey declared that Sullivan and Bradley operated a "gambling kitty" in New Orleans. Sullivan crimsoned, bit through his cigar, and then rose and started toward Huey with his fists clenched. Rightor grasped his arm and persuaded him to return to his chair. Big John sank back into it, muttering curses. The press had difficulty in reproducing his language: "You couldn't prove that in a thousand years. You, dirty, rotten ——. You rotten ——, ——, —— ——. You Sands Point ——." Bradley smiled wanly throughout the exchange.[6]

Also attending the hearing were Julius and Earl Long, who had come from Louisiana to testify that Moore was a good man and that Huey was an evil man. They took a room in a hotel, but soon Julius noticed that Earl was spending most evenings out. He asked Earl what he was doing, and the younger brother answered that he had run into Bob Brothers and that he and Bob had been getting together to drink beer and talk. One night Earl came back drunker than Julius had ever seen him and said that he had had to put Brothers to bed. Julius scoffed at the picture of an inebriated Brothers. "Do you know what he's doing now?" he asked Earl, "He's telling Huey how far he's got with buying you back. You're going to sell out."[7]

Julius's use of the term "sell out" was possibly too harsh, but he was right in his suspicion—Earl was at the point of going back to Huey. And the man who was accomplishing the reconciliation, and doing it on his own initiative, was Brothers. He had let Earl run into him and then had arranged to meet him every night. At one of these sessions, according to Brothers, Earl confessed that the antis were paying all his expenses to come to Washington. When Bob relayed this news to Huey, the Kingfish told him to give Earl four hundred dollars, and this persuaded Earl. It was not the money in itself that influenced Earl but the implied promise in back of the gift—that henceforth he would receive greater recognition in the

---

stating that the latter controlled gambling in Palm Beach and was trying to take over operations in Miami; Miami *Life*, April 7, 1934.

[6] New Orleans *Item*, April 4 and 5, 1934; *Congressional Record*, 73 Cong., 2 Sess., pp. 5882–92.

[7] Julius T. Long.

Long hierarchy. His quarrel with Huey had been completely political, whereas Julius's was personal, though in Julius's mind based on principle. Julius would never be reconciled.[8]

Huey was able to block the confirmation of both appointees. Viosca's nomination was considered by the judiciary committee, which named a committee headed by Huey to study it. Not surprisingly, the subcommittee reported unfavorably on the nomination, and the full committee accepted the report. Thus Viosca's name was not sent to the Senate for a vote. The finance committee reported Moore's appointment favorably, but Huey fought off a vote on the floor and got the recommendation returned. Again the committee sent a favorable report, and again Huey prevented a vote. His victory was, however, an empty one. Roosevelt gave Viosca another recess appointment and in place of Moore named another anti as acting collector of internal revenue. The administration had lost a battle but would continue the war.[9]

ON FEBRUARY 23, 1934, Senator Long spoke over a national radio hookup for thirty minutes. He had exciting news for his listeners. The fight to decentralize wealth in America had entered a new phase, he proclaimed: it had achieved the advantage of organization. The organization had been created by people whom he identified only as "we," and it had a name, the Share Our Wealth Society, and a slogan, Every Man a King. He exhorted his hearers to join the society, to get together in their communities and form local chapters. If they needed instructions on how to proceed, they should write him. He emphasized that in the society there would be no national dues.[1]

Huey was being prudently modest when he indicated that other persons had joined with him to form the society. It was completely his own creation, the idea for it coming to him, according to one account, at three o'clock one morning in his rooms at the Mayflower Hotel. Excited and wanting someone to discuss the idea with, he telephoned his secretary and another assistant to come over immediately. He explained his plan to them and then sat down and sketched on sheets of yellow foolscap paper the whole design of the

---

[8] Robert Brothers; James A. Noe; Jess Nugent; Julius T. Long to W. D. Robinson, August 8, 1935, in Robinson Papers.

[9] New Orleans *Times-Picayune*, May 8 and 10, 1934; New Orleans *Item*, June 19, 1934.

[1] *Congressional Record*, 73 Cong., 2 Sess., pp. 3450–3.

society—its name, motto, structure, and the principles it would advocate.[2]

The principles were not entirely new. They were essentially the same proposals that Huey had been advancing in his Senate speeches since 1932, with the addition of some features that were the result of his recent reading. The federal government would impose a capital-levy tax that would prevent a family from owning a fortune of more than five million dollars, or more than three hundred times the fortune of the average American family. The government would impose an income tax that would prohibit a family from earning more than one million dollars in a year, or more than three hundred times the income of the average family. From the revenue derived from these taxes the government would provide every family in the country with a "homestead" of five thousand dollars, or "enough for a home, an automobile, a radio, and the ordinary conveniences." The government would further guarantee that every family would receive an annual income of two thousand to three thousand dollars, or one third of the average family income. Other benefits would be furnished by the government. It would also give pensions of thirty dollars a month to the aged (this figure was later deleted and the word "adequate" substituted), finance the college education of youths of proven ability (Huey eventually suggested that the federal government and the state should jointly bear the costs of educating also children below the college level), and pay generous bonuses to veterans. Lastly, the government would exercise greater regulation over the economy. It would limit the hours of labor to thirty hours a week and eleven months a year, thus increasing the need for workers. And it would purchase and store agricultural surpluses, thus balancing farm supply with demand.[3]

Huey's announcement of the Share Our Wealth Society received wide publicity. It also set off an extensive discussion by commentators and critics as to the nature of the society's program. Was Share Our Wealth a radical formula or did it only seem radical? Was it compatible with capitalism or would it subtly transform the American system into something quite different? Some critics denounced the plan as a form of socialism, charging that the rate of taxation would eventually have the effect of eliminating all fortunes and

[2] Hermann B. Deutsch: "Long—the Last Phase," *Saturday Evening Post*, October 12, 1935, p. 90.
[3] Radio speech by Long, February 23, 1934, in *Congressional Record*, 73 Cong., 2 Sess., pp. 3450–3; radio speeches by Long, January 9 and May 2, 1935, ibid., 74 Cong., 1 Sess., pp. 410–12, 7048–50; Long, in *American Progress*, January 4, 1935.

reducing all persons to approximately the same income level. This charge Huey repeatedly and indignantly denied. The socialists advocated government ownership of wealth, which was equivalent to destruction of wealth, he said. He, on the contrary, would retain the profit motive. His plan, by preventing the concentration of great incomes in the hands of a few men, would actually create more, not fewer, millionaires. Moreover, by redistributing wealth it would remove the worst abuse of capitalism and really strengthen the system. Once he made this argument to a reporter from a leftist magazine, who suggested that the senator must mean to save the magnates whom he denounced. "That would be one of the unfortunate effects of my program," he admitted. "I'd cut their nails and file their teeth and let them live."[4]

Grasping at all opportunities to disassociate Share Our Wealth from socialism, Huey accepted in March 1934 an invitation to debate the leader of the Socialist party, Norman Thomas. The request came from a New York City group, which intended to sell tickets to the meeting and, to entice Huey, offered him a fee of five hundred dollars. The crowd that turned out must have astonished the sponsors—twenty-five hundred persons assembled to hear the debaters discuss the question: "Resolved, that capitalism is doomed and cannot now be saved by redistribution of wealth."

Thomas spoke first and advocated his philosophy of moderate socialism. His remarks were well received by the audience, which was largely made up of Socialists and urban leftists. Huey realized the mood of the crowd, and to disarm it he affected when he began a Southern rustic pose. He didn't understand what Thomas had said, he claimed, but when he did, he would write his rival a letter. Striding back and forth, he bellowed that all debts should be "ipso facto remitted." "Maybe you don't know what I mean by ipso facto," he continued. "Well, I don't neither." The audience roared with appreciative laughter. A perceptive reporter noticed that in this phase of his speech he made studied grammatical errors but that when he launched into an analysis of Share Our Wealth he talked like a college professor. At the end of the debate a mob of autograph seekers followed Huey out of the building, but no one attended Thomas.[5]

---

[4] Rose Lee: "Senator Long at Home," *New Republic*, LXXIX (May 30, 1934), 68; Boston *Transcript*, January 11, 1935; *American Progress*, July 1935.

[5] New York *Sun*, March 3, 1934; Washington *Post*, March 3, 1934; New York *Herald-Tribune*, March 3, 1934; Norman Thomas. Mr. Thomas stated that he did not think Huey was at his best in the debate.

The most telling critics of Share Our Wealth did not center their fire on its ideology but on its economics. Huey thought of wealth only in terms of money and overlooked the importance of the machinery that produced wealth, they argued. His plan would spread money, the symbol of wealth, around, but it would not increase the amount of wealth in the country. The critics doubted that the plan would even spread existing wealth very much. How, for example, they asked, would Huey proceed with an organization like the Ford Motor Company? How could he make a factory that produced cars produce houses? The government could tax Ford's profits, but the resulting revenue would provide only a small part of the benefits Huey had promised. And if the government taxed both the company's income and its assets at the rate proposed by Huey, it would end up owning most of the stock of the company, and then Mr. Ford would tell the government to run the business itself.[6]

Huey attempted to answer these criticisms. He explained that wealth would not necessarily be distributed in the form of money. It could be passed around in the form of goods. Thus a man who needed a house or a car could be given one of these items from the possessions of a man who had too many of them for his own use. Or, a poor man could be given a block of stock that had come into the hands of the government through taxation. He admitted, however, that some details of his plan remained to be worked out. "I am going to have to call in some great minds to help me," he said.[7]

Some of his enemies charged that he knew his plan would not work. He had put it forth only to catch votes for the presidency, they proclaimed. Some of his friends had the same suspicion, and they have claimed that when they questioned him about the plan, he admitted it was impractical. These men were, however, very conservative Longites, and it is possible that Huey was only assuring them that Share Our Wealth was not a radical scheme. He asserted many times that he was sincere in pushing the plan. "My enemies

[6] Walter Lippman, in New York *Herald-Tribune*, March 12, 1935; article, "Huey Proposes," in *New Republic*, LXXVIII (March 20, 1935), 147.

[7] *The New York Times*, March 9, 1935. The critics who said SOW would not create new wealth were really saying that it would not cause economic growth. But, as the American experience since World War II demonstrates, any program of large and sustained expenditure by government will expand the economy. The problem of modern government is not to create new wealth but to ensure that it is more evenly distributed. Huey, with his guaranteed "homestead" and income, went beyond anything yet done by government to achieve distribution.

believe I'm faking," he said once. "Let them think it. That's in my favor. All the time that they fight me, they fight upon a mistaken basis."[8]

He probably did believe that Share Our Wealth was a workable formula. In his moods of high elation he was likely to think that he could make any formula work. It is evident, however, that he developed doubts about some of the aspects of the plan and that he came to realize wealth could not be as easily distributed as he had thought. He would probably have modified the plan if he had become President, retaining and emphasizing the tax provisions. The plan might seem visionary, but it was a time that tempted visions. Other men also dreamed of ways to conquer the depression and advanced their plans. Father Charles Coughlin, the radio priest, assured his millions of listeners that the single expedient of inflating the currency with silver would end the depression. Dr. Francis Townsend enlisted a huge following with his scheme to increase mass purchasing power: he would give all elderly people generous monthly pensions that would have to be spent every month. Novelist Upton Sinclair, turning his talents to politics, attracted national attention with a plan to end poverty by having the government buy or lease land on which the jobless could raise their own food and rent idle factories in which the unemployed could produce their own clothes and other necessities.

Huey's plan differed from the others in being more complex and far-reaching. The plans of Coughlin, Townsend, and Sinclair were essentially only formulas for recovery. They might have lifted the country out of the depression, but they would not have changed significantly the existing economic structure or existing economic relationships. Huey's scheme was also designed to hasten recovery, but in addition it would have altered meaningfully the relations of the various segments of the economy. The federal government would have assumed a larger and permanent role in directing the economy. This fundamental aspect of the plan was not, however, the part that caught public attention. It was the promise in Share Our Wealth to abolish misery and poverty that drew people to its banner. Enough of them would come, Huey hoped, to elect him President.

The first Share Our Wealth clubs were organized in Louisiana. They were formed by local Long leaders, who acted on their own initiative or in response to a request from Huey to organize a

[8] Richard W. Leche; Henry C. Sevier; St. Louis *Post-Dispatch*, September 11, 1935.

club. These leaders set up the clubs on whatever basis seemed good to them and their followers. A club could formulate its own rules in a constitution written by a lawyer member and choose as many officers as it desired. It could, if it wished, charge local dues. Each club was independent of other clubs, although on occasion those in a parish or in several adjoining parishes might act together—to state a Long position on a particular issue or endorse a Long candidate in an election. The clubs in Louisiana were, in fact, primarily political machines rather than societies to propagate an ideology. For example, those in three contiguous southern parishes claimed twenty-three thousand members and transformed an area that had been doubtful for Huey into a Long stronghold.[9]

In other states the clubs were organized by men who were "fans" of Huey's, who were accustomed to listening to his radio speeches or reading his Senate addresses and who had been converted to his doctrine. The evidence on their background is scanty, but apparently they were men of average economic standing and with a somewhat above-average intelligence and interest in public affairs. When one of them decided to form a club, he would write to Huey's Washington office for information on how to proceed. At first the requests were answered individually, but as they grew in number, this proved impossible. Accordingly, Earle Christenberry and the staff prepared a pamphlet containing instructions on creating a club and educational material on the aims of the organization. Entitled *Share Our Wealth: Every Man a King*, it was sent free to whoever asked for it. Also sent free to club members was a copy of Huey's autobiography and what amounted to a subscription to the *American Progress*, members being placed on Huey's mailing list to receive the paper. As a further incentive to membership, Huey's office offered at cost price to clubs a button for members, an insignia the size of a dime on which was emblazoned in red, white, and blue "Every Man a King."[1]

Letters from persons wanting to form Share Our Wealth clubs flooded Huey's office. How many there were can only be conjectured. His staff claimed that forty thousand such letters were received in one week early in 1935. It is probable, however, that many of these were from persons who wrote simply to express their approval of

[9] Leonard Spinks; J. J. Fournet.

[1] Earle J. Christenberry; Burton H. Hotaling: "Huey Pierce Long as Journalist and Propagandist," *Journalism Quarterly*, XX (1943), 26; Raymond Gram Swing: *Forerunners of American Fascism* (New York, 1935), p. 98; *American Progress*, March 1, 1934; Edgar Norten.

Share Our Wealth or to request literature about it. The number of people who felt called upon to tell Huey that they liked Share Our Wealth was enormous, and to conservatives, appalling. By April 1935 his office was receiving an average of 60,000 letters a week, and in one week alone it was deluged with 140,000 letters. The volume would become even greater. After one of his radio speeches and during one of his encounters with the Roosevelt administration, more than thirty thousand letters a day poured in for twenty-four consecutive days.[2]

Huey liked to boast that every letter addressed to him received a "personal" reply. This was true in that the writer got a letter addressed to him as "Dear So and So" and signed by Huey. These answers were, however, form letters, prepared in Huey's office with a space left blank in the middle for a paragraph pertinent to the writer to be inserted. Even the insertions were fairly standardized, referring to the importance of supporting Share Our Wealth or to the volume of mail coming into the office. Because of the "hole" left in the middle, the staff called these documents the "doughnut letters."

In order to answer the ever-growing volume of letters, Huey had to enlarge his staff, which before the formation of the Share Our Wealth Society had consisted of Christenberry and four women from Louisiana. He added eighteen stenographers and typists, girls from the Washington area. Even this force could not take care of the job during a rush period, and at such times Huey put on a night shift, fourteen other girls who reported at five thirty in the afternoon and worked until almost midnight. He could not house this assemblage of typists and their machines in the two rooms allotted to a Senator as an office, and had to request the use of three more rooms, giving him the largest suite of offices used by a senator. He had to pay rent for the extra rooms, and the expense of this and the salaries of his employees far exceeded the amount of money he was allowed for office maintenance and help. He met the expense out of his own resources—from the deducts and other contributions that flowed into his possession from Louisiana.[3]

The initial response to Share Our Wealth was so encouraging that Huey decided to employ an organizer to form additional clubs in Louisiana and other states. The man he selected for this job

[2] *American Progress*, February 1, 1935; New York *Sun*, April 3, 1935; Hotaling: "Long as Journalist," *Journalism Quarterly*, XX (1943), 26; Long to Edgar Norten, Springfield, Ohio, May 4, 1935, copy furnished me by Mr. Norten.

[3] Mary B. Walle; Joseph F. Thorning: "Senator Long and Father Coughlin," *America*, LIII (1935), 8; *Time*, April 1, 1935, pp. 15–17; Theophile Landry.

gradually enlarged his role. Gerald L. K. Smith eased his way into the Long inner circle, a colorful and eventually one of the most controversial members of the group.

Smith was a minister of the Disciples of Christ religion. It might be said that he came to his calling by inheritance. He was born in a small town in Wisconsin, into a family that for three generations before him had produced ministers, and he became one himself at the age of eighteen. While pursuing his vocation, he attended colleges in Indiana, and then in 1929 he secured his first important assignment. He accepted an invitation to be the pastor of the First Christian Church in Shreveport, reputed to have the richest congregation in the city.

His parishioners were at first delighted with their acquisition. He was a superb pulpit performer. Only thirty years old, he was a handsome figure of a man, six feet in height, with wavy auburn hair and clear blue eyes. He had a magnificent voice, he spoke effortlessly, and he drew huge crowds to his sermons. But his rich hearers did not always like what he said. He had been reared in Wisconsin on doctrines of rural radicalism, and he frequently brought political themes into his exhortations. Soon he took to attending meetings of the labor unions in Shreveport, and the labor leaders set out to enlist him on their side. "We took him over," one of them said. He became more radical in his sermons and even spoke kindly of Huey Long. This last heresy was too much for his congregation, which asked him to leave. One of his labor friends took him to New Orleans to see Huey, who had previously met him and knew about his troubles with his congregation. Huey realized that he could use the oratorical talents of the minister to make converts to Share Our Wealth. He offered Smith a job as traveling organizer.[4]

Smith embarked immediately on a speaking tour of Louisiana, addressing audiences in towns and hamlets and sometimes in pastures and clearings in the countryside. He spoke to an estimated million people in the state during 1934 and in the following year extended his activities to other Southern states. He attracted large audiences wherever he appeared, and at the end of every exhortation many of those present surged forward to sign up as members of Share Our Wealth. His secular oratory was a mixture of his own

[4] Kenneth G. Crawford, in New York *Post*, February 26, 1935; Paul Y. Anderson, in St. Louis *Post-Dispatch*, March 3, 1935; Victor C. Ferkiss: "The Political and Economic Philosophy of American Fascism" (unpublished Ph.D. dissertation, University of Chicago, 1954), pp. 282–3; Mary B. Walle; E. H. (Lige) Williams; E. J. Bourg.

style and of mannerisms and phrases adopted from watching Huey. He used Huey's trick of asking those men in an audience who had four suits of clothes to hold up their hands. Of course, not a hand was raised. Next he asked how many had three suits . . . two suits. Again no hands went up. Then, with a sob catching in his throat, he revealed that J. P. Morgan owned hundreds of suits.

But for the most part he relied on his own devices, on his flow of language and his ability to paint a word picture. He depicted the happy America that would exist when the swollen fortunes were broken up, with resulting full employment. "Let's pull down these huge piles of gold until there shall be a real job," he would cry, "not a little old sow-belly, black-eyed pea job but a real spending money, beefsteak and gravy, Chevrolet, Ford in the garage, new suit, Thomas Jefferson, Jesus Christ, red, white, and blue job for every man!" He closed every address with a prayer. "Lift us out of this wretchedness, O Lord, out of this poverty, lift us who stand here in slavery tonight," he would intone. "Rally us under this young man who came out of the woods of north Louisiana, who leads us like a Moses out of the land of bondage into the land of milk and honey where every man is a king but no man wears a crown. Amen."[5]

He worshipped Huey, whom he called a "superman." His adoration was so intense that he had to be near his leader at every possible moment. He sometimes even went into a hotel room where Huey was sleeping and curled up on the floor beside the bed. Huey often gave Smith a suit of clothes that he had tired of using, and Smith wore it proudly, saying to everyone he met: "This is Huey's suit." Huey was at first amused at Smith's subservience. "He wants to be like me," Huey would say tolerantly. But gradually he became distrustful of Smith's aping of him. Perhaps the servant so wanted to be like the master that one day he would try to become the master himself. Huey finally decided, in 1935, that he would eventually have to fire Smith.[6]

Launched in February 1934, the Share Our Wealth movement spread like wildfire. Within a month it enrolled over two hundred thousand members, and by the end of the year it boasted of having over three million members. It grew even more spectacularly during 1935. Earle Christenberry informed the press that he had records showing that there were Share Our Wealth clubs in every state,

[5] F. Raymond Daniell, in *The New York Times*, February 7, 1935; *Time*, April 1, 1935, pp. 15–17; *American Progress*, August 7, 1934.

[6] Seymour Weiss; Charles Frampton; Harvey Peltier; Richard W. Leche; Theophile Landry; Frank Odom; Robert Brothers.

27,431 of them in all, with a total membership of 4,684,000 persons. He claimed that there were more members than his records showed. His staff had on file the names and addresses of 7,682,768 persons, and he thought that many of these were unaccounted-for members.

Whatever the exact membership figures, they were large enough to be impressive, and Huey and his adherents liked to boast that the Share Our Wealth clubs represented a powerful national movement, "an active, crusading force" that someday soon would sweep into control of the government. The number of members was, however, deceptive as to the movement's strength. More significant was the geographical distribution of the clubs. The best available evidence suggests that Share Our Wealth was essentially a regional phenomenon. Louisiana contained more clubs than any other state, one forth of the total number, and probably more members than any state. The next greatest concentration of clubs and members was in Arkansas and Mississippi and then in other Southern states. Outside the South the largest number of clubs was in the north-central states, led by Minnesota, and in New York and California. In these latter clubs the number of members is not known, but it was relatively small in comparison with the Southern membership. The political influence of Share Our Wealth was therefore limited to certain areas. Even if most of the members should vote as Huey asked them to, which was not at all certain, they could not conceivably carry a national election.[7]

There were some Negro Share Our Wealth clubs, most of them in Louisiana, perhaps a few in other Southern states, and a number in the larger Northern cities. The first black clubs were formed in Louisiana by local white Long leaders who called meetings in Negro churches and persuaded the congregations to sign up en masse. Although some of these leaders may have acted on their own initiative, they were more probably following Huey's instructions. He stated publicly more than once that Negroes were eligible to join the Share Our Wealth movement. "In fact, we want them," he said. The creation of Negro clubs stirred the resentment of many whites and especially of Huey's farmer followers, the Southern class most likely to react against increased rights for Negroes. These clubs might be segregated, but to organize "niggers" in a society that had political

[7] *American Progress*, March 22, 1934, January 4, 1935; *Literary Digest*, September 8, 1934. p. 9; Gerald L. K. Smith: "Or Superman?" *New Republic*, LXXXII (February 13, 1935), 15; *Time*, April 1, 1935, pp. 15–17; Carter: *American Messiahs*, pp. 22–4.

overtones was dangerous—the Negroes might be encouraged to demand the right to vote. Huey's enemies played on this fear by charging that his motive in setting up the Negro clubs was to eventually
enroll the Negroes as voters. This motive never entered his mind.
Only about two thousand Negroes out of an adult black population
of over four hundred thousand voted in Louisiana, and he made no
effort to open the gates to others. He wanted Negroes in the clubs
for a simple reason: Share Our Wealth was for poor people and the
Negroes were poor, poorer even that the poorest whites.[8]

The Negro clubs in the North were organized by black leaders
who heard Huey on the radio or read his speeches. One of the fifteen
Share Our Wealth clubs in New York City was a Negro club whose
organizer and president was a minister. The minister told an inquisitive reporter how he had organized the club, speaking glowingly if
oddly about its aims. "The Senator and me could take this town
like an epidemic," he boasted. But it was the matter of his race that
the reporter wanted to talk about. Did Huey know that he was a
Negro? "The color question never comes up," the minister said. "I
address him as a man, and he addresses me as a man."[9]

Huey addressed a member of any minority group as a man. He
was completely without prejudice in his personal relations, and he
had friends and associates in a spectrum of religious and ethnic
groups in Louisiana and other places. He liked to say that some of
his best friends, such as Seymour Weiss and Abe Shushan, were
Jews. He did not mean, as do many who use this cliché, that he liked
a few Jews who were different from the mass of their people. He
meant that in choosing his friends he did not consider such matters
as ethnic backgrounds.[1]

People of many ethnic backgrounds resided in the small towns
of south Louisiana—Lebanese, Italians, Greeks, and others. They
were either recent immigrants or the offspring of recent immigrants,
and they lived pretty much to themselves, unnoticed by their neighbors and even by the politicians. Huey was the only leader who
showed them attention. He got to know many of them, and when
he hit one of these towns in a campaign, he would, if he had time,
telephone one of his acquaintances and say: "Fix me a dish of that

[8] Baton Rouge *State-Times*, January 12, 1935; C. F. Hyde to Pat Harrison and
Theodore Bilbo, February 18, 1935, and to Bilbo, March 8, 1935, in Robinson
Papers; Associated Press dispatch, April 30, 1935, in Long Scrapbooks, XIX; Alexandria *Town Talk*, quoted in Nashville *Globe*, June 7, 1935.
[9] New York *Post*, June 14, 1935.
[1] George H. Maines; Seymour Weiss; Bernie K. Hoffer, in *Saturday Review*,
XLVII (October 17, 1964), 6–8.

lasagna [or whatever was the ethnic culinary speciality of the man being called]. I'm coming over." These visits to the homes and social affairs of the immigrants were vividly recalled by a lawyer of Lebanese descent. This man readily admitted that as a result Huey garnered the immigrant vote. "Of course, it was partly politics, but it was something more," he said. In trying to describe what else it was, he pointed up an unrecognized function of a great politician: "Huey must have liked people. He made these people feel important, and somebody should have."[2]

Huey's obvious contempt for prejudice sometimes aroused the anger of bigoted people. In 1934 the Ku Klux Klan leveled a barrage at him. The "imperial klonvocation," meeting in Atlanta, denounced him for having an "un-American attitude" toward "authority," and Dr. Hiram W. Evans, the head of the organization, announced that he was going to Louisiana to campaign against the Kingfish. Huey could easily have ignored the threat. The Klan had lost strength in the state during recent years and even if rallied personally by Evans could pose no danger to the Long machine. But it still counted thousands of adherents, many of them presumably Long supporters who would be offended if Huey took issue with Evans. Huey, nevertheless, chose to reply.

He went to the press gallery of the state senate—the legislature was in session at the time—and said that he wished to make a formal statement on Evans's projected visit to Louisiana. As accustomed as the correspondents were to Huey's language, they gasped on hearing his words: "Quote me as saying that that Imperial bastard will never set foot in Louisiana, and that when I call him a sonofabitch I am not using profanity, but am referring to the circumstances of his birth." He added that if Evans did come to the state he would leave with "his toes turned up." The newspapers did not quote the full statement, or if they did, they used blanks to indicate Huey's expletives. But Dr. Evans got the message and decided not to go to Louisiana.[3]

The largest minority group in Louisiana, and also the most sub-

---

[2] Edmund T. Reggie. Mr. Reggie stated that for years after Huey's death old Lebanese people when coming to Baton Rouge would on crossing the Mississippi by bridge or ferry look toward Huey's grave on the capitol grounds and murmur in Arabic: "God rest his soul."

[3] Associated Press dispatch, August 17, 1934, in Long Scrapbooks, XXVIII; United Press dispatch, August 21, 1934, ibid., XX; unidentified clipping, August 27, 1934, ibid., XVIII; Laurel (Miss.) *Leader-Call*, August 28, 1934; Hermann B. Deutsch: "Kingdom of the Kingfish," in New Orleans *Item*, September 19, 1933. I have been assured by reliable sources that Huey's words were as quoted here.

merged, was the Negroes. In Huey's time they were not restive in their situation, or if they were, they did not voice their feelings or demand a change in their status. They were similarly quiet throughout most of the South, and the politicians ignored them except during campaigns, when some votes could always be picked up by denouncing the "nigger danger." Huey could have ignored them too, but he did not.

He discussed the racial problem fairly frequently, and on these occasions he talked like a typical white Southerner—he was for segregation and white supremacy all the way. He repeatedly stated that he favored leaving the question of whether Negroes should vote to the respective states (in the South the Negroes were already disfranchised), and as senator he consistently opposed a federal antilynching law as unnecessary. "We just lynch an occasional nigger," he said, with apparent callousness.[4]

His extreme talk, indeed, his whole racial stance, was a strategy. By seeming to be a complete segregationist, he reserved for himself a freedom of action on racial matters—he could then do some things that breached the pattern of segregation, he could give the Negroes certain rights that he believed they should have. The rights he would extend were economic ones. He felt a genuine sympathy for the material plight of the Negro. "Now, just a word about the poor Negroes," he said while he was governor. "They're here. They've got to be cared for. . . . The poor Negroes have got to live, too." He was never very explicit as to the exact economic rights the Negroes should have, probably because he thought that these rights were so apparent they did not have to be defined. When a reporter asked him in 1935 how he would treat Negroes as President he answered: "Treat them just the same as anybody else, give them an opportunity to make a living." He added that Negroes should have "a chance to work and to make a living, and to get an education." The Negroes in Louisiana shared in the benefits of the Long program, such as the free schoolbooks, the enlarged facilities at the state hospitals, the public health services. Indeed, because they were poorer than the whites, they benefited more from the program. A homestead-exception law exempted seventy-seven per cent of the homes of white people from taxation but ninety-five per cent of the homes of Negroes. Huey realized the racial implications of his program. As one of his

[4] *Congressional Record*, 73 Cong., 2 Sess., p. 11941, speech of June 16, 1934; Boston *Transcript*, January 11, 1935; Amsterdam *News*, January 1935, clipping in Long Scrapbooks, XIX; Washington *Post*, May 5, 1935.

leaders explained his reasoning: "You can't help poor white people without helping Negroes. It has to be that way."[5]

The privileges that Huey wanted to extend to Negroes might seem small to later generations, but for his time they were large, almost revolutionary, far more than any other Southern politician was willing to give. He would carry the Negroes as far as he safely could at the time. He would raise their economic and educational standards because he could accomplish that. He would not attempt to extend the suffrage to them because if he did, he would fail as a politician, and everything else that the Negroes had won would be lost. "I have been able to do a hell of a lot of things down there because I am Huey Long," he said once. "A lot of guys would have been murdered politically for what I've been able to do quietly for the niggers."[6]

What he did do earned him the deep gratitude of Negroes, especially in the South. The Negro press of the region was unanimous in praising him. Although the papers noted that he had helped Negroes with his program, they expressed their greatest appreciation for his refusal to indulge in "nigger baiting." Unlike his predecessors in Louisiana, "he has not ridden to power on the 'Negro question,'" one editor said. More revealing of Negro opinion, and moving in their simple eloquence, are the statements of Negroes who were young persons in Huey's time and who although they live in an era when Negroes enjoy greater rights than he dreamed of, yet think of him as one who prepared the way for that era. A man who acted as a chauffeur for state officials: "There was not a finer man. Nothing wrong with him. He always treated me fine." A laboring man: "He was fair to colored people, good to all poor people. He walked the land like Jesus Christ and left nothing undone." A schoolteacher: "We felt that he had no prejudices. He gave the Negroes and all poor people hope."[7]

In 1935 Roy Wilkins, later to become a leader of his race but then a newspaperman, heard that Senator Long was in New York City and requested an interview with the Kingfish. He was invited to come to Huey's hotel suite. Somewhat to his surprise, he was greeted

[5] *Louisiana Progress*, August 18, 1931; Boston *Transcript*, January 11, 1935; Baton Rouge *State-Times*, June 3, 1935; David B. McConnell.

[6] Roy Wilkens: "Huey Long Says—An Interview with Louisiana's Kingfish," *Crisis*, XLII (February 1935), 41.

[7] Shreveport *Sun*, April 12, 1933; Nashville *Globe*, June 7, 1935; William Pickens, in New Orleans *Louisiana Weekly*, clipping, n.d., probably 1935, in Long Scrapbooks, XXVII; Charles Davidson; Rivers Livous; Vivian S. Bernard.

courteously by Huey, who did not hesitate to shake his hand although a number of white men, some of them Southerners, were in the room. Huey discussed various matters with these men, who had previous appointments, and then asked Wilkins to come into the bedroom. There he launched into a long and frank exposition of his views on the racial question. "Let me tell you about the Nigras," he began. Wilkins noted with interest that throughout the interview Huey used the words nigra, colored, nigger, but mostly nigger, which Huey did not regard as being offensive.

Huey described for Wilkins the benefits the Negroes were receiving from the Long program in Louisiana. He said that many whites in the state had wanted to keep the Negro ignorant. Planters especially desired this condition, so that they could cheat their black tenants. "So what did I do?" he asked. He had started his night schools for adult illiterates. And the whites had not wanted the niggers to go to school and had protested his action. "They kept on hollering, and I simply had to put my foot down," he shouted. "I said 'I'm the governor and I say the ignorant in this state have to learn, blacks as well as whites.' And they learned."

Huey was anxious to put over to his visitor that it was difficult to achieve measures to help Negroes in a Southern state. A politician often had to resort to stratagems to do justice. He described what he had had to do to convince whites that Negroes should share equally in the public health facilities maintained by Louisiana. "I said to them: 'You wouldn't want a colored woman watching over your children if she had pyorrhea, would you?' They see the point."

Wilkins did not see Huey's point. He was as single-minded as a segregationist, and he thought Huey was playing politics with the racial issue and that he was cynical in his views on the issue. The import of Huey's concluding words was lost on him completely. "In your article," Huey said, "don't say I'm working for niggers. I'm not, I'm for the poor man—all poor men. Black and white, they all gotta have a chance. They gotta have a home, a job, and a decent education for their children. 'Every Man a King'—that's my slogan. That means every man, niggers along with the rest, but not specially for niggers."[8]

[8] Wilkins: "Huey Long Says," *Crisis*, February 1935, pp. 41, 52.

# CHAPTER 25

# *Sit Down, Isom*

IN JANUARY 1934, shortly before he unveiled the Share Our Wealth program to the nation, Huey introduced in the Senate a bill embodying the principal features of his plan—limiting fortunes, inheritances, and income and providing pensions to needy persons over sixty years of age.

Speaking in support of his measure, he began by describing the administration's method of attacking the depression—hiring people on public works projects, putting them on what he called the "dole roll." It was very much like a farmer feeding corn to hogs, he said. The government took the money or corn from the "crib," the treasury, and scattered it to the hogs, "calling them up from here, there, and yonder, throwing them a handful of corn." But where was the money coming from to finance these projects? It was coming from the pockets of the very people being given the little rewards, because Congress had refused to lift the tax burden from the masses and shift it to the rich. "You are giving the little man a biscuit to eat, and you put a barrel of flour more taxes on top of his head to carry," he said. The administration's fragmentary approach was not helping the economic situation; it was "permanently aggravating" it. A fundamental change in the economic system had to be made, he proclaimed: a redistribution of wealth. He would strike this theme continually in his speeches during 1934. He had small hope that his plan would be enacted into law, but he was going to keep it before the Senate and the country.[1]

---

[1] *Congressional Record*, 73 Cong., 2 Sess., pp. 58, 216–19, speeches of January 4 and 8, 1934.

He denounced the administration in flaming rhetoric. "Not a single thin dime of concentrated, bloated, pompous wealth, massed in the hands of a few people, has been raked down to relieve the masses," he charged in one address. The President and the Democratic leadership were following the Republican philosophy of helping only the rich, he went on, gibing finally: "Let us bring Hoover back and enshrine him." The Democrats had to choose between two methods of fighting the depression, he declared in another speech: "One is to let it alone, to let the people starve and let them cry, let them fight and let them lie. That is one way—the old laissez faire doctrine. That is the ultra conservative way." But there was a better way, "the way by which man considers himself a part of the family of all humanity; by which one nation's problems become the problem of all its people and of all other nations," by which lofty language he meant the redistribution of wealth.[2]

He had little hope that his party would decide to take the bold way. The Democrats were not a bold party, he said. They had been elected on a promise to put down the power of Wall Street, "the bloody hands of masterful finance," but they had not touched the bankers. Instead, they had concerned themselves with enacting laws to regulate the small economic activities of small people, "from chicken feathers on up to the size of litters of hogs." He despaired of the party, but he was not yet ready to break with it. He would remain in its ranks, but as a guerrilla fighter, operating independently on its flank. In this session of Congress he voted for approximately half of the administration's bills and opposed the other half. His decision in each case was an easy one: "Whenever this administration has gone to the left I have voted with it, and whenever it has gone to the right I have voted against it."[3]

His partial support of Rooseveltian measures did not propitiate the administration, which continued to consider him an opponent. He was viewed in the same light by more objective observers, the Washington political correspondents. Most of these men conceded, however, that he had a liberal voting record and that he was, indeed, to the left of the administration. But they insisted on regarding him as primarily an obstructionist, a negative political force. He seemed to be constantly opposing programs proposed by others but offering nothing in their place. Thus in this session he introduced only one

[2] Ibid., pp. 3695, 5985–6, 6081, 8002–4, speeches of March 5, April 4 and 5, May 3, 1934.
[3] Ibid., pp. 10921–33, 11451–2, speeches of June 9 and 14, 1934.

important measure, his bill to redistribute wealth, and he made no effort to bring it to a vote.

The negativist label pinned on him was accurate only in part. He did not introduce many bills, but this was because he believed partial reforms would not save the country from the revolutionary situation it was in. Only a drastic change in the system would save it, and this was the only kind of change he wanted to lead. Nor did he associate himself as a co-sponsor of bills introduced by other senators, and consequently his name did not appear on any measures. But he helped to pass a number of important bills, including some proposed by the administration. Curiously, he sometimes speeded passage of the administration bills by denouncing them. More conservative senators, who did not particularly like the bills, voted for them because they feared the Kingfish would arouse support for something more extreme.[4]

On occasion he would take up a bill of another senator and steer it to passage—a bill that was in trouble because it seemed radical and was not supported by the administration or was covertly opposed by it. Such a bill was before the Senate in the spring of 1934. It was a measure to establish a uniform federal bankruptcy law, and to it progressive Republican Lynn Frazier of North Dakota offered an amendment—really another bill—extending bankruptcy privileges to farmers. The amendment provided that farmers unable to pay their mortgages could declare bankruptcy, have their property appraised by federal officials, and pay the appraised sum to their creditors in installments over five years.

The Frazier amendment enlisted Huey's immediate interest: it would aid farmers, the class he felt closest to; it proposed a bold procedure; and it embodied one of his favorite Biblical principles, the remission of debts. He therefore jumped into the middle of the fight for its passage, in fact, taking over the leadership of the progressives backing the bill and speaking for it more often than Frazier did. In these speeches he also discussed subjects that were not related to the bill. He denounced Roosevelt's experimenting bureaucrats, who by issuing edicts tested their theories on the people as though the people were children: "this baby-rattling system." He demanded higher taxes to reduce the great fortunes: "I would pull them down to frying size." And, of course, he advocated his plan to share wealth: "We are either going to apply the laws which were given from Heaven, or our country is not going to last."

[4] Rexford G. Tugwell: *The Democratic Roosevelt* (New York, 1957), p. 348.

Huey and his allies, despite their best efforts, were not able to get the Frazier amendment incorporated into the bankruptcy bill. But in the meantime the House was considering the bill, and a North Dakota congressman, William Lemke, succeeded in getting the amendment tacked onto it. Huey then persuaded the Senate to adopt a version of the amendment that did not go as far as the House measure. As the two chambers had passed differing bills, one of them would have to recede from its position before the bill could be enacted. Both bills had moved slowly through the houses—the administration leaders showed no enthusiasm for the amendment—and the House version was not ready to come over to the Senate until June 16, a Saturday, when the final adjournment of Congress was scheduled at midnight.

The Senate convened at one o'clock that afternoon. Huey and his cohorts had their strategy planned. When the House bill arrived, they would move that the Senate concur with the House measure. They waited throughout the afternoon and into the early evening, and still the bill was not presented, although it was known to have arrived. Finally, at seven o'clock, Huey addressed the chair. He charged that the House leadership had deliberately delayed the transmission of the bill and now that it had finally come, the Senate leadership was delaying consideration of it. "It is the queerest thing that I ever saw happen in the Senate," he shouted. "It beats anything I ever saw as long as I have been here and as long as I have been anywhere else."

Determined to force action, he moved that the bill be referred to a joint conference committee. His motion was agreed to, and he was named to the committee. He held the floor, however, announcing that he would continue talking and hold up all business until the House agreed to refer the bill to the conference committee. "They will do some sitting up over there tonight before they get out of there," he threatened. A filibuster could jam up the last-minute passage of vital bills, so the leadership hastily capitulated. Joe Robinson moved that the Senate recess until Monday. "Congress stepped up to the very door of adjournment Saturday night and met Huey Long," one correspondent wrote appreciatively.

Immediately after the recess Huey gathered up two of the House and one of the Senate conferees, a majority of the committee, and stood them up outside the door of a Senate office. "Now here is what we will do," he announced, which was to recommend the House version of the amendment. In two minutes the members reached agreement, ending what political correspondents called the fastest conference on record. The Senate would have on Monday a recommendation from the committee, which was exactly what the leadership did not want to have and had not believed could be produced so quickly.

The Senate convened on Monday, eager to whip through the most important of the administration's remaining bills and then adjourn. Hardly was the session underway when Huey, looking grim, gained the floor. He had a startling piece of news. The copy of the report of the conference committee could not be presented, since it had mysteriously been lost in the House! Holding the floor, he proclaimed: "It seems the only way we can get anything started here is for me to make a speech." His threat was all too clear to the leadership: he would hold the Senate in session indefinitely. Robinson hastily interjected that the report had been found and was on its way to the Senate. "Glory be!" Huey exclaimed. But, he said, he thought that he would keep on talking. "This Congress ought to listen to me for a while before it goes home," he said. "Many people have gotten into their buggies and driven forty miles to hear me, back home." Again, his strategy was apparent—he would talk until the report arrived and thus prevent consideration of any other legislation. Robinson, desperate now, promised that a vote would be taken on the report before adjournment. Only then did Huey desist and permit the Senate to transact its business.[5]

The conference report was agreed to, and the measure extending credit relief to farmers was known in its final form as the Frazier-Lemke Act. Frazier and Lemke were its authors, but Huey had put it through, and his name could justly have been added to the bill's title.

Huey did not confine his speaking to the theme of concentrated wealth. He encompassed, in fact, more subjects than he had in previous sessions. He took a leading part in defeating ratification of the St. Lawrence waterway treaty with Canada, demonstrating in his speeches that although he was cognizant of the danger the proposed channel posed for the commerce of the Mississippi Valley he had made a thorough study of the problems of flood control and water conservation. He was one of the leaders of the opposition to a bill granting the President authority to negotiate reciprocal trade agreements with other countries, and although he was not able to defeat

[5] *Congressional Record*, 73 Cong., 2 Sess., pp. 7992–8805, 8056–77, 8082, 10184–5, 12060–7, 12083–7, 12356–62, 12369, 12376, 13812–82, debates of May 3 and 4, June 1, 16, and 18, 1934; *American Progress*, August 7, 1934, quoting reports of various correspondents.

the measure, he showed in his frequent speeches an extensive knowledge of the working of the tariff system.

He opposed the reciprocal trade bill partly because he objected to giving additional authority to Roosevelt but mainly because he feared the President would use the power to lower duties on American-produced goods. Pridefully he declared that he was "a tariff Democrat," devoted to protecting domestic interests straight down the line. This was economic nationalism, but in speeches on foreign policy he revealed that he was also a political nationalist. He advocated that the United States should withdraw from all agreements that might involve it in other parts of the world. Thus he demanded that the government disassociate itself from cooperative efforts to settle the war debts of European nations to the United States and that the government grant immediate independence to the Philippines. "Let us get out of the entanglements of Europe and the Orient in the quickest way possible," he cried. Political correspondents surmised that he was branching out into foreign affairs to enhance his status as a presidential candidate.[6]

Huey publicly upheld nonintervention as a principle, but, if newspaper reports were true, he did not always observe his doctrine. He was said to have had two agents working in Central America to persuade the banana growers there not to market their product with the United Fruit Company, a Louisiana concern that was fighting him in state politics. It was suspected that he had had something to do with a movement in some South American countries to shut off their sales of oil to the Standard Oil Company. In this session he delivered a fierce and sustained attack on Standard Oil, charging it with financing Bolivia to conduct a war against Paraguay over oil lands. The Paraguayan government took grateful notice of the efforts of its champion, a "great crusader for justice." It named a captured Bolivian stronghold "Senator Huey Long Fort."[7]

HUEY'S ENEMIES IN Louisiana were in a confident mood during the first months of 1934. They had inflicted a series of setbacks on the Kingfish in the previous year, and they believed that his political stock was still sinking.

[6] *Congressional Record*, 73 Cong., 2 Sess., pp. 1837–43, 4233–7, 4260–7, 9108–12, 9342–7, 9488–9, 10195–200, debates of February 2, March 14, May 18 and 24, 1934; Forrest Davis: *Huey Long, A Candid Biography* (New York, 1935), pp. 278–9.

[7] *Congressional Record*, 73 Cong., 2 Sess., pp. 3375, 5096–105, speeches of February 28 and March 2, 1934; Chicago *Tribune*, August 19, 1934; Rodney Dutcher, in Jacksonville *Journal*, September 7, 1934.

Their hopes seemed justified by events. In the spring Governor Allen called, as he had promised he would, a primary election to select a congressman for the vacant seat in the sixth district. J. Y. Sanders, Jr., again announced as a candidate, but Mrs. Kemp refused to make another race. Huey, after casting around desperately for a strong candidate to oppose Sanders, finally settled on Harry Wilson, a popular resident of the district who had been elected several times to the state office of commissioner of agriculture.

The election in April did not produce a winner. Sanders led Wilson by a narrow margin but because of the presence of several minor candidates in the race did not have a majority. A second primary, involving only the two front runners, was called immediately, and in this contest Sanders won by a majority of approximately fifteen hundred votes out of a total of over thirty thousand. The result seemed to intoxicate conservatives throughout the state, who trumpeted that another victory marking the end of Longism had been won. Actually, they had small cause to rejoice. In one of the strongest anti-Long districts in the state the anti candidate had barely squeezed through to victory. Nor was it certain that the vote in the election had accurately expressed public sentiment. Bands of armed antis had patrolled the polls on election day, and although no violence occurred, their presence must have intimidated some voters. This was all but admitted by an anti leader, who said that Huey might have had the election machinery, "but we had the riflemen."[8]

Threats of violence were rife in anti circles at this time. A meeting of citizens in a town north of Baton Rouge demanded that the senator from the district be tarred and feathered if he did not oppose the Allen administration in the regular legislative session, which would meet in May. In another town in the same district a mob prevented touring lecturer Gerald Smith from speaking and then while the sheriff looked on complacently escorted him to the parish line.[9]

Made heady by their victories over Long underlings, the antis decided to move on the center of Long power—to engineer a coup that would give them the governorship itself. As a first move, at the May session of the legislature they would displace Allen Ellender as speaker of the house and reorganize the lower chamber. With the momentum of this success behind them, they would then remove

[8] New Orleans *Times-Picayune*, March 7, 9, 10, and 24, 1934; Baton Rouge *Morning Advocate*, April 22 and 25, 1934; J. Y. Sanders, Jr.; Hermann B. Deutsch: "Kingdom of the Kingfish," in New Orleans *Item*, September 1, 1939; Will Irwin: "Empire of the Kingfish," *Liberty* (March 30, 1935), p. 20.

[9] New Orleans *Times-Picayune*, May 20, 1934; New Orleans *Morning Tribune*, May 23, 1934.

John Fournet as lieutenant governor by "addressing him out of office," a process peculiar to the Louisiana constitution that permitted the legislature to remove by a two-thirds vote of both houses any official except the governor for any "reasonable cause." Such a cause could easily be manufactured, and once Fournet was out, the senate would elect an anti president pro tem. Then would come the final move in the plot. Impeachment proceedings would be instituted against Governor Allen—on grounds to be decided later—and when Allen was found guilty, the new president pro tem would become governor.

The antis had prepared their plan carefully. For two months preceding the meeting of the legislature they held secret meetings at key towns throughout the state. At these sessions were discussed ways of persuading or pressuring legislators to support the scheme. To one of the meetings came representatives of the Old Regulars, who as allies of Huey's had recently been denounced by decent conservatives but who as present enemies of the dictator were welcomed as comrades. The accession of the Old Regulars gave added impetus to the movement, and its leaders were able to secure the signatures of forty-seven legislators pledging to vote to unseat Ellender. Fifty-one votes would be required to remove the speaker, but the antis had verbal promises from five additional legislators to vote for removal. Victory seemed certain, but the anti leaders were taking no chances. They summoned five hundred picked men from throughout the state to come to Baton Rouge May 13, the day before the legislature was to meet. Most of these men came armed, and at a secret meeting on the following day they professed their readiness to support the reorganization move with force. Several of the speakers who addressed them said that if a clash developed, Huey should be the first man to be killed.[1]

Also in the capital on the eve of the session was Huey. Word of the reorganization plot had leaked out to the Long camp, and the Kingfish had come from Washington to personally direct his forces. Setting up headquarters in the Heidelberg Hotel, he called in his leaders and outlined possible strategies. He knew about the meeting of the armed antis—he had had several spies planted in it—and his first thought was to prevent his enemies from achieving their end by force. Accordingly, he instructed Governor Allen to call out the militia and cordon off the capitol. The proposal horrified Ellen-

[1] Deutsch: "Kingdom of the Kingfish," in New Orleans *Item*, September 4, 1939; T. O. Harris: *The Kingfish: Huey P. Long, Dictator* (New Orleans, 1938), pp. 160–2; Allen J. Ellender; E. H. (Lige) Williams.

der, who protested that the move would ensure his removal. "They are looking for an issue and this will furnish them with one," he argued. Huey saw the point and rescinded his order. He would have to fight his foes with political methods.[2]

His first objective was to get certain house members who had signed the ouster pledge away from the secret meetings the antis were holding, to come to his suite or go to the house floor, where he and his lieutenants could work on them. He or his aides offered large inducements to members to remove their names from the pledge— patronage, favors for their parishes, and even money. The antis were also offering inducements to hold the signers in line and persuade additional members to sign. A Long emissary who approached one legislator was told frankly: "Bill, I'm bought and paid for." The antis, according to surviving conservatives, had even secured one of Huey's principal agents. Earl Long, now reconciled with his brother, was publicly laboring to save Ellender. But Earl had made a secret deal with the antis: he would deliver three to four votes to remove Ellender if supplied with a certain amount of money, not for himself but to buy the votes. Then one day a message came to the anti leaders from Earl. One of them bitterly summarized its content: "He was on the other side. He had been offered more money."

Earl's defection was an omen of what was happening to the anti plot. One by one many of the signers of the pledge went over to Huey. "They slipped away from us," an anti leader recalled. The legislature had convened on Sunday, and the antis had planned to present a resolution to displace Ellender on Monday morning. But when Monday came, the antis, recognizing defeat, did not even offer their resolution. Most of the men who had come to Baton Rouge bearing arms went home in disgust. Those who remained considered a proposal to rush Huey's suite and force him to abdicate his power and leave the city. It was a vague, mad scheme and was abandoned. That afternoon the Kingfish, realizing that he had routed his foes, departed for Washington. He had won partly because he had been able to offer more than the antis could. But a more significant reason was that a majority of the legislature knew that despite the apparent signs to the contrary, the people still supported him and his program.[3]

[2] New Orleans *Times-Picayune*, May 13, 1934; Allen J. Ellender; E. H. (Lige) Williams.

[3] Confidential communications from two Longites and two antis; New Orleans *Item*, May 15, 1934; New Orleans *Times-Picayune*, May 16, 1934; Deutsch: "Kingdom of the Kingfish," in New Orleans *Item*, September 4, 1939; Harris: *The Kingfish*, pp. 162–4.

Huey had devised an extension of his program before he left for Washington and had laid it down to Governor Allen. The administration was to sponsor a number of new taxes: on incomes, the gross receipts of utilities, transactions on the floor of the New Orleans Cotton Exchange, chain stores, liquors, sulphur, and the gross advertising receipts of newspapers publishing twenty thousand or more copies a day. Some existing taxes were to be repealed: the poll tax, which was a requisite for voting, and the personal-property tax on automobiles; and the cost of automobile licenses was to be reduced. In addition, the state would help to bring about a reduction in local property taxes by providing a homestead-exemption fund secured by the income tax. The first two thousand dollars of assessment on an owner's dwelling would be exempt from local taxation, and the state would reimburse the localities from the fund.

The income from the new taxes would support an expansion of the Long social program, and also of the officials and boards and jobholders who administered the program, and thus the levies would indirectly expand the Long power. Other items in the list that Huey left for the administration dealt directly with power and were aimed specifically at the Old Regular machine. A bill was to be introduced taking from the commission council of New Orleans the control of the city's police force and transferring this control to a state-appointed board. A section of the bill providing for lower-priced automobile licenses deprived New Orleans of the seven hundred thousand dollar annual grant that the state provided to pave the city's streets. Lastly, a special state police force was to be created, with authority to go into parishes that were not enforcing the law, such as Orleans and other anti-Long parishes.

The various bills making up the program were introduced immediately after Huey left for Washington. They were referred to committees, and in the committees most of them were stalled. Those that got onto the floor of either house ran into a storm of denunciation. The strongest opposition was to the tax bills and the measure reorganizing the New Orleans police, and some of the loudest opponents were Long legislators. Governor Allen quailed before the outbreak. He let it be known that the administration was abandoning its support of five of the six tax bills under consideration. As for the police bill, the governor said that the administration had no desire to enact spite legislation. The sponsor of the bill thereupon withdrew it from the calendar.[4]

[4] Shreveport *Times*, June 7, 1934; New Orleans *Item*, June 9, 1934.

The sudden collapse of the Long program inspired the antis with renewed hope. Obviously Huey's victory in preventing the reorganization of the legislature had been a fluke. His machine was in disarray, and now a well-delivered blow would crumble it. The anti leaders summoned a mass meeting in Baton Rouge, to be attended by representatives from every parish. Several thousand men poured into the capital for the rally and listened to speeches by Mayor Walmsley, J. Y. Sanders, Jr., and other orators. The speakers touched on the desirability of forming a better organization to overthrow Longism, but most of them emphasized the greater efficiency of violence. "The most glorious pages of Louisiana's history are written in blood," one man cried. The session came to a roaring climax when Mayor George W. Hardy of Shreveport shouted: "If it is necessary for us to teach them fairness and justice at the end of the hempen rope, I, for one, am ready to swing that rope." Before adjourning, the meeting yelled approval of a resolution recommending the use of "force if necessary" to return the government to the people.[5]

The conservatives were misreading the situation in the legislature. The Long machine was not crumbling, but it was betraying a dangerous weakness. It could not function under subleaders. The leader himself had to be present.

THE CONSERVATIVE PRESS reported the news with only faintly concealed trepidation. On June 21 Senator Long arrived suddenly in Baton Rouge and strode grinning into the governor's office, where he and Allen were closeted for over an hour.[6]

A few hours later the house "docilely" adopted an administration appropriation bill that had been stalled. And on the following day the other administration measures that had been held up began to move through both chambers. The change in the legislative atmosphere amazed a veteran reporter, who wrote in retrospect that one could almost hear the various parts of the Long machine click back into place.[7]

Huey took direct charge of every bill that was in question. He had been particularly disturbed at the delay of the important tax

[5] New Orleans *Times-Picayune*, June 12, 1934.

[6] Baton Rouge *State-Times*, June 21, 1934.

[7] Baton Rouge *State-Times*, June 21, 1934; New Orleans *Times-Picayune*, June 22 and 25, 1934; Baton Rouge *Morning Advocate*, June 23, 1934; Deutsch: "Kingdom of the Kingfish," in New Orleans *Item*, September 4, 1939.

bills, which he blamed on the administration leaders in the house, where the bills originated. Accordingly, soon after he arrived, he re-arranged the house leadership, placing in charge of administration measures a shrewd but untried member, Isom Guillory, from a southern parish. Guillory, however, made motions only at Huey's di-rection. Huey acted as his own floorleader in both houses. He darted from chamber to chamber, giving instructions to his leaders, roam-ing the aisles, and growling threats or whispering cajoleries to doubt-ful members. "Get back there and vote," he shouted at a Longite senator who started to leave the chamber just as an important roll call was to be taken.[8]

He also took charge of those bills that had to have committee hearings, bills that had been bottled up in a committee in one house or the other or that had been passed by one house only to be stalled in a committee of the other chamber. Ostensibly, he attended these committee sessions as an interested citizen, but actually he dom-inated each meeting, acting in effect as chairman of the committee. He gave a full display of his methods at a meeting of a senate com-mittee that passed favorably or unfavorably on seven bills in ten minutes. The chairman took up first the income-tax bill. "Does any-one desire any information on this bill?" he asked. "None," Huey shouted. "If not, the bill will be reported favorably," the chair-man announced. On another bill, the chairman asked if anyone wished to speak. "No," Huey answered. The bill would be reported favorably, said the chairman. One of the bills had just been passed by the house by a vote of eighty-four yeas to six nays. "I'm against that," Huey roared. "That will mess us up." "I'm against it too," a senator said. "Senator Heywood moves an unfavorable report on this bill," Huey said. "I move an unfavorable report on the bill," Heywood echoed. "The bill is reported unfavorably," the chairman announced.[9]

Before Huey had arrived, many of the bills in the administration program had been dealt with in such a manner that they were no longer eligible for consideration. They had been voted on and killed in one house and could not be reconsidered or they had been with-drawn by their sponsors. And when Huey reached the scene, the deadline for the introduction of new bills had passed. But he was not

[8] Isom Guillory; Arthur Provost; New Orleans *Times-Picayune*, June 26 and July 6, 1934; unidentified clipping, July 4, 1934, in Long Scrapbooks, XXI; New Orleans *Item*, July 3 and 7, 1934; Greenville (S.C.) *News*, July 22, 1934.

[9] Baton Rouge *Morning Advocate*, July 3, 1934; New Orleans *Times-Picayune*, July 8, 1934; New Orleans *Item*, July 7 and 8, 1934; New Orleans *States*, July 9, 1934.

going to be stopped now by what he considered technicalities. The antis had stalled his program by stratagems and pressures and threats of violence, and he would have to use extraordinary methods to save his measures. He hit instantly on a technique to circumvent the rules of the legislature.

"They didn't know what they were voting on," he said of a tax bill that had been defeated. "We'll find another bill to write the tax provision into." His innovation was to attach an administration measure that had been voted down, or not acted on, as an amendment to a pending bill, even if the latter was totally unrelated or had been introduced by an anti. Thus, an administration bill giving the state more power to select voting commissioners was added, with inspired malice, to an anti bill regulating the use of dummy candidates. Sometimes the same technique was employed to reverse the purpose of a bill. Two antis had sponsored a bill providing that no voting records could be removed from a registrar's office except by a court order. It was designed to enable the New Orleans courts to direct the removal of registration lists from the Orleans office if necessary to prevent the Longites from doctoring them. On the eve of its passage it was amended to provide that no court could order the removal of records from a registrar's office. The disgusted sponsors asked for permission to withdraw their bill but were refused, the first time in the state's legislative history that such a request had been denied.

The most sensational use of the new technique was to revive the withdrawn bill to reorganize the New Orleans police. Huey tacked the bill on to a measure introduced by a Choctaw legislator regulating the building of boathouses on Bayou St. John in New Orleans. The bill passed in this form, to the accompaniment of outraged cries from the antis, who charged that the bill would place the city's police under state political control. The bill did deprive the city government of the right to govern its police, but it did not provide for outright state control and it was singularly free of politics. The state was to appoint a board of police commissioners chosen from representatives nominated by the faculties of Tulane and Loyola universities, the city's Chamber of Commerce, other business and civic groups, and the Central Trades and Labor Council. Huey described his purpose in permitting such a board: "I'm putting the police under a non-political board and giving the city a chance to do its own cleaning; if they don't, I will."[1]

[1] Baton Rouge *State-Times*, July 3 and 12, 1934; New Orleans *Times-Picayune*, July 8, 1934; Greenville (S.C.) *News*, July 22, 1934.

Under Huey's constant surveillance, the legislature ground out the administration program. Every bill on the original list was enacted except the measure creating a special state police force, and this bill Huey decided should be withdrawn for this session. He held his majority in line on every vote, including those on bills that had to be cast as constitutional amendments and hence required a two-thirds consent. He was able, in fact, to increase his majority as he went along, bringing over to his side ten members of the Orleans delegation and a number of country members. But to secure these recruits, and to keep his previous followers faithful, he had to do some things he did not want to do, to make demeaning commitments to certain individuals. He had trouble rounding up enough votes to pass the constitutional amendment providing for an income tax, which some of his rich legislative adherents balked at supporting. He had at last to promise one of them, whose vote was crucial, the control of state patronage in the parishes represented by this man.

He had even greater difficulty getting the votes to pass the bill to abolish the poll tax. Many legislators feared that passage of this bill, which was also a constitutional amendment, would open the way for Negroes to vote. Huey dismissed their objections: the Negroes were disfranchised by other legal devices that were more efficacious. It was the effect of the poll tax on white voting that concerned him. The tax prevented many of the poorer whites, potentially his followers, from voting. Or, conversely, it turned them into anti-Long voters; rich antis would often pay up the poll taxes of large numbers of poor whites in return for a promise of their votes. He needed finally but one vote to put his bill through the house. He sought it from an Orleans member, who refused. It so happened that this man had a brother who was a bank president and who was, along with several other presidents, under indictment for having accepted deposits after their banks had become insolvent. It also happened that a bill had been introduced to extend legislative pardon to the executives, but had been stalled. Huey suddenly gave his sanction to the bill, and got the crucial vote.[2]

[2] Russell B. Long; E. H. (Lige) Williams; confidential communication; Harris: *The Kingfish*, pp. 170–1; New Orleans *Item*, July 10, 1934; Baton Rouge *State-Times*, July 12, 1934; New Orleans *Item-Tribune*, July 15, 1934; Meigs O. Frost: "Huey Long 'Purifies' Louisiana," *Today*, II (August 4, 1934), 10–11. The Louisiana income-tax law was modeled on the New York law. Huey cut a copy of the New York act out of a *World Almanac*, made a few revisions, and gave the clipping to his legislative lieutenants; Fred Blanche.

His control of the session was an impressive display of leadership. But he had to remain in Baton Rouge for three weeks, away from the Senate and the national spotlight. And he was worn down by the constant supervision he had to exercise, even over his own leaders. A revealing incident occurred near the end of the session. One of the administration tax bills was being steered to final passage in the house by new leader Isom Guillory as Huey watched from the back of the chamber. An anti member, seeking to needle Guillory, asked if the interest on whom the tax was laid would not pass it on to the people in higher prices. Mr. Guillory received the question with amused condescension. "Isn't it a fact that every tax eventually goes back to the people?" he asked. This bit of ineptness was too much for Huey. From his place in the rear he roared, and his command was obeyed: "Sit down, Isom."[3]

The legislature adjourned in mid-July, but its ending gave Huey no rest from his Louisiana labors. He had to face new and immediate challenges from the enemy organization and keep his own organization intact before these challenges. In New Orleans, Mayor Walmsley announced that the city would not bow to the law placing its police force under state control. Going into court, the city government obtained a temporary injunction, which was shortly made permanent, restraining enforcement of the law. At the same time the city defied Huey on another issue. Two members of the seven-man Orleans board of assessors had recently died, with their terms having more than a year to run. Governor Allen, at Huey's direction, appointed two Longites to the vacant positions. But Walmsley refused to recognize the appointees, contending that the places had to be filled by a special election, and the other five assessors refused to let the Long members sit with them.

The city government had legitimate reasons to oppose the state on these issues. The city clearly should have the control of its police and the choice of its assessors. But the Old Regulars who dominated its government were moved more by politics than by principle. They upheld the previous system of choosing police because it gave them the disposition of the jobs, whereas the system proposed by Huey, on its face at least, would eliminate politics from the force. Their stand on the assessor question could be explained only as a petty

---

[3] New Orleans *Times-Picayune*, July 6, 1934; Robert Angelle. The exchange between Guillory and the anti occurred during a discussion of the tax on newspaper advertising. This measure was obviously aimed at the anti-Long metropolitan press and was thus discriminatory and was voided by the Supreme Court.

piece of opposition. The two men appointed by the state would serve only a year and would be helpless in the Choctaw majority on the board.

Huey did not bother to argue the merits of the controversy. His reaction to the city's position revealed that he was approaching a point beyond which he would tolerate no opposition—from any quarter or on any grounds. He had pushed almost to completion the great program he had set for Louisiana, and now he wanted to finish it and move on to fulfill his national ambitions. If New Orleans insisted on standing in his way, New Orleans would have to suffer. He would not be deterred now by captious interference.

He first disposed of the assessor issue, harshly, without troubling to make it appear that the disposal came from Governor Allen. Calling attention to the fact that all assessments by the Orleans board had to be reviewed by the state tax commission, he announced that the two Long appointees to the board would be named as deputies of the commission and, moreover, that five other deputies, one from each of the other districts of the city, would be appointed. And as these deputies would have the final decision on assessments, they might as well make them out to begin with, and the existing board could close up shop! At the same time he revealed that the state was appealing to the supreme court the injunction against enforcement of the police law—and warned the justices to decide the case according to law if they expected to remain in office. "There ain't any man in too high a place that he can't be pulled down by the people," he said grimly.[4]

Huey had an additional reason to give his special attention to New Orleans at this time. An election was scheduled for September 11 in the city and the parishes immediately adjoining it to choose certain national and state officials. Huey had candidates entered in this contest. Leading his slate were the two incumbent congressmen from the extreme southern districts, Joe Fernandez and Paul Maloney, who faced opponents backed by the Choctaws and the Williams faction, these once bitterly antagonistic groups having recently combined. Running for the Public Service Commission against Francis Williams was a man who was a recent recruit to Longism and whose adherence illustrated the Louisiana talent for crossing factional lines. He was James P. O'Connor, the son of a former anti-Long congressman whom Huey had supplanted with Fernandez. Lastly, Huey was supporting a candidate for a vacant seat on the

[4] New Orleans *Morning Tribune*, July 31, 1934; F. Raymond Daniell, in *The New York Times*, August 6, 1934; *The New York Times*, August 10, 1934.

supreme court, Archie T. Higgins, a respected appeals court judge, who faced an aspirant endorsed by the Choctaw-Williams coalition. O'Connor and Higgins were relatively young men, and Huey was at this time moving men like this up in his organization, possibly indicating that he was worried about the ultimate succession to the Long power.[5]

Huey desperately wanted to win this election. A Long victory would erase the effect of his defeat in the January mayoralty election, which had lowered his stock in the whole state, and would be a gigantic forward step toward his eventual goal of smashing the Old Regulars completely. Obsessed with his purpose as he was, he was partially lost to reality, and in such a mood he was likely to make a rash and radical move.

Shortly before midnight on July 30 General Raymond Fleming led fifty national guardsmen, marching in pairs, down narrow Lafayette Street to the office of the registrar of voters, opposite the city hall, where they broke the lock off the door and took possession of the office. Word of the seizure spread immediately, and within a few minutes ten automobiles filled with policemen screeched up in front of the office. Out of one of the cars stepped Mayor Walmsley. Arriving just after the cavalcade was Chief of Police George Reyer, who had been summoned by Walmsley. The mayor had no doubt as to who had ordered the incursion. Turning to Reyer, he sputtered: "He can't do that." Reyer looked at the machine guns that the guardsmen had promptly mounted in the windows of the office. "Well, if he can't, they are there," he said.

Walmsley realized the chief's point and refrained from ordering the police to attack the office. He was determined, however, to know on what legal authority the state had acted, and he demanded an explanation of Fleming. The general said merely that he was acting on the governor's orders. Not until later that night did Walmsley get his answer. It came in the form of a proclamation announcing limited martial law in the city and declaring that the militia had occupied the office only to guarantee that there would be an honest registration for the coming election. Observers noted with interest that although the proclamation was signed by Allen, it had been issued from Senator Long's suite in the Roosevelt Hotel.[6]

The news of the proclamation enraged Walmsley. Taking to the radio, he identified Huey as the instigator of the document and

[5] James P. O'Connor; Clem H. Sehrt; Herve Racevitch.
[6] Raymond H. Fleming; George Reyer; New Orleans *Times-Picayune*, July 31, 1934.

labeled his enemy variously as a screech owl, a political degenerate, a moral leper, a coward, a gangster, and a madman. Huey replied to the diatribe, also on the radio. He depicted the controversy as one between the forces of reform and vice. What had been Turkey Head's first thoughts when he heard of the movement of the troops? Huey asked. Had Walmsley thought of his soul or of his Maker? "No, here's what he did. He sent his police running down into the red-light district to warn the inmates to hide."[7]

Walmsley, after venting his anger, considered how he could repossess the registration office. The possibility of testing the legality of the state's action came immediately to his mind. The governor could call out the militia only to preserve law and order or repress insurrection, and it could be argued that neither of these needs existed. Accordingly, the city government went into one of the district courts of the parish and obtained an order directing that the troops be removed. Commanded to observe the order were General Fleming, Governor Allen, and Senator Long. The Choctaw chiefs were jubilant as their sheriff set out to serve the papers.

Serving the papers, however, turned out to be a difficult matter. The sheriff had been informed that Fleming was at his office at Jackson Barracks and proceeded there. But he was refused admission to the post and was told that the general was ill and would not emerge for an indeterminate time. The sheriff then went to the Roosevelt Hotel and demanded to see Senator Long. He was received immediately and was surprised when Huey graciously accepted the papers. But, Huey solemnly explained, he had no power in the matter. He was a national official, and this was a state situation and therefore completely under the control of Governor Allen. However, Huey continued sweetly, he would be glad to drive to Baton Rouge and ask the governor to disband the troops. He made his offer audibly so that the grinning witnesses in the room could hear him.

On reaching Baton Rouge, he went immediately to Allen's office. He emerged shortly, wearing a look of resignation. Allen had called in bodyguards and defied him; in fact, "He told me to go to hell," said Huey. He added that he had done his best to see that the court's order was obeyed and that now he would have to return to New Orleans and follow the situation as a mere observer.[8]

Huey's ruse drew furious responses from the Old Regulars. But their anger reflected frustration. The Choctaws had no way to force

[7] Unidentified clipping, August 1, 1934, in Long Scrapbooks, XVIII.
[8] Chicago *News*, August 3, 1934; Washington *News*, August 3, 1934; Daniell, in *The New York Times*, August 6, 1934.

the governor to disband the troops. They could seek an eviction order from the supreme court, but this procedure promised little. The court would undoubtedly be reluctant to interfere with the governor's power to summon the militia. And even if the court should hand down a favorable decision, it would do so only after a lengthy hearing, and time was the one thing the Choctaws could not afford. The registration books had to be closed on August 11, and it would do the machine no good to possess them after that date.

Publicly, however, Walmsley and his leaders exuded confidence and resolution. The city government, with great fanfare, swore in four hundred special deputies to augment the police force of nine hundred, and Chief Reyer announced that he had received a large shipment of machine guns, tear gas, and arsenic bombs. The special deputies, variously armed, some of them with machine guns, were deployed around the city hall and opposite the fifty guardsmen in the registration office. The rival forces glared at each other across the "no man's land" of Lafayette Street. The state retaliated to the city's show of force by summoning six hundred additional guardsmen but held them at Jackson Barracks.[9]

The "armies" had been mobilized and a collision seemed imminent. But as the days went by, nothing happened. The rival forces continued to merely watch one another, and it was obvious that neither wanted to provoke an incident. Furthermore, neither side seemed to know what objective it should fight for. From the beginning there had been an air of unreality about the whole episode, and the protagonists apparently had no rational motives for doing what they were doing. The city government certainly had no reason to raise its special force of deputies. This contingent could not have been intended for defense of the city hall, for there was no evidence that the state desired to possess the building. It could not have been intended for offense unless the city government was willing to countenance an attack on the militia, which would have been a risky venture. There were some men on the commission council who would have taken the risk, but the majority, at least then, would not. It would seem that when Huey seized the registration office, the Choctaw leaders lost their heads and responded with a theatrical but dangerous gesture. They brought an armed force into being and then did not know what to do with it.

Just as hard to explain is Huey's purpose in touching off the crisis. He did not seize the office in order to shut off Choctaw regis-

[9] United Press dispatch, August 5, 1934, in Long Scrapbooks, XVIII; Washington *Post*, August 5, 1934; Daniell, in *The New York Times*, August 6, 1934.

trants, for he instructed General Fleming to permit an absolutely free registration. He offered as an excuse for his action that the city was about to remove the books, as it had done before the mayoralty election, to prevent the registrar from scratching the names of illegal voters. His plea does not stand up. The registrar was a state appointee and had ample time, and motive, to purge the rolls. The city could not have removed the books without a court order, which because of legislation just enacted, it could not obtain, and there was no evidence that the city meant to take the books by force. There is only one possible explanation of Huey's action: he thought that by a crude display of power he could awe his opposition in New Orleans, probably in the coming election and perhaps permanently. Awing his enemies had become a preoccupation with him, as was evident from his next move.[1]

An announcement came from the governor's office on August 13 that a special session of the legislature had been called, to convene on the following day and to remain in session for only four days. The startled political correspondents did not waste time seeking information from Allen. They went straight to Huey's suite at the Roosevelt Hotel, and asked him what program of legislation the administration would sponsor in the session. Huey, still playing his role of detached observer, professed ignorance. "You know, Governor Allen doesn't tell me things like that any more," he said innocently.[2]

He dropped the role when the legislature convened. Appearing in Baton Rouge, he took charge of the administration program and made it clear that it was his program. Conservatives and some of his own people were stunned when they heard the laws he proposed. They were power laws, blunt, blatant, and unashamed. One measure would authorize the governor to call out the militia merely at his discretion, not solely to repress riot or insurrection; it would also prohibit any court from issuing writs to restrain the governor in his use of the militia. Another would empower the state-appointed boards of election supervisors in the parishes to designate as many special commissioners and deputies as might be necessary to preserve order on election days. Other measures would give the governor almost unlimited power to grant reprieves, including to persons guilty of contempt of court; authorize the governor to increase as he saw

[1] Raymond H. Fleming; New Orleans *Times-Picayune*, August 2, 1934; Daniell, in *The New York Times*, August 10, 1934.

[2] New Orleans *Morning Tribune*, August 14, 1934; New Orleans *Times-Picayune*, August 14, 1934.

fit the personnel of the bureau of criminal identification, a special enforcement agency similar to the state police but separate from it; and enable the attorney general to supersede, at his own discretion, any local district attorney and to do so without interference from any court. Huey's purpose in proposing these extraordinary laws was all too plain—they could be applied in any area of the state, but they were aimed immediately at the city that was the center of his opposition, New Orleans.[3]

The leader had put his bills forward and now he was going to put them through, fast, without risking a slip-up. He would employ methods even more frightening to conservatives than those he had used during the recent regular session. All the bills in the administration program were introduced in the house on the first day of the session and referred immediately to one committee, that on ways and means, which under the rules considered only bills dealing with monetary matters. The committee met on the following morning to hear witnesses on the bills, but only one person testified, Senator Long, who appeared as an interested citizen. The antis, either because of apathy or resignation to defeat, made no attempt to present witnesses. Huey explained each bill briefly and not always frankly, and the committee, with but one dissenting vote, stamped approval on each one. The whole process took little more than an hour.

The bills were thus ready to go to the house that afternoon. Printed copies of each had been laid on the desk of every member, and under a suspension of the rules they were ordered engrossed and passed to the third reading. The next morning they were enacted in record time. The clerk raced through the reading of the bills, going so fast that the members could not tell where one word ended and another began. Even this did not satisfy Huey, who was standing near the dais. He snapped a command to a lieutenant: "Tell him to hurry up. They don't have to hear the damn thing. All they've got to do is vote." After a short debate on each bill, a Longite would rise and move the previous question, thus shutting off further discussion. The bills were then sped to the senate, where they were referred to the finance committee, reported out, and passed by the same procedure. In a final act before adjourning, the legislature adopted a resolution authorizing the governor to appoint a committee of both houses to investigate vice in New Orleans. Huey

[3] Washington *Daily News*, August 17, 1934; *American Progress*, August 23, 1934; Hermann B. Deutsch: "Kingdom of the Kingfish," in New Orleans *Item*, September 6, 1939.

explained the need for the proposed probe. "Law and order is needed in New Orleans," he said. "The good people of the city must be protected."[4]

At the close of the session it seemed that Huey himself might need protection. Conservatives throughout the state were bitterly resentful of the power laws and were talking openly about resorting to violence. One country editor charged that the Long regime was even worse than the outside rule of Reconstruction, apologized to "the shade of those niggers and carpetbaggers," and called for a return to the methods of 1876 to remove the "scabrous growth" that had overspread Louisiana. Another editor, Hodding Carter of Hammond, declared that only the use of "ancient methods" would destroy the evils of Longism. "We hope to God that Louisiana men awake to these wrongs and to the sole remaining method of righting them," Carter trumpeted. Some Louisiana men were obviously ready to attempt the old methods. Five rifle shots were fired into the front of Huey's home on Audubon Avenue by persons who sped away before they could be identified.[5]

Governor Allen immediately appointed the joint committee to investigate vice conditions in New Orleans, a seven-man agency of out-of-city legislators. There had been a frantic scramble for places on the committee by country members, who anticipated unusually pleasant duties, but this pressure was not the reason for Allen's quick action. The committee had been created to serve an immediate political purpose: it was expected to influence the current campaign by uncovering evidence that discredited the Old Regular government, and it had to do this before the election on September 11. Organizing hurriedly, the committee as its first act employed a counsel, who to the surprise of hardly anyone, turned out to be Senator Long. The counsel promptly took charge of the committee's procedures. He announced that the inquiry would open in New Orleans on September 1 and would be broadcast over a local radio station on which the committee had bought time, since the committee wanted to make certain that the citizens of the city were properly informed as to the iniquities of their government. Observers deduced that the counsel would dominate the probe and would conduct it under whatever unusual conditions he chose to impose.

[4] Deutsch: "Kingdom of the Kingfish," in New Orleans *Item*, September 6, 1939; New York *Evening Journal*, August 11, 1934; Daniell, in *The New York Times*, August 17, 1934; Pegler, in Boston *Traveler*, August 18, 1934.

[5] Tangipahoa *Daily Parish Courier*, August 18, 1934; Pegler, in Boston *Traveler*, August 18 and 22, 1934; *The New York Times*, September 6, 1934; Rose McConnell Long.

Those conditions turned out to be even stranger than anyone had thought possible. The hearings were held in a most inaccessible place, a suite rented by a state agency high up in the Canal Bank Building. Even if an interested person made his way there, he could not enter. On Huey's orders reporters, photographers, and spectators were barred from the hearing, and to enforce his dictum, fifty national guardsmen were stationed in the corridor leading to the suite. Reporters in the corridor could not see who the witnesses were, for these persons were brought into the building and to the suite by back entrances. The witnesses were not permitted counsel and entered the room one by one. The only other people in the room were Huey and the committee members. Huey sat at a table on which were two microphones, and a witness would be directed to take a chair across the table. Once Huey was ready to begin, a "cue" signal was flashed to the radio station. The thousands of people listening heard first a few bars of dance music. Then an announcer cut in: "We will now switch you to the eighteenth floor of the Canal Bank Building where the executive investigation of the city of New Orleans will be broadcast." Next came the voice of the chairman of the committee stating that it was in session and introducing its counsel, whose voice, except for those of the witnesses, would be the only one heard thereafter.[6]

Huey promised early in the hearings that the committee would produce sensational evidence of vice. "Just listen, Turkey Head," he shouted. "You'll hear plenty." The witnesses affirmed that vice did indeed exist in the city. They testified as to the addresses and activities of gambling dens, brothels, and handbook shops. They swore that the police shook down the operators of these places for payoffs and claimed that some of the money went to Chief Reyer and to Walmsley himself. These witnesses were obscure individuals, and Huey made most of them more obscure by clothing their identities in secrecy, to protect them, he said, from police reprisal. Many of them had personal knowledge of the situations they testified to, but it was evident that they were "friendly" witnesses and had been coached as to what to say. Huey gave this away when in examining one man he said: "Well, I'm going to cut my testimony short." He corrected himself with obvious embarrassment.[7]

[6] Clem H. Sehrt; *The New York Times*, September 2, 1934; New York *Evening Journal*, September 2, 1934. The correspondent of the latter paper apparently obtained a description of the surroundings of the hearing from one of Huey's intimates.

[7] *The New York Times*, September 2, 4, and 5, 1934; Sarasota *Tribune*, September 2, 1934; Boston *Herald*, September 3, 1934; New York *Enquirer*, September 4, 1934; Washington *Evening Star*, September 5, 1934.

Whatever the validity of the testimony of the witnesses, they had implicated some big names in the alleged corruption, and observers wondered if Huey would summon before the committee the men pointed to, and especially if he would summon Walmsley. The chairman of the committee said that of course the mayor would be called, but he was speaking without Huey's permission. Huey was not going to make the mistake of calling Walmsley without having firmer incriminating evidence in his possession. He did, however, summon two officeholders who stood just below Walmsley, Chief of Police Reyer and Chief of Detectives John Grosch. These men he put through a rough grilling. He exhibited records showing payments presumably made by the underworld to two individuals identified as "R" and "G." Did these letters stand for Reyer and Grosch? he demanded of the witnesses. He then produced other records proving that the two men had accumulated large assets and properties. He asked them how they had been able to do this on their modest salaries. Reyer and Grosch denied any wrongdoing, but they sweated under the questioning. Huey was delighted with their discomfort. "Take off your coat, Chief," he said to Reyer at one point. "You look like it's getting hot in here."[8]

A few days before the election Huey adjourned the inquiry. It had accomplished its purpose. It had brought the trail of corruption close to Walmsley and the city machine. It had demonstrated that vice was prevalent and had put Walmsley and his associates in the position of seeming to defend it. And it had thoroughly intimidated the "vice vote," the people who worked for the vice interests, an estimated seven thousand persons. The effect of the probe was admitted by Chief Reyer when he was asked to recall it. He denied that Huey had proved anything on him or other Old Regulars. "But," he concluded, "the fellow was doing all right with the people."[9]

After adjourning the hearing, Huey, apparently tireless, plunged into the campaign. Moving into his suite at the Roosevelt, he had one room fitted as a radio broadcasting studio, and from it he spoke several times every day on a regular schedule. "Ladies and gentlemen," he would begin, "it's Huey P. Long again, telling you how we're going to clean out this rotten bunch of grafters."[1]

The rotten bunch, however, did not seem to realize that it was

[8] New Orleans *Times-Picayune*, September 11, 1934; Shirley Wimberly; George Reyer.

[9] George Reyer.

[1] New York *Sun*, September 10, 1934.

about to be cleaned out. At Choctaw headquarters the mood was one of confidence, and Huey, seeing this, began to have misgivings. He decided that his enemies must be planning some potent move on election day. Their most probable weapon would be their police, whom they could turn loose to intimidate voters. They had also at their disposal, for whatever use they wanted to make of them, the special deputies who had been sworn in at the time of the seizure of the registration office and who were still belligerently guarding the city hall. Huey's suspicions were fanned by a piece of news that broke on September 6. Guy Molony arrived unexpectedly in the city and reported immediately to Walmsley.

Guy Molony was likely to arouse apprehension in any opponent. In New Orleans he was a legendary figure. He had been a tough chief of police for years until he had resigned in the mid-twenties to go to Central America. There he had led military forces in several revolutions, acquiring a name as a skilled and ruthless mercenary soldier who would hire out his talents to anyone. He had returned to New Orleans during the mayoralty election and had directed a squad of thirty special policemen assigned to "keep order" at the polls. He had disappeared after the election, but now he was back for a purpose that he would not divulge. He denied the charge that he had been brought to lead Walmsley's forces on election day. But he added that he would like to lead them, implying that he might be asked to.[2]

Huey was now convinced that the Choctaws were planning to use some form of force during the election, certainly to engage in whole-sale police intimidation of voters, perhaps to attempt an armed take-over of the polls. His first guess was accurate; his second probably credited the Choctaws with too much resolve. But his fear that an uprising might occur was not entirely without reason. He had been living for months under anti threats to overthrow him by violence, and he had to recognize that some of these threats were serious. This one seemed real enough to him: the Choctaws had, at least, the physical capacity to stage an uprising. He decided he would have to meet the danger with superior force.

On September 7, four days before the election, he instructed General Fleming to move into New Orleans two thousand national guardsmen, virtually the entire militia force of the state, and to do it with utmost secrecy. (Governor Allen obligingly signed a proclamation

---

[2] New Orleans *Morning Tribune*, September 7, 1934; *The New York Times*, September 7, 1934.

authorizing the move.) Fleming brought the men in that night by train and bus and stationed them at Jackson Barracks and in buildings belonging to the Dock Board. Not until the next morning did an astonished city learn of their presence. The Choctaws raged at the "invasion," but Huey ignored their protests. He was confident that he could handle any eventuality. If his enemies tried to take over the city, he could repress them. If they set the police to pressuring voters, he could counter by setting the guardsmen on the police. He let it be known that if even a single policeman appeared at a precinct box he would dispatch two squads of soldiers to that box.[5]

The presence of the troops averted the likelihood of a Choctaw armed coup, if indeed there had ever been the possibility of one. But the danger of a collision between the opposing forces still remained. If the police and the soldiers should happen to meet at the polls, fighting and probably bloodshed could follow, and this prospect appalled some men on both sides. One of them was General Fleming, who hoped that he would not have to use his men as Huey might command him. Fleming had an idea that Reyer was equally reluctant to use force and telephoned the chief to ask if they could not come to some kind of agreement to hold their forces in check. He found that Reyer was eager to conclude such an arrangement. Fleming then suggested that neither the police nor the troopers go near the polls and said he thought he could persuade Huey to agree to such a pact. Reyer said that he believed he could persuade Walmsley.[6]

Other men were simultaneously urging Huey and the mayor not to let their forces come into conflict. Especially insistent were the business leaders, who stressed that the national publicity being given the election was hurting the city's economic prospects. Their arguments found an unexpected ready response in both Huey and Walmsley. The mayor had in fact no choice but to yield: he could not use his police effectively in the face of the superior numbers of militia Huey had mustered. Huey could yield easily: he would achieve an advantage if the police were not used. Accordingly, he advanced Fleming's suggestion that neither the police nor the troops should be allowed near the polls, and this was accepted. Someone then proposed that an arbitration committee representative of both sides be set up to supervise the election and handle all complaints. As a final touch to the agreement, the committee was empowered to appoint

[5] Raymond H. Fleming; Richard W. Leche; *The New York Times*, September 8, 1934; New York *Evening Journal*, September 8, 1934.
[6] Raymond H. Fleming.

three hundred special deputies, who would be the only persons allowed to bear arms on election day.[7]

On that day the committee set up headquarters in the municipal auditorium. Fifty specially installed telephones enabled it to keep in touch with its deputies scattered throughout the city. The Long representatives were confident, since they had arranged that most of the deputies were their men. But they were also wary, fearing that the Old Regulars would find a way to circumvent the agreement. "We were in contact with every precinct," one of them recalled, adding ambiguously: "Not many votes were stolen. But we got our votes counted." The confidence of the Long representatives mounted as the day wore on and few complaints of irregularities came into the committee. The certainty of victory was even stronger in Huey's suite at the Roosevelt, where workers reported that the Long candidates were running strongly. Late in the day a Long precinct official phoned in that some Choctaws had just stolen his ballot boxes and he demanded the deployment of soldiers. General Fleming genially told him to forget it. "Huey has won his election," Fleming said. "Let 'em steal them."[8]

Huey had indeed won his election. His candidates—Maloney, Fernandez, O'Connor, and Higgins—swept the country parishes adjoining the city and carried the city itself by a majority of some two thousand votes. They were expected to win in the country, but their unforeseen victory in the city was a blow to the Choctaws and to the city press. The latter devoted reams of copy to analyzing the results, but without much success. The most probable explanation was that the election had been, for New Orleans, a relatively honest one.[9]

Huey had been determined to elect all his candidates, but he had put forth his greatest efforts on behalf of Archie Higgins, whom he needed on the supreme court. The antis were certain to subject some of his recent laws to judicial test. The court had previously been narrowly divided, with four justices voting usually to sustain Long laws and three justices voting consistently to void these laws. The justices who had voted to sustain were H. F. Brunot and John Land, whom Huey had helped to elect, Winston Overton, a brother of the senator's, and John St. Paul, whose son was a member of the Long

[7] Richard W. Leche; Daniell, in *The New York Times*, September 9, 1934. A copy of the agreement is in the Leche Scrapbooks.

[8] Richard W. Leche; Raymond H. Fleming.

[9] Baltimore *Sun*, September 12, 1934; New York *Post*, September 12, 1934; Harris: *The Kingfish*, pp. 176–7.

city organization. The members who had voted to void were Chief Justice O'Niell, Fred M. Odom, and Wynne G. Rogers.

The four justices who supported Long laws did so for mixed motives. Brunot, Land, and Overton had political obligations to Huey, of which he reminded them before some cases, or they agreed with the political philosophy of the laws. St. Paul was an Old Regular and disliked Huey personally, but, according to his son, he believed that the court should not restrict the legislature except when the constitution was clearly violated. The motivation of the three anti-Long judges was simple: they were opposed to anything related to Longism.[1]

Justice St. Paul had suddenly decided to retire for reasons of health, with twelve years of his term yet to run, and it was for his seat that Huey had run Higgins. But another seat on the court was also at stake in this election. The term of Winston Overton, who represented the southwestern judicial district, expired on January 1, and Overton faced opposition in his bid for re-election, from anti Thomas F. Porter. Thus if Huey was going to retain his majority on the court, he had to elect Overton. Another reason for supporting the justice was that he detested Porter personally. Once when Porter's name was mentioned, Huey said: "If I owned a whorehouse, I wouldn't let him pimp for me."[2]

Since he was occupied with the New Orleans election, Huey could not campaign for Overton. He had his leaders in the district working for the justice, however, and he felt little doubt as to the result: Overton was popular with the voters and was expected to win. But suddenly, on September 9, just two days before the election, Overton died. Louisiana law governing such a situation was explicit: if a candidate died within seven days prior to an election and only one other candidate remained, the latter automatically became the party's nominee. Porter would thus become the Democratic candidate and succeed to the court, and Huey would lose his majority. The chairman of the Democratic executive committee of the district, preparing to execute the law, called a meeting of his body in Crowley on September 15 to certify Porter as the nominee.[3]

Huey was shaken at the news of Overton's death. But he rallied quickly and summoned his leaders of the southwestern district into conference. They were bitterly resentful at the turn of events, believ-

[1] Justice Fred M. Odom; Frank Peterman; John St. Paul, Jr.
[2] William Cleveland.
[3] Deutsch, dispatch in Washington *Star*, October 14, 1934; Deutsch: "Kingdom of the Kingfish," in New Orleans *Item*, September 10, 1939.

ing that their people were being deprived of the right to elect a candidate of their choice and hopeful that Huey could suggest a course of action. At first he could not. He toyed with the idea of electing Overton: "Can we elect a dead man?" he asked. The leaders thought this would be illegal and impractical. Then Huey produced the solution, which he explained, and instructed those present who were members of the executive committee to be at the Crowley meeting. He said he would be there too.

The chairman of the committee expected that meeting to be a routine one. But he had hardly gaveled it to order when Huey burst into the room, accompanied by Lieutenant Governor Fournet and Attorney General Porterie. The chairman had rude surprises coming to him. A member of the committee moved that the chairman be ousted, and he nominated for the place a stanch Longite, who then received eleven votes of the fifteen on the committee. The victor took the chair and recognized Porterie, who explained that the method of designating Porter as the nominee was illegal. A member of the committee then moved that a new primary be called for October 9, and this was carried. Porter, who had come to the meeting merely to observe his certification, now realized the trap that had been prepared for him. Jumping on a chair, he cried angrily that he was the lawful nominee and that he would take his case to court. At this, Huey, who had hitherto remained in the background, rose. He had been waiting for Porter to make such a remark. Now he discussed briefly the facts of the case, emphasizing that the people should have an opportunity to elect a justice. Then he leveled a finger at Porter and shouted: "You're afraid to face the people." Every man in the room knew that what he said was true.[4]

Porter was not going to face the people if he could help it. Rushing to Baton Rouge, he sought an order from the district court there declaring him the nominee and prohibiting the holding of another primary. The anti judge of the court promptly issued a writ directing the secretary of state to promulgate the returns of the September 11 primary, thus making Porter the nominee, and enjoining the secretary from printing ballots for the October 9 primary. But the executive committee appealed the writ to the supreme court, directing their plea to the three Long justices, Brunot, Land, and Higgins. These justices suspended the writ until a hearing on it could be held, and fixed as the date for the hearing November 26, well after the elec-

4 Wilson J. Peck; J. Cleveland Fruge; New Orleans *Item-Tribune*, September 16, 1934; Daniell, in *The New York Times*, September 16, 1934; Louis A. Jones; Trent James.

tion. Porter now had nowhere to turn. He could not get the order of the three overturned, because the supreme court was divided on a three-three basis. Unless he was willing to abdicate his claim to his seat, he would have to run in the October primary. He entered the race protesting that he should not have to be in it and thus started under a handicap—he was denying that the people had a right to choose or reject him.[5]

Porter had other handicaps. He faced a formidable rival for the nomination. Huey, knowing that he would have to field a candidate who was well known to the voters, had persuaded Lieutenant Governor Fournet to make the race. And Huey, with the New Orleans election behind him, could throw his full resources, and himself, into the campaign. He moved four sound trucks into the district and spoke for Fournet in every town and hamlet. In every speech he made the same plea: You must elect Fournet to preserve our majority on the court and the laws we have passed to benefit you. It was an argument that impressed voters. On October 9 they elected Fournet by a majority of four thousand votes. Huey had kept his hold on the supreme court. But he had done it by violating the law. An excuse for his action was offered by the Long leader who was chosen chairman of the Crowley meeting. This man said: "There was no law to authorize what Huey did, but there was no law against it." He added, however: "I thought Huey was going pretty far."[6]

AT THE END OF 1933 it had seemed that the tide of Louisiana politics was running against Huey. But in 1934 he reversed the tide. He defeated his Louisiana enemies in engagement after engagement and at the end of the year was stronger than ever. He had been able to save himself because the people still supported his program. But he was no longer willing to rely solely on their support. Faced by unrelenting foes, obsessed with his goal and his destiny, he was now determined to remain in power by creating power, by erecting a political structure that his enemies could not possibly overthrow.

[5] Baton Rouge *State-Times*, September 21, 1934; Deutsch, in Washington *Star*, October 14, 1934.
[6] John B. Fournet; Washington *Star*, October 10, 1934; J. Cleveland Fruge.

# CHAPTER 26

# *Power in Himself*

SOME COMMENTARIES ON Huey Long at the height of his power by men who had experienced that power:

An Old Regular leader who secretly admired Huey while fearing him: "If you were for him, you could have anything you wanted. If you were against him, God help you unless you were an extraordinary man."[1]

A Shreveport bank official who examined a proposed settlement of an insurance claim for a friend, who hesitated to sign it for fear he was being swindled: "Why, I never heard of a thing like that. It's awful. I wouldn't sign it even if Huey told me to."[2]

An Old Regular leader who fought Huey but finally went over to him: "Others had power in their organization, but he had power in himself. And he brought them all to their knees."[3]

HUEY COULD FIND no time to rest during the last months of 1934. From directing the campaign to elect Fournet to the supreme court he had to turn immediately to another campaign—to secure popular ratification of those recent legislative measures that had been cast in the form of amendments and that would be voted on on November 6, the date of the general congressional election. He had little doubt but that they would be approved, although in his present

[1] Edward A. Haggerty.
[2] Confidential communication.
[3] Herve Racevitch.

mood he would not trust anything to chance. He campaigned for all the amendments and particularly for the measure abolishing the poll tax as a requirement for voting, which was the only amendment that met much opposition. His enemies claimed that passage of the amendment would be an entering wedge for Negro suffrage. His answer, which was quite accurate, was that even if the tax was repealed, the Negro would still be restrained from voting by the registration laws and the white primary; the only effect of the poll tax was to keep 250,000 white men and women from voting, he claimed, charging that this was the real reason that the conservatives wanted to retain it. The voters found his argument convincing, and they ratified the poll-tax repeal and the other amendments by a majority averaging seven to one. The huge margin was renewed evidence that the people still supported the Long program—that, in fact, they wanted it extended.[4]

Huey would not have rested if he could have. He was driven now by a fear of time, an apprehension that he would not be able to execute his plans in national politics before the election of 1936. To fulfill those plans he had to be free to give his full attention to the national scene, and this he could not do unless his Louisiana base was secure. It was not secure enough even yet, he thought. He would have to reach out for still greater powers.

The amendments election fell on a Tuesday. On the following Monday, November 12, Governor Allen summoned another special session of the legislature, which was to convene that night and remain in session for five days. Senator Long was on hand when the solons gathered, and it was symptomatic of what was happening in Louisiana politics that no one was surprised that he should be present or that he should be so obviously in charge of the administration's bills. Those bills, however, did occasion surprise because of their number and their provisions. Forty-four bills were introduced in the house by administration leaders on opening night, and nearly every one of them would increase the power of the state over localities and the power of the Long organization over its enemies.

The most far-reaching of the power bills created a civil service commission composed of the governor, the lieutenant governor, the secretary of state, and four other state officials. This agency would have unprecedented authority. It could investigate the competence of all municipal police and fire chiefs except for the very few who

[4] Circulars signed by Long and by Long and Allen, in Leche Scrapbooks; *American Progress*, February 1, 1935.

were elected directly by the people, and if it decided an official was incompetent, it could remove him. It also figured in selecting his successor. A municipality had to submit to the commission the name of the man it wished to appoint or a list of names of men, of whom one would be appointed. If the commission disapproved, a new list had to be submitted within five days, and if this second list was unsatisfactory, the commission itself would appoint the head. This man could dismiss subordinates, but his action was subject to review by the commission, which on its own initiative, however, could discharge subordinates.

Other bills in the program were almost as sweeping. One authorized the governor to fill by appointment any vacancy in state or local offices resulting from death or resignation until the next regular election was held. Three bills, as a package, deprived all municipalities of the power to regulate their public utilities and placed this function in the hands of the Public Service Commission. Various bills dealt specifically with New Orleans and increased the number of state-appointed members on certain boards in the city. One measure was pure spite. Aimed at the state bar association for expelling Attorney General Porterie during his controversy with Eugene Stanley, it created a new association, a public corporation named the State Bar of Louisiana, which would have a governing board unique in the history of legal organizations. Its members, eight in number, were to be chosen not by the lawyers but by popular election, one from each congressional district in the state.

Only one bill in the program dealt with economic matters. Carrying ominous implications to some conservatives, it provided for a moratorium on debts in the state and created the office of moratorium commissioner, which would be filled by the state bank examiner; and this official was authorized to suspend for two years the collection of all debts except those owed to the state. This bill was to Huey the most significant one of the lot. He pridefully described it as "the most radical feature of my revolutionary share the wealth program."[5]

Huey had to jam this mass of bills through the legislature within five days, but in the August special session he had found a way to

---

[5] Hermann B. Deutsch: "Kingdom of the Kingfish," in New Orleans *Item*, September 11, 1939; L. Vaughan Howard: *Civil Service Development in Louisiana* (New Orleans, 1956), pp. 46–7; Ben B. Taylor, Jr.: "A Study of the Appointive and Removal Powers of the Governor of Louisiana" (unpublished M.A. thesis, Louisiana State University, 1935), p. 145; Little Rock *Gazette*, November 15, 1934.

put bills through quickly, and now he resorted to the same method. Immediately after the bills were introduced in the house, all forty-four of them were referred to the committee on ways and means. The committee met the next morning and reported them favorably in a session lasting only one hour and forty-two minutes, giving to each bill a consideration averaging only slightly more than two minutes. The bills were then rushed to the house floor, where they were enacted almost without debate and sent to the senate. In the upper chamber they were referred to the finance committee, which seemed determined to beat the house committee's record for speed. It passed favorably on the bills in one hour and twenty-one minutes. The senate showed a similar celerity in enacting the bills, passing an average of seven of them every twenty minutes.

The committee hearings were brief partly because only one witness appeared before both bodies—that interested citizen, Senator Long. Huey was in a relaxed mood at the meetings. Confident of his majorities, he replied to anti questioners with good humor and disarming frankness. Queried as to a measure increasing the number of state appointees on a New Orleans board, he grinned and said the Long organization had to have more jobs at its disposal in the city. Challenged on the civil service law, he assumed a mien of innocence: "The reformers have been crying for civil service a long time, and something ought to be done about it. We're giving them a real civil service law in this one." An opponent asked if under the law the state would go into the cities and take over the control of their officials. This was not contemplated, Huey answered. But, he added, charges of incompetency would undoubtedly be filed against Alexandria Chief of Police O'Malley, who had permitted a riot to occur in his city in 1933, when a United States senator had been egged while speaking.[6]

Huey's frankness in explaining the bills was only superficial. As he sometimes did, he ascribed to himself lower motives than he actually had. Thus, he was speaking only a partial truth when he said that his purpose in offering the power laws was to create jobs for Longites. The jobs would, indeed, be created, and because the Long machine had them to award, it would be more firmly entrenched. But the new jobs were not to be created merely as an exercise in patronage or even in power for its own sake. The ma-

[6] Miami Beach *Tribune*, November 16, 1934; Chicago *Daily News*, November 16, 1934; Boston *Daily Globe*, November 17, 1934; Deutsch: "Kingdom of the Kingfish," in New Orleans *Item*, September 11, 1939.

chine had to have power to fulfill the purpose for which it existed,
which was to enable Huey Long to control the state for his great
plan. He had to control it so that he could enact and test there the
economic program that eventually as President he would bestow on
the nation. He admitted this to correspondents after the session had
ended. "We're going to make Louisiana a utopia, the kind of a state
nobody had dreamed of," he declared. Then, he continued, after
he became President: "We'll use Louisiana as a pattern."[7]

Increasing numbers of people in the state were willing to give
him a chance to put his theories into practice, and some of them
were in unexpected quarters. A visiting reporter interviewed some
of the most prominent businessmen in New Orleans on their reactions to the recent session and found among them a surprising support for the Long program. Some manufacturers commended Huey
for using his influence with the Public Service Commission to force
utility rates down, thus helping to reduce production costs. Spokesmen for the Merchants' Association endorsed the debt-moratorium
law as a device that would take poor credit out of circulation and
disclosed that the association had had a hand in drafting this "radical" measure. The opinion of most of those interviewed was summed
up by a former president of the Board of Trade who had previously
fought Huey: "I believe the public wants Long in power, so I'm
willing to give him a chance to make good. I believe now that he is
the only politician in Louisiana who will carry out his promises."[8]

Even with the great new powers that he had grasped, Huey did
not feel secure. He had to have still more power—his appetite was
growing imperceptibly—and he knew now how to get it, quickly
and in an apparently democratic manner from a democratic instrument. On December 16, only a month after the November special
session had ended, he had Governor Allen snap the legislature into
another special session, to convene that night and transact its work
within five days. Nobody outside the Long inner circle knew what
bills would be offered this time, but the rumors of new power grabs
by the Long regime abounded. The most widely believed story was
that a measure would be proposed to place East Baton Rouge
parish, an anti-Long center, under state control by converting it into
a little District of Columbia.

As sensational as the rumors were, they did not anticipate the

[7] Washington *Star*, November 17, 1934; Washington *Herald*, November 17, 1934;
Lafayette *Advertiser*, November 19, 1934.
[8] Washington *Daily News*, November 20, 1934.

breadth of the legislation Huey had prepared. Thirty-five bills were introduced in the house on opening night. The great majority of them were designed to place still more patronage in the hands of the Long organization, and in order to do so, they extended the Long pattern of increased state control over local governments. One bill took from the parish sheriffs the right to appoint their own deputies by requiring that the names of all proposed deputies be submitted to the superintendent of the Bureau of Criminal Identification for approval. Another required that all members of municipal police and fire departments have warrants of appointment signed by the chairman of the Civil Service Commission, that is, by the governor.

Other bills were aimed at specific cities or parishes that were anti-Long centers. One of them forbade New Orleans to levy certain taxes, for the obvious purpose of making the city more dependent on, and hence more amenable to, state control. Another reconstructed the police jury of East Baton Rouge parish, which had eleven anti members to only two Long members. It authorized the governor to appoint as many additional members as there were elected members, or thirteen, the appointees to serve until the general election of 1936. East Baton Rouge parish was not going to be made into a little District of Columbia, at least as yet, but it was going to be placed under firm Long control.[9]

These bold bids for power were certainly sweeping, but even they seemed tame in comparison with another administration measure, which invaded an area of local government hitherto considered beyond the reach of the state—the right of parish public-school boards to hire teachers and other school employees of their own choosing. The bill transferred this function to the state. It created an agency to be called the state budget committee, consisting of the governor, the superintendent of education, and the state treasurer, and to this body the parish boards had to submit annually a list of all school employees whom they proposed to hire and the salaries of these employees. If the committee disapproved of any person or persons on the list, the board had to submit a revised list. If the committee still disapproved of persons on the list, it could designate other persons whom it considered qualified, and those so named had to be hired. The measure, if drastically enforced, would place the

[9] New Orleans *Item-Tribune*, December 18, 1934; L. V. Howard: *Civil Service in Louisiana*, pp. 47–8; Taylor: "Appointive Powers of the Governor," pp. 147–8; Deutsch: "Kingdom of the Kingfish," in New Orleans *Item*, September 12, 1939.

fifteen thousand public-school employees at the mercy of the Long organization.[1]

Immediately after being introduced, the bills were started on the now-accepted process of cursory enactment—reference to the house committee on ways and means for quick return to the floor and transfer to the senate. The process was, if anything, made even faster. The committee on ways and means acted on the thirty-five bills in seventy minutes, reporting all but one of them favorably. The one that failed was rejected at a suggestion from Senator Long, who was present to explain the bills, again the only witness who appeared. The senator hastened consideration by brief explanations that he delivered with mocking humor. Describing a measure that gave the state the power to appoint the employees in a certain office in New Orleans, he observed that it was a "charitable law" because it would relieve the head of the office of the "heavy burden" of hiring people himself. An opponent asked if the head had requested relief. "Not yet," Huey grinned. "We just anticipated that."

The thirty-four approved bills were brought before the house in record time. By law they had to be read to the members by the clerk. This functionary, with a beaming Huey sitting beside him, accomplished the feat in thirty-five minutes, reading only the first few words of the title of each bill. An irate anti member rose to address the obvious question to the obvious person. "When," he demanded of Senator Long, "will we know what these bills are all about?" The Kingfish smiled. "Tuesday, when they are passed," he said.[2]

He was exhibiting a confidence he did not entirely feel. He knew he would have trouble driving some of the bills through, that even his own followers would recoil from voting for the more extreme power measures. He encountered, in fact, immediate opposition on one bill, that requiring state approval of the appointment of deputy sheriffs. Country legislators saw a juicy area of patronage slipping away from local control and protested so loudly that Huey had to

[1] Guy C. Mitchell: "The Growth of State Control of Public Education in Louisiana" (unpublished Ph.D. dissertation, University of Michigan, 1942), pp. 393–5. The school bill was really enacted as two bills, one being an amendment to the other. It was objected to by Superintendent of Education Harris, who was attending a convention out of the state when it was passed. Harris feared that he would always be outvoted by the other two members of the committee.

[2] Raymond Gram Swing: *Forerunners of American Fascism* (New York, 1935), pp. 65–70; New York *Sun*, December 17, 1934; unidentified clipping, December 19, 1934, in Long Scrapbooks, XXIII.

agree to modify the bill. At least five deputies appointed by a sheriff had to be automatically approved by the state, except for the sheriffs of Orleans and East Baton Rouge parishes. The sheriffs here were required to have approval for each deputy. As most sheriffs employed fewer than five deputies, the bill would have no effect except in the two specified parishes.

On certain other measures Huey had to work hard to round up the votes to pass them. Once when he had to stall for time, he determined to start a filibuster. He sent a note to James Buie, a verbose and colorful house member who delighted to orate on patriotic themes. "Jim," he wrote, "speak on the Declaration of Independence." Thus encouraged, Mr. Buie, who hailed from a hamlet appropriately named Fort Necessity, swept aside the several bottles of beer that he customarily kept on his desk for refreshment and launched into a fervid speech. Huey shortly had his votes and sent word to Buie to stop speaking. Buie, however, was enjoying his own eloquence and refused to quit. Huey had to send another note to quiet him: "Jim, goddamn you, I said to sit down."[3]

So doubtful was Huey about the fate of some bills that he resorted to deception to pass them. These bills were not introduced on opening night but were affixed as amendments to other, less important bills, literally in the last minutes of the session, and passed in disguised form. The process was a refinement of the technique that had proved so successful in the May regular session: an innocuous bill would go through the routine of house and senate consideration and come up for final vote in the senate. Suddenly a Long leader would move an amendment changing completely the nature of the bill. The vote would then be called for, and the bill would be passed and rushed to the house, which was anxious to adjourn. The clerk of the house would mumble a few words of the title, a Long leader would call for the vote, and the bill would be enacted before the opposition realized what was happening. But for that matter, most of Huey's own followers did not know what was happening. Only his leaders would have been apprised of the amendment, and they would have passed the word to their people about how to vote. "You just followed the leaders," one Long legislator recalled with resignation.[4]

In one example of this strategy Huey struck down the municipal government of a small city that had long defied him, Alexandria. He

[3] Joseph Cawthorn; Arthur Provost.
[4] Harvey Peltier; Arthur Provost; A. P. White; Robert Angelle; James T. Burns; Robert D. Jones; Waldo H. Dugas; Harry Gilbert.

was determined to remove its officials, all antis, but he knew that a bill aimed explicitly at Alexandria probably would not get through the legislature. Country legislators would vote to punish such urban centers as New Orleans and Baton Rouge, but they might rebel against harassing a smaller place. So Huey did not name his target.

Instead, he slipped into the legislation introduced at the opening of the session a bill codifying existing laws regarding city charters. This measure, harmless to any interest and meritorious in nature, moved through both houses without comment and to final consideration in the senate. Just as the vote was about to be called, a Long leader jumped up and offered an amendment, not a minor addition dealing with charters but a major section that transformed the purpose of the bill. The amendment declared vacant certain offices in Alexandria—those of mayor, commissioner of streets and parks, and commissioner of finance and utilities—and authorized the governor to appoint successors to these offices who would serve until the general election of 1936. Few senators understood the nature of the amendment, and in the hurry and confusion of the moment the recast bill was adopted and quickly concurred in by the house.[5]

Huey reserved his most spectacular use of this device for his most formidable enemy, one that he particularly wanted to humiliate, one that even with his large majorities he was not sure he could defeat—the Standard Oil Company. He laid his plans carefully. A few days before the session opened, he called in legal assistant George Wallace and asked him to draft a bill imposing a manufacturers' license tax of five cents a barrel on crude oil refined in Louisiana —the same tax that he had tried to have enacted in 1929 and that had led to his impeachment. "I said that I would tax Standard Oil if it was the last thing I ever did," he declared. Other than Wallace, he told only a few close associates of his purpose, and from some of them he met objections. An oil-tax bill would not get through the legislature, they argued. It would be blocked by Standard Oil, whose lobbyists were constantly watching both chambers, ready to bring instant pressures on legislators. Huey brushed the objections aside. The company would not know that a bill was coming, he said. "This is the time I'll pay off the Standard Oil for the impeachment," he ended one discussion.[6]

The oil-tax bill did not appear among the bills introduced by the

[5] Deutsch: "Kingdom of the Kingfish," in New Orleans *Item*, September 12, 1939; Taylor: "Appointive Powers of the Governor," pp. 147–8.
[6] George M. Wallace; Robert J. O'Neal; A. P. White; Joseph Cawthorn.

administration. But in the package was an innocent measure providing for the codification of existing license laws. This bill went through both houses almost without notice and came up for final vote in the senate on the last day of the session. At this point the Standard Oil lobbyists who had been watching both houses concluded that nothing detrimental to the company would be offered, and the head lobbyist, Louis LeSage, went to a telephone to tell his employers that all was well. While he was gone, a Long senator rose and moved an amendment to the license bill, which was about to be called. He held a copy of the amendment in his hand, a bulky document of a hundred typed pages. The clerk of the senate took the copy and mumbled a few words from it, there were cries of "Question," and the bill and the amendment were passed and sped to the house. But anti senators had caught enough from even the short reading by the clerk to deduce that it dealt with oil and taxes, and they sent word to colleagues in the house that something peculiar was afoot. House antis tried to interrupt as the clerk was reading rapidly selected parts of the amendment. "Isn't that the oil tax bill of 1929 all over again?" one member cried. His query was drowned out in shouts of "Question," and a Long leader called for a vote on concurring with the senate bill. The Standard lobbyists scrambled back on to the floor just in time to see the oil tax enacted. The whole episode had happened within approximately ten minutes.[7]

The special sessions drew political correspondents from all over the country to Baton Rouge. The visiting observers were fascinated at what they saw—appalled and repelled by what they thought was happening, finding it hard to believe. Later writers have felt the same sense of malign charm and have had similar reactions. Had an American legislature actually been so subservient to one man? Was not the control exercised by this man a negation of the democratic process? How had he been able to secure such a control? And how did he operate it? Or what were the mechanics of a special session? The commentators raised questions about the sessions and then condemned the proceedings, but they did not supply very informative answers to their questions. There was much more to the workings of a special session than they knew, or even suspected.

It has generally been assumed that Huey called a special session as a matter of whim, whenever the fancy struck him. This supposition has stemmed from the way a session was summoned: the call to

[7] George M. Wallace; A. P. White; Joseph Cawthorn; Isom Guillory; W. A. Cooper; Richard W. Leche; Shelby Kidd; Deutsch: "Kingdom of the Kingfish," in New Orleans *Item*, September 12, 1939.

meet went out from Governor Allen's office on a Sunday, the legislature being ordered to convene that night. Therefore, it was assumed
that the Kingfish must have decided in the morning that he wanted
a session and had told his puppet governor to call it. And by night
his puppet legislators would be in Baton Rouge. None of the critics
stopped to consider that he would have had to accomplish a miracu-
lous conquest of time to bring all this about: if the legislators had
not been contacted until Sunday, only a small number of them could
have reached the capital that night.

Actually, careful planning went into the calling of a session.
Word that a meeting was coming up was sent to Long members of
the legislature three or four days before the official call was issued,
usually by telephone, sometimes by telegram. If a legislator could
not be reached by these means, persons who knew how to go about
finding someone—such as local law-enforcement officials—were
sent after him. One Long leader who was vacationing at a camp on
an island off the Gulf coast was aroused one morning by the sound
of a motor boat chugging up to his pier. Out of the craft stepped the
sheriff of the nearest parish, who had come to tell him to get to Baton
Rouge immediately. Anti Long legislators were not told of the call
for a session until Sunday, when they received a telegram, usually
at noon or later. Many of them, consequently, were unable to make
the opening session.[8]

The bills that were to be offered at a session had been drafted
days or even weeks before. Only Huey's leaders knew what was in
them when the session convened. But immediately thereafter, on
Monday morning, Huey apprised his other followers, a majority of
the legislature, of the nature of the bills. Emerging from an apartment that he had had set up on the twenty-fourth floor of the capitol,
he would descend to the court of appeals room on the fourth floor,
where his people had been summoned to await him. At this meeting, always referred to by Longites as a "caucus," he would explain each bill carefully and at length. If he did not have time to go
through all the bills or thought that his members needed additional
instructions, he would hold another caucus, or several. The bills
that seemed to go through the legislature so fast and without consideration were already familiar to the majority.[9]

At a caucus there was a measure of discussion between Huey
and his auditors on the desirability of the bills. How much differ-

[8] Arthur Provost; Harry Gilbert; James Buie; A. P. White; Robert D. Jones;
E. J. Bourg; James T. Burns; Isom Guillory; Rupert Peyton.
[9] Murphy Roden; E. J. Bourg.

ence he permitted is recounted variously by surviving legislators. Some members contended that he received no contradiction, that it was too dangerous to oppose him. "If you bucked him, you couldn't get anything for your parish," one man explained.[1]

But these members were men who disliked Huey and his program and were Longites only because they had to be. The testimony of most surviving caucusites is that there was a fair amount of discussion and some give and take on the bills. "We would talk back to Huey," one man claimed. "And I think that Huey respected us for it." Another one said: "We spoke our minds, and sometimes bills were modified because of reasonable objections." Still another one said: "He let you have your say and sometimes would even change if he was convinced."[2]

They could have their say, but few of them tried to say very much. It was not that they feared his power, although all were aware of it. Rather, as they listened to him they became strangely entranced and did not want to interrupt him. One especially perceptive legislator, recalling a caucus scene after the passage of almost thirty years, still could not repress his amazement at the memory of the spectacle: "It was remarkable. You knew you were going to vote for the bills anyway. But when he explained them you couldn't see any bad angles, even though you knew they were there. I've often wondered how so many sensible men could sit there and listen and believe for the moment what he said. It was like we were mesmerized. It wasn't just that he had power or patronage, although you knew he had. But he carried you along with him."[3]

HUEY LONG WAS A remarkably introspective politician, and he sometimes paused to contemplate the power he was grasping and wonder at his use of it. "They say they don't like my methods," he said in an address. "Well, I don't like them either. I really don't like to have to do things the way I do. I'd much rather get up before the legislature and say, 'Now this is a good law; it's for the benefit of the people, and I'd like for you to vote for it in the interest of the public welfare.' Only I know that laws ain't made that way. You've got to fight fire with fire." He offered a similar justification of his actions to a friend who asked why he ran bills through the legisla-

[1] Harry Gilbert; James Buie.

[2] Joseph Fisher; Isom Guillory; Robert D. Jones; Robert Angelle; John J. Wingrave; Harvey Peltier; Arthur Provost.

[3] James T. Burns.

ture so fast: "You sometimes fight fire with fire. The end justifies the means. I would do it some other way if there was time or if it wasn't necessary to do it this way."[4]

Two themes run through his defenses of his use of power. One, he had to put down a dangerous opposition that otherwise would defeat his program and destroy him: "fight fire with fire." He once said bitterly to his wife: "Everything I did, I've had to do with one hand, because I've had to fight with the other." And two, he had to employ power because he had to do things fast, because he had to get on to other things. "I have so many things to do and not enough time to do them," he burst out to a friend. "I may not live long enough to do everything I want to do." And to another friend he explained: "I just can't afford to be slowed up."[5]

He doubtless believed, at times, his justifications. And he had some reason to believe them. He did face a relentless opposition, one with a singleness of purpose and a dedication rarely found in organizations in democratic politics. It would consent to no compromise with him on any issue but would resist any measure that he proposed, regardless of its merits, merely because he proposed it. Its reasons for resisting were only partly political, although its members viewed themselves as conservatives and him as a radical. Their revulsion toward him was fundamentally social and personal. They might have tolerated his radicalism and even the corruption they suspected him of if he had come from the right class and had "belonged." A New Orleans dowager tried to explain this to a Northern reporter: "Huey Long is not the first scoundrel to be elected governor of Louisiana. A good many of our governors have been scoundrels. But they have always been gentlemen." But even his low origin was not the worst of it, nor the simple though unpalatable fact of his power over gentlemen. He reminded them of his power, constantly, rudely, noisily, impressing on them, as it seemed to one observer, that Huey Long of Winn parish was their master and "could do with them about as he pleased."[6]

It was a relentless opposition, but an ineffective one. It was made up of disparate elements—Old Regular spoilsmen, idealistic reformers, pained aristocrats, apprehensive big businessmen—that

[4] F. Raymond Daniell: "The Gentleman from Louisiana," *Current History*, XLI (November 1934), 172; Charles Frampton; Charles E. Dunbar.

[5] Rose McConnell Long; Trent James; H. Lester Hughes; Raymond H. Fleming.

[6] Robert Cantwell: "No Southern Gentleman," *Vanity Fair*, March 1935, excerpt in Long Scrapbooks, XXIV; Thomas L. Stokes: *Chip Off My Shoulder* (Princeton, 1940), p. 403.

were drawn into a semblance of alliance only by a common hatred of Huey. It offered no platform that would appeal to the people, no program to improve the life of the masses, but iterated only that it stood for honest and democratic government. In the legislature it was a harmless minority and was likely to remain so, for it obviously lacked the capacity to carry a state election. Conceivably it might have recuperative powers, but these were not at the moment evident. Certainly it posed little threat to Huey. He did not have to fight it with "fire," did not have to have great power to sustain himself against it. He was engaging in self-deception when he said that he did.[7]

He was rationalizing again, but in a different way, when he said that he must have power because he had to do things fast. He did have a sense of oppression by time, a characteristic of the great politician. He has goals to pursue, but lesser people impede him, insisting that he observe rules and procedures. He cannot get on with his work, and he becomes impatient with rules and willing to shortcut procedures. So it was with Huey. He convinced himself that what he had to do could not be done in time unless he used unusual means to do it.

He was completely frank in admitting his desire for power. On two different occasions interviewers asked him why, with his radical ideas, he did not affiliate with the Socialists. He gave them almost identical answers. First of all, he said, he did not agree with the tenets of Socialism. But even if he did, he would not run for office as a Socialist because he would be defeated. "Hell, I want to be in office," he said. "That's where I can do good." There was no point to be right only to be defeated, he emphasized: "First you must come into power—POWER—and then you can do things."[8]

But what were the things he wanted to do? A friend once put this question to him, a man who had known him as a youth in north Louisiana but who had left the state and who was not in politics and to whom it was profitless to lie. Huey answered by re-

[7] Hodding Carter: "Huey Long: American Dictator," in Isabel Leighton, ed.: *The Aspirin Age, 1919–1941* (New York 1949), pp. 360–1. Mr. Carter admitted in this essay that the antis erred in opposing everything that Huey was for and not sponsoring economic change themselves. Some surviving members of the anti group admit the same fault. Said one (Harry Gamble): "There were things that ought to have been done that were not even thought of being done. The trouble was that everybody thought that whatever he proposed was for the purpose of getting votes. He did those things. He was a builder—he built with our money—but he was a builder."

[8] Unidentified clipping, January 26, 1933, in Long Scrapbooks, XIX; Benjamin Stolberg: "Dr. Huey and Mr. Long," *Nation*, CXLI (September 25, 1935), 344.

calling various individuals whom they both had known in the northern parishes, men who were abjectly poor. He said, as the friend recalled his language, that he wanted to be "the champion of those little guys" and people like them everywhere. He seemed to be sincerely moved as he spoke, the friend thought, undoubtedly correctly. Huey was nearly always moved when he talked about poor people and his determination to help them. He once told the United States Senate, in his most eloquent address to that body, that nothing could deter him from his efforts. "Nonetheless, my voice will be the same as it has been," he proclaimed. "Patronage will not change it. Fear will not change it. Persecution will not change it. It cannot be changed while people suffer. The only way it can be changed is to make the lives of these people decent and respectable."[9]

He wanted to do good, but to accomplish that he had to have power. So he took power and then to do more good seized still more power, and finally the means and the end became so entwined in his mind that he could not distinguish between them, could not tell whether he wanted power as a method or for its own sake. He gave increasing attention to building his power structure, and as he built it, he did strange, ruthless, and cynical things.

He once showed an associate a list of the richest and most powerful men in the state, urging him to contact each one personally and ask what his ambition was and how far he would go for Huey Long if his ambition was gratified. The associate, recalling the incident after many years, was still shocked at the stark pragmatic request. "I told Huey I couldn't do it, that this was going too far," he said.[1]

He built up a collection of records and affidavits containing material damaging to his enemies, actual or potential. These papers he kept in a lockbox, to be produced when he needed them as threats to force men to come over to him or as weapons to discredit men who would not. He assumed that every man had something in his past to conceal. "I can frighten or buy ninety-nine out of every hundred men," he once boasted. He also kept records on his followers, using them to keep these men subordinate. Increasingly, he insisted on subordination, a characteristic that drove from him men who agreed with him politically but who cherished their independence. Said one such man: "I can't go with Huey. If you go with him, you have to let yourself be dominated." He sometimes disciplined a man in his organization merely because the man was restive under domination. "He liked to break people, especially the

[9] Gene Austin; *American Progress*, April, 1935.
[1] Harvey G. Fields.

strong, and then build them up again," one politician recalled. "But then they knew their place."[2]

He began to run his organization with even more premeditation. Controlling the number of votes cast is a technique that other strong politicians have been able to use to win an election. Huey, however, used it imaginatively to accomplish subtler purposes. Before one election, an associate suggested a method to increase the Long vote, but to his astonishment Huey rejected it. It was dangerous to get too many votes, the Kingfish explained. "If I received all of the votes in this election and the next election I received fewer votes, my enemies would say I'm beginning to slip," he said. "My politics is that I want to get a few more votes than last time but not too many more."[3]

Another example of this technique was described by one of his sisters. In a local election, a Long candidate was running, a man that Huey wanted to be sure of keeping in line. He instructed his local leaders that the candidate was to receive only a bare majority. "Just let him get by," he said. The sister marveled: "I wondered that he'd take such a chance." Sometimes he would let local Long candidates be defeated in parishes that he always carried for himself or for his state ticket; he would let them go down because he did not want them to become so strong that they might defy him. "I had to do some things behind your back," he confessed to one parish leader. An associate commented, years later: "He could stand off that way and view everything he was doing and figure all the angles." This objectivity, deliberate and thorough, made him unique as a political boss.[4]

The organization that Huey ruled at the height of his power was significantly different from the one on which he had relied in his first year as governor. It was larger, more complex, and vastly more efficient. He had built it gradually, completing its structure at about the time he became senator. It is the famous, or infamous, Long machine of the Long literature.

The term "machine" has to be applied to it with a qualification. As had been the case with the earlier Long organization, there was about this one a certain looseness, an absence of form or structure. At the top level there was no precise arrangement of authority, no chain of command. Huey simply presided over a group of associates whom he called into conference in Baton Rouge or New

[2] Robert Brothers; Charles E. Dunbar; Edward S. Robertson; Paul B. Habans.
[3] Harvey Peltier.
[4] Arthur Provost; D. J. Anders; Richard W. Leche.

Orleans when he was contemplating some move. He might or might not ask their opinions, and he might or might not accept their advice. Some men might be invited to attend one conference and not even be told of another. Only a few individuals held recognized positions or performed specific functions. Abe Shushan was known as "the collector," the man who could raise large sums of cash in an emergency. Seymour Weiss had charge of the raising and spending of campaign funds. The other members did what Huey thought they could do or what he told them to do.[5]

Huey deliberately kept his top group formless. For one reason, he could run it more easily if it lacked system: men who exercised particular functions were likely to become independent and might defy him. But beyond this personal preference, he knew that he could not bring his men together in a close arrangement—that they were of such diverse nature that they could not be combined, and that it would be dangerous to try to combine them. They were, in truth, a strange assortment of political bedfellows, men of varied backgrounds and beliefs, striking refutations of the theory that political groups are held together by a common ideology. They included radical neo-Populists from the country parishes, equally radical Share Our Wealthers, stanch conservatives with links to business from New Orleans or other cities, professional politicians who were interested primarily in spoils, and professional idealists who glimpsed in Longism a vision of a utopian Louisiana. Huey had to keep these people apart; as one associate put it, he had to keep them "on different levels." Another man when his attention was called to this problem of Huey's said: "Yes, and the wonderful thing was that he had us in our places but never let us get together so that we could fight each other and mess up his show."[6]

In contrast to the shapelessness at the top, the structure of the Long organization at the local or parish level was precise and formal, like a conventional machine. There was a Long organization in every parish, directed by a group of men who were known and recognized as Huey's leaders. They might be legislators, local office-holders or politicians, businessmen, planters, or farmers. They were assigned to their positions by Huey, who picked them through the "medium of wisdom," as one leader put it, because they had ability or influence or money. Having given them authority, he expected results. He would say to one of these supporters: "Now look, I'm giving you everything you ask for in your parish. You've got an or-

[5] Seymour Weiss; Richard Foster.
[6] George H. Maines; Richard W. Leche.

ganization. If you can't carry your parish with everything that's being done, then you're a bad leader and I'll have to get me another one."[7]

The size of the organization varied from parish to parish, but it always functioned as a group. One member of it might be recognized as the head, but his position was almost entirely titular, at Huey's insistence. "He liked the idea of several leaders so that no one of them could be too big," one leader recalled and then, as he thought about his own organization, added: "It was a committee." Huey used the committee arrangement because it divided the power that was a potential threat. The members of a parish committee watched one another and competed against one another, which kept them so busy it did not occur to them to combine against Huey. As a result of the installation of the Long system, a fundamental alteration in the structure of Louisiana politics occurred. The power of the local politician was immeasurably lessened. The significance of the change was described by a Long associate: "In the old days the leader of a parish would be the sheriff, and you had the support of that parish only as long as that leader wanted you to have it. Huey just reversed that. That man was sheriff and leader because Huey wanted him to be. Huey cut out the middleman in politics."[8]

That this subordination existed is denied by surviving parish leaders. "Huey never put any pressure on us. There was no dictation," said one. Said another: "If we said something that he wanted to do on a local issue was wrong, he would listen to us, give way." And still a third said: "He always checked with us here before he did anything that affected this parish." But these men were talking about matters that were purely local. On such issues Huey sometimes gave his leaders a long tether. He liked to say: "If you want to cook in a kitchen, use your own kitchen. You know where the tools are."[9]

Even in local matters he often pulled up the reins abruptly. A

[7] Seymour Weiss; Richard W. Leche; Joseph Fisher. The description of a Long parish machine is based on interviews with the following leaders, with their parishes in parentheses: W. V. Larcade (Acadia); J. J. Fournet, Wilson J. Peck, Edgar G. Mouton, J. Maxime Roy (Lafayette); D. J. Anders, Harry Gilbert (Franklin); Will Harvey Todd (Morehouse); Robert Angelle (St. Martin); Lessley P. Gardiner, D. J. Doucet (St. Landry); Trent James (Rapides); C. C. Barham (Lincoln); A. K. Kilpatrick, Milton Coverdale (Ouachita); John Fleury, Joseph Fisher (Jefferson); James T. Burns, Robert D. Jones (St. Tammany); Fred Blanche (East Baton Rouge); G. E. Erskine (Caldwell); and H. Lester Hughes (Natchitoches).

[8] Edgar G. Mouton; Wilson J. Peck; Robert D. Jones; John Fleury; Milton Coverdale; Richard W. Leche.

[9] Wilson J. Peck; Edgar G. Mouton; J. J. Fournet; W. V. Larcade; D. J. Anders; Joseph Fisher.

leader in one of the French parishes said with Gallic expressiveness: "He let his local leaders do what they wanted unless they stepped on his foot—you know what I mean." He meant that a leader was checked if he did something that Huey construed as defiance or thought was poor politics. Some of the same leaders who claim freedom from supervision recount almost in the next breath that on numerous occasions Huey called them in and told them to stop doing something in their parishes that he objected to. They and other leaders are uncertain as to how he had found out what they were doing—they suspect that he had informants who wrote him regularly—but they are emphatic that whatever his system was, it worked. "He knew everything about everything," one leader said. Another confessed: "He could tell me things I didn't know." In these interviews he was not the benign boss who respected the wishes of local leaders. "He didn't ask you," one leader recalled of such a session. "He told you."[1]

Huey was asked in the Overton investigation if his organization had been built up on patronage. No, he answered, it had been built down. "Our majorities were much better when we didn't have any patronage," he explained. "I wish I didn't have a job on earth. You give a job to one man and you make nine mad. Our support is from the poor devils in the forks of the creek . . . who appreciate what we have done for them." But, the questioner pressed, weren't the jobs at the disposal of the state awarded almost entirely to Long people? Huey conceded that this was the case. "You wreck your organization if you give your jobs to enemies," he said.[2]

His wish that patronage was not an adjunct of politics was an expression of the idealism that lingered in him. But he knew that in the hard world of actual politics patronage had to be used, and he had used it from the time he became governor, at first with some restraint, then more freely and with increasing zest, and finally on a scale never before witnessed in Louisiana. Contrary to what he told the Overton committee, the Long organization was built, in large part, on jobs. And because of Huey's constant expansion of state functions and power, the supply of jobs was plentiful and apparently inexhaustible. The state employed directly over thirteen thousand persons and controlled the hiring of many people in local government, having at its disposal probably twenty-five thousand jobs. This patronage gave the Long machine a running start in any state

[1] Robert Angelle; D. J. Anders; Wilson J. Peck; Will Harvey Todd; Harry Gilbert; Robert D. Jones; A. K. Kilpatrick.
[2] *Overton Hearing*, II, 1214.

election. The average employee represented five votes, those of people dependent on or beholden to him, and the machine thus entered an election with 125,000 votes almost assured, in a state where three hundred thousand was the normal vote. The reservoir of state jobs also made Huey independent of national patronage, which was why with impunity he could tell the Roosevelt administration to go to hell with its patronage. "I don't care what Washington does," he once said. No other state boss would have dared to say this. But no other boss had a machine that was so self-contained, so undependent on other sources for sustenance.[3]

The Long machine was self-sustaining financially, and it was this quality that gave it its independence and that makes it unique among American political organizations. American machines have traditionally financed themselves by asking for contributions from interests that wanted something and could afford to pay to get it—in Huey's time, from corporations—and in return the machines had to make promises. But the Long machine asked for no money from anyone. Instead, it demanded money from various sources and received it, with no commitments.

It demanded money, first of all, from the employees of the state through deductions from their salaries, collecting these systematically during a campaign. For example, in New Orleans, where most of the employees were concentrated, the collecting was assigned to the Long ward leaders and the heads of the various state agencies. Immediately after monthly pay checks were issued, a collector would contact every employee on his list and ask for a contribution of ten per cent of the amount of the check. Most employees were assessed only during the two or three months preceding an election. Some were not asked at all—those holding jobs requiring technical skills—and some who were asked did not have to pay if they could plead hardship. But most who were asked paid, because they knew Huey's rule on political gratitude: a man who did not help the organization that hired him "just doesn't stay in very long." During a campaign a fund of fifty thousand to seventy-five thousand dollars, a tremendous war chest for that time, would be amassed from this source.[4]

The machine also demanded money from various companies

[3] Ibid., I, 240, 283, 352, 557; Thomas L. Stokes, in New York *World-Telegram*, December 5, 1934; Hodding Carter: "Louisiana Limelighter," *Review of Reviews*, XCI (March 1935), 28.

[4] *Overton Hearing*, I, 283, 377–8; II, 1197; W. A. Cooper; John B. Fournet; Robert Brothers; Charles Frampton; Raymond H. Fleming; Harvey G. Fields.

and individuals that had, or wanted to get, state contracts for services or supplies: highway construction companies, truck and tractor companies, cement and gravel interests, office-supply concerns, and agencies that wrote the state's insurance. Each of these companies was expected to kick back into the machine's war chest an allocated percentage of the amount of its contract, and every one kicked back. The mechanics of collection was effectively simple. For example, when the Highway Commission awarded construction contracts, a representative of the machine, usually John Klorer of the *Progress*, sat in an adjoining room. As each contractor picked up his agreement, he passed into Klorer's room, where he was informed of his assessment. Klorer would say: "You have a $100,000 contract and you owe us $20,000," and that was that.[5]

Finally, the machine asked for money from wealthy or comfortably situated individuals who were members of the Long organization or who had a reason to stand well with it. Huey himself usually made these requests, although sometimes he entrusted the task to a lieutenant, Seymour Weiss or Abe Shushan. How many men were on his asking list is not known, or how much they were asked to give at one time. But the sum of money collected in this manner must have been huge. One associate claimed that there were a thousand or so members of the organization who would put up from one thousand to five thousand dollars each whenever Huey asked them to. "He would send for me and all these other men to come to his room in the Roosevelt," the associate recounted, "and he would say 'I need $60,000,' and we would all shell out. We would throw it on the bed."[6]

The machine's methods of collecting money were no secret in Louisiana. Huey and various associates described the methods fully. They had no hesitation in admitting them, because they saw nothing wrong in them. It was the other side that used immoral methods, they insisted. It went as a supplicant to the corporations and accepted money under the table and then had to do the bidding of the givers. But the Long machine took money in the open, was, in Huey's words, supported by "public contributions," and hence was independent and free to act for the people.[7]

The contributions, from whatever source they came, had to be in

[5] Clem H. Sehrt; Robert Brothers; Fred Blanche; Harry Gamble; Norman Lant.
[6] Joseph Fisher.
[7] *Overton Hearing*, I, 240, 282–3, II, 2113. Surviving Long leaders defend passionately the machine's methods of raising money, insisting that they were more moral than any later methods.

cash. Huey was not going to have any embarrassing checks appear in the record. Most of the money received was kept at the Roosevelt Hotel, in the charge of Seymour Weiss. Large sums were entrusted to private secretary Earle Christenberry, who carried from twenty to thirty thousand dollars on his person.

Only a part of it was expended on state elections. Large sums were paid out by Weiss or Christenberry to parish leaders who asked for help in local elections, to pay the poll taxes of their followers or for other expenses. Leaders who needed money usually telephoned Weiss or Christenberry, who then sent out a trusted agent with the amounts asked. Louie Jones once carried thirty thousand dollars to be divided among various leaders. Sometimes a leader would come to New Orleans to lay his request personally before Huey. This was a mistake, because Huey could not resist chopping down a man in front of him. One leader pleaded for money to pay poll taxes, and Huey said he could have eight hundred dollars. The man said he would have to have twelve hundred dollars. Huey turned to Weiss and said: "Give him one thousand one hundred and fifty."[8]

In many situations it was convenient to have large sums of cash available. As Huey discovered early, sometimes cash had to be used to cover up cases of financial carelessness or crookedness in the machine itself. Once he was informed that a state institution had a shortage of ninety-two thousand dollars in its accounts. Associates who were with him at the time thought he would have to let the matter become public and suffer the charges of corruption that were sure to come. But he picked up the phone and called certain "financial friends" in New Orleans, telling them that he needed ninety-two thousand dollars in cash and that he wanted it in Baton Rouge by the next day. When the money arrived, he called in a friend who was an accountant and said: "Now I want you to take this money and work it back into that institution. This hasn't cost anybody anything. It came out of our political kitty." He explained to another friend why he had resorted to this subterfuge: he had avoided a damaging scandal while saving the state from losing any money, and now he could find the guilty party and punish him by removing him from office—the ultimate punishment for wrongdoers in the Long organization.[9]

He sometimes even covered the shortages of enemies. On two

[8] Seymour Weiss; Earle J. Christenberry; Harry Gilbert; J. Cleveland Fruge; Milton Coverdale; Ira Gleason; Arthur Provost; Louis A. Jones; D. J. Anders.
[9] W. C. Pegues.

occasions he discovered discrepancies in the accounts of anti sheriffs, the amount with one of them being ten thousand dollars. Instead of making the matter public, he confronted the officials with the evidence and demanded that they resign, promising to hide the shortages if they did so. He then appointed followers of his to fill out their unexpired terms and named the offenders to minor state jobs, thus attaching them to him. Such incidents demonstrate again his ability to stand off and view himself and those around him and figure all the angles.[1]

HUEY LONG AT THE HEIGHT of his power was the subject of a fascinated national and even international literature. Everyone who could write, it sometimes seemed, wanted to examine him and measure him and put him in a category of some kind. H. G. Wells, arriving from England in 1935 for an American tour, announced that he had come to study such domestic institutions as the Tennessee Valley Authority, the Home Owners' Loan Corporation, and Huey P. Long; and after observing the Kingfish in the Senate Wells rendered an admiring, though English, verdict. Long, he said, was like "a Winston Churchill who has never been at Harrow." Another English visitor, Rebecca West, was not so favorably impressed. She saw the cold intelligence that Huey concealed behind his buffoonery—he was "the most formidable kind of brer fox"—but she also saw something dangerous lurking within him, a realization of destiny barely concealed coupled with a vitality that was almost animal.[2]

This aura of something hidden and unusual was also apparent to some American correspondents. One of them, who was especially perceptive and who spent much time with Huey, concluded that on the whole Long was to be admired. But he confessed that he did not know how to classify this man who seemed to be so simple but really was incredibly complex. There were things about Huey he did not understand and found disturbing, such as "the charged atmosphere which envelops him, the sense of danger that pervades the air around him." Huey definitely deviated from the pattern of the normal democratic politician: "If events fail to occur naturally, he produces them."[3]

[1] Wilson J. Peck; Edgar G. Mouton; A. Wilmot Dalferes; J. Maxime Roy; John B. Fournet.
[2] Unidentified clipping, 1935, in Long Scrapbooks, XVIII; H. G. Wells: *The New American* (New York, 1935), p. 29; Arthur M. Schlesinger: *The Politics of Upheaval* (New York, 1960), p. 66.
[3] Paul Y. Anderson, in St. Louis *Post-Dispatch*, February 10, 1935.

To one group of classifiers Huey was not the slightest mystery. The American Communists knew exactly what he was and in their various publications devoted reams of copy to exposing him. He was a fascist, in fact, "the personification of the fascist menace." He claimed to represent the poor but he had misled them from the time that he had entered politics. He mouthed a radical rhetoric but was really a defender of capitalism, he denounced big businessmen but hobnobbed with them secretly—and he was the man most likely to become the Hitler or Mussolini of America.[4]

Interestingly, the same diagnosis of Huey was advanced by the American fascists. Lawrence Dennis, the leading theoretician of the right-wing group, hailed the Kingfish as "the nearest approach to a national fascist leader" that the country had yet produced. Long was capable of exploiting the weaknesses of capitalism as displayed in the crisis of the depression and of acting to create an ordered fascist system, Dennis thought. He expressed a hope that Long would decide to place himself at the head of the fascist movement. "It takes a man like Long to lead the masses," Dennis said, admitting that he and other fascists could not fill the role.[5]

Other people agreed that Huey was a fascist and a potential dictator—editors and columnists, professors and intellectuals generally, and ordinary persons who knew him only through what they read. Their reaction at the time is understandable. Knowing something of European fascism and fearing its spread to America, they were inclined to see in a strong and unusual leader a possible dictator. And Huey was such a leader. He exulted in the use of power, and he had erected in Louisiana a power structure that had no counterpart in any other state. He sometimes took shortcuts to attain his ends and seemed to scorn the slow procedures of democracy. He did not have an ideology—unless Share Our Wealth was such—but he was supposed to have uttered various ominous fascistic predictions. Widely and fearfully quoted was one that in fact he never made: "When the United States gets fascism it will call it anti-fascism."[6]

It is not so understandable that the fascist label has stuck to him and become the enduring verdict on him. This contemporary

[4] The Communist view of Long is summarized in two pamphlets, Sender Garlin: The Real Huey P. Long (New York, 1935), and Alex Bittelman: The Communist Way vs. Huey Long (New York, 1935). See also the New York Daily Worker, March 12 and 15, 1935, issues devoted almost entirely to Long and containing articles by Garlin.

[5] Schlesinger: Politics of Upheaval, p. 77.

[6] Ibid., p. 67.

judgment would normally have been suspected by later scholars and subjected to scrutiny. Curiously, its accuracy has hardly been questioned. Indeed, it has been reinforced by a body of literature that attempts to prove with scholarly paraphernalia that Long was indeed a fascist. The most systematic study of American fascism asserts that he was "the precursor of fascism," the American leader best fitted to be a dictator.

The reasoning behind this conclusion goes as follows. American capitalism in the 1930's was in a crisis. The middle class, always a potential fascist group, demanded to be saved. There arose out of the middle class Huey Long, who claimed to know the will of the people better than they did, who would save the people by whatever means he had to use, and who would admit no check on himself except their general approval. He would hope to achieve his goal by conventional democratic methods but would inevitably have to resort to more drastic methods, and so by stages would become the fascist head of a fascist nation.

It was all neatly laid out and supported by examples to prove that Huey was psychologically a fascist, that he scorned democratic procedures. One typical example cited his reply to a reporter who pressed him as to what he would do as President if the Supreme Court voided a Share Our Wealth law. "Why," he said, "we'll get a law passed adding the whole membership of Congress to the Supreme Court and try the case again." Anyone who knew him could have told that he was trying to get rid of the journalist with a jocular remark.[7]

Huey hotly rejected the charge that he was a fascist on the model of certain European leaders. A bold reporter once asked him if he saw any resemblance between himself and Hitler. "Don't liken me to that sonofabitch," he roared. "Anybody that lets his public policies be mixed up with religious prejudice is a plain Goddamned fool." Commenting on the German dictator at another time, he said: "I don't know much about Hitler. Except this last thing, about the Jews. There has never been a country that put its heel down on the Jews that ever lived afterwards."[8]

He rejected too the charge that he was a dictator of native stamp. But it was characteristic of him that he gave the accusation

[7] Victor C. Ferkiss: "The Political and Economic Philosophy of American Fascism" (unpublished Ph.D. dissertation, University of Chicago, 1954), pp. 132-3, 137, 152.

[8] Allan Michie and Frank Rhylick: *Dixie Demagogues* (New York, 1939), p. 112; New Orleans *Item*, March 26, 1933.

a good deal of thought, pondering why it should be applied to him. He realized that it had originated in the grip he had fastened on Louisiana, and he was frank enough to admit that his control over his state was abnormal in an American commonwealth. But Louisiana was still a democracy, he insisted. "A perfect democracy can come close to looking like a dictatorship, a democracy in which the people are so satisfied they have no complaint," he once suggested.[9]

As he continued to dwell on the dictator charge (and he seemed unable to let it go), he developed a thesis that he was only an agent of the popular will in Louisiana. He had explained his program to the people, asked for a mandate, and received it. "A man is not a dictator when he is given a commission from the people and carries it out," he protested. The people had given him his commission and could revoke it, and hence his power was only temporary. "I believe in democracy, and the people of Louisiana ain't never going to have anything but a democracy," he told one correspondent. "You know and I know that if people want to throw me out they're going to do it. They like what I'm giving them and what they're getting."[1]

Huey Long did, indeed, have a commission from the people. He had given them things they had long yearned for and thought they would never get, and this they did not forget. "They do not merely vote for him, they worship the ground he walks on," a puzzled correspondent wrote. "He is a part of their religion." They would support him faithfully, almost blindly, not caring that he had built a ruthless political machine or that he might permit some corruption in state government or even that he might take some money himself. A Long leader trying to convey their feelings had to resort to a Biblical figure of speech: "They felt the hand of Huey," he said.[2]

It was to help the people that Huey had seized power and then more power. He was not a fascist and he did not want to be a dictator. But he had become obsessed with the conviction that he could not do what he had to do without reaching for more power. He could not tell, himself, whether he would ever have enough.

[9] Earl Sparling, in New York *World-Telegram*, March 25, 1933.
[1] Russell Owen, in *The New York Times*, February 10, 1935, magazine section; New Orleans *Times-Picayune*, March 2, 1935; James Crown, in *The New York Times*, July 21, 1935, magazine section.
[2] Anderson in St. Louis *Post-Dispatch*, March 3, 1935; Joseph Fisher.

# CHAPTER 27

# *Fighting for Their Ground*

THE HOUSTON NEWSPAPERS headlined the news: The Kingfish Is in Town.

He had come to watch his Louisiana State University football team engage Rice Institute in the second game of the 1932 season for the visiting Tigers, and he had arrived in characteristic Kingfish style, on a special train of the Missouri Pacific Railroad and at the head of the LSU band and over four hundred students. At the station to greet him were various city officials and several thousand persons, the largest local welcoming crowd to turn out since a prominent citizen had returned from Washington in 1928 after landing the Democratic convention of that year for the city. Huey jumped from his car and quickly aligned the band in marching formation and then, as the crowd pressed in, shouted at the chief of police to clear the street ahead. The startled officer complied, and Huey led the band through the cheering throng to the Rice Hotel, headquarters of the LSU contingent. Above the noise a small boy was heard to cry out: "Mama, I see the Kingfish, but where's Amos?"[1]

No pressures of politics ever caused Huey to lose interest in his university. He was a senator in 1932, occupied with national as well as state affairs, and when he came to Houston he had just been through the rigors of the Caraway and Overton campaigns and shortly he would plunge into the campaign to elect Roosevelt President. But he still could find time to root the Tiger football team to victory and lead the Tiger band.

[1] Clippings, probably Houston *Press*, October 1 and 3, 1932, in Long Scrapbooks, XVI.

Huey had high hopes for the team in 1932: this should be the winning season that all Tiger fans had long awaited, the year that LSU would at last achieve national recognition. He pinned his expectations partly on the excellent material the squad was known to possess but mainly on the reputation of the "big-time" coach who had been hired to replace the fired Russ Cohen.

He had started to search for such a coach almost before Cohen left the campus. He first approached Clark Shaughnessy of Loyola University in New Orleans, a young coach but tabbed as one of the rising stars of the profession. Shaughnessy declined the offer, however, saying that he was under contract to Loyola and would leave only to go to the University of Chicago. Huey then heard that Burt Ingwerson, formerly of Iowa, was available, and he offered the job to Ingwerson, who accepted it and signed a contract. But before the signing could be made public a complication developed, since President Smith had found another man and had committed the university to negotiate with him.

Smith had understandably thought that he should have something to do with hiring the coach, and he had come up with a man who was interested and who had a much bigger name than Ingwerson—Lawrence M. "Biff" Jones, a former star and coach at West Point who was now an army captain on tour of duty in Washington, D.C., before returning to the Academy as graduate manager of athletics. Huey would ordinarily have resented such a display of independence by Smith, but he was delighted at the chance to get Jones and authorized the president to hire him. But when Jones agreed to come, a spot had to be found for Ingwerson. Huey solved the problem by persuading Jones to retain Ingwerson as a member of the staff. Jones kept on two other LSU coaches and brought two men with him, giving the university an unusually large staff for that time. It was referred to in sporting circles, with some mockery, as the All American Staff.[2]

Smith had become interested in Jones at the suggestion of the commandant of cadets, Major Middleton, who knew Biff from army days and admired him, and it was Middleton, acting for Smith, who made the first approach to Jones. Jones was not receptive, saying that there would be too much politics, that is, too much Huey, connected with the job. But he was persuaded to come to Louisiana to check the situation personally, and in New Orleans and Baton Rouge

[2] Fred Digby; Digby, in New Orleans *Item*, December 22, 1934; Harry Rabenhorst.

he met with Smith, Middleton, and other administrators, and inspected the LSU athletic plant.

He was impressed with the facilities and the evident desire of the administration to build up LSU's football fortunes. But he still had doubts about accepting the position, and these were not reassured when at the conclusion of one interview Huey swept into the room and shouted: "Well, coach, have you got everything you want?" Jones received the question gravely: a massive man—six feet three inches and over two hundred pounds—he was always serious in manner. He finally said that if he came he would like to employ a public relations man in the athletic department to get the team national publicity. Huey laughed. "Don't worry," he said. "I'll get you all the publicity you need."

Jones left Baton Rouge without coming to a decision. On his way back to Washington he stopped at Nashville to see Cohen, who had taken a job on the Vanderbilt staff. Cohen advised him to accept the offer, saying that Jones would not have the trouble he had had because Huey now had to be in Washington much of the time. This convinced Jones. He asked Smith to grant certain conditions, and when these were met he agreed to come to LSU, but warned that the university would have to ask the army to release him from duty.[3]

The university anticipated no difficulty in effecting Jones's release. It would simply ask the army to assign him to LSU to be an instructor in the ROTC program. The move would be a subterfuge, but surely the army would be glad to oblige a large state university and a United States senator. And ordinarily the army would have been willing to cooperate in such a sleight of hand. But Jones's case presented a special problem. He was an artillery officer, and there were no artillery units in LSU's cadet corps. The ruse would be too blatant, and the army held back its approval. President Smith finally realized he would have to take the question right to the chief of staff, General Douglas MacArthur.

Smith and the chairman of the faculty committee on athletics met with MacArthur in the general's Washington office. They explained their request at length, while MacArthur sat at his desk smoking a cigarette in a long holder and gazing out of the window. Finally he turned and asked what Jones's salary would be. Seventy-five hundred dollars, Smith answered. MacArthur thought a minute and then said: "I like Biff Jones. If a poor army captain can make

---

[3] Troy H. Middleton; Lawrence M. Jones.

that much in addition to his salary, I'll let you have him." Then he swung around in his chair and snapped out: "But don't you ever come back to this office and ask for a single thing."[4]

One of the last conditions Jones had laid down to Smith, and the one that he had been most insistent on, was that Huey had to leave the team alone: he was not to sit on the bench during games and not to come to the dressing room at half time. Huey readily agreed to this arrangement, and at the first game of the 1932 season he sat in the stands. But after the game an associate came to Jones with a request from Huey: his friends were twitting him about being exiled and he begged permission to sit on the end of the bench, promising not to move beyond the thirty-five yard line. Jones granted the entreaty, and Huey observed the limit he had set for himself. He also observed Jones's dictum to stay out of the dressing room.[5]

He interfered with Jones only on rare occasions, and then harmlessly. Sometimes he would summon the coach to look at a play that he had secured from his usual mysterious sources and that he was certain would produce a touchdown. Jones took the plays and then ignored them, but he was irritated at Huey's presumptuousness. He was also annoyed at the stunts Huey still pulled on the field. Before one game he noticed the senator talking to the officials, and when he had an opportunity asked the referee what Huey had said. The official dazedly quoted Huey's words: "Look, I know you guys got to call some penalties to earn your pay. But when you call 'em on LSU, call 'em near midfield, not down near the goal line."[6]

Huey was going to give Jones a free hand because he had faith that Jones was the man to make LSU the football power it deserved to be. And in 1932 he was satisfied with the coach's accomplishment. The season was not exactly a glorious one, but it was an improvement on what had gone before and carried a bright augury for the future. The Tigers ran up six victories to three losses (one of these being to Rice in Houston) and one tie. Sweetest among the victories was a 14 to 0 verdict over Tulane. Then in 1933 the record was excellent, leading Huey to hope that LSU would be invited to play in the Rose Bowl postseason classic. The Tigers won seven games and lost none but were tied three times, including by Tulane. Unaccountably to Huey, there was no Rose Bowl bid, but LSU was ranked second in the recently formed Southeastern Conference and

[4] Troy H. Middleton.
[5] Lawrence M. Jones.
[6] Ibid.

fifth nationally. Huey bubbled with pride: next year would do it, he proclaimed.

The 1934 season opened disappointingly with two ties. But then the Tigers swept to six straight victories and came up to the always crucial Tulane game with a high national rating and a chance to be designated as the host team in the first Sugar Bowl game in New Orleans. Their reputation had spread even beyond sporting circles. The whole country, in fact, was aware of this LSU team, not so much because of its record as because of Senator Long's actions in some of the games.

On the eve of the season Huey predicted that the Tigers would set a local attendance record in the recently enlarged LSU stadium. He was therefore puzzled when he learned that the advance sales for the opening-night game with Southern Methodist were badly off. Checking around, he found that another attraction was scheduled in Baton Rouge on the day of the game—the great Ringling Brothers and Barnum and Bailey Circus, which was then in Texas and moving east on its regular circuit. The conflict caused LSU athletic authorities to lament, but they assumed that nothing could be done to prevent the circus's appearance. No such mood of resignation depressed the Kingfish, and declaring that no circus was going to compete with LSU, he acted.

He first asked some law students at the university to dig up the provisions of the compulsory animal dipping law passed in 1930 to apply to farm stock but since forgotten. Armed with this information, he telephoned the owner of the circus, John Ringling North, in Texas. Explaining the problem created by the conflict of attractions, he asked if the circus could not reschedule its showing in Baton Rouge. North said haughtily that a big-time circus operated on a fixed schedule that could not be altered. All right, Huey said amiably, but Louisiana had a dip law and as he interpreted the act, animals crossing the state line would have to be dipped and then placed in quarantine for three weeks. "Did you ever dip a tiger?" he inquired pleasantly. "Or how about an elephant?" Mr. North said the circus would go to New Orleans that Saturday night.[7]

Huey's handling of the circus crisis excited wide and incredulous

[7] Harry Rabenhorst; Clayton Coleman; Charles L. Dufour; "Trost," in Brooklyn *Eagle*, November 13, 1934; Pete Finney: "Starring the Magnificent Kingfish and LSU," *Sportfolio*, November 1967, p. 34. "Trost" mistakenly related the incident to a game with Tulane. Mr. Finney thinks Huey sprang the dip law on the advance agent of the circus, who then called North.

national comment. And he shortly furnished the skeptics with an even more spectacular demonstration of his capacity to overcome the impossible when LSU football was concerned. He moved almost the entire student body to an out-of-town game in what must rank as one of the great exoduses in football history.

The game was with Vanderbilt in Nashville and occurred soon after LSU started on its winning streak. Huey decided that the Tigers were more likely to keep the streak going if in the Tennessee city they were cheered on by a group of loyal rooters, and as he revolved the idea in his mind it got bigger and bigger. Certainly the band ought to go. But why not also the cadet corps of twenty-five hundred boys and as many other students as wanted to make the trip? The journey would have to be made by railroad, on a special train, and the mass procession would advertise LSU, and Huey Long, to the nation. He excitedly discussed his plan with several intimates and with Major Middleton, who would have to give his permission to let the cadets go. Middleton threw cold water on the idea, saying that the railroad fare for the trip would be so high that not many students could pay it. "You worry too much about expenses," Huey snapped. "I'll take care of that."

He grabbed a phone and called the traffic manager of the Illinois Central Railroad, which controlled the greater part of the route to Nashville. He was taking several thousand students to the Vanderbilt game, he said, and he wanted a quotation on a round-trip fare, which he hoped would be reasonable. The manager replied that the rates were set and could not be altered: the fare for this trip would have to be nineteen dollars. The Kingfish shouted, "That's too much. I'll give you six dollars per person." Scorning to deal further with underlings, he next called the president of the railroad in Chicago. He told this man of his desire to secure a cheap rate and then casually mentioned that the railroad owned bridges in Louisiana valued at much more than they were assessed. It was quite possible that the Tax Commission would decide to assess these properties at their true value, he said. Significantly, nobody in the Central hierarchy doubted that the Kingfish would carry out his threat. He had, in fact, already convoked a meeting of the Tax Commission. One of its members protested: "You know we don't assess bridges." "We're going to assess 'em now and everything they own," Huey answered.[8]

[8] Troy H. Middleton; James A. Noe; A. P. White; "Trost," in Brooklyn *Eagle*, November 13, 1934; Blinkey Horn, in Nashville *Tennesseean*, clipping, 1934, in Hammond Scrapbook; H. Lester Hughes.

By the next day he had his answer: the road would grant the six-dollar rate. He could not contain his elation. He dashed out to the LSU campus with a few associates and directed President Smith to suspend classes and call a student convocation in an outdoor amphitheater known as the Greek Theater. When the excited students had assembled, he told them of the cheap rate he had arranged and other details of the trip. The LSU contingent would travel in six special trains of fourteen cars each. There would be no Pullman cars, and those making the trip would have to sit up for one night going and two nights returning. They would also have to observe certain rules: there was to be no drinking or pulling of bell cords or any other form of rowdyism. And to make sure that order was preserved, he was detailing twenty-five state policemen to accompany the party and patrol the cars.

This announcement was greeted with loud cheers, and when quiet was restored he spelled out the financing of the trip. The cadet corps and the band were to be taken with all expenses paid. But, he said, he had realized that other students might not have the cash available to pay even the low rate. "If you don't have the money, we can arrange to lend it to you," he revealed: seven dollars, six for the trip and one for subsistence in Nashville. Pulling out a wad of bills, he invited those needing help to come up and get their money and sign an IOU. A mob of students engulfed him, and he soon ran out of money. Turning to the associates who had come with him, he made them empty their pockets, and when this additional amount was exhausted he sent a courier to his hotel suite to bring out more money, in a suitcase. He dispensed finally three thousand dollars and then called a halt and returned to the hotel. But many students followed him there and clamored for their share, and standing in the door of his suite he handed out another thousand dollars. It afterward developed that some students came to him several times and some signed fictitious names, and it proved impossible to collect on most of the loans. The number of people making the trip, students and others, was variously estimated as between four and five thousand.[9]

The railroad, after deciding to cooperate with Huey on the rate question, did everything else it could think of to please him. The cars that made up the special trains were painted in eye-catching colors, red, white, blue, orange, and green, and their sides were

[9] Little Rock *Arkansas Gazette*, October 24, 1934; Buffalo *Courier-Express*, October 24, 1934; *The New York Times*, October 25, 1934; New York *World-Telegram*, October 26, 1934; Carl Corbin; Gene Quaw; A. P. White.

festooned with signs proclaiming "Hurrah for Huey." He was offered a private car, but he preferred to ride in one attached to the cadet section, in which he put also various university dignitaries and their wives. The glittering caravan passed through Mississippi like a triumphal procession, greeted at every station by crowds that had waited for hours, some of them until near midnight, to see the spectacle—and the Kingfish.[1]

At Nashville a large crowd had gathered long before the specials rolled in. Huey alighted and with him piled out a number of Louisiana state policemen, who quickly formed a cordon around him. He had insisted to the Tennessee state authorities that he had to be protected by his own armed guards, and the authorities had obligingly deputized the policemen as Tennessee game wardens so that they could bear weapons. He had also secured permission to lead the LSU band and students on a parade to a park, where he was to direct the band in a concert, and he briskly ordered his followers to fall in. Along the line of march an estimated eighty thousand persons roared their applause. Huey was ecstatic, experiencing an almost mystic sense of unity with the crowd. "Look at those folks," he exclaimed. "I believe I could be elected governor of any state in the Union."

At the conclusion of the concert he led his contingent to the Vanderbilt stadium, where at half time he was to address the spectators from one of his sound trucks that he had sent up. Critics had predicted that he would use the occasion to make a political speech, but he spoke only briefly, thanking the audience for its friendly reception and hoping that they were enjoying the game. He himself enjoyed it immensely, for LSU romped to a 29 to 0 victory.[2]

As the Tigers continued on their winning streak, Huey's hopes for a bid to a postseason classic rose to a fever pitch. Although he was gratified that the team was being discussed as a Sugar Bowl possibility, he had his eye on something bigger than an invitation to New Orleans. He once proposed that LSU should play the best of the Northern teams, Minnesota or Princeton, for the mythical national championship at Yankee Stadium in New York City, with the proceeds to go to unemployment relief. But what he wanted above all was an invitation to the Rose Bowl, and he was convinced that the Tigers would be asked. He expressed his conviction with an arrogance that must have enraged the California sponsors.

---

[1] New York *World-Telegram*, October 26 and 27, 1934; Troy H. Middleton; Fred Digby.

[2] New York *World-Telegram*, October 26, 1934; *The New York Times*, October 29, 1934; Cleveland *Plain Dealer*, October 29, 1934.

"The proposition is not whether the Rose Bowl will invite us but whether we will honor the Rose Bowl by our presence," he proclaimed. If those people out there wanted LSU, they had better get "their name in the pot damn quick."[3]

A bid to a bowl depended in large measure on whether LSU could beat its traditional rival Tulane, which also had an excellent record. The Tigers went into the game favored, but Tulane upset them 13 to 12. Then on the following weekend came another unexpected reverse, to Tennessee, by a 19 to 13 score. Huey saw his dream of a lustrous season suddenly fading. A team with two losses and two ties was not likely to receive a bowl invitation. But the Tigers could still salvage something from the season. They had one game remaining, with Oregon in early December in Baton Rouge, and a victory over this intersectional foe could give them a high national ranking. At the game Huey took his usual seat on the end of the bench. He was curiously quiet. Anyone who knew him could have predicted that a storm was brewing.

During the first half Oregon ran up a 13 to 0 lead and seemed on the way to achieving a decisive victory. But Jones, taking his boys to the dressing room, decided that he could still pull off a win if he changed his game plan. In the room he went up to a blackboard and began to diagram some new plays. Suddenly he heard Huey's voice behind him, and turning he saw Huey and one of his associates and Joe Messina. "I want to talk to the team," Huey demanded. The first thought that ran through the coach's mind was that if Huey gave a pep speech and LSU won, the Kingfish would think he was responsible for the result and would take over again as he had done with Cohen. Jones knew that he had to meet the challenge. He said coldly that only he and his coaches could talk to the team. "Who's going to stop me?" Huey asked. Jones repeated his statement. Huey fell back toward the door. "All right," he snarled, "but you better win this one." At this Jones's composure broke. "I don't have to win this one," he shot back. "Win, lose, or draw, I'm going to resign at the end of this game."[4]

Just before the players went back on the field, Jones called them together. They had never seen him display much emotion, but now they noted that his cheeks were quivering. "I've never asked a personal favor of you but I am now," he said. "I want to win this game

[3] Jimmy Powers, in New York *Daily News*, November 7 and 8, 1934; New Orleans *Times-Picayune*, November 10, 1934; Lawrence M. Jones.

[4] Lawrence M. Jones; Fred Digby; Digby, in New Orleans *Item*, December 17, 1934.

more than anything else in the world." Inspired by his plea, the Tigers were a different team in the second half. They ran off two touchdowns and kicked the point after each while holding Oregon scoreless for a 14 to 13 victory.[5]

Immediately after the game Jones informed President Smith of his intention to resign. Smith tried to persuade him to reconsider, as did Major Middleton, both of them arguing that the outcome of the game would prevent Huey from attempting any more interferences. Jones refused to believe this. He said that Huey had "a long memory" and probably would not permit him to remain. His analysis of Huey's reaction was accurate. One of his friends met Huey on the following day and interceded for the coach. Huey rejected the plea. "Anytime I fire anybody I'll hire them again," he said. "But when they quit on me they're through."[6]

The Kingfish announced that LSU would begin immediately to search for a new coach, one who would not lose or even tie any games. He conducted the search himself, again contacting Clark Shaughnessy, now at Chicago, and when Shaughnessy turned him down approaching coaches at other Northern schools. He met with rejections from all of them and could not understand the reason— no name coach was going to risk the interference that had become synonymous with the job at LSU. Several of the coaches did, however, suggest to him a man he could get, an able assistant coach on Jones's staff, Bernie Moore. He finally awarded the job to Moore and vowed that he would give the new coach plenty of assistance and some new plays that he had recently secured. An unexampled experiment for him had ended. He had let somebody else run something for three years. Now he was himself again.[7]

At the same time that he started to look for a coach, he hired a new band director, his friend, Castro Carazo, the orchestra leader of the Roosevelt Hotel. He informed President Smith of his action afterward. He gave Carazo only one instruction: "I want you to build and buy the best band in the country." Provided with a lavish budget for musical fellowships and instruments, Carazo enlarged the band from 125 to 240 pieces, making it one of the two largest university bands in the country. In odd moments he and Huey worked at com-

[5] Abe Mickal.

[6] Lawrence M. Jones; Fred Digby; Troy H. Middleton; Lewis Gottlieb.

[7] Fred Digby; Clem H. Sehrt; Washington *Post*, December 18, 1934; unidentified clipping, December 20, 1934, in Long Scrapbooks, XXIII; Chicago *Tribune*, December 25, 1934. During the next two seasons LSU, partly because of the excellent material recruited under Huey, compiled victorious records, winning every game but one in 1935 and suffering only the blemish of a tie in 1936.

posing some new school songs, producing eventually two that became Tiger classics, "Touchdown for LSU" and "Darling of LSU."[8]

During the fall of 1934 Huey gave the university even more than
his usual attention. As in previous years, he seemed to be interested
only in the peripheral and most noneducational areas of the school,
the football team and the band. Actually, as before, he was concerned with the whole function of LSU, and deeply with its educational mission. He was still determined to improve its capacity to fulfill
that mission, but now he was considering giving it an additional
role, fitting it into his plan to capture the presidency by making it
a model university for poor students. His preoccupation with the
idea caused him to become even more possessive about LSU and led
him to commit one of the worst mistakes of his career.

One day in November a large group of students assembled in
the Greek Theater on the campus, summoned there by a call signed
by various student leaders, most of them known Longites. The students did not know why the meeting had been convened, but it was
rumored that something spectacular would happen and that the
Kingfish himself would be present. He soon drove up, accompanied
by Joe Messina, and took a seat on the stage. As the audience
laughed in disbelief, Messina announced himself as chairman of the
meeting and introduced a Long student leader. This youth read a
statement that had been handed to him by Huey. It recited that
since J. Y. Sanders, Jr., had assumed his place as congressman from
the sixth district, the East Baton Rouge parish senatorial seat that
Sanders had occupied was now vacant. Because it was wrong that
the parish should not be represented in the special session then sitting,
this "citizens' mass meeting" had been called to select a successor
to Sanders. The students got the drift: they were going to participate in a parody of the citizen gatherings in the sixth district that
had tried to "elect" Sanders to Congress in 1933. They were convulsed by the mocking humor of the proposal, but something even
funnier was to come. The student speaker concluded his remarks
by nominating as a candidate Abe Mickal, backfield star of the football team who was, as everybody in the audience knew, a resident
of Mississippi. With a roar of ayes the students declared him to be
the elected senator from East Baton Rouge and dispersed, chuckling
that the Kingfish had pulled off a good gag this time.[9]

A gag was all that Huey intended the affair to be. Mickal, who

[8] Castro Carazo; Washington *Post*, December 18, 1934.

[9] New Orleans *Times-Picayune*, November 11, 1934; Joseph Cawthorn; Carl
Corbin; David R. McGuire.

was out of town with the team on a trip, was on his return to present himself to the senate, be admitted in a mock ceremony, and then introduce a bill forbidding any visiting football team to beat LSU in Baton Rouge. Why Huey thought it was important to go through with the stunt is difficult to understand. As a political maneuver, it was pointless. It might cause some people to laugh at Sanders but would not damage him, and it certainly did not increase the chances of the Long people to elect later a senator from the parish. The most probable explanation of Huey's action is that he wanted to do something to honor Mickal, for whom he had a warm devotion, and he hit on this tasteless method. Mickal was the kind of person likely to elicit Huey's admiration, a poor boy who had come up on his merit. Born in Syria, he had grown up in McComb, Mississippi, where in high school he starred in football and other sports. He had been brought to LSU because of his athletic prowess and had fulfilled his every promise, developing into one of the greatest passers in the country. But he was more than just an athlete; he was also an outstanding student, colonel of the cadet corps, and president of the student body. He had determined that he would become a doctor, and it was this that particularly endeared him to Huey, who talked to him by the hour, encouraging him to pursue his ambition and discoursing on the South's need for more and better doctors.[1]

The mass meeting received wide newspaper coverage, but the accounts did not clearly indicate its burlesque character. Rather, they conveyed the impression that Huey was actually going to make Mickal a senator. In some cases this was malicious reporting by correspondents who knew better. But with most correspondents it was honest error. Huey had become the victim of his reputation. If the man who had forced a circus to cancel a showing and a railroad to lower its rates said that he was going to make a football player a senator, he was going to do it. As the episode was ballooned into a national sensation, Huey fumed helplessly. He had started something and now could not control it.

Among those who were deceived as to Huey's purpose was Mickal himself, who read of his election in Washington, D.C., where LSU was playing George Washington University, and did not discover its gag nature until later. Distressed at the prospect of participating in a farce, he consulted with Jones, who advised that he must not go to the capitol when the team returned to Baton Rouge. Jones himself went to see Huey after arriving and discovered the

[1] Abe Mickal; Fred C. Frey; Washington *Daily News*, November 6, 1934.

joke, but declared that Mickal was not going to take his seat even in a mock ceremony. Huey, eager to have the affair ended, readily agreed. But to save face he publicly announced that "senator" Mickal had been given a five-day leave of absence, by which time the special session would be concluded. Mickal's escape from the situation was scathingly commemorated by Will Rogers. "Huey Long is trying to make senators out of football players," Rogers wrote. "He better be trying to make something out of senators. I don't blame the boy for not wanting to be demoted."[2]

National interest in the episode quickly subsided, but in Louisiana some people were not prepared to let Huey forget it. In anti circles indignation at his action ran high and was especially strong among LSU students. One angry youth decided to express his feelings in a letter to the student newspaper, the semiweekly *Reveille*. His communication was brief but pointed: the recent mass meeting had been "a mockery of constitutional government and democracy." It arrived at the *Reveille* office on the campus a day before the paper was going to press and received interested consideration from the editor, Jesse Cutrer, and his seven editorial associates.

Cutrer and his editors were journalism students. The coterie was more or less anti-Long in sentiment but passively so. The members had remained aloof from the campus political factions and had kept the paper on a fairly neutral course. Cutrer, however, had recently aroused Huey's suspicion by refusing to sign the call for the mass meeting. At the same time Huey heard reports from Long student leaders that the editor was secretly working with J. Y. Sanders. Huey was inclined to believe the charge. He reflected that Jesse was a nephew of an enemy of his that he detested, a former legislator and a Baptist minister, "Preacher" Cutrer, who during the impeachment had, in Huey's opinion, sold out to the anti side. The boy was probably like his treacherous uncle, Huey thought.

When Cutrer and his editors read the protesting letter, they realized that it had political implications. But they decided that it was a legitimate expression of student opinion, a personal statement and not reflective of the position of the *Reveille*. They therefore included it in the copy that was sent that night to the downtown printing plant that put out the paper.[3]

The printers set the material and then waited, as they custom-

[2] Abe Mickal; Lawrence M. Jones; Rogers, in New Orleans *Times-Picayune*, November 11, 1934; Little Rock *Arkansas Gazette*, November 13, 1934.

[3] Joseph Cawthorn; Carl Corbin; David R. McGuire; Bruce Denbo; New Orleans *Item*, November 16, 1934.

arily did, for a journalism student to appear and read the proof. The student who came that night was an unusually alert young man. When he read the letter, he realized at once its potential explosive quality and also its news value. He decided that it should be seen by somebody else in the school of journalism. The most available person he could think of was another student, David R. McGuire, who was at the capitol doing leg work for a local correspondent covering the November special session for a wire service, Helen Gilkison. Stuffing the proof of the letter in his pocket, he headed for the capitol.

He found McGuire in the senate press box and showed him the letter. McGuire glanced at it and handed it to Miss Gilkison. She must have registered some surprise as she read it, for Huey, coming up at this moment to speak to her, grabbed the sheet from her hand and ran his eye over it. His face went red with rage, and he cursed Cutrer and his family. "That lying uncle of his sold me out for forty dollars," he cried. "That's my university and I'm not going to stand for any criticism from anybody out there." Turning to an associate, he shouted: "Get Jim Smith on the phone."[4]

His conversation with Smith must have been emphatic, for the president immediately called Cutrer and directed him not to print the offending letter. Cutrer assented, saying that he could withhold the document because it was a personal expression and not a statement of editorial opinion. This led Smith to suggest that the editor should go to the capitol and explain to Huey why he had thought it was proper to print the letter. Cutrer did so, and thought that he had assuaged the Kingfish and that the matter was ended. He was puzzled therefore when later that night he received instructions to report with one of his associates to Smith's office the next morning.

At the meeting he got a jolting explanation. Smith announced that the university was going through an "abnormal" period in its history and that during this time it could not afford to offend Senator Long. Hence he had appointed a member of the journalism faculty to "advise" the *Reveille* on what material it should print. This faculty member had just been employed, on the previous night— and it was Helen Gilkison. Cutrer and his associate were so stunned by the news that they did not protest. They said that they would have to discuss the development with their staff.

The staff reacted with stormy anger, declaring that the action

---

[4] David R. McGuire; Carl Corbin; affidavits of McGuire and Cutrer, in Baton Rouge *State-Times*, December 4, 1934.

was censorship and they would not submit to it. Cutrer agreed with them, and when Miss Gilkison asked to read the contents of the next issue, he told her that if she did, a box would appear on the front page, exposing her function. At this she became agitated, and saying she would not inspect the proof, she left. The staff, congratulating themselves on having withstood censorship, prepared the copy for publication.

Miss Gilkison must have gone to see someone in the administration, for on the next morning the entire staff was summoned to the office of the dean of administration. This official asked them whether they would not accept Miss Gilkinson as an adviser. They replied that they would not, and one of them added that they had principles. The dean looked amused. "When you get to be my age, you'll learn that principles don't mean so much," he said. He conceded, however, that they should not have to work under Miss Gilkison's supervision. But he warned them, in veiled language, that this might not be the end of the matter. The administration was under some kind of pressure about the *Reveille*, he ended.[5]

The staff did not quite understand his meaning, but within a few days it was made clear to them. They were summoned to President Smith's office and told by him that they would have to agree to some form of faculty supervision or resign. But, Smith hastened to add, the supervision would extend to only one area of the paper's operation—it could not print anything derogatory about Senator Long. The staff hardly deigned to consider the proposal. They said that it was censorship and they would resign. Then they walked out.[6]

The news of the mass resignation inevitably spread across the campus. First to hear of it were the students in the school of journalism, and they were immediately indignant. The staff had been forced to resign, they decided, and after a meeting twenty-six of them signed a petition to Smith asking for reinstatement of the editors and threatening that if the request was not granted they would refuse to contribute to the *Reveille* or any other campus publication. But except for the journalism group there was little student interest in the affair, as inquisitive reporters who converged on the campus were surprised to discover. The great mass of students read the *Reveille* only in passing and saw no issue of freedom

[5] Carl Corbin; David R. McGuire; affidavits of Cutrer, Corbin, McGuire, and other students in Baton Rouge *State-Times*, December 4, 1934.

[6] Carl Corbin; Bruce Denbo; Baton Rouge *State-Times*, November 27, 1934.

involved. Said one student spokesman: "Sure, we knew Huey's running the university. What of it? If it wasn't Huey it would be somebody else. Huey's made it a good place to go to."[7]

The outside reporters had come to the campus because the
journalism students had seen fit to give their petition to the press
before submitting it to Smith. Their motives in making the controversy public were innocent: they believed that they were upholding
a principle and they hoped to attract popular support. But the effect
of their action was to project the controversy into state politics.
Anti leaders in Baton Rouge and New Orleans now entered it, encouraging the students to increase their agitation but emphasizing
that it should be directed at the real enemy, Huey. This incitement
spurred on the *Reveille* staff, already inclined to anti sentiments.
The members went in a body to the office of a Baton Rouge attorney
and dictated affidavits recounting the controversy and then took the
documents to the editor of the anti *State-Times*, who promptly
printed them. The statements were accurate enough as to the facts
of the case, but the numerous references to Huey had bitter political
overtones.[8]

President Smith acted on the journalism petition with the assurance of an administrator who knew that he had strong backing.
He suspended indefinitely the twenty-six signers. And when he
learned of the affidavits made by the staff members, he suspended
them. These students had shown "gross disrespect," he charged, not
specifying to whom they had shown it. In the face of his retaliation
the rebellion quickly collapsed, an indication that it had never been
deeply rooted. Twenty-two of the journalism students and four of
the *Reveille* staff members expressed regret for their action and
asked for reinstatement and were taken back. Only seven of the
expelled group remained defiant, and out of school. They had been
assured, however, that they would be able to continue their education at another institution. Some unnamed individuals in New
Orleans had set up a fund from which the seven could borrow without
interest, and they shortly departed for the University of Missouri.[9]

The *Reveille* controversy excited wide comment in universities

[7] David R. McGuire; Carl Corbin; New Orleans *Times-Picayune*, November 28,
1934; New Orleans *Item-Tribune*, December 9, 1934.

[8] Confidential communication; Carl Corbin; David R. McGuire; Baton Rouge
*State-Times*, December 4, 1934.

[9] New Orleans *Times-Picayune*, November 29 and December 6, 1934; New
Orleans *Morning Tribune*, December 4, 1934; Carl Corbin; David R. McGuire;
Bruce Denbo.

throughout the country. Other student papers uniformly denounced LSU for restricting freedom of the press and charged that Senator Long was behind the restriction. The largest student organization in the country, the National Student Federation, considered at its convention a resolution to censure LSU and Huey, but after extended debate refused to vote on it—and then elected an LSU student as president. A supporter of the censure move wrote bitterly that "Huey Long's hand" had been apparent at the convention.[1]

More ominous for LSU than this student muttering, the accrediting organizations showed an inquisitive interest in the affair. The Southern Association of Colleges, meeting in December 1934, considered complaints received from "citizens" in Louisiana that Huey was running LSU. The complaints were in the form of letters, from anti-Long leaders actually, and they were, as one delegate pointed out, vague in nature and inadequately sustained. However, the association was sufficiently disturbed to ask its executive committee to investigate the charges. And in the same month the Association of American Law Schools at its convention appointed a committee to inquire into conditions at the LSU law school. Its action was prompted by a report that K. K. Kennedy, the student who had been expelled and jailed in 1930 for his complicity in the *Whangdoodle* affair, had recently been granted a law degree under strange circumstances.[2]

Kennedy, after his sentence was commuted by Governor Allen, had taken a job with a state agency and in his spare time studied his law books. He still intended to get the degree that he thought he had rightly earned: he had completed all his requirements and at the time of his expulsion had only to stand examinations in three courses. He could see no reason why the law school should not let him take these tests. But one man at the school could see every reason—its crusty dean, Robert L. Tullis, who detested Kennedy as a troublemaker and a deplorable student example of the influence of Longism. No examinations for Kennedy, the dean decreed.

The issue was apparently closed, with a victory for Tullis. But the dean did not appreciate fully the nature of the Longism he scorned, and especially its capacity to wait to strike down an enemy.

---

[1] Baton Rouge *State-Times*, December 5, 1934, which reprints editorials from many college papers; *Literary Digest*, January 12, 1935, p. 38; Joe Sugarman: "Huey Long's Hand at the N.S.F.A. Congress," *Carolina Magazine*, clipping, n.d., in Long Scrapbooks, XXIX.

[2] Baton Rouge *State-Times*, December 5, 7, and 28, 1934.

The blow fell on him without warning in 1933. At the spring meeting of the board of supervisors President Smith recommended that Tullis be placed on an emeritus status, explaining that the sixty-nine-year-old dean was physically unable to discharge his duties. The board complied with the request and then quickly adopted another presidential recommendation: that Kennedy be granted his degree after taking his required examinations. In the meantime he was to be given a special diploma—not signed by Tullis or anyone connected with the law school but by Smith and Governor Allen. It was this development that had aroused the suspicion of the American Bar Association and that would cause the organization, after further investigation, to put the law school on probation.[3]

In the *Reveille* and Kennedy affairs President Smith seemed to be the man making the decisions. But as everyone knew, Smith was being directed at every stage by Huey. It was Huey who had decided that the *Reveille* should be supervised and that Kennedy should be given a degree. Why Huey had done so seemed evident to many observers at that time and has seemed obvious to later writers. He viewed LSU as a personal or political possession and interfered with it whenever he saw fit. He had, in short, no respect for the principle of academic freedom.

Huey conceded, many times, that he had interfered with the university. But he hastened to explain what he meant by the word. He had intervened to improve the school by giving it more money. And he was going to continue this kind of interference, he vowed. In fact, in 1935 he announced that he had devised a plan that would enable every boy and girl in Louisiana who had ability to attend the university free of cost. "We should provide that education is not limited by finances, but that it should be limited by mentality," he said.[4]

On one occasion he became philosophical in discussing his role as an interferer. He was asked to speak at a conference at LSU in 1935 celebrating the university's seventy-fifth anniversary, to an audience made up largely of distinguished visiting educators. It was a discriminating group, but he charmed it with his grasp of the problems of education and his account of how he had helped LSU. At the end of his remarks he gave the educators some advice. "You

[3] Ibid., June 5, 1933; New Orleans *Times-Picayune*, May 5 and 10, 1935.
[4] *American Progress*, January, March, and April, 1935; New Orleans *Times-Picayune*, June 9, 1935; Long, radio address, July 19, 1935, in Christenberry: *Speeches by Long*.

will find that you cannot do without politicians," he said. "They are a necessary evil in this day and time. You may not like getting money from one source and spending it for another. But the thing for the school people to do is that if the politicians are going to steal, make them steal for the schools."[5]

Huey did not think he had interfered with the university in the *Reveille* and Kennedy cases. Rather, he thought that he was preventing his enemies from interfering with it. A letter critical of him had appeared in the paper edited by a nephew of a political enemy of his. Therefore, his enemies were using the *Reveille* to smear him. So he had to place the editors under responsible supervision. Kennedy was being denied a degree because he was a Longite, the victim of antis within the university. So the Kingfish would see to it that the boy got the degree.

He had interfered, of course, unwisely and improperly. But contrary to what many have thought, he did not have a philosophic hostility to the principle of academic freedom. He knew little about the principle and cared less. He did not concern himself with what the professors at LSU said in their classrooms or what visiting lecturers said in their presentations. Both the professors and the lecturers discussed fully and freely current political and economic issues. In fact, the discussion was of such proportions as to lead one outside lecturer to state that there was more questioning of existing institutions and beliefs at LSU than at any other college in the country except the ultraliberal University of Wisconsin. Huey, in one of his rare pronouncements on academic freedom, indicated that he was willing to stretch the practice to extraordinary lengths, further than it went in most states. A reporter for a national student magazine asked him what he thought of the laws being proposed in some states to require students to take loyalty oaths. "Well, there hasn't been any of that in Louisiana, and there won't be," he snapped. "All the radicals and reds in the colleges won't do any harm. It's a mighty good thing that they are beginning to do a little thinking. I wish there were a few million radicals."[6]

He drew only one line on the discussion at LSU. There must be no public criticism of Huey Long, for this would damage the creator of LSU and his design for the nation, in which the university had a

[5] New York *Post*, May 9, 1935; Rorty: "Callie Long's Boy Huey," *Forum*, XCIV (August 1935), 76.

[6] Carter: *American Messiahs* (New York, 1935), pp. 15–16; Monroe Sweetland: "The Student Movement and Huey Long," *Student Outlook*, III (April 1935), 10.

part, as a shining example of the kind of subsidized education that the creator would eventually give to the whole country.

THE NEWS STRUCK Baton Rouge right after New Year's Day in 1935: the Standard Oil Company had laid off a thousand employees and had intimated that it probably would have to move its huge refinery to another state. "Now the blow has fallen," lamented the *State-Times*, which went on to inform its readers of the reason for the company's decision. It was the five cents a barrel tax on refined oil enacted by the legislature in December at the demand of "a mad ruler, drunk with power," whose only purpose was to "wreak private vengeance" on the company.[7]

The mad ruler was immediately sought out by reporters for his reaction to the news. He professed not to be alarmed. "If they got to leave, they can go to hell and stay there," he observed genially. But becoming grimmer, he declared that Louisiana might have to operate its own refineries. It could set itself up in the business by borrowing money from the federal government and building refineries, he said. Or it could expropriate the Standard Oil plant and use the money from its operation to educate students at LSU. The company did not know how to evaluate these threats. The directors in New York City scoffed at the notion that the national government would lend money to an enterprise connected with Huey Long. But the hierarchy of the Louisiana branch was shaken by his expropriation proposal, believing that he was quite capable of forcing such a measure through the legislature. Hurriedly they obtained the consent of the New York group to try to negotiate a compromise with Huey.[8]

Huey was equally eager to compromise the issue, if the company met his conditions. His purpose in having the tax enacted was not to avenge himself on Standard Oil or even to damage it, although he took a grim satisfaction in humbling his most powerful enemy. Rather, his objective was economic, as it had always been in his jousts with the company: he wanted to force it to use more Louisiana oil in its refining operations. And this was all he demanded of the president of the Louisiana division, J. C. Hilton, when the latter came to ask for terms. The company must agree to take eighty per cent of the oil for its Baton Rouge plant from Louisiana sources,

[7] Baton Rouge *State-Times*, January 4, 5, 7, and 8, 1935.
[8] International News and Associated Press dispatches, January 5, 1935, in Long Scrapbooks, XXIII; Clem H. Sehrt.

he said. If this was done, he would see to it that the legislature passed a law rebating to the company, and to other companies following the same practice, four cents of the five cents tax on each barrel of Louisiana oil.

Hilton grasped at the proposal, which was more reasonable than he had expected, and he and Huey put it in the shape of a tentative agreement. But it was Huey who announced the settlement to the public and revealed at the same time that the company had agreed to take back the thousand employees it had laid off. It was indicative of what had happened in Louisiana politics that no one saw anything odd in a United States senator acting for the state government and committing that government to follow a particular policy.[9]

While Huey and Hilton were negotiating, some of the Standard Oil employees who had been laid off called a mass meeting of all the company's workers to protest the tax. The leader in the movement was Ernest Bourgeois, a fiery young man who was an electrical engineer at the Baton Rouge plant but who according to reports was often sent to other states to break strikes against Standard Oil. The other signers of the call were also white-collar employees, and men of this class predominated over ordinary workers in the meeting.[1]

It was, in truth, a strange assortment of persons who had assembled. In addition to the employees, there were a number of local anti-Long leaders who had heard that the meeting was directed at Huey and had come to lend their assistance and some individuals who had wandered in simply out of curiosity. Anyone who wanted to speak participated in the discussion, which was long and heated and concerned with the oil tax and the threatened closure of the refinery. After a time someone came in and announced the compromise that Huey and Hilton had arranged. At this news there were cries for adjournment, and some persons started to leave. But others stayed in their seats, setting up a chant: "Let's end the rule of Long." A man named James Mehaffey, who was not a Standard Oil employee and who had, in fact, only recently returned to Baton Rouge after a long absence, stood up and shouted: "You ought to hang every

[9] Associated Press dispatch, January 5, 1935, in Long Scrapbooks, XXIII; unidentified clipping, January 7, 1935, ibid., XVIII; Joseph Cawthorn; James A. Noe. As a minor provision of the agreement, Huey insisted that the company rehire Louis LeSage, the lobbyist whom it had fired after the passage of the oil tax.
[1] Baton Rouge *Morning Advocate*, January 17, 1935; Magnolia (Ark.) *Times* February 2, 1935; Tom Wallace, in San Francisco *Chronicle*, February 25, 1935.

legislator, commencing with your governor." His exhortation aroused roaring applause from most of the crowd. The purpose of the meeting had suddenly and subtly changed.

Those persons who had remained quickly decided to organize themselves, their celerity indicating previous planning by the leaders. They took as a name for the group the Square Deal Association, suggested by a member who said that all they wanted was square-dealing in state politics, and chose Bourgeois as president and Mehaffey as vice-president. Female employees or supporters were, with a proper adherence to Southern tradition, enrolled in a "woman's division," headed by a Mrs. J. S. Roussel. The male members were to be organized in companies as in an army and, as Bourgeois put it, "taught the rudiments of military science." To further emphasize their military character, they were to wear blue shirts, at least when on duty. But some members objected to this, probably fearing that an analogy to Hitler's brown shirts would be drawn, and it was decided to substitute identifying lapel buttons for the shirts.

The meeting ended in a dramatic climax, with members shouting through a resolution directing Governor Allen to call within ten days a special legislative session to repeal every "dictator" law. "We are not asking this," Bourgeois cried. "We are demanding it." He added that if the governor did not heed the ultimatum a mass march on the capitol would follow. Another member said: "If any attempt is made to stop this organization, there will be more bloodshed than this state has seen in its history."[2]

News of the formation of the Square Deal Association spread quickly throughout the state, and soon chapters in other cities sprang up. These units were even more frankly political than the parent group in Baton Rouge. Hardly any of the members were Standard Oil employees. The majority were anti-Long men and women of varying ranges of importance—the rolls carried such prominent names as Mayor Walmsley, former governors Parker and Pleasant, and Hilda Phelps Hammond—and the leaders openly avowed their purpose: they were going to get rid of Huey Long by whatever means they had to employ. Some of them hoped that they could achieve their goal by political action. But others declared that violence and probably assassination would be required.

As the movement swelled to statewide proportions, some observ-

[2] New York *Herald-Tribune*, January 7, 1935; unidentified clipping January 10, 1935, in Long Scrapbooks, XVIII; Los Angeles *Times*, January 18, 1935; George Healy, in Washington *Star*, January 27, 1935; James L. Mehaffey; Bonnie V. Baker.

ers concluded that somebody must be directing it, perhaps Standard Oil. Actually, it was spontaneous, an expression of anti-Longism, its leaders hoping to use the resentment felt at the oil tax as a weapon to overthrow the Kingfish. There is no evidence that the company encouraged the creation of any of the units except possibly the one at Baton Rouge. A leader of the capital chapter, when asked if Standard Oil had sponsored its formation, replied ambiguously: "I don't know. But they were interested, liked the idea of employees putting the pressure on Huey."[3]

The Baton Rouge chapter was the largest one in the state, numbering probably several hundred persons, and its threat to march on the capitol unless a special session was called aroused apprehension in some quarters of the city that bloodshed might result. Governor Allen, ignoring the ultimatum, professed not to be alarmed but still ordered extra details of state policemen posted around the capitol and the mansion. Also professing not to be alarmed was Huey. "March!" he exclaimed. "Those fellows won't march unless you get them a buggy or a jinrikisha. They're too lazy to march." He had reason to scorn the Square Dealers. He had planted in their inner councils a spy who was reporting to him their every move, a man named Sidney Songy, whose presence in the organization would shortly force it to make a big move.[4]

On January 24, 1935, the governing body of East Baton Rouge parish, its thirteen-man police jury, received an accession of members. The thirteen additional jurors that Governor Allen had been authorized by the legislature to appoint showed up at its meeting and claimed their seats. Nine anti members of the elected jury refused to attend the session and vowed that they would test the legality of the governor's action in the courts. But two anti members and the two previous Long members attended. The new jury, now with a heavy Long majority, displaced the president of the elected group with a Long leader and then raced through a number of other punitive measures. It fired all of the 225 employees of the parish, removed District Attorney John Fred Odom as its counsel and substituted for him Attorney General Porterie, and took from Sheriff

---

[3] Lafayette *Daily Advertiser*, January 12, 1935; New Orleans *Times-Picayune*, January 19, 1935; Healy, in Washington *Star*, January 27, 1935; E. H. (Lige) Williams; James L. Mehaffey; confidential communication.

[4] M. J. Kavanaugh; Boston *Transcript*, January 12, 1935; Los Angeles *Times*, January 18, 1935; New Orleans *Times-Picayune*, January 27 and June 8, 1935; E. J. Bourg.

Robert L. Pettit the custody of the courthouse and gave this function to a Long man.[5]

The jury's action did not become generally known until the following day. But even more disturbing news followed. Late in the afternoon a report spread that a Square Dealer had been arrested, presumably by the state authorities, and that he would be forced to reveal the names of a number of his colleagues who had recently attended a meeting at a certain private home and who were also to be arrested. The name of the man who had been seized by Huey Long's cossacks was said to be Songy.

This development threw the Square Dealers into an apparent frenzy. Some of them ran from house to house in certain wards crying: "All Square Dealers out! Get your guns and go to the courthouse"; others telephoned a similar message to company leaders in the city and in adjoining parishes. A force of about one hundred armed men soon gathered, some of whom reportedly had been given guns by deputies of Sheriff Pettit, and were joined by two hundred other men from nearby parishes who arrived in automobiles. The aggregation then marched to the courthouse and took possession of it, expelling the Long-appointed custodian and other employees and refusing to let any person who was not a Square Dealer enter. Women members of the association appeared with sandwiches and coffee to sustain the troops for a protracted occupation, and various speakers addressed them, denouncing Huey and declaring that he should not be permitted to arrest any of them. A young woman whose mother had been fired as secretary of the police jury tried to arrest the flow of words by crying: "There ought to be action now. There has been too much talk."

Other speakers took up the cry for action. But nobody seemed to know what action to take. Several persons proposed to march on the capitol, and this was debated at length but without a decision being reached. It was now nine o'clock at night, and the crowd had been standing around for five hours. At this point someone came in and reported that Songy had been released. Some of the men then started to leave, and the leaders quickly announced that all should go home, that their "purpose" had been "accomplished." What the purpose had been would soon be revealed.[6]

[5] Baltimore *Sun*, January 25, 1935; Hermann B. Deutsch, in New Orleans *Item*, September 13, 1939; Bonnie V. Baker.

[6] Associated Press dispatch, January 25, 1935, in Long Scrapbooks, XXIII; New Orleans *Morning Tribune*, January 26, 1935; New Orleans *Times-Picayune*, January 26, 1935; *The New York Times*, January 26 and 27, 1935; Bonnie V. Baker; James L. Mehaffey; confidential communication, on sheriff's deputies providing guns.

While the crowd still held the courthouse, a reporter met Huey in the lobby of the Heidelberg Hotel and asked the Kingfish how he intended to deal with the uprising. Huey seemed angry but confident. "If they want a fight, they'll get one," he answered. He had already acted to meet a possible crisis, instructing Governor Allen to call out the national guard and summoning its commander, General Fleming, up from New Orleans.

Fleming, at Huey's direction, prepared two proclamations that were issued at midnight or soon after. One, signed by Allen, was brief and simple, imposing martial law in Baton Rouge and East Baton Rouge parish. The other was longer and more detailed and created the "First Military District," comprising "the territory" of the city and the parish. Signed by the general commanding the district, Brigadier General Louis F. Guerre, it announced a set of regulations that were unusually stringent in the history of American martial law. The carrying of firearms was prohibited by any persons except members of the city and state police forces. No firearms could be sold, exchanged, or given away in the district or be transported into it. No publication, including newspapers, could print anything that reflected on the state government or its officers. Crowds were forbidden to gather at any time anywhere and "two or more people" constituted a crowd.[7]

The first units of the national guard arrived in the city by daybreak on the morning of January 26, a Saturday, and before noon over eight hundred troops had assembled on the capitol grounds. One squad was dispatched to take possession of the courthouse and another to assume custody of the city police station. The reason for this massing of military might was revealed by the Kingfish to reporters. He charged that he had discovered a plot to murder him, instigated by Standard Oil. The compromise he had granted the company was off unless it "stopped its violence," he snapped. He added that he would prove his charge later in the morning at a hearing called by Attorney General Porterie before District Judge J. D. Womack, a recently appointed Long stalwart.[8]

The hearing convened shortly, but not in Womack's court. It was held in a heavily guarded room in the capitol, and although Porterie represented the state, Huey conducted the questioning of

[7] New York *Sun*, January 26, 1935; New Orleans *Item-Tribune*, January 27, 1935; Raymond H. Fleming; Louis F. Guerre. General Fleming provided me with copies of the two proclamations. They are dated January 26, but Allen had issued a preliminary martial law edict just before midnight on the twenty-fifth.

[8] *The New York Times*, January 27, 1935.

witnesses. The star witness was Songy, who was revealed now as a Long spy in the Square Deal Association. Songy unfolded a sensational story. He said that he had pretended to connive in a plot to murder Senator Long with seven prominent Baton Rouge citizens: Fred Parker, a former deputy sheriff and the directing figure in the plot; John Fred Odom, the district attorney; Fred LeBlanc, his assistant; Dallas Gross, the manager of Congressman Sanders's local office; Powers Higginbotham, a recently deposed city official; Fred O'Rourke, a Square Deal officer; and Roland Kizer, an attorney. Privy to the plot, he said, were the sheriffs of two adjoining parishes, Henry Sherburne of Iberville and Sidney Debroca of West Baton Rouge.

Songy said that he had regularly conveyed the plans of the plotters to Joe Messina or Huey himself. They had first decided to kill the senator on the night of January 23, rushing his suite at the Heidelberg Hotel, but he had convinced them that the rooms were so heavily guarded they could not break through. They had then determined to strike on the following night when it was known that Huey would be going to New Orleans by automobile. They would lie in wait at a point on the road known as "Dead Man's Curve," and as Huey's car slowed up they would shoot him. Songy had apprised Huey of the plan and as proof of its reality had shown Huey the weapons he was to carry to the ambush, a pistol, a shotgun, and several gas bombs.

Huey believed him, Songy said, and had asked the city police to take him into protective custody on a trumped-up charge that he had no license plates on his car. But almost immediately, and to his dismay, he received legal counsel, Roland Kizer, who appeared at the police station and had Songy paroled to him. He was warned by Kizer to keep his mouth shut and was promised money to get out of town. But he had wanted to expose the plot and so had sought refuge in the governor's mansion and was here now to tell the truth.

When Songy concluded his testimony, Huey announced that he had wanted to examine the men named by the spy but was informed that they could not be found, that apparently they had left town. "It's a mysterious circumstance," he declared. One of the alleged plotters, Powers Higginbotham, was eventually brought in, however. But when placed on the stand he replied to every question with "I don't remember." Huey thereupon asked Womack to adjourn the hearing until the following Friday, when presumably the missing men would be located. "Those of us who practice criminal law know that men need time to polish off their recollections and memories," he said.[9]

The hearing revealed why the Square Dealers had been so strangely excited at the news of Songy's arrest and had seized the courthouse and then disbanded when they heard that he had been released. They did not know which of them he was going to accuse or of what, and responding to some kind of mass urge they had sought to protect themselves by flocking together. And now that Songy had testified, they engaged in another one of those tribal communions. Late that same Saturday afternoon some one hundred armed Square Dealers appeared at the municipal airport and milled around waiting for their leaders to tell them why they had assembled. Those leaders of the group who survive are themselves not sure what had brought them together. Vice-President Jim Mehaffey thought that they had decided to hold a rally and had fixed on the airport because of its open space. But other members declared that the gathering was not planned. They related that a number of company captains had received telephone calls from men who did not identify themselves but simply stated: "Call your men, get in your cars, and get out to the airport. Instructions will be given there." Not pausing to check the authenticity of the calls, the captains obeyed the message. The men who gave this account suspect that from some source, possibly Songy, Huey had obtained a list of the members and that lieutenants of his had made the calls to trap the Square Dealers into forming a crowd in violation of the martial law prohibition.[1]

This supposition is plausible in view of the events that followed the assembling of the crowd. Almost immediately five hundred national guardsmen and state policemen appeared, armed in addition to their rifles with machine guns and tear gas. They had been ordered there by General Fleming and Colonel E. P. Roy of the police, both of whom in recalling the episode denied any knowledge of springing a trap. They had been told only that an armed mob had taken possession of the airport, they affirmed, which is what Huey would have had them told if he was setting a snare for the Square Dealers.

[9] Deutsch, in New Orleans *Item-Tribune*, January 27, 1935, almost a verbatim report of the hearing; *The New York Times*, January 27, 1935. Songy, after the hearing, was given a job in a state agency. Powers Higginbotham, when asked to comment on the episode, asserted that Songy's story was a fabrication.

[1] James L. Mehaffey; Bonnie V. Baker; J. Y. Sanders, Jr., who was a member of the association.

The major commanding the militia deployed his men in line, and Colonel Roy summoned the Square Dealers to surrender. A few of them threw down their guns, but the rest broke and ran for a nearby wood. The troopers thereupon lobbed some tear-gas bombs over their heads, and most of them halted and surrendered. Roy took their guns and names and told them that they were under technical arrest but could go to their homes. In the meantime several hundred spectators had gathered and were shouting insults at the state force, and Roy ordered them dispersed with a volley of tear gas. The "battle of the airport," as the incident immediately became known, was over. It had been an almost bloodless engagement. One Square Dealer was wounded in the arm by a shotgun, hit from behind by one of his comrades who was hastening to escape.

A few Square Dealers did escape. Mehaffey made his way into the city but was followed and took refuge on the steps of the federal post office building. After staying there for three hours, he was glad to surrender to the same kind of technical arrest that Roy had imposed on his colleagues. Bourgeois got completely away and turned up in Mississippi. He ventured to return to Baton Rouge shortly and was arrested and resigned as president of the Square Deal Association, which now stood revealed as a not very effective organization led by not very smart men.[2]

In exposing the incapability of the Square Dealers, Huey had weakened somewhat his contention that he was threatened with murder by determined enemies. He went ahead, nevertheless, with his court hearing to prove that he had such enemies. At sessions on February 1 and 2 he produced another talkative witness, a former East Baton Rouge parish deputy sheriff, George, "Red," Davis, who testified that Fred Parker had offered him ten thousand dollars to shoot the Kingfish. He took the assignment and was furnished a car from Sheriff Pettit's office and a rifle from a hardware store owned by relatives of the sheriff. Several times he had tried to shoot Huey through a window at the capitol or the mansion but could not get close enough because of the presence of state policemen. After Davis finished, Huey summoned Parker and Fred O'Rourke, a Square Dealer, to the stand. They refused to testify on the grounds that they might incriminate themselves. Huey did not call any of the other men named by Songy and announced that he was adjourning the

[2] Raymond H. Fleming; E. P. Roy; Bonnie V. Baker; James L. Mehaffey; New Orleans *Item-Tribune*, January 27, 1935; New Orleans *Times-Picayune*, January 27, 1935; *The New York Times*, January 27, 1935; Baton Rouge *State-Times*, February 1 and March 11, 1935.

hearing indefinitely. He seemed satisfied with having fixed the suspicion of murder on his enemies.[3]

He was convinced, though, that there had been a plot to murder .him, and so were the men around him at that time, although one or two of them were skeptical of Songy's tale about an ambush at Dead Man's Curve. Some of them begged him to buy a bullet-proof vest, but he refused. "If somebody's going to shoot me, he's going to shoot me," he said. "I'm not going to worry about it."[4]

Huey seemed to be resigned to being assassinated. He once told a Senate colleague that too many people in Louisiana were plotting to kill him. "If there were just a few people plotting it, I think I might live through it," he said. "But those people are determined to kill me, and I'm not going to live through it."[5]

That his fears had a basis was substantiated by a story told by Mason Spencer, the legislator who had been manager of the impeachment in 1929. Spencer related that he was invited to a meeting in Baton Rouge that he understood was to discuss political methods of overthrowing Huey. The chairman opened the session by stating: "This meeting is called for the purpose of discussing ways and means of killing Huey Long." This was too much for the massive Spencer, bitter anti that he was. He heaved himself to his feet and said: "Let the minutes show that at this point Mason Spencer walked out."[6]

Early in February, soon after the adjournment of the murder-plot hearing, rumors circulated in Baton Rouge that Huey and Standard Oil were about to settle their differences. It was stated that the company had agreed to fire fifty employees who had been active Square Dealers and that the Kingfish would in return convoke the legislature into special session to enact the compromise previously agreed upon by him and President Hilton rebating four cents of the five cents a barrel tax on Louisiana oil. The city's mayor, Wade A. Bynum, gave official credence to the possibility of a settlement by asking the citizens to refrain from "any further gesture of armed uprising" to the end that martial law might be lifted. Also lending

[3] Daniell, in *The New York Times*, February 3, 1935; Brooklyn *Daily Eagle*, February 3, 1935.

[4] James P. O'Connor; Theophile Landry; James A. Noe; Murphy Roden; Louis F. Guerre; John B. Fournet; Trent James; Castro Carazo. Huey did not go to New Orleans on the night that the ambush was allegedly planned, but men in his group drove to the spot and found no one there. Either there was nothing planned or the arrest of Songy caused the plan to be called off.

[5] Russell B. Long, recounting a conversation with Harry Byrd.

[6] Mason Spencer; Cecil Bird.

support to the rumors was the sudden departure from the city of most of the militia.[7]

Huey denied that he was going to deal with Standard Oil. "You can't cooperate with thieves and murderers," he growled. Actually, he had already settled with it. He and Hilton had met secretly on January 22 and drawn up an agreement embodying the essence of their previous compromise on the oil tax. (Curiously, Huey signed it as the head of his faction, the Louisiana Democratic Association.) But he would not admit the existence of a pact until he was satisfied that Standard Oil had observed the parts of it agreed upon but not formally stated—the firing of the Square Deal employees. He received their assurance finally, and then he directed Governor Allen to convoke the legislature on February 26 for a session of five days. Included in the call as matters of legislation were a large number of routine measures but nothing on the oil tax. Standard Oil would soon learn the reason for the omission.[8]

The legislature raced rapidly through the bills offered by the administration, the two houses being in actual session for only nine and a half hours. Then, on February 28, two days before adjournment was scheduled, Long leaders offered a concurrent resolution in both chambers that authorized the governor to suspend any portion of the oil tax that he saw fit. Immediately after the passage of the resolution Allen suspended four cents of the tax on Louisiana oil for a fixed period. The strategy behind the resolution was all too obvious: Huey could have his governor reimpose the tax at any time that the company opposed him. The Standard Oil executives accepted the humiliation without even a whimper.[9]

Huey was very sure of everything in the early months of 1935, of himself and of his power and of all parts of his Louisiana domain. He was pushing his enemies to extinction, he believed. In a radio address to the people he said that in 1929, when he ran for governor, his enemies were fighting for "our ground." But now he said grimly: "We are fighting for their ground."[1]

[7] Daniell, in *The New York Times*, February 7, 1935; Brooklyn *Daily Eagle*, February 3, 1935, for the departure of the troops. Martial law continued until early in July, but after this withdrawal of the militia was only lightly enforced.

[8] Anderson, in St. Louis *Post-Dispatch*, February 3, 1935. The agreement is reproduced in T. O. Harris: *The Kingfish: Huey P. Long, Dictator* (New Orleans, 1938), pp. 208–9, and in a circular, "To Help Louisiana Resources and Industry," in my possession.

[9] Baton Rouge *State-Times*, February 26, 1935; Baton Rouge *Morning Advocate*, February 27, 1935; New Orleans *Morning Tribune*, March 1, 1935.

[1] Daniell, in *The New York Times*, February 7, 1935.

# CHAPTER 28

# *I Might Have a Good Parade*

O N JANUARY 4, 1935, Senator Burton K. Wheeler sent up to the clerk of the Senate a telegram he had just received and asked that it be read. The message was from Senator Long and stated: "Please announce or have announced to the Senate that on Monday or on the first day thereafter on which the Senate is in session next week, I shall speak on the propositions in the newspapers with which I am identified." A ripple of laughter ran through the chamber and the galleries at the idea of a senator claiming the floor by telegraph.[1]

Huey, occupied with his opposition in Louisiana, had not been able to attend the opening session of Congress. But now he was coming, and officials in the Roosevelt administration were apprehensive. They knew the "proposition in the newspapers" that he was going to speak on. It had been widely publicized that Governor Allen had received from the President a letter stating that all Public Works loans to the state would be withheld unless certain recent legislative enactments were repealed or clarified. Roosevelt had singled out two laws as being particularly objectionable: the act declaring a moratorium on debts except those owed to municipalities and the state and federal governments, which might jeopardize municipal bonds bought by the Public Works Administration, and a measure placing the New Orleans sewage and water board under state control, which seemed to take away the independence of the city agency.[2]

[1] New Orleans *Times-Picayune*, January 4, 1935.
[2] New Orleans *Item*, January 1, 1935; New York *Herald-Tribune*, January 2, 1935.

Huey's threat to discuss the prohibition caused the PWA to declare hastily that its lawyers now saw no danger to municipal bonds in the moratorium law and that ten million dollars in loans was being immediately released to Louisiana. This relaxation did not deter Huey. He announced in New Orleans before entraining for Washington that he would discuss the part of the ban still in effect and "similar other matters" as soon as he could gain the floor.[3]

He secured it almost immediately after arriving, on January 7. It had become known that he would speak that day, and the chamber was filled. Every Senate seat was occupied, the floor was lined with congressmen, the galleries were jammed, and in the corridors people stood in lines hoping to get in. The audience expected a circus, but Huey did not give them one. He was intensely serious, and his speech was a closely reasoned attack on the Roosevelt administration. Its theme was the ingratitude that the President had shown to the progressives who had elected him and who had then tried to steer him onto a progressive course. Instead of cherishing these men, Roosevelt had turned on them and was now trying to destroy them. He had marked specially for destruction Huey Long and hoped to accomplish his purpose by giving patronage in Louisiana only to anti-Longs, to men who would bow the knee to the administration. But it could never make him kneel, Huey vowed. "God send me to hell before I go through that kind of thing in order to get patronage," he cried.

Then, turning calm, he charged that the administration was employing against him an even fouler weapon than denial of the patronage. It was trying to secure evidence that would enable it to put him and his most trusted associates in prison. The Treasury Department had sent "hordes" of agents, 250 of them, to Louisiana to check on the income tax returns of Huey and his friends, and these inquisitors had declared that since they had convicted Al Capone, they were now going to get Huey Long. "They did not try to put any covering over this thing," he said: they had boasted that Long and his gang "were all going away."[4]

Huey had not exaggerated in declaring that the administration was trying to destroy him. The effort was, if anything, even more determined than he described it, and the President himself was di-

[3] Associated Press Dispatch, January 4, 1935, in Hilda Phelps Hammond Scrapbook, in possession of Mrs. Nauman S. Scott, Jr., Alexandria, Louisiana.
[4] *Congressional Record*, 74 Cong., 1 Sess., pp. 150–9; John O'Donnell and Doris Fleeson, in New York *Daily News*, January 8, 1935.

recting the strategy. Roosevelt had become acutely alarmed during 1934 at the spreading signs of Huey's influence. A superb judge of public opinion, he read in the signs a threat to his re-election in 1936, and from associates he received warnings that Huey represented another and more sinister threat: Long was not only a probable presidential contender but also a potential fascist leader. Roosevelt was increasingly inclined to believe the fascist charge. Huey could well be the strong man to whom the country might turn if the New Deal failed to solve the depression. The times were "not normal," the President wrote to a friend, and the people were "jumpy and ready to run after strange gods." As one weapon against his rising rival Roosevelt employed the patronage, tightening still more the denial of jobs to Huey that had long been in effect. He stated his policy emphatically at a meeting of his inner council early in 1935: "Don't put anybody in and don't help anybody that is working for Huey Long or his crowd: that is a hundred per cent!"[5]

But even as Roosevelt struck with the patronage, he realized that this weapon in itself would not bring Huey down. The Kingfish had so many state jobs at his disposal that he did not have to rely on federal favors. An additional and more effective instrument would have to be employed, and Roosevelt hit on one in 1934 that he thought would do the job. Ironically, it had been forged by Republican President Hoover, who had also desired to destroy the senator from Louisiana.

One of Hoover's officials was Elmer Irey, who headed the intelligence division of the revenue department in the Treasury. During the last two years of the Hoover administration Irey noted that he was receiving an unusually large volume of letters from Louisiana. The writers, most of whom did not sign their names, claimed that Huey Long and his associates were stealing large sums of state money and naturally not reporting the thefts in their income tax returns. The Treasury should start an investigation of these returns, the correspondents urged.

Despite the anonymity of the writers, Irey was impressed with the probable truth of their charges, and he became more impressed when former Governor Parker called at his office and demanded:

[5] Lela Stiles: *The Man Behind Roosevelt* (Cleveland, 1954), p. 285; Roosevelt to E. M. House, February 16, 1935; and E. M. House to Roosevelt, February 21, 1935, in Elliott Roosevelt, ed.: *F.D.R.: His Personal Letters* (New York, 1947–50), I, 452–4, 460–1; Arthur M. Schlesinger: *Politics of Upheaval* (New York, 1960), pp. 242–9.

"When are you going to do something about Long?" (Or so he stated later in a book describing his subsequent investigation.) But he took no action on the matter until July 1932, after Huey had been in the Senate for months and had become a principal gadfly of the Hoover administration. Then he sent an agent to Louisiana to undertake preliminary inquiry. This man spent a few weeks in the state and returned to Irey's office triumphant. "Chief," he said, "Louisiana is crawling. Long and his gang are stealing everything in the state." (Irey in his book could repeat dozens of conversations verbatim.)

Irey thereupon sent other agents to Louisiana, but as he continued the investigation he became aware that his superiors wished he would drop it. They were being pressured by Huey and were afraid of him, he suspected. He was certain of this when after Hoover's defeat in November Secretary of the Treasury Ogden Mills instructed him to suspend the probe and write a report of it that would be turned over to the incoming Democratic secretary. Huey was one of the Democrats' "babies," Mills said, and they should have to decide what to do about him.[6]

Irey was correct in thinking that Huey had used some kind of pressure to get the investigation called off, but he did not know exactly how Huey had done it. Huey revealed the inside story only to a few intimates. He related that Hoover's assistant secretary of the navy, E. L. Jahncke, who was from New Orleans, owed a bank in the city $250,000, which the bank had suddenly called. Thereupon Huey had received a telephone call from Washington from his friend Harvey Couch, now a director of the Reconstruction Finance Corporation. Couch protested the calling of Jahncke's loan and charged that as it had been done at the instruction of the state bank examiner, Huey must have ordered it. Huey denied any knowledge of the action. "I don't have anything more to do with that bank examiner than the Assistant Secretary of the Navy has to do with the Treasury Department," he said. Couch got the message. "Oh, is *that* it?" he asked. "That's exactly it," Huey replied.[7]

In March 1933 Irey's report was turned over to Roosevelt's secretary of the treasury, William H. Woodin. Irey hoped that he would receive instructions from Woodin to continue the investigation, but during the rest of the year he received no word from the secretary.

[6] Elmer Irey and William J. Slocum: *The Tax Dodgers* (New York, 1949), pp. 89–90.
[7] Wheeler: *Yankee from the West*, pp. 290–1.

Then in January 1934 Woodin resigned and was succeeded by Henry Morgenthau, Jr., and three days after the new secretary took office he summoned Irey before him. Why had the investigation of Long been stopped? Morgenthau demanded. Irey explained that he had received no instructions to reopen it, whereupon Morgenthau replied that he was receiving them now: "Get all your agents back on the Louisiana job. Start the investigation of Huey Long and proceed as though you were investigating John Doe." If the secretary had put his charge with complete frankness, he would have said: Investigate Huey Long, who is undoubtedly corrupt but had been sought by the administration as a supporter and who has now become its most powerful enemy and has to be crushed.[8]

Irey, delighted at this evidence of high support, immediately sent a battery of investigators into Louisiana, not the 250 that Huey charged with being there but still a considerable number, at least 50 men. Working secretly, the agents spent months checking the incomes of Long lieutenants and comparing these with tax returns. They reported finally that a number of Huey's leaders had received huge incomes during the last few years that had not been reported, incomes derived from bribes and kickbacks paid by contractors and other individuals doing business with the state. The evidence was such that the government could ask for indictments from a federal grand jury, the agents said.

Irey was excited at the information. Although the federal government could not prosecute the offenders for corruption, it could for income tax evasion, and in proving its case it could expose the corruption in the Long machine and weaken it and its leader. Irey decided that his strategy should be to seek first to convict a lesser Long leader and if successful, to go after a bigger one and then a still bigger one, and finally perhaps to bag the Kingfish himself. This was the strategy that had disposed of the Al Capone gang and it should work with the Long gang, Irey thought. But he realized that in these cases he would face a special difficulty: Louisiana juries might be reluctant to convict Louisiana citizens. Therefore he had to have a Southerner as prosecuting attorney. He discussed his problem with Morgenthau, who promptly took him to Roosevelt, the man who could get him such a lawyer. The President persuaded former Texas governor Dan Moody to take the cases.[9]

As a preliminary victim, Irey fixed on Representative Joe Fisher,

[8] Irey and Slocum: *The Tax Dodgers*, pp. 91–2.
[9] Ibid., pp. 92–5.

the Long leader in Jefferson parish, and as a second one, Abe Shushan, the collector for the Long organization. But the first indictment, for a reason not explained, was returned against Shushan, in October 1934. He was accused of having received over five years an income of almost half a million dollars and reporting only a fraction of it. At the same time the government indicted three road contractors who had sold materials to the state and in order to prove that they had not reported their true incomes sought to get possession of the records of the Highway Commission.[1]

Joe Fisher was indicted in December, and along with him his uncle, state senator Jules Fisher. Joe was charged with not reporting and not paying taxes on an income of $122,000 received over four years. Jules was accused of having received during the same years an income of $348,000 on which he paid a tax of only $41.18. Also indicted in December—and now Irey was really moving up in the Long hierarchy—was Seymour Weiss, who was accused of having received over five years an income of $232,000 but reporting only $55,000. The government alleged that Weiss had drawn a large part of his income from a corrupt arrangement he had forced on the Highway Commission whereby the latter agency compelled road contractors to get their bonds from a company controlled by Weiss and return twenty per cent of the bond premiums to him.[2]

It was the investigation by the Treasury agents and the resulting indictments that Huey had denounced so bitterly in his speech on January 7. His resentment caused his enemies to hope that he was worried by the persecution.

Huey did not seem worried. On the contrary, he never seemed surer of himself. At a press conference in mid-January he said that the only way to stop him from becoming President was for Congress to enact his "share our wealth" laws. "I would rather see my laws passed than be President," he affirmed. But he indicated that he expected no action from Congress and therefore would have to run. He voiced his intention again in two national radio broadcasts that he made in January. Billed as addresses on the Share Our Wealth philosophy, they were really expositions on the strength of the movement and its potential to elect a President. He ended one of these

[1] Ibid., p. 95; Walter Davenport: "Too High and Too Mighty," Collier's, XCV (January 19, 1935), 7–8; T. O. Harris: The Kingfish: Huey P. Long, Dictator (New Orleans, 1938), pp. 228–9.

[2] New Orleans Times-Picayune, December 7, 1934; New Haven Journal-Courier, December 7 and 15, 1934; Harris: The Kingfish, p. 233.

presentations by reciting some lines that he said he had recently written. They opened thus:

> Why weep or slumber, America?
>     Land of brave and true
> With castles, clothing and food for all
>     All belongs to you.
> Ev'ry man a king, ev'ry man a king.[3]

The effusion puzzled his listeners, who wondered if the Kingfish had added poetry writing to his varied repertoire. He dispelled the mystery two days after the broadcast. Arriving suddenly in New York City and summoning a press conference, he announced that he had come to find a publisher for the "song" he had recited over the air, which was to have the title of his autobiography, "Every Man a King." Was there music for the words? a reporter asked. Yes, the senator replied, provided by Castro Carazo. He said that he and Carazo had whipped up the song early one morning in Baton Rouge in less than forty-five minutes. Was it to be a campaign song? he was asked. "One of several," he answered. "We'll have half a dozen." He soon got the song published, probably subsidizing it, and also had it recorded for presentation on a national newsreel service by a nationally known band, Ina Ray Hutton and Her All Girl Orchestra.[4]

Huey's assurance that he need not fear the administration was shared by the Washington correspondents. In fact, these observers, watching him perform in the Senate during the early months of 1935, concluded that the administration should fear him. He continued to draw huge crowds whenever he spoke. One correspondent declared that the other ninety-five senators would have to do something like putting the United States off the gold standard to attract as large an audience as the Kingfish could simply by standing up and saying "Mr. President." All the reporters noted that other senators were afraid to take him on in debate. He had reduced the Senate to a

---

[3] Associated Press dispatch, January 13, 1935, in Hammond Scrapbook; radio addresses by Long, January 9 and 19, 1935, inserted in *Congressional Record*, 74 Cong., 1 Sess., pp. 410–12, 790–2.

[4] Boston *Transcript*, January 11, 1935; Daniell, in *The New York Times*, February 7, 1935; unidentified clipping, in Long Scrapbooks, XXVI; Castro Carazo. The song never became popular, even with members of the Share Our Wealth clubs. Although the air was pleasing, it lacked "punch," and the lines were pretentiously political and awkward to sing.

state of "futile anger," one writer said. Another labeled him as "smart, fast, and deadly" and next to Roosevelt "the most vital figure in public life."[5]

Huey demonstrated his parliamentary skills in January by helping to defeat an administration measure Roosevelt had thought would have easy Senate passage—a treaty providing for American adherence to the World Court. The President had sent a special message to the Senate urging ratification of the treaty, and he was shocked when it ran into a storm of opposition from a bloc of progressive Republican senators led by Borah and from Huey. The Republicans were isolationists and feared that membership in the Court would embroil the United States in the affairs of other nations. Huey, an ardent nationalist on the rare occasions that he thought about foreign policy, fully shared their views. But in joining their attack on the treaty he was motivated primarily by his detestation of Roosevelt. He was determined to defeat and humiliate the man who was trying to destroy him.

He betrayed his intention in the veiled references to Roosevelt that he made in discussing the treaty. The United States should never again become entangled in European quarrels, he said in one speech. The nation had entered the World War to make the world safe for democracy, and what had been the result? "We wound up with all of Europe under dictatorship, and we are trying to set up one in this United States at the same time," he answered. "I do not intend to have these gentlemen whose names I cannot even pronounce, let alone spell, passing upon the rights of the American people," he cried in another speech. "I do not intend to vote for this infernal thing."[6]

The fierce debate in the Senate aroused discussion of the treaty throughout the country, and formidable opposition to it quickly developed, led by Father Coughlin, the radio priest. Letters and telegrams opposing ratification, over fifty thousand in all, poured into Washington, and Democratic senators who had been relied on to vote for the treaty hastily fell away. Brought up for a vote late in January,

[5] Arthur Krock, in *The New York Times*, January 10, 1935; George Durno, in Lexington (Ky.) *Herald*, January 12, 1935; Robert S. Allen and Drew Pearson, unidentified clipping, February 26, 1935, in Long Scrapbooks, XVII; Ollie M. James, in *Herald-Post*, February 26, 1935, clipping in Long Scrapbooks, XXIII; Westbrook Pegler, in Memphis *Press-Scimitar*, March 7, 1935; John Bantry, in Boston *Post*, March 10, 1935; Raymond Clapper, in Washington *Post*, quoted in *American Progress*, March issue.

[6] *Congressional Record*, 74 Cong., 1 Sess., pp. 563–78, 1044–8, 1114–33, debates of January 17, 18, and 29, 1935.

it failed to attain the majority necessary for approval. Washington correspondents ascribed its defeat primarily to two men—Huey Long and Coughlin, who by their denunciations of the treaty had stirred the avalanche of letters that caused the Democratic senators to desert the President. Observers speculated that perhaps these two commanders of mass audiences had joined forces.[7]

The possibility of a Long–Coughlin alliance was a topic of increasing political discussion during 1935. If it could be consummated, it would have obvious effects on the election of 1936, joining together as it would the followings of two masters of radio oratory. But observers doubted that Long and Coughlin could join together. To do it, one would have to give up his pet formula, Huey his Share Our Wealth proposal or Coughlin his currency inflation panacea. And even if they succeeded in such a reconciliation, these two men of dominating personalities would find it difficult to work together. Still, they were known to be personally friendly. Coughlin came to Washington frequently and nearly always went immediately to Huey's suite at the Broadmoor Hotel and stayed there for hours. What they discussed they did not divulge. Huey denied that he and the priest had an alliance but admitted that they were fighting for "the same general objectives."[8]

Only a few persons heard the conversations between the two men—Huey's bodyguards and other employees and occasionally Louisiana followers of his who were visiting Washington. These men naturally did not follow the dialogue closely and when they were asked what was discussed, could not answer in detail. They knew only that the subject was Huey's plan to capture the presidency, and they believed that he had secured Coughlin's support. But on one matter they were certain: Huey was the dominant partner in whatever arrangement was concluded. As one of them put it, Coughlin "capitulated" to Huey.[9]

Not stated, but implied, is an impression of another aspect of the relationship, that Huey was secretly contemptuous of the priest. He undoubtedly was. Huey was a political man and was going to work toward his goal with political methods. Coughlin was a theorist, a

[7] Schlesinger: *Politics of Upheaval*, pp. 4–5; Rodney Dutcher, in Jackson (Miss.) *Daily News*, February 13, 1935.

[8] Joseph F. Thorning: "Senator Long and Father Coughlin," *America* LIII (1935), 8–9; Carter: *American Messiahs* (New York, 1935), p. 43; Victor C. Ferkiss: "The Political and Economic Philosophy of American Fascism" (unpublished Ph.D. dissertation, University of Chicago, 1954), p. 164.

[9] Theophile Landry; Robert Brothers; Murphy Roden; Earle J. Christenberry; James P. O'Connor.

voice, an instrument that the political man could use but would never completely trust. Once, in a moment of disgust with Coughlin, Huey indiscreetly gave vent to his opinion. Likening the cleric to a popular woman radio singer, he said: "Coughlin is just a political Kate Smith on the air. They'll get tired of him."[1]

HUEY, ELATED BY HIS VICTORY in the World Court fight, soon found an opportunity to attack Roosevelt on another issue where the President was vulnerable. In February 1935 the administration's work relief bill came before the Senate. Carrying an appropiation of $4,800,000, it provided for federal employment of needy persons and was presented as a measure to stimulate mass purchasing power. Immediately it met criticism from Huey and other progressives, who favored the bill generally but thought that it did not go nearly far enough toward accomplishing its purpose. They objected most strenuously to the absence of a minimum wage provision, an omission that would allow the government to pay whatever wages it wished to on public works projects. It would naturally choose to pay low wages, Huey and his progressive colleagues reasoned. Determined to prevent this injustice, they attempted to attach to the bill an amendment, the McCarran amendment, providing that public works wages should not be less than the "prevailing" rate for labor of a similar nature in areas where the projects were located.

The McCarran amendment encountered strong opposition from the administration's Senate leaders, who frankly revealed that they were acting on orders from the White House. Roosevelt feared that the prevailing wage rate would quickly exhaust the relief fund, the leaders explained. But not even presidential displeasure could check a developing sentiment for the amendment. Progressives supported it because they thought it was fair, and conservative Republicans rallied behind it in the hope that its inclusion would cause the bill to be defeated in the House. However, its sponsors realized that they faced a hard fight. Huey directed their strategy, and as a part of his preparation he came onto the floor with a list of absent senators who were paired for and against the amendment.

He revealed the purpose of the list when the vote was called. Standing by the side of Senator L. J. Dickinson, a conservative Republican leader, he instructed Dickinson how to cast Republican

[1] Benjamin Stolberg: "Dr. Huey and Mr. Long," *Nation* CXLI (September 25, 1935), 344.

pairs for the amendment. The roll call disclosed a tie, forty-three votes for the amendment and forty-three votes against it. Huey instantly recalled that Dickinson had transferred his own pair to a senator who had later come in and voted. Dickinson could not vote but he could still use his pair. Dashing over to the Republican, Huey told him to transfer his vote to the absent Mrs. Caraway. Dickinson thereupon cast her vote for the amendment and broke the tie. Huey's quick thinking dazzled even the Washington correspondents. One of them, noting that Huey had now inflicted two defeats on the President within two weeks, added thoughtfully: "He has shown his strength."[2]

Huey relished his latest victory, but he had not fought this battle just to embarrass the administration. Rather, he had taken up the McCarran amendment because of his devotion to a principle—he believed in economic justice and thought that the amendment represented a step toward this goal. He often responded to such idealistic impulses while simultaneously engaging in the crudest kind of political maneuver. It was a curious duality in him, and he illustrated it to the full during this month of February. He launched a succession of attacks on the administration that were intended to damage Roosevelt by smearing one of the President's most prominent and trusted subordinates with the taint of corruption.

He began the offensive on February 11. He announced in the Senate that he had come into possession of evidence suggesting corruption in Postmaster General Farley's administration of his department. Therefore he was offering a resolution authorizing the appointment of a special committee to investigate his charges. The resolution listed a hodgepodge of charges: that Farley had operated the Post Office Department to gratify his political and personal whims, had given away free stamps, was implicated in a racing wire service leading to gambling establishments, and had improperly solicited party funds from persons of questionable character. One charge was given special prominence—that Farley was financially interested in companies constructing buildings for the government under the Public Works program and that he had used his influence to get contracts awarded to these concerns even though they were not the low bidders. Huey admitted that the charges were varied. They had to

<hr>

[2] *Congressional Record*, 74 Cong., 1 Sess., pp. 2395–6, debates of February 21, 1935; Phelps Adams, in New York *Sun*, February 22, 1935; George Morris, in Memphis *Commercial Appeal*, February 26, 1935; Clapper in Washington *Post*, n.d., in Long Scrapbooks, XVII.

be, he said, because Farley's "slimy, roaming tentacles" were wrapped around most of the government's activities.[3]

The suddenness of Huey's attack temporarily threw administration leaders off balance. They recognized, however, that the resolution was in reality aimed at the President and that he should decide how to deal with it, and therefore they stalled for time until word could be received from the White House. The word had apparently come down two days later, for then Joe Robinson smoothly proposed that the resolution be referred for action to the committee on post offices, which was stacked with friends of Farley's. Huey opposed the motion, denouncing it as a surrender to Farley's malign influence, but it was adopted. In his remarks Huey leveled for the first time a specific charge at Farley. He asserted that Big Jim had been interested in a company that had bid on the construction of an annex to the New York City post office building. His statement gave concern to administration leaders, who wondered if he had any evidence for it or was merely firing a shot in the dark.[4]

Next, on February 14, Huey moved a resolution requesting Secretary of the Interior Harold L. Ickes to transmit to the Senate certain information gathered by an assistant of Ickes's, Louis Glavis, concerning the Public Works building program. His new move was obviously related in some way to the proposed investigation of Farley, but the leaders did not know how and hence stalled action on his motion while they again checked with the White House. The instructions came down with special speed this time, for on the following day Robinson announced that the leadership did not object to the motion and would let it pass. His concession seemed to indicate that the administration did not fear disclosure of the information in the Glavis report. But certain cabinet officials were secretly perturbed at the prospect. Huey evidently knew that Glavis had conducted for Ickes an investigation of the letting of contracts on the New York post office—but how had he managed to obtain this classified material? He naturally did not tell them that an employee of his had removed a file of documents from Ickes's office.[5]

The Glavis investigation had been a consequence of the divided lines of authority that Roosevelt delighted to set up, that he seemed to think represented the ultimate in good administration. Thus he had apportioned to Ickes's Interior Department the function of disbursing funds for the Public Works program but had assigned the role of

[3] Congressional Record, 74 Cong., 1 Sess., pp. 1782, 1894-6.
[4] Ibid., pp. 1828-41, debates of February 12, 1935.
[5] Ibid., pp. 1904, 1933-9; confidential communication.

supervising the expending of the funds to an agency in Morgenthau's Treasury Department, the division of procurement, headed by Lawrence W. Roberts, a friend of Farley's. Hence both departments had been involved in letting the contracts for the New York post office. Ickes had allocated the required sum of money to the Post Office Department, which then asked the procurement division to seek bids. Two companies submitted similar bids, but the Post Office Department informed Roberts by letter that it preferred the offer of the James Stewart Company, which had not conformed to federal financial regulations until after submitting its bid and which reportedly had some kind of relationship with Farley. Roberts promptly accepted the recommendation and destroyed the letter.

Such a gross irregularity could not be kept secret, however, and rumors of it eventually reached Ickes, who was highly disturbed at the possibility that corruption had entered the Public Works program. Calling in Glavis, he instructed the subordinate to discreetly investigate the conditions under which the bids had been let. Glavis was soon able to ascertain what seemed to be the facts—that somebody in the Post Office Department had been interested in throwing the contract to the Stewart Company and that Roberts in the procurement division had cooperated with the effort. Obeying Ickes's injunction to be circumspect, Glavis did not let Farley or Morgenthau know that he was investigating their departments. He revealed his findings only to Ickes and then, for some reason, to a Democratic senatorial friend. Ickes kept the information to himself, but the senator revealed it to Morgenthau, who was enraged that Ickes had secretly investigated his department. But Morgenthau was also frightened at Glavis's evidence against Roberts, and he quietly shifted the administration of the procurement division to another official and readvertised for bids on the New York post office. And there the episode would have ended, safely buried, if Huey had not forced it into the open.[6]

These tangled and tortuous maneuvers were not known to Roosevelt, who was as surprised as his Senate leaders at Huey's attack on Farley. Naturally disturbed, the President moved promptly to get the facts, first calling in Ickes to ask if Glavis had conducted an investigation of Farley's activities. He told Ickes that he was disposed to let Huey's resolution pass unless there was something in the Interior Department's files "seriously reflecting upon Farley" (or so Ickes, who kept a diary, unblushingly recorded his words). Ickes

[6] John Martin Blum, ed.: *From the Morgenthau Diaries: Years of Crisis, 1928–1938* (New York, 1959), pp. 87–90.

admitted that Glavis had made an investigation but insisted that his report contained nothing damaging to Farley. Heartened by this assurance, Roosevelt then met with Ickes, Morgenthau, and Farley, who had been hastily summoned to return from a vacation in Florida. The President was still seeking information and must have been troubled by some that he received—for example, the disclosure that the Post Office Department had solicited a contract for the Stewart Company—but now he was primarily interested in devising a strategy to meet Huey's attack.

He decided on one quickly. The administration could not be put in a position of denying the investigation demanded by Huey and, furthermore, had little to fear from it. Therefore it would cooperate with the inquiry. He directed that the Interior, Treasury, and Post Office departments search their files for any information bearing on the New York post office matter and send it to the Senate. He also urged Farley to voluntarily appear as a witness before the Senate post office committee, but Big Jim begged off, saying that he did not want the Kingfish to get at him. Instead, he would send a written statement to the committee denying Huey's charges.[7]

The news that the administration was going to brave the investigation through startled Washington correspondents, who knew that Huey had strong if covert support for his move from many of his colleagues. Progressive senators particularly, of both parties, hoped that he would be able to prove his charges against Farley, whom they detested as a spoilsman and a conservative. Huey would confound the administration strategy if he could come up with some real evidence against Farley, the correspondents believed.[8]

Huey, after introducing his two resolutions, had had to dash to Baton Rouge to direct the February special session of the legislature. But immediately on returning he took the floor, on March 4. Looking impudently at Vice-President Garner and Robinson, he demanded to know why the report Ickes had been asked to furnish had not been transmitted. There was obviously something "dead up the creek," he challenged. Robinson fell into the trap. The report was ready, he cried, but the Senate had had to wait for Long to return

[7] Harold L. Ickes: *The Secret Diary of Harold L. Ickes: The First Thousand Days, 1933–36* (New York, 1953), pp. 294–302, entry of February 20, 1935; James A. Farley: *Behind the Ballots* (New York, 1938), pp. 244–9. Ickes was highly circumspect in the account of the affair he extracted for his published diary, giving no indication of who in the Post Office Department had written the letter to Roberts.

[8] John T. Lambert, in Washington *Herald*, February 20, 1935; Herbert C. Plummer, in Oakland *Tribune*, dispatch of February 23, in Hammond Scrapbook.

from running his state under martial law. The Kingfish coolly replied that just one part of Louisiana was under martial law, "the Standard Oil domicile," the only part Robinson would know about. Ignoring Robinson, who was angrily waving the report at him, Huey continued that he did not care if the administration refused to produce the requested information. He had enough material under "lock and key" to prove his case against Farley, he asserted. In fact, he could inform the Senate of a sensational development that had just broken: Farley was about to resign and his successor had already been chosen by Roosevelt.

The effect of this statement on the Senate was revealing. Most of the senators accepted it without question, although it was unsupported by evidence: they were ready to believe that Huey had something on Farley. Robinson rushed from the chamber to telephone the White House and on returning stated that he could deny Huey's allegation on information from "the highest source." Huey insolently asked what the source was. "The President of the United States," Robinson shouted, banging his hands on his desk. That source had often been mistaken, Huey leered. At this Robinson's face reddened with anger, and he advanced toward Huey with clenched fist. A fight might have occurred if Garner had not shouted an order to Huey to take his seat.[9]

Huey's performance in the bitter debate was a brilliant example of political effrontery. He had produced no evidence against Farley, only implying that he had some, and yet he had managed to put the administration on the defensive, to suggest that it was trying to cover up for the postmaster general. His success enraged some men in the Roosevelt circle, who had long thought that the administration should not wait to be attacked by Huey but should attack him. Particularly aroused was Hugh S. Johnson, the former head of the National Recovery Administration, known as General Johnson from his army days, and a salty and colorful character who considered himself to be a master of political invective, fully capable of dealing with Huey Long.

Johnson carefully chose a time to deliver his attack. On the night of March 4, the day of the debate, he spoke at a banquet in New York tendered to him by the editors of a national magazine. The affair was carried by one of the radio network systems, thus assuring

[9] *Congressional Record*, 74 Cong., 1 Sess., pp. 2338–48; New York *Daily News*, March 5, 1935; New Orleans *Times-Picayune*, March 5, 1935; Duluth *Herald*, March 6, 1935.

him of a national audience. He made the most of his opportunity. Announcing that the title of his address was "The Pied Pipers," he launched into a tirade against Huey and Coughlin, the minstrels who with false promises of economic salvation were leading the nation to destruction. "You can laugh at Father Coughlin—you can snort at Huey Long—but this country was never under a greater menace," he cried.

Long and Coughlin, "the great Louisiana demagogue and this political padre," had formed an alliance, Johnson continued, and their hope was to see an "American Hitler" riding into Washington at the head of troops: "That would be definite enough to Huey because he knows what part of the horse he can be." The diatribe ran on, becoming ever more bitter in its charges and more extravagant in its comparisons—"this priest and Punchinello," these two "Catilines" were preaching "not construction but destruction—not reform but revolution." It ended at last with an exhortation to the people to stand by Roosevelt: "Our sole hope lies in him."[1]

The speech excited national attention, partly because of Johnson's prominence and association with the administration, but mainly because of its studied virulence. Observers wondered how the Kingfish would react to the attack. Would he be cowed by the polished brilliance of Johnson's language and shrink from replying? Or would he be thrown into a rage and lash back crudely and demagogically? The speculators had to wait only until the next day for their answer. At an early hour Huey gained the Senate floor and smiling benignly began what was apparently going to be a reply to Johnson.

"Last night, while I was undertaking to throw myself into the arms of Morpheus, I thought I heard my name being mentioned over the radio in the next room," Huey opened. He had thereupon turned on the radio in his room and "lo and behold" what did he get but Hugh Johnson on the pied pipers, Long and Coughlin. And who was this Johnson who had seemed so virtuous? Why, he had once been "a hired hand" of the banking house of Bernard Baruch, which had as its motto "Presidents: You make 'em; we break 'em." Johnson had been put into the administration by Baruch to do the latter's bidding and had promptly established the N.R.A., which should have been called the National Racketeering Administration or the National Ruin Administration. The N.R.A. experiment had failed and Johnson had been repudiated by the administration, yet

---

[1] *Time*, March 18, 1935, pp. 10–14; Schlesinger: *Politics of Upheaval*, pp. 244–5.

when it needed a defender it could find no one but him. How low it had sunk, to have to call upon one "rebuked in its own order."

At this point in his remarks Huey suddenly dropped Johnson, as though disdaining to attack such an inconsequential opponent, and turned to other targets—Roosevelt, who had refused to take the right course to deal with the depression, Farley, who had advised the President to take the wrong course, and Robinson, who had blindly supported the Roosevelt–Farley program in the Senate. Looking directly at Robinson and reminding the majority leader that he would come up for re-election in 1936, Huey shouted a threat: "Beware! beware! If things go on as they have been going on, you will not be here next year." Then, as the galleries rocked with laughter, he strolled nonchalantly from the chamber.

Robinson rose immediately to reply. Quivering with anger, he ignored the Senate rule that one member should not reflect upon another. "The Senate and the galleries have just witnessed a demonstration," he began. "Egotism, arrogance, and ignorance are seldom displayed in the Senate of the United States. They require a measure of talent possessed only by the Senator from Louisiana." That senator had for month after month disgusted the Senate with attacks upon "men who were superior to him," but now it was time that "the manhood of the Senate should assert itself," that the senator from Louisiana "be made to know and take his proper place in a body composed for the most part of gentlemen." Robinson reserved his most unparliamentary remark for the last: he apologized for paying attention to the "ravings of one who anywhere else than in the Senate would be called a madman."

Huey returned to the chamber as Robinson was concluding and was told by his secretary what the majority leader had said. Claiming the floor, he protested that in his remarks he had not violated the rule on reflecting on another member, whereas Robinson had flagrantly flouted it. He went on to relate that he and Robinson had been induced by a mutual friend to make a truce after the conclusion of the Overton investigation. That truce was now off. "There will be no more compromise," he vowed. "There will be no more shaking of hands." He would undoubtedly go into Arkansas to campaign against Robinson, he said, not out of personal animosity but for the sake of the Democratic party. "The Democratic party is now in the ascendancy," he ended. "It did not come into the ascendancy on the doctrines of the Senator from Arkansas." His threat to Robinson brought other conservative Democrats to their feet to shout maledictions at him, but he did not seem perturbed. At the close of the session he walked past Robinson's desk and patted the latter's shoulder indulgently.[2]

He could be patronizing because he had carried off the honors of the debate. He had been, in comparison with Robinson and other administration senators, restrained and dignified, and although he had baited them to commit their outbursts, he seemed to be a victim of crude abuse. As an additional result of the exchange, he had received an enormous amount of national publicity, and this he determined to keep going by continuing his feud with Johnson. He therefore demanded of the National Broadcasting Company, which had carried Johnson's speech, equal time to answer the general. The company, knowing a good attraction when it was offered, readily granted him thirty minutes on the night of March 7. It failed, however, to gauge his drawing power: every station on its coast-to-coast network ordered the Kingfish. When Huey learned of this development, he presented another demand to the company. He said that he thought he should be paid but that he would settle for fifteen minutes extra time. The company hastily agreed.[3]

An estimated twenty-five million persons sat at their radios on the night of his broadcast. They expected a typical Kingfish show, an eruption of abuse that would rival Johnson's. But Huey barely alluded to the general, "the late and lamented, the pampered ex-Crown Prince." "It will serve no purpose to our distressed people for me to call my opponents even more bitter names than they call me," he said. "Even were I able, I have not the time to present my side of the argument and match them in billingsgate or profanity." The trouble with the administration was that it wanted to blame Huey Long for its failures, he went on. Hence it had sent Johnson and other "spellbinders" out "gunning" for him. But it could not shift the responsibility for the continued depression from itself. He described its confused program to cope with the depression. "What is it?" he asked. "Is it government? Maybe so. It looks more like St. Vitus dance." And all the time a plan that would have worked had been available to the administration. He himself had proposed it to the President, but "Mr. Franklin De-La-No Roosefelt" would not listen. It was the Share Our Wealth plan, the plan of God.

He had taken only five minutes or so to dispose of Johnson and

[2] *Congressional Record*, 74 Cong., 1 Sess., pp. 2933–8, 2944–56, debates of March 5, 1935; *The New York Times*, March 6, 1935; *Time*, March 18, 1935, pp. 14–16.
[3] O'Donnell and Fleeson, in New York *Daily News*, March 8, 1935; Carter: *American Messiahs*, p. 8.

Roosevelt, so he had forty minutes remaining to explain Share Our Wealth to the largest audience he had yet reached. He presented his plan in detail, supported it with scholarly data, and defended it with restraint. His whole performance, in fact, was marked by restraint. Again he appeared as a man of reason and calm and made his opponents seem to be men of unreason. A perceptive correspondent, summing up the controversy, wrote that Johnson and Roosevelt between them had managed to transform the Kingfish "from a clown into a real political menace."[4]

On March 8, a Friday and the day following his broadcast, Huey unleashed a new kind of offensive against the administration. The Senate leadership had brought up for consideration the important War Department appropriation bill and was anxious to pass it quickly and then enact other pending measures before adjourning for the weekend. Huey did not speak on the bill, but he asked countless questions about it that caused other senators to speak at length. In this manner he kept the debate going for five hours, and at last it dawned on the leaders that he was trying to prevent a vote on the appropriation bill, that he was conducting a "silent filibuster." His performance disappointed a huge crowd of spectators who had been drawn by a report that he would speak on the Farley investigation, their lines stretching from the chamber out to the street. Finally the sergeant-at-arms begged him for some word to give the mob. "Tell 'em to go home," he said.

He did not take the floor until late in the afternoon, when it seemed that the Senate would balk at a continuation of his question-and-answer technique. But then he held it, discussing at length the N.R.A., Farley, and other subjects unrelated to the appropriation bill. He admitted now that he was filibustering. "The fact of the case is," he said, "I do not know what the War Department bill is." With equal frankness he admitted his purpose. Among the measures scheduled for a vote before the weekend adjournment was the Work Relief bill, which had come back from the House with a watered-down version of the McCarran prevailing-wage amendment. He was going to hold off a vote on the relief bill until Father Coughlin could make a radio address supporting the original amendment. As he could obviously accomplish his purpose, the leadership capitulated. Carter Glass said that if the Kingfish would permit passage of the War Department bill no action would be taken on the relief measure before the first part of the following week. "All right," said Huey triumphantly. "I agree. O.K."[5]

He quickly discovered that he had misjudged the public sentiment he and Coughlin could rally. The administration had quietly mobilized enough votes to defeat the McCarran amendment, and no effort that he made could save it. He ruefully admitted his error and reluctantly paid tribute to Roosevelt's political skill. The President was a more subtle operator than Hoover, he said: "Hoover is a hoot owl and Roosevelt is a scrootch owl. A hoot owl bangs into the nest and knocks the hen clean off and catches her while she's falling. But a scrootch owl slips into the roost and scrootches up to the hen and talks softly to her. And the hen just falls in love with him, and the next thing you know there ain't no hen."[6]

Roosevelt never publicly complimented Huey's political skill. But the President recognized the dexterity of his rival and in the close circle of New Deal advisers admitted his fear of the Kingfish. One night in the spring, while discussing with a few close associates the evidence of Huey's spreading influence, Roosevelt startled them by saying that he might have to take over as his own some of Long's ideas in order to, as he put it, "steal Long's thunder." He was not alarmed enough to do this as yet, and he would not do it at all if he could devise some method to destroy Huey. During the spring and summer months he devoted increasing thought to what method he could employ. For a while he considered using the constitutional guarantee of a republican form of government to the states as a basis for national action against Louisiana, but he was informed by the Justice Department that the move would be of doubtful legality. He then came up with the idea of a joint congressional investigation of affairs in Louisiana, but was told that his legislative leaders were averse to the proposal. Frustrated, Roosevelt resigned himself to using, at least for the time being, more conventional weapons against his great enemy.[7]

The President's spirits were momentarily lifted when Secretary of the Interior Ickes refurbished a weapon that had previously been used against the Kingfish. In April, at a press conference, Ickes an-

[5] *Congressional Record*, 74 Cong., 1 Sess., pp. 3206–10; *The New York Times*, March 12, 1935; Franklin L. Burdette: *Filibustering in the Senate* (Princeton, 1940), pp. 178–9.

[6] *Congressional Record*, 74 Cong., 1 Sess., pp. 3442–7, 3452, 3484, 3532–41, 3592–5, 3609–13, debates of March 12, 13, and 14, 1935; New Orleans *Item*, March 25, 1935.

[7] Raymond Moley: *After Seven Years* (New York, 1939), pp. 304–5; Schlesinger: *Politics of Upheaval*, pp. 250–1.

nounced that unless Huey ceased his efforts to put federal spending in Louisiana under state control, all federal allotments "down there" might be canceled. "No public works money is going to build up any share-the-wealth machine," the secretary vowed. Huey, obviously not worried by the threat, retorted that Louisiana was a sovereign state and that Ickes could go "slambang to hell." Ickes, a master of pungent wit who enjoyed a good exchange, snapped back that the trouble with Long was that he had "halitosis of the intellect." Huey, also enjoying the exchange and recognizing in it another opportunity to reap publicity at the expense of the administration, proclaimed that he would reply to Ickes in the Senate on April 22.[8]

His announcement drew a huge crowd of spectators to the Senate on that day, many of them Easter visitors in the capital from all over the country. The Washington correspondents, impressed in spite of themselves, estimated that the audience was the largest ever to jam the Senate chamber. From its close-packed ranks rose appreciative murmurs as Huey walked down the aisle to his seat, a model of sartorial splendor in a fawn-colored silk suit, lavender shirt, and brown shoes with white trimming.

He did not disappoint the crowd when he gained the floor, launching immediately into a spirited and satiric description of the men who were running the government in "this third year of our reigning empire of St. Vitus." They were "the prime minister," Farley, "the Nabob of New York"; "the lord high chamberlain," Ickes, "the chinch bug of Chicago"; "the expired and lamented royal block," Johnson, "the oo-la-la of Oklahoma"; and "the honorable lord destroyer," Secretary of Agriculture Henry A. Wallace (who advocated the destruction of farm products as a way of getting rid of the agricultural surplus), "the ignoramus of Iowa." And presiding over this strange court was "Prince Franklin," who when he wanted to study the problems of the depression had himself invited to go cruising on the yacht *Nourmahal* owned by his millionaire friend Vincent Astor and therefore should be known as "the knight of the Nourmahal."

This gang was not going to run his state, the Kingfish concluded. Louisiana intended to have a voice in determining how federal money was spent within its boundaries. The audience, which had roared at his sallies at the Roosevelt "court," overlooked the fact that he had said something very serious and important. At a time when the federal government was just beginning to spend large sums of

[8] New York *World-Telegram*, April 16, 1935; Ickes: *Secret Diary*, pp. 346–7, entry of April 19, 1935.

money to influence the economy he had contended that the states should be partners in the spending and had warned that if they were not they would sink in power.[9]


EARLY IN 1935 Huey began to receive invitations to speak at various places in the country. In February he addressed the Georgia legislature in the capitol at Atlanta, extolling Share Our Wealth, and later conferred with Governor Eugene Talmadge, who, though an arrant conservative, affected to be a spokesman of the farmers and as proof of his devotion to rural interests wore red suspenders. Talmadge voiced delight with Huey's attack on Roosevelt and presented his visitor with a pair of red suspenders but denied that he agreed with the Share Our Wealth doctrine or had made a deal to support Huey for President. Huey publicly praised Talmadge, but to a private gathering of Georgians he blurted out his real opinion of the governor and his organization. "It's a goddamned bush league outfit," he said.[1]

In March he appeared in Philadelphia to address a meeting sponsored by the Congress Club, an organization that had Republican leanings and that probably engaged him in the hope of hearing an attack on Roosevelt. He spoke to an audience of fifteen thousand persons, who filled every seat in the hall. Realizing that it was largely a conservative crowd, he tailored his remarks accordingly, concentrating on Roosevelt and subordinating Share Our Wealth. The speech was warmly received, and after the meeting a former mayor told reporters that if Huey ran for President he would roll up at least 250,000 votes in the city.[2]

Later in March Huey journeyed to Columbia, South Carolina, where he was to speak to a student audience at the state university. It was an invitation he had angled to get and a meeting at which he particularly wanted to make a good impression. He had decided to enroll students at universities all over the country in the Share Our Wealth organization, and he had picked the University of South Carolina as the place to start his drive. To prepare the way for him, he had sent one of his student followers from LSU on ahead to con-

[9] Baltimore *Evening Sun*, April 22, 1935; New Orleans *Item*, April 23, 1935; *Congressional Record*, 74 Cong., 1 Sess., pp. 6109–13.

[1] Atlanta *Constitution*, February 6, 1935; *The New York Times*, February 6, 1935; Reinhard H. Luthin: *American Demagogues: Twentieth Century* (Boston, 1954), p. 193; William C. Turpin.

[2] Philadelphia *Inquirer*, March 15, 1935; Philadelphia *Record*, March 15, 1935; Boston *Record*, March 15, 1935.

fer with the Carolina student leaders. He also sent Gerald Smith through the state to organize Share Our Wealth clubs.[3]

The trip began auspiciously. At Charlotte, North Carolina, where he detrained for the night to break the long trip, he was met at the railroad station by a crowd of over a thousand persons, and when he went to his hotel several hundred people followed him and sought admittance to his room. One spectator, overcome at seeing his hero, exclaimed: "Good God, if there ain't the Kingfish himself." Three bodyguards sat at the door of his room and let enter only those visitors who said that they were LSU graduates or parents of students attending LSU. He amazed the parents by identifying the students, even telling one startled father what instrument his son played in the band.[4]

But on reaching Columbia Huey found that a controversy had developed over his speaking appearance. Some members of the university faculty had declared that he was not a fit person to address students and had demanded that his meeting be canceled. Affecting to be above such petty bickering, he canceled the meeting himself, but then invited several hundred students to have lunch with him in the university dining hall, where he talked to them informally and won their signed adherence to Share Our Wealth. Later he paid a courtesy call on Governor Olin D. Johnston, who had made it obvious that he did not want to be called on, and told the governor that he would like to speak on the capitol grounds. The denial of a forum at the university had been well publicized in the local press, and Johnston could hardly deny the request. From a hastily erected platform, Huey addressed a crowd variously estimated to number from five thousand to fourteen thousand persons. His attack on Roosevelt and concentrated wealth was loudly applauded, and he told associates traveling with him that he would remain in the state and speak at other towns. "South Carolina is the strongest state for Roosevelt," he explained. "If I can sell myself here, I can sell myself anywhere."

He went to extreme lengths to sell himself as he traveled through the state. In one small town he instructed a follower to get him a bench to speak from and to find a woman obviously in dire poverty to sit on it, in order to, as he explained, steady the bench. The mystified employee complied with the request and then watched in fascination as Huey built his speech around the woman—this

[3] Joseph Cawthorn.
[4] Charlotte *Observer*, March 23, 1935; Ray Erwin.

poor creature who because wealth was concentrated had no comforts such as chairs in her home and had naturally seated herself on
the bench. At every meeting Huey's helpers would pass out post-
cards and pencils to the people and ask them to mail back the cards
after marking one of two statements on them: "I will" or "I will not
vote for Huey Long for President." Over 140,000 cards marked
"I will" were returned, and simultaneously Gerald Smith reported
that he had enrolled some 60,000 Carolinians in Share Our Wealth
clubs. The tour had been a huge success except for one flaw: the
state's officialdom from Governor Johnston down had given Huey
a big cold shoulder. A brother of the governor's told Huey the
reason—a telephone call from the White House had warned that all
federal allotments to the state would be cut off if any favor was
shown to the Kingfish.[5]

Huey was delighted at the invitations he was getting to speak;
they were a recognition of his growing national stature. But the ones
he had received so far had been from local groups, and when he
spoke he reached only a local audience. In April, he therefore eagerly accepted an invitation to address the annual conference of the
National Farmers' Holiday Association in Des Moines, Iowa, since
the organization could give him a national forum. The association
was the most militant farm organization in the country, advocating,
among other planks, that agricultural producers withhold supplies
from markets to raise prices (take a "holiday" from production), and
its president, Milo Reno, believed that the farmers would have to find
economic salvation in a third political party. Reno meant, in fact,
to weld together a new party by the election of 1936, composed of
the various radical factions in the country, and he hoped that the
party could be formed at the Des Moines conference. He invited to it
all the radical luminaries: Huey; Father Coughlin; Floyd Olson, the
Farmer-Labor governor of Minnesota; Dr. Francis Townsend, the
old-age pension prophet; and others. Every one of them but Huey
found an excuse not to attend.[6]

Huey thus was the stellar attraction at Des Moines, the center of
attention from the moment he arrived in town on April 27. He made
immediate news by declining an invitation to address the Iowa sen-

[5] Charleston *News & Courier*, March 24, 1935; Columbia *Free Press*, March 29,
1935; unidentified clipping, n.d., in Long Scrapbooks, XIX; Joseph Cawthorn.
[6] Donald R. McCoy: *Angry Voices: Left of Center Politics in the New Deal Era*
(Lawrence, Kan., 1958), p. 116; Carter: *American Messiahs*, pp. 151-2. For valuable
information on Reno and his plans, I am indebted to Professor John L. Shover, who
is writing a life of the farm leader.

ate, which had been contrived by Republicans, saying that he preferred to have breakfast in his hotel room with the queen of the Drake Relays, then in progress, and her court of honor. The queen, at least, was not favorably impressed by the Kingfish. Asked by reporters what he had talked about, she said disgustedly: "Politics and himself." Later in the day he unexpectedly appeared on the field at the Relays and was booed by the fans, who either wanted to show their disapproval of his politics or his interruption of the events.

He found a friendlier audience in the afternoon—ten thousand farmers, members of the Farm Holiday Association, gathered in the grandstand at the Iowa State Fair grounds. They cheered when he was introduced by Reno and cheered almost every part of his speech, which was a composite of several of his recent Senate and radio addresses. He repeated his listing of the Roosevelt royal court, which drew appreciative laughter, denounced Roosevelt for being no different from Hoover, and defined a New Deal liberal: "It's all right to say it, but be damn sure you don't intend to do it."

From this light and humorous beginning he launched into a long and serious analysis of Share Our Wealth, replete with statistics illustrating how wealth had been concentrated and how it could be redistributed. Maybe there were some persons in the audience who did not understand his data, he said. "Well, you don't have to. Just shut your damn eyes and don't understand it, if you don't want to," or, in short, just believe it. He concluded by asking all those in the crowd who believed in Share Our Wealth to raise their hands. The showing was unanimous. His presentation fascinated one observer, the famous University of Chicago English professor Robert Morss Lovett, who was reporting the meeting for a liberal magazine. Lovett had come to the meeting distrusting Huey but now found him oddly attractive: "an engagingly boyish figure, jovial and impudent, Tom Sawyer in a toga."[7]

No third party had emerged from the Des Moines conference, and Huey in his address had revealed nothing concerning his own plans for 1936. As he left the platform, however, he said to reporters: "I could take this state like a whirlwind."[8]

Political observers judged that he could take a number of states if he decided to run for President—certainly several Southern states, probably some in the Middle West, and perhaps some in other sec-

[7] Des Moines *Register*, April 28, 1935; New York *Herald-Tribune*, April 28, 1935; Robert Morss Lovett: "Huey Long Invades the Middle West," *New Republic*, LXXXIII (May 15, 1935), 10–12.
[8] Des Moines *Register*, April 28, 1935.

tions. He was reported to be particularly strong in California, where an estimated 672 Share Our Wealth clubs formed the nucleus of his organization, which included also many of Upton Sinclair's End Poverty in America clubs, and where the *American Progress* was ordered in lots of one thousand by the largest newsstands in Los Angeles. But how would Huey use his strength? Would he go to the Democratic convention with a bloc of delegates pledged to him and attempt to wrest the Democratic nomination from Roosevelt? Or would he run as a third-party candidate backed by all the factions of the radical left? And if he did run, what did he hope to accomplish? Did he think that he could be elected—or did he intend to take enough normally Democratic votes away from Roosevelt to throw the election to the Republicans?[9]

Huey at various times during the spring of 1935 gave differing answers to the questions about his intention. Once he told reporters that "positively" there would be a Share Our Wealth candidate in the race in 1936 but he refused to say that he would be that candidate. On another occasion he offered to support the Republicans if they would put up as their candidate a progressive like Senator Borah. But he never completely ruled out the possibility that he would run himself. "I might have a good parade to offer before we get through," he observed in a Senate speech. "I never bar myself from anybody away in advance. I am always open to propositions as they occur in these changing cycles of time."[1]

[9] John Kelley, in Portland *Morning Oregonian*, n.d., probably March 1935, and unidentified clipping, March 3, 1935, in Long Scrapbooks, XVII; *New Republic,* March 6, 1935, p. 87; Los Angeles *Evening Herald*, March 18, 1935; *Time*, April 1, 1935, pp. 15–17; *National End Poverty in America News*, April 5 and 12, 1935; unidentified clipping, April 23, 1935, in Long Scrapbooks, XVII; Baltimore *Evening Sun*, April 28, 1935.

[1] *Time*, April 1, 1935, pp. 15–17; *The New York Times*, April 25, 1935; *American Progress*, July 1935.

# CHAPTER 29

# *Lay Over, Huey*

A T THE DES MOINES conference Huey was told by reporters of a news item from New Orleans that had just come over the wire: Representative Joe Fisher had been convicted by a federal jury of income tax evasion and sentenced to serve eighteen months in the Atlanta penitentiary. The Kingfish refused to be drawn into a statement. "He's a good friend of mine," he said, "but I've got too many relatives in the pen to make any comments about it."[1]

The federal government, following Elmer Irey's schedule of moving first against a minor figure in the Long hierarchy, had brought Fisher to trial late in March. Also conforming to Irey's strategy, the government had prepared a case that not only impeached Fisher for tax evasion but also was designed to reveal evidence of corruption in the Long machine. Thus it alleged that Fisher had amassed most of his unreported income through crooked contracts with the state Highway Commission: that he had sold clam shells and other road materials to the commission at an exorbitant price, that he had done business with it under an assumed name, and that he had placed on its payrolls the names of several men who did not work and collected their salary checks. Fisher, testifying in his own defense, denied the charges and claimed that he had distributed most of the money he had received from the commission to political helpers. The bulk of his income was derived from systematic gambling,

---

[1] New Orleans *Times-Picayune*, April 28, 1935.

he asserted. "Gambling isn't fun, your honor," Joe solemnly told the court. "It's hard work."[2]

Huey's flippancy on being told of Fisher's conviction masked a concern that had been growing on him. He knew now that something had gone wrong in his organization: some of his men were taking in more money than they should. He had always permitted them to take in a little, believing that they had a right to an extra reward for their labors for him and believing also that in politics, at least in Louisiana, some "sweetening" was necessary to make the system work. "Huey assumed a certain amount of corruption," one intimate related, "relatively little stuff, enough to make a good living." But he had laid down as a rule for his organization that the grafting must be moderate, kept within strict limits. His restriction was not based on moral grounds, in the classic meaning of morality, but on a concept of what was sound politics: if the corruption got out of hand the machine, and hence the whole political structure, would be weakened. Or as he perhaps would have put it, large-scale grafting was politically immoral.[3]

But now, as a result of the federal indictments of certain of his leaders and his own observations of other leaders, he recognized that corruption was entering his machine. Angered that his rule of moderation had been violated, he summoned before him Abe Shushan, who would come up next for trial in October, and demanded to know if the charges against the "collector" were true. "Goddamn you," he shouted at Abe, "I've got a notion to put you in jail myself." Shushan, more shaken by this threat than by the federal indictment, swore by the highest authority he could think of, his dead grandmother, that he was innocent of the charges. Huey seemed satisfied, but he still nourished suspicions of other leaders. "They'll be stealing the emblems off the capitol pretty soon," he told his secretary.[4]

At times he seemed resigned to the fact that some of his men

---

[2] *The New York Times*, April 3, 1935; New Orleans *Item*, April 20, 1935; New Orleans *Item-Tribune*, n.d., but April 1935 in Long Scrapbooks, XVIII; T. O. Harris: *The Kingfish: Huey P. Long, Dictator* (New Orleans, 1938), pp. 228–9; Elmer Irey and William J. Slocum: *The Tax Dodgers* (New York, 1949), p. 95. Irey claimed that the Long hierarchy had decided to sacrifice Fisher, to, in Irey's words, "let him ride." The meaning of the statement is unclear. The Long organization could hardly have prevented the trial from being held, and Fisher was vigorously defended by an able lawyer who was close to Huey, Hugh Wilkinson. Fisher, in conversation with me, denied that he was guilty of the charges against him or that he was sacrificed. "I didn't think that they could convict me," he said, adding ruefully: "But they did."

[3] James P. O'Connor; Robert Brothers; John B. Fournet; confidential communications.

[4] George H. Maines; confidential communications; Earle J. Christenberry.

were corrupt. He remarked on several occasions that it was impossible to build an organization that was completely pure. Even Jesus
Christ had had one apostle who had gone wrong, he said. But these
moods were rare. He determined finally that he would clean up his
organization from top to bottom after the state and national elections
of 1936 were safely over. An associate who recalled his plan was
asked if many leaders would have been dismissed. "There would have
been a flood from them jumping in the Mississippi River," this man
said appreciatively.[5]

With his usual introspection, Huey tried to analyze the causes
that had produced corruption in his organization. He decided finally
that he himself was the unwitting cause: he had erected too great a
power structure in Louisiana, one that only he could operate and
that lesser men were tempted to misuse. He said despairingly to a
friend: "If I don't live long enough to undo the centralization of government I've built up in this state, all these men around me are going
to end up in the penitentiary." He repeatedly warned his associates
that if he were to die suddenly they must not attempt to use the
power that he had created. They would land in prison, he said.[6]

Curiously, Huey did not consider a related factor that helped to
produce corruption—the huge sums of money that the machine
constantly collected to remain in power. These revenues, coming
from salary deductions of state employees, donations from corporations doing business with the state, and contributions from various
backers, flowed through many hands in the organization, and inevitably some of the money stuck to the hands that gathered it—
there was so much of it that some men could not resist taking a
little and then more, and finally devising their own deals with the
state. Elmer Irey's agents were correct in suspecting that some of
Huey's associates were not reporting the revenues they received.
What the agents did not realize was that in most cases the bulk of
the unreported money went into the campaign chest of the Long
organization.

In the organization this chest was known as the "deduct box,"
because most of the contributions to it came from salary deductions.
While Huey was governor, the box was kept in a safe in his suite at
the Roosevelt Hotel. According to some associates, when he went to
Washington as senator, he took the box with him and placed it in
a safe at the Mayflower Hotel, his first residence in the capital. Later

[5] Harvey G. Fields; Rose McConnell Long; John B. Fournet; Robert Brothers;
Earle J. Christenberry.
[6] Fred Blanche; W. C. Pegues.

he removed it to a vault at the Riggs National Bank. But other friends think the box remained at the Roosevelt. The amount of money in it kept growing, and by 1935, according to associates, it had risen to a million dollars or more. The box also contained affidavits of material damaging to Roosevelt and other enemies. It was Huey's campaign chest for the election of 1936.[7]

Many persons wondered about Huey's own income. He lived lavishly, maintaining hotel quarters in Washington, Baton Rouge, and New Orleans, as well as a home in the last city. He dashed around Washington in an expensive car driven by a chauffeur, made numerous train trips to New Orleans, and was rumored to own one hundred expensive suits and dozens of costly shirts. Obviously he could not live as he did on a senator's salary. He must have other sources of income, and these must be lavish. Irey's treasury agents thought that like his subordinates he was taking corrupt money.[8]

One source of his income was public knowledge in Louisiana. In 1935 he acted as an attorney for the state in a number of legal cases and for his service in some of them received large fees. Early in the year he represented the Public Service Commission in several efforts it was making to force utility companies to lower their rates. When the companies agreed to adjust the rates without going to court, as they frequently did when he appeared in the cases, he charged the state only a small fee for his labor. But if a company chose to fight the Commission and take the matter to court, he charged a large fee if he won the case, because in that event the company had to pay the expenses of the state's lawyer. In total fees as the Commission's lawyer during 1935 he received $125,000. He did not, however, retain all of this sum. He had to pay out part of it to other lawyers who had assisted him and for various expenses connected with the case. Moreover, he returned an undeterminable amount to

[7] Seymour Weiss; Robert Brothers; Earle J. Christenberry; Harvey G. Fields; Russell B. Long. Shushan came to trial in October 1935, a month after Huey's death, and was acquitted. His defense was that the revenue he received had been political contributions which he held as agent. In May 1936 the United States attorney for Louisiana, Rene Viosca, announced that since the Shushan case had been the government's strongest, he was dismissing the indictments against the other Long leaders. It was widely charged in the press and elsewhere that the government had dropped the cases in return for a pledge from Huey's political heirs that Louisiana would support Roosevelt at the Democratic national convention. In 1939 the famous "Louisiana scandals" broke, resulting in new indictments and imprisonment of a number of Long leaders. Huey's warning to his lieutenants not to attempt to use his powers had gone unheeded.

[8] Chicago *Tribune*, May 5, 1935.

the Commission, saying that it needed money to carry on its activities. The amount that he kept for himself was probably modest.[9]

More profitable to him was an arrangement he made with the Tax Commission to act as its attorney in collecting back taxes due the state from corporations and individuals whose property had not previously been assessed or had been assessed incorrectly. To assist him in this endeavor, he formed a partnership with an Opelousas lawyer, and their fee was to be one third of the taxes collected as a result of their placing new properties on the assessment rolls. They succeeded in securing for the state during 1935 a total of $206,367, which was paid directly to Huey as the Tax Commission's lawyer. He deposited the money in an Alexandria bank, entitling the account "Huey Pierce Long, Attorney for the State of Louisiana, Tax Reclamation," and promptly turned over to the state its two thirds, or $137,578. This left as his share $68,789, of which he withdrew $18,335, possibly to compensate his partner. The remaining $50,454 he left in the special account with the odd semi-official title.[1]

Huey's relationship with the Tax Commission occasioned only moderate criticism in Louisiana. What there was came from antis, who were not so much disturbed at the arrangement as they were at the high fees they thought he was receiving. Most people thought the state had made a smart deal: he was the best lawyer that could be employed for the purpose and he was recovering large sums of tax money, much larger than his fees. It was revealing of the moral climate of Louisiana that hardly anyone questioned the propriety of his employment. Yet he had been employed at his own demand, by a state government that he controlled and that jumped to obey his every whim. Moreover, he was certain to win any tax adjustment issue that he took up, for it would be a foolhardy corporation that

[9] Anderson, in St. Louis *Post-Dispatch*, February 10, 1935; New Orleans *Item-Tribune*, March 19, 1935; New Orleans *Times-Picayune*, March 19, 1935; *Time*, April 1, 1935, pp. 15–17; New Orleans *Item*, April 2, 1935; Baton Rouge *State-Times*, September 11, 1935; Clayton Coleman. No record of an income from the Commission appears in Huey's "succession," the listing of his assets made after his death. It is possible, of course, that he spent the money or placed it in the deduct box. But in the succession there is a record of the money he received as attorney for the state in tax reclamation cases, which suggests that he retained only a fraction of his income as the Commission's lawyer. See Succession of Huey P. Long, Jr., 215,671, Division B. Civil District Court, Parish of Orleans, New Orleans, La., hereafter cited as Succession of Huey P. Long. I was assisted in securing a copy of this lengthy document by Judge Oliver P. Carriere of New Orleans.

[1] New Orleans *Item*, May 16, 1935; Chicago *Tribune*, May 17, 1935; New Orleans *Item-Tribune*, May 19, 1935; Succession of Huey P. Long.

defied him and took the case to court. His activities were within the law but highly improper. He seemed to realize this, which was perhaps why he kept his fees in a special account, as though he thought he should return them to the state at some time, or would be forced to return them.

The anti-Long press in Louisiana was certain that it knew one source of Huey's income: he and his machine were receiving large revenues from gambling interests in New Orleans and the adjoining parishes of St. Bernard and Jefferson that the state was permitting to operate even though they were illegal. According to the newspapers, the Long organization had a "take" of at least one million dollars a year from the operators of gambling houses, "bookie" joints, and, most lucrative of all, slot machines.[2]

As evidence of their charges, the papers offered that in the spring of 1935 Huey announced that the gambling places in St. Bernard and Jefferson parishes, which for years had been kept closed by the state police, could reopen. He made it clear in his statement, however, that he was relaxing the ban for completely political reasons: his leaders in the two parishes had told him that they could not hold their pleasure-loving French voters in line if gambling was not permitted. "The people seem to want gambling, so let 'em gamble," he said. "I did my part. I did my damndest to stop gambling. . . . About all that's left for me to do is to have insane asylums moved next door to the gambling houses for the convenience of those of you who are crazy enough to insist on gambling."[3]

His frank explanation did not satisfy his critics. The stories of a Long tie-in with the gambling interests persisted and in 1940 (five years after Huey's death) gained a new credence when they were apparently substantiated by gambling czar Frank Costello in a statement to a federal grand jury. Costello, who was suspected of income tax evasion, in the course of his testimony abruptly interjected that early in 1935 he had been invited to come to New Orleans to discuss a certain proposition with Huey, whom he had met previously in New York. Huey's proposition was that Costello should put one thousand slot machines into New Orleans, which would make him the dominant operator in the city, and for the privilege pay the Long

[2] Baton Rouge *State-Times*, March 29, 1935; New Orleans *Times-Picayune*, March 30, 1935; New Orleans *Item*, April 1, 1935; Hamilton Basso: "The Death and Legacy of Huey Long," *New Republic*, LXXV (January 1, 1936), 215–18.

[3] Baton Rouge *State-Times*, May 30, 1935; Hermann B. Deutsch: "Kingdom of the Kingfish," in New Orleans *Item*, September 17, 1939.

organization a yearly fee of thirty dollars a machine. It was a good deal and he had taken it, Costello stated.[4]

Costello's testimony is open to question on several points. His overeagerness to connect his entrance into the New Orleans slot-machine business with Huey suggests that he was trying to shield somebody who had permitted him to come into the city later. But there is an even bigger hole in Costello's statement. Slot-machine operators never went into a city without concluding a "protection" arrangement with the municipal government: they agreed to pay a specified sum of money in return for a promise that the police would not raid the places where the machines were installed and seize them. In 1935 Huey could not have provided this protection in New Orleans, for the city government was controlled by his bitter enemy Semmes Walmsley, who would have rushed to confiscate any machines operating under Long sponsorship. Surviving members of the Long organization pointed out this obvious inconsistency in Costello's statement, and one of them indicated another weakness. "If anything like that happened, Huey wouldn't have dealt with Costello himself," this man said. "He would have sent somebody."[5]

Elmer Irey and his agents were certain that they had uncovered an important source of Huey's income, and that the source was corrupt. It was his connection with an oil and gas company that bore the interesting title of the Win or Lose Corporation. It came to be a saying in Louisiana that the company "never lost."

The Win or Lose company was chartered by the state on November 20, 1934. Its purpose, as announced in the articles of incorporation, was to acquire, sell, or exchange lands and leases for the drilling and prospecting of oil, gas, and other minerals. The president of the company was James A., "Jimmie," Noe of Monroe, an oil man and also an Allen administrative leader in the senate; the vice-president was Seymour Weiss; and the secretary-treasurer was Earle Christenberry, Huey's secretary. The three officers had subscribed the entire capital stock of the company, which was ten thousand dollars divided into one hundred shares. Only two hundred dollars of this represented an actual cash investment. Weiss and Christenberry owned a share each, which they had purchased with cash. Noe had secured his ninety-eight shares by transferring to the company his interest in leases he held on state-owned lands in the rich oil and gas Ouachita River bed. The structure of the company

---

[4] New Orleans *Times-Picayune*, May 8, 1940.
[5] Louis A. Jones; Joseph Fisher.

was devised by Huey, who drew up the act of incorporation. He received shortly thereafter a secret transfer of thirty-one shares of the stock from Noe.[6]

Noe's leases of state lands had been negotiated only a month before Win or Lose was formed. The agreement obligated him to pay the state the customary one-eighth royalty on all oil or gas discovered but did not require him to do any actual drilling. It was immediately evident that he had never intended to drill. On November 20, the day Win or Lose was created but before it was formally chartered, he assigned to a Texas firm, for $27,500, a three-fourths interest in his lease, reserving for himself not only a one-fourth interest but twenty choice holdings of land. It was this reserved interest that he transferred to Win or Lose in payment for his stock. The corporation was off to a flying start—in one day it had acquired a respectable bank balance and valuable oil locations, all for an actual cash investment of only two hundred dollars.

But for Win or Lose this was just a beginning. Late in August 1935 it disposed of its remaining twenty locations to two gas companies that had holdings on either side of the Ouachita River for a total consideration of $320,000. The company thereupon declared its first dividend to the stockholders, $2,000 a share, Huey's cut being $62,000. The checks to each recipient were made out simply to "cash."[7]

The dividend payment was known to Irey's investigators, or so Irey would claim later in his book. Irey had turned the information over to Dan Moody, the federal prosecutor, and the two of them decided that they now had a case to indict Huey. Their reasoning is hard to fathom. Nothing that Win or Lose had done was outside the law. It had come into possession of one lease of state lands that was acquired on terms extremely favorable to it but still legally. (Louisiana law at that time did not require competitive bidding for leases.) The only possible contingency in which the government could indict Huey would be if he failed to report the dividend as income for tax purposes. Irey inadvertently admitted that he had no case when he said that the principal result of the indictment would be to destroy Huey's image as a champion of the common

[6] Articles of Incorporation of the Win or Lose Corporation, Mortgage Record Book 1493, Folio 82, in Mortgage Office; Civil Courts Building, New Orleans, La.; Robert Angelle; Fred Blanche. A copy of the act of incorporation was provided to me through the courtesy of Judge Oliver P. Carriere of New Orleans.

[7] W. R. Lance, in Shreveport *Times*, November 23, 1935; Russell B. Long; David B. McConnell.

people—it would, by Irey's curious reasoning, show up the King-fish as an ally of the oil corporations.[8]

Although Win or Lose had done nothing illegal, the morality of its operations was open to grave question. It had succeeded so sensationally because the men heading it were important governmental officials and politicians who had access to special knowledge about state oil lands and who could get from the state any lease they demanded. This letting of leases to politicians was not new in Louisiana. There had always been some favoritism shown to certain applicants, and men in the anti faction had not been above accepting favors. But nothing in the past had quite approached the magnitude of the Win or Lose operation. Huey's justification for his participation apparently was that since other individuals, some of whom were his enemies, had previously got in on oil leases, then so could he. It was a weak rationalization for a foolish action. He was violating his own rule that politicians should be moderate in taking in extra money.[9]

The income that Huey received in any given year is impossible to compute with exactness. In 1935 he declared in a Senate speech that he had made, presumably in 1934, twenty-five thousand dollars. But he was referring only to his personal income and was not including the revenue that flowed in to his political coffer. His estimate was probably accurate, and if the amount seems small it is because he was not greatly interested in having a large income to spend on himself. He took enough money from his various sources of income to enable him to live the fast life that he delighted in but put the bulk in his campaign chest. His interest in money was almost entirely political—money meant power, and therefore he would acquire huge amounts of it. He did not really, in his mind or in his bookkeeping, segregate his personal and political incomes, and this is why Irey's agents probably could not have pinned an indictment for tax evasion on him. The futility of the Treasury's case was, in fact, admitted to a New Orleans lawyer by one of the federal attorneys who was prosecuting the cases against the Long leaders. "We have no in-

---

[8] Irey and Slocum: *The Tax Dodgers*, pp. 95–7. After Huey's death in 1935 the Win or Lose company acquired interests in a number of leases on other state lands and also engaged in drilling on privately owned lands. It has been an extremely prosperous and profitable corporation.

[9] Russell B. Long; James A. Noe. Mr. Noe insisted passionately that Win or Lose's operations were legal and above moral question. The leases were obtained openly and on fair terms to the state and could have been secured by anyone who had the energy and foresight to get them. Russell Long thinks that his father wanted the money for campaign purposes.

come tax case against Huey Long," this man said. "We've traced the money coming in, but it all stops at one of his lieutenants."[1]

IN MAY 1935 Huey renewed his Senate attacks on the Roosevelt administration, stepping up both the frequency and the bitterness of his speeches. He led off his offensive by becoming one of the floor managers for a bill that the President reportedly opposed, the Patman bill to pay the veterans of World War I an immediate bonus in a special paper currency.

The Patman bill had originally been introduced during the Hoover administration, when it passed the House but failed in the Senate because of presidential pressures against it. It had recently been reintroduced, strongly backed by veterans' organizations, and had cleared the House and come before the Senate. Roosevelt, according to rumor, had threatened to veto the measure, believing that it would cause a costly drain on the budget. This hint of presidential displeasure would in itself have spurred Huey to support the bill, although he would have voted for it in any case, as he had for all previous bonus legislation.

Huey, leading the fight for the bill, sought to dispel the suspicion that the President would veto it, which was causing some senators to waver toward the opposition. Roosevelt would not interpose a veto because he was a candidate for re-election and was too good a poli-

---

[1] *Congressional Record*, 74 Cong., 1 Sess., p. 445, speech of March 26, 1935; confidential communication. The evaluation of Huey's estate made after his death placed its value at one hundred thousand dollars but listed against this total twenty-seven thousand dollars that he owed in debts, most of this sum being due on his New Orleans house; Succession of Huey P. Long. The appraisal of assets was low, as was customary for tax purposes, and does not give a completely accurate picture of Huey's wealth. As an example, his thirty-one shares of Win or Lose stock were listed at their declared value of one hundred dollars a share, or at thirty-one hundred dollars, although they were obviously worth much more and were potentially a fortune. Listed as the principal assets were his law library, twenty thousand dollars (this was the library that his enemies claimed had been bought with state money); insurance policies, twenty-seven thousand dollars; and the fifty thousand-dollar account that he had put in an Alexandria bank after collecting back taxes for the state. Not listed was the sixty-two thousand-dollar Win or Lose dividend that officials of the company said had been paid to him. Mrs. Long expected to find this money and other valuables in the safe in his suite at the Roosevelt Hotel, but when she opened the safe it was empty. Nevertheless, the Long family had to pay income tax on the dividend; Charles J. Rivet; Russell B. Long; David B. McConnell. The "deduct box" in Washington, as will be described in a later chapter, also mysteriously disappeared.

tician to do anything that would cost him votes, Huey assured. Interjecting a brief homily on the art of politics, he declared: "What the politician had better do is stay a politician. That is law number one with him—the law of self-preservation." He was stating a fundamental political truth, one that all practitioners of the trade believe but seldom admit—the politician has to do some things in which he does not believe in order to stay in power, for without power he cannot accomplish things in which he does believe. Huey was also preparing a situation from which Roosevelt could not escape with much credit. If he signed the bill, he would seem to do so for completely political reasons; if he vetoed it, he would seem to be opposing a popular measure that embodied the just aspirations of the veterans.[2]

The bill passed the Senate and thus needed only presidential approval to become law. Roosevelt, however, calmly vetoed it. Huey had evidently expected this reaction, for he immediately seized the Senate floor to demand that the veto be overridden. In a long and angry speech he reviewed American participation in the World War, a war that had been fought to save the big bankers. And now those very bankers, "old Barney Baruch" and others, were advising the President and had, in fact, influenced him to veto the Patman bill. Roosevelt had always been willing to help the bankers but would do nothing to aid the soldiers, Huey charged; and enlarging on the President's attitude he said in an obvious menacing reference: "I say it is a political monstrosity that no party can defend, and no man can defend, either in his own conscience or in a political campaign." Huey could not persuade his colleagues to override the veto and had not really wanted to. He had acquired one more issue to use against Roosevelt in 1936.[3]

From the fight over the Patman bill Huey turned to his campaign to discredit Postmaster General Farley. In March his resolution proposing a special committee to investigate Farley's activities had been adversely reported by the committee on post offices, whose Democratic majority contended that he had not produced sufficient evidence to justify an investigation. The Republican minority agreed that he had not made a case but, seeing an opportunity to embarrass the administration, argued that in view of the seriousness of his charges an inquiry should be held. The Senate had held back from acting on the report at that time, and Huey had not pressed for a vote. He was apparently satisfied to let the controversy simmer while he hunted for additional evidence to substantiate his charges.[4]

On May 13 he announced that he had that evidence and demanded a vote on his resolution. Admitting that he had not made a case against Farley to the committee on post offices, he claimed that he could not do so because the committee lacked the power to call witnesses. But, he said, if a special committee was appointed it would receive from him the names of witnesses who could prove every charge he had made. He then launched into a long rehash of these charges—that Farley was interested in a corporation that did construction business with the government and had used his influence to get contracts for this concern and had awarded government jobs in return for monetary payments and had given valuable stamp issues to his friends.

He gave special emphasis to the New York post office episode, stating that a woman who had been employed by Farley's company had given him an affidavit extremely damaging to the postmaster general. Senator McKellar of the post office committee asked where the affidavit was. Huey answered that he had placed it in a lockbox because his office had recently been rifled and several documents stolen. He claimed that he had not given it to the committee because that body was packed with Farley's supporters, who defended him because he had jobs to hand out. "Judas Iscariot would have had defenders just as Farley has them now," Huey added insultingly.

Huey's baiting remarks incited administration senators to angry rebuttal. The principal reply to him was made by Josiah Bailey of North Carolina, a conservative Democrat, and it was a somewhat odd statement. Bailey noted quite correctly that Long had failed to produce any firm evidence against Farley, advancing only a set of allegations. But Bailey did not attempt a systematic defense of Farley. Instead, he attacked Huey's motives in asking for an investigation. Long's purpose was really to blacken the character of the President and this was unpatriotic, Bailey charged. "The President of the United States is the symbol of the nation. . . . No responsible man should ever venture, should ever dare to utter a word or make a suggestion calculated to destroy the national faith in him." Bailey previously had uttered many words denouncing various Rooseveltian measures as being too radical, but apparently he did not consider that these had weakened the national faith in the President.[5]

[4] Ibid., pp. 3218–24, debates of March 8, 1935.
[5] Ibid., pp. 7354–92.

The furious debate ran on so long that a vote on Huey's resolution had to be postponed until the next day, May 14. A brief but bitter discussion preceded the taking of the roll call, with Huey charging that the administration leaders were trying to hush up his charges to save the Democratic party and the leaders charging that he was pushing his charges to make himself President. The vote disclosed a resounding defeat for Huey: his resolution was supported by but twenty senators and opposed by sixty-two. But this was only the reaction of the Senate. In opinion outside the chamber Huey had not suffered a defeat at all, had, indeed, won something of a victory. He had succeeded in casting suspicion on Farley and by implication on Roosevelt, and he had accomplished this without having any good evidence to sustain his charges, had done it by making a set of charges so varied and extreme that the administration had not been able to keep up with them or answer them. He had not proved that Farley was guilty of the charges, but neither had the administration proved that the postmaster general was innocent of wrongdoing. Huey summed up well the result of his effort when, speaking of Farley, he taunted the administration leaders: "You may have covered up the grave, but you have not buried the corpse very deep."[6]

A week after the conclusion of the Farley controversy, the issue of the Patman bonus bill boiled up again. Roosevelt requested from Congress permission to read to a joint session a special message explaining why he had vetoed the bill, with the proceedings being broadcast to the nation on the radio, and administration leaders in both houses introduced resolutions on May 21 to hold the session on the following day. In the Senate there was some angry muttering at Roosevelt's request: many senators resented the presumption of the President in proposing to use Congress as a platform from which to deliver a political speech. But the objections did not rise beyond a mutter. No senator wanted to put himself in the position of seeming to petulantly deny the President the right to speak.

No senator, that is, except Huey. The Kingfish did not care in the slightest that he might seem petulant—if he could attack the President. Seizing the floor, he tried to prevent consideration of the resolution by filibustering until the day's session was ended. He discussed any subject that came to his mind, delighting the galleries with frequent jibes at his favorite target, Senator McKellar of Tennessee, who rose finally to cry out that the senator from Lousiana had so little influence in the chamber that he could not get the

[6] Ibid., pp. 7432–42.

Lord's Prayer adopted if he tried. Unperturbed by this outburst, Huey rambled on, coming finally to a relevant subject, the proposed appearance of the President. "He is coming here to celebrate," Huey charged, "coming here to be known, coming here to be embellished, coming here to be fawned over." At six o'clock most of the senators left the chamber to go to the Senate dining room for supper. He was still talking with undiminished energy when they returned. But at the end of five hours he suggested the absence of a quorum and headed for the men's room. Immediately an administration senator made the point of order that Long had surrendered the floor, and Vice-President Garner sustained the suggestion. When Huey returned, he was refused permission to continue speaking, and the resolution to hear Roosevelt was passed by a margin of forty-four to four. But forty-eight senators abstained from voting, a possible indication that a majority agreed with Huey's position.[7]

FROM NOW ON Huey would resort more frequently to the filibustering technique. His motives in adopting it caused wide speculation among the Washington correspondents, who thought variously that he was seeking publicity or pestering the administration or asserting his mastery over the Senate. He was doing all of these things, but not for the petty reasons the correspondents ascribed to him. He saw in the filibuster an opportunity offered by no other parliamentary device to advertise himself and his ideas to the nation. He could talk and talk, and now he seemed to feel that he had to talk, as though he subconsciously felt he had but a short time left to get his message over. He would exhibit in his filibusters that abnormal, feverish energy and elation that ruled him at times of great excitement.

On June 12, 1935, he engaged in a filibuster that gripped the attention of the whole nation. It was occasioned by an administration-backed bill to extend in modified form the National Recovery Act, which had been declared unconstitutional by the Supreme Court. Huey had opposed the original N.R.A. and did not want to see it extended even if attenuated. But if the bill was going to pass, as it obviously was, he was determined to keep in it an amendment that had been adopted on the previous day but that now the administration leaders proposed to remove—the Gore amendment providing that all

[7] Ibid., pp. 7912–42; New Orleans *Times-Picayune*, May 22, 1935; Tom Connally: *My Name Is Tom Connally* (New York, 1954), pp. 168–9; Franklin L. Burdette: *Filibustering in the Senate* (Princeton, 1940), pp. 181–2.

N.R.A. personnel appointed by the President and receiving more than four thousand dollars a year had to be confirmed by the Senate. He made no secret of his purpose: he hoped to prevent the appointment of his foes to N.R.A. jobs in Louisiana. And to accomplish his end he would filibuster until the leadership agreed to retain the Gore amendment.

He talked almost continuously for fifteen and a half hours, beginning at a little after noon and continuing until almost four o'clock the following morning. An unfriendly observer felt compelled to call it one of the "great orations of obstruction" in American history. It was not the longest Senate filibuster on record. In 1918 Robert M. LaFollette, Sr., had held the floor for over eighteen hours. But LaFollette was aided by sympathetic colleagues who requested thirty quorum calls that consumed seven and a half hours. Huey got almost no help from other senators and was permitted only two quorum calls that allowed him to leave the floor for ten minutes each time. He could not take more because as he proceeded the Senate invoked a seldom-enforced rule that a member yielding the floor twice for calls could not regain it on the same legislative day.

He had to contend with another unusual restriction. A group of "freshmen" Democratic senators led by Lewis Schwellenbach of Washington and egged on by Vice-President Garner announced that they would object to any unanimous-consent requests by Huey, such as to have a document read by the clerk while he rested. "We are no longer going to permit the Senator from Louisiana to run the Senate," Schwellenbach proclaimed.[8]

The galleries were jammed when Huey took the floor—a Shriners convention was meeting in Washington and many of its members had come to the Senate expressly to hear him—and remained filled as he talked on. Whenever a section emptied because the occupants had to leave, it was immediately refilled by persons who had been waiting in line. After darkness fell, many men and women in evening clothes came in, choosing to hear the entertainment offered by the Kingfish rather than that in the night clubs where they had been going.

Huey began by announcing that he would lecture on the Constitution, which in these New Deal days had become only a collection of "ancient and forgotten lore." Then, for hour after hour, he read each section of the Constitution and discussed its origin and analyzed its meaning. (Will Rogers thought that this section of the speech was

[8] Washington *Evening Star*, June 13, 1935; New Orleans *Item*, June 13, 1935; *Time*, June 24, 1935, pp. 10–12; Burdette: *Filibustering in the Senate*, pp. 3–5, 182–6.

the "biggest and most educational novelty ever introduced in the Senate. A lot of 'em thought he was reviewing a new book.")[9] As he continued, most of the senators went to the cloakroom, and some of those that remained on the floor dozed in their chairs. Noting this, he impudently suggested to Vice-President Garner that every senator should be compelled to listen to him unless excused. "That would be unusual cruelty under the Bill of Rights," Garner ruled icily. Several times Huey paused in his lecture to announce that he would yield the floor if the leadership would agree to recess the Senate and vote on the Gore amendment the next day. The leadership was willing to give him this concession, but the young Democrats— "the young Turks," as Huey called them—showed no mercy. They shouted that they would object to an agreement of any kind by unanimous consent until Huey gave up the floor. He had to go on.

It was now after ten o'clock, but he declared that he was perfectly willing to go on. "I seem to have new inspiration," he said. "I seem to hear a voice that says, 'Speak ten hours more.'" He invited other senators to suggest subjects for him to discuss. "I will accommodate any Senator tonight on any point on which he needs advice," he promised. None of his colleagues took advantage of the offer, but reporters in the press gallery, increasingly impressed by the magnitude of his performance, sent down written requests: Speak on Frederick the Great . . . on Judah P. Benjamin, the Confederate secretary of state from Louisiana. He obliged in every case, and when these suggestions ran out he introduced topics of his own choosing. He put into the record a detailed description of how to fry oysters and then demonstrated how to prepare potlikker, holding up a wastebasket to represent a cooking pot. The Senate should print his recipes as public documents and send out several million copies, he declared, and for good measure he threw in another one on how to concoct a Roquefort cheese salad dressing.

He must have been maddened by his descriptions of these delicacies, for during the ordeal he could eat but little. At intervals his secretary would place on his desk a sandwich, which he broke into small parts and rolled into balls that he could slip into his mouth as he talked. He also sipped milk from a glass and munched candy bars and grapes. Several times he tried to secure a respite by requesting that the clerk read a document, but on each occasion the Young Turks objected. Once he asked that the Democratic platform of 1932 be read. There were shouted Democratic objections.

[9] Will Rogers, column of June 1935, unidentified clipping in Long Scrapbooks, XXVI.

"Can you beat that?" he exclaimed with mock disgust. He finally asked that the Lord's Prayer be read, but even this was objected to. "The guilty flee when no one pursueth," he quoted resignedly.

After midnight Huey obviously began to tire. His voice became hoarse, and frequently he wavered and seemed about to fall. But his greatest problem now was that he could not answer the call of nature. He had not relieved himself since eight o'clock, when he had had his second and last quorum call. At ten minutes to four he could stand it no longer. He announced that he was yielding the floor to seek a conference with the leadership and the Young Turks and that Senator Schall, the blind solon from Minnesota, would now speak on the Gore amendment. Then he headed for the men's room.[1]

By the time he returned Schall had claimed the floor to ask that his speech be read. This was at first objected to but finally permitted. At its conclusion an administration senator moved to table the Gore amendment, and this was carried. The bill to extend the N.R.A. was then passed by a vote of forty-one to thirteen but with forty-one senators abstaining. The majority sentiment of the Senate was obviously opposed to the bill, and if Huey had had any help in his filibuster he might have defeated it.[2]

Two days after his tremendous effort Huey reappeared in the Senate refreshed and unchastened. He injected himself immediately into a debate on the Social Security bill sponsored by liberal Senator Robert Wagner of New York, declaring that although he liked the measure's objectives, it did not go far enough in providing pensions for the aged. Wagner had proposed two types of assistance for these people. Those who were destitute and unable to work could receive payments of up to fifteen dollars a month from a fund created by the federal government and matched by the states. Those who were working could receive annuities ranging from ten to eighty-five dollars a month provided by taxes on their employer's payroll.

Huey pointed out, and quite correctly, that the pension provisions were halting and timid. The recipients should not be forced to contribute to their own support, he contended, and the states should not be asked to match federal funds, for then the poorer states could not participate in the program. Moreover, the bill gave too much option to local boards to decide who were eligible for pensions,

[1] *Congressional Record,* 74 Cong., 1 Sess., pp. 9091–175; New Orleans *Item,* June 13, 1935; *Time,* June 24, 1935, pp. 10–12.

[2] *Congressional Record,* 74 Cong., 1 Sess., pp. 9176–9, 9188, 9190. Huey had expected that Gore and possibly other senators would join the filibuster. Gore reportedly was persuaded not to do so by the leadership.

which in the South would result in the exclusion of Negroes. The pension program should be entirely a federal project and paid for by the federal government, he asserted, adding that he would later offer amendments to the bill providing pensions of thirty dollars a month to all persons over the age of sixty who had incomes of less than five hundred dollars a year to be paid for by heavy estates taxes on the wealthy. His amendments were defeated, but he voted for the bill, which passed, as better than nothing and a move in the right direction. His ideas seemed to be getting more popular, he said.[3]

He shortly received a more sensational testament to the drawing power of his ideas. On June 19 Roosevelt, without prior warning except to a few intimates, sent a special tax message to Congress. Condemning the existing tax structure for having failed "to prevent an unjust concentration of wealth and economic power," the President called for heavy inheritance taxes, a sharp increase in income taxes on persons receiving more than fifty thousand dollars a year, and graduated taxes on corporation incomes and surpluses. Roosevelt made it clear that he was not merely advocating an overhaul of the tax system. He was going to use taxation as an instrument of social reform, was going to alleviate social unrest by securing a "wider distribution of wealth."

In the House the Democrats responded to the reading of the message with a rising ovation. But in the Senate members of both parties listened in cool silence, except for one senator. Huey strutted around the chamber grinning smugly and telling colleagues that Roosevelt had taken over his program. At the conclusion of the reading he addressed the chair and said that he wanted to make one comment before the message was referred to the committee on finance. "I just wish to say 'Amen,'" he announced.[4]

Three days later he discussed the President's message at greater length, reading various newspaper comments charging that Roosevelt had stolen his thunder. With delight he quoted the observation of Will Rogers: "I would sure liked to have seen Huey's face when he was woke up in the middle of the night by the President, who said 'Lay over, Huey, I want to get in bed with you.'" He was glad to have Roosevelt join him at last, he said. All he wanted was a tax bill that would decentralize wealth, and if one was passed he would be willing to retire from politics. But what specifically was Roosevelt's program? he asked. He then read to the Senate a letter he had

[3] Ibid., pp. 9291–7, 9427–37, 9649–50, debates of June 14, 17, and 19, 1935.
[4] Ibid., pp. 9557–9; Arthur M. Schlesinger: *Politics of Upheaval* (New York, 1960), pp. 327–8.

written Roosevelt congratulating him on his message but demanding answers to a list of questions. If the President were to reply affirmatively, he would have to endorse every plank in the Share Our Wealth platform.[5]

Huey made his offer to retire from politics in complete confidence that he would not have to act on it. He believed that Roosevelt would refuse to support a tax bill that really decentralized wealth, and that even if the President agreed to back such a bill, his party in Congress would not pass it. He had his suspicions verified when the Senate finance committee reported a bill that would produce in revenue only 340 million dollars a year. He told the Senate that if he had his way he would frame a bill that produced 165 billion dollars a year.[6]

Roosevelt's tax message signaled a shift in his thinking about social questions. It was his much-heralded "turn to the left," and he had made it primarily because of the threat posed by Huey and the Share Our Wealth movement. But it was not a great turn, and it was not going to satisfy Huey and perhaps not the restless millions of aggrieved people who followed Huey as a savior.[7]

IN JULY HUEY was absent from the Senate for almost three weeks, most of which he spent in Louisiana tending to state political matters. Consequently he took little part in the proceedings of the Senate. Early in the month he spoke briefly in support of an administration bill to regulate utility holding companies, declaring that he favored regulation but thought that eventually government ownership of these corporations would be necessary. His only other speech was a harangue against the efforts of the federal government to control the spending of its money in Louisiana. His state did not need federal money, he said. It could borrow whatever amounts it required because its credit rating was excellent, better than that of the United States. He revealed that Louisiana was going before the next session of the Supreme Court to ask for an injunction against most of the federal boards that were operating within its boundaries and spending money for unconstitutional purposes. Other states should

[5] *Congressional Record*, 74 Cong., 1 Sess., pp. 9907–14, speech of June 22, 1935; *American Progress*, July 1935.

[6] *Congressional Record*, 74 Cong., 1 Sess., pp. 10145–50, speech of June 26, 1935.

[7] Raymond Moley: *After Seven Years* (New York, 1939), pp. 308–10; Burns: *Roosevelt*, pp. 224–6. Professor Burns believes that Roosevelt's new departure was caused primarily by resentment of the unreasoning abuse he received from the right.

follow Louisiana's example, he urged. "Defy this kind of autocracy!" he cried. "Defy this kind of tyranny!" There was considerable disorder in the galleries as he finished, and Vice-President Garner shouted angrily: "The show is over. You can get out."[8]

Late in July Huey went to New York City for several days, ostensibly for pleasure but probably to negotiate the sale of an issue of Louisiana bonds to Wall Street banking firms. As he always did when in the city, he stayed at the New Yorker Hotel, and there he engaged in a bizarre publicity stunt. Taking over the barroom one day, he introduced the Ramos gin fizz, the favorite drink of New Orleans, to New York. As newsreel cameras whirred and reporters scribbled furiously, he announced that he had been unable to get a decent gin fizz in the hotel. Therefore he had had flown up from New Orleans a man who knew how to make the drink, Sam Guarino, the head bartender at the Roosevelt Hotel. He presented Mr. Guarino and instructed him to concoct a gin fizz. He sipped it appreciatively, his first drink in almost two years ("Huey wanted that drink so damn bad," one of his bodyguards recalled) and then downed it and ordered another. "I'm merely sampling this to make sure you gentlemen are getting the real thing," he said solemnly.

He had to sample five drinks in all before he determined that it was the real thing. Holding up the last one at the end of two hours, he proclaimed: "And this is, gentlemen, my gift to New York." His demonstration caused widespread ridicule, which may have been his real purpose. He possibly was clowning to divert attention from a serious effort he had to make to prevent the federal Treasury from sabotaging the sale of the Louisiana bonds.[9]

Early in August Huey returned to the Senate and immediately seized the floor. "For some weeks I have been quiet," he declared with a straight face. "I have been a model of political perfection from the standpoint of silence and inaction." But he could not promise to remain quiet, he added. Before very long he expected to address his colleagues on one or more topics that would interest them.[1]

[8] *Congressional Record*, 74 Cong., 1 Sess., pp. 10690–1, 11452–6, speeches of July 3 and 19, 1935; *The New York Times*, July 20, 1935.

[9] Unidentified clipping, July 25, 1935, in Long Scrapbooks, XVIII; Washington *Times*, July 26, 1935; Theophile Landry; Lester P. Barlow. The suggestion that Huey was putting on an act to deceive the Treasury came from Mr. Barlow, a resident of Connecticut who had decided to support Huey for the presidency and who at this time was much in Huey's company. Barlow stated that the Treasury was about to make a "raid" on the standing of the Louisiana bonds.

[1] *Congressional Record*, 74 Cong., 1 Sess., pp. 12476–7, speech of August 5, 1935.

He more than made good his promise. On August 9 he rose and announced to a shocked chamber that he had evidence of a plot by his enemies in Louisiana to murder him. It had been hatched at a statewide meeting of antis at the DeSoto Hotel in New Orleans in mid-July, he asserted. The meeting had been called to settle on anti candidates to run for state offices and a candidate to run against him in 1936. A group of the inner leaders had met secretly in a room in the hotel and had discussed not only plans for the election but ways of killing him. But he had secured a record of their conversation, he claimed. Two henchmen of his had been concealed in an adjoining room and had listened in on the plotters with a dictograph and had taken down most of their statements in shorthand. He had been provided with a typed transcript of the conference, which had taken place over two days, and he would read to the Senate parts of the document. He stressed that some men were not in the room constantly and that while many could be identified—Mayor Walmsley, Congressmen John Sandlin and Cleveland Dear, the anti candidates for senator and governor—others could not be recognized. These latter individuals were referred to in the transcript as "a voice."

First to speak had been Oscar Whilden of New Orleans (a violent anti who had once advocated that Huey be tied to a stake and whipped by a "bluegummed nigger"), who announced: "I am out to murder, bulldoze, steal, or anything to win this election." Various persons, some identified and some not, then discussed the possibility of carrying the election in 1936. A voice said: "The entire resources of the United States [government] are at our disposal." Another voice stated that Roosevelt probably would be willing to send federal troops into the state to ensure a fair vote. But other voices declared that more than political action was required to save Louisiana. One said: "I would draw in a lottery to go out and kill Long. It would take only one man, one gun, one bullet." Another claimed: "I haven't the slightest doubt but that Roosevelt would pardon anyone who killed Long." Should the job be done in Washington? a voice asked. Another answered cryptically: "I once thought that would be necessary, but I don't think it is now."[2]

The DeSoto Hotel conference had been held in a blaze of publicity furnished by the anti-Long press. Several hundred persons had attended it, taking up an entire floor of the hotel. During the sessions a ticket for the state election of 1936 was prepared, and plans were

[2] Ibid., p. 12786; *American Progress*, August 1935.

made to carry Louisiana for Roosevelt in the national election. A much-heralded result of the conference was the issuance of a statement signed by five of the state's eight congressmen affirming their loyalty to Roosevelt and denouncing Senator Long for preventing sixty million dollars in federal grants from coming into the state. Three of the signers had always been anti-Long. But two of them, Sandlin and Numa Montet, had previously been allied with Huey, and their defection indicated that the Roosevelt administration, by offering the bait of federal money, had partially eroded the bases of Huey's power.[3]

This was the conference as it appeared to the public. But behind the façade was something else going on, something sinister? Did some anti leaders gather in a room and discuss the desirability of killing Huey? Did they propose that they should draw in some kind of lottery to determine who should do the act—and did they draw then or later? The evidence on the issue is highly contradictory and impossible to resolve. The Long men who were connected with the DeSoto episode relate the following story.

They learned that the leaders of the conference planned to discuss secretly a new and unusual strategy, and they decided that they should find out what it was. One of them, John DeArmond, secured a job as desk clerk at the DeSoto, and when he assigned the rooms, he held out one adjoining the suite of Congressman Sandlin. He smuggled into this room through the freight elevator two men, Herbert Christenberry, a brother of Huey's secretary and also a shorthand expert, and B. W. Cason. They had with them a dictograph, which they placed on the end of a pole and extended from the window of their room to the window of the conference room. Through the listening device they could hear the conversation of the plotters, and Christenberry scribbled it down in shorthand. Later he prepared a typed version that he gave to Seymour Weiss, who promptly telephoned a summary of it to Huey in Washington. Huey asked Weiss to mail him a copy, and this was the document that Huey read from to the Senate.[4]

Surviving antis who attended the DeSoto meeting, including men who were in the conference room, deny that a plot to kill Huey was

[3] Deutsch: "Kingdom of the Kingfish," in New Orleans *Item*, September 18, 1939; Harris: *The Kingfish*, pp. 221–2, 260–2.

[4] John DeArmond; Frank W. Manning; Louis A. Jones; Seymour Weiss. Mr. Weiss has the original transcript. He discussed it with me but declared: "Nobody is ever going to see it."

hatched or even discussed. The transcript was a fabrication of Huey's associates, they contend, or a misinterpretation of remarks made by some men in the room. "There was a bunch of talk about shooting Huey Long everytime that anti-Long men got together," J. Y. Sanders, Jr., said. "It was some of the wildness in the air. I think somebody said that the only way we could get rid of him was with a bullet."[5]

But another anti leader related that there was a plot, one that Huey and even the directors of the conference did not know of. "All the stories about the DeSoto conference are wrong," he claimed. "The real truth is that there were three rooms. The meeting I'm talking about was not the one reported in the [transcript]. At this meeting there were five men." They had drawn straws to see which one of them would shoot Huey and much to his regret he had not got the short straw. "We would all have killed him," he said with relish.[6]

HUEY, AFTER DESCRIBING TO THE SENATE the DeSoto plot, again relapsed into comparative silence, claiming the floor only on a few occasions and then speaking briefly. His behavior surprised but delighted Robinson and other administration leaders, who were straining to put through vital legislation before adjourning the present session and were being pushed by the President to end it as soon as possible. At Roosevelt's insistence, the leadership finally decided that since most of the important bills had been passed or were on the point of passage, Congress could adjourn at midnight on August 26.

On that day the Senate convened at six o'clock in the evening. Robinson announced that only one urgent measure had to be disposed of, a deficiency appropriation bill to compensate various governmental agencies for shortages incurred during the past fiscal year, including funds for the social security program. But certain changes would have to be made in the bill, the majority leader explained. When it had come over from the House, amendments had been added providing government subsidies to cotton and wheat farmers to ensure a minimum price for their products. There was not enough time to send the revised bill back to the House for concurrence. Therefore Robinson said that he would move to strike the cotton and wheat amendments from the bill.

[5] Harry Gamble; Roland B. Howell; John G. Appel; J. Y. Sanders, Jr.
[6] Confidential communication.

At this point Huey rose and claimed the floor. Declaring that something had to be done to relieve the plight of the cotton and wheat farmers, he threatened that he would talk until the leadership of the Senate and House agreed to let the House vote on the controversial amendments. Robinson interjected that they could not possibly be acted on before twelve o'clock. Then, Huey replied, the majority leader should "reconsider the vote by which he has undertaken to adjourn Congress." In the meantime, he would talk. "I have nothing to do," he declared. "I'm just having a high-heeled good time."

He talked about various subjects, the right of Congress to be free from presidential domination and decide when it would adjourn, the right of both chambers to vote on such important measures as the amendments, and his own right to fight for these amendments. If Democratic senators thought that he was wrong, let them come to Louisiana and try to beat him when he came up for re-election in four months. "I have not even got an opponent down there yet," he said scornfully.

Progressive senators of both parties begged him to stop, pointing out that if he prevented the bill from being brought to a vote, appropriations for old-age pensions, railroad pensions, and other worthy projects would be imperiled. Robinson even requested a quorum call so that the progressives could go to Huey's desk to entreat him. But he resisted all appeals. "All I care is what the boys at the forks of the creek think of me," he said. "They would uphold my hands."

Finally the Young Turks sprang into action, needling the orator with insistent questions. "Does the Senator intend to deprive crippled children of benefits by defeating this bill?" "Will the Senator face the responsibility of halting funds for railworkers' pensions?" Huey let the questioners irritate him. "I do not need any advice," he snapped at them. "Give advice to someone who needs it." Shortly before midnight the leader of the Turks, Lewis Schwellenbach, arose. "It is now almost twelve o'clock," he said. "I submit . . . whether or not, because of his selfish desire to get publicity for himself, the Senator from Louisiana has not defeated the hopes and aspirations and the desires of the people of this country?" Before Huey could deny the charge, Garner banged down his gavel and declared the Senate adjourned, and the chamber and the galleries quickly emptied. Huey walked out alone.[7]

[7] *Congressional Record*, 74 Cong., 1 Sess., pp. 14718–52; Baton Rouge *State-Times*, August 27, 1935; Burdette: *Filibustering in the Senate*, pp. 187–9.

He had defeated the deficiency appropriation bill, but in the opinion of most political observers he had committed a prime blunder. Indeed, some commentators declared that his filibuster was an act of political suicide, and taking their cue from the Young Turks, denounced him for denying money to the aged and the crippled. This charge was nonsense, as the critics should have known. Roosevelt had ample funds at his disposal from other appropriations to finance the administration's modest social security program and had, in fact, promised his Senate leaders to allocate the needed money if the deficiency bill held up adjournment.

Huey, rather than being weaker as a result of the filibuster, was actually stronger. He had fought dramatically for the rights of millions of cotton and wheat farmers and had increased his chances of taking the farm vote if he ran for President. And it was not he who had committed a blunder but Roosevelt. If Roosevelt had permitted his leaders to hold Congress in session for a day or so more, both the social security appropriation and the cotton and wheat amendments could have been passed. That had been the purpose of Huey's filibuster—to prove that there was no valid reason for adjourning at the moment, that Congress did not have to obey the President's will.[8]

Huey was not worried by the outcry against him. At a press conference soon after the adjournment he demonstrated a realistic grasp of the situation resulting from the filibuster. That "abortion" of a Social Security Act had not been hurt at all, he declared. "It's signed, sealed, and delivered, and that feller's got enough money to polish the North Star if he wants to." He supplied some profane opinions of the "feller" and ended grimly: "This is his last term."[9]

BY THE LATE SUMMER OF 1935 his plan to deny Roosevelt another term was almost complete. As he outlined it to intimates, he would go to the Democratic convention in 1936 as the head of the Louisiana delegation and as a candidate for the presidential nomination. Although he expected to have the support of several other Southern states, he would not be able to prevent Roosevelt's renomination. But he would receive vast national radio coverage and advertise

---

[8] Benjamin Stolberg: "Dr. Huey and Mr. Long," *Nation*, CXLI (September 25, 1935), 344; George E. Sokolsky: "Huey Long," *Atlantic Monthly*, CLVI (November 1935), 533.
[9] Los Angeles *Daily News*, August 28, 1935.

himself and his program and the division within the Democratic party to the country. Then after the convention he would dramatically announce that he was forming a third party to voice the aspirations of the millions of people who wanted an alternative to the big business-dominated major parties.

He hoped to coalesce into this party the various factions of the left, the followers of Coughlin, Townsend, Sinclair, and others, but on his terms. It would be predominantly a Share Our Wealth party. He would be its candidate, or if not he, some man that he picked, a progressive Democrat or Republican, probably from the Senate. This candidate would not win the election, but he would take enough votes and states away from Roosevelt to throw the election to the Republicans. The latter, coming into power, would make even a worse botch of handling the depression than Roosevelt had, and in 1940 the country would be crying for a radical candidate—and a strong man. Huey was inclined to think that he should not run in 1936 but back another candidate. In this way he would not have a defeat on his record and would be in a stronger position to take over in 1940. It was a bold plan and also a coldly calculated one. He was willing to let the country suffer for four years so that he could then save it.[1]

Whether he or someone else was the candidate in 1936, Huey planned to conduct a vigorous campaign. He had purchased two additional sound trucks, and with them he was going to address audiences all over the country, going if he could into all forty-eight states. He realized, however, that he could not accomplish this feat traveling by car or rail. So, although he disliked airplanes and had used them only on a few occasions, he decided that he would be a flying campaigner, the first politician to stump by air. He ordered a private plane built to carry him and his campaign party. It was to be a "sound-plane": as it flew over a town it would announce that Huey Long was on board and would shortly descend to speak.[2]

The kind of campaign that Huey envisioned would require tremendous amounts of money. But he believed that he would have ample resources to conduct it, for in addition to his own Louisiana revenues he had been promised help from an unexpected quarter. Representatives of some of the biggest corporations and banks in the

[1] Seymour Weiss; Earle J. Christenberry; Robert Brothers; Charles Frampton; Joseph Cawthorn; Lucille Long Hunt; Anderson, in St. Louis *Post-Dispatch*, February 10, 1935; Thomas L. Stokes: *Chip Off My Shoulder* (Princeton, 1940), p. 402.

[2] Clem H. Sehrt; Lester P. Barlow; Joseph Cawthorn.

country came to him secretly and pledged huge contributions, up to two million dollars or even more if he would remove Roosevelt from the White House. He was astonished at the depth of their hatred for the President and reminded one man that he was more radical than Roosevelt. "We're not for you either," the man spat out. "Just give me the money," Huey said amiably, probably reflecting to himself that these conservatives were no smarter than the ones in Louisiana.[3]

The threat of Huey's third party alarmed the Roosevelt high command. Jim Farley caused a secret poll to be taken of Huey's national strength. The result was disquieting. It disclosed that if Huey himself ran he would poll three to four million and maybe six million popular votes. Moreover, his support was not restricted to the South but was nationwide. He would, in fact, attract as big a percentage of the votes in the industrial centers of the East as he would in the rural areas, and in a close election he could tip the balance to the Republicans.[4]

In the spring of 1935 Huey had an idea to write a book describing the policies he would put in effect when he became President. *My First Days in the White House* was the title he gave to the manuscript. He dictated it in six weeks to a secretary whom he brought up from Louisiana to Washington and then turned the rough draft over to Earle Christenberry and political reporter Ray Daniell of *The New York Times* to revise. By the end of the summer they had it ready to go to a publisher.[5]

It was a curious book, a mixture of nonsense and wisdom, of frivolity and gravity, and Huey must have thoroughly enjoyed writing it. He recounted first how President Long chose his cabinet, which was truly a ministry of all the talents. He sought out the best man for each position, regardless of party, and persuaded the individual that he had to accept the appointment as a patriotic duty. Thus he convinced Senator Borah to be secretary of state and induced

[3] Robert Brothers; George H. Maines; Joseph Cawthorn.

[4] James A. Farley: *Behind the Ballots* (New York, 1938), pp. 249–50; Harold L. Ickes: *Secret Diary of Harold L. Ickes: The First Thousand Days, 1933–36* (New York, 1953), p. 462.

[5] Mabel R. Roshton; Murphy Roden; Burton H. Hotaling: "Huey Pierce Long as Journalist and Propagandist," *Journalism Quarterly*, XX (1943), 28–9; Hermann B. Deutsch: *The Huey Long Murder Case* (New York, 1963), pp. 8–9. Both Hotaling and Deutsch state that Huey had nothing to do with writing the book, which was ghosted for him by William K. Hutchinson (Hotaling) and Daniell (Deutsch). But Mrs. Roshton, the secretary who took the dictation, has several shorthand notebooks to attest that Huey was the principal author.

Herbert Hoover to be secretary of commerce. But his greatest stroke was in securing an able man with experience in nautical matters to be secretary of the navy—Franklin D. Roosevelt.

Immediately President Long set his program in motion—using his executive authority boldly and demanding needed laws of Congress. A vast public works program was created, supported by an appropriation of ten billion dollars. A central bank was authorized, by a law called the Coughlin Act. The railroads were put under "absolute government control," with the probability existing that they would be nationalized. Lavish federal aid to the states for education at all levels was provided, with a special stipulation that every boy and girl of ability must be given the opportunity to attend college. A huge public health project was launched, to ensure that for the first time in American history the federal government "would care for the health of the American people." And to crown the whole program, a special organization was established by Congress to put into effect the principal campaign promise of the President— the Federal Share Our Wealth Corporation. To help this agency perform its work, President Long appointed a National Share Our Wealth Committee. It was made up entirely of bankers and industrialists, who now put their great skills to work for the people. John D. Rockefeller, Jr., was its chairman, and even Barney Baruch agreed to serve. President Long, however, excluded representatives of one banking house from membership—the firm of J. P. Morgan.[6]

Huey hoped to find a publisher for his manuscript in New York, and after Congress adjourned in August he went to the city on a combined business and pleasure trip. One night while he was having dinner with his theatrical friend Lou Irwin, Phil Baker, the radio star, came to their table and introduced himself and his wife and the latter's niece. The niece turned out to be an artist, and at Huey's request she did a sketch of him on a napkin. It was a superb caricature of the Kingfish in action in the Senate, arms waving and hair flying. He liked it so well that on the spot he engaged her to illustrate his book with similar sketches of the men mentioned in its pages.

Later at his hotel a representative of a Harrisburg, Pennsylvania, publishing company showed up, sent by Earle Christenberry, to offer a contract to print the book. Huey negotiated with him at four o'clock in the morning and several hours later caught a train to Harrisburg and signed a contract. The publisher insisted that the 340-page manuscript was too long, and Huey readily agreed to cut

[6] Huey P. Long: *My First Days in the White House* (Harrisburg, Pa., 1935), pp. 6–7, 29, 34–6, 42, 46–8, 61–6, 88–90, 95–6, 108–11, 143–6.

out 200 pages. His headlong haste and overeagerness to cooperate suggest that he was ruled by motives of simple vanity: he wanted to see his name on another book. He must have known that this one was not going to further his political ambitions.[7]

Huey concentrated on his national plans in the assurance that his home base of operation, Louisiana, was now secure against any rebellion. During 1935 he had routed his enemies from position after position and had reduced finally even the Old Regulars. He had achieved at last his goal of overwhelming the opposition so completely that it ceased to exist.

[7] Theophile Landry. The book was published in the fall of 1935, shortly after Huey's death.

# CHAPTER 30

# *Blood on the Marble Floor*

O N APRIL 14, 1935, knowing residents of Baton Rouge observed to one another that a special session of the legislature must be in the offing, for Senator Long had arrived suddenly in town from Washington. They wondered idly what this one would be about. In other parts of the state the interpretation of Huey's return was equally indifferent. By this time Louisianians had become inured to special sessions, accepting them as recurring features of the political scene and realizing that each one would go off according to a predetermined script. Longites assumed that Huey called them to enact needed legislation and would see that it was passed. Anti-Longites recognized that they could not block legislation he was for and were resigned to seeing how vicious it was.

The call for a session went out sooner than the observers had thought possible. On the morning of the day following Huey's arrival Governor Allen summoned the legislators to convene that night for a five-day session. Listed in the call as matters they were to act upon were measures affecting the financial structure of local governments and the conduct of state and parish elections. The specific nature of these and of other proposed bills did not become known to the solons until they assembled that night and heard them introduced by Long leaders.

At this opening meeting thirty-four bills were introduced in the house and started on the usual process to quick enactment. Most of them dealt with routine matters and excited little interest. But the measures concerned with local governmental finances and with elections aroused intense reactions. Direct power grabs, they frightened

848

anti members and shocked even Long legislators. There were two local government bills, and they were designed to prevent anti-Long cities and parishes from receiving monetary aid from the federal government and thus escape state control.

One of the bills restricted municipalities from taking advantage of a recent New Deal law authorizing cities to apply to federal courts to have their indebtedness adjusted downward. New Orleans, it so happened, had just used this law to avert an attempt by the state to wreck its financial system. In January Governor Allen, at Huey's direction, had instituted before the supreme court a concursus suit charging that the city was disbursing its funds improperly and that it therefore should be thrown into receivership.[1] The Long majority on the court had appointed a district judge, a Long man, to hear the case, and he had promptly issued a temporary injunction prohibiting the city from spending any of its money except to meet payrolls and purchase supplies. But before the order could be made permanent, the city sought relief from a federal judge, who first restrained the state from pushing its suit and then in April accepted the debt resettlement plan proposed by the municipal government.

New Orleans had won a legal victory over Huey, but it would not win another by the same route. The first local government bill provided that henceforth a municipality had to obtain the consent of the governor and the attorney general before it could apply for debt adjustment. And the second of the bills made it almost impossible for New Orleans and other anti-Long centers to receive other forms of federal aid, such as Public Works loans or grants. By its terms no political subdivision of the state could incur any debt or issue any bonds without securing the approval of a newly created agency, the Bond and Tax Board, which was composed of the governor and four other state officials. Huey was making sure that Roosevelt and Ickes were not going to run Louisiana.

There were startling extensions of state power, but an even greater one was proposed in an inclusive measure to regulate the conduct of elections. Presented as a "reform" bill, it abolished the existing system of drawing election clerks, commissioners, and watchers from lists of names furnished by the candidates and placed this

[1] Associated Press dispatch, January 14, 1935, clipping in Long Scrapbooks, XVIII; George M. Wallace; Hermann B. Deutsch: "Kingdom of the Kingfish," in New Orleans *Item*, September 13, 1939. A concursus suit is based on the legal doctrine that all creditors are entitled to establish equally their rights in a single fund. As the state was a creditor of the city's, it had grounds for action. Huey thought that this was the first time in legal history an entire city had been put under concursus.

function in the hands of the parish boards of election supervisors, all of whose members were to be appointed by the governor. Every election official would, in effect, be named by the governor, and local control would cease to exist.

The election bill aroused more resentment than the local government measures and was called up before a sullen house. As the vote was about to be taken, Mason Spencer, the anti leader of impeachment days, claimed the floor. Once a frequent and eloquent speaker, he had in recent years hardly bothered to oppose the Long primacy. But now he strode to the podium, and the buzz of noise in the chamber stilled. He wanted to go on record on this bill, he declared. "When this ugly thing is boiled down in its own juices, it disfranchises the white people of Louisiana," he cried. "I am not gifted with second sight, nor did I see a spot of blood on the moon last night, but I can see blood on the polished marble of this capitol, for if you ride this thing through, you will travel with the white horse of death. White men have ever made poor slaves." As Spencer returned to his seat, the galleries broke into loud applause, moved either by his defense of local liberty or of white superiority.[2]

The bill was then passed by a vote of sixty-one to twenty-seven, and the other bills proposed by the administration were enacted by similar margins. There might have been resentment of some of them, but the members of the huge Long majority did not dare oppose the master of the organization. And now, as a result of the session, there would be fewer in the state who could oppose him. Only New Orleans remained defiant and disobedient.

On July 3 Huey abruptly left Washington and flew to New Orleans. Arriving at the airport at night, he sent word by telephone and telegraph to all Long legislators to meet him in Baton Rouge at eight o'clock on the following night for a caucus. Coincidentally with the assembling of the caucus, Governor Allen called a special session to convene that same night at ten o'clock and transact its business within five days. Nothing in the call indicated what bills would be acted upon, although the Long members had been briefed on them in the caucus. Anti members did not find out their nature until they straggled into Baton Rouge after the session was underway.

At the opening meeting twenty-six bills were introduced in the house, all by one Long leader who did not bother to explain their

[2] New Orleans *Item*, April 18, 1935; New Orleans *Times-Picayune*, April 19, 1935; Mason Spencer; Deutsch: "Kingdom of the Kingfish," in New Orleans *Item*, September 14, 1939; L. Vaughan Howard: *Civil Service Development in Louisiana* (New Orleans, 1956), pp. 48–9.

provisions. They went through the procedure of committee and floor consideration in record time. The senate finance committee approved them in twenty minutes with no discussion, and the senate enacted them in fifty minutes with no debate. In both chambers anti members recognized the hopelessness of opposing the bills and on most roll calls did not even vote. The largest number of votes cast against the bill was only five. Present in either chamber when the vote was taken was Huey, apparently only a jovial onlooker until he saw a need to intervene—and then the steel flashed. Thus he stood quietly by the secretary's desk in the senate as the administration program ground to passage, but as the vote on the last item was called he shouted: "I don't want that bill passed." Turning to the secretary, he coolly ordered that the measure be returned to the calendar.

The twenty-five bills that were passed completed the framework of the Long power structure. One act placed under the jurisdiction of the Civil Service Commission all parish and municipal officers and employees who were not popularly elected, thus almost abolishing the independence of local governments throughout the state. Another forbade parish sheriffs to dismiss or change the status of any deputy sheriff without the approval of the head of the state police (by a previous law the sheriffs had to have this official's consent to appoint deputies). A third act extended the existing state control over parish school boards, requiring the boards to submit annually to the State Budget Committee the names and salaries of all teachers they proposed to employ and authorizing the committee to revise the budget in any way and discharge any prospective teacher and direct the employment of another one in his place.

Two acts enlarged state control over the municipal government of New Orleans. One of them included the city in the extension of civil service jurisdiction to officials and employees not popularly elected. The other took from the district attorney of Orleans parish (Eugene Stanley) the right to appoint his assistants and staff and vested this power in the attorney general. Several acts had as their frank purpose forcing New Orleans into financial bankruptcy. One forbade the city to collect real estate and personal property taxes, this power being transferred to the state tax collector. Others prohibited the city from levying a manufacturers license tax, a paving assessment tax, or a gallonage tax on the sale, manufacture, or consumption of liquors. As a result of these laws, New Orleans would be deprived of $1,800,000 in annual revenues, or two thirds of its yearly income. A Long spokesman gleefully contemplating this prospect, predicted that before Huey was through with the city, Mayor Walmsley would be left with "nothing but his title and office furniture."[3]

These laws of July represented the culmination of Huey's drive to force the Old Regulars to abdicate to him. Acts passed in previous sessions had enabled him to advance partway to his goal. Already the state controlled the city's police, fire, and sewage and water departments. Various sources of its tax revenues had been taken away, and it was in such financial straits that it could not pay the salaries of most municipal employees. In June a health crisis had threatened when the garbage collectors went out on strike for two months of back pay. The city government would have had to surrender to Huey then if the federal government had not advanced funds to reimburse the garbage men.[4]

After the recent session, surrender was inevitable, and it came fast. On July 10 the Choctaw ward leaders met in special caucus and by a vote of thirteen to four demanded that Walmsley resign as mayor. Simultaneously two members of the five-man commission council announced that they were bolting the organization and going over to Huey. Two days later the thirteen ward leaders met with Huey at the Roosevelt Hotel and asked him what terms he would grant the city. He replied that he would demand a number of municipal jobs for his followers but would leave the majority of the present employees undisturbed. But before a pact could be concluded Walmsley must be forced to resign, he stressed. Then the state would provide financial aid to New Orleans. The ward leaders told reporters that they were surprised at his "magnanimity."

Walmsley, however, would not even contemplate resigning. "I will never let a draft dodger like Long run me out of office," he stated with characteristic irrelevance. "Walmsley is a political corpse and don't know it," the Kingfish retorted amiably. His analysis was quickly proved to be correct. A third member of the commission council now came over to him, leaving the major and an allied commissioner in a minority. At the same time the remaining four

[3] New Orleans *States*, July 5, 1935; Baton Rouge *State-Times*, July 5 and 6, 1935; New Orleans *Times-Picayune*, July 6, 1935; unidentified clipping, July 6, 1935, in Long Scrapbooks, XVII; New Orleans *Item-Tribune*, July 7, 1935; Camden *Courier-Post*, July 8, 1935; Deutsch: "Kingdom of the Kingfish," in New Orleans *Item*, September 17, 1939.

[4] New Orleans *Morning Tribune*, April 30, 1935; New Orleans *Item-Tribune*, June 2, 1935; Newark *Evening News*, June 22, 1935; *The New York Times*, June 22 and 30, 1935.

ward leaders deflected to him, making the Choctaw caucus a unanimous Long group. One leader explained to a reporter the reason for the mass surrender. "We are helpless," he said. "Long controls every city job through his civil service, and we are nothing unless we have jobs."

The new Long majority on the commission council promptly stripped Walmsley of his effective powers, taking particular care to deny him any control over patronage. At the same time the Choctaw caucus refused him admission to its meetings. He was now only a forlorn figurehead, and the Old Regular leaders thought that they had done enough to placate Huey. They asked him if they also had to force Walmsley to resign. He answered that he would not demand any more of them. He added that a special session of the legislature would probably meet in September and that he would request it to provide financial assistance to New Orleans.[5]

Huey had brought a great city almost to ruin so that he could enforce his will on its government, and in the writings about him this action is denounced as a supreme example of his ruthlessness and desire for power. It is not known that he made an effort to avoid the conflict with Walmsley, that he offered the mayor a compromise which in the context of Louisiana politics was reasonable and realistic.

At some time early in 1935, probably just before the February special session, he sent an emissary to Walmsley with a proposition. He chose this agent with care—he was a young New Orleans Choctaw who with a close colleague had recently made overtures to join the Long organization. The two men were excellent examples of the Louisiana political type. They did not like Huey personally and were not attracted by his ideas. But they admired him as a "great technician" who would remain in the ascendancy, and they were thoroughly contemptuous of Walmsley's political ability. They jointly recalled the result of the visit of one of them to the mayor.

The emissary stated Huey's proposition. The Kingfish now had enough votes in the legislature to pass any bills he wished concerning New Orleans. He could wreck the city and would—if this was

[5] New Orleans *Item*, July 10 and 15, 1935; New Orleans *Times-Picayune*, July 11, 14, and 30, 1935; New Orleans *Morning Tribune*, July 11 and 30, August 1, 1935; New Orleans *Item-Tribune*, July 12, 1935; *The New York Times*, July 12 and 19, 1935; Camden *Courier-Post*, July 13, 1935; New York *Herald-Tribune*, July 15, 1935; New Orleans *States*, July 16, 1935. Walmsley hung on in his job until the summer of 1936 and then resigned.

necessary to end the opposition of the Old Regulars and free him to pursue his national ambitions undisturbed by fears of a rebellion at home. But he did not want to have to destroy in order to achieve peace. Therefore he was offering a deal. The Old Regulars were to come into his organization. They would have a respectable place in it and would control a portion of the patronage in New Orleans—but he would determine the place and the portion. The proposal enraged Walmsley. "He doesn't have me licked," he said. "We've counted heads in the legislature, and he doesn't have the votes." Turning on the emissary, the mayor ripped out: "The trouble with you is you don't have any guts."

The narrators emphasized that this was the last chance to bring political peace to the state and that Walmsley had destroyed it. But, they were asked, why should he have accepted a position of enforced subordination? And as a result of the proposed arrangement wouldn't Huey have been absolute in the state? One of them answered: "He would have been. Walmsley was too stupid to accept it."[6]

After the surrender of the Old Regulars Huey was almost absolute in Louisiana. He wielded powers such as no other American boss or leader had ever had. But it was significant that he did not always use all of his powers. Even now he acted on occasion like a typical pragmatic American politician. He could be surprisingly idealistic and unselfish. He could negotiate with people who differed with him and offer concessions and accept compromises—all very unlike a dictator.

In the spring of 1935 the Federal Resettlement Administration set up operations in Louisiana and other Southern states, with the purpose of removing low-income farmers from submarginal lands and relocating them on better lands. Its directors, dedicated rural reformers, feared that Huey would try to control the appointments to local jobs and to prevent this they named as state director a tough-minded young South Carolinian, Pete Hudgens. Much to Hudgens's surprise, he was not bothered at all by Huey. But anti leaders overwhelmed him with demands for patronage plums. For months he resisted these requests, and then one day he had a surprise visit from Huey.

"You were sent down here to keep me from running this program, weren't you?" Huey began. Hudgens replied that he had been sent merely to run a good program. Huey waved this aside. He said that he had been watching the director's resistance to the pressure of the antis. "All I'm concerned about is that you help these poor people," he said. "As long as you stick to that job, I'll never bother you." Then he delivered his message: "The first time I catch you appointing somebody because one of those sons of bitches tells you to I'll drive you out of Louisiana."[7]

The law authorizing the budget committee (the governor, state treasurer, superintendent of education) to oversee the operations of parish school boards resulted in the quick dismissal of a number of teachers. Politics clearly entered into the board's action. The teachers who failed to gain approval were in anti-Long parishes (twenty were rejected in East Baton Rouge), and all of them were in one way or another connected with the anti-Long faction, either as active supporters or relatives of supporters. The antis denounced the firings, but interestingly, their reaction was also politically inspired. In the parishes affected protest meetings were called, and although the speakers paid lip service to the ideals of free schools, they invariably ended by making an anti-Long stump speech. Typical of their remarks was a statement by a member of the East Baton Rouge parish school board, who declared angrily that he objected to the schools being politicized by Huey Long: "a thief, a rat, and a scoundrel."

The operations of the law distressed particularly Superintendent of Education Harris. His objection to it sprang from mixed motives. He disliked the political influence that it introduced into the hiring of teachers, but he recognized that there had always been political influences on local school boards. In the past he had tried to abate these pressures and himself control the firing of teachers. But now he was powerless, for on the budget committee he was outvoted by the governor and the state treasurer.

Harris was in a position to make his resentment felt. Immensely popular, he was certain to be returned to office in the coming state election, and he would add strength to any ticket he ran on. In 1932 he had run on the Long slate and was expected to be on it in 1936. But now he told Huey that he would refuse to run, that he was retiring to private life. Huey was dumfounded and asked for his reasons. Harris said that it was because the schools had been turned over to the budget committee and were being politicized. Huey seemed astonished at the information. "I had no designs on the school system when I had the budget act prepared," he protested. "My purpose was to prevent parish school boards from play-

[7] Will W. Alexander, memoir in Oral History Project, Columbia University.

ing politics in the appointment of principals, teachers, janitors, and other personnel. Maybe it will work the way you fear." He pondered the matter a little and then said: "I want you to run for reelection on our ticket. You may rewrite the budget act. I'll help you to put it through the legislature. . . . You are to take charge of the present law and administer it as you see fit until it can be revised. Isn't that as much as I can do?" Following through on his pledge, he instructed Governor Allen that the other members of the budget committee were always to vote as Harris did, and the discharges of teachers abruptly stopped—except for those teachers Harris wanted to get rid of.[8]

Huey had no hesitation in choosing Harris for a place on his ticket, but he could not decide who should head the slate as candidate for governor. He considered several men, all of whom were eager to run: Allen Ellender, speaker of the house; John B. Fournet, formerly lieutenant governor and now a justice of the supreme court; James A. Noe, president of the senate; Wade O. Martin, of the Public Service Commission; and Richard W. Leche, once Governor Allen's secretary but now a rising judge on the court of appeals. As he weighed their availability, he had to recognize that although each one had strength, he also had a weakness. Martin was a Catholic and by tradition a Catholic could not be elected governor. Leche was from New Orleans, which was almost as bad as being a Catholic. Fournet was a Frenchman and might not run well in the northern parishes. Noe was too closely allied with the oil business. Ellender was too short.

Huey ruled Martin out immediately. The other four he kept under consideration, and each one got the impression that he had been chosen. The probable truth is that Huey was unable to make up his mind and let each man think that he was the one. He felt no urgency in the matter because he thought that the identity of the candidate was not important to victory in the January election. Whoever the Long candidate was, he would win. He was primarily concerned with choosing a man who would be a good governor, and his difficulty in settling on one revealed the great weakness of

[8] New Orleans *Item-Tribune*, August 18, 1935; Baton Rouge *State-Times*, August 23, September 5, 6, and 7, 1935; Baton Rouge *Morning Advocate*, September 5, 1935; Guy C. Mitchell: "The Growth of State Control of Public Education in Louisiana" (unpublished Ph.D. dissertation, University of Michigan, 1942), pp. 395–404; T. H. Harris: *The Memoirs of T. H. Harris* (Baton Rouge, 1963), pp. 168–70. Huey's statement was reproduced by Harris and undoubtedly "prettified." It does not sound like Huey.

the Long organization. It did not produce strong or dynamic leaders who could form a line of successors. Huey so dominated it that other leaders could not emerge. But then he did not want them to emerge—for who else could possibly use his powers?[9]

Huey was certain of victory in the coming election for several reasons. He would be running for renomination as senator and would carry the state ticket along with him. His organization was at the height of its power and efficiency. But above all he relied on the desire of the people to retain the Long program. They would not turn out of office the faction that was responsible for the great road and bridge program, the improved free hospital services, the free textbooks and increased appropriations to schools, the free night schools for adults, the debt moratorium and homestead exemption laws, and the abolition of the poll tax.

Huey could well take pride in his program. It was a rare achievement in a Southern state of that time. But in some quarters it encountered scorn and sharp attack. Eastern liberals, convinced that Huey was a rural demagogue and perhaps a fascist and disturbed at the possibility that he might become President, started a campaign to prove that his program lacked substance. It contained nothing for labor or urban dwellers, they charged. The Kingfish boasted of his control over the Louisiana legislature, yet he had not attempted to induce it to pass an old-age pension, minimum wage, unemployment insurance, or child labor act. Either he was hypocritical in claiming that he wanted to help the poor or he was ignorant of the needs of a modern commonwealth, the liberals concluded.[1]

Huey did not duck the issue that had been raised against him. He noted in his defense that in the Senate he had compiled a hundred per cent pro-labor voting record, although in Louisiana organized labor, which had at the most eighty-five hundred members, could give him little help in elections. But he admitted that he had not tried to induce his legislature to enact social welfare legislation. The legislators and people of his agricultural state would not accept such legislation, he asserted. "This is the kind of issue you cannot change people on," he said. "They must change it them-

[9] Allen J. Ellender, corroborated by Theophile Landry and Clara Long Knott; James A. Noe, by Joseph Cawthorn; John B. Fournet, by A. P. White; Richard W. Leche, by Seymour Weiss; Trent James and J. J. Fournet, who thought that Huey had not made a decision. The eventual candidate, chosen after Huey's death, was Leche, who was put forward by Long leaders in New Orleans.

[1] *New Republic*, March 27, 1935, p. 171; May 8, p. 353–4; Oliver Carlson: "Huey Long at Home," in New York *Post*, April 29 and 30, 1935.

selves." Or, there were things that even he, with all his powers, could not do.[2]

After the surrender of the Old Regulars Huey faced only the semblance of an organized opposition. The anti faction remained, but since it was badly weakened by the loss of its New Orleans allies, who had controlled the only source of patronage available to it, it was forced now to depend for sustenance upon job handouts from the federal government. But if Huey had little to fear from those enemies who proposed to rely on political methods, he still had to dread those other ones who were willing to use violence to overthrow him. They had not yet abandoned their plans.

On August 1, 1935, twenty-seven men met in Alexandria and under the leadership of a pugnacious little man from the neighboring town of Bunkie, David Haas, formed the Minute Men of Louisiana. A secret organization, it announced its purpose in a privately circulated Declaration of Independence, which was modeled on the document of 1776 and even used its preamble: when a government attempted to oppress its people it was the right and duty of the people to "throw off such government." Therefore the twenty-seven signers, after cataloguing the crimes of the Long government in Louisiana, declared that as "representatives of the free people" of the state they were absolving themselves and their members and all who agreed with them "from all allegiance to the present administration" of the state. As a "free and independent people," they were entitled to certain basic rights, and chief among these was the right "to levy war" against the enemies of their "State."[3]

The Minute Men were organized like an army. Haas was the commanding general, and below him colonels directed operations in their respective localities. Perhaps as many as ten thousand members were enrolled, and every man was armed. The leaders secured weapons from various sources and many from four parish sheriffs who were members and who issued even submachine guns from their official arsenals. Dave Haas, recalling these details, stated flatly that the organization was armed for aggressive purposes. The Minute Men planned to march on Baton Rouge and take over the capitol and, if necessary, kill Huey. The colonel of the Baton Rouge

[2] Philadelphia *Record*, March 11, 1935; *Congressional Record*, 74 Cong., 1 Sess., pp. 15075–6, speech of August 26, 1935. E. H. (Lige) Williams, an early Louisiana labor leader, asserted that Huey understood the problems of labor and sympathized with the labor movement. "But we were too small to get what we wanted," he added.

[3] David Haas. Mr. Haas furnished me with a photostat copy of the document.

chapter, however, told a somewhat different story. He claimed that the purpose of the organization was political, to carry elections. The members were armed in self-defense and would have used their weapons only in certain contingencies, if Huey had "started grabbing people or going too far." Asked what they would have done in such an event, he answered: "We would have gone for him whereever he was. We would have done what we had to do."[4]

These were not the only men who were contemplating a resort to violence. In Baton Rouge a remnant of Square Dealers, forty bitter men, had reorganized and resolved to kill Huey. They decided that they would meet during the week beginning September 8 and draw lots to determine who would do the deed.[5]

LATE ON THE AFTERNOON OF September 4 Huey arrived in Baton Rouge by automobile from Shreveport. It was the end of a long and circuitous journey that had begun in New York, where Huey had gone after the adjournment of Congress in August. From New York he had dashed by train to Harrisburg to sign the contract for *My First Days in the White House*, and then he went on to Oklahoma City, where he was to speak on Labor Day. In the latter city he delivered a Share Our Wealth speech to a crowd of over six thousand persons assembled at the state fair grounds and renewed acquaintance with old friends of his traveling salesman days in the state, including Kaye Dawson, the produce merchant for whom he had once worked.

After the meeting he and two bodyguards, who were his only companions on the whole trip, left for Louisiana, even though the only available train would carry them no farther than Dallas. There they rented a car and drove to Shreveport, which they reached on the night of September 3. On the following day they went on to Baton Rouge in a state police car. Huey retired to his apartment on the twenty-fourth floor of the capitol and, even though he was deadly tired, went into conference with Governor Allen and other state officials.[6]

His arrival touched off speculation that a special session of the

[4] David Haas; John G. Appel.
[5] Confidential communication.
[6] Oklahoma City *Daily Oklahoman*, September 3, 1935; New Orleans *Item-Tribune*, September 5, 1935; Baton Rouge *Morning Advocate*, September 5, 1935; Theophile Landry.

legislature would soon be called, but he refused either to confirm or deny the rumors. On September 6, a Friday, he went to New Orleans and to his suite at the Roosevelt Hotel. That night he went on the radio and in the course of his wide-ranging remarks on national and state politics he intimated that he would not call a special session. Certainly one would not be called to help New Orleans financially as long as Walmsley was mayor, he declared. But on the following morning he summoned reporters and announced that a special session would convene that night. Governor Allen presumably had been told what to put in the call.[7]

The call did not go out until well after ten o'clock on Saturday morning. It listed twenty-one subjects to be acted on and also included an omnibus clause authorizing the enactment of any legislation that could be handled in a regular session. Named as specific items were measures to extend limited financial aid to New Orleans and to rearrange existing judicial districts. One item excited particular attention: legislation was demanded to preserve and protect the powers reserved to Louisiana by the Tenth Amendment to the Constitution. The amendment stated that powers not delegated to the United States were reserved to the states. Was Huey going to provoke some kind of constitutional showdown with the federal government?

When the legislature convened that night, forty-two bills were introduced by Long leaders. Most of them were of routine importance and aroused little interest. But two of them astonished even Long legislators. One provided a mandatory fine and jail sentence for any person who violated Louisiana's reserved rights as guaranteed in the Tenth Amendment. The bill did not spell out what constituted a violation, but it was obviously aimed at federal officials in the state and was designed to prevent them from performing their functions. Any federal appointee who performed any act or disbursed any money for an alleged political purpose could be hauled into the state courts and subjected to months of legal harassment.

The bill had been drafted at Huey's request by George Wallace, who protested that it was unconstitutional. "I don't give a damn," the Kingfish snapped. "I want you to draw it up anyway." He himself doubted that the act would pass an ultimate test before the Supreme Court. But it could not reach the highest tribunal until after months of litigation, and in the meantime the national administra-

[7] Baton Rouge *State-Times*, September 7, 1935; New Orleans *Times-Picayune*, September 7, 1935.

tion could not use its patronage against the Long faction in the January election.[8]

The other bill that occasioned surprise boldly proposed to end the political career of one of Huey's bitterest enemies, Judge Benjamin Pavy of St. Landry parish. Pavy was the presiding judge of the thirteenth judicial district, composed of St. Landry and Evangeline parishes, and he had been elected and re-elected to his office for twenty-eight years. He was unbeatable because of the population distribution in his district. St. Landry was the fourth most populous parish in the state, and was anti-Long; Evangeline was thinly populated, and was pro-Long. Consequently, the district had consistently elected an anti judge, Pavy, and also an anti district attorney, Lee Garland, who had held his office for forty-four years.

The Pavy–Garland dominion was bitterly resented by Long leaders in both parishes, who directed their hostility mainly at Pavy, the younger of the two officials and the anti chief of the district. The Long leaders in Evangeline, and also their people, disliked always having judicial officers from the neighboring larger parish. The Long leaders in St. Landry hungered to grasp control of the judicial offices but could not envision a strategy that would succeed. In desperation a delegation of Longites from both parishes went to New Orleans right after the special session was called to beg Huey for help. They suggested various solutions, the most favored one being that Evangeline be placed in another judicial district. This would leave St. Landry as a separate district, and this distinction might so flatter its people that they would elect a Long judge and a Long district attorney.

Huey listened to the proposals with interest. He detested Pavy personally and politically and would willingly unseat him. But his first and overriding concern was that he must help these followers of his. "I'll attend to it," he said finally. "I'll think up something." He did, and had his solution put in a bill to be presented to the legislature on Saturday night. None of the leaders had thought of this particular solution, and some of them did not like the bill. It removed St. Landry from the thirteenth judicial district and set up little Evangeline as the only parish in the district. St. Landry, which logically should have been made a district, was placed in the fifteenth judicial district, which already had three parishes—all Long centers, Acadia, Lafayette, and Vermilion—and two district judges. Pavy,

[8] Baton Rouge *State-Times*, September 8, 1935; George M. Wallace; Seymour Weiss.

when he came up for re-election early in 1937, would have to run in a district where the votes were heavily stacked against him. The gerrymander was so obvious that one of Huey's lieutenants was moved to protest the bill. Huey explained that he could not refuse his leaders in St. Landry and Evangeline. "I live and die for my people," he said.[9]

On the Saturday that the special session was called Huey remained in New Orleans. In the afternoon he played golf with Seymour Weiss, and as the two men leisurely made their way down the course Huey discussed his plans for the state and national elections of 1936. As Weiss relates the story, Huey assured him that the organization had ample funds to carry it through both contests. The deduct box in Washington was bulging with money, he said. Weiss naturally assumed that the box was still in the Riggs National Bank.

After the game they returned to the Roosevelt Hotel and sat in Weiss's office chatting about their score, the weather, and other light topics. Suddenly Huey interjected a serious remark. "By the way, Seymour, I've moved the deduct box," he said. Before he could say more, the telephone rang, and Huey took the call. It was from one of his legislative leaders in Baton Rouge, who said that his presence was needed at the session. He said no more about the box, and early on the following morning, Sunday, September 8, he left by car for Baton Rouge.[1]

He had been begged not to go by various associates in New Orleans, who thought that he looked tired and worried and in need of rest. Besides, they had heard rumors, vague but disquieting reports whispered in hotel corridors and on street corners, that an attempt on his life would be made at the session. In Baton Rouge Colonel E. P. Roy of the state police had heard the same reports and thought he could detect a strange tenseness around the capitol. He detailed ten policemen, a larger force than usual, to accompany Huey at all times. It was a logical precaution, but, as the policemen and also the bodyguards realized, a useless one. Huey could not be protected because he always walked, ran actually, in front of his guards. "We knew that any man could kill him who was willing to give his own life," one policeman recalled.[2]

Huey on arriving went immediately to his apartment in the cap-

[9] J. Cleveland Fruge; Isom Guillory; Henry D. Larcade; Waldo H. Dugas; Harvey G. Fields.

[1] Seymour Weiss.

[2] Amos Lee Ponder; James P. O'Connor; Henry D. Larcade; E. P. Roy; Theophile Landry; M. J. Kavanaugh.

itol. As though he was trying to delay involvement in the business of the session, he summoned Castro Carazo, and for several hours the two of them worked on a new song. Carazo had been urging Huey to establish a state school of music in New Orleans for persons of talent who had not gone to college or could not afford to go, and at a pause in their labors Huey said: 'We'll go ahead with the school of music. I think I know where to find the money." He did not admit any politicians until late in the afternoon, and then he talked with a group of leaders as to who the Long candidate for governor would be. Some of those present got the impression that he was leaning toward Judge Leche. During the conversation he telephoned printer Joe David in New Orleans and said that the copy for an important circular would soon be sent down, one dealing with Judge Pavy. Finally he adjourned the meeting, telling his leaders that he would see them that evening in the house of representatives when it convened.[3]

That night Huey ate dinner in his capitol apartment, munching on cheese and crackers and fruit and talking with various politicians who drifted in and out of the room. When he judged that the house had convened, he beckoned to Jimmie O'Connor, a young Longite member of the Public Service Commission, to accompany him, and the two men went down on an elevator to the first floor and entered the house chamber.

Huey soon discovered that nothing demanded his attention—the administration program was moving smoothly to passage—and he sauntered around the chamber greeting legislators and friends. At the press table he paused to exchange a few words with his favorite and privileged reporter, Charles Frampton, who shortly left to go to Governor Allen's office to call his editor in New Orleans. Huey turned to O'Connor and asked the younger man to run down to the restaurant in the basement and buy him some cigars. O'Connor was surprised at the request, for Huey had forsworn tobacco when he gave up alcohol, but he departed on the errand. Huey then moved up to the speaker's dais and seating himself, began a conversation with Allen Ellender. It was now about nine o'clock and almost time for the house to adjourn. Huey told Ellender to come to his apartment after the session, wishing to talk, Ellender presumed, about the governorship.[4]

In the meantime Chick Frampton had ensconced himself in

[3] Castro Carazo; New Orleans *Tribune*, September 11, 1935; Deutsch: "Kingdom of the Kingfish," in New Orleans *Item*, September 19, 1939; Joseph B. David.
[4] Harry Gamble; James P. O'Connor; Charles Frampton; Allen J. Ellender.

Allen's office and called his editor, who had an exciting piece of news that he wanted followed up. A hurricane had struck the Florida coast and marooned a camp of Civilian Conservation Corps youngsters on the keys, some of them drowning, and the editor thought that surely Senator Long would wish to comment on this example of New Deal negligence. Frampton told the editor to hang on—on another phone he would call Huey at the sergeant-at-arms' office adjoining the house chamber and get a quote. He got through quickly to Huey, who delivered a blast at Roosevelt for sacrificing the C.C.C. boys and then asked where Frampton was. On being told, he said: "Wait there. I'm coming to see you." Frampton took up the other phone and told his editor to keep the line open: Huey was on his way and probably would want to add to his statement.[5]

Huey strode back into the house and told Ellender that he was going to Allen's office for a short time. As he passed by the desks of his leaders, he barked out that the Long members would caucus at nine thirty on the following morning to discuss the pending bills. Near the door he paused to tell anti member Mason Spencer a joke and then swept out into the rotunda and turned to the right into a U-shaped corridor leading to the governor's office. Behind him, racing to keep up, were Murphy Roden and three other state policemen, and farther back Joe Messina and A. P. White, Allen's secretary, and Justice Fournet, who had a matter that he wanted to discuss, and still more to the rear other policemen and politicians.[6]

Huey continued rapidly down the corridor until he came to the door of the office of the governor's secretary, or the anteroom to the governor's office. Another door, known as the main door, also opened into the governor's office but at night was kept locked. Huey pushed into the anteroom but seeing no legislators there turned back into the corridor. Most of those in the crowd following him had now caught up, and he swung around to address them. Still thinking of the caucus, he said: "We have to get all our men here tomorrow." Somebody in the group answered that the Long legislators had been notified of the meeting. Huey was standing in the middle of the corridor opposite the main door of the governor's office and facing almost in the direction from which he had come. At this moment Frampton, thinking to see if his expected visitor was on the way, opened the main door and looked out into the corridor. It was nine twenty.

[5] Charles Frampton.
[6] Allen J. Ellender; Isom Guillory; Arthur Provost; Mason Spencer.

From behind a pillar on the opposite side of the corridor a man in a white suit emerged and walked up to Huey. "He flashed among us," said John Fournet later in trying to describe the suddenness of the man's appearance, and Murphy Roden said: "He brushed through." The man had approached to within a few feet of Huey when his presence was noted, and then his right hand came up and in it was a small pistol pointed at Huey. He started to move closer but Fournet leaped forward and struck at his arm, and simultaneously the man fired. Huey screamed: "I'm shot," and wheeled and headed for the stairs leading to the basement. As he turned away, Roden sprang on the assailant and grappled him, and the two men fell on the floor, with Roden underneath. The man fired again and shot Roden's wristwatch off, and then broke away and backed off in a crouching position. Roden regained his feet and drew his gun, and another policeman had his gun out, burly Elliott Coleman, who had tried to hit the assailant as he wrestled with Roden but had failed. Roden and Coleman fired at almost the same time, with Coleman's bullet probably reaching the man first. Several other guards had unholstered their guns and were blazing away. The man crumpled and fell face downward near the wall of the corridor from which he had come.[7]

He lay there with his face resting on one arm and did not move and was obviously dead. But this did not satisfy some of the guards. Crazed with rage or grief, they stood over the body and emptied their guns into it. It was later discovered to have thirty bullet holes in the back and twenty-nine in the front (many of these were caused by the same bullet making an entry and exit), and two in the head. The face was partially shot away, and the white suit was cut to ribbons and drenched with blood. Eventually the guards drew off, and other people, reporters and capitol employees and visitors to the

[7] Murphy Roden; A. P. White; John B. Fournet; Charles Frampton; Elliott Coleman. My account is based on the statements of the above witnesses and on material in a rare document, "Transcript of the Testimony Taken Before the Coroner's Inquest held over the Body of Dr. Carl Austin Weiss . . . September 9 and 16, 1935 . . . In Baton Rouge." A typed copy of this seventy-two-page record was kindly provided to me by Senator Russell B. Long. Several witnesses to the event now dead or unavailable and Roden, Fournet, Frampton, and Coleman appeared at the inquest. The testimony of the last four men was almost identical to their statements to me. All of the witnesses were in essential agreement as to what they saw. They differed only as to how close the assailant placed his gun to Huey, a foot or so, a few inches; and as to how he drew the gun. Frampton and White thought he concealed it under a straw hat, but none of the other witnesses mention this fact. The assailant's hat, battered and crushed, was found, however, near the scene.

legislative session, came up and viewed the body. None of them knew who the man was, and the coroner of the parish, who had been summoned, did not recognize him. But finally a resident of Baton Rouge pushed forward and said in some surprise: "Why, that's Dr. Weiss." The man on the floor was Carl Austin Weiss, a young ear, nose, and throat specialist in Baton Rouge—and a son-in-law of Judge Pavy.[8]

In the basement of the capitol Jimmie O'Connor found the restaurant deserted but still open and a young lady on duty at the cashier's counter. He bought the cigars that Huey had requested and loitered to exchange a few light remarks with the attendant. Suddenly he heard what sounded like firecrackers going off on the floor just above, and then another burst of explosions. "What the hell is that?" he said, and started for the stairway leading up to the first floor. He had almost reached the foot of the stairs when he saw Huey stagger from them. In O'Connor's words, Huey was "running by himself and wheeling back and forth." O'Connor ran to him, crying: "Kingfish, what's the matter?" "Jimmie, my boy, I've been shot," Huey moaned. He had flecks of blood on his lips, which caused O'Connor to think that the wound was in the mouth. The young man placed an arm around Huey and half-carried him out the back door to the parking lot. He summoned the first man that he saw in a car and said that the senator had been hurt and had to have medical aid. Huey muttered that he should be taken to the nearby Catholic Our Lady of the Lake hospital, and the driver sped off. On the short trip Huey spoke only once, more to himself than to the occupants of the car. "I wonder why he shot me," he said.[9]

At the door to the hospital O'Connor helped Huey out of the car and into the hallway. Seeing no one on duty, he managed to place Huey on a hospital cart, and rang a bell on the reception desk. A sister soon appeared, and O'Connor suggested that Huey should be taken upstairs to a room. At this moment Charles Frampton appeared, having run all the way from the capitol. "Chick," Huey said, "who was that that shot me?" "Don't you know?" Frampton asked. Huey said that he did not. In a few minutes he was moved into a room, and shortly afterward a state policeman came in to tell him that the assassin had been identified. The name meant nothing to Huey. "Weiss, Dr. Weiss," he muttered. "What did he want to shoot me for?" A little later he was told by one of the attending doctors

[8] Margaret Dixon, in New Orleans *States*, September 9, 1935; E. P. Roy; John DeArmond; James Buie; Fred Blanche; Bryan Clemmons.

[9] James P. O'Connor.

that Weiss was a son-in-law of Judge Pavy. Huey shook his head. "I don't know him," he said.[1]

By many of those who did know him, Carl Weiss was considered to be a brilliant young doctor, perhaps a genius, who would scale great heights in the medical world. An acknowledged specialist in his field at the age of only twenty-nine, he had a grasp of other areas of medicine, and was also accomplished in music, painting, mathematics, and mechanics. Some of the doctors in Baton Rouge, while admiring his talents, thought him to be somewhat odd—a brooding and intense and unstable-man. The impression of strangeness was strengthened by his appearance. He was five feet ten inches in height but weighed only a little more than 130 pounds. He had a thin face of olive complexion, crowned by a shock of dark hair, and he peered out at the world from behind thick-lensed glasses that gave him an owlish or intellectual look. Some people thought he looked foreign.

He had, in fact, pursued part of his medical education abroad. The son of a Baton Rouge doctor, Carl Adam Weiss, he had taken his premedical course at LSU and his medical training at Tulane. On receiving his degree he interned at Touro Infirmary in New Orleans and so impressed the doctors there that they obtained for him a fellowship for two years of further internment at the American Hospital in Paris. Determined to take full advantage of this opportunity, he spent a year of study in Vienna between his two years in Paris. In his spare time he traveled around Europe, gratifying his love of art at the great galleries and buying souvenirs that struck his fancy. He was a gun collector of sorts, and on a trip in Belgium he purchased a small, 32-caliber automatic pistol.

One day in Paris he met a visitor from Louisiana, pretty young Yvonne Pavy of Opelousas, who had come with several other girls to exhibit Acadian costumes at the Louisiana stand at the International Colonial Exposition. After the exposition closed, Yvonne, a graduate of exclusive Newcomb College in New Orleans, stayed on in Paris to study French on a scholarship granted her by the French government. Very soon she and Carl became engaged, and when on the completion of his internship he returned to America, she went back to Louisiana, enrolling in the LSU graduate school. Carl served briefly at Bellevue Hospital in New York and then decided to go into practice with his father in Baton Rouge. The young couple were

---

[1] Charles Frampton; John B. Fournet; Dr. Cecil O. Lorio.

married in December 1933, and set up housekeeping in a modest dwelling two blocks from the capitol. In June 1935 Yvonne gave birth to a son.[2]

At first no one questioned the fact that Weiss had been the assassin of Senator Long. He was described as having committed the act by a number of witnesses, the bodyguards, Justice Fournet, and others, and the pistol he had bought in Belgium was found on the floor near his hand after he was shot down (it had jammed after he fired the second shot). The fact that he had come to the capitol armed seemed to prove that he had come with the intention to kill.

His guilt was accepted even by his wife and parents and members of his wife's family, who spoke frankly to the press. His mother said that she could not think what had impelled her son to shoot the senator. "All we know is that he took living seriously," she moaned. "Right with him was right. Right above everything." His father said that Carl could not have gone into the capitol to kill Long because he would have known that he was walking into suicide under the guns of the guards. "What happened there, what brought him there, will always be between him and his Maker," the father concluded. He seemed to be saying that Carl had gone to confront Huey on some matter and that something dark and evil that would always be unknown had occurred between them. A similar theory was advanced by Yvonne in a brief and sob-interrupted interview.

All three of them stressed that Carl could not have committed a premeditated crime because on Sunday his actions had been too "normal and happy." He and Yvonne, with the baby, had gone as usual to his parents' home for noon dinner, and after eating Carl had suggested that they all go out in his car to the father's camp on the Amite River. There they had spent several enjoyable hours—Carl and Yvonne went swimming—and in the early evening had returned to the city. The young Weisses dropped off the older couple at their house and went on to their own home for supper. Shortly before nine o'clock Carl said that he had to make a sick call and departed in his car. He had, his wife later discovered, taken a gun with him, but there was nothing unusual about this—many doctors carried guns for protection when on night calls.[3]

[2] New Orleans *States*, September 9, 1935; Associated Press dispatch, September 9, 1935, in Mrs. John Lungaro Scrapbook, in possession of John Lungaro, Baton Rouge, Louisiana; New Orleans *Item*, September 11, 1935; confidential communication.

[3] James Marlow, in New Orleans *States*, September 9, 1935; New Orleans *Times-Picayune*, September 10, 1935; New Orleans *Item*, September 11, 1935; Baton Rouge *State-Times*, September 13, 1935.

What then had happened in the mind of the young doctor when he entered the capitol to discuss whatever it was he wanted to discuss with Huey? An answer was supplied by Dr. F. O. Pavy, a brother of the judge. "Carl must have been temporarily deranged when he shot the Senator," Dr. Pavy said. "Carl was a deep student of political theory. I am convinced that this intensive study of the Louisiana political situation convinced him that the form of government in the state under Senator Long's dictatorship was so terrible and such a miscarriage of justice that his broodings finally unbalanced his mind. I believe that, thus mentally unbalanced on this subject, he saw as a martyr to liberty the man who would assassinate Senator Long."[4]

The theory of an unpremeditated shooting did not satisfy the Long people. They would not admit even that Weiss had planned his deed alone. Secretary Earle Christenberry issued a statement charging that the doctor had acted at the instruction of Huey's enemies. Weiss had attended the DeSoto Hotel conference at which Huey's killing was discussed, Christenberry claimed. As proof of his accusation, the secretary asserted that in the transcript of the conference secured by Huey's agents the name of a "Dr. Wise" had appeared. Huey had originally included the name in the copy of his speech to the Senate describing the plot but being uncertain of Wise's identity and not wishing to do an injustice had scratched it off. But now, said Christenberry, it was obvious that "Dr. Wise" and Dr. Weiss were the same person.[5]

The *American Progress* came to Christenberry's support by printing what purported to be a four-line excerpt from the type-script of Huey's speech. The third line read: "Dr. Wise entered the room and was introduced." Beside the line on the left-hand margin a pen-and-ink question mark appeared, and through the line a wavy penstroke was drawn. To Longites this closed the case: Weiss had shot their hero and had done it at the urging of prominent antis, Congressmen Cleveland Dear and John Sandlin and others, the men who were now leading the anti ticket in the state election. In bitter derision Longites labeled the opposition slate "the Assassination Ticket."[6]

It was a hard term for the antis to bear, and their gubernatorial candidate, Cleveland Dear, finally struck back. In the closing days of the campaign he stated in a speech that one of Long's bodyguards

[4] United Press dispatch, September 9, 1935, in Persac Scrapbook.
[5] Unidentified clipping, September 9, 1935, in Grace Scrapbook.
[6] *American Progress*, December, 1935.

had been confined to a mental hospital where he reportedly confessed that he had shot Huey by mistake. The suggestion that Huey might have been hit by a wild shot or a ricochet from the guns of the guards had been advanced privately by various individuals, but no one had taken it very seriously, for unless all the witnesses to the event were lying or mistaken, only four shots had been fired while Huey was still in the corridor, the two from Weiss's pistol that struck Huey and Roden's wristwatch respectively and the two from the revolvers of Roden and Coleman that dropped Weiss. By the time the other guards had got their guns out and started to fire Huey had run from the scene. But when the suggestion had been made publicly, various people wanted to believe it—members of Weiss's family and anti politicians, naturally; and persons of the type who sense mystery in any murder case, the kind of people who have created doubts about some of the other great American assassinations. A myth and a folklore about the Long case were about to be born, and once born would not die.[7]

The myth goes as follows. Weiss did not go to the capitol on that Sunday night to kill Huey. He passed the building while making his call and seeing it ablaze with lights he reflected that Huey must be there. Simultaneously he noticed a parking space and decided to go in and talk with Huey. What he wanted to discuss is not clearly indicated—perhaps the Pavy gerrymander or the recent firing of two schoolteacher relatives of his wife, a sister and an uncle, or a rumor he had heard that Huey had said privately and was going to say publicly that the Pavys were part Negro. (Practically all of Huey's surviving intimates state that they never heard him voice the Negro charge, and members of the Pavy family apparently had not heard of the supposed slur.)

He possibly had his pistol on him when he entered the capitol but more probably had left it in the glove compartment of his car. He may have gone briefly onto the house floor and seen Huey there and decided that the senator would go to the governor's office after

[7] Deutsch, in New Orleans *Times-Picayune*, September 8, 1963. A suspicion that a shot from one of the guards hit Huey was obviously in the mind of John Fred Odom, district attorney of East Baton Rouge parish, when he conducted the coroner's inquest on September 9 and 16. He tried to establish by testimony that the fusillade of shots in the corridor had come instantly after the first shot fired by Weiss. The same suspicion was probably held by Carl's father. Two recent books treat this assassination, the previously cited volume by Deutsch, *The Huey Long Murder Case*, and David H. Zinman: *The Day Huey Long Was Shot* (New York, 1963). Deutsch takes the view that Weiss was probably the assassin. Zinman thinks that Weiss did not go into the capitol to kill Long and that probably the latter was struck by a wild shot from the guards.

the session. At any rate, he stationed himself in the corridor near the office and waited. When he saw Huey pause outside the anteroom, he stepped forward and engaged him in conversation. Becoming angered, he struck Huey. (This explained the blood on Huey's lip. A student nurse at the hospital stated that Huey pointed to his mouth and said: "That's where he hit me." He may have been referring to Weiss or to Elliott Coleman, who had hit at Weiss.) At the blow, the guards drew their guns, and Weiss drew his, if he had one. (The mythmakers have it two ways. Weiss did not have a gun and therefore did not intend to kill Huey; he had a poor gun that jammed and therefore did not intend to kill Huey.) A fusillade of shots from the guards rang out and a wild one hit Huey. Thereupon the guards in a paroxysm of rage at their mistake riddled the helpless doctor. One wild twist to the story has it that one of the guards for some reason shot Huey deliberately and that this man, or the one that shot by error, went to Weiss's car in the parking lot and removed his gun and placed it near his hand on the floor. (Weiss's body was identified approximately half an hour after his death, and within that space of time no guard could have picked out Weiss's car from among the hundreds in the parking lot.)[8]

So THE MYTH. It is wrong—unless it is assumed that the various witnesses to the event who testified at the time collaborated in creating a gigantic lie and then with remarkable fidelity to memory repeated the lie in detail to later investigators. But what of the Long myth—that Weiss acted at the direction of powerful men, the anti leaders at the DeSoto Hotel conference?

It rests on shaky grounds. Seymour Weiss and other surviving Long intimates are certain that when Seymour read over the phone to Huey the names of the men in the conference room, he listed a "Dr. Wise" or a "Dr. Weiss." Huey replied: "You must be wrong about that one. There's no man named Weiss in politics except you, and I know you didn't attend that meeting." Seymour Weiss thought that he had secured the name in question from the transcript given to him by the two agents who had listened in on the conversation in the murder room. But on checking the transcript for another researcher, he was surprised to find that the name of Wise or Weiss occurred nowhere in it. He still insists, however, that he gave such a

---

[8] Zinman: *The Day Long Was Shot, passim*; Margaret Dixon: "Who Killed Huey Long?" in Baton Rouge *Morning Advocate*, September 9, 1951; J. Y. Sanders, Jr., James Petrie; confidential communications.

name to Huey, believing that he heard it in a verbal report. It should be added that by the testimony of his family and other witnesses Dr. Weiss was in Opelousas and Baton Rouge on the two days that the DeSoto conference met.[9]

Only one witness was found who placed Weiss at the DeSoto meeting. This is the man, previously cited, who claimed that there was a secret conference that neither Huey nor the political anti leaders know about. He was a chief of the Minute Men, and he recounted that he and three members of his organization and Weiss sat in a room and drew straws to see which one would kill Huey. "Weiss drew the short straw," he claimed. "He wanted it. He hated Huey because of the nigger business. He was the poorest choice. The rest of us had been under fire as soldiers." He and the others thought that Weiss might fail in his mission; and knowing Huey was going to north Louisiana the following week, they laid plans to kill him there with machine guns.[1]

Carl Weiss was a sincere and idealistic young man who agonized over the evils that he believed Huey Long was inflicting on his class and his state. He wept openly when he heard other people describe these evils, and he said to at least one person: "I'm going to kill Huey Long."[2] He was the kind of man who could spend a normal, happy day with his family and then commit an abnormal act. He went into the capitol that Sunday night to remove a tyrant. He went on his own and on an impulse, but one that had come to him many times before, and he went knowing that he himself would undoubtedly be killed. He did not care. He was willing to be a martyr.

[9] Seymour Weiss; Earle J. Christenberry; Robert Brothers; George H. Maines. Seymour Weiss checked his transcript for Hermann B. Deutsch; New Orleans *Times-Picayune*, September 8, 1963. If the name of Wise or Weiss was given to Huey in such a dramatic setting in late July, it is remarkable that with his phenomenal memory he did not recall it when it was repeated to him in the hospital.

[1] Confidential communication. The leader of the Square Deal group that had planned to draw lots during the week of September 8 to decide who would kill Huey was in the home of a friend on Sunday night when the news came over the radio that Huey had been shot. "That wasn't planned," he said. "The meeting was to have been tomorrow"; confidential communication.

[2] New Orleans *Item*, September 9, 1935; Baton Rouge *State-Times*, September 11, 1935; confidential communications.

# EPILOGUE

# I Have So Much to Do

**A**T OUR LADY OF THE LAKE HOSPITAL Jimmie O'Connor and the sister nurse and an intern rolled Huey to the operating room on the third floor. Here soon collected various functionaries and figures in the Long organization who had witnessed the shooting or heard of it—John Fournet, Chick Frampton, Jimmie Noe, Seymour Weiss, and others. One of the first to arrive was Dr. Arthur Vidrine, superintendent of Charity Hospital in New Orleans, who had been visiting the legislative session, and with the tacit consent of those present he became the doctor in charge. Huey's clothes were removed by cutting them off with a pocketknife that Fournet produced, and Vidrine examined the wound. He found a small bullet hole right under the ribs on the right side, and on the back near the spine another hole where the bullet had exited. (Presumably the assassin had aimed higher but had his arm deflected downward by Fournet's blow.) During the examination Huey asked for three other doctors, the noted surgeons Urban Maes and Russell Stone of New Orleans and his personal friend E. L. Sanderson of Shreveport, and someone left to phone these men.[1]

Huey remained conscious but was growing weaker, and Vidrine directed that he be placed in bed in a private room. By this time two Baton Rouge doctors had arrived in answer to calls from persons in the Long organization, Cecil Lorio, a brother of the Long leader in the parish, Clarence Lorio, also a doctor, and William H. Cook. They assisted Vidrine in checking Huey's condition, which

[1] James P. O'Connor; John B. Fournet; Hermann B. Deutsch: *The Huey Long Murder Case* (New York, 1963), pp. 118–19.

became steadily worse. His pulse rate kept climbing and his blood
pressure kept dropping, a certain indication that internal hemorrhaging had set in and that the patient would soon go into shock,
when the pulse rate and blood pressure almost met. Interestingly,
Huey was aware of this relationship. He said to Dr. Lorio: "When
they get together, I'll have to be operated on, won't I?" and when
they did approach, he said: "Getting about time to operate."[2]

Vidrine had known from the first that an operation would be
necessary, but he had hoped to delay it until Maes and Stone, more
experienced surgeons than he, could arrive. But now he realized
that he could not wait any longer, for the patient might bleed to
death. He approached the bed and said: "Huey, I'm going to have
to operate." Huey asked who would perform the operation, and
Vidrine said that he would and asked if Huey had any objections.
"No, no," Huey murmured weakly. Vidrine then made his preparations, directing that an anesthetist and a pathologist be called and
that blood tests be taken of the various people in the room so that
transfusions could be prepared. The operation began at about eleven
twenty. While it was underway, Dr. Clarence Lorio arrived, and
he and his brother and Cook did what they could to assist Vidrine.[3]

It was surely one of the most public operations in medical history. Associates and supporters of the patient stood arm to arm
around the walls of the room and stretched out into the hall. One of
them, at least, thought that there was something wrong about it. "I
thought then and have since, what a scene," he said in recalling it.
"Here was a man maybe dying, and the room was full of politicians."[4]

Vidrine, working swiftly, opened the abdomen. He was looking
for damage to the abdominal organs, and to his relief found little.
The liver, gall bladder, and stomach were free of injury. Two per-
forations appeared in the colon, the bullet having cut through one
fold and then another. Only a small amount of blood was discovered
in the abdominal cavity and a small blood clot in the small intestine.
The wounds of entrance and exit in the colon were sutured, and
the abdomen was closed. The operation had lasted about an hour
and apparently had been successful. Huey seemed in no great
danger.[5]

[2] Dr. Cecil O. Lorio.

[3] John B. Fournet; Seymour Weiss; Dr. Cecil O. Lorio; Allen J. Ellender; James
P. O'Connor; Dr. John L. Beven; James A. Noe.

[4] Fred Dent.

[5] Dr. Cecil O. Lorio; Deutsch: *Huey Long Murder Case*, pp. 118–19; Frank L.
Loria: "Historical Aspects of Penetrating Wounds of the Abdomen," *International
Abstracts of Surgery*, LXXXVII (1948), 521–49, reprint of twenty-nine pages by

At about one o'clock on Monday morning, Dr. Maes finally arrived, accompanied by another surgeon whom he had asked to come along to assist him. They had been told that a chartered plane would be available at the New Orleans airport to fly them to Baton Rouge, but they had decided that they could reach there more quickly by car. On the trip they had had an accident that caused a long delay. Somewhat later the other New Orleans surgeon who had been called, Russell Stone, arrived, and so also did Dr. E. L. Sanderson from Shreveport. Coming after the operation was completed, these doctors could only ask if certain things that should have been done had been done. They were shocked to learn that Vidrine had not catheterized the bladder to see if it contained blood. At their urging a catheter was inserted, and the urine was found to be holding a great deal of blood. A renal duct to the kidney had obviously been hit by the bullet, and Vidrine had not discovered this.[6]

It soon became evident that Huey was experiencing internal hemorrhaging from the injured kidney. But all the doctors agreed that in his weakened condition another operation to tie off the kidney would be fatal. On Monday he became steadily worse, his blood pressure dropping and his pulse becoming fainter. He had been given one blood transfusion on the preceding night and during the day was given four more, but they resulted in only a temporary improvement. At times he passed into unconsciousness and then revived and talked wildly, as though he saw visions beyond the hospital walls.[7] He saw the people out there, the poor people of America, a mass of faces, staring at him, needing him, wanting to give him power so that he could help them . . . the one-gallus farmers of the hill lands of the South . . . the white and black sharecroppers in the broad cotton fields . . . the gaunt and debt-ridden farmers of the Great Plains . . . the unemployed factory workers tramping the streets of the Northeast . . . the small businessmen all over the

Franklin H. Martin Foundation furnished me by Chief Justice John B. Fournet. Dr. Loria interviewed every doctor who attended Long, and his article is the best medical commentary on the case.

[6] Deutsch: *Huey Long Murder Case*, pp. 108–10, 120–1; David B. McConnell; John B. Fournet. Vidrine had very properly decided to operate; if he had not operated, Huey would certainly have died. But according to sources that will not be named, he was not thorough enough in his examination. They say that if he had probed further, he would have found that the kidney was impaired and could have put a clamp on it. This would have resulted in the death of the kidney, but Huey probably would have lived. Vidrine had had little training in surgery. In the words of one doctor: "If I was going to be operated on, I would not have picked Vidrine."

[7] Seymour Weiss; John B. Fournet; Earle J. Christenberry; Russell B. Long; Rose McConnell Long.

country pushed to the wall by big business . . . the pathetic elderly couples in countless towns and villages whose lifesavings had disappeared with the collapse of the banks . . . the fresh-faced boys and girls eager to gain an education . . . they looked at him and trusted him . . . and they would give him the power.

At other times he was completely rational and conversed seriously with the people in the room. Even more people were there now. In addition to the doctors and the politicians, his family was present—his wife and children, who had come up from New Orleans, his brothers, even Julius, and sisters, and briefly, his aged father. Mostly he talked with members of his family and with certain of his political chiefs. One of the latter was particularly anxious to talk to him. Seymour Weiss recalled that he had approached the bed and shook the patient and said: "Huey, you've got to tell me. Where is the deduct box?" Huey raised himself up but quickly fell back. "Later, Seymour, later," he whispered before relapsing into a coma. Weiss tried once again to get the information but received the same answer: "Later, Seymour, later."[8]

By early morning on Tuesday, September 10, it was obvious that Huey was sinking fast. His family was called into the room to witness the end, and at six minutes after four he died, some thirty hours after he had been shot and slightly more than a week since he had passed his forty-second birthday. Those persons who stood around the bed during his last hours differed afterwards as to what his dying words were. Some of them thought that he said: "What will my poor boys at LSU do without me?" But most of them remembered that he said: "God, don't let me die. I have so much to do."[9]

[8] Seymour Weiss; Harvey G. Fields: *A True History of the Life, Works, Assassination and Death of Huey P. Long* (Silver Spring, Md., 1944), p. 55. The deduct box was never located, even though Mrs. Long, who could legally claim it, sent agents to various cities in the United States and even in Canada; Earle J. Christenberry; Robert Brothers. Some Long associates think that a Long leader or leaders made off with the box; confidential communications.

[9] Seymour Weiss; James P. O'Connor; Louis A. Jones; John B. Fournet; Earle J. Christenberry.

# *Bibliographical Essay*

It would be fruitless and heartless to add to an already long book an extensive and pedantic listing of every source that I have consulted in my research or cited in my footnotes. The following essay is a selected bibliography, intended to indicate to other researchers and students and to interested readers the principal and pertinent sources on Huey P. Long.

## Oral History

As I stated in the preface, I obtained my most valuable and intimate material by interviewing persons who knew Long and recording their statements. The great majority of the 295 individuals listed below were interviewed by me personally. A few of them were interviewed for me by researchers that I employed, and a few of them supplied their recollections in letters to me. I also talked to at least ten other persons who did not wish to be interviewed but who in explaining their reasons revealed interesting bits of information. Although I was unable to interview Earl K. Long, I obtained some of his reminiscences from the recording, "Earl Long: Last of the Red Hot Papas," edited by Brooks Read and Bud Hebert and owned by News Records, Inc. I was also able to secure through the courtesy of the Columbia University Oral History Project typed excerpts of material dealing with Long from the recollections of Will W. Alexander, Samuel B. Bledsoe, Arthur Krock, and Harry Leland Mitchell.

## Persons Interviewed:

W. C. Alford, D. J. Anders, Robert Angelle, John G. Appel, Gene Austin, A. C. Bacon, Daisy Badley, L. P. Bahan, Bonnie V. Baker, Guy Baker, David Rankin Barbee, C. C. Barham, Lester P. Barlow, Norman Bauer, George E. Beckcom, Vivian S. Bernard, George Bertrand, John L. Beven, Cecil Bird, W. A. Bisso, David Blackshear, Fred Blanche, William C. Boone,

E. J. Bourg, Sidney Bowman, Harley Bozeman, B. W. Bradford, John P. Brashears, Overton Brooks, Robert Brothers, J. W. Brouillette, Alton E. Broussard, J. C. Broussard, Carroll Buck, James Buie, Francis P. Burns, James T. Burns, William T. Burton, W. E. Butler, Theo Cangelosi, Castro Carazo, Oliver P. Carriere, Myrtle M. Carroll, W. Kenneth Carroll, W. P. Carson, Joseph Cawthorn, Earle J. Christenberry, Ernest Clements, Bryan Clemmons, William Cleveland, Isidore Cohn, Clegg Cole, Clayton Coleman, Elliott Coleman, James Comiskey, James Thomas Connor, Olive Long Cooper, W. A. Cooper, R. S. Copeland, Carl Corbin, Milton Coverdale, Paul E. Cox, Perry Craddock, A. Wilmot Dalferes, Joseph B. David, Charles Davidson, Harry Davis, Lottie Long Davis, John DeArmond, J. D. DeBlieux, Norbert DeLatte, Bruce Denbo, Fred Dent, Hermann B. Deutsch, Fred Digby, William Dillon, Margaret Dixon, William J. Dodd, John J. Doles, James Domengeaux, D. J. Doucet, C. J. Dugas, Felix Dugas, Patrick Dugas, Charles L. Dufour, Charles E. Dunbar, John Dyer, Allen J. Ellender, G. E. Erskine, Ray Erwin, Mrs. George C. Everett, St. Clair Favrot, J. B. Ferchaud, Harvey G. Fields, Paul Fink, Joseph Fisher, Raymond H. Fleming, John Fleury, Paul Flowers, John M. Foote, Ralph Ford, W. S. Foshee, Richard Foster, John B. Fournet, J. J. Fournet, Charles Frampton, Fred Francis, Lether Frazar, Fred C. Frey, J. Cleveland Fruge, Harry Gamble, Lessley P. Gardiner, Leon Gary, Harry Gilbert, George J. Ginsberg, Ira Gleason, Lewis Gottlieb, Louis F. Guerre, Oscar Guidry, Isom Guillory, David Haas, Paul B. Habans, Edward A. Haggerty, Wood M. Hallack, Walter Hamlin, Rubie M. Hanks, F. Leonard Hargrove, Maud Harper, Frank Hood, John T. Hood, Jr., Roland B. Howell, H. Lester Hughes, Lucille Long Hunt, Robert A. Hunter, J. L. Hutcheson, Trent James, Lawrence M. Jones, Louis A. Jones, Robert D. Jones, Sam H. Jones, Alvin M. Josephy, Jr., Harrison Jordan, Marion Kahn, M. J. Kavanaugh, Pearl Kennedy, Shelby Kidd, A. K. Kilpatrick, Clara Long Knott, Donald Labbe, Theophile Landry, Norman Lant, Henry D. Larcade, W. V. Larcade, Lester Lautenschlaeger, Rollo C. Lawrence, Richard W. Leche, Leon LeSueur, John L. Lewis, Rivers Livous, Arthur Long, Rose McConnell Long, Julius T. Long, Otho Long, Palmer Long, Russell B. Long, Cecil O. Lorio, David B. McConnell, Vernon McCoy, Rose Long McFarland, David R. McGuire, John H. McSween, George T. Madison, Tom Mahoney, George H. Maines, Paul Maloney, Manuel Manetta, Frank W. Manning, Sidney Marchand, Mario Marmalakis, Philip H. Mecom, James L. Mehaffey, Abe Mickal, Troy H. Middleton, Matt Milam, Woody N. Miley, Harold Moise, Numa Montet, Cecil Morgan, Wayne Morse, Edgar G. Mouton, Karl Mundt, Eugene A. Nabors, Margaret F. Newberry, James A. Noe, Mrs. Alexander W. Norman, Edgar Norton, John Nuckolls, Jess Nugent, E. J. Oakes, James P. O'Connor, John J. O'Connor, Frank Odom, R. W. Oglesby, Robert J. O'Neal, Charles L. Orr, Mrs. John H. Overton, Vernon J. Parenton, Mrs. Robert Parrott, Wilson J. Peck, W. C. Pegues, Harvey A. Peltier, George E. Pereira, Leander H. Perez, Frank J. Peterman, James Petrie, Rupert Peyton, Marc Picciola, "Fats" Pichon, Mrs. Clarence Pierson, Robert Hunter

Pierson, Maurice Planche, Irving Poche, Irvin F. Polmer, Amos Lee Ponder, Marvin Pope, Mrs. Gaston Porterie, Robert L. Prophit, C. Arthur Provost, Maud Bomar Purdy, Gene Quaw, Carlos Rabby, Herve Racevitch, Harry Rabenhorst, M. J. Rathbone, Edmund T. Reggie, George Reyer, Charles J. Rivet, Jesse Roberts, Edward S. Robertson, Mabel R. Roshton, Murphy Roden, E. P. Roy, J. Maxime Roy, John St. Paul, J. Y. Sanders, Jr., Lennie Savoy, William S. Shaw, Clem H. Sehrt, Andrew Sevier, Henry C. Sevier, Frank Sheffield, Ollie H. Sheffield, J. Stewart Slack, Ed T. Slean, Charles L. Smith, Mason Spencer, Leonard Spinks, Eugene Stanley, Frank J. Stich, Edmond E. Talbot, W. Harry Talbot, Fred E. Tarman, Robert Taylor, Warren Taylor, Mrs. Theo Terzia, Norman Thomas, Orlean Thomas, O. B. Tompson, Will Harvey Todd, Leon Trice, Harry S Truman, William C. Turpin, Larry Udell, Scoville Walker, A. M. Wallace, George M. Wallace, Mary B. Walle, Kenneth Watts, Seymour Weiss, Spencer Whedon, A. P. White, Rupert S. Whitley, V. V. Whittington, William Wiegand, Hugh M. Wilkinson, E. H. (Lige) Williams, Lewellyn B. Williams, Shirley G. Wimberly, John J. Wingrave, Byrne M. Womack, James D. Womack, Lantz Womack, Mrs. D. F. Yost.

## Manuscripts

No COMPREHENSIVE BODY of Long papers has apparently survived, or, if surviving, is available. The largest extant collection is in the Department of Archives and Manuscripts of the Louisiana State University Library, Baton Rouge. Arranged in four file cabinets, these Huey P. Long Papers are classified under Public Service Commission File and Private Law Cases File. They deal mainly with the years from 1920 to 1928, and although they contain some letters by Long, they consist mostly of legal and public documents. They are valuable, however, for a study of Long's legal and early political career. There are other Long letters for this early period in Public Service Commission File No. 3, in the office of the Louisiana Public Service Commission, state capitol, Baton Rouge. Small collections of Long Papers are in the libraries of Duke University, Durham, North Carolina, and Emory University, Atlanta, Georgia. The Duke collection consists mainly of form and official letters of the Share Our Wealth organization. The Emory collection contains letters from Long to Julian Harris on the subject of potlikker. The two libraries furnished me with photostat copies of the papers. Mr. John McGuire of New Orleans owns and made available to me his collection of Long Papers, which consist mainly of letters detailing Long's relations with the press and the writing of his autobiography.

Collections of the papers of some other leaders bear on Long and his period. In the Department of Archives and Manuscripts at Louisiana State University the Jared Y. Sanders and Family Papers contain numerous though hostile references to Long. The Governor's Correspondence in the same library is disappointing: it goes up to only 1924, and for the important Parker administration was apparently screened. The John M. Parker Papers in the Southern Historical Collection, University of North Carolina Library, Chapel Hill, contains one Long letter and much pertinent Long material. Also at North Carolina is the large and rewarding collection of W. D. Robinson Papers, containing letters by Robinson, at one time Long's publicity man and then bitter enemy, Julius T. Long, and other assorted Long foes.

Three collections relating to Long are in the Duke University Library, Durham, North Carolina: the Sam Irby Papers, which are revealing as to Irby's "kidnapping" and the writing of his book; the Harry A. Slattery Papers, which indicate the reaction of "outside" progressives to Long; and the Socialist Labor Party Papers, in which is a lengthy and public but valuable letter by Long on concentrated wealth.

A search of materials in the Division of Manuscripts, Library of Congress, made for me by Mrs. Pio Uliassi, produced a number of references on Long's senatorial career in the Tom Connally and George W. Norris Papers.

## National and State Government Documents

THE BASIC SOURCES on Long's service with the Railroad Commission and the Public Service Commission are available in the office of the Louisiana Public Service Commission, state capitol, Baton Rouge. They are, for the Railroad Commission, the twenty-first, twenty-second, and twenty-third *Annual Reports* (1919–1922), the last item being also the first report of the Public Service Commission; and for the Public Service Commission, the second, third, fourth, fifth, sixth, seventh, and eighth *Annual Reports* (1923–1929). Also valuable is the Minute Book of the Railroad and Public Service Commissions (January 7, 1919–July 27, 1929), a manuscript record that lists the cases and summarizes the actions of the two agencies. Another revealing item is Case 197, Louisiana Public Service Commission *v.* Standard Oil Company of Louisiana, a folio containing the pertinent documents on one of the Commission's most important prosecutions.

Invaluable for Long's governorship is the two-volume record of his impeachment, *Official Journal of the Proceedings of the House of Representatives and the Senate of Louisiana* (fifth extraordinary session, 1929). More than an account of the specific event, it deals also with developments preceding it and is a revealing commentary on Louisiana politics. Even broader in scope and more valuable is the report of the investigation conducted by a United States Senate Committee of the election of John H. Overton, *Hearings Before the Special Committee on Investigation of Campaign Expenditures,* 72 Cong., 2 Sess., 73 Cong., 2 Sess. (2 vols.; Washington, D.C., 1933, 1934). The investigators decided to delve into almost every aspect of Long's career before the hearing, and their report of 2,755 pages is a mass of rich information.

Long's speeches and activities in the Senate of the United States from January 25, 1932, to August 26, 1935, can be followed in the close-filled pages and many volumes of the *Congressional Record*, 72 Cong., 1 Sess.–74 Cong., 1 Sess.

## Newspapers and Magazines

IT IS A CONVICTION of all Huey Long admirers that the Louisiana newspapers of his time were grossly unfair to him and that therefore they are useless as sources on him. The indictment is true only in part. Most of the papers were opposed to him and denounced him in their editorial columns and sometimes colored their news stories against him. But all of them gave him unusually full coverage, and it is obvious that many of the correspondents liked him personally and reported fairly his words and actions. The New Orleans press particularly was very politics-conscious, and its accounts of political doings are always informative and usually perceptive. Newspapers therefore constitute a valuable source on Long and his times.

My newspaper research was greatly facilitated by having access to a number of scrapbooks, some of them in public depositories, others in private hands and made available to me by the owners, to whom I am grateful. The largest and most valuable collection of this kind is the Huey P. Long Scrapbooks in the Department of Archives and Manuscripts at the Louisiana State University Library. This collection consists of fifty-seven large volumes, and of these the first thirty-five cover Long's life from 1923 to 1935, treating it from almost every aspect and containing clippings from not only Louisiana newspapers but journals throughout the country. In the same library but in the Louisiana Room is a file of unbound clippings dealing with Long, mostly for one year, 1935.

Other rewarding collections are the E. A. Conway Scrapbook Collection of Long Materials, 13 vols., Louisiana State Library, Baton Rouge; the Henry L. Fuqua Scrapbooks, 10 vols., Department of Archives and Manuscripts, Louisiana State University Library; the Lucille M. Grace Scrapbook, made available to me by Mr. Fred Dent, Baton Rouge, and later presented to the Louisiana State University Library; the Hilda Phelps Hammond Scrapbook, made available to me by Mrs. Nauman S. Scott, Jr., Alexandria, Louisiana; the S. J. Harper Scrapbook, made available to me by Miss Maud H. Harper, Winnfield, Louisiana; the Richard W. Leche Scrapbook, 2 vols., made available to me by the late Mr. Leche and later presented by his heirs to the Louisiana State University Library; the Mrs. John Lungaro Scrapbook, made available to me by Mr. John Lungaro, Baton Rouge; the New Orleans Public Service Incorporation Scrapbooks, 9 vols. and 2 folders, in the office of the New Orleans Public Service Incorporation, dealing with the bringing of natural gas to the city; the Mrs. John H. Overton Scrapbooks, 2 vols., made available to me by Mrs. Overton, Alexandria, Louisiana; the Linnie B. Persac Scrapbook, made available to me by Mrs. Persac, Baton Rouge, and later presented to the Louisiana State University Library; and the Arthur Provost Scrapbooks, 2 vols., made available to me by Mr. Provost, New Iberia, Louisiana.

In addition to using these scrapbooks, I made selected runs of the following newspapers: the Baton Rouge *Morning Advocate* and *State-Times*, 1924–35; the Donaldsonville *Chief*, 1928–9; and the New Orleans *Item, States*, and *Times-Picayune*, 1924–35. I read the complete file of the *Louisiana Progress*, 1930–2, and the *American Progress*, 1933–5, in the William B. Wisdom Collection, Tulane University Library, New Orleans.

I also made selected runs of two of the news magazines, the *Literary Digest* and *Time*, 1932–5, both of which gave Long frequent mention. *Time*'s coverage was much the fuller and was uniformly hostile.

## Articles in Periodicals and Newspapers

A VAST PERIODICAL LITERATURE on Long exists, most of it written during his lifetime. The articles are of varying value, most of them being ephemeral, and many of them are cited and some are characterized in the notes. Rising above the general level, though marked by a strong antipathy to Long, are the following evaluations by Hodding Carter: "Kingfish to Crawfish," *New Republic*, LXXXI (January 24, 1934), 302–5; "The Kingfish on His Way," ibid., LXXXI (November 21, 1934), 40–2; and "Louisiana Limelighter," *Review of Reviews*, XCI (March 1935), 23–8, 64. Also superior and rich in information are the pieces by the veteran New Orleans correspondent Hermann B. Deutsch in the *Saturday Evening Post*: "Hattie and Huey," CCV (October 15, 1932), 6–7 ff.; "Prelude to a Heterocrat," CCVII (September 7, 1935), 5–7 ff.; "Paradox in Pajamas," CCVIII (October 5, 1935), 14 ff.; and "Huey Long—the Last Phase," CCVIII (October 12, 1935), 27 ff.

Two articles in scholarly journals are deserving of special mention—M. S. Cushman: "Huey Long's First Session in the United States Senate," *Proceedings of the West Virginia Academy of Science*, XI (1937), 123–31; and Burton J. Hotaling: "Huey P. Long as Journalist and Propagandist," *Journalism Quarterly*, XX (1943), 21–9, excellent on Long's attention to forming public opinion.

The following newspaper serial articles contain excellent factual material on Long: Harley B. Bozeman, "Winn Parish As I Have Known It," in *Winn Parish Enterprise*, October 2, 1956, through 1963, invaluable for Long's life up to 1928 and his local background; Hermann B. Deutsch: "The Kingdom of the Kingfish," in New Orleans *Item*, July 19–September 20, 1939, a sprightly journalistic account of Long's entire political career; and George H. Maines, articles in Flint *News-Advertiser*, September 13, 20, 22, 27, November 11, 1935, revealing though partisan pieces by Long's public relations man.

## Books, Dissertations, and Theses

SIX PREVIOUS BIOGRAPHIES of Long have been published. First to appear was John Kingston Fineran: *The Career of a Tin Pot Napoleon* (New Orleans, 1932). Covering only a part of Long's life, it was violently prejudiced against him and is interesting chiefly as a revelation of the anti-Long mind. Next came Webster Smith: *The Kingfish* (New York, 1933). The author was a man in the Long organization writing under an assumed name. He chose, however, to draw his material from newspapers, and the book is a bland and curiously neutral account.

Two years later two more serious works came out, Forrest Davis: *Huey Long: A Candid Biography* (New York, 1935), and Carleton Beals: *The Story of Huey P. Long* (Philadelphia, 1935). Both authors confined their research mainly to periodicals and newspapers, although Davis interviewed Long and quoted the result at length, thus giving his book something of the quality of a source. They attempted, however, to see Long in some kind of perspective, and although they were too close in time to the subject to succeed, they invested their books with a certain depth.

No such effort marked the next biography, T. O. Harris: *The Kingfish* (New Orleans, 1938). The author was an anti-Long Louisiana reporter, and he wrote in a bitter anti spirit. He attempted to be solidly factual, however, and his book contains some material not found in any other accounts. The sixth biography was Harvey G. Fields: *A True History of the Life, Works, Assassination and Death of Huey Pierce Long* (Silver Spring, Md., 1944). Fields was a close associate of Long's, and the book is strongly sympathetic to the subject. But in preparing it, the author supplemented his own recollections with those of others, and the book is therefore in part a primary source.

Three books that bear on Long's career deserve mention. Harnett T. Kane: *Louisiana Hayride* (New York, 1941) is a New Orleans journalist's account of the Louisiana scandals of the post-Huey Long period, preceded by a description of the Huey Long years. It is a sprightly but surface work and is not always judicious. Allen P. Sindler: *Huey Long's Louisiana: State Politics, 1920–1952* (Baltimore, 1950), and Perry H. Howard: *Political Tendencies in Louisiana* (Baton Rouge, 1951), are studies of Long and his time by, respectively, a political scientist and a sociologist. They are invaluable for their information, especially for their data on elections. But in my opinion they suffer from a mechanistic view of history, from an assumption that Long was only a product and a reflection of his environment.

A number of unpublished theses and dissertations contain material of varying value on Long—Emile B. Ader: "An Analysis of the Campaign Techniques and Appeals of Huey Long" (M.A. thesis, Tulane University, 1942), a shallow work; Ernest Gordon Borman: "A Rhetorical Analysis of the National Radio Broadcasts of Senator Huey P. Long" (Ph.D. dissertation, State University of Iowa, 1953), a useful study; Leo Glenn Douthit: "The Governorship of Huey Long" (M.A. thesis, Tulane University, 1947), an intelligent study based on wide newspaper coverage; Adolph O. Goldsmith, "A Study of the Objectivity of Treatment of Governor Huey P. Long, by Six Daily Newspapers during Long's First Eleven Months in Office" (Ph.D. dissertation, University of Iowa, 1967), excellent on the subject; Curtiss Hodges: "The Politics of Huey P. Long" (M.A. thesis, Louisiana State University, 1940), a superficial survey; Ansel Miree Sharp: "A Study of the Counter-Cyclical Aspects of Total Government Fiscal Policy, 1929–1940" (Ph.D. dissertation, Louisiana State University, 1956), invaluable for the Long taxation policies; and Elsie B. Stallworth: "A Survey of the *Louisiana Progresses* of the 1930's" (M.A. thesis, Louisiana State University, 1948), a first-rate description and analysis.

*Index*

Roosevelt, Theodore, 131–2
Roosevelt Hotel (New Orleans),
Huey's suite at, 318, 428–9
Round Robins, and impeachment,
396–400
Roy, E. P., head of state police, 664,
789–90, 862

Saint, Percy, attorney general, 287; op-
poses Huey, 291; and severance tax,
325; and Dreher-LeBoeuf, 338–9;
and antigambling raids, 343
St. Bernard parish (La.), vote in
1932, 539–40, 599
St. Landry parish (La.), 861–2
St. Paul, John, Jr., 196, 201
St. Paul, John, Sr., justice of supreme
court, 733–4
Sanders, Jared Y., Jr., anti-Long
leader, 181, 298, 350; and impeachment, 354–5, 364, 395; Congressional candidate, 666–9, 713; and
DeSoto Hotel conference, 841
Sanders, Jared Y., Sr., 43, 138, 151,
445, 574; in gubernatorial election,
1920, 133; and highways, 144–5; in
gubernatorial election, 1924, 194;
and Democratic state convention,
1924, 216–18; in Senatorial election, 1924, 219–20; and Watson-
Williams bridge, 228–31; in Senatorial election, 1926, 235–40; in
gubernatorial election, 1928, 249,
268; fight with Huey, 271–2; and
Democratic National Convention,
*1928*, 282–3, *1932*, 578
Sanderson, E. L., attends Huey in
hospital, 873–5
Sandlin, John, and DeSoto Hotel
conference, 839–40, 869
Sands Point incident, 648–54
*Saturday Evening Post*, 116–17, 557,
558
Savoie, Clarence, Long leader, 261

Sayes, Clinton, and impeachment, 357
Schall, Thomas, U.S. Senator, 835
Schwellenbach, Lewis, U.S. Senator,
833, 842
Schwing, Calvin K., 261
Seelye, Stuart A., 166–7
severance tax: defined, 140; Parker's
bill on, 140–4; and Standard Oil,
141–2; and constitutional convention of 1921, 142–4; Huey's bill on,
1928, 308–9; court test of bill, 325–
6, 345–6, 445
Share Our Wealth Society: and plan,
692–5; criticisms of, 695–6; popular
support of, 697–8, 700–1; Negroes
in, 701–2
Shaughnessy, Clark, 764, 772
Sherburne, Henry, 788
sheriffs, power of, 130; broken by
Huey, 754
Shreveport (La.), 93; characterized,
96–7; and air base, 329–32; and
free schoolbooks, 329–32
Shreveport *Journal*, 97
Shushan, Abraham, 645, 757; Long
leader, 421, 549; and New Orleans
airport, 549–50; indictment of, 798,
820
Simpson, Oramel H., governor, 241,
569; in gubernatorial election, 1928,
244–79; and impeachment, 399–400
Sinclair, Upton, 696
sixth district Congressional election,
*1933*, 665–9, *1934*, 713
Smith, Alfred E., 283, 326–8, 572
Smith, Gerald L. K., SOW organizer,
699–700, 713, 816
Smith, James Monroe, LSU president,
500–3, 504, 507, 513, 517, 764–6,
769, 772, 776–8, 780
Smith, Thelma, 503
Snyder, J. B., Long leader, 261
Socialism, Huey on, 694, 750
Socialist party, in Winn parish, 44
Songy, Sidney, Long spy, 785, 786–9